# SECURITIES LITIGATION AND ENFORCEMENT

## CASES AND MATERIALS

By

**Donna M. Nagy**
*Associate Dean for Faculty Development*
*and Charles Hartsock Professor of Law*
*University of Cincinnati College of Law*

**Richard W. Painter**
*Professor of Law*
*University of Illinois College of Law*

**Margaret V. Sachs**
*Robert Cotten Alston Professor of Law*
*University of Georgia School of Law*

**AMERICAN CASEBOOK SERIES®**

THOMSON
WEST ™

Mat #18404265

610 Opperman Drive
P.O. Box 64526
St. Paul, MN 55164–0526
1–800–328–9352


Printed in the United States of America

**ISBN** 0–314–25953–8

*TEXT IS PRINTED ON 10% POST CONSUMER RECYCLED PAPER*

*To Brian and Caitlin*
D.M.N.

*To William H. Painter*
R.W.P.

*To my Mother and to the memory of my Father*
M.V.S

# Preface

This casebook fills a gap in currently available materials for securities law courses: the absence of materials designed specifically to acquaint students with the theoretical as well as practical aspects of federal securities litigation and enforcement. The casebook addresses important actions and issues in the clusters in which they are likely to arise in actual securities litigation, thereby maximizing student preparedness to represent clients in private litigation, in enforcement actions by the Securities and Exchange Commission, and in criminal prosecutions. Even before the corporate governance and accounting scandals at Enron, WorldCom and numerous other companies, the need for such a casebook was great. But the scandals grabbing front page headlines throughout 2002-03 have generated considerably more student interest in securities litigation and enforcement, in part because students (rightly) recognize its growing importance as an area of practice.

We have designed this casebook for use in a variety of two or three credit courses or seminars. These include a "securities litigation" course examining litigation topics under the Securities Exchange Act (e.g., Rule 10b-5, proxy fraud, tender offer fraud, class actions, and international securities fraud) as well as Securities Act liability for material misstatements and omissions, and securities arbitration. Much of this material is left uncovered—or is covered only briefly—in the more transactional-oriented securities regulation course. Another possible offering is a course in "securities litigation and enforcement" that covers some of the just-mentioned topics but also encompasses SEC enforcement issues (including the conduct of SEC investigations and the professional responsibilities of lawyers and accountants), insider trading, market manipulation, and criminal enforcement. Other possibilities are more specialized courses or seminars that focus on such areas as enforcement, insider trading, or market manipulation, or that build around the theme of "current topics in securities litigation."

A course or seminar in securities litigation and enforcement need not come after a course in securities regulation. We do not presuppose familiarity with the contents of the securities regulation course, and students who have not taken that course are at no disadvantage. But in order to challenge and stimulate more experienced students, we have included materials and problems that allow such students to explore doctrinal nuances and practical issues that they are unlikely to have encountered previously.

We have edited most of the cases and materials to keep each chapter a manageable length. Asterisks (***) indicate substantive omissions, but citations, footnotes, and concurring and dissenting opinions may have also been omitted without a specific notation that such an omission has been made. Footnotes included in cases and materials retain their number from the original source.

Throughout our work on this casebook, we have been encouraged and informed by our many friends and colleagues in law schools and in the practicing bar. We hope that they—as well as others who use our casebook—will share their comments and suggestions for future editions.

DONNA M. NAGY
RICHARD W. PAINTER
MARGARET V. SACHS

February, 2003

# Acknowledgments

Donna M. Nagy wishes to express thanks and appreciation to the many individuals who have contributed to this casebook. Dean Joseph P. Tomain and the faculty and staff at the University of Cincinnati College of Law provided constant encouragement and support, and Dean Stephen Todd and the faculty and staff of the University of Canterbury School of Law in Christchurch, New Zealand provided a warm welcome and generous resources during a sabbatical semester. Betsy Lenhart, Class of 2004, and James Flax, Class of 2003, provided excellent research assistance. Ralph C. Ferrara and other talented securities litigators at the law firm of Debevoise & Plimpton served as excellent mentors. And her husband, Brian Lewis, daughter Caitlin, and parents, Mary and Ken Nagy, provided much needed and constantly drawn-on support and encouragement from the homefront.

Richard W. Painter thanks the University of Illinois for support of his work on this casebook, including invaluable student research assistance and secretarial assistance from Dee Falls. He is also grateful for the generous support of the Ross and Helen Workman Law Research Grant for his work on this casebook during the summer of 2002.

Margaret V. Sachs is very grateful for the steadfast support she received from numerous friends and colleagues in connection with this casebook, especially Alexander M. Meiklejohn, Charles R.T. O'Kelley, and Camilla E. Watson. She also appreciates very much the invaluable technological assistance of Carol A. Watson, Reference/Computing Services Librarian, University of Georgia School of Law. In addition, she thanks her splendid secretary, Mary Louise Fielding, for her numerous contributions.

All three of us owe a huge debt of gratitude to Connie Miller at the University of Cincinnati College of Law for her stellar word processing skills and dedication to this project, and to the following students at the University of Georgia School of Law for their diligence in cite-checking the manuscript: Jason A. Alloy, Emily E. Barrier, Rebecca H. Bishop, Caroline Castle, Michelle L. Carter, Christopher A. Cosper, Christy D. Durden, Stacey G. Godfrey, Michael Grubbs, Stephanie Harris, Jonathan E. Hawkins, Michael J. Jacobs, Michelle M. Moore, Tiana S. Mykkelvedt, Timothy F. Sanders, and Colin Wright.

Finally, we acknowledge with appreciation the following authors, publishers, and journals who have graciously granted permission to reprint excerpts from their publications.

ABA Section of Business Law, Committee on the Law of Cyberspace, Achieving Legal and Business Order in Cyberspace: A Report on Global Jurisdiction Issues Created by the Internet, 55 Bus. Law 1801, 1932 (2000). Copyright ©2000 by the American Bar Association. Reprinted with permission.

ABA Committee on Federal Regulation of Securities, Report of the Task Force on SEC Settlements, 47 Bus. Law. 1083, 1091-94 (1992). Copyright ©1992 by the American Bar Association. Reprinted with permission.

John W. Avery, Securities Litigation Reform: The Long and Winding Road to the Private Securities Litigation Reform Act of 1995, 51 Bus. Law. 335, 362 (1996). Copyright ©1996 by the American Bar Association. Reprinted with permission.

Janet Cooper Alexander, Rethinking Damages in Securities Class Actions, 48 Stan. L. Rev. 1487, 1491-93 (1996). Reprinted with permission of the Stanford Law Review.

Stephen M. Bainbridge, Insider Trading Regulation: The Path Dependent Choice Between Property Rights and Securities Fraud, 52 SMU L. Rev. 1589, 1606-08 (1999). Reprinted with permission from the SMU Law Review, the Southern Methodist University School of Law, and the author.

Dennis M. Carlton and Daniel R. Fischel, The Regulation of Insider Trading, 35 Stan. L. Rev. 857, 866-68 (1983). Reprinted with permission of the Stanford Law Review.

Ralph C. Ferrara and Philip S. Khinda, SEC Enforcement Proceedings: Strategic Considerations for When the Agency Comes Calling, 51 Admin. L. Rev. 1143, 1148-1166 (1999). Copyright ©1999 by the American Bar Association. Reprinted with permission.

Daniel R. Fischel and David J. Ross, Should the Law Prohibit "Manipulation" in Financial Markets?, 105 Harv. L. Rev. 503, 508-10 (1991). Copyright ©1991 by the Harvard Law Review Association. Reprinted with permission of the Harvard Law Review and the authors.

Roberta S. Karmel, Outsider Trading on Confidential Information—A Breach in Search of A Duty, 20 Cardozo L. Rev. 83, 112-113 (1998). Reprinted with permission of the Cardozo Law Review and the author.

Henry G. Manne, In Defense of Insider Trading, Harvard Bus. Rev., Nov.-Dec., 1966 at 113-19. Reprinted with permission of Harvard Business School Publishing.

William R. McLucas, J. Lynn Taylor, Susan A. Mathews, A Practitioner's Guide to the SEC's Investigative and Enforcement Process, 70 Temple L. Rev. 53, 111-16 (1997). Reprinted with permission of the Temple Law Review and the authors.

National Association of Securities Dealers, Inc. (NASD, Inc.), Arbitration and Mediation Statistics ©2003, and Arbitration Procedures ©2001. Copyright by NASD, Inc. Reprinted with permission of NASD, Inc.

Richard W. Painter, Kimberly D. Krawiec, Cynthia A. Williams, Don't Ask, Just Tell: Insider Trading After *United States v. O'Hagan*, 84 Va. L. Rev. 153, 211-12, 219-28 (1998). Copyright ©1998 by Virginia Law Review. Reprinted with the permission of the Virginia Law Review and the authors.

Richard M. Phillips, Glenn R. Reichardt, Michael J. Missal, and Robyn J. Lipton, SEC Investigations: The Heart of SEC Enforcement Practice in Kirkpatrick & Lockhart LLP, The Securities Enforcement Manual: Tactics and Strategies (Richard M. Phillips, ed. 1997). Copyright ©1997 by the American Bar Association. Reprinted with permission of the American Bar Association.

Kim Lane Scheppele, "It's Just Not Right:" The Ethics of Insider Trading, 56 Law & Contemp. Probs. 123, 162-63 (1993). Reprinted with permission.

Andrew M. Smith, SEC Cease-and-Desist Orders, 51 Admin. L. Rev. 1197, 1217-1225 (1999). Copyright ©1999 by the American Bar Association. Reprinted with permission.

Lynn A. Stout, Type I Error, Type II Error, and the Private Securities Litigation Reform Act, 38 Ariz. L. Rev. 711, 713-14 (1996). Copyright ©1996 by the Arizona Board of Regents. Reprinted by permission of the Arizona Board of Regents and the author.

William K.S. Wang, Stock Market Insider Trading: Victims, Violators and Remedies—Including an Analogy to Fraud in the Sale of a Used Car with a Generic Defect, 45 Vill. L. Rev. 27, 28-38 (2000). Reprinted by permission of the Villanova Law Review and the author.

Min Wu, Restatements by Year 1977-2Q2002. Copyright ©2002 Min Wu, New York University, Stern School of Business. Reprinted by permission. All rights reserved.

# Summary of Contents


| | | Page |
|---|---|---|
| PREFACE | | v |
| ACKNOWLEDGMENTS | | vii |
| TABLE OF CASES | | xxvii |
| **Chapter 1.** | **An Overview of Securities Litigation and Enforcement** | **1** |
| A. | The Federal Securities Statutes | 2 |
| B. | The Courts | 11 |
| C. | The Securities and Exchange Commission | 13 |
| D. | The Department of Justice | 13 |
| E. | State Law | 14 |
| F. | Social and Economic Forces | 15 |
| G. | The Efficient Capital Markets Hypothesis | 16 |
| H. | Looking Ahead | 17 |
| **Chapter 2.** | **Section 10(b) of the Exchange Act and Rule 10b-5** | **19** |
| A. | The Requirement of Manipulation or Deception | 23 |
| B. | The Materiality Requirement | 64 |
| C. | The "In Connection With" Requirement | 86 |
| D. | The Scienter Requirement | 102 |
| E. | The Purchaser-Seller Requirement | 133 |
| F. | Causation | 147 |
| G. | Damages | 193 |
| H. | Primary and Secondary Liability | 206 |
| I. | Statute of Limitations | 236 |
| J. | The Overlap Between Rule 10b-5 and the Express Actions for Material Misstatements and Omissions | 254 |
| **Chapter 3:** | **Liability Under the Securities Act for Material Misstatements, Omissions, and Fraudulent Conduct** | **260** |
| A. | Sections 11 and 12(a)(2): Express Private Actions for Material Misstatements and Omissions | 260 |
| B. | Section 17(a): Fraud in the Offer or Sale of Securities | 320 |
| **Chapter 4.** | **Proxy Fraud—Section 14(a) of the Exchange Act and Rule 14a-9** | **326** |
| A. | Judicial Recognition of the Implied Private Action | 328 |
| B. | The Materiality Requirement | 332 |
| C. | The State of Mind Requirement | 334 |
| D. | The Causation Requirement | 338 |

**Chapter 5. Tender Offer Fraud—Section 14(e) of the Exchange Act** ..... **363**
A. An Overview of Tender Offers and the Williams Act ..... 363
B. Litigation Under Section 14(e) ..... 369
C. The Critical Role of State Law in Tender Offer Litigation ..... 391

**Chapter 6. Securities Class Actions** ..... **395**
A. The Private Securities Litigation Reform Act of 1995 ..... 395
B. The Securities Litigation Uniform Standards Act of 1998 ..... 419
C. Empirical Data on Class Actions ..... 427
D. Shifting Perceptions of the Balance of Power Between Plaintiffs and Defendants ..... 437
E. Problems ..... 442

**Chapter 7. Insider Trading** ..... **448**
A. Initial Efforts to Combat and Curtail Insider Trading ..... 449
B. The Supreme Court Speaks on Insider Trading and Rule 10b-5. 468
C. Rule 14e-3—Insider Trading in the Context of Tender Offers ..... 506
D. Congress Speaks on Insider Trading—ITSA, ITFSEA, and Subsequent Legislation ..... 516
E. Litigating Insider Trading Cases—The Problem of Circumstantial Evidence ..... 523
F. Policy Rationales for Federal Regulation of Insider Trading and the Search for a Definition ..... 549

**Chapter 8. Market Manipulation** ..... **578**
A. Practices that Create the Appearance of Active Trading ..... 579
B. Actual Trading Conducted for a Manipulative Purpose ..... 585
C. Misleading Recommendations and Material Misstatements Designed to Affect Market Prices ..... 599

**Chapter 9. SEC Enforcement of the Federal Securities Laws** ..... **617**
A. The SEC's Division of Enforcement ..... 618
B. SEC Investigations ..... 621
C. Civil Remedies for Violations of the Securities Laws ..... 657
D. Litigating with the SEC ..... 699
E. SROs as Enforcers of the Federal Securities Laws ..... 723
F. Parallel Proceedings ..... 744

**Chapter 10. Enforcement Issues Involving Attorneys and Accountants** ..... **768**
A. SEC Discipline of Professionals Under Rule 102(e) ..... 769
B. Ethical and Proper Conduct for Securities Attorneys ..... 773
C. The Regulation of Accountants Under the Sarbanes-Oxley Act of 2002 ..... 819

**Chapter 11. Criminal Enforcement** ..... **833**
A. The Securities Act and the Exchange Act ..... 834
B. The Sarbanes-Oxley Act ..... 846
C. The Mail and Wire Fraud Statutes ..... 849
D. Racketeer Influenced and Corrupt Organizations Act ..... 861

**Chapter 12. International Securities Fraud** ..... **888**
A. The Principles of Extraterritorial Jurisdiction Developed By Courts ..... 889
B. Choice of Law and Choice of Forum Clauses ..... 914
C. The Forum Non Conveniens Doctrine ..... 924
D. International Securities Fraud and the SEC ..... 934

**Chapter 13. Securities Arbitration** ..... **937**
A. The Relationship Between the Federal Arbitration Act and the Federal Securities Laws ..... 938
B. The Process of Securities Arbitration ..... 952
C. The Remaining Judicial Role in Arbitration ..... 965
D. Securities Arbitration in Perspective ..... 973

INDEX ..... 976

# Table of Contents


| | | | | Page |
|---|---|---|---|---|
| PREFACE | | | | v |
| ACKNOWLEDGMENTS | | | | vii |
| TABLE OF CASES | | | | xxvii |
| **Chapter 1. An Overview of Securities Litigation and Enforcement** | | | | **1** |
| A. | The Federal Securities Statutes | | | 2 |
| | *1.* | *The Securities Act* | | 3 |
| | | a. | The Registration Requirement | 3 |
| | | b. | Exemptions from Registration | 4 |
| | | c. | Liability Provisions | 5 |
| | *2.* | *The Exchange Act* | | 6 |
| | | a. | Section 10(b) and Rule 10b-5 | 6 |
| | | b. | Market Manipulation | 7 |
| | | c. | Disclosure Obligations: Reporting Companies | 7 |
| | | d. | Proxy Regulation | 8 |
| | | e. | Tender Offer Regulation | 8 |
| | | f. | Self-Regulatory Organizations | 9 |
| | *3.* | *The Private Securities Litigation Reform Act* | | 9 |
| | *4.* | *The Sarbanes-Oxley Act* | | 10 |
| B. | The Courts | | | 11 |
| C. | The Securities and Exchange Commission | | | 13 |
| D. | The Department of Justice | | | 13 |
| E. | State Law | | | 14 |
| F. | Social and Economic Forces | | | 15 |
| G. | The Efficient Capital Markets Hypothesis | | | 16 |
| H. | Looking Ahead | | | 17 |
| **Chapter 2. Section 10(b) of the Exchange Act and Rule 10b-5** | | | | **19** |
| A. | The Requirement of Manipulation or Deception | | | 23 |
| | *1.* | *Material Misstatements or Omissions in General* | | 24 |
| | | a. | "Mere" Breaches of Fiduciary Duty | 24 |
| | | | Santa Fe Industries, Inc. v. Green | 24 |
| | | | Notes and Questions | 30 |
| | | b. | Corporate Mismanagement and Lost State Remedies | 32 |
| | | | Healey v. Catalyst Recovery of Pennsylvania, Inc. | 32 |
| | | | Notes and Questions | 39 |
| | | | Problems 2-1 and 2-2 | 42 |
| | | c. | Secret Intention Not to Perform a Contract | 43 |
| | | | Wharf (Holdings) Ltd. v. United International Holdings, Inc. | 43 |

Notes and Questions ..... 46
2. *Material Omissions in Particular* ..... 47
a. The General Rule—Silence Is Not Deceptive Absent a Duty to Speak ..... 47
Gallagher v. Abbott Laboratories ..... 47
Notes and Questions ..... 51
b. The Duty to Disclose ..... 52
i. Line-Item and Real Time Disclosure Requirements ..... 52
Proposed Rule: Additional Form 8-K Disclosure Requirements and Acceleration of Filing Date ..... 54
Problem 2-3 ..... 55
ii. A Brief Word About Regulation FD ..... 56
iii. The Duty to Update ..... 57
iv. The Duty to Correct ..... 58
v. Fiduciary Relationships and Other Duties at Common Law ..... 60
vi. The Relation Between the Duty to Disclose and Materiality ..... 61
Problems 2-4, 2-5, 2-6 ..... 62
B. The Materiality Requirement ..... 64
1. *Materiality Defined* ..... 64
Notes and Questions ..... 65
Problems 2-7 and 2-8 ..... 66
2. *The Materiality of Soft Information* ..... 67
Basic Inc. v. Levinson ..... 67
Notes and Questions ..... 73
Problem 2-9 ..... 73
3. *Forward-Looking Statements* ..... 74
a. Rules 175 and 3b-6 ..... 74
b. The Bespeaks Caution Doctrine ..... 75
In re Donald J. Trump Casino Securities Litigation ..... 75
Notes and Questions ..... 78
c. The Statutory Safe Harbor for Forward-Looking Statements ..... 79
Harris v. Ivax Corporation ..... 80
Notes and Questions ..... 84
Problems 2-10 and 2-11 ..... 85
C. The "In Connection With" Requirement ..... 86
Notes and Questions ..... 87
Problem 2-12 ..... 87
Chemical Bank v. Arthur Andersen & Co. ..... 88
Notes and Questions ..... 94
SEC v. Zandford ..... 95
Notes and Questions ..... 100
Problem 2-13 ..... 101
D. The Scienter Requirement ..... 102
1. *The Substantive Standard* ..... 102

Ernst & Ernst v. Hochfelder ..... 102
Notes and Questions ..... 109
Problem 2-14 ..... 113
2. *Requirements for Pleading Scienter* ..... 113
Florida State Board of Administration v. Green Tree Financial Corporation ..... 114
Notes and Questions ..... 128
Problem 2-15 ..... 132
E. The Purchaser-Seller Requirement ..... 133
Blue Chip Stamps v. Manor Drug Stores ..... 133
Notes and Questions ..... 141
Cowin v. Bresler ..... 142
Notes and Questions ..... 144
Problems 2-16 and 2-17 ..... 146
F. Causation ..... 147
1. *The Reliance Requirement* ..... 147
a. The Affiliated Ute Presumption ..... 147
Notes and Questions ..... 148
Binder v. Gillespie ..... 148
Notes and Questions ..... 152
Problem 2-18 ..... 153
b. The "Fraud-on-the-Market" Presumption ..... 153
Basic Inc. v. Levinson ..... 153
Notes and Questions ..... 159
Problem 2-19 ..... 161
Panzirer v. Wolf ..... 161
Notes and Questions ..... 164
Problem 2-20 ..... 164
c. The "Fraud-Created-the-Market" Presumption ..... 164
Shores v. Sklar ..... 164
Notes and Questions ..... 170
Problem 2-21 ..... 171
d. The Justifiableness of the Reliance ..... 172
Zobrist v. Coal-X, Inc. ..... 172
Notes and Questions ..... 179
Problem 2-22 ..... 181
2. *The Loss Causation Requirement* ..... 181
AUSA Life Insurance Co. v. Ernst and Young ..... 182
Notes and Questions ..... 192
Problem 2-23 ..... 193
G. Damages ..... 193
1. *The Measurement of Damages* ..... 193
a. In General ..... 194
Rowe v. Maremont Corporation ..... 194
Notes and Questions ..... 201
Problem 2-24 ..... 202
b. Damages in the Class Action Context ..... 202
2. *Proportionate Liability* ..... 204
Problem 2-25 ..... 205
3. *Who Pays for Recoveries?* ..... 205

Notes and Questions ... 206
H. Primary and Secondary Liability ... 206
1. *Aiding and Abetting Liability* ... 207
Central Bank, N.A. v. First Interstate Bank, N.A. ... 207
Notes and Questions ... 219
2. *Primary Liability* ... 220
Wright v. Ernst & Young LLP ... 220
Notes and Questions ... 224
Problem 2-26 ... 225
3. *Controlling Person Liability* ... 226
Arthur Children's Trust v. Keim ... 227
Notes and Questions ... 233
Problems 2-27 and 2-28 ... 234
4. *Respondeat Superior Liability* ... 235
Notes and Questions ... 236
Problem 2-29 ... 236
I. Statute of Limitations ... 236
Lampf, Pleva, Lipkind, Prupis & Petigrow v. Gilbertson ... 237
Notes and Questions ... 243
Sterlin v. Biomune Systems, Inc. ... 244
Notes and Questions ... 252
Problem 2-30 ... 253
J. The Overlap Between Rule 10b-5 and the Express Actions for Material Misstatements and Omissions ... 254
Herman & MacLean v. Huddleston ... 255
Notes and Questions ... 258

**Chapter 3: Liability Under the Securities Act for Material Misstatements, Omissions, and Fraudulent Conduct ... 260**
A. Sections 11 and 12(a)(2): Express Private Actions for Material Misstatements and Omissions ... 260
1. *Section 11* ... 261
a. Standing to Sue ... 263
Lee v. Ernst & Young, LLP ... 263
Notes and Questions ... 268
Problem 3-1 ... 269
b. The Due Diligence Defenses ... 269
Escott v. Barchris Construction Corporation ... 270
Notes and Questions ... 282
Problem 3-2 ... 286
c. Damages and Negative Causation ... 286
Akerman v. Oryx Communications, Inc. ... 287
Notes and Questions ... 290
2. *Section 12(a)(2)* ... 291
a. "By Means of a Prospectus or Oral Communication" ... 292
Gustafson v. Alloyd Corporation ... 292
Notes and Questions ... 300
Problem 3-3 ... 302
b. Who Is a Seller? ... 303

Pinter v. Dahl ........ 303
Notes and Questions ........ 308
Problem 3-4 ........ 311
c. The Reasonable Care Defense ........ 311
Notes and Questions ........ 313
Problem 3-5 ........ 313
d. Damages and Negative Causation ........ 314
Notes and Questions ........ 314
Problem 3-6 ........ 315
*3. Additional Shared Features of Sections 11 and 12(a)(2).* 315
a. Materiality ........ 315
b. Statute of Limitations ........ 316
c. Controlling Person Liability ........ 316
d. Pleading Standards ........ 316
e. Concurrent State and Federal Jurisdiction ........ 317
Problem 3-7 ........ 318
B. Section 17(a): Fraud in the Offer or Sale of Securities ........ 320
*1. In General* ........ 320
Aaron v. SEC ........ 320
Notes and Questions ........ 321
*2. The (Non)Existence of An Implied Private Action* ........ 322
Maldonado v. Dominguez ........ 323
Notes and Questions ........ 324

**Chapter 4. Proxy Fraud—Section 14(a) of the Exchange Act and Rule 14a-9** ........ **326**
A. Judicial Recognition of the Implied Private Action ........ 328
J.I. Case Company v. Borak ........ 328
Notes and Questions ........ 331
B. The Materiality Requirement ........ 332
Notes and Questions ........ 334
C. The State of Mind Requirement ........ 334
Notes and Questions ........ 337
D. The Causation Requirement ........ 338
*1. The Basic Parameters* ........ 338
Mills v. Electric Auto-Lite Company ........ 338
Notes and Questions ........ 344
*2. When Management Controls Sufficient Shares to Approve the Transaction; Lost State Remedies.* . 345
Virginia Bankshares, Inc. v. Sandberg ........ 346
Notes and Questions ........ 356
Problem 4-1 ........ 357
Wilson v. Great American Industries, Inc. ........ 358
Notes and Questions ........ 361
Problem 4-2 ........ 362

**Chapter 5. Tender Offer Fraud—Section 14(e) of the Exchange Act** ........ **363**
A. An Overview of Tender Offers and the Williams Act ........ 363
*1. Tender Offers in General* ........ 363

2. *The Williams Act* .... 365
a. Section 13(d) .... 365
b. Section 14(d) .... 366
c. Section 14(f) .... 366
d. Section 13(e) .... 367
e. Section 14(e) .... 367
f. Enforcement .... 367
3. *The Definition of a Tender Offer* .... 367
Notes and Questions .... 368
B. Litigation Under Section 14(e) .... 369
1. *The Necessity of Misrepresentation or Nondisclosure* .... 370
Schreiber v. Burlington Northern, Inc. .... 371
Notes and Questions .... 376
Problem 5-1 .... 378
2. *Standing to Sue* .... 378
Piper v. Chris-Craft Industries, Inc. .... 378
Notes and Questions .... 381
Problem 5-2 .... 382
3. *(Further) Comparisons Between Section 14(e) and Rule 10b-5* .... 382
Wardrop v. Amway Asia Pacific Ltd. .... 382
Notes and Questions .... 387
Problems 5-3 and 5-4 .... 390
4. *The SEC's Rulemaking Authority* .... 391
C. The Critical Role of State Law in Tender Offer Litigation .... 391

**Chapter 6. Securities Class Actions** .... **395**
A. The Private Securities Litigation Reform Act of 1995 .... 395
1. *Selection of Lead Plaintiff and Class Counsel* .... 398
a. Minimum Standards for Lead Plaintiffs .... 398
b. Ending the Race to the Courthouse Steps .... 399
c. Presumption in Favor of the Largest Investor as Lead Plaintiff .... 400
d. Financial Incentives for Lead Plaintiffs .... 400
e. Attorney Conflicts of Interest .... 401
f. Auction of the Class Counsel's Role .... 401
2. *Mandatory Discovery Stays* .... 402
3. *Disclosure of Proposed Settlement and Attorneys' Fees* .... 403
4. *Mandatory Sanctions for Rule 11 Violations* .... 404
Gurary v. Nu-Tech Bio-Med, Inc. .... 405
Notes and Questions .... 416
5. *Aftermath of the PSLRA* .... 416
Notes and Questions .... 418
B. The Securities Litigation Uniform Standards Act of 1998 .... 419
Lazar v. Gregerson .... 421
Notes and Questions .... 425
C. Empirical Data on Class Actions .... 427
1. *Who Gets Sued?* .... 428
2. *How Many Lawsuits are Filed?* .... 428

3. *How Many of the Lawsuits Survive Motions to Dismiss?* ..... 430
4. *Which Pleading Standard are Courts Imposing With Respect to Scienter?* ..... 430
5. *How Long Does a Securities Class Action Take to Resolve?* ..... 432
6. *What Types of Allegations are Most Common in Securities Class Actions?* ..... 432
7. *How Much Does the Typical Lawsuit Settle For and Why?* ..... 433
8. *Who are the Lawyers?* ..... 434
9. *How Much Fraud is Out There?* ..... 435
Notes and Questions ..... 436

D. Shifting Perceptions of the Balance of Power Between Plaintiffs and Defendants ..... 437
1. *On Balance, Are Securities Class Actions Meritorious?* ..... 437
2. *Securities Class Action Litigation After Enron and WorldCom* ..... 439
Notes and Questions ..... 441

E. Problems ..... 442

**Chapter 7. Insider Trading** ..... **448**

A. Initial Efforts to Combat and Curtail Insider Trading ..... 449
1. *Insider Trading Under the Common Law* ..... 449
2. *A Brief Look at Section 16(b)* ..... 452
3. *Insider Trading as a Violation of Rule 10b-5* ..... 454
SEC v. Texas Gulf Sulphur Co. ..... 455
Notes and Questions ..... 464

B. The Supreme Court Speaks on Insider Trading and Rule 10b-5. ..... 468
1. *The Classical Theory of Insider Trading* ..... 468
Chiarella v. United States ..... 468
Notes and Questions ..... 475
Problems 7-1 and 7-2 ..... 477
2. *Tippees and Temporary Insiders* ..... 478
Dirks v. SEC ..... 478
Notes and Questions ..... 487
3. *The Misappropriation Theory* ..... 489
United States v. O'Hagan ..... 490
Notes and Questions ..... 501
Problems 7-3 and 7-4 ..... 503

C. Rule 14e-3—Insider Trading in the Context of Tender Offers ..... 506
United States v. O'Hagan ..... 506
Notes and Questions ..... 513
Problems 7-5, 7-6, and 7-7 ..... 515

D. Congress Speaks on Insider Trading—ITSA, ITSFEA, and Subsequent Legislation ..... 516
Problem 7-8 ..... 522

E. Litigating Insider Trading Cases—The Problem of Circumstantial Evidence ..... 523
SEC v. Moran ..... 524

Notes and Questions ..... 546
F. Policy Rationales for Federal Regulation of Insider Trading and the Search for a Definition ..... 549
1. *The Policy Debate Over the Harms and Benefits of Insider Trading* ..... 550
a. Insider Trading and its Effects on Corporate Management ..... 550
Henry G. Manne, In Defense of Insider Trading ..... 550
b. The Effects of Insider Trading on Stock Market Price Efficiency ..... 554
c. Identifying the "Victims" of Insider Trading ..... 556
William K.S. Wang, Stock Market Insider Trading: Victims, Violators and Remedies—Including an Analogy to Fraud in the Sale of a Used Car with a Generic Defect ..... 557
d. Investor Confidence in Securities Markets ..... 563
e. Fairness and Morality ..... 564
f. Protecting Private Property ..... 565
Stephen M. Bainbridge, Insider Trading Regulation, The Path Dependent Choice Between Property Rights and Securities Fraud ..... 565
2. *The Debate Over a Statutory Definition of Insider Trading* ..... 568
Legislative History: Insider Trading Sanction Act of 1984 ..... 568
Legislative History: Insider Trading and Securities Fraud Enforcement Act ..... 569
Richard W. Painter, Kimberly D. Krawiec, and Cynthia A. Williams, Don't Ask, Just Tell: Insider Trading After *United States v. O'Hagan* ..... 570
Proposal for a Directive of the European Parliament and of the Council On Insider Dealing and Market Manipulation, May 30, 2001 ..... 576

**Chapter 8. Market Manipulation** ..... **578**
A. Practices that Create the Appearance of Active Trading ..... 579
SEC v. U.S. Environmental, Inc. ..... 580
Notes and Questions ..... 583
Problem 8-1 ..... 584
B. Actual Trading Conducted for a Manipulative Purpose ..... 585
United States v. Mulheren ..... 585
Notes and Questions ..... 593
Problem 8-2 ..... 599
C. Misleading Recommendations and Material Misstatements Designed to Affect Market Prices ..... 599

1. *Scalping and "Pump and Dumps"* ..... 599
SEC v. Colt ..... 601
Notes and Questions ..... 610
2. *Conflicts of Interest on Wall Street* ..... 613
Problems 8-3 and 8-4 ..... 616

**Chapter 9. SEC Enforcement of the Federal Securities Laws** ..... **617**
A. The SEC's Division of Enforcement ..... 618
B. SEC Investigations ..... 621
Richard M. Phillips, Glenn R. Reichardt, Michael J. Missal, and Robyn J. Lipton, SEC Investigations: The Heart of SEC Enforcement Practice ..... 621
1. *The Investigatory Process* ..... 623
Ralph C. Ferrara and Philip S. Khinda, SEC Enforcement Proceedings: Strategic Considerations for When the Agency Comes Calling ..... 625
Notes and Questions ..... 631
SEC v. Jerry T. O'Brien, Inc. ..... 635
Notes and Questions ..... 641
2. *Concluding an SEC Investigation* ..... 641
William R. McLucas, J. Lynn Taylor, and Susan A. Mathews, A Practitioner's Guide to the SEC's Investigative and Enforcement Process ..... 642
Notes and Questions ..... 644
Report of Investigation Pursuant to Section 21(a) of the Securities Exchange Act of 1934 and Commission Statement on the Relationship of Cooperation to Agency Enforcement Decisions ..... 645
Notes and Questions ..... 648
3. *Consent Decrees and Settlements with the SEC* ..... 651
Report of the Task Force on SEC Settlements, Prepared by the Subcommittee on Civil Litigation and SEC Enforcement Matters of the Federal Regulation of Securities Committee of the ABA's Section on Business Law ..... 652
Notes and Questions ..... 654
C. Civil Remedies for Violations of the Securities Laws ..... 657
1. *Judicial Remedies* ..... 662
SEC v. First City Financial Corp. ..... 662
SEC v. Patel ..... 670
Notes and Questions ..... 674
2. *Administrative Remedies* ..... 680
Rizek v. SEC ..... 680
In the Matter of Jeffry L. Feldman ..... 685
Notes and Questions ..... 689
3. *Collateral Consequences of SEC Sanctions* ..... 693
Andrew M. Smith, SEC Cease-and-Desist Orders ..... 694
Notes and Questions ..... 697

Problem 9-1 ... 698
D. Litigating with the SEC ... 699
1. *The Litigation Process* ... 699
a. SEC Administrative Proceedings ... 699
b. Federal Court Proceedings ... 700
2. *Legal Issues in SEC Litigation* ... 702
a. Burden of Proof ... 702
Steadman v. SEC ... 702
Notes and Questions ... 706
b. Statutes of Limitations ... 708
Johnson v. SEC ... 709
Notes and Questions ... 715
c. Collateral Estoppel ... 716
Parklane Hosiery Co. v. Shore ... 716
Notes and Questions ... 721
E. SROs as Enforcers of the Federal Securities Laws ... 723
1. *Self-Regulation and SEC Oversight* ... 723
Legislative History: Securities Acts Amendments of 1975 ... 723
Notes and Questions ... 733
2. *SRO Investigations and Disciplinary Proceedings* ... 734
Money Penalties: Securities and Futures Regulators Collect Many Fines But Need to Better Use Industry Wide Data ... 734
United States v. Solomon ... 736
Notes and Questions ... 742
F. Parallel Proceedings ... 744
1. *Multiple Investigations of the Same Conduct or Activities* ... 744
SEC v. Dresser Industries, Inc. ... 744
Notes and Questions ... 754
2. *Multiple State, Federal, and SRO Enforcement Proceedings Against Securities Analysts and Investment Banks* ... 755
Notes and Questions ... 758
3. *Multiple Prosecutions and Sanctions and the Double Jeopardy Clause* ... 760
SEC v. Palmisano ... 761
Notes and Questions ... 766

**Chapter 10. Enforcement Issues Involving Attorneys and Accountants** ... **768**
A. SEC Discipline of Professionals Under Rule 102(e) ... 769
Notes and Questions ... 771
B. Ethical and Proper Conduct for Securities Attorneys ... 773
1. *The Legal Landscape Before the Sarbanes-Oxley Act* ... 773
In re Carter & Johnson ... 776
Notes and Questions ... 795
2. *The Enron Scandal and Questions of Professional Responsibility* ... 798

Susan P. Koniak, United States Senate Committee on the Judiciary; Accountability Issues: Lessons Learned From Enron's Fall . . . 798
Notes and Questions . . . 803
3. *Section 307 of the Sarbanes-Oxley Act and SEC Rules Thereunder* . . . 805
Standards of Professional Conduct for Attorneys Appearing & Practicing Before the Commission in the Representation of an Issuer . . . 806
Notes and Questions . . . 815
Problem 10-1 . . . 817
C. The Regulation of Accountants Under the Sarbanes-Oxley Act . 819
Legislative History: Report of the Committee on Banking, Housing, and Urban Affairs . . . 820
Notes and Questions . . . 830

**Chapter 11. Criminal Enforcement** . . . 833
A. The Securities Act and the Exchange Act . . . 834
1. *The Requirement that the Defendant Act "Willfully"* . . . 835
United States v. Peltz . . . 836
Notes and Questions . . . 839
Problem 11-1 . . . 842
2. *The Violations that Give Rise to Criminal Liability* . . . 842
Notes and Questions . . . 843
Problem 11-2 . . . 845
B. The Sarbanes-Oxley Act . . . 846
1. *The New Crime of Securities Fraud* . . . 846
Notes and Questions . . . 847
Problems 11-3, 11-4, and 11-5 . . . 847
2. *The New Crime of Failing to Certify Financial Reports* . 848
Notes and Questions . . . 848
C. The Mail and Wire Fraud Statutes . . . 849
Carpenter v. United States . . . 851
Notes and Questions . . . 854
Neder v. United States . . . 855
Notes and Questions . . . 859
Problems 11-5 and 11-6 . . . 860
D. Racketeer Influenced and Corrupt Organizations Act . . . 861
1. *Racketeering Activity* . . . 862
Notes and Questions . . . 862
2. *Pattern* . . . 864
H.J. Inc. v. Northwestern Bell Telephone Co. . . . 864
Notes and Questions . . . 872
3. *The Enterprise* . . . 873
Notes and Questions . . . 873
4. *Conducting or Participating in the Conduct of the Enterprise* . . . 874
Reves v. Ernst & Young . . . 874
Notes and Questions . . . 884
Problems 11-7 and 11-8 . . . 886

5. *Private RICO Securities Actions* ..... 887

**Chapter 12. International Securities Fraud** ..... 888

A. The Principles of Extraterritorial Jurisdiction Developed By Courts ..... 889
1. *Jurisdiction Based Upon Domestic Effects* ..... 890
Schoenbaum v. Firstbrook ..... 890
Notes and Questions ..... 894
2. *Jurisdiction Based Upon Domestic Conduct* ..... 897
Notes and Questions ..... 898
Kauthar SDN BHD v. Sternberg ..... 899
Notes and Questions ..... 904
3. *The Restatement (Third) of Foreign Relations Law* ..... 907
Europe and Overseas Commodity Traders, S.A. v. Banque Paribas London ..... 907
Notes and Questions ..... 913
Problems 12-1, 12-2, and 12-3 ..... 913
B. Choice of Law and Choice of Forum Clauses ..... 914
Lipcon v. Underwriters at Lloyd's, London ..... 915
Notes and Questions ..... 923
Problems 12-4 and 12-5 ..... 924
C. The Forum Non Conveniens Doctrine ..... 924
Alfadda v. Fenn ..... 925
Notes and Questions ..... 931
Problem 12-6 ..... 934
D. International Securities Fraud and the SEC ..... 934
Notes and Questions ..... 936

**Chapter 13. Securities Arbitration** ..... 937

A. The Relationship Between the Federal Arbitration Act and the Federal Securities Laws ..... 938
Shearson/American Express, Inc. v. McMahon ..... 940
Notes and Questions ..... 951
B. The Process of Securities Arbitration ..... 952
Securities Industry Conference on Arbitration, Arbitration Procedures ..... 953
Notes and Questions ..... 960
C. The Remaining Judicial Role in Arbitration ..... 965
1. *Arbitrability* ..... 965
First Options of Chicago, Inc. v. Kaplan ..... 965
Notes and Questions ..... 969
Problem 13-1 ..... 971
2. *Judicial Review* ..... 971
Notes and Questions ..... 972
Problem 13-2 ..... 972
D. Securities Arbitration in Perspective ..... 973

INDEX ..... 976

# Table of Cases

The principal cases are in bold type. Cases cited or discussed in the text are roman type. References are to pages. Cases cited in principal cases and within other quoted materials are not included.


**Aaron v. SEC,** 6, 109, 110, **320**, 674
Abell v. Potomac Ins. Co., 170-71
**Akerman v. Oryx Communications, Inc., 287**, 314
Acme Propane, Inc. v. Tenexco, Inc., 180, 181
Adams v. Standard Knitting Mills, Inc., 336
Advanced Res. Int'l, Inc. v. Tri-Star Petroleum Co., 145
Advanta Corp. Sec. Litig., In re, 431
Affiliated Ute Citizens v. United States, 11, 20, 147, 148, 152, 164, 171, 179, 194, 389
Agency Holding Corp. v. Malley-Duff & Assocs., Inc., 886
Aldridge v. A.T. Cross Corp., 235
**Alfadda v. Fenn, 925**
Anderson v. First Sec. Corp., 402
Andreo v. Friedlander, Gaines, Cohen, Rosenthal & Rosenberg, 885
Anixter v. Home-Stake Prod. Co., 224
Apple Computer Sec. Litig., In re, 159
**Arthur Children's Trust v. Keim, 227**
Ash v. LFE Corp., 336
Associated Randall Bank v. Griffin, Kubik, Stephens & Thompson, 312
AT & T Techs., Inc. v. Communications Workers, 970
Atlantic Fin. Mgmt., Inc., In re, 236
**AUSA Life Insurance Co. v. Ernst and Young, 182**
Austin Mun. Sec. v. Nat'l Ass'n of Sec. Dealers, 743

Baan Co. Sec. Litig., 914
Backman v. Polaroid Corp., 58, 519
Bald Eagle Area School Dist. v. Keystone Fin., 887
Banca Cremi, S.A. v. Alex Brown & Sons, Inc., 180
Barbara v. NYSE, 743
Barnes v. Osofsky, 267-68
Barth v. Fid. & Columbia Trust Co., 449
**Basic Inc. v. Levinson,** 51, 60, 65, **67**, 85, 112, **153**, 164, 171, 179, 333, 388, 389, 418, 466, 594, 860, 894
Bastian v. Petren Res. Corp., 181
Bateman, Eichler, Hill, Richards, Inc. v. Berner, 180-81
Bawden v. Taylor, 449
Bensusn Rest. Corp. v. King, 897
Bersch v. Drexel Firestone, Inc., 888, 895-96, 899, 906, 907, 913
Berger v. Bishop Inv. Corp., 258
Berger v. Compaq Computer Corp., 399
Berry v. Valence Tech., Inc., 252, 254
**Binder v. Gillespie, 148,** 160
Blackie v. Barrack, 164
**Blue Chip Stamps v. Manor Drug Stores,** 12, 20, 60, 87, **133,** 145, 160, 310, 419
Blum v. Yaretsky, 743
Brentwood v. Tenn. Secondary School, 743, 744
Brophy v. Cities Serv. Co., 451
Brown v. Hutton Group, 219, 220
Browning-Ferris Indus., Shareholder Litig., In re, 334
Brumbaugh v. Princeton Partners, 252
Bruschi v. Brown, 192
Bryan v. United States, 835
Bryant v. Avado Brands, Inc., 431
Bryant v. Dupree, 129
Burlington Coat Factory Sec. Litig., In re, 51, 65

Cady, Roberts & Co., In re, 454-55, 516, 569
Capital Real Estate Investors Fund v. Schwartzberg, 336
Carley Capital Group v. Deloitte & Touche, 224
**Carpenter v. United States**, 490, 599, 833, **851**, 859
Carr v. Cigna Sec., Inc. 179
**Carter & Johnson, In re**, 772, **776**, 804, 815
Carter-Wallace, Inc. Sec. Litig., In re, 87
Cashman v. Coopers & Lybrand, 225
Castellano v. Young & Rubicam, Inc., 61
Cavalier Carpets, Inc. v. Caylor, 152
Cedric Kushner Promotions, Ltd. v. King, 874
Cenco Inc. Sec. Litig., In re, 721
Cendant Corp. Sec. Litig., In re, 401, 433
**Central Bank, N.A. v. First Interstate Bank, N.A.,** 12, 206, **207**, 224, 225, 226, 235, 236, 440
Champion Enterprises Inc. Sec. Litig., In re, 84-85, 129
Chang v. Chen, 873
Checkosky v. SEC, 770, 771
Cheff v. Mathes, 392
Chemetron v. Bus. Funds, Inc., 259
**Chemical Bank v. Arthur Andersen & Co.,** 88, 100

**Chiarella v. United States**, 12, 51-52, 60, 236, 467, **468**, 478, 489, 501, 513, 516, 564, 594, 600, 833
Chris-Craft Indus., Inc. v. Piper Aircraft Corp., 148
Citisource, Inc. Sec. Litig, In re, 235
City Inv. Group, In the Matter of, 369
City of Philadelphia v. Fleming Cos., 431
Cleveland v. United States, 860
Coates v. Heartland Wireless Communications, Inc., 129
Cohen v. Ruckelshaus, 334
Collins Sec. Corp. v. SEC, 707
Comdisco Sec. Litig., In re, 401, 402
Consol. Gold Fields PLC v. Minorco, S.A., 896, 913
Convergent Tech. Sec. Litig., In re, 65
Cooper v. Pickett, 59
Copland v. Grumet, 519
Couch v. United States, 773
**Cowin v. Bresler, 142**, 345

D.L. Cromwell Inv., Inc. v. NASD Regulation, Inc., 742
D'Alessio v. NYSE, 743
Datek Sec. Corp. v. NASD, Inc., 743
Davis v. Avco Fin. Serv., Inc., 314
Davy v. SEC, 770
Dawson v. Nat'l Life Ins. Co., 449
Dean Witter Reynolds v. Byrd, 939
Dellastratious v. Williams, 234
Deutsche Telekom AG Sec. Litig., In re, 309
Diamond v. Oreamuno, 451-52
Diceon Electronics, Inc. v. Calvary Partners, 367
Dinsmore v. Squadron, Ellenoff, Plesent, Sheinfeld & Sorkin, 220
**Dirks v. SEC**, 52, **478**, 501, 516
DiRenzo v. Philip Serv. Corp., 933
DiRussa v. Dean Witter Reynolds, Inc., 972
Diversified Indus., Inc. v. Meredith, 649
Donohoe v. Consol. Operating & Prod. Corp., 233, 234
Dorchester Investors v. Peak Int'l Ltd., 286
Dragon Capital Partners L.P. v. Merrill Lynch Capital Servs., Inc., 925
Drasner v. Thomson McKinnon Sec., Inc., 844
Drobbin v. Nicolet Instrument Corp., 367

E. On AG, In the Matter of, 894-95
EP Medsystems, Inc. v. Echocath, Inc., 78
Eckstein v. Balcor Film Investors, 171
Edelman v. Salomon, 344
Edgington v. R.G. Dickerson & Co, 164
Eisenstadt v. Centel Corp., 59, 60
Elkind v. Liggett & Myers, Inc., 59
Elliot Assocs., L.P. v. Hayes, 46
Elliot Assocs., L.P. v. Covance, Inc., 42
Eng'g Animation Sec. Litig., In re, 130
**Ernst & Ernst v. Hochfelder**, 12, 101, **102**, 128, 236, 324, 549, 578, 579
**Escott v. Barchris Construction Corp., 270**
**Europe and Overseas Commodity Traders, S.A. v. Banque Paribus London,** 906, **907**
Evans v. Newton, 743

Faberge, In re, 467
Federal Corp., In re, 596
**Feldman, Jeffry L., In the Matter of, 685,** 797
Fidelity Funding of Calif., Inc. v. Reinhold, 885
Fidelity/Micron Sec. Litig., In re, 235
First Equity Corp. v. Standard & Poor's Corp., 112
**First Options of Chicago, Inc. v. Kaplan, 965**
First Pacific Bancorp, Inc. v. Bro, 863
Fitzgerald v. Texaco, 925
Fleet Credit Corp. v. Sion, 872
Flir Sys., Inc. Sec. Litig., In re, 402
Fla. Commercial Banks v. Culverhouse, 381-82
**Florida State Board of Administration v. Green Tree Financial Corp., 114,** 431
Foman v. Davis, 129
Freedman v. Louisiana Pacific Corp., 56
Friedlob v. Trustees of Alpine Mut. Fund Trust, 864
Fridrich v. Bradford, 466
Fryar v. Abell, 171

**Gallagher v. Abbott Laboratories, 47**, 55, 58, 59
Gaming Lottery Sec. Litig., In re, 913
Ganino v. Citizens Util. Co., 233
Garcia v. Cardova, 73
Gen. Elec. Co. v. Cathcart, 345
George Watts & Son, Inc. v. Tiffany & Co., 972
Gerstle v. Gamble-Skogmo, Inc., 335-36, 337
Glassman v. Computervision Corp., 66
Glenfed, Inc. Sec. Litig., In re, 113
Goldberg v. Meridor, 32, 40, 41, 425
Goldsmith, John D., NYSE Hearing Panel, 742
Goodwin v. Agassiz, 450, 451
Greebel v. FTP Software, Inc., 111, 128, 431
Greenberg v. Bear Stearns & Co., 972
Griffin v. Paine Webber, 309
Grubb v. FDIC, 148
Grunenthal GmbH v. Hotz, 907
Guidry v. Bank of LaPlace, 874
Gulf Oil Corp. v. Gilbert, 924
**Gurary v. Nu-Tech Bio-Med, Inc., 405**
Gurary v. Winehouse, 159
Gurfein v. Sovereign Group, 79
**Gustafson v. Alloyd Corp.**, 263, **292**, 310, 324-25

**H.J. Inc. v. Northwestern Bell Telephone Co., 864**
Hall v. Geiger-Jones Co., 2
Hallwood Realty Partners, LP v. Gotham Partners, LP, 367
Hanson Trust PLC v. SMC Corp., 368

Harkavy v. Apparel Indus., Inc., 73
**Harris v. Ivax Corp., 80**
Harris v. Ivax Corp. (11th Cir. 2000), 84
Harsco Corp. v. Segui, 179
Hartford Fire Ins. Co. v. Calif., 933-34
**Healey v. Catalyst Recovery of Pennsylvania, Inc., 32**, 425
Helwig v. Vencor, Inc., 431
**Herman & MacLean v. Huddleston**, 6, 19, 20, 21, 23, 110, 111, **255**, 269, 322, 707
Herskowitz v. Nutri/System, Inc., 336
Hertzberg v. Dignity Partners, Inc., 268
Heyman v. Heyman, 145
Hollinger v. Titan Capital Corp., 110, 234, 235
Holmes v. Secs. Investor Protection Corp., 863, 887
Horowitz v. Pownall, 390
Howe v. Goldcorp Invs., Ltd., 925
Howard v. Everex Sys., Inc., 130, 233
Howing Co. v. Nationwide Corp., 41, 362
Howsam v. Dean Witter Reynolds, Inc., 970
Hudson v. United States, 706, 761, 766

IG Holdings, Inc., In the Matter of, 369
IIT v. Cornfeld, 905-06
IIT v. Vencap, Ltd., 896, 905
Integrated Res. Real Estate Ltd., P'ships Sec. Litig., In re, 864
Int'l Brotherhood of Teamsters v. Daniel, 322
Investors Mgmt. Co., In re, 455
Iragorri v. United Techs. Corp., 933
Isquith v. Caremark Int'l, Inc., 43, 145
Itoba, Ltd. v. Lep Group PLC, 906

Jaguar Cars, Inc. v. Royal Oaks Motor Car Co., 887
James v. Gerber Prods. Co., 145
Janigan v. Taylor, 202
**J.I. Case Co. v. Borak**, 8,11, 20, 326, **328**, 356
John Hancock Life Ins. Co. v. Wilson, 971
**Johnson v. SEC**, 708, **709**, 766
Jones v. SEC, 766
Jordan v. Duff & Phelps, 61, 64

KPMG, LLP v. SEC, 691
KPMG Peat Marwick LLP, In the Matter of, 690, 691
Kahn v. Lynden, 389
Kaplan v. Rose, 159
Kardon v. Nat'l Gypsum Co., 19, 454
Kaufman v. Lawrence, 378
**Kauthar SDN BHD v. Sternberg, 899**
Kearney v. Prudential-Bache Sec., Inc., 94
Keating, Muething & Klekamp, In re, 770
Kehr Packages, Inc. v. Fidelcor, Inc., 872
Kemmerer v. Weaver, 226
Kern, George C., In re, 693, 797
Kersh v. Gen. Council of Assemblies of God, 234
Ketchum v. Green, 101
Kiernan v. Homeland Inc., 110
Kirkwood v. Taylor, 268-69
Kittilson v. Ford, 112
Kline v. First W. Gov't Sec., Inc., 179
Koppel v. 4987 Corp., 334
Koster v. Lumbermens Mut. Cas. Co., 924
Krauth v. Executive Telecard, Ltd., 344
Kronfeld v. First Jersey Nat'l Bank, 219

LHLC Corp. v. Cluett, Peabody & Co., 40
**Lampf, Pleva, Lipkind, Prupis & Petigrow v. Gilbertson**, 236, **237**, 362, 441, 708-09
Lander v. Hartford Life & Annuity Ins. Co., 427
Laventhall v. Gen. Dynamics Corp., 148, 517
**Lazar v. Gregerson, 420, 421**
Leasco Data Processing Equip. Corp. v. Maxwell, 897-98, 899, 907
Lebed, Jonathan G., In the Matter of, 612-13
Lebron v. Nat'l R.R. Passenger Corp., 743-44, 830, 831
**Lee v. Ernst & Young, 263**
Leitch GoldMines, Ltd. v. Texas Gulf Sulphur Co., 464
Lernout & Hauspie Sec. Litig., In re, 932
Lewis v. McGraw, 389
Lincoln Sav. & Loan Ass'n v. Wall, 798
**Lipcon v. Underwriters at Lloyd's, London, 915**
List v. Fashion Park, Inc., 147
Lugar v. Edmondson Oil Co., 743

MCG, Inc. v. Great W. Energy Corp., 898, 899
Magma Power Co. v. Dow Chem. Co., 453
Maher v. Durango Metals, Inc., 233
**Maldonado v. Dominguez, 323**
Malone v. Microdyne Corp., 66
Marbury Mgmt. v. Kohn, 193
Marine Bank v. Weaver, 419
Markowski v. SEC, 597, 598-99
Marx v. Computer Sciences Corp., 74
Mastrobuono v. Shearson Lehman Hutton, Inc., 960
Mayer v. Mylod, 41
McCormick v. Fund Am. Cos., 61, 475
McCulloch v. Suter, 874
McGann v. Ernst & Young, 87
McLean v. Alexander, 205
McMahan & Co. v. Wherehouse Entertainment, Inc., 286-87, 291
McNally v. United States, 854
Med. Imaging Centers of Am., Inc. v. Lichtenstein, 128
Menowitz v. Brown, 252
Merrill Lynch, Pierce, Fenner & Smith, In the Matter of, 632
Merrill Lynch, Pierce, Fenner & Smith, Inc. v. Moore, 939
Miller Indus. Inc. Sec. Litig., In re, 233
**Mills v. Electric Auto-Lite Co.**, 11, **338**, 356
Minzer v. Keegan, 357
Mistretta v. United States, 834

MobileMedia Sec. Litig., In re, 59
Montes v. Shearson Lehman Bros., 971, 973
Moran v. Household Int'l, Inc., 393
Moss v. Morgan Stanley, Inc., 466
Murray v. British Broad. Corp., 934
Musick, Peeler & Garrett v. Employers Ins., 20, 204

Napoli v. United States, 885
Nathanson v. Zonagen, Inc., 66, 110, 431
Nat'l Ass'n of Sec. Dealers, Inc., In re, 733
**Neder v. United States, 855**
Neibel v. Trans World Assurance Co., 886
Nobles v. First Carolina Communications, Inc., 388
Novak v. Kasaks, 129, 431

Occidental Life Ins. Co. v. EEOC, 709
O'Connor & Assocs. v. Dean Witter Reynolds, 517
O'Melveny & Meyers v. FDIC, 220
Oracle Sec. Litig., In re, 401
Oran v. Stafford, 65, 441
Oxford Heath Plan Sec. Litig., In re, 519

Pacific Gateway Exchange, Inc., In re, 402
Painewebber, Inc. v. Elahi, 970
Pandick, Inc. v. Rooney, 863
**Panzirer v. Wolf, 161**
Par Pharm, Inc., Sec. Litig., In re, 863
Paracor Fin., Inc. v. Gen. Elec. Capital Corp., 233
Paramount Communications v. QVC Network, Inc., 393
Paramount Communications v. Time, Inc., 393
**Parklane Hosiery Co. v. Shore,** 697, **716**
Parnes v. Gateway 2000, Inc., 66
Parsons v. Jefferson-Pilot Corp., 344
Pelletier v. Stuart-James Co., 194
Pereira v. United States, 850
Picard Chem. Inc. Profit Sharing Plan v. Perrigo Co., 224
Pinker v. Rouche Holdings, Ltd., 894, 896
**Pinter v. Dahl, 303**
**Piper v. Chris-Craft Indus., Inc., 378**
Piper Aircraft Co. v. Reyno, 924
Plaine v. McCabe, 390
Polaroid Corp. v. Disney, 381, 389-90, 391
Polydoroff v. ICC, 770
Posters N' Things, Ltd. v. United States, 850
Presstek, Inc., In re, 60
Primary Care Investors, Seven, Inc. v. PHP Healthcare Corp., 872
Primavera Familienstiftung v. Askin, 226
Prod. Res. Group L.L.C. v. Stonebridge Partners Equity Fund, LP, 94
Provenz v. Miller, 79
Pryor v. United States Steel Corp., 390

Raab v. Gen. Physics Corp., 59, 63, 66
Randall v. Loftgaarden, 194, 314
Ratzlaf v. United States, 840-41
Raychem Corp. v. Fed. Ins. Co., 206
Raytheon Sec. Litig., In re, 129
Razorfish, Inc. Sec. Litig., In re, 401
Reg'l Props., Inc. v. Fin. & Real Estate Consult. Co., 146
Reliance Sec. Litig., In re, 336, 356-57
Resolution Trust Corp. v. Stone, 872
**Reves v. Ernst & Young, 874**
Revlon v. MacAndrews and Forbes Holdings, Inc., 393
Rexplore Sec. Litig., In re, 873
Richards v. Lloyd's of London, 923
Rissman v. Rissman, 181
**Rizek v. SEC, 680,** 692
Rizek, Al, In re, 698
Robbins v. Kroger Prop., Inc., 193
Robinson v. TCI/US West Communications, Inc., 924-25
Rochez Bros. v. Rhoades, 233-34
Rodriguez de Quijas v. Shearson/Am. Exp., 951, 971
Rondeau v. Mosinee Paper Corp., 365
Ross v. A.H. Robins Co., 170, 258
Rothberg v. Rosenbloom, 490
Rotstein v. Reynolds, 66
**Rowe v. Maremont Corporation, 194**
Rubenstein v. Collins, 78

SG Cowen Sec. Corp. v. U.S. D. Ct. for N. Dist. of Cal., 128
Salit v. Stanley Works, 233, 338
San Leandro Emergency Med. Group v. Philip Morris Cos., 58
Sanders v. John Nuveen & Co., 311, 312, 313
**Santa Fe Industries, Inc. v. Green, 24,** 39, 51, 370, 377, 425, 441, 579, 594
Schaffer v. Timerland Co., 60
Scherk v. Alberto-Culver Co., 938, 939
Schmuck v. United States, 850
**Schoenbaum v. Firstbrook, 890,** 905
Scholastic Corp. Sec. Litig., In re, 131
**Schreiber v. Burlington Northern, Inc., 371,** 382, 388, 392, 579, 594
Schreiber v. Burlington Northern, Inc. (3rd Cir.), 377
SEC v. Adler, 476
SEC v. Banner Fund Int'l, 907, 934
SEC v. Bausch & Lomb, Inc., 60
SEC v. Blinder, Robinson & Co., 676
SEC v. Brigadoon Scotch Distrib. Co., 623
SEC v. Burns, 844
SEC v. C.M. Joiner Leasing Corp., 706
SEC v. Capital Gains Res. Bur., Inc., 600, 674
SEC v. Carter Hawley Hale Stores, 368
SEC v. Chenery Corp., 651
SEC v. Cherif, 490
SEC v. Clark, 100, 490
**SEC v. Colt, 601**
SEC v. Coffey, 226
**SEC v. Dresser Industries, Inc., 744**
SEC v. Elfindepan, 936

SEC v. Falbo, 502
SEC v. Falstaff Brewing Corp., 113
SEC v. Fehn, 219, 798
**SEC v. First City Financial Corp.**, 367, **662**, 664, 675, 676, 678
SEC v. First Jersey Secs. Inc., 225, 226
SEC v. Fisher, 547
SEC v. Freeman, 505
SEC v. Geon Indus., Inc., 523
SEC v. Ginsburg, 675
SEC v. Grossman, 722
SEC v. Gun Soo Oh Park (a.k.a. Tokyo Joe), 600
SEC v. Ingram, 487
**SEC v. Jerry T. O'Brien, Inc., 635**
SEC v. Kasser, 905
SEC v. Lenfest, 547
SEC v. Lorin, 707, 716
SEC v. Maoi, 514
SEC v. Materia, 489
SEC v. Mayhew, 487, 514
SEC v. MacDonald, 66
SEC v. McCaskey, 722
SEC v. Mgmt. Dynamics, Inc., 236
SEC v. Monarch Funding Corp., 722
**SEC v. Moran, 524**, 548, 707
SEC v. Moran II, 548
SEC v. Musella I, 490, 514
SEC v. Musella II, 505, 707
SEC v. Musella III, 549
SEC v. Nat'l Student Mktg. Corp., 775
**SEC v. Palmisano**, 722, **762**
**SEC v. Patel, 670**, 676, 678
SEC v. Posner, 677
SEC v. Pros Int'l, Inc., 675
SEC v. Ralston Purina, 5, 301
SEC v. Rind, 708-09, 715-16
SEC v. Sargent, 515
SEC v. Stevens, 488
SEC v. Stroud, 934
**SEC v. Texas Gulf Sulphur Co.**, 86-87, 88, 94, **455**, 475, 516
SEC v. Texas Gulf Sulphur (S.D.N.Y.), 465
SEC v. Texas Gulf Sulphur II, 465
SEC v. Thorn, 936
SEC v. Truong, 549
**SEC v. U.S. Environmental, Inc.**, 225, **580**
SEC v. Unifund SAL, 675
SEC v. Warde, 549
SEC v. Warren, 676
SEC v. Wheeling Pittsburgh Steel Corp., 624
SEC v. Willis, 549
**SEC v. Zandford, 95**
SEC v. Zandford (4th Cir.), 100
Sec. Indus. Assoc. v. Connolly, 951-92
Sec. Litig. BMC Software, Inc., In re, 130
Semerenko v. Cedant Corp., 78, 87
Seolas v. Bilzerian, 235
7547 Corp. v. Parker & Parsley Dev. Partners, L.P., 145
Shapiro v. Merrill Lynch, 466
Sharp v. Coopers & Lybrand, 152
Shaw v. Digital Equip. Corp., 61, 309, 475
**Shearson/Am. Exp., Inc. v. McMahon, 940**, 952, 972, 973, 975
**Shores v. Sklar, 164**
Silicon Graphics Inc. Sec. Litig., In re, 110, 130, 131, 429, 431
Smith v. Van Gorkom, 426
Software Toolworks, Inc. Securities Litigation, In re, 225, 283-84, 311
Stahl v. Gibraltar Fin. Corp., 345
State Teachers Ret. Bd. v. Fluor Corp., 56, 59, 63
**Steadman v. SEC, 702**
Steckman v. Hart Brewing, Inc., 440
Steinhardt Partners, In re, 649
Stephenson v. Paine Webber, Jackson & Curtis, 181
**Sterlin v. Biomune Systems, Inc., 244**
Sterlin v. Biomune Systems, Inc., (D. Utah, 2000), 253
Stewart v. Harris, 449
Stransky v. Cummins Engine Co., 58, 59
Strong v. Repide, 450
Subpoena Duces Tecum, In re, 649
Sunstrand Corp. v. Sun Chemical Corp., 110
Superintendent of Ins. of N.Y. v. Bankers Life & Cas. Co., 11, 19, 94

TBG, Inc. v. Bendis, 204
T.J. Raney & Sons, Inc. v. Fort Cobb, Oklahoma Irrigation Fuel Auth., 171
TSC Indus., Inc. v. Northway, Inc., 64, 65, 67, 315, 332, 388, 466, 859
Tabas v. Tabas, 872
Tafflin v. Leavitt, 887
Teicher v. SEC, 692-93
Terrell, Kenneth, In the Matter of, 610-11
Time Warner Sec. Litig., In re, 51, 57, 58
Torchmark Corp. v. Bixby, 381
Touche Ross & Co. v. Redington, 332
Touche Ross & Co. v. SEC, 769, 770, 771
Transamerica Mortgage Advisors, Inc. v. Lewis, 145
Treats Int'l Enter., Inc. v. SEC, 624
**Trump Casino Securities Litigation, In re, 75**
Trump Hotels & Casino Resorts, Inc. v. Mirage Resorts, Inc., 145
Tull v. United States, 701-02

United Paperworkers Int'l Union v. Int'l Paper Co., 333-334
United States v. Allen, 885
United States v. Amick, 840
United States v. Arthur Young & Co., 773
United States v. Antar, 886
United States v. Autuori, 859
United States v. Bach, 860
United States v. Benjamin, 802
United States v. Bilzerian, 65-66, 844
United States v. Bingham, 833
United States v. Bledsoe, 873

United States v. Blinder, 863
United States v. Bouyea, 860
United States v. Brown, 584, 840, 845
United States v. Bryan, 490
United States v. Carpenter, 490
United States v. Charnay, 833
United States v. Chestman, 503, 566, 833, 844
United States v. Cook, 833, 936
United States v. Coyle, 850
United States v. Davis, 860
United States v. Davuluri, 850
United States v. DeSantis, 839
United States v. Dixon, 839
United States v. Drexel Burnham Lambert, Inc., 596
United States v. English, 840
United States v. Eisenberg, 863
United States v. Falcone, 502
United States v. Flynn, 845
United States v. Gaudin, 859
United States v. Gay, 850
United States v. Gee, 859
United States v. Gleason, 833
United States v. Glecier, 872
United States v. Guadagna, 850
United States v. Haddy, 844
United States v. Hall, 597
United States v. Halper, 760, 761, 766
United States v. Holtzclaw, 833
United States v. Lang, 844
United States v. Leonard, 850
United States v. Libera, 467
United States v. Lilley, 841
United States v. Marcus Schloss, 761
United States v. Maze, 849
United States v. McDermott, 523-24
United States v. Mittelstaedt, 859
United States v. Morton Salt Co., 623
**United States v. Mulheren, 585**
United States v. Naftalin, 322, 843
United States v. Newman, 489
**United States v. O'Hagan**, 12, 52, 100-01, 391, 452, **490**, **506**, 519, 520, 556, 563, 833, 841, 843, 844
United States v. O'Hagan (8th Cir.), 514-15, 845
United States v. Oreto, 885
United States v. Patrick, 873
**United States v. Peltz, 836**, 842
United States v. Pelullo, 872
United States v. Posada-Rios, 886
United States v. Quintanilla, 886
United States v. ReBrook, 854-55
United States v. Reed, 503
United States v. Regan, 593, 594, 597
United States v. Richards, 859
United States v. Rudi, 846
United States v. Russo, 845
United States v. Shvarts, 742
United States v. Siegel, 860
United States v. Smith, 73, 476
**United States v. Solomon**, 733, **736**, 754, 830
United States v. Starrett, 886
United States v. Swift & Co., 676
United States v. Syme, 850
United States v. Teicher, 476
United States v. Turkette, 873
United States v. United Med. & Surgical Supply Corp., 845
United States v. United States Gypsum Co., 850
United States v. Utah Constr. & Mining Co., 721
United States v. Vasilios, 845
United States v. Vogt, 886
United States v. Willis, 502
Univ. of Tenn. v. Elliot, 721
Unocal Corp. v. Mesa Petroleum Co., 393, 394

Verifone Sec. Litig., In re, 79
Vine v. Beneficial Fin. Co., 145
Virginia, Ex parte, 831
**Virginia Bankshares, Inc. v. Sandberg**, 41, 327, 336-37, 338, **346**, 361, 613

Wachovia Bank & Trust Co. v. Nat'l Student Mktg. Corp., 258
Wade v. Indus. Funding Corp., 269
**Wardrop v. Amway Asia Pacific Ltd., 382**
Washington Nat'l Ins. Co. v. Morgan Stanley & Co., 225
Weinberger v. Jackson, 285
Weiner v. Quaker Oats Co., 57
Wellman v. Dickinson, 368
West v. Atkins, 743
Westinghouse Elec. Corp. v. Rep. of the Philippines, 649
Westinghouse Elec. Corp. by Levit v. Franklin, 362
**Wharf (Holdings) Ltd. v. United International Holdings, Inc.**, 24, **43**, 141, 142, 377
Wilko v. Swan, 939, 951, 971, 972
Wilson v. Comtech Telecomm. Corp., 147, 466
**Wilson v. Great American Indus., Inc.**, 41, 335, 337, **358**
Winship, In re, 834
Wool v. Tandem Computers, Inc., 129
**Wright v. Ernst & Young LLP, 220**

ZZZZ Best Sec. Litig., In re, 225
Zarzecki v. United States, 594
Zerman v. Ball, 66
Ziemba v. Cascade Int'l, Inc., 225
Zippo Mfg. Co. v. Zippo Dot Com, Inc., 897
Zlotnick v. TIE Comm., 161
**Zobrist v. Coal-X, Inc., 172**
Zoelsch v. Arthur Andersen & Co., 888
Zweig v. Hearst Corp., 235, 600

# Chapter 1

# AN OVERVIEW OF SECURITIES LITIGATION AND ENFORCEMENT

Securities litigation and enforcement is a dynamic area of legal practice with important developments occurring on a number of fronts. Massive financial frauds at Enron, WorldCom, and other large companies prompted Congress to enact the Sarbanes-Oxley Act of 2002, multi-pronged legislation that heightens corporate disclosure obligations, enhances federal regulation of attorneys and accountants, establishes several new securities crimes, and lengthens the statute of limitations for private securities fraud actions. The frauds at Enron, WorldCom, and other industry giants have also triggered a spate of private and governmental enforcement activity that is likely to occupy the attention of courts and lawyers for years to come. Indeed, securities litigation is booming generally. Private securities fraud actions reached an all-time high in 2001, despite Congress's efforts to curtail such actions in the Private Securities Litigation Reform Act of 1995. Enforcement actions by the government are likewise on the rise, as the Securities and Exchange Commission (SEC) and the Department of Justice (DOJ) contend with the high-profile financial scandals as well as with matters such as Internet fraud, insider trading, and international securities fraud.

Securities litigation and enforcement involve businesses and transactions of all sizes. Indeed, small—even one on one—securities transactions can (and do) precipitate complex litigation. Thus, lawyers in small firms and solo practitioners who represent family businesses or individual investors are almost as likely to become involved in securities litigation as are lawyers who represent parties to the transactions that make front page news.

Representing clients in all these situations requires familiarity with more than substantive securities law. It also requires knowledge of the relevant procedural rules as well as the strategies employed by plaintiffs (be they investors or the government) and by defendants (be they individuals or corporations). Likewise important to successful advocacy is awareness of the politics underlying recent legislation and case law developments.

This casebook is intended to provide a grounding in both the theoretical and practical aspects of securities litigation and enforcement. Throughout, the intention is to address important causes of action and issues in the clusters in which they are likely to arise in actual cases. This overview is followed by twelve additional chapters: Section 10(b) of the Exchange Act and Rule 10b-5 (Chapter 2); Securities Act Liability for Material Misstatements, Omissions, and

Fraudulent Conduct (Chapter 3); Proxy Fraud (Chapter 4); Tender Offer Fraud (Chapter 5); Securities Class Actions (Chapter 6); Insider Trading (Chapter 7); Market Manipulation (Chapter 8); SEC Enforcement (Chapter 9); Enforcement Issues Involving Attorneys and Accountants (Chapter 10); Criminal Enforcement (Chapter 11); International Securities Fraud (Chapter 12); and Securities Arbitration (Chapter 13).

The present Chapter provides background and perspectives that will enhance your understanding of later chapters. After a canvass of the federal securities statutes (Section A), it examines the roles played in securities litigation and enforcement by the courts (Section B), the SEC (Section C), the DOJ (Section D), state law (Section E), and social and economic forces (Section F). Section G presents the efficient capital markets hypothesis, an economic theory underlying many of the important case law and legislative developments appearing throughout the casebook. Section H concludes with some themes and questions to keep in mind in connection with the chapters that follow.

## A. THE FEDERAL SECURITIES STATUTES

The principal federal securities statutes are the Securities Act of 1933 (the Securities Act) and the Securities Exchange Act of 1934 (the Exchange Act). These two statutes were among the first laws enacted by an overwhelmingly Democratic Congress after President Franklin D. Roosevelt took office. The statutes responded to public outrage at widespread failures in American financial markets. Indeed, by 1932, the stock market had lost almost 90% of the value that it had prior to the "Great Crash" of 1929. Many Americans lost their life savings that they had either invested in stocks or placed in deposits with uninsured banks that collapsed when the market did.

The necessity of federal regulation seemed apparent given the inadequacy of state securities statutes, the so-called "blue sky" laws enacted in the early 1900s to protect investors from promoters selling stock worth only "so many feet of blue sky." *Hall v. Geiger-Jones Co.*, 242 U.S. 539, 550 (1917). State regulators had done little to halt manipulation of stock prices or other deceptive practices that had run rampant prior to the Crash, despite the fact that much of the malfeasance violated blue sky laws as well as state criminal fraud statutes.

Many of the statutory provisions that you will encounter in this casebook were part of the Securities Act and the Exchange Act as originally enacted (although some were added later). You will understand these provisions better if you bear in mind the unique historical situation from which they sprang.

In addition to the Securities Act and the Exchange Act, Congress enacted a number of specialized securities statutes during the 1930s that target specific abuses in the securities markets: the Public Utility Holding Company Act of 1935 (directed at complex and often fraudulent holding company structures used by public utility companies), the Trust Indenture Act of 1939 (regulation of the contracts between issuers of debt securities and the bank trustees retained to enforce those contracts on behalf of investors, as well as of the conflicts of interest that arise in this situation), the Investment Company Act of 1940 (regulation of mutual funds and other companies with assets consisting primarily of securities of other issuers), and the Investment Advisers

Act of 1940 (regulation of conflicts of interest and other problems affecting investment advisers). For a variety of views concerning the federal securities legislation enacted in the 1930s, see Joel Seligman, The Transformation of Wall Street (rev. ed. 1995); William O. Douglas, Protecting the Investor, 23 Yale Rev. 521 (1934); James M. Landis, The Legislative History of the Securities Act of 1933, 28 Geo. Wash. L. Rev. 29 (1959); Paul G. Mahoney, The Stock Pools and the Securities Exchange Act, 5 J. Fin. Econ. 343 (1999); Steve Thel, The Original Conception of Section 10(b) of the Securities Exchange Act, 42 Stan. L. Rev. 385 (1990).

Following a sketch of the Securities Act and the Exchange Act that highlights provisions of especial importance to litigators, we survey two major recent congressional enactments— the Private Securities Litigation Reform Act of 1995 and the Sarbanes-Oxley Act of 2002. Another such enactment, the Securities Litigation Uniform Standards Act of 1998, is discussed later in this Chapter in connection with state law.

### *1. The Securities Act*

To combat the market abuses that led to the1929 Crash, the Securities Act emphasizes both the disclosure of information and the prevention of fraud. The emphasis on disclosure reflects the influence of Justice Brandeis, who wrote: "Publicity is justly commended as a remedy for social and industrial diseases. Sunlight is said to be the best of disinfectants; electric light the most efficient policeman." Louis D. Brandeis, Other People's Money and How the Bankers Use It 62 (2d. ed. 1933). In embracing a disclosure approach, Congress rejected the so-called merit approach, which, philosophical considerations aside, would have been considerably more expensive. Under the merit approach, currently in place in various states, regulators prohibit public sales of securities by companies that they conclude are financially troubled, regardless of whether those financial troubles are publicly disclosed.

The Securities Act is primarily concerned with securities offerings by issuers and those who control them (in contrast to the Exchange Act, which focuses on the secondary trading markets). The Securities Act applies both to initial public offerings (IPOs) as well as to subsequent offerings by seasoned issuers that have long been publicly held. Section 5 of the Act requires that all offerings of securities be registered, unless an exemption from registration applies. The Act places enforcement in the hands of the SEC and the DOJ as well as investors (who have at their disposal several express private actions).

#### *a. The Registration Requirement*

An issuer wishing to make an offering of securities for which no registration exemption is available must file a registration statement with the SEC. The registration statement—the centerpiece disclosure document of the Securities Act—provides detailed information about the company's business and management along with the terms of the offering and certified financial statements. The preparation of the registration statement is less onerous for the largest companies, which are entitled to incorporate into their registration statements the annual and quarterly reports (described below) that the Exchange Act requires them to file regularly with the SEC. This fusion of

Securities Act and Exchange Act disclosure requirements is known as "integrated disclosure."

An issuer can begin selling the securities covered by a registration statement only when the SEC allows the registration statement to become effective. The wait averages four to six weeks in the case of an IPO and substantially less time in the case of an offering by a seasoned issuer. A prospectus containing substantially the same information as the registration statement must be provided to dealers selling the securities in the registered offering as well as to those who purchase in the offering.

In reviewing a registration statement, the SEC makes no affirmative investigation of the facts that the issuer sets forth. Therefore, unless there are obvious red flags, the SEC is unlikely to question the accuracy of the company's representations. Misleading disclosures thus usually do not come to light until after the sale of the securities to the public. Hence the principal deterrent against fraud or negligence consists of *ex post* enforcement actions by investors, the SEC, and the DOJ.

*b. Exemptions from Registration*

The Securities Act provides numerous exemptions from the registration requirements. Litigators need to be familiar with these exemptions for two reasons. First, suppose an issuer offers securities pursuant to an exemption without satisfying the exemption's requirements. Under these circumstances, the purchasers have a right to rescission under Section 12(a)(1) of the Act, even if no misleading statement was made to them. Second, the availability of Section 12(a)(2), a private action for material misstatements and omissions, may turn on which exemption the offering of securities was based.

The exemptions from registration rest on a variety of rationales. These include the nature of the issuer or of the investors, the size of the offering, or the fact that some other regulatory authority is in the picture.

The exemptions from registration include securities issued by the United States and by state or local governments as well as by banks and non-profit institutions. See Sections 3(a)(2) and 3(a)(4). Also exempt are intrastate offerings, which are offerings of securities sold to residents of a single state by an issuer both incorporated and doing most of its business within that state. See Section 3(a)(11) and Rule 147. The traditional rationale for the intrastate exemption is two-fold: the ability of states to regulate offerings within their borders coupled with the ability of investors to discover information about companies located in the state in which they live.

Exemptions based at least partly on the size of the offering include those provided by Rules 504 and 505 of Regulation D as well as by Regulation A. The statutory basis for each of these is Section 3(b), which authorizes the SEC to adopt exemptions for offerings not exceeding $5 million where registration is "not necessary in the public interest and for the protection of investors." A Rule 504 offering cannot exceed $1 million, can be made only by issuers not subject to the Exchange Act's reporting requirements (described infra), and does not require disclosure of information to investors. A Rule 505 offering, available to reporting companies and non-reporting companies alike, cannot exceed $5 million. Disclosure of specified information must be made to investors who are not "accredited investors" (a category which includes certain institutions, certain insiders of the issuer, and individuals with a net worth exceeding $1 million or a yearly income exceeding $200,000). A Rule 505 offering is limited to 35 purchasers, not including accredited investors. A Regulation A offering cannot exceed $5 million and can be made only by issuers not subject to the Exchange Act's reporting requirements. Often referred to as "mini-registration" or "junior registration," Regulation A requires the issuer to file with the SEC an abbreviated registration statement (that need not include audited financials) and to distribute an abbreviated prospectus to investors.

A very important exemption is the private offering exemption, set forth in Section 4(2). This exemption from the Securities Act's registration requirements encompasses "transactions by an issuer not involving any public offering." According to the Supreme Court, the private offering exemption applies only to those offerings made to persons with "access to the kind of information which registration would disclose" and with the capacity to "fend for themselves." *SEC v. Ralston Purina Co.*, 346 U.S. 119, 125-27 (1953). A quintessential private offering would be an offering to ten banks, but private offerings can also be made to sophisticated individuals. Far from clear, however, is the precise nature of the attributes that these individuals must have. Thus, the SEC has adopted a "safe harbor" rule under Section 4(2) that provides issuers with an alternative to Section 4(2) itself. The safe harbor is Rule 506, which, like Rules 504 and 505 described earlier, is part of Regulation D. Rule 506 provides an exemption for offerings of any dollar amount, to an unlimited number of accredited investors (see Rule 505 supra) and up to 35 additional investors who must each be sophisticated—that is, have "such knowledge and experience in financial and business matters that he is capable of evaluating the merits and risks of the *** investment." Rule 506(b)(2)(ii). As with Rule 505 discussed supra, disclosure of specified information must be made to investors who are not accredited investors.

Additional exemptions from registration are set forth in Regulation S, which encompasses offerings made outside the United States by either domestic or foreign issuers. Regulation S draws distinctions based on the probability that the securities in question will find their way to the United States. The greater the probability, the more restrictions the issuer must satisfy in order to obtain an exemption from registration.

### c. *Liability Provisions*

The Securities Act contains several liability provisions. First, recall that we have already mentioned Section 12(a)(1), which confers a right of recission where a private plaintiff is able to establish a violation of Section 5 of the Securities Act.

The Securities Act also includes two express private actions for material omissions and misstatements. Under Section 11, purchasers in registered offerings may sue the issuer and numerous other specified defendants (including underwriters, accountants, directors, and certain corporate officers) for material omissions and misstatements in the registration statement. Under Section 12(a)(2), those who purchase in registered offerings as well as in some exempt offerings may sue their "sellers" (a category that the Act does not define) for material omissions and misstatements made "by means of a prospectus" or, in some instances, orally. Sections 11 and 12(a)(2) impose fewer demands on plaintiffs than would a traditional common law fraud action. For example, neither Section requires proof that the defendant acted with scienter (i.e., an intent to deceive) and, under Section 11, an issuer is strictly liable for any material misrepresentations or omissions in the registration statement.

In designing Sections 11 and 12(a)(2), Congress thought much about the "gatekeeping" functions performed by those who assist issuers with securities offerings. Indeed, the so-called "due diligence defenses" available to non-issuer Section 11 defendants such as accountants and underwriters, along with the "reasonable care" defense available to Section 12(a)(2) defendants, provide substantial incentives to make the issuer's disclosures accurate and complete.

Another significant fraud provision is Section 17(a), which prohibits three sets of fraudulent acts "in the offer or sale of a security." The Supreme Court has held that subsection 17(a)(1) requires proof of scienter but that subsections 17(a)(2) and (3) do not. See *Aaron v. SEC,* 446 U.S. 680 (1980). Section 17(a) is an important enforcement tool of the SEC and the DOJ. Section 17(a) does not contain an express private action and courts have declined to recognize an implied private action.

### 2. *The Exchange Act*

As noted earlier, the Exchange Act focuses mainly on the secondary trading markets. Its wide-ranging regulation of these markets includes the following aspects of particular significance to securities litigators.

#### a. *Section 10(b) and Rule 10b-5*

From the standpoint of securities litigation and enforcement, by far the most important provision in the Exchange Act (as well as in the federal securities laws generally) is Section 10(b). That Section makes it "unlawful *** [t]o use or employ, in connection with the purchase or sale of any security ***, any manipulative or deceptive device or contrivance" in contravention of SEC rules. In 1942, the SEC adopted Rule 10b-5, which proscribes fraud in a manner virtually as wide-ranging as Section 10(b) itself. The Rule, applicable regardless of the size of the transaction or the securities issuer, serves not only as a general prohibition against fraud "in connection with the purchase or sale of any security" but also as a prohibition against insider trading (a subject addressed by Section 16(b) as well).

As originally contemplated by their drafters, Section 10(b) and Rule 10b-5 were to be enforced only by the SEC and the DOJ. Beginning in 1946, however, courts recognized an implied private action that is now established "beyond peradventure." *Herman & MacLean v. Huddleston,* 459 U.S. 375, 380 (1983). The importance of the implied private action has undoubtedly been enhanced by the limited scope and onerous burdens imposed by the Exchange Act's two express private fraud actions: an action under Section 9(e) for market manipulation and an action under Section 18(a) for material misstatements in reports filed with the SEC.

*b. Market Manipulation*

The Exchange Act contains numerous provisions that specifically target market manipulation. These include—in addition to Section 10(b) and Rule 10b-5—Section 9, which bars various types of manipulative practices involving securities registered on national exchanges; Section 10(a), which authorizes the SEC to adopt rules regulating short sales and stop-loss orders involving securities registered on national exchanges; Section 14(e), which prohibits "fraudulent, deceptive, or manipulative acts or practices, in connection with any tender offer;" and Section 15(c), which prohibits "any fraudulent, deceptive, or manipulative act or practice" by brokers and dealers in the over-the-counter markets. The Exchange Act does not define manipulation, however, and the precise meaning of the term is by no means self-evident.

*c. Disclosure Obligations: Reporting Companies*

To reduce the frequency of fraud and manipulation in public markets, the Exchange Act requires certain companies—known as reporting companies—to file reports on a regular basis with the SEC. A number of provisions important to litigators—not only in the Exchange Act but also in the Private Securities Litigation Reform Act and the Sarbanes-Oxley Act—are applicable only to reporting companies (or only to Section 12 companies, which comprise the first and second reporting company categories listed below).

Reporting companies are companies that fall into any of the following three categories:

- Companies which, as provided by Section 12(b), have a class of securities (equity or debt) listed on a national securities exchange. These companies must comply with the reporting requirements set forth in Section 13(a).
- Companies which, as provided by Section 12(g) and Rule 12g-1, have total assets exceeding $10 million and a class of equity securities held by at least 500 shareholders. These companies must comply with the reporting requirements set forth in Section 13(a).
- Companies that do not fit either of the above two categories must nonetheless satisfy the Exchange Act's reporting requirements if, as provided by Section 15(d), they have filed a registration statement under the Securities Act that has become effective.

The vast majority of publicly traded companies (also known as public companies or publicly held companies) are reporting companies. In recognition of this fact and for reasons of convenience, Congress and the SEC sometimes refer to reporting companies as "publicly traded companies." See, e.g., Section 807 of the Sarbanes-Oxley Act (entitled "criminal penalties for defrauding shareholders of publicly traded companies" but applicable to companies that either have securities registered pursuant to Section 12 or that are required to file reports pursuant to Section 15(d)). Likewise for reasons of convenience, we also occasionally employ the same shorthand throughout this casebook.

The most significant report that reporting companies must file is the annual report (the 10-K). The 10-K includes, among other things, management's discussion and analysis of the company's performance as well as audited financial statements. Reporting companies must also file quarterly reports (the 10-Q) as well as reports (the 8-K) for special occurrences, such as the dismissal of the company's accounting firm. The substance of these reports, as well the frequency with which they must be filed, stand on the verge of substantial change. Indeed, Section 13(*l*) of the Exchange Act, added in 2002 by the Sarbanes-Oxley Act, empowers the SEC to adopt rules requiring reporting companies to disclose "on a rapid and current basis such additional information concerning material changes in the financial condition or operations of the issuer."

*d. Proxy Regulation*

By enacting Section 14(a) of the Exchange Act, Congress sought to combat abuses prevalent in the 1920s involving the solicitation of proxies from a corporation's shareholders. These abuses flowed from inadequacies in state law which, while allowing shareholders to vote to elect directors and to approve mergers and other corporate transactions, did not require that they be given information relevant to deciding how to vote. Nor did state law do much to address deceitful proxy solicitations by the company's managers. Indeed, while proxy fraud was, at least theoretically, a breach of state law fiduciary duties, a state court was in fact unlikely to enter an order invalidating a shareholder vote that fraud had tainted.

Section 14(a) gives the SEC a broad mandate to adopt rules governing the solicitation of proxies in Section 12 companies—that is, companies that fit either the first or second of the reporting company categories described above. Pursuant to Section 14(a), the SEC has adopted numerous proxy rules. The proxy rules mandate that shareholders receive information on the matters as to which their votes are sought (although state law continues to control what those matters are). In addition, the proxy rules regulate such things as the form and content of proxy solicitation materials as well as the communications, both written and oral, that are used in connection with the proxy solicitation process.

Especially important is Rule 14a-9, which prohibits material omissions or misrepresentations in proxy solicitations. The Rule is enforceable not only by the SEC and the DOJ, but also by investors. To be sure, Rule 14a-9 says nothing about private enforcement. But an implied private action under the Rule has been recognized by the Supreme Court. See *J. I. Case Co. v. Borak,* 377 U.S. 426 (1964).

*e. Tender Offer Regulation*

The Exchange Act has regulated tender offers since 1968, when Congress amended the Exchange Act for this purpose. These amendments, now embodied in Sections 13(d), 13(e), and 14(d)-(f) of the Exchange Act and known as the Williams Act, were precipitated by the growing number of tender offers in the 1960s. While the Williams Act does not define a "tender offer," the phrase typically refers to a publicized offer, sometimes by a hostile bidder, to buy shares of a publicly owned company at an advertised price within a confined time period. The regulation established by the Williams Act has three principal aspects.

The first aspect involves disclosure of information. Under Section 13(d), an acquiror (whether pursuant to tender offer or otherwise) of more than 5% of a class of equity security of a Section 12 company (that is, a company that fits either the first or second of the reporting company categories described supra) must, within ten days of making the acquisition, provide a report (the Schedule 13D) to the SEC, the target company, and any exchanges on which the security is traded. Disclosures required by Schedule 13D include, among other things, the acquiror's identity, background, and source of financing as well as his purpose in making the acquisition. Section 14(d) requires similar disclosure (the Schedule TO) by anyone who makes a tender offer for more than 5% of a class of equity security of a Section 12 company.

The second aspect involves regulating the process of tender offers so as to reduce shareholder coercion. Thus, the offer must remain open for twenty business days (Rule 14e-1), the tendered shares must be accepted by the bidder on a pro rata rather than on a "first-come-first-served" basis (Section 14(d)(6) and Rule 14d-8), tendered shares may be withdrawn by the shareholders during the period that the tender offer remains open (Section 14(d)(5) and Rule 14d-7) and all tendering shareholders must be paid the same price (Section 14(d)(7) and Rule 14d-10).

Finally, and of greatest importance to securities litigators, the Williams Act prohibits fraud in connection with any tender offer. This prohibition is contained in Section 14(e), a provision modeled on Rule 10b-5 and applicable to tender offers in all companies (whether they are Section 12 companies or not). Section 14(e) is enforceable by the SEC and the DOJ as well as by private parties. While Section 14(e) does not create an express private action, courts have recognized such an action by implication.

#### *f. Self-Regulatory Organizations*

The Exchange Act gives the stock exchanges and the National Association of Securities Dealers the status of self-regulatory organizations (SROs). SROs exercise considerable regulatory authority while at the same time are themselves the object of regulation by the SEC. SROs also provide the forum for almost all securities arbitrations.

### *3. The Private Securities Litigation Reform Act*

The Private Securities Litigation Reform Act of 1995 (PSLRA) imposes numerous restrictions on private securities actions. Enacted in the wake of the 1994 Republican landslide, the PSLRA took aim at purportedly frivolous securities class actions which, in the view of Congress, were filed by lawyers desirous of simply reaching a settlement and collecting a fee. While some PSLRA restrictions apply to class actions specifically, others apply more broadly. Moreover, while some restrictions are substantive, others are procedural.

On the substantive side, the PSLRA gives certain issuers a "safe harbor" which, when satisfied, shields them from claims that they made fraudulent forward-looking statements (that is, predictions of earnings or other matters). See Securities Act Section 27A and Exchange Act Section 21E. The safe harbor was enacted in response to complaints by issuers, particularly Silicon Valley high-technology companies whose share prices depend heavily on estimated future earnings, that the threat of litigation inhibited them from making forecasts necessary in order for the market to place a value on their stock. Other substantive changes wrought by the PSLRA include requirements that plaintiffs prove loss causation (Securities Act Section 12(b); Exchange Act Section 21D(b)(4)); an adjustment to the calculation of damages (Exchange Act Section 21D(e)); and a system of proportionate liability that in many circumstances replaces joint and several liability (Exchange Act Section 21D(f); see also Securities Act Section 11(f)(2)).

Probably the two most important procedural hurdles that the PSLRA imposes on plaintiffs are (i) heightened pleading requirements mandating the setting forth of specific facts (Exchange Act Section 21D(b)(1)-(2)) and (ii) a stay on discovery pending resolution of a defendant's motion to dismiss on the pleadings (Exchange Act Section 21D(b)(3); Securities Act Section 27(b)). The combined effect of these two provisions is that a plaintiff who files a lawsuit without the facts necessary to show a strong likelihood of prevailing on the merits is likely to have his lawsuit dismissed before he has the opportunity to acquire additional facts through discovery.

The PSLRA also establishes numerous procedural requirements on class actions specifically, including barring the use of repeat "professional plaintiffs;" creating a presumption that the largest shareholder of an issuer is the most adequate lead plaintiff; barring lawyers from giving financial incentives to lead plaintiffs; prohibiting sealed settlements that conceal attorneys' fees and other information about a settlement; barring attorneys from receiving a disproportionate share of settlement awards; and requiring courts to impose sanctions on parties and their counsel if there has been a breach of Rule 11 of the Federal Rules of Civil Procedure (applicable in general as a means to sanction frivolous pleadings in federal court). See Securities Act Section 27(a), (c); Exchange Act Section 21D(a), (c). Despite their curtailment under the PSLRA, however, securities class actions remain a cornerstone of securities litigation.

President Clinton perceived the PSLRA to be overwhelmingly pro-defendant. Accordingly, he vetoed the bill in November 1995. (Plaintiffs' lawyers were among his most loyal campaign contributors and class action lawyer William Lerach, now lead counsel in the Enron litigation, was rumored to have visited the White House the day before the PSLRA veto). Silicon Valley high-technology companies, other corporate issuers and accounting firms, however, were not remiss in their own political contributions to congressional campaigns, and by contrast lawyers for securities plaintiffs had relatively few friends in Congress. On December 20, 1995, the House voted to override the President's veto by a vote of 319-100, and on December 22, the Senate voted to override by a vote of 68-30. The bill became law.

#### *4. The Sarbanes-Oxley Act*

In the wake of the massive accounting frauds at Enron, WorldCom, and other large publicly traded companies, Congress enacted the Sarbanes-Oxley Act of 2002. Among other things, the Act heightens corporate disclosure obligations (Section 409); places the accounting industry under the oversight of a Board appointed by and under the supervision of the SEC (Sections 101-109); requires the SEC to adopt professional responsibility rules for securities lawyers, including a rule that compels a lawyer to report evidence of securities violations up-the-ladder to her client's board of directors (Section 307 and Rule 205); establishes several new securities crimes (e.g., Sections 807 and 906(c)); toughens the penalties for some already existing securities crimes; and extends the statute of limitations for private actions for securities fraud (Section 804).

Whether the changes wrought by the Sarbanes-Oxley Act will reduce the incidence of corporate fraud remains to be seen. It is nonetheless instructive to consider what that Act did not do, namely, repeal even one of the many restrictions on private securities actions established by the PSLRA.

## B. THE COURTS

Besides providing a forum for securities actions, the federal courts play a substantial role in shaping the substantive law of securities litigation. This is so mainly for two reasons.

The first reason has to do with the federal securities laws themselves. As you will see throughout this casebook, the federal securities laws are written in broad language. For example, Section 10(b) of the Exchange Act prohibits "any manipulative or deceptive device or contrivance" and Rule 10b-5 prohibits "any device, scheme, or artifice to defraud." Moreover, definitions of critical terms are frequently lacking, such as what makes misstatements or omissions "material" (as they must be under Rule 10b-5, Rule14a-9, and Section 14(e) of the Exchange Act as well as under Sections 11 and 12(a)(2) of the Securities Act); what it means for a defendant to commit his violation "willfully" (a prerequisite for criminal conviction under the Securities Act and the Exchange Act); and what qualifies as a "tender offer" (the focus of regulation under the Williams Act). As Congress undoubtedly expected, courts step in to supply the missing content.

The second reason involves a happenstance of timing. Many questions of foundational importance for securities litigation reached the courts in the 1960s and 1970s, an era of judicial activism across the legal landscape. Thus, in the 1960s and 1970s, a period when the Supreme Court discovered constitution entitlements to privacy and abortion and issued other expansive rulings in the areas of civil liberties and criminal defense, it also upheld implied private actions under Rule 10b-5 and Rule 14a-9 and established presumptions of reliance or causation on behalf of investors who sued under those provisions. See *Affiliated Ute Citizens v. United States,* 406 U.S. 128, 152-54 (1972) (upholding presumption of reliance under Rule 10b-5); *Superintendent of Ins. v. Bankers Life & Cas. Co.,* 404 U.S. 6, 13 n. 9 (1971) (upholding implied private action under Rule 10b-5); *Mills v. Elec. Auto-Lite Co.,* 396 U.S. 375, 384-85 (1970) (upholding presumption of causation under Rule 14a-9); *J. I. Case Co. v. Borak,* 377 U.S. 426 (1964) (upholding implied private action under Rule 14a-9). Likewise during this period, the lower federal courts recognized an implied private action under Section 14(e) of the Exchange Act, read Rule 10b-5 to prohibit insider trading (a subject to which the Rule does not refer), and accorded Rule 10b-5 a substantial international reach (despite the absence of virtually any guidance on this matter from Congress).

These decisions from the 1960s and 1970s had the effect of further expanding judicial power. Indeed, having recognized implied private actions, the courts could not avoid shaping their elements. Similarly, having concluded that Rule 10-5 encompasses insider trading and international transactions, the courts could not avoid plumbing the meaning of insider trading and the reach of extraterritoriality.

To be sure, judicial activism in securities law subsided and some of the expansive interpretations from the 1960s and 1970s were cut back by later decisions and legislative developments. But the rights and duties that courts recognized in the 1960s and 1970s have largely remained in place. The private actions under Rule 10b-5, Rule 14a-9, and Section 14(e) continue to be highly important enforcement tools. Moreover, Rule 10b-5's applicability to insider trading and to international transactions appears rock solid.

As the above discussion demonstrates, the lower federal courts play a pivotal role in developing securities law. Although all of the federal appeals and district courts contribute in this regard, the Second Circuit has over the years issued some of the most influential decisions and has long been regarded as the "Mother Court" of securities law. *Blue Chip Stamps v. Manor Drug Stores,* 421 U.S. 723, 762 (1975) (Blackmun, J., dissenting). Recently, however, the Ninth Circuit has emerged as an influential force in securities law because of the large number of class actions brought against high-technology companies in the Silicon Valley and elsewhere in the western United States during the 1980s and 1990s. On some important issues, the Second Circuit and the Ninth Circuit disagree. Most recently, the Ninth Circuit has adopted a decidedly more pro-defendant position than the Second Circuit with respect to the PSLRA pleading standards as well as with respect to the substantive standard for scienter under Rule 10b-5. Until the Supreme Court resolves these issues, courts and lawyers elsewhere in the country will jostle over whether the reasoning of the Second Circuit or the Ninth Circuit is more persuasive.

The Supreme Court has an impact by virtue of not only what it decides but also what it fails to decide (and thereby leaves to the lower courts for resolution). Important issues, such as the viability of the misappropriation theory of insider trading or the existence of aiding and abetting liability under Rule 10b-5, remained unresolved for years after first being raised, and then left open, by Supreme Court decisions decided on other grounds. Compare *Chiarella v. United States,* 445 U.S. 222, 235-37 (1980) (acknowledging, but not addressing, the misappropriation theory) with *United States v. O'Hagan*, 521 U.S. 642, 665 (1997) (upholding the misappropriation theory); compare *Ernst & Ernst v. Hochfelder*, 425 U.S. 185, 191 n. 7 (1976) (reserving the question of aiding and abetting liability under Rule 10b-5) with *Central Bank, N.A. v. First Interstate Bank, N.A.,* 511 U.S. 164 (1994) (rejecting aiding and abetting liability in private actions under Rule 10b-5). Moreover, the Court has yet to say whether recklessness satisfies Rule 10b-5's scienter requirement, even though more than twenty years have elapsed since the Court posed but declined to answer that question. See *Ernst v. Ernst v. Hochfelder*, supra, 425 U.S. at 193 n. 12.

As you proceed through this casebook, notice the many Supreme Court decisions in which the Court splits 5-4. This suggests that many of the same political and jurisprudential divisions operative in the Court's decisions in other substantive areas affect its securities decisions as well.

Congress has only occasionally overridden the courts. While the most striking example is probably the wide range of procedural and substantive changes brought about by the PSLRA, other instances include two amendments to the Exchange Act. The first, enacted in 1988 in the wake of a surge of insider trading scandals, overrode a Second Circuit decision barring private actions based on the misappropriation theory of insider trading. See Exchange Act Section 20A. The other, enacted in 1995, clarified the SEC's right to sue aiders and abetters following a 1994 Supreme Court decision that called the agency's right to do so into question. See Exchange Act Section 20(e).

## C. THE SECURITIES AND EXCHANGE COMMISSION

A major accomplishment of the Exchange Act was the establishment of the SEC (also known as the Commission), an independent agency charged with enforcing the federal securities laws. The SEC is composed of five commissioners appointed by the President and confirmed by the Senate for five year terms, no more than three of whom can come from the same political party. Since its founding, the SEC has played a formidable and multi-faceted role in the development of the federal securities laws.

First, the SEC is empowered to adopt rules that implement those laws. Among the most important rules ever adopted by the SEC are Rules 10b-5 and 14a-9.

Second, the SEC has the power both to initiate administrative actions against securities law violators as well as to adjudicate those actions. In this capacity, the SEC may from time to time issue important rulings on statutory questions as to which the courts have not yet had the opportunity to speak.

Third, the SEC frequently brings enforcement actions in the federal courts. It thus shapes the law through its decisions regarding which cases to prosecute.

Fourth, the SEC often files amicus briefs on federal securities issues in private actions in which it is not a party. The courts are at least attentive to the SEC's positions although they do not by any means always follow them.

Finally, the SEC's Chairperson and sometimes other Commissioners or staff testify before Congress, as well as provide informal input, when Congress considers legislation amending the securities laws. In this instance as well, the SEC does not by any means always get its way.

The SEC consists of four principal divisions, the most important of which from the standpoint of securities litigators is the Enforcement Division. That Division conducts investigations and, where appropriate, files administrative or court actions against securities law violators. Where criminal prosecution appears warranted, the matter is referred to the DOJ.

## D. THE DEPARTMENT OF JUSTICE

The DOJ has exclusive authority over criminal enforcement of the federal securities laws. While (as previously noted) the SEC sometimes refers cases to the DOJ, it is the DOJ (and not the SEC) that makes the final decision as to whether to bring criminal charges. Moreover, the DOJ prosecutes numerous securities cases that did not originate with the SEC.

The federal securities laws contain only a few stand-alone crimes. Thus, for the most part, the DOJ prosecutes people for the securities violations that can also trigger actions by the SEC (as well as sometimes by private parties). To be sure, criminal liability requires proof that the defendant acted "willfully." In addition, the DOJ must establish its case by "proof beyond a reasonable doubt" rather than by the preponderance standard applicable to civil actions.

The SEC and the DOJ from time to time prosecute the same offenses simultaneously. These parallel SEC civil actions and DOJ criminal actions may engender procedural conflicts as well as the application of inconsistent substantive legal standards to the same facts.

Moreover, a conflict sometimes arises between the goals of criminal enforcement (punishment of wrongdoers, including corporations, whose directors or employees violate the law) and the goals of class action plaintiffs (maximum recovery from a defendant which, if it is a corporation, must remain a going concern in order to generate cash flow sufficient to pay damages). The recent criminal prosecution of the accounting firm of Arthur Andersen is illustrative.

## E. STATE LAW

Although this casebook focuses on the federal securities laws, state law constitutes a significant aspect of securities litigation. Sometimes the state law at issue is that of the state of incorporation; at other times it is the law of the state where the securities were sold. Each state continues to have its own blue sky laws and state officials may bring both civil and criminal actions under those statutes. See generally Mark A. Sargent, A Future for Blue Sky Laws, 62 U. Cin. L. Rev. 471 (1993).

As originally enacted, the Securities Act and the Exchange Act preserved state law actions brought by private parties as well as by state governments. In the years that followed, courts assumed that this preservation extended to class actions filed in state court under state law. Nonetheless, after the enactment of the PSLRA in 1995, its supporters complained that plaintiffs' lawyers were avoiding its restrictions, including the bar on discovery pending resolution of motions to dismiss, by filing class actions in state court (mostly in California). Preemption of these state class actions was supported by the high-technology companies of Silicon Valley, who were often defendants in securities class actions, as well as by the major accounting firms.

In 1998 Congress enacted the Securities Litigation Uniform Standards Act (SLUSA), which preempted class actions for securities fraud under the common law and statutes of all fifty states. Investors, with the exception of state and local governments and their pension funds, are now barred from bringing in state court or under state law a class action alleging fraud in connection with the purchase or sale of a "nationally traded security" (encompassing those listed on the New York Stock Exchange, the American Stock Exchange, or the NASDAQ). SLUSA also authorizes federal courts to stay discovery in state court of any private action (whether or not a class action) while a federal action is pending. The Act does, however, preserve state jurisdiction over certain types of corporate law claims (the so-called "Delaware carve-out").

Congress has also received complaints from Wall Street firms of excessive prosecutorial zeal by state attorneys general, most notably the New York Attorney General Eliot Spitzer, who in 2002 led an investigation that culminated in a $100 million settlement with Merrill Lynch & Co., Inc. involving overly optimistic recommendations by securities analysts who allegedly sought to win lucrative investment banking business for their firm. Although bills were introduced in Congress that would have preempted such state enforcement activities, the SEC's well-publicized agreement to join forces with Spitzer and other state attorneys general appears to have tempered these calls for legislative action.

## F. SOCIAL AND ECONOMIC FORCES

Social and economic forces have always had a substantial impact on securities litigation and enforcement. Blue sky laws were enacted in response to widespread financial scandals of the 1890s and the crash of 1907. Moreover, as noted previously, the crash of 1929 and the disastrous bear market of 1929-1932 led to the enactment of the Securities Act, the Exchange Act, and other federal securities statutes. Nor has the impact of social and economic forces on securities law abated since.

Beginning in the 1970s, widespread concern developed in American society, and particularly in the business community, over the extent of government regulation, the volume of litigation, and the prevalence of judicial activism. Responding to these concerns from the mid-1970s through the mid-1990s, the Supreme Court restricted the scope of the implied private actions previously recognized under the federal securities laws as well as of certain express private actions under those laws. This period is often referred to as one of "retrenchment."

In adopting at least some of these restrictions, the Supreme Court may well have been influenced by the fact that the stock market was rising. Indeed, when the economy is booming, concern about protecting investors can take a back seat to other priorities, such as curtailing what was perceived to be excessive litigation. Similarly, the rising stock market no doubt likewise made possible Congress's restraints on private securities actions in the PSLRA.

The Internet brings huge consequences as well. Consider its two-fold impact. First, the Internet creates new opportunities for deception, since vast audiences can now be reached by tricksters who operate anonymously. Second, the Internet's global reach generates substantial jurisdictional questions. For example, suppose a foreign national, operating in a foreign country, posts on the Internet fraudulent corporate information that affects the investment decisions of United States residents. Do the federal securities fraud provisions reach this far? What about personal jurisdiction over the foreign national? See generally John C. Coffee, Jr., Brave New World? The Impact(s) of the Internet on Modern Securities Regulation, 52 Bus. Law. 1195, 1223 (1997) (identifying the Internet's two-fold impact).

Indeed, even putting the Internet to the side, the internationalization of the securities markets that began in the 1960s has had—and continues to have—significant ramifications for securities litigation and enforcement. United States investors now trade vast quantities of foreign securities, and foreign investors trade vast quantities of United States securities as well. As a result, federal securities fraud litigation now involves foreign plaintiffs, foreign defendants, and foreign securities in various permutations as well as fraud that occurred in whole or in part on foreign soil. Courts are engaged in an ongoing struggle to determine which such cases they are entitled to hear and which lie beyond the scope of their jurisdiction.

Finally, revelations of large-scale accounting frauds at a number of the country's largest companies—including Enron, Global Crossings, Sunbeam, Waste Management, and WorldCom—will undoubtedly bring consequences for years to come. These revelations have not only led to Congress's enactment of the Sarbanes-Oxley Act (which will have numerous ramifications of its own) but have also apparently generated an at least somewhat increased judicial receptivity to securities litigation brought by private parties. And of course, many of the repercussions of the Enron-WorldCom debacles are undoubtedly as yet unknown.

## G. THE EFFICIENT CAPITAL MARKETS HYPOTHESIS

The Efficient Capital Market Hypothesis (ECMH) is a highly influential economic theory that has had (and continues to have) a substantial impact on both securities law in general and securities litigation and enforcement in particular. For example, the fraud-on-the-market doctrine and the puffery doctrine that you will encounter in later chapters are based on the ECMH, as is the statutory safe harbor for forward-looking statements that Congress enacted as part of the PSLRA. While the fraud-on-the-market doctrine is a boon to plaintiffs (because it gives them a presumption of reliance), most of the doctrines and legislation predicated on the ECMH benefit defendants instead.

The ECMH comes in three versions: weak, semi-strong, and strong. The weak version, which commands virtual universal acceptance, posits only that security prices are determined by currently available information rather than historical market trends. The widely accepted semi-strong version, on which the doctrines and legislation draw, posits that once information becomes public, it is quickly impounded into securities prices. The highly controversial strong version posits that even nonpublic information is routinely impounded into security prices through leaks and insider trading.

Markets become efficient as the result of heavy trading by sophisticated investors, many of them institutions, based on what they and their advisers cull from available public sources about the securities and the companies that issue them. Not all public markets are efficient markets by any means. Before assuming that the ECMH, or any legal doctrine based on the ECMH, applies, it is important to assess the likely efficiency of the securities market in question. Public markets that are thinly traded or have few or no institutional investors are unlikely to be efficient because they lack the ingredients of market efficiency. See generally Lawrence A. Cunningham, From Random Walks to Chaotic Crashes: The Linear Geneology of the Efficient Capital Market

Hypothesis, 62 Geo. Wash. L. Rev. 546 (1994); Ronald J. Gilson & Reinier H. Kraakman, The Mechanisms of Market Efficiency, 70 Va. L. Rev. 549 (1984). The IPO market is prototypically inefficient, whereas the market for New York Stock Exchange-traded securities is prototypically efficient.

Yet a certain amount of skepticism may be in order as to the efficiency of the markets for even the largest companies, since it appears that some publicly available information about Enron and WorldCom was not reflected in their stock prices prior to their collapse. Indeed, debates swirl over whether and to what extent markets are inefficient because of trading driven by psychological factors such as faddishness, overestimation or underestimation of risk, anchoring (allowing sometimes arbitrary numbers to exert a gravitational pull on estimations of value), and attempts to outguess the market. See, e.g., Brad M. Barber & Terrance Odean, Boys Will Be Boys: Gender, Overconfidence, and Common Stock Investment, 116 Q. J. Econ. 261 (2001); Andrei Shleifer & Lawrence H. Summers, The Noise Trader Approach to Finance, 4 J. Econ. Persp. 19 (1990); Lynn A. Stout, How Efficient Markets Undervalue Stocks: CAPM and ECMH Under Conditions of Uncertainty and Disagreement, 19 Cardozo L. Rev. 475 (1997); Amos Tversky & Daniel Kahneman, Judgment Under Uncertainty: Heuristics and Biases, 185 Science 1124 (1974).

## H. LOOKING AHEAD

As with any area of the law, securities litigation and enforcement involves a number of recurrent themes. Some of those themes are reflected in the following questions, which you should ponder in connection with the chapters that lie ahead:

- **Congress vs. the Courts.** What accounts for Congress's tendency to defer to the courts on matters of securities litigation and enforcement? Under what circumstances has Congress been unwilling to defer?
- **The Many Roles of the SEC.** What types of issues are raised by the fact that the SEC – as a single administrative body—has the power to make law (through rulemaking), to enforce the law (through prosecutorial decisions), and to interpret the law (through adjudicating administrative proceedings)?
- **SEC Actions vs. Private Actions.** What are the respective advantages and disadvantages of relying on SEC actions rather than private actions to deter violations of the federal securities laws? Why have both Congress and the courts been more hospitable to SEC actions than to private actions for the past 25 years?
- **Implied Private Actions**. What difficulties are confronted by courts in interpreting, and by parties in litigating, implied private actions, such as those under Section 10(b) and Rule 10b-5, Section 14(a) and Rule 14a-9, and Section 14(e) of the Exchange Act?
- **Civil vs. Criminal.** When interpreting a securities provision in a civil action, must the court take account of the fact that the provision is also enforceable in a criminal action? If so, what should be the impact upon interpretation?

- **The Scope of Judicial Power.** Do courts exceed their authority when they "update" the federal securities laws to accommodate changes that have occurred since the 1930s, such as the greater ease of detecting insider trading or the increased internationalization of the securities markets? Why don't courts leave such updating to Congress?

- **Federal Law vs. State Law.** When interpreting the federal securities laws, how do courts distinguish between the competency of federal law and state corporate law? Does it make sense to distinguish between disclosure issues (covered by federal securities law) and fiduciary duty issues (covered by the law of the issuer's state of incorporation), particularly in view of the fact that disclosure is often an element of fiduciary duty and the additional fact that most breaches of fiduciary duty are concealed by the perpetrator? What are the implications for courts, and for counsel, of having numerous cases heard simultaneously in both state court (where fiduciary duty issues are resolved) and federal court (where disclosure issues under the federal securities laws are resolved)? What are the implications of introducing, on top of this dual forum litigation, the possibility of litigation under the blue sky laws of states where the issuer's securities are sold?

# Chapter 2

# SECTION 10(b) OF THE EXCHANGE ACT AND RULE 10b-5

Rule 10b-5 is the leading anti-fraud weapon in the federal securities laws. Its reach is vast, embracing fraud in the context of large publicly traded corporations as well as tiny close corporations. Likewise varied are its forms of enforcement: individual and class actions by investors, civil and administrative actions by the Securities and Exchange Commission (SEC or Commission), and criminal actions by the Department of Justice (DOJ).

The Commission adopted Rule 10b-5 in 1942 pursuant to Section 10(b) of the Exchange Act. Section 10 reads in pertinent part:

> It shall be unlawful for any person, directly or indirectly, by the use of any means or instrumentality of interstate commerce or of the mails, or of any facility of any national securities exchange— ***
>
> (b) To use or employ, in connection with the purchase or sale of any security registered on a national securities exchange or any security not so registered, *** any manipulative or deceptive device or contrivance in contravention of such rules and regulations as the Commission may prescribe as necessary or appropriate in the public interest or for the protection of investors.

Rule 10b-5 (which largely mirrors the language of Section 17(a) of the Securities Act) encompasses virtually as much as Section 10(b) itself:

> It shall be unlawful for any person, directly or indirectly, by the use of any means or instrumentality of interstate commerce, or of the mails or of any facility of any national securities exchange,
>
> (a) to employ any device, scheme, or artifice to defraud,
>
> (b) to make any untrue statement of a material fact or to omit to state a material fact necessary in order to make the statements made, in the light of the circumstances under which they were made, not misleading, or
>
> (c) to engage in any act, practice, or course of business which operates or would operate as a fraud or deceit upon any person,
>
> in connection with the purchase or sale of any security.

As is apparent, Rule 10b-5 and Section 10(b) say nothing about private enforcement. Beginning with *Kardon v. Nat'l Gypsum Co.*, 69 F. Supp. 512 (E.D. Pa. 1946), however, lower federal courts recognized an implied private action for violations of the Rule. The Supreme Court upheld the implied private action in a footnote in *Superintendent of Ins. v. Bankers Life & Cas. Co.*, 404 U.S. 6, 13 n. 9 (1971). See also *Herman & MacLean v. Huddleston,* 459 U.S. 375, 380 (1983) (describing the implied private action under Rule 10b-5 as "beyond peradventure"). But the Court offered no rationale for so doing, later observing that "the theory *** [was] to supplement" actions by the SEC and the DOJ. See *Musick, Peeler & Garrett v. Employers Ins.*, 508 U.S. 286, 291 (1993). See also *J.I. Case Co. v. Borak,* 377 U.S. 426, 432 (1964) (observing that "[p]rivate enforcement of the proxy rules provides a necessary supplement to Commission action").

Indeed, the courts (rather than the Commission) have been the principal interpreters of Rule 10b-5. Recognizing the implied private action has been only one aspect of this interpretative project (albeit an important one). Another aspect has been identifying the elements of the implied private action as well as those of SEC and criminal actions and giving the elements substantive content. Courts construing Rule 10b-5 have faced (and continue to face) formidable challenges given the confluence of the following:

• *Broad Language.* Section 10(b) and Rule 10b-5 are broadly worded, offering few bright lines as to how far the Rule's prohibition extends. Moreover, the language of the Section and the Rule is especially uninstructive with respect to matters that bear exclusively on the implied private action (such as standing or reliance), since neither provision was written with private actions in mind.

• *Limited History.* In the course of enacting the Exchange Act in 1934, Congress made only scant references to Section 10(b) in the floor debates and official reports. Moreover, when the SEC commissioners approved Rule 10b-5, the only comment made was "we are against fraud, aren't we?" Conference on Codification of the Federal Securities Laws, 22 Bus. Law. 793, 921-22 (1967) (comments of Milton Freeman).

• *Multiple Enforcement Contexts.* As mentioned, Rule 10b-5 is enforceable in criminal actions as well as in various types of civil actions. Interpretations of the Rule in one context may have undesirable ramifications when applied in other contexts.

• *Shifting Policies.* Until the mid-1970s, the Supreme Court gave Section 10(b) and Rule 10b-5 a relatively liberal reading in order to protect gullible investors from exploitation. See, e.g., *Affiliated Ute v. United States,* 406 U.S. 128, 151-54 (1972). Thereafter, the Court came to see at least some investors as essentially puppets of lawyers who filed securities actions irrespective of their merit simply to reach a settlement and collect a fee. Curtailing frivolous private actions thus became an important judicial policy. See, e,g., *Blue Chip Stamps v. Manor Drug Stores,* 421 U.S. 723, 739-47 (1975). But (perhaps not surprisingly) that policy has not invariably determined the result in specific cases. See, e.g., *Herman & MacLean v. Huddleston,* 459 U.S. 375, 387 (1983) (allowing a Rule 10b-5 action challenging conduct that was also actionable under Section 11 of the Securities Act). In addition, beginning in the 1970s, the Court adopted approaches to statutory interpretation that have carried significant consequences for the interpretation of Section 10(b) and Rule 10b-5: strict construction, constriction of implied private actions, and disregard for legislative history.

• *The Influence of the Efficient Capital Markets Hypothesis.* Recall from Chapter 1.G the efficient capital markets hypothesis (ECMH), which posits that the price of a security traded in an efficient market reflects all publicly available information. Courts have developed various Rule 10b-5 doctrines based on the

ECMH. One such doctrine is that of "fraud-on-the-market," which may undermine the policy of curtailing frivolous private actions mentioned above. Indeed, the fraud-on-the-market doctrine (where applicable) spares the plaintiffs the necessity of proving their individual reliance on the defendant's fraud by giving them a presumption of reliance on the integrity of the market price. Other Rule 10b-5 doctrines based on the ECMH include the "truth-on-the-market" defense (relevant when the information the defendant failed to disclose reaches the market through another source, such as a trade magazine) and the "puffery" defense (relevant when the alleged fraud amounts to overheated rhetoric lacking the specificity necessary to impact the market).

• *The Absence of Dependable Analogies.* Because Section 10(b) and Rule 10b-5 prohibit fraud, they virtually invite judicial analogies to common law deceit. But the deceit analogy is far from perfect, since Congress intended the federal securities laws to "rectify perceived deficiencies in the available common-law protections." *Herman & MacLean v. Huddleston,* 459 U.S. 375, 389 (1983). Another obvious potential analogy is Rule 14a-9, which you will study in Chapter 4. Adopted by the Commission pursuant to Section 14(a) of the Exchange Act, Rule 14a-9 prohibits material misstatements and omissions in proxy solicitations and, like Rule 10b-5, is enforceable in implied private actions as well as in SEC and criminal actions. Yet the proxy voting context involves distinctive considerations that may render Rule 14a-9 (at least some of the time) a less than reliable benchmark for interpreting Rule 10b-5.

• *Subsequent Congressional Enactments.* Congress has not ceded control of Section 10(b) and Rule 10b-5 entirely to the courts. Its most significant contribution in this regard has been the Private Securities Litigation Reform Act of 1995 (PSLRA), which makes maintenance of private securities actions more difficult by stiffening the pleading requirements, providing a safe harbor for fraud involving forward-looking statements, establishing an affirmative requirement of loss causation, adjusting the calculation of damages, and creating a scheme of proportionate liability. This Chapter addresses these matters, while Chapter 6 considers additional aspects of the PSLRA applicable exclusively to class actions.

Likewise important for Rule 10b-5 purposes is the Sarbanes-Oxley Act of 2002. Not only has that Act lengthened the statute of limitations for private actions under the Rule. In addition, it has expanded the scope of the "duty to disclose" upon which Rule 10b-5 liability often turns by directing the SEC to adopt "real time" disclosure rules for reporting companies. (For a discussion of reporting companies see Chapter 1.A.2.c.) This Chapter addresses the new statute of limitations and "real time" disclosure. Other aspects of the Sarbanes-Oxley Act are considered in connection with SEC enforcement (Chapter 9) and SEC regulation of accountants and attorneys (Chapter 10).

This Chapter examines the elements of Rule 10b-5, with emphasis upon the Rule's private enforcement. It is divided into ten sections: the requirement of manipulation or deception; the materiality requirement; the "in connection with" requirement; the scienter requirement; the purchaser-seller requirement; causation (encompassing both reliance and loss causation); damages; primary and secondary liability; the statute of limitations; and the overlap between Rule 10b-5 and the express private actions for material misstatements and omissions. Later chapters draw upon the elements of Rule 10b-5 in connection with securities class actions (Chapter 6); insider trading (Chapter 7); market manipulation (Chapter 8); SEC enforcement (Chapter 9); criminal enforcement (Chapter 11); and international securities fraud (Chapter 12).

As you proceed through the present Chapter, consider the following. Would Section 10(b) and Rule 10b-5 benefit from greater congressional involvement? Why have Congress's interventions (thus far at least) been for the most part marginal? Why do courts pay so little attention to the language of Rule 10b-5 and fixate instead on the language of Section 10(b)? To what extent does the policy of curbing frivolous private actions influence the outcome of decisions even when it is not mentioned explicitly? How (if at all) will the scandals at companies such as Enron and WorldCom impact the interpretation of Section 10(b) and Rule 10b-5? Have courts done enough to make the implied private action live up to the ostensible purpose for which it was created—to serve as a viable supplement to SEC and criminal actions?

In considering Rule 10b-5, it is important to keep in mind certain critical procedural matters. These involve pleading, dismissal of actions, discovery stays, and the burden of proof.

*Pleading.* The Federal Rules of Civil Procedure apply to all civil complaints filed in federal court. Although Rule 8 provides that plaintiffs need only plead "a short and plain statement of the claim showing that [they are] entitled to relief," Rule 9 sets the standard for "Pleading Special Matters," with Rule 9(b) providing that in "all averments of fraud or mistake, the circumstances constituting fraud or mistake shall be stated with particularity." Courts generally construe Rule 9(b) to require particularity in the pleading of what material misstatements or omissions were made, who made them, and where and when they were made.

The pleading burdens on private plaintiffs grew even greater with the enactment of the PSLRA, which added a new Section 21D(b)(1) to the Exchange Act:

**Section 21D(b)(1)—Misleading Statements and Omissions**

> In any private action arising under [the Exchange Act] in which the plaintiff alleges that the defendant—
>
> (A) made an untrue statement of a material fact; or
>
> (B) omitted to state a material fact necessary in order to make the statements made, in the light of the circumstances in which they were made, not misleading;
>
> the complaint shall specify each statement alleged to have been misleading, the reason or reasons why the statement is misleading, and, if an allegation regarding the statement or omission is made on information and belief, the complaint shall state with particularity all facts on which that belief is formed.

While at first blush this Section appears to pertain only to the pleading of material omissions and misstatements, its reach is actually broader. For example, the requirement to plead "the reason or reasons why the statement is misleading" bears on materiality and reliance. (The PSLRA also substantially raised a private plaintiff's burden of pleading scienter by adding Section

21D(b)(2) to the Exchange Act. We address this provision in connection with the scienter requirement in Section D of this Chapter).

*Dismissal of Actions and Discovery Stays.* The above-mentioned heightened pleading requirements for private plaintiffs must be considered in light of two additional provisions added to the Exchange Act as part of the PSLRA. One is Section 21D(b)(3)(A), which states that in any private action arising under the Exchange Act, "the court shall, on the motion of any defendant, dismiss the complaint" if the heightened requirements in Section 21D(b) are not met. The other equally significant addition is Section 21D(b)(3)(B), which requires a court to stay discovery during the pendency of any such motion to dismiss. This mandatory stay of discovery while a dismissal motion is pending permits only a limited exception when a "court finds upon motion of any party that particularized discovery is necessary to preserve evidence or to prevent undue prejudice to that party." As you read this Chapter, consider how Fed. R. Civ. P. 9(b) and the PSLRA's requirements for heightened pleading and mandatory stays of discovery interact with a plaintiff's ability to state a claim under Rule 10b-5.

*Burden of Proof.* For the small percentage of Rule 10b-5 civil actions that reach the trial stage, the proof must meet a "preponderance-of-the-evidence" standard. See *Herman & MacLean v. Huddleston,* 459 U.S. 375, 390 (1983).

## A. THE REQUIREMENT OF MANIPULATION OR DECEPTION

Section 10(b) of the Exchange Act prohibits, in connection with the purchase or sale of a security, "any manipulative or deceptive device or contrivance" in contravention of rules promulgated by the SEC for the protection of investors. Therefore, the scope of Section 10(b)—and hence also of Rule 10b-5—turns on the meaning of the phrase "manipulative or deceptive," regardless of whether the action is brought by a private party, the SEC, or the DOJ.

The term "manipulative" has a specialized meaning (as the following materials show) and is explored thoroughly in Chapter 8. The meaning of the term "deceptive"—traditionally the more nettlesome problem for the securities litigator—is our focal point here.

Deception includes outright misrepresentations as well as statements that mislead by omission, even if such statements are literally true (so-called half-truths). Rule 10b-5(b) explicitly prohibits both types of deception:

> It shall be unlawful for any person *** [t]o make any untrue statement of a material fact or to omit to state a material fact necessary in order to make the statements made, in the light of the circumstances under which they were made, not misleading *** in connection with the purchase or sale of a security.

As this language suggests, omissions and misstatements are actionable only when they are "material" (a requirement considered in depth in the next section of this Chapter). Subsections (a) and (c) of Rule 10b-5 also apply to material misstatements and omissions, although they are phrased more broadly than is Subsection (b).

Almost all of the recent litigation generated by the high-profile accounting scandals at WorldCom, Xerox, Rite Aid, Enron, and other industry giants focuses on material misstatements and omissions in the companies' annual and quarterly SEC filings and, more specifically, in their audited financial statements. The dollar amounts of those misstatements have been staggering: WorldCom (alleged to have inflated revenues by over $7 billion); Xerox ($1.9 billion); Rite Aid ($1.6 billion); and Enron ($1.2 billion). And while those scandals raise a host of interesting and complex doctrinal questions, it would (to say the least) be exceedingly difficult to argue that deception was not present.

This section of the Chapter addresses aspects of the deception element that are far less settled. The first part explores issues involving material misstatements and omissions in general, whereas the second part focuses on issues involving material omissions in particular.

### *1. Material Misstatements or Omissions in General*

We begin with *Santa Fe Industries, Inc. v. Green*, 430 U.S. 462 (1977), the critical starting point for understanding the meaning of the term "deceptive" in Section 10(b). That decision allows us to examine the circumstances capable of transforming a breach of fiduciary duty or other act of corporate mismanagement into deception that is actionable under Section 10(b) and Rule 10b-5. As we will see, such transformation requires, among other things, that the aggrieved investors show that they lost a state remedy. We then consider *Wharf v. United International Holdings, Inc.*, 532 U.S. 588 (2001), which addresses whether deception encompasses a secret intention not to perform a contract.

#### *a. "Mere" Breaches of Fiduciary Duty*

## SANTA FE INDUSTRIES, INC. v. GREEN

430 U.S. 462 (1977)

JUSTICE WHITE:

The issue in this case involves the reach and coverage of §10(b) of the Securities Exchange Act of 1934 and Rule 10b-5 thereunder in the context of a Delaware short-form merger transaction used by the majority stockholder of a corporation to eliminate the minority interest.

I

In 1936, petitioner Santa Fe Industries, Inc. (Santa Fe), acquired control of 60% of the stock of Kirby Lumber Corp. (Kirby), a Delaware corporation. Through a series of purchases over the succeeding years, Santa Fe increased its control of Kirby's stock to 95%; the purchase prices during the period 1968- 1973 ranged from $65 to $92.50 per share. In 1974, wishing to acquire 100% ownership of Kirby, Santa Fe availed itself of § 253 of the Delaware Corporation Law, known as the "short-form merger" statute. Section 253 permits a parent corporation owning at least 90% of the stock of a subsidiary to merge with that subsidiary, upon approval by the parent's board of directors, and to make payment in cash for the shares of the minority stockholders. The statute does not require the consent of, or advance notice to, the minority stockholders.

However, notice of the merger must be given within 10 days after its effective date, and any stockholder who is dissatisfied with the terms of the merger may petition the Delaware Court of Chancery for a decree ordering the surviving corporation to pay him the fair value of his shares, as determined by a court-appointed appraiser subject to review by the court. Del. Code Ann., Tit. 8, §§ 253, 262 (1975 ed. and Supp.1976).

Santa Fe obtained independent appraisals of the physical assets of Kirby land, timber, buildings, and machinery and of Kirby's oil, gas, and mineral interests. These appraisals, together with other financial information, were submitted to Morgan Stanley & Co. (Morgan Stanley), an investment banking firm retained to appraise the fair market value of Kirby stock. Kirby's physical assets were appraised at $320 million (amounting to $640 for each of the 500,000 shares); Kirby's stock was valued by Morgan Stanley at $125 per share. Under the terms of the merger, minority stockholders were offered $150 per share.

The provisions of the short-form merger statute were fully complied with. The minority stockholders of Kirby were notified the day after the merger became effective and were advised of their right to obtain an appraisal in Delaware court if dissatisfied with the offer of $150 per share. They also received an information statement containing, in addition to the relevant financial data about Kirby, the appraisals of the value of Kirby's assets and the Morgan Stanley appraisal concluding that the fair market value of the stock was $125 per share.

Respondents, minority stockholders of Kirby, objected to the terms of the merger, but did not pursue their appraisal remedy in the Delaware Court of Chancery. Instead, they brought this action in federal court on behalf of the corporation and other minority stockholders, seeking to set aside the merger or to recover what they claimed to be the fair value of their shares. The amended complaint asserted that, based on the fair market value of Kirby's physical assets as revealed by the appraisal included in the information statement sent to minority shareholders, Kirby's stock was worth at least $772 per share. The complaint alleged further that the merger took place without prior notice to minority stockholders; that the purpose of the merger was to appropriate the difference between the "conceded pro rata value of the physical assets," and the offer of $150 per share to "freez[e] out the minority stockholders at a wholly inadequate price;" and that Santa Fe, knowing the appraised value of the physical assets, obtained a "fraudulent appraisal" of the stock from Morgan Stanley and offered $25 above that appraisal "in order to lull the minority stockholders into erroneously believing that [Santa Fe was] generous." This course of conduct was alleged to be "a violation of Rule 10b-5 because defendants employed a 'device, scheme, or artifice to defraud' and engaged in an 'act, practice or course of business which operates or would operate as a fraud or deceit upon any person, in connection with the purchase or sale of any security.'" Morgan Stanley assertedly participated in the fraud as an accessory by submitting its appraisal of $125 per share although knowing the appraised value of the physical assets.

The District Court dismissed the complaint for failure to state a claim upon which relief could be granted. As the District Court understood the complaint, respondents' case rested on two distinct grounds. First, federal law was assertedly violated because the merger was for the sole purpose of eliminating the minority from the company, therefore lacking any justifiable business purpose, and because the merger was undertaken without prior notice to the minority shareholders. Second, the low valuation placed on the shares in the cash-exchange offer was itself said to be a fraud actionable under Rule 10b-5. ***

A divided Court of Appeals for the Second Circuit reversed. *** As to the first aspect of the case, the Court of Appeals did not disturb the District Court's conclusion that the complaint did not allege a material misrepresentation or nondisclosure with respect to the value of the stock; and the court declined to rule that a claim of gross undervaluation itself would suffice to make out a Rule 10b-5 case. With respect to the second aspect of the case, however, the court fundamentally disagreed with the District Court as to the reach and coverage of Rule 10b-5. The Court of Appeals' view was that, although the Rule plainly reached material misrepresentations and nondisclosures in connection with the purchase or sale of securities, neither misrepresentation nor nondisclosure was a necessary element of a Rule 10b-5 action; the Rule reached "breaches of fiduciary duty by a majority against minority shareholders without any charge of misrepresentation or lack of disclosure." The court went on to hold that the complaint, taken as a whole, stated a cause of action under the Rule:

> We hold that a complaint alleges a claim under Rule 10b-5 when it charges, in connection with a Delaware short-form merger, that the majority has committed a breach of its fiduciary duty to deal fairly with minority shareholders by effecting the merger without any justifiable business purpose. The minority shareholders are given no prior notice of the merger, thus having no opportunity to apply for injunctive relief, and the proposed price to be paid is substantially lower than the appraised value reflected in the Information Statement.

We granted the petition for certiorari challenging this holding because of the importance of the issue involved to the administration of the federal securities laws. We reverse.

II

Section 10(b) of the 1934 Act makes it "unlawful for any person ... to use or employ ... any manipulative or deceptive device or contrivance in contravention of [Securities and Exchange Commission rules]"; Rule 10b-5, promulgated by the SEC under § 10(b), prohibits, in addition to nondisclosure and misrepresentation, any "artifice to defraud" or any act "which operates or would operate as a fraud or deceit." The court below construed the term "fraud" in Rule 10b-5 by adverting to the use of the term in several of this Court's decisions in contexts other than the 1934 Act and the related Securities Act of 1933. The Court of Appeals' approach to the interpretation of Rule 10b-5 is inconsistent with that taken by the Court last Term in *Ernst & Ernst v. Hochfelder*, 425 U.S. 185 (1976).

*Ernst & Ernst* makes clear that in deciding whether a complaint states a cause of action for "fraud" under Rule 10b-5, "we turn first to the language of § 10(b), for '[t]he starting point in every case involving construction of a statute is the language itself.'" Id., at 197, quoting *Blue Chip Stamps v. Manor Drug Stores*, 421 U.S. 723, 756 (1975) (Powell, J., concurring). In holding that a cause of action under Rule 10b-5 does not lie for mere negligence, the Court began with the principle that "[a]scertainment of congressional intent with respect to the standard of liability created by a particular section of the [1933 and 1934] Acts must ... rest primarily on the language of that section," 425 U.S. at 200, and then focused on the statutory language of § 10(b) "[t]he words 'manipulative or deceptive' used in conjunction with 'device or contrivance.'" Id., at 197. The same language and the same principle apply to this case.

To the extent that the Court of Appeals would rely on the use of the term "fraud" in Rule 10b-5 to bring within the ambit of the Rule all breaches of fiduciary duty in connection with a securities transaction, it interpretation would, like the interpretation rejected by the Court in *Ernst & Ernst*, "add a gloss to the operative language of the statute quite different from its commonly accepted meaning." Id., at 199. But, as the Court there held, the language of the statute must control the interpretation of the Rule:

> "Rule 10b-5 was adopted pursuant to authority granted the [Securities and Exchange] Commission under § 10(b). The rulemaking power granted to an administrative agency charged with the administration of a federal statute is not the power to make law. Rather, it is " 'the power to adopt regulations to carry into effect the will of Congress as expressed by the statute' " [The scope of the Rule] cannot exceed the power granted the Commission by Congress under § 10(b)." Id., at 212-214.

The language of § 10(b) gives no indication that Congress meant to prohibit any conduct not involving manipulation or deception. Nor have we been cited to any evidence in the legislative history that would support a departure from the language of the statute. "When a statute speaks so specifically in terms of manipulation and deception, ... and when its history reflects no more expansive intent, we are quite unwilling to extend the scope of the statute...." Id., at 214. Thus the claim of fraud and fiduciary breach in this complaint states a cause of action under any part of Rule 10b-5 only if the conduct alleged can be fairly viewed as 'manipulative or deceptive' within the meaning of the statute.

III

It is our judgment that the transaction, if carried out as alleged in the complaint, was neither deceptive nor manipulative and therefore did not violate either § 10(b) of the Act or Rule 10b-5.

As we have indicated, the case comes to us on the premise that the complaint failed to allege a material misrepresentation or material failure to disclose. The finding of the District Court, undisturbed by the Court of Appeals, was that there was no "omission" or "misstatement" in the information statement accompanying the notice of merger. On the basis of the information provided, minority shareholders could either accept the price offered or reject it and seek an appraisal in the Delaware Court of Chancery. Their choice was fairly presented, and they were furnished with all relevant information on which to base their decision.[14]

We therefore find inapposite the cases relied upon by respondents and the court below, in which the breaches of fiduciary duty held violative of Rule 10b-5 included some element of deception. Those cases forcefully reflect the principle that "[§] 10(b) must be read flexibly, not technically and restrictively" and that the statute provides a cause of action for any plaintiff who "suffer[s] an injury as a result of deceptive practices touching its sale [or purchase] of securities. ..." *Superintendent of Insurance v. Bankers Life & Cas. Co.*, 404 U.S. 6, 12-13 (1971). But the cases do not support the proposition, adopted by the Court of Appeals below and urged by respondents here, that a breach of fiduciary duty by majority stockholders, without any deception, misrepresentation, or nondisclosure, violates the statute and the Rule.

It is also readily apparent that the conduct alleged in the complaint was not 'manipulative' within the meaning of the statute. "Manipulation" is "virtually a term of art when used in connection with securities markets." *Ernst & Ernst*, 425 U.S., at 199. The term refers generally to practices, such as wash sales, matched orders, or rigged prices, that are intended to mislead investors by artificially affecting market activity. See, e. g., § 9 of the 1934 Act (prohibiting specific manipulative practices). Section 10(b)'s general prohibition of practices deemed by the SEC to be "manipulative"—in this technical sense of artificially affecting market activity in order to mislead investors—is fully consistent with the fundamental purpose of the 1934 Act " 'to substitute a philosophy of full disclosure for the philosophy of *caveat emptor*....' " *Affiliated Ute Citizens v. United States*, 406 U.S. 128, 151 (1972), quoting *SEC v. Capital Gains Research Bureau*, 375 U.S. 180, 186 (1963). Indeed, nondisclosure is usually essential to the success of a manipulative scheme. No doubt Congress meant to prohibit the full range of ingenious devices that might be used to manipulate securities prices. But we do not think it would have chosen this "term of art" if it had meant to bring within the scope of § 10(b) instances of corporate mismanagement such as this, in which the essence of the complaint is that shareholders were treated unfairly by a fiduciary.

---

14. In addition to their principal argument that the complaint alleges a fraud under clauses (a) and (c) of Rule 10b-5, respondents also argue that the complaint alleges nondisclosure and misrepresentation in violation of clause (b) of the Rule. Their major contention in this respect is that the majority stockholder's failure to give the minority advance notice of the merger was a material nondisclosure, even though the Delaware short-form merger statute does not require such notice. Brief for Respondents 27. But respondents do not indicate how they might have acted differently had they had prior notice of the merger. Indeed, they accept the conclusion of both courts below that under Delaware law they could not have enjoined the merger because an appraisal proceeding is their sole remedy in the Delaware courts for any alleged unfairness in the terms of the merger. Thus, the failure to give advance notice was not a material nondisclosure within the meaning of the statute or the Rule. Cf. *TSC Industries, Inc. v. Northway, Inc.*, 426 U.S. 438 (1976).

IV

The language of the statute is, we think, "sufficiently clear in its context" to be dispositive here, *Ernst & Ernst*, supra, at 201; but even if it were not, there are additional considerations that weigh heavily against permitting a cause of action under Rule 10b-5 for the breach of corporate fiduciary duty alleged in this complaint. Congress did not expressly provide a private cause of action for violations of § 10(b). Although we have recognized an implied cause of action under that section in some circumstances, *Superintendent of Insurance v. Bankers Life & Cas. Co.*, supra, [404 U.S.] at 13 n. 9, we have also recognized that a private cause of action under the antifraud provisions of the Securities Exchange Act should not be implied where it is "unnecessary to ensure the fulfillment of Congress' purposes" in adopting the Act. *Piper v. Chris-Craft Industries*, 430 U.S., at 41, 97. Cf. *J. I. Case Co. v. Borak*, 377 U.S. 426, 431-433 (1964). As we noted earlier, the Court repeatedly has described the "fundamental purpose" of the Act as implementing a "philosophy of full disclosure"; once full and fair disclosure has occurred, the fairness of the terms of the transaction is at most a tangential concern of the statute. Cf. *Mills v. Electric Auto-Lite Co.*, 396 U.S. 375, 381-385 (1970). As in *Cort v. Ash*, 422 U.S. 66, 80 (1975), we are reluctant to recognize a cause of action here to serve what is "at best a subsidiary purpose" of the federal legislation.

A second factor in determining whether Congress intended to create a federal cause of action in these circumstances is "whether 'the cause of action [is] one traditionally relegated to state law. ...'" *Piper v. Chris-Craft Industries, Inc.*, 430 U.S., at 40, quoting *Cort v. Ash*, supra, at 78. The Delaware Legislature has supplied minority shareholders with a cause of action in the Delaware Court of Chancery to recover the fair value of shares allegedly undervalued in a short- form merger. Of course, the existence of a particular state-law remedy is not dispositive of the question whether Congress meant of provide a similar federal remedy, but as in *Cort* and *Piper*, we conclude that "it is entirely appropriate in this instance to relegate respondent and others in his situation to whatever remedy is created by state law." 422 U.S., at 84; 430 U.S., at 41.

The reasoning behind a holding that the complaint in this case alleged fraud under Rule 10b-5 could not be easily contained. It is difficult to imagine how a court could distinguish, for purposes of Rule 10b-5 fraud, between a majority stockholder's use of a short-form merger to eliminate the minority at an unfair price and the use of some other device, such as a long-form merger, tender offer, or liquidation, to achieve the same result; or indeed how a court could distinguish the alleged abuses in these going private transactions from other types of fiduciary self-dealing involving transactions in securities. The result would be to bring within the Rule a wide variety of corporate conduct traditionally left to state regulation. In addition to posing a "danger of vexatious litigation which could result from a widely expanded class of plaintiffs under Rule 10b-5," *Blue Chip Stamps v. Manor Drug Stores*, 421 U.S., at 740, this extension of the federal securities laws would overlap and quite possibly interfere with state corporate law. Federal courts applying a "federal fiduciary principle" under Rule 10b-5 could be expected to depart from state fiduciary standards at least to the extent necessary to ensure uniformity within the federal system. Absent a clear indication of congressional intent, we are reluctant to federalize the substantial portion of the law of corporations that deals with transactions in securities, particularly where established state policies of corporate regulation would be overridden. As the Court stated in *Cort v. Ash*, supra: "Corporations are creatures of state law, and investors commit their funds to corporate directors on the understanding that, except where federal law *expressly* requires certain responsibilities of directors with respect to stockholders, state law will govern the internal affairs of the corporation." 422 U.S., at 84 (emphasis added).

We thus adhere to the position that "Congress by § 10(b) did not seek to regulate transactions which constitute no more than internal corporate mismanagement." *Superintendent of Insurance v. Bankers Life & Cas. Co.*, 404 U.S., at 12. There may well be a need for uniform federal fiduciary standards to govern mergers such as that challenged in this complaint. But those standards should not be supplied by judicial extension of § 10(b) and Rule 10b-5 to "cover the corporate universe."[17]

The judgment of the Court of Appeals is reversed, and the case is remanded for further proceedings consistent with this opinion. ***

## *NOTES AND QUESTIONS*

***1. Federal vs. State Law.*** The Court distinguished between a breach of fiduciary duty (governed by the corporate governance law of the issuer's state of incorporation) and conduct involving deception in connection with the purchase or sale of a security (governed by the federal securities laws as well as by state blue sky laws). The United States is unique among major industrialized countries in drawing such a sharp jurisdictional as well as doctrinal distinction between "corporate law" and "securities law." Do these distinctions make sense? Does it make sense to litigate them in different fora?

Is the distinction between conduct involving deception and conduct "merely" involving a breach of fiduciary duty as obvious as the Court makes it seem? See Donald C. Langevoort, Seeking Sunlight in *Santa Fe*'s Shadow: The SEC's Pursuit of Managerial Accountability, 79 Wash. U. L.Q. 449, 451 (2001) (emphasizing that "[t]here are not many instances of governance abuse that are disclosed with complete candor" and that "[h]idden breaches of fiduciary obligation can almost always be characterized in terms of fraud or misrepresentation"). See also Jennifer O'Hare, Director Communications and the Uneasy Relationship Between the Fiduciary Duty of Disclosure and the Anti-Fraud Provisions of the Federal Securities Laws, 70 U. Cin. L. Rev. 475 (2002); Faith Stevelman Kahn, Transparency and Accountability: Rethinking Corporate Fiduciary Law's Relevance to Corporate Disclosure, 34 Ga. L. Rev. 505 (2000); Lawrence A. Hamermesh, Calling Off the Lynch Mob: The Corporate Director's Fiduciary Disclosure Duty, 49 Vand. L. Rev. 1087 (1996). Assume that you

---

17. Cary, Federalism and Corporate Law: Reflections Upon Delaware, 83 Yale L.J. 663, 700 (1974) (footnote omitted). Professor Cary argues vigorously for comprehensive federal fiduciary standards, but urges a "frontal" attack by a new federal statute rather than an extension of Rule 10b-5. He writes: "It seems anomalous to jigsaw every kind of corporate dispute into the federal courts through the securities acts as they are presently written." Ibid.

represent plaintiffs in a Rule 10b-5 action similar to *Santa Fe*. Given the *Santa Fe* precedent, what facts would you try to develop in order to insure that the action remains in federal court as a Rule 10b-5 action?

*2. **Judicial Economy.*** Was the *Santa Fe* decision justified by considerations of judicial economy? Consider the ramifications if the Court had held breach of fiduciary duty claims to be actionable under Section 10(b) and Rule 10b-5. Under these circumstances, would federal courts have generated a federal common law of fiduciary duties or would they have endeavored to follow state corporate law? If the latter, what would have happened if federal and state courts arrived at different interpretations of state law? What consequences would have ensued if the same fiduciary duty issue arose in federal and state courts simultaneously?

*3. **Reconsidering Fairness.*** As part of its sweeping legislation precipitated by the corporate and accounting scandals that rocked the securities markets in 2001-02, Congress required, and the SEC subsequently adopted, broad new rules mandating the certification of the annual and quarterly filings that must be made by reporting companies under the Exchange Act. Under these new rules, the issuer's chief executive officer and chief financial officer (or persons performing similar functions) must make a number of certifications, including that:

> (1) He or she has reviewed the report being filed; [and]
>
> (2) Based on his or her knowledge, the report does not contain any untrue statement of a material fact or omit to state a material fact necessary to make the statements made, in light of the circumstances under which such statements were made, not misleading with respect to the period covered by the report; [and]
>
> (3) Based on his or her knowledge, the financial statements, and other financial information included in the report, fairly present in all material respects the financial condition, results of operations and cash flows of the issuer as of, and for, the periods presented in the report.

Exchange Act Rules 13a-14 and 15d-14. See also Section 302 of the Sarbanes-Oxley Act.

Consider how (or whether) a report that satisfies the truthfulness condition in subsection (2) could nonetheless violate the fairness condition in subsection (3). Ascertaining the meaning of this fairness requirement will clearly be a top corporate priority, particularly because another provision of the Sarbanes-Oxley Act imposes similar certification requirements upon CEOs and CFOs and authorizes stiff criminal fines and prison terms for a "knowing" certification of a noncomplying report. See Section 906 of the Sarbanes-Oxley Act (codified at 18 U.S.C. § 1350 and providing for fines of up to $1 million and prison terms of not more than 10 years, or both, when the certification is "knowing" and fines up to $5 million and prison terms of not more than 20 years, or both, when the certification is not only "knowing" but done "willfully"). Note also that in its release adopting Rules 13a-14 and 15d-14, the SEC specifically stated that "an officer providing a false certification potentially could be subject to *** both Commission and private actions for violating Section 10(b) of the Exchange Act and Exchange Act Rule 10b-5." Final Rules:

Certification of Disclosure in Companies' Quarterly and Annual Reports, Exchange Act Release No. 46427 (Aug. 29, 2002).

What is the difference between the fairness representation now required by CEOs and CFOs and the fairness issue that arose in *Santa Fe*?

---

*b. Corporate Mismanagement and Lost State Remedies*

In its landmark decision in *Goldberg v. Meridor*, 567 F.2d 209 (2d Cir. 1977), the Second Circuit built on footnote 14 in *Santa Fe* to hold that Section 10(b)'s deception requirement encompasses a breach by directors of their fiduciary duty to minority shareholders regarding an impending corporate transaction in the situation where the directors misstated or omitted the existence of the breach and because of that misstatement or omission, the minority shareholders lost the opportunity to have the transaction enjoined under state law. The following decision discusses *Goldberg*. Which opinion do you find more persuasive—that of the majority or the dissent?

## HEALEY v. CATALYST RECOVERY OF PENNSYLVANIA, INC.

616 F.2d 641 (3rd Cir. 1980)

SEITZ, CHIEF JUDGE:

Five individual and three corporate defendants appeal from a judgment entered against them on a jury verdict awarding the plaintiff damages for violation of §10(b) of the Securities Exchange Act of 1934 and rule 10b-5.

*I. Factual Background*

In the spring of 1972, the plaintiff became a 20% shareholder and president of Catalyst Regeneration Services, Inc. (CRS), a Texas corporation. CRS set up its only plant in Pennsylvania and began regenerating oil refining catalysts (a process by which the catalyst is cleaned for reuse).

In early 1975, defendant P. K. Maher, a research chemist in the field of petroleum catalysts, decided to acquire an existing company and enter the regeneration market. Maher began contacting people in the Baltimore area in his search for investors for his plan. The first investor to join him was defendant Robert H. Levi, vice chairman of the board of directors at Mercantile Safe Deposit & Trust Co. (Mercantile). Levi then introduced Maher to defendant Lawrence P. Naylor, III, who also invested.

At about the same time, Maher began soliciting legal and business help in setting up and running his company, which was incorporated in Maryland and became known as SCR, Inc. (SCR). [SCR later changed its name to Catalyst Recovery, Inc.] He persuaded defendant Dennis J. Shaughnessy, a vice president at Mercantile, and defendant Wilbert H. Sirota, a partner in a Baltimore law firm, to assist him with planning the acquisition of an existing company. Eventually, Maher, Naylor, Shaughnessy, and Sirota became officers and/or directors of SCR and its subsidiary companies, all of which were made defendants.

In July of 1975, after studying the existing regeneration companies, Maher decided to purchase CRS, the plaintiff's company. Shaughnessy began negotiating a stock purchase with the major shareholder of CRS. The negotiations over the price to be paid for the stock continued for the next four months. In November of 1975, all the shareholders of CRS other than the plaintiff agreed in principle to sell their 80% at a price of $5.25 per share. The plaintiff knew of this agreement and the previous offers and counteroffers but did not join in the agreement.

Next, in December, Maher, Naylor, and Sirota discussed with the plaintiff on behalf of SCR a possible purchase from him of the remaining 20% of the CRS stock. Plaintiff testified that he requested certain information at these December meetings that he never received. This information included long and short range plans for SCR, the identity of SCR board members and shareholders, and other similar information. The defendants admit that some of the information was never given to the plaintiff. In the course of the negotiations, the plaintiff submitted a proposed purchase option and a request for an employment contract. Sirota replied by letter on December 24 that SCR would only buy the plaintiff's shares on the same terms as the other 80%. ***

On March 2, 1976, SCR purchased 80% of the CRS stock pursuant to the agreement the previous November. On March 15, a new board of directors for CRS was elected without the plaintiff being reelected. For the rest of March, the plaintiff and Maher continued discussions but could not agree on a price.

In early April, a decision was made by SCR to form a new company and effect a merger between it and CRS. Accordingly, Catalyst Recovery of Pennsylvania, Inc. (CRPa) was incorporated in Maryland as a wholly owned subsidiary of SCR. SCR then transferred its own preferred shares to CRPa.

On April 12, 1976, Maher gave the plaintiff a copy of the proposed merger between CRS and CRPa along with a notice of a CRS shareholders meeting to be held on May 3 to vote to approve the merger, a description of the SCR preferred stock, and an SCR balance sheet. Under the merger proposal, if the CRS shareholders voted to approve (which was inevitable under Texas law given SCR's 80% ownership of CRS), then the CRS shareholders would transfer their CRS shares to CRPa in return for the SCR preferred.

On April 27, the plaintiff's attorney sent a letter to Sirota requesting six categories of information,[2] objecting to the merger, and threatening legal action.

---

2. The letter stated:

The information received about the proposed merger is woefully inadequate and is deficient in at least the following respects:

1. Failure to disclose the rationale for fixing the rate of exchange of the [CRS] common stock for the SCR preferred stock as called for in the merger proposal.

2. Failure to disclose the identity of the persons who fixed the exchange rate called for in the merger proposal and whether any conflicts of interest exist that could affect the judgment of the persons who fixed the rate of exchange.

3. Failure to furnish copies of recent audited financial statements of SCR so that a shareholder of [CRS] will have available to him material information he requires to determine whether to accept or reject the exchange offer called for in the merger proposal.

4. The failure to obtain and provide to shareholders of [CRS] an independent evaluation of their [CRS] stock.

On April 28, the plaintiff sent a letter to Maher objecting to the merger and expressing his "intention to exercise his right to dissent."

On April 29, SCR did two things. First, Donovan M. Hamm, Jr., a member of Sirota's law firm, called one of the plaintiff's lawyers and stated a willingness to provide information and said the merger still would go through. Second, the same day Hamm sent a letter to the plaintiff's lawyer. Among other things, it answered some of the questions in the plaintiff's attorney's April 27 letter and confirmed the telephone offer to permit inspection of SCR documents and records by the plaintiff.[3]

On May 3, 1976, SCR voted its 80% of the CRS stock to approve the CRS-CRPa merger. On May 11, the plaintiff's attorney again wrote a letter to Sirota asking for a chance to inspect the information as had been suggested in Hamm's April 29 letter. No such inspection ever occurred. See note 3 supra.

The merger became effective June 30, 1976, and the plaintiff filed this suit seeking an injunction and damages under § 10(b) and rule 10b-5. The plaintiff also filed an appraisal petition in Texas court in September 1976, which was dismissed without prejudice in August 1977. After a lengthy jury trial in federal court, the jury found for the plaintiff for $189,400 plus prejudgment interest. This appeal followed.

*II. Existence of a Cause of Action*

The major contention of the defendants concerns a recurring problem of recent years: the role of rule 10b-5 in the context of mergers effected under state law. At trial, the plaintiff argued that if he had been given the information he requested, he would have tried to enjoin the merger in state court.[4] He relied

---

5. The failure to obtain and provide to shareholders of [CRS] an independent evaluation of the SCR preferred stock.

6. The general failure to provide other material information about SCR which would enable a shareholder to make an informed investment decision.

3. The defendants argue that this offer means there was no omission of information. The jury could have believed, however, either that the offer came too late (it was four days before the CRS shareholders meeting) or that the plaintiff reasonably felt that the defendants were not serious. ***

4. The plaintiff testified:

Q: Can you tell us why you wanted this information?. . . .
A: Yes. I had to make a decision before May 3rd. What was I going to do? My lawyers told me that I could have tried to obtain an injunction to stop the merger vote.
Q: What's an injunction?
A: This is an order from a court that would have stopped that merger.
Q: Did you consider that at the time?
A: Yes, we considered that.
Q: Okay. Did you go and seek one?
A: No, we did not.
Q: Why not?
A: We didn't have enough information to go to a judge and tell him that there's sufficient reason.

on *Goldberg v. Meridor*, 567 F.2d 209 (2d Cir. 1977), which held that such a theory states a basis for a cause of action under rule 10b-5. The defendants argue that under *Goldberg*, the plaintiff must prove that he would have obtained the injunction had he been given the information in question. Although *Goldberg* did not expressly consider this issue, the defendants' position was adopted in *Kidwell ex rel. Penfold v. Meikle*, 597 F.2d 1273 (9th Cir. 1979).

Initially, we must determine whether this circuit should adopt the reasoning of *Goldberg*. Some have argued that *Goldberg* is inconsistent with the Supreme Court's opinion in *Santa Fe Industries, Inc. v. Green*, 430 U.S. 462 (1977). E.g., Note, *Goldberg v. Meridor*: The Second Circuit's Resurrection of Rule 10b-5 Liability for Breaches of Corporate Fiduciary Duties to Minority Shareholders, 64 Va.L.Rev. 765 (1978).

In *Santa Fe*, minority shareholders brought suit under rule 10b-5 challenging the fairness of the terms of a short form merger effectuated under Delaware law. The Court noted: "[T]he complaint failed to allege a material misrepresentation or material failure to disclose. The finding of the District Court ... was that there was no 'omission' or 'misstatement'. ..." 430 U.S. at 474. The Court therefore held that because the language of both § 10(b) and rule 10b-5 required some kind of improper flow of information, whether deception, misrepresentation, manipulation, or nondisclosure, the complaint failed to state a cause of action. Id. at 474-77.

Although the statutory language in *Santa Fe* was "'sufficiently clear in its context' to be dispositive here," id. at 477 (quoting *Ernst & Ernst v. Hochfelder*, 425 U.S. 185, 201 (1976)), the Court in Part IV of its opinion went on to examine other reasons for its refusal to find a cause of action under rule 10b-5. Noting that the essence of the complaint was a breach of fiduciary duty by the majority shareholders, the Court characterized this as "corporate conduct traditionally left to state regulation." Id. at 478. The Court concluded: "Absent a clear indication of congressional intent, we are reluctant to federalize the substantial portion of the law of corporations that deals with transactions in securities, particularly where established state policies of corporate regulation would be overridden." Id. at 479.

In *Santa Fe*, the minority's only possible state law remedy was appraisal. See id. at 474 n.14,. The United States Court of Appeals for the Second Circuit distinguished the case in part on this ground in *Goldberg v. Meridor*, 567 F.2d 209 (2d Cir. 1977). In that case, under New York law the plaintiffs could seek an injunction against the merger in addition to their appraisal rights. Thus the information in the case was material to a reasonable investor because he could have used it to attempt to obtain an injunction.

It is important to note at the outset the difference between *Goldberg* and *Santa Fe*. The mere existence of a state injunctive remedy would be insufficient, by itself, to distinguish *Santa Fe*. The crucial difference is whether there was misrepresentation or omission in the flow of information between the majority and minority shareholders. In *Santa Fe*, the Supreme Court expressly noted that there had been no misinformation connected with the merger. By contrast, in *Goldberg*, the plaintiffs claimed that a parent corporation had either not disclosed or misleadingly disclosed information concerning its sale of the overvalued assets of its controlled subsidiary, some of the shares of which were held by the public.

We believe that this distinction concerning the flow of information between the majority and minority shareholders is persuasive. There is a strong federal interest, evidenced by the entire field of federal securities regulation, in ensuring a proper flow of information between the parties to a securities transaction. The Supreme Court has sanctioned a private cause of action under rule 10b-5 on behalf of sellers to enforce that federal interest. See *Santa Fe*, supra, 430 U.S. at 477, citing *Superintendent of Insurance v. Bankers Life & Casualty Co.*, 404 U.S. 6, 13 n.9 (1971). All that *Goldberg* holds is that if some misrepresentation or omission by the defendant prevents the plaintiff from stopping the merger through a state injunction, then there is a cause of action under rule 10b-5. Because this result flows from misinformation that harms the plaintiff, it is precisely the type of situation to which rule 10b-5 is addressed.

Nor do we perceive an inconsistency between this result and Part IV of *Santa Fe*. Part IV should not be read out of context. What was objectionable in *Santa Fe* was use of rule 10b-5 by the federal courts to override traditional areas of state law "[a]bsent a clear indication of congressional intent." 430 U.S. at 479. Thus the problem in *Santa Fe* was not merely federal judicial intrusion into areas of state law, but rather federal judicial invasion of areas of state law without explicit federal statutory authority.

Here, by contrast, the plaintiff alleges that the defendants engaged in conduct expressly forbidden by the statute and the rule: an omission of certain information claimed to be material. That the harm to the plaintiff from the omission was deprivation of a state remedy in no sense diminishes the federal interest in preventing the omission and thereby ensuring full disclosure of all material information in securities transactions. Indeed, deprivation of state rights and remedies often forms the basis for federal claims. See, e. g., Hart & Wechsler's The Federal Courts and the Federal System 500-06 (2d ed. 1973).

Moreover, the federal courts have a duty under the supremacy clause of the Constitution to ensure that federal interests are vindicated. The Supreme Court has permitted use of the securities laws in the merger context where there has been misinformation that violates a specific federal provision. See, e.g., *TSC Industries, Inc. v. Northway, Inc.*, 426 U.S. 438 (1976) (proxy rules). Thus we do not feel that *Santa Fe* can be read to force us to stay our hand from remedying the harm that flows from the very type of conduct to which specific federal statutory and regulatory provisions are addressed.

Accordingly, we hold that where a misrepresentation or omission of material information deprives a proper plaintiff minority shareholder of an opportunity under state law to enjoin a merger, there is a cause of action under rule 10b-5. ***

Having determined that the plaintiff has a cause of action, we now consider the defendants' [contention] *** that a plaintiff must make some type of showing on the question of whether he would have actually been granted the injunction had he been given the information in question. The United States

Court of Appeals for the Ninth Circuit in *Kidwell ex rel. Penfold v. Meikle*, 597 F.2d 1273 (9th Cir. 1979), adopted this rule on the theory that to hold otherwise would be inconsistent with *Santa Fe*'s concern over federal judicial encroachment on areas of law traditionally left to the states.

We feel it is better to view this question as an aspect of the materiality requirement. As already noted, once a sufficient disruption in the flow of information is alleged, as in *Goldberg* and here, the concerns expressed in Part IV of *Santa Fe* are not present. Therefore, *Santa Fe* is not particularly helpful in deciding whether there must be proof that the plaintiff had some chance of success in his injunctive suit. The theory of *Goldberg* is that the plaintiff wanted the information to make a decision whether to apply for a state injunction. Accordingly, we think a doctrine that is geared to the plaintiff's decisionmaking process is more suitable for analyzing the question the defendants have raised here.

*** Seen as a question of materiality, the issue of the plaintiff's ability to secure an injunction is easily resolved. Unless there is a reasonable probability that a shareholder could have used the information to obtain an injunction, then the information would not be important to the decisionmaking process of a reasonable investor. We therefore hold that in a case such as this the plaintiff must demonstrate that at the time of the misrepresentation or omission, there was a reasonable probability of ultimate success in securing an injunction had there been no misrepresentation or omission. Although *Meikle* speaks in terms of actual success, we frame the test in terms of a reasonable probability for two reasons. First, we believe absolute certainty to be both an impossible goal as well as an impracticable standard for a jury to implement. Second, in most cases the state remedy will be a preliminary injunction, which looks to the likelihood of ultimate success.

It is important to stress here the relationship of the information to the injunction. As already noted, the mere existence of an injunctive remedy is not enough; the information must be of a type that if the plaintiff had the information not supplied, he could use it to seek an injunction. For example, in a case of omitted information, the question is whether, if the plaintiff had received the information, it would have been significant to the determination of the reasonable probability of ultimate success.

Applying these principles to the facts here, we find that a remand is necessary. One can enjoin a merger for any of several reasons: fraud, illegality, ultra vires act, or unfairness. See generally W. Cary, Cases and Materials on Corporations 1707-12 (4th ed. 1969). It is unclear which, if any, of these doctrines would apply under Texas law. See, e. g., Texas Bus.Corp.Act Ann. art. 5.16.E(5) (Vernon Cum. Supp.1978-1979); *Governing Board v. Pannill*, 561 S.W.2d 517 (Tex.Civ.App.1977); *Inter-Continental Corp. v. Moody*, 411 S.W.2d 578 (Tex.Civ.App. 1966); *Farnsworth v. Massey*, 365 S.W.2d 1 (Tex.1963).

In any event, we cannot decide the question here because the district court did not address this issue and it has not been briefed in this court. Therefore, we remand to the district court to consider in the first instance whether there was sufficient evidence to create a jury issue on the question of the plaintiff's reasonable probability of ultimate success under Texas law. This requires a two-step inquiry. First, the court should determine what information the jury could reasonably believe was withheld. Second, it should determine whether any of that information could have been used to obtain a Texas injunction. If there was as a matter of law no reasonable probability of ultimate success, the information is not material. ***

ALDISERT, CIRCUIT JUDGE, DISSENTING:

*** Healey's private action does not further the policies embodied in the securities laws. As the Court noted in *Santa Fe*, "the 'fundamental purpose' of the Act [is to implement] a 'philosophy of full disclosure'; once full and fair disclosure has occurred, the fairness of the terms of the transaction is at most a tangential concern of the statute." 430 U.S. at 477-78 (citation omitted). Although Healey does allege nondisclosure, the entire thrust of his state claim for injunctive relief would have been that the terms of the merger were unfair to him. By requiring him to demonstrate a reasonable probability of success in the state action, the majority require him to demonstrate unfairness to prevail on his federal claim. The majority thus deem concern for fairness, under the guise of nondisclosure, sufficient under the federal statutory schema to serve as a passport into a federal courtroom. Apart from its unjustified assumption that the concern for fairness cannot be vindicated in the state court system, the failure of this approach is dramatically demonstrated by the effect of the federal action. Healey's action serves only to protect his state breach of fiduciary duty action, which deals with a concern—fairness—that is "'at best a subsidiary purpose' of the federal legislation." 430 U.S. at 478. Thus, Healey has succeeded in slipping through the back door what federal courts are loathe to let him do directly: He challenges the fairness of a state corporate transaction, using the majority's test of "a reasonable probability of ultimate success" in the state action, by asserting his claim under the federal securities laws.

Not only do I fail to see how federal evaluation of the transaction's fairness serves the purpose of the federal schema, I also fail to see how Healey's action promotes full disclosure. By creating a federal action under these facts, the majority do not provide a remedy in damages that is unavailable under state law. The measure of damages is the same; no additional monetary relief can be forthcoming under rule 10b-5. If the plaintiff here is successful in the federal action, the defendants will be required to pay the plaintiff the fair value of his stock. This measure of damages is the same one available under state law, because if no federal action were implied, plaintiff would be limited to the parallel state court appraisal action, in which the defendants would also be required to pay the plaintiff the fair value of his stock. If there is no additional relief in the federal forum, I fail to see how the availability of federal relief vindicates the commendable objective of full disclosure. Moreover, by the time the federal action accrues, the merger will be completed and injunctive relief will be impossible under both state and federal law. Thus, if a state appraisal proceeding, giving relief virtually identical to the federal action, does not currently promote sufficient disclosure for Healey's injunction action, I cannot understand how a federal rule 10b-5 action will.

*** Healey's action also enters an area traditionally relegated to state law, *** [and a] clearer instance of a plaintiff asking federal courts to usurp state functions is difficult to imagine. The allegation is that the defendants violated federal law by withholding information critical to Healey's state claim. Not only does Healey's claim present an unpersuasive case for a federal remedy, it creates a startling irony. Under the majority's formulation, only if a plaintiff has a state claim for an injunction can he recover under federal rule 10b-5 for breach of fiduciary duty. If state injunctive relief is unavailable, as in *Santa Fe*, the plaintiff also has no federal remedy. Thus, rather than aiding plaintiffs under federal law who have no state remedy, the majority's formulation provides federal relief to plaintiffs who have state remedies, but denies federal relief to plaintiffs who have no state remedy! See Note, *Goldberg v. Meridor*: The Second Circuit's Resurrection of Rule 10b-5 Liability for Breaches of Corporate Fiduciary Duties to Minority Shareholders, 64 Va.L.Rev. 765, 776 (1978).

In *Santa Fe* the Court admonished against "extension of the federal securities laws" to the extent that they "overlap and quite possibly interfere with state corporate law." 430 U.S. at 479. By recognizing a federal action for the mere failure to release information relevant to a state action, the majority risk interference with state corporate law. ***

Most bothersome, however, is the implicit assumption by the majority that only federal courts can grant proper relief to an injured party whenever transactions in securities are involved. Traditional state remedies guarantee the plaintiff an appraisal procedure through which he can obtain the fair value of his stock. An action under rule 10b-5 guarantees him no more. Because it assures the plaintiff of no greater recovery than he could obtain in his state action, I cannot see how it promotes greater disclosure than the state action. Absent explicit legislative sanction, therefore, federal encroachment into this area is justified only if the federal courts do a superior job of administering the remedy. *** Because I cannot begin to accept the notion that federal judges have better expertise in state corporate law than state judges, I have no qualms about deferring to the state judiciaries and legislatures. Deference is supported by the admonitions of the Supreme Court regarding the breadth of the securities laws and its statements regarding the relationship of federal and state judiciaries.

Accordingly, because I cannot justify the majority's bold action in "federaliz[ing a] substantial portion of the law of corporations that deals with transactions in securities," *Santa Fe Industries, Inc. v. Green*, 430 U.S. at 479, I dissent. I would vacate the judgment of the district court and remand these proceedings with a direction to dismiss the action for lack of federal subject matter jurisdiction.

### *NOTES AND QUESTIONS*

***1. A Back Door Through* Santa Fe.** The dissenting opinion asserts that the majority effectively gives plaintiffs a means of overcoming the Supreme Court's *Santa Fe* decision. Is it correct in so asserting?

***2. Characterizing State Law as Federal Law.*** Were you convinced by the *Healey* court's transformation of a state law fiduciary duty issue into a federal securities disclosure issue? Will a court that follows the *Healey* approach have to decide state law issues in order to determine if there is an actionable failure to disclose?

*3. **Demonstrating the Loss of a State Remedy.*** Under what circumstances is a plaintiff most likely to succeed in showing that he lost a state remedy? Is a plaintiff in a stronger position if he shows an undisclosed breach of fiduciary duty coupled with (i) a lost opportunity to seek an appraisal, (ii) a lost opportunity to seek an injunction against a transaction, and/or (iii) a lost opportunity to sue for damages? Is the appropriate standard *Healey*'s "reasonable probability of ultimate success" in the state action? Would a higher standard be better ? A lower one?

*4. **Pleading and Preparing a Lost-State-Remedy Case.*** In pleading loss of a state remedy, you might consider including (i) a specific description of the remedy lost by your client and an explanation of why it would have been available under state procedural and substantive law; (ii) an explanation of how the undisclosed information related to the availability of the state remedy; (iii) an explanation of how the undisclosed information affected a reasonable investor's decision about whether to seek a state remedy; and (iv) your client's likelihood of prevailing in state court had she sought the state remedy in question. How much emphasis would you give to each of these factors? In determining your strategy, be sure to consider the heightened pleading requirements in Section 21D(b)(1) of the Exchange Act (set forth at the beginning of this Chapter).

*5. **Litigation Decisions vs. Investment Decisions.*** *Goldberg* and *Healey* present one approach to whether undisclosed breaches of fiduciary duty are actionable under Rule 10b-5. The Seventh Circuit has rejected that approach in favor of an alternative which looks to whether the alleged misstatements or omissions affect "an investment decision." Consider Judge Easterbrook's analysis:

> ***What should happen when the missing information affected a decision not to file a lawsuit about the securities, as in *Goldberg v. Meridor*?
>
> We have suggested in recent years that the appropriate inquiry is whether the information disclosed or withheld affected an investment decision. E.g., *Harris Trust & Savings Bank v. Ellis*, 810 F.2d 700, 704 (7th Cir.1987). See also *Rand v. Anaconda-Ericsson, Inc.*, 794 F.2d 843, 847-48 (2d Cir.1986). The securities laws single out investment decisions concerning financial instruments from among the many decisions people must make. Whether to buy a house or go to school or take a job or file a suit may be important, but the securities laws do not apply to these decisions. The securities laws deal with instruments that have at least the potential to be traded in liquid markets, see *Marine Bank v. Weaver*, 455 U.S. 551, 560 (1982). Information about these instruments should be compiled and released by a single source, usually the issuer, to facilitate both trading among passive investors and the ability to compare the prospects of one firm against the prospects of others—a comparison essential if capital is to flow to its most valuable uses. If a person is locked into possession of a security, however, disclosure serves neither of these functions. Capital has been committed, and trading will not occur. Decisions concerning the securities then are not fundamentally different from decisions concerning works of art. The buyer of a purported Rembrandt who learns that the painting was only by "the studio of" the artist faces a tough decision, but not an investment decision.

*LHLC Corp. v. Cluett, Peabody & Co.*, 842 F.2d 928, 931-32 (7th Cir. 1988). Is the Seventh Circuit's approach preferable?

At issue in *LHLC* was a misrepresentation involving a valuation of inventory that was made in connection with the sale of securities. Judge Easterbrook concluded that "[t]he [misrepresented] information, even if conventionally 'material,' did not affect the investment decision." Id. at 931. When the focus is on the "investment decision," what other elements of a Rule 10b-5 action are implicated? Does the following note suggest at least a partial answer?

***6. A Possible Proxy Fraud Analogy.*** A problem analogous to that in *Healey* arose in *Virginia Bankshares, Inc. v. Sandberg*, 501 U.S. 1083 (1991), an action under Section 14(a) of the Exchange Act and Rule 14a-9. In *Virginia Bankshares* (which is a principal case in Chapter 4), the plaintiff challenged a material misstatement in a proxy statement urging approval of a merger. That approval was assured based on the shares controlled by management, regardless of how the minority shareholders voted. Id. at 1099. At issue was whether the plaintiff could show, notwithstanding the superfluousness of the minority shareholders' vote, a causal connection between the fraudulent proxy statement and her injury. See id. The plaintiff attempted to establish this connection by arguing that the fraudulent proxy statement insulated management from a state law proceeding that the minority shareholders would have initiated in order to void the merger on conflict of interest grounds. See id. at 1101. The Court concluded that "[t]his case does not *** require us to decide whether § 14(a) provides a cause of action for lost state remedies, since there is no indication in the law or facts before us that the proxy solicitation resulted in any such loss." Id. at 1107. Does the Court's reservation of this question involving Rule 14a-9 causation undercut *Goldberg* and *Healey*?

Following *Virginia Bankshares,* lower federal courts have allowed causation to be established in Rule 14a-9 cases based on the loss of a state remedy. See, e.g., *Wilson v. Great Am. Indus., Inc.*, 979 F.2d 924 (2d Cir. 1992). See also *Howing Co. v. Nationwide Corp.*, 972 F.2d 700, 709-710 (6th Cir. 1992) (accepting a lost state remedy argument in connection with claim made under Section § 13(e) of the Exchange Act). Do such lower court rulings bolster *Goldberg* and *Healey*?

***7. Deceptive Opinions.*** The *Virginia Bankshares* decision described in the preceding note bears on Section 10(b)'s deception element in yet another respect. The challenged misrepresentation in *Virginia Bankshares* consisted of the directors' opinion as to what would be a fair price for the shares, thereby raising the question whether an opinion is a "fact" the misrepresentation of which can be actionable under Rule 14a-9. Id. at 1091. The Court concluded that while an opinion constitutes a "fact," it is not actionable simply because it is material and "misstate[s] the speaker's reasons." Id. at 1095. It must also be "false or misleading about its subject." Id. at 1095-96. Thus, the directors' assertion that $42 per share was a "fair price" for the stock would be actionable under Rule 14a-9 only so long as (i) the directors did not believe that $42 was a fair price and (ii) the price was not fair in fact. Cf. id. at 1109 (Scalia, J., concurring in part and concurring in the judgment).

These requirements from *Virginia Bankshares* are routinely imported into Rule 10b-5 decisions involving deceptive opinions. See, e.g., *Mayer v. Mylod,* 988 F.2d 635, 639 (6th Cir. 1993) (emphasizing that "[m]aterial statements which contain the speaker's opinion are actionable under Section 10(b) *** if the speaker does not believe the opinion and the opinion is not factually well-grounded"); *Elliott Assocs., L.P. v. Covance, Inc.*, 2000 WL 1752848 at *9 (S.D.N.Y. 2000) (stating that "unless plaintiffs can sufficiently plead that the speakers were aware of contrary information at the time they expressed their opinions regarding the status of the merger, such statements are not actionable under section 10(b) or Rule 10b-5"). Is it appropriate to import these requirements from Rule 14a-9 into Rule 10b-5? Are these requirements apt to be difficult to satisfy? In thinking about this question, consider the effect of the heightened pleading requirements in Section 21D(b)(1) of the Exchange Act (set forth at the beginning of this Chapter).

### *PROBLEM 2-1*

Barrington International, Inc., is one of the country's largest pharmaceutical manufacturers. At one time, the company owned all of the shares of Wellmark Corp., a subsidiary that distributed many of the prescription drugs manufactured by Barrington. In 1998, when Wellmark was still a part of Barrington, the government began investigating Wellmark for Medicaid and Medicare fraud. The management of Barrington feared the worst, and opted to insulate Barrington from any potential liability by spinning off Wellmark. This spin off was to be accomplished by transferring the ownership of the Wellmark subsidiary from Barrington to Barrington's shareholders, who each were to receive shares of Wellmark proportional to their shares in Barrington. As a result of the spinoff, Wellmark would no longer be a subsidiary, but an independent company.

In announcing this planned spinoff to the media, Barrington's CEO stated that the purpose of the spinoff was "to avoid a looming competitive conflict between Wellmark and other lines of Barrington's business" and that Barrington shareholders were getting a "great deal." Barrington later repeated this statement of purpose in a document that it was required to file with the SEC in connection with the spinoff. The spinoff—which required neither SEC approval nor the consent of Barrington shareholders—was effectuated in May 1999, and Barrington shareholders thereafter held one Wellmark share for every four shares of Barrington that they owned. At first, the combined market value of Barrington and Wellmark stock exceeded the pre-spinoff value of Barrington stock, but when the investing public learned of the government's investigation of Wellmark, Wellmark's stock price plummeted. In May 2000, Wellmark pleaded guilty to criminal charges of fraud and paid the government $160 million.

In April 2001, those who were shareholders of Barrington at the time of the spinoff filed a class action lawsuit. They claimed that the transfer to them of Wellmark shares was deceptive and fraudulent because, had the true purpose of the spinoff been revealed, they would have been able to convince a court to enjoin it. Barrington would then have been kept intact; and Barrington stock would today be worth more than the current combined value of Barrington and Wellmark stock, because the spinoff destroyed valuable synergies between Barrington and its Wellmark subsidiary. The complaint alleged that the true purpose of the spinoff was to minimize the liability of Barrington's shareholders for Wellmark's fraud, and that several of Barrington's key executives sold significant portions of their own stock holdings in Wellmark in the months following the spinoff. The complaint therefore alleged that the CEO's statements of a competitive purpose and a "great deal" were lies to the shareholders of Barrington.

Have the plaintiffs stated a cause of action for deception in violation of Rule 10b-5?

Cf. *Isquith v. Caremark Int'l, Inc.*, 136 F.3d 531 (7th Cir. 1998).

### *PROBLEM 2-2*

Susan and Tim Anderson are minority shareholders of Apex, Inc., a closely held corporation with 15 shareholders. In February 2001, Susan and Tim learned of the board of directors' decision to sell all of Apex's stock in a wholly-owned subsidiary to the Betta Group for one million dollars. Four months later, the couple was stunned to discover that the Betta Group is owned by 2 of the 3 directors of Apex. Susan then did additional research revealing that the fair market value of the former subsidiary was more than three million dollars. Are the Andersons able to state a Rule 10b-5 claim against the directors for deception?

### c. *Secret Intention Not to Perform a Contract*

## WHARF (HOLDINGS) LTD. v. UNITED INTERNATIONAL HOLDINGS, INC.

532 U.S. 588 (2001)

BREYER, JUSTICE:

This securities fraud action focuses upon a company that sold an option to buy stock while secretly intending never to honor the option. The question before us is whether this conduct violates §10(b) of the Securities Exchange Act of 1934, which prohibits using "any manipulative or deceptive device or contrivance" "in connection with the purchase or sale of any security." See also [Rule] 10b-5. We conclude that it does.

I

Respondent United International Holdings, Inc., a Colorado-based company, sued petitioner The Wharf (Holdings) Limited, a Hong Kong firm, in Colorado's Federal District Court. United said that in October 1992 Wharf had sold it an option to buy 10% of the stock of a new Hong Kong cable system. But, United alleged, at the time of the sale Wharf secretly intended not to permit United to exercise the option. United claimed that Wharf's conduct amounted to a fraud "in connection with the ... sale of [a] security," prohibited by §10(b), and violated numerous state laws as well. A jury found in United's favor. The Court of Appeals for the Tenth Circuit upheld that verdict. And we granted certiorari to consider whether the dispute fell within the scope of §10(b).

The relevant facts, viewed in the light most favorable to the verdict winner, United, are as follows. In 1991, the Hong Kong government announced that it would accept bids for the award of an exclusive license to operate a cable television system in Hong Kong. Wharf decided to prepare a bid. Wharf's chairman, Peter Woo, instructed one of its managing directors, Stephen Ng, to find a business partner with cable system experience. Ng found United. And United sent several employees to Hong Kong to help prepare Wharf's application, negotiate contracts, design the system, and arrange financing.

United asked to be paid for its services with a right to invest in the cable system if Wharf should obtain the license. During August and September 1992, while United's employees were at work helping Wharf, Wharf and United negotiated about the details of that payment. Wharf prepared a draft letter of intent that contemplated giving United the right to become a co-investor, owning 10% of the system. But the parties did not sign the letter of intent. And in September, when Wharf submitted its bid, it told the Hong Kong authorities that Wharf would be the system's initial sole owner, although Wharf would also "consider" allowing United to become an investor.

In early October 1992, Ng met with a United representative, who told Ng that United would continue to help only if Wharf gave United an enforceable right to invest. Ng then orally granted United an option with the following terms: (1) United had the right to buy 10% of the future system's stock; (2) the price of exercising the option would be 10% of the system's capital requirements minus the value of United's previous services (including expenses); (3) United could exercise the option only if it showed that it could fund its 10% share of the capital required for at least the first 18 months; and (4) the option would expire if not exercised within six months of the date that Wharf received the license. The parties continued to negotiate about how to write documents that would embody these terms, but they never reduced the agreement to writing.

In May 1993, Hong Kong awarded the cable franchise to Wharf. United raised $66 million designed to help finance its 10% share. In July or August 1993, United told Wharf that it was ready to exercise its option. But Wharf refused to permit United to buy any of the system's stock. Contemporaneous internal Wharf documents suggested that Wharf had never intended to carry out its promise. For example, a few weeks before the key October 1992 meeting, Ng had prepared a memorandum stating that United wanted a right to invest that it could exercise if it was able to raise the necessary capital. A handwritten note by Wharf's Chairman Woo replied, "No, no, no, we don't accept that." In September 1993, after meeting with the Wharf board to discuss United's investment in the cable system, Ng wrote to another Wharf executive, "How do we get out?" In December 1993, after United had filed documents with the Securities Exchange Commission (SEC) representing that United was negotiating the acquisition of a 10% interest in the cable system, an internal Wharf memo stated that "[o]ur next move should be to claim that our directors got quite *upset* over these representations.... Publicly, we *do not* acknowledge [United's] opportunity" to acquire the 10% interest. In the margin of a December 1993 letter from United discussing its expectation of investing in the cable system, Ng wrote, "[B]e careful, must deflect this! [H]ow?" Other Wharf documents referred to the need to "back ped[al]," and "stall."

These documents, along with other evidence, convinced the jury that Wharf, through Ng, had orally sold United an option to purchase a 10% interest in the future cable system while secretly intending not to permit United to exercise the option, in violation of §10(b) of the Securities Exchange Act and various state laws. The jury awarded United compensatory damages of $67 million and, in light of "circumstances of fraud, malice, or willful and wanton conduct," punitive damages of $58.5 million on the state-law claims. As we have said, the Court of Appeals upheld the jury's award. And we granted certiorari to determine whether Wharf's oral sale of an option it intended not to honor is prohibited by §10(b).

II

Section 10(b) of the Securities Exchange Act makes it "unlawful for any person ... [t]o use or employ, in connection with the purchase or sale of any security ..., any manipulative or deceptive device or contrivance in contravention of such rules and regulations as the [SEC] may prescribe."

Pursuant to this provision, the SEC has promulgated Rule 10b-5. That Rule forbids the use, "in connection with the purchase or sale of any security," of (1) "any device, scheme, or artifice to defraud"; (2) "any untrue statement of a material fact"; (3) the omission of "a material fact necessary in order to make the statements made ... not misleading"; or (4) any other "act, practice, or course of business" that "operates ... as a fraud or deceit."

To succeed in a Rule 10b-5 suit, a private plaintiff must show that the defendant used, in connection with the purchase or sale of a security, one of the four kinds of manipulative or deceptive devices to which the Rule refers, and must also satisfy certain other requirements not at issue here. See, e.g., [Exchange Act Section 10(b)] (requiring the "use of any means or instrumentality of interstate commerce or of the mails, or of any facility of any national securities exchange"); *Ernst & Ernst v. Hochfelder*, 425 U.S. 185, 193 (1976) (requiring scienter, meaning "intent to deceive, manipulate, or defraud"); *Basic Inc. v. Levinson*, 485 U.S. 224, 231-232 (1988) (requiring that any misrepresentation be material); id., at 243 (requiring that the plaintiff sustain damages through reliance on the misrepresentation).

In deciding whether the Rule covers the circumstances present here, we must assume that the "security" at issue is not the cable system stock, but the option to purchase that stock. That is because the Court of Appeals found that Wharf conceded this point. That concession is consistent with the language of the Securities Exchange Act, which defines "security" to include both "any ... option ... on any security" and "any ... right to ... purchase" stock. [Exchange Act Section 3(a)(10)]; see also *Blue Chip Stamps v. Manor Drug Stores*, 421 U.S. 723, 751 (1975) ("holders of ... options, and other contractual rights or duties to purchase ... securities" are " 'purchasers' ... of securities for purposes of Rule 10b-5"). *** Consequently, we must decide whether Wharf's secret intent not to honor the option it sold United amounted to a misrepresentation (or other conduct forbidden by the Rule) in connection with the sale of the option.

Wharf argues that its conduct falls outside the Rule's scope for two basic reasons. First, Wharf points out that its agreement to grant United an option to purchase shares in the cable system was an oral agreement. And it says that §10(b) does not cover oral contracts of sale. *** [The Court rejected this contention in a part of the opinion set out in Section E of this Chapter.]

Second, Wharf argues that a secret reservation not to permit the exercise of an option falls outside §10(b) because it does not "relat[e] to the value of a security purchase or the consideration paid"; hence it does "not implicate [§10(b)'s] policy of full disclosure." Brief for Petitioners 25, 26 (emphasis deleted). But even were it the case that the Act covers only misrepresentations likely to affect the value of securities, Wharf's secret reservation was such a misrepresentation. To sell an option while secretly intending not to permit the option's exercise is misleading, because a buyer normally presumes good faith. Cf., e.g., Restatement (Second) of Torts § 530, Comment *c* (1976) ("Since a promise necessarily carries with it the implied assertion of an intention to perform[,] it follows that a promise made without such an intention is fraudulent"). For similar reasons, the secret reservation misled United about the option's value. Since Wharf did not intend to honor the option, the option was, unbeknownst to United, valueless.

Finally, Wharf supports its claim for an exemption from the statute by characterizing this case as a "disput[e] over the ownership of securities." Brief for Petitioners 24. Wharf expresses concern that interpreting the Act to allow recovery in a case like this one will permit numerous plaintiffs to bring federal securities claims that are in reality no more than ordinary state breach-of-contract claims—actions that lie outside the Act's basic objectives. United's claim, however, is not simply that Wharf failed to carry out a promise to sell it securities. It is a claim that Wharf sold it a security (the option) while secretly intending from the very beginning not to honor the option. And United proved that secret intent with documentary evidence that went well beyond evidence of a simple failure to perform. Moreover, Wharf has not shown us that its concern has proven serious as a practical matter in the past. Cf. *Threadgill v. Black*, 730 F.2d 810, 811- 812 (CADC) (per curiam) (suggesting in 1984 that contracting to sell securities with the secret reservation not to perform one's obligations under the contract violates § 10(b)). Nor does Wharf persuade us that it is likely to prove serious in the future. Cf. Private Securities Litigation Reform Act of 1995, §21D(b)(2) [of the Exchange Act] (imposing, beginning in 1995, stricter pleading requirements in private securities fraud actions that, among other things, require that a complaint "state with particularity facts giving rise to a strong inference that the defendant acted with the required [fraudulent] state of mind").

For these reasons, the judgment of the Court of Appeals is affirmed.

## *NOTES AND QUESTIONS*

***1. Timing is Everything.*** Shortly before the Supreme Court's decision in *Wharf*, a federal district court held that a company's refusal to convert convertible preferred shares into common stock constituted a breach of contract, but not a violation of Rule 10b-5, unless the company had a secret intention not to convert at the time it made the conversion contract. See *Elliott Assocs., L.P. v. Hayes*, 141 F. Supp.2d 344, 354 (S.D.N.Y 2000), aff'd mem., 26 Fed. Appx 83 (2d Cir. 2002). Is this result consistent with *Wharf*?

***2. Pleading Intent Not to Perform.*** What types of facts might a plaintiff plead in order to demonstrate the defendant's intent not to perform at the time of agreeing to do so? Is there any way to show such intent without the benefit of extensive discovery (for example, as to e-mails or other internal communications among defendants)? If not, should conclusory allegations of intent not to perform suffice at the pleading stage? Would conclusory allegations of this sort satisfy Section 21D(b)(1)'s heightened pleading requirements for private plaintiffs? Would such conclusory allegations satisfy the pleading requirements of Fed. R. Civ. P. 9(b) in a Rule 10b-5 action brought by the SEC?

---

### 2. *Material Omissions in Particular*

We now focus specifically on material omissions. In other words, when does a person's silence about material facts in a securities transaction satisfy Section 10(b)'s deception element?

#### a. *The General Rule—Silence is Not Deceptive Absent a Duty to Speak*

## GALLAGHER v. ABBOTT LABORATORIES

269 F.3d 806 (7th Cir. 2001)

EASTERBROOK, CIRCUIT JUDGE:

Year after year the Food and Drug Administration inspected the Diagnostic Division of Abbott Laboratories, found deficiencies in manufacturing quality control, and issued warnings. The Division made efforts to do better, never to the FDA's satisfaction, but until 1999 the FDA was willing to accept Abbott's promises and remedial steps. On March 17, 1999, the FDA sent Abbott another letter demanding compliance with all regulatory requirements and threatening severe consequences. This could have been read as more saber rattling—Bloomberg News revealed the letter to the financial world in June, and Abbott's stock price did not even quiver—but later developments show that it was more ominous. By September 1999 the FDA was insisting on substantial penalties plus changes in Abbott's methods of doing business. On September 29, 1999, after the markets had closed, Abbott issued a press release describing the FDA's position, asserting that Abbott was in "substantial" compliance with federal regulations, and revealing that the parties were engaged in settlement talks. Abbott's stock fell more than 6%, from \$40 to \$37.50, the next business day. On November 2, 1999, Abbott and the FDA resolved their differences, and a court entered a consent decree requiring Abbott to remove 125 diagnostic products from the market until it had improved its quality control and to pay a \$100 million civil fine. Abbott took an accounting charge of \$168 million to cover the fine and worthless inventory. The next business day Abbott's stock slumped \$3.50, which together with the earlier drop implied that shareholders saw the episode as costing Abbott (in cash plus future compliance costs and lost sales) more than \$5 billion. ***

Plaintiffs in these class actions under § 10(b) of the Securities Exchange Act of 1934 and the SEC's Rule 10b-5 contend that Abbott committed fraud by deferring public revelation. The classes comprise all buyers of Abbott's securities between March 17 and November 2. (One class consists of persons who bought securities in ALZA, a firm that Abbott proposed to acquire through an exchange of securities and whose market price thus tracked Abbott's. For simplicity we treat these plaintiffs as purchasers of Abbott stock.) The district judge dismissed the complaints under Fed.R.Civ.P. 12(b)(6) for failure to state a claim on which relief may be granted *** [though] the judge's reasons seem more akin to an invocation of Fed.R.Civ.P. 9(b), which requires fraud to be pleaded with particularity, or the extra pleading requirements for securities cases created by the Private Securities Litigation Reform Act of 1995. But it is not necessary to decide whether Rule 12(b)(6), Rule 12(c), Rule 9(b), or the Reform Act supplies the best basis of decision. Nor is it necessary to decide whether the news was "material" before the FDA's negotiating position stiffened, to decide whether Abbott acted with the state of mind necessary to support liability under Rule 10b-5, or to address other potential stumbling blocks. What sinks plaintiffs' position is their inability to identify any false statement—or for that matter any truthful statement made misleading by the omission of news about the FDA's demands.

Much of plaintiffs' argument reads as if firms have an absolute duty to disclose all information material to stock prices as soon as news comes into their possession. Yet that is not the way the securities laws work. We do not have a system of continuous disclosure. Instead firms are entitled to keep silent (about good news as well as bad news) unless positive law creates a duty to disclose. See, e.g., *Basic, Inc. v. Levinson*, 485 U.S. 224, 239 n. 17 (1988); *Dirks v. SEC*, 463 U.S. 646, 653-54 (1983); *Chiarella v. United States*, 445 U.S. 222, 227-35 (1980); *Stransky v. Cummins Engine Co.*, 51 F.3d 1329, 1331 (7th Cir.1995); *Backman v. Polaroid Corp.*, 910 F.2d 10, 16 (1st Cir.1990) (en banc). Until the Securities Act of 1933 there was no federal regulation of corporate disclosure. The 1933 Act requires firms to reveal information only when they issue securities, and the duty is owed only to persons who buy from the issuer or an underwriter distributing on its behalf; every other transaction is exempt under § 4. (No member of either class contends that he purchased securities from Abbott, or an underwriter on Abbott's behalf, between March 17 and November 2.) Section 13 of the Securities Exchange Act of 1934 adds that the SEC may require issuers to file annual and other periodic reports—with the emphasis on *periodic* rather than continuous. Section 13 and the implementing regulations contemplate that these reports will be snapshots of the corporation's status on or near the filing date, with updates due not when something "material" happens, but on the next prescribed filing date.

Regulations implementing §13 require a comprehensive annual filing, the Form 10-K report, and less extensive quarterly supplements on Form 10-Q. The supplements need not bring up to date everything contained in the annual 10-K report; counsel for the plaintiff classes conceded at oral argument that nothing in Regulation S-K (the SEC's list of required disclosures) requires either an updating of Form 10-K reports more often than annually, or a disclosure in a quarterly Form 10-Q report of information about the firm's regulatory problems. The regulations that provide for disclosures on Form 10-Q tell us which items in the annual report must be updated (a subset of the full list), and how often (quarterly).

Many proposals have been made to do things differently—to junk this combination of sale-based disclosure with periodic follow-up and replace it with a system under which *issuers* rather than *securities* are registered and disclosure must be continuous. E.g., American Law Institute, Federal Securities Code xxvii-xxviii, § 602 & commentary (1978); Securities and

Exchange Commission, Report of the Advisory Committee on the Capital Formation and Regulatory Process 9-14, 36-38 (1996). Regulation S-K goes some distance in this direction by defining identical items of disclosure for registration of stock and issuers' subsequent reports, and by authorizing the largest issuers to use their annual 10-K reports as the kernels of registration statements for new securities. But Regulation S-K does not replace periodic with continuous disclosure, and the more ambitious proposals to do this have not been adopted.

The ALI's proposal, for example, was embraced by the SEC, see 1933 Act Release No. 6242 (Sept. 18, 1980); 1933 Act Release No. 6377 (Jan. 31, 1982), but never seriously pursued, and revisions of Regulation S-K satisfied many of the original supporters of the ALI's proposal. The advisory committee report, prepared by a distinguished group of scholars and practitioners under the leadership of Commissioner Steven M.H. Wallman, did not persuade the SEC's other members and was not taken up by the agency as a legislative plan or even as the basis of a demonstration project. Whatever may be said for and against these proposals, they must be understood as projects for legislation (and to a limited extent for the use of the SEC's rulemaking powers); judges have no authority to scoop the political branches and adopt continuous disclosure under the banner of Rule 10b-5. *Especially* not under that banner, for Rule 10b-5 condemns only fraud, and a corporation does not commit fraud by standing on its rights under a periodic-disclosure system. The Supreme Court has insisted that this judicially created right of action be used only to implement, and not to alter, the rules found in the text of the 1933 and 1934 Acts. See *Central Bank of Denver, N.A. v. First Interstate Bank of Denver, N.A.*, 511 U.S. 164, 173 (1994) ("We have refused to allow [private] 10b-5 challenges to conduct not prohibited by the text of the statute.").

Trying to locate some statement that was either false or materially misleading because it did not mention the FDA's position, plaintiffs pointed in the district court to several reports filed or statements made by Abbott before November 2, 1999. All but two of these have fallen by the wayside on appeal. What remain are Abbott's Form 10-K annual report for 1998 filed in March 1999 and an oral statement that Miles White, Abbott's CEO, made at the annual shareholders' meeting the next month.

Plaintiffs rely principally on Item 303(a)(3)(ii) of Regulation S-K, which provides that registration statements and annual 10-K reports must reveal

> any known trends or uncertainties that have had or that the registrant reasonably expects will have a material favorable or unfavorable impact on net sales or revenues or income from continuing operations.

The FDA's letter, and its negotiating demands, are within this description, according to the plaintiff classes. We shall assume that this is so. The 10-K report did state that Abbott is "subject to comprehensive government regulation" and that "[g]overnment regulatory actions can result in ... sanctions." Plaintiffs say that this is too general in light of the FDA's letter and Abbott's continuing inability to satisfy the FDA's demands. Again we shall assume that plaintiffs are right. But there is a fundamental problem: The 10-K report was filed on March 9, 1999, and the FDA's letter is dated March 17, eight days later. Unless Abbott had a time machine, it could not have described on March 9 a letter that had yet to be written.

Attempting to surmount this temporal problem, plaintiffs insist that Abbott had a "duty to correct" the 10-K report. Yet a statement may be "corrected" only if it was *in*correct when made, and nothing said as of March 9 was incorrect. In order to maintain the difference between periodic-disclosure and continuous-disclosure systems, it is essential to draw a sharp line between duties to correct and duties to update. We drew just this line in *Stransky* and adhere to it now. If, for example, the 10-K report had said that Abbott's net income for 1998 was $500 million, and the actual income was $400 million, Abbott would have had to fix the error. But if the 10-K report had projected a net income of $125 million for the first quarter of 1999, and accountants determined in May that the actual profit was only $100 million, there would have been nothing to correct; a projection is not rendered false when the world turns out otherwise. See *Wielgos v. Commonwealth Edison Co.*, 892 F.2d 509 (7th Cir.1989). Amending the 10-K report to show the results for 1999 as they came in—or to supply a running narrative of the dispute between Abbott and the FDA—would *update* the report, not *correct* it to show Abbott's actual condition as of March 9.

Updating documents has its place in securities law. A registration statement and prospectus for a new issue of securities must be accurate when it is used to sell stock, and not just when it is filed. Section 12(a)(2) of the '33 Act; Regulation S-K, Item 512(a). Material changes in a company's position thus must be reflected in a registration statement promptly. But this does not imply changes in a 10-K annual report, even when that report is used (as it can be with securities registered on Form S-3, or for a shelf offering under Rule 415) as the principal disclosure document. Instead of changing the 10-K report weekly or monthly, the issuer must file and distribute an addendum to that document bringing matters up to date. See Form S-3, Item 11. Anyway, as we've already mentioned, Abbott did not sell any stock to the class members during the period from March 17 to November 2, 1999.

As for White's statements at the annual meeting: he said very little that was concrete (as opposed to puffery), and everything concrete was true. White said, for example:

> The outcome [of our efforts] has been growth more than five times faster than the diagnostics market. We expect this trend to continue for the foreseeable future, due to the unprecedented state of our new product cycle. By supplementing our internal investment with opportunistic technology acquisitions, Abbott's diagnostics pipeline is fuller than ever before.

The statement about past performance was accurate, and the plaintiffs have not given us any reason to doubt that White honestly believed that similar growth would continue, or that White honestly believed "Abbott's diagnostics pipeline [to be] fuller than ever before." Even with the benefit of hindsight these statements cannot be gainsaid. Here is where Rule 9(b) pinches: Plaintiffs have done nothing to meet the requirements for pleading fraud with respect to the annual meeting, even if it were possible (which we doubt) to treat as "fraud" the predictive components in White's boosterism. See *DiLeo v. Ernst & Young*, 901 F.2d 624 (7th Cir.1990). ***

## NOTES AND QUESTIONS

*1. **The Right to Remain Silent.*** In *Abbott*, the Seventh Circuit joined a long line of other courts, including the Supreme Court, in emphasizing that remaining silent about both good news and bad is a right that a securities issuer may exercise in the absence of a positive duty to disclose that information. See, e.g., *Basic Inc. v. Levinson*, 485 U.S. 224, 239 n.17 (1988) ("[s]ilence, absent a duty to disclose, is not misleading under Rule 10b-5"); *In re Time Warner Sec. Litig.*, 9 F.3d 259, 267 (2d Cir. 1993) ("a corporation is not required to disclose a fact merely because a reasonable investor would very much like to know that fact"); *In re Burlington Coat Factory Sec. Litig.*, 114 F.3d 1410, 1432 (3d Cir. 1997) ("there is no general duty on the part of a company to provide the public with all material information"). Note that this general rule in Rule 10b-5 cases is consistent with the common law, where the principle of caveat emptor generally governs in the absence of some affirmative duty giving rise to an obligation of disclosure. See, e.g., Restatement (Second) of Torts § 551(1) (emphasizing that liability for fraudulent nondisclosure attaches "if, but only if, [one party to a transaction] is under a duty to the other to exercise reasonable care to disclose the matter in question").

*2. **Silence as Deception in Insider Trading Cases.*** The Supreme Court's discussion of silence as deception has occurred largely in insider trading cases. But cf. *Basic Inc. v. Levinson*, 485 U.S. 224, 239 n. 17 (1988) (noting in the context of a fraud-on-the-market action that "[s]ilence, absent a duty to disclose, is not misleading under Rule 10b-5"). The Court's most important discussion of silence as deception occurred in *Chiarella v. United States*, 445 U.S. 222 (1980). As we shall see in Chapter 7 (which is devoted exclusively to insider trading), Chiarella was a financial printer who bought stock in target companies prior to the public announcement of the tender offers, based on information he had learned from confidential documentation supplied to his employer by the acquiring companies. In deciding whether Chiarella could legally trade target company securities without disclosing the material nonpublic information in his possession, the Court emphasized the following:

> At common law, misrepresentation made for the purpose of inducing reliance upon the false statement is fraudulent. But one who fails to disclose material information prior to the consummation of a transaction commits fraud only when he is under a duty to do so.

Id. at 227-28. The Court eventually concluded that Chiarella did not in fact deceive the target company shareholders because "the element required to make [his] silence fraudulent—a duty to disclose—is absent in this case." Id. at 232. The Court explained:

> Section 10(b) is aptly described as a catchall provision, but what it catches must be fraud. When an allegation of fraud is based on a nondisclosure, there can be no fraud absent a duty to speak. We hold that a duty to disclose under § 10(b) does not arise from the mere possession of nonpublic market information. The contrary result is without support in the legislative history of § 10(b) and would be inconsistent with the careful plan that Congress has enacted for regulation of the securities markets. Cf. *Santa Fe Industries, Inc. v. Green*, 430 U.S., at 479.

*Chiarella*, 445 U.S. at 234-35. In elaborate dicta, the Court observed that Chiarella's silence would have constituted deception had he been an officer or director of one of the target companies in which he bought shares. See id. at 228-29 (noting that the relationship between corporate insiders and shareholders "gives rise to a duty to disclose because of the 'necessity of preventing a corporate insider from ... tak[ing] unfair advantage of the uninformed minority stockholders' "). See also *Dirks v. SEC*, 463 U.S. 646, 656 n. 14 (1983) (extending the duty to disclose to corporate "outsiders" such as lawyers or accountants who "have entered into a special confidential relationship in the conduct of the business of the enterprise and are given access to information solely for corporate purposes"). The *Chiarella* Court declined to rule on whether the defendant could be held liable based on his misappropriation of the information from his employer and his employer's client. In the Court's view, the government had not adequately presented the misappropriation theory to the jury. See *Chiarella*, supra, 445 U.S. at 235-37. The Court thereafter upheld the misappropriation theory in *United States v. O'Hagan*, 521 U.S. 642, 665 (1997) (applying the theory to an attorney who worked in the law firm retained by the tender offeror and who traded in the target company's securities).

Note that *Abbott* cited *Chiarella* and *Dirks* in support of its statement that "firms are entitled to keep silent (about good news as well as bad news) unless positive law creates a duty to disclose."

#### *b. The Duty to Disclose*

The general rule that silence under Rule 10b-5 does not constitute deception without a duty to disclose is merely an empty vessel absent analysis of the numerous ways in which a duty to disclose can arise. The *Chiarella* Court began to fill this vessel by focusing on the fiduciary relationship between corporate insiders and shareholders, and in *Abbott* Judge Easterbrook added further substance by focusing on the disclosure requirements of the Securities Act and the Exchange Act and the so-called duties to update and correct. The balance of the material in this subpart explores these and other sources of disclosure duties.

##### i. Line-Item and Real Time Disclosure Requirements

As noted in *Abbott*, the Securities Act's registration requirement as well as the Exchange Act's periodic reporting requirements impose on securities issuers an affirmative duty to disclose information about a wide range of matters including results of business operations, financial position, transactions involving directors and other related persons, and known trends or uncertainties (including pending litigation) that the issuer expects will have a favorable or unfavorable impact on net sales or revenues. Most of these disclosures take the form of "line-items" in Regulations S-X (for accounting-related information) and S-K (for all other information), and these line-items must be included in any registration statements filed with the SEC (on a Form S-1, for example) as well as in a reporting company's annual report (Form 10-K) and quarterly reports (Form 10-Qs). Particularly sweeping are the disclosure requirements set out in Item 303(a) of Regulation S-K, which is often referred to as MD & A disclosures ("Management's Discussion and Analysis").

Additional disclosure obligations under the Exchange Act are imposed for specific transactions or events. For example, Section 14(a) imposes disclosure requirements in connection with proxy solicitations in connection with a security registered under Section 12. Section 13(d) requires disclosure in connection with the acquisition of more than 5% of a class of equity security of a Section 12 company; Section 14(d) requires disclosure when a tender offer is the means of accomplishing the acquisition of more than 5% of a class of equity security of a Section 12 company; and Section 14(e) prohibits fraud in connection with tender offers in all companies. The schedules that must be filed with the SEC on the occurrence of these transactions or events (i.e., Schedule 14A, Schedule 13D, or a Schedule TO) contain highly detailed line-item requirements, many of which simply draw upon the line-items set out in Regulations S-X and S-K.

To be sure, when *Abbott* was decided in 2001, reporting companies were under only a minimal obligation to update information previously disclosed in annual and quarterly reports because only six "momentous" events had to be reported on a Form 8-K: changes in control of the issuer; acquisition or disposition of significant assets not in the ordinary course of business; bankruptcy or receivership; changes in accountants; resignation of directors; and change in fiscal year. See Items 1, 2, 3, 4, 6, and 8 of Form 8-K. Although such companies were entitled to utilize Form 8-K to report the occurrence of any other event deemed "of importance to securities holders," such reporting was voluntary rather than mandatory. See Form 8-K, General Instructions.

But *Abbott*'s blanket statement that "[w]e do not have a system of continuous disclosure" has been called into question by the Sarbanes-Oxley Act, the July 2002 legislation prompted by the corporate and accounting scandals that grabbed front page headlines in the months preceding its enactment. Specifically, Section 409 of the Sarbanes-Oxley Act adds a new Section 13(*l*) to the Exchange Act, providing:

> **Section 13(*l*) REAL TIME ISSUER DISCLOSURES**—Each issuer reporting under section 13(a) or 15(d) shall disclose to the public on a rapid and current basis such additional information concerning material changes in the financial condition or operations of the issuer, in plain English, which may include trend and qualitative information and graphic presentations, as the Commission determines, by rule, is necessary or useful for the protection of investors and in the public interest.

Even before Congress delivered this real time disclosure mandate, the SEC had been contemplating for some time an overhaul of the periodic disclosure system. See, e.g., Harvey L. Pitt, How to Prevent Future Enrons, Wall St. J. at A18 (December 11, 2001) ("[i]nvestors need current information, not just periodic disclosures, along with clear requirements for public companies to make affirmative disclosures of, and to provide updates to, unquestionably material information in real time"); SEC Chairperson Harvey L. Pitt, Written Testimony Concerning Accounting and Investor Protection Issues Raised by Enron and Other Public Companies, Before the U.S. Sen. Comm. on Banking, Housing and Urban Affairs (March 21, 2002) (stating that "[w]e intend to formulate revisions to our rules that would impose a duty on companies quickly to disclose events that are unquestionably significant to investors").

Specifically, a little more than a month before the enactment of the Sarbanes-Oxley Act, the SEC proposed significant revisions to the types of disclosures required of reporting companies on a Form 8-K, and further proposed a shortening of the time period for such reporting. The following proposals therefore provide much insight into the types of "real time" disclosure rules that the SEC is likely to enact pursuant to its new rulemaking power under Exchange Act Section 13(*l*).

## PROPOSED RULE: ADDITIONAL FORM 8-K DISCLOSURE REQUIREMENTS AND ACCELERATION OF FILING DATE

Exchange Act Release No. 46084 (June 17, 2002)

*** We propose to add 11 new items to the list of events that require a company to file a current report on Form 8-K. In addition, we propose to make significant changes to existing Form 8-K items and to move two items from other Exchange Act reports to Form 8-K. Through our extensive experience with, and reviews of, filings, as well as comment letters from the public, we believe that these items represent events that presumptively have, or can have, such significance that timely disclosure is necessary for the market to perform properly and efficiently. The following is a list of the new disclosure items that we propose to add to Form 8-K:

- Entry into a material agreement not made in the ordinary course of business;
- Termination of a material agreement not made in the ordinary course of business;
- Termination or reduction of a business relationship with a customer that constitutes a specified amount of the company's revenues;
- Creation of a direct or contingent financial obligation that is material to the company;
- Events triggering a direct or contingent financial obligation that is material to the company, including any default or acceleration of an obligation;
- Exit activities including material write-offs and restructuring charges;
- Any material impairment;
- A change in a rating agency decision, issuance of a credit watch or change in a company outlook;
- Movement of the company's securities from one exchange or quotation system to another, delisting of the company's securities from an exchange or quotation system, or a notice that a company does not comply with a listing standard;
- Conclusion or notice that security holders no longer should rely on the company's previously issued financial statements or a related audit report; and

- Any material limitation, restriction or prohibition, including the beginning and end of lock-out periods, regarding the company's employee benefit, retirement and stock ownership plans.

We also propose to move the following two items from other Exchange Act reports to Form 8-K:

- Unregistered sales of equity securities by the company; and
- Material modifications to rights of holders of the company's securities.

Finally, we propose to expand the current Form 8-K item that requires disclosure about the resignation of a director to also require disclosure regarding the departure of a director for reasons other than a disagreement or removal for cause, the appointment or departure of a principal officer, and the election of new directors. We also would combine the current Form 8-K item regarding a change in a company's fiscal year with a new requirement to disclose any material amendment to a company's articles of incorporation or bylaws. ***

The proposed amendments would require domestic issuers that are subject to the reporting requirements of Section 13(a) and Section 15(d) of the Exchange Act to file required current reports on Form 8-K within two business days of a triggering event. *** This would shorten significantly the deadlines of five business days or 15 calendar days, depending on the nature of the event currently requiring a Form 8-K filing. Disclosure of all of the proposed new items also would have to be made within the two business day timeframe. We are proposing such changes given the significance of "real time" disclosure of these events to participants in the secondary markets. ***

### *PROBLEM 2-3*

Reconsider the facts of *Gallagher v. Abbott Laboratories*. If the proposals noted in the above SEC Release had been codified in SEC rules at the time when Abbott had received the FDA's March 17, 1999 letter demanding compliance and threatening severe consequences, would Abbott have owed its shareholders a duty to disclose this information? If so, is it now correct to say that we have (or are soon to have) a system of continuous disclosure for reporting companies? If not, do you think that result would be consistent with the congressional intentions behind Section 13(*l*)'s real time disclosure directive? In other words, does the SEC have an obligation to build on the proposals set forth in its June 2002 release?

---

Note that even if the SEC adopts rules requiring a company to disclose information such as the FDA letter in *Abbott*, rules of this sort will produce a system of "real time" disclosure only to the extent that they are rigorously enforced. Instructive on this point are the experiences of the New York Stock Exchange, the American Stock Exchange, and the National Association of Securities Dealers Automated Quotation System (NASDAQ) which, for decades, have required listed companies to comply with what was, in effect, a continuous disclosure requirement. Consider, for example, Section 202.05 in the NYSE Listed Company Manual:

> A listed company is expected to release quickly to the public any news or information which might reasonably be expected to materially affect the market for its securities. This is one of the most important and fundamental purposes of the listing agreement which the company enters into with the Exchange.

Listed companies that violate the exchanges or the NASDAQ's disclosure requirements risk the imposition of sanctions by the exchange or NASDAQ including an order to halt trading in the company's securities. Yet it is widely believed that a listed company's risk of sanction is minimal, given the negligible enforcement efforts made by the exchanges and the NASDAQ. One particularly staunch critic of this practice is Professor Dale Oesterle, who has stated:

> [O]ur most important market, the NYSE, has a continuous disclosure requirement that is extraordinary in its breadth, its lack of any exception for sensitive information, and its imprecision. However, the sloppiness is revealing. An exchange that does not specifically enforce the language of its rules can afford to be imprecise and over-broad because no-ones cares. It is a classic bargain of mutual convenience: lawyers advise firms that the language is not enforced, and firms safely ignore it. The exchanges enjoy whatever positive public relations come from having the language in their listing manuals.

Dale Arthur Oesterle, The Inexorable March Toward a Continuous Disclosure Requirement for Publicly Traded Corporations: "Are We There Yet?" 20 Cardozo L. Rev. 135, 163 (1998). And while the shareholders of these listed companies would no doubt be ready and willing to pursue such enforcement efforts through private litigation, courts have generally been consistent in holding that Rule 10b-5 does not provide a private right of action for violating the continuous disclosure provisions of the exchanges and the NASDAQ. See *Freedman v. Louisiana-Pacific Corp.*, 922 F. Supp. 377, 390 (D. Or. 1996) ("[p]laintiffs' citations to the NYSE Manual *** are irrelevant with respect to establishing [defendant's] duty to disclose under § 10(b) and Rule 10b-5"). See also *State Teachers Retirement Bd. v. Fluor Corp.*, 654 F.2d 843, 852-53 (2d Cir. 1981).

Does the SEC's rhetoric both before and after passage of the Sarbanes-Oxley Act of 2002 provide a basis for predicting its intentions with respect to enforcing any newly-crafted system of real time disclosure? In addition to actions instituted by the government, what else is likely to encourage compliance with the new SEC rules?

ii. A Brief Word About Regulation FD

Another important issue relating to the duty to disclose under the federal securities laws involves Regulation FD (for "Fair Disclosure"), adopted by the SEC in August 2000 and applicable to companies required to file reports under Sections 13(a) and 15(d) of the Exchange Act. See Regulation FD, Rules 100-03. To be sure, Regulation FD does not compel these companies to make public disclosure of information. But it does prohibit them from engaging in selective disclosure of information to securities analysts or to other favored constituencies by requiring any such disclosure to be shared with the general public. The Regulation is, however, enforceable only in an action brought by the SEC, and by its specific terms "[n]o failure to make a public disclosure required solely by [Regulation FD] shall be deemed to be a violation of Rule 10b-5 under the Securities Exchange Act." Id., Rule 102. Why was the Regulation drafted so as to sever any connection to Rule 10b-5? We will consider Regulation FD again in connection with insider trading in Chapter 7.

iii. The Duty to Update

For years prior to Congress's recent embrace of "real time" disclosure, a number of federal appeals courts had recognized a so-called "duty to update" as an exception to a securities issuer's general right to remain silent about new material information. See, e.g, *Weiner v. Quaker Oats Co.*, 129 F.3d 310, 318 (3d Cir. 1997). The case law on the duty to update remains important even now that the Sarbanes-Oxley Act is on the books. First, because the SEC's real time disclosure rules will apply only to reporting companies, the duty continues to be relevant as a source of obligation for non-reporting companies as well as for individuals. Second, even for reporting companies, the SEC's "real time" rules are apt to leave uncertain the necessity of disclosing many types of information. The duty to update may therefore continue to function as an additional source of disclosure obligation.

In the federal circuits in which it is recognized, the duty to update imposes a duty, typically on a securities issuer, to modify or supplement a prior statement that, although accurate when made, has since become inaccurate or misleading in light of subsequent developments. Such past disclosures, however, need be updated only to the extent that they remain "alive" in the minds of reasonable investors. See *Weiner v. Quaker Oats Co.*, supra, 129 F.3d at 318 (concluding that "[t]he complaint alleges facts on the basis of which a reasonable factfinder could determine that Quaker's statements regarding its total debt-to-total-capitalization ratio guideline would have been material to a reasonable investor, and hence that Quaker had a duty to update such statements when they became unreliable").

One of the most notable cases recognizing a securities issuer's duty to update is *In re Time Warner Sec. Litig.*, 9 F.3d 259 (2d Cir. 1993). In that case, Time Warner had voluntarily disclosed to its shareholders that it was negotiating with unnamed "strategic partners," mostly in Europe, who would provide Time Warner with cash flow needed to pay off debt from its recent highly leveraged merger (consummated, among other reasons, in order to fend off a hostile takeover bid for Time from Paramount Communications). When negotiations with these "strategic partners" failed, Time Warner had to raise the necessary cash with a rights offering, which diluted the value of the shares held by the company's existing stockholders. Some of these stockholders alleged that Time Warner's failure to disclose that it had been considering the rights offering as an alternative to the strategic partnerships made the prior public disclosures about negotiations for these partnerships materially misleading. Although the district court dismissed this claim, the Second Circuit reversed, holding that "when a corporation is pursuing a specific business goal and announces that goal as well as an intended approach for reaching it, it may come under an obligation to disclose other approaches to reaching the goal when those approaches are under active and serious consideration." Id. at 268. In effect, the Second Circuit found that an issuer's public statement about a specific plan can trigger a duty to update when the issuer begins seriously to consider an alternative plan to achieve the same goal in a different way. But a subsequent Second Circuit decision cautioned against construing the duty to update in a manner that amounts to a requirement of continuous disclosure. See *San Leandro Emergency Med. Group Profit Sharing Plan v. Philip Morris Cos.*, 75 F.3d 801, 810 (2d Cir. 1996) (noting that *Time Warner* "went nearly to the outer limit of the line that separates disclosable plans from plans that need not be disclosed," and concluding that Philip Morris did not have a duty to disclose its alternative plan for marketing cigarettes, even though the new plan constituted a radical change from its previously announced pricing strategy that would reduce the company's profits for the upcoming year by more than $2 million dollars).

Rather than attempting to distinguish between which subsequent plans or events require disclosure and which do not, the Seventh Circuit has rejected outright the existence of a duty to update. In *Stransky v. Cummins Engine Co.*, 51 F.3d 1329 (7th Cir. 1995), the Seventh Circuit refused to impose on an issuer a duty to update its projections merely because subsequent events showed them to be inaccurate. The court based its refusal on Rule 10b-5(b)'s language prohibiting "any untrue statement of material fact or [omitting] to state a material fact necessary in order to make the statements made, *in the light of the circumstances under which they were made*, not misleading" (emphasis added). Id. at 1332. In the court's opinion, this language "implicitly precludes basing liability on circumstances that arise after the speaker makes the statements." Id. The court therefore concluded that a "projection can lead to liability under Rule 10b-5 only if it was not made in good faith or was made without a reasonable basis." Id. at 1333. The court found that such an approach "remains true" to Rule 10b-5's text and restricts the imposition of liability "to the small number of statements that are most harmful in the marketplace." Id. Significantly, *Stransky* did not confine its rejection of the duty to update to prior statements involving projections or other soft information (subjects covered in connection with the materiality requirement in Section B of this Chapter). Indeed, recall that *Abbott* cited *Stransky* to buttress its conclusion that there was no obligation to disclose the existence of the FDA letter threatening sanctions.

Does recognition of a duty to update inevitably emasculate the general rule that silence is not actionable absent a duty to speak? Can a valid line be drawn between subsequent plans or events as to which updating is necessary and those as to which disclosure should be voluntary? It appears that the court in *San Leandro* drew a distinction between financing strategy that had been the subject of much corporate "hype" (*Time Warner*) and more ordinary business decisions such as Philip Morris's plans to change its marketing. Is this distinction a workable one? Finally, consider the First Circuit's policy argument that "[f]ear that statements of historical fact might be claimed to fall within [the duty to update], could inhibit disclosures altogether." See *Backman v. Polaroid Corp.*, 910 F.2d 10, 17 (1st Cir. 1990). Is this a valid concern?

#### iv. The Duty to Correct

The duty to correct arises when a statement already made is later discovered to have been false when made. The duty to correct thus requires a company to redress intentional or negligent misrepresentations as well as statements that it believed to be true when made but subsequently learned were materially false, incomplete, or misleading.

Most courts recognize some form of a duty to correct when the prior false statements were made by the issuer or one of its officials. See *Abbott*, supra. See also *Stransky v. Cummins Engine Co.*, 51 F.3d 1329, 1331 (7th Cir. 1995) (stating that the duty to correct arises "when a company makes a historical statement that, at the time made, the company believed to be true, but as revealed by subsequently discovered information actually was not"); *In re MobileMedia Sec. Litig.*, 28 F. Supp.2d 901 (D.N.J. 1998) (finding that MobileMedia's discovery of past instances of noncompliance with FCC regulation placed the company under a duty to correct prior statements made in FCC filings as to the company's full compliance).

There is substantially more doubt, however, as to whether (and when) issuers may be under a duty to correct false statements made by third parties. Virtually all courts agree that issuers are not under a duty to correct third party statements (including inaccurate rumors) when such statements cannot be attributed to the issuer or its officials. See *State Teachers Retirement Bd. v. Fluor Corp.*, 654 F.2d 843, 850 (2d Cir.1981) ("[a] company has no duty to correct or verify rumors in the marketplace unless those rumors can be attributed to the company"). See also *Eisenstadt v. Centel Corp.*, 113 F.3d 738, 744 (7th Cir. 1997) (stating that "[o]bviously a corporation has no duty to correct rumors planted by third parties" and speculating that "[t]he rumor might be planted by the target of a hostile takeover and be designed to elicit, if there is a legal duty to correct inaccurate rumors, a premature disclosure of the takeover firm's intentions").

An issuer may, however, assume an obligation to correct a third party's misstatement of material facts where the issuer had become "entangled" with the third party statement. Typically this situation arises in connection with material misstatements or omissions in an analyst's report as to which the issuer provided extensive assistance. One of the more notable decisions on the so-called entanglement theory is *Elkind v. Liggett & Myers, Inc.*, 635 F.2d 156 (2d Cir. 1980). In that decision, the Second Circuit made the following statement:

> We have no doubt that a company may so involve itself in the preparation of reports and projections by outsiders as to assume a duty to correct material errors in those projections. This may occur when officials of the company have, by their activity, made an implied representation that the information they have reviewed is true or at least in accordance with the company's views.

Id. at 163. See also *Raab v. General Physics Corp.*, 4 F.3d 286, 289 (4th Cir. 1993) (in order to be liable for statements in an analyst's report, a company must "sufficiently entangle[ ] itself with the analyst['s] forecasts to render those predictions attributable to it," quoting *Elkind*, supra); *Cooper v. Pickett*, 122 F.3d 1186, 1193-94 (9th Cir. 1997) (holding plaintiffs' allegations regarding entanglement sufficient to survive motion to dismiss).

A duty to correct may be based not only on an entanglement theory but also on the theory that the issuer "adopted" the third-party statement after its publication. Similar to the entanglement theory, this so-called "adoption" theory is premised on an issuer's implied representation to the market that the statement published by the securities analyst is accurate. See *In re Presstek, Inc.*, Exchange Act Release No. 39472, 66 SEC Docket 328 (Dec. 22, 1997) (cease-and-desist order stating that "[s]uch adoption occurs 'when a company conveys the suggestion that the analyst's forecasts are accurate or at least in accordance with its views,' " quoting *In re Cypress Semiconductor Sec. Litig.*, 891 F. Supp. 1369, 1377 (N.D. Cal. 1995), aff'd mem. sub nom. *Eisenstadt v. Allen*, 113 F.3d 1240 (9th Cir. 1997)). See also *Schaffer v. Timberland Co.*, 924 F. Supp. 1298, 1310 (D.N.H. 1996) (liability may attach to an analyst's statements where the defendants "have expressly or impliedly adopted the statements, placed their imprimatur on the statements, or have otherwise entangled themselves with the analysts to a significant degree").

Not surprisingly, cases involving theories of "entanglement" or "adoption" have presented a continuing source of frustration for courts, issuers, and attorneys. See generally D. Joseph Meister, Note, Securities Issuer Liability for Third Party Misstatements: Refining the Entanglement Standard, 53 Vand. L. Rev. 947 (2000). Cf. *SEC v. Bausch & Lomb, Inc.*, 565 F.2d 8, 9 (2d Cir. 1977) (stating that "[m]any a corporate executive, conscious of the antifraud provisions of the Securities Acts, may analogize an encounter with a financial analyst to a fencing match conducted on a tightrope").

v. Fiduciary Relationships and Other Duties at Common Law

Any discussion of duties to disclose under Rule 10b-5 must include the disclosure duties imposed by the common law on the parties to a business transaction. Courts frequently draw on these common law duties when interpreting Rule 10b-5. Thus, in *Chiarella v. United States*, 445 U.S. 222 (1980), the Supreme Court observed that officers and directors who trade in their company's securities while failing to disclose material information are liable under Rule 10b-5 because their fiduciary obligations to shareholders under the common law include a disclosure duty:

> [O]ne who fails to disclose material information prior to the consummation of a transaction commits fraud only when he is under a duty to do so. And the duty to disclose arises when one party has information "that the other [party] is entitled to know because of a fiduciary or other similar relation of trust and confidence between them."

Id. at 228, quoting Restatement (Second) of Torts § 551(2)(a) (1976). Cf. *Basic Inc. v. Levinson*, 485 U.S. 224, 253 (1988) (White, J., concurring in part and dissenting in part) (emphasizing that "[i]n general, the case law developed in this Court with respect to § 10(b) and Rule 10b-5 has been based on doctrines with which we, as judges, are familiar: common-law doctrines of fraud and deceit"); *Blue Chip Stamps v. Manor Drug Stores*, 421 U.S. 723, 744 (1975) (stating that "it is not inappropriate to advert briefly to the tort of misrepresentation and deceit, to which a claim under Rule 10b-5 certainly has some relationship").

In relying on Section 551(2)(a) of the Restatement (Second) of Torts, the *Chiarella* Court focused on one of five situations set forth in Section 551(2) in which one party to a business transaction has a common law duty to disclose to the other party. The five situations consist of the following:

> (a) matters known to him that the other is entitled to know because of a fiduciary or other similar relation of trust and confidence between them; and
>
> (b) matters known to him that he knows to be necessary to prevent his partial or ambiguous statement of the facts from being misleading; and
>
> (c) subsequently acquired information that he knows will make untrue or misleading a previous representation that when made was true or believed to be so; and
>
> (d) the falsity of a representation not made with the expectation that it would be acted upon, if he subsequently learns that the other is about to act in reliance upon it in a transaction with him; and
>
> (e) facts basic to the transaction, if he knows that the other is about to enter into it under a mistake as to them, and that the other, because of the relationship between them, the customs of the trade or other objective circumstances, would reasonably expect a disclosure of those facts.

Restatement of Torts (Second) §551(2)(a)-(e). Reconsider the duties to disclose that we have seen thus far under Rule 10b-5. Which of these duties receives additional support from the common law? Note also that Rule 10b-5's prohibition against half-truths is reflected in Section 551(2)(b).

Moreover, courts rely on common law disclosure duties to impose Rule 10b-5 liability not only on officers and directors but also on securities issuers who buy or sell their own securities while withholding material information from the public. See *Castellano v. Young & Rubicam, Inc.*, 257 F.3d 171, 179 (2d Cir. 2001) (maintaining that "under §10(b) and Rule 10b-5, closed corporations that purchase their own stock have a special obligation to disclose to sellers all material information"); *Shaw v. Digital Equip. Corp.*, 82 F.3d 1194 (1st Cir. 1996) (maintaining that issuer engaged in a stock offering may not sell stock if it is in possession of undisclosed information); *Jordan v. Duff & Phelps, Inc.*, 815 F.2d 429, 435-39 (7th Cir. 1987) (maintaining that issuer may not purchase employee's securities without disclosing material information in its possession); *McCormick v. Fund Am. Cos.*, 26 F.3d 869, 875-876 (9th Cir. 1994) (maintaining that issuer's purchases triggered a duty to disclose all material information, but concluding that alleged omissions were not material). But see Deborah A. DeMott, Beyond Metaphor: An Analysis of Fiduciary Obligation, 1988 Duke L.J. 879, 916-921 (1988) (contending that issuers do not owe "fiduciary duties" to their shareholders, but acknowledging that the insiders in control of the issuer owe such duties and the corporation may be vicariously liable for their breaches).

#### vi. The Relation Between the Duty to Disclose and Materiality

To be actionable under Rule 10b-5, omitted information must be material as well as be subject to a disclosure duty. It is important to keep the materiality question and the duty question distinct. Consider Professor Langevoort's observations:

> Courts sometimes confuse materiality and duty issues, sometimes in the direction of declaring something immaterial—even though shareholders would find it important—on grounds that it is not the sort of thing the issuer should have to disclose. That should be the work of the "duty" analysis. Materiality should be the question of what the reasonable investor would likely find

> significant, nothing more, nothing less. However, it is also important to avoid the converse error: assuming a duty simply because materiality is present.

Donald C. Langevoort, Seeking Sunlight in *Santa Fe*'s Shadow: The SEC's Pursuit of Managerial Accountability, 79 Wash. U. L.Q. 449, 458 (2001).

We examine materiality (which is applicable to misstatements as well) in the very next section of this Chapter. But because we have yet to do so, you should focus as much as possible on the duty question rather than on the materiality question in the problems that follow.

### *PROBLEM 2-4*

General Physics Corporation, a company whose shares are listed on the NYSE, provides technical services to the nuclear power industry as well as to the U.S. Department of Energy (DOE) and to contractors who assist DOE with production and maintenance of nuclear weapons and disposal of waste from nuclear weapons. A portion of General Physics's DOE contracts involve peaceful use of nuclear energy, but a significant number of its contracts are tied to DOE expenditures on nuclear weapons programs. After the end of the Cold War in the early 1990s, General Physics's management believes that there will likely be a significant slowdown in nuclear weapons contracts from DOE.

General Physics has made the following public statements in its Annual Report to shareholders about its peacetime nuclear energy contracts with DOE:

> (1) "Regulatory changes resulting from [nuclear power accidents at Three Mile Island and Chernobyl] combined with the rising importance of environmental restoration and waste management, have created a marketplace for the DOE Services Group with an expected annual growth rate of 10% to 30% over the next several years;"
>
> (2) "Helping the DOE prime contractors respond to these directives is expected to be an increasing segment of General Physics' business in 1992;" and
>
> (3) "With experienced management, engineers, scientists and technicians in place, the DOE Services Group is poised to carry the growth and success of 1991 well into the future."

On the same day this Annual Report was issued, General Physics also released a statement to its shareholders stating that the first quarter earnings were likely to be half of analysts' estimates and that "the lower than anticipated earnings resulted primarily from administrative delays in contract awards by [DOE] and the resultant increased overhead costs associated with retaining professional staff pending contract awards by the DOE," but that General Physics believed that "conditions in the 1st quarter are temporary and that results during the remainder of 1992 should be in line with analysts' current projections."

About a month earlier, a Goldman Sachs research report recommended purchase of shares in the company, stating "General Physics has indicated that the pace of contract awards has increased significantly in recent weeks." The report, however, did not specify a source for this comment.

a) Was General Physics's Annual Report materially misleading under Rule 10b-5? Were the Annual Report and the statement to shareholders, taken together, materially misleading?

b) Is General Physics's required to disclose management's concern that DOE contracts would decline for nuclear weapons related projects?

c) Was it materially misleading for the company to report its belief that the slowdown in DOE contracts was temporary?

d) Is General Physics under a duty to correct the statement in the Goldman Sachs report that was attributed to a company official?

e) If General Physics's company website had provided a hyperlink to the Goldman Sachs report, and General Physics's general counsel later learns of the hyperlink and removes it from the company's website, must General Physics do anything more to comply with its obligations under Rule 10b-5.?

See *Raab v. General Physics Corp.*, 4 F.3d 286 (4th Cir. 1993).

### *PROBLEM 2-5*

Fluor Corporation, whose common shares are listed on the NYSE, receives a $1 billion contract for engineering work from a South African utility company, SASOL. SASOL, however, requires Fluor to delay announcing the contract until SASOL has had an opportunity to line up financing from investment bankers in France. In the meantime, rumors start to circulate that Fluor has entered into a contract with SASOL and there is a significant upswing in Fluor's stock price.

a) Is Fluor under a duty to disclose the existence of the SASOL contract? Can Fluor's officials deny these rumors in a press conference if SASOL officials specifically request that they do so?

b) If Fluor responds "no comment" to the rumors, is Fluor still liable under Rule 10b-5 to investors who sold Fluor stock if Fluor, a NYSE listed company, violated NYSE rules that require listed companies to either disclose significant developments such as the SASOL contract or request suspension of trading in their shares?

c) How should a company in Fluor's position reconcile the business reasons for confidentiality with the regulatory demands of a system of "real time" disclosure? Should the SEC promulgate a rule that allows a company in Fluor's situation to delay disclosure of such material developments for a reasonable period of time? How would you draft such a rule?

See *State Teachers Retirement Bd. v. Fluor Corp.*, 654 F.2d 843 (2d Cir. 1981).

### *PROBLEM 2-6*

David Davis began working for Hammerville Furniture Company, a closely held corporation, in 1990. He worked diligently at the company's Chicago office for a number of years, and in 1993, Hammerville's management offered David the opportunity to buy 200 shares of Hammerville common stock.

(The company had 39 other shareholders with 20,000 shares of stock outstanding). David was delighted with the opportunity and agreed to purchase his 200 shares at "book value" (the accounting net worth of Hammerville divided by the number of shares outstanding), resulting in a price of $40 per share. Prior to the purchase, David signed a contract with Hammerville committing him to sell back his shares to the company upon termination of his employment with Hammerville, for any reason, including resignation, discharge, retirement, or death (thereby committing his estate to the resale). The contract provided that David would receive for the resale of his 200 shares the adjusted book value of the shares on December 31 of the year preceding when the termination took place.

In May 2002, David decided to resign his position with Hammerville to move his family to Houston because David's wife did not get along with David's mother in Chicago. On May 15, pursuant to his contract with Hammerville, David resold his shares to the company, and received $23,225 for his 200 shares (approximately $116 a share).

Less than a week later, David was stunned by Hammerville's announcement to the media of a merger between Hammerville and one of the country's largest furniture manufacturers. Under the terms of the merger, which was agreed to in principle at a meeting between the companies on May 12, Hammerville was valued at $25 million, such that the acquiring company was willing to pay $1,250 per outstanding share.

Did Hammerville violate Rule 10b-5 by re-purchasing David's shares while remaining silent about the merger negotiations?

See *Jordan v. Duff & Phelps, Inc.*, 815 F.2d 429 (7th Cir. 1987).

## B. THE MATERIALITY REQUIREMENT

To be actionable under Section 10(b) and Rule 10b-5, the omitted or misstated information must be "material" in nature. The materiality requirement has its origins in common law deceit and appears explicitly in Rule 10b-5(b).

Our examination of materiality begins with the basic definition and proceeds to the complexities that arise when the information at issue is "soft" rather than "hard." We then give special attention to an important subcategory of soft information—forward-looking statements—and the administrative, judicial, and statutory approaches that surround them.

### 1. *Materiality Defined*

The definition of materiality applicable to Rule 10b-5 comes from *TSC Indus., Inc. v. Northway, Inc.*, 426 U.S. 438 (1976). In *Northway*, an action under Section 14(a) of the Exchange Act and Rule 14a-9, the plaintiff alleged that a proxy statement seeking shareholder approval of a merger contained material omissions (involving control of the acquired corporation and the advantageousness of the deal proposed to the shareholders). Regarding the materiality of those omissions, the Supreme Court had this to say:

> The question of materiality, it is universally agreed, is an objective one, involving the significance of an omitted or misrepresented fact to a reasonable

> investor. Variations in the formulation of a general test of materiality occur in the articulation of just how significant a fact must be or, put another way, how certain it must be that the fact would affect a reasonable investor's judgment.
>
> The Court of Appeals in this case concluded that material facts include "all facts which a reasonable shareholder *might* consider important." (emphasis added). This formulation of the test of materiality has been explicitly rejected by at least two courts as setting too low a threshold for the imposition of liability under Rule 14a-9. *Gerstle v. Gamble-Skogmo, Inc.*, 478 F.2d 1281, 1301-1302 (C.A.2 1973); *Smallwood v. Pearl Brewing Co.*, 489 F.2d 579, 603-604 (C.A.5 1974). In these cases, panels of the Second and Fifth Circuits opted for the conventional tort test of materiality—whether a reasonable man *would* attach importance to the fact misrepresented or omitted in determining his course of action. See Restatement (Second) of Torts § 538(2) (a) (Tent.Draft No. 10, Apr. 20, 1964). ***
>
> The general standard of materiality that we think best comports with the policies of Rule 14a-9 is as follows: An omitted fact is material if there is a substantial likelihood that a reasonable shareholder would consider it important in deciding how to vote. *** It does not require proof of a substantial likelihood that disclosure of the omitted fact would have caused the reasonable investor to change his vote. What the standard does contemplate is a showing of a substantial likelihood that, under all the circumstances, the omitted fact would have assumed actual significance in the deliberations of the reasonable shareholder. Put another way, there must be a substantial likelihood that the disclosure of the omitted fact would have been viewed by the reasonable investor as having significantly altered the "total mix" of information made available. ***

Id. at 445-49. See *Basic Inc. v. Levinson,* 485 U.S. 224, 232 (1988) (adopting *Northway* definition of materiality for purposes of Rule 10b-5).

---

## *NOTES AND QUESTIONS*

***1. Might vs. Would.*** As *Northway* acknowledged, the lower courts had been divided over whether to define materiality in terms of facts the reasonable investor "would consider important" in making her decision and facts she "might consider important." Which position carried the day in *Northway*?

***2. The "Total Mix" and Efficient Markets.*** According to *Northway,* a fact is material if it "significantly alters the 'total mix' of information." When the Rule 10b-5 action involves securities traded in an efficient market (see Chapter 1.G), the "total mix" of information encompasses information known to the market. See, e.g., *In re Burlington Coat Factory Sec. Litig.,* 114 F.3d 1410, 1425 (3d Cir. 1997) (market awareness concerning sales from 53rd week in fiscal year); *In re Convergent Techs. Sec. Litig.,* 948 F.2d 507, 513 (9th Cir. 1991) (market awareness concerning likely lessening of demand for computer work stations). Thus, if a company whose securities are traded in an efficient market makes a public announcement correcting a prior fraudulent disclosure and in the wake of the announcement there is a change in the market price of the securities, the change is evidence of the materiality of the fraud. Similarly, if a company makes such an announcement after which there is no change in the market price, the absence of a change is evidence of a lack of materiality. See, e.g., *Oran v. Stafford,* 226 F.3d 275, 282 (3d Cir. 2000); *United States v.*

*Bilzerian*, 926 F.2d 1285, 1298 (2d Cir. 1991); *SEC v. MacDonald*, 699 F.2d 47, 49-50 (1st Cir. 1983) (en banc). Should price movements (or their absence) constitute merely evidence of materiality or should they be dispositive of the materiality question?

*3. **Puffery.*** A misrepresentation is immaterial if it constitutes "puffery"—that is, if it is so vague as to be meaningless. The puffery doctrine (sometimes called the puffery defense) arose initially in securities cases involving brokers. See, e.g., *Zerman v. Ball*, 735 F.2d 15, 21 (2d Cir. 1984) (characterizing as puffery the statement "when E.F. Hutton Talks, People Listen"); *Rotstein v. Reynolds & Co.*, 359 F. Supp. 109, 113 (N.D. Ill. 1973) (characterizing as puffery the statement that a stock was "red-hot"). Now expanded in scope, the puffery doctrine is today frequently invoked by corporations and their managers in connection with statements about the operation of their firms. See, e.g., *Nathenson v. Zonagen, Inc.*, 267 F.3d 400, 419 (5th Cir. 2001) (characterizing as puffery the statement that a drug was a "fast-acting, improved formulation"); *Parnes v. Gateway 2000, Inc.*, 122 F.3d 539, 547 (8th Cir. 1997) (characterizing as puffery a prediction of "significant growth").

A frequent rationalization for the puffery doctrine is that puffing statements by their very nature cannot have an impact on market price. See, e.g., *Raab v. General Physics Corp.*, 4 F.3d 286, 290 (4th Cir. 1993). Courts divide, however, as to how to assess the likely impact on the market of the statement in question. Some courts appear to focus simply on the statement itself. See, e.g., id; *Malone v. Microdyne Corp.*, 26 F.3d 471, 479-80 (4th Cir. 1994). Other courts attempt to place the statement in its larger context. See, e.g., *Glassman v. Computervision Corp.*, 90 F.3d 617, 635-36 (1st Cir. 1996) (dismissing a statement as puffery only after considering it in light of other contemporaneous company statements and the fact that it pertained to a new product). Which approach to puffery appears more sound? For discussions of puffery, see Jennifer O'Hare, The Resurrection of the Dodo: The Unfortunate Re-emergence of the Puffery Defense in Private Securities Fraud Actions, 59 Ohio St. L. J. 1697 (1998); R. Gregory Roussel, Note, Securities Fraud or Mere Puffery: Refinement of the Corporate Puffery Defense, 51 Vand. L. Rev. 1049 (1998).

### *PROBLEM 2-7*

Playday, Inc., a toy manufacturer and reporting company under the Exchange Act, was in the midst of making a private offering of securities to raise money for a new plant. Mary was contemplating buying shares in the offering upon the advice of her broker. Mary is strongly committed to equal rights for women and seeks to invest only in those companies that make use of women's talents. Accordingly, she asked Joe, a Playday vice president and a neighbor, whether the Playday board had any female members. Sensing that Mary would purchase securities in the offering only if she found his answer satisfactory, Joe told her that 30% of the board was female. In fact, the board was entirely male. Did Joe make a material misrepresentation to Mary?

### *PROBLEM 2-8*

Are the following statements puffery? Why or why not?

a. A stock broker, who knows the issuer of a stock has severe liquidity problems that are not yet publicly known, tells one of his customers: "This stock is one of the best buys out there right now."

b. The same broker describes the same company to his customer as "a sound company that is rolling in cash."

c. An issuer's CEO says to a group of analysts, "our earnings are poised for growth," a day before the issuer announces that earnings are 50% below that of the previous year.

d. The same CEO says "our market share is likely to increase dramatically in the next few years." All the internal projections the CEO has received from his marketing officers suggest that the company's market share is likely to remain flat for the next five years, and at several board meetings the directors have based strategic planning on the assumption that the company's market share will remain flat for the foreseeable future.

---

### *2. The Materiality of Soft Information*

Materiality is typically easier to assess when the information at issue is "hard" rather than "soft." Hard information is information rooted in historical or objective fact (e.g., the plant burned to the ground yesterday). Soft information, on the other hand, is information with a subjective or futurist aspect (e.g., the corporation is considering a merger; a competitor's new product may soon put the corporation out of business). The Supreme Court addressed the materiality of soft information in the following decision, which also explicitly adopted the *Northway* definition of materiality for purposes of Rule 10b-5.

## BASIC INC. v. LEVINSON

485 U.S. 224 (1988)

JUSTICE BLACKMUN:

This case requires us to apply the materiality requirement of § 10(b) of the Securities Exchange Act of 1934 (1934 Act) and the Securities and Exchange Commission's Rule 10b-5, promulgated thereunder, in the context of preliminary corporate merger discussions. We must also determine whether a person who traded a corporation's shares on a securities exchange after the issuance of a materially misleading statement by the corporation may invoke a rebuttable presumption that, in trading, he relied on the integrity of the price set by the market. [*The Court's treatment of this presumption is set forth in Section F.1.b of this Chapter, which addresses the reliance requirement*].

I

Prior to December 20, 1978, Basic Incorporated was a publicly traded company primarily engaged in the business of manufacturing chemical refractories for the steel industry. As early as 1965 or 1966, Combustion Engineering, Inc., a company producing mostly alumina-based refractories, expressed some interest in acquiring Basic, but was deterred from pursuing this inclination seriously because of antitrust concerns it then entertained. In 1976, however, regulatory action opened the way to a renewal of Combustion's interest. The "Strategic Plan," dated October 25, 1976, for Combustion's Industrial Products Group included the objective: "Acquire Basic Inc. $30 million."

Beginning in September 1976, Combustion representatives had meetings and telephone conversations with Basic officers and directors, including petitioners here, concerning the possibility of a merger. During 1977 and 1978, Basic made three public statements denying that it was engaged in merger negotiations.[4] On December 18, 1978, Basic asked the New York Stock Exchange to suspend trading in its shares and issued a release stating that it had been "approached" by another company concerning a merger. On December 19, Basic's board endorsed Combustion's offer of $46 per share for its common stock, and on the following day publicly announced its approval of Combustion's tender offer for all outstanding shares.

Respondents are former Basic shareholders who sold their stock after Basic's first public statement of October 21, 1977, and before the suspension of trading in December 1978. Respondents brought a class action against Basic and its directors, asserting that the defendants issued three false or misleading public statements and thereby were in violation of § 10(b) of the 1934 Act and of Rule 10b-5. Respondents alleged that they were injured by selling Basic shares at artificially depressed prices in a market affected by petitioners' misleading statements and in reliance thereon.

The District Court *** granted summary judgment for the defendants. It held that, as a matter of law, any misstatements were immaterial: there were no negotiations ongoing at the time of the first statement, and although negotiations were taking place when the second and third statements were issued, those negotiations were not "destined, with reasonable certainty, to become a merger agreement in principle."

The United States Court of Appeals for the Sixth Circuit *** reversed the District Court's summary judgment, and remanded the case. *** In the

---

4. On October 21, 1977, after heavy trading and a new high in Basic stock, the following news item appeared in the Cleveland Plain Dealer:

> [Basic] President Max Muller said the company knew no reason for the stock's activity and that no negotiations were under way with any company for a merger. He said Flintkote recently denied Wall Street rumors that it would make a tender offer of $25 a share for control of the Cleveland- based maker of refractories for the steel industry.

On September 25, 1978, in reply to an inquiry from the New York Stock Exchange, Basic issued a release concerning increased activity in its stock and stated that "management is unaware of any present or pending company development that would result in the abnormally heavy trading activity and price fluctuation in company shares that have been experienced in the past few days."

On November 6, 1978, Basic issued to its shareholders a "Nine Months Report 1978." This Report stated: "With regard to the stock market activity in the Company's shares we remain unaware of any present or pending developments which would account for the high volume of trading and price fluctuations in recent months."

Court of Appeals' view, Basic's statements that no negotiations were taking place, and that it knew of no corporate developments to account for the heavy trading activity, were misleading. With respect to materiality, the court rejected the argument that preliminary merger discussions are immaterial as a matter of law, and held that "once a statement is made denying the existence of any discussions, even discussions that might not have been material in absence of the denial are material because they make the statement made untrue." ***

We granted certiorari to resolve the split among the Courts of Appeals as to the standard of materiality applicable to preliminary merger discussions ***

II

*** The Court previously has addressed various positive and common-law requirements for a violation of § 10(b) or of Rule 10b-5. The Court also explicitly has defined a standard of materiality under the securities laws, see *TSC Industries, Inc. v. Northway, Inc.*, 426 U.S. 438 (1976), concluding in the proxy-solicitation context that "[a]n omitted fact is material if there is a substantial likelihood that a reasonable shareholder would consider it important in deciding how to vote." Id., at 449. Acknowledging that certain information concerning corporate developments could well be of "dubious significance," id., at 448, the Court was careful not to set too low a standard of materiality; it was concerned that a minimal standard might bring an overabundance of information within its reach, and lead management "simply to bury the shareholders in an avalanche of trivial information—a result that is hardly conducive to informed decisionmaking." Id., at 448-449. It further explained that to fulfill the materiality requirement "there must be a substantial likelihood that the disclosure of the omitted fact would have been viewed by the reasonable investor as having significantly altered the 'total mix' of information made available." Id., at 449. We now expressly adopt the *TSC Industries* standard of materiality for the § 10(b) and Rule 10b-5 context.

III

The application of this materiality standard to preliminary merger discussions is not self-evident. Where the impact of the corporate development on the target's fortune is certain and clear, the *TSC Industries* materiality definition admits straightforward application. Where, on the other hand, the event is contingent or speculative in nature, it is difficult to ascertain whether the "reasonable investor" would have considered the omitted information significant at the time. Merger negotiations, because of the ever-present possibility that the contemplated transaction will not be effectuated, fall into the latter category.[9]

9. We do not address here any other kinds of contingent or speculative information, such as earnings forecasts or projections. See generally Hiler, The SEC and the Courts' Approach to Disclosure of Earnings Projections, Asset Appraisals, and Other Soft Information: Old Problems, Changing Views, 46 Md.L.Rev. 1114 (1987).

A

Petitioners urge upon us a Third Circuit test for resolving this difficulty. Under this approach, preliminary merger discussions do not become material until "agreement-in-principle" as to the price and structure of the transaction has been reached between the would-be merger partners. See *Greenfield v. Heublein, Inc.*, 742 F.2d 751, 757 (CA3 1984). By definition, then, information concerning any negotiations not yet at the agreement-in-principle stage could be withheld or even misrepresented without a violation of Rule 10b-5.

Three rationales have been offered in support of the "agreement-in-principle" test. The first derives from the concern expressed in *TSC Industries* that an investor not be overwhelmed by excessively detailed and trivial information, and focuses on the substantial risk that preliminary merger discussions may collapse: because such discussions are inherently tentative, disclosure of their existence itself could mislead investors and foster false optimism. The other two justifications for the agreement-in-principle standard are based on management concerns: because the requirement of "agreement-in-principle" limits the scope of disclosure obligations, it helps preserve the confidentiality of merger discussions where earlier disclosure might prejudice the negotiations; and the test also provides a usable, bright-line rule for determining when disclosure must be made. See *Greenfield v. Heublein, Inc.*, 742 F.2d, at 757; *Flamm v. Eberstadt*, 814 F.2d 1169, 1176-1178 (CA7 1987).

None of these policy-based rationales, however, purports to explain why drawing the line at agreement-in-principle reflects the significance of the information upon the investor's decision. The first rationale, and the only one connected to the concerns expressed in *TSC Industries,* stands soundly rejected, even by a Court of Appeals that otherwise has accepted the wisdom of the agreement-in-principle test. "It assumes that investors are nitwits, unable to appreciate—even when told—that mergers are risky propositions up until the closing." *Flamm v. Eberstadt*, 814 F.2d, at 1175. Disclosure, and not paternalistic withholding of accurate information, is the policy chosen and expressed by Congress. We have recognized time and again, a "fundamental purpose" of the various Securities Acts, "was to substitute a philosophy of full disclosure for the philosophy of *caveat emptor* and thus to achieve a high standard of business ethics in the securities industry." *SEC v. Capital Gains Research Bureau, Inc.*, 375 U.S. 180, 186 (1963). The role of the materiality requirement is not to "attribute to investors a child-like simplicity, an inability to grasp the probabilistic significance of negotiations," *Flamm v. Eberstadt*, 814 F.2d, at 1175, but to filter out essentially useless information that a reasonable investor would not consider significant, even as part of a larger "mix" of factors to consider in making his investment decision.

The second rationale, the importance of secrecy during the early stages of merger discussions, also seems irrelevant to an assessment whether their existence is significant to the trading decision of a reasonable investor. To avoid a "bidding war" over its target, an acquiring firm often will insist that negotiations remain confidential, see, e.g., *In re Carnation Co.*, Exchange Act Release No. 22214 (1985), and at least one Court of Appeals has stated that "silence pending settlement of the price and structure of a deal is beneficial to most investors, most of the time." *Flamm v. Eberstadt*, 814 F.2d, at 1177.

We need not ascertain, however, whether secrecy necessarily maximizes shareholder wealth—although we note that the proposition is at least disputed as a matter of theory and empirical research—for this case does not concern the *timing* of a disclosure; it concerns only its accuracy and completeness. We face here the narrow question whether information concerning the existence and status of preliminary merger discussions is significant to the reasonable investor's trading decision. Arguments based on the premise that some disclosure would be "premature" in a sense are more properly considered under the rubric of an issuer's duty to disclose. The "secrecy" rationale is simply inapposite to the definition of materiality.

The final justification offered in support of the agreement- in-principle test seems to be directed solely at the comfort of corporate managers. A bright-line rule indeed is easier to follow than a standard that requires the exercise of judgment in the light of all the circumstances. But ease of application alone is not an excuse for ignoring the purposes of the Securities Acts and Congress' policy decisions. Any approach that designates a single fact or occurrence as always determinative of an inherently fact- specific finding such as materiality, must necessarily be overinclusive or underinclusive. In *TSC Industries* this Court explained: "The determination [of materiality] requires delicate assessments of the inferences a 'reasonable shareholder' would draw from a given set of facts and the significance of those inferences to him...." 426 U.S., at 450. After much study, the Advisory Committee on Corporate Disclosure cautioned the SEC against administratively confining materiality to a rigid formula. Courts also would do well to heed this advice.

We therefore find no valid justification for artificially excluding from the definition of materiality information concerning merger discussions, which would otherwise be considered significant to the trading decision of a reasonable investor, merely because agreement-in-principle as to price and structure has not yet been reached by the parties or their representatives.***

C

Even before this Court's decision in *TSC Industries*, the Second Circuit had explained the role of the materiality requirement of Rule 10b-5, with respect to contingent or speculative information or events, in a manner that gave that term meaning that is independent of the other provisions of the Rule. Under such circumstances, materiality "will depend at any given time upon a balancing of both the indicated probability that the event will occur and the anticipated magnitude of the event in light of the totality of the company activity." *SEC v. Texas Gulf Sulphur Co.*, 401 F.2d [833, 849 (CA2 1968)]. Interestingly, neither the Third Circuit decision adopting the agreement-in-principle test nor petitioners here take issue with this general standard. Rather, they suggest that with respect to preliminary merger discussions, there are good reasons to draw a line at agreement on price and structure.

In a subsequent decision, the late Judge Friendly, writing for a Second Circuit panel, applied the *Texas Gulf Sulphur* probability/magnitude approach in the specific context of preliminary merger negotiations. After acknowledging that materiality is something to be determined on the basis of the particular facts of each case, he stated:

> Since a merger in which it is bought out is the most important event that can occur in a small corporation's life, to wit, its death, we think that inside information, as regards a merger of this sort, can become material at an earlier stage than would be the case as regards lesser transactions—and this even though the mortality rate of mergers in such formative stages is doubtless high.

*SEC v. Geon Industries, Inc.*, 531 F.2d 39, 47-48 (1976). We agree with that analysis.

Whether merger discussions in any particular case are material therefore depends on the facts. Generally, in order to assess the probability that the event will occur, a factfinder will need to look to indicia of interest in the transaction at the highest corporate levels. Without attempting to catalog all such possible factors, we note by way of example that board resolutions, instructions to investment bankers, and actual negotiations between principals or their intermediaries may serve as indicia of interest. To assess the magnitude of the transaction to the issuer of the securities allegedly manipulated, a factfinder will need to consider such facts as the size of the two corporate entities and of the potential premiums over market value. No particular event or factor short of closing the transaction need be either necessary or sufficient by itself to render merger discussions material.[17]

As we clarify today, materiality depends on the significance the reasonable investor would place on the withheld or misrepresented information.[18] The fact-specific inquiry we endorse here is consistent with the

---

17. To be actionable, of course, a statement must also be misleading. Silence, absent a duty to disclose, is not misleading under Rule 10b-5. "No comment" statements are generally the functional equivalent of silence. See *In re Carnation Co.*, supra. See also New York Stock Exchange Listed Company Manual § 202.01 (premature public announcement may properly be delayed for valid business purpose and where adequate security can be maintained).

It has been suggested that given current market practices, a "no comment" statement is tantamount to an admission that merger discussions are underway. See *Flamm v. Eberstadt*, 814 F.2d, at 1178. That may well hold true to the extent that issuers adopt a policy of truthfully denying merger rumors when no discussions are underway, and of issuing "no comment" statements when they are in the midst of negotiations. There are, of course, other statement policies firms could adopt; we need not now advise issuers as to what kind of practice to follow, within the range permitted by law. Perhaps more importantly, we think that creating an exception to a regulatory scheme founded on a prodisclosure legislative philosophy, because complying with the regulation might be "bad for business," is a role for Congress, not this Court.

18. We find no authority in the statute, the legislative history, or our previous decisions for varying the standard of materiality depending on who brings the action or whether insiders are alleged to have profited. See, e.g., *Pavlidis v. New England Patriots Football Club, Inc.*, 737 F.2d 1227, 1231 (CA1 1984) ("A fact does not become more material to the shareholder's decision because it is withheld by an insider, or because the insider might profit by withholding it"); cf. *Aaron v. SEC*, 446 U.S. 680, 691 (1980) ("[S]cienter is an element of a violation of § 10(b) and Rule 10b-5, regardless of the identity of the plaintiff or the nature of the relief sought"). ***

approach a number of courts have taken in assessing the materiality of merger negotiations. Because the standard of materiality we have adopted differs from that used by both courts below, we remand the case for reconsideration of the question whether a grant of summary judgment is appropriate on this record. ***

### *NOTES AND QUESTIONS*

1. ***Assessing Magnitude and Probability.*** Assessments of magnitude are sometimes relatively easy, since corporate events such as mergers are frequently of clearcut importance. Assessments of probability, however, are often considerably more challenging. Transactions such as mergers, leveraged buyouts, or initial public offerings are often conditioned on numerous factors that cannot be predicted (e.g., market conditions, availability of financing, resolution of antitrust and other regulatory issues). How can such uncertainties be overcome when applying the probability/magnitude test?

2. ***The Problem of Hindsight Bias.*** Further confounding assessments of probability is the fact that these assessments are typically made after the merger or other event in question has occurred (or failed to occur). The event's occurrence contributes to the perception that the probability at the relevant earlier point was higher than it may actually have been, just as the event's non-occurrence has the opposite effect. This phenomenon—known as hindsight bias—can impact the fact-finding of a judge or jury (or even the SEC or the DOJ). It arises not only in securities cases but in other areas of the law as well. See generally Jeffrey J. Rachlinski, A Positive Psychological Theory of Judging in Hindsight, 65 U. Chi. L. Rev. 571 (1998). Is there any way to avoid hindsight bias when applying the probability/magnitude test? Should a defense lawyer flag the risk of hindsight bias for the judge or jury?

3. ***Reaching Beyond Merger Negotiations.*** Prior to *Basic,* lower federal courts applied the probability/magnitude test not only to merger negotiations but also to other contingent events. See, e.g., *Harkavy v. Apparel Indus., Inc.,* 571 F.2d 737, 740-42 (2d Cir. 1978) (applying the probability/magnitude test to assess the materiality of a clothing manufacturer's possible introduction of a new line of sportswear). Does *Basic* confine the test to merger negotiations? Compare *United States v. Smith,* 155 F.3d 1051, 1065 (9th Cir. 1998) (not confined) with *Garcia v. Cordova,* 930 F.2d 826, 829 n.1 (10th Cir. 1991) (confined). Is such confinement sensible?

### *PROBLEM 2-9*

Vroom Corporation is a drug company with an aggressive research and marketing agenda developed by its president (Marvin). This agenda was extensively described in the company's SEC's filings as well as in press releases throughout the past year. None of those documents, however, revealed a matter known to the board and top officers—that Marvin (who until recently had 20/20 vision) was contemplating resigning because of a degenerative eye disease. Indeed, for some months he had been able to function professionally only by wearing unusually thick glasses. By year's end, Marvin submitted his resignation, effective immediately. Would Vroom's failure to disclose Marvin's situation be regarded as material in a Rule 10b-5 action against the company? Is there additional information that would be useful to have in answering this question?

---

### 3. *Forward-Looking Statements*

Until the 1970s, the Commission generally barred the inclusion of earnings projections, statements of future plans and other forward-looking statements from documents required to be filed under the Securities Act or the Exchange Act. Forward-looking information could, however, be disseminated in other ways, such as in speeches or press releases. Cf. *Marx v. Computer Sciences Corp.*, 507 F.2d 485, 488 (9th Cir. 1974) (Rule 10b-5 action challenging a forecast contained in vice president's speech). The Commission's rationale—that forward-looking statements were unreliable and likely to mislead gullible investors—received blistering criticism. See, e.g., Homer Kripke, The SEC, the Accountants, Some Myths and Some Realities, 45 N.Y.U. L. Rev. 1151, 1197-99 (1970).

In an about-face in 1973, the Commission announced that it would "take the first steps toward integrating projections into the disclosure system." Securities Act Release No. 5362, 1 SEC Docket 4 (Feb. 2, 1973). In 1978, it issued a release urging companies to provide projections both in filed documents and otherwise. See Securities Act Release No. 5992, 16 SEC Docket 112 (Nov. 7, 1978). Moreover, beginning in 1980, it required companies complying with certain Securities Act and Exchange Act disclosure requirements to set forth "any known trends or uncertainties" likely to impact their performance. See Item 303 of Regulation S-K. It simultaneously distinguished such "presently known data which will impact upon future operating results" from "forward-looking information," which companies were "encouraged, but not required, to supply." Instruction 7 to ¶ 303(a), Regulation S-K. See also Item10(b), Regulation S-K.

But companies worried that by disclosing forward-looking information, they would make themselves vulnerable to fraud actions when their predictions failed to materialize. We consider the solutions provided by the SEC, the courts, and Congress to address this concern: (i) SEC Rules 175 and 3b-6; (ii) the judicial bespeaks caution doctrine; and (iii) the statutory safe harbor for forward-looking statements.

#### a. *Rules 175 and 3b-6*

Adopted by the Commission in 1979, Rule 175 (under the Securities Act) and Rule 3b-6 (under the Exchange Act) do little to allay companies' anxieties about releasing forward-looking information. First, the rules do not provide insulation from fraud liability when a forward-looking statement "was made or reaffirmed without a reasonable basis or was disclosed other than in good faith." Because the existence of bad faith and a reasonable basis are generally questions of fact for which a hearing is necessary, these rules do not ordinarily enable defendants to obtain a dismissal at an early stage of the proceedings.

Second, the rules apply only to forward-looking statements that appear in SEC filings.

### b. *The Bespeaks Caution Doctrine*

Courts developed the bespeaks caution doctrine partly as a response to the limitations inherent in Rules 175 and 3b-6. Consider the following decision.

## IN RE DONALD J. TRUMP CASINO SEC. LITIG.

7 F.3d 357 (3rd Cir. 1993)

BECKER, CIRCUIT JUDGE:

*** In November, 1988 the Trump defendants offered to the public $675 million in first mortgage investment bonds (the "bonds") with Merrill Lynch acting as the sole underwriter. The interest rate on the bonds was 14%, a high rate in comparison to the 9% yield offered on quality corporate bonds at the time. The Trump defendants issued the bonds to raise capital to: (1) purchase the Taj Mahal, a partially-completed casino/hotel located on the boardwalk, from Resorts International, Inc. (which had already invested substantial amounts in its construction); (2) complete construction of the Taj Mahal; and (3) open the Taj Mahal for business.

As is well-known, the Taj Mahal was widely touted as Atlantic City's largest and most lavish casino resort. When ultimately opened in April, 1990 it was at least twice the size of any other casino in Atlantic City. It consisted of a 42-story hotel tower that contained approximately 1,250 guest rooms and an adjacent low-rise building encompassing roughly 155,000 square feet of meeting, ballroom and convention space, a 120,000 square foot casino, and numerous restaurants, lounges and stores. The entire structure occupied approximately seventeen acres of land.

The prospectus accompanying the bonds estimated the completion cost of the Taj Mahal, including the payment of interest on the bonds for the first fifteen months of operation, at $805 million. It explained that, to obtain that amount, the Trump defendants were relying on the $675 million in bond proceeds, a $75 million capital contribution by Donald Trump, investment income derived from those sums, a contingent additional loan of $25 million from the Trump Line of Credit, and loans from other sources.

Plaintiffs ground their lawsuits in the text of the prospectus. ***

The defendants moved to dismiss the complaints pursuant to Rule 12(b)(6), asserting that the plaintiffs had failed to state actionable securities fraud claims ***. The district court granted the defendants' motion ***.

*** The plaintiffs allege that the prospectus contained material misrepresentations. Their principal claim is that the defendants had neither an honest belief in nor a reasonable basis for one statement in the MD & A section of the prospectus: "The Partnership believes that funds generated from the operation of the Taj Mahal will be sufficient to cover all of its debt service (interest and principal)." Before the district court and again before us, the plaintiffs concentrate on this statement and its allegedly misleading character. ***

The statement the plaintiffs assail as misleading is contained in the MD & A section of the prospectus, which follows the sizable "Special Considerations" section, a section notable for its extensive and detailed disclaimers and cautionary statements. More precisely, the prospectus explained that, because of its status as a new venture of unprecedented size and scale, a variety of risks inhered in the Taj Mahal which could affect the Partnership's ability to repay the bondholders. For example, it stated:

> The casino business in Atlantic City, New Jersey has a seasonal nature of which summer is the peak season.... Since the third interest payment date on the Bonds [(which constitutes the first interest payment not paid out of the initial financing)] occurs before the summer season, the Partnership will not have the benefit of receiving peak season cash flow prior to the third interest payment date, which could adversely affect its ability to pay interest on the Bonds.
>
> ... The Taj Mahal has not been completed and, accordingly, has no operating history. The Partnership, therefore, has no history of earnings and its operations will be subject to all of the risks inherent in the establishment of a new business enterprise. Accordingly, the ability of the Partnership to service its debt to [Taj Mahal Funding Inc., which issued the bonds,] is completely dependent upon the success of that operation and such success will depend upon financial, business, competitive, regulatory and other factors affecting the Taj Mahal and the casino industry in general as well as prevailing economic conditions....
>
> The Taj Mahal will be the largest casino/hotel complex in Atlantic City, with approximately twice the room capacity and casino space of many of the existing casino/hotels in Atlantic City. [No] other casino/hotel operator has had experience operating a complex the size of the Taj Mahal in Atlantic City. Consequently, no assurance can be given that, once opened, the Taj Mahal will be profitable or that it will generate cash flow sufficient to provide for the payment of the debt service....

Prospectus at 8.

The prospectus went on to relate, as part of its "Security for the Bonds" subsection, the potential effect of the Partnership's default on its mortgage payments. For example, this subsection unreservedly explained that if a default occurred prior to completion of the Taj Mahal, "there would not be sufficient proceeds [from a foreclosure sale of the Taj Mahal] to pay the principal of, and accrued interest on, the Bonds." Prospectus at 9.

The "Special Considerations" section also detailed the high level of competition for customers the completed Taj Mahal would face once opened to the public:

> Competition in the Atlantic City casino/hotel market is intense. At present, there are twelve casino/hotels in Atlantic City.... Some Atlantic City casino/hotels recently have completed renovations or are in the process of expanding and improving their facilities.... *The Partnership believes* that, based upon historical trends, *casino win per square foot of casino space will decline in 1990* as a result of a projected increase in casino floor space, including the opening of the Taj Mahal.

Prospectus at 14 (emphasis added). In a section following the MD & A section, the prospectus reiterated its reference to the intense competition in the Atlantic City casino industry:

> Growth in Atlantic City casino win is expected to be restrained until further improvements to the City's transportation system and infrastructure are undertaken and completed and the number of non-casino hotel rooms and existing convention space are increased. No assurance can be given with respect to either the future growth of the Atlantic City gaming market or the ability of the Taj Mahal to attract a representative share of that market.

Prospectus at 33. The prospectus additionally reported that there were risks of delay in the construction of the Taj Mahal and a risk that the casino might not receive the numerous essential licenses and permits from the state regulatory authorities.

In this case the Partnership did not bury the warnings about risks amidst the bulk of the prospectus. Indeed, it was the allegedly misleading statement which was buried amidst the cautionary language. At all events, in addition to reading the allegedly misleading statement setting forth the Partnership's belief that it could repay the principal and interest on the bonds, a prospective investor would have also read the dire warnings and cautionary statements a sampling of which we have just outlined. Moreover, an investor would have read the sentence immediately following the challenged statement, which cautioned: "[n]o assurance can be given, however, that actual operating results will meet the Partnership's expectations."

*** [W]e must consider an alleged misrepresentation within the context in which the speaker communicated it. Here the context clearly and precisely relayed to the bondholders the substantial uncertainties inherent in the completion and operation of the Taj Mahal. The prospectus contained both general warnings that the Partnership could not assure the repayment of the bonds as well as specific discussions detailing a variety of risk factors that rendered the completion and profitable operation of the Taj Mahal highly uncertain. Within this broad context the statement at issue was, at worst, harmless.

### *C. The Bespeaks Caution Doctrine*

The district court applied what has come to be known as the "bespeaks caution" doctrine. In so doing it followed the lead of a number of courts of appeals which have dismissed securities fraud claims under Rule 12(b)(6) because cautionary language in the offering document negated the materiality of an alleged misrepresentation or omission. See *Sinay v. Lamson & Sessions Co.*, 948 F.2d 1037, 1040 (6th Cir. 1991); *I. Meyer Pincus & Assocs. v. Oppenheimer & Co.*, 936 F.2d 759, 763 (2d Cir. 1991); *Romani v. Shearson Lehman Hutton*, 929 F.2d 875, 879 (1st Cir. 1991); *Polin v. Conductron Corp.*, 552 F.2d 797, 806 n.28 (8th Cir. 1977). We are persuaded by the *ratio decidendi* of these cases and will apply bespeaks caution to the facts before us.

The application of bespeaks caution depends on the specific text of the offering document or other communication at issue ***. Nevertheless, we can state as a general matter that, when an offering document's forecasts, opinions or projections are accompanied by meaningful cautionary statements, the forward-looking statements will not form the basis for a securities fraud claim if those statements did not affect the "total mix" of information the document provided investors. In other words, cautionary language, if sufficient, renders the alleged omissions or misrepresentations immaterial as a matter of law.

The bespeaks caution doctrine is, as an analytical matter, equally applicable to allegations of both affirmative misrepresentations and omissions concerning soft information. Whether the plaintiffs allege a document contains an affirmative prediction/opinion which is misleading or fails to include a forecast or prediction which failure is misleading, the cautionary statements included in the document may render the challenged predictive statements or opinions immaterial as a matter of law. Of course, a vague or blanket (boilerplate) disclaimer which merely warns the reader that the investment has risks will ordinarily be inadequate to prevent misinformation. To suffice, the cautionary statements must be substantive and tailored to the specific future projections, estimates or opinions in the prospectus which the plaintiffs challenge.

Because of the abundant and meaningful cautionary language contained in the prospectus, we hold that the plaintiffs have failed to state an actionable claim regarding the statement that the Partnership believed it could repay the bonds. We can say that the prospectus here truly bespeaks caution because, not only does the prospectus generally convey the riskiness of the investment, but its warnings and cautionary language directly address the substance of the statement the plaintiffs challenge. That is to say, the cautionary statements were tailored precisely to address the uncertainty concerning the Partnership's prospective ability to repay the bondholders. ***

*D. Conclusion*

*** [W]e think it clear that the accompanying warnings and cautionary language served to negate any potentially misleading effect that the prospectus' statement about the Partnership's belief in its ability to repay the bonds would have on a reasonable investor. The prospectus clearly and precisely cautioned that the bonds represented an exceptionally risky, perhaps even speculative, venture and that the Partnership's ability to repay the bonds was uncertain. Given this context, we believe that no reasonable jury could conclude that the subject projection materially influenced a reasonable investor. ***

For the foregoing reasons we will affirm the orders of the district court dismissing the plaintiffs' complaints under Rule 12(b)(6). ***

## *NOTES AND QUESTIONS*

***1. Materiality vs. Reliance.*** Does *Trump* characterize "bespeaks caution" as a materiality doctrine or as a reliance doctrine? Courts divide as to which characterization is more appropriate. See, e.g., *EP Medsystems, Inc. v. Echocath, Inc.*, 235 F.3d 865, 876 n. 4 (3d Cir. 2000) (materiality, not reliance); *Semerenko v. Cendant Corp.*, 223 F.3d 165, 182-83 (3d Cir. 2000) (reliance); *Rubinstein v. Collins,* 20 F.3d 160, 167 (5th Cir. 1994) (both). Is this a distinction that makes a difference? Why or why not?

***2. Reaching Efficient Markets.*** The *Trump* court applied the bespeaks caution doctrine to an IPO, which (as you will recall from Chapter 1.G) is ordinarily not sold in an efficient market. Should the doctrine apply in the efficient market context as well?

*3. The Relevance of the Defendant's Bad Faith.* Should a court dismiss an action based on the bespeaks caution doctrine if the plaintiff can show that the defendant did not believe the forecast at the time he made it? Consider the following argument against applying the doctrine in such circumstances:

> [O]ne could construct a completely inaccurate and fraudulent offering memorandum, yet be shielded from a fraud claim as long as there was language in the document cautioning investors of the specific risks. To the extent that such a rule would allow, if not encourage, fraud and non-disclosure on the part of corporate actors, it clearly is not a viable application of the "bespeaks caution" doctrine.

*Gurfein v. Sovereign Group,* 826 F. Supp. 890, 908 n. 20 (E.D. Pa. 1993). Are you persuaded? What (if anything) does *Trump* suggest about the relevance of the defendant's bad faith to the application of "bespeaks caution"?

*4. Omitted Forecasts.* The *Trump* court maintains that the bespeaks caution doctrine applies when forecasts are omitted as well as misrepresented. A claim involving an omitted forecast is subject to dismissal based not only on the bespeaks caution doctrine but also on the absence of a duty to disclose. See, e.g., *In re VeriFone Sec. Litig.*, 11 F.3d 865, 869-70 (9th Cir. 1993) (omitted sales forecasts not actionable under Rule 10b-5 because no duty to disclose existed). But cf. *Provenz v. Miller*, 102 F.3d 1478, 1488-89 (9th Cir. 1996) (trial necessary to determine whether omitted forecast rendered disclosed forecast false and misleading).

*5. Justifications.* While the bespeaks caution doctrine may increase companies' willingness to make forward-looking statements, it may do something else as well—eliminate weak actions prior to the discovery phase of the litigation and thereby spare the defendants the time and expense that discovery entails. Are you comfortable with this justification? Are there other Rule 10b-5 doctrines that emerge from a desire to weed out tenuous actions rather than from substantive considerations?

---

### c. *The Statutory Safe Harbor for Forward-Looking Statements*

In 1995, a newly elected Republican majority in Congress enacted the Private Securities Litigation Reform Act (PSLRA) over President Clinton's veto. The override received significant support from Democrats as well, without whom it would not have been possible.

The PSLRA added a safe harbor for forward-looking statements to the Exchange Act (Section 21E) as well as to the Securities Act (Section 27A). Other changes wrought by the PSLRA are addressed later in this Chapter as well as in subsequent Chapters (especially Chapter 6 on class actions).

The statutory safe harbor is explicitly limited to private actions (and thus does not come into play in actions brought by the SEC or the DOJ). Moreover, it applies only when the firm that issued the securities is a reporting company under the Exchange Act (see Chapter 1.A.2.c). It is not available to certain types of firms (for example, partnerships and limited liability companies) or transactions (for example, initial public offerings and tender offers).

The statutory safe harbor authorizes three independent bases for dismissal of a fraud action involving a forward-looking statement. The first ground, modeled on the judicial bespeaks caution doctrine, requires that the forward-looking statement be "identified as a forward-looking statement, and [be] accompanied by meaningful cautionary statements identifying important factors that could cause actual results to differ materially from those in the forward-looking statement." Section 21E(c)(1)(A)(i). The second ground requires that the forward-looking statement be "immaterial." Section 21E(c)(1)(A)(ii). The third ground authorizes dismissal when the plaintiff fails to show that the defendant made the forward-looking statement "with actual knowledge." Section 21E(c)(1)(B). The third ground has the effect of making "actual knowledge" the requisite state of mind in private Rule 10b-5 actions involving forward-looking statements. Note also that dismissals based on the third ground are proper regardless of whether the fraud is material.

Two other points merit mention. First, a special subsection of the statutory safe harbor specifically addresses oral forward-looking statements. See Section 21E(c)(2). Second, during the pendency of a motion to dismiss, discovery is stayed. See Section 21E(f).

Courts struggle with numerous aspects of the statutory safe harbor. Consider the following case.

## HARRIS v. IVAX CORPORATION

182 F.3d 799 (11th Cir. 1999)

COX, CIRCUIT JUDGE:

This appeal invites application of the safe harbor for forward-looking statements added to the Securities Exchange Act of 1934 by the Private Securities Litigation Reform Act of 1995 (PSLRA). We affirm the district court's dismissal of the complaint under Fed.R.Civ.P. 12(b)(6).

### I. BACKGROUND

*** Ivax Corporation is a manufacturer of generic drugs, a highly volatile business. Ivax was profitable in 1995, but lost money in the second quarter of 1996. On August 2, 1996 Ivax issued a press release that, while acknowledging business problems, also showed some optimism.[2] Ivax stock rose. On September 30, the last day of the quarter, Ivax announced in another

---

2. *** Ordinarily, the full text of such a release would not be part of the record under review for a dismissal under Fed.R.Civ.P. 12(b)(6) unless it was attached to the complaint. But a document central to the complaint that the defense appends to its motion to dismiss is also properly considered, provided that its contents are not in dispute. See, e.g., *Brooks v. Blue Cross & Blue Shield of Fla., Inc.*, 116 F.3d 1364, 1369 (11th Cir.1997). The PSLRA, moreover, contains a provision that directs the district court to consider not only "any statement cited in the complaint" but also "any cautionary statement accompanying the forward-looking statement, which are [*sic* ] not subject to material dispute, cited by the defendant." PSLRA § 102(b), codified at 15 U.S.C. § 78u-5(e). The usual rules for considering 12(b)(6) motions are thus bent to permit consideration of an allegedly fraudulent statement in its context.

press release that it anticipated a $43 million loss. On November 11, Ivax announced a $179 million loss for the third quarter, $104 million of which was a reduction in the carrying value of the goodwill ascribed to certain of Ivax's businesses. Neither of the earlier press releases had mentioned the possibility of this goodwill writedown based on third-quarter results. The price of Ivax stock plummeted. ***

II. DISCUSSION

*A. Overview*

*** The district court concluded that all of the statements alleged in the complaint to be fraudulent were forward-looking, and that the statements' "cautionary language" was "meaningful." The court thus concluded that Ivax's statements were anchored within the statutory safe harbor, and that the cautionary language shielded Ivax from liability. The court went further to conclude in the alternative that the complaint stumbled on the new pleading standards by failing to allege adequate facts to support a "strong inference," as the statute requires, that the defendants made the forward-looking statements with actual knowledge of their falsity.

The plaintiffs *** argue that the statements they allege to be fraudulent were either not forward-looking or were unaccompanied by sufficient cautionary language. For this reason, they contend that the district court should not have dismissed the current complaint. ***

For the more detailed reasons that follow, we reject the plaintiffs' arguments. All of the statements that the plaintiffs claim to be false or misleading are forward-looking. They were accompanied, moreover, by "meaningful cautionary language." Because we reach this conclusion, we need not in this case enter the thicket of the PSLRA's new pleading requirements for scienter; if a statement is accompanied by "meaningful cautionary language," the defendants' state of mind is irrelevant. See H.R. Conf. Rep. 104-369, at 44 (1995)("The first prong of the safe harbor requires courts to examine only the cautionary statement accompanying the forward-looking statement. Courts should not examine the state of mind of the person making the statement."). ***

*B. Were the August 2 and September 30 Statements in the Safe Harbor for Forward-Looking Statements?*

*** The plaintiffs' core theories appear rather to be two: first, that Ivax's hopeful outlooks concealed an intent to write down goodwill by $104 million in the third quarter of 1996, and second, that a limited list of clouds on the horizon deliberately omitted the risk of a goodwill writedown. In judging whether the statements on which alleged liability rests are forward- looking, our focus is accordingly on the remaining four excerpts from the press releases, discussed below, that contain those outlooks and that list. ***

*2. The "unique challenges."*

The August 2, 1996 press release also announced optimistically that "the challenges unique to this period in our history are now behind us." Taken in context, this statement is forward-looking. The two paragraphs of the press release preceding this statement describe two problems that contributed to a loss in the second quarter: excessive customer inventories, which reduced new orders, and a technical default in a revolving credit facility. Both problems, the statement said, were being resolved; inventories were becoming depleted, and the bank syndicate was expected to waive the default. Thus, the chairman and CEO announced that things were looking up.

"Forward-looking statement[s]" include "statements of future economic performance." 15 U.S.C. § 78u-5(i)(l)(C). The chairman and CEO's hopeful conclusion that conditions are better because of two anticipated improvements in business conditions is a prediction of economic performance, however couched. The plaintiffs' purely grammatical argument to the contrary—that a present-tense statement cannot predict the future—is unpersuasive; a statement about the state of a company whose truth or falsity is discernible only after it is made necessarily refers only to future performance. Whether the worst of Ivax's challenges were behind it was a matter verifiable only after the chairman so declared. This statement was thus forward-looking and in the safe harbor.

*3. Intact strategies.*

The August 2, 1996 press release continued with another hopeful outlook from Ivax's chairman and CEO, Phillip Frost, that "[o]ur fundamental business and its underlying strategies remain intact.... Only a limited number of companies are positioned to meaningfully participate in this rapidly growing market and, among them, IVAX is certainly very well positioned." Like the previous statement, this one is a prediction "of future economic performance." While it is true that the *state* of Ivax's "fundamental business" and "underlying strategies" is a question of present condition, whether they are intact is a fact only verifiable by seeing how they hold up in the future. Likewise, whether Ivax is "well positioned" is a statement whose truth can only be known after seeing how Ivax's future plays out. That puts this statement in the safe harbor, as well.

*4. The laundry list.*

The September 30, 1996 press release, which predicted third quarter results, contained a list of factors "relating to [Ivax's] generic drug business [that] will influence [Ivax's] third quarter results." Those five factors included high customer inventory levels and low orders; declining prices; "shelf stock adjustments" for existing customers; higher reserves for returns; and the bankruptcy of a major customer who owed Ivax $16 million. The list is a mixed bag, with some sentences that are forward-looking and some that are not. The statement's choice of language suggests that three of the factors had already been observed: "customer re-orders remain depressed"; "prices have continued to decline"; and "a wholesaler customer who owed us approximately $16 million filed a Chapter 11 bankruptcy petition." Observed facts of this kind are not "assumptions," and they are not any kind of prediction, either, that would put them within the definition of a forwardlooking statement. These sentences are not, therefore, forward-looking. Two other factors, however, are worded as assumptions about future events: "we expect reserves for returns and inventory writeoffs to be well above typical quarters" and "lower prices ... will increase shelf stock adjustments." As "assumptions underlying" the predictions elsewhere in the press release, these sentences are forward-looking. 15 U.S.C. § 78u-5(i)(l)(D).

The mixed nature of this statement raises the question whether the safe harbor benefits the entire statement or only parts of it. Of course, if any of the individual sentences describing known facts (such as the customer's bankruptcy) were allegedly false, we could easily conclude that that smaller, non-forward-looking statement falls outside the safe harbor. But the allegation here is that the list *as a whole* misleads anyone reading it for an explanation of Ivax's projections, because the list omits the expectation of a goodwill writedown. If the allegation is that the whole list is misleading, then it makes no sense to slice the list into separate sentences. Rather, the list becomes a "statement" in the statutory sense, and a basis of liability, as a unit. It must therefore be either forward-looking or not forward-looking in its entirety. The next issue is what the character of the list is as a whole—forward-looking or not.

We conclude that the entire list is due forward-looking treatment. To begin with, there is no question under the statute that a material and misleading omission can fall within the forward-looking safe harbor. And while the statute does not tell us exactly what to do with a mixed statement, extrinsic sources of congressional intent point strongly toward treating the entire list as forward-looking. Congress enacted the safe-harbor provision in order to loosen the "muzzling effect" of potential liability for forward-looking statements, which often kept investors in the dark about what management foresaw for the company. See H.R. Conf. Rep. 104-369, at 42 (1995). Forward-looking conclusions often rest both on historical observations and assumptions about future events. Thus, were we to banish from the safe harbor lists that contain both factual and forward-looking factors, we would inhibit corporate officers from fully explaining their outlooks. Indeed, liability-conscious officers would be relegated to citing only the factors that could individually be called forward-looking. That would hamper the communication that Congress sought to foster.

Treating mixed lists as forward-looking may open a loophole for misleading omissions, but there are two circumstances that should put investors on guard, anyway. First, a list or explanation will only qualify for this treatment if it contains assumptions underlying a forward-looking statement. Investors should know, under the current statutory scheme, that relying on assumptions is dangerous; there will often be no legal recourse even if the assumption is false. Second, a defendant can fully benefit from the safe harbor's shelter only when it has disclosed risk factors in a warning accompanying the forward- looking statement. This disclosure as well should warn investors against blind reliance on mixed lists.

For these reasons, we hold that when the factors underlying a projection or economic forecast include both assumptions and statements of known fact, and a plaintiff alleges that a material factor is missing, the entire list of factors is treated as a forward-looking statement. This list is therefore in the safe harbor.

*C. Cautionary Language*

The district court was correct that adequate cautionary language accompanies the forward-looking statements here. The italicized warning that Ivax appended to both press releases is detailed and informative; it tells the reader in detail what kind of misfortunes could befall the company and what the effect could be. We can reject out of hand, therefore, the plaintiffs' arguments that the cautionary statements are "mere boilerplate." That leaves, however, another question: the plaintiffs here allege fraud by material omission. Neither of the statements mentions the possibility of a large goodwill writedown. To be "meaningful," must the cautionary language explicitly mention *the* factor that ultimately belies a forward-looking statement?

We think not. The statute requires the warning only to mention "important factors that could cause actual results to differ materially from those in the forward-looking statement." It does not require a listing of *all* factors. The conference report, moreover, that accompanied the PSLRA specified that "[f]ailure to include the particular factor that ultimately causes the forward-looking statement not to come true will not mean that the statement is not protected by the safe harbor." H.R. Conf. Rep. 104-369, at 44 (1995). In short, when an investor has been warned of risks of a significance similar to that actually realized, she is sufficiently on notice of the danger of the investment to make an intelligent decision about it according to her own preferences for risk and reward. This statement satisfies Ivax's burden to warn under the statute, and it excuses Ivax from liability. ***

III. CONCLUSION

For the foregoing reasons, we affirm the district court's dismissal of the complaint. ***

---

## *NOTES AND QUESTIONS*

*1.* ***Waiting for Data.*** The court suggested that a statement is forward-looking when its ultimate accuracy or inaccuracy turns on data that have yet to be gathered. Is this a sound approach?

*2.* ***Omitting the Factor that "Dwarfs" the Others.*** The Commission submitted a brief in partial support of a petition for rehearing in *Ivax,* in which it argued that the decision "erroneously implies that a 'cautionary statement[ ]' could *** shield a company from liability *** even if the cautionary statement knowingly omits a fact that is such a market-driver that it dwarfs" the other factors in terms of importance. See *Harris v. Ivax Corp.,* 209 F.3d 1275, 1276 (11th Cir. 2000). The court denied the petition with the observation that the "argument [made by the Commission] had not been made to the panel, and *** we have therefore not considered it." Id. If the argument had been made to the panel, would the outcome of the case likely have been different?

*3.* ***Incorporating Factors by Reference.*** Does the statutory safe harbor apply where the document containing the forward-looking statement refers investors to factors discussed in documents on file with the Commission? Cf. *In re Champion Enters. Inc. Sec. Litig.,* 144 F. Supp. 2d 848, 862 (E.D. Mich.

2001) (answering this question in the affirmative). In thinking about this question, consider the possible relevance of the reference to a "readily available written document" in the special safe harbor for oral forward-looking statements set forth in Section 21E(c)(2).

*4. The Relevance of the Defendant's State of Mind.* The *Ivax* court cited the Conference Report for the proposition that meaningful cautionary language accompanying a forward-looking statement renders the defendant's state of mind "irrelevant." Why would Congress authorize dismissal of an action against a defendant who deliberately defrauded investors?

*5. The Impact of the Safe Harbor.* A study conducted by business school faculty members suggests that the statutory safe harbor has led to the dissemination of more forward-looking statements. The study examined disclosures made by firms in the computer, software, and drug industries the year before and the year following enactment of the PSLRA and concluded that with respect to the first two industries that "there was a significant post-Act increase in both the frequency of firms issuing forecasts and the mean number of forecasts issued." Marilyn Johnson et al., The Impact of Securities Litigation Reform on the Disclosure of Forward-Looking Information by High Technology Firms 23, Research Paper 1471R, University of Michigan Business School and Stanford University School of Business (March 1999). An equally important question has as yet no definitive answer: Has the statutory safe harbor precipitated the release of more forward-looking statements that are materially misleading?

*6. Bespeaks Caution Revisited.* Given the statutory safe harbor, in what respects does the bespeaks caution doctrine continue to be relevant?

### *PROBLEM 2-10*

Decide whether the following statements are forward-looking:

*a.* Our new shampoo is in the process of becoming an industry benchmark.

*b.* Our loan loss reserves are adequate.

*c.* We expect that Phase 2 of our building plan will begin in 5 months.

*d.* The misrepresentation at issue in *Basic Inc. v. Levinson,* 485 U.S. 224 (1988), which you read earlier in this section of the Chapter.

### *PROBLEM 2-11*

Luna, Inc. is an electronics parts manufacturer whose stock is listed on the New York Stock Exchange. Needing capital to expand its production capacity, Luna decided to make a registered stock offering. This offering began on December 15, 2001 and concluded on January 15, 2002.

The registration statement for the offering described the planned capacity expansion in its "Use of the Proceeds" section. The registration statement also stated the following in a section entitled "Description of Business": "Management plans to complete its expansion of current production facilities by the end of March 2002, and expects both an increase in manufacturing orders from its existing customers and an influx of manufacturing orders from new customers. See 'Risk Factors.' " In a "Risk Factors" section, the registration statement stated only that "all statements regarding completion of our new production facilities and our increase in revenue from additional manufacturing orders are merely projections and may not be realized."

The expansion project was completed on schedule, but shortly thereafter, Luna's largest customer (Alva) announced that it was planning to relocate almost all of its manufacturing offshore, and would therefore be placing no future orders with the company. Luna issued a press release announcing its cessation of business with Alva and adding that the competition it now faced from electronics parts manufacturers outside the continental United States might significantly impact the projected revenue from its capacity expansion.

As a result of the press release, the price of Luna stock fell significantly, and shareholders who purchased in the registered offering instituted a class action lawsuit against Luna under Rule 10b-5 based on alleged material misstatements in the registration statement's "Description of Business" section.

On plaintiff's motion to a very sympathetic judge, the trial court allowed a limited amount of pre-trial discovery to prevent "undue prejudice." This limited pre-trial discovery revealed that, prior to the filing of the registration statement as well as during the entire period of the offering, Luna's management assumed without any investigation that its existing customers would renew their short-term contracts and had no plans to move offshore. Had Luna's management investigated, they would have learned that Alva had been placing at least some new orders with offshore electronics parts manufacturers beginning at least two months before the public offering.

At the conclusion of this phase of limited discovery, Luna made a motion for summary judgment, claiming that it was not liable as a matter of law under the statutory safe harbor for forward-looking statements. Discuss the likely outcome of this motion. How (if at all) would your answer differ if the motion had been based on the bespeaks caution doctrine?

## C. THE "IN CONNECTION WITH" REQUIREMENT

The "in connection with" requirement emerges from the language of Section 10(b) and Rule 10b-5, which prohibit fraud "in connection with" the purchase or sale of any security. The language is silent, however, about what the nature of that connection must be, as is the legislative history. Courts have supplied a variety of answers to this question.

One important answer comes from the Second Circuit's landmark en banc decision in *SEC v. Texas Gulf Sulphur Co.*, 401 F.2d 833 (2d Cir. 1968). At issue was whether a corporation's issuance of a fraudulent press release violated Rule 10b-5. Concluding that the Rule was violated, the court had this to say:

> Congress when it use the phrase "in connection with the purchase or sale of any security" intended only that the device employed *** be of a sort that would cause reasonable investors to rely thereon, and, in connection therewith, so relying, cause them to purchase or sell a corporation's securities. *** We do not believe that Congress intended that the proscriptions of the Act would not be violated unless the makers of a misleading statement also participated in pertinent securities transactions in connection therewith ***.

> *** [W]e hold that Rule 10b-5 is violated whenever assertions are made *** in a manner reasonably calculated to influence the investing public, e.g., by means of the financial media, if such assurances are false or misleading ***.

Id. at 860-62. Relying on *Texas Gulf Sulphur,* courts have found the "in connection with" requirement satisfied by a corporation's submission of fraudulent quarterly or annual reports to the Commission or by release of fraudulent information to the news media. See, e.g., *Semerenko v. Cendant Corp.,* 223 F.3d 165, 176 (3d Cir. 2000) (collecting cases). See also *McGann v. Ernst & Young,* 102 F.3d 390, 397 (9th Cir. 1996) (holding the "in connection with" requirement met where an accounting firm issued a fraudulent audit report that it knew would be incorporated into the company's annual report).

## *NOTES AND QUESTIONS*

***1. Non-Trading Defendants.*** Under *Texas Gulf Sulphur,* the "in connection with" requirement can be satisfied regardless of whether the defendant traded the security in question. But as we shall see, *Blue Chip Stamps v. Manor Drug Stores,* 421 U.S. 723 (1975), imposes a purchaser-seller requirement for private plaintiffs at least partly on the basis of the "in connection with" language. Is requiring plaintiffs but not defendants to be buyers or sellers troublesome as a matter of either policy or statutory construction?

***2. Advertisements in Trade Publications.*** The Second Circuit has relied on *Texas Gulf Sulphur* to uphold application of Rule 10b-5 to a drug company's fraudulent advertisements in medical journals:

> In an economy that produces highly sophisticated products, technical information is of enormous importance to financial analysts *** . The fact that such information is found in a specialized medical journal *** rather than in a statement addressed to participants in financial markets *** seems to us irrelevant, so long as the journals are used by analysts studying the prospects of drug companies. ***
>
> We hold, therefore, that false advertisements in technical journals may be "in connection with" a securities transaction if the proof at trial establishes that the advertisements were used by market professionals in evaluating the stock of the company.

*In re Carter-Wallace, Inc. Sec. Litig.,* 150 F.3d 153, 156-57 (2d Cir. 1998). Is the court's conclusion unavoidable?

## *PROBLEM 2-12*

George is the lawyer for Martha, who was dismissed from her position as senior vice president of Designer Dresses, Inc., a large company whose shares are listed on the New York Stock Exchange. George's negotiations with the company on Martha's behalf have not been going well. George told a reporter for a national newspaper that Martha would soon file a class action charging the company with gender discrimination. George's assertion appeared in the newspaper and caused the price of the company's stock to drop. In fact, George (and Martha) have no intention of filing a class action. If George is named as a defendant in a Rule 10b-5 action, will the "in connection with" requirement be satisfied?

---

In the decision that follows, the court adopted an approach to the "in connection with" requirement that differed markedly from that of *Texas Gulf Sulphur*.

## CHEMICAL BANK v. ARTHUR ANDERSEN & CO.

726 F.2d 930 (2d Cir. 1984)

FRIENDLY, CIRCUIT JUDGE:

Arthur Andersen & Co. (Andersen) appeals, pursuant to 28 U.S.C. § 1292(b), from so much of an order *** as denied its motion to dismiss the claims alleging violations of the federal securities laws in three actions brought by four commercial banks which had made loans to Frigitemp Corporation (Frigitemp) and its wholly owned subsidiary, Elsters, Inc. (Elsters). ***

Frigitemp was a publicly held company whose stock was listed on the American Stock Exchange. The company was primarily in the business of selling, manufacturing and installing interior furnishings in hotels, restaurants, institutions and ships. During the early and mid-1970's, Frigitemp embarked on a course of rapid expansion, acquiring a number of other companies. It acquired Elsters *** as of December 31, 1976. *** The company's rapid expansion *** required larger amounts of capital to sustain its operations. After having mixed success in forays into the public debt and equity markets, Frigitemp looked to the Banks for financing.

By a contract dated December 31, 1975 (the Secured Credit Agreement), the Banks agreed to provide Frigitemp with a line of credit up to $8 million. Pursuant to the Secured Credit Agreement, the Banks advanced $6.5 million to Frigitemp beginning in 1976. The loans were evidenced by Frigitemp's promissory notes maturing on July 1, 1977, and were secured by a pledge of Frigitemp customer notes receivable.

In September, 1976, the Banks and Frigitemp began discussing the need to restructure Frigitemp's debt. Pending such restructuring, three banks in September, 1976, advanced $1.5 million evidenced by Frigitemp's one month promissory note to each bank; in October, 1976, they advanced an additional $3.5 million. Frigitemp gave each bank a promissory note maturing on February 28, 1977, which included the $1.5 million owed on the September financing. This maturity was later extended to April 30, 1977. In February, 1977, Frigitemp received an additional $4 million unsecured loan from all four banks, evidenced by promissory notes also maturing April 30, 1977. ***

The restructuring transaction occurred in early August, 1977. Although evidenced by three different agreements, an officer of Manufacturers Hanover averred that these "were structured as, and were intended to be, part of one single, integrated refinancing package", and we shall assume for present purposes that this was the case.

Under one set of agreements, the Banks extended the maturity date of the $6.5 million of notes issued under the Secured Credit Agreement from July 1, 1977 to July 1, 1978; the notes were amended by endorsements dated August 9, 1977 (the Note Endorsements). Under a second set of agreements, substituting for the $9 million of unsecured notes which had become due on April 30, 1977, Frigitemp issued to the Banks the same amount of unsecured notes dated August 9, 1977 and maturing March 31, 1978 (the Replacement Notes). Finally, the Banks advanced $4 million to Elsters for which they received promissory notes dated August 8, 1977, maturing March 31, 1978; Frigitemp guaranteed these notes and pledged as security 100% of Elsters' common stock, 750 shares, pursuant to a Pledge and Security Agreement.

Frigitemp filed a petition in bankruptcy on March 20, 1978. *** At the same time Elsters ceased engaging in business. ***

In this action, commenced in 1979, the Banks seek to hold Andersen and three principal officers of Frigitemp liable for their losses. The complaints allege that the Banks entered into the transactions with Frigitemp and Elsters in reliance on Frigitemp's financial statements audited and certified by Andersen for the years 1973-1976.[6] The Banks allege that Andersen knew that Frigitemp's financial statements were false and misleading in numerous respects *** The first claim in the complaints alleges that in making such certifications Andersen violated or aided and abetted in the violation of *** § 10(b) of the Securities Exchange Act of 1934, and Rule 10b-5 issued thereunder. Three other claims in the complaints allege violations of state law.

After answer and extensive discovery Andersen moved *** for an order *** dismissing the actions for lack of subject matter jurisdiction or, in the alternative, granting summary judgment in its favor *** and, in either event, dismissing the pendent claims.

After receiving briefs and hearing argument, Judge Goettel filed a comprehensive opinion denying Andersen's motion. ***

*** He ended his opinion by saying:

> Although the Court believes that the present state of the law in this circuit precludes dismissal of the Banks' claims under the securities laws, it recognizes that there is substantial ground for difference of opinion on the jurisdictional questions—whether the Replacement Notes are securities and whether the pledge of Elsters stock is sufficient to support jurisdiction over this lawsuit. Because these are controlling legal questions, it appears that an immediate appeal from this decision will materially advance the ultimate termination of this litigation. Consequently, the Court will certify an interlocutory appeal on the jurisdictional questions *** and will stay further proceedings pending the outcome of the appeal.

552 F. Supp. 457-58. A panel of this court granted leave to appeal.

## DISCUSSION

### *The Replacement Notes as Securities*

*** [W]e hold *** that thc context requires that they not be considered securities within § 10(b) of the 1934 Act. ***

---

6. Andersen was not the auditor for Elsters and certified no financial statements for it.

*Whether the pledge of the Elsters stock brings the August 1977 restructuring within the federal securities laws*

*** Andersen's initial brief did not directly challenge the proposition that a pledge is a sale and purchase of a security under § 10(b), as we squarely held in *Mallis v. Federal Deposit Insurance Corp.*, supra, 568 F.2d at 830. *** We see no reason to disavow *Mallis.* ***

With this much established, we are ready to consider Andersen's more serious point with respect to the pledge of the Elsters stock. This is that the complaint does not allege that Andersen made any misrepresentation concerning Elsters. Andersen contends, correctly so far as we have been able to ascertain, that all the cases imposing liability for violations of *** § 10(b) of the 1934 Act or Rule 10b-5, in respect of pledges, are cases where the defendant committed a proscribed act with respect to the pledged securities. It argues therefore that even if it made any untrue statement of a material fact with respect to Frigitemp or omitted to state a material fact concerning Frigitemp necessary in order to make the statements made, in the light of the circumstances under which they were made, not misleading, this was not "in connection with" the Banks' "purchase" or Frigitemp's "sale" of the Elsters stock by way of the pledge to secure the $4,000,000 loan made to Elsters. The Banks' principal answer is that the Elsters loan was guaranteed by Frigitemp; that misrepresentations with respect to Frigitemp thus affected the entire Elsters transaction since Frigitemp's guarantee was less valuable than the Banks had thought and they would have to rely more heavily on the pledged Elsters stock; and that since all three of the August, 1977 transactions were integrated and the Elsters loan involved the purchase or sale of a security, the misrepresentations affected all.

Section 10(b) of the 1934 Act was obviously drawn from § 17(a) of the 1933 Act; its principal effect *** was to cover frauds practiced on the seller as well as on the buyer. The legislative history sheds no light why Congress instead of simply expanding "in the offer or sale" phraseology of § 17(a) to read "in the offer, sale or purchase," adopted the "in connection with the purchase or sale" phraseology of § 10(b). Although arguably "in connection with" has a somewhat broader sweep than "in", it may be just as true that the "in connection with" phraseology simply fit better with the rest of § 10(b). Cf. *United States v. Naftalin,* 441 U.S. 768, 773 n.4 (1979) (The Court is "not necessarily persuaded that 'in' is narrower than 'in connection with.'"). ***

The difficulty has been somewhat increased by Justice Douglas' reference, in the Supreme Court's first brush with Rule 10b-5, to the plaintiff's having "suffered an injury as a result of deceptive practices *touching* its sale of securities as an investor." *Superintendent of Insurance v. Bankers Life & Casualty Co.,* supra, 404 U.S. 6, 12-13 (emphasis supplied). We are inclined to agree with Professor Loss, that "there is no reason to believe that the Justice's use of 'touching' was anything more than his variation of 'in connection with' as a matter of literary style." Loss, supra, [Fundamentals of Securities Regulation (1983)] at 903-04. There is no need for us to recapitulate the oft-described complex facts of the *Superintendent of Insurance* case. It suffices to point out that the Court had found, long before the "touching" reference, that "[t]here certainly was an 'act' or 'practice' ... which operated as a 'fraud or deceit' on

Manhattan, the seller of [securities]", in that although "the full market price was paid for these bonds ... the seller was duped into believing that it, the seller, would receive the proceeds." 404 U.S. at 9. Thus, the Court had concluded that "Manhattan was injured as an investor through a deceptive device which deprived it of any compensation for the sale of its valuable block of securities." Id. at 10.

A leading treatise on § 10(b) and Rule 10b-5 suggests that the "connection" between fraud and a securities transaction "can be very tenuous," 2 Bromberg & Lowenfels, Securities Fraud & Commodities Fraud § 4.7(574)(3), at 88.34 (1982) ***. However, statements to this effect have usually been made in cases *** where the connection was anything but tenuous. In cases near the borderline, courts have warned that "[i]t is important that the standard be fleshed out by a cautious case-by-case approach." *Smallwood v. Pearl Brewing Co.*, 489 F.2d 579, 595 (5 Cir.1974) (Wisdom, J.) We ourselves have stated that *Superintendent of Insurance* "pushed the perimeters rather far", *IIT v. Vencap, Ltd.*, 519 F.2d 1001, 1014 n.26 (2 Cir.1975).

As earlier stated, in August, 1977, Frigitemp not only was unable to repay the $6.5 million of secured notes and the $9 million unsecured notes but needed $4 million more. The Banks had to decide whether to let Frigitemp go under or to make the loans needed to keep it afloat and hopefully to survive. The complaints adequately allege that in deciding to renew the loans to Frigitemp and to loan $4 million to Elsters guaranteed by Frigitemp, the Banks relied on information concerning Frigitemp furnished by Andersen with knowledge of its falsity. This, however, would not bring the transaction within § 10(b) and Rule 10b-5 since neither the notes nor the guarantee were a "security." Does the case come within it because the Banks also obtained a pledge of 100% of the stock of Elsters[21] when there is no allegation that Andersen, which had never been Elsters' auditor, misrepresented the value of Elsters or its stock? In *Rubin*, supra, 449 U.S. at 429, n.6, the Supreme Court stated that it "need not decide whether misrepresentations or omissions involved in a securities transaction but not pertaining to the securities themselves can form the basis of a violation of § 17(a)." We are here compelled to decide that question, with respect to § 10(b) and Rule 10b-5 *** ; our answer is in the negative.

The purpose of § 10(b) and Rule 10b-5 is to protect persons who are deceived in securities transactions—to make sure that buyers of securities get what they think they are getting and that sellers of securities are not tricked into parting with something for a price known to the buyer to be inadequate or for a consideration known to the buyer not to be what it purports to be. Andersen is not alleged to have deceived the Banks with respect to the pledge

21. At first blush it is hard to see what added security a lender obtains by a pledge of the stock of the borrower when it already has a claim against the borrower's assets ranking prior to the stock. However, in an answer to an interrogatory, Chemical averred that "[b]anks commonly take the stock of a company as collateral in order to obtain additional protection," which itself tells us nothing, and that it was felt "that, in the event of default, recovery realized on the foreclosure and sale of the equity would be higher than that realized on piecemeal foreclosure and sale of various assets of Elsters."

of the Elsters stock; the Banks got exactly what they expected. Their showing is simply that but for Andersen's description of Frigitemp they would not have renewed the Frigitemp loans or made the Elsters loan which Frigitemp guaranteed, and that if they had not done this, there would have been no pledge of Elsters' stock. Such "but-for" causation is not enough.[23] The Act and Rule impose liability for a proscribed act in connection with the purchase or sale of a security; it is not sufficient to allege that a defendant has committed a proscribed act in a transaction of which the pledge of a security is a part.

None of the many cases relied on by the Banks goes as far as they would take us here.[24] *** We cannot believe that if a person misrepresents his financial condition in order to borrow $100,000 from a bank to which he gives a one month note partially secured by a pledge of GM stock, the case comes within § 10(b) and Rule 10b-5, although but for the pledge it would not. Yet this seems the inevitable consequence of the Banks' position here.[26] While, as the Banks argue, the misrepresentations as to the borrower's financial condition would require greater resort to the GM stock, and result in greater loss to the extent that the loan was not fully repaid, this is not enough to make the misrepresentations in connection with the purchase or sale of a security. It would be anomalous to hold that commercial bank loans procured by fraud are generally not within § 10(b) and Rule 10b-5, but that they become so, even though of a sort that no one would have considered to constitute a security, if collateralized with a security, although no misrepresentation was made with respect to the latter. It would be even more anomalous to hold that alleged misrepresentations concerning Frigitemp but not Elsters subject Andersen to liability for transactions *** in which no security played a part. ***

We thus hold *** while the pledge of the Elsters stock was a sale of a security by Frigitemp and a purchase by the Banks, Andersen's alleged misrepresentations concerning Frigitemp (but not Elsters) were not in connection with the sale or purchase of the Elsters stock under § 10(b) of the 1934 Act and Rule 10b-5 issued thereunder ***.

---

23. Borrowing the phraseology this court used in *Schlick v. Penn-Dixie Cement Corp.*, 507 F.2d 374, 380 (2 Cir.1974), the Banks' "but-for" allegation merely established "transaction causation." As described below, they have failed to establish the "loss causation" necessary for a legally sufficient claim under § 10(b) and Rule 10b-5.

24. *** Here the pledge of the Elsters stock, as to which no fraud is alleged, was merely an incident in a transaction not otherwise involving the purchase or sale of securities.

26. The dissent does not deal satisfactorily with this hypothetical. Its position, that a misrepresentation by a borrower with respect to a loan which is not itself a security renders the transaction subject to § 10(b) and Rule 10b-5 if it also involves a pledge, would cover the hypothetical. *** Admittedly the bank in the hypothetical would have had better ways of evaluating the GM stock than the Banks here had with respect to the Elsters stock. But the point remains that Andersen is not charged with having made or aided or abetted the making of any false representations about the Elsters stock.

VAN GRAAFEILAND, CIRCUIT JUDGE, CONCURRING AND DISSENTING:

I concur in Judge Friendly's customary well-reasoned opinion, except for that portion which holds as a matter of law that Arthur Andersen & Co. did not violate section 10(b). As to that portion I respectfully dissent. Because Arthur Andersen & Co. is alleged to be an aider and abettor of Frigitemp Corporation, discussion of the issue which prompts this dissent will be simplified by assuming that Frigitemp rather than Arthur Andersen is the defendant.[1]

*** Although Elsters' stock was not traded on any exchange and had no accurately ascertainable market value, appellees loaned Elsters $4 million as their part of the "sales" transaction. We have no way of knowing how much the banks would have loaned Elsters solely on the basis of Elsters' estimated net worth. It is undisputed, however, that they would not have advanced $4 million unless Frigitemp guaranteed that the money would be repaid. In short, then, the consideration for the $4 million loan was Elsters' promise of repayment plus a pledged asset and a guarantee of Elsters' allegedly solvent parent company.

This was a single transaction, a package deal, no part of which could have stood alone. To say, therefore, that there was no connection between the fraudulent misstatement of solvency and the "sale" of the asset and that "the Banks got exactly what they expected" is simply to blink at reality. When a company sells something it owns, the purchaser does not get what he expects unless he receives the benefits of the warranties and guaranties that accompany the sale. ***

With all due respect to my learned colleagues, I find little analogy to the present case in the situation posited by the majority in which a person pledges shares of General Motors stock as security for a $100,000 bank loan. In the first place, General Motors stock is nationally traded and has an established market value. In the second place, unlike Frigitemp, the would be borrower of $100,000 does not control the corporation whose stock he is pledging and to whom the loan is being made. The relationship between parent and subsidiary corporations has been a matter of continuing concern to the Supreme Court. An in-depth review of the many decisions in this area is not needed to establish that the obligations which Frigitemp owed to "the entire community of interests" in Elsters, *see Superintendent of Ins. v. Bankers Life & Casualty Co.*, supra, 404 U.S. at 12 (quoting *Pepper v. Litton,* 308 U.S. 295, 307 (1939)), are not fairly comparable to those which the holder of a few shares of General Motors owes to that company's "community of interests."

I am satisfied that Frigitemp's fraudulent guarantee of the Elsters loan and its pledge of the Elsters stock were integral parts of a "single seamless web", id., in which appellee banks were ensnared and that a clear 10(b) connection existed between them. This being so, there is no need to decide at this point whether the lending negotiations between Frigitemp and the banks were so integrated that the 10(b) connection carried over to the Frigitemp loans as well as that of Elsters. Because there was only one fraudulent scheme, so long as the district court has acquired jurisdiction of a portion of it that clearly

1. Suit against Frigitemp was precluded by its bankruptcy.

is securities related, there is no reason why the court should not be permitted to dispose of the entire action.

### *NOTES AND QUESTIONS*

*1. The Utility of* **Texas Gulf Sulphur.** Would *Texas Gulf Sulphur*'s approach to the "in connection with" requirement have been of use in *Chemical Bank*? Why or why not?

*2. An Incidental Connection.* What was the court's basis for concluding that only an incidental connection existed between the fraud and the pledge of the Elsters' stock? Professor Loss and Dean Seligman note that while the court's analysis in *Chemical Bank* has proven popular, the dissent's analysis is "more persuasive." 8 Louis Loss & Joel Seligman, Securities Regulation 3684 n. 563 (3d ed. 1991). Do you agree? If so, why would the more persuasive reasoning not carry the day?

*3. Critique.* Consider whether you agree with the following critique of *Chemical Bank*'s approach to the "in connection with" requirement:

> Whether the securities transaction is a relatively small part of a larger wrongdoing or is the very heart of the wrongdoing makes no difference. In either case, the primary concern addressed by the anti-fraud provisions of the federal securities laws—investor protection—is implicated.

C. Edward Fletcher III, The "In Connection With" Requirement of Rule 10b-5, 16 Pepp. L. Rev. 913, 975 (1989). Can you identify any other difficulties with *Chemical Bank*'s approach?

*4. A Limited Life for* **Bankers Life?** According to *Chemical Bank*, what light (or heat) does *Superintendent of Ins. v. Bankers Life & Cas. Co.*, 404 U.S. 6 (1971), shed on the "in connection with" requirement?

*5. Causation.* In the view of some courts, *Chemical Bank* equates the "in connection with" requirement with causation. See, e.g., *Kearney v. Prudential-Bache Sec., Inc.*, 701 F. Supp. 416, 425 n. 10 (S.D.N.Y. 1988). Is this accurate? You will study the causation aspects of Rule 10b-5 later in this chapter. Bear in mind, however, that insofar as the "in connection with" requirement merges into other aspects of the action, it in effect disappears.

*6. Fraud Pertaining to the Value of the Securities.* *Chemical Bank* has been read as holding that the fraud must pertain to the value of the securities. See, e.g., *Prod. Res. Group L.L.C. v. Stonebridge Partners Equity Fund, L.P.*, 6 F. Supp. 2d 236, 239 (S.D.N.Y. 1998). Is this a valid interpretation of *Chemical Bank*? Is it a plausible way to construe the "in connection with" requirement? Reconsider this question after reading the next case.

---

Ask yourself whether the unanimous Supreme Court decision that follows amounts to a comprehensive statement about the "in connection with" requirement or a relatively narrow holding.

## SEC v. ZANDFORD

535 U.S. 813 (2002)

JUSTICE STEVENS:

The Securities and Exchange Commission (SEC) filed a civil complaint alleging that a stockbroker violated both § 10(b) of the Securities Exchange Act of 1934 and the SEC's Rule 10b-5, by selling his customer's securities and using the proceeds for his own benefit without the customer's knowledge or consent. The question presented is whether the alleged fraudulent conduct was "in connection with the purchase or sale of any security" within the meaning of the statute and the rule.

I

Between 1987 and 1991, respondent was employed as a securities broker in the Maryland branch of a New York brokerage firm. In 1987, he persuaded William Wood, an elderly man in poor health, to open a joint investment account for himself and his mentally retarded daughter. According to the SEC's complaint, the "stated investment objectives for the account were 'safety of principal and income.'" The Woods granted respondent discretion to manage their account and a general power of attorney to engage in securities transactions for their benefit without prior approval. Relying on respondent's promise to "conservatively invest" their money, the Woods entrusted him with $419,255. Before Mr. Wood's death in 1991, all of that money was gone.

In 1991, the National Association of Securities Dealers (NASD) conducted a routine examination of respondent's firm and discovered that on over 25 separate occasions, money had been transferred from the Woods' account to accounts controlled by respondent. In due course, respondent was indicted in the United States District Court for the District of Maryland on 13 counts of wire fraud in violation of 18 U.S.C. § 1343. The first count alleged that respondent sold securities in the Woods' account and then made personal use of the proceeds. Each of the other counts alleged that he made wire transfers between Maryland and New York that enabled him to withdraw specified sums from the Woods' accounts. Some of those transfers involved respondent writing checks to himself from a mutual fund account held by the Woods, which required liquidating securities in order to redeem the checks. Respondent was convicted on all counts, sentenced to prison for 52 months, and ordered to pay $10,800 in restitution.

After respondent was indicted, the SEC filed a civil complaint in the same District Court alleging that respondent violated § 10(b) and Rule 10b-5 by engaging in a scheme to defraud the Woods and by misappropriating approximately $343,000 of the Woods' securities without their knowledge or consent. The SEC moved for partial summary judgment after respondent's criminal conviction, arguing that the judgment in the criminal case estopped respondent from contesting facts that established a violation of § 10(b).[1] Respondent filed

1. The scope of Rule 10b-5 is coextensive with the coverage of § 10(b), see *United States v. O'Hagan*, 521 U.S. 642, 651 (1997); *Ernst & Ernst v. Hochfelder*, 425 U.S. 185, 214 (1976); therefore, we use § 10(b) to refer to both the statutory provision and

a motion seeking discovery on the question whether his fraud had the requisite "connection with" the purchase or sale of a security. The District Court refused to allow discovery and entered summary judgment against respondent. It enjoined him from engaging in future violations of the securities laws and ordered him to disgorge $343,000 in ill-gotten gains.

The Court of Appeals for the Fourth Circuit reversed the summary judgment and remanded with directions for the District Court to dismiss the complaint. It first held that the wire fraud conviction, which only required two findings—(1) that respondent engaged in a scheme to defraud and (2) that he used interstate wire communications in executing the scheme—did not establish all the elements of a § 10(b) violation. Specifically, the conviction did not necessarily establish that his fraud was "in connection with" the sale of a security. Id., at 562.

The court then held that the civil complaint did not sufficiently allege the necessary connection because the sales of the Woods' securities were merely incidental to a fraud that "lay in absconding with the proceeds" of sales that were conducted in "a routine and customary fashion." Respondent's "scheme was simply to steal the Woods' assets" rather than to engage "in manipulation of a particular security." Ultimately, the court refused "to stretch the language of the securities fraud provisions to encompass every conversion or theft that happens to involve securities." Adopting what amounts to a "fraud-on-the-market" theory of the statute's coverage, the court held that without some "relationship to market integrity or investor understanding," there is no violation of § 10(b).

We granted the SEC's petition for a writ of certiorari to review the Court of Appeals' construction of the phrase "in connection with the purchase or sale of any security." Because the Court of Appeals ordered the complaint dismissed rather than remanding for reconsideration, we assume the allegations contained therein are true and affirm that disposition only if no set of facts would entitle petitioner to relief. We do not reach the question whether the record supports the District Court's grant of summary judgment in the SEC's favor—a question that requires all potential factual disputes to be resolved in respondent's favor. We merely hold that the allegations of the complaint, if true, entitle the SEC to relief; therefore, the Court of Appeals should not have directed that the complaint be dismissed.

II

Section 10(b) of the Securities Exchange Act makes it "unlawful for any person ... [t]o use or employ, in connection with the purchase or sale of any security ..., any manipulative or deceptive device or contrivance in contravention of such rules and regulations as the [SEC] may prescribe." Rule 10b-5, which implements this provision, forbids the use, "in connection with the purchase or sale of any security," of "any device, scheme, or artifice to defraud" or any other "act, practice, or course of business" that "operates ... as a fraud or deceit." Among Congress' objectives in passing the Act was "to insure honest securities

---

the Rule. ***

markets and thereby promote investor confidence" after the market crash of 1929. *United States v. O'Hagan,* 521 U.S. 642, 658 (1997). More generally, Congress sought "'to substitute a philosophy of full disclosure for the philosophy of *caveat emptor* and thus to achieve a high standard of business ethics in the securities industry.'" *Affiliated Ute Citizens of Utah v. United States,* 406 U.S. 128, 151 (1972) (quoting *SEC v. Capital Gains Research Bureau, Inc.,* 375 U.S. 180, 186 (1963)).

Consequently, we have explained that the statute should be "construed 'not technically and restrictively, but flexibly to effectuate its remedial purposes.'" 406 U.S., at 151 (quoting *Capital Gains Research Bureau, Inc.,* 375 U.S., at 195). In its role enforcing the Act, the SEC has consistently adopted a broad reading of the phrase "in connection with the purchase or sale of any security." It has maintained that a broker who accepts payment for securities that he never intends to deliver, or who sells customer securities with intent to misappropriate the proceeds, violates § 10(b) and Rule 10b-5. See, e.g., *In re Bauer,* 26 S.E.C. 770 (1947); *In re Southeastern Securities Corp.,* 29 S.E.C. 609 (1949). This interpretation of the ambiguous text of § 10(b), in the context of formal adjudication, is entitled to deference if it is reasonable, see *United States v. Mead Corp.,* 533 U.S. 218, 229-230, and n. 12 (2001). For the reasons set forth below, we think it is. While the statute must not be construed so broadly as to convert every common-law fraud that happens to involve securities into a violation of § 10(b), *Marine Bank v. Weaver,* 455 U.S. 551, 556 (1982) ("Congress, in enacting the securities laws, did not intend to provide a broad federal remedy for all fraud"), neither the SEC nor this Court has ever held that there must be a misrepresentation about the value of a particular security in order to run afoul of the Act.

The SEC claims respondent engaged in a fraudulent scheme in which he made sales of his customer's securities for his own benefit. Respondent submits that the sales themselves were perfectly lawful and that the subsequent misappropriation of the proceeds, though fraudulent, is not properly viewed as having the requisite connection with the sales; in his view, the alleged scheme is not materially different from a simple theft of cash or securities in an investment account. We disagree.

According to the complaint, respondent "engaged in a scheme to defraud" the Woods beginning in 1988, shortly after they opened their account, and that scheme continued throughout the 2-year period during which respondent made a series of transactions that enabled him to convert the proceeds of the sales of the Woods' securities to his own use. The securities sales and respondent's fraudulent practices were not independent events. This is not a case in which, after a lawful transaction had been consummated, a broker decided to steal the proceeds and did so. Nor is it a case in which a thief simply invested the proceeds of a routine conversion in the stock market. Rather, respondent's fraud coincided with the sales themselves.

Taking the allegations in the complaint as true, each sale was made to further respondent's fraudulent scheme; each was deceptive because it was neither authorized by, nor disclosed to, the Woods. With regard to the sales of shares in the Woods' mutual fund, respondent initiated these transactions by writing a check to himself from that account, knowing that redeeming the check would require the sale of securities. Indeed, each time respondent "exercised his power of disposition for his own benefit," that conduct, "without more," was a fraud. *United States v. Dunn,* 268 U.S. 121, 131 (1925). In the aggregate, the sales are properly viewed as a "course of business" that operated as a fraud or deceit on a stockbroker's customer.

Insofar as the connection between respondent's deceptive practices and his sale of the Woods' securities is concerned, the case is remarkably similar to *Superintendent of Ins. of N.Y. v. Bankers Life & Casualty Co.,* 404 U.S. 6 (1971). In that case the directors of Manhattan Casualty Company authorized the sale of the company's portfolio of treasury bonds because they had been "duped" into believing that the company would receive the proceeds of the sale. Id., at 9. We held that "Manhattan was injured as an investor through a deceptive device which deprived it of any compensation for the sale of its valuable block of securities." Id., at 10. In reaching this conclusion, we did not ask, as the Fourth Circuit did in this case, whether the directors were misled about the value of a security or whether the fraud involved "manipulation of a particular security." In fact, we rejected the Second Circuit's position in *Superintendent of Ins. of N.Y. v. Bankers Life & Casualty Co.* that because the fraud against Manhattan did not take place within the context of a securities exchange it was not prohibited by § 10(b). 404 U.S., at 10. We refused to read the statute so narrowly, noting that it "must be read flexibly, not technically and restrictively." Id., at 12. Although we recognized that the interest in "'preserving the integrity of the securities markets,'" was one of the purposes animating the statute, we rejected the notion that § 10(b) is limited to serving that objective alone. Ibid.

Like the company directors in *Bankers Life,* the Woods were injured as investors through respondent's deceptions, which deprived them of any compensation for the sale of their valuable securities. They were duped into believing respondent would "conservatively invest" their assets in the stock market and that any transactions made on their behalf would be for their benefit for the "'safety of principal and income.'" The fact that respondent misappropriated the proceeds of the sales provides persuasive evidence that he had violated § 10(b) when he made the sales, but misappropriation is not an essential element of the offense. Indeed, in *Bankers Life,* we flatly stated that it was "irrelevant" that "the proceeds of the sale that were due the seller were misappropriated." It is enough that the scheme to defraud and the sale of securities coincide.

The Court of Appeals below distinguished *Bankers Life* on the ground that it involved an affirmative misrepresentation, whereas respondent simply failed to inform the Woods of his intent to misappropriate their securities. We are not persuaded by this distinction. Respondent was only able to carry out his fraudulent scheme without making an affirmative misrepresentation because the Woods had trusted him to make transactions in their best interest without prior approval. Under these circumstances, respondent's fraud represents an even greater threat to investor confidence in the securities industry than the misrepresentation in *Bankers Life.* Not only does such a fraud prevent investors from trusting that their brokers are executing transactions for their benefit, but it undermines the value of a discretionary account like that held by the Woods. The benefit of a discretionary account is that it enables individuals, like the

Woods, who lack the time, capacity, or know-how to supervise investment decisions, to delegate authority to a broker who will make decisions in their best interests without prior approval. If such individuals cannot rely on a broker to exercise that discretion for their benefit, then the account loses its added value. Moreover, any distinction between omissions and misrepresentations is illusory in the context of a broker who has a fiduciary duty to her clients. See *Chiarella v. United States,* 445 U.S. 222, 230 (1980) (noting that "silence in connection with the purchase or sale of securities may operate as a fraud actionable under § 10(b)" when there is "a duty to disclose arising from a relationship of trust and confidence between parties to a transaction"); *Affiliated Ute Citizens of Utah v. United States,* 406 U.S., at 153.

More recently, in *Wharf (Holdings) Ltd. v. United Int'l Holdings, Inc.,* 532 U.S. 588 (2001), our decision that the seller of a security had violated § 10(b) focused on the secret intent of the seller when the sale occurred. The purchaser claimed "that Wharf sold it a security (the option) while secretly intending from the very beginning not to honor the option." Although Wharf did not specifically argue that the breach of contract underlying the complaint lacked the requisite connection with a sale of securities, it did assert that the case was merely a dispute over ownership of the option, and that interpreting § 10(b) to include such a claim would convert every breach of contract that happened to involve a security into a violation of the federal securities laws. We rejected that argument because the purchaser's claim was not that the defendant failed to carry out a promise to sell securities; rather, the claim was that the defendant sold a security while never intending to honor its agreement in the first place. Similarly, in this case the SEC claims respondent sold the Woods' securities while secretly intending from the very beginning to keep the proceeds. In *Wharf,* the fraudulent intent deprived the purchaser of the benefit of the sale whereas here the fraudulent intent deprived the seller of that benefit, but the connection between the deception and the sale in each case is identical.

In *United States v. O'Hagan,* 521 U.S. 642 (1997), we held that the defendant had committed fraud "in connection with" a securities transaction when he used misappropriated confidential information for trading purposes. We reasoned that "the fiduciary's fraud is consummated, not when the fiduciary gains the confidential information, but when, without disclosure to his principal, he uses the information to purchase or sell securities. The securities transaction and the breach of duty thus coincide. This is so even though the person or entity defrauded is not the other party to the trade, but is, instead, the source of the nonpublic information." Id., at 655-656. The Court of Appeals distinguished *O'Hagan* by reading it to require that the misappropriated information or assets not have independent value to the client outside the securities market. We do not read *O'Hagan* as so limited. In the chief passage cited by the Court of Appeals for this proposition, we discussed the Government's position that "[t]he misappropriation theory would not ... apply to a case in which a person defrauded a bank into giving him a loan or embezzled cash from another, and then used the proceeds of the misdeed to purchase securities," because in that situation "the proceeds would have value to the malefactor apart from their use in a securities transaction, and the fraud would be complete as soon as the money was obtained." 521 U.S., at 656. Even if this passage could be read to introduce a new requirement into § 10(b), it would not affect our analysis of this case, because the Woods' securities did not have value for respondent apart from their use in a securities transaction and the fraud was not complete before the sale of securities occurred.

As in *Bankers Life, Wharf,* and *O'Hagan,* the SEC complaint describes a fraudulent scheme in which the securities transactions and breaches of fiduciary duty coincide. Those breaches were therefore "in connection with" securities sales within the meaning of § 10(b).[4] Accordingly, the judgment of the Court of Appeals is reversed, and the case is remanded for further proceedings consistent with this opinion. ***

### *NOTES AND QUESTIONS*

***1.* Chemical Bank *Revisited.*** The lower court in *Zandford* had relied on *Chemical Bank* to reach the conclusion that the "in connection with" requirement had not been satisfied. See *SEC v. Zandford,* 238 F.3d 559, 563-64 (4th Cir. 2001) (finding that "Zandford's securities sales were incidental to his scheme to defraud"). Do you agree that the application of *Chemical Bank* produces this result? What impact (if any) does the Supreme Court's decision in *Zandford* have on *Chemical Bank*?

***2. In Search of Coincidences.*** Suppose Woods had presented various stock certificates to Zandford and asked him to sell the shares. Would the "in connection with" requirement have been satisfied if Zandford formed his plan to steal the proceeds (i) immediately upon hearing Woods's request; (ii) the day before completing the sales; (iii) three weeks after completing of the sales?

***3. Reality or Rhetoric.*** By expressing concern about investor confidence and advocating flexibility in interpretation, does *Zandford* tell us to read the "in connection with" requirement broadly in all settings? Or was the Court simply providing rhetorical packaging for a narrow holding? If the latter, how is the choice of packaging to be explained?

***4. Differentiating Private Actions.*** Prior to *Zandford,* some courts took the position that in order to discourage vexatious private litigation, the "in connection with" requirement should be made more difficult for private plaintiffs than for government plaintiffs. See, e.g., *SEC v. Clark,* 915 F.2d 439, 449 n. 18 (9th Cir. 1990). What impact (if any) does *Zandford* have in this regard?

***5. Coextensive Coverage.*** *Zandford* asserts that "[t]he scope of Rule 10b-5 is co-extensive with the coverage of § 10(b)" and cites as support *United*

---

4. Contrary to the Court of Appeals' prediction, our analysis does not transform every breach of fiduciary duty into a federal securities violation. If, for example, a broker embezzles cash from a client's account or takes advantage of the fiduciary relationship to induce his client into a fraudulent real estate transaction, then the fraud would not include the requisite connection to a purchase or sale of securities. Likewise if the broker told his client he was stealing the client's assets, that breach of fiduciary duty might be in connection with a sale of securities, but it would not involve a deceptive device or fraud. Cf. *Santa Fe Industries, Inc. v. Green,* 430 U.S. 462 (1977).

*States v. O'Hagan,* 521 U.S. 642 (1997), and *Ernst & Ernst v. Hochfelder,* 425 U.S. 185 (1976). But do these decisions actually say something somewhat different? See *O'Hagan,* supra, 521 U.S. at 651 ("Liability under Rule 10b-5 *** does not extend beyond conduct encompassed by § 10(b)'s prohibition"); *Hochfelder,* supra, 425 U.S., at 214 (the Rule's "scope cannot exceed the power granted the Commission by Congress under § 10(b)"). What effect (if any) is *Zandford's* position on coextensiveness likely to have on the interpretation of the Rule?

*6. One Approach or Many.* Is it possible to have a single approach to the "in connection with" requirement that would apply in all circumstances?

### *PROBLEM 2-13*

Zartman, Inc. is a closely held corporation. Its shareholders have a written agreement requiring each of them to be employed as an officer of the company. The agreement further provides that if an officer's employment ends due to death, retirement, or disability, he or she (or a representative) will receive a per share price determined by a specified formula, but if that employment ends for any other reason, only 1/3 of such price will be paid.

As of May 2002, Phoebe was Zartman's president and Peter the vice president. Both were also directors of the company and between them owned 45% of the shares. The other five directors (the "director group") owned 48% of the shares. At the end of May, the director group decided to remove Phoebe and Peter as officers. They also decided that they would not disclose the removal plan until the last minute.

In June, the board appointed a nominating committee to select nominees for director and officer positions. The committee, consisting of Phoebe, Peter, and two members of the director group, compiled a list of nominees consisting of all the incumbent officers and directors, including Phoebe and Peter. The list was received at a directors' meeting on June 20.

The next day, the annual shareholders' meeting was held. Phoebe and Peter assumed that the director group would support all of the committee's nominees. They thus joined with the director group and the other shareholders to reelect unanimously the incumbent directors. The result of the election was to return the director group to its majority position on the board.

At a subsequent directors' meeting, the director group made known for the first time its intention to remove Phoebe and Peter as officers. Acting as a majority of the board, the group rejected the committee's nominations of Phoebe as president and Peter as vice president and placed two other individuals in those positions. The group then adopted a resolution to purchase the shares of Phoebe and Peter in accordance with the shareholders' agreement.

Phoebe and Peter have surrendered their stock certificates and accepted payment for their shares. But they would like to bring a Rule 10b-5 action. If they do so, would the "in connection with" requirement be satisfied?

Cf. *Ketchum v. Green,* 557 F.2d 1022 (3d Cir. 1977).

## D. THE SCIENTER REQUIREMENT

Scienter, a Latin word for "knowingly," is a term used to describe a person's state of mind at the time he or she took action or failed to take action. An action taken with scienter is taken intentionally, or at least recklessly. On the other hand, an action taken negligently, or even grossly negligently, is said to lack scienter.

The first part of this section explores *Ernst & Ernst v. Hochfelder*, 425 U.S. 185 (1976), which held that scienter is necessary to establish liability under Section 10(b) and Rule 10b-5. The second part focuses on the requirements for pleading scienter that apply to all plaintiffs in Rule 10b-5 cases, as well as on the heightened pleading requirements for private plaintiffs enacted as part of the Private Securities Litigation Reform Act of 1995 (PSLRA).

### *1. The Substantive Standard*

### ERNST & ERNST v. HOCHFELDER
425 U.S. 185 (1976)

JUSTICE POWELL:

The issue in this case is whether an action for civil damages may lie under § 10(b) of the Securities Exchange Act of 1934 and Securities and Exchange Commission Rule 10b-5 in the absence of an allegation of intent to deceive, manipulate, or defraud on the part of the defendant.

I

Petitioner, Ernst & Ernst, is an accounting firm. From 1946 through 1967 it was retained by First Securities Company of Chicago (First Securities), a small brokerage firm and member of the Midwest Stock Exchange and of the National Association of Securities Dealers, to perform periodic audits of the firm's books and records. In connection with these audits Ernst & Ernst prepared for filing with the Securities and Exchange Commission (Commission) the annual reports required of First Securities under § 17(a) of the 1934 Act. It also prepared for First Securities responses to the financial questionnaires of the Midwest Stock Exchange (Exchange).

Respondents were customers of First Securities who invested in a fraudulent securities scheme perpetrated by Leston B. Nay, president of the firm and owner of 92% of its stock. Nay induced the respondents to invest funds in "escrow" accounts that he represented would yield a high rate of return. Respondents did so from 1942 through 1966, with the majority of the transactions occurring in the 1950's. In fact, there were no escrow accounts as Nay converted respondents' funds to his own use immediately upon receipt. These transactions were not in the customary form of dealings between First Securities and its customers. The respondents drew their personal checks payable to Nay or a designated bank for his account. No such escrow accounts were reflected on the books and records of First Securities, and none was shown on its periodic accounting to respondents in connection with their other investments. Nor were they included in First Securities' filings with the Commission or the Exchange.

This fraud came to light in 1968 when Nay committed suicide, leaving a note that described First Securities as bankrupt and the escrow accounts as "spurious." Respondents subsequently filed this action for damages against Ernst & Ernst in the United States District Court for the Northern District of Illinois under § 10(b) of the 1934 Act. The complaint charged that Nay's escrow scheme violated § 10(b) and Commission Rule 10b-5, and that Ernst & Ernst had "aided and abetted" Nay's violations by its "failure" to conduct proper audits of First Securities. As revealed through discovery, respondents' cause of action rested on a theory of negligent nonfeasance. The premise was that Ernst & Ernst had failed to utilize "appropriate auditing procedures" in its audits of First Securities, thereby failing to discover internal practices of the firm said to prevent an effective audit. The practice principally relied on was Nay's rule that only he could open mail addressed to him at First Securities or addressed to First Securities to his attention, even if it arrived in his absence. Respondents contended that if Ernst & Ernst had conducted a proper audit, it would have discovered this "mail rule." The existence of the rule then would have been disclosed in reports to the Exchange and to the Commission by Ernst & Ernst as an irregular procedure that prevented an effective audit. This would have led to an investigation of Nay that would have revealed the fraudulent scheme. Respondents specifically disclaimed the existence of fraud or intentional misconduct on the part of Ernst & Ernst.

After extensive discovery the District Court granted Ernst & Ernst's motion for summary judgment and dismissed the action. The court rejected Ernst & Ernst's contention that a cause of action for aiding and abetting a securities fraud could not be maintained under § 10(b) and Rule 10b-5 merely on allegations of negligence. It concluded, however, that there was no genuine issue of material fact with respect to whether Ernst & Ernst had conducted its audits in accordance with generally accepted auditing standards.

The Court of Appeals for the Seventh Circuit reversed and remanded, holding that one who breaches a duty of inquiry and disclosure owed another is liable in damages for aiding and abetting a third party's violation of Rule 10b-5 if the fraud would have been discovered or prevented but for the breach.[7] The court reasoned that Ernst & Ernst had a common-law and statutory duty of inquiry into the adequacy of First Securities' internal control system because it had contracted to audit First Securities and to prepare for filing with the Commission the annual report of First Securities' financial condition required under § 17 of the 1934 Act and Rule 17a-5. The court further reasoned that respondents were beneficiaries of the statutory duty to inquire and the related duty to disclose any material irregularities that were discovered. The court concluded that there were genuine issues of fact as to whether Ernst & Ernst's failure to discover and comment upon Nay's mail rule constituted a breach of its

7. *** In view of our holding that an intent to deceive, manipulate, or defraud is required for civil liability under § 10(b) and Rule 10b-5, we need not consider whether civil liability for aiding and abetting is appropriate under the section and the Rule, nor the elements necessary to establish such a cause of action. [Editor's Note: Almost two decades later, the Supreme Court held that Section 10(b) and Rule 10b-5 do not encompass aiding and abetting liability. See *Central Bank, N.A. v. First Interstate Bank, N.A.*, 511 U.S. 164 (1994), a principal case in Section H of this Chapter.]

duties of inquiry and disclosure and whether inquiry and disclosure would have led to the discovery or prevention of Nay's fraud.

We granted certiorari to resolve the question whether a private cause of action for damages will lie under § 10(b) and Rule 10b-5 in the absence of any allegation of "scienter"—intent to deceive, manipulate, or defraud.[12] We conclude that it will not and therefore we reverse.

II

*** Although § 10(b) does not by its terms create an express civil remedy for its violation, and there is no indication that Congress, or the Commission when adopting Rule 10b-5, contemplated such a remedy, the existence of a private cause of action for violations of the statute and the Rule is now well established. *Blue Chip Stamps v. Manor Drug Stores*, 421 U.S. 723, 730 (1975); *Affiliated Ute Citizens v. United States*, 406 U.S. 128, 150-154 (1972); *Superintendent of Insurance v. Bankers Life & Cas. Co.*, 404 U.S. 6, 13, n. 9 (1971). During the 30-year period since a private cause of action was first implied under § 10(b) and Rule 10b-5, a substantial body of case law and commentary has developed as to its elements. Courts and commentators long have differed with regard to whether scienter is a necessary element of such a cause of action, or whether negligent conduct alone is sufficient. In addressing this question, we turn first to the language of § 10(b), for "(t)he starting point in every case involving construction of a statute is the language itself." *Blue Chip Stamps*, supra, at 756 (Powell, J., concurring).

A

Section 10(b) makes unlawful the use or employment of "any manipulative or deceptive device or contrivance" in contravention of Commission rules. The words "manipulative or deceptive" used in conjunction with "device or contrivance" strongly suggest that § 10(b) was intended to proscribe knowing or intentional misconduct. See *SEC v. Texas Gulf Sulphur Co.*, 401 F.2d 833, 868 (CA2 1968) (Friendly, J., concurring); Loss, Summary Remarks, 30 Bus. Law. 163, 165 (Special Issue 1975).

In its *amicus curiae* brief, however, the Commission contends that nothing in the language "manipulative or deceptive device or contrivance" limits its operation to knowing or intentional practices. In support of its view, the

---

12. Although the verbal formulations of the standard to be applied have varied, several Courts of Appeals have held in substance that negligence alone is sufficient for civil liability under § 10(b) and Rule 10b. *** But few of the decisions announcing that some form of negligence suffices for civil liability under § 10(b) and Rule 10b-5 actually have involved only negligent conduct.

In this opinion the term "scienter" refers to a mental state embracing intent to deceive, manipulate, or defraud. In certain areas of the law recklessness is considered to be a form of intentional conduct for purposes of imposing liability for some act. We need not address here the question whether, in some circumstances, reckless behavior is sufficient for civil liability under § 10(b) and Rule 10b-5.

Since this case concerns an action for damages we also need not consider the question whether scienter is a necessary element in an action for injunctive relief under § 10(b) and Rule 10b-5.

Commission cites the overall congressional purpose in the 1933 and 1934 Acts to protect investors against false and deceptive practices that might injure them. See *Affiliated Ute Citizens v. United States*, supra, at 151; *Superintendent of Insurance v. Bankers Life & Cas. Co.*, supra, 404 U.S., at 11-12; *J. I. Case Co. v. Borak*, 377 U.S. 426, 432-433 (1964). The Commission then reasons that since the "effect" upon investors of given conduct is the same regardless of whether the conduct is negligent or intentional, Congress must have intended to bar all such practices and not just those done knowingly or intentionally. The logic of this effect-oriented approach would impose liability for wholly faultless conduct where such conduct results in harm to investors, a result the Commission would be unlikely to support. But apart from where its logic might lead, the Commission would add a gloss to the operative language of the statute quite different from its commonly accepted meaning. The argument simply ignores the use of the words "manipulative," "device," and "contrivance" terms that make unmistakable a congressional intent to proscribe a type of conduct quite different from negligence.[20] Use of the word "manipulative" is especially significant. It is and was virtually a term of art when used in connection with securities markets. It connotes intentional or willful conduct designed to deceive or defraud investors by controlling or artificially affecting the price of securities.[21]

In addition to relying upon the Commission's argument with respect to the operative language of the statute, respondents contend that since we are dealing with "remedial legislation," *Tcherepnin v. Knight,* 389 U.S. 332, 336 (1967), it must be construed "'not technically and restrictively, but flexibly to effectuate its remedial purposes.'" *Affiliated Ute Citizens v. United States*, 406 U.S., at 151, quoting *SEC v. Capital Gains Research Bureau*, supra, 375 U.S., at 195. They argue that the "remedial purposes" of the Acts demand a construction of § 10(b) that embraces negligence as a standard of liability. But in seeking to accomplish its broad remedial goals, Congress did not adopt uniformly a negligence standard even as to express civil remedies. In some circumstances and with respect to certain classes of defendants, Congress did create express liability predicated upon a failure to exercise reasonable care. E. g., 1933 Act § 11(b)(3)(B) (liability of "experts," such as accountants for misleading statements in portions of registration statements for which they are responsible). But in other situations good faith is an absolute defense. 1934 Act § 18 (misleading statements in any document filed pursuant to the 1934 Act).

---

**20.** Webster's International Dictionary (2d ed. 1934) defines "device" as "(t)hat which is devised, or formed by design; a contrivance; an invention; project; scheme; often, a scheme to deceive; a stratagem; an artifice," and "contrivance" in pertinent part as "(a) thing contrived or used in contriving; a scheme, plan, or artifice." In turn, "contrive" in pertinent part is defined as "(t)o devise; to plan; to plot ... (t)o fabricate ... design; invent ... to scheme...." The Commission also ignores the use of the terms "(t)o use or employ," language that is supportive of the view that Congress did not intend § 10(b) to embrace negligent conduct.

**21.** Webster's International Dictionary, supra, defines "manipulate" as "to manage or treat artfully of fraudulently; as to manipulate accounts.... 4. *Exchanges.* To force (prices) up or down, as by matched orders, wash sales, fictitious reports ...; to rig."

And in still other circumstances Congress created express liability regardless of the defendant's fault, 1933 Act § 11(a) (issuer liability for misleading statements in the registration statement).

It is thus evident that Congress fashioned standards of fault in the express civil remedies in the 1933 and 1934 Acts on a particularized basis. Ascertainment of congressional intent with respect to the standard of liability created by a particular section of the Acts must therefore rest primarily on the language of that section. Where, as here, we deal with a judicially implied liability, the statutory language certainly is no less important. In view of the language of § 10(b), which so clearly connotes intentional misconduct, and mindful that the language of a statute controls when sufficiently clear in its context, further inquiry may be unnecessary. We turn now, nevertheless, to the legislative history of the 1934 Act to ascertain whether there is support for the meaning attributed to § 10(b) by the Commission and respondents.

B

Although the extensive legislative history of the 1934 Act is bereft of any explicit explanation of Congress' intent, we think the relevant portions of that history support our conclusion that § 10(b) was addressed to practices that involve some element of scienter and cannot be read to impose liability for negligent conduct alone. ***

C

The 1933 and 1934 Acts constitute interrelated components of the federal regulatory scheme governing transactions in securities. See *Blue Chip Stamps*, 421 U.S., at 727-730. As the Court indicated in *SEC v. National Securities, Inc.*, 393 U.S. 453, 466 (1969), "the interdependence of the various sections of the securities laws is certainly a relevant factor in any interpretation of the language Congress has chosen...." Recognizing this, respondents and the Commission contrast § 10(b) with other sections of the Acts to support their contention that civil liability may be imposed upon proof of negligent conduct. We think they misconceive the significance of the other provisions of the Acts.

The Commission argues that Congress has been explicit in requiring willful conduct when that was the standard of fault intended, citing § 9 of the 1934 Act which generally proscribes manipulation of securities prices. Sections 9(a)(1) and (a)(2), for example, respectively prohibit manipulation of security prices "(f)or the purpose of creating a false or misleading appearance of active trading in any security ... or ... with respect to the market for any such security," and "for the purpose of inducing the purchase or sale of such security by others." See also § 9(a)(4). Section 9(e) then imposes upon "(a)ny person who willfully participates in any act or transaction in violation of" other provisions of § 9 civil liability to anyone who purchased or sold a security at a price affected by the manipulative activities. From this the Commission concludes that since § 10(b) is not by its terms explicitly restricted to willful, knowing, or purposeful conduct, it should not be construed in all cases to require more than negligent action or inaction as a precondition for civil liability.

The structure of the Acts does not support the Commission's argument. In each instance that Congress created express civil liability in favor of purchasers or sellers of securities it clearly specified whether recovery was to be premised on knowing or intentional conduct, negligence, or entirely innocent mistake. See 1933 Act §§ 11, 12, 15; 1934 Act §§ 9, 18, 20. For example, § 11 of the 1933 Act unambiguously creates a private action for damages when a registration statement includes untrue statements of material facts or fails to state material facts necessary to make the statements therein not misleading. Within the limits specified by § 11(e), the issuer of the securities is held absolutely liable for any damages resulting from such misstatement or omission. But experts such as accountants who have prepared portions of the registration statement are accorded a "due diligence" defense. In effect, this is a negligence standard. An expert may avoid civil liability with respect to the portions of the registration statement for which he was responsible by showing that "after reasonable investigation" he had "reasonable ground(s) to believe" that the statements for which he was responsible were true and there was no omission of a material fact. § 11(b)(3)(B)(i). The express recognition of a cause of action premised on negligent behavior in § 11 stands in sharp contrast to the language of § 10(b), and significantly undercuts the Commission's argument.

We also consider it significant that each of the express civil remedies in the 1933 Act allowing recovery for negligent conduct, see §§ 11, 12(2), 15, is subject to significant procedural restrictions not applicable under § 10(b). Section 11(e) of the 1933 Act, for example, authorizes the court to require a plaintiff bringing a suit under §11, § 12(2), or § 15 thereof to post a bond for costs, including attorneys' fees, and in specified circumstances to assess costs at the conclusion of the litigation. Section 13 specifies a statute of limitations of one year from the time the violation was or should have been discovered, in no event to exceed three years from the time of offer or sale, applicable to actions brought under §11, § 12(2), or § 15. These restrictions, significantly, were imposed by amendments to the 1933 Act adopted as part of the 1934 Act. *** We think these procedural limitations indicate that the judicially created private damages remedy under § 10(b)—which has no comparable restrictions—cannot be extended, consistently with the intent of Congress, to actions premised on negligent wrongdoing. Such extension would allow causes of action covered by §§ 11, 12(2), and 15 to be brought instead under § 10(b) and thereby nullify the effectiveness of the carefully drawn procedural restrictions on these express actions. We would be unwilling to bring about this result absent substantial support in the legislative history, and there is none.

D

We have addressed, to this point, primarily the language and history of § 10(b). The Commission contends, however, that subsections (b) and (c) of Rule 10b-5 are cast in language which—if standing alone—could encompass both intentional and negligent behavior. These subsections respectively provide that it is unlawful "(t)o make any untrue statement of a material fact or to omit to state a material fact necessary in order to make the statements made, in the light of the circumstances under which they were made, not misleading...." and "(t)o engage in any act, practice, or course of business which operates or would operate as a fraud or deceit upon any person.... " Viewed in isolation the language of subsection (b), and arguably that of subsection (c), could be read as proscribing, respectively, any type of material misstatement or omission, and any course of conduct, that has the effect of defrauding investors, whether the wrongdoing was intentional or not.

We note first that such a reading cannot be harmonized with the administrative history of the Rule, a history making clear that when the Commission adopted the Rule it was intended to apply only to activities that involved scienter. More importantly, Rule 10b-5 was adopted pursuant to authority granted the Commission under § 10(b). The rulemaking power granted to an administrative agency charged with the administration of a federal statute is not the power to make law. Rather, it is "'the power to adopt regulations to carry into effect the will of Congress as expressed by the statute.'" *Dixon v. United States*, 381 U.S. 68, 74 (1965), quoting *Manhattan General Equipment Co. v. Commissioner*, 297 U.S. 129, 134 (1936). Thus, despite the broad view of the Rule advanced by the Commission in this case, its scope cannot exceed the power granted the Commission by Congress under § 10(b). *** When a statute speaks so specifically in terms of manipulation and deception, and of implementing devices and contrivances—the commonly understood terminology of intentional wrongdoing—and when its history reflects no more expansive intent, we are quite unwilling to extend the scope of the statute to negligent conduct.

III

Recognizing that § 10(b) and Rule 10b-5 might be held to require proof of more than negligent nonfeasance by Ernst & Ernst as a precondition to the imposition of civil liability, respondents further contend that the case should be remanded for trial under whatever standard is adopted. Throughout the lengthy history of this case respondents have proceeded on a theory of liability premised on negligence, specifically disclaiming that Ernst & Ernst had engaged in fraud or intentional misconduct. In these circumstances, we think it inappropriate to remand the action for further proceedings. ***

JUSTICE BLACKMUN, WITH WHOM JUSTICE BRENNAN JOINS, DISSENTING:

Once again—see *Blue Chip Stamps v. Manor Drug Stores*, 421 U.S. 723, 730 (1975)—the Court interprets § 10(b) of the Securities Exchange Act of 1934 and the Securities and Exchange Commission's Rule 10b-5 restrictively and narrowly and thereby stultifies recovery for the victim. This time the Court does so by confining the statute and the Rule to situations where the defendant has "scienter," that is, the "intent to deceive, manipulate, or defraud." Sheer negligence, the Court says, is not within the reach of the statute and the Rule, and was not contemplated when the great reforms of 1933, 1934, and 1942 were effectuated by Congress and the Commission.

Perhaps the Court is right, but I doubt it. The Government and the Commission doubt it too, as is evidenced by the thrust of the brief filed by the Solicitor General on behalf of the Commission as *amicus curiae*. The Court's opinion, to be sure, has a certain technical consistency about it. It seems to me, however, that an investor can be victimized just as much by negligent conduct as by positive deception, and that it is not logical to drive a wedge between the two, saying that Congress clearly intended the one but certainly not the other.***

### *NOTES AND QUESTIONS*

***1. Driving Wedges.*** Do you agree with the majority that in drafting Section 10(b), Congress intended to "drive a wedge" (to borrow Justice Blackmun's phrase) between conduct that is intentional and conduct that is merely negligent or even grossly negligent? Is Justice Blackmun correct in focusing on the ultimate effect of a material misrepresentation on investors? In pondering this question, consider the observation of Professor Loss and Dean Seligman that "[a] pedestrian fatally hit by a negligent driver is just as dead as if the driver had been roaring drunk, but that does not convict the negligent driver of manslaughter." 8 Louis Loss and Joel Seligman, Securities Regulation 3664 (3d ed. 1991). How would Justice Blackmun likely respond to this analogy? To what extent was the majority's allegiance to intent apt to have been influenced by the critical role played by Rule 10b-5 in private securities litigation?

***2. Don't Close That Dictionary!*** Note that in footnotes 20 and 21, the Court draws on Webster's International Dictionary for definitions of the terms "device," "contrivance" and "manipulative." Note particularly the lack of definition for the term "deceptive." Had the Court continued its march through the dictionary, would it have made a difference to the outcome of the case?

Professor James Cox's analysis of this question suggests that this is a distinct possibility. See James D. Cox, *Ernst & Ernst v. Hochfelder*: A Critique and an Evaluation of Its Impact upon the Scheme of the Federal Securities Laws, 28 Hastings L. J. 569 (1977). In that article, Professor Cox contended that the word deceptive "suggests no established state of mind. It instead describes the potential impact of conduct upon a person's perception, regardless of the actor's mental state." Id. at 575. As authority, he cited to the dictionary definition of deceptive: "[t]ending to deceive; having the power to mislead." Id. at 575 n. 30. He also noted that "[a]lthough the common meaning of 'device' or 'contrivance' suggests deliberate conduct by the participants, in the context of section 10(b) both nouns definitively exclude only transactions or conduct initiated solely by accident or inadvertence." Id. at 574. He therefore concluded:

> The broader meaning of "deceptive" has obvious significance for the purpose of determining whether congressional intent was clear; the enabling statute used the disjunctive, not the conjunctive, thereby leaving open the possibility of a much broader scope than that attributed to the statute in *Ernst & Ernst*.

Id. at 575.

***3. The Element of Scienter in Government-Initiated Rule 10b-5 Cases.*** Does the scienter requirement upheld in *Hochfelder* in the context of a Rule 10b-5 private action apply as well to actions under the Rule initiated by the SEC or the DOJ? When faced with this question in *Aaron v. SEC*, 446 U.S. 680 (1980), a six member majority of the Supreme Court stated:

> In our view, the rationale of *Hockfelder* [sic] ineluctably leads to the conclusion that scienter is an element of a violation of § 10(b) and Rule 10b-5, regardless of the identity of the plaintiff or the nature of the relief sought. ***

Id. at 691. In what had become a predictable pattern in federal securities decisions, Justice Blackmun, joined by Justices Brennan and Marshall, dissented from the majority's holding, emphasizing again the effect on investors:

> If the Commission is denied the ability effectively to nip in the bud the misrepresentations and deceptions that its investigations have revealed, honest investors will be the ones who suffer. Often they may find themselves stripped of their investments through reliance on information that the Commission knew was misleading but lacked the power to stop or contain.

Id. at 704 (Blackmun, J., concurring in part and dissenting in part). Is there an effective response to Justice Blackmun's concerns? Consider this question again in the Chapter 3, particularly when you study Sections 17(a)(2) and (3) of the Securities Act.

*4. **Recklessness as a Form of Scienter.*** The Supreme Court has declined on three occasions to address whether reckless conduct establishes scienter under Section 10(b) and Rule 10b-5. See *Ernst & Ernst*, supra, at n. 12; *Aaron v. SEC*, 446 U.S. 680, 686 n. 5 (1980); *Herman & MacLean v. Huddleston*, 459 U.S. 375, 378 n. 4 (1983). Yet, every federal court of appeals to confront the question has held recklessness sufficient for these purposes. See *Hollinger v. Titan Capital Corp.*, 914 F.2d 1564, 1568 n. 6 (9th Cir. 1990) (citing appellate cases from all federal circuits except for the 4th Circuit, and citing district court cases from the 4th Circuit). Although the circuits vary in their precise formulation of the recklessness standard, the following definition is cited frequently:

> [R]eckless conduct may be defined as ... highly unreasonable [conduct], involving not merely simple, or even inexcusable negligence, but an extreme departure from the standards of ordinary care, and which presents a danger of misleading buyers or sellers that is either known to the defendant or is so obvious that the actor must have been aware of it.

*Sunstrand Corp. v. Sun Chem. Corp.*, 553 F.2d 1033, 1045 (7th Cir. 1977). Courts have also both ratcheted up and ratcheted down from this basic definition. Compare *Nathenson v. Zonagen Inc.*, 267 F.3d 400, 408 (5th Cir. 2001) (plaintiffs must prove the defendant's "severe recklessness," which is "limited to those highly unreasonable omissions or misrepresentations that involve not merely simple or even inexcusable negligence, but an extreme departure from the standard of ordinary care, and that present a danger of misleading buyers or sellers which is either known to the defendant or is so obvious that the defendant must have been aware of it") (quoting *Broad v. Rockwell Int'l Corp.*, 642 F.2d 929, 961-62 (5th Cir. 1981)) with *Keirnan v. Homeland, Inc.*, 611 F.2d 785, 788 (9th Cir. 1980) (stating that recklessness exists when defendants "had reasonable grounds to believe material facts existed that were misstated or omitted, but nonetheless failed to obtain and disclose such facts although they could have done so without extraordinary effort"). Note also that in response to Congress's decision to heighten the pleading requirements for private plaintiffs in federal securities fraud cases (a subject that is addressed in detail in the next part of this section of the Chapter), the Ninth Circuit adopted a standard for recklessness that is arguably the most restrictive in the country. See *In re Silicon Graphics Inc. Sec. Litig.*, 183 F.3d 970, 985 (9th Cir. 1999) (requiring plaintiffs to plead with particularity "facts giving rise to a strong inference of the required state of mind, i.e., at least deliberate recklessness"). See also id. at 977 (stating that "recklessness only satisfies scienter under § 10(b) to the extent that it reflects some degree of intentional or conscious misconduct").

All that being said, businesses that are frequently named in Rule 10b-5 actions, such as high-technology companies and accounting firms, have long insisted that a showing of recklessness does not satisfy Section 10(b)'s requirement of scienter. On several occasions, most notably in 1995 and 1998, lobbyists supporting defendants' interests sought to persuade Congress that Rule 10b-5 liability should not attach absent proof of a defendant's actual intent to deceive. From your study of the PSLRA thus far, what evidence can you identify that Congress recognizes—and implicitly approves of—recklessness as a mental state sufficient to establish liability under Rule 10b-5? Consider this question again in Section G of this Chapter when you study the scheme for proportionate liability now set forth in Section 21D(f) of the Exchange Act.

*5. **Circumstantial Evidence as Proof of Scienter.*** As the Supreme Court recognized in *Herman & MacLean v. Huddleston*, 459 U.S. 375 (1983), proof of scienter in Rule 10b-5 cases "is often a matter of inference from circumstantial evidence." Id. at 390 n. 30. In *Greebel v. FTP Software, Inc.*, 194 F.3d 185 (1st Cir. 1999), the First Circuit compiled the following list of factors that evidence scienter:

- insider trading [at suspicious times or in suspicious amounts];
- divergence between internal reports and external statements on the same subject;
- closeness in time of an allegedly fraudulent statement or omission and the later disclosure of inconsistent information;
- evidence of bribery by a top company official;
- existence of an ancillary lawsuit charging fraud by a company and the company's quick settlement of that suit;
- disregard of the most current factual information before making statements;
- disclosure of accrual basis information in a way which could only be understood by someone with a high degree of accounting skill;
- the personal interest of certain directors in not informing disinterested directors of an impending sale of stock; and
- the self-interested motivation of defendants in the form of saving their salaries or jobs.

Id. at 196-97. Consider the actual showing that a plaintiff would need to make to establish one or more of these factors. Which factors can be proven based on evidence that is publicly available to a shareholder-plaintiff? Which factors can be proven based on evidence that is likely to be found in internal corporate documents? Which factors can be proven based on evidence most apt to be obtainable from civil interrogatories or depositions?

In addition to the factors listed by the *Greebel* court, what other types of evidence might support a circumstantial case that the defendant acted with scienter, i.e., with recklessness or intent to deceive ? Are there ways of proving scienter other than by using circumstantial evidence?

*6. Seeking State Law Alternatives.* Some state courts have held that plaintiffs suing under anti-fraud provisions contained in blue sky laws must prove only that the defendant acted negligently. See e.g. *Kittilson v. Ford*, 93 Wash. 2d 223, 226, 608 P.2d 264, 265 (1980) ("We believe the holding in *Ernst & Ernst v. Hochfelder* [is] inapplicable to our Securities Act."). For this reason, blue sky laws may sometimes provide a more attractive vehicle for securities plaintiffs than does federal litigation under Rule 10b-5. Note, however, that in 1998, Congress constricted this state law option by preempting securities class actions brought under state law counterparts to Rule 10b-5 where the action involves a security listed on a stock exchange or traded on the NASDAQ. See discussion of the Securities Litigation Uniform Standards Act of 1998, infra, Chapter 6.B.

*7. The Problem of Corporate Scienter.* A plaintiff can establish the scienter of a corporate defendant by showing the individual scienter of the corporation's directors or high ranking officers. Should a plaintiff also be able to show a corporation's scienter based upon "the piecemeal knowledge of various actors," even without any single individual's having the requisite scienter? See Donald C. Langevoort, The Epistemology of Corporate-Security Lawyering: Beliefs, Biases and Organizational Behavior, 63 Brook. L. Rev. 629, 660-61 (1997). See generally Craig L. Griffin, Corporate Scienter Under the Securities Exchange Act of 1934, 45 BYU L. Rev. 1227 (1989).

Proving corporate scienter by aggregating the knowledge of several individuals remains a largely untested approach because few Rule 10b-5 cases have presented courts with an "amalgamation" type of fact pattern, and many courts have suggested that corporate liability for Rule 10b-5 follows only if an individual agent has the requisite scienter. See Donald C. Langevoort, Organized Illusions: A Behavioral Theory of Why Corporations Mislead Stock Market Investors (And Cause Other Social Harms), 146 U. Pa. L. Rev. 101, 127 n. 87 (1997), citing *First Equity Corp. v. Standard & Poor's Corp.*, 690 F. Supp. 256, 260 (S.D.N.Y. 1988) ("A corporation can be held to have a particular state of mind only when that state of mind is possessed by a single individual"). What benefits and/or drawbacks would come about from allowing an aggregation approach to corporate scienter?

*8. Good Motives vs. Bad.* Does a person act with scienter if he or she intentionally misrepresents (or omits) a material fact with an arguably laudable motive? Consider, for example, the CEO of a potential takeover target who denies to a reporter the existence of merger negotiations to prevent a run-up in the stock price (which would make the transaction substantially less attractive to a potential bidder).

Securities fraud cases generally draw the same distinction between motive and intent that is common in the criminal law. That is, proof of motive often evidences an intent to deceive, but such intent does not require a nefarious motive. Recall that in *Basic Inc. v. Levinson*, 485 U.S. 224 (1988), the Supreme Court expressed a clear unwillingness to insulate "white lies" from Rule 10b-5 liability, stating "we think that creating an exception to a regulatory scheme founded on a prodisclosure legislative philosophy, because complying with the regulation might be 'bad for business,' is a role for Congress, not this Court." Id. at 240, n. 17. See also *SEC v. Falstaff Brewing Corp.*, 629 F.2d 62, 77 (D.C. Cir. 1980) (when a defendant "[knows] the nature and consequences of his actions, he act[s] with scienter"); Restatement (Second) of Torts § 8A (1965) ("If the actor knows that the consequences are certain, or substantially certain, to result from his act, and still goes ahead, he is treated by the law as if he had in fact desired to produce the result").

The normative question of whether the lie told with "good motives" should be insulated from liability under the federal securities laws has provoked interesting commentary. See, e.g., Ian Ayres, Back to *Basics*: Regulating How Corporations Speak to the Market, 77 Va. L. Rev. 945, 946 (1991) (arguing that "corporations should be given the option of lying [to the market] but that corporations that contemplate lying should be forced to disclose that they do not warrant the truth of their statements"); Marcel Kahan, Games, Lies and Securities Fraud, 67 N.Y.U. L. Rev. 750 (1992) (using game theory to suggest that some lies told in the context of corporate negotiations should not trigger liability); Jonathan R. Macey & Geoffrey P. Miller, Good Finance, Bad Economics: An Analysis of the Fraud-on-the-Market Theory, 42 Stan. L. Rev. 1059, 1091 (1990) (arguing that "valuable corporate information should not be disclosed if, in the business judgment of the officers and directors involved, such disclosure would jeopardize the aggregate value of the firm's shares"). Should Congress act on any of these suggestions?

### *PROBLEM 2-14*

Reconsider the facts of Problems 2-1 and 2-6 in Section A of this Chapter. What difficulties, if any, will the plaintiffs encounter in establishing scienter? If the corporation in Problem 2-5 had denied the existence of the contract in accordance with the foreign government's request, would the plaintiffs be able to establish scienter?

### 2. *Requirements for Pleading Scienter*

As noted at the beginning of this Chapter, all complaints alleging violations of Rule 10b-5 must satisfy the pleading requirements of Rule 9(b) of the Federal Rules of Civil Procedure:

> In all averments of fraud or mistake, the circumstances constituting fraud or mistake shall be stated with particularity. Malice, intent, knowledge, and other condition of mind of a person may be averred generally.

By allowing general allegation regarding a "condition of mind," Rule 9(b) may at first blush seem to set a rather low hurdle for pleading scienter in Rule 10b-5 cases. But in cases involving claims of securities fraud, many courts put additional teeth into Rule 9(b), requiring plaintiffs (including the SEC) to allege in their complaints specific facts giving rise to a strong inference of scienter. Other courts, most particularly in the Ninth Circuit (at least prior to 1995), read Rule 9(b)'s requirements more literally and allowed plaintiffs in securities fraud cases to plead scienter generally. See *In re Glenfed, Inc. Sec. Litig.*, 42 F.3d 1541, 1547 (9th Cir. 1994) ("We conclude that plaintiffs may aver scienter *** simply by saying that scienter existed").

In 1995, Congress established a uniform standard for the pleading of state of mind in complaints filed in federal court under the Exchange Act by private plaintiffs seeking money damages. Specifically, the PSLRA added a new Section 21D(b)(2) to the Exchange Act:

> **Section 21D(b)(2)**—*Required State of Mind.*—In any private action arising under [the Exchange Act] in which the plaintiff may recover money damages only on proof that the defendant acted with a particular state of mind, the complaint shall, with respect to each act or omission alleged to violate [the Exchange Act], state with particularity facts giving rise to a strong inference that the defendant acted with the required state of mind.

Congress also added to the Exchange Act a new Section 21D(b)(3)(A), which requires a court, on the motion of any defendant, to dismiss a complaint for failure to meet Section 21D(b)'s pleading requirements, and a new Section 21D(b)(3)(B), which imposes an automatic stay on discovery during the pendency of dismissal motions, unless the court finds that "particularized discovery is necessary to preserve evidence or to prevent undue prejudice to that party."

In the case that follows, the district court determined that the allegations in the plaintiffs' complaints did not satisfy Section 21D(b)(2)'s heightened pleading requirements and ordered the plaintiffs' complaints dismissed. The Eighth Circuit reversed the district court's finding and remanded the case for further proceedings. As you read through the extensive allegations detailed in the plaintiffs' complaints, consider how you would have ruled on the question of whether the plaintiffs satisfied Section 21D(b)(2)'s pleading requirements.

## FLORIDA STATE BOARD OF ADMINISTRATION v. GREEN TREE FINANCIAL CORPORATION

270 F.3d 645 (8th Cir. 2001)

GIBSON, CIRCUIT JUDGE:

In this case we must assess the sufficiency of three complaints under the new pleading standards made applicable to securities fraud cases by the Private Securities Litigation Reform Act of 1995. The Florida State Board of Administration, which invests state employees' pension funds, and two putative classes of investors, one for stock purchasers and one for option traders, have each brought Rule 10b-5 actions against Green Tree Financial Corporation, its CEO, Lawrence Coss, and other executives, on the theory that they fraudulently overstated Green Tree's financial value. The investors allege that they bought securities in a market affected by this fraud and that when the true facts came to light, Green Tree's stock price tumbled and they lost their money. The district court held that none of the three complaints pleaded facts giving rise to a strong inference of knowing or reckless misconduct, and so the court dismissed the complaints with prejudice. *Florida State Bd. of Admin. v. Green Tree Fin. Corp. (In re Green Tree Fin. Corp. Stock Litig*), 61 F.Supp.2d 860, 878 (D.Minn.1999). The Florida Board and both investor classes appeal, contending that their complaints were indeed sufficient to plead securities fraud. We reverse.

I.

For the purpose of a motion to dismiss, we take the facts from the complaints. Green Tree is a financial services corporation that originally specialized in lending money on house trailers, referred to as "manufactured housing," although it later diversified into other kinds of lending. Because manufactured housing loans are classified as "sub-prime," the interest rates are very high—as much as 200 to 400 basis points (two to four percentage points) above residential mortgage rates. Green Tree rose to prominence by pioneering the securitization of manufactured housing loans, which means that it pooled large numbers of these loans and put them into a trust, which sold securities for which the loans served as collateral. The securities entitled the purchaser to fixed interest and principal payments under the loans. Importantly, Green Tree did not relinquish all rights under the securitized loans; instead, it retained the right to keep a portion of the loan payments and it retained the obligation to service the loans. Green Tree's profit was therefore the spread between the interest it charged the borrowers and the interest it promised the instrument-holders, minus Green Tree's costs of servicing the loans. However, Green Tree retained the risk of losses from loan defaults, as well as the risk that borrowers would prepay their loans before incurring interest charges, so that the expected interest would never materialize. By absorbing these risks, Green Tree could take high-interest-rate manufactured-housing loans and turn them into low-interest-rate securities, thereby creating the profitable spreads that fueled Green Tree's growth.

As it securitized each loan pool, Green Tree booked a current gain on the transaction, even though the expected profits would not actually come into its coffers until much later and even though the amount of those profits would fluctuate with Green Tree's success in collecting the loan payments. This "gain-on-sale revenue" was the force that drove Green Tree's reported earnings during the periods covered by the complaints. Gain-on-sale receivables made up 63.8% of the net revenue that Green Tree originally reported for 1996. In addition to the income, Green Tree also recorded the present value of the securitizations as balance sheet assets called "Excess Servicing Rights Receivable" or "Interest Only Securities." In 1996 "Excess Servicing Rights Receivable" was the greatest single asset on Green Tree's balance sheet.

In order to estimate the present value of the securitizations, Green Tree had to assume three things: (1) the discount rate (reflecting the lesser value of a dollar to be paid in the future than a dollar paid today); (2) the loan default rate; and (3) the loan prepayment rate. The numbers chosen for these assumptions played a crucial role in deciding the amount Green Tree would report as earnings on the securitizations and as the value of the Excess Servicing Rights Receivable. Choosing a figure for prepayment rate was especially difficult because if interest rates fell substantially or if other lenders competed aggressively, borrowers would be likely to refinance in large numbers. If that happened, the loans and consequently, the expected profit on them, would simply disappear. A discrepancy between assumed prepayment rates and actual prepayment experience could have a serious effect on Green Tree's earnings and balance sheet.

The crux of this suit is the investors' allegation that Green Tree used "unrealistic and unreasonable" assumptions in its gain-on-sale accounting, thus overvaluing its assets and overstating its earnings. In particular, the investors allege that the actual prepayment experience from 1995 to 1997 varied so much from the prepayment rate Green Tree assumed in its gain-on-sale accounting for 1994 and 1995 securitizations that Green Tree's financials and other publicly filed reports during the 1995-1997 period were materially false. The investors concede that Green Tree publicly disclosed its actual prepayment experience. However, they allege the defendants refused to disclose what prepayment assumptions Green Tree had used in its gain-on-sale accounting and that this constituted omission of a material fact necessary to prevent its financial reports from being misleading. Green Tree stated in its public filings with the SEC that its management regularly reevaluated Green Tree's prepayment assumptions in light of actual experience. According to the complaints, the defendants either knew that the discrepancy between the actual prepayment experience and the assumed rates rendered the financials materially false, or alternatively, recklessly disregarded this fact.

In any event, Green Tree's assumptions about prepayment rates turned out to be seriously inadequate. Green Tree announced on November 13, 1997, that it planned to increase the prepayment reserve in its 1997 financials by an estimated $125-150 million because of higher than expected prepayment rates on manufactured housing loans. This announcement caused a precipitous decline in Green Tree's stock price, from $42 to $30.75. The day after the announcement, in a conference call with industry analysts, CEO Coss disclosed the prepayment assumptions Green Tree had been using for the 1994 and 1995 pools. He assured analysts, "I don't see any set of circumstances that would cause us to [write down the 1994-1995 loan pools] again. And if we thought there was any set of circumstances that would, we would have provided more." He also stated that a revision of prior earnings was not appropriate.

On January 27, 1998, Green Tree took an addition to its reserves of $190 million, rather than the $125-150 million addition to reserves anticipated in the November announcement. At the same time, it took a $200 million reduction of its previously reported 1996 earnings. In the press release accompanying the financials, Green Tree explained the decision to make larger adjustments than it had announced before; in reviewing its financial modeling, it "determined it had not fully considered the effect upon its interest only securities of partial prepayments (principal curtailments) and the impact that higher prepayments have on projected future interest due to investors on a weighted average basis." Green Tree's stock fell as low as $18.

On April 7, 1998, about two months after the close of the class periods, Green Tree announced that it would be acquired by Conseco, Inc., in a merger. On July 6, 1998, Conseco took charges totaling $350 million to write down the carrying value of Green Tree's interest-only securities, reflecting adjustment to assumptions for prepayment rates, discount rates, and default rates.

The investors allege that several motives prompted the defendants to spread misleading financial information through the market. First, they allege that the compensation of defendant Coss and other Green Tree executives was tied to Green Tree's financial results, which made the defendants want to maximize Green Tree's reported earnings. In particular, CEO Coss had a remarkable contract awarding him 2.5% of Green Tree's pre-tax income (minus other executives' bonuses). Coss's contract was to expire December 31, 1996. Accordingly, it was in Coss's personal interest to report as much income as possible before the expiration of his lucrative contract. Other motives alleged are: (1) the defendants' desire to maintain a high corporate credit rating to maximize the selling price of the loan pools; and (2) Green Tree's need to demonstrate exemplary financial results in order to fend off a pending derivative suit alleging that the company wasted corporate assets by paying excessive executive compensation.

The stock purchasers allege that class members bought Green Tree stock from July 15, 1995 through January 27, 1998, and the options traders claim to have traded options from July 15, 1995 though January 26, 1998. The Florida State Board alleges that it bought Green Tree stock from January 30, 1996 through January 27, 1998. The investors contend that they bought stock or traded options in a market in which the stock price was artificially inflated because of the defendants' misrepresentations about Green Tree's financial condition and that they lost money when the truth came out and the stock price fell.

II.

The stock purchasers' class, the option traders' class and the Florida State Board of Administration each filed a complaint alleging that Green Tree and the defendant officers of Green Tree violated section 10(b) of the Securities Exchange Act of 1934 and Rule 10b-5. ***

The defendants moved to dismiss the complaints for failure to state a claim under Fed.R.Civ.P. 12(b)(6) and 9(b) and the pleading provisions of the Private Securities Litigation Reform Act of 1995 [Exchange Act Sections 21D(b)(1) & (2)].

Applying [Exchange Act Section 21D(b)(1)], which requires that a complaint specify with particularity each statement alleged to have been misleading, the district court held that most of the investors' factual allegations regarding the misleading statements and omissions were sufficiently particular to survive the dismissal motion. ***

The district court then turned to the central issue in this case-whether the complaints met the Reform Act's requirements for pleading scienter, [Exchange Act Section 21D(b)(2)]. The district court held that the complaints failed to plead facts giving rise to a strong inference of scienter, as required by statute. ***

III.

*** Although not explicitly mentioned in the text of the rule, scienter is nevertheless an essential element of a Rule 10b-5 claim. *Alpern v. UtiliCorp United, Inc.*, 84 F.3d 1525, 1534 (8th Cir.1996). Scienter means "the intent to deceive, manipulate, or defraud." See *Carlon v. Thaman* (*In re NationsMart Corp. Sec. Litig.*), 130 F.3d 309, 320 (8th Cir.1997) (quoting *Ernst & Ernst v. Hochfelder*, 425 U.S. 185, 193 (1976)). Our Circuit ruled before enactment of the Reform Act that recklessness satisfied the Rule 10b-5 scienter requirement, see *Alpern*, 84 F.3d at 1534, and the defendants do not contend that the Reform Act changed the substantive nature of the scienter requirement.***

The question before us is whether the facts pleaded in the complaints adequately plead scienter. At the outset we must determine what pleading standard the investors have to satisfy. Complaints brought under Rule 10b-5 and section 10(b) are governed by special pleading rules unique to securities cases, which Congress adopted in the Private Securities Litigation Reform Act of 1995 as part of its attempt to curb abuses of securities fraud litigation. In the Reform Act, Congress [added a new Section 21D(b)(2) to the Exchange Act that] *** requires that the complaint state "with particularity" facts giving rise to a "strong inference" that the defendant acted with the scienter required for the cause of action.

There is disagreement in the various circuits about the meaning of the strong-inference-of-scienter pleading standard. Our circuit has not yet decided the question, and the district court declined to decide it because the court concluded the investors had not framed an adequate complaint under any of the possible standards. ***

The strong inference standard [in Section 21D(b)(2)] has its genesis in case law antedating the Reform Act.*** Even though Rule 9(b) said that state of mind could be averred generally (rather than with particularity), some circuits began to apply a special standard in securities cases, requiring pleading of facts that would indicate scienter, rather than the mere conclusion that the defendant acted with scienter. See, e.g., *Romani v. Shearson, Lehman, Hutton*, 929 F.2d 875, 878 (1st Cir.1991); *In re Time Warner Inc. Securities Litig.*, 9 F.3d 259, 268 (2d Cir.1993).

In particular, the Second Circuit began to require plaintiffs in fraud cases to plead facts that "give rise to a 'strong inference' that the defendants possessed the requisite fraudulent intent." *Beck v. Manufacturers Hanover Trust Co.*, 820 F.2d 46, 50 (2d Cir.1987). In *Beck*, Judge Newman elaborated in a discussion that became the black-letter law of the Second Circuit:

> A common method for establishing a strong inference of scienter is to allege facts showing *a motive for committing fraud and a clear opportunity for doing so.* See e.g., *Goldman v. Belden*, 754 F.2d 1059, 1070 (2d Cir.1985). Where motive is not apparent, it is still possible to plead scienter by identifying *circumstances indicating conscious behavior by the defendant, though the strength of the circumstantial allegations must be correspondingly greater.*

Id. (citations omitted and emphasis added). ***

The rule that pleading motive and opportunity alone would give rise to a strong inference of scienter was remarkable for two reasons. First, having the motive and opportunity to do wrong are certainly not the same as having the intent to do it. See *In re Comshare, Inc. Sec. Litig.*, 183 F.3d 542, 551 (6th Cir.1999). The rule, taken literally, presumes that anyone who has the chance to profit by wrongdoing is likely to do so. This is a large leap.

The second remarkable thing about the assertion that pleading motive and opportunity alone gives rise to a strong inference of fraud is the size of the breach it would leave in a pleading standard that was said to be stringent and tough. Nearly every highly ranked executive of a company could be said to have the motive and the opportunity to profit by misstatements. "Greed is a ubiquitous motive, and corporate insiders and upper management always have the opportunity to lie and manipulate." *Bryant v. Avado Brands, Inc.*, 187 F.3d 1271, 1286 (11th Cir.1999).

Apparently because of the potentially wide applicability of "motive and opportunity," the Second Circuit soon retreated from a literal application of the rule. "Motive and opportunity" evolved into a term of art, meaning something far narrower than what it appears to mean. *** [T]he Second Circuit [thus] held that allegations of commonly held motives, even powerful ones such as the desire to stay CEO of a company, would not supply scienter under Rule 9(b):

> If motive could be pleaded by alleging the defendant's desire for continued employment, and opportunity by alleging the defendant's authority to speak for the company, the required showing of motive and opportunity would be no realistic check on aspersions of fraud, and mere misguided optimism would become actionable under the securities laws.

*Shields v. Citytrust Bancorp, Inc.*, 25 F.3d 1124, 1130 (2d Cir.1994). Nor would it constitute a pleading of "motive" to allege that the defendant wanted to maintain his or her company's profitability or credit rating, either for its own sake or to increase thereby the defendant's own compensation, see *Chill v. Gen. Elec. Co.*, 101 F.3d 263, 268 (2d Cir.1996), even though common sense would suggest that these may be the very motives that prompt many cases of deceptive misstatements. Instead, the Second Circuit came to interpret "motive and opportunity" as requiring allegations that the "defendants benefitted in some concrete and personal way from the purported fraud," *Novak v. Kasaks*, 216 F.3d 300, 307 (2d Cir. 2000), with the prototypic case being insider trading. Id. ("[I]n the ordinary case, adequate motive arose from the desire to profit from extensive insider sales."). ***

Whatever the difficulties in applying the Second Circuit's strong-inference-of-scienter standard, when Congress decided to reform securities litigation to eliminate strike suits, it regarded the Second Circuit standard as the "most stringent pleading standard" in the country. S. Rep. No. 104-98, at 15 (1995). The Senate Committee intended to impose the Second Circuit standard in securities fraud cases in all circuits. The Committee chose to accomplish this by requiring, "In any private action to recover money damages, the plaintiff must, for each misstatement or omission, specifically allege facts giving rise to a strong inference that the defendant acted with the required state of mind." S. Rep. 104-98, at 26. However, the Committee expressly chose not "to codify the Second Circuit's caselaw interpreting this pleading standard, although courts may find this body of law instructive." Id. at 15.

The subsequent legislative history shows a great deal of confusion about whether the strong-inference-of-fraud standard was the same standard with the motive-and-opportunity test as without it. Senator Specter clearly thought it was not. He introduced an amendment to add the motive-and-opportunity language into the text of the bill. 141 Cong. Rec. 17,286 (1995). He reasoned that without this caveat, the strong-inference-of-scienter standard posed an impossible task for plaintiffs. "How do you get into somebody else's head?" he asked. 141 Cong. Rec. 17,424 (1995). It is not clear, however, if Senator Specter's objection was that the standard was simply so vague that it might be interpreted unevenly or whether he believed the motive-and-opportunity language was a substantive relaxation of the strong-inference standard.

The Specter amendment passed on the Senate floor, 141 Cong. Rec. 17,425 (1995), only to be deleted in the Conference Committee. The Conference Report stated: "Because the Conference Committee intends to strengthen existing pleading requirements, it does not intend to codify the Second Circuit's case law interpreting this pleading standard." H. Conf. Rep. No. 104-369, at 41 (1995). In a footnote, the report adverted to the deletion of the Specter amendment: "For this reason, the Conference Report chose not to include in the pleading standard certain language relating to motive, opportunity, or recklessness." Id. at 48 n. 23.

Although the import of the Conference Report seems to be that any reference to the motive-and-opportunity test applied in the Second Circuit was disapproved, the legislative history does not support that reading. Admittedly, the opponents of the bill, including President Clinton, characterized the deletion of the Specter amendment as a decision to raise the pleading standard above the Second Circuit standard. E.g., 141 Cong. Rec. at 38,194 (Clinton veto message); 141 Cong. Rec. at 38,205-07 (Senator Specter); 141 Cong. Rec. at 35,299 (Senator Biden). However, Senator Dodd, a manager of the bill, contended that the Specter amendment was not deleted because the Conference Committee wanted to disavow the Second Circuit's case law, but because the Specter amendment did not codify the case law accurately. 141 Cong. Rec. at 35,266. *** Taken at face value, Senator Dodd's defense of the bill suggests that he had no objection to the motive-and-opportunity part of the Specter amendment. ***

In sum, the legislative history provides nothing but uncertainty about whether the motive-and-opportunity test is an inherent part of the strong inference standard or whether it modifies and relaxes that standard. Ultimately, the Act as passed does not resolve this question.

The Circuits that have interpreted the Reform Act have fallen into (at least) three camps. The Ninth Circuit inferred from the deletion of the Specter amendment by the Conference Committee that Congress expressly rejected the Second Circuit's "two-pronged test" and raised the pleading standard to a level beyond that in the Second Circuit. *In re Silicon Graphics Inc. Sec. Litig.*, 183 F.3d 970, 978-79 (9th Cir.1999).

At the other end of the spectrum, the Second and Third Circuits have held that in using the "strong inference" language, the Reform Act adopted a pleading standard "approximately equal in stringency to that of the Second Circuit," *In re Advanta Corp. Sec. Litig.*, 180 F.3d 525, 534 (3d Cir.1999); *Novak v. Kasaks*, 216 F.3d 300, 310 (2d Cir.2000), including the motive-and-opportunity formulation, *Advanta*, 180 F.3d at 534-35; *Ganino v. Citizens Util. Co.*, 228 F.3d 154, 168-70 (2d Cir.2000). The Second Circuit qualified its conclusion by stating that "Congress's failure to include language about motive and opportunity suggests that we need not be wedded to these concepts in articulating the prevailing standard," *Novak*, 216 F.3d at 310, but that courts should nevertheless be guided by the motive-and-opportunity cases. The Second and Third Circuits also agree that the Reform Act's additional requirement that facts pertaining to scienter be pleaded "with particularity" represents a "heightening of the [pleading] standard." *Novak*, 216 F.3d at 310-11; *Advanta*, 180 F.3d at 534.

Occupying the middle ground, the First, Fifth, Sixth, Tenth, and Eleventh Circuits have held that the primary effect of the Reform Act is to require a pleading to state facts giving rise to a "strong inference of scienter." Allegations of motive and opportunity may or may not rise to that level in a particular case. See *Nathenson v. Zonagen Inc.*, 267 F.3d 400, 409-11 (5th Cir.2001); *City of Philadelphia v. Fleming Cos.*, 264 F.3d 1245, 1261-63 (10th Cir.2001); *Helwig v. Vencor, Inc.*, 251 F.3d 540, 551 (6th Cir.2001) (en banc); *Greebel v. FTP Software, Inc.*, 194 F.3d 185, 197 (1st Cir.1999); *Bryant v. Avado Brands, Inc.*, 187 F.3d 1271, 1282-83 (11th Cir.1999). "While it is true that motive and opportunity are not substitutes for a showing of recklessness, they can be catalysts to fraud and so serve as external markers to the required state of mind.... '[M]otive' and 'opportunity' are simply recurring patterns of evidence." *Helwig*, 251 F.3d at 550.

Putting aside the Ninth Circuit standard, which gives the deletion of the Specter amendment a more pointed reading than it will bear, the split in the other Circuits is more apparent than real. As we discussed above, supra, the Second Circuit has dramatically constricted the types of "motive and opportunity" that it will recognize as sufficient to plead scienter. It will not allow plaintiffs to proceed based on widely held motives such as "(1) the desire to maintain a high corporate credit rating or otherwise sustain 'the appearance of corporate profitability, or of the success of an investment, [or] (2) the desire to maintain a high stock price in order to increase executive compensation or prolong the benefits of holding corporate office." *Novak*, 216 F.3d at 307. Even complaints based on insider trading must allege more than that the defendant benefitted from trading because of a false statement or misleading omission; the insider trades have to be "unusual," either in the amount of profit made, the amount of stock traded, the portion of stockholdings sold, or the number of insiders involved, before they will give rise to the required inference of scienter. See *Rothman v. Gregor*, 220 F.3d 81, 94 (2d Cir.2000); *In re Advanta*, 180 F.3d at 540-541; *Oran v. Stafford*, 226 F.3d 275, 290 (3d Cir.2000). This is the same kind of inquiry undertaken by courts that do not adhere to the motive-and-opportunity formulation. See *Nathenson*, 267 F.3d at 420; *Helwig*, 251 F.3d at 552; *Greebel*, 194 F.3d at 198. The search in the Second Circuit line of cases, as well as in the other circuits, is for facts that give a strong reason to believe that there was reckless or intentional wrongdoing. See *Greebel*, 194 F.3d at 197 (facts must support strong inference of scienter, rather than merely reasonable inference). Taken as a whole, the cases simply do not substantiate the fear that courts applying the motive-and-opportunity formulation will permit pleadings to go forward without facts strongly suggesting wrongdoing.

The Reform Act itself adopted only the strong-inference-of-scienter standard, without codifying the particular methods of satisfying the standard. The Second Circuit cases interpreting that language, both leading up to the Reform Act and after its enactment, give us valuable guidance about what factors help to establish such an inference. At the same time, we also look to case law from other circuits developing their own criteria for the badges of fraud. E.g., *Greebel*, 194 F.3d at 196-98; *Helwig*, 251 F.3d at 552. Ultimately, however, we must take care to use subsidiary formulae as an aid to interpreting the strong-inference standard and not as a substitute for it.

Therefore, we can say three things about motive and opportunity allegations. First, motive and opportunity are generally relevant to a fraud case, and a showing of unusual or heightened motive will often form an important part of a complaint that meets the Reform Act standard. Second, in some cases the same circumstantial allegations that establish motive and opportunity also give additional reason to believe the defendant's misrepresentation was knowing or reckless. For instance, in insider trading cases, the timing of trades shows motive and opportunity, but it may also provide additional circumstantial evidence that the defendant knew of an advantage. Such allegations may meet the Reform Act standard, but if so it is because they give rise to a strong inference of scienter, not merely because they establish motive and opportunity. Third, when the complaint does not show motive and opportunity of any sort-either the unusual, heightened motive highlighted in the Second Circuit cases, or even an everyday motive such as keeping one's job-then other allegations tending to show scienter would have to be particularly strong in order to meet the Reform Act standard. Cf. *Matsushita Elec. Indus. Co. v. Zenith Radio Corp.*, 475 U.S. 574, 587 (1986) (in Sherman Act context, where there appeared to be no rational motive to break the law, a plaintiff would have to adduce a particularly strong case in order to survive summary judgment).

IV.

This case was decided under both the Federal Rules of Civil Procedure and the Reform Act. The Reform Act modifies the ordinary Rule 12(b)(6) dismissal mechanism in two limited ways. First, whereas under Rule 12(b)(6), we must assume all factual allegations in the complaint are true, see *Goss v. City of Little Rock*, 90 F.3d 306, 308 (8th Cir.1996), under the Reform Act, we disregard "catch-all" or "blanket" assertions that do not live up to the particularity requirements of the statute. See *Advanta*, 180 F.3d at 535.

Second, under Fed.R.Civ.P. 12(b)(6), the plaintiff is entitled to all reasonable inferences that may be drawn from the allegations of the complaint. *Young v. City of St. Charles*, 244 F.3d 623, 627 (8th Cir.2001). However, under the Reform Act, a securities fraud case cannot survive unless its allegations collectively add up to a strong inference of the required state of mind.

> Congress has effectively mandated a special standard for measuring whether allegations of scienter survive a motion to dismiss. While under Rule 12(b)(6) all inferences must be drawn in plaintiffs' favor, inferences of scienter do not survive if they are merely reasonable .... Rather, inferences of scienter survive a motion to dismiss only if they are both reasonable and "strong" inferences.

*Greebel*, 194 F.3d at 195-96. See *Helwig*, 251 F.3d at 553 ("[T]he strong inference requirement means that plaintiffs are entitled only to the most plausible of competing inferences.").

We review de novo the district court's dismissal of complaints pursuant to Rule 12(b)(6), *Breedlove v. Earthgrains Baking Cos.*, 140 F.3d 797, 799 (8th

Cir.1998), and by analogy we will apply the same standard of review to dismissal pursuant to the Reform Act, [Exchange Act Section 21D(b)(3)(a)].

V.

We must evaluate the cogency of the investors' allegations against the strong inference standard. The investors argue that Coss and the other executives' performance-based compensation gave the defendants a motive not to disclose the prepayment problems. The stock purchasers class, for example, alleged:

> In 1995 and 1996, Green Tree had the highest paid business executive in the entire United States. In 1995 and 1996, defendant Coss was paid, in cash and deeply discounted stock, $65 million and $102 million, respectively. Under the terms of his 1991 employment agreement, which was in effect until the end of 1996, Coss was paid 2.5% of the Company's pre-tax income, in addition to a base salary of over $430,000. After Green Tree restated its 1996 earnings, Coss was required to repay $25.9 million of his 1996 bonus.
>
> ...
>
> As a result of the approaching expiration of the 1991 employment agreement, Coss knew that 1996 would be the last year for which he would receive bonus compensation valued in the tens of millions of dollars.... Coss's 1997 compensation was valued at approximately $4.8 million, about $97 million less than the value of his original 1996 compensation.

Even in the Second Circuit, pleading that a defendant's compensation depends on corporate value or earnings does not, by itself, establish motive to fraudulently misrepresent corporate value or earnings. *Novak v. Kasaks*, 216 F.3d 300, 307 (2d Cir.2000). Here, the investors allege that Coss's arrangement established a legally significant motive because the amount of his compensation was based on a percentage of Green Tree's pre-tax earnings, and his contract was set to expire at the end of 1996, making it urgent for Coss to maximize Green Tree's earnings for that year. Green Tree originally booked earnings for 1996 that allowed Coss to earn $102 million. Roughly a year later, Green Tree found it necessary to revise its 1996 earnings retrospectively.

We conclude that the magnitude of Coss's compensation package, together with the timing coincidence of an overstatement of earnings at just the right time to benefit Coss, provides an unusual, heightened showing of motive to commit fraud. The motive and opportunity allegations regarding Coss are therefore an important part of a circumstantial case against him and consequently, against Green Tree, which was subject to Coss's control.

The defendants contend that Coss's compensation is irrelevant because Coss wound up giving back a proportional amount of his 1996 compensation after the 1996 earnings were restated in January 1998. But Coss did not necessarily know at the time of the alleged misrepresentations and omissions that it would turn out that way. He could have acted recklessly to pile up earnings before his contract ran out, gambling that he would get away with it. The ultimate profitability of a course of conduct is not conclusive of intent. Just as we cannot countenance pleading fraud by hindsight, neither can we infer innocence by hindsight because the alleged misdeeds did not pay off.

The district court held that, even without such hindsight, such a gamble was so unlikely to succeed that the court would not infer that Coss tried it:

> [T]here is no allegation in the pleadings from which it can be inferred that defendants could have concealed (forever) a significant gap between projected and actual earnings, even if prepayment speeds eventually had slowed. Furthermore, this alleged motive is premised on mere hope: even assuming that defendants knew that the company's earnings were inflated and that a later turnaround could have been used to conceal past poor performance, plaintiffs allege no facts which suggest that defendants had reason to believe that economic forces beyond their control would change dramatically enough to correct the alleged earnings woes.

61 F.Supp.2d at 873-74. To the contrary, the allegations provide powerful support for the idea that defendants hoped that the prepayment problem would come out in the wash—why else would they have waited until 1998 to reveal and remedy the problem? The complaints plead that defendants knew their assumed prepayment rate and they knew their actual rates as those rates were unfolding. This amounts to knowledge of the prepayment discrepancy. If the valuation of the interest-only securities turned out to be significantly wrong, there can be no question that it would be material to the accuracy of Green Tree's financials. Assuming the defendants knew of the prepayment discrepancy, if we deprive them of the expectation that this discrepancy would be offset by other factors or later experience, we deprive them of an innocent explanation for their failure to correct their financials. Indeed, the *defendants'* theory of this case is that they failed to correct the financials because the accounting was sufficiently complex that they reasonably believed the financials were fairly stated despite the prepayment discrepancy. Somewhere in between the defendants' theory that the assumptions were still reasonable and the district court's theory that the defendants could not have hoped to conceal the inadequacy of the assumptions, lies the investors' theory. The investors allege that the defendants knew facts that showed the assumptions were materially inadequate, but the defendants recklessly attempted to sweep the problem under the rug hoping a change in the economy would ameliorate the problem. We cannot conclude that this is a case in which the motive theory is too irrational to add to the weight of other circumstantial allegations, and we therefore must disagree with the district court's determination to the contrary.

Notably, the complaints do not allege that the executives sold their stock during the class periods. Indeed, the defendants point to documents filed with the S.E.C. indicating that the executive defendants owned more Green Tree stock at the end of the class period than at the beginning. Defendants Finn, Gottesman, and Potts bought more than $870,000 in Green Tree stock during the stock and option class period. Apparently, only Richard Evans sold stock during the class period. The defendants argue that these purchases are so inconsistent with the idea that defendants intentionally inflated the value of Green Tree stock that they "defeat" the investors' pleading of motive.

*** [T]he documents detailing defendants' trading history *** do not neutralize the motive allegations because they do not directly contradict them. In cases in which plaintiffs sought to use stock transactions as evidence of motive, the Second Circuit has held that certain defendants' abstention from trading stock so undercut the investors' allegations of motive that the complaints failed to state a claim. *Acito,* 47 F.3d at 54; *San Leandro Emerg. Med. Plan v. Philip Morris Cos.*, 75 F.3d 801, 814 (2d Cir.1996). In this case, however, the investors do not rely on allegations of inside transactions, but on other motives, such as the hope of huge bonuses, that are not directly undermined by their abstention from trading. ***

The other executives besides Coss object that they did not share Coss's lucrative employment contract and that it is not plausible that they would commit fraud to enrich someone else. The compensation allegations against the other executives are obviously weaker evidence of motive than those against Coss and Green Tree. The investors did not plead that the other executives had incentive contracts that were about to expire or that their compensation was comparable to Coss's. Potts was alleged to have received a bonus of $1.25 million in 1996 and Richard Evans $350,000. The option traders argue, "The primary motive was to enrich Coss, and along the way a trickle down effect would be felt in the bonuses of the other executives." This falls short of alleging the "concrete and personal" benefit that would add significantly to the allegations against the other executives.

The investors also allege that the defendants were motivated by the desire to maintain a high credit rating for Green Tree so that its securitizations would continue to sell at good prices. The desire to maintain a high credit rating is universally held among corporations and their executives and consequently does not contribute significantly to an inference of scienter. *Novak,* 216 F.3d at 307; *San Leandro,* 75 F.3d at 814. ***

The options traders' class and the shareholders' class also argue in their briefs that the defendants were motivated to overstate Green Tree's financial results in order to make it more attractive to a potential buyer. They did not plead any such facts. The district court said that even if they had pleaded this theory, it would have been too implausible to suggest that Green Tree hoped a buyer would purchase the company without performing its own examination of Green Tree's financial status. Another problem with the theory is that the only merger on the horizon was the merger with Conseco, Inc., a transaction announced April 7, 1988-months after the November 1997 and January 1998 revelations. This is too thin a reed on which to hang an inference of scienter existing during the class period. Cf. *Rothman,* 220 F.3d at 94 (whether motive to inflate stock sufficiently pleaded by alleging impending acquisition "might well depend on the particular circumstances of the case").

While this is not the kind of case in which the facts showing motive and opportunity alone create a strong inference of scienter, nevertheless, Coss's extraordinary compensation package, on the very eve of expiring, created a powerful incentive to see to it that Green Tree made plenty of money before his contract expired. For Coss and for Green Tree, this factor is an important part of the overall picture of scienter. It appears that the investors' motive allegations against the other executives are basically derivative from their case against Coss. They argue that "Coss was the dominant force at Green Tree" and that the Green Tree board of directors lacked independence from Coss. Although these contentions do not amount to a showing of an unusual, heightened motive for the other executives, they at least paint a rational and plausible picture of why the executives would have gone along with the alleged fraud. Thus, if the motive allegations do not add much to the investors' claims against the other executives, neither is there an utter lack of rational motive, which would require the investors to make a stronger circumstantial case than would otherwise be necessary.

VI.

In addition to the motive-and-opportunity allegations, the complaints contain other facts that give rise to a strong inference of fraud. In broad outline, the investors pleaded with particularity that defendants knew the prepayment assumptions on which their gain-on-sale accounting for the 1994 and 1995 pools were based, they knew that actual experience in 1995, 1996 and the first three quarters of 1997 deviated from those premises greatly, and they issued financials that did not take account of the disparity between the assumptions and actual experience. Specifically, Green Tree's gain-on-sale accounting assumed that the 1994 and 1995 pools would experience prepayment at a rate referred to as "100 MHP," ["Manufactured Housing Prepayment"] meaning roughly that after twenty-four months the borrowers would be prepaying the loans at the rate of 6% per annum. In fact, the loans were being prepaid at a much faster rate, with the majority of the pools running well above the 6% per annum rate at ten months. "At 24 months, the loans were being prepaid at a rate of between 9.0% and 16.30%." The shareholders have appended to their complaint a chart indicating that the problem was pronounced as early as July 1995. The complaints alleged that the defendants were informed of the actual prepayment rates "on at least a monthly basis." Green Tree's SEC filings stated: "Actual default and prepayment experience are reviewed quarterly." In the November 14, 1997 conference call with industry analysts, Coss stated that Green Tree had been taking additional reserves in connection with this prepayment problem since the fourth quarter of 1996. There is no dispute that the prepayment problem led to Green Tree's $390 million write-down in January 1998.

One of the classic fact patterns giving rise to a strong inference of scienter is that defendants published statements when they knew facts or had access to information suggesting that their public statements were materially inaccurate. See *Novak v. Kasaks*, 216 F.3d 300, 311 (2d Cir. 2000); *In re Scholastic Corp. Sec. Litig.*, 252 F.3d 63, 76 (2d Cir.2001); *Howard v. Everex Sys. Inc.*, 228 F.3d 1057, 1064 (9th Cir.2000); *City of Philadelphia v. Fleming Cos.*, 264 F.3d 1245, 1260-61 (10th Cir.2001) (in case of omissions, scienter proved by knowledge of omitted fact plus knowledge that omission likely to mislead). Here, the investors alleged that defendants published statements with knowledge of facts indicating crucial information in the statements was based on discredited assumptions. These allegations give rise to a strong inference of scienter. See *Rothman v. Gregor*, 220 F.3d 81, 91 (2d Cir.2000) (where defendants regularly assessed likelihood of recouping investment in asset, failure to expense investment that obviously would not be recouped supported strong inference of scienter). Additionally, the sheer size of the $390 million write-down adds to the inference that the defendants must have been aware the problem was brewing. See *Rothman*, 220 F.3d at 92; *In re Scholastic Corp.*, 252 F.3d at 77.

The defendants respond that this is too simplistic a view of a case involving sophisticated financial transactions in which the accounting decisions were difficult and even very large mistakes could fall within the realm of good faith. The defendants contend:

> [T]he securities that Green Tree issues are complex, with multiple layers (tranches) of debt at varying rates, making all of Green Tree's valuation calculations complex. For example, with respect to the 'weighted average' interest rate issue [which Green Tree cited as causing greater write-downs than anticipated in November 1997], prepayments cause high priority tranches of the securities (which bear lower interest rates) to pay down more quickly, so the weighted average interest rate to be paid out to investors in the future increases.

Undoubtedly, the accounting issues are complex; whether they were handled within the parameters of good faith decision-making or whether the decisions amounted to recklessness will surely be the focus of any trial of this case. We will not prejudge that issue. But neither the district court, nor we, can conduct a battle of experts on a motion to dismiss. Rather, we must assume the truth of the allegations pleaded with particularity in the complaint. The strong-inference pleading standard does not license us to resolve disputed facts at this stage of the case.

The defendants contend that they did respond to the discrepancy between actual and assumed prepayment rates by adding to their reserves. This response does not rob the investors' allegations of their effect. First, although adding to reserves could correct the discrepancy, in light of the $390 million write-down announced in January 1998, it is clear that whatever response defendants took was not adequate. It was, after all, necessary to amend the 1996 financials retrospectively in 1998 to reduce reported earnings by $200 million. Moreover, in the November 14, 1997 conference call, Coss said that Green Tree had begun increasing reserves in response to the prepayment problem in the third quarter of 1996. This supports the inference that Green Tree did not begin responding to the prepayment problem until the end of 1996, whereas the investors have alleged that the problem was apparent by July 1995. Coss also characterized those additions to reserves as "relatively modest." Whether defendants could have believed during the class period that the reserves were an adequate response is a question of fact that cannot render the complaints inadequate, lest the heightened pleading requirements of the Reform Act replace the function of a trial.

The investors have pleaded that during the various class periods, the defendants had in their possession facts that rendered their financial results materially false when they published them. Additionally, the investors have pleaded facts giving Coss, the dominant force within Green Tree, a substantial and urgent reason to delay owning up to the prepayment problem. Although the defendants other than Green Tree and Coss had less of a personal interest in putting off the hour of reckoning, the investors' theory that the others were subject to domination by Coss fits within a highly plausible theory of fraud. While the defendants have many good arguments explaining how and why they thought their statements proper, none of these arguments saps the investors' allegations of their force at this procedural stage. The facts pleaded with particularity add up to a strong inference of scienter, thus meeting the Reform Act standard. ***

We reverse the district court's dismissal of the investors' complaints and remand for further proceedings consistent with this opinion.

## *NOTES AND QUESTIONS*

***1. Heightened Pleading and Stays of Discovery.*** Return to note 5 following the Supreme Court's *Hochfelder* decision and the list of factors evidencing scienter compiled by the *Greebel* court. Much of the evidence necessary to establish these factors is uniquely within the defendants' possession and control.

Prior to the passage of the PSLRA, district courts in Rule 10b-5 cases typically allowed the civil discovery process to continue while the defendant's motion to dismiss was pending. And the process of discovery generally allowed the plaintiffs to garner additional evidence which they added to their cases in the form of amended complaints. See Hillary A. Sale, Heightened Pleading and Discovery Stays: An Analysis of the Effect of the PSLRA's Internal-Information Standard on '33 Act and '34 Act Claims, 76 Wash. U. L.Q. 537, 562 (1998) (emphasizing that prior to the PSLRA, plaintiffs routinely "amended their complaints while the discovery process progressed, resulting in several amended and consolidated complaints and concomitant motions to dismiss"). Many of the PSLRA's strongest proponents argued that allowing discovery to be utilized in this way promoted frivolous litigation by encouraging plaintiffs to "file-first-and-research-the-complaint-later." Id. at 553.

Did Congress swing the pendulum too far in a pro-defendant direction when it coupled the heightened pleading requirements in Section 21D(b)(1) and (2) with the automatic stay of discovery in Section 21(b)(3)(B)? Recall that this stay provision permits "particularized discovery" upon a district judge's finding that it is "necessary to preserve evidence or to prevent undue prejudice." How should a court determine whether barring discovery constitutes "undue prejudice?" Compare *Medical Imaging Centers of America, Inc. v. Lichtenstein*, 917 F. Supp. 717, 721 n. 3 (S.D. Cal. 1996) (maintaining that a stay of discovery can result in undue prejudice when it effectively "shield[s] *** [defendants] from eventual liability for any material violations of the securities laws") with *SG Cowen Sec. Corp. v. United States Dist. Court for the N. Dist. of Cal.*, 189 F.3d 909, 913 (9th Cir. 1999) (holding "as a matter of law, failure to muster facts sufficient to meet the [PSLRA's] pleading requirements cannot constitute the requisite 'undue prejudice' to the plaintiff justifying a lift of the discovery stay under [Section 21D(b)(3)(B)]").

Assume that a plaintiff is unable to pursue civil discovery. What other avenues of fact-gathering remain open that may allow him to satisfy his burden of pleading specific facts that establish a strong inference of the defendant's scienter?

***2. Leaves to Amend.*** In her article mentioned in the immediately preceding note, Professor Sale shows that prior to the PSLRA, judges were generally quite permissive in allowing securities plaintiffs leave to amend their complaints. See Sale, supra, 76 Wash. U. L.Q. at 554. How should courts today determine whether to grant a plaintiff's request for leave to amend a complaint that has failed to satisfy the PSLRA's heightened pleading requirements?

Under Rule 15(a) of the Federal Rules of Civil Procedure, leave to amend "shall be freely given when justice so requires." Yet a district court need not allow an amendment (1) where there has been undue delay, bad faith, dilatory motive, or repeated failures to cure deficiencies by previously permitted amendments; (2) where permitting amendment would cause undue prejudice to the opposing party; or (3) where amendment would be futile. See *Foman v. Davis*, 371 U.S. 178, 182 (1962). Do these criteria in effect guarantee that most plaintiffs alleging securities fraud will have at least one attempt to amend a complaint before a district judge issues a dismissal with prejudice? What about multiple re-pleadings? Compare *Byrant v. Dupree*, 252 F.3d 1161 (11th Cir. 2001) (holding that district court abused its discretion when it denied plaintiff the opportunity to amend a complaint for a second time) with *In re Champion Enters., Inc. Sec. Litig.*, 145 F. Supp. 2d 871, 872-73 (E.D. Mich. 2001) (emphasizing that "the Reform Act restricts Rule 15 in Securities Fraud cases" and that the heightened pleading standards are "meaningless if judges on a case-by-case basis grant leave to amend numerous times").

*3. **Group Pleading and Anonymous Sources.*** Prior to the enactment of the PSLRA, the majority of courts recognized the so-called "group pleading" doctrine:

> In cases of corporate fraud where the false or misleading information is conveyed in prospectuses, registration statements, annual reports, press releases, or other "group-published information," it is reasonable to presume that these are the collective actions of the officers. Under such circumstances, a plaintiff fulfills the particularity requirement of Rule 9(b) by pleading the misrepresentations with particularity and where possible the roles of the individual defendants in the misrepresentations.

*Wool v. Tandem Computers, Inc.*, 818 F.2d 1433, 1440 (9th Cir.1987). Does the group pleading doctrine survive the enactment of the PSLRA's heightened pleading standards? Or must a complaint against a securities issuer and its top officers today specifically attribute the allegedly fraudulent statements to the particular officer-defendants? Most courts to address this issue have upheld the continued viability of the doctrine. See *In re Raytheon Sec. Litig.*, 157 F. Supp.2d 131, 153 (D. Mass. 2001) (collecting cases and noting that "the rationale behind the group pleading doctrine remains sound in the wake of the passage of the PSLRA"). But some courts have concluded otherwise. See, e.g., *Coates v. Heartland Wireless Communications, Inc.*, 26 F. Supp.2d 910, 916 (N.D. Tex. 1998) (stating that "[i]t is nonsensical to require that a plaintiff specifically allege facts regarding scienter as to each defendant, but to allow him to rely on group pleading in asserting that the defendant made the statement or omission").

A somewhat related issue concerns the PSLRA's impact on the fairly common practice of citing unnamed or confidential sources in a securities fraud complaint. And, once again, courts have offered differing conclusions, with the majority of courts continuing to permit the practice. Compare *Novak v. Kasaks*, 216 F.3d 300, 314 (2d Cir. 2000) (maintaining that the imposition of "a general requirement of disclosure of confidential sources serves no legitimate pleading purpose while it could deter informants from providing critical information to investigators in meritorious cases or invite retaliation against them") with *In re Eng'g Animation Sec. Litig.*, 110 F. Supp.2d 1183, 1192 (S.D. Iowa 2000) (stating that "[w]here 'allegations of fraud are *** based only on information and belief, *the complaint must set forth the source of the information* and the reasons for the belief' "). In a portion of the *Green Tree* opinion not included in the excerpt that you read, the Eighth Circuit permitted an unnamed source to be included in the complaint at the pleading stage, reasoning that sanctions under Fed. R. Civ. P. 11 already provided a mechanism "to deter and punish fabrication." See *Green Tree*, supra, 270 F.3d at 668. But the *Green Tree* court observed that there was no need to name the source in the complaint, since the source would "soon have to be disclosed under Fed. R. Civ. P. 26(a)(1)(A) if the shareholders intend to make use of it." Id.

***4. The Relation Between Heightened Pleading and the Substantive Scienter Standard.*** In the wake of the PSLRA, a heated controversy arose as to whether Congress intended Section 21D(b)(2)'s heightened pleading requirements to raise the substantive standard for scienter in Rule 10b-5 cases. The controversy was fueled by *In re Silicon Graphics Inc. Sec. Litig.*, 183 F.3d 970 (9th Cir. 1999), which held that under the PSLRA, plaintiffs must plead a strong inference of "deliberate recklessness." Id. at 974. Many regarded the *Silicon Graphics* standard as the functional equivalent of actual intent. See, e.g., *In re Sec. Litig. BMC Software, Inc.*, 183 F. Supp. 2d 860, 897 (S.D. Tex. 2001).

The controversy has largely evaporated. Indeed, all of the circuits that have considered the issue agree that Section 21D(b)(2) did not alter Section 10(b)'s substantive scienter standard. See *Green Tree*, 270 F.3d 645, 653 n. 7 (citing cases from the First, Second, Third, Fourth, Fifth, Sixth, Ninth, Tenth, and Eleventh Circuits). Moreover, the Ninth Circuit has since restricted *Silicon Graphics* to a pleading requirement. See *Howard v. Everex Sys., Inc.*, 228 F.3d 1057, 1064 (9th Cir. 2000) (observing that "the PSLRA did not alter the substantive requirements for scienter under § 10(b)").

Congress also attempted to resolve this question, although its method for doing so remains dubious. Three years after enacting the PSLRA, Congress enacted the Securities Litigation Uniform Standards Act of 1998 (SLUSA), a significant piece of legislation that prevents state courts from hearing most securities class actions. (See Chapter 6.B infra.) At the SEC's urging, Congress agreed to provide in the SLUSA what amounted to "retroactive legislative history" on the PSLRA. The result was the following statement (entitled "Statement by the Managers") from the conference committee that had reconciled the House and Senate versions of the SLUSA: "It is the clear understanding of the managers that Congress did not, in adopting the Reform Act, intend to alter the standards of liability under the Exchange Act." H.R. Conf. Rep. No. 105-803, at 15 (1998); see also S. Rep. No. 182, at 5-6 (1998) ("The Committee understands that *** certain Federal district courts have interpreted the Reform Act as having altered the scienter requirement. In that regard, the Committee emphasizes that the clear intent in 1995 and our continuing intent in this legislation is that neither the Reform Act nor [the SLUSA] in any way alters the scienter standard in Federal securities fraud suits."). What weight should courts give to these statements of the SLUSA "managers" in interpreting Section 21D(b)(2) of the Exchange Act?

5. ***Insider Trading as a "Motive and Opportunity" For Fraud.*** As was recognized by *Green Tree,* insiders who are themselves trading in an issuer's securities presumably have a motive to conceal material information from other investors until they have executed their own trades, and their control over an issuer's disclosure policies provides them with a clear opportunity to deceive shareholders. Thus, both before and after the PSLRA, many plaintiffs in Rule 10b-5 cases have sought to satisfy the requirements for pleading scienter by providing evidence that corporate officials were trading in the issuer's stock at the time of the material misstatement or omission alleged in the complaint.

Moreover, there is significant empirical evidence that the PSLRA has precipitated a stark increase in the number of complaints containing claims of insider trading in addition to the ostensibly primary claims of material misstatements or omissions. For example, a 2002 study by National Economic Research Associates concluded:

> [P]robably as a result of the strengthening of the scienter requirements by the Reform Act, the number of complaints that plead insider trading appears to have increased. Plaintiffs often look for a pattern of officers and directors liquidating their ownership positions during the class period to plead motive and opportunity. A sample of post-PSLRA filings shows that about 53% of post-PSLRA complaints contain insider-trading allegations.

Todd S. Foster et al., Recent Trends VII: PSLRA, Six Years Later 9 (January 2002). See also Hillary A. Sale, Judging Heuristics, 35 U.C. Davis L. Rev. 903, 924 (2002) (noting that in 1996 there were two judicial opinions on motions to dismiss securities suits with insider trading allegations, but 12 in 1997, 23 in 1998, 28 in 1999, and 44 in 2000).

Yet, as was also recognized in *Green Tree,* courts faced with claims of an "insider trading motive" typically subject that claim to a substantial degree of scrutiny. See Sale, supra, 35 U.C. Davis L. Rev. at 925 (noting that in the 1996-2000 period, 68 motions to dismiss a Rule 10b-5 complaint were granted despite insider-trading allegations and only 41 such motions were denied). Professor Sale's study thus shows "although trades are included in complaints in the hope that their presence will decrease the likelihood of a successful motion to dismiss, approximately 62 percent of the complaints containing such allegations are dismissed." Id.

Indeed, most courts are quick to observe that the "strong inference" pleading requirement may be satisfied only if the complaint includes specific facts demonstrating that the insider trading is "unusual" and "suspicious." See, e.g., *In re Silicon Graphics Sec. Litig.*, 183 F.3d 970, 986 (9th Cir. 1999) (stating that "[a]lthough 'unusual' or 'suspicious' stock sales by corporate insiders may constitute circumstantial evidence of scienter, insider trading is suspicious only when it is 'dramatically out of line with prior trading practices at times calculated to maximize the personal benefit from undisclosed inside information' "); *In re Scholastic Corp. Sec. Litig.*, 252 F.3d 63, 74-75 (2d Cir. 2001) (noting that "[f]actors considered in determining whether insider trading activity is unusual include the amount of profit from the sales, the portion of stockholdings sold, the change in volume of insider sales, and the number of insiders selling"). The problem that follows provides an opportunity to explore these factors.

## *PROBLEM 2-15*

Shareholders of Katteller Corporation have filed a class action lawsuit against the company and four of its current or former officers and directors, alleging violations of Rule 10b-5 through the numerous intentional or reckless omissions of material adverse information and through the intentional or reckless dissemination of false and misleading statements over a period of time from March through August 2002. Plaintiffs seek to satisfy Section 21D(b)(2)'s heightened pleading requirement through the allegation of specific facts demonstrating insider trading on the part of three of the named officials. That is, plaintiffs claim that "massive insider selling on the part of the company's three principal officers is evidence of the defendants' motive to commit fraud through inflating the stock price of company shares."

The plaintiff's complaint includes the following allegations:

1. Officer A, the company's president until May 31, 2002 and a current director, sold 390,000 shares of Katteller stock between April and May 2002 for approximately $11.7 million dollars. These stock sales constituted more than 60% of the president's holdings in the company. Previously, the president had never sold more than 10% of his Katteller holdings in any given year.

2. Officer B, the company's chief executive officer and chairman of its board of directors, sold 1.2 million shares of Katteller stock between April and August 2002, for over $30 million dollars. This constituted more than 39% of his holdings in the company. Previously, the CEO had never sold more than 5% of his Katteller holdings in any given year.

3. Officer C, the company's chief financial officer and director of the company, sold 7,000 shares of Katteller stock on April 20, 2002, for approximately $220,000. This constituted 9% of the CFO's holdings in Katteller, and he had made no other Katteller stock sales in the previous five years.

4. During the class period, the price of Katteller's stock ranged from $22 to $32 per share. On September 1, 2002, when all of defendants' material omissions and misrepresentations came to light, Katteller's stock price fell to approximately $10 a share, and currently trades in the range of $12-15.

5. When combined, the sales of officers A, B, and C amounted to approximately 35% of all outstanding shares of Katteller's stock.

In their affidavits supporting their motion to dismiss under Section 21D(b)(3)(a) of the Exchange Act, defendants attest to the following additional facts:

1. Officer A's stock sales immediately preceded his retirement from the company on May 31, 2002, and individuals leaving employment with a company frequently sell a large percentage of their shares.

2. Officer B purchased 10,000 shares of Katteller stock on April 1, 2002.

3. Officer C sold his Katteller stock in order to free up cash to assist his daughter and her new husband with a down payment for the purchase of their first home. During the period of the alleged fraud, Officer C continued to hold more than 28,000 shares of common stock in the company.

4. Officer D, the company's president as of June 1, 2002 and previously on the board of directors, sold no shares of Katteller stock during the class period, though he owned more than 500,000 shares in the company.

If you were the district judge ruling on defendants' motion to dismiss plaintiffs' complaint under Section 21D(b)(3)(A), would you find that the plaintiffs had satisfied their pleading burden under Section 21D(b)(2)?

## E. THE PURCHASER-SELLER REQUIREMENT

Private plaintiffs suing for damages under Rule 10b-5 must satisfy the purchaser-seller requirement. This requirement need not be satisfied, however, in actions under the Rule brought by the SEC or by the DOJ.

The Supreme Court upheld the purchaser-seller requirement in the following landmark decision. The decision is noteworthy also for articulating a policy that has played a critical role in the interpretation of Rule 10b-5—the necessity of curbing vexatious private actions.

### BLUE CHIP STAMPS v. MANOR DRUG STORES

421 U.S. 723 (1975)

JUSTICE REHNQUIST:

This case requires us to consider whether the offerees of a stock offering, made pursuant to an antitrust consent decree and registered under the Securities Act of 1933 (1933 Act) may maintain a private cause of action for money damages where they allege that the offeror has violated the provisions of Rule 10b-5 ***, but where they have neither purchased nor sold any of the offered shares.

I

In 1963 the United States filed a civil antitrust action against Blue Chip Stamp Co. (Old Blue Chip), a company in the business of providing trading stamps to retailers, and nine retailers who owned 90% of its shares. In 1967 the action was terminated by the entry of a consent decree. The decree contemplated a plan of reorganization whereby Old Blue Chip was to be merged into a newly formed corporation, Blue Chip Stamps (New Blue Chip). The holdings of the majority shareholders of Old Blue Chip were to be reduced, and New Blue Chip, one of the petitioners here, was required under the plan to offer a substantial number of its shares of common stock to retailers who had used the stamp service in the past but who were not shareholders in the old company. ***

The reorganization plan was carried out, the offering was registered with the SEC as required by the 1933 Act, and a prospectus was distributed to all offerees as required by § 5 of that Act. Somewhat more than 50% of the offered units were actually purchased. In 1970, two years after the offering, respondent, a former user of the stamp service and therefore an offeree of the

1968 offering, filed this suit ***. Defendants below and petitioners here are Old and New Blue Chip, eight of the nine majority shareholders of Old Blue Chip, and the directors of New Blue Chip (collectively called Blue Chip).

Respondent's complaint alleged *** that the prospectus prepared and distributed by Blue Chip in connection with the offering was materially misleading in its overly pessimistic appraisal of Blue Chip's status and future prospects. It alleged that Blue Chip intentionally made the prospectus overly pessimistic in order to discourage respondent and other members of the allegedly large class whom it represents from accepting what was intended to be a bargain offer, so that the rejected shares might later be offered to the public at a higher price. The complaint alleged that class members because of and in reliance on the false and misleading prospectus failed to purchase the offered units. Respondent therefore sought on behalf of the alleged class some $21,400,000 in damages representing the lost opportunity to purchase the units; the right to purchase the previously rejected units at the 1968 price; and in addition, it sought some $25,000,000 in exemplary damages.

The only portion of the litigation thus initiated which is before us is whether respondent may base its action on Rule 10b-5 *** without having either bought or sold the securities described in the allegedly misleading prospectus. ***

II

*** Section 10(b) does not by its terms provide an express civil remedy for its violation. Nor does the history of this provision provide any indication that Congress considered the problem of private suits under it at the time of its passage. See, e.g., Note, Implied Liability Under the Securities Exchange Act 61 Harv. L. Rev. 858, 861 (1948); A. Bromberg, Securities Law: Fraud—SEC Rule 10b-5 § 2.2(300)-(340) (1968)(hereinafter Bromberg); S. Rep. No.792, 73d Cong., 2d Sess., 5-6 (1934). Similarly there is no indication that the Commission in adopting Rule 10b-5 considered the question of private civil remedies under this provision. SEC Securities Exchange Act Release No. 3230 (1942).

Despite the contrast between the provisions of Rule 10b-5 and the numerous carefully drawn express civil remedies provided in the Acts of both 1933 and 1934,[4] it was held in 1946 by the United States District Court for the Eastern District of Pennsylvania that there was an implied private right of action under the Rule. *Kardon v. National Gypsum Co.*, 69 F. Supp. 512. This Court had no occasion to deal with the subject until 25 years later, and at that time we confirmed with virtually no discussion the overwhelming consensus of the District Courts and Courts of Appeals that such a cause of action did exist. *Superintendent of Insurance v. Bankers Life & Cas. Co.*, 404 U.S. 6, 13 n. 9 (1971); *Affiliated Ute Citizens v. United States*, 406 U.S. 128, 150-154 (1972). Such a conclusion was, of course, entirely consistent with the Court's recognition in *J. I. Case Co. v. Borak*, 377 U.S. 426, 432 (1964), that private enforcement of Commission rules may "[provide] a necessary supplement to Commission action."

4. See, e.g., §§ 11, 12, 15 of the 1933 Act; §§ 9, 16, 18, 20 of the 1934 Act.

Within a few years after the seminal *Kardon* decision the Court of Appeals for the Second Circuit concluded that the plaintiff class for purposes of a private damage action under § 10(b) and Rule 10b-5 was limited to actual purchasers and sellers of securities. *Birnbaum v. Newport Steel Corp.*, [193 F.2d 461 (2d Cir. 1952)].

*** But in this case a majority of the Court of Appeals found that the facts warranted an exception to the *Birnbaum* rule. For the reasons hereinafter stated, we are of the opinion that Birnbaum was rightly decided, and that it bars respondent from maintaining this suit under Rule 10b-5. ***

III

*** Just as this Court had no occasion to consider the validity of the *Kardon* holding that there was a private cause of action under Rule 10b-5 until 20-odd years later, nearly the same period of time has gone by between the *Birnbaum* decision and our consideration of the case now before us. As with *Kardon*, virtually all lower federal courts facing the issue in the hundreds of reported cases presenting this question over the past quarter century have reaffirmed *Birnbaum's* conclusion that the plaintiff class for purposes of § 10(b) and Rule 10b-5 private damage actions is limited to purchasers and sellers of securities.

In 1957 and again in 1959, the Securities and Exchange Commission sought from Congress amendment of § 10(b) to change its wording from "in connection with the purchase or sale of any security" to "in connection with the purchase or sale of, *or any attempt to purchase or sell*, any security." 103 Cong.Rec. 11636 (1957) (emphasis added); SEC Legislation, Hearings on S. 1178-1182 before a Subcommittee of the Senate Committee on Banking & Currency, 86th Cong., 1st Sess., 367-368 (1959); S. 2545, 85th Cong., 1st Sess. (1957); S. 1179, 86th Cong., 1st Sess. (1959). In the words of a memorandum submitted by the Commission to a congressional committee, the purpose of the proposed change was "to make section 10(b) also applicable to manipulative activities in connection with any attempt to purchase or sell any security." Hearings on S. 1178-1182, supra, at 331. Opposition to the amendment was based on fears of the extension of civil liability under § 10(b) that it would cause. Id. at 368. Neither change was adopted by Congress.

The longstanding acceptance by the courts, coupled with Congress' failure to reject *Birnbaum's* reasonable interpretation of the wording of § 10(b), wording which is directed toward injury suffered "in connection with the purchase or sale" of securities, argues significantly in favor of acceptance of the *Birnbaum* rule by this Court.

Available evidence from the texts of the 1933 and 1934 Acts as to the congressional scheme in this regard, though not conclusive, supports the result reached by the *Birnbaum* court. The wording of § 10(b) directed at fraud "in connection with the purchase or sale" of securities stands in contrast with the parallel antifraud provision of the 1933 Act, § 17(a) reaching fraud "in the offer of sale" of securities. Cf. § 5 of the 1933 Act. When Congress wished to provide a remedy to those who neither purchase nor sell securities, it had little trouble in doing so expressly. Cf. § 16(b) of the 1934 Act. ***

The principal express nonderivative private civil remedies, created by Congress contemporaneously with the passage of § 10(b), for violations of various provisions of the 1933 and 1934 Acts, are by their terms expressly limited to purchasers or sellers of securities. Thus § 11(a) of the 1933 Act confines the cause of action it grants to "any person acquiring such security" while the remedy granted by § 12 of that Act is limited to the "person purchasing such security." Section 9 of the 1934 Act, prohibiting a variety of fraudulent and manipulative devices, limits the express civil remedy provided for its violation to "any person who shall purchase or sell any security" in a transaction affected by a violation of the provision. Section 18 of the 1934 Act, prohibiting false or misleading statements in reports or other documents required to be filed by the 1934 Act, limits the express remedy provided for its violation to "any person . . . who . . . shall have purchased or sold a security at a price which was affected by such statement . . ." It would indeed be anomalous to impute to Congress an intention to expand the plaintiff class for a judicially implied cause of action beyond the bounds it delineated for comparable express causes of action.

Having said all this, we would by no means be understood as suggesting that we are able to divine from the language of § 10(b) the express "intent of Congress" as to the contours of a private cause of action under Rule 10b-5. When we deal with private actions under Rule 10b-5, we deal with a judicial oak which has grown from little more than a legislative acorn. Such growth may be quite consistent with the congressional enactment and with the role of the federal judiciary in interpreting it, see *J. I. Case Co. v. Borak*, supra, but it would be disingenuous to suggest that either Congress in 1934 or the Securities and Exchange Commission in 1942 foreordained the present state of the law with respect to Rule 10b-5. It is therefore proper that we consider, in addition to the factors already discussed, what may be described as policy considerations when we come to flesh out the portions of the law with respect to which neither the congressional enactment nor the administrative regulations offer conclusive guidance.

Three principal classes of potential plaintiffs are presently barred by the *Birnbaum* rule. First are potential purchasers of shares, either in a new offering or on the Nation's post-distribution trading markets, who allege that they decided not to purchase because of an unduly gloomy representation or the omission of favorable material which made the issuer appear to be a less favorable investment vehicle than it actually was. Second are actual shareholders in the issuer who allege that they decided not to sell their shares because of an unduly rosy representation or a failure to disclose unfavorable material. Third are shareholders, creditors, and perhaps others related to an issuer who suffered loss in the value of their investment due to corporate or insider activities in connection with the purchase or sale of securities which violate Rule 10b-5. It has been held that shareholder members of the second and third of these classes may frequently be able to circumvent the *Birnbaum* limitation through bringing a derivative action on behalf of the corporate issuer if the latter is itself a purchaser or seller of securities. See, e.g., *Schoenbaum v. Firstbrook*, 405 F.2d 215, 219 (CA2 1968). But the first of these classes, of which respondent is a member, cannot claim the benefit of such a rule.

A great majority of the many commentators on the issue before us have taken the view that the *Birnbaum* limitation on the plaintiff class in a Rule 10b-5 action for damages is an arbitrary restriction which unreasonably prevents some deserving plaintiffs from recovering damages which have in fact been caused by violations of Rule 10b-5. See, e.g., Lowenfels, The Demise of the *Birnbaum* Doctrine: A New Era for Rule 10b-5, 54 Va. L. Rev. 268 (1968). The Securities and Exchange Commission has filed an *amicus* brief in this case espousing that same view. We have no doubt that this is indeed a disadvantage of the *Birnbaum* rule, and if it had no countervailing advantages it would be undesirable as a matter of policy, however much it might be supported by precedent and legislative history. But we are of the opinion that there are countervailing advantages to the *Birnbaum* rule, purely as a matter of policy, although those advantages are more difficult to articulate than is the disadvantage.

There has been widespread recognition that litigation under Rule 10b-5 presents a danger of vexatiousness different in degree and in kind from that which accompanies litigation in general. This fact was recognized by Judge Browning in his opinion for the majority of the Court of Appeals in this case, 492 F.2d at 141, and by Judge Hufstedler in her dissenting opinion when she said:

> The purchaser-seller rule has maintained the balances built into the congressional scheme by permitting damage actions to be brought only by those persons whose active participation in the marketing transaction promises enforcement of the statute without undue risk of abuse of the litigation process and without distorting the securities market. Id. at 147.

Judge Friendly in commenting on another aspect of Rule 10b-5 litigation has referred to the possibility that unduly expansive imposition of civil liability "will lead to large judgments, payable in the last analysis by innocent investors, for the benefit of speculators and their lawyers...." *SEC v. Texas Gulf Sulphur Co.*, 401 F.2d 833, 867 (CA2 1968) (concurring opinion).

We believe that the concern expressed for the danger of vexatious litigation which could result from a widely expanded class of plaintiffs under Rule 10b-5 is founded in something more substantial than the common complaint of the many defendants who would prefer avoiding lawsuits entirely to either settling them or trying them. These concerns have two largely separate grounds.

The first of these concerns is that in the field of federal securities laws governing disclosure of information even a complaint which by objective standards may have very little chance of success at trial has a settlement value to the plaintiff out of any proportion to its prospect of success at trial so long as he may prevent the suit from being resolved against him by dismissal or summary judgment. The very pendency of the lawsuit may frustrate or delay normal business activity of the defendant which is totally unrelated to the lawsuit. See, e.g., Sargent, The SEC and the Individual Investor: Restoring His Confidence in the Market, 60 Va. L. Rev. 553, 562-572 (1974); Dooley, The Effects of Civil Liability on Investment Banking and the New Issues Market, 58 Va. L. Rev. 776, 822-843 (1972).

Congress itself recognized the potential for nuisance or "strike" suits in this type of litigation, and in Title II of the 1934 Act amended § 11 of the 1933 Act to provide that:

> In any suit under this or any other section of this title the court may, in its discretion, require an undertaking for the payment of the costs of such suit, including reasonable attorney's fees.... § 206(d).

Senator Fletcher, Chairman of the Senate Banking and Finance Committee, in introducing Title II of the 1934 Act on the floor of the Senate, stated in explaining the amendment to § 11(e): "This amendment is the most important of all." 78 Cong. Rec. 8669. Among its purposes was to provide "a defense against blackmail suits." Ibid.

Where Congress in those sections of the 1933 Act which expressly conferred a private cause of action for damages, adopted a provision uniformly regarded as designed to deter "strike" or nuisance actions, that fact alone justifies our consideration of such potential in determining the limits of the class of plaintiffs who may sue in an action wholly implied from the language of the 1934 Act.

The potential for possible abuse of the liberal discovery provisions of the Federal Rules of Civil Procedure may likewise exist in this type of case to a greater extent than they do in other litigation. The prospect of extensive deposition of the defendant's officers and associates and the concomitant opportunity for extensive discovery of business documents, is a common occurrence in this and similar types of litigation. To the extent that this process *** permits a plaintiff with a largely groundless claim to simply take up the time of a number of other people, with the right to do so representing an *in terrorem* increment of the settlement value, rather than a reasonably founded hope that the process will reveal relevant evidence, it is a social cost rather than a benefit. ***

Without the *Birnbaum* rule, an action under Rule 10b-5 will turn largely on which oral version of a series of occurrences the jury may decide to credit, and therefore no matter how improbable the allegations of the plaintiff, the case will be virtually impossible to dispose of prior to trial other than by settlement. ***

The *Birnbaum* rule, on the other hand, permits exclusion prior to trial of those plaintiffs who were not themselves purchasers or sellers of the stock in question. The fact of purchase of stock and the fact of sale of stock are generally matters which are verifiable by documentation, and do not depend upon oral recollection, so that failure to qualify under the *Birnbaum* rule is a matter that can normally be established by the defendant either on a motion to dismiss or on a motion for summary judgment. ***

*** The *Birnbaum* rule undoubtedly excludes plaintiffs who have in fact been damaged by violations of Rule 10b-5, and to that extent it is undesirable. But it also separates in a readily demonstrable manner the group of plaintiffs who actually purchased or actually sold, and whose version of the facts is therefore more likely to be believed by the trier of fact, from the vastly larger world of potential plaintiffs who might successfully allege a claim but could seldom succeed in proving it. And this fact is one of its advantages.

The second ground for fear of vexatious litigation is based on the concern that, given the generalized contours of liability, the abolition of the *Birnbaum* rule would throw open to the trier of fact many rather hazy issues of historical fact the proof of which depended almost entirely on oral testimony. We in no way disparage the worth and frequent high value of oral testimony when we say that dangers of its abuse appear to exist in this type of action to a peculiarly high degree. ***

But in the absence of the *Birnbaum* rule, it would be sufficient for a plaintiff to prove that he had failed to purchase or sell stock by reason of a defendant's violation of Rule 10b-5. *** Plaintiff's proof would not be that he purchased or sold stock, a fact which would be capable of documentary verification in most situations, but instead that he decided not to purchase or sell stock. Plaintiff's entire testimony could be dependent upon uncorroborated oral evidence of many of the crucial elements of his claim, and still be sufficient to go to the jury. The jury would not even have the benefit of weighing the plaintiff's version against the defendant's version, since the elements to which the plaintiff would testify would be in many cases totally unknown and unknowable to the defendant. The very real risk in permitting those in respondent's position to sue under Rule 10b-5 is that the door will be open to recovery of substantial damages on the part of one who offers only his own testimony to prove that he ever consulted a prospectus of the issuer, that he paid any attention to it, or that the representations contained in it damaged him. The virtue of the *Birnbaum* rule, simply stated, in this situation, is that it limits the class of plaintiffs to those who have at least dealt in the security to which the prospectus, representation, or omission relates. And their dealing in the security, whether by way of purchase or sale, will generally be an objectively demonstrable fact in an area of the law otherwise very much dependent upon oral testimony. In the absence of the *Birnbaum* doctrine, bystanders to the securities marketing process could await developments on the sidelines without risk, claiming that inaccuracies in disclosure caused nonselling in a falling market and that unduly pessimistic predictions by the issuer followed by a rising market caused them to allow retrospectively golden opportunities to pass. ***

Thus we conclude that what may be called considerations of policy, which we are free to weigh in deciding this case, are by no means entirely on one side of the scale. Taken together with the precedential support for the *Birnbaum* rule over a period of more than 20 years, and the consistency of that rule with what we can glean from the intent of Congress, they lead us to conclude that it is a sound rule and should be followed.

IV

The majority of the Court of Appeals in this case *** noted that prior cases have held that persons owning contractual rights to buy or sell securities are not excluded by the *Birnbaum* rule. Relying on these cases, it concluded that respondent's status as an offeree pursuant to the terms of the consent decree served the same function, for purposes of delimiting the class of plaintiffs, as is normally performed by the requirement of a contractual relationship.

The Court of Appeals recognized, and respondent concedes here, that a well-settled line of authority from this Court establishes that a consent decree is not enforceable directly or in collateral proceedings by those who are not parties to it even though they were intended to be benefited by it. *United States v. Armour & Co.*, 402 U.S. 673 (1971); *Buckeye Coal & R. Co. v. Hocking Valley Co.*, 269 U.S. 42 (1925).

A contract to purchase or sell securities is expressly defined by § 3(a) of the 1934 Act, as a purchase or sale of securities for the purposes of that Act. Unlike respondent, which had no contractual right or duty to purchase Blue Chip's securities, the holders of puts, calls, options, and other contractual rights or duties to purchase or sell securities have been recognized as "purchasers" or "sellers" of securities for purposes of Rule 10b-5, not because of a judicial conclusion that they were similarly situated to "purchasers" or "sellers," but because the definitional provisions of the 1934 Act themselves grant them such a status.

Even if we were to accept the notion that the *Birnbaum* rule could be circumvented on a case-by-case basis through particularized judicial inquiry into the facts surrounding a complaint, this respondent and the members of its alleged class would be unlikely candidates for such a judicially created exception. While the Birnbaum rule has been flexibly interpreted by lower federal courts,[14] we have been unable to locate a single decided case from any court in the 20-odd years of litigation since the *Birnbaum* decision which would support the right of persons who were in the position of respondent here to bring a private suit under Rule 10b-5. Respondent was not only not a buyer or seller of any security but it was not even a shareholder of the corporate petitioners. ***

*** As a purely practical matter, it is doubtless true that respondent and the members of its class, as offerees and recipients of the prospectus of New Blue Chip, are a smaller class of potential plaintiffs than would be all those who might conceivably assert that they obtained information violative of Rule 10b-5 and attributable to the issuer in the financial pages of their local newspaper. And since respondent likewise had a prior connection with some of petitioners as a result of using the trading stamps marketed by Old Blue Chip, and was intended to benefit from the provisions of the consent decree, there is doubtless more likelihood that its managers read and were damaged by the allegedly misleading statements in the prospectus than there would be in a case filed by a complete stranger to the corporation.

But respondent and the members of its class are neither "purchasers" nor "sellers," as those terms are defined in the 1934 Act, and therefore to the extent that their claim of standing to sue were recognized, it would mean that the lesser practical difficulties of corroborating at least some elements of their proof would be regarded as sufficient to avoid the *Birnbaum* rule. While we have noted that these practical difficulties, particularly in the case of a complete

14. Our decision in *SEC v. National Securities, Inc.*, 393 U.S. 453 (1969), established that the purchaser-seller rule imposes no limitation on the standing of the SEC to bring actions for injunctive relief under § 10(b) and Rule 10b-5.

stranger to the corporation, support the retention of that rule, they are by no means the only factor which does so. *** Were we to agree with the Court of Appeals in this case, we would leave the *Birnbaum* rule open to endless case-by-case erosion depending on whether a particular group of plaintiffs was thought by the court in which the issue was being litigated to be sufficiently more discrete than the world of potential purchasers at large to justify an exception. We do not believe that such a shifting and highly fact-oriented disposition of the issue of who may bring a damages claim for violation of Rule 10b-5 is a satisfactory basis for a rule of liability imposed on the conduct of business transactions. Nor is it as consistent as a straightforward application of the *Birnbaum* rule with the other factors which support the retention of that rule. ***

JUSTICE POWELL, WITH WHOM JUSTICE STEWART AND JUSTICE MARSHALL JOIN, CONCURRING:

Although I join the opinion of the Court, I write to emphasize the significance of the texts of the Acts of 1933 and 1934 and especially the language of § 10(b) and Rule 10b-5. ***

The starting point in every case involving construction of a statute is the language itself. The critical phrase in both the statute and the Rule is "in connection with the *purchase* or *sale* of any security." (emphasis added). Section 3(a)(14) of the 1934 Act provides that the term "sale" shall "include any contract to sell or otherwise dispose of" securities. There is no hint in any provision of the Act that the term "sale," as used in § 10(b), was intended—in addition to its long-established legal meaning—to include an "offer to sell." Respondent, nevertheless, would have us amend the controlling language in § 10(b) to read:

> in connection with the purchase or sale of, or an offer to sell, any security.

Before a court properly could consider taking such liberty with statutory language there should be, at least, unmistakable support in the history and structure of the legislation. None exists in this case. ***

## *NOTES AND QUESTIONS*

***1. Curbing Vexatious Private Litigation.*** How does the purchaser-seller requirement curb vexatious litigation? At what cost? To what extent did the Court act like a legislature in taking this policy consideration into account? Did the Court suggest that policy considerations are always relevant when construing Rule 10b-5?

***2. Standing to Sue For Contract Holders.*** According to *Blue Chip Stamps*, standing to sue under Rule 10b-5 can rest on a contract to buy or sell securities because the Exchange Act defines "purchase" to include a contract to purchase and "sale" to include a contract to sell. See Exchange Act Sections 3(a)(13)-(14). Is this conclusion unavoidable as a matter of statutory construction? Does it follow from the Court's policy analysis?

***3. Oral Contracts.*** In *Wharf (Holdings) Ltd. v. United Int'l Holdings, Inc.*, 532 U.S. 588 (2001), the Supreme Court held that a contract to buy or sell securities provides standing to sue under Rule 10b-5 even if it is oral:

> *Blue Chip Stamps* said nothing to suggest that oral purchases or sales fall outside the scope of the Act. Rather, the Court's concern was about "the abuse potential and proof problems inherent in suits by investors who neither bought nor sold, but asserted they would have traded absent fraudulent conduct by others." *United States v. O'Hagan*, 521 U.S. 642, 664 (1997). Such a "potential purchase" claim would rest on facts, including the plaintiff's state of mind, that might be "totally unknown and unknowable to the defendant," depriving the jury of "the benefit of weighing the plaintiff's version against the defendant's version." *Blue Chip Stamps*, supra, at 746. An actual sale, even if oral, would not create this problem, because both parties would be able to testify as to whether the relevant events had occurred.
>
> Neither is there any other convincing reason to interpret the Act to exclude oral contracts as a class. The Act itself says that it applies to "any contract" for the purchase or sale of a security. [Exchange Act §§ 3(a)(13),(14)]. Oral contracts for the sale of securities are sufficiently common that the Uniform Commercial Code and statutes of frauds in every State now consider them enforceable. Any exception for oral sales of securities would significantly limit the Act's coverage, thereby undermining its basic purposes.
>
> Wharf makes a related but narrower argument that the Act does not encompass oral contracts of sale that are unenforceable under state law. But we do not reach that issue. The Court of Appeals held that Wharf's sale *** was not covered by the then-applicable Colorado statute of frauds, and hence was enforceable under state law. Though Wharf disputes the correctness of that holding, we ordinarily will not consider such a state-law issue, and we decline to do so here.

532 U.S. at 594-96. By allowing standing to sue based on an oral contract, has the *Wharf* Court undermined the policy of curbing vexatious litigation articulated in *Blue Chip Stamps*?

***4. Exceptions?*** Does the Court in *Blue Chip Stamps* shut the door on all exceptions to the purchaser-seller requirement? In thinking about this question, revisit Part IV of the opinion, which acknowledges that there are at least plausible arguments for creating an exception on behalf of the plaintiffs in this case. Is it significant that the Court chose a case in which such arguments could be made as its vehicle for upholding the purchaser-seller requirement? You will have the opportunity to consider these matters further in connection with the next case.

---

## COWIN v. BRESLER

741 F.2d 410 (D.C. Cir. 1984)

BORK, CIRCUIT JUDGE:

Bresler & Reiner, Inc. is a publicly-owned company incorporated in the State of Delaware and engaged in the development and management of residential and commercial properties in the District of Columbia. In late 1980, Daniel Cowin, a Bresler & Reiner shareholder, sued the company and its directors on his own behalf. Cowin has a minority interest in the company. The individual directors-appellees, with their families, own in excess of 79% of the company's stock. Appellees Bresler and Reiner together hold more than 70% of the company's outstanding shares, and their control of the corporation is undisputed.

The thrust of Cowin's charges is that the appellees have manipulated the business for their personal profit at the expense of the minority shareholders. The complaint alleges numerous instances of corporate mismanagement, fraud, and self-dealing, all in breach of the common law fiduciary duty owed by the directors of the company to the appellant as a shareholder. ***

The remainder of the complaint charges appellees with violations of the federal securities laws ***. Specifically, Cowin claims that Bresler and Reiner caused the company to "disseminate reports to the public shareholders which were materially deceptive" and concealed material information in violation of Rule 10b-5 and section 10(b) ***

Appellant's federal claims raise novel questions under the Securities Exchange Act of 1934. Although Cowin did not buy or sell his stock in connection with the allegedly misleading reports issued by the company, he relies upon section 10(b) of the Act and Rule 10b-5 in seeking to prevent appellees from "depress[ing] the value of [his] stock and ... eliminat[ing] the public market in that stock through dissemination of deceptive statements." In short, appellant claims not that he was wrongfully induced to buy or sell stock by appellees' misrepresentations but rather that his stock was made less valuable by appellees' misrepresentations to the investing public generally. He does not seek damages but an injunction requiring an end to the alleged misrepresentations and disclosure of past misrepresentations. It is clear from *Blue Chip Stamps v. Manor Drug Stores,* 421 U.S. 723 (1975), that appellant could not maintain an action for damages under section 10(b) or Rule 10b-5. The question before us is whether he may bring suit for an injunction. ***

Cowin argues that the purchaser-seller limitation does not apply to actions seeking equitable relief. He points to a pre-*Blue Chip* line of cases holding that a private party who seeks only injunctive relief need not have bought or sold securities to sue under Rule 10b-5, see, e.g., *Kahan v. Rosenstiel,* 424 F.2d 161 (3d Cir.1970); *Mutual Shares Corp. v. Genesco, Inc.,* 384 F.2d 540 (2d Cir.1967), and contends that the "exception" to the purchaser-seller rule in those cases survives *Blue Chip* because the Supreme Court limited its holding in that case to private damage actions. We appear to be the first court of appeals squarely to address this issue, and we think *Blue Chip* cannot be so limited. ***

The relaxed standing requirement urged on us by appellant would be contrary to the rationale of section 10(b) and Rule 10b-5 as perceived by the Supreme Court in *Blue Chip.* While it may be possible to discern differences between an action for damages and a suit for an injunction, most of the Supreme Court's argument in *Blue Chip* applies quite as much to the latter as to the former. The scope of section 10(b) and Rule 10b-5 is limited to fraud "in connection with the purchase or sale of a security." Congress was asked on two different occasions to expand the jurisdictional reach of those provisions but chose not to. In contrast, Congress did choose to define the scope of other provisions in the 1933 and 1934 Acts in terms that clearly reflected a broader jurisdictional reach. Congress also limited standing in those instances where it did create express remedies under the Act to a class of persons including only purchasers or sellers. Thus, the purchaser-seller limitation is "sufficiently supported by the statutory structure of the Securities Act." The Supreme Court, 1974 Term, supra, 89 Harv. L. Rev. at 269. These features also constrain us to accept, in the context of an injunctive suit, the common meaning of the terms "purchase or sale" and reject an expansive construction of the Rule, as *Blue Chip* did for damage actions.

Attempting to fashion a different concept of standing for cases like this would involve us in distinctions altogether too awkward to be persuasive. As *Blue Chip* noted, the "wording of § 10(b) ... is surely badly strained when construed to provide a cause of action, not to purchasers and sellers of securities, but to the world at large." 421 U.S. at 733 n. 5. The Court also stated that it "would indeed be anomalous to impute to Congress an intention to expand the plaintiff class for a judicially implied cause of action beyond the bounds it delineated for comparable express causes of action." Id. at 737.

Our analysis might well end here. However, because *Blue Chip* went beyond statutory analysis to examine certain "policy considerations," 421 U.S. at 737, Cowin argues that relaxing the purchaser-seller requirement in his case is proper because that would not contradict the several policies relied upon by *Blue Chip.* Several lower courts, including the lower court in this case, have distinguished the Supreme Court's opinion in this fashion. See, e.g., *Fuchs v. Swanton Corp.,* 482 F.Supp. 83, 89-90 (S.D.N.Y.1979); *Hundahl v. United Benefit Life Insurance Co.,* 465 F.Supp. 1349, 1357-59 (N.D.Tex.1979).

If we thought this question open, we might conclude that injunctive suits present many of the same problems of vexatiousness, "strike" suits, abuse of discovery, and the like that damage actions do. We need not decide that, however, for we think the approach appellant suggests is foreclosed by *Blue Chip* itself. There, the plaintiff had contended that two policies articulated by the Court—the difficulties in corroborating the elements of Rule 10b-5 proof and the potential for an unlimited class of plaintiffs—were simply not raised on the facts of the case. If plaintiffs were allowed to sue, the Court said, "it would mean that the lesser practical difficulties of corroborating at least some elements of their proof would be regarded as sufficient to avoid the *Birnbaum* rule." 421 U.S. at 754-55. The Court rejected this result stating that while its decision to affirm *Birnbaum* was in part based on these "practical difficulties," the consistency of the rule with "the statutes involved and their legislative history [were] likewise bases for retaining the rule." Id. at 755. To take such arguments into account "would leave the *Birnbaum* rule open to endless case-by-case erosion." Id. Thus, while "policy considerations" did play a role in the *Blue Chip* decision, when those policy considerations were inconsistent with the retention of a flat rule and with the other grounds on which the decision rested—the statute and its history—they were not strong enough to create an exception. ***

## NOTES AND QUESTIONS

*1. Unlikely Vehicle?* Was there anything about *Cowin* that made it an unlikely vehicle for establishing an injunction exception to the purchaser-seller requirement?

2. ***Open Question.*** *Cowin* notwithstanding, the viability of the injunction exception remains an open question in other circuits. See, e.g., *Trump Hotels & Casino Resorts, Inc. v. Mirage Resorts, Inc.*, 140 F.3d 478, 486 (3d Cir. 1998); *Advanced Resources Int'l, Inc. v. Tri-Star Petroleum Co.*, 4 F.3d 327, 332 (4th Cir. 1993). What are the arguments for retaining this exception in the wake of *Blue Chip Stamps*?

3. ***Forced Seller Exception.*** Another exception to the purchaser-seller requirement that was on the books prior to *Blue Chip Stamps* involved forced sellers. Consider *Vine v. Beneficial Fin. Co.*, 374 F.2d 627 (2d Cir. 1967), which involved an alleged multi-part scheme consisting of a deceptive tender offer followed by a short form merger that squeezed out those who had not previously tendered their shares. The plaintiff had not, however, tendered his own shares. Nor had he, at the time of the lawsuit, exchanged his shares for cash pursuant to the short form merger. The court nonetheless held that he had standing to sue under Rule 10b-5:

> [O]nce the conditions for a short form merger had been achieved, appellant's rights in his own stock were frozen. He had and still has only the options of exchanging his stock *** pursuant to appellee's offer, or pursuing his right of appraisal, which would result in cash from appellee. *** Since, in order to realize any value for his stock, appellant must exchange the shares for money from appellee, as a practical matter appellant must eventually become a party to a "sale" *** [R]equiring him to do so as a condition to suit seems a needless formality.

Id. at 634. Lower courts are currently divided about whether the "forced seller" exception survives *Blue Chip Stamps*. Compare *7547 Corp. v. Parker & Parsley Dev. Partners, L.P.*, 38 F.3d 211, 229 (5th Cir. 1994) (exception survives) with *Isquith v. Caremark Int'l, Inc.*, 136 F.3d 531, 536 (7th Cir. 1998) (exception unlikely to have survived). What arguments support its survival? What arguments support its elimination?

4. ***De Facto Seller Exception.*** Likewise granted standing to sue under Rule 10b-5 prior to *Blue Chip Stamps* were "de facto sellers"—trust beneficiaries who alleged fraud in connection with trades made by their trustees. See, e.g., *James v. Gerber Prods. Co.*, 483 F.2d 944, 948-50 (6th Cir. 1973); *Heyman v. Heyman*, 356 F. Supp. 958, 965 (S.D.N.Y. 1973). Should the de facto seller exception survive *Blue Chip Stamps*?

5. ***The Section 29(b) Alternative.*** At least some plaintiffs who are unable to satisfy the purchaser-seller requirement may nonetheless be able to bring an action under Section 29(b) of the Exchange Act, which reads in pertinent part:

> Every contract made in violation of any provision of this Act or rule or regulation thereunder, and every contract *** the performance of which involves the violation of *** any provision of this Act or rule or regulation thereunder, shall be void ***.

According to the Supreme Court, this language "confers a 'right to rescind' a contract void under the criteria of the statute." *Transamerica Mortgage Advisors, Inc. v. Lewis*, 444 U.S. 11, 19 (1979), quoting *Mills v. Electric Auto-Lite Co.*, 396 U.S. 375, 388 (1970).

To obtain this right, the plaintiff must show that "(1) the contract involved a 'prohibited transaction,' (2) he is in contractual privity with the defendant, and (3) he is 'in the class of persons the Act was designed to protect.'" *Reg'l Props., Inc. v. Fin. & Real Estate Consulting Co.*, 678 F.2d 552, 559 (5th Cir. 1982). See generally Samuel H. Gruenbaum & Marc I. Steinberg, Section 29(b) of the Securities Exchange Act of 1934: A Viable Remedy Awakened, 48 Geo. Wash. L. Rev. 1 (1979). In *Regional*, the court found these elements satisfied by a real estate developer which wished to rescind its contracts with a securities broker for the marketing of limited partnerships. Because the broker had not complied with the Exchange Act's broker registration requirement, performance of the contracts constituted a "prohibited transaction." *Reg'l Props., Inc.*, 678 F. 2d at 561. The court held that the developer was within the class of people the Act was designed to protect even though he was not an investor:

> The statute does not in terms limit the class of persons who may invoke its contractual voidness provisions to investors. *** If a party to these contracts could not attack them, it would be yet more difficult to find reason to permit assault by the nonparty issuers and investors whom, according to *** [the defendant], the Act was designed to protect.

Id. at 561. Why couldn't the plaintiff in *Regional* have brought an action under Rule 10b-5 based on his contract?

### *PROBLEM 2-16*

Endring Corporation was a large publicly traded company with 3,000 employees and a longstanding track record of profitability. In 1990, the company's board of directors established the Endring Retirement Stock Fund. Employees were entitled to contribute a portion of their salaries to the Fund (which was invested exclusively in Endring stock) and they retained the right to liquidate their contributions in whole or in part whenever they chose to do so.

Last year, Endring assured the world in general and their employees in particular that the company was strong, its future bright. In reality, a small circle of senior executives were cooking the books to hide the fact that the company was in dire straits. Early this year, the truth about Endring emerged, and the market price of Endring stock plummeted to near zero. The numerous employees who had made contributions to the Fund were aghast that important information had been withheld from them. They have said that if they had known the company's actual situation, they would have liquidated their Fund accounts. Do they have standing to sue under Rule 10b-5?

### *PROBLEM 2-17*

Amy sent Dewey, her broker, a check to cover the cost of stock in several companies, all of which Dewey had told her were great investments. Amy's monthly statement from Dewey itemized these purchases, but the companies were in fact altogether fictitious. Amy has now discovered the fraud. Does she have standing to sue under Rule 10b-5? What about an action under Section 29(b)?

## F. CAUSATION

Rule 10b-5 has two causation requirements. One is the reliance requirement, also known as the transaction causation requirement or but/for causation. The other is the loss causation requirement, also known as proximate causation or simply as causation. Both causation requirements apply to private actions only and do not come into play in SEC or criminal actions.

### *1. The Reliance Requirement*

The reliance requirement focuses on whether the plaintiff relied on the defendant's fraud when buying or selling the securities in question. Courts imported the reliance requirement from tort law in order to restrict the implied private action. One court put it this way:

> [T]he aim of *** rule [10b-5] *** is to qualify *** the doctrine of caveat emptor—not to establish a scheme of investors' insurance. Assuredly, to abandon the requirement of reliance would be to facilitate *** proof of *** fraud ***. But this strikes us as an inadequate reason for reading out of the rule so basic an element of tort law as the principle of causation in fact.

*List v. Fashion Park, Inc.*, 340 F.2d 457, 463 (2d Cir. 1965). See, e.g., *Wilson v. Comtech Telecommunications Corp.*, 648 F.2d 88, 94 (2d Cir. 1981) (denying recovery to a plaintiff who relied on his broker's advice in making his purchases rather than on the defendant's fraud).

While upholding the reliance requirement, courts nonetheless grant plaintiffs presumptions of reliance under various circumstances. We examine (i) the *Affiliated Ute* presumption; (ii) the fraud-on-the-market presumption; and (iii) the fraud-created-the-market presumption. These presumptions facilitate class actions by eliminating the need for mini-trials on the reliance of each plaintiff, but apply equally to individual actions. We conclude our study of reliance by considering when the plaintiff must show that her reliance was justifiablc.

#### *a. The* Affiliated Ute *Presumption*

This presumption originated in the Supreme Court's decision in *Affiliated Ute Citizens v. United States*, 406 U.S. 128 (1972). In that case the plaintiffs, Native Americans of the Ute tribe, brought a Rule 10b-5 action against a bank and two bank employees. The bank served as the transfer agent for the stock of the corporation established to allocate tribal assets. The plaintiffs alleged that the defendants had purchased their shares without informing them that the stock was trading at a higher price in a secondary market that the defendants had established. The Court held that the plaintiffs could maintain their action without having to prove that they sold their shares in reliance on what the defendants had failed to tell them:

> The defendants may not stand mute while they facilitate the mixed-bloods' sales to those seeking to profit in the non-Indian market the defendants had developed and encouraged ***. The sellers had the right to know that the defendants were in a position to gain financially from their sales and that their shares were selling for a higher price in that market.
>
> Under the circumstances of this case, involving primarily a failure to disclose, positive proof of reliance is not a prerequisite to recovery. All that is

> necessary is that the facts withheld be material ***. This obligation to disclose and this withholding of a material fact establish the requisite element of causation in fact.

Id. at 153-54.

### *NOTES AND QUESTIONS*

1. ***Presumption?*** Did the Court give the plaintiffs a rebuttable presumption of reliance or did it hold that the "circumstances" conclusively established reliance as a matter of law? If it intended to create a rebuttable presumption, as is now universally assumed, why didn't it say so? Cf. *Chris-Craft Indus., Inc. v. Piper Aircraft Corp.*, 480 F.2d 341, 400 (2d Cir. 1973) (Mansfield, J., concurring and dissenting) (arguing that by failing to "expressly or impliedly speak in terms of a 'presumption,' " *Affiliated Ute* indicated that reliance had been established as a matter of law).

2. ***The "[C]ircumstances" to Which the Presumption Applies.*** What were the "circumstances" in *Affiliated Ute* that prompted the Court to spare the plaintiffs the necessity of proving reliance? According to some courts, the circumstances were that the defendants had a relationship with the plaintiffs that was akin to a fiduciary duty and that the defendants and the plaintiffs dealt with each other face-to-face. See, e.g., *Laventhall v. Gen. Dynamics Corp.*, 704 F.2d 407, 413 n. 4 (8th Cir. 1983). Most courts, however, have focused on the fact that an omission rather than a misrepresentation was principally at issue. The rationale for a presumption in the case of an omission (unstated by *Affiliated Ute*) is said to be the "impossibility" of proving reliance on the absence of something. See, e.g., *Grubb v. FDIC*, 868 F.2d 1151, 1163 (10th Cir. 1989). Is it truly so much easier to prove reliance on a misrepresentation? Does the presumption apply in cases in which omissions and misrepresentations are both present? Consider these questions in connection with the next case.

---

## BINDER v. GILLESPIE

184 F.3d 1059 (9th Cir. 1999)

SKOPIL, CIRCUIT JUDGE:

Albert Binder brought this action against Aqua Vie Beverage Corporation (AVBC), various AVBC officers and directors, and the accounting firm of Deloitte & Touche (Deloitte), asserting, on his own behalf and as a representative for a class of investors, that defendants violated federal and state securities laws. The district court decertified the class and declined to exercise supplemental jurisdiction over the related state law class claims. *** Final judgments were entered pursuant to Federal Rule of Civil Procedure 54(b). We affirm.

Tom Gillespie and Marie Mullen Gillespie formed AVBC in 1991 by purchasing a publicly owned shell corporation and merging it with their Hawaii-based beverage company, KWC, Inc. They moved their operations to Sun Valley, Idaho. Shortly thereafter, Diane Karban joined the company as Chief Financial Officer and Deloitte was hired as the company's accounting firm. AVBC stock soon began trading publicly on the over-the-counter (OTC) market.

In the summer of 1991, Cottell Bottling agreed to manufacture, and Golden Brands agreed to distribute, AVBC's product—"lightly flavored," noncarbonated spring water. Industry publications touted AVBC as a promising, if speculative, investment, and AVBC stock sold for $2.75 per share by August. On September 24, 1991, Binder purchased 3000 shares at $4.00 per share. A month later, AVBC's bid price reached its peak at $4.50 per share.

AVBC began production in 1992. Chief of quality control John Good, however, warned CEO Tom Gillespie and consultant Gordon Sim that there was instability in the product formula. Sixty days after it was bottled, the water turned brown. AVBC adjusted the formula but continued to experience problems with the product's shelf life. By the end of the year, AVBC was forced to repurchase the defective water from Golden Brands, which eventually resigned as AVBC's distributor and sued for past-due debts.

In 1993, AVBC struggled to raise funds and to establish a distribution network for its product. On December 29, 1993, Binder sold his 3000 shares at less than one dollar per share. In 1994, AVBC suspended operations, and Binder filed this action. *** In February 1995, the action against AVBC was stayed pending Chapter 11 bankruptcy proceedings. ***

The district court reasoned that the class would have to satisfy the reliance element through a presumption; otherwise individual questions of reliance would predominate over questions common to the class. See Fed. R. Civ. P. 23(b)(3); *Basic Inc. v. Levinson,* 485 U.S. 224, 242 (1988) (noting that individualized proof of reliance by each class member would preclude a class action). The court concluded that no presumption was available under the facts of the case, and, accordingly, decertified the class[.] ***

Binder argues that the class is eligible for a presumption of reliance pursuant to *Affiliated Ute Citizens v. United States,* 406 U.S. 128, 153-54 (1972). Such a presumption is generally available to plaintiffs alleging violations of section 10(b) based on omissions of material fact. The district court, however, characterized Binder's action as "not primarily an omissions case" and held that the *Affiliated Ute* presumption was unavailable. We agree with the district court's characterization of Binder's action. Binder's complaint contains both allegations of omissions and misrepresentations, and at the very least, must be characterized, as the district court noted, as "a mixed case of misstatements and omissions."

We have applied the *Affiliated Ute* presumption to cases that "are, or can be, cast in omission or non-disclosure terms." *Blackie v. Barrack,* 524 F.2d 891, 905 (9th Cir.1975). We have not squarely decided, however, whether the presumption may be invoked in a case involving misrepresentations or both omissions and misrepresentations. Nevertheless, in *Blackie,* we embraced the presumption because of the difficulty of proving "a speculative negative"—that the plaintiff relied on what was not said. *Blackie,* 524 F.2d at 908. This suggests to us that *Affiliated Ute* should be confined to cases that primarily allege omissions.

Most circuits have limited the presumption accordingly. A handful of circuits have addressed mixed cases, concluding that the preferred approach is to do as the magistrate judge did here and "analytically characterize [the] action as either primarily a nondisclosure case (which would make the presumption applicable), or a positive misrepresentation case." *Finkel v. Docutel/Olivetti Corp.*, 817 F.2d 356, 359 (5th Cir.1987); see also *Austin v. Loftsgaarden*, 675 F.2d 168, 178 n. 21 (8th Cir.1982).

We agree with these circuits that the *Affiliated Ute* presumption should not be applied to cases that allege both misstatements and omissions unless the case can be characterized as one that primarily alleges omissions. *** Accordingly, we agree with the district court that Binder's plaintiff class is not entitled to the *Affiliated Ute* presumption of reliance. ***

REINHARDT, CIRCUIT JUDGE, DISSENTING IN PART:

Because the plaintiffs are entitled to a presumption of reliance under the doctrine of *Affiliated Ute Citizens v. United States*, 406 U.S. 128, 153-54 (1972), I would reverse the district court's decision to decertify the class of investors represented by Binder. I therefore respectfully dissent.

In today's decision, the majority decides that the *Affiliated Ute* presumption does not apply to cases involving both material misrepresentations and material omissions, "unless the case can be characterized as one that primarily alleges omissions." In so holding, the majority resolves a question that we have previously, and explicitly, reserved: "whether *Affiliated Ute Citizens* applies equally to misrepresentations." *Kramas v. Security Gas & Oil, Inc.*, 672 F.2d 766, 769 n. 2 (9th Cir.1982). To reach this conclusion, the majority simply adopts the procedure followed by two other circuits. See *Finkel v. Docutel/Olivetti Corp.*, 817 F.2d 356, 359 (5th Cir.1987); *Cavalier Carpets, Inc. v. Caylor*, 746 F.2d 749, 756 (11th Cir.1984). Those circuits have determined that, in mixed cases, it is necessary to "analytically characterize [the] action as either primarily a nondisclosure case ... or a positive misrepresentation case." *Finkel*, 817 F.2d at 359. I believe, however, that the logic behind the *Affiliated Ute* decision and the reasoning contained in our decisions implementing *Affiliated Ute* make it clear that the presumption applies equally to misrepresentations, and that it is irrelevant whether the case is primarily a misrepresentations case or primarily an omissions case. In either event, the plaintiff is entitled to a presumption of reliance.

In *Blackie v. Barrack*, 524 F.2d 891, 908 (9th Cir.1975), on which the majority relies, we examined a material omissions case in which the plaintiff bought stock based in part on material omissions made by the defendant. We examined the *Affiliated Ute* rule and concluded that the *Blackie* plaintiffs did not need to prove reliance. We explained that such proof would require "proof of a speculative negative." Id. In other words, to establish reliance, the plaintiff would have to prove the following proposition: "I would not have bought had I known." Id. We rejected such a requirement because:

> Direct proof would inevitably be somewhat pro-forma, and impose a difficult evidentiary burden, because addressed to a speculative possibility in an area where motivations are complex and difficult to determine.... Here, the requirement [of proving reliance] is redundant—the same causal nexus can be adequately established indirectly, by proof of materiality coupled with the common sense that a stock purchaser does not ordinarily seek to purchase a loss in the form of artificially inflated stock.

Id. Because *Blackie* was a pure omissions case, we did not have occasion to determine whether the same reasoning would apply to material misrepresentations.

One year later, however, in *Little v. First California Co.*, 532 F.2d 1302, 1305 n. 4 (9th Cir.1976), we stated the rather obvious proposition that "[t]he categories of 'omission' and 'misrepresentation' are not mutually exclusive." As we wrote:

> All misrepresentations are also nondisclosures, at least to the extent that there is a failure to disclose which facts in the representation are not true. Thus, the failure to report an expense item on an income statement, when such a failure is material in the *Affiliated Ute* sense, can be characterized as (a) an omission of a material expense item, (b) a misrepresentation of income, or (c) both.

Id. This observation, besides being binding upon us as a matter of law, is clearly correct as a matter of logic. Omissions and misrepresentations both deprive the investor of truthful information relevant to the investment decision, and both result in the artificial pricing of a stock.

Most important for our purposes here, it is *equally* difficult to establish reliance on a misrepresentation and on an omission. While a plaintiff in an omissions case—absent the *Affiliated Ute* presumption—would bear the daunting task of proving 'I would not have bought/sold had I known what you failed to tell me' see *Blackie,* 524 F.2d at 908, the plaintiff in a misrepresentation case bears the equally daunting burden of proving 'I would not have bought/sold had I known what you failed to tell me; namely, the truth.' In either case, the plaintiff must prove that he would have acted differently if he had known something that he did not actually know, i.e., the full truth.

In an omissions case, the plaintiff does not know the truth because the defendant said nothing; in a misrepresentations case the plaintiff does not know the truth because the defendant lied. But as far as the plaintiff's ability to demonstrate reliance, this is a distinction without a difference. In either case, the plaintiff must attempt to prove that he would have acted differently had he known the truth. The evidentiary burden is therefore equally difficult in either case, and there is no logical reason to afford the presumption of reliance to plaintiffs in omissions cases but not in misrepresentations cases. The rule we announced in *Blackie,* that the "causal nexus can be adequately established indirectly, by proof of materiality coupled with the common sense that a stock purchaser does not ordinarily seek to purchase a loss in the form of artificially inflated stock," id., applies with equal force of logic to misrepresentations. ***

*** I would therefore hold that plaintiffs in mixed cases are entitled to the *Affiliated Ute* presumption of reliance whether the case is primarily an omissions case or primarily a misrepresentations case. Accordingly, whether this case is properly classified simply as a mixed omissions and misrepresentations case, or as "primarily" a misrepresentations case, I would hold that the

Binder class was entitled to a presumption of reliance, and would therefore reverse the decertification of the class.[3]

## *NOTES AND QUESTIONS*

1. ***"Primarily Alleg[ing] Omissions."*** *Binder* concluded that the *Affiliated Ute* presumption applies only when the complaint "primarily alleges omissions." In deciding whether this standard has been satisfied, must the court take the complaint at face value? Cf. *Cavalier Carpets, Inc. v. Caylor*, 746 F.2d 749, 757 (11th Cir. 1984) (noting that the complaint alleged three omissions and three misrepresentations and therefore was "not primarily an omission case"). If so, what impact is such an approach likely to have on the drafting of complaints?

2. ***An Alternative Approach.*** Instead of taking the complaint at face value, consider the approach taken in *Sharp v. Coopers & Lybrand,* 649 F.2d 175 (3d Cir. 1981). In *Sharp,* plaintiffs challenged as fraudulent an accounting firm's tax opinion letter issued in connection with the sale of limited partnerships offered by Westmoreland Minerals Corp. (WMC). Acknowledging that the letter contained both omissions and misrepresentations, the court found the *Affiliated Ute* presumption applicable based on the following reasoning:

> We conclude that the proper approach *** is to analyze the plaintiff's allegations, in light of the likely proof at trial, and determine the most reasonable placement of the burden of proof of reliance. ***
>
> We agree with the district court that the burden in this case should fall on Coopers & Lybrand. The opinion letter issued by Coopers & Lybrand was intended to influence the investment decisions of persons interested in WMC partnerships. *** [Coopers & Lybrand] undoubtedly foresaw that it would have that effect. As in *Affiliated Ute,* Coopers & Lybrand by its action facilitated the transactions at issue but failed to disclose certain facts. Its misrepresentation of other facts should not alleviate its burden of proving nonreliance.

Id. at 188-89. What are the advantages and disadvantages of the *Sharp* approach?

3. ***The Dual Instruction Possibility.*** Rather than attempting to determine whether a complaint "primarily alleges omissions," a court could simply instruct the jury to presume reliance when it comes to the omission claims but to require proof of reliance when it comes to the misrepresentation claims. Is this approach preferable to those identified in notes 1 and 2?

4. ***Misrepresentations Alone.*** The dissenting opinion in *Binder* supports a presumption of reliance even in cases in which the plaintiffs allege only misrepresentations. Do you agree? How likely is it that the stated disagreements between the dissenting and the majority opinions mask unstated disagreements about the value of private securities actions?

---

3. A different question, one not presented here, is whether plaintiffs are entitled to a presumption of reliance in pure misrepresentation cases. *** In light of the logic of *Affiliated Ute,* and for the reasons I have outlined above, I would hold (were I called upon to reach the question) that plaintiffs are entitled to a presumption of reliance even in pure misrepresentation cases.

### *PROBLEM 2-18*

Healthy Foods, Inc. produces frozen vegetarian entrees for sale in grocery stores. Its brochures seek to lure new investors with the statement that "our research department is always in the process of developing multiple new entrees." In fact, its research "department" consists of one person who focuses on one new entree project at a time, while simultaneously considering which of many other new projects he will move to next. Kim received a Healthy Foods brochure in the mail and thereafter bought stock in the company. She now wishes to bring a Rule 10b-5 action that challenges the brochure as fraudulent. Would she be entitled to a presumption of reliance based on *Affiliated Ute*?

*b. The Fraud-on-the-Market Presumption*

## BASIC INC. v. LEVINSON

485 U.S. 224 (1988)

JUSTICE BLACKMUN:

[*The facts of this case were set out supra in Section B.2 of this Chapter in the discussion of materiality. In brief, the plaintiffs brought a class action against Basic Inc., the shares of which were listed on the New York Stock Exchange. At issue were Basic's three public statements denying that it was involved in merger negotiations. After holding those denials to have been material misstatements, the Court turned to reliance and fraud-on-the-market.*]

IV

A

We turn to the question of reliance and the fraud-on-the-market theory. Succinctly put:

> The fraud-on-the-market theory is based on the hypothesis that, in an open and developed securities market, the price of a company's stock is determined by the available material information regarding the company and its business.... Misleading statements will therefore defraud purchasers of stock even if the purchasers do not directly rely on the misstatements.... The causal connection between the defendants' fraud and the plaintiffs' purchase of stock in such a case is no less significant than in a case of direct reliance on misrepresentations."

*Peil v. Speiser,* 806 F.2d 1154, 1160-1161 (CA3 1986). Our task, of course, is not to assess the general validity of the theory, but to consider whether it was proper for the courts below to apply a rebuttable presumption of reliance, supported in part by the fraud-on-the-market theory.

This case required resolution of several common questions of law and fact concerning the falsity or misleading nature of the three public statements made by Basic, the presence or absence of scienter, and the materiality of the misrepresentations, if any. In their amended complaint, the named plaintiffs alleged that in reliance on Basic's statements they sold their shares of Basic stock in the depressed market created by petitioners. *** Requiring proof of individualized reliance from each member of the proposed plaintiff class effectively would have prevented respondents from proceeding with a class action, since individual issues then would have overwhelmed the common ones.

The District Court found that the presumption of reliance created by the fraud-on-the-market theory provided "a practical resolution to the problem of balancing the substantive requirement of proof of reliance in securities cases against the procedural requisites of [Federal Rule of Civil Procedure] 23." The District Court thus concluded that with reference to each public statement and its impact upon the open market for Basic shares, common questions predominated over individual questions, as required by Federal Rules of Civil Procedure 23(a)(2) and (b)(3).

Petitioners and their *amici* complain that the fraud-on-the-market theory effectively eliminates the requirement that a plaintiff asserting a claim under Rule 10b-5 prove reliance. They note that reliance is and long has been an element of common-law fraud, see, e.g., Restatement (Second) of Torts § 525 (1977); Prosser and Keeton on Law of Torts § 108 (5th ed. 1984), and argue that because the analogous express right of action includes a reliance requirement, see, e.g., § 18(a) of the 1934 Act, so too must an action implied under § 10(b).

We agree that reliance is an element of a Rule 10b-5 cause of action. See *Ernst & Ernst v. Hochfelder,* 425 U.S. [196, 206 (1976)] (quoting Senate Report). Reliance provides the requisite causal connection between a defendant's misrepresentation and a plaintiff's injury. See, e.g., *Wilson v. Comtech Telecommunications Corp.,* 648 F.2d 88, 92 (CA2 1981); *List v. Fashion Park, Inc.,* 340 F.2d 457, 462 (CA2 1965). There is, however, more than one way to demonstrate the causal connection. Indeed, we previously have dispensed with a requirement of positive proof of reliance, where a duty to disclose material information had been breached, concluding that the necessary nexus between the plaintiffs' injury and the defendant's wrongful conduct had been established. See *Affiliated Ute Citizens v. United States,* 406 U.S. [128, 153-154 (1972)]. Similarly, we did not require proof that material omissions or misstatements in a proxy statement decisively affected voting, because the proxy solicitation itself, rather than the defect in the solicitation materials, served as an essential link in the transaction. See *Mills v. Electric Auto-Lite Co.,* 396 U.S. 375, 384-385 (1970).

The modern securities markets, literally involving millions of shares changing hands daily, differ from the face-to-face transactions contemplated by early fraud cases,[21] and our understanding of Rule 10b-5's reliance requirement must encompass these differences.[22]

---

21. Prosser and Keeton on Law of Torts 726 (5th ed. 1984) ("The reasons for the separate development of [the tort action for misrepresentation and nondisclosure], and for its peculiar limitations, are in part historical, and in part connected with the fact that in the great majority of the cases which have come before the courts the misrepresentations have been made in the course of a bargaining transaction between the parties. Consequently the action has been colored to a considerable extent by the ethics of bargaining between distrustful adversaries") (footnote omitted).

22. Actions under Rule 10b-5 are distinct from common-law deceit and misrepresentation claims, see *Blue Chip Stamps v. Manor Drug Stores,* 421 U.S. 723, 744-745 (1975), and are in part designed to add to the protections provided investors by the common law, see *Herman & MacLean v. Huddleston,* 459 U.S. 375, 388-389 (1983).

> In face-to-face transactions, the inquiry into an investor's reliance upon information is into the subjective pricing of that information by that investor. With the presence of a market, the market is interposed between seller and buyer and, ideally, transmits information to the investor in the processed form of a market price. Thus the market is performing a substantial part of the valuation process performed by the investor in a face-to-face transaction. The market is acting as the unpaid agent of the investor, informing him that given all the information available to it, the value of the stock is worth the market price.

*In re LTV Securities Litigation,* 88 F.R.D. 134, 143 (ND Tex.1980).

B

Presumptions typically serve to assist courts in managing circumstances in which direct proof, for one reason or another, is rendered difficult. The courts below accepted a presumption, created by the fraud-on-the-market theory and subject to rebuttal by petitioners, that persons who had traded Basic shares had done so in reliance on the integrity of the price set by the market, but because of petitioners' material misrepresentations that price had been fraudulently depressed. Requiring a plaintiff to show a speculative state of facts, i.e., how he would have acted if omitted material information had been disclosed, see *Affiliated Ute Citizens v. United States,* 406 U.S., at 153-154, or if the misrepresentation had not been made, see *Sharp v. Coopers & Lybrand,* 649 F.2d 175, 188 (CA3 1981), would place an unnecessarily unrealistic evidentiary burden on the Rule 10b-5 plaintiff who has traded on an impersonal market. Cf. *Mills v. Electric Auto-Lite Co.,* 396 U.S., at 385.

Arising out of considerations of fairness, public policy, and probability, as well as judicial economy, presumptions are also useful devices for allocating the burdens of proof between parties. The presumption of reliance employed in this case is consistent with, and, by facilitating Rule 10b-5 litigation, supports, the congressional policy embodied in the 1934 Act. In drafting that Act, Congress expressly relied on the premise that securities markets are affected by information, and enacted legislation to facilitate an investor's reliance on the integrity of those markets:

> No investor, no speculator, can safely buy and sell securities upon the exchanges without having an intelligent basis for forming his judgment as to the value of the securities he buys or sells. The idea of a free and open public market is built upon the theory that competing judgments of buyers and sellers as to the fair price of a security brings *[sic]* about a situation where the market price reflects as nearly as possible a just price. Just as artificial manipulation tends to upset the true function of an open market, so the hiding and secreting of important information obstructs the operation of the markets as indices of real value. H.R.Rep. No. 1383, at 11.

The presumption is also supported by common sense and probability. Recent empirical studies have tended to confirm Congress' premise that the market price of shares traded on well-developed markets reflects all publicly available information, and, hence, any material misrepresentations.[24] It has been noted that "it is hard to imagine that there ever is a buyer or seller who does not rely on market integrity. Who would knowingly roll the dice in a crooked crap game?" *Schlanger v. Four-Phase Systems Inc.,* 555 F.Supp. 535, 538 (SDNY 1982). Indeed, nearly every court that has considered the proposition has concluded that where materially misleading statements have been disseminated into an impersonal, well-developed market for securities, the reliance of individual plaintiffs on the integrity of the market price may be presumed.[25] Commentators generally have applauded the adoption of one variation or another of the fraud-on-the-market theory.[26] An investor who buys or sells stock at the price set by the market does so in reliance on the integrity of that price. Because most publicly available information is reflected in market price, an investor's reliance on any public material misrepresentations, therefore, may be presumed for purposes of a Rule 10b-5 action.

C

The Court of Appeals found that petitioners "made public, material misrepresentations and [respondents] sold Basic stock in an impersonal, efficient market. Thus the class, as defined by the district court, has established the threshold facts for proving their loss." The court acknowledged that petitioners may rebut proof of the elements giving rise to the presumption, or show that the misrepresentation in fact did not lead to a distortion of price or that an individual plaintiff traded or would have traded despite his knowing the statement was false.

Any showing that severs the link between the alleged misrepresentation and either the price received (or paid) by the plaintiff, or his decision to trade at a fair market price, will be sufficient to rebut the presumption of reliance. For example, if petitioners could show that the "market makers" were privy to the truth about the merger discussions here with Combustion, and thus that the market price would not have been affected by their misrepresentations, the

---

**24.** See *In re LTV Securities Litigation,* 88 F.R.D. 134, 144 (ND Tex.1980) (citing studies); Fischel, Use of Modern Finance Theory in Securities Fraud Cases Involving Actively Traded Securities, 38 Bus. Law. 1, 4, n. 9 (1982) (citing literature on efficient-capital-market theory); Dennis, Materiality and the Efficient Capital Market Model: A Recipe for the Total Mix, 25 Wm. & Mary L. Rev. 373, 374-381, and n. 1 (1984). We need not determine by adjudication what economists and social scientists have debated through the use of sophisticated statistical analysis and the application of economic theory. For purposes of accepting the presumption of reliance in this case, we need only believe that market professionals generally consider most publicly announced material statements about companies, thereby affecting stock market prices.

**25.** See, e.g. *Peil v. Speiser,* 806 F.2d 1154, 1161 (CA3 1986); *Blackie v. Barrack,* 524 F.2d 891, 905-908 (CA9 1975).

**26.** See, e.g., Black, Fraud on the Market: A Criticism of Dispensing with Reliance Requirements in Certain Open Market Transactions, 62 N.C. L. Rev. 435 (1984); Note, The Fraud-on-the-Market Theory, 95 Harv. L. Rev. 1143 (1982); Note, Fraud on the Market: An Emerging Theory of Recovery Under SEC Rule 10b-5, 50 Geo. Wash. L. Rev. 627 (1982).

causal connection could be broken: the basis for finding that the fraud had been transmitted through market price would be gone.[28] Similarly, if, despite petitioners' allegedly fraudulent attempt to manipulate market price, news of the merger discussions credibly entered the market and dissipated the effects of the misstatements, those who traded Basic shares after the corrective statements would have no direct or indirect connection with the fraud.[29] Petitioners also could rebut the presumption of reliance as to plaintiffs who would have divested themselves of their Basic shares without relying on the integrity of the market. For example, a plaintiff who believed that Basic's statements were false and that Basic was indeed engaged in merger discussions, and who consequently believed that Basic stock was artificially underpriced, but sold his shares nevertheless because of other unrelated concerns, e.g., potential antitrust problems, or political pressures to divest from shares of certain businesses, could not be said to have relied on the integrity of a price he knew had been manipulated. ***

JUSTICE WHITE, WITH WHOM JUSTICE O'CONNOR JOINS, CONCURRING IN PART AND DISSENTING IN PART:

*** I dissent *** because I do not agree that the "fraud-on-the-market" theory should be applied in this case. ***

Even when compared to the relatively youthful private cause-of-action under § 10(b), see *Kardon v. National Gypsum Co.*, 69 F.Supp. 512 (E.D. Pa. 1946), the fraud-on-the-market theory is a mere babe. Yet today, the Court embraces this theory with the sweeping confidence usually reserved for more mature legal doctrines. In so doing, I fear that the Court's decision may have many adverse, unintended effects as it is applied and interpreted in the years to come. ***

*** Even if I agreed with the Court that "modern securities markets ... involving millions of shares changing hands daily" require that the "understanding of Rule 10b-5's reliance requirement" be changed, I prefer that such changes come from Congress in amending § 10(b). The Congress, with its superior resources and expertise, is far better equipped than the federal courts for the task of determining how modern economic theory and global financial markets require that established legal notions of fraud be modified. In choosing to make these decisions itself, the Court, I fear, embarks on a course that it does not genuinely understand, giving rise to consequences it cannot foresee. ***

---

28. By accepting this rebuttable presumption, we do not intend conclusively to adopt any particular theory of how quickly and completely publicly available information is reflected in market price. Furthermore, our decision today is not to be interpreted as addressing the proper measure of damages in litigation of this kind.

29. We note there may be a certain incongruity between the assumption that Basic shares are traded on a well-developed, efficient, and information-hungry market, and the allegation that such a market could remain misinformed, and its valuation of Basic shares depressed, for 14 months, on the basis of the three public statements. Proof of that sort is a matter for trial, throughout which the District Court retains the authority to amend the certification order as may be appropriate. ***

At the bottom of the Court's conclusion that the fraud-on-the-market theory sustains a presumption of reliance is the assumption that individuals rely "on the integrity of the market price" when buying or selling stock in "impersonal, well-developed market[s] for securities." Even if I was prepared to accept (as a matter of common sense or general understanding) the assumption that most persons buying or selling stock do so in response to the market price, the fraud-on-the-market theory goes further. For in adopting a "presumption of reliance," the Court *also* assumes that buyers and sellers rely—not just on the market price—but on the "*integrity* " of that price. It is this aspect of the fraud-on-the-market hypothesis which most mystifies me.

To define the term "integrity of the market price," the majority quotes approvingly from cases which suggest that investors are entitled to "'rely on the price of a stock as a reflection of its value.'" Ante (quoting *Peil v. Speiser,* 806 F.2d 1154, 1161 (CA3 1986)). But the meaning of this phrase eludes me, for it implicitly suggests that stocks have some "true value" that is measurable by a standard other than their market price. While the scholastics of medieval times professed a means to make such a valuation of a commodity's "worth," I doubt that the federal courts of our day are similarly equipped.

Even if securities had some "value"—knowable and distinct from the market price of a stock—investors do not always share the Court's presumption that a stock's price is a "reflection of [this] value." Indeed, "many investors purchase or sell stock because they believe the price *inaccurately* reflects the corporation's worth." See Black, Fraud on the Market: A Criticism of Dispensing with Reliance Requirements in Certain Open Market Transactions, 62 N.C.L.Rev. 435, 455 (1984) (emphasis added). If investors really believed that stock prices reflected a stock's "value," many sellers would never sell, and many buyers never buy (given the time and cost associated with executing a stock transaction). As we recognized just a few years ago: "[I]nvestors act on inevitably incomplete or inaccurate information, [consequently] there are always winners and losers; but those who have 'lost' have not necessarily been defrauded." *Dirks v. SEC,* 463 U.S. 646, 667, n. 27 (1983). Yet today, the Court allows investors to recover who can show little more than that they sold stock at a lower price than what might have been.[7]

I do not propose that the law retreat from the many protections that § 10(b) and Rule 10b-5, as interpreted in our prior cases, provide to investors.

---

7. This is what the Court's rule boils down to in practical terms. For while, in theory, the Court allows for rebuttal of its "presumption of reliance"—a proviso with which I agree, in practice the Court must realize, as other courts applying the fraud-on-the-market theory have, that such rebuttal is virtually impossible in all but the most extraordinary case. See *Blackie v. Barrack,* 524 F.2d, at 906-907, n. 22; *In re LTV Securities Litigation,* 88 F.R.D. 134, 143, n. 4 (ND Tex.1980).

Consequently, while the Court considers it significant that the fraud-on-the-market presumption it endorses is a rebuttable one, the majority's implicit rejection of the "pure causation" fraud-on-the-market theory rings hollow. In most cases, the Court's theory will operate just as the causation theory would, creating a nonrebuttable presumption of "reliance" in future Rule 10b-5 actions.

But any extension of these laws, to approach something closer to an investor insurance scheme, should come from Congress, and not from the courts. ***

And who will pay the judgments won in such actions? I suspect that all too often the majority's rule will "lead to large judgments, payable in the last analysis by innocent investors, for the benefit of speculators and their lawyers." Cf. *SEC v. Texas Gulf Sulphur Co.*, 401 F.2d 833, 867 (CA2 1968) (en banc) (Friendly, J., concurring). This Court and others have previously recognized that "inexorably broadening ... the class of plaintiff[s] who may sue in this area of the law will ultimately result in more harm than good." *Blue Chip Stamps v. Manor Drug Stores*, supra, at 747-748. See also *Ernst & Ernst v. Hochfelder*, 425 U.S., at 214. Yet such a bitter harvest is likely to be reaped from the seeds sewn by the Court's decision today. ***

## *NOTES AND QUESTIONS*

*1.* ***The Truth-on-the-Market Defense.*** *Basic* says that defendants can rebut the fraud-on-the-market presumption by proving that truthful information on the matter in question "credibly entered the market and dissipated the effects of the misstatements." Apple Computer succeeded in making such a rebuttal (sometimes known as the truth-on-the-market defense) in an action claiming that it had defrauded the market with respect to its Lisa computer:

> The press portrayed Lisa as a gamble, with the potential for either enormous success or enormous failure. At least twenty articles stressed the risks Apple was taking, and detailed the underlying problems producing those risks. Many of the optimistic statements challenged by plaintiffs appeared in those same articles, essentially bracketed by the facts which plaintiffs claim Apple wrongfully failed to disclose. The market could not have been made more aware of Lisa's risks.

*In re Apple Computer Sec. Litig.*, 886 F.2d 1109, 1116 (9th Cir. 1989). But cf. *Kaplan v. Rose*, 49 F.3d 1363, 1377 (9th Cir. 1995) (rebuttal of the presumption did not succeed where the articles submitted by the defendant "came from obscure sources, and only a few mention any specific problems"). Successful rebuttals are quite rare. See Elliott J. Weiss & John S. Beckerman, Let the Money Do the Monitoring: How Institutional Investors Can Reduce Agency Costs in Securities Class Actions, 104 Yale L. J. 2053, 2076 (1995). Why would this be so? Does the rarity of successful rebuttals suggest that the fraud-on-the-market presumption in effect gives us the scheme of investors' insurance that the reliance requirement was created to avoid?

*2.* ***Rebuttals as to Specific Plaintiffs.*** *Basic* also says that defendants can rebut the presumption for those plaintiffs who bought or sold "without relying on the integrity of the market." See, e.g., *Gurary v. Winehouse*, 1998 WL 54641 (S.DN.Y. 1998) (a company insider supplied the plaintiff with the information unknown to the market), aff'd in part, vac. on other grounds, 190 F.3d 37, 44 (2d Cir. 1999). Can a defendant rebut by showing that the plaintiff sold her stock because she was desperate for money? See generally Barbara Black, The Strange Case of Fraud on the Market: A Label in Search of a Theory, 52 Alb. L. Rev. 923 (1988).

*3. The Necessity of an Efficient Market.* The fraud-on-the-market presumption applies only when the securities in question are traded in an efficient market. Is it good policy to withhold the presumption from investors who purchased securities traded in inefficient markets and thereby impede the ability of these investors to bring class actions?

In order to obtain the presumption, the plaintiff must establish the efficiency of the market in which the securities were traded. To determine whether the plaintiff has met this burden, a number of courts look to the following five factors:

> first, whether the stock trades at a high weekly volume; second, whether securities analysts follow and report on the stock; third, whether the stock has market makers and arbitrageurs; fourth, whether the company is eligible to file SEC registration form S-3, as opposed to S-1 or S-2; and fifth, whether there are "empirical facts showing a cause and effect relationship between unexpected corporate events or financial releases and an immediate response in the stock price."

*Binder v. Gillespie*, 184 F.3d 1059, 1065 (9th Cir. 1999) (quoting *Cammer v. Bloom*, 711 F. Supp. 1264, 1286-87 (D.N.J. 1989)). In applying these factors, what questions are apt to arise? Why didn't the *Basic* plaintiffs have difficulty in proving market efficiency?

*4. Inattentive Investors.* One of the main goals of the federal securities laws is to compel disclosure of information and thereby to equip investors to make well-grounded decisions. Yet plaintiffs can invoke the fraud-on-the-market presumption regardless of whether they have read the documents they challenge as fraudulent. Would it be better to limit use of the presumption to those who have done the reading?

**5. Blue Chip Stamps *Revisited.*** Recall from Section E of this Chapter the Supreme Court's decision in *Blue Chip Stamps v. Manor Drug Stores*, 421 U.S. 723 (1975), which upheld the purchaser-seller requirement. *Blue Chip Stamps*, you will remember, lamented the vexatiousness of private Rule 10b-5 litigation. Does the fraud-on-the-market presumption upheld in *Basic* have the tendency to promote vexatious litigation? If so, what accounts for the *Basic* Court's seeming lack of concern about this matter?

*6. Four Justices Only.* Justice Blackmun's opinion for the Court on fraud-on-the-market was joined only by Justices Brennan, Marshall, and Stevens. Justices Rehnquist, Scalia, and Kennedy played no role in *Basic*. What significance should be attached to the fact that only four members of the Court endorsed the fraud-on-the-market presumption?

*7. The Role of Congress.* Do you agree with Justice White that the decision about whether to adopt the fraud-on-the-market presumption should have been left to Congress? In the course of enacting the PSLRA, Congress at least contemplated overturning *Basic*. What about *Basic* do you suppose generated congressional concern? Why do you suppose that Congress decided against overturning the decision?

### *PROBLEM 2-19*

After scrutinizing all available public information regarding Spotlight, Inc., investor Boris Box decided that the company's stock was overvalued. He based this decision on the company's earnings coupled with the threat posed by the competition. He became a short seller—selling shares of Spotlight he did not own (borrowed from a broker) and gambling that he would make money on his eventual obligatory purchase when the price went down. After Box's short sale, Spotlight issued a fraudulent press release that misrepresented the company's earnings and competitive situation. The effect was to artificially inflate the stock price. After a number of months, the price climbed higher than ever. Seeking to cut his losses, Box made the purchase required by his short position and in so doing lost $50,000. Thereafter, as the result of more accurate information distributed by Spotlight, the stock price tumbled. If Box sued Spotlight under Rule 10b-5, is he entitled to the fraud-on-the-market presumption?

Cf. *Zlotnick v. TIE Communications, Inc.*, 836 F.2d 818 (3d Cir. 1988).

---

As you read the following decision, consider how the presumption which it upholds differs from the presumption upheld by *Basic.*

## PANZIRER v. WOLF

663 F.2d 365 (2d Cir. 1981)

LUMBARD, CIRCUIT JUDGE:

Allied Artists Industries, Inc., issued an allegedly false annual report in August 1978. Zelda Panzirer purchased Allied stock thereafter upon reading an article in The Wall Street Journal. She never saw the annual report. When Allied started bankruptcy proceedings in 1979, she sued Allied officers and Price Waterhouse & Co., Allied's accountants, under § 10(b) and Rule 10b-5 ***. The district court, per Motley, J., dismissed Zelda Panzirer's suit on summary judgment ***. We reverse ***. Plaintiff relied on an article in The Wall Street Journal which she claims would have presented the company in a less favorable light had the annual report been accurate. She has stated a causal connection between her loss and the annual report which, on this record, cannot be dismissed on summary judgment. ***

On this appeal from summary judgment, the allegations of the complaint, as supplemented by plaintiff's deposition and numerous affidavits submitted by all parties, describe the story of Zelda Panzirer's losing investment in Allied common stock. She read about Allied in The Wall Street Journal while driving up to Vermont on September 29, 1978. The "Heard on the Street" column in that day's Journal covered the video cassette market, and devoted two paragraphs to Allied:

> Several analysts contend that Allied Artists is in a good position to take advantage of the growing demand for video tapes, having pioneered the development of pre-recorded cassettes.
>
> Andrew G. Racz of Philips, Appel & Walden, Inc. says Allied Artists, besides having a head start in video tapes and cassettes, is negotiating with TV

> networks, other film producers and makers of educational films to put their films on video cassettes. "The educational and informational area constitutes a tremendous market for video cassettes," says Mr. Racz, adding: "We continue to be bullish on Allied Artists. It's an attractive turn-around situation."

Zelda Panzirer had been a substitute school teacher. The item on the educational use of video cassettes caught her eye. She checked the price of Allied common stock, which was listed on the American Stock Exchange and had traded at between $5 and $6 1/8 on September 28. Her husband Leo Panzirer stopped the car. Zelda Panzirer called her broker, Michael Blum, at E. F. Hutton's office in Hackensack, N.J. She asked if there was any negative news about Allied. Blum said that neither he nor E. F. Hutton followed the company, but after several minutes delay and a glance at Standard & Poor's tear sheet on Allied, said there was no negative news. Zelda Panzirer ordered 200 shares of Allied common stock. Later on her trip, after discussing the purchase with her husband, she phoned Blum a second time to raise her order to 500 shares. E. F. Hutton purchased the shares for Zelda Panzirer at a September 29 market price of $7 per share.

The Standard & Poor's tear sheet abstracted information from Allied's annual report for the fiscal year ending March 31, 1978. The report was issued on August 18, 1978, and allegedly contained numerous misrepresentations and omissions. The principal misrepresentation was the report of profits for that year based in part on receipts from Allied's film, "The Betsy." In fact, Allied had to split those receipts with the film's overseas distributor, United Artists, and thus lost money in 1978. The principal omission was the annual report's failure to include a qualification by Allied's accountants stating their doubts as to Allied's ability to function as a going concern. Allied common stock closed at $2 7/8 per share the day the annual report was issued. It peaked at $7 3/8 per share on October 2, 1978,[2] and declined thereafter. Allied filed a Chapter XI petition in bankruptcy on April 4, 1979.

Zelda Panzirer never saw the annual report. In her complaint, she alleges that she relied on the "integrity of the market." She asserts that the annual report affected the market, and therefore she had relied on the report through her reliance on the integrity of the market. Judge Motley, however, found that plaintiff "primarily" relied on The Wall Street Journal column about Allied's prospects in the video cassette market and that plaintiff placed only secondary reliance on the integrity of the market. She held that secondary reliance was insufficient to support a 10b-5 claim. We cannot agree. We find no support in the law for the district court's distinction between primary and secondary reliance.

The function of requiring the plaintiff to show reliance in a 10b-5 action is to permit only those injured by fraud to sue. If plaintiff can link her injury to defendant's fraud by showing the fraud was a "substantial" or "significant

---

2. *** Whether the subsequent appreciation in price was due to the annual report or to Allied's entry into the video cassette market is irrelevant to our decision, as we do not depend on Zelda Panzirer's knowledge of the market price. Though Michael Blum stated in his affidavit that he mentioned the activity of Allied common to plaintiff, she nowhere refers to the stock's activity as a reason for her purchase.

contributing cause," plaintiff has shown sufficient reliance to support her 10b-5 claim. *Wilson v. Comtech Telecommunications Corp.*, 648 F.2d 88, 92 (2d Cir. 1981). Plaintiff has on this record stated a sufficient connection between her loss and the allegedly fraudulent annual report to withstand a motion for summary judgment.

As we read the record, Zelda Panzirer's purchase of the Allied stock was caused by her perusal of The Wall Street Journal column. Her knowledge of the price of the stock and her conversation with her broker were merely neutral factors as they presented no impediment to her acting on the favorable notice in The Wall Street Journal.[3] Consequently, the plaintiff argues that if Allied's report had been accurate, the stock analysts interviewed by the Journal would not have mentioned the company favorably, the Journal would not have devoted two paragraphs to Allied's prospects in the video cassette market, and plaintiff would not have been led by the article to buy her stock. Defendants have introduced no evidence to contradict this chain of causation. Though, at trial, the validity of the chain of causation will be tested, on summary judgment questions about this chain of causation must be resolved in favor of plaintiff, who in the case of a material fraud-on-the-market enjoys a presumption of reliance. Where the plaintiff acts upon information from those working in or reporting on the securities markets, and where that information is circulated after a material misrepresentation or omission, plaintiff has stated a sufficient claim of reliance on the misrepresentation or omission. ***

Where, as is here alleged, the fraud consists of a failure to disclose, the difficult nature of plaintiff's claim—that if there had been disclosure, plaintiff would not have been harmed—has led the Supreme Court to hold that if the omission is material, reliance upon the omission will be presumed. *Affiliated Ute Citizens v. United States*, 406 U.S. 128, 153-54 (1972). Proving reliance is necessarily difficult where the fraud has affected the market and damaged the plaintiff only through its effect on the market. Relying on *Affiliated Ute*, this and other circuits do not require direct reliance where the fraud affects the market, on the ground that an investor relies generally on the supposition that the market price is validly set and that no unsuspected fraud has affected the price. See *Ross v. A.H. Robins Co.*, 607 F.2d 545, 554 (2d Cir. 1979); *Blackie v. Barrack*, 524 F.2d 891, 906-07 (9th Cir. 1975). As in *Affiliated Ute, Blackie* held that the materiality of a fraud creates a presumption of reliance through its presumed effect on the market.

Our holding is no more than an extension of *Blackie*. Zelda Panzirer did not rely on the integrity of the market price because she did not rely on price, but she did rely on the integrity of the market in producing the information reported in The Wall Street Journal. Just as a material misrepresentation or omission is presumed to affect the price of the stock, so it should be presumed

---

3. Plaintiff refers to the price of Allied common stock once in her deposition: "If the price was outrageous, something very high, I wouldn't have been interested. The price was attractive." If anything, her testimony indicates that a lower price accurately reflecting Allied's true financial position might have led her to buy more stock.

to affect the information "heard on the street" which led Zelda Panzirer to make her losing investment. ***

### *NOTES AND QUESTIONS*

*1. Merely an Extension of* **Basic/Blackie***?* The court describes its holding as "no more than an extension of *Blackie* [*v. Barrack*, 524 F.2d 891 (9th Cir. 1975)]," a fraud-on-the-market case similar to (and cited favorably by) *Basic*. Is this characterization accurate? Or is it arguable that *Panzirer* is not a fraud-on-the-market case at all? That is, might the result in *Panzirer* have been the same even if Allied stock had not been traded in an efficient market? Cf. *Edgington v. R.G. Dickinson & Co.*, 1992 WL 24747 at *3 (D. Kan. 1992) (noting that "most of the courts that have applied *** [*Panzirer*] have done so in the limited context of fraud-on-the-market claims").

*2. Rebutting the Presumption.* The *Panzirer* court noted that "at trial, the validity of the chain of causation will be tested." What would be sufficient to break the chain?

*3.* **Affiliated Ute** *Revisited.* Why couldn't Zelda Panzirer have invoked the presumption upheld in *Affiliated Ute*?

*4. What Might Have Been.* The Supreme Court granted certiorari in *Panzirer*. See 458 U.S. 1105 (1982). But in the wake of a settlement by the parties, the Court vacated the judgment and directed dismissal of the complaint with prejudice. See 459 U.S. 1027 (1982). Would the *Basic* Court have affirmed *Panzirer*?

### *PROBLEM 2-20*

Apex Co., a manufacturer of paper products, is listed on the New York Stock Exchange. In January, Apex issued a fraudulent earnings statement, on the basis of which it received favorable comments in the Wall Street Journal. In February, Eliza bought shares of Apex on the recommendation of her brother-in-law, a sophisticated investor. He based his recommendation on his belief that paper product manufacturers were a safe investment in uncertain times. In April, Apex issued a corrected earnings statement and the price fell. If Eliza sued Apex under Rule 10b-5, would she be entitled to a presumption of reliance?

c. *The Fraud-Created-the-Market Presumption*

## SHORES v. SKLAR

647 F.2d 462 (5th Cir. 1981) (en banc)

CHARLES CLARK, CIRCUIT JUDGE:

Clarence E. Bishop, Jr., was one of a number of purchasers of First Mortgage Revenue Bonds of the Industrial Development Board of Frisco City, Alabama [Bonds"] The lessee of the industrial business premises, the sole source of the income necessary to amortize the revenue Bonds, almost immediately defaulted in the payment of rent, causing the value of the Bonds to drop precipitously.[1] Bishop sued most of those involved with the issuance of the Bonds, alleging that he was the victim of a pervasive scheme to defraud members of the investing public in violation of the securities laws. In essence, the complaint alleged that the defendants had fabricated a materially misleading Offering Circular in order to induce the Industrial Development Board ("Board") to issue, and the public to buy, fraudulently marketed bonds.[2] ***

The bond issue in question had its genesis in 1972 when J. C. Harrelson, president and chief shareholder of Alabama Supply and Equipment Company (ASECo), and Clarence Hamilton, president of Investors Associates of America, Inc., a Tennessee underwriter, decided to seek industrial development financing to construct and equip a facility for the construction of mobile homes in Frisco City, Alabama. Alabama law provides for such financing pursuant to the Wallace-Cater Act, which authorizes the incorporation of an Industrial Development Board in a municipality in order to induce industry to locate in Alabama. Such a board has the authority to issue tax-exempt bonds. With the proceeds of such an issue, a board can build an industrial facility, which it may then lease to a manufacturing, industrial, or commercial enterprise. The amount of rental payments is calculated to amortize the interest and principal of the bonds and is ostensibly lower than that which could be obtained without tax-free financing. ***

Neither Harrelson nor ASECo was a paragon of financial integrity or industrial ability. Harrelson had been only moderately successful in previous business ventures and had little experience in the development of plants for the construction of modular or mobile homes. ASECo's management was inept and unsophisticated, its projections for the sales of mobile homes were mere marketing assumptions, and its financial condition was weak. Indeed, Harrelson and Hamilton both knew that ASECo did not have the financial capability to engage in the manufacture of mobile homes and related products or to pay the rent necessary to amortize the principal and interest on the Bonds. Nevertheless, they determined to induce the Town of Frisco City to create an Industrial Development Board to finance ASECo's facility as a scheme to defraud the investing public.

Hamilton retained defendant Jerald H. Sklar, a Tennessee attorney, as bond counsel. ***

Sklar also drafted the Offering Circular, based on material furnished to him by the underwriter, the lessee company, and those associated with them, but he intentionally or recklessly disregarded other facts of which he was aware. Sklar omitted from the Offering Circular, for example, that the Securities and

---

1. After the sale of the lessee's plant, the identifiable Bond holders received $373.33 per $1000 bond.

2. Throughout the opinion we refer to these Bonds as being "fraudulently marketed." This means the fraudulent scheme alleged by Bishop was so pervasive that without it the issuer would not have issued, the dealer could not have dealt in, and the buyer could not have bought these Bonds, because they would not have been offered on the market at any price.

Exchange Commission had investigated and commenced a civil action against Hamilton and Investors Associates (and against Jackson Municipals, Inc., the assignee who ultimately underwrote the issue) for violations of the securities laws; he even failed to name the underwriter in the Offering Circular. He misleadingly portrayed ASECo as the owner of 519 acres of Florida real estate valued at $2,284,000, already approved for development, recklessly disregarding not only that ASECo had filed no development plans but also that it had no ownership or equity interest in the property. Although Sklar knew that Harrelson had been only moderately successful at past efforts, he falsely represented Harrelson in the Offering Circular as a successful and experienced developer of modular home manufacturing plans with well-established mobile home sales. Furthermore, Sklar relied on an opinion letter that no actions were pending against or threatening ASECo, even though the opinion letter was obviously deficient and was prepared by a lawyer other than the one originally selected to give an opinion, as Sklar knew. In fact, an action affecting the Florida investment real estate listed on ASECo's balance sheet was pending at the time of the opinion letter.

Part of the information Sklar incorporated into the Offering Circular was a financial statement prepared by George C. Rakard, a certified public accountant from Salem, Illinois. Rakard's financial statement was materially false and misleading because of numerous misrepresentations and omissions. It included as assets of ASECo a number of items of doubtful worth. Open notes and capital stock subscriptions from Harrelson and his wife were valued at $376,000, in reckless disregard of their true value and without taking into account the Harrelsons' probable inability to satisfy these obligations. Three-quarters of the assets were investment properties, including the Florida real estate in which ASECo in fact had no interest. Moreover, although Rakard's forwarding letter accompanying the financial statement stated that the audit fairly presented the financial condition of ASECo, Rakard knew or recklessly disregarded the fact that the financial statement constituted mere "window dressing" that did not fairly present ASECo's financial condition.

By the time Sklar incorporated Rakard's financial statement into the Offering Circular, he knew or recklessly disregarded the fact that Harrelson was already in default on at least one of the notes listed as an asset of ASECo and that ASECo was in default on its obligation in the lease to maintain at least $400,000 in working capital.

Meanwhile, Investors Associates had determined that it did not possess sufficient capital to underwrite the proposed issue and assigned the right to underwrite the issue to Jackson Municipals, Inc., a Tennessee underwriting firm headed by Cecil Lamberson. Jackson Municipals and Lamberson proceeded to offer the Bonds for sale to the public on the basis of the Offering Circular, even though they knew it contained materially false misrepresentations and omissions. They knew Harrelson was inexperienced and unsophisticated, contrary to the Offering Circular's representation. They purported to rely on Hamilton and Investors Associates, but because they were all defendants in the same SEC action (which the Offering Circular failed to disclose) they knew that Investors Associates needed to induce another firm to underwrite the bond issue or it would lose the value of all the time and effort it had put into the issue thus far.

Lamberson and Jackson Municipals knew that while Harrelson was not as financially secure as represented, 95% of ASECo's current assets consisted of open notes from Harrelson and over 75% of ASECo's listed assets was the Florida real estate, but failed to investigate the true value of either of these assets. They knew that the financial statement did not reflect ASECo's true assets. They even failed to inquire whether Harrelson had paid $200,000 due ASECo on a stock subscription, knowing that ASECo would be in default if Harrelson had not. In spite of this knowledge, Jackson Municipals bought the bond issue from the Board in three increments, commencing on December 14, 1972, and resold the Bonds to securities dealers.

The Phenix National Bank *** had been chosen to act as trustee of the Bond proceeds. The Bank's responsibility was to ensure that the lessee complied with the terms and conditions of the lease, one of which was that ASECo at all times have working capital in the amount of $400,000.00 or more. The Bank had the duty to determine the existence of any default in the lease requirements by the lessee, and to demand a cure of the default or else declare the Bonds due and payable upon failure to cure. *** The Bank knew or recklessly disregarded *** that ASECo was in breach of the lease requirement that it maintain $400,000.00 in working capital. ***

Bishop purchased three of the Bonds in January, paying $3,052.67, and one more in February, for $1,043.37. *** The district court found Bishop purchased as part of the primary offering. ***

Bishop never saw the Offering Circular nor knew one existed. He bought the Bonds based solely on his broker's oral representations. ***

After the ASECo plant had been constructed, the lessee ceased all operations at the plant and, on April 15, 1974, defaulted in payment of rent under the lease. Although Harrelson had unconditionally guaranteed the performance of the lease by ASECo, he did not have sufficient assets to back up his guarantee. The Trustee Bank declared the lease in default. ***

Bishop's original complaint sought relief for himself and for the class of all purchasers of the Bonds under *** the Securities Exchange Act of 1934, rule 10b-5, and an unspecified Alabama law. The court *** permitted Bishop to amend his complaint twice in order to allege that he relied on the Offering Circular. Bishop's inability to make such an allegation resulted in the dismissal here on appeal. ***

Bishop alleged that the Offering Circular contained material misrepresentations and failed to state material facts necessary to make the statements made not misleading. At the same time, he admitted that he never read or otherwise relied on the Offering Circular. If the *Ute* presumption applies to these nondisclosures, Bishop's admission rebuts it. Bishop's claim that he was deceived by the misrepresentations and omissions of the Offering Circular was correctly dismissed by the district court because of his failure to read or even seek to read the Offering Circular. ***

The district court erred, however, in construing the remainder of Bishop's complaint as narrowly confined to charges of misrepresentations and omissions in the Offering Circular that would have defrauded investors who did rely. It would permit proof that the defendants engaged in an elaborate scheme to create a bond issue that would appear genuine but was so lacking in basic requirements that the Bonds would never have been approved by the Board nor presented by the underwriters had any one of the participants in the scheme not acted with intent to defraud or in reckless disregard of whether the other defendants were perpetrating a fraud. Rather than containing the entire fraud, the Offering Circular was assertedly only one step in the course of an elaborate scheme.

*** Bishop's 10b-5(2) claim *** cannot withstand his admitted lack of reliance on the Offering Circular. However, his 10b-5(1) and (3) claims *** assert something more that prevents dismissal at this preliminary stage.

*** His pleadings would permit him to show that he was willing to accept any marketable risk. If a municipal authority was willing to authorize the issuance of the Bond, and the underwriters were willing to present the issue to the market, that was sufficient for Bishop's purposes. His pleadings allow him to show that he sought to make investments in securities which were entitled to be marketed.

*** The requisite element of causation in fact would be established if Bishop proved the scheme was intended to and did bring the Bonds onto the market fraudulently and proved he relied on the integrity of the offerings of the securities market. His lack of reliance on the Offering Circular, only one component of the overall scheme, is not determinative. *Blackie v. Barrack*, 524 F.2d 891, 906 (9th Cir. 1975).

Bishop has alleged the necessary elements of an action under 10b-5(1) or (3). In the literal words of rule 10b-5, he must be able to show a "scheme ... to defraud ... or ... [an] act, practice or course of business which operates as a fraud or deceit upon [him] ... in connection with the sale of [the Bonds]...." Bishop's burden of proof will be to show that (1) the defendants knowingly conspired to bring securities onto the market which were not entitled to be marketed, intending to defraud purchasers, (2) Bishop reasonably relied on the Bonds' availability on the market as an indication of their apparent genuineness, and (3) as a result of the scheme to defraud, he suffered a loss. ***

The thrust of the arguments against our holding is that a recovery in this circumstance is not consonant with the central purpose of the securities laws, which, it is argued, is to provide full disclosure so that investors may make informed investment decisions. It is asserted that allowing recovery to one who has never read the Offering Circular minimizes the importance of such documents and discourages investors from reading them.

We disagree. First, the purpose of the securities acts and rule 10b-5 are far broader than merely providing full disclosure or fostering informed investment decisions. The Supreme Court has held that the acts were designed "to protect investors against fraud ... and to promote ethical standards of honesty and fair dealing. See H.R. Rep. No. 85, 73d Cong., 1st Sess., 1-5

(1933)." *Ernst & Ernst v. Hochfelder*, 425 U.S. 185, 195 (1976). *** Full disclosure is only one means, albeit a central one, of enhancing our goals.

Second, the role of the Offering Circular will continue undiminished even if Bishop proves his allegations and recovers. He has alleged that the fraud caused the Bonds to be offered for sale on the market. If Bishop proves no more than that the bonds would have been offered at a lower price or a higher rate, rather than that they would never have been issued or marketed, he cannot recover. Thus, a purchaser of securities will still have the strongest incentive to read the disclosure statement if he wants to ensure he gets full value for his securities purchases.

Under Bishop's broader theory, it would have availed him nothing to have read the Offering Circular. This theory is not that he bought inferior bonds, but that the Bonds he bought were fraudulently marketed. The securities laws allow an investor to rely on the integrity of the market to the extent that the securities it offers to him for purchase are entitled to be in the market place.

Finally, we reject the contention that our holding imposes new burdens on defendants or enhances their liability. Lawyers, underwriters, and accountants who participate in bond issues in good faith are unaffected by our decision. Liability results only if they act with intent to deceive or defraud. ***

The dissent asserts that we adopt a "new theory" because we separate Bishop's claim under 10b-5(2) that the Offering Circular was misleading from his claim under 10b-5(1) and (3) that defendants' fraudulently marketed Bonds caused his loss. It is not our "theory" but the words of rule 10b-5 which confer the right of action we hold Bishop is entitled to try to prove. ***

*** Whenever the rule 10b-5 issue shifts from misrepresentation or omission in a document to fraud on a broader scale, the search for causation must shift also. The "reliance" that produces causation in the latter type of case cannot come from reading a document. *** The rule is recognized also to provide the basis for a federal cause of action for more elaborate, intentional schemes which deceive or defraud purchasers of securities. ***

The judgment dismissing plaintiff's complaint is vacated and the cause remanded for further proceedings not inconsistent with this opinion. The district court also ruled that this action could not be maintained as a class action because of lack of typicality, lack of adequate representation, and lack of a showing that common questions of fact would predominate. All three of these determinations, however, were premised on the belief that reliance on the Offering Circular was crucial to Bishop's claim. On remand, the court must reconsider the maintainability of this action as a class action as to members of a properly defined class of Bond purchasers who did not so rely. ***

RANDALL, CIRCUIT JUDGE, WITH WHOM BROWN, RONEY, GEE, TJOFLAT, HILL, FAY, RUBIN, REAVLEY, AND HATCHETT, CIRCUIT JUDGES, JOIN, DISSENTING:

The majority opinion today adopts a new theory of recovery in federal court under Rule 10b-5. It holds that a purchaser of securities offered to the public by means of a misleading offering circular, who has heretofore been foreclosed from recovering in federal court under Rule 10b-5 because of his admitted lack of reliance on the offering circular, will not henceforth be foreclosed from recovering under the Rule if he is able to prove that the defendants knowingly conspired to bring securities onto the market which were not "entitled to be marketed" and that he reasonably relied on the availability of the securities on the market as an indication of their entitlement to be marketed.

This newly-devised route to recovery under Rule 10b-5 is completely without supporting precedent; indeed, it conflicts with the prior decisions of this and every other circuit and with the clear implication of recent Supreme Court decisions in the securities field. But even if the majority were writing on a blank slate, its novel holding would be profoundly unwise for several reasons. First, it introduces into the law under Rule 10b-5 a distinction between securities that are "entitled to be marketed," i. e., securities that may be the subject of a fraudulent marketing scheme, but which, absent the fraud, could be sold at *some* price, and securities that are not "entitled to be marketed," i. e., securities that are the subject of a fraudulent marketing scheme and that, absent the fraud, could not be sold at *any* price. The requirements for recovery under Rule 10b-5 in any case hinge upon which category of securities the defrauded plaintiff purchased. If he purchased a security that was entitled to be marketed, he must have relied on the defendants' misrepresentations or omissions in order to recover. If, however, he can show that he purchased a security which was not entitled to be marketed, he can recover in spite of his nonreliance on the defendants' misrepresentations or omissions if he can show that he reasonably relied on the integrity of the marketplace to offer him securities that were entitled to be marketed. This novel theory permits recovery under the Rule to one who has elected not even to seek to read what the seller is obligated by the Rule to disclose, thereby defeating the primary objective of the Rule—the making of an informed investment decision. Second, the majority opinion has great potential for increasing the volume of litigation under Rule 10b-5 by providing a federal forum to those plaintiffs who by their own actions would otherwise have forfeited the protection of the Rule and have relegated themselves to state court actions for conversion. Finally, the majority opinion also has great potential for protracting much Rule 10b-5 litigation that would heretofore have terminated at the summary judgment stage. For these reasons, I respectfully dissent. ***

## *NOTES AND QUESTIONS*

***1. The Meaning of "Unmarketable."*** To obtain a presumption based on fraud-created-the-market, plaintiffs must show that the securities in question were "unmarketable." Courts have defined that term in the following ways. What are the advantages and disadvantages of each definition? Which definitions (if any) are consistent with *Shores*?

(a) *Economic Unmarketability.* This definition requires that the securities in question "could 'not have been offered on the market at any price' absent the fraudulent scheme." *Ross v. Bank South, N.A.*, 885 F.2d 723, 729 (11th Cir. 1989), quoting *Shores v. Sklar* at n. 2.

(b) *"Patently Worthless" Enterprise.* This definition requires that the enterprise offering the securities be a "sham" or a "hoax." *Abell v. Potomac Ins.*

*Co.*, 858 F.2d 1104, 1122 (5th Cir. 1988) (arguing that in *Shores*, the defendants "never intended to start a legitimate" business), judgment vac. on other grounds sub nom. *Fryar v. Abell*, 492 U.S. 914 (1989).

(c) *Legal Unmarketability*. This definition requires the existence of a legal bar to the marketing of the securities in question. *T.J. Raney & Sons, Inc. v. Fort Cobb, Oklahoma Irrigation Fuel Auth.*, 717 F.2d 1330, 1333 (10th Cir. 1983) (finding that the municipal authority that issued the bonds was barred by state law from doing so).

2. ***Rebutting the Presumption***. How can a defendant rebut a presumption of fraud-created-the-market?

3. ***Disharmony Among the Circuits.*** The Seventh Circuit decided not to follow *Shores* on these grounds:

> The *existence* of a security does not depend on, or warrant, the adequacy of disclosure. Many a security is on the market even though the issuer or some third party made incomplete disclosures. Federal securities law does not include "merit regulation." Full disclosure of adverse information may lower the price, but it does not exclude the security from the market. Securities of bankrupt corporations trade freely; some markets specialize in penny stocks.

*Eckstein v. Balcor Film Investors*, 8 F.3d 1121, 1130-1131 (7th Cir. 1993). Are you persuaded?

4. ***"Fraud on a Broader Scale."*** The *Shores* court justified its presumption partly on the ground that the allegations involved not merely a "misrepresentation or omission in a document" but rather "fraud on a broader scale." Are you comfortable with this justification?

5. ***Fraud-on-the-Market Compared.*** To what extent (if any) does *Shores* follow from *Basic*?

6. ***Recalling* Blue Chip Stamps.** According to the dissenting opinion in *Shores*, the presumption recognized by the majority will foment vexatious litigation. Do you agree?

7. ***The Presumptions and the Reliance Requirement.*** Consider not only the fraud-created-the-market presumption but also the fraud-on-the-market presumption and the *Affiliated Ute* presumption. To what extent do these presumptions have the effect of decimating the reliance requirement altogether?

## *PROBLEM 2-21*

By means of the Internet and the telephone, Dwayne persuaded numerous investors to buy shares of Spring Cure Company. According to Dwayne, Spring Cure has developed a treatment for pollen allergies that is far superior to any treatment currently available. In fact, both the cure and the company are a complete fiction. Investors whom Dwayne has defrauded have brought an action against him under Rule 10b-5. Can these investors satisfy the reliance requirement?

### d. *The Justifiableness of the Reliance*

In private Rule 10b-5 actions, courts imported from tort law not only the reliance requirement but the additional (albeit connected) requirement that the reliance be justifiable. The justifiable reliance requirement (also known as the reasonable reliance requirement or due diligence or the duty of care) is steeped in controversy on a number of fronts. Consider the following decision.

## ZOBRIST v. COAL-X, INC.

708 F.2d 1511 (10th Cir. 1983)

BARRETT, CIRCUIT JUDGE:

Phil Rasmussen *** and Neil Rasmussen and Herman Zobrist *** brought an action pursuant to section 10(b) *** and rule 10b-5 *** against Coal-X, Inc., Emmet L. Shultz, and Paul B. Baker (defendants). *** In No. 82-1055, the defendants appeal from the judgment in favor of Phil Rasmussen, while in No. 82-1104, Neil Rasmussen and Herman Zobrist appealed from the judgment in favor of the defendants. ***

Both appeals arise from the same business transaction, the organization of Coal-X, Ltd./'76 (Coal-X '76), a Utah limited partnership formed to raise venture capital for a coal mining operation in West Virginia. Coal-X, Inc. is the general partner in Coal-X '76. At the time relevant here, the summer of 1976, Emmet Shultz was the president and a director of Coal-X, Inc., while Paul Baker was a vice-president and a director of that entity. While employed by the Huntsman Coal Company, Shultz, with the assistance of independent geologists, evaluated a certain coal property in West Virginia. Based on those evaluations, the Huntsman Coal Company entered into a sublease which granted it the right to develop the coal on that property. The company prepared a private placement memorandum and certain projections in anticipation of selling limited partnership interests to finance the development of the property. Later, for disputed reasons, Huntsman Coal Company abandoned the project and sold its entire interest in the project, including the private offering materials, to Shultz for $5,000. Shultz subsequently left Huntsman Coal Company and prepared to develop the coal property through Coal-X '76.

Pursuant to section 4(2) of the Securities Act of 1933, *** interests in Coal-X '76 were marketed through a private placement offering. *** Herman Zobrist, Neil Rasmussen, and Phil Rasmussen were among the investors contacted by the defendants to purchase interests in Coal-X '76.

Shultz and Baker, and their representatives, met with Zobrist and the Rasmussens several times over a period of about thirty to forty-five days before any interests were sold. At those meetings, the defendants described the investment as a good opportunity and provided oral and written projections which presented the potential benefits of the investment. Although there was conflict in the evidence, the jury apparently determined that Baker represented to Phil Rasmussen that the investment "couldn't miss" and was a "sure thing". When Phil Rasmussen challenged those assertions, the defendants assured him that there were "no risks" in the investment and that they would guarantee with their stock that the investment would work out as projected.

Either prior to the time the Rasmussens and Zobrist purchased their interests in Coal-X '76, or shortly thereafter, the defendants provided each of those investors with a Private Placement Memorandum. The memorandum clearly and specifically stated the risks involved in the investment, including the lack of a firm output contract, the speculative nature of coal mining, the fluctuation of metallurgical coal prices in response to fluctuations in steel production, and competition from larger, more experienced coal mining companies. Prior to the time of their purchases, Zobrist and the Rasmussens each signed an "Application Form and Subscription Agreement" which included a statement that the investor recognized that the investment was subject to the risks set forth in the Private Placement Memorandum. Phil Rasmussen also completed and signed an "Investment Questionnaire" wherein he responded affirmatively to questions inquiring whether he had read the memorandum and whether he understood the nature of the investment and the risks involved. It is undisputed, nevertheless, that Zobrist and the Rasmussens in fact did not read the Private Placement Memorandum prior to investing in Coal-X '76.

Herman Zobrist and Phil Rasmussen each purchased two units in Coal-X '76 at $35,000 per unit and Neil Rasmussen purchased one unit. *** Due to permitting problems and unusually severe weather, Coal-X '76 did not commence commercial production until 1977. After production began, labor strikes impeded the development of the venture and declining steel production depressed the price offered for metallurgical coal. Consequently, Coal-X '76 lost between $800,000 and $900,000 between 1977 and 1979, which in turn reduced the value of a limited partnership interest in Coal-X ' 76. Gulf Energy, a parent of Coal-X, Inc., loaned over $800,000 to Coal-X '76 to keep the mine in operation. The mine remains in operation today and has produced at levels exceeding what was originally projected.

In 1979, however, the Rasmussens and Zobrist became convinced that the investment had missed, and filed this action ***. Phil Rasmussen claimed that the defendants' assertions and guarantees that the investment involved no risk were misrepresentations of material facts in violation of rule 10b-5. In addition, the Rasmussens and Zobrist asserted that the defendants violated rule 10b-5 by failing to disclose material facts. The jury, in a special verdict, found that each of the defendants knowingly violated rule 10b- 5 by misrepresenting material facts to Phil Rasmussen, that he justifiably relied on those misrepresentations, and that as a result, he suffered $50,000 in damages. With respect to Neil Rasmussen and Herman Zobrist, however, the jury found that while the defendants violated rule 10b-5 by knowingly failing to disclose material facts to those investors, the investors had not justifiably relied on those failures to disclose. Thus, the jury found that Neil Rasmussen and Zobrist were not entitled to any damages.

On appeal, the primary contention of the defendants is that, as a matter of law, Phil Rasmussen's reliance on the misrepresentations that the investments involved no risk could not be "justifiable" when those representations were contradicted by the warnings in the Private Placement Memorandum, which he failed to read. *** Neil Rasmussen and Zobrist contend that because the defendants failed to disclose material facts, reliance should have been presumed. ***

We will first examine the contention of the defendants that Phil Rasmussen did not "justifiably rely" on the misrepresentations as to the risk involved in the investments. In a misrepresentation case under rule 10b-5, a plaintiff generally must establish that in connection with the purchase or sale of a security, the defendant, with scienter, made a false representation of a material fact upon which the plaintiff justifiably relied to his or her detriment. See *Holdsworth v. Strong,* 545 F.2d 687, 694 (10th Cir.1976) (en banc). In the instant case, the jury found that the defendants did make the "no risk" representations, that Phil Rasmussen relied on those misrepresentations, and that such reliance was justifiable. The defendants argue that since Phil Rasmussen was a sophisticated businessman with prior investment experience, his reliance on the no risk representations without reading the Private Placement Memorandum, which expressly warned of risks, was not justifiable as a matter of law. Phil Rasmussen responds that the jury examined the defendants' entire course of conduct in finding that his reliance was justifiable. If the effect of such conduct can be mitigated by "boiler plate" recitations of risk in a prospectus, he contends, the prospectus will become a shield behind which promoters can safely hide while boldly making fraudulent misstatements to investors. ***

In essence, both parties request that this court examine the prospectus and the conduct of the parties independent of one another and seek to focus our attention on the elements which support their respective contentions. To determine whether reliance was justifiable, however, we must examine all of the elements of the transaction. Justifiable reliance is not a theory of contributory negligence; rather, it is a limitation on a rule 10b-5 action which insures that there is a causal connection between the misrepresentation and the plaintiff's harm. *Holdsworth v. Strong,* supra, at 694-95. Only when the plaintiff's conduct rises to a level of culpable conduct comparable to that of the defendant's will reliance be unjustifiable. Id. at 693. In this circuit, such conduct must amount to at least reckless behavior. See *Hackbart v. Holmes,* 675 F.2d 1114, 1117 (10th Cir.1982).

Courts have examined a number of factors in determining whether reliance on misrepresentations is justifiable in a particular fact situation. In *Holdsworth v. Strong,* for example, the plaintiff was an attorney and accountant who had access to the relevant corporate books and records. On the basis of misrepresentations by a close business and personal friend, the plaintiff sold his stock in the corporation without first examining the corporate books and records. Three judges of an equally divided court concluded that under those circumstances, the plaintiff's reliance was justifiable, despite his sophistication and failure to investigate, because the defendant had carefully cultivated the plaintiff's trust and confidence over a long period of time, and then used that trust to encourage the sale. Id. at 696-97. It must be noted, however, that the judges also concluded that an examination of the corporate books and records would not have revealed the falsity of the defendant's representations. Id. at 697.

Similarly, a review of the cases from other circuits indicates that the following are all relevant factors in determining whether reliance was justifiable: (1) the sophistication and expertise of the plaintiff in financial and securities matters; (2) the existence of long standing business or personal relationships; (3) access to the relevant information; (4) the existence of a fiduciary relationship; (5) concealment of the fraud; (6) the opportunity to detect the fraud; (7) whether the plaintiff initiated the stock transaction or sought to expedite the transaction; and (8) the generality or specificity of the misrepresentations. See *G.A. Thompson & Co. v. Partridge,* 636 F.2d 945, 955 (5th Cir.1981); *Straub v. Vaisman & Co.,* 540 F.2d 591, 598 (3d Cir.1976). No single factor is determinative; all relevant factors must be considered and balanced to determine whether reliance was justified. See, e.g., *Holdsworth v. Strong,* supra at 696-97.

This court has not articulated a standard by which it can be determined whether in light of the circumstances the reliance was justifiable. At a minimum, though, "a plaintiff may not reasonably or justifiably rely on a misrepresentation where its falsity is palpable." *Holdsworth v. Strong,* 545 F.2d at 694. The trial court here instructed the jury that the test to be applied was whether the plaintiff's

> reliance was justified; that he did not intentionally close his eyes and refuse to investigate, concerning the circumstances, in disregard of a risk known to him, or so obvious that he must be taken to have been aware of it, and so great as to make it highly probable that harm would follow.

[Joint App., Vol. I, p. 288]. This standard is followed by the Fifth Circuit Court of Appeals, *Gower v. Cohn,* 643 F.2d 1146, 1156 (5th Cir.1981), and we consider it appropriate to apply in the instant case. ***

In considering the factors and applying the test to determine whether Phil Rasmussen's reliance was justified, however, we are confronted with an unusual factual situation. While in other cases the plaintiff failed to investigate information to which he had access, *Holdsworth v. Strong,* supra at 692, or to read information which the defendants provided, *Nye v. Blyth Eastman Dillon & Co.,* supra at 1197, we have found no relevant cases wherein the plaintiff failed to read a prospectus or equivalent document which disclosed information in accordance with the requirements of the Securities Act of 1933.[7] It is our view that while the full and fair disclosure of information in the Private Placement Memorandum is a relevant factor which favors the defendants here, such disclosure is not determinative, even though Phil Rasmussen was a sophisticated and knowledgeable investor.

We observe, however, that had Phil Rasmussen read the Private Placement Memorandum, he undeniably would have been notified of the risks of the investment. Indeed, prominently displayed on the first page of the Private Placement Memorandum was the following warning:

---

7. In *Shores v. Sklar,* 647 F.2d 462, 468-70 (5th Cir.1981), the plaintiff was held to have stated a cause of action *** despite his failure to read an offering circular. The plaintiff's claim, however, was based on alleged misrepresentations and non-disclosures contained in the circular. The issue was whether, despite his failure to read, the plaintiff could recover for those misrepresentations and omissions, not whether he could recover for other misrepresentations, despite full and accurate disclosure in the circular.

> THESE SECURITIES INVOLVE A HIGH DEGREE OF RISK. See "Risk and Special Factors" and "Who Should Invest."

The section entitled "Who Should Invest" began on page 8 *** and included several monitions, beginning with the following:

> Investment in the Units offered hereby may be considered to involve a high degree of risk, and is suitable only for investors of substantial net worth who are willing to purchase an investment which cannot be easily liquidated and may not provide immediate cash returns. ***

In the four pages under the heading of "Risks and Special Factors", the risks associated with coal mining and the limited partnership form were succinctly presented. In addition, early in the memorandum the following warning appeared: "No person has been authorized to give any information or to make any representations not contained in this Memorandum ... and, if given or made, such information or representations must not be relied upon."

Of course, we do not imply that the defendants can disclaim responsibility for their misrepresentations simply by disclosing the risks in the memorandum and therein warning investors not to rely on representations not contained within the memorandum. Had Phil Rasmussen read the memorandum, though, there would be a substantial question whether his reliance on the original misrepresentations of no risk, absent further inquiry, would be justifiable. Since the memorandum expressly contradicted the representations, he would have to show compelling reasons for passively accepting the contradictions. In the sense of proving justifiable reliance, Phil Rasmussen is consequently in a better position than he would have been had he read the memorandum and yet relied on the original misrepresentations. While we are not certain that this result would encourage investors to throw caution and prospectuses to the wind, we see no reason to reward investors who do so. See *Straub v. Vaisman & Co.,* 540 F.2d at 597-98. Thus, it is our view that knowledge of information contained in a prospectus or an equivalent document authorized by statute or regulation, should be imputed to investors who fail to read such documents. We thus hold that Phil Rasmussen must be charged with constructive knowledge of the risks and warnings contained in the Private Placement Memorandum.

Charging Phil Rasmussen with constructive knowledge does no more than place him in a position equal to that of a cautious investor. We are imputing knowledge of information only to the extent to which such information actually was disclosed. That is, we do not charge him with information that a knowledgeable investor would infer from the printed words or numbers; we impute knowledge of the printed words or numbers only. Nor does such constructive knowledge alter the standard of justifiable reliance. The only consequence of imputing knowledge of the contents of the Private Placement Memorandum to Phil Rasmussen is that when the various factors are considered in evaluating justifiable reliance, his conduct must be examined as if he were aware of the warnings contained in the memorandum. ***

Under the circumstances of this case, when we impute to Phil Rasmussen knowledge of the warnings contained in the Private Placement Memorandum, it becomes clear that, as a matter of law, his reliance on the misrepresentations was not justified. We reach this conclusion after a consideration of the above noted factors. It is true that Phil Rasmussen previously participated in investments with Baker, but there was no evidence of any long standing business or personal relationship that, in light of the patent contradiction between Baker's representations and the express warnings disclosed in the Private Placement Memorandum, would justify Rasmussen's reliance on Baker's representations without further inquiry. Not only did the defendants not conceal their fraud from Rasmussen, they provided him with information and warnings which exposed the representations as false. It was not necessary for Rasmussen to delve into voluminous books and records, or to decipher balance sheets and financial statements; the warning on the first page of the memorandum contradicted the representations of no risk, and there were four full pages devoted to concise, informative descriptions of the risks inherent in coal mining and partnerships.

In short, there is simply no evidence which provides a valid reason for Rasmussen's reliance on the general misrepresentations as to risk when he is considered to have knowledge of the specific warnings contained in the memorandum. We do not say that such reliance might not be justified under different factual circumstances. We simply conclude that, in this case, when knowledge of the disclosed risks is imputed to Phil Rasmussen, it is evident that he acted recklessly by intentionally closing his eyes to and failing to investigate the contradiction between the misrepresentations and the information in the memorandum. As a matter of law, Phil Rasmussen could not rely on the misrepresentations without further inquiry. ***

The cross-appellants, Neil Rasmussen and Herman Zobrist, contend that the defendants wilfully and knowingly failed to disclose material information.[8] Zobrist and Neil Rasmussen contend that the information was material as a matter of law. Consequently, they argue, under *Affiliated Ute Citizens of Utah v. United States,* 406 U.S. 128 (1972), reliance should be presumed. We do not dispute the cross-appellant's contentions; indeed, the trial court correctly instructed the jury on these matters and the jury expressly found that the information was material. Pursuant to another instruction, however, the jury also found that Neil Rasmussen and Zobrist did not prove "reliance". The cross-appellants challenge the jury's conclusion by vaguely arguing that the trial court's "reliance" instruction can be read to suggest that the cross-appellants had to prove actual reliance. The cross-appellants do not specify any defect in the instruction, nor can we discern any.

After describing reliance and justifiable reliance in terms of a case of misrepresentation, the trial court instructed the jury on the element of reliance in a case of omission or failure to disclose:

> The plaintiff's burden of proof is different with regard to the element of reliance when there is an intentional omission of a material fact, which makes a

8. The information that the defendants failed to disclose was that the Huntsman Coal Company abandoned the project that Coal-X '76 later operated after spending $250,000 preparing to develop the property, and sold their rights and materials to Shultz for $5,000. In addition, the defendants failed to disclose that if they sold a sufficient number of limited partnership unit interests, Coal-X '76 would be merged with Gulf Energy Corporation to the substantial personal benefit of the defendants.

> statement made misleading. With regard to such a claimed material omission, the burden of proof on the issue of reliance is different. If there had been an intentional omission of material fact, it would be difficult for the plaintiffs to prove that they relied on something they did not know and the law infers that the plaintiffs would have relied upon facts which are shown to be material and are intentionally withheld. Accordingly, *if you find from a preponderance of the evidence that there were material facts intentionally not disclosed to the plaintiffs in connection with the transactions in question, then the defendants and not the plaintiffs have the burden to demonstrate that even if the material facts had been disclosed, the plaintiffs' investment decision would not have been different.*

[Jt.App.Vol. I at p. 288] (Emphasis added). We hold that this instruction properly informed the jury of the allocation of the burden of proof on the reliance issue in a case of failure to disclose.

In accordance with *Affiliated Ute,* the instruction informed the jury that reliance could be inferred from a showing of materiality. The inference of reliance, however, is not conclusive. Most courts, as did the trial court here, simply shift the burden of proof of non-reliance to the defendant. See *Shores v. Sklar,* 647 F.2d at 468. The trial court correctly instructed the jury that the defendant meets this burden when he establishes that the plaintiff's investment decision would not have been different even had the defendant disclosed the omitted material facts. Id. It is clear that the jury dutifully followed the trial court's instruction and found that although the omitted facts were material, the defendants proved that even if the information were disclosed the cross-appellants would not have acted differently. Inasmuch as the cross-appellants did not read the Private Placement Memorandum, there was substantial evidence to support the jury's verdict. ***

HOLLOWAY, CIRCUIT JUDGE, CONCURRING AND DISSENTING:

I concur in the affirmance of the judgment based on the jury's verdict in No. 82-1104. However, I must respectfully dissent from the opinion as to No. 82- 1055. *** [T]he majority's resolution of this issue defeats the main purpose of the securities law to protect from fraud and misrepresentation, unsoundly striking the balance in favor of the wrongdoers by penalizing a plaintiff for his neglect or recklessness in not discovering the defendants' intentional wrongs. All this is done without questioning the jury's well supported findings on the defendants' knowing misrepresentations or omissions.

The majority opinion *** correctly notes that *Holdsworth* held that the plaintiff's conduct in Rule 10b-5 cases will bar recovery only when it "rises to a level of culpable conduct *comparable to that of the defendant* ...." (Emphasis added). To me, however, the majority opinion's application of this rule is illogical. It observes that a defendant's liability must be based on misbehavior rising (or sinking) at least to the level of recklessness. The opinion labels plaintiff Phil Rasmussen's behavior "reckless" and hence denies recovery. What is wanting is recognition of the fact that in light of the jury's unquestioned findings here, the defendants' conduct cannot be sanitized so as to say it was merely comparable to the plaintiff's conduct.

*** The jury's findings are overturned only by imputing to the plaintiff constructive knowledge of the Private Placement Memorandum. Thus the knowing misrepresentations or omissions are accepted as proven. The case then comes down to whether the important policies of the securities law and the regulation are served by imposing a loss on the plaintiff by imputing knowledge to him of the printed exculpatory statements and by exonerating the defendants who were found guilty of "knowing" wrongful conduct. ***

## *NOTES AND QUESTIONS*

*1.* ***The Eight Factors.*** To what extent did the eight factors listed by the court determine the result? Would it have made a difference if Phil had not been sophisticated (the first factor)? Cf. *Carr v. Cigna Sec., Inc.*, 95 F.3d 544, 547 (7th Cir. 1996) (deeming the *Zobrist* holding relevant to any "literate, competent adult"). Do any of the factors (whether or not applied by the court) suggest that Phil Rasmussen's reliance was justifiable?

*2.* ***Misrepresentations vs. Omissions.*** The court imposed the burden of proving justifiable reliance on Phil Rasmussen (who claimed misrepresentations) but made the defendants plead lack of justifiable reliance when it came to the other plaintiffs (who claimed omissions). The basis for this distinction was probably *Affiliated Ute Citizens v. United States*, 406 U.S.128 (1972), which, as you will recall, provides a rebuttable presumption of reliance in omissions cases. Should *Affiliated Ute*'s presumption of reliance encompass a presumption of justifiable reliance as well?

*3.* ***Fraud-on-the-Market Again.*** Earlier you also encountered *Basic Inc. v. Levinson*, 485 U.S. 224 (1988), which gives certain plaintiffs a presumption that they relied on the integrity of the market price, thereby sparing them the need to prove reliance on the defendant's fraud. Where the plaintiff has this presumption, should she nonetheless have the burden of proving justifiable reliance? Or should that burden shift to the defendant to prove lack of justifiable reliance? Cf. *Harsco Corp. v. Segui*, 91 F.3d 337, 342 n. 5 (2d Cir. 1996) (maintaining that the burden shifts). Can you identify factual situations in which a plaintiff entitled to a fraud-on-the-market presumption should nonetheless be barred from recovery for lack of justifiable reliance? Is there any philosophical tension between the fraud-on-the-market presumption and the justifiable reliance requirement?

*4.* ***Element or Defense.*** Justifiable reliance is most often treated as an element of the plaintiff's prima facie case, as it was in *Zobrist*, but lack of justifiable reliance is at least sometimes treated as an affirmative defense. See, e.g., *Kline v. First W. Gov't Sec., Inc.*, 24 F.3d 480, 488 (3d Cir. 1994). Does it make more sense to require the plaintiff to establish her justifiable reliance or instead to require the defendant to establish the plaintiff's lack of justifiable reliance?

*5.* ***Justifying Justifiable Reliance.*** Courts have offered each of the following as rationales for the justifiable reliance requirement. Which (if any) do you find persuasive?

*(a) Causation.* The justifiable reliance requirement "insures that there is a causal connection between the misrepresentation and the plaintiff's harm." *Zobrist*, supra.

*(b) Protecting Defendants.* Without a justifiable reliance requirement, "even the most careful seller is at risk, for it is easy to claim: 'Despite what the

written documents say, one of your agents told me something else.' " *Acme Propane, Inc. v. Tenexco, Inc.*, 844 F.2d 1317, 1322 (7th Cir. 1988).

*(c) Anti-Fraud.* Justifiable reliance "requir[es] plaintiffs to invest carefully" and thereby "'promotes the anti-fraud policies' of the securities acts by making fraud more readily discoverable." *Banca Cremi, S.A. v. Alex. Brown & Sons, Inc.*, 132 F.3d 1017, 1028 (4th Cir. 1997) (quoting *Dupuy v. Dupuy*, 551 F.2d 1005, 1014 (5th Cir. 1977)).

***6. Conflict?*** Consider whether the justifiable reliance requirement can be reconciled with *Bateman Eichler, Hill Richards, Inc. v. Berner*, 472 U.S. 299 (1985). In *Bateman*, the plaintiffs brought a Rule 10b-5 action against a corporate insider and a broker for allegedly providing them with fraudulent nonpublic information. The defendants invoked the defense of *in pari delicto* (Latin for "equal fault"): their argument was that by trading on the information in question, the plaintiffs had themselves violated the securities laws and thus should be barred from recovery. The Supreme Court held that an *in pari delicto* defense to a federal securities action can succeed only when two conditions are satisfied: "(1) as a direct result of his own actions, the plaintiff bears at least substantially equal responsibility for the violation he seeks to redress and (2) preclusion of suit would not significantly interfere with the effective enforcement of the securities laws and protection of the investing public." Id. at 310-311.

Examining the first condition, the Court held that at least as a general rule, an insider and a broker bear greater responsibility than do their tippees. The Court acknowledged that the plaintiffs "may well have violated the securities laws." Id. at 314. But it observed that "there are important distinctions between the relative culpabilities of tippers, securities professionals, and tippees in these circumstances." Id. at 312-313. First, the Court noted that the tippee is apt to be less culpable because his liability is "solely derivative" from the tipper. Id. at 313. Second, the Court observed that insiders and brokers who tip may commit additional offenses in which their tippees are not involved, such as violating fiduciary duties owed the issuer. Id. at 313. The Court termed these offenses "particularly egregious when committed by a securities professional." Id. at 314.

Examining the second condition, the Court held that barring the lawsuit would undermine enforcement of Rule 10b-5. The Court observed that given the Commission's limited resources, disallowance of private actions by tippees against tippers would mean that many tippers would escape prosecution altogether. Lawsuits against tippers are a vital weapon against insider trading, the Court asserted, because they target the "sources" of inside information. Id. at 315-16.

One of your casebook authors has argued that the justifiable reliance requirement cannot be reconciled with *Bateman*:

> Although *Bateman* addressed only the *in pari delicto* defense, the decision applies equally to other common law doctrines. If this defense is subordinate to enforcement considerations, there is no principled basis for preventing subordination of other common law doctrines that are antithetical to enforcement.

> ***The duty of care requires that courts dismiss the claims of careless plaintiffs who have not themselves violated Rule 10b-5. Defendants in these actions, however, have violated Rule 10b-5. Dismissing suits against violators in order to penalize nonviolators undermines the enforcement of section 10(b) in direct violation of *Bateman* ***.

Margaret V. Sachs, The Relevance of Tort Law Doctrines to Rule 10b-5: Should Careless Plaintiffs Be Denied Recovery?, 71 Cornell L. Rev. 96, 135, 137 (1985). On the other hand, the Fifth Circuit has expressed a very different view:

> The due diligence standard *** ultimately foster[s] the same law enforcement goal as *Bateman* Eichler[.] *** These standards relating to a plaintiff's conduct encourage an investor to complain promptly about violations of his or her rights and, in so doing, to enable those with authority to control wrongdoing before additional investors are injured.

*Stephenson v. Paine Webber, Jackson & Curtis*, 839 F.2d 1095, 1099 (5th Cir. 1988).

7. **Zobrist *and Materiality.*** Can *Zobrist* be understood as a materiality case? A few courts have said yes. See, e.g., *Acme Propane, Inc. v. Tenexco, Inc.*, 844 F.2d 1317, 1322 & n. * (7th Cir. 1988). What are the consequences of characterizing justifiable reliance issues as materiality issues?

### *PROBLEM 2-22*

Topcat, Inc. is a toy manufacturer, founded in 1968 by Hughie and his brother Louie. Hughie and Louie each own 50% of the stock and have shared in the running of the business. In 2000, Louie sold his shares to Hughie for $3 million. In their negotiations leading to the sale, Hughie promised orally that he would never sell Topcat to anyone outside their family. Louie asked Hughie to incorporate this promise into their written contract, but Hughie declined to do so. Their contract contained a clause providing that Louie "executed the agreement without relying on any representation except as set forth in the agreement." Thereafter, Hughie sold the company to Bluster, Inc. for $50 million. Louie has now brought a Rule 10b-5 action based on the oral fraud. Can Louie satisfy the justifiable reliance requirement?

Cf. *Rissman v. Rissman,* 213 F.3d 381 (7th Cir. 2000).

### 2. *The Loss Causation Requirement*

The loss causation requirement focuses on whether the plaintiff's loss is attributable in significant measure to the defendant's fraud rather than to market or industry conditions or other factors extraneous to the fraud. One court has offered the following rationale for the requirement:

> No social purpose would be served by encouraging everyone who suffers an investment loss because of an unanticipated change in market conditions to pick through offering memoranda with a fine-tooth comb in the hope of uncovering a misrepresentation. Defrauders are a bad lot and should be punished, but Rule 10b-5 does not make them insurers against national economic calamities.

*Bastian v. Petren Res. Corp.*, 892 F.2d 680, 685 (7th Cir. 1990).

Courts originally imported the loss causation requirement into Rule 10b-5 from tort law. But in 1995 Congress codified the requirement as part of the PSLRA: "In any private action arising under this Act, the plaintiff shall have the burden of proving that the act or omission of the defendant alleged to violate this Act caused the loss for which the plaintiff seeks to receive damages." Section 21D(b)(4) of the Exchange Act. As is apparent from this language, Congress did not specify the nature of the required causative connection. In the following case, the court split three ways on that issue.

## AUSA LIFE INSURANCE CO. v. ERNST AND YOUNG

206 F.3d 202 (2d Cir. 2000)

OAKES, CIRCUIT JUDGE:

*** The appellants are insurance companies that invested in the securities of JWP, Inc., a company which ultimately went belly-up, causing the appellants to lose most of their investments. The appellee is the accounting firm that served as the independent auditor for JWP from 1985 through 1992, the period during which the appellants invested in JWP and the period during which the allegedly fraudulent activity was occurring.

The appellants made their initial purchases of JWP's notes in November of 1988. Through March 1992, they purchased additional JWP notes, the investments totaling $149 million. The notes were purchased in accordance with agreements ("Note Agreements") which included, among other things, the financial representations made by JWP at the time of the notes' issuances, future procedures to which JWP agreed to adhere for certifying JWP's maintained financial viability, procedures to be followed in the event of a default on the notes, and the like.

In purchasing the notes, appellants relied on JWP's past financial statements, including annual reports certified by E & Y. These financial statements were required, under the Note Agreements, to be kept in accordance with generally accepted accounting principles ("GAAP"). Also, at the time of each annual audit by E & Y, E & Y was required under the Note Agreements to furnish to JWP a letter for JWP to transmit to noteholders, referred to as a "no-default certificate" or a "negative assurance letter," which stated that E & Y had audited JWP's financial statements and that JWP was in compliance with the financial covenants in the Note Agreements.

In this instance and consistently, E & Y's statements about JWP's financial health were less than accurate and were not always in accordance with GAAP or GAAS ("generally accepted auditing standards"). However, E & Y did not fail to notice that often JWP's financial representations about itself were not in accordance with GAAP; rather, E & Y consistently noticed, protested, and then acquiesced in these misrepresentations:

> E & Y's failure lay in the seeming spinelessness of John LaBarca [the partner in charge of the JWP audit] and the other E & Y accountants in their dealings with JWP, and particularly with its CEO, Ernest Grendi.... Grendi almost invariably succeeded in either persuading or bullying them to agree that JWP's books required no adjustment. Part of the problem was undoubtedly the close personal relationship between Grendi and LaBarca. Grendi had been a partner of LaBarca in E & Y's predecessor firm and they continued to be good friends, regularly jogging together in preparation for the New York City Marathon.

*AUSA*, 991 F.Supp. at 248. "It became a well-worn inside joke to refer to the lax accounting standards at JWP as 'EGAAP,' an acronym for Ernest Grendi's Accepted Accounting Practices." Id. at 253.

JWP rapidly expanded between 1984 and 1992 with many aggressive acquisitions. The expansion was mainly financed by private placements of debt securities, which put JWP in an increasingly leveraged position. JWP's final, fatal acquisition was that of Businessland, Inc., in 1991. Businessland was a retailer of computers and a supplier of software. It had lost an average of ten million dollars a month over the ten months prior to the acquisition, and its auditors had issued a "going concern" qualification on its most recent audited financial statement, which indicated that the auditors doubted the company could survive.

Notwithstanding the gloomy financial picture, JWP executives saw potential. They believed that Businessland's structure could be converted into that of a "value-added" systems integrator; they thought that Businessland could be meshed into JWP's existing business which was heavily involved in installing wiring for computer networks; and they intended to capitalize on Businessland's trained sales force and existing clientele.

Unfortunately, this ambitious business venture did not evolve as envisioned. Upon JWP's acquisition of Businessland, JWP was forced to advance money to Businessland to meet the latter's operating expenditures. As well, the planned closure of most of Businessland's retail stores took longer than was initially anticipated. During the same general time period (the early 1990s), the retail computer market was the battleground for the "PC price wars," periods of intense competition, on bases including price. To nail the coffin shut, there was a downward trend in office construction which negatively impacted the electrical construction division of JWP.

In early 1992, David Sokol, JWP's new President and Chief Operating Officer, took note of what appeared to be serious accounting irregularities in JWP's records and statements. In August of 1992, JWP retained Deloitte & Touche ("D & T"), another major accounting firm, to review thoroughly JWP's books and E & Y's audits.

D & T concluded that JWP's annual reports for 1990-1992 should be restated to reduce the 1990 after-tax net income by 15% (from $59 million to $50 million), that the 1991 after-tax income should be reduced by 52% from $60 million to $29 million, and that 1992 loss of $612 million with a corresponding net worth of negative $176 million should be reflected. E & Y concurred.

JWP was able to continue paying the interest due on its notes through 1992, and JWP made partial payments through April 1993. However, JWP ultimately defaulted and was placed in involuntary bankruptcy in December 1993. Some appellants sold their notes at a huge loss in 1993 and 1994, and some appellants partially exchanged some of their notes for cash and securities of a lesser total value than the original notes. At the end of the day, appellants sustained at least a loss of approximately $100 million in lost principal and unpaid interest. ***

The [district] court found definitively that the plaintiffs did not prove the causation element *** because the plaintiffs were not able to show loss causation—the plaintiffs could not establish that E & Y's egregious accounting idiosyncracies caused plaintiffs' losses because JWP ultimately imploded due to Businessland's operations and the uncontrollable effects of the PC price wars. ***

We agree with the district court that E & Y did not perform the most efficacious accounting in this situation. See *AUSA,* 991 F.Supp. at 253- 254 ("John LaBarca [senior E & Y accountant] and his associates apparently lacked the backbone to stand up to the intransigent and intimidating Ernest Grendi and insist upon the changes necessary for compliance with GAAP"). However, we part company with the district court on its determination that it was "unforeseeable post-audit developments [that] caused JWP's insolvency and default even if its financial condition had been fully as healthy as was represented in those reports." Id. at 254.

*** How far back should the line be drawn in the causal chain, before which, "because of convenience, of public policy, of a rough sense of justice," proximate cause cannot be found? *Palsgraf v. Long Island R. Co.,* 248 N.Y. 339, 352 (1928). In the vernacular, where does the buck stop?

*** [T]he district court found that "JWP would not have defaulted on its debt obligations but for its acquisition of Businessland, which turned out to be a veritable sinkhole for cash." But *** had JWP's financial situation been accurately represented by E & Y, and had E & Y revealed the undisputed GAAP violations, JWP would have been in default on its notes prior to its acquisition of Businessland. Therefore, the acquisition of Businessland could not have taken place without a cure of the default or the investors' waivers of the default.

The appellee maintains—and the district court agreed—that the events leading to the demise of JWP and the loss of appellants' investments were due to external events for which appellee cannot be held accountable, and therefore loss causation was not established. The district court said specifically that

> JWP's insolvency and resulting default on its note obligations were caused not by the differences between its actual financial condition and that reflected in its audited annual reports, but by much more significant factors, including JWP's disastrous acquisition of the failing Businessland, in combination with the downturn in commercial construction and fierce competition in the PC market.

[991 F. Supp] at 250. We disagree, however, with this conclusion of the district court to the extent that the district court did not fully consider the legal definition of "loss causation" and the requisite factual points in determining whether loss causation was established. ***

We have consistently said that "loss causation in effect requires that the damage complained of be one of the foreseeable consequences of the misrepresentation." *Manufacturers Hanover [Trust Co. v. Drysdale Sec. Corp.,* 801 F.2d 13,] 21 [2d Cir. 1986]. However, Prosser and Keeton on the Law of Torts states that "it must be repeated that the question [of foreseeability or reasonably foreseeable risk] is primarily not one of causation, and never arises until causation has been established." Prosser and Keeton on the Law of Torts § 43, at 280-81 (5th ed.1984). In essence, this position contends that the foreseeability question need not be reached until causation is established, and foreseeability should then be used as a curb on all-encompassing liability, as a determination "of the fundamental policy of the law, as to whether the defendant's responsibility should extend to such results." Id. at 281. This position strikes us as entirely sensible. However, given the language in *** *Manufacturers Hanover* that seems to collapse the foreseeability inquiry into the proximate cause inquiry, and given that we are disinclined to retreat from an analysis that we have consistently employed, we will continue to treat loss causation qua proximate causation as a concept which embodies notions of foreseeability. ***

The foreseeability query is whether E & Y could have reasonably foreseen that their certification of false financial information could lead to the demise of JWP, by enabling JWP to make an acquisition that otherwise would have been subjected to higher scrutiny, which led to harm to the investors. Given that the district court did not make factual findings as to foreseeability specifically, we remand for more factual findings. In accordance with the factual findings, the court is then instructed to reconsider proximate cause in the context of its factual determinations on foreseeability.

By way of offering a tow rope to assist the district court through this Serbonian Bog, we note the following: A foreseeability finding turns on fairness, policy, and, as before, "a rough sense of justice." *Palsgraf,* 248 N.Y. at 352. "A 'reasonably foreseeable act' might well be regarded as an act that a reasonable person who knew everything that the defendant knew at the time would have been able to know in advance with a fair degree of probability." *United States v. LaCroix,* 28 F.3d 223, 229 (1st Cir.1994). Where foreseeability is less than immediately obvious, it is appropriate to make a judgment based on "some social idea of justice or policy." *First Nationwide Bank* [*v. Gelt Funding Corp.*, 27 F.3d 763, 770 (2d Cir. 1994]; id. at 772 ("proximate cause determination necessarily involves a component of policy"). These considerations should be coupled with the recognition that proximate cause is a common law concept, and such concepts evolve in a manner that reflects "economic, social, and political developments." *Cullen v. BMW of North America, Inc.*, 691 F.2d 1097, 1102 (2d Cir.1982) (Oakes, J. dissenting). Therefore, it is appropriate to examine the underlying policy of the securities laws involved and the climate of securities regulation as it has evolved and as it currently exists.

"During the Great Depression, Congress enacted the 1933 and 1934 [Securities] Acts to promote investor confidence in the United States securities markets and thereby to encourage the investment necessary for capital formation, economic growth, and job creation." Private Securities Litigation Reform Act of 1995, S.Rep. No. 104-98 (June 19, 1995). The 1934 Act was intended "to impose regular reporting requirements on companies whose stock is listed on national securities exchanges." *Ernst & Ernst v. Hochfelder*, 425 U.S. 185, 195 (1976). This was part of an overall broad scheme of federal regulation enacted in the early 1930s, through which Congress wanted investors to have access to comprehensive, accurate information about the companies in which they were investing. See id. (citing legislative reports of both the Securities Act of 1933 and the Securities Act of 1934).

In recent years, concern over potentially meritless securities lawsuits filed by "professional" plaintiffs abounded. See S.Rep. No. 104-98 (1995). It was feared that these suits were filed in the hopes of obtaining quick settlements by anxious defendants who were adverse to litigation. See id. It was further feared that these suits and the potential resultant settlements would increase the cost of raising capital and would chill corporate disclosure. See id. Therefore, in response to these and other concerns, Congress enacted the Private Securities Litigation Reform Act of 1995 (the "1995 Act").

The purposes of the 1995 Act are threefold: "(1) to encourage the voluntary disclosure of information by corporate issuers; (2) to empower investors so that they—and not their lawyers—exercise primary control over private securities litigation; and (3) to encourage plaintiffs' lawyers to pursue valid claims for securities fraud and to encourage defendants to fight abusive claims." See S.Rep. No. 104-98 (1995). The first and the third of the purposes merit our consideration from a policy standpoint in addressing the instant factual situation. The first purpose makes clear that Congress continues to be concerned with disclosure. The third purpose indicates that Congress recognizes that not all plaintiffs' claims are valid, plaintiffs are often disinclined to come forward and make otherwise valid claims, and defendants sometimes fail to aggressively fight abusive claims.

These two considerations weigh in favor of finding loss causation has been established in the instant case. As to the first purpose, E & Y specifically hindered disclosure. As to the third purpose, though some might argue that the risk of abusive claims would increase should the district court ultimately find loss causation here, we disagree. Certainly there may be claims against an auditor that are meritless and abusive. However, this opinion, and a potential finding of loss causation by the district court on remand, will not open the barn door for such. ***

We conclude that the district court failed to make sufficient factual findings relevant to the foreseeability aspects of loss causation. We therefore vacate and remand. ***

JACOBS, CIRCUIT JUDGE, CONCURRING:

*** The three opinions on this appeal argue for three different results, a division that would cause the appeal to misfire and leave the case undecided—an unacceptable outcome in a reviewing court.

In order to allow the Court to issue a mandate, I have shifted my vote on the issue of loss causation—from affirmance, to vacatur with a remand for further findings. If, as I think, the district court has implicitly decided the fact question that is now being remanded for consideration, the district court's express adoption of those findings of fact will under this mandate result in the same judgment that the district court has entered and that I would affirm on the present record and findings. If, as Judge Oakes thinks, the fact question is open, I am content to let the district court decide it, whatever the result. Vacatur under the terms of the mandate that Judge Oakes has drawn and that I join will result in a correct outcome as to loss causation. ***

Judge Oakes believes that the district court's discussion of loss causation fails to decide whether JWP would have been able to purchase Businessland absent E & Y's misstatements. I think that is the wrong question. It has been found—and all opinions on appeal agree—that JWP's acquisition of Businessland was a calamity that overwhelmed all other financial circumstances and brought about JWP's bankruptcy. Therefore, I think that the loss causation inquiry should be: Was it foreseeable that E & Y's misstatement of accounts would cause the plaintiffs to suffer losses caused by the disastrous Businessland acquisition? In my view, the question is sufficiently answered by the district court's findings that the plaintiffs' chief investment concern was JWP's *actual* cash flow (which was perfectly adequate to fund plaintiffs' bonds and was unaffected by the misrepresentations) and that the disastrous nature of the Businessland investment was unforeseeable. ***

Judge Oakes frames the foreseeability question in terms of "whether E & Y could have reasonably foreseen that their certification of false financial information could lead to the demise of JWP, by enabling JWP to make an acquisition that otherwise would have been subjected to higher scrutiny, which led to harm to the investors." I think that this "enabling" issue is a variant of but-for causation, and that the relevant inquiry (considering that JWP's failure and bankruptcy is the proximate cause of the bondholders' loss) is whether E & Y's misrepresentations could foreseeably have led to the failure of the company. As to this question, the district court's factual findings are clear enough[.] ***

Whether or not the acquisition was a foreseeable consequence of the misrepresentations cannot matter unless the misrepresentations are shown to have caused the resulting collapse. Even if one assumes (a stretch) that E & Y's misrepresentations allowed JWP to buy Businessland, E & Y's misrepresentations were not the reason for the resulting company's failure: JWP's ruin is easily attributable to business factors that were more potent than E & Y's misrepresentations, and were unrelated to them. The dispositive question is whether the JWP/Businessland combination would have collapsed even if JWP's books were accurately stated.

*** I think it would be a mistake to *** say (as I think my colleagues say) that *** loss causation can be satisfied by a nondisclosure that does no more than cause the investor to buy and hold during a drop in the market price induced by other causes. ***

To collapse loss causation into transaction causation would distort the traditional application of Section 10(b). *** By requiring both transaction causation and loss causation, Section 10(b) sets a high bar for recovery, and deliberately so. There is a particular reluctance to expand liability in any direction, see *Santa Fe Indus., Inc. v. Green,* 430 U.S. 462, 464 (1977); *Ernst & Ernst,* 425 U.S. at 197, let alone merge the required elements of the cause of action.

The misrepresentations in JWP's books (concerning treatment of acquisition costs, small tool inventories, net operating losses, and software costs) were not the proximate cause—*i.e.,* the loss causation—for the plaintiffs' loss. Those misrepresentations affected JWP's *apparent* cash flow, but they had no effect on JWP's *actual* cash flow. This is a critical distinction. While JWP's equity investors were rightfully concerned with the discrepancies in the company's books (because such variances would have affected the company's stock price), JWP's debt holders—the plaintiffs—would not necessarily have had cause for alarm. The primary concern of a debt holder is actual cash flow, the ability of the debt issuer to pay interest and principal as required. Indeed, even after JWP's annual reports were restated, the company continued to meet its interest payment schedule.

The district court's findings suggest that the plaintiffs would have remained invested in JWP notwithstanding the Businessland acquisition even if they had known of the discrepancies in JWP's books, because prior to acquisition there was no indication that Businessland would become the "sinkhole for cash" that it became. Id. There is also no allegation that the plaintiffs would have somehow prevented JWP from acquiring Businessland had they known of JWP's true financial condition. Therefore, JWP would still have been able to proceed with the acquisition that would have led to its insolvency and the plaintiffs' losses.

Moreover, it is hard to see how, had the auditors done a proper job, the bondholders would have been better situated or made more prescient. If, as it should have, E & Y had resisted JWP's pressure to misrepresent the company's financial condition, the bondholders would have received an accurate statement of accounts. But E & Y would not have been required to disclose management's thwarted desire to dress up the numbers. The job of the accountant is to ensure, within the parameters of the audit letter, that accounts comply with sound accounting practice. The accountant's duty is to do this regardless of pressure from managers to present the company's financial status as favorably as they can. But that obligation does not require disclosure of management's pressure to make the overly favorable representation. See *Santa Fe Indus., Inc. v. Green,* 430 U.S. 462, 477-78 (1977). ***

WINTER, CHIEF JUDGE, DISSENTING:

*** With regard to loss causation, I would hold that the facts found by the district court demonstrate loss causation as a matter of law. ***

Both the district court and my colleagues view the loss causation issue more narrowly than I do. The district court's reasoning went more or less as follows. Because of the misleading financial statements and no-fault letters, appellants had a view of JWP's financial condition that was more rosy than the truth. However, the true financial condition of JWP was not so different from the rosy view that a fully informed reasonable investor would have apprehended a significantly greater risk of default. Rather, in the court's view, because the collapse was largely caused by the risky and mistaken business decision to acquire Businessland, it was not sufficiently connected to the misrepresentations to be deemed a foreseeable consequence of them.

*** I would ask the following question: Would a reasonable investor—knowing in 1990 (i) that a firm's financial statements have deliberately and systematically misstated its condition over at least a two-year period, (ii) that the firm's auditor has supinely acquiesced in those statements, and (iii) that the auditor had also issued fraudulent no-fault letters on outstanding notes—reasonably apprehend a new and significant danger that business decisions involving volatile risks might be made and that one such decision might lead to financial collapse without the investor having a timely opportunity to make an informed decision as to the exercise of contractual rights that might cap its losses? I would answer the question in the affirmative.

The core of my disagreement with my colleagues goes to the scope of the matters on which appellants were misled by what the district court aptly described as E&Y's "lap dog" approach to the auditing of JWP and to the preparation of the no-fault letters. ***

First, the various financial statements and no-default letters misstated the firm's financial condition and compliance with the terms of the notes, not only for the current year but also for prior years. *** If aware of those facts, a reasonable lender would have inferred that JWP had a management quite willing to lie systematically to investors and an auditor willing to certify the lies. A reasonable lender would then have discounted JWP's creditworthiness not only because of its less favorable financial condition but also, far more devastatingly, because of the questionable quality of its management and auditor. Reasonable investors surely view firms with an untrustworthy management and auditor far more negatively than they view financially identical firms with honest management and a watch-dog auditor. Moreover, a reasonable lender informed of the truth would also have known that outstanding notes held by the investor were actually in default. Such defaults would have prompted serious consideration of the exercise of contractual remedies. Indeed, had the defaults been known, the Businessland acquisition could not have occurred without either a cure by JWP detailing the years of fraud or a waiver by appellants.

Second, the concealed information about JWP's management and E & Y's performance as an auditor would have alerted a reasonable lender to JWP's incentives to make risky decisions such as the Businessland acquisition. When the management of a firm and its auditor knowingly issue a series of certified annual financial statements that depict a financial condition more favorable than the truth, a dilemma is created. Both know that the truth will ultimately emerge. All things being equal, the value of the firm's outstanding securities will then decline, and fresh capital will be more costly or simply unavailable without installing a new management and auditor. Only a deal so profitable as to improve the firm's financial condition sufficiently to offset both the financial implications of the false statements and the decline in confidence in management will preserve the firm's standing in capital markets. The "huge-deal" solution to the firm's dilemma, however, puts lenders at risk. Unknown to them, the firm is far less risk averse than would be expected from the publicly available financial statements, and the chances of a default resulting from a deal with high volatility risk—like the Businessland acquisition—are much greater. The collapse here was therefore a foreseeable risk resulting from the series of false financial statements, and loss causation has been shown. ***

*** Judge Oakes correctly notes that "foreseeability" is the touchstone of loss causation. However, the concept of foreseeability may vary according to legal context. ***

In the case of securities fraud, the limits of "foreseeability" must be derived from the purposes of the federal securities laws. Those laws *** impose a duty on firms to provide investors with truthful information relevant to the value of certain investments. "The purpose of [Section] 10(b) and Rule 10b-5 is to protect persons who are deceived in securities transactions—to make sure that buyers of securities get what they think they are getting...." *Chemical Bank v. Arthur Andersen & Co.,* 726 F.2d 930, 943 (2d Cir.1984) (Friendly, J.). The securities laws are, of course, not an insurance policy against all losses by investors, and the concept of proximate cause limits recovery to plaintiffs and to losses for which the intent of the laws is served by recovery and denies recovery when that intent is not served.

If the meaning of proximate cause in the present context is to be derived from the statutory purpose of making sure that firms provide the truthful information necessary to allow investors to "get what they think they are getting," then much of the requisite analysis must come from the definition of materiality under federal securities law, which governs the scope and content of the information that the firm is under a duty to provide. The test of materiality is whether a reasonable investor would consider the particular information significant or, put another way, whether the information would affect the "total mix" of information available to the investor. See *TSC Indus., Inc. v. Northway, Inc.,* 426 U.S. 438, 449 (1976). The "foreseeability" of a loss in this context, therefore, turns upon the significance of the misrepresentations or omissions to the total mix of information available to the investor. Of course, in the context of common law negligence, it is generally foreseeability from the defendant's point of view that is at stake. In securities law, however, the critical issue is what a reasonable investor would have considered significant, and foreseeability is generally from the plaintiff's point of view because, once reliance and scienter are proven, the defendant is presumed to anticipate the apprehensions of a reasonable investor.

Loss causation in the context of federal securities law thus requires consideration of the significance to a reasonable investor of the truth compared to the content of the misrepresentations or omissions. If the significance of the truth is such as to cause a reasonable investor to consider seriously a zone of risk that would be perceived as remote or highly unlikely by one believing the fraud, and the loss ultimately suffered is within that zone, then a misrepresentation or omission as to that information may be deemed a foreseeable or proximate cause of the loss. This is all that is meant by our rule "that the damage complained of be one of the foreseeable consequences of the misrepresentation." *Manufacturers Hanover,* 801 F.2d at 21.

*** The issue is not whether a misstatement "caused" a loss. Rather, the issues are: (i) whether a reasonable investor would find the total mix of information so significantly altered by the truth as to apprehend a zone of risk that would seem remote to an investor still under the spell of misstatements, and (ii) whether the ultimate loss falls within that zone of risk. For example, losses due to insolvency, much less insolvency itself, are not "caused" by misrepresentations. Currently insolvent firms may (often do) survive and ultimately prosper if skillfully managed. But if a firm is not so fortunate after an investor has been misled as to solvency, the investor should not be denied recovery on the ground that it was management's lack of skill rather than the false assurances of solvency that "caused" the loss.

*** When appellants invested in JWP, they bargained for a certain risk profile that governed the decision to lend and matters such as maturity and interest rate. They also bargained for E & Y to monitor JWP's compliance with GAAP and for contractual rights, including acceleration, that might cap their losses should JWP default. E & Y's conduct deprived them of all these bargains and subjected them to concealed risks that resulted in losses.

It appears to have been the district court's view that E & Y misrepresented only particular financial information. It found that JWP's misrepresentations as to its financial condition had a calculable effect on the solvency of the firm so marginal that the risk of a default was not significantly understated by the misrepresentations. The court concluded that the risky and mistaken acquisition of Businessland was therefore not within the risks related to those misrepresentations. If the only material information misrepresented were the treatment of certain financial matters, I would agree. E & Y's conduct , however, misrepresented far more. ***

The note purchases at issue here began in 1990. The fraud had been ongoing since 1987, and, by the time of the 1990 purchases, some of the appellants already owned millions of dollars of JWP notes. A reasonable investor receiving the financial statements (and in two cases no-default letters) would have concluded that: (i) the risk profile established by prior financial statements was accurate and stable; (ii) E & Y was monitoring JWP's compliance with GAAP in its financial statements, and no default on the outstanding notes had occurred; and (iii) the ongoing monitoring by E & Y might afford some opportunity for appellants to cap their losses should JWP encounter unexpected difficulties. None of these conclusions would have been correct.

If the true facts had become known in 1990, *** a reasonable investor *** would have concluded that JWP had a management quite willing to certify the misrepresentations.[5] The note provisions requiring the auditor to misrepresent systematically its financial condition and an auditor willing to certify the lack of a default annually would have been deemed worthless. Absent an auditor willing to do its duty, such an investor would attribute no value to contractual rights to take certain action in the event of default because a fully-informed exercise would not be possible. The purchase of yet more JWP notes would have been out of the question in light of the true information. *** A reasonable noteholder would also have seriously contemplated the wisdom of retaining its present JWP notes and the need to invoke its powers under those notes, including acceleration.

5. Judge Jacobs speculates that E & Y could have issued a corrected statement of accounts for several years but would not have had to disclose that management had corruptly insisted on the earlier false statements. Even if that is so—and I am not sure that it is—such an extensive correcting of earlier years' books without any explanation would likely have had the same consequences as a full explanation for their need. Of course, any explanation that omitted a reference to management's role would have been yet another fraudulent misstatement.

The pattern of such misrepresentations itself created another risk to appellants that a reasonable investor would take into account. The management of a firm like JWP would have apprehended that, while such misstatements would reduce borrowing costs for a time, in all likelihood corrections in statements for prior years would eventually have to be made. The true financial condition of the firm would then be exposed, as would the misdeeds of JWP's management and E & Y. Investors' and analysts' evaluation of JWP would reflect both facts. Moreover, JWP's management and auditor would know that the corrections would reveal defaults on outstanding notes and perhaps trigger the exercise of the noteholders' contractual rights, including acceleration. (Indeed, the Businessland acquisition could not have proceeded if the default on the notes had been known, absent a cure by JWP—admission of years of fraud—or waiver by appellants).

For a management facing such circumstances, the temptation to seek salvation in a risky deal is greatly heightened. Only a very profitable new venture could offset the effect of revelations of past financial misstatements and systematic fraud by existing management and the firm's auditor. To be sure, such a deal would also have a vast downside, but even the prospect of a financial collapse might not seem to management all that different from the circumstances that would prevail if profitability were not substantially increased before disclosure of the fraud.

In short, when appellants began in 1990 to purchase the notes at issue, they were investing in a firm with compelling incentives that rendered it far less risk averse than the information certified by E & Y suggested. The chance that a highly risky venture would be undertaken that might lead to a default was far greater than could have been reasonably inferred from the false financial statements and no-default letters, and the contractual rights that might have minimized such a loss were in reality worthless. ***

## *NOTES AND QUESTIONS*

*1. The Foreseeability Approach.* Does the foreseeability approach endorsed by Judge Oakes blur the line between loss causation and transaction causation, as Judge Jacobs suggests? If so, is that blurring necessarily a bad thing?

*2. The Materialization of the Risk Approach.* Does the materialization of the risk approach favored by Judge Winter conflate loss causation with materiality? If so, is that a bad thing?

*3. The Proximate Cause Approach.* Does the proximate cause approach endorsed by Judge Jacobs require the plaintiff to prove that market or industry conditions (or other factors unconnected to the fraud) did not cause his loss? Would requiring such proof amount to too tough a standard?

*4. Making Comparisons.* Which approach to loss causation does the best job of disallowing losses due to extraneous conditions while allowing those due to the fraud?

*5. The Role of Policy.* Is the division among the judges in *AUSA* at bottom a function of underlying policy disputes? Cf. *Bruschi v. Brown*, 876 F.2d 1526, 1530 n. 6 (11th Cir. 1989) (maintaining that "policy considerations external to the transaction between the parties *** govern the courts' decisions" on loss causation). If so, what are the disputes at issue?

*6. The Significance of Codification.* As mentioned earlier, the PSLRA codified the loss causation requirement. What difference (if any) does codification make?

*7. Damages Contrasted.* Although you will study Rule 10b-5 damages in the section that immediately follows, you may find the following distinction helpful at this stage:

> To satisfy the loss causation requirement, a plaintiff need not show that a misrepresentation was the sole reason for the investment's decline in value. Ultimately, however, a plaintiff will be allowed to recover only damages actually caused by the misrepresentation. *** Consequently, as long as the misrepresentation is one substantial cause of the investment's decline in value, other contributing forces will not bar recovery under the loss causation requirement. But in determining recoverable damages, these contributing forces must be isolated and removed.

*Robbins v. Koger Properties, Inc.*, 116 F.3d 1441, 1447 n. 5 (11th Cir. 1997).

### *PROBLEM 2-23*

Thalia purchased shares of various companies on the advice of Jed, an employee of Starr & Co., a brokerage house. Jed had told Thalia that he was a stockbroker and had given Thalia a business card indicating that he was a portfolio management specialist. In fact, Jed was merely a trainee. When the stocks that Jed recommended began declining in value, he assured Thalia that they would rebound. Once Thalia learned that Jed was not in fact a stockbroker, she sold the stocks purchased on his advice. If Thalia sues Jed under Rule 10b-5, will she be able to satisfy the loss causation requirement?

Cf. *Marbury Mgmt., Inc. v. Kohn,* 629 F.2d 705 (2d Cir. 1980).

## G. DAMAGES

To recover damages under Rule 10b-5, a private plaintiff is obliged to prove them. This section examines three aspects of damages: their measurement; the system of proportionate liability established by the PSLRA; and the question of who supplies the money that plaintiffs recover.

In Rule 10b-5 actions brought by the SEC or the DOJ, no proof of damages is required. Thus, the material in this section of the Chapter applies to private actions only.

### *1. The Measurement of Damages*

Section 10(b) and Rule 10b-5 say nothing about how to measure damages. Given that the drafters of those provisions did not anticipate private enforcement, this silence is not surprising. Lower federal courts must therefore look elsewhere for guidance.

One benchmark is Section 28(a) of the Exchange Act, which provides that "no person permitted to maintain a suit for damages under the provisions of this Act shall recover, through satisfaction of judgment in one or more actions, a total amount in excess of his actual damages on account of the act complained of." As its language suggests, Section 28(a) precludes multiple recoveries for the same wrong. The Section has also been routinely held to prohibit punitive damages. See, e.g., *Pelletier v. Stuart-James Co.*, 863 F.2d 1550, 1557 (11th Cir. 1989) (Rule 10b-5 action). Moreover, according to the Supreme Court, the Section does not limit recovery to "net economic harm" and therefore does not require reduction of a Rule 10b-5 plaintiff's recovery by the amount of tax benefits received. See *Randall v. Loftsgaarden,* 478 U.S. 647, 663 (1986).

Another benchmark consists of two Supreme Court decisions that specifically reference methods of measuring damages. The first such decision is *Affiliated Ute v. United States,* 406 U.S. 128 (1972), which you will recall from your study of the reliance requirement in Section F.1.a of this Chapter. In *Affiliated Ute*, the Court designated as the default measure for Rule 10b-5 actions the "out of pocket rule" from common law deceit, with disgorgement (originating in contract law) as an alternative measure:

> In our view, the correct measure of damages under § 28 of the Act, is the difference between the fair value of all that the [plaintiff] received and the fair value of what he would have received had there been no fraudulent conduct, except for the situation where the defendant received more than the [plaintiff's] actual loss. In the latter case damages are the amount of the defendant's profit.

*Affiliated Ute*, supra, 406 U.S. at 155. Later, the Court opened up the possibilities still further by assuming (but not actually upholding) the at least occasional appropriateness of rescission—the unwinding of the transaction in question (or the monetary equivalent). See *Randall v. Loftsgaarden,* 478 U.S. 647, 662 (1986). See also id. at 666 (reserving the question of "whether, assuming that a rescissory recovery may sometimes be proper under § 10(b), plaintiffs in such cases should invariably be free to elect a rescissory measure of damages rather than out-of-pocket damages"). Recall that rescission (another remedy originating in contract law) is the remedy for actions under Section 29(b) of the Exchange Act. See supra Chapter 2.E (note 5 following *Cowin v. Bresler*). It is likewise the remedy for actions under Sections 11 and 12(a)(2) of the Securities Act, which you will study in Chapter 3.

Given these minimalist constraints, lower federal courts exercise enormous discretion in deciding how to measure Rule 10b-5 damages. Consider the consequences of this discretion as we focus first, on the measurement of Rule 10b-5 damages generally, and, second, on the special complexities raised by class actions.

#### *a. In General*

As you read the following decision, ask yourself whether the court reached a just result.

## ROWE v. MAREMONT CORPORATION

850 F.2d 1226 (7th Cir. 1988)

MANION, CIRCUIT JUDGE:

Herbert J. Rowe, his wife, Ann M. Rowe, and the Continental Illinois National Bank sued Maremont Corporation for securities fraud under Section 10(b) of the Securities and Exchange Act of 1934 and SEC Rule 10b-5. The suit arose from a face-to-face transaction in July, 1977 in which Maremont purchased 225,986 shares of stock in Pemcor, Inc. from the Rowes. After a bench trial, the district court entered judgment for the Rowes for $745,423.80 plus prejudgment interest and costs. Maremont appeals the district court's judgment. The Rowes cross-appeal, claiming that the district court awarded inadequate damages. We reject the contentions made in both the appeal and cross-appeal, and affirm.

I.

*** In early 1977, Herbert and Ann Rowe owned 8,921 shares of stock in Pemcor, Inc. The Rowes were also co-trustees, with Continental Illinois Bank, of a trust Mrs. Rowe's father had established in his will. The trust owned 216,965 shares of Pemcor stock. Together, the Rowes' and the trust's shares comprised 11 1/2 percent of Pemcor's outstanding stock. (We will refer to the shares collectively as the "Rowe shares" or "Rowe block," as did the district court.)

Although Pemcor was listed on the New York Stock Exchange, the Rowes could not sell their shares on the open market because the shares were not registered. The Rowe shares were also subject to an agreement between the Rowes and Potter-Englewood Corporation (the corporate predecessor to Pemcor) providing that the Rowes would not sell the shares before notifying Pemcor and receiving an opinion from Pemcor's counsel that the sale would not violate the 1933 Securities Act.

By early 1977, the Rowes had decided to sell their Pemcor shares. The Rowes explored selling the shares both by private placement and by a secondary public offering. In a secondary offering, the Rowe shares would have fetched between $5 and $6 1/2 per share. At that time, Pemcor's market price was around $12-$13 per share.

The investment bankers whom the Rowes had contacted concerning a private placement were having no luck finding a buyer. However, at around the same time the Rowes became interested in selling their shares, Maremont had become interested in expanding its operations by acquiring new companies. As part of this expansion program, Maremont retained Skadden, Arps, Slate, Meagher & Flom, a New York law firm active in mergers and acquisitions. In January, 1977, Maremont executed a commission agreement with The Illinois Company, a Chicago brokerage firm. The Illinois Company recommended Pemcor to Maremont as a potential acquisition and arranged meetings between Pemcor's and Maremont's executives. Although the meetings were cordial, Pemcor was not interested in a merger or affiliation at that time.

Around July 13, 1977, The Illinois Company informed Richard Black, Maremont's president, that the Rowe shares might be available. On July 18, pursuant to Black's instructions, Gordon Teach of The Illinois Company offered, on behalf of an undisclosed principal, to purchase the Rowe shares for that day's closing market price, $13 per share. Although Mrs. Rowe agreed the price was good (it was, in fact, an all-time high), she refused to sell the shares without knowing the purchaser's name. Therefore, Mrs. Rowe arranged to fly from her home in Virginia to Chicago the next day to meet Teach.

Over the next three days, the Rowes and their representatives met with Maremont representatives to negotiate the stock sale. On July 19, Mrs. Rowe, the Rowes' attorney, Robert Fuchs, and two Continental Illinois trust department officers, Darryl Hoovel and Gordon Martin, met with Teach in Chicago. After Mrs. Rowe insisted on knowing the purchaser's name, Teach told her that Maremont was the purchaser. Teach asked the Rowes not to disclose Maremont's name to anybody until twenty-four hours after the sale. Teach also told the Rowes that Maremont had recently sold a division, that it wanted the Rowe shares as an investment, that it wanted to protect its investment by electing a director, and that it wanted to purchase up to 20 percent of Pemcor's stock. At the close of the meeting, Mrs. Rowe agreed to sell the Rowes' Pemcor shares to Maremont for $13 per share. Before the Rowes and Maremont could close the deal, however, they needed to agree to and prepare written documents. Therefore, further meetings were necessary. ***

During the afternoon of July 20, Robert Pirie and Milton Strom, two Skadden Arps lawyers, arrived to handle the transaction for Maremont. Although Maremont had specifically retained Skadden Arps to work on a possible Pemcor acquisition, Shapiro [, Maremont's Treasurer,] introduced Pirie and Strom as two New York lawyers in Chicago on other business who were "stopping by" to help Maremont with the Rowe transaction.

Sometime during one of the meetings, on July 20 or 21, Marvin Temple, Fuchs' law partner, asked Shapiro whether Maremont was going to make a tender offer for Pemcor. Shapiro replied, "No." ***

By the end of the afternoon on July 21, the Rowes and Maremont had agreed on the final form of the documents necessary to complete the sale. *** Maremont and the Rowes subsequently executed all the documents.

During the days immediately following the execution of the Rowe contract, Maremont took steps to acquire the rest of Pemcor's stock. Black contacted Edward Anixter, Pemcor's president, to discuss a friendly takeover. Anixter was not receptive to the idea; a hostile tender offer thus seemed the most likely course. Skadden Arps' attorneys drafted "anticipatory tender offer documents" so that Maremont could move quickly. Maremont also arranged financing for its offer. On Friday, July 29, Black sent Anixter a "bear hug" letter advising Anixter that Maremont intended to offer $16.75 per share for all Pemcor shares. Pemcor did not respond to the letter. On August 1, Maremont publicly announced that it intended to make a tender offer. Pemcor opposed the tender offer. *** On August 3, Pemcor sued both Maremont and the Rowes to prevent the Rowes from transferring the shares to Maremont. Pemcor's complaint sought $30 million in damages and injunctive relief.

In the meantime, the Rowes *** went about the business of trying to complete the sale of their Pemcor stock. Immediately after the documents were signed, Fuchs phoned Chuck Kaufman, Pemcor's outside counsel, to ask Kaufman to cooperate in obtaining the necessary opinion letter. During that conversation, Kaufman asked Fuchs whether Maremont would make a tender offer. Fuchs replied that Maremont had advised him there would be no tender offer. ***

Fuchs and the Rowes learned about Maremont's tender offer on August 2. The Rowes were angry, and told Fuchs they wanted their stock back. Gordon Martin of Continental Illinois complained to Fuchs that the Rowes and the trust had been "taken." Fuchs, however, decided to move cautiously and to keep the Rowes' options open. The Rowes thus moved on a dual track, taking the necessary steps to complete the transaction while at the same time exploring the possibility of rescission.

*** On August 15, Fuchs spoke by phone with Pirie. *** At trial, Fuchs testified that he *** told Pirie that it was "incredible" that Maremont had not disclosed that it was going to make a tender offer, and that the Rowes were entitled to rescission. Fuchs did not, however, formally request rescission at that time. On August 23, Fuchs sent Maremont a letter formally requesting rescission. Although the rescission letter mentioned several alleged misstatements and omissions by Maremont (e.g., the representation that Maremont planned to obtain only up to 20 percent of Pemcor's stock), the letter did not mention Shapiro's statement that Maremont would not make a tender offer.

On August 30, the Rowes filed a counterclaim against Pemcor. Part of the relief the Rowes requested was an order directing Pemcor to transfer the Rowe shares to Maremont. On October 27, 1977, the Rowes filed a cross-claim against Maremont, alleging securities fraud (among other things). The cross-claim, like the rescission letter, did not mention the "No" tender offer representation.

*** On April 8, 1978, the escrow agent (over the Rowes' objections) delivered the Rowe shares to Maremont. Pemcor successfully rebuffed all merger attempts by Maremont until a white knight, Esmark, came to Pemcor's rescue. Pemcor merged into Esmark, and Maremont exchanged the Rowe shares for a block of Esmark shares. In August, 1979, Maremont sold the Esmark shares for $7,039,439. Thus, Maremont made a total profit of $4,056,834 from purchasing the Rowe shares.

II.

[*The Court of Appeals affirmed the district court's determination that Rule 10b-5 had been violated.*]

III.

The district court awarded the Rowes $745,423.80 in damages. Both the Rowes and Maremont challenge the district court's damage award. The Rowes complain that the district court did not award enough damages; Maremont contends that the district court should not have awarded any damages. ***

The district court made several key findings regarding damages. The court found that the Rowes were eager to sell, and that they would not have held onto their Pemcor stock even had Maremont not come along. The court also found that had the Rowes known the truth, they would have negotiated for a 25 percent premium from Maremont. The court found no evidence that Maremont would have rejected a demand for a premium, and noted that "Maremont had been willing to pay [the Rowes] market price for their [restricted] stock ... and might have been willing to pay more had plaintiffs negotiated for the same." Implicit in the above findings is a finding that

Maremont would have paid a premium over market price for the Rowe shares had the Rowes asked for it. In fact, the court noted that the price per share it awarded as damages was close to the 25 percent premium Fuchs testified he would have sought had he known the truth.

The Supreme Court has broadly stated that in Rule 10b-5 cases involving defrauded sellers, "the correct measure of damages ... is the difference between the fair value of all the ... seller received and the fair value of what he would have received had there been no fraudulent conduct, except for the situation where the defendant received more than the seller's actual loss. In the latter case damages are the amount of the defendant's profit." *Affiliated Ute Citizens of Utah v. United States,* 406 U.S. 128, 155 (1972). Based on this statement in *Affiliated Ute,* the Rowes argue that the district court should have ordered Maremont to pay them the over $4,000,000 profit it eventually made from purchasing the Rowe shares.

Despite its broad language in *Affiliated Ute,* the Court has not set any hard and fast rule concerning disgorgement of profits. Cf. *Randall v. Loftsgaarden,* 478 U.S. 647 (1986) (leaving open the question whether plaintiffs in Rule 10b-5 actions are "invariably" free to elect disgorgement). It is within the district court's discretion to determine whether disgorgement or some other damage measure is appropriate. *Arrington v. Merrill Lynch, Pierce, Fenner, & Smith,* 651 F.2d 615, 621 (9th Cir.1981). "The court's function is to fashion the remedy best suited to the harm." Id.*; Nye v. Blyth Eastman Dillon & Co.,* 588 F.2d 1189, 1198 (8th Cir.1978).

The district court properly rejected the Rowes' disgorgement request. Being a rescissionary measure of damages, disgorgement is meant to place a defrauded seller in the same position he would have occupied had the buyer's fraud not induced him to enter the transaction. See *Nelson v. Serwold,* 576 F.2d 1332, 1339 (9th Cir.1978). Disgorgement also prevents a defendant from being unjustly enriched by his fraud. *Randall,* 106 S.Ct. at 3153*; Hackbart,* [*v. Holmes,* 675 F.2d at 1114, 1122 (10th Cir. 1982)]. Making Maremont disgorge all its profit from purchasing the Rowe shares would accomplish neither of these purposes. Since the Rowes would have sold their Pemcor stock absent Maremont's fraud none of the profit Maremont made from the Rowe shares (besides that representing the higher purchase price the Rowes would have received from Maremont had the Rowes known the truth) would have accrued to the Rowes; thus, disgorgement is not necessary to place the Rowes in the same position they would have occupied but for the fraud. See *Capital Investments, Inc. v. Bank of Sturgeon Bay,* 430 F.Supp. 534, 537 (E.D.Wis.1977) ("[W]here it is shown that the seller would not have retained the securities had full disclosure been made, there is no reason to allow the plaintiff accrued profits as damages"), aff'd, 577 F.2d 745 (7th Cir.1978). And since Maremont would have obtained the stock from the Rowes even absent its fraud, any profit it earned above the premium it would have paid the Rowes absent the fraud is not unjust enrichment.

The Rowes argue that what would have happened if they had not sold to Maremont is speculative and in such a case courts should give plaintiffs—the defrauded parties—the benefit of the doubt and require defendants to disgorge their profits. We have no quarrel with this general principle—after all, "[i]t is more appropriate to give the defrauded party the benefit even of windfalls than to let the fraudulent party keep them." *Janigan v. Taylor,* 344 F.2d 781, 786 (1st Cir.1965). The problem here is that the district court did not have to "speculate"—in the legal sense—about the Rowes' course of conduct absent the fraud. There was more than sufficient evidence to support the court's finding that the Rowes would have sold their stock even absent Maremont's fraud.

The Rowes also argue that what they would have done absent the fraud is irrelevant because disgorgement is based on "simple equity" and on deterring fraudulent conduct. Deterrence is an important consideration in allowing disgorgement, see *Randall,* 106 S.Ct. at 3154, but "[d]isgorgement is remedial and not punitive." [*SEC v. MacDonald,* 699 F.2d at 47, 54 (1st Cir. 1983) (en banc)]. To make Maremont pay back profits that it would have made even if it told the truth is harsh and punitive. Equity requires only that a defendant give up its *unjust* enrichment. The district court did not err in rejecting full disgorgement as a measure of damages.

Maremont argues that the district court erred in awarding the Rowes any damages at all. The district court found that if Maremont had not come along, the Rowes would have sold their stock at a secondary offering for much less than the $13 per share they received from Maremont. Since the Rowes received more by selling their shares to Maremont than they would have if they had not sold to Maremont, Maremont contends that its fraud did not damage the Rowes. The problem with this argument is that Maremont *did* come along, and *did* induce the Rowes to sell their stock for $13 per share by lying about its intent to acquire Pemcor. Therefore, the district court correctly determined that it could base a damage award on the difference between what the Rowes actually received and what the Rowes would have received had Maremont not committed fraud. See *Affiliated Ute,* 406 U.S. at 155.

Maremont also argues that no evidence supports the district court's damage award. In determining how much the Rowes would have received if they had known the truth, the district court examined evidence of Pemcor's performance in the market to determine the value the market placed on the tender offer information. The district court found that

> Maremont's purchase of the Rowe shares was publicly announced the same day that Pemcor announced a substantial improvement in earnings: the stock (which had been inching up the entire period of the Rowe-Maremont negotiations) jumped over one point the next trading day to a high of 16.5. The stock then dropped to around 15, but climbed up again to 16.3 shortly after Maremont announced its tender offer. The stock price thereafter fluctuated and dropped below 16 until mid-November. Not until November 22, 1977 did the stock price again exceed 16.3.

650 F.Supp. at 1114-15. From this market evidence, the court concluded that by the market's evaluation of the information 16.3 represented a likely negotiated price between the Rowes and Maremont, and that the difference between 16.3 and the $13 per share Maremont paid the Rowes was the proper damage amount.

Maremont argues that the district court could not rely on the market information because the Rowes offered no expert testimony to demonstrate how much of the rise in Pemcor's stock price was caused by the tender offer information. While it is true that Pemcor's stock price rose to 16.5 after it announced substantial increases in dividends and earnings, the price fell to 15 during the next week and did not rise again until after Maremont announced its intention to make a tender offer. This raises the inference that the tender offer was a substantial factor in Pemcor's increased price. Even if other factors caused part of the price increase, it was Maremont's burden to present evidence to segregate those factors. See *Daniels Towing Service, Inc. v. Nat Harrison Associates,* 432 F.2d 103, 106 (5th Cir.1970) ("once illicit damage of consequence is established, the burden of segregating damages should be on the [defendant]"); *Meyers v. Moody,* 475 F.Supp. 232, 248 (N.D.Tex.1979), aff'd, 693 F.2d 1196 (5th Cir.1982) (applying *Daniels* in a Rule 10b-5 action). Maremont did not meet this burden.

Moreover, Maremont's attack on the district court's use of the market evidence misses the mark because the market evidence was not the only evidence the district court relied on in determining damages. The district court also relied on evidence that the Rowes would have received a 25 percent (or $3.25 per share) premium from Maremont had Maremont disclosed its intent to make a tender offer. This evidence reinforces the inference raised by the market evidence that the Rowes would have been able to negotiate for a price near $16.30 per share had they known the truth.

Maremont protests that there was no evidence that the Rowes would have received, or that Maremont would have paid, more than $13 per share. However, several of the Rowes' witnesses, including Fuchs, testified that they would have negotiated for a premium had they known the truth. Jerry Williams, who headed Maremont's corporate planning department, testified by deposition that Maremont normally paid a 25 percent premium for control stock. There was no evidence that Maremont would not have paid a premium if the Rowes had asked for one.

Maremont points out that the Rowes' stock was unregistered and restricted, and therefore incapable of being sold on the market. But Maremont did not want the stock for resale; it wanted the stock for control. Maremont could vote the stock like any other stock, and the Rowe shares represented the largest single bloc of Pemcor stock. Maremont had been pursuing Pemcor for some time, so it seems unlikely that Maremont would have simply given up and walked away from the bargaining table had the Rowes asked for more money. Given Maremont's control intentions, it was reasonable to conclude that the Rowe shares were just as (or almost as) valuable to Maremont as any other Pemcor stock (for which Maremont was willing to pay $16.75 per share); therefore, the district court could conclude that Maremont would have paid a premium over market to get the Rowe shares, even though the stock was not marketable.

Taken together, the market evidence and the evidence that Maremont likely would have paid a premium if it had told the truth support the district court's damage award. Although a damages award based on a purchase price of $16.30 per share is slightly higher than the 25 percent premium the Rowes testified they would have asked for, this difference does not require us to reduce the damages. A district court need not calculate damages with mathematical precision; it is enough that the evidence be sufficient to allow the district court to intelligently estimate damages. See *Feldman v. Pioneer Petroleum, Inc.*, 813 F.2d 296, 301 (10th Cir. 1987); *Freight Terminals, Inc. v. Ryder System, Inc.*, 461 F.2d 1046, 1053 (5th Cir.1972). ***

## *NOTES AND QUESTIONS*

*1.* ***Overlapping Measures?*** What measure did the court apply—out of pocket, disgorgement, rescission, or perhaps a blend?

*2.* ***The Role of Deterrence.*** Did the court give appropriate weight to deterrence? Judge Easterbrook and Professor Fischel have argued that from a deterrence standpoint, "the optimal sanction is the net harm that activity imposes on other people divided by the probability that the activity will be detected and prosecuted successfully." Frank H. Easterbrook and Daniel R. Fischel, Optimal Damages in Securities Cases, 52 U.Chi. L. Rev. 611, 618 (1985). Application of this formula is likely to be difficult. What is the net social harm, say, of the fraud attributed to Enron Corporation? Even more challenging, at the time of the commission of such fraud, what was the probability that it would eventually be discovered?

*3.* ***The Hole in the Out of Pocket Measure.*** The out of pocket measure seeks to ascertain what the fraud cost the plaintiff on the date he bought or sold the security in question. But the fraud's impact as of that date is not easy to pinpoint. The best evidence of that impact, at least for securities traded in an efficient market (see Chapter 1.G), is apt to be the market price following the announcement acknowledging the fraud. But the market price on the announcement date (invariably after the plaintiff's trade date) likely reflects not only the market's response to the fraud but also to numerous extraneous factors unrelated to the fraud. See generally Robert B. Thompson, "Simplicity and Certainty" in the Measure of Recovery Under Rule 10b-5, 51 Bus. Law. 1177, 1181 (1996). To be sure, courts can and do hear testimony from experts about how to discount the extraneous factors, but the invariable disagreement among the experts makes the scope (if not also the existence) of plaintiff's recovery impossible to ascertain in advance. How do you suppose this lack of predictability affects Rule 10b-5 litigation?

*4.* ***Market Overreactions.*** Conceivably an announcement acknowledging fraud may cause the market to overreact temporarily. As part of the PSLRA, Congress addressed this concern by adding Section 21D(e) to the Exchange Act:

> *** [I]n any private action arising under this title in which the plaintiff seeks to establish damages by reference to the market price of a security, the award of damages to the plaintiff shall not exceed the difference between the purchase price or sale price paid or received, as appropriate, by the plaintiff for the subject security and the mean trading price of that security during the 90-day period beginning on the date on which the information correcting the misstatement or omission that is the basis for the action is disseminated to the market.

Section 21D(e)(1). See also Section 21D(e)(2) (addressing how to proceed "if the plaintiff sells or repurchases the subject security prior to the expiration of the 90 day period described in" subsection (1)). As numerous commentators have noted, Section 21D(e) never operates to the detriment of defendants (or to the benefit of plaintiffs). See, e.g., Jonathan C. Dickey and Marcia Kramer Mayer,

Effect on Rule 10b-5 Damages of the 1995 Private Securities Litigation Reform Act: A Forward-Looking Assessment, 51 Bus. Law. 1203, 1209 (1996). How so? Is such an imbalance defensible?

Consider also the question of to which actions Section 21D(e) applies. Is it limited to actions based on the fraud-on-the-market theory? Does it apply to all actions that look to the market price (whether exclusively or partly) to set damages? Had it been on the books at the time, would it have applied in *Rowe*?

***5. Loss Causation Revisited.*** Recall that as part of the PSLRA, Congress codified a loss causation requirement by adding Section 21D(b)(4) to the Exchange Act. See supra Section F.2. Would the *Rowe* plaintiffs have satisfied this requirement had it been on the books at the time of their lawsuit? To what extent would their proof of loss causation have overlapped their proof of damages?

### *PROBLEM 2-24*

Fred is the president of Bosley, Inc., a closely held corporation and a widget manufacturer. Fred developed a plan for producing more and better widgets that he believed would double the company's profits. Not wanting to share these profits with anyone else, Fred asked the other shareholders to sell him their stock. At a shareholders' meeting called to discuss the matter, one of the other shareholders (Carl) asked Fred whether anything had recently occurred or was about to occur that should cause them to adopt a different view of the company. Fred replied that there was none. Shortly thereafter, Fred purchased the stock of the other shareholders for $100,000, a price determined in an appraisal commissioned for this purpose. Immediately after becoming the sole owner, Fred began putting into place his plan for more and better widgets. Execution of the plan required enormous effort and imagination on his part. As the result of the plan, the company's profits quadrupled. Shortly thereafter, he sold Bosley for $10 million.

Upon learning what Fred had done, Carl and the other shareholders sued Fred under Rule 10b-5. They allege that his denial to them concerning any impending changes constituted fraud. Assuming that they satisfy the other elements of Rule 10b-5, how should their damages be measured?

Cf. *Janigan v. Taylor*, 344 F.2d 781 (1st Cir. 1965).

#### *b. Damages in the Class Action Context*

In the context of a class action, the measurement of damages becomes especially complex. Consider Professor Alexander's description of those complexities:

> The class damages are supposed to consist of the sum of the individual damages of each member of the class. Calculating the total class damages is a two-step process. The first step is to determine the "per-share damages," the amount of the actual market price attributable to the nondisclosure on each day of the class period. The second step is to determine the aggregate damages of the class. To determine per-share damages, an expert economic witness constructs a "value line" which represents the "true value" of the stock—what purchasers would have been willing to pay if they had known the undisclosed information—on each day of the class period. The damages sustained by any particular

member of the class can then, in theory, be determined by comparing the price actually paid with the value line for the date of the transaction.

The value line is a hypothetical construct. The most common method of estimating per-share damages is to start with the share price after disclosure of the relevant information, and then, through an event study,[9] to isolate the effects of the withheld information from other factors, unrelated to the litigation, that may have affected the stock price between the time of the purchase and the time of the disclosure. Determining the value line is the least problematic aspect of the class action damages calculation, but it is subject to serious difficulties. The event study methodology depends on various debatable factual assumptions. As a result, the value line calculations of the experts for the two sides can differ greatly, even when they are using the same methodology. Moreover, even at its best the event study methodology can only calculate the price effect of the disclosure, which is not necessarily the same as the price effect of the information that was withheld.

From the value line, one can determine each class member's damages. A member of the class who bought shares during the class period and held them until the close of the class period (typically the date when the bad news was finally disclosed) suffered damages of the difference between the price paid and the value line, multiplied by the number of shares purchased. If a plaintiff resold the shares during the class period, however, both the purchase price and the selling price were inflated by the nondisclosure. The windfall the plaintiff received on the sale must therefore be offset against the loss incurred on the purchase. If the value of the undisclosed information remained constant during the class period, these amounts would cancel each other out, and those who bought and sold during the class period ("in-and-out traders") would have no damages. If the value of the information fluctuated during the class period, in-and-out investors' damages would depend on the dates of their transactions.

Related to this issue is the question of the number of shares in the class. Because some shares are bought and sold, often repeatedly, within the class period, the number of shares in the class is not simply the sum of the daily volume of trading during the class period. Indeed, the total daily trading volume may exceed the total number of shares outstanding. The methodology for calculating aggregate class damages must therefore include a procedure to account for in-and-out traders and to net out their windfalls against their losses. This step, however, introduces a fatal amount of uncertainty. The parties cannot reconstruct a share-by-share trading history of the shares traded during the class period, because most shares are held by brokers in street name. Individual buyers are not in fact matched to individual sellers, and individualized records of such transactions are not kept. Therefore, the parties cannot determine directly either the number of shares in the class or the precise damages attributable to each share in the class. Adjusting for in-and-out traders requires the use of a statistical model which estimates how many of the shares that traded on a given day had traded before during the class period, and on what days. The results of such models depend critically on empirical

---

9. Event studies begin with the change in the share price on the day of disclosure. Using regression analysis, the study eliminates events that are not firm specific (for example, an across the board fall in market prices) and isolates the extent to which the price change can be attributed to the disclosure. Working backwards, the study then establishes a hypothetical price for each day from the date of actual disclosure to the date that the information should have been disclosed. Ronald J. Gilson & Bernard S. Black, The Law and Finance of Corporate Acquisitions 185-228 (2d ed. 1995).

> assumptions about trading patterns. Those assumptions, in turn, are subject to considerable doubt. It is possible that the most widely used model overstates actual aggregate class damages by 100 percent or more, even in a relatively short class period.
>
> Thus, while the doctrinal statement of the measure of damages is relatively straightforward, the practical and methodological difficulties of calculating aggregate class damages make the damages inquiry in class actions complex and the ultimate outcome at trial uncertain. ***

Janet Cooper Alexander, Rethinking Damages in Securities Class Actions, 48 Stan. L. Rev. 1487, 1491-93 (1996). What is the likely impact of these uncertainties on the filing of class actions? What might explain Congress's failure to tackle the problem of class action damages in the PSLRA?

### 2. *Proportionate Liability*

Prior to the enactment of the PSLRA, courts maintained that defendants were jointly and severally liable for damages under Rule 10b-5. See, e.g., *TBG, Inc. v. Bendis,* 36 F.3d 916, 927 (10th Cir. 1994). Consequently, the plaintiff was entitled to recoup the entire amount of the damages from any defendant (who in turn could bring contribution actions against the others). See id. See also *Musick Peeler & Garrett v. Employers Ins.,* 508 U.S. 286 (1993) (recognizing an implied right to contribution among those who violate Rule 10b-5).

The PSLRA radically upended this state of affairs with its addition of Section 21D(f) to the Exchange Act. That Section establishes a scheme of proportionate liability under which a defendant (with limited exceptions) is liable exclusively for the fraction of the judgment for which she bears responsibility. Joint and several liability remains for those defendants who commit their violations "knowingly" (and who may seek contribution from each other pursuant to an express action enacted for this purpose). Whether each defendant acted knowingly as well as how much responsibility he bears for the total wrong are jury questions to be answered pursuant to special interrogatories. In deciding upon each defendant's respective share, the jury is to take account of "each of the other persons claimed by any of the parties to have caused or contributed to the loss incurred by the plaintiff, including persons who have entered into settlements with the plaintiff." Section 21D(f)(3). There is an explicit prohibition against disclosing to the jury how their decisions will affect the award of damages. See Section 21D(f)(6).

The PSLRA's proportionate liability scheme has been highly controversial. One commentator has summarized the debate as follows:

> Advocates of proportionate liability argued that joint and several liability is inequitable because it forces parties who are only partially responsible for the harm to bear more than their proportionate share of the damages. The accounting profession, in particular, argued that the current system provides plaintiffs with an incentive to join as many "deep pocket" defendants as possible, and compels defendants to settle weak claims in order to avoid disproportionate liability.
>
> The response to this argument is that, although the traditional doctrine of joint and several liability may cause accountants and others to bear more than their proportional share of liability in particular cases, this is because the

> system is based on equitable principles that operate to protect innocent investors. As between defrauded investors and defendants who are found knowingly or recklessly to have participated in a fraud, the risk of loss should fall on the latter. Proportionate liability would inevitably have the greatest effect on investors in the most serious cases, such as those in which the issuer becomes bankrupt after a fraud is exposed.

John W. Avery, Securities Litigation Reform: The Long and Winding Road to the Private Securities Litigation Reform Act of 1995, 51 Bus. Law. 335, 362 (1996).

Congress enacted the PSLRA 's proportionate liability scheme largely in response to lobbying from accounting firms. In a *quid pro quo*, the accounting firms endorsed an amendment to the Exchange Act requiring them to report illegal conduct to the issuer's directors and to the SEC. See Section 10A of that Act.

The pivotal role played by accountants in the Enron scandal has led some to argue that Congress should repeal Section 21D(f). Does proportionate liability make sense or does it encourage auditors and other collateral participants to be more reckless in the face of client fraud? To what extent is it necessary to abolish joint and several liability in order to protect defendants from having to pay more of the judgment than is just? On the latter question, see Donald C. Langevoort, The Reform of Joint and Several Liability Under the Private Securities Litigation Reform Act of 1995: Proportionate Liability, Contribution Rights, and Settlement Effects, 51 Bus. Law. 1157, 1158-59 (1996).

### *PROBLEM 2-25*

The president of Worldwide Corporation perpetrated a massive fraud from which the company's outside law and accounting firms kept their distance. The company is now bankrupt, as is the president. As the attorney for the shareholders, you have brought a Rule 10b-5 action against the law and accounting firms. You worry, however, that a jury will hold these firms responsible for only a small fraction of the harm done to your clients. What are your alternatives?

### *3. Who Pays for Recoveries?*

When plaintiffs recover damages under Rule 10b-5, from where does the money come? Can corporations indemnify their officers and directors? The answers turn largely on whether the litigation ends in a judgment of liability (relatively rare) or in a settlement without a judgment of liability (far more common).

When a court finds a defendant liable for intentional violations of the federal securities laws, courts have long prohibited indemnification on public policy grounds. See *McLean v. Alexander*, 449 F. Supp. 1251, 1266 (D. Del. 1978) (collecting cases). Such a defendant may nonetheless be protected by insurance. See id. at 1266 n. 51 (noting that exclusionary clauses notwithstanding, "some policies may be more expansive than the courts would permit through indemnification"), rev'd on other grounds, 599 F.2d 1190 (3rd Cir. 1979). In the case of a corporate defendant, recovery may come either from insurance or from the corporate treasury (and therefore ultimately from the shareholders themselves).

Where the litigation is settled without a finding of wrongdoing, the situation changes in several respects. Corporations are entitled to indemnify their officers and directors. See, e.g., *Raychem Corp. v. Fed. Ins. Co.,* 853 F. Supp. 1170, 1176-77 (N.D. Calif. 1994) (collecting cases). In addition, insurance coverage is more likely to be applicable. The availability of indemnification and insurance has meant that many individual defendants have not had to contribute personally to settlements. In addition, many settlements contain a condition that the individual defendants' personal assets cannot be tapped. Thus, a study of securities class actions over a five year period revealed that a settlement of an action against a company and its officers and directors is typically funded 70% by insurance, and 29.7% by the company, with only .3% coming from the officers and directors themselves. See Denise N. Martin et al., Recent Trends IV: What Explains Filings and Settlements in Shareholder Class Actions? iv (National Economic Research Associates, Nov. 1996). This pattern may be on the verge of change. The Enron and WorldCom scandals involve not only huge shareholder losses as to which indemnification and insurance are almost certainly insufficient but also individual defendants with vast personal assets. Under these circumstances, the plaintiffs are unlikely to be willing to agree to settlements that place those assets out of their reach. See Richard B. Schmitt & Henry Sender, CEO's Wealth May Be at Stake in Investor Suits, Wall St. J. at B1 (Aug. 9, 2002).

### *NOTES AND QUESTIONS*

*1.* ***Public Policy.*** If indemnification is objectionable on public policy grounds, what makes insurance any different?

*2.* ***Deciding Whether to Settle.*** Do the rules regarding indemnification and insurance make settlement more or less likely?

*3.* ***Tinkering at the Margins.*** As part of the PSLRA, Congress codified a right to recover attorneys' fees and costs on behalf of a defendant "that prevails in any private action" insofar as "a contractual relation permits." See Section 21D(f)(2)(B)(ii) of the Exchange Act. Does this small change signify that Congress otherwise approves of the indemnification/insurance schema as it currently operates?

## H. PRIMARY AND SECONDARY LIABILITY

A Rule 10b-5 violation typically involves a number of participants, be they individuals, business entities, or a combination. Which of these participants may be held liable for the violation? To answer this question, it is necessary to examine (i) the Supreme Court's decision in *Central Bank, N.A. v. Interstate Bank, N.A.,* 511 U.S. 164 (1994), which held that Section 10(b) and Rule 10b-5 do not encompass aiding and abetting liability; (ii) "primary liability," a category introduced by *Central Bank;* (iii) controlling person liability, a form of secondary liability explicitly authorized by the Exchange Act; and (iv) the possible relevance of the tort law doctrine of respondeat superior.

### 1. *Aiding and Abetting Liability*

In the 5-4 decision that follows, the Supreme Court overturned decisions in every circuit holding that liability under Section 10(b) and Rule 10b-5 extended to aiders and abettors.

## CENTRAL BANK, N.A. v. FIRST INTERSTATE BANK, N.A.

511 U.S. 164 (1994)

JUSTICE KENNEDY:

*** In this case, we must answer a question reserved in two earlier decisions: whether private civil liability under § 10(b) extends as well to those who do not engage in the manipulative or deceptive practice, but who aid and abet the violation. See *Herman & MacLean v. Huddleston,* 459 U.S. 375, 379, n. 5 (1983); *Ernst & Ernst v. Hochfelder,* 425 U.S. 185, 191-192, n. 7 (1976).

I

In 1986 and 1988, the Colorado Springs-Stetson Hills Public Building Authority (Authority) issued a total of $26 million in bonds to finance public improvements at Stetson Hills, a planned residential and commercial development in Colorado Springs. Petitioner Central Bank of Denver served as indenture trustee for the bond issues.

The bonds were secured by landowner assessment liens, which covered about 250 acres for the 1986 bond issue and about 272 acres for the 1988 bond issue. The bond covenants required that the land subject to the liens be worth at least 160% of the bonds' outstanding principal and interest. The covenants required AmWest Development, the developer of Stetson Hills, to give Central Bank an annual report containing evidence that the 160% test was met.

In January 1988, AmWest provided Central Bank with an updated appraisal of the land securing the 1986 bonds and of the land proposed to secure the 1988 bonds. The 1988 appraisal showed land values almost unchanged from the 1986 appraisal. Soon afterwards, Central Bank received a letter from the senior underwriter for the 1986 bonds. Noting that property values were declining in Colorado Springs and that Central Bank was operating on an appraisal over 16 months old, the underwriter expressed concern that the 160% test was not being met.

Central Bank asked its in-house appraiser to review the updated 1988 appraisal. The in-house appraiser decided that the values listed in the appraisal appeared optimistic considering the local real estate market. He suggested that Central Bank retain an outside appraiser to conduct an independent review of the 1988 appraisal. After an exchange of letters between Central Bank and AmWest in early 1988, Central Bank agreed to delay independent review of the appraisal until the end of the year, six months after the June 1988 closing on the bond issue. Before the independent review was complete, however, the Authority defaulted on the 1988 bonds.

Respondents First Interstate Bank of Denver and Jack K. Naber had purchased $2.1 million of the 1988 bonds. After the default, respondents sued the Authority, the 1988 underwriter, a junior underwriter, an AmWest director, and Central Bank for violations of § 10(b) of the Securities Exchange Act of

1934. The complaint alleged that the Authority, the underwriter defendants, and the AmWest director had violated § 10(b). The complaint also alleged that Central Bank was "secondarily liable under § 10(b) for its conduct in aiding and abetting the fraud."

The United States District Court for the District of Colorado granted summary judgment to Central Bank. The United States Court of Appeals for the Tenth Circuit reversed.

The Court of Appeals first set forth the elements of the § 10(b) aiding and abetting cause of action in the Tenth Circuit: (1) a primary violation of § 10(b); (2) recklessness by the aider and abettor as to the existence of the primary violation; and (3) substantial assistance given to the primary violator by the aider and abettor.

*** [T]he Court of Appeals found that Central Bank was aware of concerns about the accuracy of the 1988 appraisal. Central Bank knew both that the sale of the 1988 bonds was imminent and that purchasers were using the 1988 appraisal to evaluate the collateral for the bonds. Under those circumstances, the court said, Central Bank's awareness of the alleged inadequacies of the updated, but almost unchanged, 1988 appraisal could support a finding of extreme departure from standards of ordinary care. The court thus found that respondents had established a genuine issue of material fact regarding the recklessness element of aiding and abetting liability. On the separate question whether Central Bank rendered substantial assistance to the primary violators, the Court of Appeals found that a reasonable trier of fact could conclude that Central Bank had rendered substantial assistance by delaying the independent review of the appraisal. ***

II

*** In our cases addressing § 10(b) and Rule 10b-5, we have confronted two main issues. First, we have determined the scope of conduct prohibited by § 10(b). See, e.g., *Dirks v. SEC*, 463 U.S. 646 (1983); *Chiarella v. United States*, 445 U.S. 222 (1980); *Santa Fe Industries, Inc. v. Green*, 430 U.S. 462 (1977); *Ernst & Ernst v. Hochfelder*, 425 U.S. 185 (1976). Second, in cases where the defendant has committed a violation of § 10(b), we have decided questions about the elements of the 10b-5 private liability scheme: for example, whether there is a right to contribution, what the statute of limitations is, whether there is a reliance requirement, and whether there is an *in pari delicto* defense. See *Musick, Peeler & Garrett v. Employers Ins. of Wausau*, 508 U.S. 286 (1993); *Lampf, Pleva, Lipkind, Prupis & Petigrow v. Gilbertson*, 501 U.S. 350 (1991); *Basic Inc. v. Levinson*, 485 U.S. 224 (1988); *Bateman Eichler, Hill Richards, Inc. v. Berner*, 472 U.S. 299 (1985).

The latter issue, determining the elements of the 10b-5 private liability scheme, has posed difficulty because Congress did not create a private § 10(b) cause of action and had no occasion to provide guidance about the elements of a private liability scheme. We thus have had "to infer how the 1934 Congress would have addressed the issue[s] had the 10b-5 action been included as an express provision in the 1934 Act." *Musick, Peeler*, supra, at 294.

With respect, however, to the first issue, the scope of conduct prohibited by § 10(b), the text of the statute controls our decision. In § 10(b), Congress prohibited manipulative or deceptive acts in connection with the purchase or sale of securities. It envisioned that the SEC would enforce the statutory prohibition through administrative and injunctive actions. Of course, a private plaintiff now may bring suit against violators of § 10(b). But the private plaintiff may not bring a 10b-5 suit against a defendant for acts not prohibited by the text of § 10(b). To the contrary, our cases considering the scope of conduct prohibited by § 10(b) in private suits have emphasized adherence to the statutory language, "'[t]he starting point in every case involving construction of a statute.'" *Ernst & Ernst,* supra, 425 U.S., at 197 (quoting *Blue Chip Stamps,* 421 U.S., at 756 (Powell, J., concurring)). We have refused to allow 10b-5 challenges to conduct not prohibited by the text of the statute.

In *Ernst & Ernst,* we considered whether negligent acts could violate § 10(b). We first noted that "[t]he words 'manipulative or deceptive' used in conjunction with 'device or contrivance' strongly suggest that § 10(b) was intended to proscribe knowing or intentional misconduct." 425 U.S., at 197. The SEC argued that the broad congressional purposes behind the Act—to protect investors from false and misleading practices that might injure them—suggested that § 10(b) should also reach negligent conduct. Id., at 198. We rejected that argument, concluding that the SEC's interpretation would "add a gloss to the operative language of the statute quite different from its commonly accepted meaning." Id., at 199. ***

Later, in *Chiarella,* we considered whether § 10(b) is violated when a person trades securities without disclosing inside information. We held that § 10(b) is not violated under those circumstances unless the trader has an independent duty of disclosure. In reaching our conclusion, we noted that "not every instance of financial unfairness constitutes fraudulent activity under § 10(b)." We stated that "the 1934 Act cannot be read more broadly than its language and the statutory scheme reasonably permit," and we found "no basis for applying ... a new and different theory of liability" in that case. "Section 10(b) is aptly described as a catchall provision, but what it catches must be fraud. When an allegation of fraud is based upon nondisclosure, there can be no fraud absent a duty to speak." ***

Our consideration of statutory duties, especially in cases interpreting § 10(b), establishes that the statutory text controls the definition of conduct covered by § 10(b). That bodes ill for respondents, for "the language of Section 10(b) does not in terms mention aiding and abetting." Brief for SEC as *Amicus Curiae* 8 (hereinafter Brief for SEC). To overcome this problem, respondents and the SEC suggest (or hint at) the novel argument that the use of the phrase "directly or indirectly" in the text of § 10(b) covers aiding and abetting.

The federal courts have not relied on the "directly or indirectly" language when imposing aiding and abetting liability under § 10(b), and with good reason. There is a basic flaw with this interpretation. According to respondents and the SEC, the "directly or indirectly" language shows that "Congress ... intended to reach all persons who engage, even if only indirectly, in proscribed activities connected with securities transactions." Ibid. The problem, of course, is that aiding and abetting liability extends beyond persons who engage, even indirectly, in a proscribed activity; aiding and abetting liability reaches persons who do not engage in the proscribed activities at all, but who give a degree of aid to those who do. A further problem with respondents' interpretation of the "directly or indirectly" language is posed by the numerous provisions of the 1934 Act that use the term in a way that does not impose aiding and abetting liability. See § 7(f)(2)(C) (direct or indirect ownership of stock); § 9(b)(2)-(3) (direct or indirect interest in put, call, straddle, option, or privilege); § 13(d)(1), (direct or indirect ownership); § 16(a) (direct or indirect ownership); § 20 (direct or indirect control of person violating Act). In short, respondents' interpretation of the "directly or indirectly" language fails to support their suggestion that the text of § 10(b) itself prohibits aiding and abetting.

Congress knew how to impose aiding and abetting liability when it chose to do so. See, e.g., 18 U.S.C. § 2 (general criminal aiding and abetting statute); Packers and Stockyards Act, 7 U.S.C. § 192(g) (civil aiding and abetting provision). If, as respondents seem to say, Congress intended to impose aiding and abetting liability, we presume it would have used the words "aid" and "abet" in the statutory text. But it did not.

We reach the uncontroversial conclusion, accepted even by those courts recognizing a § 10(b) aiding and abetting cause of action, that the text of the 1934 Act does not itself reach those who aid and abet a § 10(b) violation. Unlike those courts, however, we think that conclusion resolves the case. It is inconsistent with settled methodology in § 10(b) cases to extend liability beyond the scope of conduct prohibited by the statutory text. To be sure, aiding and abetting a wrongdoer ought to be actionable in certain instances. The issue, however, is not whether imposing private civil liability on aiders and abettors is good policy but whether aiding and abetting is covered by the statute. ***

III

Because this case concerns the conduct prohibited by § 10(b), the statute itself resolves the case, but even if it did not, we would reach the same result. When the text of § 10(b) does not resolve a particular issue, we attempt to infer "how the 1934 Congress would have addressed the issue had the 10b-5 action been included as an express provision in the 1934 Act." *Musick, Peeler,* 508 U.S., at 294. For that inquiry, we use the express causes of action in the securities Acts as the primary model for the § 10(b) action. The reason is evident: Had the 73d Congress enacted a private § 10(b) right of action, it likely would have designed it in a manner similar to the other private rights of action in the securities Acts. See id., at 294-297. ***

Following that analysis here, we look to the express private causes of action in the 1933 and 1934 Acts. ***

From the fact that Congress did not attach private aiding and abetting liability to any of the express causes of action in the securities Acts, we can infer that Congress likely would not have attached aiding and abetting liability to § 10(b) had it provided a private § 10(b) cause of action. There is no reason to think that Congress would have attached aiding and abetting liability only to § 10(b) and not to any of the express private rights of action in the Act. ***

Our reasoning is confirmed by the fact that respondents' argument would impose 10b-5 aiding and abetting liability when at least one element critical for recovery under 10b-5 is absent: reliance. A plaintiff must show reliance on the defendant's misstatement or omission to recover under 10b-5. *Basic Inc. v. Levinson,* 485 U.S., at 243. Were we to allow the aiding and abetting action proposed in this case, the defendant could be liable without any showing that the plaintiff relied upon the aider and abettor's statements or actions. Allowing plaintiffs to circumvent the reliance requirement would disregard the careful limits on 10b-5 recovery mandated by our earlier cases.

IV

Respondents make further arguments for imposition of § 10(b) aiding and abetting liability, none of which leads us to a different answer.

A

The text does not support their point, but respondents and some *amici* invoke a broad-based notion of congressional intent. They say that Congress legislated with an understanding of general principles of tort law and that aiding and abetting liability was "well established in both civil and criminal actions by 1934." Brief for SEC 10. Thus, "Congress intended to include" aiding and abetting liability in the 1934 Act. Id., at 11. A brief history of aiding and abetting liability serves to dispose of this argument.

Aiding and abetting is an ancient criminal law doctrine. See *United States v. Peoni,* 100 F.2d 401, 402 (CA2 1938); 1 M. Hale, Pleas of the Crown 615 (1736). Though there is no federal common law of crimes, Congress in 1909 enacted what is now 18 U.S.C. § 2, a general aiding and abetting statute applicable to all federal criminal offenses. Act of Mar. 4, 1909, § 332, 35 Stat. 1152. The statute decrees that those who provide knowing aid to persons committing federal crimes, with the intent to facilitate the crime, are themselves committing a crime. *Nye & Nissen v. United States,* 336 U.S. 613, 619 (1949).

The Restatement of Torts, under a concert of action principle, accepts a doctrine with rough similarity to criminal aiding and abetting. An actor is liable for harm resulting to a third person from the tortious conduct of another "if he ... knows that the other's conduct constitutes a breach of duty and gives substantial assistance or encouragement to the other...." Restatement (Second) of Torts § 876(b) (1977). The doctrine has been at best uncertain in application, however. As the Court of Appeals for the District of Columbia Circuit noted in a comprehensive opinion on the subject, the leading cases applying this doctrine are statutory securities cases, with the common-law precedents "largely confined to isolated acts of adolescents in rural society." *Halberstam v. Welch,* 705 F.2d 472, 489 (1983). ***

*** Congress has not enacted a general civil aiding and abetting statute—either for suits by the Government (when the Government sues for civil penalties or injunctive relief) or for suits by private parties. Thus, when Congress enacts a statute under which a person may sue and recover damages from a private defendant for the defendant's violation of some statutory norm, there is no general presumption that the plaintiff may also sue aiders and abettors. ***

With this background in mind, we think respondents' argument based on implicit congressional intent can be taken in one of three ways. First, respondents might be saying that aiding and abetting should attach to all federal civil statutes, even laws that do not contain an explicit aiding and abetting provision. But neither respondents nor their *amici* cite, and we have not found, any precedent for that vast expansion of federal law. It does not appear Congress was operating on that assumption in 1934, or since then, given that it has been quite explicit in imposing civil aiding and abetting liability in other instances. We decline to recognize such a comprehensive rule with no expression of congressional direction to do so.

Second, on a more narrow ground, respondents' congressional intent argument might be interpreted to suggest that the 73d Congress intended to include aiding and abetting only in § 10(b). But nothing in the text or history of § 10(b) even implies that aiding and abetting was covered by the statutory prohibition on manipulative and deceptive conduct.

Third, respondents' congressional intent argument might be construed as a contention that the 73d Congress intended to impose aiding and abetting liability for all of the express causes of action contained in the 1934 Act—and thus would have imposed aiding and abetting liability in § 10(b) actions had it enacted a private § 10(b) right of action. As we have explained, however, none of the express private causes of action in the Act imposes aiding and abetting liability, and there is no evidence that Congress intended that liability for the express causes of action.

Even assuming, moreover, a deeply rooted background of aiding and abetting tort liability, it does not follow that Congress intended to apply that kind of liability to the private causes of action in the securities Acts. In addition, Congress did not overlook secondary liability when it created the private rights of action in the 1934 Act. Section 20 of the 1934 Act imposes liability on "controlling person[s]"—persons who "contro[l] any person liable under any provision of this chapter or of any rule or regulation thereunder." This suggests that "[w]hen Congress wished to create such [secondary] liability, it had little trouble doing so." *Pinter v. Dahl,* 486 U.S., at 650. Aiding and abetting is "a method by which courts create secondary liability" in persons other than the violator of the statute. *Pinter v. Dahl,* supra , 486 U.S. at 648, n. 24. The fact that Congress chose to impose some forms of secondary liability, but not others, indicates a deliberate congressional choice with which the courts should not interfere.

We note that the 1929 Uniform Sale of Securities Act contained a private aiding and abetting cause of action. And at the time Congress passed the 1934 Act, the blue sky laws of 11 States and the Territory of Hawaii provided a private right of action against those who aided a fraudulent or illegal sale of securities. See Abrams, The Scope of Liability Under Section 12 of the Securities Act of 1933: "Participation" and the Pertinent Legislative Materials, 15 Ford.Urb.L.J. 877, 945, and n. 423 (1987) (listing provisions). Congress enacted the 1933 and 1934 Acts against this backdrop, but did not provide for aiding and abetting liability in any of the private causes of action it authorized. ***

B

When Congress reenacts statutory language that has been given a consistent judicial construction, we often adhere to that construction in interpreting the reenacted statutory language. See, e.g., *Keene Corp. v. United States,* 508 U.S. 200, 212-213 (1993); *Lorillard v. Pons,* 434 U.S. 575, 580-581 (1978). Congress has not reenacted the language of § 10(b) since 1934, however, so we need not determine whether the other conditions for applying the reenactment doctrine are present.

Nonetheless, the parties advance competing arguments based on other post-1934 legislative developments to support their differing interpretations of § 10(b). Respondents note that 1983 and 1988 Committee Reports, which make oblique references to aiding and abetting liability, show that those Congresses interpreted § 10(b) to cover aiding and abetting. H.R.Rep. No. 100-910, pp. 27-28 (1988); H.R.Rep. No. 355, p. 10 (1983). But "[w]e have observed on more than one occasion that the interpretation given by one Congress (or a committee or Member thereof) to an earlier statute is of little assistance in discerning the meaning of that statute." *Public Employees Retirement System of Ohio v. Betts,* 492 U.S. 158, 168 (1989).

Respondents observe that Congress has amended the securities laws on various occasions since 1966, when courts first began to interpret § 10(b) to cover aiding and abetting, but has done so without providing that aiding and abetting liability is not available under § 10(b). From that, respondents infer that these Congresses, by silence, have acquiesced in the judicial interpretation of § 10(b). We disagree. This Court has reserved the issue of 10b-5 aiding and abetting liability on two previous occasions. *Herman & MacLean v. Huddleston,* 459 U.S., at 379, n. 5; *Ernst & Ernst,* 425 U.S., at 191-192, n.7. Furthermore, our observations on the acquiescence doctrine indicate its limitations as an expression of congressional intent. "It does not follow ... that Congress' failure to overturn a statutory precedent is reason for this Court to adhere to it. It is 'impossible to assert with any degree of assurance that congressional failure to act represents' affirmative congressional approval of the [courts'] statutory interpretation.... Congress may legislate, moreover, only through the passage of a bill which is approved by both Houses and signed by the President. See U.S. Const., Art. I, § 7, cl. 2. Congressional inaction cannot amend a duly enacted statute." *Patterson v. McLean Credit Union,* 491 U.S. 164, 175, n. 1 (1989) (quoting *Johnson v. Transportation Agency, Santa Clara Cty.,* 480 U.S. 616, 672 (1987) (Scalia, J., dissenting)).; see *Helvering v. Hallock,* 309 U.S. 106, 121 (1940) (Frankfurter, J.) ("[W]e walk on quicksand when we try to find in the absence of corrective legislation a controlling legal principle").

Central Bank, for its part, points out that in 1957, 1959, and 1960, bills were introduced that would have amended the securities laws to make it "unlawful ... to aid, abet, counsel, command, induce, or procure the violation of any provision" of the 1934 Act. S. 1179, 86th Cong., 1st Sess. § 22 (1959); see also S. 3770, 86th Cong., 2d Sess. § 20 (1960); S. 2545, 85th Cong., 1st Sess. § 20 (1957). These bills prompted "industry fears that private litigants, not only the

SEC, may find in this section a vehicle by which to sue aiders and abettors," and the bills were not passed. SEC Legislation: Hearings before a Subcommittee of the Senate Committee on Banking and Currency on S. 1178, S. 1179, S. 1180, S. 1181, and S. 1182, 86th Cong., 1st Sess., 288, 370 (1959). According to Central Bank, these proposals reveal that those Congresses interpreted § 10(b) not to cover aiding and abetting. We have stated, however, that failed legislative proposals are "a particularly dangerous ground on which to rest an interpretation of a prior statute." *Pension Benefit Guaranty Corporation v. LTV Corp.,* 496 U.S. 633, 650 (1990). "Congressional inaction lacks persuasive significance because several equally tenable inferences may be drawn from such inaction, including the inference that the existing legislation already incorporated the offered change." Ibid.

It is true that our cases have not been consistent in rejecting arguments such as these. Compare *Merrill Lynch, Pierce, Fenner & Smith, Inc. v. Curran,* 456 U.S. 353, 381-382 (1982), with *Aaron v. SEC,* 446 U.S., at 694, n. 11. As a general matter, however, we have stated that these arguments deserve little weight in the interpretive process. Even were that not the case, the competing arguments here would not point to a definitive answer. We therefore reject them. As we stated last Term, Congress has acknowledged the 10b-5 action without any further attempt to define it. *Musick, Peeler,* 508 U.S., at 293-294. We find our role limited when the issue is the scope of conduct prohibited by the statute. Id., at 291-292. That issue is our concern here, and we adhere to the statutory text in resolving it.

C

The SEC points to various policy arguments in support of the 10b-5 aiding and abetting cause of action. It argues, for example, that the aiding and abetting cause of action deters secondary actors from contributing to fraudulent activities and ensures that defrauded plaintiffs are made whole.

Policy considerations cannot override our interpretation of the text and structure of the Act, except to the extent that they may help to show that adherence to the text and structure would lead to a result "so bizarre" that Congress could not have intended it. *Demarest v. Manspeaker,* 498 U.S. 184, 191 (1991); *Santa Fe Industries,* 430 U.S., at 477 (language sufficiently clear to be dispositive). That is not the case here. ***

In addition, "litigation under Rule 10b-5 presents a danger of vexatiousness different in degree and in kind from that which accompanies litigation in general." *Blue Chip Stamps,* supra, 421 U.S., at 739. Litigation under 10b-5 thus requires secondary actors to expend large sums even for pretrial defense and the negotiation of settlements. See 138 Cong. Rec. S12605 (Aug. 12, 1992) (remarks of Sen. Sanford) (asserting that in 83% of 10b-5 cases major accounting firms pay $8 in legal fees for every $1 paid in claims).

This uncertainty and excessive litigation can have ripple effects. For example, newer and smaller companies may find it difficult to obtain advice from professionals. A professional may fear that a newer or smaller company may not survive and that business failure would generate securities litigation against the professional, among others. In addition, the increased costs incurred by professionals because of the litigation and settlement costs under

10b-5 may be passed on to their client companies, and in turn incurred by the company's investors, the intended beneficiaries of the statute. See Winter, Paying Lawyers, Empowering Prosecutors, and Protecting Managers: Raising the Cost of Capital in America, 42 Duke L.J. 945, 948-966 (1993).

We hasten to add that competing policy arguments in favor of aiding and abetting liability can also be advanced. The point here, however, is that it is far from clear that Congress in 1934 would have decided that the statutory purposes would be furthered by the imposition of private aider and abettor liability.

D

At oral argument, the SEC suggested that 18 U.S.C. § 2 is "significant" and "very important" in this case. At the outset, we note that this contention is inconsistent with the SEC's argument that recklessness is a sufficient scienter for aiding and abetting liability. Criminal aiding and abetting liability under § 2 requires proof that the defendant "in some sort associate[d] himself with the venture, that he participate[d] in it as in something that he wishe[d] to bring about, that he [sought] by his action to make it succeed." *Nye & Nissen,* 336 U.S., at 619. But recklessness, not intentional wrongdoing, is the theory underlying the aiding and abetting allegations in the case before us.

Furthermore, while it is true that an aider and abettor of a criminal violation of any provision of the 1934 Act, including § 10(b), violates 18 U.S.C. § 2, it does not follow that a private civil aiding and abetting cause of action must also exist. We have been quite reluctant to infer a private right of action from a criminal prohibition alone; in *Cort v. Ash,* 422 U.S. 66, 80 (1975), for example, we refused to infer a private right of action from "a bare criminal statute." And we have not suggested that a private right of action exists for all injuries caused by violations of criminal prohibitions. See *Touche Ross,* 442 U.S., at 568 ("[Q]uestion of the existence of a statutory cause of action is, of course, one of statutory construction"). If we were to rely on this reasoning now, we would be obliged to hold that a private right of action exists for every provision of the 1934 Act, for it is a criminal violation to violate any of its provisions. [Exchange Act § 32]. And thus, given 18 U.S.C. § 2, we would also have to hold that a civil aiding and abetting cause of action is available for every provision of the Act. There would be no logical stopping point to this line of reasoning: Every criminal statute passed for the benefit of some particular class of persons would carry with it a concomitant civil damages cause of action. ***

V

Because the text of § 10(b) does not prohibit aiding and abetting, we hold that a private plaintiff may not maintain an aiding and abetting suit under § 10(b). The absence of § 10(b) aiding and abetting liability does not mean that secondary actors in the securities markets are always free from liability under the securities Acts. Any person or entity, including a lawyer, accountant, or bank, who employs a manipulative device or makes a material misstatement (or omission) on which a purchaser or seller of securities relies may be liable as a primary violator under 10b-5, assuming *all* of the requirements for primary liability under Rule 10b-5 are met. See Fischel, 69 Calif.L.Rev., at 107-108. In any complex securities fraud, moreover, there are likely to be multiple violators; in this case, for example, respondents named four defendants as primary violators.

Respondents concede that Central Bank did not commit a manipulative or deceptive act within the meaning of § 10(b). Instead, in the words of the complaint, Central Bank was "secondarily liable under § 10(b) for its conduct in aiding and abetting the fraud." Because of our conclusion that there is no private aiding and abetting liability under § 10(b), Central Bank may not be held liable as an aider and abettor. The District Court's grant of summary judgment to Central Bank was proper, and the judgment of the Court of Appeals is reversed.

JUSTICE STEVENS, WITH WHOM JUSTICES BLACKMUN, GINSBERG, AND SOUTER, JOIN, DISSENTING:

*** In *hundreds* of judicial and administrative proceedings in every Circuit in the federal system, the courts and the SEC have concluded that aiders and abettors are subject to liability under § 10(b) and Rule 10b-5. See 5B A. Jacobs, Litigation and Practice Under Rule 10b-5 § 40.02 (rev. ed. 1993) (citing cases). While we have reserved decision on the legitimacy of the theory in two cases that did not present it, all 11 Courts of Appeals to have considered the question have recognized a private cause of action against aiders and abettors under § 10(b) and Rule 10b-5. The early aiding and abetting decisions relied upon principles borrowed from tort law; in those cases, judges closer to the times and climate of the 73d Congress than we concluded that holding aiders and abettors liable was consonant with the Exchange Act's purpose to strengthen the antifraud remedies of the common law. ***

*** If indeed there has been "continuing confusion" concerning the private right of action against aiders and abettors, that confusion has not concerned its basic structure, still less its "existence." Indeed, in this case, petitioner *assumed* the existence of a right of action against aiders and abettors, and sought review only of the subsidiary questions whether an indenture trustee could be found liable as an aider and abettor absent a breach of an indenture agreement or other duty under state law, and whether it could be liable as an aider and abettor based only on a showing of recklessness. These questions, it is true, have engendered genuine disagreement in the Courts of Appeals. But instead of simply addressing the questions presented by the parties, on which the law really was unsettled, the Court *sua sponte* directed the parties to address a question on which even the petitioner justifiably thought the law was settled, and reaches out to overturn a most considerable body of precedent.

Many of the observations in the majority's opinion would be persuasive if we were considering whether to recognize a private right of action based upon a securities statute enacted recently. Our approach to implied causes of action, as to other matters of statutory construction, has changed markedly since the Exchange Act's passage in 1934. At that time, and indeed until quite recently, courts regularly assumed, in accord with the traditional common-law presumption, that a statute enacted for the benefit of a particular class conferred on members of that class the right to sue violators of that statute. *** There is a risk of anachronistic error in applying our current approach to implied causes of action, to a statute enacted when courts commonly read statutes of this kind broadly to accord with their remedial purposes and regularly approved rights to sue despite statutory silence.

Even had § 10(b) not been enacted against a backdrop of liberal construction of remedial statutes and judicial favor toward implied rights of action, I would still disagree with the majority for the simple reason that a "settled construction of an important federal statute should not be disturbed unless and until Congress so decides." *Reves v. Ernst & Young,* 494 U.S. 56, 74 (1990) (Stevens, J., concurring). See *Blue Chip Stamps v. Manor Drug Stores,* 421 U.S. 723, 733 (1975) (the "longstanding acceptance by the courts" and "Congress' failure to reject" rule announced in landmark Court of Appeals decision favored retention of the rule). A policy of respect for consistent judicial and administrative interpretations leaves it to elected representatives to assess settled law and to evaluate the merits and demerits of changing it. Even when there is no affirmative evidence of ratification, the Legislature's failure to reject a consistent judicial or administrative construction counsels hesitation from a court asked to invalidate it. Here, however, the available evidence suggests congressional *approval* of aider and abettor liability in private § 10(b) actions. In its comprehensive revision of the Exchange Act in 1975, Congress left untouched the sizeable body of case law approving aiding and abetting liability in private actions under § 10(b) and Rule 10b-5.[8] The case for leaving aiding and abetting liability intact draws further strength from the fact that the SEC itself has consistently understood § 10(b) to impose aider and abettor liability since shortly after the rule's promulgation. See *Ernst & Young,* 494 U.S., at 75

8. By 1975, the renowned decision in *Brennan v. Midwestern United Life Ins. Co.,* 259 F.Supp. 673, 680 (ND Ind.1966), had been on the books almost a decade and several Courts of Appeals had recognized aider and abettor liability in private actions brought under § 10(b) and Rule 10b-5. See *Kerbs v. Fall River Industries, Inc.,* 502 F.2d 731, 739- 740 (CA10 1974); *Strong v. France,* 474 F.2d 747, 752 (CA9 1973). See also Ruder, Multiple Defendants in Securities Law Fraud Cases: Aiding and Abetting, Conspiracy, *In Pari Delicto,* Indemnification, and Contribution, 120 U. Pa. L. Rev. 597, 620-638 (1972). We have noted the significance of the 1975 amendments in another case involving a "consistent line of judicial decisions" on the implied right of action under § 10(b) and Rule 10b-5. See *Herman & MacLean v. Huddleston,* 459 U.S. 375, 384-386 (1983). Those amendments emerged from "'the most searching reexamination of the competitive, statutory, and economic issues facing the securities markets, the securities industry, and, of course, public investors, since the 1930's.'" Id., at 385, n. 20 (quoting H.R. Conf. Rep. No. 94-229, p. 91 (1975)).

Congress' more recent visits to the securities laws also suggest approval of the aiding and abetting theory in private § 10(b) actions. The House Report accompanying an aiding and abetting provision of the 1983 Insider Trading Sanctions Act contains an approving reference to "judicial application of the concept of aiding and abetting liability to achieve the remedial purposes of the securities laws," H.R. Rep. No. 98-355, p. 10 (1983), and notes with favor *Rolf v. Blyth, Eastman Dillon & Co.,* 570 F.2d 38 (CA2 1978), which affirmed a judgment against an aider and abettor in a private action under § 10(b) and Rule 10b-5. Moreover, § 5 of the Insider Trading and Securities Fraud Enforcement Act of 1988 contains an express "acknowledgment," *Musick, Peeler & Garrett v. Employers Ins. of Wausau,* 508 U.S. 286, 294 (1993), of causes of action "implied from a provision of this title."

(Stevens, J., concurring). In short, one need not agree as an original matter with the many decisions recognizing the private right against aiders and abettors to concede that the right fits comfortably within the statutory scheme, and that it has become a part of the established system of private enforcement. We should leave it to Congress to alter that scheme.

The Court would be on firmer footing if it had been shown that aider and abettor liability "detracts from the effectiveness of the 10b-5 implied action or interferes with the effective operation of the securities laws." See *Musick, Peeler & Garrett v. Employers Ins. of Wausau,* 508 U.S. 286, 298 (1993). However, the line of decisions recognizing aider and abettor liability suffers from no such infirmities. *** Allowing aider and abettor claims in private § 10(b) actions can hardly be said to impose unfair legal duties on those whom Congress has opted to leave unregulated: Aiders and abettors of § 10(b) and Rule 10b-5 violations have always been subject to *criminal* liability under 18 U.S.C. § 2. [Exchange Act § 32]. Although the Court canvasses policy arguments against aider and abettor liability, it does not suggest that the aiding and abetting theory has had such deleterious consequences that we should dispense with it on those grounds. The agency charged with primary responsibility for enforcing the securities laws does not perceive such drawbacks, and urges retention of the private right to sue aiders and abettors.

As framed by the Court's order redrafting the questions presented, this case concerns only the existence and scope of aiding and abetting liability in suits brought by private parties under § 10(b) and Rule 10b-5. The majority's rationale, however, sweeps far beyond even those important issues. The majority leaves little doubt that the Exchange Act does not even permit the SEC to pursue aiders and abettors in civil enforcement actions under § 10(b) and Rule 10b-5. Aiding and abetting liability has a long pedigree in civil proceedings brought by the SEC under § 10(b) and Rule 10b-5, and has become an important part of the SEC's enforcement arsenal. Moreover, the majority's approach to aiding and abetting at the very least casts serious doubt, both for private and SEC actions, on *other* forms of secondary liability that, like the aiding and abetting theory, have long been recognized by the SEC and the courts but are not expressly spelled out in the securities statutes.[12] The principle the Court espouses today—that liability may not be imposed on parties who are not within the scope of § 10(b)'s plain language—is inconsistent with long-established SEC and judicial precedent. ***

---

12. The Court's rationale would sweep away the decisions recognizing that a defendant may be found liable in a private action for *conspiring* to violate § 10(b) and Rule 10b-5. See, e.g., *U.S. Industries, Inc. v. Touche Ross & Co.,* 854 F.2d 1223, 1231 (CA10 1988); *Dasho v. Susquehanna Corp.,* 380 F.2d 262, 267, n. 2 (CA7 1967) See generally Kuehnle, 14 J.Corp.L., at 343-348. *** In addition, many courts, concluding that § 20(a)'s "controlling person" provisions are not the exclusive source of secondary liability under the Exchange Act, have imposed liability in § 10(b) actions based upon *respondeat superior* and other common-law agency principles. See, e.g., *Hollinger v. Titan Capital Corp.,* 914 F.2d 1564, 1576-1577, and n. 27 (CA9 1990) (en banc) (citing and following decisions to this effect from six other Circuits). These decisions likewise appear unlikely to survive the Court's decision.

### *NOTES AND QUESTIONS*

*1. The Court's Methodology.* The Court announced that Section 10(b) and Rule 10b-5 are construed differently depending on whether the issue involves the scope of prohibited conduct (in which case Section 10(b)'s text is determinative) or aspects of the implied private action (in which case the focus is on what Congress would have done had it explicitly created a private action under Section 10(b)). Have the decisions you have read thus far in this Chapter applied this methodology? See generally Jill E. Fisch, The Scope of Private Securities Litigation: In Search of Liability Standards for Secondary Defendants, 99 Colum. L. Rev. 1293 (1999).

*2. The Text of Section 10(b).* Is it arguable that Section 10(b)'s text encompasses aiding and abetting liability, the Court's insistence to the contrary notwithstanding? See Donald C. Langevoort, Words From On High About Rule 10b-5: *Chiarella*'s History, *Central Bank*'s Future, 20 Del. J. Corp. L. 865, 886-87 (1995) (focusing on the language "us[ing] or employ[ing] *** a manipulative or deceptive device or contrivance").

*3. Moving Beyond the Text.* While maintaining that aiding and abetting liability is a "scope" matter as to which the statutory text is dispositive, the Court nonetheless devoted considerable space to a discussion of whether such liability could be sustained based on the express causes of action, legislative history, and statutory policy. Are extra-textual considerations relevant to scope matters after all? Should they be?

*4. The Impact of* **Central Bank** *on SEC Actions.* What does *Central Bank* suggest about the Commission's authority to sue those who aid and abet Rule 10b-5 violations? To safeguard the Commission's authority in this regard, Congress enacted Exchange Act Section 20(e), which reads as follows:

> For purposes of any action brought by the Commission under paragraph (1) or (3) of section 21(d) [authorizing injunction actions and money penalties], any person that knowingly provides substantial assistance to another person in violation of a provision of this Act, or of any rule or regulation issued under this Act, shall be deemed to be in violation of such provision to the same extent as the person to whom such assistance is provided.

See *SEC v. Fehn,* 97 F.3d 1276 (9th Cir. 1996) (enjoining attorney under Section 20(e) for aiding and abetting violations of Rule 10b-5 and other Exchange Act provisions that were committed by the company that retained him and its promoter). Does Section 20(e) require the Commission to establish the defendant's "actual knowledge" of the underlying violation or does his recklessness suffice? In thinking about this question, consider the definition of "knowingly" in Exchange Act Section 21D(f)(2), which relates to joint and several liability for damages. (Note that there was no need to safeguard the DOJ's authority to proceed on an aiding and abetting theory, given the separate criminal aiding and abetting provision, 18 U.S.C. § 2).

*5. Conspiracy Liability.* Prior to *Central Bank,* conspiracies to violate Rule 10b-5 were actionable. See, e.g., *Brown v. Hutton Group,* 795 F. Supp. 1317, 1324 (S.D.N.Y. 1992); *Kronfeld v. First Jersey Nat'l Bank,* 638 F. Supp. 1454, 1468 (D.N.J. 1986). To establish a conspiracy, the plaintiff had to show "(i) an agreement between the conspirator and the wrongdoer and (ii) a wrongful act committed in furtherance of the conspiracy." *Brown,* supra, 795 F. Supp. at 1324. Following *Central Bank,* most courts have concluded that Rule 10b-5 conspiracy claims are no longer viable. See *Dinsmore v. Squadron, Ellenoff, Plesent, Sheinfeld & Sorkin,* 135 F.3d 837, 841 (2d Cir. 1998) (collecting cases). Do you agree? Can conspiracy claims be premised on the language of Rule 10b-5(a), which prohibits any person from "employ[ing] any device, *scheme,* or artifice to defraud" (emphasis added)? Do conspiracy allegations in private actions stand on a different footing from conspiracy allegations in Commission actions? (Note that the DOJ has the authority to allege criminal conspiracies based on provisions that you will study in Chapter 11).

*6. **State Law Alternatives.*** Aiding and abetting liability remains an option under the blue sky laws of many states as well as under common law fraud. Moreover, collateral participants in securities fraud (such as lawyers) are sometimes sued for malpractice or breach of fiduciary duty by the client/primary violator after the latter becomes insolvent and enters receivership. See *O'Melveny & Myers v. FDIC,* 512 U.S. 79 (1994). Money recovered in such litigation is then passed on to the investors, who are claimants of the insolvent entity's estate.

---

### 2. *Primary Liability*

In Part V of *Central Bank,* the Court made clear that at least some of those previously liable as aiders and abettors remain liable to suit as "primary violators." What are the components of primary liability? Consider that question as you read the following decision.

## WRIGHT v. ERNST & YOUNG LLP

152 F.3d 169 (2d Cir. 1998)

MESKILL, CIRCUIT JUDGE:

Plaintiff-appellant Irene Wright appeals from a final judgment rendered in the United States District Court *** dismissing her amended class action complaint charging defendant accounting firm Ernst & Young LLP with making materially false representations in connection with BT Office Products' sale of common stock, all in violation of § 10(b) of the Securities Exchange Act of 1934 (the Act), and *** Rule 10b- 5. *** The question we must answer is whether, under the Act, persons who purchase stock in a company that issued a press release containing false and misleading financial information, with a notation that the information is unaudited and without mention of its outside auditor, can recover from the auditor for its private approval of the information contained in the press release. We conclude that under these circumstances, primary liability is foreclosed by *Central Bank of Denver v. First Interstate Bank of Denver,* 511 U.S. 164 (1994), and by our recent decision in *Shapiro v. Cantor,* 123 F.3d 717 (2d Cir.1997). Accordingly, we affirm the judgment of the district court dismissing the amended complaint.

BACKGROUND

The appellee, Ernst & Young LLP (Ernst & Young or the firm), is a firm engaged in the business of providing various accounting services, including auditing and financial analysis. At all relevant times, Ernst & Young was the outside auditor for BT Office Products, Inc. (BT), a corporation engaged in the distribution and sale of office products. The gravamen of the amended complaint is that Ernst & Young violated the antifraud provisions of the Act by orally approving BT's materially false and misleading financial statements that BT in turn disseminated to the public in a January 30, 1996 press release. Plaintiff-appellant Irene Wright (Wright) represents a class of investors who purchased BT common stock during the period between BT's January 30, 1996 press release and BT's public statement on March 28, 1996 disavowing the financial statements contained in that release (the class period). Wright claims that because "the market knew and relied on the fact that these financial statements were approved by [Ernst & Young]," Ernst & Young is liable for losses suffered once BT's true financial picture emerged. Wright also filed a class action suit *** against BT alleging securities fraud in connection with the same set of circumstances. In March 1997, the class reached a settlement with BT under which the company agreed to pay $1,480,000 to the class.

As set forth in the amended complaint against Ernst & Young, BT embarked on a series of acquisitions in 1987, including the purchase of a stationer known as Summit Office Supply (BT-Summit). As BT expanded, its management decided to engage Ernst & Young to audit its year-end financial statements. Ernst & Young issued audit opinions certifying the accuracy of BT's financial statements for the years ending December 31, 1993 and December 31, 1994. Later, in July 1995, the firm updated and re-released the December 31, 1994 audit opinion as a "Report of Independent Auditors" for use in BT's initial public offering prospectus, which included a statement of BT's first quarter earnings for 1995. The audit upon which that report was based included a "full-scope" audit of several BT subsidiaries, but only a "limited review" of BT-Summit's accounts.

In the fall of 1995, the firm began a new "full-scope" audit of BT-Summit. Pursuant to this effort, it discovered an under-accrual of BT-Summit's accounts payable and alerted BT management. Upon consideration, however, Ernst & Young concluded that the under-accrual was not material and advised BT that it was probably a carryover of a similar under-accrual from the year before. Accordingly, the amended complaint avers that "on January 22, 1996 [Ernst & Young] signed off on BT Office Products' 1995 financial statements ... and authorized [BT] to release its 1995 year end results with full knowledge of the fact that the market would and did interpret the release of these figures as having been approved by [Ernst & Young]." The amended complaint further states that based on Ernst & Young's oral assurances, BT issued a press release on January 30, 1996 that set forth BT's 1995 financial results and indicated strong growth during 1995. The press release also stated, however, that the figures were "unaudited" and it made no mention of Ernst & Young.

In late February and March of 1996, it became apparent to both BT and Ernst & Young that the under-accrual problem at BT-Summit was more serious than previously believed. A further investigation revealed not only that BT-Summit employees used improper accounting techniques, but substantial company funds had been embezzled. In light of these discoveries, BT announced on March 28, 1996 that it was restating its 1995 financial results from a previously announced profit of $1.5 million to a loss of $200,000. With that announcement, BT's stock lost more than 25% of its value, injuring Wright and the other class members.

The amended complaint alleges that "due to [the firm's] recklessness and failure to follow Generally Accepted Auditing Standards ('GAAS') [Ernst & Young, by electing to perform only a limited review of BT-Summit,] did not uncover the massive 'accounting and financial reporting irregularities' at BT-Summit." Allegedly because of this recklessness, Wright and other class members purchased stock at an artificially inflated price and later suffered injury once BT's true financial picture emerged.

*** Ernst & Young filed a motion to dismiss, arguing *** that because it did not itself make any false statement to the public, the amended complaint alleged nothing more than "aiding and abetting" liability, a form of Rule 10b-5 liability that the Supreme Court abolished in *Central Bank of Denver v. First Interstate Bank of Denver*, 511 U.S. 164 (1994). In opposing that motion, Wright argued that the amended complaint properly alleged a 10b-5 violation because it alleged that Ernst & Young provided false and misleading advice to BT, knowing that the advice would be passed on to investors. Moreover, because Ernst & Young allegedly "signed-off" or approved the financial information within that press release, Wright averred that the market understood the press release as an implied statement by Ernst & Young that the financial information contained therein was accurate. In reply, Ernst & Young pointed out that BT's January 30, 1996 press release did not purport to repeat any statement made by Ernst & Young and that the press release expressly stated that the 1995 financial results were "unaudited."

On September 9, 1997 Judge Scheindlin granted the motion to dismiss. In doing so, she rejected Wright's argument that BT's press release constituted an implied statement to the public that Ernst & Young had approved BT's financial statements, noting that such a claim was refuted by BT's statement in the press release that the 1995 financial results were "unaudited." Further, the court observed that transforming that disclaimer into a guarantee of the statement's accuracy would "seriously deter disclosure of unaudited financial information." Id. The court also observed that sustaining the amended complaint in light of Ernst & Young's "clearly tangential role in the alleged fraud would effectively revive aiding and abetting liability under a different name, and would therefore run afoul of the Supreme Court's holding in *Central Bank*." ***

DISCUSSION

*** Wright first argues that because a defendant can incur primary liability under the Act for false statements that are not directly communicated to the public, there is no requirement that the false statement be attributed to the defendant at the time of its dissemination. Thus, Wright maintains that although BT's press release attributes no statement to Ernst & Young, the amended complaint nevertheless alleges a false statement within the meaning of § 10(b) because it alleges that Ernst & Young "assured" BT of the accuracy of its 1995 financial results, knowing that BT would, in turn, promptly disseminate those results to investors in the press release.

Further, Wright argues that even if the amended complaint does not allege conduct amounting to a false statement, it does state a § 10(b) cause of action under post-*Central Bank* authority because Ernst & Young is alleged to have "substantially participated" in the fraud. See *SEC v. First Jersey Securities,* 101 F.3d 1450, 1471 (2d Cir.1996) ("Primary liability may be imposed 'not only on persons who made fraudulent misrepresentations but also on those who had knowledge of the fraud and assisted in its perpetration.'" (citation omitted)). We disagree on both counts.

We conclude that Wright's arguments are foreclosed by *Central Bank* and by our recent decision in *Shapiro v. Cantor,* 123 F.3d 717 (2d Cir.1997). ***

In *Central Bank,* *** the Court did not hold that secondary actors are always free from liability under the Act. Rather, secondary actors like accountants may be held liable as primary violators if *all* the requirements for primary liability are met, including "a material misstatement (or omission) on which a purchaser or seller of securities relies." 511 U.S. at 191.

In the wake of *Central Bank,* federal courts have differed over the threshold required for a secondary actor's conduct to implicate primary liability. As Judge Gleeson of the Eastern District of New York observed,

> [s]ome courts have held that a third party's review and approval of documents containing fraudulent statements is not actionable under Section 10(b) because one must *make* the material misstatement or omission in order to be a primary violator. See, e.g., *In re Kendall Square Research Corporation Securities Litigation,* 868 F.Supp. 26, 28 (D.Mass.1994) (accountant's "review and approval" of financial statements and prospectuses insufficient); *Vosgerichian v. Commodore International,* 862 F.Supp.1371, 1378 (E.D.Pa.1994) (allegations that accountant "advised" and "guid[ed]" client in making allegedly fraudulent misrepresentations insufficient).
>
> Other [courts] have held that third parties may be primarily liable for statements made by others in which the defendant had significant participation. See, e.g., *In re Software Toolworks,* 50 F.3d 615, 628 n. 3 (9th Cir.1994) (accountant may be primarily liable based on its "significant role in drafting and editing" a letter sent by the issuer to the SEC); ... *In re ZZZZ Best Securities Litigation,* 864 F.Supp. 960, 970 (C.D.Cal.1994) (an accounting firm that was "intricately involved" in the creation of false documents and their "resulting deception" is a primary violator of section 10(b)).

*In re MTC Electronic Technologies Shareholders Litigation,* 898 F.Supp. 974, 986 (E.D.N.Y.1995). These two differing approaches have been characterized respectively as the "bright line" test and the "substantial[ ] participat[ion]" test. Id.

In *Shapiro,* we followed the "bright line" test after observing that "'[i]f *Central Bank* is to have any real meaning, a defendant must actually make a false or misleading statement in order to be held liable under Section 10(b). Anything short of such conduct is merely aiding and abetting, and no matter how substantial that aid may be, it is not enough to trigger liability under Section 10(b).'" We also observed that because § 10(b) and Rule 10b-5 focus on fraud made in connection with the sale or purchase of securities, a defendant must "'know or should know'" that *his* representation would be communicated to investors. Id. at 720 (quoting *Anixter,* 77 F.3d at 1226). "There is no requirement that the alleged violator directly communicate misrepresentations to [investors] for primary liability to attach." *Anixter,* 77 F.3d at 1226. However, contrary to Wright's argument, a secondary actor cannot incur primary liability under the Act for a statement not attributed to that actor at the time of its dissemination. Such a holding would circumvent the reliance requirements of the Act, as "[r]eliance only on representations made by others cannot itself form the basis of liability." Id. at 1225. Thus, the misrepresentation must be attributed to that specific actor at the time of public dissemination, that is, in advance of the investment decision.

In this case, BT's press release did not attribute any assurances to Ernst & Young and, in fact, did not mention Ernst & Young at all. Thus, Ernst & Young neither directly nor indirectly communicated misrepresentations to investors. Therefore, the amended complaint failed to allege that Ernst & Young made "a material misstatement (or omission) on which a purchaser or seller of securities relie[d]." *Central Bank,* 511 U.S. at 191. Moreover, as the district court aptly recognized, because the press release contained a clear and express warning that no audit had yet been completed, there is no basis for Wright to claim that Ernst & Young had endorsed the accuracy of those results. We therefore agree with the district court that holding Ernst & Young primarily liable under the Act "in spite of its clearly tangential role in the alleged fraud would effectively revive aiding and abetting liability under a different name, and would therefore run afoul of the Supreme Court's holding in *Central Bank.*" ***

Finally, Wright argues that we should follow other jurisdictions that have adopted the substantial participation test. See *In re Software Toolworks Inc. Securities Litigation,* 50 F.3d at 628 n. 3; *In re ZZZZ Best Securities Litigation,* 864 F.Supp. at 970 n. 12. We decline to do so. Moreover, even under the "substantial participation" test, we would be hard pressed to conclude that the amended complaint alleged an actionable misrepresentation within the meaning of § 10(b). ***

## *NOTES AND QUESTIONS*

*1. **Bad Facts.*** Was there anything about the facts of *Wright* that might have contributed to the court's disinclination to embrace a more expansive approach to primary liability?

*2. **The Bright Line Test.*** Do you agree with *Wright* that *Central Bank* provides support for the bright line test rather than for the substantial participation test? Does the bright line test follow from the reliance requirement, to which *Central Bank* refers? What impact is the bright line test likely to have upon the content of disclosure?

*3. **The Substantial Participation Test.*** This test comes in several varieties. Under the more restrictive version, the defendant must have been the initial source of the fraud. See, e.g., *Anixter v. Home-Stake Prod. Co.,* 77 F.3d 1215, 1226 (10th Cir. 1996); *Carley Capital Group v. Deloitte & Touche, LLP,* 27 F. Supp. 2d 1324, 1334 (N.D. Ga. 1998); *Picard Chem. Inc. Profit Sharing Plan v. Perrigo Co.,* 940 F. Supp. 1101, 1120 (W.D. Mich .1996). Under the more expansive version, the defendant need not have originated the fraud but must have figured significantly in drafting or editing the fraudulent document. See, e.g., *In re Software Toolworks Sec. Litig.*, 50 F.3d 615, 628 n. 3 (9th Cir. 1994); *Cashman v. Coopers & Lybrand*, 877 F. Supp. 425, 432 (N.D. Ill. 1995); *In re ZZZZ Best Sec. Litig.*, 864 F. Supp. 960, 970 (C.D. Calif 1994). Is either version consistent with *Central Bank*? With the reliance requirement? Is either version good policy? Which version is easier to apply? Would Ernst & Young have been liable under either version?

***4. The Necessity of a Fraudulent Statement.*** Can a defendant be primarily liable if he has not made a fraudulent statement? The Second Circuit addressed this question in a decision issued shortly after *Wright*:

> [A] primary violator is one who "participated in the fraudulent scheme" or other activity proscribed by the securities laws. *SEC v. First Jersey Secs., Inc.*, 101 F.3d 1450, 1471 (2d Cir. 1996).
>
> *** Romano "participated in the fraudulent scheme," i.e., the manipulation of USE's stock, by effecting the very buy and sell orders that artificially manipulated USE's stock price upward. Indeed, if the trader who executes manipulative buy and sell orders is not a primary violator, it is difficult to inquire who would remain liable after *Central Bank*. ***
>
> *** Romano is a primary violator despite the fact that someone else directed the market manipulation scheme. The Supreme Court in *Central Bank* never intended to restrict § 10(b) liability to supervisors or directors of securities fraud schemes while excluding from liability subordinates who also violated the securities laws.

*SEC v. U.S. Envt'l, Inc.*, 155 F.3d 107, 111-12 (2d Cir. 1998). Is *U.S. Envt'l* consistent with *Central Bank*?

***5. Primary Liability and Attorneys.*** The ability to hold primarily liable those who have not made fraudulent statements carries significance for the liability of attorneys in particular. Indeed, attorneys who have not themselves made fraudulent statements sometimes orchestrate schemes to violate Rule 10b-5. See, e.g., *Wash. Nat'l Ins. Co. v. Morgan Stanley & Co.*, 1999 WL 461796 at * 12 (S.D.N.Y. 1999) (denying summary judgment to a defendant law firm in part "because of [its] possible activities in planning and carrying out the whole program of taxable municipal bond issues"). But see *Ziemba v. Cascade Int'l, Inc.*, 256 F.3d 1194, 1206-07 (11th Cir. 2001) (evaluating law firm's primary liability solely with reference to whether it made an actionable misrepresentation or omission to investors).

***6. Primary Liability and* Central Bank.** Would Central Bank have been liable under the bright line test? Under either version of the substantial participation test? Under the approach to primary liability advocated by *U.S. Envt'l*?

### *PROBLEM 2-26*

Granger, Inc. is a drug company whose stock is listed on the New York Stock Exchange. The company has not been doing well recently, but it hopes that its new diabetes drug (Dibex), now in the final stages of testing, will turn things around. Unfortunately for Granger, Dibex has encountered difficulty in these last stages.

A major national newspaper assigned Sheila to write a feature article on diabetes. Sheila's article focused in significant measure on Dibex and the relief it stands to bring to millions. Sheila wanted her first feature article to be as good as possible. Accordingly, she submitted her final draft for review by several Granger employees with whom she had spoken. These employees failed to correct statements in the draft favorable to Granger that they knew to be wrong. In addition, they added statements favorable to Granger that they also knew to be wrong (which Sheila unwittingly included). The article did not refer to any Granger employees by name.

The article caused Granger's stock to rise in price. The price tumbled, however, several months thereafter once Granger announced that Dibex had encountered difficulties and might have to be scuttled entirely.

Ben is a Granger shareholder who bought his stock within a week of the article's publication. Can he sue Granger under Rule 10b-5 based on the fraudulent newspaper article?

---

### 3. *Controlling Person Liability*

Controlling person liability is the only form of secondary liability explicitly authorized by the Exchange Act (excepting SEC actions under Section 20(e) for aiding and abetting). The authorization is set forth in Section 20(a), which reads as follows:

> Every person who, directly or indirectly, controls any person liable under any provision of this Act or any rule or regulation thereunder shall also be liable jointly and severally with and to the same extent as such controlled person to any person to whom such controlled person is liable, unless the controlling person acted in good faith and did not directly or indirectly induce the act or acts constituting the violation or cause of action.

Controlling person liability has become more important in private actions under Rule 10b-5 in the wake of the Supreme Court's elimination of aiding and abetting liability in *Central Bank v. Interstate Bank,* 511 U.S. 164 (1994). Courts are divided, however, over whether the Commission can use Section 20(a). Compare *SEC v. First Jersey Sec., Inc.*, 101 F.3d 1450, 1472 (2d Cir. 1996) (holding that Section 20(a)'s text allows use by the Commission) with *SEC v. Coffey*, 493 F.2d 1304, 1318 (6th Cir. 1974) (holding that Section 20(a)'s text does not allow use by the Commission). What do you think?

As Section 20(a) indicates, controlling person liability requires a primary violation committed by a controlled person. The controlled person need not, however, be joined as a defendant. See, e.g., *Kemmerer v. Weaver,* 445 F.2d 76, 78 (7th Cir. 1971); *Primavera Familienstiftung v. Askin,* 1996 WL 580917 at *2 (S.D.N.Y. 1996).

Note also that Section 20(a) does not provide a definition of control. As you read the following case, ask yourself why the court found the defendant to be a controlling person as well as how the defendant might establish his good faith defense at trial.

## ARTHUR CHILDREN'S TRUST v. KEIM

994 F.2d 1390 (9th Cir. 1993)

NOONAN, CIRCUIT JUDGE:

*** The underlying action against Keim is for securities fraud in violation of *** Rule 10b-5. He is alleged to have been a control person *** of an issuer of fraudulent securities. *** We reverse the summary judgment in favor of Keim ***.

### *FACTS*

In January 1985 an agreement for a joint venture called Los Caballos Development Associates (the Venture) was entered into by Los Caballos de Santa Fe, Inc., a New Mexico corporation (the Santa Fe Company) and Parkland Development Corporation, an Arizona corporation (Parkland). The agreement provided that the Santa Fe Company would "initially contribute" certain real estate and services to the Venture "in the form of administrative and development expertise" and that Parkland would "initially contribute" certain real estate and services "in the form of administrative, and financing and development expertise." A Management Committee was created whose duties were stated in the agreement as follows:

> Except as expressly provided herein, neither of the Venturers shall have the authority to act for the other Venturer, but instead the management of the business affairs of the Venture shall be vested in a Management Committee ... Any major or significant business decisions affecting the Venture shall be made by the Management Committee, including, but not limited to ... incurring of any obligation on behalf of the Venture in excess of Twenty Thousand Dollars ($20,000), the employment of professionals and other employees, and any other decision which may materially affect the Venture.

A special section of the agreement, entitled "Additional Funds," provided:

> If in the judgment of the Management Committee additional funds are required for the Venture's operations and purposes from time to time, and if the Management Committee determines that the funds are not to be borrowed, then the additional funds required shall be contributed by the Venturers fifty percent (50%) each upon ten (10) days' advanced notice, and shall be treated as additional capital contributions to the Venture.

The Management Committee was to consist of eight members, with each venturer nominating four and Parkland having the right to designate the chairman, whose vote in case of a tie would be decisive and who was to be responsible for "the day-to-day business decisions and operations." Parkland nominated John Hill, Michael Smith, Timothy Sprague and Larry LaPrade, with LaPrade designated as chairman. The Santa Fe company nominated its chairman, Burton Melton; its president, Don Burt; and two of its directors, Mark Conkling and Keim.

The purpose of the Venture was a real estate development south of Santa Fe which, when completed, would include private residences, retail shops, a hotel and—as a centerpiece—a stadium and accompanying facilities to constitute a major equestrian convention center—hence the project's appealing name, "The Horses," in Spanish.

LaPrade and Smith began the task of money-raising, using as a vehicle Incor, a corporation controlled by them. As a result of Incor's solicitation the Investors, mostly pension plans for doctors, were led to purchase the Venture's notes. All the representations made to the Investors were made by Incor, LaPrade or Smith. The Venture put no restrictions on their methods. No representations to the Investors were made by Keim.

On March 1, 1985 the Venture issued a promissory note for $3,760,000 *** The interest was 16 percent on the unpaid principal balance beginning April 1, 1985, with a balloon payment of the entire unpaid principal balance plus all unpaid interest due 12 months from the date of the note. The note was secured by a second mortgage by the Venture on its real estate in Santa Fe. The mortgage and the note were executed by the Venture with the signatures of Los Caballos de Santa Fe, Inc., joint venturer, by Peter C. Webb, its secretary-treasurer, and Parkland Development Corporation, joint venturer, by Michael Smith, its treasurer.

Soon after this financing had been accomplished, the Venture was in difficult straits. According to a memorandum of July 3, 1985 from Peter Webb, controller of the Santa Fe company, to the members of the Management Committee of the Venture, including Keim, the committee on June 17, 1985 discussed the "precarious situation regarding our financial capabilities to meet our obligations to the Incor investors and our other contractual obligations." The Venture's current deposits were "adequate to cover our Incor interest obligations," but if "we continue to pay our development obligations we could be out of money as soon as October." Michael Smith had stated that if construction financing were not in place by October he "would address the problem." In light of this statement, "it was agreed" that Webb "should continue to pay our obligations as they are incurred or due using all available funds including those previously earmarked for interest payments to Incor's investors."

According to the minutes of the Management Committee for July 10, 1985, at which Keim was present, a large number of topics were discussed. Among other things:

> Larry LaPrade emphasized the profit portion of Sheet 16 [of the Financial Package]. The lenders are interested in hard numbers, and the profit that will be generated.
>
> Financing package was discussed. Sprague stated that we had to raise from three to five million dollars worth of equity. He suggested to the Management Committee that they should begin putting names, addresses of potential investors. He said that there were tax considerations to think of, perhaps potential pension fund money. Three and one half million dollars raised by ourselves, the rest banks. Great tax shelters for prospective investors. Keim felt tax benefits would be there. Pension Plan money is easier to tap.

Following a discussion of "the appraisal," Larry LaPrade raised the possibility of a bridge loan, "starting in August." Keim said "he was prepared to give all out whatever it takes. Pension Plan 15%."

In addition to being a member of the Management Committee of the Venture, Keim was chairman of its Development Committee. He had a 10 percent equity interest in the enterprise. He was also owed a $100,000 "development fee" by the Santa Fe company, a fee which he asserted in a letter to Larry LaPrade of November 27, 1985 had been assumed by LaPrade, apparently meaning that the Venture had assumed it. A budget of the Venture reflects only one fee for development—$100,000 owed Keim.

According to the affidavit of Timothy Sprague:

> [V]arious discussions were had between members of the management committee, including Howard Keim, with respect to the raising of seed capital for the project. As time progressed throughout 1985, the project having continued to incur significant development expenses and no construction or permanent financing having been obtained for the project, these discussions among the members of the management committee included "rolling over" previous loans secured for the project by Michael Smith and Larry LaPrade, together with the raising of new monies through additional loans.
>
> Mr. Keim—who was constantly pressing the venture for payment of his own fees—was generally an advocate of Smith and LaPrade's lending activities, his comments essentially being to get it done.

Sprague further swore that at the July 1985 meeting or prior thereto, Smith advised the members of the Management Committee that "he was borrowing monies for the project from doctor pension plans by offering to secure their loans by the project's real property, on a 50% loan to value ratio. Previously, at the time of the original loan, it was discussed that it would also be secured by the personal guarantees of all the Los Caballos venturers, excluding defendant Keim, who I understand refused to provide one." On a flight from Albuquerque to Phoenix in July 1985 Sprague also described to Keim "Smith and LaPrade's manner of raising funds."

On March 1, 1986 the Venture again executed a promissory note, secured by a mortgage on its real estate, in the amount of $5,400,000. *** The interest was 16 percent on the unpaid principal balance, due beginning April 1, 1986, "with a balloon payment of the entire unpaid principal plus all unpaid interest due and payable six months from the date of receipt of invested funds." The note and mortgage were executed by the same entities and persons as the note and mortgage of March 1, 1985. The proceeds of this issue were used to repay the 1985 note.

All of the foregoing facts are not disputed, with one large exception. According to Keim's deposition, he had no knowledge of how LaPrade and Smith were raising the money and no knowledge of who was providing it.

The Venture was a financial disaster. LaPrade and Smith entered bankruptcy. The Investors lost their money.

*PROCEEDINGS*

On December 21, 1988 the Investors filed suit under the Securities Exchange Act of 1934 against six of the members of the Management Committee, including Keim, and against several others associated with the enterprise. *** The third claim for relief asserted that the defendants who had been members of the Management Committee of the Venture were controlling persons in the sense that section 20(a) *** defines "controlling persons." They were alleged to have known the dire financial straits of the Venture and, knowing it, to have also known that no one would have invested in it unless provided incentives which no defendant had reason to believe were being promised or unless there were false representations. In this situation, knowing that millions of dollars were being raised for their project from private investors, the control persons allegedly undertook no action to implement controls on LaPrade, Smith and Sprague; they allegedly exercised no "internal control or supervision" to prevent violation of the securities law; they allegedly either did not inquire as to the representations made to induce the loans or knew that the loans were induced by fraudulent representations. ***

On May 30, 1991, the district court found that Keim had no control over the financing and was therefore not a control person. Moreover, the court found "nothing to indicate that Keim knew anything about 'false representations.' Therefore, he is not liable as a controlling person." *** The court granted Keim's motion for summary judgment *** .

*ANALYSIS*

*The Case Against Keim*

*The Issuer.* The notes and mortgages given to the Investors by the Venture in 1985 and 1986 were investment contracts constituting securities under the Securities Act of 1933. *SEC v. Howey Co.,* 328 U.S. 293, 301 (1946). Accordingly, the Venture was an issuer under the statute.

*The Issuer's Scienter.* If the representations made by LaPrade were false, the issuer had the scienter that *Ernst & Ernst v. Hochfelder,* 425 U.S. 185 (1976) requires for Rule 10b-5 liability. Id. at 212-14. The issuer is chargeable with the knowledge of LaPrade, the head of its Management Committee, acting to market the issuer's securities. That LaPrade acted through Incor cannot insulate the issuer from his knowledge. The issuer is equally possessed of scienter if the providing of the appraisal reports to Incor for fund-raising is found to have been the providing of information not fraudulently but recklessly. *Hollinger v. Titan Capital Corp.,* 914 F.2d 1564, 1568-69 (9th Cir.1990). ***

*The Controlling Persons of the Issuer.* In general, the determination of who is a controlling person for purposes of liability under [Section 20] is an intensely factual question. See 4 Louis Loss & Joel Seligman, Securities Regulation 1724 (1990). A director is not automatically liable as a controlling person. *Burgess v. Premier Corp.,* 727 F.2d 826, 832 (9th Cir.1984) (a director who was uninvolved in the company's day-to-day cattle business and was without experience in the business and had nothing to do with the prospectuses issued to the doctor investors was not a controlling person, nor was a director who had minimal interaction with the company, due partly to ill health). Citing *Burgess,* Loss and Seligman observe: "Accordingly, although a person's being an officer or director does not create any *presumption* of control, it is a sort of red light." 4 Loss & Seligman, supra, at 1724 (emphasis in original). It is not uncommon for control "to rest with a group of persons, such as the members of the corporation's management." Id. at 1722.

Here the persons controlling the issuer in every material respect were the Management Committee, whose decisions, as the Joint Venture Agreement specifies, were "binding on the Venturers." The "major or significant business decisions affecting the Venture" were to be made by the Management

Committee. Every decision which might "materially affect the Venture" was the Management Committee's to make. A line was drawn by the agreement between decisions of this kind which were confided to the committee and "day-to-day business decisions and operations."

The terms and representations on which the Venture's financing were obtained were not a day-to-day affair. They were "major" or "significant." They materially affected the Venture. They had to be determined by the Management Committee.

In the words of the agreement, Parkland was "initially" to contribute "administrative, and financing and development expertise." The agreement did not specify that this obligation of Parkland was to continue beyond the beginning of the Venture. In particular, the raising of additional funds was expressly left to "the judgment of the Management Committee" which was to determine whether "additional funds are required for the Venture's operations and purposes from time to time." It was further expressly provided in the agreement that neither of the Venturers had "the authority to act for the other Venturer," so Parkland had no authority to raise money by itself. As the agreement puts it, "instead the management of the business affairs of the Venture shall be vested in a Management Committee." The members of this committee were "a narrowly defined group" charged with the task of making these decisions, hence "it is reasonable to presume that [they] had the power to control." *Wool v. Tandem Computers Inc.*, 818 F.2d 1433, 1441 (9th Cir.1987).

Webb's memorandum of July 3, 1985 shows that the Management Committee on June 17, 1985 specifically discussed the "precarious situation regarding our financial capabilities to meet our obligations to the Incor investors." According to that memorandum, the members of the Management Committee, including Keim, were informed that the Venture would run out of money as soon as October 1985. The Management Committee then decided to use for current obligations funds "previously earmarked for interest payments to Incor's investors."

According to the minutes of the Management Committee for July 10, 1985, which Keim attended, there was explicit discussion of the "financing package"—necessarily a reference to the package to be put together by Incor, the company doing the financing. Sheet 16 of that package, dealing with the residential property of the project, was discussed in terms of expected profits. The amount to be raised was discussed. Keim specifically addressed the tapping of pension plan money. Keim also took the lead in stating what rate of interest should be paid.

Webb's memorandum of the June 17, 1985 meeting and the minutes of the meeting of July 10, 1985 show the Management Committee acting by consensus, not by vote. The committee does not appear to have been dominated by LaPrade or by the Parkland members as a whole. Keim appears as a vocal and active participant in the management of the Venture.

Keim states that in fact he had no control over LaPrade, Smith and Incor and argues that this undisputed fact should relieve him of liability as a controlling person. Keim misunderstands the basis on which his liability is alleged. He is sued not because he controlled those marketing the investment contracts but because he was one of the persons controlling the issuer of the investment contracts.

*The Controlling Person's Scienter.* To establish the liability of a controlling person, the plaintiff does not have the burden of establishing that person's scienter distinct from the controlled corporation's scienter. If the plaintiff had this obligation, the controlling person provision "would hardly make anyone liable who would not be so otherwise." *G.A. Thompson & Co. v. Partridge,* 636 F.2d 945, 960 (5th Cir.1981). But a defendant who is a controlling person of an issuer with scienter has the burden of proving his absence of scienter. *Hollinger,* 914 F.2d at 1575; *Partridge,* 636 F.2d at 960. Under the controlling person statute that means that Keim, as a person controlling the issuer, was subject to liability unless he establishes that he "acted in good faith and did not directly or indirectly induce the act or acts constituting the violation or cause of action."

Some of our earlier cases took the position that in proving the liability of a controlling person, the plaintiff has the burden of showing that the defendant does not come within the good faith exception. E.g., *Christoffel v. E.F. Hutton & Co.,* 588 F.2d 665, 668-69 (9th Cir.1978). But it has now been established that this burden falls upon the controlling person. *Hollinger,* 914 F.2d at 1575. Although *Hollinger* is specifically directed to a broker-dealer in relation to its registered securities salesman, id. at 1575 n. 24, we have extended the holding beyond this context. See *San Mateo County Transit Dist. v. DeArman, Fitzgerald and Roberts, Inc.,* 979 F.2d 1356 (9th Cir.1992). There is no reason to construe the statute as though it were restricted only to broker-dealers and their salespersons. Congress was well aware of the special duties owed by a broker-dealer and could have put the rules on control person liability solely in that context if it so desired. Congress did not act in this restricted way. Those controlling an issuer of securities are liable for the conduct of the issuer and so are liable if an issuer intentionally or recklessly permitted the fraudulent marketing of its securities.

Consequently, Keim has the burden of proving his good faith. His own declaration of innocence does not meet that burden when the Investors have offered evidence disputing his ignorance of the financing; when Webb's memo of July 3, 1985 shows Keim was aware that Incor had recruited the Investors and that the interest payments to them were in jeopardy; when the minutes of the Management Committee for July 10, 1985 show him as a participant in the discussion of financing; when his letter to LaPrade of November 27, 1985 and the affidavit of Sprague show him pressing for his $100,000 developer's fee; when Sprague's affidavit shows him influential enough to avoid giving the personal guarantee extracted from the others; when Sprague has deposed that Keim was told that the loans from the Investors were to be secured on the basis that they would be half the value of the property; and when his responsibilities as a member of the Management Committee necessarily made him familiar with the cash needs and cash resources of the Venture. In the face of these proffered facts, Keim's alleged good faith and his not having directly or indirectly induced the allegedly fraudulent marketing of the Venture's notes could not be determined by summary judgment. Accordingly, summary judgment in his favor is reversed. ***

### *NOTES AND QUESTIONS*

1. ***Defining "Controlling Person."*** The following definitions of controlling person currently receive at least some support in the cases. Which (if any) are consistent with the result reached in *Keim*?

*a. Two-Pronged Definition.* Most courts assess the defendant's control over (i) the overall operations of the primary violator as well as (ii) the specific activity underlying the litigation. With respect to the first prong, courts divide over whether the actual exercise of control is necessary or whether the mere power to control should suffice. See *Maher v. Durango Metals, Inc.*, 144 F.3d 1302, 1305-06 n. 8 (10th Cir. 1998) (collecting cases in support of each view). What are the arguments for each side? With respect to the second prong, the consensus is that the mere power to control the activity is sufficient. See, e.g., *Donohoe v. Consol. Operating & Prod. Corp.*, 30 F.3d 907, 911-12 (7th Cir. 1994). Why not require actual control?

*b. Status-Based Definition.* Some courts assume that the defendant is a controlling person simply because he is an officer or director. See, e.g., *In re Miller Indus. Inc. Sec. Litig.*, 12 F. Supp. 2d 1323, 1333 (N.D. Ga. 1998); *Salit v. Stanley Works*, 802 F. Supp. 728, 734-35 (D. Conn. 1992). Is this approach too harsh? Should it be tenable only for the purpose of determining whether the complaint states a cause of action? Cf. *Miller*, supra, 12 F. Supp. 2d at 1333 (using status-based approach for this purpose); *Salit*, supra, 802 F. Supp. 2d at 735 (same). Should an outside director ever be deemed to be a controlling person merely by virtue of being a director?

*c. The Commission's Definition.* Rule 12b-2 of the Exchange Act defines "control" as follows for purposes of the registration and reporting requirements: "the possession, direct or indirect, of the power to direct or cause the direction of the management and policies of a person, whether through ownership of voting securities, by contract, or otherwise." While courts sometimes acknowledge this definition in connection with controlling person liability under Rule 10b-5, they do not typically apply it. See, e.g., *Howard v. Everex Sys., Inc.*, 228 F.3d 1057, 1065 n. 9 (9th Cir. 2000). Cf. *Paracor Fin., Inc. v. Gen. Elec. Capital Corp.*, 96 F. 3d 1151, 1162 (9th Cir. 1996) (stressing the importance of focusing on "management and policies"). Why do you suppose that courts don't make more use of the Commission's definition?

2. ***Culpable Participation.*** In addition to requiring the defendant to possess "control," some courts also require that he have been "in some meaningful sense a culpable participant in the fraud perpetrated by the controlled person." *Ganino v. Citizen Utils. Co.*, 228 F.3d 154, 170 (2d Cir. 2000) (quoting *SEC v. First Jersey Sec., Inc.*, 101 F.3d 1450, 1472 (2d Cir. 1996)). Consider whether you are persuaded by the following justification for so doing:

> Judge Adams *** reviewed the legislative history of Rule 10b-5 and concluded that Congress, through the use of words such as " 'cunning,' 'manipulative,' 'deceptive,' 'fraudulent,' 'illicit,' 'fraud,' and lack of 'good faith' " intended that liability would not attach unless the element of culpability was present. Since the standard of culpability is ever-present in the securities laws, it is reasonable that the same standard should be included in Section 20(a).

*Rochez Bros. v. Rhoades,* 527 F.2d 880, 885 (3d Cir. 1975). Can you identify any additional justifications for the culpable participation requirement? Is the requirement consistent with the language of Section 20(a)? What is the likely impact of the requirement on the behavior of those who otherwise possess "control"? Would Keim qualify as a "culpable participant"?

*3. **The Statutory Defense.*** To determine whether the statutory defense has been established, courts typically "examine what the defendants could have done under the circumstances to prevent the violation, and then to ask whether the defendants—aware that they could take such measures—decided not to." *Donohoe v. Consol. Operating & Prod. Corp.,* 30 F.3d 907, 912 (7th Cir. 1994). The defense must meet a higher standard, however, when the defendant is a broker-dealer firm sued in connection with an employee's primary violation. In this instance, the defendant must show that "its supervisory system was adequate and that it reasonably discharged its responsibilities under the system." *Hollinger v. Titan Capital Group,* 914 F.2d 1564, 1576 (9th Cir. 1990) (en banc). Why is the bar raised for broker-dealer firms? Should other defendants likewise be required to have supervisory systems in place? One court has said that the answer should turn on the following considerations:

> a) whether the controlling person derives direct financial gain from the activity of the controlled person, b) the extent to which the controlled person is tempted to act unlawfully because of the controlling person's policies (e.g., compensation system), c) the extent to which statutory or regulatory law or the defendant's own policies require supervision, d) the relationship between the plaintiff and the controlling person, and e) the demonstration of some public policy need to impose such a requirement.

*Kersh v. Gen. Council of Assemblies of God,* 804 F.2d 546, 550 (9th Cir. 1986). Cf. *Dellastratious v. Williams,* 242 F.3d 191, 195-96 (4th Cir. 2001) (evaluating whether directors established their defense by looking at directors' obligations under state law). If the *Kersh* factors had been applied to *Keim,* would the defendant have had to establish maintenance of an adequate supervisory system?

*4. **Proportionate Liability Revisited.*** Recall that in Section G.2 of this Chapter you examined Section 21D(f) of the Exchange Act, which establishes a scheme of proportionate liability under which a defendant (with limited exceptions) is liable exclusively for the fraction of the judgment for which she bears responsibility. If a defendant is found liable as a controlling person, how does Section 21D(f) apply to her? In thinking about this question, be sure to take into account the text of Section 20(a).

### *PROBLEM 2-27*

Inkwell, Inc. is a publicly traded company that manufactures pens and pencils. Forty percent of its shares are owned by George (the son of the company's founder), who has not involved himself with the company's operation. In a recent press release, Inkwell claimed that a new product had caught on well with consumers, whereas in fact the opposite was the case. In a Rule 10b-5 action against Inkwell challenging the fraudulent press release, would George qualify as a controlling person?

See *Aldridge v. A.T. Cross Corp.*, 284 F.3d 72 (1st Cir. 2002).

### *PROBLEM 2-28*

Sam Sivard has been employed for a year as a financial reporter for a major daily newspaper owned by Quibble, Inc. In March 2000, Sam wrote a column praising the management and potential of Vroom, Inc., a company he claimed to have stumbled on during the previous week. In fact, Sam had been a Vroom shareholder for five years. The newspaper knew nothing about Sam's investment portfolio (or that of the other reporters). Nor did the newspaper attempt to confirm the accuracy of the facts stated in Sam's column (or the columns of other reporters).

In the wake of Sam's column, the price of Vroom shares rose drastically. Sam sold most of his shares at a substantial profit. Assume that Sam's conduct violates Rule 10b-5 and that an action has been brought against Quibble as a controlling person. Can Quibble avoid liability on the basis of the statutory defense?

Cf. *Zweig v. Hearst Corp.*, 521 F.2d 1129 (9th Cir. 1975).

---

### *4. Respondeat Superior Liability*

For many years, courts imported into Rule 10b-5 the tort law doctrine of respondeat superior, which renders an employer vicariously liable for the primary violation of an employee committed within the scope of employment or pursuant to apparent authority. See, e.g., *Hollinger v. Titan Capital Corp.*, 914 F.2d 1564, 1577-78 (9th Cir. 1990); *In re Citisource, Inc. Sec. Litig.*, 694 F. Supp. 1069, 1078 (S.D.N.Y. 1988). Such courts regarded respondeat superior liability and controlling person liability as complementary:

> When both remedies are available, then the agent who personally committed the wrong is primarily liable *** ; the principal who acts through the agent (assuming the agent is acting within the scope of his employment) is secondarily liable; and other persons who are not subject to respondeat superior but who nevertheless control the wrongdoer can be held liable under § 20(a).

*Hollinger,* supra, 914 F.2d at 1577-78. But does respondeat superior liability survive the Supreme Court's decision in *Central Bank*? The dissenting opinion in *Central Bank,* you will recall, said no. Not all lower courts have agreed, however. Consider the following view:

> Unlike *** *Central Bank* ***, the issue in this case—whether respondeat superior is a legitimate basis of liability under § 10(b)—is not a question of defining the scope of affirmative conduct proscribed by the statute. Instead, the issue is "deciding on whose shoulders to place responsibility for conduct indisputably proscribed" by the statute. [*AT&T v. Winback & Conserve Program,* 42 F.3d 1421, 1430-31 (3d Cir.1994)].

*Seolas v. Bilzerian,* 951 F. Supp. 978, 983 (D. Utah 1997). But see *In re Fidelity/Micron Sec. Litig.*, 964 F. Supp. 539, 544 (D. Mass. 1997) (doctrine does not survive); compare Robert A. Prentice, Conceiving the Inconceivable and Judicially Implementing the Preposterous: the Premature Demise of Repondeat Superior Liability Under Section 10(b), 58 Ohio St. L. J. 1325 (1997) (doctrine survives) with Joel Seligman, The Implications of *Central Bank*, 49 Bus. Law. 1429, 1430 (1994) (doctrine does not survive).

## *NOTES AND QUESTIONS*

*1. **Viability.*** Do you think that respondeat superior liability survives *Central Bank*? Is the answer the same for private actions and Commission actions? Putting *Central Bank* aside, to what extent does respondeat superior liability undermine Section 20(a)?

*2. **The Relevance of the Statutory Definition of "Person."*** Also arguably relevant to the viability of respondeat superior liability is that Section 10(b) and Rule 10b-5 apply to "any person" and the Exchange Act defines a "person" to include "a corporation." See Exchange Act Section 3(a)(9). The Second Circuit has made this observation:

> Congress evidently intended that a corporation might be liable in some instances as a "person"; and this can only be by virtue of agency principles, since a corporation can act only through its agents. Were §§ 15 [of the Securities Act] and 20(a) the sole measures of corporate liability *** the inclusion of corporations under the definitions of "person" would be not only unnecessary but also misleading.

*SEC v. Mgmt. Dynamics, Inc.*, 515 F.2d 801, 812 (2d Cir. 1975). See *In re Atlantic Fin. Mgmt., Inc.*, 784 F.2d 29, 33-34 (1st Cir. 1986) (Breyer, J.) (endorsing reasoning of *Mgmt. Dynamics*). Thus, one commentator has predicted that "if the courts reject respondeat superior as such, we will soon see a blossoming of the law of what constitutes primary wrongdoing by organizational entities." Donald C. Langevoort, Words From On High About Rule 10b-5: *Chiarella's* History, *Central Bank's* Future, 20 Del. J. Corp. L. 865, 894 (1995).

## *PROBLEM 2-29*

Reconsider Problem 2-28. Would Quibble be liable on a respondeat superior theory in a jurisdiction in which that form of liability is still viable?

## I. STATUTE OF LIMITATIONS

This section addresses the statute of limitations only for private actions under Rule 10b-5. The limitations periods for SEC and criminal actions under the Rule will be considered in Chapters 9 and 11 respectively.

As originally enacted, the Exchange Act did not contain a limitations period applicable to private Rule 10b-5 actions. This omission was to be expected, given that Congress did not have private actions in mind when it enacted Section 10(b). To supply the limitations period, lower courts for years routinely borrowed the most analogous statute of limitations from the common law or blue sky law of the relevant state. See *Ernst & Ernst v. Hochfelder*, 425 U.S. 185, 210 n. 29 (1976) (acknowledging practice of state law borrowing and observing that "it is not always certain which state statute of limitations should be followed").

This practice came to a halt with the Supreme Court's decision in *Lampf, Pleva, Lipkind, Prupis & Petigrow v. Gilbertson*, 501 U.S. 350 (1991). In *Lampf*, the Court held that the limitations period for private actions under Rule 10b-5 must be borrowed from federal law and that the appropriate federal benchmark for these purposes was Section 9(e) of the Exchange Act. See id. at 355, 364 n. 9. Section 9(e) reads in pertinent part:

> No action shall be maintained to enforce any liability created under this section, unless brought within one year after the discovery of the facts constituting the violation and within three years after such violation.

The ground shifted again with the enactment of the Sarbanes-Oxley Act of 2002. Section 804 of that Act amended 28 U.S.C. § 1658, until then a single sentence providing for a four year statute of limitations for civil actions created by Congress after December 1, 1990 as to which no other limitations period specifically governed. Recasting that sentence as subsection (a) of Section 1658, Section 804 of the Sarbanes-Oxley Act added to Section 1658 the following new subsection (b), applicable to all actions filed on the Act's enactment date or later:

> Notwithstanding subsection (a), a private right of action that involves a claim of fraud, deceit, manipulation, or contrivance in contravention of a regulatory requirement concerning the securities laws, as defined in section 3(a)(47) of the Securities Exchange Act of 1934, may be brought not later than the earlier of—
>
> (1) 2 years after the discovery of the facts constituting the violation; or
>
> (2) 5 years after such violation.

The phrase "securities laws" is defined in Exchange Act Section 3(a)(47) as "the Securities Act of 1933, the Securities Exchange Act of 1934, the Sarbanes-Oxley Act of 2002, the Public Utility Holding Company Act of 1935, the Trust Indenture Act of 1939, the Investment Company Act of 1940, the Investment Advisers Act of 1940, and the Securities Investor Protection Act of 1970."

Congress thus appears to have replaced the one year/three year structure of Rule 10b-5's limitations period with a two year/five year structure. Why did it elect to accomplish this goal by amending 28 U.S.C. § 1658 rather than the federal securities laws?

Moreover, the uncertainties surrounding operation of the one year/three year structure carry over to the new two year/five year structure. For example, does the period begin running when the plaintiff receives actual notice of the fraud? Or is the pivotal date that of inquiry notice – when the plaintiff receives notice that fraud might exist? What about the availability of equitable estoppel and equitable tolling? The Supreme Court's *Lampf* decision continues to be relevant as a source of answers.

## LAMPF, PLEVA, LIPKIND, PRUPIS & PETIGROW v. GILBERTSON

501 U.S. 350 (1991)

JUSTICE BLACKMUN DELIVERED THE OPINION OF THE COURT, EXCEPT AS TO PART II-A:

In this litigation we must determine which statute of limitations is applicable to a private suit brought pursuant to *** Rule 10b-5.

I

The controversy arises from the sale of seven Connecticut limited partnerships formed for the purpose of purchasing and leasing computer hardware and software. Petitioner Lampf, Pleva, Lipkind, Prupis & Petigrow is a West Orange, N.J., law firm that aided in organizing the partnerships and that provided additional legal services, including the preparation of opinion letters addressing the tax consequences of investing in the partnerships. The several plaintiff-respondents purchased units in one or more of the partnerships during the years 1979 through 1981 with the expectation of realizing federal income tax benefits therefrom.

The partnerships failed, due in part to the technological obsolescence of their wares. In late 1982 and early 1983, plaintiff-respondents received notice that the United States Internal Revenue Service was investigating the partnerships. The IRS subsequently disallowed the claimed tax benefits because of overvaluation of partnership assets and lack of profit motive.

On November 3, 1986, and June 4, 1987, plaintiff-respondents filed their respective complaints in the United States District Court for the District of Oregon, naming as defendants petitioner and others involved in the preparation of offering memoranda for the partnerships. The complaints alleged that plaintiff-respondents were induced to invest in the partnerships by misrepresentations in the offering memoranda, in violation of, among other things, § 10(b) of the 1934 Act and Rule 10b-5. The claimed misrepresentations were said to include assurances that the investments would entitle the purchasers to substantial tax benefits; that the leasing of the hardware and software packages would generate a profit; that the software was readily marketable; and that certain equipment appraisals were accurate and reasonable. Plaintiff-respondents asserted that they became aware of the alleged misrepresentations only in 1985 following the disallowance by the IRS of the tax benefits claimed.

After consolidating the actions for discovery and pretrial proceedings, the District Court granted summary judgment for the defendants on the ground that the complaints were not timely filed. Following precedent of its controlling court, see, e.g., *Robuck v. Dean Witter & Co.*, 649 F.2d 641 (CA9 1980), the District Court ruled that the securities claims were governed by the state statute of limitations for the most analogous forum-state cause of action. The court determined this to be Oregon's 2-year limitations period for fraud claims. The court found that reports to plaintiff-respondents detailing the declining financial status of each partnership and allegations of misconduct made known to the general partners put plaintiff-respondents on "inquiry notice" of the possibility of fraud as early as October 1982. The court also ruled that the distribution of certain fiscal reports and the installation of a general partner previously associated with the defendants did not constitute fraudulent concealment sufficient to toll the statute of limitations. Applying the Oregon statute to the facts underlying plaintiff-respondents' claims, the District Court determined that each complaint was time barred.

The Court of Appeals for the Ninth Circuit reversed and remanded the cases. In its unpublished opinion, the Court of Appeals found that unresolved factual issues as to when plaintiff-respondents discovered or should have discovered the alleged fraud precluded summary judgment. Then, as did the District Court, it selected the 2-year Oregon limitations period. In so doing, it implicitly rejected petitioner's argument that a federal limitations period should apply to Rule 10b-5 claims. In view of the divergence of opinion among the Circuits regarding the proper limitations period for Rule 10b-5 claims,[1] we granted certiorari to address this important issue.

II

Plaintiff-respondents maintain that the Court of Appeals correctly identified common-law fraud as the source from which § 10(b) limitations should be derived. They submit that the underlying policies and practicalities of § 10(b) litigation do not justify a departure from the traditional practice of "borrowing" analogous state-law statutes of limitations. Petitioner, on the other hand, argues that a federal period is appropriate, contending that we must look to the "1-and-3-year" structure applicable to the express causes of action in § 13 of the Securities Act of 1933, and to certain of the express actions in the 1934 Act.[2] The Solicitor General, appearing on behalf of the Securities and Exchange Commission, agrees that use of a federal period is indicated, but urges the application of the 5-year statute of repose specified in § 20A of the 1934 Act, as added by § 5 of the Insider Trading and Securities Fraud Enforcement Act of 1988. *** For the reasons discussed below, we agree that a uniform federal period is indicated, but we hold that the express causes of action contained in the 1933 and 1934 Acts provide the source.

A

It is the usual rule that when Congress has failed to provide a statute of limitations for a federal cause of action, a court "borrows" or "absorbs" the local time limitation most analogous to the case at hand. *Wilson v. Garcia*, 471 U.S. 261, 266-267 (1985); *Campbell v. Haverhill*, 155 U.S. 610, 617 (1895). This practice *** has enjoyed sufficient longevity that we may assume that, in enacting remedial legislation, Congress ordinarily "intends by its silence that we borrow state law." *Agency Holding Corp. v. Malley-Duff & Associates, Inc.*, 483 U.S. 143, 147 (1987).

The rule, however, is not without exception. We have recognized that a state legislature rarely enacts a limitations period with federal interests in mind, *Occidental Life Ins. Co. of Cal. v. EEOC*, 432 U.S. 355, 367 (1977), and when the operation of a state limitations period would frustrate the policies embraced by the federal enactment, this Court has looked to federal law for a suitable period. See, e.g., *DelCostello v. Teamsters*, 462 U.S. 151 (1983). These departures from the state-borrowing doctrine have been motivated by this Court's conclusion that it would be "inappropriate to conclude that Congress

1. See, e.g., *Nesbit v. McNeil*, 896 F.2d 380 (CA9 1990)(applying state limitations period governing common-law fraud); *O'Hara v. Kovens*, 625 F.2d 15 (CA4 1980) (applying state blue sky limitations period); *In re Data Access Systems Securities Litigation*, 843 F.2d 1537 (CA3 1988) (establishing uniform federal period).

2. Although not identical in language, all these relate to one year after discovery and to three years after violation.

would choose to adopt state rules at odds with the purpose or operation of federal substantive law." *DelCostello*, 462 U.S. at 161.

Rooted as it is in the expectations of Congress, the "state-borrowing doctrine" may not be lightly abandoned. We have described federal borrowing as "a closely circumscribed exception," to be made "only 'when a rule from elsewhere in federal law clearly provides a closer analogy than available state statutes, and when the federal policies at stake and the practicalities of litigation make that rule a significantly more appropriate vehicle for interstitial lawmaking.'" *Reed v. United Transportation Union*, 488 U.S. 319, 324 (1989), quoting *DelCostello*, 462 U.S., at 172.

Predictably, this determination is a delicate one. Recognizing, however, that a period must be selected, our cases do provide some guidance as to whether state or federal borrowing is appropriate and as to the period best suited to the cause of action under consideration. From these cases we are able to distill a hierarchical inquiry for ascertaining the appropriate limitations period for a federal cause of action where Congress has not set the time within which such an action must be brought.

First, the court must determine whether a uniform statute of limitations is to be selected. Where a federal cause of action tends in practice to "encompass numerous and diverse topics and subtopics," *Wilson v. Garcia*, 471 U.S. at 273, such that a single state limitations period may not be consistently applied within a jurisdiction, we have concluded that the federal interests in predictability and judicial economy counsel the adoption of one source, or class of sources, for borrowing purposes. Id., at 273-275. This conclusion ultimately may result in the selection of a single federal provision, see *Agency Holding Corp.*, supra, or of a single variety of state actions. See *Wilson v. Garcia* (characterizing all actions under 42 U.S.C. § 1983 as analogous to a state-law personal injury action).

Second, assuming a uniform limitations period is appropriate, the court must decide whether this period should be derived from a state or a federal source. In making this judgment, the court should accord particular weight to the geographic character of the claim:

> The multistate nature of [the federal cause of action at issue] indicates the desirability of a uniform federal statute of limitations. With the possibility of multiple state limitations, the use of state statutes would present the danger of forum shopping and, at the very least, would "virtually guarante[e] ... complex and expensive litigation over what should be a straightforward matter."

*Agency Holding Corp.*, 483 U.S., at 154, quoting Report of the Ad Hoc Civil RICO Task Force of the ABA Section of Corporation, Banking and Business Law 392 (1985).

Finally, even where geographic considerations counsel federal borrowing, the aforementioned presumption of state borrowing requires that a court determine that an analogous federal source truly affords a "closer fit" with the cause of action at issue than does any available state-law source. Although considerations pertinent to this determination will necessarily vary depending upon the federal cause of action and the available state and federal analogues, such factors as commonality of purpose and similarity of elements will be relevant.

B

In the present litigation, our task is complicated by the nontraditional origins of the § 10(b) cause of action. The text of § 10(b) does not provide for private claims. Such claims are of judicial creation, having been implied under the statute for nearly half a century. Although this Court repeatedly has recognized the validity of such claims, we have made no pretense that it was Congress' design to provide the remedy afforded. It is therefore no surprise that the provision contains no statute of limitations.

In a case such as this, we are faced with the awkward task of discerning the limitations period that Congress intended courts to apply to a cause of action it really never knew existed. Fortunately, however, the drafters of § 10(b) have provided guidance.

We conclude that where, as here, the claim asserted is one implied under a statute that also contains an express cause of action with its own time limitation, a court should look first to the statute of origin to ascertain the proper limitations period. We can imagine no clearer indication of how Congress would have balanced the policy considerations implicit in any limitations provision than the balance struck by the same Congress in limiting similar and related protections. See *DelCostello*, 462 U.S., at 171. When the statute of origin contains comparable express remedial provisions, the inquiry usually should be at an end. Only where no analogous counterpart is available should a court then proceed to apply state-borrowing principles.

In the present litigation, there can be no doubt that the contemporaneously enacted express remedial provisions represent "a federal statute of limitations actually designed to accommodate a balance of interests very similar to that at stake here—a statute that is, in fact, an analogy to the present lawsuit more apt than any of the suggested state-law parallels." *DelCostello*, 462 U.S. at 169. The 1934 Act contained a number of express causes of action, each with an explicit limitations period. With only one more restrictive exception,[5] each of these includes some variation of a 1-year period after discovery combined with a 3- year period of repose. [Exchange Act §§ 9(e) and 18(c)]. In adopting the 1934 Act, the 73d Congress also amended the limitations provision of the 1933 Act, adopting the 1-and-3- year structure for each cause of action contained therein. [Securities Act § 13].

Section 9 of the 1934 Act, pertaining to the willful manipulation of security prices, and § 18, relating to misleading filings, target the precise dangers that are the focus of § 10(b). Each is an integral element of a complex web of regulations. Each was intended to facilitate a central goal: "to protect investors against manipulation of stock prices through regulation of transactions upon securities exchanges and in over-the-counter markets, and to impose

---

5. Section 16(b) sets a 2-year rather than a 3-year period of repose. Because that provision requires the disgorgement of unlawful profits and differs in focus from § 10(b) and from the other express causes of action, we do not find § 16(b) to be an appropriate source from which to borrow a limitations period here.

regular reporting requirements on companies whose stock is listed on national securities exchanges." *Ernst & Ernst*, 425 U.S., at 195, citing S.Rep. No. 792, 73d Cong., 2d Sess., 1-5 (1934). ***

We therefore conclude that we must reject the Commission's contention that the 5-year period contained in § 20A, added to the 1934 Act in 1988, is more appropriate for § 10(b) actions than is the 1-and-3-year structure in the Act's original remedial provisions. The Insider Trading and Securities Fraud Enforcement Act of 1988, which became law more than 50 years after the original securities statutes, focuses upon a specific problem, namely, the "purchasing or selling [of] a security while in possession of material, nonpublic information," that is, "insider trading." Recognizing the unique difficulties in identifying evidence of such activities, the 100th Congress adopted § 20A as one of "a variety of measures designed to provide greater deterrence, detection and punishment of violations of insider trading." H.R.Rep. No. 100-910, p. 7 (1988). There is no indication that the drafters of § 20A sought to extend that enhanced protection to other provisions of the 1934 Act. Indeed, the text of § 20A indicates the contrary. Section 20A(d) states: "Nothing in this section shall be construed to limit or condition the right of any person to bring an action to enforce a requirement of this chapter or the availability of any cause of action implied from a provision of this chapter." ***

Finally, the Commission contends that the adoption of a 3-year period of repose would frustrate the policies underlying § 10(b). The inclusion, however, of the 1-and-3-year structure in the broad range of express securities actions contained in the 1933 and 1934 Acts suggests a congressional determination that a 3-year period is sufficient.

Thus, we agree with every Court of Appeals that has been called upon to apply a federal statute of limitations to a § 10(b) claim that the express causes of action contained in the 1933 and 1934 Acts provide a more appropriate statute of limitations than does § 20A.

Necessarily, we also reject plaintiff-respondents' assertion that state-law fraud provides the closest analogy to § 10(b). The analytical framework we adopt above makes consideration of state-law alternatives unnecessary where Congress has provided an express limitations period for correlative remedies within the same enactment.

III

Finally, we address plaintiff-respondents' contention that, whatever limitations period is applicable to § 10(b) claims, that period must be subject to the doctrine of equitable tolling. Plaintiff-respondents note, correctly, that "[t]ime requirements in lawsuits ... are customarily subject to 'equitable tolling.'" *Irwin v. Department of Veterans Affairs*, 498 U.S. 89, 95 (1990), citing *Hallstrom v. Tillamook County*, 493 U.S. 20, 27 (1989). Thus, this Court has said that in the usual case, "where the party injured by the fraud remains in ignorance of it without any fault or want of diligence or care on his part, the bar of the statute does not begin to run until the fraud is discovered, though there be no special circumstances or efforts on the part of the party committing the fraud to conceal it from the knowledge of the other party." *Bailey v. Glover*, 21 Wall. 342, 348 (1875). Notwithstanding this venerable principle, it is evident that the equitable tolling doctrine is fundamentally inconsistent with the 1-and-3-year structure.

The 1-year period, by its terms, begins after discovery of the facts constituting the violation, making tolling unnecessary. The 3-year limit is a period of repose inconsistent with tolling. One commentator explains: "[T]he inclusion of the three-year period can have no significance in this context other than to impose an outside limit." Bloomenthal, The Statute of Limitations and Rule 10b-5 Claims: A Study in Judicial Lassitude, 60 U.Colo.L.Rev. 235, 288 (1989). See also ABA Committee on Federal Regulation of Securities, Report of the Task Force on Statute of Limitations for Implied Actions 645, 655 (1986) (advancing "the inescapable conclusion that Congress did not intend equitable tolling to apply in actions under the securities laws"). Because the purpose of the 3-year limitation is clearly to serve as a cutoff, we hold that tolling principles do not apply to that period.

IV

Litigation instituted pursuant to § 10(b) and Rule 10b-5 therefore must be commenced within one year after the discovery of the facts constituting the violation and within three years after such violation.[9] As there is no dispute that the earliest of plaintiff-respondents' complaints was filed more than three years after petitioner's alleged misrepresentations, plaintiff- respondents' claims were untimely. ***

The judgment of the Court of Appeals is reversed. ***

## NOTES AND QUESTIONS

***1. Equitable Tolling vs. Equitable Estoppel.*** Why is equitable tolling "fundamentally inconsistent with the one and three year structure?" Does *Lampf* preclude equitably estopping a defendant from asserting a statute of limitations defense where the defendant has prevented the plaintiff from discovering the fraud? Under the limitations period in 28 U.S.C. § 1658(b), can a plaintiff maintain an action for more than five years after the violation on the basis of equitable estoppel?

***2. Unresolved Question?*** Does *Lampf* resolve the question whether the limitations period begins to run from the time the plaintiff actually discovers the fraud ("actual notice") or from the time she receives notice that fraud might exist ("inquiry notice")? Consider this question in connection with the next case.

---

9. The Commission notes, correctly, that the various 1-and-3-year periods contained in the 1934 and 1933 Acts differ slightly in terminology. To the extent that these distinctions in the future might prove significant, we select as the governing standard for an action under § 10(b) the language of § 9(e) of the 1934 Act.

## STERLIN v. BIOMUNE SYSTEMS, INC.

154 F.3d 1191 (10th Cir. 1998)

MURPHY, CIRCUIT JUDGE:

Appellant Roman Sterlin ("Plaintiff") brought this securities fraud class action suit against Biomune Systems, Inc. ("Biomune"), David Derrick, Aaron Gold, Charles J. Quantz, Jack Solomon, Genesis Investment Corporation ("Genesis"), and the Institute for Social and Scientific Development ("Institute") (collectively, "Defendants"). The district court dismissed the action, concluding that Plaintiff's claims were barred by the statute of limitations. From this dismissal, Plaintiff appeals. This court reverses and remands.

### I. BACKGROUND

Biomune is a biotech company which, during the relevant time period, was developing a protein called Immuno-C to be used in enhancing human immune systems. David Derrick was Biomune's President, CEO, Chairman of the Board, and main spokesperson. Aaron Gold and Charles Quantz were directors of Biomune. Jack Solomon founded Biomune, the Institute, and Genesis, and was a member of Biomune's Business Advisory Board. Genesis manages Genesis Trust, whose beneficiaries are Solomon's family members. Genesis Trust was at one time Biomune's largest shareholder. Both Derrick and Gold were directors of Genesis. The Institute, a Utah corporation, was also a shareholder of Biomune. Gold served as a director of the Institute.

Plaintiff asserts this "action arises from a fraud of massive proportions," generally consisting of a "scheme to obtain Biomune's listing on NASDAQ, manipulate Biomune's finances and inflate the price of Biomune stock in order to dump thousands of Biomune shares on the market and earn million[s] of dollars in profits." Plaintiff's specific allegations in the Amended Complaint fall into two general categories: those concerning Biomune's NASDAQ listing and those concerning Biomune's alleged misrepresentations regarding the efficacy of Immuno-C.

NASDAQ Listing. Plaintiff alleges that Biomune faced two obstacles in its attempt to obtain a NASDAQ listing. First, Biomune had to convince the Securities and Exchange Commission ("SEC") that Solomon, who was subject to a consent decree for previous securities violations, did not maintain control over the company. Second, Biomune had to sufficiently increase its capital and surplus so that it could qualify for listing.

On March 7, 1994, NASDAQ notified Biomune that it was deferring consideration of its application pending a review by the NASDAQ Listing Qualifications Committee. NASDAQ was concerned with disciplinary actions taken against "a principal shareholder," which Plaintiff alleges was Solomon. According to Plaintiff, Derrick drafted numerous affidavits, executed by himself and Gold, falsely attesting that Solomon did not maintain a control relationship with Biomune.

With respect to the manipulation of Biomune's capital and surplus, Plaintiff alleges that a "fraud network," consisting of relatives and friends of Solomon and Derrick, effectuated a "cleanup" of Biomune's balance sheet. Plaintiff alleges this plan took place in three parts during mid to late 1993. The first part involved an illegal Regulation S offering of securities to increase Biomune's capital and surplus. The second part of the plan consisted of Biomune's purchase of Furtek Technologies from Brian Furtek, a long-time friend of Derrick, at an inflated price in an attempt to increase Biomune's asset base. The third and final part was intended to eliminate Biomune's long-term debt by entering into a phony settlement agreement with Genesis Trust. Plaintiff alleges that all of these transactions were entered into for the purpose of manipulating Biomune's finances so that Biomune could obtain a NASDAQ listing. Plaintiff further alleges that during 1993 and 1994, Defendants made false and misleading statements regarding the financial stability and commercial success of Biomune.

Immuno-C Misrepresentations. Plaintiff alleges that in late 1993, Biomune retained Dr. Stephen Upton from the University of Kansas to perform Immuno-C testing on mice (the "Upton Study"). Plaintiff further alleges that Dr. Upton's work was preliminary and contained a number of biases. Although several tests were unsuccessful, in one preliminary test Dr. Upton found that Immuno-C seemed to reduce the parasite level in mice, indicating that Immuno-C may be effective in the treatment of intestinal disorders. Plaintiff alleges that beginning with a press release on March 21, 1994, Defendants "launched their series of false and misleading announcements about the efficacy of Immuno-C based upon Dr. Upton's results."

Plaintiff further alleges that in late June or early July 1994, Defendants retained Dr. Mark Healey to perform additional testing of Immuno-C on mice. Dr. Healey completed his testing, which included both in vitro and in vivo tests, in early September 1994. The in vivo tests indicated that Immuno-C "did not demonstrate therapeutic efficacy," though Dr. Healey suggested that further in vivo tests be performed. Dr. Healey's in vitro tests, however, confirmed that Immuno-C may be effective, though once again he recommended that further testing be done.

Despite Dr. Healey's recommendations, Defendants decided not to proceed with additional in vivo testing nor did they immediately disclose the results of the in vivo studies. Instead, Plaintiff alleges, Defendants disseminated several press releases emphasizing and exaggerating the importance of Dr. Upton's preliminary study results and Dr. Healey's in vitro test results. Plaintiff further alleges that as a consequence of Defendants' misleading statements, Biomune's stock consistently traded at over $12.00 per share (pre-split).

On January 13, 1995, Biomune filed its Form 10-KSB for the fiscal year ending September 30, 1994. In the Form 10-K, Biomune disclosed the results of the Healey in vivo study. Plaintiff alleges that as a result of this disclosure, Biomune's stock fell to $7.50 per share (pre-split) and has never recovered.

On October 12, 1995, Plaintiff brought this class action Complaint on behalf of *** all persons who purchased Biomune common stock during the period September 15, 1993 through January 12, 1995 ***. In Count I, against all defendants, Plaintiff alleges a violation of § 10(b) of the Securities Exchange Act of 1934 ("1934 Act") and Rule 10b-5 promulgated thereunder. In Count II, against Derrick, Gold, Quantz, and Solomon, Plaintiff alleges that each individual defendant is a control person of Biomune and is therefore liable under § 20(a) of the 1934 Act for the allegedly fraudulent conduct of Biomune. Count III, against Derrick, Genesis, and the Institute, alleges a violation of § 10(b) and Rule 10b-5 based on the defendants' conduct in their positions as officers, advisors, and/or major stockholders. ***

After Plaintiff filed his Complaint, Defendants moved to dismiss, arguing *** the suit was barred by the applicable one-year statute of limitations. The district court agreed and dismissed the action. *** Plaintiff appeals, arguing his Complaint was timely filed.

II. DISCUSSION

This court reviews de novo the district court's determination that Plaintiff's claims are barred by the statute of limitations. In conducting our review, we accept all well-pleaded allegations in the Complaint as true and construe them in the light most favorable to Plaintiff.

In *Lampf, Pleva, Lipkind, Prupis & Petigrow v. Gilbertson,* 501 U.S. 350 (1991), the Supreme Court *** concluded that actions under § 10(b) "must be commenced within one year after the discovery of the facts constituting the violation and within three years after such violation." Id. at 364. ***

Shortly after the Supreme Court's decision in *Lampf,* this court stated that the one-year discovery period set forth in *Lampf* commences when the plaintiff is put on "inquiry notice" of possible misrepresentations. *Anixter v. Home-Stake Prod. Co. [Anixter I],* 939 F.2d 1420, 1437 (10th Cir.), amended on reh'g, 947 F.2d 897 (10th Cir.1991), vacated sub nom. *Dennler v. Trippet,* 503 U.S. 978 (1992). The court noted that those facts triggering inquiry notice have been characterized as "'sufficient storm warnings to alert a reasonable person to the possibility that there were either misleading statements or significant omissions involved in the sale.'" Id. (quoting *Cook v. Avien, Inc.,* 573 F.2d 685, 697 (1st Cir.1978)).

A. Proceedings Below

The district court concluded that an article published in Barron's on August 1, 1994, put Plaintiff on inquiry notice, thus commencing the one-year statute of limitations period. See *Sterlin,* 960 F.Supp. at 1537. The Barron's article expressed doubt about the veracity of Biomune's claims regarding Immuno-C and was generally critical of Biomune's founders. See id. (citing Kathryn M. Welling, A Question of Immunity, Barron's, Aug. 1, 1994, at 5, 5-6).

Plaintiff argues the district court erred in concluding the Barron's article put him on inquiry notice of his claims. Among other things, Plaintiff argues that because he could not have discovered the results of the Healey study, and thus Defendants' misrepresentations concerning the efficacy of Immuno-C, until Defendants publicly disclosed the Healey study results in January 1995, he could not have been on notice of his claims as of August 1, 1994, the date the article was published. In other words, Plaintiff essentially argues that inquiry notice cannot exist until the facts underlying the cause of action are discoverable. Defendants, on the other hand, contend that the one-year statute of limitations period commences upon inquiry notice, without regard to when a plaintiff could reasonably have discovered the facts underlying his claims. ***

B. Tenth Circuit Case Law

*** The *Anixter I* court stated that the one-year statute of limitations period commenced when plaintiffs were put on inquiry notice, which the court described as sufficient facts to put a reasonable investor on notice of the possibility of fraud. See id. at 1437. Under a strict application of this standard, the one year limitations period may begin to run before a reasonably diligent investor should have discovered the facts underlying the alleged fraudulent activity. In its opinion partially granting the plaintiffs' petition for rehearing, however, the court seemed to equate inquiry notice with the time when the plaintiffs reasonably should have discovered the facts underlying the alleged fraud. See *Anixter v. Home-Stake Prod. Co. [Anixter II]*, 947 F.2d 897, 899 (10th Cir. 1991), vacated sub nom. *Dennler v. Trippet*, 503 U.S. 978 (1992). *** The court concluded, however, that its "its previous analysis of when plaintiffs were on notice of the violation remain[ed] applicable to their § 10(b) claims." *Anixter II*, 947 F.2d at 899. ***

C. Other Circuits' Case Law

Cases from other circuits generally apply an inquiry notice standard.[14] coupled with some form of reasonable diligence requirement in determining whether a plaintiff's securities claims are timely filed. The circuits are not consistent, however, in their determination of exactly when the one-year limitations period accrues. Moreover, this inconsistency exists not only among circuits but also within circuits.[15]

Some courts have indicated the one-year limitations period begins to run once the plaintiff is put on inquiry notice, so long as the plaintiff could acquire actual knowledge of the facts underlying the fraudulent activity with the

---

14. Not all circuits have addressed whether, under the Supreme Court's analysis in *Lampf*, an inquiry notice standard, as opposed to an actual notice standard, should apply to § 10(b) claims. ***

15. This inconsistency may be largely attributable to the fact that in many cases the court need not decide exactly when the one-year limitations period began to run, i.e., upon inquiry notice or only when the plaintiff reasonably should have discovered the facts underlying the alleged fraud. See, e.g., *Cooperativa de Ahorro y Credito Aguada v. Kidder, Peabody & Co.*, 129 F.3d 222, 225 (1st Cir.1997) (recognizing First Circuit precedent supported two different accrual dates but concluding court need not decide between dates because even assuming later accrual date, plaintiff still filed too late); *Law v. Medco Research, Inc.*, 113 F.3d 781, 785 (7th Cir.1997) (citing Seventh Circuit cases applying inconsistent standards and noting that "none of the cases treats the difference between the two formulas as an issue," perhaps because "it made no difference in those cases or the parties had chosen not to make it an issue"). Thus, although there appear to be different standards for determining when the one-year limitations period should accrue, these differences may be more semantic than substantive.

exercise of reasonable diligence.[16] For example, in *Great Rivers Cooperative v. Farmland Industries, Inc.,* 120 F.3d 893 (8th Cir.1997), the Eighth Circuit stated that "[i]nquiry notice exists when the victim is aware of facts that would lead a reasonable person to investigate and consequently acquire actual knowledge of the defendant's misrepresentations." Id. at 896. ***

Other courts have indicated the one-year limitations period commences when the plaintiff is placed on inquiry notice, unless the plaintiff can show the actual exercise of reasonable diligence to discover the fraud. If the plaintiff can show the exercise of such diligence, the limitations period begins to run when the plaintiff actually discovers the facts underlying the alleged fraud. If, however, the plaintiff cannot show such actual diligence, constructive knowledge of the fraud is imputed to the plaintiff as of the date of inquiry notice. For example, in *Dodds v. Cigna Securities, Inc.,* 12 F.3d 346 (2d Cir.1993), the Second Circuit stated that "when the circumstances would suggest to an investor of ordinary intelligence the probability that she has been defrauded, a duty of inquiry arises, and knowledge will be imputed to the investor who does not make such an inquiry." Id. at 350. ***

The Seventh Circuit, essentially merging the inquiry notice and reasonable diligence standards into one governing standard, has indicated that a plaintiff is not put on inquiry notice until the plaintiff reasonably should have discovered the fraud. See *Marks v. CDW Computer Ctrs., Inc.,* 122 F.3d 363, 368 (7th Cir.1997) ("[I]nquiry notice does not begin to run unless and until the investor is able, with the exercise of reasonable diligence (whether or not actually exercised), to ascertain the information needed to file suit."). ***

The First Circuit, based on the same rationale as the Seventh Circuit, has stated that while " 'storm warnings' of the possibility of fraud trigger a plaintiff's duty to investigate in a reasonably diligent manner, ... his cause of action is deemed to accrue on the date when he *should have discovered* the alleged fraud." *Maggio v. Gerard Freezer & Ice Co.,* 824 F.2d 123, 128 (1st Cir.1987) In *Cooperativa de Ahorro y Credito Aguada v. Kidder, Peabody & Co.,* 129 F.3d 222 (1st Cir.1997), however, the First Circuit stated that it "need not decide whether the statute of limitations begins to run on the date the storm warnings appear or the later date on which an inquiring investor would through reasonable diligence have discovered the fraud. The time between the two dates in most cases is not likely to be long enough to affect the outcome." Id. at 225 (citing First Circuit cases supporting both accrual dates).

D. Determination of Proper Standard

In this case the time between the date Plaintiff was allegedly placed on inquiry notice and the date Plaintiff claims he could reasonably have discovered the facts underlying the alleged fraud does affect the outcome. If this court accepts the district court's determination that Plaintiff was on inquiry notice as of August 1, 1994, the date the Barron's article was published, but agrees with Plaintiff that a reasonable investor should not have discovered the facts

16. Courts generally have not specified under this standard within what time frame the plaintiff must be able to discover the facts.

underlying the fraud until January 1995, then the timeliness of Plaintiff's October 1995 filing hinges on the resolution of whether the limitations period begins to run when an investor is placed on inquiry notice or instead when the investor should reasonably have discovered the fraud.

This court concludes that inquiry notice *** triggers an investor's duty to exercise reasonable diligence and that the one-year statute of limitations period begins to run once the investor, in the exercise of reasonable diligence, should have discovered the facts underlying the alleged fraud. We reach this conclusion after a considered analysis of this circuit's precedent, other circuit's case law, and the policies underlying the securities laws.

*** Delaying the accrual of the one-year limitations period until this time is also consistent with the Supreme Court's statement in *Lampf* that equitable tolling is "unnecessary" because the doctrine is already reflected in the one-year discovery period. *Lampf*, 501 U.S. at 363.

Our holding *** strikes a balance between two competing policies underlying the securities laws. While we recognize there is a strong federal interest in requiring plaintiffs to file suit soon after they are put on notice of their claims, the applicable statute of limitations should not precipitate groundless or premature suits by requiring plaintiffs to file suit before they can discover with the exercise of reasonable diligence the necessary facts to support their claims.

The purpose behind commencing the one-year limitations period upon inquiry notice is to discourage investors from adopting a wait-and-see approach. See [*Anixter v. Home-Stake Prod Co.* [*Anixter IV*], 977 F.2d 1549, 1552 (10th Cir. 1992)] (stating securities laws are intended "'to protect the innocent investor, not one who loses his innocence and then waits to see how his investment turns out before he decides to invoke the provisions of the Act'" (quoting *Volk v. D.A. Davidson & Co.*, 816 F.2d 1406, 1413 (9th Cir.1987))). Adopting inquiry notice as the point when the one-year limitations period begins to run, however, could lead to valid suits being barred because the plaintiff, although on inquiry notice, could not reasonably have discovered within one year sufficient facts to file a suit which satisfies the particularized pleading requirements of § 9(b). The objective of encouraging investors to file suit as soon as possible is not undermined by delaying the accrual of the statute of limitations until the plaintiffs, in the exercise of reasonable diligence, should have discovered the facts underlying the alleged fraud. Delaying the accrual of the one-year limitations period until this time does, however, ensure that plaintiffs are given the opportunity to adequately develop the facts and determine whether those facts merit bringing suit, thus giving meaning to the term "inquiry."

E. Application of Standard

1. Inquiry Notice

The district court determined that an article published in Barron's on August 1, 1994, entitled "A Question of Immunity," put Plaintiff on inquiry notice of his claims. In support of its conclusion, the district court quoted the following passages from the article:

> The story you're about to read is true. And in its broad outlines, alas, oft-told. Not even the names have been changed. Maybe its retelling will protect a few innocents.
>
> [The main body of the article is critical of Biomune's research and claims regarding the effectiveness of Immuno-C.]
>
> Concludes Hatch, who studied under one of Biomune's founders at Brigham Young University in the mid-Seventies, 'I don't rule out the one in 100 chance that Biomune actually has something. But if I were betting, I'd say the other 99% is going to rule.'
>
> And that's a bet, it turns out, based on considerably more than the scientific evidence. As Hatch knows—and anyone else who cares to take the trouble to research Biomune's corporate history can discover—ever since its December 1981 founding as New Age Corp.—the company's true raison d'etre hasn't been shrimp farming in Ecuador or tomato cultivation in Egypt or immunity enhancers or any of the other ventures it's run through. It's been to sell shares—or, at the least, to use shares as currency to keep any number of its promoters' ventures afloat.
>
> And who are those promoters? The list is long and their connections colorful, but we will list only one. Biomune founder and consultant of long-standing is a Salt Lake City philanthropist, Jack D. Solomon. He owns no Biomune shares, according to the company's SEC filings. But a byzantine array of entities in one way or another affiliated with Solomon own more than 35% of its stock. As it happens, way back when—in 1983—the federal district court in Nevada permanently enjoined Solomon from violations of the registration, antifraud, stock ownership reporting and proxy solicitation provisions of the securities laws. Without admitting or denying the charges, Solomon consented to the filing of that injunction rather than fight SEC charges that, as president and chairman of Advanced Patent Technology Inc., he had illegally sold about 8.7 million shares of unregistered stock in purported private placements between 1975 and late 1980 to raise money for APT's purchase of a Las Vegas slot machine route business and other gaming-related enterprises. Over that span, APT's shares climbed from pennies to just under \$10—and they subsequently went back to pennies, before being delisted from Nasdaq.
>
> There's a lesson there somewhere.

*Sterlin*, 960 F.Supp. at 1533-34 (quoting Kathryn M. Welling, A Question of Immunity, Barron's, Aug. 1, 1994, at 5, 5-6).

Plaintiff argues the district court erred in concluding the Barron's article put him on inquiry notice. He characterizes the article as "consist[ing] primarily of sarcastic comments"[21] and asserts that nothing in the article even "raises the possibility" that Defendants made knowing misrepresentations about Immuno-C or knowingly manipulated the market for Biomune stock. With respect to the alleged misrepresentations about Immuno-C, Plaintiff contends that any storm warnings raised by the article were premature, as the article was published only nine days after the Healey study commenced and over six weeks before the Healey results became available. Likewise, with

21. Defendants correctly note that many of these supposedly "sarcastic comments" made their way into Plaintiff's original Complaint.

respect to the fraud claim premised on Biomune's NASDAQ listing, i.e., the illegal Regulation S offering, the acquisition of Furtek Technologies, and the settlement arrangement with Genesis, Plaintiff asserts that because the article did not even mention these transactions, "it would have been impossible" for the article to put him on notice. Finally, Plaintiff argues that two "dear shareholder" letters written by Derrick a few days after the Barron's article was published sufficiently negated any suspicions raised by the article so that Plaintiff could not have been placed on inquiry notice.

Plaintiff misunderstands the nature of inquiry notice. As this court in *Anixter I* recognized, Plaintiff "'need not ... have fully discovered the nature and extent of the fraud before [he was] on notice that something may have been amiss. Inquiry notice is triggered by evidence of the possibility of fraud, not full exposition of the scam itself.'" 939 F.2d at 1438 (quoting *Kennedy v. Josephthal & Co.*, 814 F.2d 798, 802 (1st Cir.1987)). ***

The district court correctly ruled that the Barron's article, as a whole, created sufficient "storm warnings" to put a reasonable investor on notice of the possibility of fraudulent activity. Importantly, the Barron's article questioned whether Biomune's purpose was to create a viable product, Immuno-C, or whether it was in business simply to "sell shares." The article pointed out that Solomon, who, according to Biomune's SEC filings, owned no stock, actually owned more than 35% of Biomune's stock through a "byzantine array of entities." This statement related directly to Plaintiff's claim that Defendants fraudulently represented to the SEC that Solomon owned no Biomune stock in order to obtain Biomune's NASDAQ listing. The article also stated that Solomon had been permanently enjoined in 1983 from violating various provisions of the securities laws. While insufficient by itself to establish inquiry notice, Solomon's prior history may be considered in determining whether Plaintiff was on inquiry notice. Cf. *Lenz v. Associated Inns & Restaurants Co. of Am.*, 833 F.Supp. 362, 375 (S.D.N.Y.1993) ("[A]wareness of other lawsuits or criminal fraud convictions involving a defendant puts a plaintiff on inquiry notice of the probability of fraud within another transaction involving the defendant."). The article further raised serious questions about Biomune's claims regarding the FDA approval process and expressed skepticism about Biomune's assertions regarding the efficacy of Immuno-C. Finally, as Plaintiff acknowledges in his Complaint, the market apparently took notice of the Barron's article, as the price of Biomune's stock "suffered a slide" after the article was published.[22]

Contrary to Plaintiff's assertions, the Barron's article need not discuss each and every aspect of the alleged fraudulent activity to put him on notice of the need to inquire. See *In re Valence Tech., Inc. Sec. Litig.*, 987 F.Supp. 796,

---

22. Although the determination of whether Plaintiff was on inquiry notice is judged by an objective standard, this court notes that Plaintiff's own buying pattern of Biomune stock supports our conclusion that the Barron's article was sufficient to put Plaintiff on inquiry notice. In the 11 months prior to the date the article was published, Plaintiff made 10 purchases of Biomune stock totaling approximately 13,000 shares. The day the article was published, August 1, 1994, Plaintiff purchased 333.33 shares, and after that date, he purchased only 33.33 shares.

802-03 (N.D.Cal.1997) (rejecting plaintiffs' argument that because Forbes article did not address core allegations, it could not have put them on inquiry notice). Rather, the article need only alert a reasonable investor to the possibility of fraud. See *Anixter I,* 939 F.2d at 1438.

Once the storm clouds gathered, the "dear shareholder" letters from Derrick refuting the claims in the article could not dissipate them.[23] *Lenz,* 833 F.Supp. at 376 n. 12 (noting that "reassurances accompanying the relevant notice" do not "relieve[ ] the plaintiff of his duty to undertake reasonable inquiry").

In sum, a reasonable investor would have investigated further after reading the Barron's article. Contrary to Plaintiff's assertions, the "dear shareholder" letters did not relieve him of his duty to investigate. This court therefore concludes the article put Plaintiff on inquiry notice, triggering the duty to exercise reasonable diligence.

2. Reasonable Diligence

The district court did not address whether, in the exercise of reasonable diligence, Plaintiff should have discovered the facts underlying the alleged fraudulent activity prior to October 12, 1994, one year before he filed suit. Rather, the district court held the statute began to run on August 1, 1994, the date the *Barron's* article was published. We therefore remand to the district court to determine whether Plaintiff's Complaint was timely filed under the standard adopted herein. ***

### *NOTES AND QUESTIONS*

***1. Inquiry Notice vs. Actual Notice.*** *Sterlin's* preference for inquiry notice over actual notice is shared by most other circuit courts to consider the issue. See, e.g., *Menowitz v. Brown,* 991 F.2d 36, 41-42 (2d Cir. 1993); *Brumbaugh v. Princeton Partners,* 985 F.2d 157, 162 (4th Cir. 1993). But cf. *Berry v. Valence Tech., Inc.,* 175 F.3d 699, 704 (9th Cir. 1999) (affirmatively not deciding between inquiry and actual notice). If it is at least arguable that *Lampf* points towards actual notice, how can the case law be explained? See Lewis D. Lowenfels and Alan R. Bromberg, SEC Rule 10b-5 and Its New Statute of Limitations: The Circuits Defy the Supreme Court, 51 Bus. Law. 309, 332-33 (1996). Does the wording of the explicit two year limitation period in 28 U.S.C. § 1658(b) resolve the controversy?

***2. Inquiry Notice and Policy Considerations.*** The *Sterlin* court justified its use of inquiry notice partly on the ground that it would "discourage investors from adopting a wait-and-see approach." One commentator has challenged this justification as follows:

> Suppose the investor suspects or knows of fraud, but delays suit. In the interim, the price of the stock rises from factors unrelated to the fraud, inducing the investor not to sue. Who is harmed? It is not the investor, who has profited or at least limited his loss. It is certainly not the prospective defendant, who has

23. This court expresses no opinion on Plaintiff's argument that the "dear shareholder" letters affected his ability to discover the facts underlying the fraud.

> escaped a lawsuit for fraud. Courts, certainly, will not be heard to complain if another securities fraud suit is *not* brought to their attention. If the price of the stock does not recover and the investor sues, the defendant cannot complain.

Charles B. Nutley, Comment, Triggering One-Year Limitations on Section 10(b) and Rule 10b-5 Actions: Actual or Inquiry Discovery?, 30 San Diego L. Rev. 917, 955-56 (1993). Do you agree? What policy considerations favor use of actual notice?

***3. Mr. Sterlin's Reasonable Diligence.*** On remand, the district court concluded that Mr. Sterlin should have ascertained the underlying facts before October 12, 1994:

> Although plaintiff contacted Ms. Welling, the author of the *Barron's* article, as well as Mr. Solomon, a representative of Biomune, such contacts alone were not enough to discharge his duty. A reasonably diligent investor upon reading the *Barron's* article immediately would have checked out the sources provided by Ms. Welling, including Form 10-K for the year 1993 filed by Biomune with the SEC, the Arthur Andersen audit report contained in the 1993 SEC report, the 1994 first quarterly SEC Form 10-QSB, and the Nevada Court records and injunction against Solomon. In addition, a reasonable investor would have contacted the independent doctors involved in the clinical studies of Immuno-C, particularly Dr. Upton, whose studies plaintiff had reason to believe were misrepresented by Biomune *** A reasonable investor would have scrutinized the transactions described in SEC documents referred to by Ms. Welling, which transactions had eliminated Biomune's debt and enabled public trading on the NASDAQ. Plaintiff did not do any of these things or even attempt to do so until much later than Octboer 12, 1994.

*Sterlin v. Biomune Sys., Inc.*, 114 F. Supp.2d 1163, 1172 (D. Utah 2000). If a plaintiff lacks the time, money, or business acumen to undertake an investigation of this nature, should he nonetheless be precluded from suing?

### *PROBLEM 2-30*

Volt, Inc. was founded in 1997 to develop new battery technology. In February 1999, Volt raised $33 million in a registered offering in the wake of its announcement that it had in the final stages of production a revolutionary new battery that was better performing and longer-lasting than any battery on the market. In May 1999, Volt announced a $100 million contract with Phonex, a leading cellular telephone manufacturer, which would begin using Volt's batteries in its phones by 2002.

On September 15, 1999, an article about Volt entitled "Story Stock" appeared on the front page of the business section of a major newspaper with a national circulation. Although press coverage of Volt had been quite positive up until then, the article was more skeptical. It directed attention to "the curious merry-go-round of insiders, underwriters and journalists that keeps Volt stock spinning." It referred to "a triad that included insiders unloading shares for a price hundreds of times what they paid, an underwriting firm that pulls in fees for helping them do that, and journalists who are only too willing to take at face value the boastful pronouncements of the company's publicity department." Thus, "there is no reliable evidence that they will work as advertised." According to the article, the contract with Phonex was "less than meets the eye," since Phonex had agreed to buy batteries only if they operated as Volt claimed they would. The article also took aim at Jed, Volt's largest shareholder, noting that he had profited from two other companies even though the companies themselves suffered financially.

Electra, Volt's CEO, responded by sending a letter to the newspaper's editor that described the article as "inaccurate." Her letter in addition insisted that Volt's contract with Phonex was a "basic purchase agreement" and not "less than meets the eye" as the article had claimed. The newspaper published the letter on September 17 and Volt immediately distributed the letter to its shareholders.

There was a modest press follow-up to the article. A major finance magazine published a story on September 22, 1999, repeating the claim in the newspaper article that "there was no reliable evidence that the batteries will work as advertised." In contrast, on September 23, an important business wire service reported on Electra's letter in a story entitled "Volt CEO Calls Article 'Inaccurate'." Later press coverage resumed its largely positive tone and did not mention the September 15 newspaper article.

The week after September 15, 1999, Volt 's stock dropped from about $15.00 per share to $12.50 per share. It bounced back to $15.00 three weeks later, however.

On October 3, 2002, Volt announced that it was unable to meet Phonex's specifications and would not be delivering batteries under that contract as planned. On that day, Volt's stock dropped to $5.25. On October 10, 2002, Volt announced that it was abandoning its new battery technology. Its stock then dropped to $1.

On December 3, 2002, Thalia filed a Rule 10b-5 action against Volt. She had purchased stock in Volt's February 1999 offering and claimed that, in connection with that offering, Volt had misrepresented its new battery's likelihood of success. Volt has now made a motion to dismiss Thalia's action on statute of limitations grounds. What arguments support Volt's motion? What counter-arguments are available to Thalia? Should the court grant Volt's motion or deny it?

Cf. *Berry v. Valence Tech., Inc.*, 175 F.3d 699 (9th Cir. 1998).

## J. THE OVERLAP BETWEEN RULE 10b-5 AND THE EXPRESS ACTIONS FOR MATERIAL MISSTATEMENTS AND OMISSIONS

Sometimes the conduct at issue in an implied private action under Rule 10b-5 also provides the predicate for invoking an express private action that provides liability for material misstatements and omissions—Sections 11 or 12(a)(2) of the Securities Act or Sections 9(e) or 18(a) of the Exchange Act. Under these circumstances, should the implied action be barred?

In the decision that follows, the Supreme Court addressed a private plaintiff's use of Rule 10b-5 to challenge conduct actionable under Section 11. Ask yourself what guidance this decision gives us when the overlap is between Rule 10b-5 and an express action other than Section 11.

## HERMAN & MACLEAN v. HUDDLESTON

459 U.S. 375 (1983)

JUSTICE MARSHALL:

*** In 1969 Texas International Speedway, Inc. ("TIS"), filed a registration statement and prospectus with the Securities and Exchange Commission offering a total of $4,398,900 in securities to the public. The proceeds of the sale were to be used to finance the construction of an automobile speedway. The entire issue was sold on the offering date, October 30, 1969. TIS did not meet with success, however, and the corporation filed a petition for bankruptcy on November 30, 1970.

In 1972 plaintiffs Huddleston and Bradley instituted a class action in the United States District Court for the Southern District of Texas on behalf of themselves and other purchasers of TIS securities. The complaint alleged violations of Section 10(b) of the 1934 Act and SEC Rule 10b-5 promulgated thereunder. Plaintiffs sued most of the participants in the offering, including the accounting firm, Herman & MacLean, which had issued an opinion concerning certain financial statements and a pro forma balance sheet that were contained in the registration statement and prospectus. Plaintiffs claimed that the defendants had engaged in a fraudulent scheme to misrepresent or conceal material facts regarding the financial condition of TIS, including the costs incurred in building the speedway.

After a 3-week trial, the District Judge submitted the case to the jury on special interrogatories relating to liability. The judge instructed the jury that liability could be found only if the defendants acted with scienter. *** After the jury rendered a verdict in favor of the plaintiffs on the submitted issues, the judge concluded that Herman & MacLean and others had violated § 10(b) and Rule 10b-5 by making fraudulent misrepresentations in the TIS registration statement. The court then determined the amount of damages and entered judgment for the plaintiffs.

On appeal, the United States Court of Appeals for the Fifth Circuit held that a cause of action may be maintained under § 10(b) of the 1934 Act for fraudulent misrepresentations and omissions even when that conduct might also be actionable under § 11 of the 1933 Act. ***

We granted certiorari to consider whether an implied cause of action under § 10(b) of the 1934 Act will lie for conduct subject to an express civil remedy under the 1933 Act, an issue we have previously reserved ***. We now affirm the Court of Appeals' holding that plaintiffs could maintain an action under § 10(b) of the 1934 Act ***.

II.

The Securities Act of 1933 and the 1934 Act "constitute interrelated components of the federal regulatory scheme governing transactions in securities." *Ernst & Ernst v. Hochfelder,* 425 U.S. 185, 206 (1976). The Acts created several express private rights of action, one of which is contained in § 11 of the 1933 Act. In addition to the private actions created explicitly by the 1933 and 1934 Acts, federal courts have implied private remedies under other provisions of the two laws. Most significantly for present purposes, a private right of action under § 10(b) of the 1934 Act and Rule 10b-5 has been consistently recognized for more than 35 years. The existence of this implied remedy is simply beyond peradventure.

The issue in this case is whether a party should be barred from invoking this established remedy for fraud because the allegedly fraudulent conduct would apparently also provide the basis for a damage action under § 11 of the 1933 Act. The resolution of this issue turns on the fact that the two provisions involve distinct causes of action and were intended to address different types of wrongdoing.

Section 11 of the 1933 Act allows purchasers of a registered security to sue certain enumerated parties in a registered offering when false or misleading information is included in a registration statement. The section was designed to assure compliance with the disclosure provisions of the Act by imposing a stringent standard of liability on the parties who play a direct role in a registered offering. If a plaintiff purchased a security issued pursuant to a registration statement, he need only show a material misstatement or omission to establish his prima facie case. Liability against the issuer of a security is virtually absolute, even for innocent misstatements. Other defendants bear the burden of demonstrating due diligence.

Although limited in scope, § 11 places a relatively minimal burden on a plaintiff. In contrast, § 10(b) is a "catchall" antifraud provision, but it requires a plaintiff to carry a heavier burden to establish a cause of action. While a § 11 action must be brought by a purchaser of a registered security, must be based on misstatements or omissions in a registration statement, and can only be brought against certain parties, a § 10(b) action can be brought by a purchaser or seller of "*any* security" against "*any* person" who has used "*any* manipulative or deceptive device or contrivance" in connection with the purchase or sale of a security. However, a § 10(b) plaintiff carries a heavier burden than a § 11 plaintiff. Most significantly, he must prove that the defendant acted with scienter, *i.e.*, with intent to deceive, manipulate, or defraud.

Since § 11 and § 10(b) address different types of wrongdoing, we see no reason to carve out an exception to § 10(b) for fraud occurring in a registration statement just because the same conduct may also be actionable under § 11. Exempting such conduct from liability under § 10(b) would conflict with the basic purpose of the 1933 Act: to provide greater protection to purchasers of registered securities. It would be anomalous indeed if the special protection afforded to purchasers in a registered offering by the 1933 Act were deemed to deprive such purchasers of the protections against manipulation and deception that § 10(b) makes available to all persons who deal in securities.

While some conduct actionable under § 11 may also be actionable under § 10(b), it is hardly a novel proposition that the 1934 Act and the 1933 Act "prohibit some of the same conduct." *United States v. Naftalin,* 441 U.S. 768, 778 (1979) (applying § 17(a) of the 1933 Act to conduct also prohibited by § 10(b) of the 1934 Act in an action by the SEC). " 'The fact that there may well be some overlap is neither unusual nor unfortunate.' " Ibid, quoting *SEC v. National Securities., Inc.,* 393 U.S. 453, 468 (1969). In savings clauses included in the 1933 and 1934 Acts, Congress rejected the notion that the express remedies of the securities laws would preempt all other rights of action. Section 16 of the 1933 Act states unequivocally that "[t]he rights and remedies provided by this title shall be in addition to any and all other rights and remedies that may exist at law or in equity." Section 28(a) of the 1934 Act contains a parallel provision. These provisions confirm that the remedies in each Act were to be supplemented by "any and all" additional remedies.

This conclusion is reinforced by our reasoning in *Ernst & Ernst v. Hochfelder,* which held that actions under § 10(b) require proof of scienter and do not encompass negligent conduct. In so holding, we noted that each of the express civil remedies in the 1933 Act allowing recovery for negligent conduct is subject to procedural restrictions not applicable to a § 10(b) action.[18] We emphasized that extension of § 10(b) to negligent conduct would have allowed causes of action for negligence under the express remedies to be brought instead under § 10(b), "thereby nullify[ing] the effectiveness of the carefully drawn procedural restrictions on these express actions." In reasoning that scienter should be required in § 10(b) actions in order to avoid circumvention of the procedural restrictions surrounding the express remedies, we necessarily assumed that the express remedies were not exclusive. Otherwise there would have been no danger of nullification. Conversely, because the added burden of proving scienter attaches to suits under § 10(b), invocation of the § 10(b) remedy will not "nullify" the procedural restrictions that apply to the express remedies.

This cumulative construction of the remedies under the 1933 and 1934 Acts is also supported by the fact that, when Congress comprehensively revised the securities laws in 1975, a consistent line of judicial decisions had permitted plaintiffs to sue under § 10(b) regardless of the availability of express remedies. In 1975 Congress enacted the "most substantial and significant revision of this country's Federal securities laws since the passage of the Securities Exchange Act in 1934." See Securities Acts Amendments of 1975, 89 Stat. 97. When Congress acted, federal courts had consistently and routinely permitted a plaintiff to proceed under § 10(b) even where express remedies under § 11 or other provisions were available. In light of this well-established judicial interpretation, Congress' decision to leave § 10(b) intact suggests that Congress ratified the cumulative nature of the § 10(b) action.

A cumulative construction of the securities laws also furthers their broad remedial purposes. In enacting the 1934 Act, Congress stated that its purpose was "to impose requirements necessary to make [securities] regulation and control reasonably complete and effective." 15 U.S.C. § 78b. In furtherance of that objective, § 10(b) makes it unlawful to use "*any* manipulative or deceptive device or contrivance" in connection with the purchase or sale of any security. The effectiveness of the broad proscription against fraud in § 10(b) would be undermined if its scope were restricted by the existence of an express remedy under § 11. Yet we have repeatedly recognized that securities laws combating fraud should be construed "not technically and restrictively, but flexibly to effectuate [their] remedial purposes." *SEC v. Capital Gains Research*

18. For example, a plaintiff in a § 11 action may be required to post a bond for costs ***. In contrast, § 10(b) contains no provision requiring plaintiffs to post security for costs. ***

*Bureau, Inc.*, 375 U.S. 180, 195 (1963). We therefore reject an interpretation of the securities laws that displaces an action under § 10(b).

Accordingly, we hold that the availability of an express remedy under § 11 of the 1933 Act does not preclude defrauded purchasers of registered securities from maintaining an action under § 10(b) of the 1934 Act. ***

### *NOTES AND QUESTIONS*

1. ***Cumulativeness Across the Board?*** Does the Court in effect call for adoption of a cumulative approach whenever the implied private action under Rule 10b-5 overlaps with an express private action under the federal securities laws? If not, what circumstances must be present in order to render the express action exclusive?

2. ***The Case for Codification.*** The Court acknowledged that the existence of an implied private action under Rule 10b-5 was "beyond peradventure." Should Congress codify the action and thereby eliminate any remaining uncertainties over cumulativeness?

3. ***Rule 10b-5 and Section 12(a)(2).*** Section 12(a)(2) of the Securities Act, a principal subject of Chapter 3, allows purchasers in a public offering to sue their sellers when a prospectus or oral communication contains a material misstatement or omission. Like Section 11, Section 12(a)(2) does not require scienter. Largely for this reason, courts have taken a cumulative approach to Rule 10b-5 and Section 12(a)(2). See, e.g., *Berger v. Bishop Inv. Corp.*, 695 F.2d 302, 308 (8th Cir. 1982). Does *Huddleston* counsel otherwise?

4. ***Rule 10b-5 and Section 18(a).*** Section 18(a) of the Exchange Act provides an action for anyone who buys or sells a security in reliance on a material misstatement in an SEC filing "at a price affected by such misstatement." While a plaintiff need not establish scienter, she must nonetheless satisfy several other demanding requirements: actual reliance on the document in question, a causal relationship between reliance and damages, and a causal relationship between the misstatement and the price paid. Courts have taken a cumulative approach to Section 18(a) and Rule 10b-5 on the ground that Rule 10b-5 requires scienter but Section 18(a) does not. See, e.g., *Wachovia Bank & Trust Co. v. Nat'l Student Mktg. Corp.*, 650 F.2d 342, 356-58 (D.C. Cir. 1980); *Ross v. A. H. Robbins Co.*, 607 F.2d 545, 556 (2d Cir. 1979). Is the likely result the nullification of Section 18(a) and thereby the contravention of *Huddleston*?

As you contemplate the appropriate relationship between Section 18(a) and Rule 10b-5, consider what would happen if Section 18(a) stood as the exclusive remedy for material misstatements in documents filed with the SEC. According to Professor Aldave, the consequences would be anomalous:

> [P]ersons deceived by misstatements in documents that were not filed with the SEC would have a more effective remedy than persons deceived by misstatements in documents filed with the SEC, even though Congress enacted Section 18 as part of its effort to ensure that filed documents would be accurate and complete.

Barbara Bader Aldave, "Neither Unusual Nor Unfortunate": The Overlap of Rule 10b-5 With the Express Liability Sections of the Securities Acts, 60 Tex. L. Rev. 719, 749 (1982).

*5. **Rule 10b-5 and Section 9(e).*** Section 9(e) of the Exchange Act, a principal subject of Chapter 8, provides a remedy to purchasers and sellers of securities on national securities exchanges who are injured by specified forms of market manipulation. The plaintiff must meet a demanding two-pronged causation requirement: the manipulation must not only cause the plaintiff's damages but also affect the price at which he bought or sold. Moreover, unlike any other private federal securities remedy, the plaintiff must show that the defendant acted "willfully." Does *Huddleston* support a cumulative approach to Rule 10b-5 and Section 9(e)? The majority of a Fifth Circuit panel gave an affirmative answer. See *Chemetron Corp. v. Business Funds, Inc.*, 718 F.2d 725 (5th Cir. 1983). The active judges voted for a rehearing en banc. See id. at 730. The case was settled, however, and thus the rehearing en banc did not occur. For analysis of whether a cumulative approach to Rule 10b-5 and Section 9(e) is warranted, see Marc I. Steinberg, The Propriety and Scope of Cumulative Remedies Under the Federal Securities Laws, 67 Cornell L. Rev. 557, 588-94 (1982).

*6. **The Savings Clauses.*** To support its cumulative approach to Section 11 and Rule 10b-5, the *Huddleston* Court referred to the language in Section 16 of the Securities Act and Section 28(a) of the Exchange Act stating that the statutory "rights and remedies" are "in addition to any and all other rights and remedies that may exist at law and equity." While this language may or may not have been designed to insure cumulation of express and implied remedies, it was clearly designed to insure cumulation of federal and state remedies. Why would Congress have taken this approach in the 1930s? The approach remained in place until 1998, when the Securities Litigation Uniform Standards Act amended Sections 16 and 28(a) to preempt state law class actions involving nationally traded securities. See infra Chapter 6.B.

*7. **The More the Merrier?*** Section 28(a) of the Exchange Act provides that "no person permitted to maintain a suit for damages under the provisions of [the Exchange Act] shall recover, through satisfaction of judgment in one or more actions, a total amount in excess of his actual damages on account of the act complained of." Thus, even if a plaintiff establishes the requisite elements of multiple provisions (be they state and federal securities provisions or federal securities provisions exclusively), his recovery cannot exceed his "actual damages." Are there nonetheless strategic advantages to suing under multiple provisions?

# Chapter 3

# LIABILITY UNDER THE SECURITIES ACT FOR MATERIAL MISSTATEMENTS, OMISSIONS, AND FRAUDULENT CONDUCT

---

This Chapter examines provisions of the Securities Act that authorize liability for material misstatements, omissions, and fraudulent conduct. Two of these provisions—Sections 11 and 12(a)(2)—create express private actions. The third—Section 17(a)—is enforceable by the government only.

To be sure, the Securities Act also contains a provision—Section 12(a)(1)—that creates an express private action for violations of Section 5 of the Securities Act. But because this Chapter does not focus principally on registration, Section 12(a)(1) is considered only insofar as it sheds light on its statutory sibling, Section 12(a)(2).

## A. SECTIONS 11 AND 12(a)(2): EXPRESS PRIVATE ACTIONS FOR MATERIAL MISSTATEMENTS AND OMISSIONS

Sections 11 and 12(a)(2) both authorize express private actions to challenge material misstatements and omissions. We examine these actions separately and then consider briefly certain features that they share.

Sections 11 and 12(a)(2) both apply to offerings registered under Section 5 of the Securities Act (although, as we will see, the reach of Section 12(a)(2) is broader than this). Therefore, before turning to these Sections specifically, we identify the persons responsible for the accuracy of the registration statement—the document filed with the SEC in a registered offering (part one of which is the prospectus distributed to investors):

**The Issuer.** This is the company whose securities are sold to the public pursuant to the registration statement. The issuer's officers and directors are responsible for the content of the registration statement and for cooperating with the auditor and underwriters in their efforts to confirm the truthfulness of the registration statement.

**The Auditor.** This is the accounting firm that must conduct a detailed audit of the issuer and certify that the issuer's financial statements have been prepared in accordance with Generally Accepted Accounting Principles (GAAP).

**The Underwriters.** Occasionally, a small offering (known as a direct public offering) will be sold directly to investors without an underwriter. More commonly, however, the issuer retains one or more investment banks as underwriters. The investment bank leading the effort to sell the securities is known as the managing underwriter (or lead underwriter), and the other underwriters are "major bracket" or "minor bracket" underwriters, depending on the amount of securities for which they agree to be responsible.

The issuer and the underwriters sometimes agree to a "firm commitment" underwriting, pursuant to which the underwriters buy the securities from the issuer and resell them. In so doing, the underwriters assume the market risk prior to resale as well as the risk of being unable to resell. Firm commitment underwriting is typically utilized when the issuer is well-established.

Alternatively, the issuer and the underwriter may agree to a "best efforts" underwriting, pursuant to which the underwriters do not purchase the securities from the issuer but instead utilize their "best efforts" in helping the issuer sell the securities. A "best efforts" underwriting may be canceled, and the money returned to investors, if a predetermined amount of the securities are not sold.

Regardless of whether the underwriting is of the "firm commitment" or "best efforts" variety, the underwriters are compensated with a "spread"—the percentage difference (often about 5% for an equity offering, but less for a debt offering) between the consideration paid by investors for the securities and the proceeds from the offering received by the issuer. One problem with this compensation system is that underwriters, unlike auditors and for the most part unlike lawyers, are paid only if the offering is consummated or "closed," thereby giving the underwriters an incentive to close an offering even if they know that the registration statement is misleading. One way in which the Securities Act addresses this problem is to subject underwriters to substantial liability under Section 11 if securities are sold pursuant to a misleading registration statement.

The brokers who distribute the securities to investors comprise the "selling group." In contrast to the underwriters, the brokers are not in privity of contract with the issuer.

**The Lawyers.** The issuer as well as the managing underwriter typically retain lawyers to assist with the preparation of the registration statement and related duties. The issuer's lawyer usually takes the principal role in drafting the registration statement, although the underwriters' lawyer usually also has a significant involvement. As we will see, neither Section 11 nor Section 12(a)(2) imposes liability on lawyers based on their drafting of the registration statement or their investigation of its accuracy.

As you examine Sections 11 and 12(a)(2), ask yourself the following. Why did Congress enact these private actions in the first place? How do they complement each other? What advantages and disadvantages do they offer investors as compared with the implied private action under Section 10(b) and Rule 10b-5?

### *1. Section 11*

Section 11(a) is undoubtedly one of the longest single sentences in the federal securities laws. An examination of that sentence, however, reveals a straightforward cause of action: a purchaser of a security sold pursuant to a registration statement may sue any enumerated defendant if the registration statement contained a material misstatement or omission on the date it became effective. The enumerated defendants include the following:

- Signers of the registration statement. (Note that Section 6(a) of the Securities Act lists those who must sign the registration statement, and that the required signers include the issuer);
- Every person who was a director of the issuer at the time of registration;
- Every future director who, with his or her consent, was named in the registration statement;
- Any accountant who certified any financial statement contained in the registration statement, where at least one of the material misstatements or omissions at issue appears in the statement that he certified;
- Any other person who certified a part of the registration statement (say, an attorney who attested to the validity of patents), where at least one of the material misstatements or omissions at issue appears in the statement that he certified; and
- Every underwriter involved in the offering.

Why did Congress cast the net of liability so widely? To what extent was it seeking to ensure that the issuer's officers and directors took seriously the disclosure obligations of a registered offering? To what extent was it prodding the underwriters and accountants to fulfill their roles as gatekeepers?

For the issuer, liability under Section 11 is strict. That is, unless the issuer proves that the plaintiff knew of the misstatement or omission at issue at the time of purchasing the security (see Section 11(a)) or unless the statute of limitations has run (see Section 13), the issuer has no defenses. To be sure, an issuer may be able to reduce (or even eliminate) damages by showing negative causation—sometimes known as the negative causation defense (see Section 11(e)).

Defendants other than the issuer have "due diligence" defenses. In accordance with Section 11(b), these defendants can avoid liability by establishing that they acted diligently in investigating the facts set forth in the registration statement. Such defendants may also avoid liability based on the plaintiff's knowledge of the misstatement or omission, the statute of limitations, or negative causation.

Contrast the elements of a Section 11 action and the implied private action under Section 10(b) and Rule 10b-5. Unlike Rule 10b-5, Section 11 does not require the plaintiff to prove scienter or causation. Nor does Section 11 require the plaintiff to establish reliance on the material misstatement or omission, except in the rare circumstance in which a plaintiff bought the securities after the issuer distributed audited financial statements covering the 12 month period after the effective date of the registration statement (see Section 11(a)).

A Section 11 plaintiff does not establish a prima facie case merely by showing that the registration statement contains one or more material misstatements or omissions. In addition, she must demonstrate her standing to sue, which, as we will see, constitutes a significant hurdle. We begin with standing to sue and then consider the defenses of due diligence and negative causation.

*a. Standing to Sue*

In the following decision, the court confronted the question whether Section 11 provides a cause of action only for the original purchasers in a registered offering, or whether those who thereafter purchase such shares may sue as well. While the court did give subsequent purchasers the right to sue, it required that they "trace" their shares back to the registration statement in question.

Notice that in reaching its conclusions, the court contrasted Section 11 with Section 12(a)(2) and drew upon *Gustafson v. Alloyd Co.*, 513 U.S. 561 (1995), a Supreme Court decision involving Section 12(a)(2) that we will examine later in this Chapter. In so doing, the court demonstrated that Sections 11 and 12(a)(2) have important similarities and differences.

## LEE v. ERNST & YOUNG, LLP

294 F.3d 969 (8th Cir. 2002)

MCMILLIAN, CIRCUIT JUDGE:

This appeal arises from consolidated securities fraud lawsuits filed against Summit Medical Systems, Inc. ("Summit"), Summit's officers and directors, and Summit's public accountant-independent auditor, Ernst & Young ("E & Y") (collectively "defendants") by Summit shareholders ("plaintiffs") in the United States District Court for the District of Minnesota. Following the entry of final judgment, plaintiffs appeal from orders of the district court resulting in the dismissal, pursuant to Fed.R.Civ.P. 12(b)(6), of their claim against E & Y for allegedly violating § 11 of the Securities Act of 1933 ("the 1933 Act") by making materially false and misleading statements and omissions in Summit's registration statement filed with the Securities and Exchange Commission ("SEC") in connection with Summit's initial public offering in August 1995. For reversal, plaintiffs argue that the district court *** erred in holding as a matter of law that standing to bring the § 11 claim exists only for those plaintiffs who acquired their stock in the initial public offering. *** For the reasons discussed below, we reverse the district court's holding on the § 11 standing issue *** and remand the case to the district court for further proceedings consistent with this opinion. ***

Background

Summit is a corporation headquartered in Minneapolis, Minnesota, which provides "clinical outcomes" medical database software and related products and services. According to the first amended complaint, 2.5 million shares of Summit common stock began trading publicly on August 4, 1995, at $9.00 per share. Following the initial public offering, the Summit stock price increased even though no profit was shown by Summit. A secondary public offering was made in June 1996. At the end of 1996, the Summit stock price began to decline, and it eventually fell below the price at which the stock was initially offered to the public. On March 3, 1997, Summit publicly disclosed that it had been improperly recognizing revenues. Following an investigation, Summit announced that it planned to restate its financial results dating back to 1994. On April 4, 1997, Summit filed revised statements with the SEC showing the total revenues for the years 1994 and 1995, and the first nine months of 1996, to be $5.6 million less than originally reported, representing an 11% cumulative shortfall.

Following Summit's public disclosures, numerous lawsuits were brought against defendants, resulting in the present consolidated action. *** According to the first amended complaint, the registration statement identified E & Y as an "expert" which had audited and certified Summit's financial statements, and it set forth E & Y's opinion that Summit's consolidated financial statements "presented fairly, in all material respects, the consolidated financial position of [Summit] for the 1993 and 1994 fiscal years, and the results of [Summit's] consolidated operations and its consolidated cash flows for 1992, 1993, and 1994, 'in conformity with generally accepted accounting principles [ ("GAAP")].'" In Count III of the first amended complaint, plaintiffs asserted that, because of Summit's premature recognition of revenue in violation of GAAP and Summit's own publicly-stated revenue recognition policies, the registration statement contained materially false and misleading statements and omissions regarding Summit's actual financial status and accounting practices from as early as 1994. ***

Defendants, including E & Y, moved to dismiss the first amended complaint on several grounds. The district court granted in part and denied in part defendants' motion to dismiss. As to the § 11 claim against E & Y, the district court held, as a matter of law, that only those plaintiffs who purchased their stock in the Summit initial public offering had standing to sue. In support of this holding, the district court relied upon *Gustafson v. Alloyd Co.*, 513 U.S. 561 (1995) (holding that aftermarket purchasers of securities did not have a claim under § 12(2) of the 1933 Act). The district court explained that the 1933 Act must be read as a whole and that, based upon the shared legislative history and legislative intent behind § 11 and § 12(2) of the 1933 Act, "the standing principles announced in *Gustafson* apply equally to Section 11 and 12 claims." ***

Following an agreement by the parties to settle the remaining claims against Summit and its officers and directors, the district court entered an order approving the terms of the settlement and entering final judgment. This appeal [on the § 11 claims against E & Y] followed.

Discussion

*** We review the district court's interpretation of a federal statute *de novo*. Plaintiffs, with the support of the SEC as an amicus curiae, argue that the district court erroneously interpreted § 11 of the 1933 Act when it held that only those plaintiffs who acquired stock in the Summit August 1995 initial public offering have standing to sue under § 11. Plaintiffs argue that aftermarket purchasers may bring a claim under § 11 so long as they can "trace" their securities to the public offering under the registration statement alleged to be false and misleading. See, e.g., *Kirkwood v. Taylor*, 590 F.Supp. 1375 (D. Minn. 1984) (allowing an aftermarket purchaser to establish standing by "direct tracing"—that is, by showing that the security was issued under the registration statement alleged to be defective, and not under a different registration statement), aff'd, 760 F.2d 272 (8th Cir.1985) (unpublished table decision). Plaintiffs maintain that the district court erroneously relied on the Supreme Court's decision in *Gustafson* in rendering its decision. Plaintiffs contend that, because *Gustafson* involved § 12(2) of the 1933 Act, not § 11, its holding is limited to the question of what constitutes a "prospectus" under § 12. Plaintiffs note that the majority of federal courts that have addressed this issue, including the only two circuit courts of appeals to have ruled on it since *Gustafson* was decided, have concluded that the *Gustafson* holding does not extend to § 11 claims. See Brief for Appellants at 14-16 (citing, e.g., *Joseph v. Wiles*, 223 F.3d 1155, 1159-61 (10th Cir. 2000); *Hertzberg v. Dignity Partners, Inc.*, 191 F.3d 1076, 1080-82 (9th Cir. 1999)). ***

*** This court has yet to rule upon the § 11 standing issue in a published opinion. By affirming the district court's pre-*Gustafson* decision in *Kirkwood v. Taylor*, we have, however, upheld an interpretation of § 11 which allows aftermarket stock purchasers to establish standing by tracing their securities to the registration statement alleged to be defective.

*** Prior to *Gustafson*, the First and Second Circuits had indicated a similar view. See *Versyss Inc. v. Coopers & Lybrand*, 982 F.2d 653, 657-58 (1st Cir.1992); *Barnes v. Osofsky*, 373 F.2d 269, 271-72 (2d Cir.1967) (assuming that § 11 allows claims based upon tracing to the registration statement in question, but rejecting the even broader interpretation urged by the appellant, which would provide a cause of action for purchasers of securities "of the same nature" as those issued pursuant to the registration statement in question). ***

Section 11(a) provides in relevant part:

> In case any part of the registration statement, when such part became effective, contained an untrue statement of a material fact or omitted to state a material fact required to be stated therein or necessary to make statements therein not misleading, *any person acquiring such security* (unless it is proved that at the time of such acquisition he knew of such untruth or omission) may, either at law or in equity, in any court of competent jurisdiction, sue .... (emphasis added)

The phrase "any person acquiring such security" is not only broad on its face but, more importantly, is broad when compared to the language of § 12(2), the provision at issue in the *Gustafson* decision. Section 12(2) provides that any person who "offers or sells a security" by means of a "prospectus or oral communication" containing a materially false or misleading statement or omission shall be liable "to the person purchasing such security from him" (subject to exceptions not pertinent herein). Section 12(2), therefore, expressly requires privity between the issuer and the purchaser of the security at issue. Section 11, by contrast, has no comparable language—it simply refers to "any person acquiring such security," with "such security" referring to a security registered under the registration statement alleged to be defective. We perceive the absence in § 11 of limiting language similar to that found in § 12(2) to indicate Congress's intent to convey a relatively broader meaning. In other words, we read § 11's plain language to state unambiguously that a cause of action exists for any person who purchased a security that was originally registered under the allegedly defective registration statement—so long as the security was indeed issued under *that* registration statement and not another. Therefore, even in light of *Gustafson*, § 11 is broad enough to encompass some aftermarket purchasers, subject, of course, to the long-recognized requirement that the plaintiff must directly trace his or her security to the allegedly defective registration statement at issue in the case, as was required in *Kirkwood v. Taylor*. In addition, we note that, under § 11(e), damages are generally calculated as the difference between the amount paid for the security, *not exceeding the price at which the security was offered to the public*, and the price of the security at the time the lawsuit was filed or the security was disposed of in the market. It would be unnecessary to limit the price to no more than the price offered to the public if the cause of action were limited to participants in the initial public offering. Similarly, § 11(g)—which expressly caps the maximum amount recoverable to the price offered to the public—would likewise be superfluous if only those who participated in the initial public stock offering could bring a § 11 claim.

We next consider whether there is clear legislative intent contrary to our interpretation of § 11. The purpose and scope of the 1933 Act was to regulate the initial distribution of securities. Central to the regulatory scheme was the requirement that publicly-offered securities be registered with the SEC. The importance of the registration statement to Congress's regulatory and enforcement framework is indicated by the standard imposing liability for materially false and misleading misstatements or omissions, without a scienter requirement. By making the cause of action available to anyone who purchased stock that was originally issued under the registration statement in question, not just those who actually participated in the initial public offering, Congress enhanced the incentive for compliance and bolstered the mechanism for enforcing § 11. Our interpretation of § 11 is also consistent with the recognition that a material misstatement or omission in connection with an initial public offering can adversely affect aftermarket purchasers. However, to protect issuers of publicly- traded securities against abuses of the process, Congress additionally incorporated a requirement for certain aftermarket purchasers to prove that they *relied* on the registration statement in question. See [Section 11(a)] ("If such person acquired the security after the issuer has made generally available to its security holders an earning statement covering a period of at least twelve months beginning after the effective date of the registration statement, then the right of recovery under this subsection shall be conditioned on proof that such person acquired the security relying upon the such untrue statement in the registration statement or relying upon such registration statement and not knowing of such omission, but such reliance may be established without proof of the reading of the registration statement by such person."). Finally, requiring aftermarket purchasers to show that their securities can be traced to the allegedly defective registration statement further ensures fidelity to the statutory purpose, and we again emphasize that tracing is a requirement of aftermarket purchaser standing under § 11 in this circuit. See, e.g., *Kirkwood v. Taylor*, 590 F.Supp. at 1378-79.

Conclusion

We hold in the present case that standing to pursue a claim against E & Y pursuant to § 11 of the 1933 Act exists for aftermarket purchasers of Summit stock who can make a prima facie showing that the Summit shares they purchased can be traced to the registration statement alleged to be false and misleading. Accordingly, we reverse the district court's holding to the contrary. In light of our holding on the § 11 standing issue, we reverse the dismissal of plaintiff's § 11 claim *** The case is remanded to the district court for further proceedings consistent with this opinion.

---

Section 11's tracing requirement can itself be traced to *Barnes v. Osofsky*, 373 F.2d 269 (2d Cir. 1967). In *Barnes*, Judge Friendly interpreted the language of Section 11 to limit standing to those shareholders who had acquired securities "issued pursuant to the registration statement" in question. Consider his reasons for so doing as well as his reasons for rejecting the plaintiff's broader reading of the statutory language:

> The key phrase [in Section 11(a)] is "any person acquiring such security"; the difficulty, presented when as here the registration is of shares in addition to those already being traded, is that "such" has no referent. Although the narrower reading—"acquiring a security issued pursuant to the registration statement"—would be the more natural, a broader one—"acquiring a security of the same nature as that issued pursuant to the registration statement"—would not be such a violent departure from the words that a court could not properly adopt it if there were good reason for doing so. Appellants claim there is. Starting from the seemingly correct premise that an unduly optimistic prospectus will affect the price of shares already issued to almost the same extent as those of the same class about to be issued, they say it would therefore be unreasonable to distinguish newly registered shares from those previously traded. In addition, they contend that once it is agreed that § 11 is not limited to the original purchasers, to read that section as applying only to purchasers who can trace the lineage of their shares to the new offering makes the result turn on mere accident since most trading is done through brokers who neither know nor care whether they are getting newly registered or old shares. Finally, appellants argue that it is often impossible to determine whether previously traded shares are old or new, and that tracing is further complicated when stock is held in margin accounts in street names since many brokerage houses do not identify specific shares with particular accounts but instead treat the account as having an undivided interest in the house's position. Therefore, they urge that the narrower construction offends the cardinal principle of equal treatment for persons whose entitlement is not significantly different ***.
>
> Appellants' broader reading would be inconsistent with the over-all statutory scheme. The Securities Act of 1933 had two major purposes, "[t]o provide full and fair disclosure of the character of securities sold in interstate and foreign commerce and through the mails, and to prevent frauds in the sale thereof, *** " 48 Stat. 74 (1933). These aims were "to be achieved by a general antifraud provision and by a registration provision." 1 Loss, Securities Regulation 178-79 (1961). Section 11 deals with civil liability for untrue or misleading statements or omissions in the registration statement; its stringent penalties are to insure full and accurate disclosure through registration. Since, under §§ 2(1) and 6, only individual shares are registered, it seems unlikely that the section developed to insure proper disclosure in the registration statement

> was meant to provide a remedy for other than the particular shares registered. *** Beyond this, the over-all limitation of § 11(g) that "In no case shall the amount recoverable under this section exceed the price at which the security was offered to the public," and the provision of § 11(e) whereby, with qualifications not here material, an underwriter's liability shall not exceed "the total price at which the securities underwritten by him and distributed to the public were offered to the public," point in the direction of limiting § 11 to purchasers of the registered shares, since otherwise their recovery would be greatly diluted when the new issue was small in relation to the trading in previously outstanding shares.

Id. at 271-72.

## *NOTES AND QUESTIONS*

***1. A Substantial Hurdle.*** Often, a securities issuer will have issued fungible securities pursuant to multiple registration statements. Under these circumstances, an investor is likely to have a difficult—if not impossible—time tracing her securities to the registration statement at issue in her lawsuit. Indeed, many investors own in "street" name and their brokers typically do not either segregate newly-issued from previously-issued shares of the same issuer or assign particular shares to particular investors.

The tracing requirement is relatively easy to meet when the securities sold pursuant to the registration statement are the only securities that the issuer ever sold to the public. See *Hertzberg v. Dignity Partners, Inc.*, 191 F.3d 1076, 1080 (9th Cir. 1999). But it does not follow that tracing is invariably easy in every IPO. Indeed, even in an IPO, there may be secondary market trading in securities of the issuer, fungible with those sold in the IPO, that were previously sold pursuant to offerings exempt from the registration requirement.

If a plaintiff cannot meet the tracing requirement, what remedies might be available to her in place of Section 11?

***2. Judicial Creation?*** Judge Friendly sought to anchor the tracing requirement in the language of Section 11(a), but he nonetheless acknowledged that the language would also support a broader reading. Does it follow that the tracing requirement was a judicial creation?

***3. The Roads Not Taken.*** Would it have been better if Judge Friendly had adopted the broader reading of Section 11(a)? What would have been the drawbacks of the broader reading? Assuming that the narrower reading was preferable, does it necessarily follow that the plaintiff should have the burden of proof on the tracing issue?

***4. Methods of Tracing.*** In *Kirkwood v. Taylor*, 590 F. Supp. 1375 (D. Minn. 1984), aff'd mem., 760 F.2d 272 (8th Cir. 1985), the court discussed four methods of tracing. It approved "direct tracing," which requires tracing the plaintiff's securities to the registration statement. It rejected "fungible-mass tracing," which uses statistics to demonstrate the likelihood that the plaintiff's shares were sold pursuant to the registration statement. In the court's view, proof of such a likelihood was insufficient for Section 11 purposes. The court also rejected "contrabroker tracing," which links the plaintiffs' shares to an underwriter involved in the registration statement. The court explained that if this method were accepted, "anyone who ever purchased from a participant in the underwriting after the offering date could claim he or she bought 'new' stock." Id. at 1381. Finally, the court rejected "heritage tracing," at least for purposes of the case before it. "Heritage tracing" seeks to show that code numbers of stock certificates registered in the plaintiffs' names matched those issued in the registered offering. The *Kirkwood* plaintiffs had trouble with the matching, however, and thus their proof failed in this regard as well. Id. at 1378-83.

The *Kirkwood* decision and the four methods of tracing identified therein are discussed in Hillary A. Sale, Disappearing Without a Trace: Sections 11 and 12(a)(2) of the 1933 Securities Act, 75 Wash. L. Rev. 429, 447-53 (2000). Professor Sale argues that the tracing requirement contravenes Congress's intent and should be reexamined. She favors a statistical approach to tracing similar to that rejected by the *Kirkwood* court. Id. at 484-94. What would be the advantages and disadvantages of adopting such an approach?

5. ***The Relevance of Timing.*** A few courts have found the tracing requirement satisfied where the plaintiff purchased her shares within days of the registered offering at issue. See, e.g., *Wade v. Indus. Funding Corp.*, 1993 WL 650837 (N.D. Cal. 1993). Is this approach sound?

6. ***Tracing and the Preponderance Standard.*** A plaintiff must prove her securities case by a preponderance of the evidence. See *Herman & MacLean v. Huddleston,* 459 U.S. 375, 390 (1983). Does judicial insistence on direct tracing in effect exceed that standard? See Sale, supra, 75 Wash. L. Rev. at 484 n. 351.

### *PROBLEM 3-1*

Garrett, a securities broker, met with his clients Molly and Polly, identical twins, and recommended that they purchase stock in the upcoming registered offering by Peacock, Inc. Garrett showed them the Peacock preliminary prospectus, which captured their fancy. When the offering occurred, Molly and Polly purchased 1000 Peacock shares each, obtaining stock certificates in their own names (rather than in "street" name).

Thereafter, it became apparent that the Peacock registration statement was fraudulent. Molly and Polly consulted with Garrett, who ascertained that Molly had received newly registered shares, whereas Polly had received shares that had been issued pursuant to a registered offering that Peacock had made six months earlier.

Does Molly have standing to bring a Section 11 action? What about Polly?

#### *b. The Due Diligence Defenses*

As mentioned previously, Section 11 imposes strict liability on the issuer. Often, however, the issuer has become bankrupt, and therefore judgment proof, prior to the time the Section 11 action is filed. Under these circumstances, the plaintiff's ability to recover may turn on whether the non-issuer defendants can establish their due diligence defenses under Section 11(b).

Section 11(b) distinguishes between the expertised and non-expertised portions of the registration statement. The expertised portions are portions to which an expert (such as an accountant) has expressly certified. The non-expertised portions (the bulk of the registration statement) has no such certification attached.

Consider a director who wishes to establish his due diligence defenses. With respect to the non-expertised portions, the director must show that:

> he had, after reasonable investigation, reasonable ground to believe and did believe, at the time such part of the registration statement became effective, that the statements therein were true and that there was no omission to state a material fact required to be stated therein or necessary to make the statements therein not misleading.

Section 11(b)(3)(A). With respect to the expertised portions, the director has a lesser showing, namely that:

> he had no reasonable ground to believe and did not believe, at the time such part of the registration statement became effective, that the statements therein were untrue or that there was an omission to state a material fact required to be stated therein or necessary to make the statements therein not misleading, or that such part of the registration statement did not fairly represent the statement of the expert or was not a fair copy of or extract from the report or valuation of the expert.

Section 11(b)(3)(C).

An expert can be liable only in connection with those portions of the registration statement that he has certified. For example, an accountant who wishes to establish his due diligence defense with respect to the financial statements that he has certified must show that:

> (i) he had, after reasonable investigation, reasonable ground to believe and did believe, at the time such part of the registration statement became effective, that the statements therein were true and that there was no omission to state a material fact required to be stated therein or necessary to make the statements therein not misleading, or (ii) such part of the registration statement did not fairly represent his statement as an expert or was not a fair copy of or extract from his report or valuation as an expert.

Section 11(b)(3)(B).

The following decision contains a comprehensive discussion of the due diligence defenses. This decision is a landmark familiar to all securities litigators.

## ESCOTT v. BARCHRIS CONSTRUCTION CORPORATION

283 F.Supp. 643 (S.D.N.Y. 1968)

McLEAN, DISTRICT JUDGE:

This is an action by purchasers of 5 1/2 per cent convertible subordinated fifteen year debentures of BarChris Construction Corporation (BarChris). ***

The action is brought under Section 11 of the Securities Act of 1933. Plaintiffs allege that the registration statement with respect to these debentures *** contained material false statements and material omissions. ***

*** At the time relevant here, BarChris was engaged primarily in the construction of bowling alleys, somewhat euphemistically referred to as "bowling centers." ***

BarChris was an outgrowth of a business started as a partnership by Vitolo and Pugliese in 1946.***

The introduction of automatic pin setting machines in 1952 gave a marked stimulus to bowling. It rapidly became a popular sport, with the result that "bowling centers" began to appear throughout the country in rapidly increasing numbers. BarChris benefitted from this increased interest in bowling. Its construction operations expanded rapidly. It is estimated that in 1960 BarChris installed approximately three per cent of all lanes built in the United States. ***

In general, BarChris's method of operation was to enter into a contract with a customer, receive from him at that time a comparatively small down payment on the purchase price, and proceed to construct and equip the bowling alley. When the work was finished and the building delivered, the customer paid the balance of the contract price in notes, payable in installments over a period of years. BarChris discounted these notes with a factor and received part of their face amount in cash. The factor held back part as a reserve.

*** BarChris was compelled to expend considerable sums in defraying the cost of construction before it received reimbursement. As a consequence, BarChris was in constant need of cash to finance its operations, a need which grew more pressing as operations expanded.

In December 1959, BarChris sold 560,000 shares of common stock to the public at $3.00 per share. ***

By early 1961, BarChris needed additional working capital. The proceeds of the sale of the debentures involved in this action were to be devoted, in part at least, to fill that need.

The registration statement of the debentures, in preliminary form, was filed with the Securities and Exchange Commission on March 30, 1961. A first amendment was filed on May 11 and a second on May 16. The registration statement became effective on May 16. The closing of the financing took place on May 24. On that day BarChris received the net proceeds of the financing.

By that time BarChris was experiencing difficulties in collecting amounts due from some of its customers. Some of them were in arrears in payments due to factors on their discounted notes. As time went on those difficulties increased. Although BarChris continued to build alleys in 1961 and 1962, it became increasingly apparent that the industry was overbuilt. Operators of alleys, often inadequately financed, began to fail. Precisely when the tide turned is a matter of dispute, but at any rate, it was painfully apparent in 1962.

In May of that year BarChris made an abortive attempt to raise more money by the sale of common stock. It filed with the Securities and Exchange Commission a registration statement for the stock issue which it later withdrew. In October 1962 BarChris came to the end of the road. On October 29, 1962, it filed in this court a petition for an arrangement under Chapter XI of the Bankruptcy Act. BarChris defaulted in the payment of the interest due on November 1, 1962 on the debentures.

*The Debenture Registration Statement*

In preparing the registration statement for the debentures, [director and outside counsel] Grant acted for BarChris. He had previously represented BarChris in preparing the registration statement for the common stock issue. In connection with the sale of common stock, BarChris had issued purchase warrants. In January 1961 a second registration statement was filed in order to update the information pertaining to these warrants. Grant had prepared that statement as well.

Some of the basic information needed for the debenture registration statement was contained in the registration statements previously filed with respect to the common stock and warrants. Grant used these old registration statements as a model in preparing the new one, making the changes which he considered necessary in order to meet the new situation.

The underwriters were represented by the Philadelphia law firm of Drinker, Biddle & Reath. John A. Ballard, a member of that firm, was in charge of that work, assisted by a young associate named Stanton.

Peat, Marwick, BarChris's auditors, who had previously audited BarChris's annual balance sheet and earnings figures for 1958 and 1959, did the same for 1960. These figures were set forth in the registration statement. In addition, Peat, Marwick undertook a so-called "S-1 review," the proper scope of which is one of the matters debated here.

*** The prospectus [included in the registration statement] contained, among other things, a description of BarChris's business, a description of its real property, some material pertaining to certain of its subsidiaries, and remarks about various other aspects of its affairs. It also contained financial information. It included a consolidated balance sheet as of December 31, 1960, with elaborate explanatory notes. These figures had been audited by Peat, Marwick. It also contained unaudited figures as to net sales, gross profit and net earnings for the first quarter ended March 31, 1961, as compared with the similar quarter for 1960. In addition, it set forth figures as to the company's backlog of unfilled orders as of March 31, 1961, as compared with March 31, 1960, and figures as to BarChris's contingent liability, as of April 30, 1961, on customers' notes discounted and its contingent liability under the so-called alternative method of financing.

Plaintiffs challenge the accuracy of a number of these figures. They also charge that the text of the prospectus, apart from the figures, was false in a number of respects, and that material information was omitted. ***

[*The court found that the registration statement, including the financial statements attached thereto, did contain material false statements of fact and omitted to state material facts which should have been stated in order to prevent it from being misleading.*]

*The "Due Diligence" Defenses*

*** Before considering the evidence, a preliminary matter should be disposed of. The defendants do not agree among themselves as to who the "experts" were or as to the parts of the registration statement which were expertised. ***

*** To say that the entire registration statement is expertised because some lawyer prepared it would be an unreasonable construction of the statute. Neither the lawyer for the company nor the lawyer for the underwriters is an expert within the meaning of Section 11. The only expert, in the statutory sense, was Peat, Marwick, and the only parts of the registration statement which purported to be made upon the authority of an expert were the portions which purported to be made on Peat, Marwick's authority.

*** I turn now to the question of whether defendants have proved their due diligence defenses. The position of each defendant will be separately considered.

*Russo*

Russo was, to all intents and purposes, the chief executive officer of BarChris. He was a member of the executive committee. He was familiar with all aspects of the business. He was personally in charge of dealings with the factors. He acted on BarChris's behalf in making the financing agreements with Talcott and he handled the negotiations with Talcott in the spring of 1961. He talked with customers about their delinquencies.

Russo prepared the list of jobs which went into the backlog figure. He knew the status of those jobs. ***

It was Russo who arranged for the temporary increase in BarChris's cash in banks on December 31, 1960, a transaction which borders on the fraudulent. He was thoroughly aware of BarChris's stringent financial condition in May 1961. He had personally advanced large sums to BarChris of which $175,000 remained unpaid as of May 16.

In short, Russo knew all the relevant facts. He could not have believed that there were no untrue statements or material omissions in the prospectus. Russo has no due diligence defenses. ***

*Kircher*

Kircher was treasurer of BarChris and its chief financial officer. He is a certified public accountant and an intelligent man. He was thoroughly familiar with BarChris's financial affairs. He knew the terms of BarChris's agreements with Talcott. He knew of the customers' delinquency problem. He participated actively with Russo in May 1961 in the successful effort to hold Talcott off until the financing proceeds came in. He knew how the financing proceeds were to be applied and he saw to it that they were so applied. ***

Moreover, as a member of the executive committee, Kircher was kept informed as to those branches of the business of which he did not have direct charge. *** In brief, Kircher knew all the relevant facts.

Kircher worked on the preparation of the registration statement. He conferred with Grant and on occasion with Ballard. He supplied information to them about the company's business. He read the prospectus and understood it. He knew what it said and what it did not say.

Kircher's contention is that he had never before dealt with a registration statement, that he did not know what it should contain, and that he relied wholly on Grant, Ballard and Peat, Marwick to guide him. He claims that it was their fault, not his, if there was anything wrong with it. He says that all the facts were recorded in BarChris's books where these "experts" could have seen them if they had looked. He says that he truthfully answered all their questions. In effect, he says that if they did not know enough to ask the right questions and to give him the proper instructions, that is not his responsibility.

There is an issue of credibility here. In fact, Kircher was not frank in dealing with Grant and Ballard. He withheld information from them. But even if he had told them all the facts, this would not have constituted the due diligence contemplated by the statute. Knowing the facts, Kircher had reason to believe that the expertised portion of the prospectus, i.e., the 1960 figures, was in part incorrect. He could not shut his eyes to the facts and rely on Peat, Marwick for that portion.

As to the rest of the prospectus, knowing the facts, he did not have a reasonable ground to believe it to be true. On the contrary, he must have known that in part it was untrue. Under these circumstances, he was not entitled to sit back and place the blame on the lawyers for not advising him about it.

Kircher has not proved his due diligence defenses. ***

*Birnbaum*

Birnbaum was a young lawyer, admitted to the bar in 1957, who, after brief periods of employment by two different law firms and an equally brief period of practicing in his own firm, was employed by BarChris as house counsel and assistant secretary in October 1960. Unfortunately for him, he became secretary and a director of BarChris on April 17, 1961, after the first version of the registration statement had been filed with the Securities and Exchange Commission. He signed the later amendments, thereby becoming responsible for the accuracy of the prospectus in its final form.

Although the prospectus, in its description of "management," lists Birnbaum among the "executive officers" *** the fact seems to be that he was not an executive officer in any real sense. He did not participate in the management of the company. As house counsel, he attended to legal matters of a routine nature. ***

Birnbaum examined contracts. In that connection he advised BarChris that the T-Bowl contracts were not legally enforceable. He was thus aware of that fact.

One of Birnbaum's more important duties, first as assistant secretary and later as full-fledged secretary, was to keep the corporate minutes of BarChris and its subsidiaries. This necessarily informed him to a considerable extent about the company's affairs. ***

It seems probable that Birnbaum did not know of many of the inaccuracies in the prospectus. He must, however, have appreciated some of them. In any case, he made no investigation and relied on the others to get it right. *** [H]e was entitled to rely upon Peat, Marwick for the 1960 figures, for as far as appears, he had no personal knowledge of the company's books of account or financial transactions. But he was not entitled to rely upon Kircher, Grant and Ballard for the other portions of the prospectus. As a lawyer, he should have known his obligations under the statute. He should have known that he was required to make a reasonable investigation of the truth of all the statements in the unexpertised portion of the document which he signed. Having failed to make such an investigation, he did not have reasonable ground to believe that all these statements were true. Birnbaum has not established his due diligence defenses except as to the audited 1960 figures.

*Auslander*

Auslander was an "outside" director, i.e., one who was not an officer of BarChris. He was chairman of the board of Valley Stream National Bank in Valley Stream, Long Island. In February 1961 Vitolo asked him to become a director of BarChris. Vitolo gave him an enthusiastic account of BarChris's progress and prospects. As an inducement, Vitolo said that when BarChris received the proceeds of a forthcoming issue of securities, it would deposit $1,000,000 in Auslander's bank.

In February and early March 1961, before accepting Vitolo's invitation, Auslander made some investigation of BarChris. He obtained Dun & Bradstreet reports which contained sales and earnings figures for periods earlier than December 31, 1960. He caused inquiry to be made of certain of BarChris's banks and was advised that they regarded BarChris favorably. He was informed that inquiry of Talcott had also produced a favorable response.

On March 3, 1961, Auslander indicated his willingness to accept a place on the board. *** Auslander observed that BarChris's auditors were Peat, Marwick. They were also the auditors for the Valley Stream National Bank. He thought well of them.

Auslander was elected a director on April 17, 1961. The registration statement in its original form had already been filed, of course without his signature. On May 10, 1961, he signed a signature page for the first amendment to the registration statement which was filed on May 11, 1961. This was a separate sheet without any document attached. Auslander did not know that it was a signature page for a registration statement. He vaguely understood that it was something "for the SEC."

Auslander attended a meeting of BarChris's directors on May 15, 1961. At that meeting he, along with the other directors, signed the signature sheet for the second amendment which constituted the registration statement in its final form. Again, this was only a separate sheet without any document attached. Auslander never saw a copy of the registration statement in its final form.

At the May 15 directors' meeting, however, Auslander did realize that what he was signing was a signature sheet to a registration statement. This was the first time that he had appreciated that fact. A copy of the registration statement in its earlier form as amended on May 11, 1961 was passed around at the meeting. Auslander glanced at it briefly. He did not read it thoroughly.

At the May 15 meeting, Russo and Vitolo stated that everything was in order and that the prospectus was correct. Auslander believed this statement.

In considering Auslander's due diligence defenses, a distinction is to be drawn between the expertised and non-expertised portions of the prospectus. As to the former, Auslander knew that Peat, Marwick had audited the 1960 figures. He believed them to be correct because he had confidence in Peat, Marwick. He had no reasonable ground to believe otherwise.

As to the non-expertised portions, however, Auslander is in a different position. He seems to have been under the impression that Peat, Marwick was responsible for all the figures. This impression was not correct, as he would have realized if he had read the prospectus carefully. Auslander made no investigation of the accuracy of the prospectus. He relied on the assurance of Vitolo and Russo, and upon the information he had received in answer to his inquiries back in February and early March. These inquiries were general ones, in the nature of a credit check. The information which he received in answer to them was also general, without specific reference to the statements in the prospectus, which was not prepared until some time thereafter.

It is true that Auslander became a director on the eve of the financing. He had little opportunity to familiarize himself with the company's affairs. The question is whether, under such circumstances, Auslander did enough to establish his due diligence defense with respect to the non-expertised portions of the prospectus.

*** Section 11 imposes liability in the first instance upon a director, no matter how new he is. He is presumed to know his responsibility when he becomes a director. He can escape liability only by using that reasonable care to investigate the facts which a prudent man would employ in the management of his own property. In my opinion, a prudent man would not act in an important matter without any knowledge of the relevant facts, in sole reliance upon representations of persons who are comparative strangers and upon general information which does not purport to cover the particular case. To say that such minimal conduct measures up to the statutory standard would, to all intents and purposes, absolve new directors from responsibility merely because they are new. This is not a sensible construction of Section 11, when one bears in mind its fundamental purpose of requiring full and truthful disclosure for the protection of investors.

I find and conclude that Auslander has not established his due diligence defense with respect to the misstatements and omissions in those portions of the prospectus other than the audited 1960 figures. ***

*Grant*

Grant became a director of BarChris in October 1960. His law firm was counsel to BarChris in matters pertaining to the registration of securities. Grant drafted the registration statement for the stock issue in 1959 and for the warrants in January 1961. He also drafted the registration statement for the debentures. ***

Grant is sued as a director and as a signer of the registration statement. This is not an action against him for malpractice in his capacity as a lawyer. Nevertheless, in considering Grant's due diligence defenses, the unique position which he occupied cannot be disregarded. As the director most directly concerned with writing the registration statement and assuring its accuracy, more was required of him in the way of reasonable investigation than could fairly be expected of a director who had no connection with this work.

*** Having seen [Grant] testify at length, I am satisfied as to his integrity. I find that Grant honestly believed that the registration statement was true and that no material facts had been omitted from it.

In this belief he was mistaken, and the fact is that for all his work, he never discovered any of the errors or omissions which have been recounted at length in this opinion, with the single exception of Capitol Lanes. He knew that BarChris had not sold this alley and intended to operate it, but he appears to have been under the erroneous impression that Peat, Marwick had knowingly sanctioned its inclusion in sales because of the allegedly temporary nature of the operation.

Grant contends that a finding that he did not make a reasonable investigation would be equivalent to a holding that a lawyer for an issuing company, in order to show due diligence, must make an independent audit of the figures supplied to him by his client. I do not consider this to be a realistic statement of the issue. There were errors and omissions here which could have been detected without an audit. The question is whether, despite his failure to detect them, Grant made a reasonable effort to that end.

Much of this registration statement is a scissors and paste-pot job. Grant lifted large portions from the earlier prospectuses, modifying them in some instances to the extent that he considered necessary. But BarChris's affairs had changed for the worse by May 1961. Statements that were accurate in January were no longer accurate in May. Grant never discovered this. He accepted the assurances of Kircher and Russo that any change which might have occurred had been for the better, rather than the contrary.

It is claimed that a lawyer is entitled to rely on the statements of his client and that to require him to verify their accuracy would set an unreasonably high standard. This is too broad a generalization. It is all a matter of degree. To require an audit would obviously be unreasonable. On the other hand, to require a check of matters easily verifiable is not unreasonable. Even honest clients can make mistakes. The statute imposes liability for untrue statements regardless of whether they are intentionally untrue. The way to prevent mistakes is to test oral information by examining the original written record.

There were things which Grant could readily have checked which he did not check. For example, he was unaware of the provisions of the agreements between BarChris and Talcott. He never read them. Thus, he did not know, although he readily could have ascertained, that BarChris's contingent liability on Type B leaseback arrangements was 100 per cent, not 25 per cent. He did not appreciate that if BarChris defaulted in repurchasing delinquent customers' notes upon Talcott's demand, Talcott could accelerate all the customer paper in its hands, which amounted to over $3,000,000.

As to the backlog figure, Grant appreciated that scheduled unfilled orders on the company's books meant firm commitments, but he never asked to see the contracts which, according to the prospectus, added up to $6,905,000. Thus, he did not know that this figure was overstated by some $4,490,000. ***

The application of proceeds language in the prospectus was drafted by Kircher back in January. It may well have expressed his intent at that time, but his intent, and that of the other principal officers of BarChris, was very different in May. Grant did not appreciate that the earlier language was no longer appropriate. He never learned of the situation which the company faced in May. He knew that BarChris was short of cash, but he had no idea how short. He did not know that BarChris was withholding delivery of checks already drawn and signed because there was not enough money in the bank to pay them. He did not know that the officers of the company intended to use immediately approximately one-third of the financing proceeds in a manner not disclosed in the prospectus, including approximately $1,000,000 in paying old debts. ***

As far as customers' delinquencies is concerned, although Grant discussed this with Kircher, he again accepted the assurances of Kircher and Russo that no serious problem existed. He did not examine the records as to delinquencies, although BarChris maintained such a record. Any inquiry on his part of Talcott or an examination of BarChris's correspondence with Talcott in April and May 1961 would have apprised him of the true facts. ***

Grant was entitled to rely on Peat, Marwick for the 1960 figures. He had no reasonable ground to believe them to be inaccurate. But the matters which I have mentioned were not within the expertised portion of the prospectus. As to this, Grant, was obliged to make a reasonable investigation. I am forced to find that he did not make one. After making all due allowances for the fact that Bar Chris's officers misled him, there are too many instances in which Grant failed to make an inquiry which he could easily have made which, if pursued, would have put him on his guard. *** Each case must rest on its own facts. I conclude that Grant has not established his due diligence defenses except as to the audited 1960 figures.

*The Underwriters and Coleman*

The underwriters other than Drexel made no investigation of the accuracy of the prospectus. *** They all relied upon Drexel as the "lead" underwriter.

Drexel did make an investigation. The work was in charge of Coleman, a partner the firm, assisted by Casperson, an associate. Drexel's attorneys acted as attorneys for the entire group of underwriters. Ballard did the work, assisted by Stanton.

On April 17, 1961 Coleman became a director of BarChris. He signed the first amendment to the registration statement filed on May 11 and the second amendment, constituting the registration statement in its final form, filed on May 16. He thereby assumed a responsibility as a director and signer in addition to his responsibility as an underwriter. ***

*** [Coleman] was first introduced to BarChris on September 15, 1960. Thereafter he familiarized himself with general conditions in the industry ***.

Coleman continued his general investigation. He obtained a Dun & Bradstreet report on BarChris on March 16, 1961. He read BarChris's annual report for 1960 which was available in March. ***

After Coleman was elected a director on April 17, 1961, he made no further independent investigation of the accuracy of the prospectus. He assumed that Ballard was taking care of this on his behalf as well as on behalf of the underwriters. ***

Like Grant, Ballard, without checking, relied on the information which he got from Kircher. He also relied on Grant who, as company counsel, presumably was familiar with its affairs. ***

*** [I]t is clear that no effectual attempt at verification was made. The question is whether due diligence required that it be made. Stated another way, is it sufficient to ask questions, to obtain answers which, if true, would be thought satisfactory, and to let it go at that, without seeking to ascertain from the records whether the answers in fact are true and complete?

I have already held that this procedure is not sufficient in Grant's case. Are underwriters in a different position, as far as due diligence is concerned?

The underwriters say that the prospectus is the company's prospectus, not theirs. Doubtless this is the way they customarily regard it. But the Securities Act makes no such distinction. The underwriters are just as responsible as the company if the prospectus is false. And prospective investors rely upon the reputation of the underwriters in deciding whether to purchase the securities.

There is no direct authority on this question, no judicial decision defining the degree of diligence which underwriters must exercise to establish their defense under Section 11.

There is some authority in New York for the proposition that a director of a corporation may rely upon information furnished him by the officers without independently verifying it. See *Litwin v. Allen*, 25 N.Y.S.2d 667 (Sup.Ct.1940).

In support of that principle, the court in *Litwin* (25 N.Y.S.2d at 719) quoted from the opinion of Lord Halsbury in *Dovey v. Cory*, (1901) App.Cas. 477, 486, in which he said:

> "The business of life could not go on if people could not trust those who are put into a position of trust for the express purpose of attending to details of management."

Of course, New York law does not govern this case. The construction of the Securities Act is a matter of federal law. But the underwriters argue that *Litwin* is still in point, for they say that it establishes a standard of reasonableness for the reasonably prudent director which should be the same as the standard for the reasonably prudent underwriter under the Securities Act.

In my opinion the two situations are not analogous. An underwriter has not put the company's officers "into a position of trust for the express purpose of attending to details of management." The underwriters did not select them. In a sense, the positions of the underwriter and the company's officers are adverse. It is not unlikely that statements made by company officers to an underwriter to induce him to underwrite may be self-serving. They may be unduly enthusiastic. As in this case, they may, on occasion, be deliberately false.

The purpose of Section 11 is to protect investors. To that end the underwriters are made responsible for the truth of the prospectus. If they may escape that responsibility by taking at face value representations made to them by the company's management, then the inclusion of underwriters among those liable under Section 11 affords the investors no additional protection. To effectuate the statute's purpose, the phrase "reasonable investigation" must be construed to require more effort on the part of the underwriters than the mere accurate reporting in the prospectus of "date presented" to them by the company. It should make no difference that this data is elicited by questions addressed to the company officers by the underwriters, or that the underwriters at the time believe that the company's officers are truthful and reliable. In order to make the underwriters' participation in this enterprise of any value to the investors, the underwriters must make some reasonable attempt to verify the data submitted to them. They may not rely solely on the company's officers or on the company's counsel. A prudent man in the management of his own property would not rely on them.

It is impossible to lay down a rigid rule suitable for every case defining the extent to which such verification must go. It is a question of degree, a matter of judgment in each case. In the present case, the underwriters' counsel made almost no attempt to verify management's representations. I hold that that was insufficient.

On the evidence in this case, I find that the underwriters' counsel did not make a reasonable investigation of the truth of those portions of the prospectus which were not made on the authority of Peat, Marwick as an expert. Drexel is bound by their failure. It is not a matter of relying upon counsel for legal advice. Here the attorneys were dealing with matters of fact. Drexel delegated to them, as its agent, the business of examining the corporate minutes and contracts. It must bear the consequences of their failure to make an adequate examination.

The other underwriters, who did nothing and relied solely on Drexel and on the lawyers, are also bound by it. It follows that although Drexel and the other underwriters believed that those portions of the prospectus were true, they had no reasonable ground for that belief, within the meaning of the statute. Hence, they have not established their due diligence defense, except as to the 1960 audited figures.

The same conclusions must apply to Coleman. Although he participated quite actively in the earlier stages of the preparation of the prospectus, and contributed questions and warnings of his own, in addition to the questions of counsel, the fact is that he stopped his participation toward the end of March 1961. He made no investigation after he became a director. When it came to verification, he relied upon his counsel to do it for him. Since counsel failed to do it, Coleman is bound by that failure. Consequently, in his case also, he has not established his due diligence defense except as to the audited 1960 figures.

*Peat, Marwick*

*** The part of the registration statement purporting to be made upon the authority of Peat, Marwick as an expert was, as we have seen, the 1960 figures. But because the statute requires the court to determine Peat, Marwick's belief, and the grounds thereof, "at the time such part of the registration statement became effective," for the purposes of this affirmative defense, the matter must be viewed as of May 16, 1961, and the question is whether at that time Peat, Marwick, after reasonable investigation, had reasonable ground to believe and did believe that the 1960 figures were true and that no material fact had been omitted from the registration statement which should have been included in order to make the 1960 figures not misleading. In deciding this issue, the court must consider not only what Peat, Marwick did in its 1960 audit, but also what it did in its subsequent "S- 1 review." The proper scope of that review must also be determined. ***

Peat, Marwick's work was in general charge of a member of the firm, Cummings, and more immediately in charge of Peat, Marwick's manager, Logan. Most of the actual work was performed by a senior accountant, Berardi, who had junior assistants, one of whom was Kennedy.

Berardi was then about thirty years old. He was not yet a C.P.A. He had had no previous experience with the bowling industry. This was his first job as a senior accountant. He could hardly have been given a more difficult assignment.

After obtaining a little background information on BarChris by talking to Logan and reviewing Peat, Marwick's work papers on its 1959 audit, Berardi examined the results of test checks of BarChris's accounting procedures which one of the junior accountants had made, and he prepared an "internal control questionnaire" and an "audit program." Thereafter, for a few days subsequent to December 30, 1960, he inspected BarChris's inventories and examined certain alley construction. Finally, on January 13, 1961, he began his auditing work which he carried on substantially continuously until it was completed on February 24, 1961. Toward the close of the work, Logan reviewed it and made various comments and suggestions to Berardi. ***

Berardi made the S-1 review in May 1961. He devoted a little over two days to it, a total of 20 1/2 hours. He did not discover any of the errors or omissions pertaining to the state of affairs in 1961 which I have previously discussed at length, all of which were material. The question is whether, despite his failure to find out anything, his investigation was reasonable within the meaning of the statute.

What Berardi did was to look at a consolidating trial balance as of March 31, 1961 which had been prepared by BarChris, compare it with the audited December 31, 1960 figures, discuss with Trilling certain unfavorable developments which the comparison disclosed, and read certain minutes. He did not examine any "important financial records" other than the trial balance. As to minutes, he read only what minutes Birnbaum gave him, which consisted only of the board of directors' minutes of BarChris. He did not read such minutes as there were of the executive committee. He did not know that there was an executive committee, hence he did not discover that Kircher had notes of executive committee minutes which had not been written up. He did not read the minutes of any subsidiary.

In substance, what Berardi did is similar to what Grant and Ballard did. He asked questions, he got answers which he considered satisfactory, and he did nothing to verify them. ***

Accountants should not be held to a standard higher than that recognized in their profession. I do not do so here. Berardi's review did not come up to that standard. *** Most important of all, he was too easily satisfied with glib answers to his inquiries.

This is not to say that he should have made a complete audit. But there were enough danger signals in the materials which he did examine to require some further investigation on his part. Generally accepted accounting standards required such further investigation under these circumstances. It is not always sufficient merely to ask questions.

*** I conclude that Peat, Marwick has not established its due diligence defense. ***

## *NOTES AND QUESTIONS*

***1. Due Diligence and the* Barchris *Defendants.*** In applying Section 11 to the defendants, the court may (or may not) have made various distinctions. Consider the following.

*(a) Outside vs. Inside Directors.* To what extent did the court draw a distinction between the duties of inside and outside directors?

*(b) Attorney Directors.* Were directors who were also attorneys held to a higher standard? Did the court apply the same standard to Grant and Birnbaum? Should it have?

*(c) Outside Directors vs. Outside Directors.* Were Grant and Auslander held to the same standard? Should they have been?

*(d) Underwriter Directors.* Would Coleman have established his due diligence defense as to the non-expertised portion of the registration statement had he not been an underwriter?

*(e) Underwriters.* According to the court, to what extent are underwriters entitled to rely on management's representations? Should there be a distinction between underwriters and directors in this regard?

*(f) Accountants.* The court maintained that "accountants should not be held to a standard higher than that recognized in their profession." Is this a sound approach?

***2. Piling It On?*** Note that once the court determined that a particular (non-expert) defendant had failed to satisfy his due diligence defense as to the non-expertised portion of the registration statement, it did not stop there. Instead, it went on to consider the defendant's liability as to the expertised portion. If a defendant is already liable as to the non-expertised portion, why bother ascertaining his liability as to the expertised portion as well?

*3. A Kinder, Gentler Approach to Underwriters?* Recent case law suggests a somewhat kinder, gentler approach to underwriters than was evident in *BarChris*. Consider the court's analysis in *In re Software Toolworks, Inc. Sec. Litig.*, 50 F.3d 615 (9th Cir. 1994):

> The plaintiffs argue that the prospectus was false and misleading because it stated that Toolworks' "Nintendo software products have not been subject to price reductions," when, in fact, Toolworks had begun a price- cutting promotion days before the offering. The plaintiffs, however, presented no direct evidence that the Underwriters knew of this promotion. Indeed, the record illustrates that Toolworks' management consistently assured the Underwriters that the company would not reduce prices. The plaintiffs nevertheless assert that summary judgment was inappropriate because a jury might infer that the Underwriters knew about the price cuts because Toolworks' management discussed the promotion while on a private plane with the Underwriters. All personnel who were on the plane, however, testified that no conversations regarding price cutting reached the Underwriters. As such, any inference that the Underwriters knew about the sales would not be based in fact and would be unreasonable. The district court properly granted summary judgment in favor of the Underwriters on this issue.
>
> The plaintiffs also claim that the prospectus was false and misleading because it stated that Toolworks "does not currently provide any product return rights to its retail Nintendo customers," when, in fact, the company had booked several consignment sales prior to the offering. Again, however, the plaintiffs offered no direct evidence that the Underwriters knew about the sales, which represented a significant departure from prior Toolworks' policy. In fact, the record illustrates that the Underwriters made a substantial effort to ascertain Toolworks' return policy, both before and after the consignment sales occurred. The plaintiffs nevertheless assert that circumstantial evidence permits an inference that the Underwriters knowingly "watered down" the prospectus' risk-disclosure statement about merchandise returns and ignored a memorandum from one Toolworks customer ("Walmart") describing an unlimited right-of-return. This argument, however, misconstrues the full record. ***
>
> The plaintiffs next attack the Underwriters' due diligence efforts for the period after Toolworks filed a preliminary prospectus and before the effective date of the offering. ***
>
> The district court held that the Underwriters satisfied their due diligence obligations during this period primarily by relying on Toolworks' representations to the SEC. For the following reasons, we conclude that disputed issues of material fact exist regarding the Underwriters' efforts and, accordingly, we reverse and remand for a trial on the merits. ***
>
> *** [T]he plaintiffs raise the issue of Toolworks' July 4, 1990 letter to the SEC, which described the company's June quarter performance. In the letter, Toolworks represented that, although preliminary financial data was not available, Toolworks anticipated revenue for the quarter between $21 and $22 million. The plaintiffs claim that Toolworks deliberately falsified these estimates and that the Underwriters knew of this deceit.
>
> The Underwriters claim that they were not involved in drafting the July 4 SEC letter and that, as a result, they have no responsibility for its contents. The plaintiffs presented evidence, however, that the letter was a joint

effort of all professionals working on the offering, including the Underwriters. ***

The Underwriters argue that, even if they participated in initial discussions about the letter, they never knew that Toolworks' financial data actually was available and that, as a result, they could not have known that the letter (and the prospectus) were misleading. Given the Underwriters participation in drafting both documents, however, we think this is an unresolved issue of material fact. A reasonable factfinder could infer that, as members of the drafting group, the Underwriters had access to all information that was available and deliberately chose to conceal the truth. We therefore hold that summary judgment was inappropriate on this issue.

After suffering lagging sales in the first two months of the June quarter, Toolworks booked several large consignment sales in late June, the quarter's final month, thereby enabling the company to meet its earning projections. Toolworks later had to reverse more than $7 million of these sales in its final financial statements for the quarter. The plaintiffs presented evidence that the Underwriters knew that Toolworks had performed poorly in April, that Toolworks had no orders for the month as of June 8, that the June quarter is traditionally the slowest of the year for Nintendo sales, and that the late June sales accounted for more revenue than the cumulative total of Toolworks' Nintendo sales for the prior two and a half months. For its due diligence investigation of these sales, however, the Underwriters did little more than rely on Toolworks' assurances that the transactions were legitimate. A reasonable inference from this evidence is that Toolworks fabricated the June sales to ensure that the offering would proceed and that the Underwriters knew, or should have known, of this fraud. As a result, we conclude that summary judgment regarding the Underwriters' diligence on this issue was also inappropriate. See *Feit v. Leasco Data Processing Equip. Corp.*, 332 F.Supp. 544, 582 (E.D.N.Y.1971) ("Tacit reliance on management is unacceptable; the underwriters must play devil's advocate.").

Id. at 622-26. Does the court hold the underwriters to a negligence standard? To a recklessness or an intentionality standard? Does the court in effect presume their due diligence absent proof to the contrary? Under what circumstances (if any) do these underwriters appear to be entitled to rely on representations made by the issuer? What similarities and differences do you see between the *Toolworks* and *BarChris* approaches?

***4. A Kinder, Gentler Approach to Outside Directors?*** Recent case law likewise suggests a somewhat kinder, gentler approach to outside directors. Consider the following analysis:

Since Valentine was an outside director, he was not obliged to conduct an independent investigation into the accuracy of all the statements contained in the registration statement. He could rely upon the reasonable representations of management, if his own conduct and level of inquiry were reasonable under the circumstances. He was reasonably familiar with the company's business and operations. He regularly attended board meetings at which the board discussed every aspect of the company's business. And he reviewed the company's financial statements. He was familiar with the company's development of its new product lines. He was involved with various company decisions. He reviewed six drafts of the registration statement and saw nothing suspicious or inconsistent with the knowledge that he had acquired as a director. And he discussed certain aspects of the registration statement with management.

> With respect to the alleged misrepresentations about shipment of the lines of products, he could not reasonably have noticed any ambiguity in the phrase "in quantity" in light of his understanding of the company's business and its practice of increasing production from the time a new model is first introduced. With respect to alleged misrepresentations regarding the availability of software, Valentine knew what the prospectus stated, that is, that software was provided by outside vendors, and that application software might not be available for new models when they are first introduced.
>
> Plaintiffs argue that Valentine did not make specific inquiries of the company's management with respect to the representations contained in the prospectus. But he had no duty to do so as long as the prospectus statements were consistent with the knowledge of the company which he had reasonably acquired in his position as director. He was also given comfort by the fact that the prospectus and the information in it were reviewed by underwriters, counsel and accountants. This met the standards of due diligence and reasonable inquiry.
>
> Judgment should therefore be granted in favor of defendant Valentine and against plaintiffs.

*Weinberger v. Jackson,* 1990 WL 260676 at *4-*5 (N.D. Cal. 1990). Would the *BarChris* court have reached a different result? How did the treatment of Auslander in *BarChris* compare with that of Valentine in *Weinberger*?

***5. The (In)Significance of Rule 176.*** In 1982, the SEC adopted Rule 176 as an aid in determining whether a Section 11 defendant has satisfied his due diligence defenses:

> In determining whether or not the conduct of a person constitutes a reasonable investigation or a reasonable ground for belief meeting the standard set forth in section 11(c), relevant circumstances include, with respect to a person other than the issuer:
>
> (a) The type of issuer;
>
> (b) The type of security;
>
> (c) The type of person;
>
> (d) The office held when the person is an officer;
>
> (e) The presence or absence of another relationship to the issuer when the person is a director or proposed director;
>
> (f) Reasonable reliance on officers, employees, and others whose duties should have given them knowledge of the particular facts (in the light of the functions and responsibilities of the particular person with respect to the issuer and the filing);
>
> (g) When the person is an underwriter, the type of underwriting arrangement, the role of the particular person as an underwriter and the availability of information with respect to the registrant; and
>
> (h) Whether, with respect to a fact or document incorporated by reference, the particular person had any responsibility for the fact or document at the time of the filing from which it was incorporated.

Rule 176 has had relatively little impact on Section 11 case law. Why do you suppose that is? Would you favor the adoption of a rule that provided defendants with more definitive protection? If so, what would that rule look like?

*6. **Expanding the Categories of Defendants.*** Section 11 liability attaches only to the specific categories of defendants named in Section 11(a). Attempts by plaintiffs to expand these categories have typically not met with success. Consider *Dorchester Investors v. Peak Int'l Ltd.*, 134 F. Supp. 2d 569 (S.D. N.Y. 2001), a Section 11 action brought in connection with the IPO of the Peak TrENDS Trust (TrENDS). Attached to the TrENDS prospectus was the Peak Share Offering Prospectus (accompanied by the notation that it was not incorporated by reference into the TrENDS prospectus). The plaintiffs argued that a defendant in the Peak Share Offering could, by virtue of the attachment, likewise be sued in connection with the TrENDS offering, but the court rejected the argument.

*7. **The Costs of Due Diligence.*** Who bears the costs of the simultaneous due diligence required of issuers, underwriters and auditors under Section 11? Do recent accounting scandals suggest that the gatekeepers are not taking their responsibilities seriously enough?

### *PROBLEM 3-2*

Trapeze, Inc., one of the largest publicly traded companies in the country, is, by virtue of its size, entitled by SEC regulations to incorporate by reference into its registration statement the quarterly and annual reports that it has previously filed with the SEC. See generally supra Chapter 1.A.1.a. Trapeze followed this procedure in connection with its registered offering in July 2002.

As is typical in such situations, no comprehensive investigation was performed. Such an investigation would have brought to light certain material information that was omitted from the non-expertised portion of the registration statement.

A Section 11 action has been filed based on the failure to disclose this information. Can the underwriters establish their due diligence defenses under these circumstances? What about an outside director who is also a lawyer as well as the author of a law review article on the difficulty of reconciling incorporation-by-reference procedures with the performance of due diligence obligations under Section 11?

#### c. *Damages and Negative Causation*

Section 11(e) provides a set formula for the calculation of damages that allows the plaintiff to recover:

> the difference between the amount paid for the security (not exceeding the price at which the security was offered to the public) and (1) the value thereof as of the time such suit was brought, or (2) the price at which such security shall have been disposed of in the market before suit, or (3) the price at which such security shall have been disposed of after suit but before judgment if such damages shall be less than [the damages specified in (1) above].

See also Section 11(g) ( providing that “”[i]n no case shall the amount recoverable under this section exceed the price at which the security was offered to the public”); *McMahan & Co. v. Wherehouse Entertainment, Inc.*, 65 F.3d 1044, 1048 (2d Cir. 1995) (noting that courts must “apply the prescribed formula in every section 11 case”).

Section 11(e) also contains a so-called "negative causation" defense pursuant to which a defendant can reduce—or even eliminate entirely—the amount of damages he might otherwise owe:

> [I]f the defendant proves that any portion or all of such damages represents other than the depreciation in value of such security resulting from such part of the registration statement, with respect to which his liability is asserted, not being true or omitting to state a material fact required to be stated therein or necessary to make the statements therein not misleading, such portion of or all such damages shall not be recoverable.

Cf. *McMahan & Co.,* supra, 65 F.3d at 1048 (reversing the district court because it had not permitted the defendant to establish negative causation).

Consider the court's application of these provisions in the following decision.

## AKERMAN v. ORYX COMMUNICATIONS, INC.

810 F.2d 336 (2d Cir. 1987)

MESKILL, CIRCUIT JUDGE:

*** This case arises out of a June 30, 1981, initial public offering of securities by Oryx, a company planning to enter the business of manufacturing and marketing abroad video cassettes and video discs of feature films for home entertainment. Oryx filed a registration statement and an accompanying prospectus dated June 30, 1981 *** for a firm commitment offering of 700,000 units. Each unit sold for $4.75 and consisted of one share of common stock and one warrant to purchase an additional share of stock for $5.75 at a later date.

The prospectus contained an erroneous *pro forma* unaudited financial statement relating to the eight month period ending March 31, 1981. It reported net sales of $931,301, net income of $211,815, and earnings of seven cents per share. Oryx, however, had incorrectly posted a substantial transaction by its subsidiary to March instead of April when Oryx actually received the subject sale's revenues. The prospectus, therefore, overstated earnings for the eight month period. Net sales in that period actually totaled $766,301, net income $94,529, and earnings per share three cents.

Oryx's price had declined to four dollars per unit by October 12, 1981, the day before Oryx revealed the prospectus misstatement to the SEC. The unit price had further declined to $3.25 by November 9, 1981, the day before Oryx disclosed the misstatement to the public. After public disclosure, the price of Oryx rose and reached $3.50 by November 25, 1981, the day this suit commenced. ***

Section 11(a) of the 1933 Act imposes civil liability on the signatories of a registration statement if the registration statement contains a material untruth or omission of which a "person acquiring [the registered] security" had no knowledge at the time of the purchase. Plaintiffs in the Akermans' situation, if successful, would be entitled to recover the difference between the original purchase price and the value of the stock at the time of suit. A defendant may, under section 11(e), reduce his liability by proving that the depreciation in value resulted from factors other than the material misstatement in the registration statement. A defendant's burden in attempting to reduce his liability has been characterized as the burden of "negative causation." *Beecher v. Able*, 435 F. Supp. 397, 409 (S.D.N.Y. 1975).

The district court determined that plaintiffs established a prima facie case under section 11(a) by demonstrating that the prospectus error was material "as a theoretical matter." The court, however, granted defendants' motion for summary judgment on damages under section 11(e), stating: "[Defendants] have carried their heavy burden of proving that the [Oryx stock price] decline was caused by factors other than the matters misstated in the registration statement." The precise issue on appeal, therefore, is whether defendants carried their burden of negative causation under section 11(e).

Defendants' heavy burden reflects Congress' desire to allocate the risk of uncertainty to the defendants in these cases. Defendants' burden, however, is not insurmountable; section 11(e) expressly creates an affirmative defense of disproving causation. ***

The misstatement resulted from an innocent bookkeeping error whereby Oryx misposted a sale by its subsidiary to March instead of April. Oryx received the sale's proceeds less than one month after the reported date. The prospectus, moreover, expressly stated that Oryx "expect[ed] that [the subsidiary's] sales will decline." Indeed, Morris Akerman conceded that he understood this disclaimer to warn that Oryx expected the subsidiary's business to decline.

Thus, although the misstatement may have been "theoretically material," when it is considered in the context of the prospectus' pessimistic forecast of the performance of Oryx's subsidiary, the misstatement was not likely to cause a stock price decline. Compare *Escott v. BarChris Construction Corp.*, 283 F.Supp. 643 (S.D.N.Y. 1968) (failure to disclose facts clearly indicating impending financial demise). Indeed, the public not only did not react adversely to disclosure of the misstatement, Oryx's price actually *rose* somewhat after public disclosure of the error.

The applicable section 11(e) formula for calculating damages is "the difference between the amount paid for the security (not exceeding the price at which the security was offered to the public) and ... the value thereof as of the time such suit was brought." The relevant events and stock prices are:

| *Date* | *Event* | *Orynx Stock Price* |
|---|---|---|
| June 30, 1981 | Initial public offering | $4.75 |
| October 15, 1981 | Disclosure of error to SEC | $4.00 |
| November 10, 1981 | Disclosure of error to public | $3.25 |
| November 25, 1981 | Date of suit | $3.50 |

The price decline before disclosure may not be charged to defendants. See *Beecher v. Able*, 435 F. Supp. 397, 407 (S.D.N.Y.1975) (price decline before misstatement revealed not attributable to defendants under section 11(e)); *Fox v. Glickman Corp.*, 253 F. Supp. 1005, 1010 (S.D.N.Y.1966) (same). At first blush, damages would appear to be zero because there was no depreciation in Oryx's value between the time of public disclosure and the time of suit.

The Akermans contended at trial, however, that the relevant disclosure date was the date of disclosure to the SEC and not to the public. Under plaintiffs' theory, damages would equal the price decline subsequent to October 15, 1981, which amount to fifty cents per share. Plaintiffs attempted to support this theory by alleging that insiders privy to the SEC disclosure—Oryx's officers, attorneys and accountants, and underwriters and SEC officials—sold Oryx shares and thereby deflated its price before public disclosure. *** After extensive discovery, however, plaintiffs produced absolutely no evidence of insider trading. Plaintiffs' submissions and oral argument before us do not press this theory. ***

The district court invited statistical studies from both sides to clarify the causation issue. Defendants produced a statistical analysis of the stocks of the one hundred companies that went public contemporaneously with Oryx. The study tracked the stocks' performances for the period between June 30, 1981 (initial public offering date) and November 25, 1981 (date of suit). The study indicated that Oryx performed at the exact statistical median of these stocks and that several issues suffered equal or greater losses than did Oryx during this period. Defendants produced an additional study which indicated that Oryx stock "behaved over the entire period ... consistent[ly] with its own inherent variation."

Plaintiffs offered the following rebuttal evidence. During the period between SEC disclosure and public disclosure, Oryx stock decreased nineteen percent while the over-the-counter (OTC) composite index rose five percent (the first study). During this period, therefore, the OTC composite index outperformed Oryx by twenty-four percentage points. Plaintiffs also produced a study indicating that for the time period between SEC disclosure and one week after public disclosure, eighty-two of the one hundred new issues analyzed in the defendants' study outperformed Oryx's stock.

Plaintiffs' first study compared Oryx's performance to the performance of the OTC index in order to rebut a comparison offered by defendants to prove that Oryx's price decline resulted not from the misstatement but rather from an overall market decline. As previously stated, defendants' comparison indicated that the OTC index generally declined for the period between Oryx's offering date and the date of suit. The parties' conflicting comparisons, however, lack credibility because they fail to reflect any of the countless variables that might affect the stock price performance of a single company. ***

The studies comparing Oryx's performance to the other one hundred companies that went public in May and June of 1981 are similarly flawed. The studies do not evaluate the performance of Oryx stock in relation to the stock of companies possessing any characteristic in common with Oryx, e.g., product, technology, profitability, assets or countless other variables which influence stock prices, except the contemporaneous initial offering dates.

Perhaps more important, the Akermans' study of the one hundred new issues focuses on a time frame which controverts one of their own theories explaining the public's failure to react adversely to disclosure. The Akermans argue that the thin market in Oryx stock prevented immediate public reaction to disclosure of the prospectus error. Their study, however, measures Oryx's performance from SEC disclosure to *one week* after public disclosure. A thin market, according to the Akermans' own explanation, would not reflect the impact of bad news in such a short time period (one week). This internal inconsistency seriously undercuts the probative value of the Akermans' study.

Finally, we note that this time period drew its relevance from the Akermans' theory that insider trading deflated Oryx's price during this period. As previously stated, this theory has no support even after extensive discovery and is not pressed on appeal.

Granting the Akermans every reasonable, favorable inference, the battle of the studies is at best equivocal; the studies do not meaningfully point in one direction or the other. ***

Defendants met their burden, as set forth in section 11(e), by establishing that the misstatement was barely material and that the public failed to react adversely to its disclosure. With the case in this posture, the plaintiffs had to come forward with "specific facts showing that there is a genuine issue for trial." *Anderson* [*v. Liberty Lobby, Inc.*, 106 S. Ct. 2505, 2511 (1986]). Despite extensive discovery, plaintiffs completely failed to produce any evidence, other than unreliable and sometimes inconsistent statistical studies and theories, suggesting that Oryx's price decline actually resulted from the misstatement. Summary judgment was properly granted. ***

### *NOTES AND QUESTIONS*

***1. Allocating the Burden of Proving Negative Causation.*** Section 11(e) places the burden of proving negative causation on the defendant. Did the court comply? If not, why not? Did the court's allocation of the burden of proof on this issue affect the result?

***2. Negative Causation vs. Loss Causation Under Rule 10b-5.*** Recall that Rule 10b-5 plaintiffs must satisfy the loss causation requirement set forth in Exchange Act Section 21D(b)(4). See supra Chapter 2.F.2. What are the differences between Rule 10b-5's loss causation requirement and Section 11's negative causation defense?

***3. Theoretical Materiality.*** In *Akerman*, the court described the misstatement at issue as "theoretically material" but nonetheless as "not likely to cause a stock price decline." Can information be material on the one hand but have no impact on the market price on the other hand? Cf. supra Chapter 2.B.1 (discussing the definition of materiality).

***4. To Sell or Not to Sell.*** Look again at Section 11(e)'s formula for calculating damages. Once a plaintiff files her Section 11 action, is she best advised to sell or retain her shares?

***5. Focusing on "Value."*** Note that Section 11(e) looks to "the difference between the amount paid for the security" and "the *value* thereof at the time such suit was brought." (emphasis added). Congress's use of the word "value" is significant:

> Congress' [s] use of the term "value," as distinguished from the terms "amount paid" and "price" indicates that, under certain circumstances, the market price may not adequately reflect the security's value. See *Beecher v. Able*, 435 F.Supp. 397, 404-05 (S.D.N.Y 1977) (adjusting the market price to account for panic selling in the market that was unrelated to the misrepresentations in the registration statements); *Grossman v. Waste Management, Inc.*, 589 F.Supp. 395, 415-16 (N.D.Ill.1984) (holding that subsequent fraud on the market may make market price an unreliable indication of the security's value). However, instances where the market price of a security will be different from its value are "unusual and rare" situations. *** Moreover, even where market price is not completely reliable, it serves as a good starting point in determining value. See *Beecher*, 435 F.Supp. at 406.

*McMahan & Co. v. Wherehouse Entertainment, Inc.*, 65 F.3d 1044, 1048-49 (2d Cir. 1995).

***6. Joint and Several Liability and Contribution.*** Most Section 11 defendants are jointly and severally liable for the damages that may be awarded. See Section 11(f)(1). Under this arrangement, any defendant may be liable for all the damages, but may thereafter obtain contribution from anyone who, "if sued separately, would have been liable to make the same payment, unless the person who has become liable was, and the other was not, guilty of fraudulent misrepresentation." Id. Two categories of defendants, however, are treated differently: underwriters and outside directors.

The exception for underwriters is set forth in Section 11(e). That provision states that unless an underwriter received a benefit from the issuer not received by the other underwriters, his liability under Section 11 is capped at "the total price at which the securities underwritten by him and distributed to the public were offered to the public." Thus, in a $300 million offering, an underwriter who sold $50 million in securities would be liable only for $50 million.

The exception for outside directors—set forth in Section 11(f)(2)(A)—was added by the Private Securities Litigation Reform Act of 1995 (PSLRA). Pursuant to this provision, a Section 11 defendant who is an outside director is subject to proportionate (rather than joint and several) liability so long as he did not act "knowingly." See generally Chapter 2.G.2 (discussing proportionate liability in the context of Rule 10b-5).

---

### 2. *Section 12(a)(2)*

Section 12(a)(2) creates an express private action for securities purchasers against their sellers for material misstatements and omissions made "by means of a prospectus" or, in some instances, orally. It reads as follows:

> Any person who—***
>
> (2) offers or sells a security (whether or not exempted by the provisions of section 3, other than paragraphs (2) and (14) of subsection (a) thereof), by the use of any means or instruments of transportation or communication in interstate commerce or of the mails, by means of a prospectus or oral communication, which includes an untrue statement of a material fact or omits to state a material fact necessary in order to make the statements, in the light of the

> circumstances under which they were made, not misleading (the purchaser not knowing of such untruth or omission), and who shall not sustain the burden of proof that he did not know, and in the exercise of reasonable care could not have known, of such untruth or omission, shall be liable *** to the person purchasing such security from him, who may sue either at law or in equity in any court of competent jurisdiction, to recover the consideration paid for such security with interest thereon, less the amount of any income received thereon, upon the tender of such security, or for damages if he no longer owns the security.

Prior to 1995, Section 12(a)(2) was codified as Section 12(2) and some courts continue to refer to it in that fashion.

Like Section 11, Section 12(a)(2) waters down the traditional elements of common law fraud. Thus, under Section 12(a)(2), the plaintiff does not have to prove scienter or causation. Nor does she have to prove reliance (similar to Section 11, except that Section 11 does require the plaintiff to prove reliance in the rare circumstance noted earlier).

Section 12(a)(2) provides the defendant with a defense of reasonable care (which we will contrast with the due diligence defenses under Section 11). The defendant may also reduce, or conceivably avoid, liability based on negative causation (see Section 12(b)).

Sections 12(a)(2) and 11 overlap only in part. To be sure, both apply to registered offerings (although the misleading statement must appear in "a prospectus or oral communication" for purposes of Section 12(a)(2) but in the registration statement for purposes of Section 11). Unlike Section 11, however, Section12(a)(2) also applies to certain exempt offerings as well as to offerings in violation of Section 5 (i.e., offerings that were neither exempted nor registered). In addition, Sections 12(a)(2) and 11 involve different defendants. Indeed, some Section 11 defendants cannot be sued under Section 12(a)(2), just as some Section 12(a)(2) defendants cannot be sued under Section 11.

We begin with two Supreme Court decisions. The first restricts the transactional reach of Section 12(a)(2) based on its interpretation of the statutory phrase "by means of a prospectus or oral communication." The second addresses who may be sued. We then consider the reasonable care defense, damages, and negative causation.

#### *a. "By Means of a Prospectus or Oral Communication"*

The following controversial decision, which split the Supreme Court 5-4, held Section 12(a)(2) inapplicable to private offerings as well as to secondary market trading. Prior to this decision, Section 12(a)(2) had been widely regarded as applicable to both.

## GUSTAFSON v. ALLOYD CORPORATON
513 U.S. 561 (1995)

JUSTICE KENNEDY:

Under § 12(2) of the Securities Act of 1933 buyers have an express cause of action for rescission against sellers who make material misstatements or omissions "by means of a prospectus." The question presented is whether this right of rescission extends to a private, secondary transaction, on the theory that recitations in the purchase agreement are part of a "prospectus."

I

Petitioners Gustafson, McLean, and Butler (collectively Gustafson) were in 1989 the sole shareholders of Alloyd, Inc., a manufacturer of plastic packaging and automatic heat sealing equipment. Alloyd was formed, and its stock was issued, in 1961. In 1989, Gustafson decided to sell Alloyd and engaged KPMG Peat Marwick to find a buyer. In response to information distributed by KPMG, Wind Point Partners II, L. P., agreed to buy substantially all of the issued and outstanding stock through Alloyd Holdings, Inc., a new corporation formed to effect the sale of Alloyd's stock. The shareholders of Alloyd Holdings were Wind Point and a number of individual investors.

In preparation for negotiating the contract with Gustafson, Wind Point undertook an extensive analysis of the company, relying in part on a formal business review prepared by KPMG. Alloyd's practice was to take inventory at year's end, so Wind Point and KPMG considered taking an earlier inventory to use in determining the purchase price. In the end they did not do so, relying instead on certain estimates and including provisions for adjustments after the transaction closed.

On December 20, 1989, Gustafson and Alloyd Holdings executed a contract of sale. Alloyd Holdings agreed to pay Gustafson and his coshareholders $18,709,000 for the sale of the stock plus a payment of $2,122,219, which reflected the estimated increase in Alloyd's net worth from the end of the previous year, the last period for which hard financial data were available. Article IV of the purchase agreement, entitled "Representations and Warranties of the Sellers," included assurances that the company's financial statements "present fairly ... the Company's financial condition" and that between the date of the latest balance sheet and the date the agreement was executed "there ha[d] been no material adverse change in ... [Alloyd's] financial condition." The contract also provided that if the year-end audit and financial statements revealed a variance between estimated and actual increased value, the disappointed party would receive an adjustment.

The year-end audit of Alloyd revealed that Alloyd's actual earnings for 1989 were lower than the estimates relied upon by the parties in negotiating the adjustment amount of $2,122,219. Under the contract, the buyers had a right to recover an adjustment amount of $815,000 from the sellers. Nevertheless, on February 11, 1991, the newly formed company (now called Alloyd Co., the same as the original company) and Wind Point brought suit in the United States District Court for the Northern District of Illinois, seeking outright rescission of the contract under § 12(2) of the Securities Act of 1933 (1933 Act or Act). Alloyd (the new company) claimed that statements made by Gustafson and his coshareholders regarding the financial data of their company were inaccurate, rendering untrue the representations and warranties contained in the contract. The buyers further alleged that the contract of sale was a "prospectus," so that any misstatements contained in the agreement gave rise to liability under § 12(2) of the 1933 Act. Pursuant to the adjustment clause, the defendants remitted to the purchasers $815,000 plus interest, but the adjustment did not cause the purchasers to drop the lawsuit.

Relying on the decision of the Court of Appeals for the Third Circuit in *Ballay v. Legg Mason Wood Walker, Inc.*, 925 F.2d 682 (1991), the District Court granted Gustafson's motion for summary judgment, holding "that section 12(2) claims can only arise out of the initial stock offerings." Although the sellers were the controlling shareholders of the original company, the District Court concluded that the private sale agreement "cannot be compared to an initial offering" because "the purchasers in this case had direct access to financial and other company documents, and had the opportunity to inspect the seller's property."

On review, the Court of Appeals for the Seventh Circuit vacated the District Court's judgment and remanded for further consideration in light of that court's intervening decision in *Pacific Dunlop Holdings Inc. v. Allen & Co. Inc.*, 993 F.2d 578 (1993). In *Pacific Dunlop* the court reasoned that the inclusion of the term "communication" in the Act's definition of prospectus meant that the term "prospectus" was defined "very broadly" to include all written communications that offered the sale of a security. Id., at 582. Rejecting the view of the Court of Appeals for the Third Circuit in *Ballay*, the Court of Appeals decided that § 12(2)'s right of action for rescission "applies to any communication which offers any security for sale ... including the stock purchase agreement in the present case." 993 F.2d, at 595. We granted certiorari to resolve this Circuit conflict, and we now reverse.

II

*** As this case reaches us, we must assume that the stock purchase agreement contained material misstatements of fact made by the sellers and that Gustafson would not sustain its burden of proving due care. On these assumptions, Alloyd would have a right to obtain rescission if those misstatements were made "by means of a prospectus or oral communication." The Courts of Appeals agree that the phrase "oral communication" is restricted to oral communications that relate to a prospectus. See *Pacific Dunlop*, supra, at 588; *Ballay*, supra, at 688. The determinative question, then, is whether the contract between Alloyd and Gustafson is a "prospectus" as the term is used in the 1933 Act.

Alloyd argues that "prospectus" is defined in a broad manner, broad enough to encompass the contract between the parties. This argument is echoed by the dissents. Gustafson, by contrast, maintains that prospectus in the 1933 Act means a communication soliciting the public to purchase securities from the issuer.

Three sections of the 1933 Act are critical in resolving the definitional question on which the case turns: § 2(10), which defines a prospectus; § 10, which sets forth the information that must be contained in a prospectus; and § 12, which imposes liability based on misstatements in a prospectus. In seeking to interpret the term "prospectus," we adopt the premise that the term should be construed, if possible, to give it a consistent meaning throughout the Act. That principle follows from our duty to construe statutes, not isolated provisions.

A

We begin with § 10. It provides, in relevant part:

> Except to the extent otherwise permitted or required pursuant to this subsection or subsections (c), (d), or (e) of this section—
>
> (1) a prospectus relating to a security other than a security issued by a foreign government or political subdivision thereof, shall contain the information contained in the registration statement ...;
>
> (2) a prospectus relating to a security issued by a foreign government or political subdivision thereof shall contain the information contained in the registration statement...

Section 10 does not provide that some prospectuses must contain the information contained in the registration statement. Save for the explicit and well-defined exemptions for securities listed under § 3 (exempting certain classes of securities from the coverage of the Act), its mandate is unqualified: "[A] prospectus ... shall contain the information contained in the registration statement."

Although § 10 does not define what a prospectus is, it does instruct us what a prospectus cannot be if the Act is to be interpreted as a symmetrical and coherent regulatory scheme, one in which the operative words have a consistent meaning throughout. There is no dispute that the contract in this case was not required to contain the information contained in a registration statement and that no statutory exemption was required to take the document out of § 10's coverage. It follows that the contract is not a prospectus under § 10. That does not mean that a document ceases to be a prospectus whenever it omits a required piece of information. It does mean that a document is not a prospectus within the meaning of that section if, absent an exemption, it need not comply with § 10's requirements in the first place.

An examination of § 10 reveals that, whatever else "prospectus" may mean, the term is confined to a document that, absent an overriding exemption, must include the "information contained in the registration statement." By and large, only public offerings by an issuer of a security, or by controlling shareholders of an issuer, require the preparation and filing of registration statements. It follows, we conclude, that a prospectus under § 10 is confined to documents related to public offerings by an issuer or its controlling shareholders.

This much (the meaning of prospectus in § 10) seems not to be in dispute. Where the courts are in disagreement is with the implications of this proposition for the entirety of the Act, and for § 12 in particular. We conclude that the term "prospectus" must have the same meaning under §§ 10 and 12. In so holding, we do not, as the dissent by Justice Ginsburg suggests, make the mistake of treating § 10 as a definitional section. Instead, we find in § 10 guidance and instruction for giving the term a consistent meaning throughout the Act. ***

The conclusion that prospectus has the same meaning, and refers to the same types of communications (public offers by an issuer or its controlling shareholders), in both §§ 10 and 12 is reinforced by an examination of the structure of the 1933 Act. Sections 4 and 5 of the Act together require a seller to file a registration statement and to issue a prospectus for certain defined types of sales (public offerings by an issuer, through an underwriter). Sections 7 and 10 of the Act set forth the information required in the registration statement and the prospectus. Section 11 provides for liability on account of false registration statements; § 12(2) for liability based on misstatements in prospectuses. Following the most natural and symmetrical reading, just as the liability imposed by § 11 flows from the requirements imposed by §§ 5 and 7 providing for the filing and content of registration statements, the liability imposed by § 12(2) cannot attach unless there is an obligation to distribute the prospectus in the first place (or unless there is an exemption). ***

The primary innovation of the 1933 Act was the creation of federal duties—for the most part, registration and disclosure obligations—in connection with public offerings. We are reluctant to conclude that § 12(2) creates vast additional liabilities that are quite independent of the new substantive obligations the Act imposes. It is more reasonable to interpret the liability provisions of the 1933 Act as designed for the primary purpose of providing remedies for violations of the obligations it had created. Indeed, §§ 11 and 12(1)—the statutory neighbors of § 12(2)—afford remedies for violations of those obligations. ***

On the other hand, accepting Alloyd's argument that any written offer is a prospectus under § 12 would require us to hold that the word "prospectus" in § 12 refers to a broader set of communications than the same term in § 10. *** Nowhere in the statute, however, do the terms "formal prospectus" or "informal prospectus" appear. Instead, the Act uses one term —"prospectus"—throughout. In disagreement with the Court of Appeals and the dissenting opinions, we cannot accept the conclusion that this single operative word means one thing in one section of the Act and something quite different in another. The dissenting opinions' resort to terms not found in the Act belies the claim of fidelity to the text of the statute.

Alloyd, as well as Justice Thomas in his dissent, respond that if Congress had intended § 12(2) to govern only initial public offerings, it would have been simple for Congress to have referred to the § 4 exemptions in § 12(2). The argument gets the presumption backwards. Had Congress meant the term "prospectus" in § 12(2) to have a different meaning than the same term in § 10, that is when one would have expected Congress to have been explicit. Congressional silence cuts against, not in favor of, Alloyd's argument. The burden should be on the proponents of the view that the term "prospectus" means one thing in § 12 and another in § 10 to adduce strong textual support for that conclusion. And Alloyd adduces none.

B

Alloyd's contrary argument rests to a significant extent on § 2(10), or, to be more precise, on one word of that section. Section 2(10) provides that "[t]he term 'prospectus' means any prospectus, notice, circular, advertisement, letter, or communication, written or by radio or television, which offers any security for sale or confirms the sale of any security." Concentrating on the word "communication," Alloyd argues that any written communication that offers a security for sale is a "prospectus." Inserting its definition into § 12(2), Alloyd insists that a material misstatement in any communication offering a security for sale gives rise to an action for rescission, without proof of fraud by the seller or reliance by the purchaser. In Alloyd's view, § 2(10) gives the term "prospectus" a capacious definition that, although incompatible with § 10, nevertheless governs in § 12.

The flaw in Alloyd's argument, echoed in the dissenting opinions, is its reliance on one word of the definitional section in isolation. To be sure, § 2(10) defines a prospectus as, *inter alia,* a "communication, written or by radio or television, which offers any security for sale or confirms the sale of any security." The word "communication," however, on which Alloyd's entire argument rests, is but one word in a list, a word Alloyd reads altogether out of context. ***

There is a better reading. From the terms "prospectus, notice, circular, advertisement, [or] letter," it is apparent that the list refers to documents of wide dissemination. In a similar manner, the list includes communications "by radio or television," but not face-to-face or telephonic conversations. Inclusion of the term "communication" in that list suggests that it too refers to a public communication.

When the 1933 Act was drawn and adopted, the term "prospectus" was well understood to refer to a document soliciting the public to acquire securities from the issuer. See Black's Law Dictionary 959 (2d ed. 1910) (defining "prospectus" as a "document published by a company ... or by persons acting as its agents or assignees, setting forth the nature and objects of an issue of shares ... and inviting the public to subscribe to the issue"). In this respect, the word "prospectus" is a term of art, which accounts for congressional confidence in employing what might otherwise be regarded as a partial circularity in the formal, statutory definition. See [Section 2 (10)] ("The term 'prospectus' means any prospectus ..."). The use of the term "prospectus" to refer to public solicitations explains as well Congress' decision in § 12(2) to grant buyers a right to rescind without proof of reliance.

The list of terms in § 2(10) prevents a seller of stock from avoiding liability by calling a soliciting document something other than a prospectus, but it does not compel the conclusion that Alloyd urges us to reach and that the dissenting opinions adopt. Instead, the term "written communication" must be read in context to refer to writings that, from a functional standpoint, are similar to the terms "notice, circular, [and] advertisement." The term includes communications held out to the public at large but that might have been thought to be outside the other words in the definitional section. ***

D

It is understandable that Congress would provide buyers with a right to rescind, without proof of fraud or reliance, as to misstatements contained in a document prepared with care, following well-established procedures relating to investigations with due diligence and in the context of a public offering by an issuer or its controlling shareholders. It is not plausible to infer that Congress created this extensive liability for every casual communication between buyer and seller in the secondary market. It is often difficult, if not altogether impractical, for those engaged in casual communications not to omit some fact that would, if included, qualify the accuracy of a statement. Under Alloyd's view any casual communication between buyer and seller in the aftermarket could give rise to an action for rescission, with no evidence of fraud on the part of the seller or reliance on the part of the buyer. In many instances buyers in practical effect would have an option to rescind, impairing the stability of past transactions where neither fraud nor detrimental reliance on misstatements or omissions occurred. We find no basis for interpreting the statute to reach so far. ***

In sum, the word "prospectus" is a term of art referring to a document that describes a public offering of securities by an issuer or controlling shareholder. The contract of sale, and its recitations, were not held out to the public and were not a prospectus as the term is used in the 1933 Act.

The judgment of the Court of Appeals is reversed, and the case is remanded for further proceedings consistent with this opinion.

JUSTICE THOMAS, WITH WHOM JUSTICE SCALIA, JUSTICE GINSBURG, AND JUSTICE BREYER JOIN, DISSENTING:

From the majority's opinion, one would not realize that § 12(2) *** was involved in this case until one had read more than halfway through. In contrast to the majority's approach of interpreting the statute, I believe the proper method is to begin with the provision actually involved in this case, § 12(2), and then turn to the 1933 Act's definitional section, § 2(10), before consulting the structure of the Act as a whole. Because the result of this textual analysis shows that § 12(2) applies to secondary or private sales of a security as well as to initial public offerings, I dissent. ***

There is no reason to seek the meaning of "prospectus" outside of the 1933 Act, because Congress has supplied just such a definition in § 2(10). That definition is extraordinarily broad:

> When used in this subchapter, unless the context otherwise requires—
>
> . . . . .
>
> (10) The term 'prospectus' means any prospectus, notice, circular, advertisement, letter, or communication, written or by radio or television, which offers any security for sale or confirms the sale of any security.

For me, the breadth of these terms forecloses the majority's position that "prospectus" applies only in the context of initial distributions of securities. Indeed, § 2(10)'s inclusion of a prospectus as only one of the many different documents that qualify as a "prospectus" for statutory purposes indicates that Congress intended "prospectus" to be more than a mere "term of art." Likewise, Congress' extension of prospectus to include documents that merely *confirm* the sale of a security underscores Congress' intent to depart from the term's ordinary meaning. Section 2(10)'s definition obviously concerns different types of communications rather than different types of transactions. Congress left the job of exempting certain classes of transactions to §§ 3 and 4, not to § 2(10). We should use § 2(10) to define "prospectus" for the 1933 Act, rather than, as the majority does, use the 1933 Act to define "prospectus" for § 2(10). ***

The majority's analysis of § 12(2) is motivated by its policy preferences. Underlying its reasoning is the assumption that Congress could never have intended to impose liability on sellers engaged in secondary transactions.

Adopting a chiding tone, the majority states that "[w]e are reluctant to conclude that § 12(2) creates vast additional liabilities that are quite independent of the new substantive obligations that the Act imposes." Yet, this is exactly what Congress did in § 17(a) of the 1933 Act as well as in § 10(b) of the 1934 Act. Later, the majority says: "It is not plausible to infer that Congress created this extensive liability for every casual communication between buyer and seller in the secondary market." It is not the usual practice of this Court to require Congress to explain why it has chosen to pursue a certain policy. Our job simply is to apply the policy, not to question it.

*** The majority is concerned that a contrary reading would have a drastic impact on the thousands of private and secondary transactions by imposing new liabilities and new transaction costs. But the majority forgets that we are only enforcing *Congress'* decision to impose such standards of conduct and remedies upon sellers. If the majority believes that § 12(2)'s requirements are too burdensome for the securities markets, it must rely upon the other branches of Government to limit the 1933 Act.

Unfortunately, the majority's decision to pursue its policy preferences comes at the price of disrupting the process of statutory interpretation. *** I doubt that the majority would read in so narrow and peculiar a fashion most other statutes, particularly one intended to restrict causes of action in securities cases. ***

JUSTICE GINSBURG, WITH WHOM JUSTICE BREYER JOINS, DISSENTING:

A seller's misrepresentation made "by means of a prospectus or oral communication" is actionable under § 12(2) of the Securities Act of 1933. To limit the scope of this civil liability provision, the Court maintains that a communication qualifies as a prospectus only if made during a public offering.[1] Communications during either secondary trading or a private placement are not "prospectuses," the Court declares, and thus are not covered by § 12(2). ***

To construe a legislatively defined term, courts usually start with the defining section. Section 2(10) defines prospectus capaciously as "any prospectus, notice, circular, advertisement, letter, or communication, written or by radio or television, which offers any security for sale or confirms the sale of any security." The items listed in the defining provision, notably "letters" and "communications," are common in private and secondary sales, as well as in public offerings. The § 2(10) definition thus does not confine the § 12(2) term "prospectus" to public offerings.

The Court bypasses § 2(10), and the solid support it gives the Court of Appeals' disposition. Instead of beginning at the beginning, by first attending to the definition section, the Court starts with § 10, a substantive provision. The Court correctly observes that the term "prospectus" has a circumscribed meaning in that context. A prospectus within the contemplation of § 10 is a formal document, typically a document composing part of a registration statement; a § 10 prospectus, all agree, appears only in public offerings. The Court then

1. I understand the Court's definition of a public offering to encompass both transactions that must be registered under § 5, and transactions that would have been registered had the securities involved not qualified for exemption under § 3.

proceeds backward; it reads into the literally and logically prior definition section, § 2(10), the meaning "prospectus" has in § 10.

To justify its backward reading—proceeding from § 10 to § 2(10) and not the other way round—the Court states that it "cannot accept the conclusion that [the operative word 'prospectus' ] means one thing in one section of the Act and something quite different in another." Our decisions, however, constantly recognize that "a characterization fitting in certain contexts may be unsuitable in others." *NationsBank of N.C., N.A. v. Variable Annuity Life Ins. Co.*, [513 U.S. 251, 262 (1995)]. ***

According "prospectus" discrete meanings in § 10 and § 12(2) is consistent with Congress' specific instruction in § 2 that definitions apply "unless the context otherwise requires." As the Court of Appeals construed the Act, § 2(10)'s definition of "prospectus" governs § 12(2), which accommodates without strain the definition's broad reach; by contrast, the specific context of § 10 requires a correspondingly specific reading of "prospectus." ***

Most provisions of the Securities Act govern only public offerings, and the legislative history pertaining to the Act as a whole shares this orientation. Section 17(a) of the Act, however, is not limited to public offerings; that enforcement provision, this Court has recognized, also covers secondary trading. See *United States v. Naftalin*, 441 U.S. 768 (1979). The drafting history is at least consistent with the conclusion that § 12(2), like § 17(a), is not limited to public offerings. ***

In light of the text, drafting history, and longstanding scholarly and judicial understanding of § 12(2), I conclude that § 12(2) applies to a private resale of securities. If adjustment is in order, as the Court's opinion powerfully suggests it is, Congress is equipped to undertake the alteration. Accordingly, I dissent from the Court's opinion and judgment.

## *NOTES AND QUESTIONS*

***1. A Failing Grade in Statutory Construction?*** To ascertain the meaning of "prospectus," the Court focused its attention on the use of that term in Section 10 rather than on the statutory definition in Section 2(a)(10). Commentators have been thunderously critical. See, e.g., Stephen M. Bainbridge, Securities Act Section 12(2) After the *Gustafson* Debacle, 50 Bus. Law. 1231, 1231-32 (1995) (describing *Gustafson* as "the most poorly-reasoned, blatantly results-driven, securities opinion in recent memory"); Ted J. Fiflis, *Gustafson v. Alloyd Co., Inc.*: Judicial vs. Legislative Power, 23 Sec. Reg. L. J. 423, 425 (1996) (observing that "[t]he reasoning used by the majority *** is so flawed that its full implications will not be known for some time"); Kimberly D. Krawiec, *Gustafson v. Alloyd Co.*: The Wrong Decision, But It Is Still Business as Usual in the Securities Markets, 31 Tulsa L.J. 509, 514 (1996) (maintaining that *Gustafson* "violates nearly every rule of statutory construction"). Are the commentators correct in their assertions? Or is the Court's methodology defensible?

***2. Section 12(a)(2) and "Public Offerings."*** *Gustafson* tells us that Section 12(a)(2) applies to "public offerings," but does not tell us precisely what public offerings are. Certainly, public offerings include registered offerings as well as illegal offerings that were neither registered nor exempt from registration. But what about exempt offerings? Consider the following possible approaches (in connection with which you may wish to reread the overview of registration exemptions in Chapter 1.A.1.b):

- *Bright Line Approach.* Under this approach, Section 12(a)(2) embraces offerings exempt under Securities Act Section 3 (except for subsections (2) and (14) thereof, excluded on the face of Section 12(a)(2)) but not those exempt under Securities Act Section 4. Offerings exempt under Section 3 would include Section 3's progeny, such as Rule 147, Regulation A, and Rules 504 and 505 of Regulation D. Similarly, offerings exempt under Section 4 would include Section 4's progeny, such as Rule 506 of Regulation D.

- *Functional Approach.* Under this approach, Section 12(a)(2) embraces any exempt offering that amounts to a "public offering," with the statutory source of the exemption being not necessarily dispositive. To determine whether an exempt offering is "public," the benchmark is Section 4(2), often called the private offering exemption, which exempts from registration "transactions by an issuer not involving any public offering." In *SEC v. Ralston Purina Co.*, 346 U.S. 119, 125-27 (1953), the Supreme Court held Section 4(2) applicable only to offerings made to those with "access to the kind of information which registration would disclose" and with the capacity "to fend for themselves."

  Accordingly, Section 12(a)(2) would not apply to an offering exempted by Section 3 if that particular offering simultaneously satisfied the private offering exemption set forth in Section 4(2). On the other hand, Section 12(a)(2) would apply to a Rule 506 offering if the offering would not satisfy Section 4(2) absent the Rule 506 safe harbor. For example, such a situation might arise where a purchaser was an accredited investor based on net worth but who failed to satisfy the *Ralston Purina* criteria.

Which of these approaches seems more consistent with *Gustafson* itself? Which makes more sense from a policy standpoint? See generally Stephen M. Bainbridge, Securities Act Section 12(2) After the *Gustafson* Debacle, 50 Bus. Law. 1231, 1260-69 (1995); Janet E. Kerr, *Ralston* Redux: Determining Which Section 3 Offerings are Public Under Section 12(2) After *Gustafson*, 50 SMU L. Rev. 175 (1996); Elliot J. Weiss, Securities Act Section 12(2) After *Gustafson v. Alloyd Co.*: What Questions Remain?, 50 Bus. Law. 1209, 1220-23 (1995). See also Stephen J. Choi, Gatekeepers and the Internet: Rethinking the Regulation of Small Business Capital Formation, 2 J. Small & Emerging Bus. Law 27, 32 n. 27 (1998) (characterizing the application of Section 12(a)(2) to exempt offerings as unresolved).

3. ***Section 12(a)(2) and Registered Offerings.*** While those who purchase securities in registered offerings may utilize Section 12(a)(2), recall that such plaintiffs may also utilize Section 11. Under what circumstances would a plaintiff who purchased in a registered offering utilize Section 12(a)(2) rather than (or in addition to) Section 11?

*4. Section 12(a)(2) and Oral Communications.* Section 12(a)(2) refers not only to a "prospectus" but also to an "oral communication." The *Gustafson* Court endorsed lower court decisions holding that an "oral communication" is actionable under Section 12(a)(2) only where it "relate[s] to a prospectus." Is this limitation significant? Is it likely to require difficult line-drawing? Is it sound from the standpoint of statutory construction? From the standpoint of policy?

*5. Section 12(a)(2) and the Aftermarket.* If, as *Gustafson* held, Congress did not intend Section 12(a)(2) to reach secondary market trading, it would seem to follow that Congress did not intend investors in the aftermarket to have any fraud cause of action at all. Indeed, recall that Section 11 has only a highly limited application to the aftermarket (and in any event applies only to misleading statements in the registration statement). And while it is true that Section 17(a) of the Securities Act prohibits fraud in the aftermarket, that Section does not authorize an express private action and is widely thought not to give rise to an implied private action. See infra Section 2.B. Nor did Congress assume that Section 10(b) of the Exchange Act would be available to aftermarket investors: "No one could have anticipated in 1934 that rule 10b-5 would be adopted eight years later, let alone that the courts would imply a private right of action for its violation ***." Louis Loss, The Assault on Securities Act Section 12(2), 105 Harv. L. Rev. 908, 915-16 (1992). Did Congress in the early 1930s actually intend to relegate aftermarket investors to state law private actions? Or is *Gustafson* mistaken in its conclusion?

*6. Does* **Gustafson** *matter?* To what extent should it matter to securities litigators that *Gustafson* narrowed the scope of Section 12(a)(2)? Cf. Kimberly D. Krawiec, *Gustafson v. Alloyd Co.*: The Wrong Decision, But It is Still Business as Usual in the Securities Markets, 31 Tulsa L.J. 509, 518-19 (1996) (maintaining that *Gustafson* does not alter the advice that a transactional attorney should give to a client regarding the importance of full disclosure). After all, Rule 10b-5 remains available to address fraud in private placements and secondary market transactions. But is Rule 10b-5 as attractive as Section 12(a)(2)? Why might a plaintiff prefer Section 12(a)(2) to Rule 10b-5 (or to blue sky law)?

### *PROBLEM 3-3*

Decide whether Section 12(a)(2) is available to the following after *Gustafson*:

a. An issuer sold interests in a cooperative agricultural venture to a large number of investors in a single state. Cf. *SEC v. Howey Co.*, 328 U.S. 293 (1946) (holding an offering of interests in cultivated orange groves to be an offering of securities under the Securities Act). The offering is exempt from the Securities Act's registration requirements pursuant to the intrastate offering exemption set forth in Securities Act Section 3(a)(11). There are no written offering materials other than the subscription agreement and a single page newspaper advertisement. Both state in bold letters at the top of the page as follows: "This intrastate sale of securities is exempt from registration under federal securities laws and this document is not a prospectus."

b. An issuer made a $5 million Regulation A offering but failed to attract any individual investors. All of the purchasers were large institutions.

c. Shortly after the completion of an IPO by Box, Inc., a purchaser (Mary) learned not only that the prospectus was materially misleading but also that Box stood on the brink of bankruptcy. Mary thereupon decided to sell the Box stock that she had just purchased. Rather than selling the stock on the open market, she negotiated a private sale to an institutional investor to whom she sent a copy of the Box prospectus, accompanied by a cover letter stating as follows: "Enclosed is the Box prospectus for the sale of the stock that I purchased, which is to the best of my knowledge true and accurate." The institutional investor bought Mary's stock, relying on the prospectus that she had sent.

d. Assume in (c) that Mary instead sold her Box stock on the open market to someone who had read the Box prospectus after downloading it from the Internet.

---

*b. Who is a Seller?*

Section 12(a)(2) imposes liability on the person who sold the securities in question, but does not tell us who qualifies as a "seller." In the decision that follows, the Supreme Court answered this question in the context of Section 12(a)(1). Ask yourself whether the Court's answer is equally applicable to Section 12(a)(2).

## PINTER v. DAHL

486 U.S. 622 (1988)

JUSTICE BLACKMUN:

*** Th[is] controversy arises out of the sale prior to 1982 of unregistered securities (fractional undivided interests in oil and gas leases) by petitioner Billy J. "B.J." Pinter to respondents Maurice Dahl and Dahl's friends, family, and business associates. Pinter is an oil and gas producer in Texas and Oklahoma, and a registered securities dealer in Texas. Dahl is a California real estate broker and investor, who, at the time of his dealings with Pinter, was a veteran of two unsuccessful oil and gas ventures. In pursuit of further investment opportunities, Dahl employed an oil field expert to locate and acquire oil and gas leases. This expert introduced Dahl to Pinter. Dahl advanced $20,000 to Pinter to acquire leases, with the understanding that they would be held in the name of Pinter's Black Gold Oil Company and that Dahl would have a right of first refusal to drill certain wells on the leasehold properties. Pinter located leases in Oklahoma, and Dahl toured the properties, often without Pinter, in order to talk to others and "get a feel for the properties." Upon examining the geology, drilling logs, and production history assembled by Pinter, Dahl concluded, in the words of the District Court, that "there was no way to lose."

After investing approximately $310,000 in the properties, Dahl told the other respondents about the venture. Except for Dahl and respondent Grantham, none of the respondents spoke to or met Pinter or toured the properties. Because of Dahl's involvement in the venture, each of the other respondents decided to invest about $7,500.

Dahl assisted his fellow investors in completing the subscription-agreement form prepared by Pinter. Each letter-contract signed by the purchaser stated that the participating interests were being sold without the benefit of registration under the Securities Act, in reliance on Securities and Exchange Commission (SEC or Commission) Rule 146. In fact, the oil and gas interests involved in this suit were never registered with the Commission. Respondents' investment checks were made payable to Black Gold Oil Company. Dahl received no commission from Pinter in connection with the other respondents' purchases.

When the venture failed and their interests proved to be worthless, respondents brought suit against Pinter in the United States District Court for the Northern District of Texas, seeking rescission under § 12(1) of the Securities Act, for the unlawful sale of unregistered securities.

In a counterclaim, Pinter alleged that Dahl, by means of fraudulent misrepresentations and concealment of facts, induced Pinter to sell and deliver the securities. Pinter averred that Dahl falsely assured Pinter that he would provide other qualified, sophisticated, and knowledgeable investors with all the information necessary for evaluation of the investment. Dahl allegedly agreed to raise the funds for the venture from those investors, with the understanding that Pinter would simply be the "operator" of the wells. ***

The District Court, after a bench trial, granted judgment for respondent-investors. The court concluded that Pinter had not proved that the oil and gas interests were entitled to the private-offering exemption from registration. Accordingly, the court ruled that, because the securities were unregistered, respondents were entitled to rescission pursuant to § 12(1). The court also concluded that the evidence was insufficient to sustain Pinter's counterclaim against Dahl. ***

A divided panel of the Court of Appeals for the Fifth Circuit affirmed. ***

The Court of Appeals *** considered whether Dahl was himself a "seller" of the oil and gas interests within the meaning of § 12(1), for if he was, the court assumed, he could be held liable in contribution for the other plaintiffs' claims against Pinter.[9] Citing Fifth Circuit precedent, the court described a statutory seller as "(1) one who parts with title to securities in exchange for consideration or (2) one whose participation in the buy-sell transaction is a substantial factor in causing the transaction to take place." While acknowledging that Dahl's conduct was a "substantial factor" in causing the other plaintiffs to purchase securities from Pinter, the court declined to hold that Dahl was a "seller" for

9. *** Unlike § 11 of the Securities Act, § 12 does not expressly provide for contribution. The Court of Appeals did not reach the question whether Pinter is entitled to contribution under § 12(1) because it found that Dahl was not a seller for purposes of § 12(1), and therefore would not be the proper subject of a contribution claim. The parties have not raised or addressed the contribution issue before this Court, and we express no view as to whether a right of contribution exists under § 12(1).

purposes of § 12(1). Instead, the court went on to refine its test to include a threshold requirement that one who acts as a "promoter" be "motivated by a desire to confer a direct or indirect benefit on someone other than the person he has advised to purchase." The court reasoned that "a rule imposing liability (without fault or knowledge) on friends and family members who give one another gratuitous advice on investment matters unreasonably interferes with well-established patterns of social discourse." Accordingly, since the court found no evidence that Dahl sought or received any financial benefit in return for his advice, it declined to impose liability on Dahl for "mere gregariousness." ***

III

*** In determining whether Dahl may be deemed a "seller" for purposes of § 12(1), such that he may be held liable for the sale of unregistered securities to the other investor-respondents, we look first at the language of § 12(1). That statute provides, in pertinent part: "Any person who ... offers or sells a security" in violation of the registration requirement of the Securities Act "shall be liable to the person purchasing such security from him." This provision defines the class of defendants who may be subject to liability as those who offer or sell unregistered securities. But the Securities Act nowhere delineates who may be regarded as a statutory seller, and the sparse legislative history sheds no light on the issue. The courts, on their part, have not defined the term uniformly.

At the very least, however, the language of § 12(1) contemplates a buyer-seller relationship not unlike traditional contractual privity. Thus, it is settled that § 12(1) imposes liability on the owner who passed title, or other interest in the security, to the buyer for value. Dahl, of course, was not a seller in this conventional sense, and therefore may be held liable only if § 12(1) liability extends to persons other than the person who passes title.[20]

A

In common parlance, a person may offer or sell property without necessarily being the person who transfers title to, or other interest in, that property. We need not rely entirely on ordinary understanding of the statutory language, however, for the Securities Act defines the operative terms of § 12(1). Section 2(3) defines "sale" or "sell" to include "every contract of sale or disposition of a security or interest in a security, for value," and the terms "offer to sell," "offer for sale," or "offer" to include "every attempt or offer to dispose of, or solicitation of an offer to buy, a security or interest in a security, for value." Under these definitions, the range of persons potentially liable under § 12(1) is not limited to persons who pass title. The inclusion of the phrase "solicitation

20. The "offers or sells" and the "purchasing such security from him" language that governs § 12(1) also governs § 12(2), which provides a securities purchaser with a similar rescissionary cause of action for misrepresentation. Most courts and commentators have not defined the defendant class differently for purposes of the two provisions.

The question whether anyone beyond the transferor of title, or immediate vendor, may be deemed a seller for purposes of § 12 has been litigated in actions under both § 12(1) and § 12(2). Decisions under § 12(2) addressing the "seller" question are thus relevant to the issue presented to us in this case, and, to that extent, we discuss them here. Nevertheless, this case does not present, nor do we take a position on, the scope of a statutory seller for purposes of § 12(2).

of an offer to buy" within the definition of "offer" brings an individual who engages in solicitation, an activity not inherently confined to the actual owner, within the scope of § 12. ***

An interpretation of statutory seller that includes brokers and others who solicit offers to purchase securities furthers the purposes of the Securities Act—to promote full and fair disclosure of information to the public in the sales of securities. In order to effectuate Congress' intent that § 12(1) civil liability be *in terrorem,* the risk of its invocation should be felt by solicitors of purchases. The solicitation of a buyer is perhaps the most critical stage of the selling transaction. It is the first stage of a traditional securities sale to involve the buyer, and it is directed at producing the sale. In addition, brokers and other solicitors are well positioned to control the flow of information to a potential purchaser, and, in fact, such persons are the participants in the selling transaction who most often disseminate material information to investors. Thus, solicitation is the stage at which an investor is most likely to be injured, that is, by being persuaded to purchase securities without full and fair information. Given Congress' overriding goal of preventing this injury, we may infer that Congress intended solicitation to fall under the mantle of § 12(1).

Although we conclude that Congress intended § 12(1) liability to extend to those who solicit securities purchases, we share the Court of Appeals' conclusion that Congress did not intend to impose rescission based on strict liability on a person who urges the purchase but whose motivation is solely to benefit the buyer. When a person who urges another to make a securities purchase acts merely to assist the buyer, not only is it uncommon to say that the buyer "purchased" from him, but it is also strained to describe the giving of gratuitous advice, even strongly or enthusiastically, as "soliciting." Section 2(3) defines an offer as a "solicitation of an offer to buy ... for value." The person who gratuitously urges another to make a particular investment decision is not, in any meaningful sense, requesting value in exchange for his suggestion or seeking the value the titleholder will obtain in exchange for the ultimate sale. The language and purpose of § 12(1) suggest that liability extends only to the person who successfully solicits the purchase, motivated at least in part by a desire to serve his own financial interests or those of the securities owner. If he had such a motivation, it is fair to say that the buyer "purchased" the security from him and to align him with the owner in a rescission action.[23]

B

Petitioner is not satisfied with extending § 12(1) primary liability to one who solicits securities sales for financial gain. Pinter assumes, without explication, that liability is not limited to the person who actually parts title with the securities, and urges us to validate, as the standard by which additional defendant-sellers are identified, that version of the "substantial factor" test

---

23. *** [T]here is no reason to think that Congress wanted to bind itself to the common-law notion of the circumstances in which rescission is an appropriate remedy. *** [W]e may infer that Congress, in order to effectuate its goals, chose to impose this relief on any defendant it classified as a statutory seller, regardless of the fact that such imposition was somewhat inconsistent with the use of rescission at common law. Congress chose rescission for its effects; there is no indication that Congress employed the remedy for its delineation of potential defendants.

utilized by the Fifth Circuit before the refinement espoused in this case. Under that approach, grounded in tort doctrine, a nontransferor § 12(1) seller is defined as one "whose participation in the buy-sell transaction is a substantial factor in causing the transaction to take place." *Pharo v. Smith*, 621 F.2d 656, 667 (CA5 1980). The Court of Appeals acknowledged that Dahl would be liable as a statutory seller under this test.

We do not agree that Congress contemplated imposing § 12(1) liability under the broad terms petitioners advocate. There is no support in the statutory language or legislative history for expansion of § 12(1) primary liability beyond persons who pass title and persons who "offer," including those who "solicit" offers. Indeed, § 12's failure to impose express liability for mere participation in unlawful sales transactions suggests that Congress did not intend that the section impose liability on participants collateral to the offer or sale. When Congress wished to create such liability, it had little trouble doing so.[26] ***

The substantial-factor test reaches participants in sales transactions who do not even arguably fit within the definitions set out in § 2(3); it "would add a gloss to the operative language of [§ 12(1)] quite different from its commonly accepted meaning." *Ernst & Ernst v. Hochfelder*, 425 U.S., at 199. We conclude that Congress did not intend such a gross departure from the statutory language. Accordingly, we need not entertain Pinter's policy arguments. Being merely a "substantial factor" in causing the sale of unregistered securities is not sufficient in itself to render a defendant liable under § 12(1).

C

We are unable to determine whether Dahl may be held liable as a statutory seller under § 12(1). The District Court explicitly found that "Dahl solicited each of the other plaintiffs (save perhaps Grantham) in connection with the offer, purchase, and receipt of their oil and gas interests." We cannot conclude that this finding was clearly erroneous. It is not clear, however, that Dahl had the kind of interest in the sales that make him liable as a statutory seller. We do know that he received no commission from Pinter in connection with the other sales, but this is not conclusive. Typically, a person who solicits the purchase will have sought or received a personal financial benefit from the

---

**26.** Congress knew of the collateral participation concept and employed it in the Securities Act and throughout its unified program of securities regulation. Liabilities and obligations expressly grounded in participation are found elsewhere in the Act, see, e.g., [Section 2(11)] (defining "underwriter," who is liable under § 5, as including direct and indirect participants), and in the later Roosevelt administration securities Acts. For example, § 9 of the 1934 Act, passed by the same Congress that enacted the Securities Act, creates a private right of action that expressly imposes liability on participants.

Section 11 of the Securities Act lends strong support to the conclusion that Congress did not intend to extend § 12 primary liability to collateral participants in the unlawful securities sales transaction. That section provides an express cause of action for damages to a person acquiring securities pursuant to a registration statement that misstates or omits a material fact. Section 11(a) explicitly enumerates the various categories of persons involved in the registration process who are subject to suit under that section, including many who are participants in the activities leading up to the sale. There are no similar provisions in § 12, and therefore we may conclude that Congress did not intend such persons to be defendants in § 12 actions.

sale, such as where he "anticipat[es] a share of the profits," *Lawler v. Gilliam*, 569 F.2d, at 1288, or receives a brokerage commission, *Cady v. Murphy*, 113 F.2d, at 990. But a person who solicits the buyer's purchase in order to serve the financial interests of the owner may properly be liable under § 12(1) without showing that he expects to participate in the benefits the owner enjoys.

The Court of Appeals apparently concluded that Dahl was motivated entirely by a gratuitous desire to share an attractive investment opportunity with his friends and associates. This conclusion, in our view, was premature. The District Court made no findings that focused on whether Dahl urged the other purchases in order to further some financial interest of his own or of Pinter. Accordingly, further findings are necessary to assess Dahl's liability. ***

The judgment of the Court of Appeals is vacated, and the case is remanded for further proceedings consistent with this opinion.

JUSTICE STEVENS, DISSENTING:

*** I am unable to join Part III because I am persuaded that the discussion of the § 12(1) term "seller" in the context of a contribution suit is both advisory, because no such suit was brought in this case, and misleading, because it assumes that the class of persons who sell securities to purchasers (i.e., § 12(1) "sellers") is coextensive with the class of potential defendants in claims for contribution, not brought directly under § 12(1), asserted by § 12(1) sellers. ***

## *NOTES AND QUESTIONS*

***1. Not Only Title Passers.*** The Court held that "seller" status extends beyond the person who passed title. Look again at the language of Section 12(a)(2) and compare it with that of Section 11. Is there reason to suppose, *Pinter* notwithstanding, that Congress intended to limit "seller" status under Section 12(a)(2) to the person who passed title?

***2. The Meaning of Solicitation.*** The Court held that a seller must "successfully solicit the purchase," but it did not define solicitation. What light does *Pinter* shed regarding the meaning of solicitation? Does someone who solicits have to intend to do so?

***3. The Meaning of Financial Interests.*** According to *Pinter*, a seller must engage in solicitation "motivated at least in part by a desire to serve his own financial interests or those of the securities owner." What sorts of financial interests would qualify in this regard? On remand, what showing might Pinter make in order to establish Dahl's requisite financial interests?

***4. Seller Status and Types of Underwriting.*** Return to the beginning of this Chapter and the discussion of the role of underwriters in the preparation of the registration statement. Note the distinction between "firm commitment" underwriting (where the underwriters buy the securities from the issuer and resell them) and "best efforts" underwriting (where the underwriters do not purchase the securities but instead use their best efforts to effectuate the distribution).

Consider first a "best efforts" underwriting. Title to the securities remains with the issuer, who is thus the passer of title and hence a "seller" for purposes of Section 12(a)(2). The underwriter may also be a seller, so long as it engages in "solicitation," since its activities on behalf of the issuer's sale are motivated by the underwriting commission it will receive if the offering is successful.

Next consider "firm commitment" underwriting. One court has provided the following explanation for why the issuer does not face liability under Section 12(a)(2) in this situation:

> Because the issuer in a firm commitment underwriting does not pass title to the securities, DEC and its officers cannot be held liable as "sellers" under Section 12(2) unless they actively "solicited" the plaintiffs' purchase of securities to further their own financial motives, in the manner of a broker or vendor's agent. See *Pinter,* 486 U.S. at 644-47. Absent such solicitation, DEC can be viewed as no more than a "seller's seller," whom plaintiffs would have no right to sue under Section 12(2). See id. at 644 n. 21; Louis Loss & Joel Seligman, Fundamentals of Securities Regulation 1000-01 (3d ed. 1995) ("[I]t seems quite clear that § 12 contemplates only an action by a buyer against *his or her immediate seller*. That is to say, in the case of the typical 'firm-commitment underwriting,' the ultimate investor can recover only from the dealer who sold to him or her.") (emphasis in original; footnotes omitted).

*Shaw v. Digital Equip. Corp.*, 82 F.3d 1194, 1215-16 (1st Cir. 1996). See *In re Deutsche Telekom AG Sec. Litig.*, 2002 WL 244597 at *4-*5 (S.D.N.Y. 2002) (rejecting seller status for a control person in a registered offering handled on a firm commitment basis). Does this result encourage issuer carelessness in the preparation of prospectuses? Would the issuer likewise avoid liability in an exempt offering underwritten on a firm commitment basis? Is the unavailability of Section 12(a)(2) significant given the availability of Rule 10b-5? Cf. *Shaw*, supra, 82 F.3d at 1225 (dismissing Section 12(a)(2) claim but not Rule 10b-5 claim).

***5. Suing the Right Underwriter.*** Recall that Section 11 allows the plaintiff to sue all the underwriters in the registered offering. Section 12(a)(2) is different in this regard. Under Section 12(a)(2), the plaintiff may sue only the underwriter or underwriters who were his sellers, that is, who passed him title or solicited his purchase for financial gain. Consider *Griffin v. PaineWebber, Inc.*, 2001 WL 740764 (S.D.N.Y. 2001), a Section 12(a)(2) class action against, among others, an underwriter (CIBC) who had neither transferred title to the named plaintiff nor solicited his purchase. The court dismissed the action:

> [B]ecause Griffin's complaint makes clear that he does not have an individual claim against CIBC that would allow him to represent the class of plaintiff who may have such a claim, his standing to maintain the action cannot be established. Accordingly, the claim against CIBC is dismissed on the basis of Griffin's lack of standing to bring the claim. Plaintiffs will be granted leave to amend the complaint *** to identify, in connection with the Offering, a named plaintiff who actually purchased Livent securities from, or was solicited directly by, CIBC.

Id. at *2. What steps might a plaintiff's lawyer in a class action take in advance in order to avoid the problem that arose in *Griffin*? If a Section 12(a)(2) class action alleges sales by more than one underwriter to more than one named plaintiff, are there likely to be sufficient questions of law and fact common to the class to allow certification of the class?

*6.* **Gustafson** ***Revisited.*** Reconsider the Supreme Court's decision in *Gustafson v. Alloyd, Inc.*, 513 U.S. 561 (1995). Is it arguable that *Gustafson* has the effect of qualifying who is a seller for purposes of Section 12(a)(2)?

***7. The Question of Contribution.*** Unlike Section 11, Section 12(a)(2) makes no mention of contribution. Note, however, that *Pinter* left the question open in a footnote. See generally Mark I. Steinberg & Christopher D. Olive, Contribution and Proportionate Liability Under the Federal Securities Laws in Multidefendant Securities Litigation After the Private Securities Litigation Reform Act of 1995, 50 SMU L. Rev. 337, 352 n. 76 (1996) (discussing the possible right of contribution under Section 12(a)(2) and noting that the case law following *Pinter* has declined to recognize such a right).

Assume that you represent a defendant in a Section 12(a)(2) action in a jurisdiction that has not yet decided whether a defendant in such an action is entitled to obtain contribution from others who meet the *Pinter* "seller" criteria. What arguments could you make in support of your client's right to do so?

***8. Rationalizing Restrictiveness.*** The Supreme Court's decisions in *Pinter* and *Gustafson* restricted the reach of Section 12(a)(2), just as Supreme Court decisions such as *Blue Chip Stamps, Hochfelder,* and *Central Bank* that you read in Chapter 2 restricted the reach of the implied private action under Rule 10b-5. Compare the reasons given by the Court for imposing restrictions in these two sets of decisions. Are they similar or different? Consistent or inconsistent?

***9. Section 12(a)(2) vs. Rule 10b-5.*** Why do you suppose that Rule 10b-5, and not Section 12(a)(2), is the centerpiece of most large securities fraud class actions?

***10. Using Section 12(a)(2) as a Litigation Strategy.*** While plaintiffs suing under Section 12(a)(2) do not have to plead or prove scienter, plaintiffs suing under Rule 10b-5 face dismissal if they fail to plead scienter with adequate specificity. See supra Chapter 2.D.2. Thus, a Section 12(a)(2) action, if it survives a motion to dismiss, may be useful for obtaining discovery as to scienter that can facilitate the amendment of the complaint, or a new complaint, that alleges Rule 10b-5 claims against a broader class of defendants (including persons who would not meet the *Pinter* definition of "seller") on behalf of a broader class of plaintiffs (including persons who purchased shares on the secondary market and thus under *Gustafson* would be ineligible to sue under Section 12(a)(2)).

Should courts allow plaintiffs to use Section 12(a)(2) to make an end-run around the stay on discovery in private Rule 10b-5 actions that becomes operative upon the filing of a motion to dismiss? See Exchange Act Section 21D(b)(3)(B), discussed supra Chapter 2.D.2. Is there language in either the Securities Act or the Exchange Act, or in the PSLRA, pursuant to which the discovery stay provision was added to the Exchange Act, suggesting that such a tactic should be disallowed?

### *PROBLEM 3-4*

Determine which of the following meets the *Pinter* definition of "seller" for purposes of Section 12(a)(2):

a. A lawyer who prepared the prospectus on behalf of the issuer in a registered offering.

b. A lawyer who prepared the prospectus on behalf of the issuer in a registered offering and who was compensated for his work on the prospectus with shares of the issuer's stock, the value of which will substantially increase if the offering is successful.

c. A lawyer who prepared the prospectus on behalf of the issuer in a registered offering and who also made telephone calls to several institutional investors in which he encouraged them to buy the issuer's stock.

d. A broker who, as a member of the selling group in a registered offering, solicited a plaintiff's purchase of the securities from one of the underwriters. The broker was paid a commission for soliciting the purchase.

e. In a firm commitment underwriting, an issuer posted a copy of the prospectus on its Web page, accompanied by a statement that encouraged prospective purchasers to contact the underwriter or members of the selling group.

---

#### c. *The Reasonable Care Defense*

Unlike Rule 10b-5, which requires the plaintiff to prove that the defendant acted with scienter (that is, intentionally or recklessly), Section 12(a)(2) does not require the plaintiff to prove the defendant's state of mind. Section 12(a)(2) does, however, allow the defendant to avoid liability by establishing a reasonable care defense, namely, that "he did not know, and in the exercise of reasonable care could not have known," about the materially misleading misstatement or omission.

How does Section 12(a)(2)'s reasonable care defense compare with Section 11's due diligence defenses? Courts struggle with this issue. See, e.g., *In re Software Toolworks, Inc. Sec. Litig.*, 50 F.3d 615, 621 (9th Cir. 1994) (describing them as "similar, if not identical"). Consider *Sanders v. John Nuveen & Co.*, 619 F.2d 1222 (7th Cir. 1980), a Section 12(a)(2) action against the exclusive underwriter of an exempt offering of unsecured promissory notes as to which the issuer (WH) had defaulted. The default had been the result of a fraud perpetrated by WH and its accountants over a ten year period. The underwriter "was not aware of the fraud and held 'the mistaken but honest belief that financial statements (of WH) prepared by certified public accountants correctly represented the condition of' WH." Id. at 1224 (quoting *Sanders v. John Nuveen & Co.*, 524 F.2d 1064, 1066 (7th Cir. 1975)). The court concluded that the underwriter had not established its reasonable care defense:

> It is not at all clear that Congress intended to impose a higher standard of care under § 11 than under § 12(2). The difference in language appeared in the House bill and was retained in the Act as agreed to by the Joint Conference Committee and as passed by both Houses. The Conference Committee report,

> in its discussion of the standard of liability imposed for a misleading registration statement, describes the standard adopted not as one of "reasonable investigation," but one of "reasonable care." More specifically, Congress does not appear to have intended that a different standard apply to underwriters. Thus, the House Report draws no distinction between an underwriter's burden in the case of misleading statements in a prospectus, for which it can be liable only under § 12(2), and its § 11 duty to conduct a "reasonable investigation." The difference in language can be explained not as an attempt to impose different duties of care under §§ 11 and 12, but by the fact that § 12(2) imposes the duty on all sellers of securities, while § 11 imposes liability only on specified groups of persons having such a close relationship with the registration statement that the 1933 Act, before it was amended the following year, treated them as fiduciaries. See Securities Act, § 11(c); Securities Exchange Act § 206(c). Thus the general duty of reasonable care, the specific requirements of which are determined by the circumstances of the case, was to be applied in § 11 only to persons who had a stronger connection with a registration statement than a seller necessarily has to a prospectus, so a more stringent articulation of the standard was appropriate.
>
> In the circumstances of this case, the reasonable care standard required [a] reasonable investigation *** . Since what constitutes reasonable care under § 12(2) depends upon the circumstances, we, of course, do not intimate that the duty of a seller under § 12(2) is always the same as that of an underwriter in a registration offering under § 11.

Id. at 1228.

In a dissent from the Supreme Court's denial of certiorari (in which Justice Rehnquist joined), Justice Powell maintained that the Seventh Circuit's view of the reasonable care defense was mistaken:

> The Court of Appeals' opinion may be read as holding that petitioner's duty of "reasonable care" under § 12(2) required it independently to *investigate* the accuracy and completeness of the certified financial statements. It was customary, however—and in my view entirely reasonable—for petitioner to rely on these statements as accurately reflecting W&H's financial condition. Even under § 11 of the Act, an underwriter is explicitly absolved of the duty to investigate with respect to "any part of the registration statement purporting to be made on the authority of an expert" such as a certified accountant if "he had no reasonable ground to believe and did not believe" that the information therein was misleading. § 11(b)(3)(C) of the Act; see § 11(a)(4). This provision is in the Act because, almost by definition, it *is* reasonable to rely on financial statements certified by public accountants. Yet, in this case, the Court of Appeals nevertheless seems to have imposed the higher duty prescribed by § 11 to investigate, but denied petitioner the right to rely on "the authority of an expert" that also is provided by § 11. ***
>
> *** Dealers may believe that they must undertake extensive independent financial investigations rather than rely on the accuracy of the certified financial statements. If this is so, the efficiency of the short- term financial markets will be impaired. I would grant certiorari.

450 U.S. 1005, 1009-11 (1981). Cf. *Associated Randall Bank v. Griffin, Kubik, Stephens & Thompson, Inc.*, 3 F.3d 208, 213 (7th Cir. 1993) (noting that no court has "pursued the implication of [the Seventh Circuit in] *Sanders*, that broker-dealers must investigate the securities they sell").

## *NOTES AND QUESTIONS*

*1.* **Sanders—*the Seventh Circuit's View.*** What does the Seventh Circuit suggest in *Sanders* concerning the nature of the reasonable care defense? Does it endorse equating the defense with the due diligence defenses under Section 11? If Congress intended such an equation, why didn't it use the same language in each Section?

*2.* **Sanders—*the Seventh Circuit vs. Justice Powell.*** Which position do you find more persuasive, that of the Seventh Circuit or that of Justice Powell?

*3.* ***A Facts and Circumstances Approach?*** Consider the views of Professor Maynard on the *Sanders* decision in particular and the reasonable care defense in general:

> *Sanders* suggests that the reasonable care standard of section 12(2) should be interpreted flexibly and that the nature of the defendant is a crucial factor in defining the relevant standard. Moreover, *Sanders* suggests that the exercise of reasonable care may, but does not automatically, require the defendant-seller to conduct an investigation to establish her exercise of reasonable care. Again, the nature of the defendant-seller is a critical factor in determining whether there is an affirmative obligation to make a reasonable investigation to establish the section 12(2) reasonable care defense. Finally, *Sanders* indicates that, where an investigation is required to show the defendant's exercise of reasonable care, the scope of any required investigation will be defined in substantial part by the nature of the defendant-seller and her involvement in, and relationship to, the plaintiff's purchase of the securities at issue. ***
>
> Since section 12(2) essentially embodies a negligence standard, the exercise of reasonable care will presumably be defined by the facts and circumstances of each case.

Therese H. Maynard, The Affirmative Defense of Reasonable Care Under Section 12(2) of the Securities Act of 1933, 69 Notre Dame L. Rev. 57, 94-95 (1993). Do you agree with her interpretation of *Sanders*? Does she suggest a workable approach to the reasonable care defense?

## *PROBLEM 3-5*

From February through July of 2000, Ace Loan Company provided secured loans to people who wanted to purchase interests in "Dare to be Great" (DTBG), a fraudulent pyramid scheme. Interests in DTBG constitute securities under the federal securities laws.

After Ace had made some of these loans, DTBG contacted an Ace employee (Joe) about future loan business. Joe attended several DTBG meetings, at which he supplied those in attendance with Ace loan applications. He also gave a speech at each of these meetings about obtaining financing through Ace. In these speeches, he represented that DTBG was a "good quality" investment.

In July 2000, Joe's supervisor (Drew) became aware of Joe's activities involving DTBG. Drew quickly realized that DTBG was a sham. He thereupon ordered Joe to stop engaging in such activities immediately.

DTBG declared bankruptcy in November 2000. Shortly thereafter, Fred, who purchased an interest in DTBG based on a loan from Ace obtained through Joe, brought a Section 12(a)(2) action against Joe. Is Joe an appropriate defendant? Assuming that he is, can he establish his reasonable care defense?

Cf. *Davis v. Avco Fin. Serv., Inc.*, 739 F.2d 1057 (6th Cir. 1984).

#### *d. Damages and Negative Causation*

Damages under Section 12(a)(2) are rescissory in nature, regardless of whether the plaintiff has sold the securities in question. Thus, if the plaintiff has not sold the securities, he is entitled to "the consideration paid for such security with interest thereon, less the amount of any income received." If the plaintiff has sold the securities, he has the right to rescissory damages—"a return of the consideration paid, reduced by the amount realized when he sold the security and any 'income received' on the security." *Randall v. Loftsgaarden*, 478 U.S. 647, 655-56 (1986). See also id. at 667 (holding that recovery under Section 12(a)(2), as well as under Rule 10b-5, need not be offset by tax benefits received).

A defendant in a Section 12(a)(2) action can reduce—or even eliminate entirely—the amount of money that the plaintiff would otherwise recover. Authorization comes from Section 12(b):

> [I]f the person who offered or sold such security proves that any portion or all of the amount recoverable under subsection (a)(2) represents other than the depreciation in value of the subject security resulting from such part of the prospectus or oral communication, with respect to which the liability of that person is asserted, not being true or omitting to state a material fact required to be stated therein or necessary to make the statement not misleading, then such portion or amount, as the case may be, shall not be recoverable.

This "negative causation" defense—enacted in 1995 as part of the PSLRA—is analogous to Section 11's negative causation defense and thus *Akerman v. Oryx Communications, Inc.*, 810 F.2d 336 (2d Cir. 1987), which you read in connection with Section 11, is relevant to Section 12(a)(2) as well. By enacting Section 12(b), Congress confirmed that a Section 12(a)(2) plaintiff has no obligation to prove causation.

### *NOTES AND QUESTIONS*

1. ***Obligatory Resale?*** Once a plaintiff discovers the material misstatement or omission at issue, is she obliged to sell her securities in order to mitigate damages under Section 12(a)(2)? See 9 Louis Loss & Joel Seligman, Securities Regulation 4205 (3d ed. 1992) (raising the question).

2. ***Delaying Tactics.*** As mentioned, the Supreme Court held in *Randall v. Loftsgaarden*, 478 U.S. 647, 667 (1986), that recovery under Section 12(a)(2) need not be offset by the amount of a tax benefit already received. But suppose a plaintiff intentionally delays filing his Section 12(a)(2) action in order to realize a tax benefit not yet received from the securities in question. Would the court be entitled to take this delay into account for purposes of calculating the amount of his recovery? What other risks are incurred by a plaintiff who pursues such a strategy?

3. ***Making Comparisons.*** How does the measure of calculating damages under Section 12(a)(2) compare with that of Section 11? With that of Rule 10b-5?

---

### *PROBLEM 3-6*

a. On the recommendation of her broker, Thalia purchased 1000 shares of Dog.com that were sold at $5 per share in a firm commitment initial public offering (IPO) in which the broker's firm acted as underwriter. The broker did not tell Thalia that analysts at the broker's firm had been giving Dog.com a "buy" recommendation under heavy pressure from the underwriting side of the firm. He told Thalia that he himself thought the stock was a "great buy," but he made no other material misrepresentations to her about Dog.com. There were also no material misrepresentations in the prospectus. Two months later, Dog.com stock had become worthless. Can Thalia sue her broker and his firm under Section 12(a)(2)?

b. Assume instead that Thalia bought the Dog.com stock on the secondary market in large part relying upon oral statements made on the television show Wall Street Beat by a renowned Internet stock analyst, James Botchit. Botchit does not work for the firm that sold Thalia her stock; instead, he works for another broker-dealer that also participated in the underwriting. Can Thalia sue Botchit and his firm under Section 12(a)(2)?

### *3. Additional Shared Features of Sections 11 and 12(a)(2)*

Sections 11 and 12(a)(2) have the following features in common: (i) a materiality requirement; (ii) a statute of limitations requirement; (iii) an applicable provision for the liability of controlling persons; (iv) pleading standards; and (v) concurrent state and federal jurisdiction. We will briefly consider each of these.

#### *a. Materiality*

To be actionable under Sections 11 and 12(a)(2), the misstatement or omission at issue must be material in nature. As is true under Rule 10b-5, the basic definition of materiality comes from *TSC Indus., Inc. v. Northway, Inc.*, 426 U.S. 438 (1976): "a substantial likelihood that a reasonable shareholder would consider [the information] *** important" or "a substantial likelihood that the disclosure of the omitted fact would have been viewed by the reasonable investor as having significantly altered the 'total mix' of information made available." Id. at 449. See generally supra Chapter 2.B (discussing the materiality requirement under Rule 10b-5). In addition, the bespeaks caution doctrine (Chapter 2.B.3.b supra) and the puffery doctrine (see note 3 on page 66) are typically available under Sections 11 and 12(a)(2) in circumstances in which they would also be available under Rule 10b-5.

Sections 11 and 12(a)(2) also share a statutory safe harbor for forward-looking statements that is set forth in Section 27A of the Securities Act. This safe harbor closely resembles its Exchange Act counterpart—Section 21E—

which you examined with reference to Rule 10b-5 in Chapter 2.B.3.c. As is with Section 21E, Section 27A applies only when the issuer is subject to the reporting requirements of the Exchange Act. See Section 27A(a)(1). See also Chapter 1.A.2.c (discussing Exchange Act reporting requirements). Likewise as with Section 21E, Section 27A does not apply to IPOs and to certain other transactions. See Section 27A(b).

### b. *Statute of Limitations*

The statute of limitations for both Sections 11 and 12(a)(2) is set forth in Section 13 of the Securities Act:

> No action shall be maintained to enforce any liability created under Section 11 or Section 12(a)(2) unless brought within one year after the discovery of the untrue statement or the omission, or after such discovery should have been made by the exercise of reasonable diligence ***. In no event shall any such action be brought to enforce a liability created under Section 11 *** more than three years after the security was bona fide offered to the public, or under Section 12(a)(2) more than three years after the sale.

With the enactment of the Sarbanes-Oxley Act of 2002, however, an interesting and important question arises. Recall that the Sarbanes-Oxley Act replaced the one year/three year structure of Rule 10b-5's limitations period with a two year/five year structure. See Section 804 of the Sarbanes-Oxley Act, enacted as 28 U.S.C. § 1658(b). See also supra Chapter 2.I (setting forth 28 U.S.C. § 1658(b) on page 237 and discussing the two year/five year structure with reference to Rule 10b-5). Can it be argued that the new statute of limitations enacted by the Sarbanes-Oxley Act applies to some or all Section 11 or Section 12(a)(2) claims?

### c. *Controlling Person Liability*

Persons who control those who violate Sections 11 and 12(a)(2) are liable under Section 15 of the Securities Act, which reads as follows:

> Every person who, by or through stock ownership, agency, or otherwise, or who, pursuant to or in connection with an agreement or understanding with one or more other persons by or through stock ownership, agency, or otherwise, controls any person liable under Sections 11 or 12, shall also be liable jointly and severally with and to the same extent as such controlled person to any person to whom such controlled person is liable, unless the controlling person had no knowledge of or reasonable ground to believe in the existence of the facts by reason of which the liability of the controlled person is alleged to exist.

You have previously examined Section 15's Exchange Act counterpart—Section 20(a)—in connection with Rule 10b-5. See Chapter 2.H.3.

### d. *Pleading Standards*

Sections 11 and 12(a)(2) are also identically situated with respect to applicable pleading standards. These standards include Fed. R. Civ. P. 8, which governs all civil complaints filed in federal court and provides that plaintiffs need plead only "a short and plain statement of the claim showing that [they are] entitled to relief."

Section 11 and 12(a)(2) claims should not, however, have to satisfy Fed. R. Civ. P. 9(b), which requires particularity in the pleading of fraud or mistake. Sections 11 and 12(a)(2) are not "fraud" actions since they do not require proof that the defendant acted with scienter. See Hillary A. Sale, Heightened Pleading and Discovery Stays: An Analysis of the Effect of the PSLRA's Internal-Information Standard on '33 and '34 Act Claims, 76 Wash.U.L.Q. 537, 584-86 (1998) (discussing the inapplicability of Rule 9(b) to Sections 11 and 12(a)(2) actions and criticizing cases that have dismissed such actions for failure to comply with Rule 9(b)). See also Brian Murray and Donald J. Wallace, You Shouldn't Be Required to Plead More than You Have to Prove, 53 Baylor L. Rev. 783 (2001).

Nor are Sections 11 and 12(a)(2) subject to the heightened pleading requirements enacted as part of the PSLRA. Indeed, the PSLRA added the heightened pleading requirements to the Exchange Act (see Exchange Act Section 21D(b)) but not to the Securities Act. Therefore the conclusion seems unavoidable that the heightened pleading requirements—applicable to private claims under Rule 10b-5—do not apply to claims under Sections 11 and 12(a)(2). See Sale, supra, 76 Wash. U. L. Q. at 586-93 (showing that this result follows from the PSLRA as well as from the nature of the Securities Act itself).

Note, however, that Section 11 and Section 12(a)(2) claims are subject to Section 27(b) of the Securities Act. Section 27(b) empowers a court to stay discovery in all private actions under the Securities Act during the pendency of a motion to dismiss. You previously encountered Section 27(b)'s Exchange Act counterpart—Exchange Act Section 21D(b)(3)(B)—in connection with Rule 10b-5. See supra Chapter 2.D.2.

#### e. *Concurrent State and Federal Jurisdiction*

Section 11 and 12(a)(2) claims may be brought in state or federal court in accordance with Section 22(a) of the Securities Act. If, however, the complaint is a class action and alleges a material misstatement or omission in connection with the sale of a "nationally traded security" (encompassing those listed on the New York Stock Exchange, the American Stock Exchange, or the NASDAQ), it may be filed in federal court only. See Section 16 of the Securities Act.

In contrast to the Securities Act, the Exchange Act has always provided for exclusive federal jurisdiction. Why does the Exchange Act embrace exclusive federal jurisdiction, in contrast to not only the Securities Act but also to all the other federal securities statutes? See Margaret V. Sachs, Exclusive Federal Jurisdiction for Implied Rule 10b-5 Actions: The Emperor Has No Clothes, 49 Ohio St. L.J. 559, 580-81 (1988) (linking the Exchange Act's exclusive federal jurisdiction with the onerousness of that Act's express private actions).

### *PROBLEM 3-7*

On March, 2002, Worldscam Communications, a long distance telephone company, sold $300 million in subordinated debentures in a registered public offering. The registration statement became effective on March 10, 2002 and the debentures were sold over the next two weeks.

The registration statement contained the following forward looking statements, which were also in the prospectus for the offering:

> a. Worldscam is highly confident that its total debt will not exceed $2 billion at any time during the three year period ending in October 2005. Only exceptional and highly unlikely circumstances—for example, a substantial deterioration of profit margins in the telecommunications market—could cause Worldscam's debt to exceed this projected level. However, investors should be aware that, although unlikely, these or other factors could cause debt levels to exceed projections.
>
> b. Worldscam projects that its total share of the long distance telephone service market, now 25%, will exceed 40% by October 2005 and that Worldscam will be able to obtain this market share without a deterioration in its profit margins. Market share, however, is unpredictable, and investors are cautioned that a variety of factors, including unexpected price cutting from competitors, could slow the growth of Worldscam's market share.

On March 1, 2002, the Worldscam Chief Financial Officer (CFO) had sent senior management a memorandum stating that (i) in his opinion, the company would have to incur total debt of $3 billion by 2003, and probably even more debt in 2004, in order to make improvements in its telecommunications network necessary to keep up with competitors; (ii) that for Worldscam to forgo some or all of these improvements would, in his opinion, seriously undermine its competitive position and its share of the long distance telephone market; and (iii) that the CFO had discussed these projected expenditures with several senior operations officers of the company and that they had agreed with him. Although the CFO's memorandum recommended disclosure of his projections in the registration statement for the debentures, the Chief Executive Officer (CEO) of Worldscam disagreed on the ground that the projections were "too speculative." Accordingly, the projections were mentioned neither in the registration statement nor in the prospectus for the debentures.

On March 11, 2002, one day after the registration statement for the debentures became effective, but before 90% of the debentures were actually sold, Worldscam was informed by the federal government's General Services Administration (GSO) that all of Worldscam's long distance telephone contracts with federal government agencies would be cancelled as of January, 2003 because of substantial allegations that Worldscam had engaged in fraudulent overbilling. The GSO told Worldscam's senior management that the overbilling allegations would be referred to the United States Attorney for investigation and possible criminal charges, and that the GSO would publicly announce the cancellation of Worldscam's government contracts in approximately two weeks.

Federal government contracts represented 30% of Worldscam's business, and Worldscam's market share thus would most likely decrease significantly rather than grow over the next few years, without these government contracts.

Several in-house lawyers at Worldscam recommended amending the registration statement for the debentures (through an additional filing with the SEC) to reflect the possible loss of Worldscam's government contracts. Alternatively, the lawyers argued that, if the registration statement was not amended, at least the prospectus should be "stickered" to note that Worldscam's federal contracts were in jeopardy. Once again, however, Worldscam's CEO successfully persuaded senior management that this was just a "dispute over billing technicalities with GSO bureaucrats that need not be disclosed at the present time." The CEO emphasized that Worldscam had considerable political influence "with U.S. Senators and others who call the shots," and that Worldscam had not yet used "informal channels" to resolve its dispute with the GSO. The registration statement was not amended, the prospectus was not stickered, and no other effort was made to inform purchasers of the debentures about this development.

The GSO made its public announcement on March 28, 2002, but by then all of the debentures had been sold. The debentures sold pursuant to the March 2002 registration statement fell in price on public trading markets from 98% of par to 85% of par within hours.

On May 10, 2002, Worldscam publicly announced that it had revised internal projections of both its market share and total debt load over the next three years. Worldscam projected that its market share would remain flat through 2005 and that its total debt would peak at somewhere between $3.5 billion and $4.0 billion in late 2003. The market trading price of the debentures that had been sold pursuant to the March 2002 registration statement fell again in price, this time to 70% of par.

Worldscam was indicted for fraudulent billing of federal government contracts on July 15, 2002 and filed for protection under Section 11 of the bankruptcy code on August 1, 2002. By September 1, 2002, the debentures were trading at 50% of par.

Mike Lerooch, a plaintiffs' attorney, filed a class action on September 2, 2002 on behalf of purchasers of the debentures against Worldscam, its directors and senior officers, and its underwriters. The complaint included claims under both Section 11 and Section 12(a)(2) of the Securities Act.

(a) Are any of these facts potentially actionable under Section 12(a)(2) but not under Section 11? Why or why not?

(b) Are the two forward-looking statements in the registration statement and prospectus protected by a safe harbor under Section 11? Under Section 12(a)(2)?

(c) Can all of the defendants named in the complaint be sued under Section 11? Under Section 12(a)(2)?

(d) If the plaintiffs are successful, how are damages likely to be calculated under Section 11? Under Section 12(a)(2)?

## B. SECTION 17(a): FRAUD IN THE OFFER OR SALE OF SECURITIES

Section 17(a) prohibits fraud in the offer or sale of securities. We begin with a general consideration of Section 17(a), which is frequently invoked by both the SEC and the DOJ. We then consider the (non)existence of an implied private action under the Section.

### *1. In General*

Section 17(a) of the Securities Act provides as follows:

> It shall be unlawful for any person in the offer or sale of any securities by ... the use of any means or instruments of transportation or communication in interstate commerce or by the use of the mails, directly or indirectly—
>
> (1) to employ any device, scheme, or artifice to defraud, or
>
> (2) to obtain money or property by means of any untrue statement of a material fact or any omission to state a material fact necessary in order to make the statements made, in the light of the circumstances under which they were made, not misleading, or
>
> (3) to engage in any transaction, practice, or course of business which operates or would operate as a fraud or deceit upon the purchaser.

The similarity between Section 17(a) and Rule 10b-5 is no accident. When drafting Rule 10b-5 in 1942, the SEC used Section 17(a) as a model.

In the decision that follows, the Supreme Court addressed whether Section 17(a) requires proof of scienter.

### AARON v. SEC
446 U.S. 680 (1980)

JUSTICE STEWART:

*** We granted certiorari to resolve the conflict in the federal courts as to whether the Commission is required to establish scienter—an intent on the part of the defendant to deceive, manipulate, or defraud [5]—as an element of a Commission enforcement action to enjoin violations of § 17(a), § 10(b), and Rule 10b-5. ***

[*The Court held that the SEC must prove scienter under Rule 10b-5*].

*** The language of Section 17(a) strongly suggests that Congress contemplated a scienter requirement under § 17(a)(1), but not under § 17(a)(2) or § 17(a)(3). The language of § 17(a)(1), which makes it unlawful "to employ

5. The term "scienter" is used throughout this opinion, as it was in *Ernst & Ernst v. Hochfelder*, 425 U.S. 185, 194, n. 12 (1976), to refer to "a mental state embracing intent to deceive, manipulate, or defraud." We have no occasion here to address the question, reserved in *Hochfelder*, ibid., whether, under some circumstances, scienter may also include reckless behavior.

any device, scheme, or artifice to defraud," plainly evinces an intent on the part of Congress to proscribe only knowing or intentional misconduct. Even if it be assumed that the term "defraud" is ambiguous, given its varied meanings at law and in equity, the terms "device," "scheme," and "artifice" all connote knowing or intentional practices.[13] Indeed, the term "device," which also appears in § 10(b), figured prominently in the Court's conclusion in *Hochfelder* that the plain meaning of Section 10(b) embraces a scienter requirement.

By contrast, the language of § 17(a)(2), which prohibits any person from obtaining money or property "by means of any untrue statement of a material fact or any omission to state a material fact," is devoid of any suggestion whatsoever of a scienter requirement. As a well-known commentator has noted, "[t]here is nothing on the face of Clause (2) itself which smacks of *scienter* or intent to defraud." 3 L. Loss, Securities Regulation 1442 (2d ed. 1961). In fact, this Court in *Hochfelder* pointed out that the similar language of Rule 10b-5(b) "could be read as proscribing ... any type of material misstatement or omission ... that has the effect of defrauding investors, whether the wrongdoing was intentional or not." 425 U.S., at 212.

Finally, the language of § 17(a)(3), under which it is unlawful for any person "to engage in any transaction, practice, or course of business which *operates* or *would operate* as a fraud or deceit," (emphasis added) quite plainly focuses upon the *effect* of particular conduct on members of the investing public, rather than upon the culpability of the person responsible. This reading follows directly from *Capital Gains*, which attributed to a similarly worded provision in § 206(2) of the Investment Advisers Act of 1940 a meaning that does not require a "showing [of] deliberate dishonesty as a condition precedent to protecting investors." 375 U.S., at 200.

It is our view, in sum, that the language of § 17(a) requires scienter under § 17(a)(1), but not under § 17(a)(2) or § 17(a)(3). Although the parties have urged the Court to adopt a uniform culpability requirement for the three subparagraphs of § 17(a), the language of the section is simply not amenable to such an interpretation. *** Indeed, since Congress drafted § 17(a) in such a manner as to compel the conclusion that scienter is required under one subparagraph but not under the other two, it would take a very clear expression in the legislative history of congressional intent to the contrary to justify the conclusion that the statute does not mean what it so plainly seems to say. ***

### *NOTES AND QUESTIONS*

*1. **The Scienter Question.*** The Court held that the Commission must prove scienter when proceeding under Section 10(b) of the Exchange Act and Rule 10b-5, but not under Sections 17(a)(2) and (3) of the Securities Act. Yet the

13. Webster's International Dictionary (2d ed. 1934) defines (1) "device" as "[t]hat which is devised, or formed by design; a contrivance; an invention; project; scheme; often, a scheme to deceive; a stratagem; an artifice," (2) "scheme" as "[a] plan or program of something to be done; an enterprise; a project; as, a business scheme[, or] [a] crafty, unethical project," and (3) "artifice" as a "[c]rafty device; trickery; also, an artful stratagem or trick; artfulness; ingeniousness."

latter provisions are almost identical to Rule 10b-5 (and, along with Section 17(a)(1), served as the model for drafting Rule 10b-5). How can virtually identical language give rise to such a sharp difference with respect to the scienter requirement?

*2. Broad Scope.* Section 17(a) is not limited to initial offerings of securities, despite the fact that such offerings are the principal focus of the Securities Act. As the Supreme Court explained in *United States v. Naftalin,* 441 U.S. 768 (1979):

> Although it is true that the 1933 Act was primarily concerned with the regulation of new offerings, *** the antifraud prohibition of § 17(a) was meant as a major departure from that limitation. Unlike much of the rest of the act, it was intended to cover any fraudulent scheme in an offer or sale of securities, whether in the course of an initial distribution or in the course of ordinary market trading. This is made abundantly clear both by the statutory language, which makes no distinctions between the two kinds of transactions, and by the Senate Report ***. Respondent is undoubtedly correct that the two Acts prohibit some of the same conduct. But "[t]he fact that there may well be some overlap is neither unusual nor unfortunate." *SEC v. National Securities, Inc.,* 393 U.S., at 468.

Id. at 777-78 (applying Section 17(a) to a customer who defrauded his broker through a short-selling scheme).

*3. Powerful Weapon for the Government.* Section 17(a) provides the SEC with a powerful litigation weapon. Not only can liability be imposed on someone who was merely careless (under Sections 17(a)(2) and (a)(3)), whether in the context of an initial offering or in secondary market trading. In addition, the material misstatement or omission need not appear in (or be linked to) an official document such as a registration statement or prospectus. Thus, it makes sense for the SEC, whenever it can, to allege violations of Section 17(a) together with violations of Rule 10b-5.

The DOJ likewise makes use of Section 17(a)'s broad scope in bringing criminal securities actions. But unlike the SEC, the DOJ cannot sidestep proof of scienter when proceeding under Section 17(a). The reason lies with Section 24 of the Securities Act, which conditions criminal liability for all Securities Act violations on proof that the defendant acted "willfully." See generally infra Chapter 11.A.1.

### *2. The (Non)Existence of An Implied Private Action*

Section 17(a) says nothing about a private action. The Supreme Court has reserved the question of whether to recognize a private action by implication. See *Herman & MacLean v. Huddleston,* 459 U.S. 375, 378 n. 2 (1983); *Int'l Bhd. of Teamsters v. Daniel,* 439 U.S. 551, 557 n. 9 (1979). The consensus among the lower federal courts, however, is that Section 17(a) should be available to the government only. Consider the following decision.

## MALDONADO v. DOMINGUEZ

137 F.3d 1 (1st Cir. 1998)

TORRUELLA, CHIEF JUDGE:

Plaintiffs invested in and became directors of a corporation called the Puerto Rico International Bank ("PRIBANK"), which was designed to create huge profits for its investor-directors by leveraging its collateral with low interest loans in order to purchase higher interest mortgage obligations. When PRIBANK failed, the plaintiffs brought this suit, claiming that the investment bankers marketing the PRIBANK stock defrauded them by failing to mention the possibility that PRIBANK's securities would be "called" in the event of an interest rate adjustment. The investors filed this suit under sections 12(2) and 17(a) of the Securities Act of 1933, as well as section 10(b) of the Securities Act of 1934, and Rule 10(b)(5) ***. The district court dismissed all of these claims on a motion to dismiss. We affirm. ***

*Section 17(a) of the 1933 Act*

*** Courts and law enforcement agencies have the authority to enforce section 17(a) of the 1933 Act via injunction and criminal prosecution. However, for years circuit courts have struggled with the question of whether an implied private right of action to enforce section 17(a) also exists. The Supreme Court has never answered the question. ***

This issue has caused confusion because, while neither the language nor the history of section 17(a) clearly indicates a congressional intent to create a private right of action, see *Newcome v. Esrey*, 862 F.2d 1099, 1103-07 (4th Cir.1988), section 10(b) of the 1934 Act—with substantially similar language—has always been interpreted to provide for a private right of action. See *Herman & MacLean v. Huddleston*, 459 U.S. 375, 385-87 (1983) (expressly interpreting section 10(b)'s private right of action as consistent with securities laws' "broad remedial purposes"). While some courts did not find the requisite congressional intent to infer a private right of action from section 17(a), see *Touche Ross & Co. v. Redington*, 442 U.S. 560, 574-76 (1979) (legislative intent is the primary factor to consider when addressing whether a private right of action exists), other circuits found no meaningful distinction between section 17(a) and section 10(b). Compare *Daniel v. Teamsters*, 561 F.2d 1223, 1244-46 (7th Cir.1977) (holding that a private right of action exists), and *SEC v. Texas Gulf Sulphur Co.*, 401 F.2d 833, 867 (2d Cir.1968) (Friendly, J., concurring) (same), with *Landry v. All American Assur. Co.*, 688 F.2d 381, 384-91 (5th Cir.1982) (holding that no private right of action exists), and *Stephenson v. Calpine Conifers II, Ltd.*, 652 F.2d 808, 815 (9th Cir.1981) (same).

However, in *Aaron v. SEC*, 446 U.S. 680, 695-97 (1980), the Supreme Court held that, unlike section 10(b) of the Exchange Act, section 17(a) of the Securities Act does not require proof of scienter. Thus, while the implied cause of action under 10(b) would expose only the deceitful to private causes of action, an implied cause of action under 17(a) would impose such liability on merely negligent wrongdoers. Furthermore, the Court had ruled four years earlier that a judicially created cause of action, such as the one implied under section 10(b), could not be extended to actions premised on negligent wrongdoing. See *Ernst & Ernst v. Hochfelder*, 425 U.S. 185, 210 (1976).

*Aaron* and *Ernst* highlighted for courts a significant distinction between implying private causes of action under the two sections. While the 10(b) implied cause of action has continued to enjoy unanimous recognition and the imprimatur of a unanimous Supreme Court in *Huddleston*, the 17(a) cause of action has been held up to renewed scrutiny. In recent years, every circuit to have addressed the issue has refused to recognize a private right of action under section 17(a), including four circuits which originally had held otherwise. We now come to the same conclusion.

In determining whether an implied private right of action exists in a statute, we look to congressional intent, see *Touche Ross*, 442 U.S. at 574-76, keeping in mind that there is a strong presumption against such inferences. In this case, we do not find sufficient evidence of congressional intent to overcome the presumption. As the district court observed, Congress *explicitly* provided for private causes of action in sections 11 and 12 of the 1933 Act. While the fact that other provisions of a complex statutory scheme create express remedies does not in itself prove that Congress did not imply a private remedy in another section, see *Cannon v. University of Chicago*, 441 U.S. 677, 690 n. 13 (1979), where the explicit remedies in the same statute address much of the same conduct and benefit the same parties as a potential implied private cause of action, the circumstances militate against that inference. Furthermore, the legislative history of section 17(a) does not, on the whole, favor an implied private right of action. See *Newcome*, 862 F.2d at 1103-07 (conducting an in-depth examination of the legislative history of this provision). Therefore, the district court did not err in dismissing the plaintiffs' claim under section 17(a) of the 1933 Act. ***

### *NOTES AND QUESTIONS*

*1. **Result-Oriented Reasoning?*** The Court asserts that *Hochfelder* held that "a judicially created cause of action, such as the one implied under section 10(b), could not be extended to actions premised on negligent wrongdoing." Is this an accurate characterization of *Hochfelder*?

Does the court refuse to recognize an implied private action under Section 17(a) based on *Aaron's* rejection of a scienter requirement for some Section 17(a) actions and *Hochfelder*'s imposition of a scienter requirement for the implied private action under Rule 10b-5? Do these two issues—the existence of an implied private action and the existence of a scienter requirement—have anything to do with each other? Is this decision an example of result-oriented reasoning?

***2. The Impact of* Gustafson.** Recall that prior to the Supreme Court's *Gustafson* decision, Section 12(a)(2) was widely considered applicable to private offerings as well as to secondary trading. Thus, most of the decisions cited by *Maldonado* were issued at a time when Sections 12(a)(2) and 17(a) encompassed many of the same types of transactions, thereby making recognition of an implied action under Section 17(a) arguably unnecessary. After *Gustafson*, however, this argument loses much of its force, a fact not acknowledged (or perhaps not even recognized) by *Maldonado*.

Is it likely that Congress would have left purchasers in private offerings and secondary markets without a private action for material misstatements and omissions under the Securities Act? If *Gustafson* was rightly decided, does it follow that the courts are now wrong in refusing to recognize a private action under Section 17(a)? Alternatively, should courts recognize an implied private action under Section 17(a) in order to right the wrong of *Gustafson* (assuming that the decision constitutes a wrong)? Or should the task of restoring a private action under the Securities Act for private offering and secondary market purchasers be left to Congress? Is a private action needed, given the availability of the implied private action under Rule 10b-5? In considering this question, recall from Chapter 2 the many obstacles that a Rule 10b-5 plaintiff must face.

# Chapter 4

# PROXY FRAUD—SECTION 14(a) OF THE EXCHANGE ACT AND RULE 14a-9

Shareholders in public corporations typically vote by proxy when electing directors or approving mergers or other corporate transactions. Section 14(a) and Rule 14a-9 help to protect the integrity of shareholder decision-making on these matters.

Consider first Section 14(a), which gives the SEC a broad mandate to adopt rules bearing on the solicitation of proxies:

> It shall be unlawful for any person, by the use of the mails or by any means or instrumentality of interstate commerce or of any facility of a national securities exchange or otherwise, in contravention of such rules and regulations as the Commission may prescribe as necessary or appropriate in the public interest or for the protection of investors, to solicit or to permit the use of his name to solicit any proxy or consent or authorization in respect of any security (other than an exempted security) registered pursuant to section 12 of this title.

SEC rules adopted pursuant to this mandate require (among other things) that shareholders receive, in conjunction with a proxy solicitation, a "proxy statement" disclosing specified information about the matter as to which their votes are sought. SEC rules also allow shareholders who satisfy explicit criteria to submit proposals for inclusion in management's proxy statement. See generally Jill E. Fisch, From Legitimacy to Logic: Reconstructing Proxy Regulation, 46 Vand. L. Rev. 1129 (1993). On the other hand, it is state law that determines the matters on which shareholders are entitled to vote and the percentage of shares necessary to approve each of those matters.

Among the rules adopted by the SEC under Section 14(a) is Rule 14a-9, which prohibits material omissions or misrepresentations in proxy solicitations:

> (a) No solicitation subject to this regulation shall be made by means of any proxy statement, form of proxy, notice of meeting or other communication, written or oral, containing any statement which, at the time and in the light of the circumstances under which it is made, is false or misleading with respect to any material fact, or which omits to state any material fact necessary in order to make the statements therein not false or misleading or necessary to correct any statement in any earlier communication with respect to the solicitation of a proxy for the same meeting or subject matter which has become false or misleading.

While nothing in the Rule (or Section 14(a)) authorizes private enforcement, the Supreme Court held in *J. I. Case Co. v. Borak*, 377 U.S. 426 (1964), that a private action under the Rule exists by implication.

As is no doubt becoming obvious, Rule 14a-9 resembles Rule 10b-5 in several critical respects. Like Rule 10b-5, Rule 14a-9 bars material omissions and misrepresentations and has given rise to a judicially created private action. Moreover, like Rule 10b-5, Rule 14a-9 can be enforced not only in private actions (of either the individual or class variety) but also in SEC and criminal actions. Finally, like Rule 10b-5, Rule 14a-9 has been construed primarily by the courts rather than by the Commission.

Yet Rule 14a-9 and Rule 10b-5 likewise have several very important differences. First, Rule 10b-5 applies regardless of the size of the corporation that has issued the securities, whereas Rule 14a-9 applies only to Section 12 companies.(For a discussion of Section 12 companies, see supra Chapter 1.A.2.c). Second, Rule 10b-5 applies when investors buy or sell securities, whereas Rule 14a-9 applies when their proxies are solicited, regardless of whether they (or others) are engaged in securities trading at the time. A third difference between Rules 10b-5 and 14a-9 involves the form that enforcement is likely to take. While SEC and criminal actions are relatively commonplace under Rule 10b-5, they are quite rare under Rule 14a-9. Hence, to a far greater degree than with Rule 10b-5, the enforcement of Rule 14a-9 falls largely to investors.

The evolution of Rule 14a-9 has been enormously affected by that of Rule 10b-5 (and to some extent vice versa). Thus, judicial hostility to private Rule 10b-5 actions appears to have aggravated judicial hostility to private Rule 14a-9 actions. See, e.g, *Virginia Bankshares, Inc. v Sandberg,* 501 U.S. 1083, 1105 (1991) (evaluating the threat of vexatious Rule 14a-9 litigation by analogizing to the threat of such litigation under Rule 10b-5).

Moreover, the Private Securities Litigation Reform Act (PSLRA), aimed primarily at Rule 10b-5, has enveloped Rule 14a-9 as well. Thus, like private Rule 10b-5 actions, private Rule 14a-9 actions are subject to Exchange Act provisions that authorize a safe harbor for misleading forward-looking statements (Section 21E); require the plaintiff to establish loss causation when seeking money damages (Section 21D(b)(4)); create a scheme of proportionate liability (Section 21D(f)); and stiffen pleading requirements (Section 21D(b)). In addition, Rule 14a-9 class actions must comply with PSLRA class action provisions that you will encounter in Chapter 6.

This Chapter examines the elements of Rule 14a-9 with emphasis on the implied private action. We begin with judicial recognition of the implied private action (Section A) and then address the requirements of materiality (Section B), state of mind (Section C), and causation (Section D). Later chapters draw upon these elements in connection with class actions (Chapter 6); SEC enforcement (Chapter 9); and criminal enforcement (Chapter 11).

As you consider Section 14(a) and Rule 14a-9, think about the following questions. Should courts draw sharper distinctions between Rule 14a-9 and Rule 10b-5 than they do at present? To what extent is judicial interpretation of Rule 14a-9 affected by fear of the possible impact on Rule 10b-5, even if that fear is not stated explicitly? When interpreting Rule 14a-9, what weight (if any) should be given to the fact that investors are the Rule's principal enforcers? What accounts for the seeming lack of interest in Rule 14a-9 on the part of the SEC and the Department of Justice (DOJ)?

## A. JUDICIAL RECOGNITION OF THE IMPLIED PRIVATE ACTION

In the landmark decision that follows, the Supreme Court recognized an implied private action for violations of Rule 14a-9.

### J. I. CASE COMPANY v. BORAK

377 U.S. 426 (1964)

JUSTICE CLARK:

This is a civil action brought by respondent, a stockholder of petitioner J. I. Case Company, charging deprivation of the pre-emptive rights of respondent and other shareholders by reason of a merger between Case and the American Tractor Corporation. It is alleged that the merger was effected through the circulation of a false and misleading proxy statement by those proposing the merger. The complaint was in two counts, the first based on diversity and claiming a breach of the directors' fiduciary duty to the stockholders. The second count alleged a violation of §14(a) of the Securities Exchange Act of 1934 with reference to the proxy solicitation material. The trial court held that as to this count it had no power to redress the alleged violations of the Act but was limited solely to the granting of declaratory relief thereon under § 27 of the Act.[2] The court held Wis. Stat. 1961, § 180.405(4), which requires posting security for expenses in derivative actions, applicable to both counts, except that portion of Count 2 requesting declaratory relief. It ordered the respondent to furnish a bond in the amount of $75,000 thereunder and, upon his failure to do so, dismissed the complaint, save that part of Count 2 seeking a declaratory judgment. On interlocutory appeal the Court of Appeals reversed on both counts, holding that the District Court had the power to grant remedial relief and that the Wisconsin statute was not applicable. *** We consider only the question of whether § 27 of the Act authorizes a federal cause of action for rescission or damages to a corporate stockholder with respect to a consummated merger which was authorized pursuant to the use of a proxy statement alleged to contain false and misleading statements violative of § 14(a) of the Act. ***

I.

Respondent, the owner of 2000 shares of common stock of Case acquired prior to the merger, brought this suit based on diversity jurisdiction seeking to enjoin a proposed merger between Case and the American Tractor Corporation (ATC). *** The injunction was denied and the merger was thereafter consum-

---

2. Section 27 of the Act provides in part:

> The district courts of the United States, the Supreme Court of the District of Columbia, and the United States courts of any territory or other place subject to the jurisdiction of the United States shall have exclusive jurisdiction of violations of this title or the rules and regulations thereunder, and of all suits in equity and actions at law brought to enforce any liability or duty created by this title or the rules and regulations thereunder. Any criminal proceeding may be brought in the district wherein any act or transaction constituting the violation occurred. Any suit or action to enforce any liability or duty created by this title or rules and regulations thereunder, or to enjoin any violation of such title or rules and regulations, may be brought in any such district or in the district wherein the defendant is found or is an inhabitant or transacts business, and process in such cases may be served in any other district of which the defendant is an inhabitant or wherever the defendant may be found.

mated. *** The claims pertinent to the asserted violation of the Securities Exchange Act were predicated on diversity jurisdiction as well as on § 27 of the Act. They alleged: that petitioners, or their predecessors, solicited or permitted their names to be used in the solicitation of proxies of Case stockholders for use at a special stockholders' meeting at which the proposed merger with ATC was to be voted upon; that the proxy solicitation material so circulated was false and misleading in violation of § 14(a) of the Act and Rule 14a-9 *** ; that the merger was approved at the meeting by a small margin of votes and was thereafter consummated; that the merger would not have been approved but for the false and misleading statements in the proxy solicitation material; and that Case stockholders were damaged thereby. The respondent sought judgment holding the merger void and damages for himself and all other stockholders similarly situated, as well as such further relief "as equity shall require." ***

II.

It appears clear that private parties have a right under § 27 to bring suit for violation of § 14(a) of the Act. Indeed, this section specifically grants the appropriate District Courts jurisdiction over "all suits in equity and actions at law brought to enforce any liability or duty created" under the Act. The petitioners make no concessions, however, emphasizing that Congress made no specific reference to a private right of action in § 14(a); that, in any event, the right would not extend to derivative suits and should be limited to prospective relief only. In addition, some of the petitioners argue that the merger can be dissolved only if it was fraudulent or non-beneficial, issues upon which the proxy material would not bear. But the causal relationship of the proxy material and the merger are questions of fact to be resolved at trial, not here. We therefore do not discuss this point further.

III.

While the respondent contends that his Count 2 claim is not a derivative one, we need not embrace that view, for we believe that a right of action exists as to both derivative and direct causes.

The purpose of § 14(a) is to prevent management or others from obtaining authorization for corporate action by means of deceptive or inadequate disclosure in proxy solicitation. The section stemmed from the congressional belief that "[f]air corporate suffrage is an important right that should attach to every equity security bought on a public exchange." H.R.Rep. No. 1383, 73d Cong., 2d Sess., 13. It was intended to "control the conditions under which proxies may be solicited with a view to preventing the recurrence of abuses which ... [had] frustrated the free exercise of the voting rights of stockholders." Id., at 14. "Too often proxies are solicited without explanation to the stockholder of the real nature of the questions for which authority to cast his vote is sought." S. Rep. No.792, 73d Cong., 2d Sess., 12. These broad remedial purposes are evidenced in the language of the section which makes it "unlawful for any person ... to solicit or to permit the use of his name to solicit any proxy or consent or authorization in respect of any security ... registered on any national securities exchange in contravention of such rules and regulations as the Commission may prescribe as necessary or appropriate in the public interest *or for the protection of investors*." (Italics supplied.) While this language makes no specific reference to a private right of action, among its chief purposes is "the protection of investors," which certainly implies the availability of judicial relief where necessary to achieve that result.

The injury which a stockholder suffers from corporate action pursuant to a deceptive proxy solicitation ordinarily flows from the damage done the corporation, rather than from the damage inflicted directly upon the stockholder. The damage suffered results not from the deceit practiced on him alone but rather from the deceit practiced on the stockholders as a group. To hold that derivative actions are not within the sweep of the section would therefore be tantamount to a denial of private relief. Private enforcement of the proxy rules provides a necessary supplement to Commission action. As in anti-trust treble damage litigation, the possibility of civil damages or injunctive relief serves as a most effective weapon in the enforcement of the proxy requirements. The Commission advises that it examines over 2,000 proxy statements annually and each of them must necessarily be expedited. Time does not permit an independent examination of the facts set out in the proxy material and this results in the Commission's acceptance of the representations contained therein at their face value, unless contrary to other material on file with it. Indeed, on the allegations of respondent's complaint, the proxy material failed to disclose alleged unlawful market manipulation of the stock of ATC, and this unlawful manipulation would not have been apparent to the Commission until after the merger.

We, therefore, believe that under the circumstances here it is the duty of the courts to be alert to provide such remedies as are necessary to make effective the congressional purpose. As was said in *Sola Electric Co. v. Jefferson Electric Co.*, 317 U.S. 173, 176 (1942):

> When a federal statute condemns an act as unlawful, the extent and nature of the legal consequences of the condemnation, though left by the statute to judicial determination, are nevertheless federal questions, the answers to which are to be derived from the statute and the federal policy which it has adopted.

It is for the federal courts "to adjust their remedies so as to grant the necessary relief" where federally secured rights are invaded. "And it is also well settled that where legal rights have been invaded, and a federal statute provides for a general right to sue for such invasion, federal courts may use any available remedy to make good the wrong done." *Bell v. Hood*, 327 U.S. 678, 684 (1946). Section 27 grants the District Courts jurisdiction "of all suits in equity and actions at law brought to enforce any liability or duty created by this title...." In passing on almost identical language found in the Securities Act of 1933, the Court found the words entirely sufficient to fashion a remedy to rescind a fraudulent sale, secure restitution and even to enforce the right to restitution against a third party holding assets of the vendor. *Deckert v. Independence Shares Corp.*, 311 U.S. 282 (1940). This significant language was used:

> The power *to enforce* implies the power to make effective the right of recovery afforded by the Act. And the power to make the right of recovery effective implies the power to utilize any of the procedures or actions normally available to the litigant according to the exigencies of the particular case. At 288 of 311 U.S.

Nor do we find merit in the contention that such remedies are limited to prospective relief. This was the position taken in *Dann v. Studebaker-Packard Corp.*, 6 Cir., 288 F.2d 201, where it was held that the "preponderance of questions of state law which would have to be interpreted and applied in order to grant the relief sought ... is so great that the federal question involved ... is really negligible in comparison." At 214. But we believe that the overriding federal law applicable here would, where the facts required, control the appropriateness of redress despite the provisions of state corporation law, for it "is not uncommon for federal courts to fashion federal law where federal rights are concerned." *Textile Workers Union of America v. Lincoln Mills*, 353 U.S. 448, 457 (1957). In addition, the fact that questions of state law must be decided does not change the character of the right; it remains federal. As Chief Justice Marshall said in *Osborn v. Bank of United States*, 9 Wheat. 738 (1824):

> If this were sufficient to withdraw a case from the jurisdiction of the federal Courts, almost every case, although involving the construction of a law, would be withdrawn.... At 819-820 of 9 Wheat.

Moreover, if federal jurisdiction were limited to the granting of declaratory relief, victims of deceptive proxy statements would be obliged to go into state courts for remedial relief. And if the law of the State happened to attach no responsibility to the use of misleading proxy statements, the whole purpose of the section might be frustrated. Furthermore, the hurdles that the victim might face (such as separate suits *** , security for expenses statutes, bringing in all parties necessary for complete relief, etc.) might well prove insuperable to effective relief.

IV.

Our finding that federal courts have the power to grant all necessary remedial relief is not to be construed as any indication of what we believe to be the necessary and appropriate relief in this case. We are concerned here only with a determination that federal jurisdiction for this purpose does exist. Whatever remedy is necessary must await the trial on the merits. ***

### *NOTES AND QUESTIONS*

*1.* ***The Advantages of Federal Court.*** Why did Borak prefer to litigate his claims in federal court rather than in state court?

*2.* ***"[B]oth Derivative and Direct."*** The Court observed that "[t]he injury which a stockholder suffers from corporate action pursuant to a deceptive proxy solicitation ordinarily flows from the damage done the corporation, rather than from the damages inflicted directly upon the stockholder." Why then did the Court hold that Borak's action was "both derivative and direct" rather than simply derivative? In what sense was his action direct?

*3.* ***Rationalizing the Implied Private Action.*** The Court offered two grounds for its recognition of an implied private action under Rule 14a-9: (i) Section 27 of the Exchange Act and (ii) the view that a private action "would provide a necessary supplement to Commission action." Years later, when faced with the question of whether to recognize an implied private action under Section 17(a) of the Exchange Act, the Court revisited both of these grounds and disavowed them:

> Section 27 grants jurisdiction to the federal courts and provides for venue and service of process. It creates no cause of action of its own force and effect; it imposes no liabilities. The source of plaintiffs' rights must be found, if at all, in the substantive provisions of the 1934 Act which they seek to enforce, not in the jurisdiction provision. The Court in *Borak* found a private cause of action implicit in Section 14(a). We do not now question the actual holding of that case, but we decline to read the opinion so broadly that virtually every provision of the securities Acts gives rise to an implied private cause of action.
>
> The invocation of the "remedial purposes" of the 1934 Act is similarly unavailing. Only last Term, we emphasized that generalized references to the "remedial purposes" of the 1934 Act will not justify reading a provision "more broadly than its language and the statutory scheme reasonably permit." *SEC v. Sloan,* 436 U.S. 103, 116 (1978). Certainly the mere fact that § 17(a) was designed to provide protection for brokers' customers does not require the implication of a private damages action in their behalf. To the extent our analysis in today's decision differs from that of the Court in *Borak,* it suffices to say that in a series of cases since *Borak* we have adhered to a stricter standard for the implication of private causes of action, and we follow that stricter standard today. The ultimate question is one of congressional intent, not one of whether this Court thinks that it can improve upon the statutory scheme that Congress enacted into law.

*Touche Ross & Co. v. Redington,* 442 U.S. 560, 577-78 (1979). It is sensible for judicial recognition of an implied private action to turn on congressional intent? If Congress intends a private action, why would it fail to create one explicitly?

***4. The Future of the Rule 14a-9 Private Action.*** As the preceding note shows, the Supreme Court has undercut the two grounds set forth in *Borak* for recognizing an implied private action under Rule 14a-9. Does it follow that the Court will eventually disavow the Rule 14a-9 implied private action itself? See generally C. Steven Bradford, The Possible Future of Private Rights of Action for Proxy Fraud: The Parallel Between *Borak* and *Wilko,* 70 Neb. L. Rev. 306 (1991) (answering this question in the affirmative). As you read the Supreme Court (and other) decisions that follow, ask yourself whether there is any indication that the action is at risk.

## B. THE MATERIALITY REQUIREMENT

The Supreme Court addressed the definition of materiality under Rule 14a-9 in *TSC Indus., Inc. v. Northway, Inc.,* 426 U.S. 438 (1976):

> In formulating a standard of materiality under Rule 14a-9, we are guided, of course, by *** the Rule's broad remedial purpose. That purpose is not merely to ensure by judicial means that the transaction, when judged by its real terms, is fair and otherwise adequate, but to ensure disclosures by corporate management in order to enable the shareholders to make an informed choice. *** And particularly in view of the prophylactic purpose of the Rule and the fact that the content of the proxy statement is within management's control, it is appropriate that these doubts be resolved in favor of those the statute is designed to protect.
>
> We are aware, however, that the disclosure policy embodied in the proxy regulations is not without limit. Some information is of such dubious significance that insistence on its disclosure may accomplish more harm than good. The potential liability for a Rule 14a-9 violation can be great indeed, and if the standard of materiality is unnecessarily low, not only may the corporation

> and its management be subjected to liability for insignificant omissions or misstatements, but also management's fear of exposing itself to substantial liability may cause it simply to bury the shareholders in an avalanche of trivial information—a result that is hardly conducive to informed decisionmaking. ***
>
> The general standard of materiality that we think best comports with the policies of Rule 14a-9 is as follows: An omitted fact is material if there is a substantial likelihood that a reasonable shareholder would consider it important in deciding how to vote. *** It does not require proof of a substantial likelihood that disclosure of the omitted fact would have caused the reasonable investor to change his vote. What the standard does contemplate is a showing of a substantial likelihood that, under all the circumstances, the omitted fact would have assumed actual significance in the deliberations of the reasonable investor as having significantly altered the "total mix" of information available. ***

Id. at 448-49. This definition of materiality is apt to sound somewhat familiar to you, since the Supreme Court later adopted it for Rule 10b-5 purposes in *Basic Inc. v. Levinson,* 485 U.S. 224 (1988), which you read in Chapter 2.B.2.

The materiality definition under Rules 14a-9 and 10b-5 may not be altogether co-extensive in application, however. Recall that when a Rule 10b-5 action involves securities traded in an efficient market, the "total mix" of information encompasses information known to the market, regardless of whether it was also known to the shareholder bringing the action. See supra Chapter 2.B.1. With this background in mind, consider *United Paperworkers Int'l Union v. Int'l Paper Co.,* 985 F.2d 1190 (2d Cir. 1993). In *United Paperworkers*, shareholders claimed that management had violated Rule 14a-9 with its response to a shareholder proposal that urged the company to adopt certain environmental policies. Management's response to the shareholder proposal had presented the company's environmental record in a positive light, failing to state that the company had pled guilty to various environmental felonies, was a defendant in numerous pending environmental actions, and had been barred from doing business with the government because of its environmental transgressions. At issue was whether, in assessing the materiality of these alleged omissions and misrepresentations, the "total mix" of information should include news reports as well as disclosures made in the company's 10-K report filed with the SEC. The Second Circuit ruled as follows:

> Corporate documents that have not been distributed to the shareholders entitled to vote on the proposal should rarely be considered part of the total mix of information reasonably available to those shareholders.
>
> *** [W]hen the subject of a proxy solicitation has been widely reported in readily available media, shareholders may be deemed to have constructive notice of the facts reported, and the court may take this into consideration in determining whether representations in or omissions from the proxy statement are materially misleading. However, the mere presence in the media of sporadic news reports does not give shareholders sufficient notice that proxy solicitation statements sent directly to them by the company may be misleading, and such reports should not be considered to be part of the total mix of information that would clarify or place in proper context the company's representations in its proxy materials.
>
> In the present case, the district court properly rejected Paper Co.'s contention that public press reports and its 10-K Report should be viewed as

> part of the total mix of information reasonably available to shareholders. Though the Company argued that news articles should be considered, the articles were few in number, narrow in focus, and remote in time. ***
>
> Nor was the Company's 10-K Report part of the reasonably available mix. That report was filed with the SEC, not distributed to shareholders. Nothing in any of the documents sent to shareholders highlighted the 10-K Report. ***

Id. at 1199. See *Koppel v. 4987 Corp.*, 167 F.3d 125, 132 (2d Cir. 1999) (finding that the "total mix" did not include a document that the proxy solicitation indicated was available in a specified New York City office partly because of "[t]he difficulty of obtaining the *** [document]—particularly for those *** who do not live in New York City" but noting that even if the document were considered, the conclusion as to materiality would remain unchanged). But cf. *In re Browning-Ferris Indus., Inc. Shareholder Derivative Litig.*, 830 F. Supp. 361, 367 n.2 (S. D. Tex. 1993) (holding that the plaintiffs' Rule 14a-9 claims were barred, among other things, by disclosures in 10-K reports), aff'd mem. sub. nom. *Cohen v. Ruckelshaus*, 20 F.3d 465 (5th Cir. 1994).

### *NOTES AND QUESTIONS*

***1. 10-K Reports and the "Total Mix."*** Do you agree that the 10-K report in *United Paperworkers* should have been excluded from the "total mix"? Note the court's suggestion that in unusual circumstances, the total mix could embrace corporate documents that had not been mailed to shareholders. What might such unusual circumstances be?

***2. News Reports and the "Total Mix."*** In *United Paperworkers*, does the court suggest that it would sooner classify news reports than 10-K reports as part of the "total mix"? If so, is this distinction sound?

***3. Puffery Revisited.*** Recall the puffery doctrine that you encountered in connection with materiality under Rule 10b-5. See note 3 on page 66. Is that doctrine applicable to Rule 14a-9?

## C. THE STATE OF MIND REQUIREMENT

In an influential opinion written by Judge Friendly, the Second Circuit contrasted Rule 14a-9 and Rule 10b-5 with respect to the state of mind requirement. The court concluded that even though negligence does not suffice under Rule 10b-5, it does suffice under Rule 14a-9:

> Although the language of Rule 14a-9(a) closely parallels that of Rule 10b-5, and neither says in so many words that scienter should be a requirement, one of the primary reasons that this court has held that this is required in a private action under Rule 10b-5 is a concern that without some such requirement the Rule might be invalid as exceeding the Commission's authority under section 10(b) to regulate "manipulation or deceptive devices." In contrast, the scope of the rulemaking authority granted under section 14(a) is broad, extending to all proxy regulation "necessary or appropriate in the public interest or for the protection of investors" and not limited by any words connoting fraud or deception. This language suggests that rather than emphasizing the prohibition of fraudulent conduct on the part of insiders to a securities transaction, as we think section 10(b) does, in section 14(a) Congress was somewhat more concerned with protection of the outsider whose proxy is being solicited. *** We note also that while an open-ended reading of Rule 10b-5 would render the

express civil liability provisions of the securities acts largely superfluous, *** a reading of Rule 14a-9 as imposing liability without scienter in a case like the present is completely compatible with the statutory scheme.[18]

Although this does not mean that scienter should never be required in an action under Rule 14a-9, a number of considerations persuade us that it would be inappropriate to require plaintiffs to prove it in the context of this case. First, many 10b-5 cases relate to statements issued by corporations, without legal obligation to do so, as a result of what the SEC has properly called "a commendable and growing recognition on the part of industry and the investment community of the importance of informing security holders and the public generally with respect to important business and financial developments." Securities Act Release No. 3844 (Oct. 8, 1957). Imposition of too liberal a standard with respect to culpability would deter this, particularly in light of the almost unlimited liability that may result. Such considerations do not apply to a proxy statement required by the Proxy Rules, especially to one, like that in the present case, which serves many of the same functions as a registration statement. Rather, a broad standard of culpability here will serve to reinforce the high duty of care owed by a controlling corporation to minority shareholders in the preparation of a proxy statement seeking their acquiescence in this sort of transaction, a consideration which is particularly relevant since liability in this case is limited to the stockholders whose proxies were solicited. While "privity" is not required for most actions under the securities laws, its existence may bear heavily on the appropriate standard of culpability.

Furthermore, the common law itself finds negligence sufficient for tort liability where a person supplies false information to another with the intent to influence a transaction in which he has a pecuniary interest. This is particularly so when the transaction redounded directly to the benefit of the defendant, in which case the common law would provide the remedies of rescission and restitution without proof of scienter. It is unlikely that section 14(a) and Rule 14a-9 contemplated less.

*Gerstle v. Gamble-Skogmo, Inc.*, 478 F.2d 1281, 1299-1300 (2d Cir. 1973). See *Wilson v. Great Am. Indus., Inc.*, 855 F.2d 987, 995 (2d Cir. 1988) (applying *Gerstle* to inside directors).

*Gerstle* notwithstanding, considerable uncertainty remains with respect to the state of mind applicable to Rule 14a-9 actions (i) that seek equitable relief; (ii) that are brought against accountants or other outside professionals; and (iii) that involve omitted or misrepresented opinions, beliefs, or reasons.

---

18. It has been argued that imposing liability for negligent misrepresentations or omissions under Rule 14a-9 would be inconsistent with the congressional intent in enacting section 18 of the 1934 Act, which expressly creates liability in a private civil action for making materially false or misleading statements in any document filed with the Commission but provides that no liability shall be imposed if the defendant "acted in good faith and had no knowledge that such statement was false and misleading." But section 18 applies broadly to any document filed with the Commission, whereas section 14 was specifically directed at proxy regulation. Moreover, most of the documents within the scope of section 18 are not distributed to stockholders for the purpose of inducing action; we see nothing anomalous about applying a different standard of culpability in actions concerning misrepresentations in proxy statements which are so distributed than in those involving reports which were merely filed with the Commission. ***

(i) *Actions Seeking Equitable Relief.* The Third Circuit has held that when the plaintiff seeks equitable relief, state of mind is irrelevant: "Whatever may be the rule with respect to scienter when other remedies such as damages or rescission of a sale are sought, we have no hesitancy in recognizing that for prospective relief looking to the protection of the franchise, the test for the purposes of Rule 14a-9 is the objective sufficiency of the disclosure." *Ash v. LFE Corp.*, 525 F.2d 215, 220 (3d Cir. 1975). Other courts, however, grant equitable relief only if the defendant acted negligently. See, e.g., *Capital Real Estate Investors Tax Exempt Fund Ltd. P'ship v. Schwartzberg,* 917 F. Supp. 1050, 1062 (S.D.N.Y. 1996) (preliminary injunction granted).

(ii) *Actions Brought Against Accountants or Other Outside Professionals.* The Sixth Circuit requires scienter in private actions against outside accountants:

> [W]e conclude that scienter should be an element of liability in private suits under the proxy provisions as they apply to outside accountants.
>
> It is not simply a question of statutory interpretation. Federal courts created the private right of action under section 14, and they have a special responsibility to consider the consequences of their rulings and to mold liability fairly to reflect the circumstances of the parties. Although we are not called on in this case to decide the standard of liability of the corporate issuer of proxy material, we are influenced by the fact that the accountant here, unlike the corporate issuer, does not directly benefit from the proxy vote and is not in privity with the stockholder. Unlike the corporate issuer, the preparation of financial statements to be appended to proxies and other reports is the daily fare of accountants, and the accountant's potential liability for relatively minor mistakes would be enormous under a negligence standard.

*Adams v. Standard Knitting Mills, Inc.*, 623 F.2d 422, 428 (6th Cir. 1980). But the Third Circuit has rejected scienter in a private action against an investment banker: "[S]ince an investment banker rendering a fairness opinion in connection with a leveraged buyout knows full well that it will be used to solicit shareholder approval, and is well paid for the service it performs, we see no compelling reason for not holding it to the same standard of liability as the management it is assisting." *Herskowitz v. Nutri/System, Inc.*, 857 F.2d 179, 190 (3d Cir. 1988).

*(iii) Actions Involving Omitted or Misrepresented Opinions, Beliefs, or Reasons.* In *Virginia Bankshares, Inc. v. Sandberg,* 501 U.S. 1083, 1095 (1991), the Supreme Court held that opinions, beliefs, or reasons constitute facts which, when misrepresented or omitted, are actionable under Rule 14a-9. Some courts and commentators have inferred from *Virginia Bankshares* that at least when an opinion, reason, or belief is at issue, liability under Rule 14a-9 requires more than negligence. See, e.g., *In re Reliance Sec. Litig.*, 135 F. Supp.2d 480, 515 (D.Del. 2001) (concluding that after *Virginia Bankshares,* liability for a misleading opinion requires that the defendants act "recklessly or intentionally"); Marc I. Steinberg & William A. Reece, The Supreme Court, Implied Rights of Action, and Proxy Regulation, 54 Ohio St. L. J. 67, 92-93 (1993) (concluding from *Virginia Bankshares* that "the culpability level [under Rule 14a-9] may no longer be simple negligence, at least in certain instances"). As you read the following excerpt from *Virginia Bankshares,* decide whether you agree:

> *** We consider first the actionability *per se* of statements of reasons, opinions, or belief. Because such a statement by definition purports to express what is consciously on the speaker's mind, we interpret the jury verdict as finding that the directors' statements of belief and opinion were made with knowledge that the directors did not hold the beliefs or opinions expressed, and we confirm our discussion to statements so made.[5] That such statements may be materially significant raises no serious question. ***
>
> *** Provable facts either furnish good reasons to make a conclusory commercial judgment, or they count against it, and expressions of such judgments can be uttered with knowledge of truth or falsity just like more definite statements, and defended or attacked through the orthodox evidentiary process that either substantiates their underlying justifications or tends to disprove their existence. ***
>
> *** Under § 14(a), then, a plaintiff is permitted to prove a specific statement of reason knowingly false or misleadingly incomplete, even when stated in conclusory terms. ***

Id. at 1090, 1093-94.

Note that the PSLRA has had a several-fold impact on the state of mind requirement in private actions under Rule 14a-9. First, there is the matter of pleading. A plaintiff seeking money damages under the Rule must "state with particularity facts giving rise to a strong inference that the defendant acted with the required state of mind." Exchange Act Section 21D(b)(2). See generally Chapter 2.D.2 (discussing this standard with respect to Rule 10b-5). Second, a plaintiff can prevail on a Rule 14a-9 claim involving a forward-looking statement only by showing that the defendants made the statement with "actual knowledge" of its falsity. See Exchange Act Section 21E(c)(1)(B). See generally Chapter 2.B.3.c (addressing liability for fraudulent forward-looking statements under Rule 10b-5). Finally, the plaintiff can hold the defendants jointly and severally liable only if she shows that they acted "knowingly." In the absence of such proof, their liability is proportionate to their participation in the wrong. See Exchange Act Section 21D(f). See generally Chapter 2.G.2 (addressing proportionate liability as well as joint and several liability in the context of Rule 10b-5).

## *NOTES AND QUESTIONS*

***1. Establishing Negligence.*** "Negligence" for Rule 14a-9 purposes may mean different things to different courts in different contexts. For example, the Second Circuit has stated that "[a]s a matter of law, the preparation of a proxy statement by corporate insiders containing materially false or misleading statements or omitting a material fact is sufficient to satisfy the *Gerstle* negligence standard." *Wilson v. Great Am. Indus., Inc.*, 855 F.2d 987, 995 (2d Cir. 1988). Does this amount to strict liability by another name? On the other hand, one federal district court explained the plaintiffs' failure to establish the negligence of outside directors in the following terms:

---

5. In *TSC Industries, Inc. v. Northway, Inc.*, 426 U.S. 438, 444 n. 7 (1976), we reserved the question whether scienter was necessary for liability generally under § 14(a). We reserve it still.

> Where plaintiffs have not pled that the individual defendants knew of the facts allegedly omitted from the proxy statement (and, not being alleged to have been personally involved in its issuance, therefore, had no duty to see that they were included in the statement), plaintiffs have insufficiently pled a negligence claim.

*Salit v. Stanley Works*, 802 F. Supp. 728, 733 (D. Conn. 1992). Would this in effect amount to a scienter standard in most instances?

***2. Opinions, Reasons, or Beliefs.*** Does *Virginia Bankshares* impose a scienter requirement when the fact allegedly omitted or misrepresented is an opinion, reason, or belief? What would be the rationale for a heightened state of mind requirement under these circumstances?

***3. Uniformity—Virtue or Straightjacket.*** What are the advantages and disadvantages of allowing the state of mind requirement to vary with the circumstances, such as whether the plaintiff has requested equitable relief or has challenged an opinion?

***4. State of Mind and SEC Actions.*** Suppose the Rule 14a-9 plaintiff is the Commission rather than an investor. What impact (if any) should that have on the state of mind requirement?

## D. THE CAUSATION REQUIREMENT

In a private action under Rule 14a-9, must the plaintiff show that the misleading proxy statement caused her injury? The Supreme Court addressed this question in *Mills v. Electric Auto-Lite Co.*, 396 U.S. 375 (1970) and also in *Virginia Bankshares, Inc. v. Sandberg*, 501 U.S. 1083 (1991). *Mills* laid down the basic parameters of Rule 14a-9 causation analysis. *Virginia Bankshares* addressed causation in the situation where management controls enough shares to obtain approval of the transaction, thereby rendering the votes of the public shareholders unnecessary.

### 1. *The Basic Parameters*

The Supreme Court decision that follows is significant not only for its analysis of causation under Rule 14a-9 but also for its analysis of the scope of relief available in private actions under the Rule.

## MILLS v. ELECTRIC AUTO-LITE COMPANY

396 U.S. 375 (1970)

JUSTICE HARLAN:

This case requires us to consider a basic aspect of the implied private right of action for violation of § 14(a) of the Securities Exchange Act of 1934, recognized by this Court in *J. I. Case Co. v. Borak*, 377 U.S. 426 (1964). As in *Borak* the asserted wrong is that a corporate merger was accomplished through the use of a proxy statement that was materially false or misleading. The question with which we deal is what causal relationship must be shown between such a statement and the merger to establish a cause of action based on the violation of the Act.

I

Petitioners were shareholders of the Electric Auto-Lite Company until 1963, when it was merged into Mergenthaler Linotype Company. They brought suit on the day before the shareholders' meeting at which the vote was to take place on the merger against Auto-Lite, Mergenthaler, and a third company, American Manufacturing Company, Inc. The complaint sought an injunction against the voting by Auto-Lite's management of all proxies obtained by means of an allegedly misleading proxy solicitation; however, it did not seek a temporary restraining order, and the voting went ahead as scheduled the following day. Several months later petitioners filed an amended complaint, seeking to have the merger set aside and to obtain such other relief as might be proper.

In Count II of the amended complaint, which is the only count before us, petitioners predicated jurisdiction on § 27 of the 1934 Act. They alleged that the proxy statement sent out by the Auto-Lite management to solicit shareholders' votes in favor of the merger was misleading, in violation of § 14(a) of the Act and SEC Rule 14a-9 thereunder. Petitioners recited that before the merger Mergenthaler owned over 50% of the outstanding shares of Auto-Lite common stock, and had been in control of Auto-Lite for two years. American Manufacturing in turn owned about one-third of the outstanding shares of Mergenthaler, and for two years had been in voting control of Mergenthaler and, through it, of Auto-Lite. Petitioners charged that in light of these circumstances the proxy statement was misleading in that it told Auto-Lite shareholders that their board of directors recommended approval of the merger without also informing them that all 11 of Auto-Lite's directors were nominees of Mergenthaler and were under the "control and domination of Mergenthaler." Petitioners asserted the right to complain of this alleged violation both derivatively on behalf of Auto-Lite and as representatives of the class of all its minority shareholders.

On petitioners' motion for summary judgment with respect to Count II, the District Court *** ruled as a matter of law that the claimed defect in the proxy statement was, in light of the circumstances in which the statement was made, a material omission. The District Court concluded, from its reading of the *Borak* opinion, that it had to hold a hearing on the issue whether there was "a causal connection between the finding that there has been a violation of the disclosure requirements of § 14(a) and the alleged injury to the plaintiffs" before it could consider what remedies would be appropriate.

After holding such a hearing, the court found that under the terms of the merger agreement, an affirmative vote of two-thirds of the Auto-Lite shares was required for approval of the merger, and that the respondent companies owned and controlled about 54% of the outstanding shares. Therefore, to obtain authorization of the merger, respondents had to secure the approval of a substantial number of the minority shareholders. At the stockholders' meeting, approximately 950,000 shares, out of 1,160,000 shares outstanding, were voted in favor of the merger. This included 317,000 votes obtained by proxy from the minority shareholders, votes that were "necessary and indispensable to the approval of the merger." The District Court concluded that a causal relationship had thus been shown, and it granted an interlocutory judgment in favor of petitioners on the issue of liability, referring the case to a master for consideration of appropriate relief.

The District Court made the certification required by 28 U.S.C. § 1292(b), and respondents took an interlocutory appeal to the Court of Appeals for the Seventh Circuit. That court affirmed the District Court's conclusion that the proxy statement was materially deficient, but reversed on the question of causation. The court acknowledged that, if an injunction had been sought a sufficient time before the stockholders' meeting, "corrective measures would have been appropriate." However, since this suit was brought too late for preventive action, the courts had to determine "whether the misleading statement and omission caused the submission of sufficient proxies," as a prerequisite to a determination of liability under the Act. If the respondents could show, "by a preponderance of probabilities, that the merger would have received a sufficient vote even if the proxy statement had not been misleading in the respect found," petitioners would be entitled to no relief of any kind.

The Court of Appeals acknowledged that this test corresponds to the common-law fraud test of whether the injured party relied on the misrepresentation. However, rightly concluding that "[r]eliance by thousands of individuals, as here, can scarcely be inquired into," the court ruled that the issue was to be determined by proof of the fairness of the terms of the merger. If respondents could show that the merger had merit and was fair to the minority shareholders, the trial court would be justified in concluding that a sufficient number of shareholders would have approved the merger had there been no deficiency in the proxy statement. In that case respondents would be entitled to a judgment in their favor. ***

II

As we stressed in *Borak*, § 14(a) stemmed from a congressional belief that "[f]air corporate suffrage is an important right that should attach to every equity security bought on a public exchange." H.R.Rep.No.1383, 73d Cong., 2d Sess., 13. The provision was intended to promote "the free exercise of the voting rights of stockholders" by ensuring that proxies would be solicited with "explanation to the stockholder of the real nature of the questions for which authority to cast his vote is sought." Id. at 14; S.Rep.No.792, 73d Cong., 2d Sess., 12; see 377 U.S., at 431. The decision below, by permitting all liability to be foreclosed on the basis of a finding that the merger was fair, would allow the stockholders to be by-passed, at least where the only legal challenge to the merger is a suit for retrospective relief after the meeting has been held. A judicial appraisal of the merger's merits could be substituted for the actual and informed vote of the stockholders.

The result would be to insulate from private redress an entire category of proxy violations—those relating to matters other than the terms of the merger. Even outrageous misrepresentations in a proxy solicitation, if they did not relate to the terms of the transaction, would give rise to no cause of action under § 14(a). Particularly if carried over to enforcement actions by the Securities and Exchange Commission itself, such a result would subvert the congressional purpose of ensuring full and fair disclosure to shareholders.

Further, recognition of the fairness of the merger as a complete defense would confront small shareholders with an additional obstacle to making a successful challenge to a proposal recommended through a defective proxy statement. The risk that they would be unable to rebut the corporation's evidence of the fairness of the proposal, and thus to establish their cause of action, would be bound to discourage such shareholders from the private enforcement of the proxy rules that "provides a necessary supplement to Commission action." *J. I. Case Co. v. Borak*, 377 U.S., at 432.[5]

Such a frustration of the congressional policy is not required by anything in the wording of the statute or in our opinion in the *Borak* case. Section 14(a) declares it "unlawful" to solicit proxies in contravention of Commission rules, and SEC Rule 14a-9 prohibits solicitations "containing any statement which ... is false or misleading with respect to any material fact, or which omits to state any material fact necessary in order to make the statements therein not false or misleading..." Use of a solicitation that is materially misleading is itself a violation of law, as the Court of Appeals recognized in stating that injunctive relief would be available to remedy such a defect if sought prior to the stockholders' meeting. *** In the present case there has been a hearing specifically directed to the causation problem. The question before the Court is whether the facts found on the basis of that hearing are sufficient in law to establish petitioners' cause of action, and we conclude that they are.

Where the misstatement or omission in a proxy statement has been shown to be "material," as it was found to be here, that determination itself indubitably embodies a conclusion that the defect was of such a character that it might have been considered important by a reasonable shareholder who was in the process of deciding how to vote.[6] This requirement that the defect have a significant *propensity* to affect the voting process is found in the express terms

---

5. The Court of Appeals' ruling that "causation" may be negated by proof of the fairness of the merger also rests on a dubious behavioral assumption. There is no justification for presuming that the shareholders of every corporation are willing to accept any and every fair merger offer put before them; yet such a presumption is implicit in the opinion of the Court of Appeals. That court gave no indication of what evidence petitioners might adduce, once respondents had established that the merger proposal was equitable, in order to show that the shareholders would nevertheless have rejected it if the solicitation had not been misleading. Proof of actual reliance by thousands of individuals would, as the court acknowledged, not be feasible, see R. Jennings & H. Marsh, Securities Regulation, Cases and Materials 1001 (2d ed. 1968); and reliance on the *nondisclosure* of a fact is a particularly difficult matter to define or prove, see 3 L. Loss, Securities Regulation 1766 (2d ed. 1961). In practice, therefore, the objective fairness of the proposal would seemingly be determinative of liability. But, in view of the many other factors that might lead shareholders to prefer their current position to that of owners of a larger, combined enterprise, it is pure conjecture to assume that the fairness of the proposal will always be determinative of their vote.

6. In this case, where the misleading aspect of the solicitation involved failure to reveal a serious conflict of interest on the part of the directors, the Court of Appeals concluded that the crucial question in determining materiality was "whether the minority shareholders were sufficiently alerted to the board's relationship to their adversary to be on their guard." An adequate disclosure of this relationship would have warned the stockholders to give more careful scrutiny to the terms of the merger than they might to one recommended by an entirely distinterested board. Thus, the failure to make such a disclosure was found to be a material defect "as a matter of law," thwarting the informed decision at which the statute aims, regardless of whether the terms of the merger were such that a reasonable stockholder would have approved the transaction after more careful analysis.

of Rule 14a-9, and it adequately serves the purpose of ensuring that a cause of action cannot be established by proof of a defect so trivial, or so unrelated to the transaction for which approval is sought, that correction of the defect or imposition of liability would not further the interests protected by § 14(a).

There is no need to supplement this requirement, as did the Court of Appeals, with a requirement of proof of whether the defect actually had a decisive effect on the voting. Where there has been a finding of materiality, a shareholder has made a sufficient showing of causal relationship between the violation and the injury for which he seeks redress if, as here, he proves that the proxy solicitation itself, rather than the particular defect in the solicitation materials, was an essential link in the accomplishment of the transaction. This objective test will avoid the impracticalities of determining how many votes were affected, and, by resolving doubts in favor of those the statute is designed to protect, will effectuate the congressional policy of ensuring that the shareholders are able to make an informed choice when they are consulted on corporate transactions.[7]

III

Our conclusion that petitioners have established their case by showing that proxies necessary to approval of the merger were obtained by means of a materially misleading solicitation implies nothing about the form of relief to which they may be entitled. We held in *Borak* that upon finding a violation the courts were "to be alert to provide such remedies as are necessary to make effective the congressional purpose," noting specifically that such remedies are not to be limited to prospective relief. In devising retrospective relief for violation of the proxy rules, the federal courts should consider the same factors that would govern the relief granted for any similar illegality or fraud. One important factor may be the fairness of the terms of the merger. Possible forms of relief will include setting aside the merger or granting other equitable relief, but, as the Court of Appeals below noted, nothing in the statutory policy "requires the court to unscramble a corporate transaction merely because a violation occurred." In selecting a remedy the lower courts should exercise " 'the sound discretion which guides the determinations of courts of equity'," keeping in mind the role of equity as "the instrument for nice adjustment and reconciliation between the public interest and private needs as well as between competing private claims." *Hecht Co. v. Bowles*, 321 U.S. 321, 329-330 (1944), quoting from *Meredith v. Winter Haven*, 320 U.S. 228, 235 (1943). ***

Monetary relief will, of course, also be a possibility. Where the defect in the proxy solicitation relates to the specific terms of the merger, the district court might appropriately order an accounting to ensure that the shareholders

---

7. We need not decide in this case whether causation could be shown where the management controls a sufficient number of shares to approve the transaction without any votes from the minority. Even in that situation, if the management finds it necessary for legal or practical reasons to solicit proxies from minority shareholders, at least one court has held that the proxy solicitation might be sufficiently related to the merger to satisfy the causation requirement, see *Laurenzano v. Einbender*, 264 F. Supp. 356 (E.D.N.Y.1966). But see *Hoover v. Allen*, 241 F. Supp. 213, 231-232 (S.D.N.Y.1965).

receive the value that was represented as coming to them. On the other hand, where, as here, the misleading aspect of the solicitation did not relate to terms of the merger, monetary relief might be afforded to the shareholders only if the merger resulted in a reduction of the earnings or earnings potential of their holdings. In short, damages should be recoverable only to the extent that they can be shown. If commingling of the assets and operations of the merged companies makes it impossible to establish direct injury from the merger, relief might be predicated on a determination of the fairness of the terms of the merger at the time it was approved. These questions, of course, are for decision in the first instance by the District Court on remand, and our singling out of some of the possibilities is not intended to exclude others.

IV

*** The absence of express statutory authorization for an award of attorneys' fees in a suit under § 14(a) does not preclude such an award in cases of this type. In a suit by stockholders to recover short-swing profits for their corporation under § 16(b) of the 1934 Act, the Court of Appeals for the Second Circuit has awarded attorneys' fees despite the lack of any provision for them in § 16(b), "on the theory that the corporation which has received the benefit of the attorney's services should pay the reasonable value thereof." *Smolowe v. Delendo Corp.*, 136 F.2d 231, 241 (2d Cir. 1943). The court held that Congress' inclusion in §§ 9(e) and 18(a) of the Act of express provisions for recovery of attorneys' fees in certain other types of suits "does not impinge [upon] the result we reach in the absence of statute, for those sections merely enforce an additional penalty against the wrongdoer." ***

While the general American rule is that attorneys' fees are not ordinarily recoverable as costs, both the courts and Congress have developed exceptions to this rule for situations in which overriding considerations indicate the need for such a recovery. A primary judge-created exception has been to award expenses where a plaintiff has successfully maintained a suit, usually on behalf of a class, that benefits a group of others in the same manner as himself. To allow the others to obtain full benefit from the plaintiff's efforts without contributing equally to the litigation expenses would be to enrich the others unjustly at the plaintiff's expense. This suit presents such a situation. The dissemination of misleading proxy solicitations was a "deceit practiced on the stockholders as a group," *J. I. Case Co. v. Borak*, 377 U.S., at 432, and the expenses of petitioners' lawsuit have been incurred for the benefit of the corporation and the other shareholders.

The fact that this suit has not yet produced, and may never produce, a monetary recovery from which the fees could be paid does not preclude an award based on this rationale. ***

*** [I]n shareholders' derivative actions, where the courts increasingly have recognized that the expenses incurred by one shareholder in the vindication of a corporate right of action can be spread among all shareholders through an award against the corporation, regardless of whether an actual money recovery has been obtained in the corporation's favor. For example, awards have been sustained in suits by stockholders complaining that shares of their corporation had been issued wrongfully for an inadequate consideration. A successful suit of this type, resulting in cancellation of the shares, does not bring a fund into court or add to the assets of the corporation, but it does benefit the holders of the remaining shares by enhancing their value. ***

*** [A]n increasing number of lower courts have acknowledged that a corporation may receive a "substantial benefit" from a derivative suit, justifying an award of counsel fees, regardless of whether the benefit is pecuniary in nature. A leading case is *Bosch v. Meeker Cooperative Light & Power Assn.*, 257 Minn. 362 (1960), in which a stockholder was reimbursed for his expenses in obtaining a judicial declaration that the election of certain of the corporation's directors was invalid. ***

In many suits under § 14(a), particularly where the violation does not relate to the terms of the transaction for which proxies are solicited, it may be impossible to assign monetary value to the benefit. Nevertheless, the stress placed by Congress on the importance of fair and informed corporate suffrage leads to the conclusion that, in vindicating the statutory policy, petitioners have rendered a substantial service to the corporation and its shareholders. Whether petitioners are successful in showing a need for significant relief may be a factor in determining whether a further award should later be made. But regardless of the relief granted, private stockholders' actions of this sort "involve corporate therapeutics," and furnish a benefit to all shareholders by providing an important means of enforcement of the proxy statute. To award attorneys' fees in such a suit to a plaintiff who has succeeded in establishing a cause of action is not to saddle the unsuccessful party with the expenses but to impose them on the class that has benefitted from them and that would have had to pay them had it brought the suit. ***

### *NOTES AND QUESTIONS*

*1.* ***The Presumption of Causation.*** What is the Court's rationale for presuming causation once the plaintiff establishes the materiality of the omission or misrepresentation? Are defendants entitled to rebut this presumption? If so, how can they do so?

*2.* ***Damages and Fairness.*** The Court observed that in fashioning relief, "[o]ne important factor may be the terms of the merger." Seizing upon this statement on remand, the Seventh Circuit held "that the terms of the merger were fair and that the plaintiffs should recover no damages." *Mills v. Electric Auto-Lite Co.*, 552 F.2d 1239, 1249 (7th Cir. 1977). Does it follow that the *Mills* litigation was not worthwhile?

*3.* ***Equitable Relief.*** No doubt due to the flexible approach to relief in *Mills,* lower courts have granted a variety of forms of equitable relief in Rule 14a-9 cases. See, e.g., *Krauth v. Executive Telecard, Ltd.*, 890 F. Supp. 269, 292 (S.D.N.Y. 1995) (ordering new disclosures to cure the earlier fraud); *Parsons v. Jefferson-Pilot Corp.*, 789 F. Supp. 697, 704 (M.D.N.C. 1992) (nullifying stock grants made pursuant to an employee stock option plan approved by the shareholders); *Edelman v. Salomon,* 559 F. Supp. 1178, 1188 (D. Del. 1983) (granting a preliminary injunction deferring the election of directors and requiring resolicitation of proxies prior to the election).

*4. The Relevance of Individual Reliance.* Suppose a shareholder who was not misled by a fraudulent proxy statement voted against the merger or other matter as to which her approval was sought. Would she nonetheless be entitled to challenge the fraud in a Rule 14a-9 action? The D.C. Circuit has given an affirmative answer:

> The injury Cowin alleges was not caused by his individual reliance on deceptive proxy solicitations. Rather, his claim is that other shareholders elected appellees as directors because they were misled by the proxy materials. The installation of appellees as directors and their subsequent actions has injured appellant. This injury is totally divorced from any reliance, or lack of reliance, on Cowin's part and falls precisely into the scope of injury Congress sought to protect. Requiring reliance in these circumstances would serve no legitimate policy and we decline to do so.

*Cowin v. Bresler,* 741 F.2d 410, 427 (D.C. Cir. 1984). See *Stahl v. Gibraltar Fin. Corp.,* 967 F.2d 335 (9th Cir.1992 ) (following *Cowin*). Do you agree? Should a shareholder who was not herself misled be able to sue only derivatively rather than both derivatively and directly?

*5. Loss Causation.* What relationship must exist between the omission or misrepresentation and the plaintiff's losses? If the defendants misrepresented the qualifications of directors in connection with their reelection, can the plaintiff recover for transactions authorized by those directors upon being reelected? The Third Circuit has given a negative answer:

> The pecuniary harm to General Electric that Levitt alleges resulted from the appellees' purported mismanagement. Yet the mere fact that omissions in proxy materials, by permitting directors to win re-election, *indirectly* lead to financial loss through mismanagement will not create a sufficient nexus with the alleged monetary loss. Rather, damages are recoverable under Section 14(a) only when the votes for a specific corporate transaction requiring shareholder authorization, such as a corporate merger, are obtained by a false proxy statement, and that transaction was the direct cause of the pecuniary injury for which recovery is sought.
>
> Thus, the appellees' re-election as directors did not create any cognizable harm because the shareholders' votes did not authorize the transactions that caused the losses.

*Gen. Elec. Co. v. Cathcart,* 980 F.2d 927, 933 (3d Cir. 1992). Does the court's conclusion follow from *Mills*? Is it consistent with the loss causation requirement set forth in Section 21D(b)(4) of the Exchange Act? (That Section was enacted in 1995 as part of the PSLRA and therefore was not yet on the books when *Cathcart* was decided).

### 2. *When Management Controls Sufficient Shares to Approve the Transaction; Lost State Remedies*

In footnote 7 of *Mills,* the Supreme Court left open whether it is appropriate to presume causation in those situations where management controls enough shares to obtain approval of the transaction without the votes of the public shareholders. The Court divided 5-4 on this question in the decision that follows.

## VIRGINIA BANKSHARES, INC. v. SANDBERG

501 U.S. 1083 (1991)

JUSTICE SOUTER:

*** In December 1986, First American Bankshares, Inc. (FABI), a bank holding company, began a "freeze-out" merger, in which the First American Bank of Virginia (Bank) eventually merged into Virginia Bankshares, Inc. (VBI), a wholly owned subsidiary of FABI. VBI owned 85% of the Bank's shares, the remaining 15% being in the hands of some 2,000 minority shareholders. FABI hired the investment banking firm of Keefe, Bruyette & Woods (KBW) to give an opinion on the appropriate price for shares of the minority holders, who would lose their interests in the Bank as a result of the merger. Based on market quotations and unverified information from FABI, KBW gave the Bank's executive committee an opinion that $42 a share would be a fair price for the minority stock. The executive committee approved the merger proposal at that price, and the full board followed suit.

Although Virginia law required only that such a merger proposal be submitted to a vote at a shareholders' meeting, and that the meeting be preceded by circulation of a statement of information to the shareholders, the directors nevertheless solicited proxies for voting on the proposal at the annual meeting set for April 21, 1987.[3] In their solicitation, the directors urged the proposal's adoption and stated they had approved the plan because of its opportunity for the minority shareholders to achieve a "high" value, which they elsewhere described as a "fair" price, for their stock.

Although most minority shareholders gave the proxies requested, respondent Sandberg did not, and after approval of the merger she sought damages in the United States District Court for the Eastern District of Virginia from VBI, FABI, and the directors of the Bank. She pleaded two counts, one for soliciting proxies in violation of § 14(a) and Rule 14a-9, and the other for breaching fiduciary duties owed to the minority shareholders under state law. Under the first count, Sandberg alleged, among other things, that the directors had not believed that the price offered was high or that the terms of the merger were fair, but had recommended the merger only because they believed they had no alternative if they wished to remain on the board. At trial, Sandberg invoked language from this Court's opinion in *Mills v. Electric Auto-Lite Co.,* 396 U.S. 375, 385 (1970), to obtain an instruction that the jury could find for her without a showing of her own reliance on the alleged misstatements, so long as they were material and the proxy solicitation was an "essential link" in the merger process.

The jury's verdicts were for Sandberg on both counts, after finding violations of Rule 14a-9 by all defendants and a breach of fiduciary duties by the Bank's directors. The jury awarded Sandberg $18 a share, having found that she would have received $60 if her stock had been valued adequately. ***

---

3. Had the directors chosen to issue a statement instead of a proxy solicitation, they would have been subject to an SEC antifraud provision analogous to Rule 14a-9. See 17 CFR § 240.14c-6 (1990). See also 15 U.S.C. § 78n(c).

On appeal, the United States Court of Appeals for the Fourth Circuit affirmed the judgments, holding that certain statements in the proxy solicitation were materially misleading for purposes of the Rule, and that respondents could maintain their action even though their votes had not been needed to effectuate the merger. 891 F.2d 1112 (1989).[4] ***

III

The second issue before us, left open in *Mills v. Electric Auto-Lite Co.*, 396 U.S., at 385, n. 7, is whether causation of damages compensable through the implied private right of action under § 14(a) can be demonstrated by a member of a class of minority shareholders whose votes are not required by law or corporate bylaw to authorize the transaction giving rise to the claim. *J.I. Case Co. v. Borak*, 377 U.S. 426 (1964), did not itself address the requisites of causation, as such, or define the class of plaintiffs eligible to sue under § 14(a). But its general holding, that a private cause of action was available to some shareholder class, acquired greater clarity with a more definite concept of causation in *Mills*, where we addressed the sufficiency of proof that misstatements in a proxy solicitation were responsible for damages claimed from the merger subject to complaint.

Although a majority stockholder in *Mills* controlled just over half the corporation's shares, a two-thirds vote was needed to approve the merger proposal. After proxies had been obtained, and the merger had carried, minority shareholders brought a *Borak* action. *Mills*, 396 U.S., at 379. The question arose whether the plaintiffs' burden to demonstrate causation of their damages traceable to the § 14(a) violation required proof that the defect in the proxy solicitation had had "a decisive effect on the voting." Id., at 385. The *Mills* Court avoided the evidentiary morass that would have followed from requiring individualized proof that enough minority shareholders had relied upon the misstatements to swing the vote. Instead, it held that causation of damages by a material proxy misstatement could be established by showing that minority proxies necessary and sufficient to authorize the corporate acts had been given in accordance with the tenor of the solicitation, and the Court described such a causal relationship by calling the proxy solicitation an "essential link in the accomplishment of the transaction." Ibid. In the case before it, the Court found the solicitation essential, as contrasted with one addressed to a class of minority shareholders without votes required by law or bylaw to authorize the action proposed, and left it for another day to decide whether such a minority shareholder could demonstrate causation. Id., 396 U.S., at 385, n. 7.

In this case, respondents address *Mills'* open question by proffering two theories that the proxy solicitation addressed to them was an "essential link" under the *Mills* causation test. They argue, first, that a link existed and was essential simply because VBI and FABI would have been unwilling to proceed with the merger without the approval manifested by the minority shareholders'

---

4. The Court of Appeals reversed the District Court, however, on its refusal to certify a class of all minority shareholders in Sandberg's action. Consequently, it ruled that petitioners were liable to all of the Bank's former minority shareholders for $18 per share. 891 F.2d, at 1119.

proxies, which would not have been obtained without the solicitation's express misstatements and misleading omissions. On this reasoning, the causal connection would depend on a desire to avoid bad shareholder or public relations, and the essential character of the causal link would stem not from the enforceable terms of the parties' corporate relationship, but from one party's apprehension of the ill will of the other.

In the alternative, respondents argue that the proxy statement was an essential link between the directors' proposal and the merger because it was the means to satisfy a state statutory requirement of minority shareholder approval, as a condition for saving the merger from voidability resulting from a conflict of interest on the part of one of the Bank's directors, Jack Beddow, who voted in favor of the merger while also serving as a director of FABI. Under the terms of Va.Code Ann. § 13.1-691(A) (1989), minority approval after disclosure of the material facts about the transaction and the director's interest was one of three avenues to insulate the merger from later attack for conflict, the two others being ratification by the Bank's directors after like disclosure and proof that the merger was fair to the corporation. On this theory, causation would depend on the use of the proxy statement for the purpose of obtaining votes sufficient to bar a minority shareholder from commencing proceedings to declare the merger void.

Although respondents have proffered each of these theories as establishing a chain of causal connection in which the proxy statement is claimed to have been an "essential link," neither theory presents the proxy solicitation as essential in the sense of *Mills'* causal sequence, in which the solicitation links a directors' proposal with the votes legally required to authorize the action proposed. As a consequence, each theory would, if adopted, extend the scope of *Borak* actions beyond the ambit of *Mills* and expand the class of plaintiffs entitled to bring *Borak* actions to include shareholders whose initial authorization of the transaction prompting the proxy solicitation is unnecessary.

Assessing the legitimacy of any such extension or expansion calls for the application of some fundamental principles governing recognition of a right of action implied by a federal statute, the first of which was not, in fact, the considered focus of the *Borak* opinion. The rule that has emerged in the years since *Borak* and *Mills* came down is that recognition of any private right of action for violating a federal statute must ultimately rest on congressional intent to provide a private remedy, *Touche Ross & Co. v. Redington,* 442 U.S. 560, 575 (1979). From this the corollary follows that the breadth of the right once recognized should not, as a general matter, grow beyond the scope congressionally intended.

This rule and corollary present respondents with a serious obstacle, for we can find no manifestation of intent to recognize a cause of action (or class of plaintiffs) as broad as respondents' theory of causation would entail. At first blush, it might seem otherwise, for the *Borak* Court certainly did not ignore the matter of intent. Its opinion adverted to the statutory object of "protection of investors" as animating Congress' intent to provide judicial relief where "necessary," 377 U.S., at 432, and it quoted evidence for that intent from House and Senate Committee Reports, id., at 431-432. *Borak's* probe of the congressional mind, however, never focused squarely on private rights of action, as distinct from the substantive objects of the legislation, and one Member of the *Borak* Court later characterized the "implication" of the private right of action as resting modestly on the Act's "'exclusively procedural provision' affording access to a federal forum." *Bivens v. Six Unknown Fed. Narcotics Agents,* 403 U.S. 388, 403, n. 4 (1971) (Harlan, J., concurring in judgment). In fact, the importance of enquiring specifically into intent to authorize a private cause of action became clear only later, see *Cort v. Ash,* 422 U.S., at 78,, and only later still, in *Touche Ross,* was this intent accorded primacy among the considerations that might be thought to bear on any decision to recognize a private remedy. There, in dealing with a claimed private right under § 17(a) of the Act, we explained that the "central inquiry remains whether Congress intended to create, either expressly or by implication, a private cause of action." 442 U.S., at 575-576.

Looking to the Act's text and legislative history mindful of this heightened concern reveals little that would help toward understanding the intended scope of any private right. According to the House Report, Congress meant to promote the "free exercise" of stockholders' voting rights, H.R.Rep. No. 1383, 73d Cong., 2d Sess., 14 (1934), and protect "[f]air corporate suffrage," id., at 13, from abuses exemplified by proxy solicitations that concealed what the Senate Report called the "real nature" of the issues to be settled by the subsequent votes, S.Rep. No. 792, 73d Cong., 2d Sess., 12 (1934). While it is true that these Reports, like the language of the Act itself, carry the clear message that Congress meant to protect investors from misinformation that rendered them unwitting agents of self-inflicted damage, it is just as true that Congress was reticent with indications of how far this protection might depend on self-help by private action. The response to this reticence may be, of course, to claim that § 14(a) cannot be enforced effectively for the sake of its intended beneficiaries without their participation as private litigants. *Borak,* supra, 377 U.S., at 432. But the force of this argument for inferred congressional intent depends on the degree of need perceived by Congress, and we would have trouble inferring any congressional urgency to depend on implied private actions to deter violations of § 14(a), when Congress expressly provided private rights of action in §§ 9(e), 16(b), and 18(a) of the same Act.[11]

The congressional silence that is thus a serious obstacle to the expansion of cognizable *Borak* causation is not, however, a necessarily insurmountable barrier. This is not the first effort in recent years to expand the scope of an action originally inferred from the Act without "conclusive guidance" from Congress, see *Blue Chip Stamps v. Manor Drug Stores,* 421 U.S., at 737, and we may look to that earlier case for the proper response to such a plea for expansion. There, we accepted the proposition that where a legal structure of private statutory rights has developed without clear indications of congressional

---

11. The object of our enquiry does not extend further to question the holding of either *J. I. Case Co. v. Borak,* 377 U.S. 426 (1964), or *Mills v. Electric Auto-Lite Co.,* 396 U.S. 375 (1970), at this date, any more than we have done so in the past, see *Touche Ross & Co. v. Redington,* 442 U.S. 560, 577 (1979). Our point is simply to recognize the hurdle facing any litigant who urges us to enlarge the scope of the action beyond the point reached in *Mills.*

intent, the contours of that structure need not be frozen absolutely when the result would be demonstrably inequitable to a class of would-be plaintiffs with claims comparable to those previously recognized. Faced in that case with such a claim for equality in rounding out the scope of an implied private statutory right of action, we looked to policy reasons for deciding where the outer limits of the right should lie. We may do no less here, in the face of respondents' pleas for a private remedy to place them on the same footing as shareholders with votes necessary for initial corporate action.

A

*Blue Chip Stamps* set an example worth recalling as a preface to specific policy analysis of the consequences of recognizing respondents' first theory, that a desire to avoid minority shareholders' ill will should suffice to justify recognizing the requisite causality of a proxy statement needed to garner that minority support. It will be recalled that in *Blue Chip Stamps* we raised concerns about the practical consequences of allowing recovery, under § 10(b) of the Act and Rule 10b-5, on evidence of what a merely hypothetical buyer or seller might have done on a set of facts that never occurred, and foresaw that any such expanded liability would turn on "hazy" issues inviting self-serving testimony, strike suits, and protracted discovery, with little chance of reasonable resolution by pretrial process. Id., at 742-743. These were good reasons to deny recognition to such claims in the absence of any apparent contrary congressional intent.

The same threats of speculative claims and procedural intractability are inherent in respondents' theory of causation linked through the directors' desire for a cosmetic vote. Causation would turn on inferences about what the corporate directors would have thought and done without the minority shareholder approval unneeded to authorize action. A subsequently dissatisfied minority shareholder would have virtual license to allege that managerial timidity would have doomed corporate action but for the ostensible approval induced by a misleading statement, and opposing claims of hypothetical diffidence and hypothetical boldness on the part of directors would probably provide enough depositions in the usual case to preclude any judicial resolution short of the credibility judgments that can only come after trial. Reliable evidence would seldom exist. Directors would understand the prudence of making a few statements about plans to proceed even without minority endorsement, and discovery would be a quest for recollections of oral conversations at odds with the official pronouncements, in hopes of finding support for *ex post facto* guesses about how much heat the directors would have stood in the absence of minority approval. The issues would be hazy, their litigation protracted, and their resolution unreliable. Given a choice, we would reject any theory of causation that raised such prospects, and we reject this one.[12]

---

12. In parting company from us on this point, Justice Kennedy emphasizes that respondents in this particular case substantiated a plausible claim that petitioners would not have proceeded without minority approval. FABI's attempted freeze-out merger of a Maryland subsidiary had failed a year before the events in question when the subsidiary's directors rejected the proposal because of inadequate share price, and there was evidence of FABI's desire to avoid any renewal of adverse comment. The issue

B

The theory of causal necessity derived from the requirements of Virginia law dealing with postmerger ratification seeks to identify the essential character of the proxy solicitation from its function in obtaining the minority approval that would preclude a minority suit attacking the merger. Since the link is said to be a step in the process of barring a class of shareholders from resort to a state remedy otherwise available, this theory of causation rests upon the proposition of policy that § 14(a) should provide a federal remedy whenever a false or misleading proxy statement results in the loss under state law of a shareholder plaintiff's state remedy for the enforcement of a state right. Respondents agree with the suggestions of counsel for the SEC and FDIC that causation be recognized, for example, when a minority shareholder has been induced by a misleading proxy statement to forfeit a state-law right to an appraisal remedy by voting to approve a transaction, cf. *Swanson v. American Consumers Industries, Inc.*, 475 F.2d 516, 520-521 (CA7 1973), or when such a shareholder has been deterred from obtaining an order enjoining a damaging transaction by a proxy solicitation that misrepresents the facts on which an injunction could properly have been issued. Cf. *Healey v. Catalyst Recovery of Pennsylvania, Inc.*, 616 F.2d 641, 647-648 (CA3 1980); *Alabama Farm Bureau Mutual Casualty Co. v. American Fidelity Life Ins. Co.*, 606 F.2d 602, 614 (CA5 1979). Respondents claim that in this case a predicate for recognizing just such a causal link exists in Va. Code Ann. § 13.1-691(A)(2) (1989), which sets the conditions under which the merger may be insulated from suit by a minority shareholder seeking to void it on account of Beddow's conflict.

This case does not, however, require us to decide whether § 14(a) provides a cause of action for lost state remedies, since there is no indication in the law or facts before us that the proxy solicitation resulted in any such loss. The contrary appears to be the case. Assuming the soundness of respondents' characterization of the proxy statement as materially misleading, the very terms of the Virginia statute indicate that a favorable minority vote induced by the solicitation would not suffice to render the merger invulnerable to later attack on the ground of the conflict. The statute bars a shareholder from seeking to avoid a transaction tainted by a director's conflict if, *inter alia*, the minority shareholders ratified the transaction following disclosure of the material facts of the transaction and the conflict. Va. Code Ann. § 13.1-691(A)(2) (1989). Assuming that the material facts about the merger and Beddow's interests were not accurately disclosed, the minority votes were inadequate to ratify the merger under state law, and there was no loss of state remedy to connect the proxy

---

before us, however, is whether to recognize a theory of causation generally, and our decision against doing so rests on our apprehension that the ensuing litigation would be exemplified by cases far less tractable than this. Respondents' burden to justify recognition of causation beyond the scope of *Mills* must be addressed not by emphasizing the instant case but by confronting the risk inherent in the cases that could be expected to be characteristic if the causal theory were adopted.

solicitation with harm to minority shareholders irredressable under state law.[13] Nor is there a claim here that the statement misled respondents into entertaining a false belief that they had no chance to upset the merger, until the time for bringing suit had run out.[14]

JUSTICE KENNEDY, WITH WHOM JUSTICE MARSHALL, JUSTICE BLACKMUN, AND JUSTICE STEVENS JOIN, CONCURRING IN PART AND DISSENTING IN PART:

A

*** The severe limits the Court places upon possible proof of nonvoting causation in a § 14(a) private action are justified neither by our precedents nor by any case in the courts of appeals. These limits are said to flow from a shift in our approach to implied causes of action that has occurred since we recognized the § 14(a) implied private action in *J.I. Case Co. v. Borak,* 377 U.S. 426 (1964).

I acknowledge that we should exercise caution in creating implied private rights of action and that we must respect the primacy of congressional intent in that inquiry. Where an implied cause of action is well accepted by our own cases and has become an established part of the securities laws, however, we should enforce it as a meaningful remedy unless we are to eliminate it altogether. As the Court phrases it, we must consider the causation question in light of the underlying "policy reasons for deciding where the outer limits of the right should lie."

According to the Court, acceptance of non-voting causation theories would "extend the scope of *Borak* actions beyond the ambit of *Mills.*" But *Mills v. Electric Auto-Lite Co.,* 396 U.S. 375 (1970), did not purport to limit the scope of *Borak* actions, and as footnote 7 of *Mills* indicates, some courts have applied nonvoting causation theories to *Borak* actions for at least the past 25 years.

To the extent the Court's analysis considers the purposes underlying § 14(a), it does so with the avowed aim to limit the cause of action and with undue emphasis upon fears of "speculative claims and procedural intractability." The result is a sort of guerrilla warfare to restrict a well-established implied right of action. If the analysis adopted by the Court today is any guide, Congress and those charged with enforcement of the securities laws stand forewarned that unresolved questions concerning the scope of those causes of action are likely to be answered by the Court in favor of defendants.

---

13. In his opinion dissenting on this point, Justice Kennedy suggests that materiality under Virginia law might be defined differently from the materiality standard of our own cases, resulting in a denial of state remedy even when a solicitation was materially misleading under federal law. Respondents, however, present nothing to suggest that this might be so.

14. Respondents do not claim that any other application of a theory of lost state remedies would avail them here. It is clear, for example, that no state appraisal remedy was lost through a § 14(a) violation in this case. *** "Va. Code § 6.1-43 specifically excludes bank mergers from application of § 13.1-730 [the Virginia appraisal statute]." ***

B

The Court seems to assume, based upon the footnote in *Mills* reserving the question, that Sandberg bears a special burden to demonstrate causation because the public shareholders held only 15 percent of the stock of First American Bank of Virginia (Bank). Justice Stevens is right to reject this theory. Here, First American Bankshares, Inc. (FABI), and Virginia Bankshares, Inc. (VBI), retained the option to back out of the transaction if dissatisfied with the reaction of the minority shareholders, or if concerned that the merger would result in liability for violation of duties to the minority shareholders. The merger agreement was conditioned upon approval by two-thirds of the shareholders, and VBI could have voted its shares against the merger if it so decided. To this extent, the Court's distinction between cases where the "minority" shareholders could have voted down the transaction and those where causation must be proved by nonvoting theories is suspect. Minority shareholders are identified only by a *post hoc* inquiry. The real question ought to be whether an injury was shown by the effect the nondisclosure had on the entire merger process, including the period before votes are cast.

The Court's distinction presumes that a majority shareholder will vote in favor of management's proposal even if proxy disclosure suggests that the transaction is unfair to minority shareholders or that the board of directors or majority shareholder is in breach of fiduciary duties to the minority. If the majority shareholder votes against the transaction in order to comply with its state-law duties, or out of fear of liability, or upon concluding that the transaction will injure the reputation of the business, this ought not to be characterized as nonvoting causation. Of course, when the majority shareholder dominates the voting process, as was the case here, it may prefer to avoid the embarrassment of voting against its own proposal and so may cancel the meeting of shareholders at which the vote was to have been taken. For practical purposes, the result is the same: Because of full disclosure the transaction does not go forward and the resulting injury to minority shareholders is avoided. The Court's distinction between voting and nonvoting causation does not create clear legal categories.

III

Our decision in *Mills v. Electric Auto-Lite Co.*, supra, at 385, rested upon the impracticality of attempting to determine the extent of reliance by thousands of shareholders on alleged misrepresentations or omissions. A misstatement or an omission in a proxy statement does not violate § 14(a) unless "there is a substantial likelihood that a reasonable shareholder would consider it important in deciding how to vote." *TSC Industries, Inc. v. Northway, Inc.*, 426 U.S. 438, 449 (1976). If minority shareholders hold sufficient votes to defeat a management proposal and if the misstatement or omission is likely to be considered important in deciding how to vote, then there exists a likely causal link between the proxy violation and the enactment of the proposal; and one can justify recovery by minority shareholders for damages resulting from enactment of management's proposal.

If, for sake of argument, we accept a distinction between voting and nonvoting causation, we must determine whether the *Mills* essential link theory applies where a majority shareholder holds sufficient votes to force adoption of a proposal. The merit of the essential link formulation is that it rests upon the likelihood of causation and eliminates the difficulty of proof. Even where a minority lacks votes to defeat a proposal, both these factors weigh in favor of finding causation so long as the solicitation of proxies is an essential link in the transaction.

A

The Court argues that a nonvoting causation theory would "turn on 'hazy' issues inviting self-serving testimony, strike suits, and protracted discovery, with little chance of reasonable resolution by pretrial process." The Court's description does not fit this case and is not a sound objection in any event. Any causation inquiry under § 14(a) requires a court to consider a hypothetical universe in which adequate disclosure is made. Indeed, the analysis is inevitable in almost any suit when we are invited to compare what was with what ought to have been. The causation inquiry is not intractable. On balance, I am convinced that the likelihood that causation exists supports elimination of any requirement that the plaintiff prove the material misstatement or omission caused the transaction to go forward when it otherwise would have been halted or voted down. This is the usual rule under *Mills,* and the difficulties of proving or disproving causation are, if anything, greater where the minority lacks sufficient votes to defeat the proposal. A presumption will assist courts in managing a circumstance in which direct proof is rendered difficult. See *Basic Inc. v. Levinson,* 485 U.S. 224, 245 (1988) (discussing presumptions in securities law).

B

There is no authority whatsoever for limiting § 14(a) to protecting those minority shareholders whose numerical strength could permit them to vote down a proposal. One of § 14(a)'s "chief purposes is 'the protection of investors.'" *J. I. Case Co. v. Borak,* 377 U.S., at 432. Those who lack the strength to vote down a proposal have all the more need of disclosure. The voting process involves not only casting ballots but also the formulation and withdrawal of proposals, the minority's right to block a vote through court action or the threat of adverse consequences, or the negotiation of an increase in price. The proxy rules support this deliberative process. These practicalities can result in causation sufficient to support recovery.

The facts in the case before us prove this point. ***

The theory that FABI would not have pursued the transaction if full disclosure had been provided and the shareholders had realized the inadequacy of the price is supported not only by the trial testimony but also by notes of the meeting of the Bank's board, which approved the merger. The inquiry into causation can proceed not by "opposing claims of hypothetical diffidence and hypothetical boldness," but through an examination of evidence of the same type the Court finds acceptable in its determination that directors' statements of reasons can lead to liability. Discussion at the board meeting focused upon matters such as "how to keep PR afloat" and "how to prevent adverse reac[tion]/perception," demonstrating the directors' concern that an unpopular merger proposal could injure the Bank.

Only a year or so before the Virginia merger, FABI had failed in an almost identical transaction, an attempt to freeze out the minority shareholders of its Maryland subsidiary. FABI retained Keefe, Bruyette & Woods (KBW) for that transaction as well, and KBW had given an opinion that FABI's price was fair. The subsidiary's board of directors then retained its own adviser and concluded that the price offered by FABI was inadequate. The Maryland transaction failed when the directors of the Maryland bank refused to proceed; and this was despite the minority's inability to outvote FABI if it had pressed on with the deal.

In the Virginia transaction, FABI again decided to retain KBW. Beddow, who sat on the boards of both FABI and the Bank, discouraged the Bank from hiring its own financial adviser, out of fear that the Maryland experience would be repeated if the Bank received independent advice. Directors of the Bank testified they would not have voted to approve the transaction if the price had been demonstrated unfair to the minority. Further, approval by the Bank's board of directors was facilitated by FABI's representation that the transaction also would be approved by the minority shareholders. ***

I conclude that causation is more than plausible; it is likely, even where the public shareholders cannot vote down management's proposal. Causation is established where the proxy statement is an essential link in completing the transaction, even if the minority lacks sufficient votes to defeat a proposal of management.

IV

The majority avoids the question whether a plaintiff may prove causation by demonstrating that the misrepresentation or omission deprived her of a state-law remedy. I do not think the question difficult, as the whole point of federal proxy rules is to support state-law principles of corporate governance. Nor do I think that the Court can avoid this issue if it orders judgment for petitioners. The majority asserts that respondents show no loss of a state-law remedy, because if "the material facts about the merger and Beddow's interests were not accurately disclosed, the minority votes were inadequate to ratify the merger under state law." This theory requires us to conclude that the Virginia statute governing director conflicts of interest, Va. Code Ann. § 13.1-691(A)(2) (1989), incorporates the same definition of materiality as the federal proxy rules. I find no support for that proposition. If the definitions are not the same, then Sandberg may have lost her state-law remedy. For all we know, disclosure to the minority shareholders that the price is $42 per share may satisfy Virginia's requirement. If that is the case, then approval by the minority without full disclosure may have deprived Sandberg of the ability to void the merger.

In all events, the theory that the merger would have been voidable absent minority shareholder approval is far more speculative than the theory that FABI and the Bank would have called off the transaction. Even so, this possibility would support a remand, as the lower courts have yet to consider the question. We are not well positioned as an institution to provide a definitive resolution to state-law questions of this kind. Here again, the difficulty of knowing what would have happened in the hypothetical universe of full disclosure suggests that we should "resolv[e] doubts in favor of those the statute is designed to protect" in order to "effectuate the congressional policy of ensuring that the shareholders are able to make an informed choice when they are consulted on corporate transactions." *Mills,* 396 U.S., at 385. ***

## NOTES AND QUESTIONS

1. ***The Corollary.*** *Virginia Bankshares* announced a "corollary" to its rule that a court should recognize an implied private action only when Congress intended the action to exist: an implied private action "should not, as a general matter, grow beyond the scope Congress intended." How important was the corollary to the *Virginia Bankshares* decision? What is the likely impact of the corollary on judicial interpretation of Rule 14a-9?

2. ***Vexatious Litigation Threat?*** The Court suggested that Rule 14a-9 presents a threat of vexatious litigation essentially comparable to that of Rule 10b-5. Do you agree?

3. ***Solicitations to Foster Shareholder Relations.*** The plaintiff claimed that management had solicited proxies in order to foster shareholder relations, but the Court rejected this argument as too speculative. Is it any more speculative than the reasoning that led to the presumption of causation in *Mills*?

4. ***Lost State Remedies.*** Are causation arguments based on lost state remedies viable in the wake of *Virginia Bankshares*? If so, must the plaintiff show that she would have prevailed on her state law remedy? Or would it be sufficient for her to show that she had a prima facie case for the remedy? Must she show that she would have pursued the state law remedy if the proxy statement had not been misleading?

5. ***Varieties of State Law.*** State laws can vary considerably with respect to the remedies provided to shareholders in any given situation. Thus, assume two corporations (X and Y) incorporated in different states, each of which issued a proxy statement to its shareholders containing a comparable material misrepresentation. The shareholders of X Corporation might be able to claim loss of a state remedy (and hence entitlement to sue under Rule 14a-9), whereas the shareholders of Y Corporation might not have had a state remedy to lose (and hence lack entitlement to sue under Rule 14a-9). Does this state of affairs conflict with the last paragraph of Part III of *Borak*? From the standpoint of policy, should the vagaries of state law determine whether Rule 14a-9 is available?

6. ***How Bright a Line?*** Can a plaintiff distinguish *Virginia Bankshares* (and thereby avail himself of the *Mills* presumption) by proving that at least some of the shares under management's "control" would have been voted against the merger if the proxy statement had not been misleading? One district court has given a negative answer:

> *Virginia Bankshares* *** apparently establishes a bright line rule that courts should not look behind an affirmative shareholder vote where a majority of the shareholders indicate in the proxy statement *** their intent to cast an affirmative vote in the face of speculative claims that, absent some statement in the proxy materials, a controlling shareholder would have voted differently.

*In re Reliance Sec. Litig.*, 135 F. Supp. 2d 480, 517 (D. Del. 2001). Do you agree?

7. ***A Wider Role for* Virginia Bankshares?** The Second Circuit relied upon *Virginia Bankshares* to dismiss a Rule 14a-9 action brought by shareholders whose votes were necessary to the approval of a merger:

> We may assume that the omitted information would have been important to a reasonable shareholder in determining how to vote on the proposed merger with Astoria and thus meets the standard definition of materiality. See *TSC Indus., Inc. v. Northway, Inc.*, 426 U.S. 438, 449 (1976). However, in the proxy context this definition of materiality assumes that the omitted information would have influenced a reasonable shareholder against the proposed transaction for which proxies were sought. Here, the omitted information would not have made a reasonable shareholder any less likely to favor the objected to transaction, and such an omission, material or not, could not have caused the injury for which damages are sought.
>
> In *Virginia Bankshares, Inc. v. Sandberg*, 501 U.S. 1083 (1991), the Supreme Court held that a materially misleading proxy solicitation was not actionable where the controlling shareholder had enough votes to approve the objected-to transaction without seeking proxies. See id. at 1099-1108. The rationale of that holding applies equally to cases where the omissions would have caused a reasonable shareholder to favor rather than disfavor the transaction. In *Virginia Bankshares*, the omissions were not actionable because the disputed transaction would have occurred even if the proxy statement had been complete and accurate. See id. at 1107-08. That is also the case here. Had a reasonable Greater New York shareholder been fully informed, that shareholder would not have been any less likely to vote for the Astoria merger knowing of the cataloged information than being ignorant of it.

*Minzer v. Keegan*, 218 F.3d 144, 149-50 (2d Cir. 2000). Could the court have reached the same result without invoking *Virginia Bankshares*?

### *PROBLEM 4-1*

Whiz, Inc. is a manufacturer of surgical supplies, including a device (the "direx") used in the performance of abortions. Whiz's stock is listed on the New York Stock Exchange.

Eliza, a Whiz shareholder, submitted a shareholder proposal recommending to the board that it halt manufacture of the direx. The proxy statement containing Eliza's proposal included an argument from management urging shareholders to vote against her proposal. Management's argument was that the direx was not used exclusively in connection with abortions. Rather, management maintained, the direx had multiple surgical uses outside the abortion context. This argument had no basis in fact.

The shareholders defeated Eliza's proposal. Eliza then filed a Rule 14a-9 action that challenged management's statement regarding the direx. She asked the court to declare void the shareholder vote on her proposal and to order the company to resubmit her proposal to the shareholders at the next annual meeting.

Whiz responded with a motion to dismiss Eliza's action for failure to state a claim. According to Whiz, the board would have been entitled to disregard Eliza's proposal even if a majority of the shareholders had voted for it. Thus, Whiz argued, the proxy solicitation was not "an essential link in the accomplishment of [a corporate] action," as the Supreme Court requires.

Should the court grant Whiz's motion?

---

In the decision that follows, the court confronted an argument mentioned but not addressed in *Virginia Bankshares*—that the shareholders would have pursued their appraisal rights if the proxy statement had not been misleading.

## WILSON v. GREAT AMERICAN INDUSTRIES, INC.

979 F.2d 924 (2d Cir. 1992)

CARDAMONE, CIRCUIT JUDGE:

Defendants appeal and plaintiffs cross appeal from two decisions and orders of the United States District Court *** that awarded damages to plaintiffs because of misrepresentations contained in a joint proxy/prospectus issued in connection with a merger of defendant Chenango Industries, Incorporated (Chenango) into defendant Great American Industries, Incorporated (Great American). Defendants assert that the intervening Supreme Court decision in *Virginia Bankshares, Inc. v. Sandberg,* 501 U.S. 1083, (1991), compels dismissal of plaintiffs' causes of action on the grounds that as minority shareholders, without power to influence the proposed merger, they suffered no compensable damages under § 14(a) of the Security Exchange Act, notwithstanding that their votes were solicited by proxies containing material misrepresentations. Defendants and plaintiffs also claim the district court incorrectly calculated damages. ***

*** The thrust of plaintiffs' complaint is that the material misstatements induced them to exchange their shares of Chenango common stock for new preferred stock in Great American. Defendants at the time of the merger owned 73 percent of Chenango's stock, well over the two thirds necessary under New York law to approve a corporate merger. New York law only required that defendants hold a shareholders' meeting prior to which Chenango was required to give each shareholder notice of the meeting accompanied by a "copy of the plan of merger." N.Y.Bus.Corp. Law § 903(a)(1) (McKinney 1986). Because Chenango stock was registered under § 12(g) of the Act, defendants were also required to provide shareholders with an "Information Statement" pursuant to § 14(c) of the Act. Nonetheless, defendants mailed out joint proxy and registration statements seeking Chenango minority shareholders' approval of the merger.

The misrepresentations or omissions contained in the proxy created an unfair exchange ratio, plaintiffs assert, by overvaluing Great American's stock and undervaluing Cherango's stock. ***

I.

A. *Intervening Supreme Court Decision*

The Supreme Court in *Virginia Bankshares* did not hold that minority shareholders whose votes number too few to affect the outcome of a shareholder vote may *never* recover damages under § 14(a) or that *no* implied private cause of action for such shareholders is provided under that section of the Act. And, it expressly declined to decide whether § 14(a) provides an implied federal remedy for minority shareholders deprived of certain state remedies as a result of deceptive proxy solicitations. 501 U.S. at [1108] & n. 14. To the extent that this Circuit recognizes such a remedy, defendants incorrectly contend therefore that *Virginia Bankshares* precludes plaintiffs from seeking such relief. ***

B. *Plaintiff's Theories of Recovery*

*** Plaintiffs set forth two theories of causation to support their claims. They assert first that an implied action under any of the four securities law provisions pleaded should be recognized because 85 percent of the voting shares, or 12 percent of the minority shareholders in addition to the controlling majority shareholders, had to approve the merger in order for the exchange of stock to take place without tax consequences. Although an opinion letter stated the merger might have tax-free consequences for the majority shareholders if 85 percent of the shareholders approved it, such an approval level was not a requirement of the merger. If it was not an express condition of the merger, the higher rate of dissenting voters could only prevent the merger were it to influence the controlling majority. Such a speculative and hypothetical causal connection would make liability "turn on 'hazy' issues [and invite] self-serving testimony, strike suits, and protracted discovery, with little chance of reasoned resolution by pretrial process." *Virginia Bankshares,* 501 U.S. at 1105 (rejecting causal theory promised on majority's desire for "cosmetic" vote and avoidance of minority shareholders' ill-will). Thus, we reject this theory of causation.

Plaintiffs' second theory of causation--one with more merit and upon which § 14(a) causes of action have been sustained in the past--is that their deceptively procured vote in favor of the merger deprived them of their state appraisal rights under N.Y. Bus. Corp. Law §§ 623(a), (b); § 910(a)(1). We and other courts have recognized that plaintiffs might prevail on such a § 14(a) theory. See *Cole v. Schenley Indus., Inc.,* 563 F.2d 35, 39-40 (2d Cir.1977) (on a motion to dismiss complaint, implied right recognized when insignificant minority shareholders had state law alternatives to accepting merger); *Schlick v. Penn-Dixie Cement Corp.,* 507 F.2d 374, 381-84 (2d Cir.1974) (though insignificant minority shareholders had no appraisal rights under state law, deprivation of measures other than casting proxies may support implied right to recovery under § 14(a)).

As noted, *Virginia Bankshares* left open the possibility that § 14(a) might include this type of implied right to recover and did not address whether the causal relationship between a deceptive proxy and lost state remedies was sufficient to support a federal remedy. Defendants, having failed to contest causation prior to the present appeal, should hardly be allowed to argue the point now, especially when to permit such puts them in a better position than if they had made this objection earlier and lost.

We continue to believe that a minority shareholder, who has lost his right to a state appraisal because of a materially deceptive proxy, may make "a sufficient showing of causal relationship between the violation and the injury for which he seeks redress." *Mills,* 396 U.S. at 385. The transaction effected by a proxy involves not only the merger of the corporate entities, and the attendant exchange of stock, but also the forfeiture of shareholders' appraisal rights. The injury sustained by a minority shareholder powerless to affect the outcome of the merger vote is not the merger but the loss of his appraisal right. The deceptive proxy plainly constitutes an "essential link" in accomplishing the forfeiture of this state right.

That the causal nexus between the merger and the proxy is absent when the minority stockholder's vote cannot affect the merger decision does not necessarily mean a causal link between the proxy and some other injury may not exist. We recognize that loss causation or economic harm to plaintiffs must be shown, as well as proof that the misrepresentations induced plaintiffs to engage in the subject transaction, that is, transaction causation. Here loss causation may be established when a proxy statement prompts a shareholder to accept an unfair exchange ratio for his shares rather than recoup a greater value through a state appraisal. And transaction causation may be shown when a proxy statement, because of material misrepresentations, causes a shareholder to forfeit his appraisal rights by voting in favor of the proposed corporate merger. See *Schlick,* 507 F.2d at 380; Note, Causation and Liability in Private Actions for Proxy Violations, 80 Yale L.J. 107, 123-27 (1970).

Even though the proxy was not legally required in this case, when defendants choose to issue a proxy plaintiffs have a right to a truthful one. With the Securities Exchange Act of 1934, Congress sought to promote fair corporate suffrage with respect to "'every equity security'" by requiring an "'explanation to the stockholder of the real nature of the questions for which authority to cast his vote is sought.'" *Mills,* 396 U.S. at 381 (quoting H.R. Rep. No. 1383, 73d Cong., 2d Sess. 13-14 (1934)); see also *J.I. Case Co. v. Borak,* 377 U.S. 426, 431-32 (1964). Congress' interest in the protection of investors and the "'free exercise of [their] voting rights,'" *Borak,* 377 U.S. at 431 (quoting H.R. Rep. No. 1383, 73d Cong., 2d Sess. 14 (1934)), should not vary in degree according to the ability of the shareholder to affect the merger, if the vote nevertheless may result in a different sort of injury which full disclosure might have avoided.

The statute does not suggest that the prohibition of material misrepresentation in a proxy extends only to necessary proxies that are mailed to shareholders the solicitation of whose votes may affect the outcome of the proposed corporate action. That a controlling group of shareholders may accomplish any corporate change they want does not insulate them from liability for injury occasioned when they commit the sort of fraud that § 14(a) seeks to prevent. See *Swanson v. American Consumer Indus., Inc.,* 415 F.2d 1326, 1331-32 (7th Cir.1969). To decline to extend the protection of § 14(a) to plaintiffs, we think, might sanction overreaching by controlling shareholders when the minority shareholders most need § 14(a)'s protection. See *Schlick,* 507 F.2d at 383. At the same time, allowing the action does not pose a threat of "speculative claims and procedural intractability," *Virginia Bankshares,* 501 U.S. at 1105, because the forfeiture of state appraisal rights is a question separate from the effectuation of the merger and does not require courts to guess how or whether the majority shareholders would have proceeded in the face of minority dissent.

Although a finding of materiality in a proxy solicitation may satisfy the elements of loss and transaction causation for forfeited state appraisal rights, plaintiffs must also prove that they in fact lost state appraisal rights. See *Virginia Bankshares,* at [1108] & n. 14. *** Accordingly, we must remand this matter for the limited purpose of determining whether the proxy solicitation actually resulted in the loss of any remedies available to plaintiffs under New York law. ***

II

Given the possibility that on remand defendants may again have liability imposed against them under § 14(a), we think it prudent to reach those aspects of the appeal and cross-appeal that challenge the trial court's calculation of damages. ***

The benefit of the bargain rule set forth in *Janigan v. Taylor,* 344 F.2d 781 (1st Cir. 1965), is the appropriate measure of damages in this matter. *Janigan* held a shareholder induced by fraud into selling his shares for less than fair consideration may recover future accretions in value of the stock, even if those damages are not foreseeable. Id. at 786-87. This rule applies to mergers involving fraudulent proxies as well as to face-to-face transactions under § 10(b). See *Osofsky v. Zipf,* 645 F.2d 107, 114 (2d Cir.1981). The goal of preventing the speculative fraud resulting when damages are awarded only for the difference in the values of the exchanged stocks, see id. (citing Restatement (Second) of Torts § 549(2), cmts. g, i (1977)), applies with as much force when appraisal rights are fraudulently forfeited as it does when a merger is fraudulently effected.

But to place plaintiffs in substantially the same position they would have occupied absent the fraud, they should be entitled to the profits attributable to the extra stock they would have received had the proxy provided a fair exchange ratio. Although the fraud may not be the proximate cause of the merger, it did cause the forfeiture of appraisal rights, which in turn prevented plaintiffs from realizing a fair exchange ratio. Thus the injury caused by the fraud cannot be measured by the shares that were exchanged, rather by the value of the additional shares that should have been exchanged but because of the fraud were not. The benefit of the bargain rule in the context of lost state appraisal rights would apply only to the stock never received, and not to the shares actually received. ***

### *NOTES AND QUESTIONS*

*1.* ***Speculativeness Again.*** As a general matter, shareholders pursue appraisal rights relatively rarely because to do so is expensive and time-consuming and may result in their receipt of a per share price that is less than that offered in the merger. See generally Robert B. Thompson, Exit, Liquidity, and Majority Rule: Appraisal's Role in Corporate Law, 84 Geo. L. J. 1 (1995). Does allowing shareholders to recover for lost appraisal rights entail a level of speculativeness that is unacceptable in light of *Virginia Bankshares*?

*2. The Benefit of the Bargain.* Should the *Wilson* court have limited the plaintiffs' recovery to the amount likely to have been forthcoming from the appraisal action that they did not pursue?

*3. The Statute of Limitations.* Revisit 18 U.S.C. § 1658(b), the statute of limitations enacted in 2002 as part of the Sarbanes-Oxley Act and set forth supra in on page 237. Does Section 1658(b) apply to Rule 14a-9 actions? Is it at least sometimes applicable? If not, what is the statute of limitations for Rule 14a-9 actions? Is the one year/three year structure adopted by the Supreme Court for Rule 10b-5 purposes prior to the enactment of the Section 1658(b) relevant in this regard? See *Lampf, Pleva, Lipkind, Prupis & Petigrow v. Gilbertson,* 501 U.S. 350 (1991), set forth supra in Chapter 2.I. Cf. *Westinghouse Elec. Corp. by Levit v. Franklin,* 993 F.2d 349, 353 (3d Cir. 1993) (applying *Lampf*'s one year/three year structure to Rule 14a-9).

## *PROBLEM 4-2*

Quincy Corporation issued a proxy statement that urged its shareholders to approve a merger with Dunster Corporation. The proxy statement included a forward-looking statement containing a material misrepresentation. Approval of the merger was a given, since management controlled eighty percent of the shares.

Jillian, one of the public shareholders, voted against the merger but did not perfect her appraisal rights. After the merger was consummated, she brought a Rule 14a-9 action that challenged the forward-looking statement. She claimed that had the proxy statement not been misleading, she would have perfected her appraisal rights and initiated an appraisal proceeding.

Quincy Corporation moved to dismiss Jillian's action. It contended that Jillian's causation argument is supported neither by *Virginia Bankshares* nor *Wilson* and therefore should be rejected.

Should the court grant the motion?

Cf. *Howing Co. v. Nationwide Corp.*, 972 F.2d 700 (6th Cir. 1992).

# Chapter 5

# TENDER OFFER FRAUD—SECTION 14(e) OF THE EXCHANGE ACT

---

Section 14(e) of the Exchange Act prohibits fraud in connection with tender offers. An important weapon in contests for corporate control, Section 14(e) did not appear in the Exchange Act as originally enacted. It was added in 1968, along with a number of other provisions on tender offer regulation. The 1968 amendments, encompassing Section 14(e) together with Sections 13(d), 13(e), 14(d), and 14(f), are known collectively as the Williams Act.

We begin our study of Section 14(e) with an overview of tender offers and the Williams Act (Section A). We then turn to litigation under Section 14(e) and contrast it with litigation under other fraud provisions of the federal securities laws, especially Section 10(b) and Rule 10b-5 (Section B). The Chapter concludes with a brief discussion of the critical role of state law in tender offer litigation (Section C).

## A. AN OVERVIEW OF TENDER OFFERS AND THE WILLIAMS ACT

The material that follows is intended to provide a context for our discussion of Section 14(e). Some students may have encountered this material previously in courses in corporations or mergers and acquisitions, whereas others will find it altogether new.

### *1. Tender Offers in General*

A tender offer enables a company (the "bidder") to acquire control of another company (the "target"). In a tender offer, the bidder offers to purchase all or some of the target's shares directly from the target's shareholders, typically at a premium over the market price. The bidder and the target are usually different companies, although occasionally a company makes a tender offer for its own shares in a transaction known as a "self tender offer."

Like a proxy contest, a tender offer provides a means of accomplishing an acquisition that is opposed by the target's management. An acquisition supported by the target's management is usually achieved through a "friendly" merger rather than a friendly tender offer. A "friendly" tender offer is by no means unknown, however.

When the bidder's goal is to control the target, a tender offer is often preferable to a proxy contest. Indeed, the winner in a proxy contest obtains seats on the board, whereas a successful bidder in a tender offer owns the shares and hence is guaranteed the control that such ownership provides. But a tender offer has the disadvantage of being expensive, both because the bidder has to buy the shares and also because the target's management can commence litigation against the bidder or implement defensive tactics designed to frustrate the offer.

Prior to the enactment of the Williams Act, tender offers were only minimally regulated by the federal securities laws (or by state law). To be sure, the registration and civil liability provisions of the Securities Act came into play in "exchange" offers—tender offers in which shareholders are asked to exchange their shares for securities rather than for cash. But these provisions do not apply when, as is common, cash is the sole consideration. And while it is true that fraud in connection with the bidder's purchase of the tendered shares is prohibited by Section 10(b) of the Exchange Act and Rule 10b-5, those provisions do nothing for the defrauded non-tendering shareholder.

The relative absence of federal regulation of tender offers contrasted sharply with the comprehensive federal regulation of proxy contests provided by Section 14(a) of the Exchange Act and SEC rules promulgated thereunder. Thus, by using a tender offer, hostile acquirers could avoid the mandatory disclosure and procedural regulations to which they would have been subject if they had instead conducted a proxy contest.

Without laws mandating disclosure, bidders often provided little information regarding such matters as their background and their plans for the target. Accordingly, shareholders were forced to decide whether to tender with little knowledge of the relevant facts. Congress recognized their plight when discussing the need for federal tender offer regulation in 1967:

> [A shareholder] has many alternatives. He can tender all of his shares immediately and hope they are all purchased. However, if the offer is for less than all the outstanding shares, perhaps only a part of them will be taken. In these instances, he will remain a shareholder in the company, under a new management which he has helped to install without knowing whether it will be good or bad for the company.
>
> The shareholder, as another alternative, may wait to see if a better offer develops, but if he tenders late, he runs the risk that none of his shares will be taken. He may also sell his shares in the market or hold them and hope for the best. Without knowledge of who the bidder is and what he plans to do, the shareholder cannot reach an informed decision.

S. Rep. 90-550 at 2 (1967).

Moreover, prior to the enactment of the Williams Act, a lack of information was not the only difficulty besetting shareholders faced with a tender offer. Common practices included giving shareholders only a short time to decide whether to tender, prohibiting withdrawals of tendered shares, giving some shareholders a better price than others, and offering to buy less than 100% of the shares (a "partial tender offer") while purchasing shares on a "first come, first served" basis. Partial tender offers coupled with "first come, first served" purchases caused Congress particular concern because bidders frequently used two-tiered transactions—first, a partial tender offer at an inadequate amount of cash per share, typically for a percentage of shares sufficient to give the bidder control, followed shortly thereafter by a second transaction squeezing out the remaining shareholders on even less desirable terms (e.g., junk bonds rather than cash). Confronting the decision whether to tender in the first tier, shareholders found themselves in a situation analogous to the prisoner's dilemma commonly used in game theory. Indeed, because the price paid in the first tier surpassed the price paid in the second tier, they were often coerced into tendering quickly, even though all shareholders would have been better off if none of them tendered.

Of course, even with disclosure, the decision whether to tender is frequently not an easy one to make. Consider a partial tender offer by a bidder with a good track record who has no present plans to acquire the remaining shares. A shareholder might plausibly refuse to tender in order to reap the benefits of a company controlled by responsible management. But she cannot be certain that the bidder will receive enough shares in the tender offer to achieve control in the first place.

### 2. *The Williams Act*

Prompted by an upsurge in tender offers in the 1960s, Congress enacted the Williams Act in 1968. That Act amended the Exchange Act to require disclosure and impose various other substantive and procedural protections on behalf of shareholders faced with the decision whether to tender their shares.

While providing shareholders with these protections, Congress sought to avoid playing favorites in the contest for control. In the words of the Supreme Court:

> The purpose of the Williams Act is to insure that public shareholders who are confronted by a cash tender offer for their stock will not be required to respond without adequate information regarding the qualifications and intentions of the offering party. By requiring disclosure of information to the target corporation as well as the Securities and Exchange Commission, Congress intended to do no more than give incumbent management an opportunity to express and explain its position. The Congress expressly disclaimed an intention to provide a weapon for management to discourage takeover bids or prevent large accumulations of stock which would create the potential for such attempts. Indeed, the Act's draftsmen commented upon the "extreme care" which was taken "to avoid tipping the balance of regulation either in favor of management or in favor of the person making the takeover bid." S. Rep. No. 550, 90th Cong., 1st Sess., 3 (1967); H.R. Rep. No. 1711, 90th Cong., 2d Sess., 4 (1968).

*Rondeau v. Mosinee Paper Corp.*, 422 U.S. 49, 58-59 (1975).

The Williams Act does not regulate the defensive tactics employed by the target's management. Such tactics are instead governed by the law of the target's state of incorporation (see Section C infra).

The Williams Act is embodied in Sections 13(d), 13(e), 14(d), 14(e), and 14(f) of the Exchange Act. Some of these Sections apply to acquisitions accomplished by any means, whereas others apply to tender offers only. Thus, after examining the various Sections and the manner of their enforcement, we will take a look at how "tender offer" is defined.

#### a. *Section 13(d)*

Section 13(d) provides the marketplace with an early indication that control of a company may be "in play." The Section applies to any acquirer (whether by tender offer or otherwise) of more than 5% of the shares of a class of equity security of a Section 12 company. (For a discussion of Section 12 companies, see Chapter 1.A.2.c). Such an acquirer must, within 10 days of making the acquisition, provide a report (the Schedule 13D) to the SEC, the target, and any exchanges on which the security is traded. Schedule 13D requires the acquirer to disclose his identity, background, source of financing, and any plans to make a later tender offer for the target.

The filing of a Schedule 13D has a several-fold impact. First, such a filing is likely to trigger an immediate sharp increase in the target's share price, particularly if it discloses that a tender offer is in the offing. Thus, if a tender offer does occur, the offering price is apt to be higher than it would have been in the absence of the Schedule 13D. Hence Schedule 13D makes tender offers more expensive for bidders and arguably for this reason may deter some tender offers altogether. Moreover, by mandating disclosure of future plans to launch a tender offer, Schedule 13D gives the target's management the opportunity to undertake defensive measures.

*b. Section 14(d)*

Unlike Section 13(d), Section 14(d) applies to tender offers specifically. Regulation under Section 14(d) takes several forms.

Under Section 14(d)(1), anyone who makes a tender offer for more than 5% of a class of equity security of a Section 12 company must file a Schedule TO with the SEC. Schedule TO requires disclosure of many items called for by Schedule 13D, along with the terms of the offer and the bidder's financial statements if "material" to the offer. Rules 14d-4 and 14d-6 govern the disclosures that must be made to the target's shareholders about the tender offer.

Under Section 14(d)(4), anyone (including the target) who makes a solicitation or recommendation to the target's shareholders concerning a tender offer must file a Schedule 14D-9 with the SEC. Schedule 14D-9 mandates many of the same disclosures called for by Schedule TO. In addition, it requires the target to indicate whether it is negotiating with another bidder (a "white knight").

Other subsections of Section 14(d) are designed to reduce shareholder coercion. Thus, the bidder must accept the tendered shares on a pro rata rather than a first-come-first-served basis (Section 14(d)(6) and Rule 14d-8); the shareholders may withdraw their tendered shares during the period that the tender offer remains open (Section 14(d)(5) and Rule 14d-7); and all tendering shareholders must be paid the same price (Section 14(d)(7) and Rule 14d-10). Shareholder coercion is also reduced by Rule 14e-1. That Rule, promulgated under Section 14(e), requires that the offer remain open for twenty business days. We return to Rule 14e-1 later in this Chapter when we discuss the SEC's rule-making authority under Section 14(e).

*c. Section 14(f)*

Section 14(f) applies to acquisitions governed by both Sections 13(d) and 14(d). Section 14(f) requires disclosure of arrangements involving a change in the membership of a majority of the target's board of directors that occurs other than by a vote of the shareholders. The disclosure must be made to the SEC as well as to the shareholders denied their franchise not less than 10 days before the new directors assume office.

*d. Section 13(e)*

Sections 13(d) and 14(d) are each inapplicable when a company purchases its own stock. Such purchases fall instead under Section 13(e), which prohibits a Section 12 company from "purchas[ing] any equity security issued by it" if doing so would violate rules adopted by the SEC. Thus, Section 13(e) and the rules adopted pursuant to it regulate issuer "buy-backs," so-called "going private transactions" (often structured as leveraged buyouts (LBOs)), and issuer self-tender offers.

*e. Section 14(e)*

Section 14(e) prohibits fraud in connection with any tender offer. In 1970, Congress added a final sentence to the Section that gives the SEC rule-making authority. Section 14(e) is the exclusive focus of the next section of this Chapter.

In contrast to Sections 13(d), 13(e), and 14(d), Section 14(e) applies to all tender offers regardless of whether the target of the acquisition is a Section 12 company. Moreover, in contrast to Sections 13(d) and 14(d), Section 14(e) applies regardless of whether the offer is for more than 5% of the shares.

*f. Enforcement*

Enforcement of the Williams Act can take several forms. The SEC enforces the Williams Act by means of administrative and judicial actions. See, e.g., *SEC v. First City Fin. Corp.*, 890 F.2d 1215 (D.C. Cir. 1989) (affirming injunctive and disgorgement orders for violations of Section 13(d) in connection with attempted hostile takeover of Ashland Oil Co.), set forth in Chapter 9.C.1. There is also the possibility (albeit remote) of a criminal prosecution by the Department of Justice (DOJ).

The Williams Act says nothing, however, about private enforcement. While courts have recognized implied private actions, their willingness to do so is in general greater when the relief sought is an injunction rather than damages. See, e.g., *Diceon Electronics, Inc. v. Calvary Partners, LP*, 772 F. Supp. 859, 865 (D. Del. 1991) (upholding target's right to sue for an injunction under Section 13(d) and collecting cases to this effect); *Hallwood Realty Partners, LP v. Gotham Partners, LP*, 2001 WL 46978 at *1 (S.D.N.Y. 2001) (rejecting target's right to sue for damages under Section 13(d) and collecting cases to this effect as well as cases denying target shareholders such a right to sue); *Drobbin v. Nicolet Instrument Corp.*, 631 F. Supp. 860, 908-914 (S.D.N.Y. 1986) (assuming that shareholders have right to sue for injunction under Section 14(f)). In the next section of this Chapter, we will give close attention to the implied private action under Section 14(e).

### *3. The Definition of a Tender Offer*

As noted, some Williams Act provisions apply to tender offers specifically. Questions sometimes arise concerning the application of these provisions to transactions which, while admittedly not conventional tender offers, nonetheless arguably call for the sort of regulation that the Williams Act provides. These questions cannot be answered by reference to a statutory definition of "tender offer" because the Williams Act does not provide one. Instead, the Act delegates the definition question to the courts, which in turn have generated two principal approaches.

One approach, known as the *Wellman v. Dickinson* eight-factor approach, determines the existence of a tender offer by reference to the following:

> (1) active and widespread solicitation of public shareholders for the shares of an issuer;
>
> (2) solicitation made for a substantial percentage of the issuer's stock;
>
> (3) offer to purchase made at a premium over the prevailing market price;
>
> (4) terms of the offer are firm rather than negotiable;
>
> (5) offer contingent on the tender of a fixed number of shares, often subject to a fixed maximum number to be purchased;
>
> (6) offer open only for a limited period of time;
>
> (7) offeree subjected to pressure to sell his stock;
>
> (8) public announcements of a purchasing program concerning the target company precede or accompany rapid accumulation of a large amount of target company's securities.

See *Wellman v. Dickinson,* 475 F. Supp. 783, 823-25 (S.D.N.Y. 1979) (applying the factors to solicitations made privately to institutions and to individuals), aff'd on other grounds, 682 F.2d 355 (2d Cir. 1982). See *SEC v. Carter Hawley Hale Stores,* 760 F.2d 945 (9th Cir. 1985) (applying the factors to a target's purchases of its own stock on the open market in response to a hostile tender offer). All of the *Wellman* factors do not have to be present in order to conclude that a tender offer has occurred. See *Wellman,* supra, 475 F. Supp. at 824 ("depending upon the circumstances ***, one or more of the [factors] may be more compelling and determinative than the others").

The other approach to the definition of a tender offer, set forth in *Hanson Trust PLC v. SMC Corp.*, 774 F.2d 47 (2d Cir. 1985), looks to whether the offerees require Williams Act protection:

> [T]he question of whether a solicitation constitutes a "tender offer" *** turns on whether, viewing the transaction in the light of the totality of the circumstances, there appears to be a likelihood that unless the pre-acquisition filing structures of that statutes are followed there will be a substantial risk that solicitees will lack information needed to make a carefully considered appraisal of the principal put before them.

Id. at 57 (applying this approach to five privately negotiated purchases and one open market purchase).

### *NOTES AND QUESTIONS*

*1. **Enforcing the Williams Act.*** What accounts for the complete absence of express private actions in the Williams Act? Did Congress drop the ball? Did it assume that courts would recognize implied private actions under some (or all) of the Act's provisions? Or did it intend to leave enforcement of the Williams Act to the SEC (and to the DOJ)?

*2. Victims of Noncompliance.* Consider Sections 13(d), 13(e), 14(d), and 14(f). Who is harmed, potentially, when the requisite disclosures are not made? Who is harmed the most? Whose interests did Congress most seek to protect? Other than an implied private action, what litigation vehicles are available to private plaintiffs who wish to challenge the failure to make the disclosures called for by the Williams Act?

*3. The Breadth of Section 14(e).* Recall that Section 14(e) applies to a tender offer regardless of whether the target is a Section 12 company and regardless of whether the bidder seeks more than 5% of the target's shares. The Section's broad reach may have been an instance of congressional foresight. Consider "mini-tender offers"—tender offers that seek to sidestep the strictures of Section 14(d) by seeking less than 5% of the shares of the target (which in addition is frequently not a Section 12 company). Some bidders offer a below-market price in mini-tender offers and thereby take advantage of uninformed shareholders who assume that a tender offer always involves a premium. See generally Commission Guidance on Mini-Tender Offers and Limited Partnership Tender Offers, Exchange Act Release No. 43069, 72 SEC Docket 2245 (July 24, 2000). The SEC has brought and settled a number of Section 14(e) actions against such bidders. See, e.g., *In the Matter of City Inv. Group, LLC*, Exchange Act Release No. 42919, 72 SEC Docket 1536 (June 12, 2000); *In the Matter of IG Holdings, Inc.*, Exchange Act Release No. 41759, 70 SEC Docket 832 (Aug. 19, 1999). Is it sensible for the SEC to use Section 14(e) in the mini-tender offer context? Or should these investors be expected to protect themselves by ascertaining the market price of their stock before deciding to tender?

## B. LITIGATION UNDER SECTION 14(e)

Section 14(e) comes into play in the vast majority of contested tender offers. It reads as follows:

> It shall be unlawful for any person to make any untrue statement of a material fact or omit to state any material fact necessary in order to make the statements made, in the light of the circumstances under which they are made, not misleading, or to engage in any fraudulent, deceptive, or manipulative acts or practices, in connection with any tender offer or request or invitation for tenders, or any solicitation of security holders in opposition to or in favor of any such offer, request, or invitation. The Commission shall, for the purposes of this subsection, by rules and regulations define, and prescribe means reasonably designed to prevent, such acts and practices as are fraudulent, deceptive, or manipulative.

Compare Section 14(e) with the Exchange Act's general antifraud provisions (Section 10(b) and Rule 10b-5) and its proxy antifraud provisions (Section 14(a) and Rule 14a-9). Compare Section 14(e) also with the Securities Act's general antifraud provision (Section 17(a)). What are the similarities and differences? Why does Section 14(e) say nothing about the use of interstate commerce, in contrast to Sections 10(b), 14(a), and 17(a)? Does this omission carry significance?

In turning to litigation under Section 14(e), we leave aside such litigation insofar as it involves insider trading. We take up that subject in Chapter 7.C.

Section 14(e) has much in common with Section 10(b) and Rule 10b-5. To begin with, both bar misstatements and omissions, apply regardless of the size of the company issuing the securities, and are enforceable in an implied private action (as well as in actions by the SEC and the DOJ). Moreover, private actions under Section 14(e), like those under Rule 10b-5, must satisfy various Exchange Act provisions that were enacted in 1995 as part of the PSLRA. These provisions require the plaintiff to establish loss causation when seeking damages (Section 21D(b)(4)), create a scheme of proportionate liability (Section 21D(f)), and stiffen pleading requirements (Section 21D(b)). In addition, Section 14(e) class actions must satisfy PSLRA class action provisions that you will encounter in Chapter 6.

Yet as we shall see, Section 14(e) and Rule 10b-5 part company in various respects as well. One example involves the safe harbor for forward-looking statements set forth in Section 21E of the Exchange Act. That safe harbor plays an important role in private litigation under Rule 10b-5 (see generally Chapter 2.B.3.c), but it specifically does not apply to litigation involving tender offers (see Section 21E(b)(2)(c)). Another difference involves the form that enforcement is likely to take. While the SEC and the DOJ bring Rule 10b-5 actions relatively frequently, they bring actions under Section 14(e) relatively infrequently (at least where insider trading is not at issue). Thus, much more than is the case with Rule 10b-5, Section 14(e) is enforced largely by investors. In this respect at least, Section 14(e) resembles Section 14(a) and Rule 14a-9. See generally Chapter 4.

Our examination of litigation under Section 14(e) is divided into three parts. They are (1) the necessity of proving misrepresentation or nondisclosure; (2) standing to sue; and (3) (further) comparisons between Section 14(e) and Rule 10b-5.

As you consider Section 14(e), think about the following questions. Should courts analogize Section 14(e) as much (or more) to Rule 14a-9 as to Rule 10b-5? Is judicial interpretation of Section 14(e) compromised by fear of the possible impact on Rule 10b-5, even if that fear is not expressly stated? When interpreting Section 14(e), what significance should be attached to the fact that it is a statute and not a rule? To the fact that it is enforced mainly in private actions? What accounts for the seeming lack of interest in tender offer fraud on the part of the SEC and the DOJ (at least when insider trading is not at issue)? Do the pleading requirements imposed by the PSLRA create any special difficulties in the context of tender offers?

### *1. The Necessity of Misrepresentation or Nondisclosure*

In the following decision, the Supreme Court addressed whether Section 14(e) requires proof of a misrepresentation or nondisclosure. The Court had previously resolved this issue for purposes of Rule 10b-5 in *Santa Fe Indus., Inc. v. Green*, 430 U.S. 462 (1977), set forth supra in Chapter 2.A.1.a. Notice how the Court used the *Santa Fe* precedent in particular and the Rule 10b-5 analogy in general.

## SCHREIBER v. BURLINGTON NORTHERN, INC.

472 U.S. 1 (1985)

CHIEF JUSTICE BURGER:

We granted certiorari to resolve a conflict in the Circuits over whether misrepresentation or nondisclosure is a necessary element of a violation of § 14(e) of the Securities Exchange Act of 1934.

I

On December 21, 1982, Burlington Northern, Inc., made a hostile tender offer for El Paso Gas Co. Through a wholly owned subsidiary, Burlington proposed to purchase 25.1 million El Paso shares at $24 per share. Burlington reserved the right to terminate the offer if any of several specified events occurred. El Paso management initially opposed the takeover, but its shareholders responded favorably, fully subscribing the offer by the December 30, 1982, deadline.

Burlington did not accept those tendered shares; instead, after negotiations with El Paso management, Burlington announced on January 10, 1983, the terms of a new and friendly takeover agreement. Pursuant to the new agreement, Burlington undertook, inter alia, to (1) rescind the December tender offer, (2) purchase 4,166,667 shares from El Paso at $24 per share, (3) substitute a new tender offer for only 21 million shares at $24 per share, (4) provide procedural protections against a squeeze-out merger[1] of the remaining El Paso shareholders, and (5) recognize "golden parachute"[2] contracts between El Paso

---

1. A "squeeze-out" merger occurs when Corporation A, which holds a controlling interest in Corporation B, uses its control to merge B into itself or into a wholly owned subsidiary. The minority shareholders in Corporation B are, in effect, forced to sell their stock. The procedural protection provided in the agreement between El Paso and Burlington required the approval of non-Burlington members of El Paso's board of directors before a squeeze-out merger could proceed. Burlington eventually purchased all the remaining shares of El Paso for $12 cash and one-quarter share of Burlington preferred stock per share. The parties dispute whether this consideration was equal to that paid to those tendering during the January tender offer.

2. Petitioner alleged in her complaint that respondent Burlington failed to disclose that four officers of El Paso had entered into "golden parachute" agreements with El Paso for "extended employment benefits in the event El Paso should be taken over, which benefits would give them millions of dollars of extra compensation." The term "golden parachute" refers generally to agreements between a corporation and its top officers which guarantee those officers continued employment, payment of a lump sum, or other benefits in the event of a change of corporate ownership. As described in the Schedule 14D-9 filed by El Paso with the Securities and Exchange Commission on January 12, 1983, El Paso entered into "employment agreements" with two of its officers for a period of not less than five years, and with two other officers for a period of three years. The Schedule 14D-9 also disclosed that El Paso's Deferred Compensation Plan had been amended "to provide that for the purposes of such Plan a participant shall be deemed to have retired at the instance of the Company if his duties as a director, officer or employee of the Company have been diminished or curtailed by the Company in any material respect."

and four of its senior officers. By February 8, more than 40 million shares were tendered in response to Burlington's January offer, and the takeover was completed.

The rescission of the first tender offer caused a diminished payment to those shareholders who had tendered during the first offer. The January offer was greatly oversubscribed and consequently those shareholders who retendered were subject to substantial proration. Petitioner Barbara Schreiber filed suit on behalf of herself and similarly situated shareholders, alleging that Burlington, El Paso, and members of El Paso's board of directors violated § 14(e)'s prohibition of "fraudulent, deceptive, or manipulative acts or practices ... in connection with any tender offer." She claimed that Burlington's withdrawal of the December tender offer coupled with the substitution of the January tender offer was a "manipulative" distortion of the market for El Paso stock. Schreiber also alleged that Burlington violated § 14(e) by failing in the January offer to disclose the "golden parachutes" offered to four of El Paso's managers. She claims that this January nondisclosure was a deceptive act forbidden by § 14(e).

The District Court dismissed the suit for failure to state a claim. The District Court reasoned that the alleged manipulation did not involve a misrepresentation, and so did not violate § 14(e). The District Court relied on the fact that in cases involving alleged violations of § 10(b) of the Securities Exchange Act, this Court has required misrepresentation for there to be a "manipulative" violation of the section.

The Court of Appeals for the Third Circuit affirmed. The Court of Appeals held that the acts alleged did not violate the Williams Act, because "§ 14(e) was not intended to create a federal cause of action for all harms suffered because of the proffering or the withdrawal of tender offers." The Court of Appeals reasoned that § 14(e) was "enacted principally as a disclosure statute, designed to insure that fully-informed investors could intelligently decide how to respond to a tender offer." It concluded that the "arguable breach of contract" alleged by petitioner was not a "manipulative act" under § 14(e).

We granted certiorari to resolve the conflict.[3] We affirm.

II

A

We are asked in this case to interpret § 14(e) of the Securities Exchange Act. The starting point is the language of the statute. ***

Petitioner relies on a construction of the phrase, "fraudulent, deceptive, or manipulative acts or practices." Petitioner reads the phrase "fraudulent, deceptive, or manipulative acts or practices" to include acts which, although

---

3. The Court of Appeals for the Sixth Circuit has held that manipulation does not always require an element of misrepresentation or nondisclosure. *Mobil Corp. v. Marathon Oil Co.*, 669 F.2d 366 (1981). The Courts of Appeals for the Second and Eighth Circuits have applied an analysis consistent with the one we apply today. *Feldbaum v. Avon Products, Inc.*, 741 F.2d 234 (C.A.8 1984); *Buffalo Forge Co. v. Ogden Corp.*, 717 F.2d 757 (C.A.2 1983).

fully disclosed, "artificially" affect the price of the takeover target's stock. Petitioner's interpretation relies on the belief that § 14(e) is directed at purposes broader than providing full and true information to investors.

Petitioner's reading of the term "manipulative" conflicts with the normal meaning of the term. We have held in the context of an alleged violation of § 10(b) of the Securities Exchange Act:

> Use of the word "manipulative" is especially significant. It is and was virtually a term of art when used in connection with the securities markets. It connotes intentional or willful conduct *designed to deceive or defraud* investors by controlling or artificially affecting the price of securities. *Ernst & Ernst* v. *Hochfelder*, 425 U.S. 185, 199 (1976) (emphasis added).

Other cases interpreting the term reflect its use as a general term comprising a range of misleading practices:

> The term refers generally to practices, such as wash sales, matched orders, or rigged prices, that are intended to mislead investors by artificially affecting market activity.... Section 10(b)'s general prohibition of practices deemed by the SEC to be "manipulative"—in this technical sense of artificially affecting market activity in order to mislead investors—is fully consistent with the fundamental purpose of the 1934 Act "'to substitute a philosophy of full disclosure for the philosophy of *caveat emptor*....'"... Indeed, nondisclosure is usually essential to the success of a manipulative scheme.... No doubt Congress meant to prohibit the full range of ingenious devices that might be used to manipulate securities prices. But we do not think it would have chosen this 'term of art' if it had meant to bring within the scope of § 10(b) instances of corporate mismanagement such as this, in which the essence of the complaint is that shareholders were treated unfairly by a fiduciary. *Santa Fe Industries, Inc.* v. *Green*, 430 U.S. 462, 476-477 (1977).

The meaning the Court has given the term "manipulative" is consistent with the use of the term at common law,[4] and with its traditional dictionary definition.[5]

She argues, however, that the term "manipulative" takes on a meaning in § 14(e) that is different from the meaning it has in § 10(b). Petitioner claims that the use of the disjunctive "or" in § 14(e) implies that acts need not be deceptive or fraudulent to be manipulative. But Congress used the phrase "manipulative or deceptive" in § 10(b) as well, and we have interpreted

---

4. For example, the seminal English case of *Scott v. Brown, Doering, McNab & Co.*, [1892] 2 Q.B. 724 (C.A.), which broke new ground in recognizing that manipulation could occur without the dissemination of false statements, nonetheless placed emphasis on the presence of deception. As Lord Lopes stated in that case, "I can see no substantial distinction between false rumours and false and fictitious acts." Id., at 730. See also *United States v. Brown*, 5 F. Supp. 81, 85 (S.D.N.Y. 1933) ("[E]ven a speculator is entitled not to have any present fact involving the subject matter of his speculative purchase or the price thereof misrepresented by word or act").

5. See Webster's Third New International Dictionary 1376 (1971) (Manipulation is "management with use of unfair, scheming, or underhanded methods").

"manipulative" in that context to require misrepresentation.[6] Moreover, it is a "'familiar principle of statutory construction that words grouped in a list should be given related meaning.'" *Securities Industry Assn. v. Board of Governors, FRS,* 468 U.S. 207, 218 (1984). All three species of misconduct, *i. e.*, "fraudulent, deceptive, or manipulative," listed by Congress are directed at failures to disclose. The use of the term "manipulative" provides emphasis and guidance to those who must determine which types of acts are reached by the statute; it does not suggest a deviation from the section's facial and primary concern with disclosure or congressional concern with disclosure which is the core of the Act.

B

Our conclusion that "manipulative" acts under § 14(e) require misrepresentation or nondisclosure is buttressed by the purpose and legislative history of the provision. Section 14(e) was originally added to the Securities Exchange Act as part of the Williams Act. "The purpose of the Williams Act is to insure that public shareholders who are confronted by a cash tender offer for their stock will not be required to respond without adequate information." *Rondeau v. Mosinee Paper Corp.*, 422 U.S. 49, 58 (1975).

It is clear that Congress relied primarily on disclosure to implement the purpose of the Williams Act. Senator Williams, the bill's Senate sponsor, stated in the debate:

> Today, the public shareholder in deciding whether to accept or reject a tender offer possesses limited information. No matter what he does, he acts without adequate knowledge to enable him to decide rationally what is the best course of action. This is precisely the dilemma which our securities laws are designed to prevent. 113 Cong. Rec. 24664 (1967).

The expressed legislative intent was to preserve a neutral setting in which the contenders could fully present their arguments.[8] The Senate sponsor went on to say:

> We have taken extreme care to avoid tipping the scales either in favor of management or in favor of the person making the takeover bids. S. 510 is designed solely to require full and fair disclosure for the benefit of investors.

---

6. *Santa Fe Industries, Inc. v. Green*, 430 U.S. 462, 476-477, 97 (1977); *Piper v. Chris-Craft Industries, Inc.*, 430 U.S. 1, 43 (1977); *Ernst & Ernst v. Hochfelder*, 425 U.S. 185, 199 (1976).

8. The process through which Congress developed the Williams Act also suggests a calculated reliance on disclosure, rather than court-imposed principles of "fairness" or "artificiality," as the preferred method of market regulation. For example, as the bill progressed through hearings, both Houses of Congress became concerned that corporate stock repurchases could be used to distort the market for corporate control. Congress addressed this problem with §13(e), which imposes specific disclosure duties on corporations purchasing stock and grants broad regulatory power to the Securities and Exchange Commission to regulate such repurchases. Congress stopped short, however, of imposing specific substantive requirements forbidding corporations to trade in their own stock for the purpose of maintaining its price. The specific regulatory scheme set forth in § 13(e) would be unnecessary if Congress at the same time had endowed the term "manipulative" in § 14(e) with broad substantive significance.

> The bill will at the same time provide the offeror and management equal opportunity to present their case. Ibid.

To implement this objective, the Williams Act added §§ 13(d), 13(e), 14(d), 14(e), and 14(f) to the Securities Exchange Act. Some relate to disclosure; §§ 13(d), 14(d), and 14(f) all add specific registration and disclosure provisions. Others—§§ 13(e) and 14(d)—require or prohibit certain acts so that investors will possess additional time within which to take advantage of the disclosed information.

Section 14(e) adds a "broad antifraud prohibition," *Piper v. Chris-Craft Industries, Inc.*, 430 U.S. 1, 24 (1977), modeled on the antifraud provisions of § 10(b) of the Act and Rule 10b-5.[10] It supplements the more precise disclosure provisions found elsewhere in the Williams Act, while requiring disclosure more explicitly addressed to the tender offer context than that required by § 10(b).

While legislative history specifically concerning § 14(e) is sparse, the House and Senate Reports discuss the role of § 14(e). Describing § 14(e) as regulating "fraudulent transactions," and stating the thrust of the section:

> This provision would affirm the fact that persons engaged in making or opposing tender offers or otherwise seeking to influence the decision of investors or the outcome of the tender offer are under an obligation to make *full disclosure* of material information to those with whom they deal." H. R. Rep. No. 1711, 90th Cong., 2d Sess., 11 (1968) (emphasis added); S. Rep. No. 550, 90th Cong., 1st Sess., 11 (1967) (emphasis added).

Nowhere in the legislative history is there the slightest suggestion that § 14(e) serves any purpose other than disclosure, or that the term "manipulative" should be read as an invitation to the courts to oversee the substantive fairness of tender offers; the quality of any offer is a matter for the marketplace.

To adopt the reading of the term "manipulative" urged by petitioner would not only be unwarranted in light of the legislative purpose but would be at odds with it. Inviting judges to read the term "manipulative" with their own sense of what constitutes "unfair" or "artificial" conduct would inject uncertainty into the tender offer process. An essential piece of information—whether the court would deem the fully disclosed actions of one side or the other to be "manipulative"—would not be available until after the tender offer had closed. This uncertainty would directly contradict the expressed congressional desire to give investors full information.

Congress' consistent emphasis on disclosure persuades us that it intended takeover contests to be addressed to shareholders. In pursuit of this goal, Congress, consistent with the core mechanism of the Securities Exchange

---

10. *** Because of the textual similarities, it is often assumed that § 14(e) was modeled on § 10(b) and Rule 10b-5. See, e.g., *Panter v. Marshall Field & Co.*, 646 F.2d 271, 283 (7th Cir. 1981). For the purpose of interpreting the term "manipulative," the most significant changes from the language of § 10(b) were the addition of the term "fraudulent," and the reference to "acts" rather than "devices." Neither change bears in any obvious way on the meaning to be given to "manipulative."

Similar terminology is also found in § 15(c) of the Securities Exchange Act [and] § 17(a) of the Securities Act of 1933 ***.

Act, created sweeping disclosure requirements and narrow substantive safeguards. The same Congress that placed such emphasis on shareholder choice would not at the same time have required judges to oversee tender offers for substantive fairness. It is even less likely that a Congress implementing that intention would express it only through the use of a single word placed in the middle of a provision otherwise devoted to disclosure.

C

We hold that the term "manipulative" as used in § 14(e) requires misrepresentation or nondisclosure. It connotes "conduct designed to deceive or defraud investors by controlling or artificially affecting the price of securities." *Ernst & Ernst* v. *Hochfelder*, 425 U.S., at 199. Without misrepresentation or nondisclosure, § 14(e) has not been violated.

Applying that definition to this case, we hold that the actions of respondents were not manipulative. The amended complaint fails to allege that the cancellation of the first tender offer was accompanied by any misrepresentation, nondisclosure, or deception. The District Court correctly found: "All activity of the defendants that could have conceivably affected the price of El Paso shares was done openly."

Petitioner also alleges that El Paso management and Burlington entered into certain undisclosed and deceptive agreements during the making of the second tender offer. The substance of the allegations is that, in return for certain undisclosed benefits, El Paso managers agreed to support the second tender offer. But both courts noted that petitioner's complaint seeks only redress for injuries related to the cancellation of the first tender offer. Since the deceptive and misleading acts alleged by petitioner all occurred with reference to the making of the second tender offer—when the injuries suffered by petitioner had already been sustained—these acts bear no possible causal relationship to petitioner's alleged injuries. The Court of Appeals dealt correctly with this claim.

III

The judgment of the Court of Appeals is affirmed.

## *NOTES AND QUESTIONS*

***1. Section 14(e)'s Two Prongs.*** Notice that Section 14(e) has two prongs. The first prong prohibits making a material misstatement or omission in connection with a tender offer. The second prong—separated from the first prong by an "or"—prohibits "engag[ing] in any fraudulent, deceptive, or manipulative acts or practices." Does the Court acknowledge the existence of these two prongs? If not, why not? What do you suppose prompted Congress to draft the statute in this fashion?

***2. "Fraudulent, Deceptive, or Manipulative."*** The Court suggested that the terms "fraudulent," "manipulative," and "deceptive" were duplicative. Why would Congress have intended duplication? But if Congress didn't intend duplication, why did it use all three terms? Might the term "fraudulent" have been intended to embrace the concept of constructive fraud, which would prohibit at least some acts of corporate mismanagement?

Why didn't Burlington's withdrawal of the December tender offer, coupled with substitution of the January tender offer at a lower price, not amount to a "manipulative" distortion of the market, as plaintiff alleged? Why did it not amount to deception, as the plaintiff also alleged?

*3. The* **Santa Fe** *Precedent.* Did the Supreme Court's *Santa Fe* decision render the result in *Schreiber* inevitable? Why or why not? To what extent do *Santa Fe* and *Schreiber* involve similar reasoning? To what extent is their reasoning different?

*4. The Road Not Taken.* The lower court in *Schreiber* had likewise upheld the necessity of proving a misrepresentation or nondisclosure, but primarily for reasons of policy rather than statutory language. Consider its analysis:

> Absent a requirement of deception, the Williams Act would mandate that the federal courts supervise the substantive fairness of practically all tender offers. Mindful of the Supreme Court's instruction in *Santa Fe* that we should be reluctant to federalize state corporate law, we decline to adopt *Mobil's* expansive view of § 14(e) and hold that deception is an essential element of a manipulative act.

*Schreiber v. Burlington Northern, Inc.,* 731 F.2d 163, 166 (3d Cir. 1984). Is it likely that the Supreme Court was also averse to federalizing state corporate law? If so, why did the Court not make its aversion explicit?

*5. The Nondisclosure Allegation.* Notice the plaintiff's allegation that Burlington had failed to disclose the "golden parachute" agreements. Why did this allegation fail to state a claim under Section 14(e)?

*6. Analogizing to Rule 10b-5.* To what extent does *Schreiber* direct lower courts to analogize to Rule 10b-5 when interpreting Section 14(e)?

*7. False Tender Offers.* Suppose Burlington had made the December tender offer without intending to consummate it but simply for the purpose of extracting the "golden parachute" agreements that accompanied the January tender offer. Would such conduct have constituted a violation of Section 14(e) as construed by *Schreiber*? Cf. *Wharf (Holdings) Ltd. v. United Int'l Holdings, Inc.,* 532 U.S. 588 (2001) (holding that a secret intention not to honor an option to buy stock satisfies the deception element of Section 10(b) and Rule 10b-5). In 1999, the SEC adopted Rule 14e-8, which reads as follows:

> It is a fraudulent, deceptive or manipulative act or practice within the meaning of section 14(e) of the Act for any person to publicly announce that the person (or a party on whose behalf the person is acting) plans to make a tender offer that has not yet been commenced, if the person:
>
> > (a) Is making the announcement of a potential tender offer without the intention to commence the offer within a reasonable time and complete the offer;
> >
> > (b) Intends, directly or indirectly, for the announcement to manipulate the market price of the stock of the bidder or subject company; or
> >
> > (c) Does not have the reasonable belief that the person will have the means to purchase securities to complete the offer.

What types of evidence would assist the SEC or private plaintiffs in pleading and proving a violation of Rule 14e-8?

*8. **Two-Track Litigation Framework.*** In the wake of *Schreiber*, claims involving breach of fiduciary duty in a tender offer must be filed in state court. Section 14(e) claims must be filed in federal court, however, since Section 27 of the Exchange Act calls for exclusive federal jurisdiction. Who benefits from this two-track litigation framework? Does it promote judicial economy?

### *PROBLEM 5-1*

WRG is an advertising firm established in 1987. The majority of the shares belonged to the WRG directors until 1995, when the company made a public offering. The directors netted $5 million in that offering.

In the years following, WRG was highly profitable. Its common stock traded at $30-35 a share, but fell to about $5 a share in a depressed market.

It was at the time of the depressed market that the directors decided to take the company private by making a tender offer for the publicly owned shares. Given the depressed market, the directors were able to offer a much lower price than would have been possible under other circumstances. The offering price was $3 cash plus an $8 note.

Glenn, a WRG shareholder, filed an action under Section 14(e) to enjoin the tender offer. He claimed that the offer to buy back the publicly held shares at a price much lower than that paid by the public shareholders violated Section 14(e). He also challenged the failure of the offering documents to state the price at which the WRG directors bought the shares prior to the IPO.

Defendants made a motion to dismiss for failure to state a claim under Section 14(e). Should the court grant the motion?

Cf. *Kaufmann v. Lawrence*, 386 F. Supp. 12 (S.D.N.Y. 1974).

### *2. Standing to Sue*

In the decision that follows, the Supreme Court addressed whether to grant a bidder standing to sue for damages. In so doing, it shed light on the general question of standing to sue under Section 14(e).

## PIPER v. CHRIS-CRAFT INDUSTRIES, INC.

430 U.S. 1 (1977)

[Chris Craft and Bangor Punta battled for control of Piper, and Bangor Punta prevailed. Chris Craft sued Bangor Punta and Piper for damages under Section 14(e). Chris Craft claimed that they had made fraudulent representations which had undermined its efforts to gain control of Piper.]

*** [W]e must consider whether § 14(e), which is entirely silent as to private remedies, permits this Court to read into the statute a damages remedy for unsuccessful tender offerors. To resolve that question we turn to the legislative history to discern the congressional purpose underlying the specific statutory prohibition in § 14(e). Once we identify the legislative purpose, we must then determine whether the creation by judicial interpretation of the implied cause of action asserted by Chris-Craft is necessary to effectuate Congress' goals. ***

The legislative history *** shows that Congress was intent upon regulating takeover bidders, theretofore operating covertly, in order to protect the shareholders of target companies. ***

Congress was indeed committed to a policy of neutrality in contests for control, but its policy of evenhandedness does not go either to the purpose of the legislation or to whether a private cause of action is implicit in the statute. Neutrality is, rather, but one characteristic of legislation directed toward a different purpose—the protection of investors. ***

*** In *Borak*, the Court emphasized that § 14(a), the proxy provision, was adopted expressly for "the protection of investors," the very class of persons there seeking relief. The Court found no difficulty in identifying the legislative objective and concluding that remedies should be available if necessary "to make effective the congressional purpose." *Borak* did not involve, and the statements in the legislative history relied upon by Chris-Craft do not implicate, the interests of parties such as offeror-bidders who are outside the scope of the concerns articulated in the evolution of this legislation.[22] ***

The legislative history *** shows that the sole purpose of the Williams Act was the protection of investors who are confronted with a tender offer. *** We find no hint in the legislative history *** that Congress contemplated a private cause of action for damages by one of several contending offerors against a successful bidder or by a losing contender against the target corporation.

*** It is clear *** that Chris-Craft has not asserted standing under § 14(e) as a Piper shareholder. The reason is not hard to divine. As a tender offeror actively engaged in competing for Piper stock, Chris-Craft was not in the posture of a target shareholder confronted with the decision of whether to tender or retain its stock. Consequently, Chris-Craft could scarcely have alleged a need for the disclosures mandated by the Williams Act. In short, the fact that Chris-Craft necessarily acquired Piper stock as a means of taking over Piper adds nothing to its § 14(e) standing arguments. ***

Chris-Craft argues, however, that Congress intended standing under § 14(e) to encompass tender offerors since the statute, unlike §10(b), does not contain the limiting language, "in connection with the purchase or sale" of securities. Instead, in § 14(e), Congress broadly proscribed fraudulent activities "in connection with any tender offer ... or any solicitation ... in opposition to or in favor of any such offer...."

---

22. In this connection, Chris-Craft emphasizes Congress' intent to treat tender offers in the same way as proxy solicitations, since both are devices for seeking corporate control. This argument, however, does not support the proposition that Chris-Craft should have a cause of action for damages, since this Court had not then held, nor has it since, that defeated insurgents in a proxy fight, suing in a capacity other than that of a shareholder, have a cause of action for damages. There is no occasion to resolve that question in this case.

The omission of the purchaser-seller requirement does not mean, however, that Chris-Craft has standing to sue for damages under § 14(e) in its capacity as a takeover bidder. It may well be that Congress desired to protect, among others, shareholder-offerees who decided not to tender their stock due to fraudulent misrepresentations by persons opposed to a takeover attempt. See generally 1 A. Bromberg, Securities Law: Fraud § 6.3 (1021), p. 122.17 (1969). See also Senate Report 2; House Report 3. These shareholders, who might not enjoy the protection of § 10(b) under *Blue Chip Stamps v. Manor Drugs Stores*, 421 U.S. 723 (1975), could perhaps state a claim under § 14(e), even though they did not tender their securities.[25] But increased protection, if any, conferred upon the class of shareholder-offerees by the elimination of the purchaser-seller restriction can scarcely be interpreted as giving protection to the entirely separate and unrelated class of persons whose conduct the statute is designed to regulate.

*** As a disclosure mechanism aimed especially at protecting shareholders of target corporations, the Williams Act cannot consistently be interpreted as conferring a monetary remedy upon regulated parties, particularly where the award would not redound to the direct benefit of the protected class. Although it is correct to say that the $36 million damages award indirectly benefits those Piper shareholders who became Chris-Craft shareholders when they accepted Chris-Craft's exchange offer, it is equally true that the damages award injures those Piper shareholders who exchanged their shares for Bangor Punta's stock and who, as Bangor Punta shareholders, would necessarily bear a large part of the burden of any judgment against Bangor Punta. The class sought to be protected by the Williams Act are the shareholders of the *target* corporation; hence it can hardly be said that their interests as a class are served by a judgment in favor of Chris-Craft and against Bangor Punta. Moreover, the damages are awarded to the very party whose activities Congress intended to curb; Chris-Craft did not sue in the capacity of an injured Piper shareholder, but as a defeated tender offeror.

Nor can we agree that an ever-present threat of damages against a successful contestant in a battle for control will provide significant additional protection for shareholders in general. The deterrent value, if any, of such awards can never be ascertained with precision. More likely, however, is the prospect that shareholders may be prejudiced because some tender offers may never be made if there is a possibility of massive damages claims for what courts subsequently hold to be an actionable violation of § 14(e).[26] Even a contestant who "wins the battle" for control may well wind up exposed to a costly "war" in a later and successful defense of its victory. Or at worst on Chris-Craft's

---

25. These cases, of course, do not present that issue, and we express no view on it.

26. *** The legal uncertainties that inevitably pervade this area of the law call into question whether "deterrence" of § 14(e) violations is a meaningful goal, except possibly with respect to the most flagrant sort of violations which no reasonable person could consider lawful. Such cases of flagrant misconduct, however, are not apt to occur with frequency, and to the extent that the violations are obvious and serious, injunctive relief at an earlier stage of the contest is apt to be the most efficacious form of remedy.

damages theory the victorious tender offeror or the target corporation might be subject to a large substantive judgment, plus high costs of litigation. ***

*** [A]warding damages to parties other than the protected class of shareholders has only a remote, if any, bearing upon implementing the congressional policy of protecting shareholders who must decide whether to tender or retain their stock.[28] Indeed, as we suggested earlier, a damages award of this nature may well be inconsistent with the interests of many members of the protected class and of only indirect value to shareholders who accepted the exchange offer of the defeated takeover contestant.

We therefore conclude that Chris-Craft, as a defeated tender offeror, has no implied cause of action for damages under § 14(e). ***

## *NOTES AND QUESTIONS*

***1. The Bidder and Standing to Sue.*** While holding that a bidder lacks standing to sue for damages under Section 14(e), the Court did not resolve whether a bidder has standing to sue for an injunction. What (if anything) did it imply about this matter? Subsequent to *Piper*, various lower courts have upheld a bidder's standing to sue for an injunction. One such court has synthesized the reasons for so doing as follows:

> Three tenets are relied on *** in reaching the conclusion that tender offerors have standing to seek injunctive relief under the Williams Act. First, in corporate control contests, injunctive relief at an early stage is "apt to be the most efficacious form of remedy." *Chris-Craft*, 430 U.S. at 40 n. 26. Second, tender offerors are more likely to be in a position to discover violations of the Act than other shareholders. Finally, if the plaintiffs' allegations are proven, the target company's shareholders benefit when the requested relief is granted.

*Torchmark Corp. v. Bixby*, 708 F. Supp. 1070, 1079 (W.D. Mo. 1988). Is this reasoning sound? Is it consistent with *Piper?* Is it sensible to disallow standing in a damages action but to allow standing in an injunctive action?

***2. The Target and Standing to Sue.*** In the wake of *Piper,* a number of courts have upheld a target's standing to sue for injunctive relief under Section 14(e) (typically for corrected disclosures). See, e.g., *Polaroid Corp. v. Disney,* 862 F.2d 987, 1003 (3d Cir. 1988) (collecting cases). One court explained its reasons for so doing as follows:

> In most cases, shareholders simply cannot protect their own interests; they lack the resources to confirm the accuracy of information in a Schedule 13D of 14D-1. The SEC simply cannot police every tender offer or major acquisition subject to the Williams Act. The issuer is frequently in the best position to seek corrective disclosures within a time frame that will optimize the benefit to shareholders of such disclosures. See *GAF Corp. v. Milstein,* 453 F.2d 709, 721 (2d Cir.1971).

---

28. Our holding is a limited one. Whether shareholder-offerees, the class protected by § 14(e), have an implied cause of action under § 14(e) is not before us, and we intimate no view on the matter. Nor is the target corporation's standing to sue in issue in this case. We hold only that a tender offeror, suing in its capacity as a takeover bidder, does not have standing to sue for damages under § 14(e). ***

> We conclude that it is necessary to grant this private right of action to issuers in order for the Williams Act to be effective.

*Florida Commercial Banks v. Culverhouse,* 772 F.2d 1513, 1519 (11th Cir. 1985). Is this reasoning sound? Is it consistent with *Piper?* Would *Piper* allow a court to grant a target standing to sue for damages?

*3. **The Target's Shareholders and Standing to Sue.*** What does *Piper* suggest about whether to grant the target's shareholders standing to sue? Does *Schreiber* shed light on this question? What is the value of Section 14(e) to a tendering shareholder, given the availability of Rule 10b-5?

### *PROBLEM 5-2*

Apex, Inc., owned 7% of the stock of Lincoln, Inc. Apex initiated a tender offer for Lincoln, making misrepresentations concerning its own history in connection with that offer. Shortly thereafter, Apex withdrew the tender offer. In fact, Apex never intended to make the tender offer for Lincoln. Its reason for initiating the offer was to enable it to sell its Lincoln shares at artificially inflated prices on the open market.

April is a Lincoln shareholder who refrained from selling her shares on the open market in anticipation of tendering her shares. Does she have standing to sue Apex for damages under Section 14(e)?

---

### *3. (Further) Comparisons Between Section 14(e) and Rule 10b-5*

Thus far in our consideration of Section 14(e), we have made a number of comparisons with Section 10(b) and Rule 10b-5. We pursue additional such comparisons in connection with the following decision, which was affirmed by the Second Circuit in unpublished order.

## WARDROP v. AMWAY ASIA PACIFIC LTD.

2001 WL 274067 (S.D.N.Y. 2001), aff'd, 2002 WL 126322 (2d Cir. 2002)

CHIN, DISTRICT JUDGE:

This proposed class action arises from a tender offer for stock of defendant Amway Asia Pacific, Ltd. ("AAP") at $18 per share. The tender offer was announced on November 15, 1999, the same day that an agreement between China and the United States permitting China to join the World Trade Organization (the "WTO") was announced. The news of the WTO agreement caused the market value of companies with business related to China to increase. Plaintiffs brought this action, before the tender offer period expired, alleging that $18 per share was not a fair price and that defendants engaged in fraud by not considering the impact of the WTO agreement on the value of AAP's stock. Defendants move to dismiss the amended complaint for failure to state a claim pursuant to Fed. R. Civ. P. 12 (b)(6) and failure to comply with Fed. R. Civ. P. 9(b).

The motion is granted, for the federal securities laws require not that a tender offer price be substantively fair, but only that full and accurate disclosure be made. Here, plaintiffs do not allege that defendants withheld any material information, nor do plaintiffs contend that defendants acted on the basis of any inside information. Rather, the factors that purportedly affected the value of the stock—the WTO agreement and China's impending entry into the WTO—were announced to the public. Moreover, plaintiffs brought suit before their time to tender expired. In other words, plaintiffs knew that the stock was purportedly underpriced before the time to tender their shares had expired, and thus they could have rejected the offer and chosen not to sell their shares. The amended complaint is dismissed for failure to state a claim upon which relief may be granted.

*BACKGROUND*

A. *Facts*

The facts alleged in the amended complaint are assumed to be true for the purposes of this motion and are as follows:

1. *The Parties*

Plaintiffs are former shareholders of AAP stock who sold their shares in connection with the tender offer. Plaintiffs sue individually and as proposed class representatives on behalf of all persons, excluding defendants, who held shares of AAP common stock on November 18, 1999, and sold their shares as a result of the tender offer.

Defendants include the "Principal Shareholders" of AAP, directors and officers of AAP, members of a special committee appointed by the AAP board of directors to consider the fairness of the tender offer price, and Goldman, Sachs & Co. ("Goldman, Sachs"), which was retained to render an opinion as to the fairness of the tender offer price.

AAP, a Bermuda company, is the exclusive distributor in the Asian Pacific region for Amway Corporation ("Amway"), a manufacturer and retailer of home and personal care products.

2. *The Tender Offer*

In 1998, the Principal Shareholders began discussions about taking AAP private. In October 1999, AAP's board formed a special committee to evaluate and negotiate any such proposal. On November 15, 1999, AAP and the Principal Shareholders announced that the Principal Shareholders intended to commence a cash tender offer to purchase, for $18 per share, the 15% of AAP stock that they did not own. Pursuant to the Offer to Purchase, which was issued on November 18th, shareholders had the opportunity to tender their shares or revoke a decision to tender their shares for one month, until the tender offer period expired on December 17, 1999. The Offer to Purchase represented that the special committee and disinterested directors had determined that the offer was fair. As stated in the Offer to Purchase, under Bermuda law shareholders who questioned the fairness of the tender offer price could apply to the Bermuda court for a court appraisal of the fair market value of the shares.

3. *The WTO Agreement*

After 13 years of discussions, China and the United States reached an agreement permitting China to join the WTO. The agreement and the $18 per share tender offer were both announced on November 15, 1999. As a result of the WTO announcement, companies with business related to China increased in value.

B. *Procedural History*

Plaintiffs commenced this action by filing a complaint on December 16, 1999 alleging that defendants committed securities fraud pursuant to § 14(e) of the Securities Exchange Act of 1934 (the "Exchange Act"). On June 26, 2000, plaintiffs filed an amended complaint, adding claims for violations of § 10(b) of the Exchange Act, Rule 10b-5, and § 20(a) of the Exchange Act, against the individual defendants. Plaintiffs also added a claim based on Bermuda common law against the Principal Shareholders. Plaintiffs allege that defendants knew that the market would react strongly to the news about the WTO and that defendants sought to announce the $18 tender offer price before the WTO news was made public. Plaintiffs further allege that defendants committed securities fraud by failing to consider the anticipated impact of China's entry into the WTO in determining a fair tender offer price, and by failing to recalculate a fair price after the WTO agreement was reached. Plaintiffs seek rescission, damages, and costs.

This motion followed.

*DISCUSSION*

A. *Applicable Law*

1. *Motions to Dismiss*

When reviewing a motion to dismiss, a court must accept as true the facts presented in the complaint and must view the pleadings in the light most favorable to, and draw reasonable inferences in favor of, the non-moving party. A court shall dismiss a complaint only when "it appears beyond doubt that the plaintiff can prove no set of facts in support of his claim which would entitle him to relief." *Conley v. Gibson,* 355 U.S. 41, 45-56 (1957). The issue "is not whether a plaintiff will ultimately prevail but whether the claimant is entitled to offer evidence to support its claims." *Village Pond, Inc. v. Darien,* 56 F.3d 375, 378 (2d Cir. 1995). In considering a motion to dismiss, a court may consider only the allegations of the pleadings and documents that are integrated in the pleading by reference.

2. *Securities Laws*

Plaintiffs sue under §§ 10(b), 14(e), and 20(a) of the Exchange Act and Rule 10b-5 and Bermuda common law.

To state a cause of action under § 10(b) and Rule 10b-5, plaintiffs must allege: (1) in connection with a purchase or sale of securities; (2) each defendant, acting with scienter; (3) made a material false representation, or omitted to disclose material information, or engaged in a scheme to defraud; (4) to each plaintiff's detrimental reliance. *Ganino v. Citizens Utils. Co.,* 228 F.3d 154, 161

(2d Cir. 2000). Section 14(e) is modeled after § 10(b) and applies specifically to tender offers. *Schreiber v. Burlington N., Inc.*, 472 U.S. 1, 10 (1985). Accordingly, as with a claim under § 10(b), to properly plead a violation of § 14(e), plaintiffs must assert that they relied upon defendants' alleged misrepresentation and that this reliance caused them injury. *Lewis v. McGraw*, 619 F.2d 192, 194-95 (2d Cir. 1980).

Section 20(a) of the Exchange Act provides that "every person who ... controls any person liable [for violation of §§ 10(b), 14(e) or Rule 10b-5] ... shall also be liable jointly and severally with and to the same extent as such controlled person." To withstand a motion to dismiss a § 20(a) claim, plaintiffs must allege: (1) an underlying primary violation by the controlled person; (2) control over the controlled person; and (3) particularized facts as to the controlling person's culpable participation in the fraud perpetrated by the controlled person. *Securities and Exchange Comm'n v. First Jersey Secs., Inc.*, 101 F.3d 1450, 1472 (2d Cir. 1996). Plaintiffs' allegation of a § 20(a) violation will not survive a motion to dismiss unless plaintiffs properly allege an underlying primary violation. ***

B. *Application*

Defendants move to dismiss, inter alia, on the following grounds: plaintiffs' allegations do not fall within the scope of the federal securities laws; plaintiffs fail to allege a prima facie claim of a federal securities fraud violation; and the Court should not exercise supplemental jurisdiction over plaintiffs' Bermuda law claim.

1. *Scope of §§ 10(b) and 14(e)*

Defendants argue that plaintiffs' claims do not fall within the scope of the federal securities laws relied on in this case. I agree.

Plaintiffs allege that defendants violated §§ 10(b) and 14(e) because they failed to factor into the tender offer price the impact of the anticipated outcome of the negotiations regarding China's entry into the WTO. According to plaintiffs, it was apparent that if China were to join the WTO, the value of AAP stock would increase, and that had defendants considered the possibility that an agreement would soon be reached, a fair tender offer price would have exceeded $18 per share. Plaintiffs further allege that presenting $18 per share as a fair offer was materially false and misleading. Plaintiffs also assert that defendants violated the federal securities laws by failing to reconsider the fairness of the tender offer price during the three days between the announcement of China's inclusion in the WTO and the date that the Offer to Purchase went into effect.

These claims, however, fall outside the ambit of §§ 10(b) and 14(e). The fundamental purpose of the Exchange Act is to ensure full disclosure so that investors may make intelligent and informed decisions. *Santa Fe Indus., Inc. v. Green*, 430 U.S. 462, 477-78 (1977) (in § 10(b) case, describing the Exchange Act as "implementing a philosophy of full disclosure"); see also *Schreiber*, 472 U.S. at 5 (stating the same regarding § 14(e)). The scope of § 10(b) does not include instances of corporate mismanagement. *Santa Fe*, 430 U.S. at 477. The Supreme Court, in examining the scope of § 14(e), observed that "nowhere in the legislative history is there the slightest suggestion that § 14(e) serves any purpose other than disclosure ... or that the ... [provision] should be read as an invitation to the courts to oversee the substantive fairness of tender offers; the quality of any offer is a matter for the marketplace." *Schreiber*, 472 U.S. at 11-12. This Court has held that an "allegation that defendants falsely characterized the tender offer price as fair and failed to disclose that it was unfair does not state a claim under § 14(e)." *In re Phlcorp Secs. Tender Offer Litig.*, 700 F. Supp. 1265, 1269 (S.D.N.Y. 1988).

Plaintiffs' claims that defendants failed to factor the WTO negotiations and agreement into the determination of the tender offer price are not allegations of nondisclosure. Even assuming that the defendants did anticipate that the WTO news would increase the value of AAP shares, but did not reveal this information, plaintiffs have not stated a claim of fraud because the news of the WTO agreement was publicly available. As the Supreme Court has held, a private cause of action under the antifraud provisions of the Exchange Act may be brought only where it is necessary to ensure the fulfillment of Congress's intent to implement full disclosure. *Santa Fe*, 430 U.S. at 477-78. Here, where the information that defendants allegedly failed to disclose was publicly disseminated, investors did not need to rely on disclosure statutes to ensure that they were fully informed.

While plaintiffs' allegations arguably may constitute claims of negligence or breach of fiduciary duty, they do not fall within the purview of the federal securities laws relied on in this case. See *Santa Fe*, 430 U.S. at 479-80 ("There may well be a need for uniform federal fiduciary standards to govern mergers ... but those standards should not be supplied by judicial extension of § 10(b) and Rule 10b-5 to cover the corporate universe."); *Chiarella v. United States*, 445 U.S. 222, 232 (1980) ("not every instance of financial unfairness constitutes fraudulent activity under § 10(b)").

For the reasons stated above, plaintiffs' §§ 10(b) and 14(e) and Rule 10b-5 claims are dismissed.

2. *Requisite Elements of §§ 10(b) and 14(e) Claims*

Plaintiffs' allegations of federal securities fraud are also dismissed for failure to sufficiently plead the requisite elements.

To properly plead a cause of action pursuant to §§ 10(b) and 14(e), plaintiffs must allege detrimental reliance on defendants' alleged misrepresentation. See *Lewis*, 619 F.2d at 194-95. Here, even assuming defendants knowingly and falsely represented that $18 per share was a fair price by omitting information about the impending entry of China into the WTO, plaintiffs could not have reasonably relied to their detriment on that misrepresentation. First, the announcement of the WTO agreement was made the same day the tender offer was announced. Hence, the allegedly withheld information was publicly available in any event. Second, plaintiffs could have chosen not to sell their shares. They had until December 17, 1999 to tender their shares or to withdraw any shares that had been tendered. Plaintiffs' attorneys executed the original complaint on December 15th and filed it on December 16th. Accordingly, plaintiffs were aware of the alleged fraud before the tender offer period expired. Indeed, plaintiffs filed the complaint asserting these allegations when they still had a choice: they could have chosen not to tender their shares. Moreover, in those instances where they had already tendered, they still could have revoked their decision to tender.

Plaintiffs argue that reliance is not a necessary element of their claims or alternatively that reliance is presumed. The cases cited by plaintiffs, however, are distinguishable. For example, plaintiffs cite to *Lewis*, 619 F.2d 192, for the proposition that reliance should be presumed. In *Lewis*, however, the Second Circuit held that reliance may be presumed in situations in which "reliance is possible, and even likely, but is unduly burdensome to prove." *Lewis*, 619 F.2d at 195. The Second Circuit further held that "we presume reliance only where it is logical to do so.... Where no reliance was possible under any imaginable set of facts, such a presumption would be illogical in the extreme." Id. Here, plaintiffs could not have relied on the alleged false and misleading representation because the information was publicly available and plaintiffs filed the complaint before the tender offer period expired. Similarly, plaintiffs also cite to *Herbst v. International Tel. & Tel. Corp.*, 495 F.2d 1308 (2d Cir. 1974), and *Affiliated Ute Citizens v. United States*, 406 U.S. 128, 153-54 (1972). Those cases are also distinguishable. The issue in *Herbst* was whether proof of reliance by each class member is necessary for recovery of a securities fraud class action. That, however, is not the issue here. The issue in the instant case is whether plaintiffs alleged reliance sufficient for a well-pleaded securities fraud case, not whether class action is appropriate. The Supreme Court's ruling in *Affiliated Ute*, is also not relevant because *Affiliated Ute* involved a situation where some of the plaintiffs could have relied (and, in fact, likely did rely) on the defendants' misrepresentation. In the instant case, however, none of the plaintiffs could have relied on the alleged misrepresentation. Accordingly, plaintiffs' claims pursuant to §§ 10(b) and 14(e) and Rule 10b-5 are also dismissed for failing to sufficiently allege reliance.

3. *Section 20(a)*

Because plaintiffs do not allege a viable federal securities claim under §§ 10(b) or 14(e) or the corresponding rules, plaintiffs' § 20(a) claim is also dismissed. See *First Jersey Secs.*, 101 F.3d at 1472.

4. *Bermuda Common Law*

Plaintiffs assert a claim of oppression of minority shareholders under Bermuda common law against the Principal Shareholders. In light of the dismissal of plaintiffs' federal causes of action, I decline to exercise supplemental jurisdiction over plaintiffs' Bermuda law claim. With no federal claims and no allegation of diversity jurisdiction, plaintiffs' Bermuda law claim is dismissed without prejudice for lack of subject matter jurisdiction. ***

## *NOTES AND QUESTIONS*

***1. Inside Information?*** According to the court, the plaintiffs did not claim that the defendants "acted on the basis of any inside information." Do you agree?

***2. The Materiality Requirement.*** Courts employ the same definition of materiality under Section 14(e) that they employ under Rule 14a-9 and Rule 10b-5: "An omitted [or misrepresented] fact is material if there is a "substantial likelihood that a reasonable shareholder would consider it important" or if there is a substantial likelihood that *** the omitted [or misrepresented] fact would have *** significantly altered the 'total mix' of information made available." *TSC Indus., Inc. v. Northway, Inc.,* 426 U.S. 438, 448-49 (1976) (decision under Rule 14a-9). See *Basic Inc. v. Levinson,* 485 U.S. 224 (1988) (adopting *Northway* standard for Rule 10b-5 purposes); *Nobles v. First Carolina Communications, Inc,* 929 F.2d 141, 145 (4th Cir. 1991) (applying *Northway to* Section 14(e)).

In an apparent reference to the materiality requirement, *Wardrop* concluded that "plaintiffs have not stated a claim of fraud because the news of the WTO agreement was publicly available." Is the court suggesting that the information was already part of the "total mix" of information available to shareholders deciding whether to tender? Or is it suggesting instead that by virtue of being publicly available, the information would already have been impounded in the market price? Possibly both? Is the court's failure to clarify this point simply accidental?

*3.* ***Forward-Looking Statements.*** As noted at the beginning of this Chapter, the Exchange Act's safe harbor for forward-looking statements explicitly excludes tender offers. See Exchange Act Section 21E(b)(2)(c). What is the rationale for this exclusion? The SEC has the authority to expand the safe harbor and override this (or any) statutory exclusion from it. See Exchange Act Section 21E(b). Should it override the exclusion for tender offers?

Recall the bespeaks caution doctrine, another shield for defendants charged with making fraudulent forward-looking statements. See generally Chapter 2.B.3.b (discussing the bespeaks caution doctrine in the context of Rule 10b-5). Does that doctrine suffice for purposes of protecting defendants who are charged with making fraudulent forward-looking statements in the tender offer context?

*4.* ***The Scienter Requirement.*** Does *Wardrop* suggest that Section 14(e) contains a scienter requirement? Professor Loss and Dean Seligman maintain that the relevance of scienter to Section 14(e) turns on which portion of the Section is at issue:

> Section 14(e), though not quite as broad as Rule 14a-9, is similar to § 17(a) of the 1933 Act; and, unlike Rule 10b-5, is a statute—not a rule. Therefore the Supreme Court's construction of § 17(a) [in *Aaron v. SEC,* 446 U.S.680 (1980)] should govern so as to conclude that scienter (whatever its meaning) is required by the "fraudulent" and "deceptive" clause of § 14(e), which more or less tracks § 17(a)(1) of the 1933 Act and § 10(b) of the 1934 Act, but not by the untrue statement clause, which *precisely* tracks § 17(a)(2).

5 Louis Loss & Joel Seligman, Securities Regulation 2255 (3d ed. 1990). Does this analysis clash with that of *Schreiber*? Should the definition of scienter for Section 14(e) purposes be the same as it is for Rule 10b-5 purposes?

*5.* ***The Reliance Requirement.*** In its unpublished order in *Wardrop,* the Second Circuit stated as follows: "The district court did not err in dismissing the complaint on the ground, inter alia, that it failed adequately to plead the reliance element of plaintiffs' claims or to present any logical basis on which reliance could be proven or presumed." 2002 WL 126322 at * 1 (2d Cir. 2002). Do you agree?

To support its view as to the impossibility of reliance in *Wardop*, the district court cited *Lewis v. McGraw*, 619 F.2d 192, 194-95 (2d Cir. 1980), where reliance had been literally impossible because the tender offer had been withdrawn. Was reliance in *Wardrop* literally impossible?

Assume that the named plaintiffs in *Wardrop* did not rely on the fraud. Is it arguable that they were nonetheless injured by the decisions of less knowledgeable shareholders who did rely? Cf. *Kahn v. Lynden, Inc.*, 705 F. Supp. 1458, 1463-64 (W.D. Wash. 1989) (noting that "[w]hile the plaintiffs themselves had adequate information, their cause of action [under Section 14(e)] is based on the allegation that the other public shareholders did not and that the defendants' fraud consequently caused the majority to tender and assured the success of the tender offer, forcing the plaintiffs to sell [in a subsequent squeeze-out merger] and resulting in their injury").

Recall that in actions for proxy fraud under Rule 14a-9, plaintiffs do not need to establish their own individual reliance. See generally Chapter 4.D.1. So far as concerns reliance under Section 14(e), should courts analogize to Rule 14a-9 rather than to Rule 10b-5? Why or why not?

*6. **Presumptions of Reliance.*** In *Wardrop*, both the Second Circuit and the district court indicate a general willingness to presume reliance under Section 14(e). Under what circumstances would a presumption be appropriate? What about a presumption when the allegation involves the omission of material information, as there is under Rule 10b-5? See *Affiliated Ute v. United States*, 406 U.S. 128 (1972). See generally Chapter 2.F.1.a. What about a presumption based on fraud-on-the-market, as there is under Rule 10b-5? See *Basic Inc. v. Levinson*, 485 U.S. 224 (1988). See generally Chapter 2.F.1.b. The latter presumption assumes the existence of an efficient market. See generally id. In the context of a tender offer, is the market efficient? More efficient than usual? Less so, or only efficient regarding some types of information?

*7. **The Reasonable Reliance Requirement.*** *Wardrop* also suggests that the plaintiff's reliance must be "reasonable." Why should there be a reasonable reliance requirement under Section 14(e)? Is the requirement based on an analogy to Rule 10b-5 (where it is sometimes called the justifiable reliance requirement)? See generally Chapter 2.F.1.d. In the Rule 10b-5 context, reasonable reliance issues arise primarily in the context of face-to-face transactions. See generally id. Is it sensible to import such a requirement into the tender offer context?

*8. **Damages.*** Section 14(e) says nothing about how to measure damages in a private action. This silence is not surprising, given that the private action under the Section is implied. Courts typically require a Section 14(e) plaintiff to establish specific damages that flowed from the defendant's violation. The burden of so doing can be daunting. One court put it this way: "While Congress has determined that accurate disclosure is important to shareholders, it would often be impossible for shareholders to prove that on the facts of their particular tender offer accurate disclosure would have affected their decision making in a particular way with concomitant quantifiable monetary loss." *Polaroid Corp. v. Disney*, 862 F.2d 987, 1006-07 (3d Cir. 1988) (directing the lower court to order a preliminary injunction on behalf of the target, partly because of the difficulty in establishing damages). Moreover, when it comes to damages sought by shareholders, a court may take into account whether the price they received for their shares was fair: "While the issue of fairness is relevant to the issue of damages, it does not necessarily defeat a plaintiff's claim of injury." *Plaine v. McCabe,* 797 F.2d 713, 721 (9th Cir. 1986). See also *Horowitz v. Pownall,* 582 F. Supp. 665, 668 (D. Md. 1984) (nontendering shareholders must show damages resulting from retention of their shares).

*9. **The Relevance of Policy Debates.*** Debates swirl over whether shareholders benefit from the regulation of tender offers. See, e.g., Gregg A. Jarrell & Michael Bradley, The Economic Effects of Federal and State Regulations of Cash Tender Offers, 23 J. L. & Econ. 371 (1980) (tender offer regulation increases premiums paid in tender offers); Roberta Romano, A Guide to Takeovers: Theory, Evidence and Regulation, 9 Yale J. on Reg. 119 (1992) (overview of the academic literature). Because this is not a casebook on mergers and acquisitions, we do not systematically address these economic and policy issues. But a lawyer who is familiar with these issues can enhance a litigation team in a tender offer case. Indeed, policy reasons for and against regulatory intervention can be used to strengthen legal arguments, particularly with respect to damages or injunctive remedies once a violation is found to have occurred.

### *PROBLEM 5-3*

Red, Inc., made a partial tender offer for the shares of Blue, Inc. Shares had to be delivered by midnight on December 10, 2002 in order to be in the proration pool. On December 11, Red issued a press release stating that the pool consisted of 50 million Blue shares.

Zoe, a Blue shareholder, relied on the size of the pool as stated in the press release to calculate the number of shares that would be returned to her. Knowing that the market price for the unpurchased and returned shares would be substantially lower than the price being paid under the tender offer, she attempted to reduce her losses by engaging in various hedging transactions involving the shares to be returned, including selling calls and/or buying puts as well as option transactions and short sales.

The actual size of the proration pool turned out to be 70 million shares. Thus, on January 15, 2003, more shares were returned unpurchased to Zoe and other Blue shareholders than could have been expected based on the press release.

On February 1, 2003, Zoe sued Red under Section 14(e). She claimed that the press release misrepresented the size of the proration pool and that by relying on that misrepresentation, she incurred losses in connection with her hedging transactions and thus with the disposition of her unpurchased shares.

Red responded with a motion to dismiss. It argues that because there is no claim that its statements affected a decision whether to tender or to withdraw tendered shares, Section 14(e) does not apply. Should Red's motion be granted?

Cf. *Pryor v. United States Steel Corp.,* 591 F. Supp. 942 (S.D.N.Y. 1984).

### *PROBLEM 5-4*

Catherine filed a damages action under Section 14(e) 18 months after receiving notice of the fraud described in Problem 5-3, supra. Is her claim barred on statute of limitations grounds?

#### *4. The SEC's Rulemaking Authority*

Recall the final sentence of Section 14(e): "The Commission shall, for the purposes of this subsection, by rules and regulations define, and prescribe means reasonably designed to prevent, such acts and practices as are fraudulent, deceptive, or manipulative." Thus, the SEC's rulemaking authority has two aspects—definition and prevention.

The above-quoted sentence constitutes a departure from Section 10(b), which allows the SEC merely to prohibit "manipulative or deceptive device[s] or contrivance[s]." The sentence instead parallels Exchange Act Section 15(c)(2)(D), which focuses on broker-dealers in the over the counter market. Under Section 15(c)(2)(D), the SEC is authorized to "define, and prescribe means reasonably designed to prevent, such [broker-dealer] practices as are fraudulent, deceptive, and manipulative." See *United States v. O'Hagan*, 521 U.S. 642, 672 n.16 (1997) (identifying examples of SEC rulemaking under Section 15(c)(2)(D) that "reach beyond common law fraud").

The Supreme Court considered the SEC's rulemaking authority under Section 14(e) in *United States v. O'Hagan*, supra. At issue in *O'Hagan* was the validity of Rule 14e-3(a), which prohibits insider trading in connection with a tender offer. The Court upheld the Rule as an appropriate exercise of the SEC's power to prevent fraud. The Court was thus able to avoid addressing the government's argument that the SEC's authority to define fraud under Section 14(e) was broader than its authority to define fraud under Section 10(b). (The *O'Hagan* decision receives extensive attention in Chapter 7 on insider trading.)

The SEC's rulemaking authority is an important issue under Section 14(e) outside the insider trading context. Recall that earlier in this Chapter we mentioned Rule 14e-1, adopted by the SEC pursuant to its authority under Section 14(e). Rule 14e-1 requires a bidder to keep the tender offer open for at least twenty business days, presumably to give shareholders sufficient time to ponder the disclosures that are required to be made under Section 14(d). It would seem, however, to be a stretch to say that a tender offer that is held open for 10 days—or 19 days—is a fraudulent, deceptive, or manipulative tender offer. If Rule 14e-1 is a valid exercise of the SEC's rulemaking authority under Section 14(e), it must be as a prophylactic measure to prevent fraud, not as a prohibition of fraud itself. See generally *Polaroid Corp. v. Disney*, 862 F.2d 987 (3d Cir. 1988) (considering SEC's authority to adopt Rule 14d-10, which requires that all shareholders in a tender offer receive the same price for their shares). Why do you suppose that the SEC adopted the twenty day rule under Section 14(e) rather than under Section 14(d)?

## C. THE CRITICAL ROLE OF STATE LAW IN TENDER OFFER LITIGATION

In most hostile tender offers, litigation between the target and the bidder can generally be expected. In many instances, target shareholders may also become parties to the lawsuit, with shareholders who wish to accept the bidder's offer aligning with the bidder, and other shareholders sometimes aligning with the target's management.

Litigation over the offer is in many cases simultaneously conducted in federal court (under the Williams Act) and in state court (under state law governing the fiduciary duties of the target's management in responding to the tender offer). In situations where the bidder does not have standing to sue the target, a target shareholder often sues the target management, sometimes with the bidder's encouragement.

Directors of target corporations routinely respond to hostile tender offers with a wide variety of measures designed to thwart the bidder's plan to take control of the company. These defensive measures, often described in artful words and phrases, include seeking a friendly acquirer (a "white knight"); granting preferential options on stock or assets to white knights or persons other than the hostile bidder ("lock-up options"); selling the corporation's most valuable assets ("sale of crown jewels"); implementing rights plans that entitle existing shareholders to large amounts of stock, debt securities, or cash if a hostile bidder gains control ("poison pills"); launching a bid for the bidder itself (the "Pac Man Defense"); paying off the hostile bidder in return for it agreeing to go away ("green mail"); and contractually binding the target corporation to make large severance payments to incumbent managers in the event of a change of control ("golden parachutes").

Because of the *Schreiber* decision, state law continues to govern these defensive tactics. The law that applies is that of the state of incorporation (typically Delaware, which is the traditional favorite of large corporations), and the forum for litigating these defensive tactics is almost always state court (again typically Delaware), in contrast to the federal court forum that is used for Section 14(e) litigation.

When the bidder and/or target shareholders challenge the validity of these defensive measures, courts in Delaware as well as other states apply a "modified business judgment rule" that requires the target's directors to show that after a "good faith and reasonable investigation," they saw a danger to corporate policy and effectiveness. See *Cheff v. Mathes,* 199 A.2d 548 (Del. 1964). The business judgment rule applied in the tender offer context thus is different from the business judgment rule applied to most other decisions by corporate directors. Courts recognize that hostile tender offers present target directors with an inherent conflict of interest (their jobs are probably on the line) and have accordingly modified the traditional business judgment rule to reflect this reality. Although Delaware courts justify the enhanced scrutiny of defensive tactics as a means to protect target company shareholders, many decisions defer to those tactics and thereby protect incumbent management. Unlike federal courts addressing claims under the Williams Act, which is supposedly neutral between the bidder and target company management, state courts hearing fiduciary duty claims can and do take sides.

Delaware courts generally apply a two part test to determine whether a target's defensive tactics survive review under this modified business judgment rule. Both parts of the test were set out in *Unocal Corp. v. Mesa*

*Petroleum Co.*, 493 A.2d 946, 955 (Del. 1985), where the court looked to (i) whether directors had reasonable grounds for perceiving a threat to the corporation from the takeover bid, and (ii) whether the defensive measures used were "reasonable in relation to the threat posed." Thus, an injunction against a target's defensive measures may be warranted where a bidder's hostile offer does not appear to threaten the corporation, its shareholders, or non-shareholder constituencies (e.g., the offer is all cash, substantially above market price and for 100% of the target company's stock, and the bidder does not plan to radically restructure the company). A court might also enjoin a defensive measure that is very costly to the corporation or its shareholders (e.g., a lock-up option or sale of crown jewels at an unreasonably low price), particularly if the threat that existed was not very great. Even in these situations, however, courts accord substantial deference to the judgment of target company directors. Indeed, most decisions under *Unocal* have permitted defensive measures to remain in place. See, e.g., *Moran v. Household Int'l, Inc.*, 500 A.2d 1346 (Del. 1985) (upholding a "flip over" poison pill providing that if an acquirer sought to merge the corporation into itself after a hostile tender offer, the remaining shareholders would be entitled to buy $200 worth of the acquirer's stock for $100).

Yet when a corporation is faced with multiple bidders, Delaware courts impose additional restrictions on directors' conduct. Under *Revlon v. MacAndrews & Forbes Holdings, Inc.*, 506 A.2d 173 (Del. 1985), once the board concludes that a sale of the company is inevitable, or the board takes steps to put the corporation up for sale (such as structuring a leveraged buyout, a sale of substantially all the corporation's assets, or a merger with a white knight), the role of the board changes substantially. At that point, a corporation is in the "*Revlon* mode," and the directors must obtain the highest price for the shareholders. Defensive measures that were permissible when the company was in the *Unocal* mode may now be a breach of directors' fiduciary duty, and directors have less discretion to take into consideration interests of non-shareholder stakeholders (e.g., employees or customers).

Delaware courts are therefore faced with the challenge of distinguishing between transactions that put a company into the *Revlon* mode from transactions that do not. Compare *Paramount Communications v. QVC Network, Inc.*, 637 A.2d 34 (Del. 1994) with *Paramount Communications v. Time, Inc.*, 571 A.2d 1140 (Del. 1989). Generally, a transaction that contemplates a change in control of the target company triggers *Revlon* duties, whereas a transaction that involves no change of control does not. Directors who seek to sell a control block of the target's stock to a single person or corporation (as in *QVC*) thus have an obligation to sell to the highest bidder, whereas directors who sell less than a control block, transfer a control block to a white knight's dispersed public shareholders, or cause the target company to incur massive debt to buy the stock of another corporation (as in *Time*) retain the far greater discretion allowed under a *Unocal* analysis.[a]

---

**a.** This modified business judgment rule of Delaware and other American jurisdictions stands in sharp contrast to the regulatory regime under the London City Code and other European jurisdictions which prohibit target company directors from deploying defensive measures without prior authorization obtained from target company

How do the goals sought by the Delaware legislature and courts compare with those sought by Congress in the Williams Act? Is the resultant regime for the regulation of tender offers an intelligible one? Are lawyers the primary beneficiaries?

---

shareholders after commencement of the tender offer (the "strict neutrality rule"). See Christian Kirchner & Richard W. Painter, A European Modified Business Judgment Rule for Takeover Law, 2 Eur. Bus. Org. L. Rev. 353 (2000) (comparing this strict neutrality rule with the American modified business judgment rule and proposing that continental Europe consider adopting a variation of the latter).

# Chapter 6

# SECURITIES CLASS ACTIONS

In the vast majority of countries with developed securities markets, violators of securities laws are punished, and defrauded investors are made whole, by government enforcement actions. At most, investors have a right to sue violators on an individual basis or in small groups. Securities class action lawsuits on a large scale, with hundreds of thousands of plaintiff class members, are unique to the American legal landscape.

Some scholars have lambasted securities class actions as a waste of resources and a drain on entrepreneurs, the securities industry, and ultimately on shareholders. See, e.g., Joseph A. Grundfest, Why Disimply?, 108 Harv. L. Rev. 727, 742-43 (1995); Roberta Romano, The Shareholder Suit: Litigation without Foundation?, 7 J.L. Econ. & Org. 55, 84 (1991); Janet Cooper Alexander, Do the Merits Matter? A Study of Settlements in Securities Class Actions, 43 Stan. L. Rev. 497, 527-57 (1991).

Others have championed securities class actions as necessary to supplement SEC enforcement efforts and to protect investors. See, e.g., James D. Cox, Making Securities Fraud Class Actions Virtuous, 39 Ariz. L. Rev. 497 (1997); Joel Seligman, The Merits Do Matter: A Comment on Professor Grundfest's "Disimplying Private Rights of Action Under the Federal Securities Laws: The Commission's Authority," 108 Harv. L. Rev. 438 (1994).

This Chapter explores the debate over securities class action litigation and the impact that various arguments raised in that debate have had on legislation and case law. The Chapter is divided into five sections. The first two sections address important federal legislation on securities class actions—the Private Securities Litigation Reform Act of 1995 (in Section A) and the Securities Litigation Uniform Standards Act of 1998 (in Section B). Section C provides an empirical overview of securities class actions, and Section D discusses the impact on such actions of the Sarbanes-Oxley Act of 2002. It also surveys other legislative changes that have been proposed, but not yet enacted, in the wake of the WorldCom, Enron, and other recent corporate and accounting scandals at publicly traded companies. The Chapter concludes with three problems in which students acting as law firms draft class action complaints and motions to dismiss, with the professor acting as judge.

## A. THE PRIVATE SECURITIES LITIGATION REFORM ACT OF 1995

The 104th Congress, elected in a Republican landslide in 1994, enacted the Private Securities Litigation Reform Act of 1995 (PSLRA), part of a package of tort reform and other legislation that had been promised by Republican candidates as one aspect of Representative Newt Gingrich's "Contract with America." The PSLRA sought to curb what some members of Congress believed was frivolous securities class action litigation in federal courts by plaintiffs' lawyers out to earn substantial fees from quick settlements.

Before enacting the legislation, Congress heard testimony about abusive practices, such as the following:

> (1) the routine filing of lawsuits against issuers of securities and others whenever there is a significant change in an issuer's stock price, without regard to any underlying culpability of the issuer, and with only faint hope that the discovery process might lead eventually to some plausible cause of action; (2) the targeting of deep pocket defendants, including accountants, underwriters, and individuals who may be covered by insurance, without regard to their actual culpability; (3) the abuse of the discovery process to impose costs so burdensome that it is often economical for the victimized party to settle; and (4) the manipulation by class action lawyers of the clients whom they purportedly represent.

H.R. Conf. Rep. No. 104-369, at 31 (1995).

Responding to such general concerns, Congress targeted specific problems in the PSLRA, including: 1) attorneys' use of the so-called "professional plaintiff;" 2) the inadequacy of some class representatives (lead plaintiffs); (3) financial incentives given to lead plaintiffs by attorneys; 4) sealed settlements that conceal attorneys' fees and other information; 5) the failure to provide meaningful information about settlements to class members; 6) receipt by attorneys of a disproportionate share of settlement awards; 7) the high cost of discovery; 8) meritless lawsuits; and 9) attorney conflicts of interest.

Many changes introduced by the PSLRA apply to both individual actions and class actions. Some of these were discussed in Chapter 2: (1) the "safe harbor" for misleading forward-looking statements made by certain issuers; (2) heightened pleading standards requiring plaintiffs to set forth specific facts in support of allegedly misleading statements or omissions as well as facts supporting "a strong inference that the defendant acted with the required state of mind;" (3) the requirement that plaintiffs seeking damages prove loss causation; (4) the replacement (in many circumstances) of joint and several liability with liability proportionate to the defendant's participation in the wrong; and (5) a "90-day bounce back" rule that reduces damages to the extent that the market price of the security recovers following public disclosure correcting the misstatement or omission.

Additional provisions of the PSLRA apply only to class actions and are discussed in detail in this Chapter. These include:

- minimum standards for lead plaintiffs and a presumption that an issuer's largest shareholder, rather than the first shareholder to file suit, shall be permitted to be the "lead plaintiff" and to control a class action; and
- a provision requiring judges to scrutinize settlement terms to assure that lawyers' fees are not excessive in proportion to the damages awarded to a plaintiff class.

This Chapter also discusses:

- a provision mandating a stay of discovery during the pendency of a dismissal motion made by the defendant; and
- a provision requiring courts to make written findings concerning compliance with Rule 11 of the Federal Rules of Civil Procedure, and requiring them also to impose sanctions on parties and their counsel if there has been a breach of Rule 11.

Although each of the latter two PSLRA provisions applies to individual actions as well as to class actions, it is in the class action context that they arise most frequently.

In enacting all of these changes to the federal securities laws, Congress made no secret of its belief that opportunistic trial lawyers were the underlying cause of the problems posed. See H.R. Conf. Rep. No. 104-369 (1995) ("The private securities litigation system is too important to the integrity of American capital markets to allow this system to be undermined by those who seek to line their pockets by bringing abusive and meritless suits"). To be sure, skeptics would argue that the PSLRA was special interest legislation for companies frequently sued for securities fraud (including many high-technology companies with volatile stock prices), as well as underwriters and accounting firms also facing such litigation. See Jeffrey Taylor, Congress Sends Business a Christmas Gift, Wall St. J. at A2 (Dec. 26, 1995).

Many of the matters addressed by the PSLRA had previously been left to the discretion of courts, such as the appointment of a lead plaintiff in class actions and Rule 11 sanctions for meritless claims. Congress also explicitly encroached on a matter previously addressed by the Commission when it created the statutory safe harbor for forward-looking statements. Nonetheless, the Commission reluctantly supported the final version of the bill. The SEC's position thus "appeared to be a change in direction for an agency that in the past had zealously defended the utility of private litigation as an aid to enforcement." Edward A. Fallone, Section 10(b) and the Vagaries of Federal Common Law: The Merits of Codifying the Private Cause of Action under A Structuralist Approach, 1997 U. Ill. L. Rev. 71, 79. The PSLRA passed by overwhelming majorities in both houses of Congress.

The bill was vetoed by President Clinton. In his veto message, the President stated his specific criticisms of the bill as follows:

> I made clear my willingness to support the bill passed by the Senate with appropriate "safe harbor" language, even though it did not include certain provisions that I favor-such as enhanced provisions with respect to joint and several liability, aider and abettor liability, and statute of limitations. *** Specifically, I object to the following elements of this bill. First, I believe that the pleading requirements of the Conference Report with regard to a defendant's state of mind impose an unacceptable procedural hurdle to meritorious claims being heard in Federal courts. I am prepared to support the *** standards of the Second Circuit, but I am not prepared to go beyond that. Second, remove the language in the Statement of Managers that waters down the nature of the cautionary language that must be included to make the safe harbor safe. Third, restore the Rule 11 language to that of the Senate bill.

Veto Message from the President of the United States on the Private Securities Litigation Reform Act of 1995, 141 Cong. Rec. H15, 214-06 (1995).

The House voted 319-100 to override the President's veto, 141 Cong. Rec. H15, 214-06 (1995), as did the Senate two days later by a vote of 68-30, 141 Cong Rec. S19, 180-01 (1995). The PSLRA then became law.

### *1. Selection of Lead Plaintiff and Class Counsel*

#### *a. Minimum Standards For Lead Plaintiffs*

Class actions are conducted by one or more "lead plaintiffs" who sue on behalf of, and represent, the class. In enacting the PSLRA, Congress expressed concern that the same lead plaintiffs appeared too often in securities class actions, that lead plaintiffs were selected by class counsel rather than the other way around, and that lead plaintiffs had relatively little control over the litigation. Thus, professional plaintiffs "who own a nominal number of shares in a wide array of public companies permit lawyers readily to file abusive securities class action lawsuits." Conference Report 369 at 32. Congress worried that class counsel made bounty payments to lead plaintiffs, thereby further encouraging frivolous filings. Moreover, Congress believed that many lead plaintiffs did not adequately represent the interests of other class members. In debate on the PSLRA, one Senator sarcastically observed that "many of the 'world's unluckiest investors'" repeatedly appear as lead plaintiffs in securities class action lawsuits." Id. at 32-33.

The PSLRA includes provisions against "professional plaintiffs" and other provisions designed to assure that the lead plaintiff actually has an interest in, and a role in directing, the class action. The PSLRA thus requires the lead plaintiff to file a sworn certified statement that:

> (i) states that the plaintiff has reviewed the complaint and authorized its filing;
>
> (ii) states that the plaintiff did not purchase the security that is the subject of the complaint at the direction of plaintiff's counsel or in order to participate in any private action arising under this title;
>
> (iii) states that the plaintiff is willing to serve as a representative party on behalf of a class, including providing testimony at deposition and trial, if necessary;
>
> (iv) sets forth all of the transactions of the plaintiff in the security that is the subject of the complaint during the class period specified in the complaint;
>
> (v) identifies any other action under this title, filed during the 3-year period preceding the date on which the certification is signed by the plaintiff, in which the plaintiff has sought to serve, or served, as a representative party on behalf of a class; and
>
> (vi) states that the plaintiff will not accept any payment for serving as a representative party on behalf of a class beyond the plaintiff's pro rata share of any recovery, except as ordered or approved by the court in accordance with paragraph (4).

Securities Act Section 27(a)(2) and Exchange Act Section 21D(a)(2).

In the wake of the PSLRA, courts have also cracked down on token lead plaintiffs. For example, in *Berger v. Compaq Computer Corp.*, 257 F.3d 475 (5th Cir. 2001), the Fifth Circuit observed out that

> [t]he district court unquestionably adopted an incorrect legal standard by stating that "the adequacy of the putative representatives and of plaintiffs' counsel is presumed in the absence of specific proof to the contrary." This is error; the party seeking certification bears the burden of establishing that *all* requirements of [F.R.C.P.] rule 23(a) have been satisfied.

Id. at 481. The court also held that "it follows that in complex class action securities cases governed by the PSLRA, the adequacy standard must reflect the governing principles of the Act and, particularly, Congress's emphatic command that competent plaintiffs, rather than lawyers, direct such cases." Id. at 484. The Fifth Circuit then dismissed the action because the lead plaintiff was unfamiliar with the basic allegations underlying the complaint. Among other difficulties, the lead plaintiff was unable to verify any facts to support his allegation that Compaq's former chief executive knowingly misstated revenue targets. Id. at 480 n. 10.

*b. Ending the Race to the Courthouse Steps*

Lawyers often rush to sue an issuer immediately following disclosure of unfavorable information or a drop in the issuer's stock price. Congress blamed this state of affairs on the courts' failure to consider factors other than the filing date in making decisions regarding the appointment of class counsel and the lead plaintiff:

> First, courts traditionally appoint counsel in class action lawsuits on a "first come, first serve" basis. Courts often afford insufficient consideration to the most thoroughly researched, but later filed, complaint. The second incentive involves the court's decision as to who will become lead plaintiff. Generally, the first lawsuit filed also determines the lead plaintiff.

Conference Report 369 at 33. In such an environment, lawyers can be "fleet of foot and sleight of hand." Id.

To remedy this problem, the PSLRA added Section 27(a)(3) to the Securities Act and Section 21D(a)(3) to the Exchange Act. These sections require a plaintiff to publish notice to members of the class within 20 days after the filing of the complaint. Then, within 60 days of publication of notice, any class member may make a motion to serve as lead plaintiff. Id. The PSLRA further provides that:

> Not later than 90 days after the date on which a notice is published under subparagraph (A)(i), the court shall consider any motion made by a purported class member in response to the notice, including any motion by a class member who is not individually named as a plaintiff in the complaint or complaints, and shall appoint as lead plaintiff the member or members of the purported plaintiff class that the court determines to be most capable of adequately representing the interests of class members (hereafter in this paragraph referred to as the "most adequate plaintiff") in accordance with this subparagraph.

Securities Act Section 27(a)(3)(B)(i) and Exchange Act Section 21D(a)(3)(B)(i).

*c. Presumption in Favor of the Largest Investor as Lead Plaintiff*

The presumption that the issuer's largest shareholder should be the lead plaintiff originated in a law review article by Professors Elliott Weiss and John Beckerman. See Elliott J. Weiss & John S. Beckerman, Let the Money Do the Monitoring: How Institutional Investors Can Reduce Agency Costs in Securities Class Actions, 104 Yale L.J. 2053 (1995). Congress believed such a presumption would be an improvement over "[t]he current system [which] often works to prevent institutional investors from selecting counsel or serving as lead plaintiff in class actions," Conference Report 369 at 34, and that active institutional participation in class actions "protects investors who join class actions against lawyer-driven lawsuits by giving control of the litigation to lead plaintiffs with substantial holdings of the securities of the issuer." Id. at 32.

The PSLRA thus codifies a rebuttable presumption that "the most adequate plaintiff *** is the person or group of persons that *** in the determination of the court, has the largest financial interest in the relief sought by the class." See Securities Act § 27(a)(3)(B)(iii)(I)(bb) and Exchange Act § 21D(a)(3)(B)(iii)(I)(bb). The PSLRA also provides that "[t]he most adequate plaintiff shall, subject to the approval of the court, select and retain counsel to represent the class." See Securities Act § 27(a)(3)(B)(v) and Exchange Act § 21D(a)(3)(B)(v). Congress made it clear, however, that this rule "does not intend to disturb the court's discretion under existing law to approve or disapprove the lead plaintiff's choice of counsel when necessary to protect the interests of the plaintiff class." Conference Report 369 at 35.

To be sure, it is possible that large investors might conspire with the management of the defendant company. The PSLRA does little specifically to avoid this possibility. But it does provide that the presumption favoring the person or group with the largest financial stake as the lead plaintiff may be rebutted by evidence that the plaintiff will not fairly and adequately protect the interests of the class; or " *** is subject to unique defenses that render such plaintiff incapable of adequately representing the class." Securities Act § 27(a)(3)(B)(iii)(II)(bb) and Exchange Act § 21D(a)(3)(B)(iii)(II)(bb).

Furthermore, while Congress barred anyone from serving as a lead plaintiff more than three times in five years, see Exchange Act Section 21D(a)(3)(B)(vi) and Securities Act Section 27(a)(3)(B)(vi), it authorized a flexible approach in the case of institutional investors. Thus, the law

> grants courts discretion to avoid the unintended consequence of disqualifying institutional investors from serving more than five times in three years. The Conference Committee does not intend for this provision to operate at cross purposes with the "most adequate plaintiff" provision. The Conference Committee does expect, however, that it will be used with vigor to limit the activities of professional plaintiffs.

Conference Report 369 at 35.

*d. Financial Incentives for Lead Plaintiffs*

The PSLRA provides that: "The share of any final judgment or of any settlement that is awarded to a representative party serving on behalf of a class shall be equal, on a per share basis, to the portion of the final judgment or settlement awarded to all other members of the class." Securities Act Section

27(a)(4) and Exchange Act Section 21D(a)(4). This provision prohibits lawyers from offering additional financial incentives to persons who become lead plaintiffs. However, courts retain discretion with respect to reimbursement of lead plaintiffs for reasonable costs: "Nothing in this paragraph shall be construed to limit the award of reasonable costs and expenses (including lost wages) directly relating to the representation of the class to any representative party serving on behalf of the class." Id.

*e. Attorney Conflicts of Interest*

Section 27(a)(8) of the Securities Act and Section 21D(a)(9) of the Exchange Act address attorneys' conflicts of interest. These provisions state that where an attorney "directly owns or otherwise has a beneficial interest in the securities that are the subject of the litigation the court shall make a determination of whether such ownership or other interest constitutes a conflict of interest sufficient" to warrant disqualification.

*f. Auction of the Class Counsel's Role*

Even before the PSLRA, some courts sought to assure efficient representation of a class by holding court-sponsored auctions of the class counsel position. See, e.g., *In re Oracle Sec. Litig.*, 131 F.R.D. 688 (N.D.Cal. 1990) (one of the first such auctions). See also Nanette L. Stasko, Comment, Competitive Bidding in the Courthouse: *In re Oracle Securities Litigation*, 59 Brook. L. Rev. 1667 (1994) (describing competitive bidding process used in *Oracle Securities*); Jonathan R. Macey & Geoffrey P. Miller, The Plaintiffs' Attorney's Role in Class Action and Derivative Litigation: Economic Analysis and Recommendations for Reform, 58 U. Chi. L. Rev. 1 (1991) (describing consequences of divergence of interest between attorneys and class members and proposing that the right to represent the class be auctioned).

Court-sponsored auctions have continued after the PSLRA, although they may conflict with the PSLRA's lead plaintiff provision, which is intended to strengthen, rather than diminish, the role of lead plaintiffs in controlling litigation, including the selection of class counsel. Thus, in *In re Cendant Corp. PRIDES Litig*, 243 F.3d 722 (3rd Cir. 2001), the Third Circuit held that a court-sponsored auction resulted in the payment of excessive legal fees to class counsel and conflicted with the PSLRA's lead plaintiff provision. Moreover, in *In re Razorfish, Inc. Sec. Litig.*, 143 F. Supp. 2d 304 (S.D.N.Y. 2001), the court declined to allow an auction because "[u]nder the approach mandated by the Reform Act *** the primary focus must always be, not on the selection of counsel, but on the selection of lead plaintiff." Id. at 311. The court observed that under a competitive bidding process, "the presumptive lead counsel is the cheapest lawyer, who is then more or less forced upon the largely irrelevant lead plaintiff." Id. at 310. Accordingly, the court concluded that judicial power under the PSLRA to review the selection of lead counsel should not thus "be transmogrified into a right to arrange a shot-gun marriage between strangers." Id.

In *In Re Comdisco Sec. Litig.*, 141 F. Supp. 2d 951 (N.D. Ill. 2001), however, the court allowed an auction on the grounds that "optimum class benefit is directly related to how much of any gross recovery obtained from defendants must go to lawyers' fees, rather than into the pockets of the class members." Id. at 952-53. The court observed that, if the presumptive lead plaintiff were to choose a lawyer who would represent the class for one-third of the total recovery, and another reputable law firm was willing to represent the class for less, "any court would be remiss if it were to foist that one-third contingency arrangement on all of the other class members who had not themselves chosen that law firm to be their advocate." Id. at 953 (quoting *In re Bank One Shareholders Class Actions*, 96 F. Supp. 2d 780, 784 (N.D. Ill. 2000)). For additional analysis, see Jill E. Fisch, Lawyers on the Auction Block: Evaluating the Selection of Class Counsel by Auction, 102 Colum. L. Rev. 650 (2002).

### 2. *Mandatory Discovery Stays*

In enacting the PSLRA, Congress took note of the substantial expense imposed by discovery: "[D]iscovery costs account for roughly 80% of total litigation costs in security fraud cases." Conference Report 369 at 37 (citing testimony of Philip A. Lacavara before the Telecommunications and Finance Subcommittee of the House Committee on Energy and Commerce, hearing on H.R. 3185). Congress was also concerned that the vast amount of time required to respond to discovery requests results in "coercive settlements" and that discovery often "resembles a fishing expedition." Id.

One of the most important, and disputed, aspects of the PSLRA is a mandatory stay on discovery until the court has ruled on a motion to dismiss. Courts must stay all discovery "during the pendency of any motion to dismiss, unless the court finds, upon the motion of any party, that the particularized discovery is necessary to preserve evidence or to prevent undue prejudice to that party." Securities Act Section 27(b)(1) and Exchange Act Section 21D(b)(3)(B). In the meantime, in order to preserve relevant evidence, the parties:

> shall treat all documents, data compilations (including electronically recorded or stored data), and tangible objects that are in the custody or control of such person and that are relevant to the allegations, as if they were the subject of a continuing request for production of documents from an opposing party under the Federal Rules of Civil Procedure.

Securities Act Section 27(b)(2) and Exchange Act Section 21D(b)(3)(C). Willful destruction of relevant evidence is unlawful and the aggrieved party "may apply to the court for an order awarding appropriate sanctions." Securities Act Section 27(b)(3) and Exchange Act Section 21D(b)(3)(C)(ii). The Conference Committee, however, stated that this provision "does not impose liability where parties inadvertently or unintentionally destroy what turn out later to be relevant documents." Conference Report 369 at 37.

Some courts have lifted or partially lifted the discovery stay when plaintiffs make the required showing "that particularized discovery is necessary to preserve evidence or to prevent undue prejudice to that party." See *In re Pacific Gateway Exch., Inc., Sec. Litig.*, 2001 WL 1334747, at *2 (N.D. Cal. 2001) (granting plaintiffs' motion for a partial lifting of the discovery stay); *Anderson v. First Sec. Corp.*, 157 F. Supp. 2d 1230, 1242-43 (D. Utah 2001) (same); *In re Comdisco Sec. Litig.*, 166 F. Supp. 2d 1260, 1263 (N.D. Ill. 2001) (same); *In re Flir Sys., Inc. Sec. Litig.*, 2000 WL 33201904 (D. Or. 2000) (permitting plaintiffs to depose a former employee of the defendant).

The mandatory stay of discovery, coupled with the PSLRA's stringent pleading requirements, however, can make it very difficult to survive a motion to dismiss in circumstances where the plaintiff, at the time the complaint is drafted, does not have access to sufficient information to plead specific facts giving rise to a strong inference of important elements of the claim (including, in actions under Rule 10b-5, the defendant's scienter). For this reason, the discovery stay remains one of the most controversial provisions of the PSLRA. See Hillary A. Sale, Heightened Pleading and Discovery Stays: An Analysis of the Effect of the PSLRA's Internal-Information Standard on '33 Act and '34 Act Claims, 76 Wash. U. L. Q. 537 (1998).

### *3. Disclosure of Proposed Settlements and Attorneys' Fees*

Most securities class actions settle after defendants and plaintiffs' counsel present a proposed settlement for court approval and class members are given a chance to object. When enacting the PSLRA, Congress worried that class members had no meaningful opportunity to object to a settlement because of their "lack [of] meaningful information about the terms of the proposed settlement." Conference Report 369 at 36 (citing testimony of Patricia Reilly before the Securities Subcommittee of the Senate Committee on Banking, Housing, and Urban Affairs, June 17, 1993). The PSLRA thus requires more detailed disclosure of settlement terms to class members, including a statement of the amount of recovery and a statement discussing the potential outcome of the case if it were litigated. See Securities Act Section 27(a)(7)(A-B) and Exchange Act Section 21D(a)(7)(A-B). Regarding this potential outcome, the notice must contain: 1) "a statement concerning the average amount of *** potential damages per share," and 2) where parties have disagreed, "a statement from each settling party concerning the issue or issues on which the parties disagree." Id. The notice must also state the amount of attorneys' fees and costs contemplated by the settlement and provide information on where the attorneys may be reached (i.e., telephone number, address). Securities Act Section 27(a)(7)(C-D) and Exchange Act Section 21D(a)(7)(C-D).

Discussing attorneys' fees, the PSLRA Conference Report observed that "[u]nder current practice, courts generally award attorneys' fees based on the so-called "lodestar" approach—i.e., court multiply the attorney's hours by a reasonable hourly fee, which may be increased by an additional amount based on risk or other relevant factors. Under this approach, attorneys' fees can constitute 35% or more of the entire settlement awarded to the class." Conference Report 369 at 36 (citing Majority Staff Report, May 17, 1994). The PSLRA instead requires that fees awarded to class counsel in any settlement or judicial resolution of a case be a "reasonable percentage of the amount of damages and prejudgment interest actually paid to the class." See Securities Act Section 27(a)(6) and Exchange Act Section 21D(a)(6).

The PSLRA also provides that "[t]he terms and provisions of any settlement agreement of a class action shall not be filed under seal, except that on motion of any party to the settlement," a court may order filing under seal if good cause is shown. See Securities Act Section 27(a)(5) and Exchange Act Section 21D(a)(5). Congress intended "good cause" to mean "that the publication of a portion or portions of the settlement agreement would result in direct and substantial harm to any party, whether or not a party to the action."

Conference Report 369 at 35. Furthermore, Congress intended " 'direct and substantial harm' to include proof of reputational injury to a party." Id.

### *4. Mandatory Sanctions for Rule 11 Violations*

Rule 11 of the Federal Rules of Civil Procedure provides that a lawyer's signature on pleadings filed in federal court certifies that the contentions therein are supported by facts known to the lawyer after due investigation and either by existing law or by a good faith argument for the modification or extension of existing law. Rule 11 further provides that imposition of sanctions for violation is at the discretion of the court. In its critique of Rule 11, the Conference Committee stated:

> Existing Rule 11 has not deterred abusive securities litigation.*** Courts often fail to impose Rule 11 sanctions even where such sanctions are warranted. When sanctions are awarded, they are generally insufficient to make whole the victim of a Rule 11 violation: the amount of the sanction is limited to an amount that the court deems sufficient to deter repetition of the sanctioned conduct, rather than imposing a sanction that equals the costs imposed on the victim by the violation. Finally, courts have been unable to apply Rule 11 to the complaint in such a way that the victim of the ensuing lawsuit is compensated for all attorneys' fees and costs incurred in the entire action.

Conference Report 369 at 39.

In the PSLRA, Congress puts teeth into Rule 11 by requiring courts to determine whether the parties had complied with the Rule, and by making sanctions mandatory. Thus, Section 27(c)(3)(C) of the Securities Act and Section 21D(c)(3)(C) of the Exchange Act provide that if a violation of Rule 11 is established, "the court *shall* award the sanctions that the court deems appropriate pursuant to Rule 11 of the Federal Rules of Civil Procedure." (emphasis added). Unless the sanctioned party or attorney can prove that "the award of attorneys' fees and other expenses will impose an unreasonable burden on that party or attorney and would be unjust *** or that the violation of Rule 11(b) was de minimus," there is a presumption in favor of awarding attorneys' fees and costs of the opposing party. See Securities Act Section 27(c)(3)(B) and Exchange Act Section 21(D)(c)(3)(B).

Furthermore, to ensure "the viability of potential sanctions as a deterrent to meritless litigation," Conference Report 369 at 40, the PSLRA also provides that:

> In any private action arising under this title that is certified as a class action pursuant to the Federal Rules of Civil Procedure, the court may require an undertaking from the attorneys for the plaintiff class, the plaintiff class, or both, or from the attorneys for the defendant, the defendant, or both, in such proportions and at such times as the court determines are just and equitable, for the payment of fees and expenses that may be awarded under this subsection.

Exchange Act, Section 21D(a)(8). These Rule 11-related provisions of the PSLRA were criticized by President Clinton in his veto message, but survived when Congress overrode his veto.

Although Rule 11 sanctions in securities class actions are still rare, a few courts have begun to crack down on complaints filed without sufficient grounding in law or fact. The case below is one of those few.

## GURARY v. NU-TECH BIO-MED, INC.

303 F.3d 212 (2d Cir. 2002)

CALABRESI, CIRCUIT JUDGE:

Responding to what it perceived to be an unwillingness on the part of courts to impose discretionary sanctions on parties who brought abusive securities fraud lawsuits, Congress passed Section 21D(c) of the Private Securities Litigation Reform Act of 1995 (PSLRA). While the mischief that Congress was addressing is clear, the statutory language Congress employed is not.

The PSLRA dictates sanctions for frivolous securities fraud complaints and emphasizes the need not only to deter such abusive lawsuits, but also to compensate fully victims of this kind of abusive litigation. It requires district courts overseeing securities fraud suits to make specific findings, upon final adjudication of the action, as to whether all parties and all attorneys have complied with each requirement of Rule 11(b) of the Federal Rules of Civil Procedure. [Exchange Act Section 21D(c)(1)]. If the court determines that a violation has occurred, the imposition of sanctions is mandatory. [Section 21D(c)(2)]. The PSLRA further establishes a presumption that, "for *substantial* failure of any complaint to comply with any requirement" of Rule 11(b), the award shall be the full amount of the reasonable attorneys' fees and costs.[1] [Section 21D(c)(3)(A)] (emphasis added). Under the statute, this presumption may be rebutted only upon proof that "the violation of [Rule 11(b)] was de minimis" or that the sanctions "will impose an unreasonable burden on that party or attorney and would be unjust, and the failure to make such an award would not impose a greater burden on the party in whose favor sanctions are to be imposed." [Section 21D(c)(3)(B)].

On their own terms these provisions present problems. Thus, one might well read the requirement that the violation be a "substantial failure," for

---

1. Rule 11(b) states, in relevant part, that:

By presenting to the court (whether by signing, filing, submitting, or later advocating) a pleading, written motion, or other paper, an attorney or unrepresented party is certifying that to the best of the person's knowledge, information, and belief, formed after an inquiry reasonable under the circumstances,—

> (1) it is not being presented for any improper purpose ...
>
> (2) the claims, defenses, and other legal contentions therein are warranted by existing law or by a nonfrivolous argument for the extension, modification, or reversal of existing law or the establishment of new law;
>
> (3) the allegations and other factual contentions have evidentiary support or, if specifically so identified, are likely to have evidentiary support after a reasonable opportunity for further investigation or discovery....

Fed. R. Civ. P. 11(b).

purposes of applying the presumption of an award of full fees and costs, to mean that the violation must not be de minimis. But such a reading would make hash of the statute's subsequent provision that a party may rebut this presumption by showing that the violation was de minimis. We must, therefore, read the requirement of a "substantial failure" to mean something else. But what? The matter is made more complex by the fact that the words "substantial failure" and "de minimis" give no guidance as to the proper extent of mandated sanctions when frivolous counts or allegations are part of a suit in which some of the other counts or allegations are not only not frivolous, but may actually have merit. The present case requires us to address these matters.

Attorney David Jaroslawicz and his law firm, Jaroslawicz & Jaros, appeal a judgment from the United States District Court for the Southern District of New York (Stanton, J.), imposing sanctions on Jaroslawicz and his law firm pursuant to Rule 11(b) and § 21D(c) of the PSLRA in the amount of $62,556.28, or approximately one-half of defendant Nu-Tech's costs and attorneys fees. The sanctions arose out of an action brought by Gurary, a purchaser of common stock in Nu-Tech, in which Gurary alleged securities fraud violations by Nu-Tech and Isaac Winehouse. Gurary claimed that Winehouse was the leader of a "cartel" that purchased convertible preferred stock and manipulated stock prices by short selling in violation of Section 10b of the Securities Exchange Act of 1934 and "Rule 10b-5", as well as § 349 of the General Business Law of the State of New York. According to Gurary's various theories of recovery, Nu-Tech knew of the short selling and committed fraud by concealing material information and providing misinformation in violation of Rule 10b-5.

The district court dismissed the complaint and we affirmed that dismissal. *Gurary v. Winehouse ("Gurary I")*, 190 F.3d 37 (2d Cir.1999). We subsequently directed the imposition of sanctions with respect to two of Gurary's four claims against Nu-Tech, *Gurary v. Winehouse ("Gurary II")*, 235 F.3d 792 (2d Cir.2000). On remand, the district court ordered sanctions against attorney Jaroslawicz and his firm in an amount equal to approximately one-half of Nu-Tech's attorneys fees and costs in the action. Before us, Jaroslawicz challenges several aspects of the district court's sanctions ruling. At the same time, Nu-Tech claims, in a cross-appeal, that the court committed legal error by not imposing sanctions equal to all of Nu-Tech's costs and fees.

BACKGROUND

In his securities lawsuit, Gurary alleged that in November of 1996 Nu-Tech privately issued 14,000 shares of "Series A Convertible Preferred Stock" for a total price of $14 million. Gurary claimed that Winehouse and his cartel arranged to buy a large part of the Convertible Stock in the name of third parties. The Winehouse cartel then allegedly began selling Nu-Tech common stock short, using various accounts to conceal the identity of its members. It could sell short in relative safety because of its ownership of the Convertible Preferred Stocks. According to Gurary, the cartel's purpose was to manipulate the market and drive down the price of Nu-Tech shares.

In his complaint, Gurary states that on four occasions he purchased shares of Nu-Tech common: (1) 1,000 shares on October 31, 1996, for $14.60 per share; (2) 5,500 shares on November 7, 1996, for $15.50; (3) 1,000 shares on December 24, 1996, for $11.75; and (4) 8,350 shares on February 18, 1997, for $11.57. In December 1996, after Gurary's first two purchases, the stock price began to decline, presumably as a result of the short selling. Gurary further alleges that Marvin Feigenbaum, chairman of Nu-Tech, assured Gurary that Feigenbaum had informed Winehouse that Nu-Tech would refuse to register any stock that would be converted from Convertible Preferred Stock to common stock unless Winehouse stopped shorting the common. Gurary states that he made his third purchase of common stock on December 24, 1996 based upon Feigenbaum's assurances.

Gurary continues that upon learning that Winehouse and his associates had persisted in shorting the stock, Gurary again spoke with Feigenbaum on February 18, 1997. Feigenbaum explained that he had met with Winehouse's group and offered to repurchase their stock at cost plus ten percent if the group would cease its activities. Winehouse rejected the offer, but Feigenbaum reemphasized that Nu-Tech would refuse to register the short sellers' shares. Apparently comforted by this information, Gurary made his fourth purchase later that same day.

On March 12, 1997, Feigenbaum made an unsuccessful attempt to negotiate an agreement with Winehouse that would end the short selling. The Nu-Tech stock dropped approximately $6 a share over the next two days. Nu-Tech issued a press release on March 14, 1997, which stated that the price decline could be attributed to "possible sales by shareholders," but Nu-Tech did not mention the discussions with Winehouse. During a conversation a few days later, Winehouse admitted to Gurary that he deliberately had shorted the stock to drive prices down and that he intended to continue doing so.

On May 23, 1997, Gurary began this action against Winehouse and Nu-Tech. Gurary charged Winehouse with manipulation of the common stock in violation of Rule 10b-5, by purchasing the Convertible Preferred and shorting the common. He alleged that Nu-Tech had engaged in fraud by concealing material information and providing misinformation in violation of Rule 10b-5. And he asserted that both of the defendants' conduct constituted fraudulent business practice in violation of § 349 of the General Business Law of the State of New York.

The district court granted the defendants' motion for summary judgment on the federal claims, but implicitly denied their motion for sanctions pursuant to Rule 11(b) and the PSLRA. *Gurary v. Winehouse*, 1998 WL 54641, at *2-3 (S.D.N.Y. Feb. 10, 1998). It also declined to exercise jurisdiction over the state law claim in light of the disposition of the federal allegations. Id. at *3. Gurary appealed and Nu-Tech cross-appealed. We affirmed the dismissal of the federal as well as the state claims, and vacated and remanded with respect to the denial of sanctions because "the district court [had] made no findings regarding compliance with Rule 11(b)" as mandated by the PSLRA. *Gurary I*, 190 F.3d at 39, 47.

On remand, the district court determined that sanctions were not warranted because Gurary could colorably argue that an extension of existing case law supported his Rule 10b-5 causes of action. *Gurary v. Winehouse*, 2000 WL 20706, at *1 (S.D.N.Y. Jan. 12, 2000). Only Nu-Tech appealed this denial.

In *Gurary II*, the district court's ruling was affirmed in part, and vacated and remanded in part. *Gurary II*, 235 F.3d at 797. We held that sanctions were warranted because the claims against Nu-Tech, based upon Gurary's first two purchases (October 31 and November 6, 1996), were frivolous. We also held, however, that sanctions could not be grounded on the nonfrivolous, but meritless, claims (also against Nu-Tech) involving the last two purchases (December 24, 1996 and February 18, 1997). Our opinion concluded that "[b]ased upon the plain language of section 10(b) and well-settled case law, Gurary's October 31, 1996 purchase could not under any circumstances give rise to a Rule 10b-5 cause of action because that purchase occurred before any alleged deception began, and therefore could not be in connection with the purchase or sale of a security" as required by the statute. Id. at 799. The November 7, 1996 purchase similarly failed to state a colorable claim because the short selling scheme, which began November 6, 1996, had actually depressed the price of the common stock, to Gurary's benefit. Id. These frivolous claims were, therefore, sanctionable pursuant to the PSLRA and Rule 11(b).

With respect to the claims based upon the last two purchases, we held that if the district court had afforded Gurary the opportunity to amend his complaint, as he requested, "Gurary could have asserted a cognizable claim under Rule 10b- 5." Id. at 801-02. We noted that in his original complaint and affidavits Gurary had "failed to adequately plead the requisite reliance on false statements made by Feigenbaum with scienter." Id. at 801; see also [Rule 10b-5]; *Ganino v. Citizens Util. Co.*, 228 F.3d 154, 161 (2d Cir.2000) ("[P]laintiff must plead that the defendant, in connection with the purchase or sale of securities, made a materially false statement or omitted a material fact, with scienter, and that plaintiff's reliance on the defendant's action caused [his] injury.").

This failure to comply with the PSLRA's heightened pleading requirements did not, however, necessarily result in a Rule 11 violation. In opposition to the motion to dismiss, Jaroslawicz, as mentioned above, had requested the opportunity to amend the complaint. The district court implicitly denied this request by granting summary judgment for the defendants. Gurary did not challenge the denial. But on appeal from the dismissal of his complaint Gurary, for the first time, asserted the theory that Feigenbaum's fraudulent statements had been made with malice and that Gurary had relied on them in making his last two purchases. Accordingly, we concluded that "[a]lthough Gurary's claim may not have survived summary judgment even with further discovery because of the inherent difficulty in establishing the subjective intent of Feigenbaum, ... Gurary's failure to sufficiently plead the necessary elements of a cognizable 10b-5 claim does not warrant sanctions under the PSLRA," since losing, though not frivolous, claims could have been made by amending the complaint with respect to these two purchases. Id. at 802. We then remanded the case to the district court to impose appropriate sanctions pursuant to the PSLRA for the claims based upon the first two purchases.

The district court, on this remand, stated that the "substantial failure of Gurary's complaint to comply with Fed.R.Civ.P. 11(b) invoked the presumption required by" the PSLRA. *Gurary v. Winehouse*, 153 F.Supp.2d 489, 491 (S.D.N.Y.2001). The court further noted that "when the failure to comply with Rule 11 is substantial, the whole costs and attorneys' fees of the adversary are awarded as the sanction, unless plaintiff's attorney proves that the burden on him will be unreasonable and unjust, or that the violation was de minimis." Id. (footnote omitted).

Relying upon our decision in *Simon DeBartolo Group v. Richard E. Jacobs Group, Inc.*, 186 F.3d 157 (2d Cir.1999), the lower court then found that the presumptive sanctions would impose an unreasonable burden. *Gurary*, 153 F. Supp. 2d at 493. The court reasoned that, because two out of the four claims were potentially nonfrivolous, "to impose the whole costs of the case on [a] plaintiff would in the statutory language 'impose an unreasonable burden on that party or attorney and would be unjust, and the failure to make such an award would not impose a greater burden on the party in whose favor sanctions are to be imposed.' " Id. at 492-93 (quoting [Exchange Act Section 21D(c)(3)(B)i]). Although it found the presumption rebutted because it would create an unreasonable burden, the court rejected Gurary's contention that the violation was de minimis. Equating the "substantial failure" analysis with the de minimis inquiry, the court noted that "[a]s the Court of Appeals made clear, the violation was substantial," and, hence, it could not be de minimis. Id. at 493. The court assessed sanctions upon Jaroslawicz, Gurary's attorney, and his firm in the amount equal to approximately one-half of the fees and costs—including the expenses associated with the sanctions application itself—incurred in the entire action. Id.

On appeal, Jaroslawicz argues that the district court abused its discretion because, if sanctions are imposed, they should be limited to the fees and costs actually borne as a result of the frivolous claims rather than be charged at one-half of the total expenses. He also contends that the district court erred by including in the award the legal fees and costs for work performed for the sanctions application itself. Nu-Tech cross-appeals, claiming that, given the district court's finding of a substantial violation of Rule 11, Jaroslawicz's evidence was insufficient to rebut the PSLRA"s presumption that full fees and costs were the proper sanction amount. According to Nu-Tech, the district court, therefore, exceeded its authority under the statute in reducing the award.

## DISCUSSION

We review the district court's conclusions of law de novo, *Connecticut v. Physicians Health Servs. of Conn., Inc.*, 287 F.3d 110, 114 (2d Cir.2002), and its imposition of sanctions under the PSLRA and Rule 11 for abuse of discretion, *Simon DeBartolo*, 186 F.3d at 167.

The language of the PSLRA does not make clear whether a complaint containing both frivolous and nonfrivolous allegations triggers the statutory presumption, and, if so, whether the presence of nonfrivolous allegations, by itself, rebuts that presumption by constituting evidence either that the violation is de minimis or that the assessment of full sanctions is an unreasonable and unjust burden. After examining the meaning of "substantial failure," "de minimis," and "unreasonable burden" in the context of complaints involving both frivolous and nonfrivolous charges, we hold that, in the circumstances of this case, the violation was substantial, and that the plaintiff failed to rebut the presumption that full compensation is the proper sanction.

I. The Meaning of the PSLRA Sanction Provisions

A. The Underlying Purpose of the PSLRA

As we stated in *Simon DeBartolo*, "[r]ecognizing what it termed 'the need to reduce significantly the filing of meritless securities lawsuits without hindering the ability of victims of fraud to pursue legitimate claims,' and commenting that the '[e]xisting Rule 11 has not deterred abusive securities litigation,' the 104th Congress included in the [PSLRA] a measure intended to put 'teeth' in Rule 11." Id. at 166-67 (quoting H.R. Conf. Rep. No. 104-369 (1995), at 39). The PSLRA's sanction regime was one of several provisions designed to reduce the economic incentives for bringing these actions.

Congress was concerned about the failure of courts to impose sanctions pursuant to Rule 11, even in cases in which penalties were warranted. Accordingly, the PSLRA required (a) mandatory findings regarding compliance with Rule 11(b), [Section 21D(c)(1)] ("In any private action arising under this chapter, upon final adjudication of the action, the court shall include in the record specific findings regarding compliance by ... each attorney representing any party with each requirement of [Rule 11(b)] as to any complaint ...."), and (b) mandatory sanctions whenever any portion of the complaint violated Rule 11, [Section 21D(c)(2)] ("If the court makes a finding under paragraph (1) that a[n] ... attorney violated any requirement of [Rule 11(b)] as to any complaint ..., the court shall impose sanctions on such ... attorney in accordance with [Rule 11(b)].").

Congress was also troubled by the fact that under existing Rule 11 practice, when a court did award Rule 11 sanctions, the award was "generally insufficient to make whole the victim of a Rule 11 violation; the amount of the sanction [was] limited to an amount that the court deem[ed] sufficient to deter repetition of the sanctioned conduct, rather than imposing a sanction that equals the costs imposed on the victim of the violation." H. Conf. Rep. No. 104-349, at 39. This concern led to the establishment of the presumption in the PSLRA that full fees and costs were the proper sanction for a violation of Rule 11.

The mandatory and broad nature of the presumption, however, was tempered by limiting it only to those cases in which the failure to comply with Rule 11 was "substantial." During the drafting of the legislation, the addition of the qualifier "substantial" was suggested by Judge Anthony Scirica of the United States Court of Appeals for the Third Circuit as a means of indicating that the presumption was reserved for only a "serious offense—filing an unfounded action." See 141 Cong. Rec. S19044, S19055 (Dec. 21, 1995) (Letter to the Senate Committee on Banking, Housing and Urban Affairs from Judge Anthony J. Scirica). But Judge Scirica further noted that, without an additional modification to indicate the consequences of a small offense, "a gap is left in the statutory scheme." Id. And while Congress adopted Judge Scirica's "substantial failure" language, the legislators failed to address his second concern and did not define clearly what was meant by a "substantial failure."

This failure left uncertain the applicability of the PSLRA's presumption in cases in which the security fraud complaint presents both frivolous and nonfrivolous claims, a problem that Congress did not seem to have in mind. Thus, the legislative history of the PSLRA focused for the most part on abusive securities litigation without considering the possibility that these suits might also contain nonfrivolous claims. The only acknowledgment of this issue is the congressional statement that when one claim in a twenty-count complaint is frivolous, the violation is de minimis and, hence, the presumption is rebutted. See H.R. Conf. Rep. No. 104-349, at 39-40.

A securities complaint may, however, present frivolous claims joined with nonfrivolous claims in a wide variety of ways, including the combination of frivolous claims with (1) valid, winning claims; (2) claims lost before a jury but which are meritorious enough to survive summary dismissal; (3) claims that, though properly dismissed at summary judgment because capable of resolution as a matter of law, presented novel legal issues that could well have gone in the plaintiff's favor; and (4) summarily dismissed claims that, while not legally frivolous, lack any merit. The statutory language leaves unclear which of these situations create a substantial violation of Rule 11. It is possible that in certain of these scenarios a complaint is not, in Judge Scirica's language, "unfounded," and, hence, should not be deemed a substantial violation. In others, instead, the violation may well remain substantial despite the presence of nonfrivolous claims. Further, the PSLRA's language does not indicate whether the mere presence of a nonfrivolous claim can suffice either to make even a substantial violation de minimis or to make the imposition of full sanctions unreasonable and unjust, thereby rebutting the statutory violation.

B. De Minimis Violations

Appellant Jaroslawicz argues that a complaint containing any nonfrivolous allegation (a) is not a substantial violation that gives rise to the PSLRA's presumption, and, (b) even if it were, falls both within the de minimis and the unreasonable burden defenses. But to accept these contentions would permit the very mischief that Congress manifestly intended to prohibit. Plaintiffs could avoid mandatory sanctions, and return to the prior discretionary regime, simply by including one colorable claim amid a myriad of abusive allegations.

Accepting Jaroslawicz's definition of de minimis, moreover, also runs counter to unusually clear legislative history. Once a substantial violation has been found and the presumption established, the Conference Committee wrote:

> [the presumption] does not mean that a party who is sanctioned for only a partial failure of the complaint under Rule 11, such as one count out of a 20-count complaint, must pay for all of the attorney's fees and costs associated with the action. The Conference Committee expects that courts will grant relief from the presumption where a de minimis violation of the Rule has occurred.

H.R. Conf. Rep. No. 104-369 at 39-40.

C. Unreasonable Burden

Jaroslawicz contends that even if the de minimis clause cannot be read as limiting sanctions in complaints that contain any nonfrivolous allegations, the unreasonable burden prong of the PSLRA's rebuttal provision should be understood to mean that the entire fees and costs ought not to be granted when only part of the complaint was frivolous. But, as indicated above, this, as much or more than an expansive reading of de minimis, would negate the congressional intent underlying the PSLRA's sanction scheme. For the presence of any nonfrivolous claim would again mean that, rather than being bound by the mandates of the PSLRA, courts would be free to engage in the ordinary Rule 11 analysis, which Congress found too often resulted in the failure to compensate fully victims of abusive securities litigation.

Moreover, both the ordinary meaning of "unreasonable burden" and its context in the PSLRA indicate that the statute's unreasonable burden prong requires the sanctioned party to offer, through financial statements or other proof, evidence that the award is unreasonable and unjust, given the party's economic or other like status. Thus, the district court is required to compare the burden on the sanctioned party to the burden placed on the victim of the litigation, given the victim's financial or similar status. See [Section21D(c)(3)(B)] ("The presumption ... may be rebutted only upon proof ... that (I) the award of attorneys' fees and other expenses will impose an unreasonable burden on that ... attorney and would be unjust, and the failure to make such an award would not impose a greater burden on the [victim of the abusive litigation] ...."); see also S.Rep. No. 104-98, at 14 (noting that under this prong, courts should "take into account the relevant circumstances of each case" as proven by the parties).

We conclude that, once a substantial violation is found, the existence of some nonfrivolous claims does not suffice to rebut the statutory presumption on the ground that full sanctions would be an unreasonable and unjust burden.

D. Substantial Violation

All this returns us to the statutory requirement that, in making the mandatory findings under the PSLRA, the district court should initially determine whether or not a violation of Rule 11 occurred, and if it has, whether the failure to comply with Rule 11 was *substantial*. And, as we have emphasized, only if the failure is substantial does the presumption of full sanctions arise. What then is a substantial violation?

Nu-Tech argues that a substantial violation occurs whenever the nonfrivolous claims that are joined with frivolous ones are insufficiently meritorious to save the complaint as a whole from being abusive. Under this interpretation, the district court must examine the qualitative substance of the nonfrivolous claims in order to assess whether these claims were, in fact, legitimate filings that had the potential of prevailing or whether they patently lacked merit and only narrowly avoided being deemed frivolous themselves.

There is much to be said for this reading of the statute, and we adopt it today. First, it gives a meaning to "substantial failure" that is not simply the opposite of de minimis. It thereby avoids what would be a paradoxical result—that the presumption is rebutted by evidence that the presumption was inapplicable in the first instance. Second, it is fully consistent with Congress's desire to punish abusive litigation severely, without discouraging, to any increased degree, parties who wish to present serious, even if ultimately unsuccessful, claims. See H.R. Conf. Rep. No. 104-369, at 39. Third, it accords with our prior holdings.

Thus, in *Simon DeBartolo*, where a nonfrivolous claim that presented a novel legal argument was joined to a single frivolous claim, we remanded for consideration of whether the violation was or was not substantial. Under such circumstances, we found that the rebuttable presumption requiring full costs might well not come into play. The nonfrivolous claim in *Simon DeBartolo* involved only questions of law and, hence, was subject to summary dismissal. But the legal questions raised were legitimate and could well have been decided in favor of the plaintiff. See *Simon DeBartolo*, 186 F.3d at 178; see also *Polar Int'l Brokerage Corp. v. Reeve*, 120 F.Supp.2d 267, 270-71 & n. 7 (S.D.N.Y.2000), aff'd sub nom. *Corroon v. Reeve*, 258 F.3d 86 (2d Cir.2001). The suit as a whole might, therefore, not be abusive and, accordingly, the presumption of full sanctions might be inappropriate.

As was implicit in *Simon DeBartolo*, however, in such cases, even if no substantial failure existed under the PSLRA, partial sanctions might still be assessable under ordinary Rule 11 standards to punish not the bringing of the whole suit, but only of the frivolous claim. In contrast, if summary judgment had been granted because the nonfrivolous claims were altogether meritless, and presented no plausible novel legal or factual contentions, the complaint as a whole would properly be viewed as prima facie abusive and, hence, as substantially failing to comply with Rule 11. Such a complaint would not avoid the statutory presumption that a penalty of full fees and costs is appropriate.

* * * *

To summarize: in cases of this sort, the district court must first determine whether frivolous claims in violation of Rule 11 have been brought. If they have, the court must examine whether nonfrivolous claims have been joined and, if so, whether these claims—whatever their number—are of a quality sufficient to make the suit as a whole nonabusive and the Rule 11 violation not substantial. If no such weighty nonfrivolous claims are attached, the statutory presumption applies. The court must then determine whether the violation was de minimis, for, if it was, the presumption is rebutted. Alternatively, financial statements or other relevant evidence may establish that the full sanction award unjustly creates an unreasonable burden on the sanctioned party and that a partial award would not "impose a greater burden on the party in whose favor sanctions are to be imposed." [Section 21D(c)(3)(B)(i)]. In this situation, too, the presumption is rebutted and *full* sanctions are not warranted.

This framework is, we believe, consistent with the statutory language, with Congress's intention that the PSLRA "impose upon courts the affirmative duty to scrutinize filings closely" when imposing sanctions for any substantial violation of Rule 11(b), H.R. Conf. Rep. No. 104-369 at 40; see also S.Rep. No. 104-98 at 14, and with the legislature's desire to sanction abusive litigations severely, while not discouraging suits that have potential merit. It is also consistent with the jurisprudence of this Circuit.

II. The Present Sanctions

Applying this statutory analysis to the present case, we find no plausible, nonfrivolous allegation in the complaint against Nu-Tech that saves it from being rightly viewed as an abusive securities lawsuit. In doing so, we do not need to decide precisely how strong the nonfrivolous counts or arguments must be in order to limit sanctions only to the frivolous portions of the complaint. It may be that the presence of claims that survive summary judgment is sufficient. It may be that more is needed. But less may also be enough when, as in *Simon DeBartolo*, the only nonfrivolous claim was a question of law, and so summary judgment was appropriate, but that claim was deemed to be a novel and plausible one.

None of that need be decided today. In the case before us, the claims grounded on the first two purchases were frivolous, while the Rule 10b-5 causes of action based upon the last two purchases—though not frivolous—patently lacked merit. The denial of an opportunity to amend the complaint precluded their being deemed frivolous, and barred imposition of Rule 11 sanctions against Jaroslawicz on their account. Because we found it possible that Jaroslawicz could have raised a potentially cognizable claim under the facts of the case with respect to these two claims, we declined to deem them abusive in *themselves*. But the legal strength, or lack thereof, of the possibly cognizable claim that was not presented in the complaint, and that was itself unlikely to succeed on the merits, cannot suffice to relieve the present complaint from being an unfounded action *as a whole*. See *Gurary I*, 190 F.3d at 44; cf. *Gurary II*, 235 F.3d at 800 (noting that Gurary misconstrued our holding in *Simon DeBartolo*, in which we found that the plaintiff's 10b-5 action was not frivolous because, unlike Gurary's 10b-5 claims, the *existing* allegations and facts in the *Simon DeBartolo*'s plaintiff's complaint supported each element of a 10b-5 cause of action). It follows that the complaint substantially violated Rule 11 and that the PSLRA presumption applied.

Jaroslawicz, moreover, has not made out the rebuttal defenses. He argues that his violation was de minimis because two out of the four allegations were deemed nonfrivolous. We need not specify precisely how minimal the frivolous components of a suit must be, in themselves or perhaps in relation to the other parties' conduct, to constitute only a de minimis violation. The legislative history of the PSLRA makes clear that two claims out of four, without any other possible saving grace, is not enough. The violation in the present case was manifestly not de minimis.

Jaroslawicz also argues that the sanctions should be reduced because he recently contracted a disabling disease and operates a small law firm. In the view of the district court, these "facts"—because Jaroslawicz refused to submit financial statements, medical bills, and other documents which would allow the court to assess the impact of his health problems—did not establish that the sanction would create an unreasonable burden. On appeal, Jaroslawicz argues that he should not have to endure an invasion of his privacy in order to receive relief from the burden created by the sanctions. But, once the presumption applies, Jaroslawicz bears precisely that burden, and he must be willing to offer some financial or other like statements, reflecting the claimed impact of his illness and the consequences of imposing the sanctions award, if that is to be the basis of his rebuttal. This he has not done.

III. Recovery of Expenses Incurred in Seeking the Sanctions

One final issue requires attention. In the present appeal, Jaroslawicz argues, for the first time, that the district court erred by including in the award the legal fees and costs incurred by Nu-Tech as a result of the sanctions application itself. These include the expenses for work related to the three decisions issued below as well as the two earlier proceedings in this Court.

Unless manifest injustice will result from refusing to consider the newly raised issue, it is not properly before this panel. *Myack v. Honeywell*, 953 F.2d 798, 803 (2d Cir.1992); see also *Gurary I*, 190 F.2d at 44. If Jaroslawicz were correct, the sanction award would be reduced by approximately $28,000. In light of his multiple opportunities to raise the issue previously, and the limited monetary difference, the point Jaroslawicz now advances does not raise concerns of manifest injustice.

Even if we were to consider the merits of this claim, it is unlikely that Jaroslawicz would prevail. We are remanding for imposition of sanctions pursuant to subsection (c)(3)(A)(ii), which states that under the statutory presumption, the sanction shall be the "reasonable attorneys' fees and other expenses incurred *in the action*." (emphasis added). As a result, the statutory language can support a reading that permits the fees and expenses incurred in pursuing the sanctions to be included in the award. As Nu-Tech argues, the present lengthy litigation exemplifies how costly pursuing sanctions may become, particularly in the case of strike suits. Were sanctions limited to recovering only the costs and fees for the initial action, which is often dismissed on the merits early in the litigation process, many defendants would fail to submit sanctions applications or to pursue them on appeal.

Such a result would undermine the PSLRA's statutory purpose. Unlike the fee-shifting provisions in other statutes that are there to promote litigation, see, e.g., 42 U.S.C. §§ 1988(b), 2000e 5(k), Congress passed the statutory presumption in the PSLRA sanctions scheme in order to encourage "defendants to fight abusive claims," see S.Rep. No. 104-98, at 4, and to compensate wholly victims of frivolous litigation, see H.R. Conf. Rep. No. 104-369, at 39 ("Finally, courts have been unable to apply Rule 11 to the complaint in such a way that the victim of the ensuing lawsuit is compensated for all attorneys' fees and costs incurred in *the entire action*." (emphasis added)). The strict statutory presumption against plaintiffs is limited to those securities fraud cases that are unfounded and abusive. Once the presumption is triggered and is not rebutted, however, it seems most likely that Congress meant for the defendant to receive fees and costs incurred in seeking sanctions pursuant to [Section 21D(c)(3)(A)(ii)], including all reasonable expenses related to appellate proceedings.

CONCLUSION

We hold that Jaroslawicz's complaint, which contains frivolous claims that were summarily dismissed and no claims of such merit as to make his suit as a whole nonabusive, subjects him to full sanctions, including appellate expenses. We hold further that the presence of some nonfrivolous claims in an otherwise frivolous complaint is not sufficient, standing alone, to establish that either the violation of Rule 11 was de minimis or that the sanctions would create an unreasonable burden, for purposes of overcoming the statutory presumption of the PSLRA.

The judgment of the district court is, therefore, vacated and remanded for further proceedings consistent with this opinion.

### *NOTES AND QUESTIONS*

*1. **Frivolousness.*** Was Jaroslawicz's lawsuit frivolous? How so? Does a lawsuit have to be frivolous in order to violate Rule 11?

*2. **The Applicable Standards.*** What is the difference between a pleading that is "frivolous," a pleading that is not "frivolous" but represents a "substantial failure" to comply with Rule 11, and a pleading that is merely a "failure" to comply with Rule 11? What different consequences follow from filing a pleading that meets each of these standards? Are these standards easy for a court to apply?

*3. **Loser Pays.*** In early drafts of the PSLRA, there was a "loser pays" provision (otherwise known as the "English Rule" because loser-pays is prevalent in Great Britain), under which the loser in a private securities action would be required to pay the legal fees and costs of the winner. If this provision had been enacted in the PSLRA, mandatory Rule 11 sanctions in many cases would have been superfluous. The loser pays provision, however, was removed from the PSLRA after strong opposition from the SEC and many members of Congress. How would a loser-pays provision have affected the securities litigation landscape? Would it have been a good idea?

*4. **The President's Concerns.*** President Clinton stated in his veto message that he objected to the Rule 11 language in the PSLRA. What, if anything, is troublesome about this language?

*5. **Sanctioning Defendants.*** Rule 11 and the statutory language in the PSLRA, on their face, can be applied to defendants as aggressively as to plaintiffs. Is it likely that Rule 11 will be enforced evenhandedly?

*6. **Incentives to Comply.*** Besides monetary penalties under Rule 11, what other incentives not to file frivolous lawsuits, motions or other pleadings does the litigation system contain? What additional incentives were put in place by the PSLRA?

---

### 5. *Aftermath of the PSLRA*

The impact of the PSLRA on securities litigation was the subject of extensive debate in the years immediately following the Act's passage. Many scholars believed that the PSLRA would deter frivolous lawsuits, but that it would also make litigation on behalf of defrauded investors more difficult. See, e.g., John C. Coffee, Jr., The Future of the Private Securities Litigation Reform Act: Or, Why the Fat Lady Has Not Yet Sung, 51 Bus. Law. 975, 995 (1996) (the PSLRA favors defendants "at virtually every juncture"). Some scholars clearly believed that the PSLRA had gone too far. See, e.g., Joel Seligman, The Private Securities Litigation Reform Act of 1995, 38 Ariz. L. Rev. 717 (1996); Lynn A. Stout, Type I Error, Type II Error, and the Private Securities Litigation Reform Act, 38 Ariz. L. Rev. 711 (1996). Finally, others were concerned that the PSLRA had not gone far enough, and that litigation was merely shifting to state courts. See, e.g., Joseph A. Grundfest & Michael A. Perino, The Pentium Papers: A Case Study of Collective Institutional Investor Activism in Litigation, 38 Ariz. L. Rev. 559 (1996).

A 1997 SEC Staff Report on the impact of the PSLRA on securities litigation observed that many of the Act's provisions seemed to be achieving their stated objectives. See Report to the President and the Congress on the First Year of Practice Under the Private Securities Litigation Reform Act of 1995 (April 1997). Still, even seven years later the Act's full impact on securities litigation is in some ways unclear, and indeed some of the statutory language itself is also unclear. For example, the federal circuit courts have yet to reach consensus on how to interpret the PSLRA's heightened pleading standards (see Chapter 2.D.2 supra).

Plaintiffs' lawyers responded to the restrictions of the PSLRA with a number of strategies, such as alleging insider trading by defendants more frequently in order to satisfy the PSLRA's heightened requirements for pleading scienter, and filing in state court more shareholder suits based on the common law or state blue sky law. This latter strategy proved to be especially controversial.

Indeed, in the aftermath of the PSLRA, much attention was focused on the legislation's effect on the volume of securities litigation in state court. And many of the PSLRA's most fervent supporters were quick to contend that plaintiffs' lawyers were taking advantage of a "loophole" in the statute by filing actions under state law in order to avoid the PSLRA's numerous restrictions. See Statement of Senator Alfonse D'Amato, 144 Cong. Rec. S 4780-03 (May 13, 1998) (floor debate on S. 1260) ("The problem to which I refer is a loophole that strike lawyers have found in the [PSLRA]***").

Bolstering the contention that much securities litigation was shifting from federal court to state court in the wake of the PSLRA was statistical data compiled by Professors Joseph Grundfest and Michael Perino. Based on their study, Professors Grundfest and Perino maintained that:

> State court class action securities fraud litigation against publicly-traded issuers has become a material factor in the litigation process since passage of the Act. These cases were rare prior to the Act's passage. *** In the first eighteen months after the Reform Act, a total of ninety-two issuers were sued in state court proceedings. ***[T]here has been some decline in state court filings in 1997, but overall approximately ninety-two of 238 post-Reform Act litigations (38.6%) involve at least some state component. There is widespread agreement that these figures represent a substantial increase in state court litigation. Two phenomena seem to explain the bulk of this shift. First, there appears to be a "substitution effect" whereby plaintiffs' counsel file state court complaints when the underlying facts appear not to be sufficient to satisfy new, more stringent federal pleading requirements, or otherwise seek to avoid the substantive or procedural provisions of the Act. Second, plaintiffs appear to be

> resorting to increased parallel state and federal litigation in an effort to avoid federal discovery stays or to establish alternative state court venues for the settlement of federal claims.

See Joseph A. Grundfest and Michael A. Perino, Prepared Testimony before the Senate Banking, Housing and Urban Affairs Committee, Subcommittee on Securities (July 24, 1997). See also Michael A. Perino, Fraud and Federalism: Preempting Private State Securities Fraud Causes of Action, 50 Stan. L. Rev. 273, 302-14 (1998) (reciting statistics showing an increase in state court filings after the PSLRA).

Other securities scholars, however, including one of your casebook authors, expressed skepticism as to whether the increase in state court filings in the immediate aftermath of the PSLRA indicated a continuing trend. See Professor Richard W. Painter, Prepared Testimony before the Senate Banking Committee (February 23, 1998) (stating that "[t]he alarm that has been sounded about a surge in state court filings after 1995 and a movement of litigation from federal to state court, has been a false alarm"). In particular, Professor Painter argued:

> The upswing in class actions filed in state court in 1996 *** may *** be attributable both to temporary disenchantment with the federal forum and to incentives to file in state court created by the Supreme Court's 1996 holding in *Matsushita Electrical Industrial Co. v. Epstein*, [516 U.S. 367 (1996)], that parties can settle federal class action claims as part of state class actions. *** [It is also] a mistake to rely solely on 1996 statistics [because] first, plaintiffs' lawyers may have found state court litigation more cumbersome than they expected; and second, they may have found the 1995 Reform Act to be less onerous than they expected.

See Richard W. Painter, Responding to a False Alarm: Federal Preemption of State Securities Fraud Causes of Action, 84 Cornell L. Rev. 1, 44-45 (1998).

Congress weighed in on this debate when it enacted the Securities Litigation Uniform Standards Act of 1998. As we will see in the section of this Chapter that immediately follows, in so doing it was apparently more convinced by the cries of fire than the warnings of a false alarm.

### *NOTES AND QUESTIONS*

1. ***Steering Clear of the Fraud-on-the-Market Theory.*** Congress could have dealt securities class actions a mortal blow by overturning the Supreme Court's decision in *Basic Inc. v. Levinson*, 485 U.S. 224 (1988), which you studied in Chapter 2. That decision gives plaintiffs a presumption of reliance on the integrity of the market price at which they purchased or sold a security (thereby sparing them the necessity of proving individual reliance on the defendant's fraud). Why do you suppose Congress did not strike down the fraud-on-the-market theory as part of the PSLRA?

2. ***Legislating in a Bull Market.*** When Congress enacted the PSLRA, investors were (as a general matter) reaping large profits and had been for some time. How (if at all) does that fact help explain what Congress did? How might Congress have acted differently in a bear market?

*3. Blaming the PSLRA.* Some observers have blamed the PSLRA for precipitating Enron, WorldCom and other recent securities frauds. See, e.g., Susan P. Koniak, Prepared Testimony before the Senate Committee on the Judiciary, Accountability Issues: Lessons Learned From Enron's Fall (February 6, 2002) (excerpted in Chapter 10.B.2. infra). Many plaintiffs' lawyers and Democrats in Congress have also ascribed such blame. Do you think the PSLRA could have been responsible, in part, for accounting abuses and other incidents of fraud? If so, which provisions of the PSLRA do you believe most likely encouraged fraud? Did the PSLRA contribute to an overall climate that might make fraud more likely? Which aspects of the PSLRA, if any, do you believe would be the best candidates for modification in light of Enron, WorldCom and other recent scandals?

*4. Fire vs. False Alarm.* Do you believe that state court securities litigation would have continued to displace federal litigation in the absence of preemption by Congress? In the wake of the PSLRA, was it accurate to characterize the filing of securities class actions in state court as using a "loophole?" Consider these questions again in light of the material in the following section.

## B. THE SECURITIES LITIGATION UNIFORM STANDARDS ACT OF 1998

As originally enacted, both the Securities Act and the Exchange Act contained broad anti-preemption provisions, ensuring that the newly enacted causes of action under federal law would supplement—rather than supplant—existing remedies under the common law and blue sky laws of the states. See Section 16(a) of the Securities Act ("the rights and remedies provided by this title shall be in addition to any and all other rights and remedies that may exist at law or in equity"); and Section 28(a) of the Exchange Act ("the rights and remedies provided by this title shall be in addition to any and all other rights and remedies that may exist at law or in equity"). And courts that subsequently interpreted federal securities remedies routinely emphasized the availability of alternative state remedies. See, e.g., *Marine Bank v. Weaver*, 455 U.S. 551, 556 (1982) ("[W]e are satisfied that Congress, in enacting the securities laws, did not intend to provide a broad federal remedy for all fraud."); *Blue Chip Stamps v. Manor Drug Stores*, 421 U.S. 723, 738, n. 9 (1975) (observing that the disadvantages of requiring the plaintiff to be a purchaser or seller of securities in order to have standing under Rule 10b-5 are "attenuated to the extent that remedies are available to nonpurchasers and nonsellers under state law").

Despite this long history of co-existing federal and state remedies, in 1998 Congress enacted the Securities Litigation Uniform Standards Act (SLUSA) to effectively preempt most class actions for securities fraud under the common law and securities statutes of all fifty states. See Pub. L. No. 105-353, 112 Stat. 3227 (1998). The Senate passed S. 1260 by a vote of 79 to 21 on May 13, 1998. See 144 Cong. Rec. D497-02 (1998). The House passed HR 1689, as amended to conform to S. 1260, by a vote of 340 to 83 on July 22, 1998. See 144 Cong. Rec. H6119-20 (1998). The bill was then signed by President Clinton (who, although he had vetoed the PSLRA, supported this legislation). The result is that investors, with the exception of state and local governments and their pension funds, are now barred from bringing in state court or under state law a class action alleging fraud in connection with nationally traded securities (encompassing those listed on the New York Stock Exchange, the American Stock Exchange, or the NASDAQ).

This sweeping preemption of state law was rooted in a post-PSLRA development discussed in the previous section of this Chapter: the documented shift in securities class action litigation from federal court to state court in 1996. Whether this shift would have continued was the subject of a contentious political debate. On one side stood the high-technology companies of Silicon Valley, one of the largest groups of defendants in securities fraud class actions, making substantial campaign contributions and strongly supporting legislation that would cut off the path to state court (with a particular eye to the California courts). On the other side of the debate stood consumer groups, public finance officials, plaintiffs' lawyers, and states' rights advocates, who were concerned about federal encroachment on state law. Congress, however, with the eventual backing of the SEC, went ahead with the SLUSA and preempted state law class actions concerning nationally traded securities.

The SLUSA, now incorporated into Section 16(b) of the Securities Act and Section 28(f) of the Exchange Act, provides that

> [n]o covered class action based upon the statutory or common law of any State or subdivision thereof may be maintained in any State or Federal court by any private party alleging—(1) an untrue statement or omission of a material fact in connection with the purchase or sale of a covered security; or (2) that the defendant used or employed any manipulative or deceptive device or contrivance in connection with the purchase or sale of a covered security.

In essence, this language preempts a class action claim that could also be couched as a federal claim under Section 10(b) of the Exchange Act and Rule 10b-5 thereunder.

The SLUSA defines a "covered class action" as a single lawsuit on behalf of more than 50 persons or by one or more named parties seeking to recover on a representative basis on behalf of themselves and others, or any group of lawsuits in the same court involving common questions of law or fact in which damages are sought on behalf of more than 50 persons and the lawsuits are joined, consolidated or otherwise allowed to proceed as a single action. See Securities Act Section 16(f), Exchange Act Section 28(f)(5). A "covered security" is defined as it is in Sections 18(b)(1) and (2) of the Securities Act (added by 1996 amendments preempting state registration requirements for "covered securities," which are defined to include nationally traded securities). Id.

Other aspects of the SLUSA bear mention as well. These include a carve-out in Section 16(d)(1) of the Securities Act and Section 28(f)(3)(A) of the Exchange Act that preserves corporate law claims under the law of the issuer's state of incorporation, including claims that misleading statements were made to obtain shareholder approval of a transaction (the so-called "Delaware carve-out" that is discussed in more detail in the *Lazar* case below). There is also a provision that permits federal courts to stay discovery in *any* private action, including an action by an individual plaintiff, in state court while a federal action is pending. See Section 27(b)(4) of the Securities Act and Section

21(D)(b)(3)(D) of the Exchange Act. The latter provision enables a federal court to prevent plaintiffs from using state court litigation not preempted by the SLUSA as a way to circumvent the discovery stay provisions of the PSLRA in parallel federal litigation. Finally, the SLUSA, in a floor amendment proposed by Senator Sarbanes, exempts from preemption those lawsuits under state law that are brought by states, their political subdivisions and state pension plans, either individually or as class actions comprised solely of such entities. See Section 16(d)(2) of the Securities Act; Section 28(f)(3)(B) of the Exchange Act.

Courts have encountered difficulty in interpreting some aspects of the SLUSA. Consider the following case.

## LAZAR v. GREGERSON

2002 WL 535405 (N.D.Cal. 2002)

ILLSTON, DISTRICT JUDGE:

On April 5, 2002, the Court heard argument on plaintiff's motion for remand and defendants' motion to dismiss. Having considered the arguments of counsel and the papers submitted, and for the reasons set forth below, the Court hereby GRANTS plaintiff's motion, REMANDS this action to the San Francisco Superior Court where it was filed, and DENIES defendants' motion to dismiss as moot.

### BACKGROUND

This putative class action lawsuit was brought on behalf of former holders of stock in PeerLogic, Inc. ("PeerLogic") against PeerLogic's former chairman, Daniel Gregerson, following the acquisition of PeerLogic by Critical Path, Inc. ("Critical Path"). The complaint, filed on November 9, 2001 in San Francisco Superior Court, alleges causes of action of breach of fiduciary duty and breach of the duty of candor and full disclosure. Class actions on behalf of an overlapping class of plaintiffs were also filed in federal court, commencing in February, 2001.

On February 6, 2002, defendants removed this action pursuant to the Securities Litigation Uniform Standards Act of 1998 ('SLUSA" or "the Act") [Securities Act Section 16] and 28 U.S.C. 1441(a). Thereafter, defendants filed a motion to dismiss, arguing that plaintiff's claims are preempted by SLUSA; and plaintiffs moved to remand, arguing that removal under SLUSA was improper. Both motions are presently before this Court.

### LEGAL STANDARD

The removal statute, 28 U.S.C. § 1441(a), provides in relevant part that "any civil action brought in a state court of which district courts of the United States have original jurisdiction, may be removed by the defendant or the defendants to the district court of the United States for the district and division embracing a place where such action is pending." Federal law provides that a district court shall remand any action in which subject matter jurisdiction is lacking. Courts must strictly construe the removal statute against removal jurisdiction. Federal jurisdiction must be rejected if there is any doubt as to the right of removal in the first instance. The burden of establishing grounds for federal jurisdiction rests on the removing party.

DISCUSSION

Defendants argue that plaintiff's claims are preempted by federal securities laws, and that dismissal is therefore required. Plaintiff argues that defendants' removal of this action was improper, because plaintiff's complaint only alleges violations of state law, and because the claims fall under a provision of SLUSA excepting certain actions from preemption.

In 1995, Congress enacted the Private Securities Litigation Reform Act ("PSLRA"), which imposed heightened procedural and substantive standards on class action plaintiffs in private securities actions in federal courts. See Pub. L. No. 104-67. Three years later, to prevent circumvention of the PSLRA by bringing securities lawsuits in state rather than federal courts, Congress enacted SLUSA. SLUSA provides as follows:

> No covered class action based upon the statutory or common law of any State or subdivision thereof may be maintained in any State or Federal court by any private party alleging—
>
> (1) an untrue statement or omission of a material fact in connection with the purchase or sale of a covered security; or
>
> (2) that the defendant used or employed any manipulative or deceptive device or contrivance in connection with the purchase or sale of a covered security.

[Securities Act § 16(b).] SLUSA goes on to state: "Any covered class action brought in any State Court involving a covered security ... shall be removable to the Federal district court for the district in which the action is pending." [Securities Act § 16(c)].

The following subsection of the Act, [Securities Act § 16(d)(1)] entitled "Preservation of certain actions," permits certain covered class actions to be maintained in state court:

> (A) Actions Preserved.—...[A] covered class action described in subparagraph (B) of this paragraph that is based upon the statutory or common law of the State in which the issuer is incorporated ... may be maintained in a State or Federal court by a private party.
>
> (B) Permissible Actions.—A covered class action is described in this subparagraph if it involves:
>
> (i) the purchase or sale of securities by the issuer or an affiliate of the issuer exclusively from or to holders of equity securities of the issuer; or
>
> (ii) any recommendation, position, or other communication with respect to the sale of securities of the issuer that—
>
> (I) is made by or on behalf of the issuer or an affiliate of the issuer to holders of equity securities of the issuer; and
>
> (II) concerns decisions of those equity holders with respect to voting their securities, acting in response to a tender or exchange offer, or exercising dissenters' or appraisal rights.

[Securities Act, § 16(d)(1)].

If an action is a "covered class action" that does not fall under this exemption, it is properly removed and dismissed. See, e.g., *Gilmore v. MONY Life Ins. Co. of America*, 165 F. Supp. 2d 1276, 1278 (M.D. Ala. 2001). If a covered action is determined to be "preserved" under the so-called "Delaware carve-out" exemption provision of SLUSA, it must be remanded to state court. See, e.g., *Gibson v. PS Group Holdings, Inc.*, 2000 U.S. Dist. LEXIS 3158 at * (S.D. Cal. Mar. 8, 2000). Neither party seriously argues that this is not a "covered class action" under SLUSA. The sole issue presented by the parties' motions is, therefore, whether plaintiffs' complaint falls within the scope of the "Delaware carve-out" exemption.

Turning to the complaint itself, it alleges that Gregerson and the Doe defendants breached their duties of loyalty, due care and candor to plaintiff by failing to ensure that the acquisition agreement reached between PeerLogic and Critical Path was fair and in the best interests of PeerLogic's shareholders; failing to ensure that merger materials disseminated to the class did not contain material misrepresentations of fact; and failing to conduct a reasonable investigation prior to the acquisition. Plaintiff alleges that "Defendants' willingness to ignore Critical Path's fraudulent accounting practices and false financial statements" resulted from their desire "to obtain significant payments for themselves via lucrative 'employment contracts,' 'severance agreements,' 'non-compete contracts' and/or 'consulting' agreements which were contemporaneously negotiated by defendants for their own benefit."

Specifically, the complaint alleges that on August 8, 2000, Critical Path and PeerLogic issued a joint statement announcing that an acquisition would occur and stating that the acquisition did not impact Critical Path's "commitment to fourth quarter 2000 profitability." The complaint alleges that defendants were provided with Critical Path financial information in the course of due diligence in preparation for the acquisition, and that defendants "failed to confirm the accuracy of the figures, assumptions or estimates provided by Critical Path." It alleges that, on the day after the acquisition, Critical Path issued a release touting the strengths of the new combination.

The complaint further alleges that the merger materials disseminated to PeerLogic shareholders incorporated false financial data provided by Critical Path to the PeerLogic board. This information included Critical Path's financial statements, a statement for the combined companies for a one year period, and documents filed with the SEC stating that the financial statements were prepared in accordance with GAAP and fairly represented Critical Path's financial condition. The complaint alleges that, by releasing these materials, PeerLogic's board exposed its shareholders to undisclosed risks and uncertainties. The complaint also alleges that PeerLogic's board of directors falsely stated that the acquisition was in the best interests of the company and its shareholders.

Finally, the complaint describes the loss of 55% of the value of Critical Path stock when, on January 19, 2001, Critical Path announced a loss for the forth quarter of 2000 and projected losses into 2001. Critical Path formed a committee to investigate its financial disclosures, and on February 15, 2001, admitted that its fourth quarter 2000 results were false. On April 5, 2001, Critical Path admitted that its third quarter 2000 revenues were overstated.

The complaint alleges that these third and forth quarter statements violated GAAP principles. Based on these factual allegations, the complaint asserts causes of action for breach of the fiduciary duties of due care and loyalty, and breach of the duty of candor and full disclosure, against PeerLogic CEO Gregerson and 100 Doe defendants.

The complaint thus "is based upon the statutory or common law" of California, which is the state in which PeerLogic was incorporated. It is undisputed that no federal question appears on the face of the complaint. The complaint seeks relief based on common law duties, not federal securities law. SLUSA establishes federal courts' exclusive jurisdiction over actions brought "to enforce any liability or duty created by [the Securities Exchange Act of 1934] or the rules and regulations thereunder." [Exchange Act Section 27]. Even though the complaint alleges false statements and omissions made by defendants in connection with the acquisition, plaintiff is not seeking to "enforce any liability or duty" arising under federal securities law. See *Klein v. Southwest Gas Corp.*, 1999 U.S. Dist. LEXIS 22979 (S.D. Cal. 1999) at *15-*16.

Defendants argue that the Court should look behind the claims to find that the "gravamen of the complaint is that Critical Path made misrepresentations to PeerLogic and its shareholders." Although the factual basis for plaintiff's claims undeniably involves actions taken by Critical Path, the Court finds that, on the whole, the gravamen of the complaint concerns alleged wrongdoing by PeerLogic's board. Specifically, plaintiff alleges that Gregerson failed sufficiently to inquire into Critical Path's financial state, disseminated false information about the acquisition to PeerLogic shareholders, and falsely advised them that the acquisition was in their "best interests," all to secure personal benefits from the transaction. The Court therefore rejects defendants' invitation to recast plaintiff's complaint as a federal securities action.

Plaintiff's claims, moreover, fall directly under the explicit exclusionary language of [Section 16(d)]. Plaintiff and other former holders of PeerLogic stock claim that defendants breached their duties to PeerLogic shareholders, and that this breach occurred in defendants' communications concerning a proposed acquisition. Under SLUSA, such a claim is not removable. Defendants' argument to the contrary is essentially the same as their argument concerning the gravamen of the complaint, namely, that plaintiff's claims are fundamentally that she was harmed by Critical Path's alleged misstatements, not PeerLogic's.

The instant case is substantially similar to *Klein v. Southwest Gas Corp*, in which a district court remanded a shareholder class action suit alleging violations of fiduciary duties by Southwest Gas board members in connection with their decision to merge with ONEOK, Inc. See *Klein*, 1999 U.S. Dist. LEXIS 22979 at *2-*5. The Southwest Gas board rejected an unsolicited, higher bid from another company, and Southwest shareholders sought a temporary restraining order enjoining the defendants from completing the merger. Id. at *3. Plaintiffs alleged that the defendants breached their fiduciary duties by approving the allegedly inferior offer; breached their duty of candor by failing to disclose and/or misrepresenting facts about the existence and nature of the competing offer; and violated California statutory law by approving a merger providing for disparate payment to certain board member shareholders. Id. at

*14. The court found that these claims fell under the exception laid out in [Securities Act Section 16d]). Id. at *19. See, also, *Gibson v. PS Group Holdings, Inc.*, 2000 U.S. Dist. LEXIS 3158 (S.D. Cal. 2000) (finding the action was a "covered class action," but that the claims fell under the [Securities Act Section 16(d)] exemption). For the reasons described above, defendants' attempt to distinguish *Klein* based on their assertion that "the bulk of the Complaint is predicated on Critical Path's statements or omissions," is unpersuasive.

Finally, plaintiff requests that she be awarded fees and costs in connection with defendants' removal under 28 U.S.C. § 1447(c). An award of attorney's fees is not mandatory and is within the discretion of the court, "to be exercised based on the nature of the removal and the nature of remand." *Moore v. Permanente Medical Group, Inc.*, 981 F.2d 443, 446 (9th Cir. 1992). Under the circumstances, the Court finds that an award of fees and costs is unjustified, and plaintiff's request is denied. ***

### *NOTES AND QUESTIONS*

***1. Tracing the Source of Alleged Misrepresentations.*** The *Lazar* defendants argued that the court should look behind the claims to find that the "gravamen of the complaint is that Critical Path made misrepresentations to PeerLogic and its shareholders." The court found otherwise. Why does it make a difference whether Critical Path or PeerLogic made the bulk of the misrepresentations alleged in the complaint?

***2. Likely Candidates for Preemption.*** Which of the misrepresentations alleged in the *Lazar* complaint would most likely fall outside the state law carve-out and thus, particularly if standing alone in a complaint, be most apt to be preempted?

***3. The SLUSA Without the Carve-out.*** Earlier drafts of the SLUSA did not include the carve-out for state law fiduciary duty claims. What would have been the effect on state law fiduciary duty cases if the "Delaware carve-out" had not been included? Given that the SLUSA impacts only class actions (not derivative actions), in what types of situations would the SLUSA minus the carve-out have had a particularly severe impact on plaintiffs?

***4. Issuers Prefer Delaware.*** Securities issuers were generally in favor of including the Delaware carve-out in the SLUSA. See Rachel Witmer, Special Report: SEC, Private Bar Working to Address Flaw in Litigation Reform Bills, 30 Sec. Reg. & L. Rep. 169 (BNA) (Jan. 30, 1998). Why might this have been the case?

***5. Breach of Duty vs. Failure to Disclose.*** The carve-out seeks to define the same boundary set forth in *Santa Fe Indus., Inc. v. Green,* 430 U.S. 462 (1977), (see Chapter 2.A.1 supra) between federal disclosure requirements and state fiduciary duty law. As noted in the *Goldberg* and *Healey* line of cases after *Santa Fe,* this boundary is not easy to define because breach of fiduciary duty is often accompanied by failure to disclose, and failure to disclose is itself a breach of fiduciary duty. See Jennifer O'Hare, Director Communications and the Uneasy Relationship Between the Fiduciary Duty of Disclosure and the Anti-Fraud Provisions of the Federal Securities Laws, 70 U. Cin. L. Rev. 475 (2002); Faith Stevelman Kahn, Transparency and Accountability: Rethinking

Corporate Fiduciary Law's Relevance to Corporate Disclosure, 34 Ga. L. Rev. 505 (2000); Lawrence A. Hamermesh, Calling Off the Lynch Mob: The Corporate Director's Fiduciary Disclosure Duty, 49 Vand. L. Rev. 1087 (1996). Does the distinction drawn by the carve-out in the SLUSA make sense?

*6. Derivative Actions Under State Law.* In the wake of both the PSLRA and the SLUSA, many commentators have observed an increase in the number of federal securities class actions and state law derivative actions that are filed simultaneously by plaintiffs' attorneys as a part of a litigation strategy to maximize the chances of successful settlements or verdicts. See Dale Barnes & Mary Huser, PSLRA Has Resulted in Rise in Derivative Claims, Nat'l L.J., at B10 (November 1, 1999) (stating that "[a]pparently in reaction to the limitations on securities investor class actions imposed by Congress in both the [PSLRA and the SLUSA] plaintiffs increasingly have been turning to shareholder derivative suits to pursue legal remedies").

The strategy of filing multiple actions for the same underlying claims is possible because, as noted above, many securities fraud claims can be cast not only as violations of the federal securities laws, but also as breaches of fiduciary duty under the law of the issuer's state of incorporation. State law claims such as these are typically filed as derivative actions (the shareholder sues on behalf of the issuer corporation instead of on behalf of a class of shareholders), but in some circumstances, fiduciary duty claims can also be filed as class actions. See *Smith v. Van Gorkom*, 488 A.2d 858 (Del. 1985) (lawsuit alleging breach of duty of care by directors filed as class action because the subject corporation no longer existed). And federal preemption is generally not a problem because the SLUSA preempts only class actions, and not derivative actions, and in any event the SLUSA contains an exception for class actions that allege breaches of fiduciary duty under the law of the issuer's state of incorporation.

Note an important distinction between derivative actions and class actions under state law. In a state court derivative action, the plaintiff must allege and prove injury to the corporation, not just to individual investors. Thus, a causal connection must generally be shown between a defendant's concealment of material information or other conduct and a decision by shareholders or directors that affected the management of the corporation. An auditing firm, for example, could be sued in connection with an effort by senior officers to hide accounting violations from the corporation's directors and shareholders. However, in contrast to a class action, the claim would not be that shareholders bought or sold stock without knowledge of the violations, but rather that deceived shareholders and directors were denied an opportunity to save the corporation from further injury. On the other hand, in a shareholder class action under state law, like the *Van Gorkom* case, the plaintiff can allege direct injury to the plaintiff in a shareholder class without reference to harm to the corporation.

In light of both the tenor and substance of the debate surrounding both the PSLRA and the SLUSA, would you expect to see state courts more or less receptive to the breach of fiduciary claims asserted in derivative litigation?

*7. The Definition of "Covered Security."* Some securities that one does not ordinarily think of as nationally traded securities still fit the technical definition of a covered security under the SLUSA. See *Lander v. Hartford Life & Annuity Ins. Co.*, 251 F.3d 101 (2d Cir. 2001) (upholding the removal to federal court of a class action alleging fraud in connection with variable annuity contracts because the accounts used to market such contracts had to be registered with the SEC and therefore qualified as "covered securities"). How important is it that issuers and investors know ahead of time that they are dealing with a "covered security"?

*8. **Preemption vs. Federalism.*** Did Congress make the correct decision in enacting the SLUSA? How would you assess the benefits and costs of the uniformity that comes as the result of the SLUSA?

## C. EMPIRICAL DATA ON CLASS ACTIONS

Policy debates over private securities litigation often revolve around empirical data on the frequency of lawsuits, dismissal rates, settlement rates and amounts, and other characteristics of the litigation landscape. Each time a bill is proposed in Congress that would make class actions easier or more difficult for plaintiffs, members of Congress are deluged with data purporting to show whether there is too much litigation or too little, whether too few class actions are dismissed or too many, and whether most lawsuits are or are not frivolous. Members of Congress also keep a close eye on who the defendants are. Investment banking firms, accounting firms, Silicon Valley high-technology companies and other groups are particularly influential on Capitol Hill, and a surge in litigation against these defendants can lead to swift congressional reaction. On the other hand, many voters are also investors, and members of Congress are sensitive to increases in the number of earnings restatements and other indicators of fraud in the marketplace.

Empirical data on class actions both before and after the PSLRA is available from a wide variety of sources, and it should be emphasized that many of these sources are themselves interested in one side or another of the securities class action debate. While the presence of self-interest does not render the data meaningless, it does underscore the importance of using data from more than one source, where possible, to support any conclusions that are drawn.

Sources used below include the Stanford Law School Securities Class Action Clearinghouse (in cooperation with Cornerstone Research) (hereinafter "Stanford/Cornerstone"),[a] National Economic Research Associates (NERA) and PricewaterhouseCoopers LLP, as well as various studies compiled by academics

---

a. Stanford Law School Securities Class Action Clearinghouse is a World Wide Web site that was launched in December 1996. As stated on its homepage:

> The Securities Class Action Clearinghouse provides detailed information relating to the prosecution, defense, and settlement of federal class action securities fraud litigation. The Clearinghouse maintains an Index of Filings of 1693 issuers that have been named in federal class action securities fraud lawsuits since passage of the Private Securities Litigation Reform Act of 1995. The Clearinghouse also contains copies of more than 2000 complaints, briefs, filings, and other litigation-related materials filed in these cases.

http://securities.stanford.edu.

using data from one or more of these sources, sometimes in addition to independent observations. Some of the general trends that can be identified from this data are discussed below.

### 1. *Who Gets Sued?*

Most studies of federal securities class actions identify high-technology firms as the defendant most likely to be sued. For example, data recorded by Professors Joseph Grundfest and Michael Perino found that high-technology companies were roughly 34% of all issuers named as defendants in class action lawsuits both before and after the PSLRA. See Joseph A. Grundfest & Michael A. Perino, Securities Litigation Reform: The First Year's Experience at 23 (Feb. 27, 1997). And in 2000, the high-technology sector was still the most common defendant, with the computer services and telecommunications fields representing 41% of the new federal class actions filed. See PricewaterhouseCoopers LLP 2000 Securities Litigation Study at 3-4.

Studies also show that underwriters and accounting firms have been the most often named co-defendants. See Mukesh Bajaj et al., Securities Class Action Settlements: An Empirical Analysis at 10 (November 16, 2000) (reporting that 171 in a sample of 807 class action lawsuits involved underwriters as co-defendants; 82 involved accounting firms). Prestigious underwriting firms are particularly likely to be sued, a development that some legal scholars, at least before the PSLRA, interpreted to be evidence that strike suits were pervasive. See James Bohn & Stephen Choi, Fraud in the New-Issues Market: Empirical Evidence on Securities Class Actions, 144 U. Pa. L. Rev. 903, 952-55 (1996) (suggesting that IPOs handled by high-reputation underwriters may be more likely to be the subject of class action securities fraud suits than IPOs handled by lower-reputation underwriters). But see James D. Cox, Making Securities Fraud Class Actions Virtuous, 39 Ariz. L. Rev. 497, 507 (1997) (contending that Bohn and Choi's "overall data merely confirms that larger offerings attract not only higher quality underwriters but also cost-conscious class action lawyers").

### 2. *How Many Lawsuits are Filed?*

Most studies of federal securities class actions report a slight increase in the number of lawsuits since the PSLRA's enactment, with a temporary surge in filings in 2001 (explained below). The number of class actions in state court has, of course, fallen dramatically in the wake of the SLUSA.

**Stanford/Cornerstone**

| | | | |
|---|---|---|---|
| **1991** | 164 | **1997** | 174 |
| **1992** | 202 | **1998** | 233 |
| **1993** | 163 | **1999** | 209 |
| **1994** | 231 | **2000** | 213 |
| **1995** | 188 | **2001** | 489 |
| **1996** | 109 | **2002** | 259 |

http://securities.stanford.edu (visited last February 1, 2003)

National Economic Research Associates, Inc. (NERA)

| | |
|---|---|
| **Avg. 1991-1995** | 191 |
| **1996** | 127 |
| **1997** | 193 |
| **1998** | 269 |
| **1999** | 240 |
| **2000** | 223 |
| **2001** | 498 |

See Todd S. Foster et al., Recent Trends VII: PSLRA, Six Years Later, National Economic Research Associates, Inc. at Figure 1A (Jan. 2002) (hereinafter NERA 2002 Study).

Note that both Stanford/Cornerstone and NERA report a surge of securities class action filings in 2001 and offer the same explanation. The NERA 2002 Study points out that 300 of the filings in 2001 involved claims that underwriters engaged in "laddering" to increase artificially the aftermarket trading price of IPOs. (As we will see in Chapter 8.A, "laddering" is the practice of making generous allocations of shares sold in an IPO to favored clients on the condition that they commit to buying additional shares in the aftermarket at progressively higher prices). Thus, although the total number of filings rose dramatically in 2001, the number of filings in 2001 would have been only 198 if the laddering cases were excluded. See id. at 1. See also Stanford/Cornerstone, supra, homepage (pointing out that 2001 "differs from prior experience because of the proliferation of 'IPO Allocation' lawsuits" and noting that such IPO allocation lawsuits "do not allege that issuers have engaged in fraud when describing their own business or financial circumstances").

The NERA 2002 Study also calls attention to the Ninth Circuit's decision *in In Re Silicon Graphics Inc. Sec. Litig.*, 183 F.3d 970 (9th Cir.1999), which imposed strict pleading requirements on private plaintiffs and was discussed in Chapter 2.D.2. According to the study, the decision in *Silicon Graphics* is a reasonable explanation for the decline in non-laddering class action lawsuits from 1998 to 2001: "In the first six months of 1999, 23 cases were filed per month (implying approximately 280 filings for the year); following the *Silicon Graphics* decision, the monthly filing rate dropped by approximately 6 cases to 17 per month (bringing the actual filings to 240 for the year)." Id.

Before the SLUSA, there were some state court class actions alleging securities fraud, but not very many, and most of these were brought in California. See Richard W. Painter, Responding to a False Alarm: Federal Preemption of State Securities Fraud Causes of Action, 84 Cornell L. Rev. 1, 36 and App. A (1998) (reporting Pricewaterhouse statistics of 67 state cases in 1994, 52 in 1995, 66 in 1996 and 44 in 1997). Congress's enactment of SLUSA in 1998 ensures that almost all private class actions for securities fraud are brought in federal court.

### 3. *How Many of the Lawsuits Survive Motions to Dismiss?*

Statistics on dismissal rates vary widely depending on the sample used, the definition of involuntary dismissal (for example whether dismissal with leave to amend the complaint counts as a dismissal) and other factors. Focusing on the pre-PSLRA time period, Professor James Cox points to one study where "11-16% of securities class actions were dismissed on pretrial motions between 1991-1993;" another study where "38% of securities fraud cases in 1990 and 1991 were dismissed on pretrial motions" and a third study concluding that "pretrial motions are ineffective in reducing incidence of securities class actions because many peripheral claims survive and the courts generally provide leave to amend the complaint." See Cox, supra, 39 Ariz. L. Rev. at 520 n. 78 (citing Frederick C. Dunbar & Vinita M. Juneja, Recent Trends II: What Explains Settlements in Shareholder Actions?, in Private Litigation Under the Federal Securities Laws: Hearings Before the Subcomm. on Securities of the Senate Comm. on Banking, Housing, and Urban Affairs, 103d Cong., 1st Sess. at 750 tb.1 (June 17 & July 21, 1993); Joel Seligman, The Merits Do Matter: A Comment on Professor Grundfest's "Disimplying Private Rights of Action Under the Federal Securities Laws: The Commission's Authority," 108 Harv. L. Rev. 438, 455 (1994); and Janet Cooper Alexander, Do the Merits Matter? A Study of Settlements in Securities Class Actions, 43 Stan. L. Rev. 497, 544 (1991). Professor Cox, however, predicted in his 1997 article that the PSLRA's forceful pleading requirements "will allow courts to dismiss a larger number of cases than have heretofore been dismissed under more lax pleading standards." Cox, supra, 39 Ariz. L. Rev. at 519-20.

The NERA 2002 Study validates Professor Cox's prediction. The study found a "marked increase" in the percentage of federal securities fraud class actions dismissed since the enactment of the PSLRA:

> Excluding voluntary dismissals, dismissals as a percent of dispositions have approximately doubled with the PSLRA's heightened pleading requirements a likely contributing factor. Prior to the PSLRA, dismissals comprised 12% of dispositions; this has rose to 24% in the post-PSLRA period. However, many of these recent dismissals allowed plaintiffs to replead, so the ultimate disposition of these cases is unknown. In the post-PSLRA era, cases as a percentage of filings, are also being dismissed at a higher rate.

NERA 2002 Study at 4 (citing Figures 12 and 13). See also Hillary A. Sale, Judging Heuristics, 35 U.C. Davis L. Rev. 903, 904 (2002) (concluding that "district courts have eagerly and overwhelmingly accepted the 'opportunity' Congress offered them by creating and using heuristics to eliminate cases on motions to dismiss ***").

### 4. *Which Pleading Standard are Courts Imposing with Respect to Scienter?*

The PSLRA tightened the standard for pleading scienter with ambiguous statutory language requiring the plaintiff to plead specific facts giving rise to a "strong inference" that the defendant acted with the requisite state of mind. See Exchange Act Section 21D(b)(2). And behind this provision stands even more ambiguous legislative history. As we have seen previously, the federal circuit courts have offered divergent interpretations of this PSLRA pleading requirement, and the Supreme Court has yet to resolve the issue. (See Chapter 2.D.2, supra.)

The three distinct interpretations of the PSLRA pleading standard applied by federal courts are:

(i) The Second and Third Circuit standard, which allows a plaintiff to satisfy the heightened requirements by pleading a defendant's "motive and opportunity" to commit fraud. See *Novak v. Kasaks*, 216 F.3d 300, 310 (2d Cir. 2000); *In re Advanta Corp. Sec. Litig.*, 180 F.3d 525, 534 (3d Cir. 1999).

(ii) An "intermediate standard" followed by the First, Fifth, Sixth, Eighth, Tenth, and Eleventh Circuits, which holds that the "mere" pleading of motive and opportunity will not suffice, but where specific facts demonstrating a defendant's "motive and opportunity" to commit fraud may provide the necessary "strong inference" of recklessness or intent. See *Greebel v. FTP Software, Inc.*, 194 F.3d 185, 197 (1st Cir. 1999); *Nathenson v. Zonagen Inc.*, 267 F.3d 400, 409-11 (5th Cir. 2001); *Helwig v. Vencor, Inc.*, 251 F.3d 540, 551 (6th Cir. 2001) (en banc); *Fla. St. Bd. of Admin. v. Green Tree Fin. Corp.*, 270 F.3d 645 (8th Cir. 2001); *City of Philadelphia v. Fleming Cos.*, 264 F.3d 1245, 1261-63 (10th Cir. 2001); *Bryant v. Avado Brands, Inc.*, 187 F.3d 1271, 1282-83 (11th Cir.1999).

(iii) The so-called *Silicon Graphics* standard applied by the Ninth Circuit, which holds that pleading motive and opportunity will not suffice, and that plaintiffs must plead specific facts giving rise to a strong inference of either "deliberate recklessness" or fraudulent intent on the part of the defendant. See *In re Silicon Graphics Inc. Sec. Litig.*, 183 F.3d 970 (9th Cir. 1999).

See Joseph A. Grundfest & A. C. Pritchard, Statutes with Multiple Personality Disorders: The Value of Ambiguity in Statutory Design and Interpretation, 54 Stan. L. Rev. 627, 670 (2002) (discussing these three interpretations).

Professors Grundfest and Pritchard have found that in 66 decisions, or 39.2% of their sample, courts avoided choosing a distinct interpretation of the PSLRA pleading standard by either finding that the case was so well pled that it would meet any of the above standards (22 cases or 13.2% of the total) or so poorly pled that it met none of them (44 cases or 26.3% of the total). Id. at 688. In the remaining cases, courts opted for the Second Circuit standard in 50 cases (29.9% of the total), for the intermediate standard in 28 cases (16.8% of the total), and for the *Silicon Graphics* standard in 23 cases (13.8% of the total). Id. at 688. The courts that do choose a standard thus appear in aggregate, "to be evenly divided as to whether the 'strong inference' pleading requirement incorporates the Second Circuit standard or calls for a stronger interpretation. Further, the opinions that call for a stronger standard are closely split between the intermediate standard and the *Silicon Graphics* standard." Id. at 689-90.

### 5. *How Long Does a Securities Class Action Take to Resolve?*

The NERA 2002 Study addressed the amount of time securities class actions took to settle or otherwise conclude:

> Of pre-Reform Act cases filed, about 59% were disposed of within three years of filing. Only 39% of post-Reform Act filings were disposed of within that length of time. We hypothesize that this trend is the result of the PSLRA provisions regarding the selection of lead plaintiff and the automatic stay of discovery while a motion to dismiss is pending.

Id. at 3.

Thus, while the PSLRA appears to have lead to higher dismissal rates, disposition of cases under the PSLRA—whether by judgment, dismissal, or settlement—appears to take longer than in the pre-PSLRA period.

### 6. *What Types of Allegations Are Most Common in Securities Class Actions?*

Even before the scandals at Enron, WorldCom, and the numerous other public company scandals grabbing headlines in 2002, there had been a steady increase in the number of securities class actions alleging accounting violations. One study reports that in 2001, 57% of the class action complaints filed included an alleged accounting irregularity. See PricewaterhouseCoopers 2001 Litigation Study at 3. The study further notes that "[i]mproper revenue recognition continues to be the most commonly alleged accounting abuse." Id.

Reflecting a similar trend, the NERA 2002 Study observes that:

> The percentage of securities class actions involving allegations of accounting fraud increased substantially since passage of PSLRA. In the five years preceding the PSLRA an average of 38% of all cases involved accounting fraud. This average jumped to 51% in the 6 years following the Act's passage. *** Many of these accounting cases involve restatements. While the growth in restatement cases occurred both before and after the passage of PSLRA, the percentage of cases involving a restatement has grown from 9% pre-PSLRA to 20% post-PSLRA.

Id. at 3 (citing Figures 4 and 5).

Earlier studies had pointed to allegations of misleading statements by a company's management as the most common type of securities fraud alleged in class action lawsuits. See Bajaj et al., Securities Class Action Settlements: An Empirical Analysis (Nov. 16, 2000). The authors of this study examined 177 class action lawsuits filed in 1999, and concluded that 55% (97) had alleged misleading statements by company management. Id. at 4. The remaining 80 cases involved at least one of the following categories of allegations:

Defendant failed to disclose material information.

Defendant violated corporate disclosure rules.

Defendant breached fiduciary responsibilities.

Registration/proxy statement included false or misleading statements.

Officers of defendant firm violated insider-trading rules.

Defendant made false revenue disclosures, which required a restatement.

The statements made at the IPO were false or misleading.

Defendant was involved in improper accounting practices.

Defendants were involved in improper Revenue recognition.

Id. at 3. Yet, consistent with the trend observed by PricewaterhouseCoopers and NERA, the Bajaj study noted that two of the above categories, revenue restatement-related cases and revenue recognition-related cases, saw significant increases in the post-PSLRA period (revenue restatement cases went from 10 pre-reform to 41 filed since 1996; and revenue recognition cases increased from 9 pre-reform to 27 filed since 1996). Id. at 4.

### 7. *How Much Does the Typical Lawsuit Settle For and Why?*

Outcomes of litigation are measured by settlement results because almost all cases settle. Yet, as illustrated below, there is some disagreement among different data providers on the figures for settlements and the conclusions that can be drawn from these figures. Also, several large accounting restatements–some of them even larger than the restatement in Enron–have resulted in remarkably large settlements. The Cendant litigation, for example, broke all previous records, with a total settlement of $3.19 billion. See *In re Cendant Sec. Litig.*, 109 F. Supp. 2d 235, 239 (D.N.J. 1999). And because the Cendant litigation's settlement figure is disproportionately high, a number of studies choose to exclude it in computing settlement averages. Other notably large settlements include Waste Management (combined total of $667 million); Bank of America ($490 million); 3Com ($259 million); Rite Aid ($193 million); MicroStrategy ($192.5 million); Informix ($136.5 million); and Sunbeam ($125 million). See Stanford/Cornerstone at http://securities.stanford.edu/Settlements/largest_post_reform_act.html.

**Stanford/Cornerstone**

**Summary Statistics of Settlement Amounts Through Year-End 2001[a]**

| | **Pre-Reform** | **Post-Reform** |
|---|---|---|
| **Minimum** | $80,000 | $100,000 |
| **Median** | $4.0 million | $5.5 million |
| **Average** | $7.8 million | $14.4 million excluding Cendant; ($24.9 million including Cendant) |
| **Maximum** | $67.5 million | $3.19 billion (Cendant) |

a. Stanford/Cornerstone notes that 303 cases comprise its Post-Reform sample of settlements; its Pre-Reform Act sample consists of 125 Rule 10b-5 cases filed between January 1, 1991 and December 31, 1994.

**Distribution of Settlement Amounts by Percentage of Cases**

| | Pre-Reform | Post-Reform |
|---|---|---|
| Less than $1 million | about 9% | about 9% |
| From $1 to $4.9 million | about 50% | about 35% |
| From $5 to $9.9 million | about 22% | about 22% |
| Greater than $10 million | about 19% | about 34% |

http://securities.stanford.edu/Settlements/REVIEW_1995-2001/REVIEW_1995-2001.html

Stanford/Cornerstone's data indicates that, both before and after the PSLRA, most securities class actions settled for less than $10 million But the number of cases settling for more than $10 million is significantly higher in the Post-Reform period.

The NERA's 2002 Study offers a similar conclusion that "[a]verage settlements increased significantly since the Reform Act was passed." See NERA 2002 Study at 4. However, the NERA Report reflects different settlement figures, with pre-PSLRA settlements averaging $8.4 million and post-PSLRA settlements averaging $13.3 million excluding Cendant ($31.7 million including Cendant).

### *8. Who are the Lawyers?*

A small number of law firms bring most securities class actions: Milberg Weiss Bershad Specthrie & Lerach (New York); Abbey & Ellis (New York); Stull, Stull and Brody (New York); Berger & Montague (Philadelphia); Much, Shelist, Freed, Denbenberg, Ament & Eiger (Chicago); and Wolf, Popper, Ross, Wolf & Jones (New York). See Jonathan R. Macey & Geoffrey P. Miller, The Plaintiffs Attorney's Role in Class Action and Derivative Litigation: Economic Analysis and Recommendations for Reform, 58 U. Chi. L. Rev. 1, 67 n. 197 (1991). Of these, Milberg Weiss is the largest and files the greatest percentage of cases. See Bajaj et. al, supra, Securities Class Action Settlements at 13 (sampling 1,203 federally filed cases and 92 state court cases in the 1988-1999 time period and reporting that Milberg Weiss filed 408 (31%) and settled 259 (32%)). Moreover, Milberg Weiss's percentage of cases has risen significantly since the enactment of the PSLRA. See Laura E. Simmons, Cornerstone Research, Post-Reform Act Securities Lawsuits: Settlements Reported Through December 2001 at 10 (reporting that Milberg Weiss "has been involved as lead or co-lead plaintiff counsel in approximately half of all post-Reform Act cases settled to date").

Milberg Weiss's increasing share of class action filings has been confirmed in law review commentary, some of it by Milberg Weiss lawyers themselves. Indeed, William Lerach (now lead counsel in the Enron securities fraud class action) has stated that prior to PSLRA, Milberg Weiss appeared in approximately 31% of securities fraud class actions, whereas after the PSLRA, this percentage increased to 59%. See William S. Lerach, "The Private Securities Litigation Reform Act of 1995—27 Months Later:" Securities Class

Action Litigation Under the Private Securities Litigation Reform Act's Brave New World, 76 Wash. U. L.Q. 597, 606 (1998). See also Randall S. Thomas, et al., Megafirms, 80 N.C. L. Rev. 115, 194 (2001) (noting that "Milberg Weiss's success in obtaining the role of lead counsel has been accompanied by significant growth in the size of this law firm").

### 9. *How Much Fraud is Out There?*

This question is probably the most difficult to answer because available data do not give a precise picture of how often issuers, underwriters, broker-dealers, auditors and other persons violate federal securities laws. The number of securities class actions could be indicative of the amount of fraudulent activity in securities markets, but other factors such as the PSLRA and changes in case law have influenced the attractiveness of these lawsuits for plaintiffs, for the most part negatively. Therefore the number of lawsuits may understate the amount of fraud. Alternatively, one could look at the number of SEC investigations. See David Wessel, What's Wrong?, Venal Sins: Why the Bad Guys of the Boardroom Emerged en Masse, Wall St. J. at A-1 (June 20, 2002) (stating that "[t]he SEC opened 570 investigations last year. That's more than in any of the previous 10 years—but just 10 more than in 1994."). SEC enforcement statistics, however, can also be misleading because SEC staffing and resources determine the amount of SEC enforcement activity. In times of pervasive fraud, the SEC may leave some smaller cases to be addressed by state securities regulators or private litigants.

Probably the most often-cited statistic in recent years has been the number of earnings restatements by publicly traded companies. Earnings restatements are at least a good indicator of the amount of securities fraud involving auditor malfeasance. Dr. Min Wu of New York University's Stern School of Business has compiled statistics on earnings restatements from 1995 to 2000:

**Restatements by Year 1977-2Q2002**

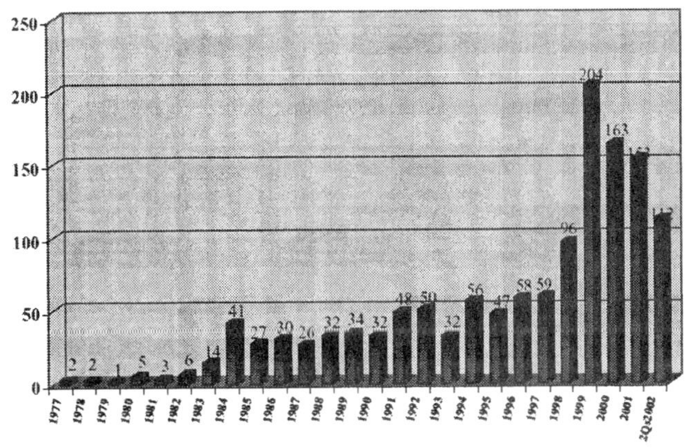



Note: Year 2001 and 2002 numbers are preliminary.

Reprinted with permission.

Business Week, citing this data, recently observed that, while the number of earnings restatements has soared, most publicly traded companies remain unaffected:

> If restatements continue at the first quarter's pace, they will reach a record 240 this year alone. Until the mid-1980s, it was unusual for financial restatements to top more than half a dozen in any given year. Then, after regularly running about 50 or so a year from the early 1990s, these redos skyrocketed to a high of 204 by 1999. Even so, from 1995 through 2000, restatements accounted for only three-quarters of one percent of the average annual number of reporting companies, according to Financial Executives International.

John A. Byrne, Commentary: Let's Really Clean Up Those Numbers—Now, Bus. Wk. Online (July 15, 2002).

One explanation for the recent surge in restatements could be that, with the restatements from a few companies such as WorldCom and Xerox being so disproportionately large, other companies conclude that they had best make their own earnings restatements now when they are likely to fall under the radar. See id. (quoting Dr. Min Wu as saying that "[t]here is so much other bad news out there, it might be a good time to release a restatement, ***. In good times, one piece of bad news would get you hammered more severely"). See also Adam Levy, Cisco, AOL, More U.S. Companies May Revise Accounting, Bloomberg Financial News (July 1, 2002) (stating that "U.S. companies are filing financial restatements to correct false or faulty accounting at a record pace this year. *** The current record is 158, set last year. Restatements almost tripled from 1997 to 2001").

### *NOTES AND QUESTIONS*

*1. **High-Tech Firm Defendants.*** Why are high-technology firms sued so often? How would you expect the burst of the dot.com bubble to affect the statistics over the next several years?

*2. **Future Statistical Trends.*** What future trends do you anticipate in light of Enron, WorldCom and similar accounting scandals? How will the bear market affect securities class actions?

*3. **Market Concentration for Plaintiffs' Legal Representation.*** Is it desirable for such a large share of plaintiffs' work to be done by a single law firm? What aspects of the PSLRA might have encouraged this development?

*4. **Causes of Securities Fraud.*** What explains the large number of earnings restatements and other incidents of fraud in the late 1990s and early 2000s? We have previously discussed the differing opinions with respect to the PSLRA (see Section A.3 supra (note 3)). What other factors could be responsible? For example, could the bull market of the late 1990s have invited fraud? See Gretchen Morgenson, Don't be a Victim: The Bull Market in Stocks has Bred a Bull Market in Fraud, Forbes at 42 (June 2, 1997); David Barboza, Large Returns are Now Bringing in Stock Promoters with Rap Sheets, N.Y. Times at B-1(May 10, 1997); Paul Beckett, Bull Market Adds to Regulators' Woes, Wall St. J. at B7B (Mar. 3, 1997). Were opportunities for fraud created by the proliferation of exemptions from the Securities Act's registration and prospectus delivery requirements that were adopted by the SEC in the 1980s and 1990s?

## D. SHIFTING PERCEPTIONS OF THE BALANCE OF POWER BETWEEN PLAINTIFFS AND DEFENDANTS

### 1. *On Balance, Are Securities Class Actions Meritorious?*

Obviously, not all securities class actions are meritorious. Neither are all such actions frivolous. Litigating class actions is expensive, and arguably too much of the benefit from litigation goes to lawyers at the expense of investors. On the other hand, securities class actions may increase investor confidence, and eventually stock prices, because of their deterrent and compensatory value. The question thus remains hotly debated as to whether private class actions, a phenomenon unique to American securities markets, are on balance worth it.

This issue came to the forefront of academic debate in the years before the PSLRA, most notably in the debate between Professor Janet Alexander and Dean Joel Seligman. Professor Alexander of Stanford Law School pointed to empirical data showing that securities class actions all settle for about the same proportion of alleged losses, meaning that the actual merits of each case were a weak proxy for settlement value. See Janet Cooper Alexander, Do the Merits Matter? A Study of Settlements in Securities Class Actions, 43 Stan. L. Rev. 497 (1991). Professor Joseph Grundfest, also of Stanford and a former SEC Commissioner, joined in on this side of the debate. See Joseph A. Grundfest, Disimplying Private Rights of Action Under the Federal Securities Laws: The Commission's Authority, 107 Harv. L. Rev. 963 (1994) (suggesting that many securities class actions lack merit and that the SEC should exercise its authority to abolish implied private rights of action under Rule 10b-5). Dean Joel Seligman, however, disputed Professor Alexander's results and suggested that a lawsuit's merit actually did influence settlement value. See Joel Seligman, The Merits Do Matter: A Comment on Professor Grundfest's "Disimplying Private Rights of Action under the Federal Securities Laws: The Commission's Authority," 108 Harv. L. Rev. 438 (1994).

Later, after enactment of the PSLRA, Professor Lynn Stout reiterated the concerns of Dean Seligman and other skeptics about the movement to "reform" securities litigation. Stout described the required balancing of interests as a tradeoff between corrective measures for two different types of error in the litigation system:

> [S]cholars generally divide error into two categories. The first category of legal error is called Type I error, or the "false positive." In securities litigation, an example of a Type I false positive would be a judicial finding that a defendant had fraudulently misrepresented something, when in fact no fraud occurred. The second type of error is called Type II error, or the "false negative." A Type II false negative occurs when a court trying to decide whether the defendant has committed fraud mistakenly finds there has been no fraud, even though fraud actually occurred.

Lynn A. Stout, Type I Error, Type II Error, and the Private Securities Litigation Reform Act, 38 Ariz. L. Rev. 711, 711 (1996). Much of the debate over class actions is a debate over which of these two types of error is more likely. Professor Stout observes that Congress, in drafting the PSLRA, and in particular the pleading requirements in Section 21D(b)(2) of the Exchange Act, "was particularly concerned about a form of Type I error: the so-called 'strike suit.'" Id.

Many critics of the PSLRA argue that the statute went too far in protecting defendants from strike suits. They point to statistical and anecdotal evidence that securities fraud is on the rise. See, e.g., Charles M. Yablon, A Dangerous Supplement? Longshot Claims and Private Securities Litigation, 94 Nw. U. L. Rev. 567 (2000) (arguing that most securities fraud suits are not frivolous strike suits of the type condemned by proponents of the PSLRA); James D. Cox, Making Securities Fraud Class Actions Virtuous, 39 Ariz. L. Rev. 497 (1997) (criticizing parts of the PSLRA and pointing out that many securities fraud lawsuits are meritorious). See also William S. Lerach, "The Private Securities Litigation Reform Act of 1995—27 Months Later:" Securities Class Action Litigation Under the Private Securities Litigation Reform Act's Brave New World, 76 Wash. U. L.Q. 597 (1998) (discussing statistical data on fraud and class action litigation).

Professor Hillary Sale, for example, points out that one specific provision of the PSLRA, the heightened standard for pleading state of mind, could decrease Type I error, or "false positives" and increase Type II error, or "false negatives." This effect is exacerbated by the fact that the PSLRA pleading standard had been developed by pre-PSLRA courts in the course of reviewing complaints revised by plaintiffs based on defendants' documentary evidence. Such evidence is now denied to plaintiffs pursuant to the PSLRA's stay on discovery pending resolution of a motion to dismiss. Hillary A. Sale, Judging Heuristics, 35 U.C. Davis L. Rev. 903, 908-909 (2002).

Professor Stout makes another argument criticizing the PSLRA when she notes the disproportionately low aggregate cost of Type I error (in the millions of dollars) relative to the impact of Type II error on capital markets in which trillions of dollars of securities are outstanding:

> Let us first talk about Type I error: the strike suit. If you listen to the rhetoric coming from Capitol Hill, you will swiftly reach the conclusion that the problem of strike suits is endemic and horribly costly. ***
>
> When the proponents of securities litigation reform start to talk dollars and cents, however, you very quickly get a better idea of the magnitude of the social losses supposedly flowing from strike suits. Most often, corporate losses from defending against meritless strike suits are described as running in the millions or tens of millions of dollars. When the proponents of securities litigation reform get really ambitious, they will sometimes mention figures in the hundreds of millions ***
>
> ***[Turning to Type II error,] fraud is bad for securities markets because it erodes investor confidence. This occurs because fraud makes it difficult for investors to detect differences in the quality of the securities they buy. Companies issuing bad securities—poorly run firms that throw away money and do a poor job for their investors—can sell their securities at about the same price as well-managed firms, because fraud makes it impossible for investors to easily distinguish between high-quality and low-quality firms.
>
> ***Although the figure is constantly rising, the market value of publicly-held equities issued by United States corporations presently exceeds $8 *trillion*. That's just stocks, of course. According to federal Flow of Funds

> accounts, the market value of corporate bonds currently outstanding is another $2 or $3 trillion. Throw in commercial paper, and some of the non-bond debt forms corporations issue, and I think it safe and fair to say that the market value of United States corporate securities outstanding today significantly exceeds $10 trillion.
>
> ***When I look at Congress worrying about firms losing hundreds of millions of dollars from strike suits, I cannot help but think about the foolishness of trading in hundreds of *millions* of dollars of Type I error costs for, potentially, hundreds of *billions* of dollars of Type II costs. ***

Stout, supra, 38 Ariz. L. Rev., at 712-14.

Proponents of restricting private rights of action point to statistical evidence of their own, including the large number of class action lawsuits that are eventually dismissed. See subsection C.3 supra (discussing dismissal rates). Critics of class action litigation also point to the correlation of filings with fluctuations in the market.

Then there is the significant number of lawsuits that settle for "nuisance value." Joseph A. Grundfest, Why Disimply?, 108 Harv. L. Rev. 727, 742-43 (1995) (assuming that settlements of less than $2 million generally involve "nuisance" suits, and citing three studies suggesting "that from 22% to 60% of observed settlements are sufficiently low that the merits may not have mattered at all in the resolution of the litigation"). But see Cox, supra, 39 Ariz. L. Rev. at 512 (citing congressional testimony indicating that while 96% of securities class actions are within insurance policy limits, insurance appears to be purchased for an appropriate amount of risk ); Joel Seligman, The Merits Do Matter: A Comment on Professor Grundfest's "Disimplying Private Rights of Action Under the Federal Securities Laws: The Commission's Authority," 108 Harv. L. Rev. 438 (1994), at 452-53 & n.65 (noting that many studies are based on unreliable estimates of plaintiffs' potential damage recoveries).

Finally, proponents of the PSLRA argued that Type I error has a hidden cost to capital markets: issuers which never go to market out of fear of strike suits. Type I error, issuers and their allies matintain, far outweighs Type II error in a society that has become obsessed with litigation.

### 2. *Securities Class Action Litigation After Enron and WorldCom*

After Enron's demise in late 2001, Enron's Board of Directors appointed a Special Investigative Committee that issued a report in February 2002. See William C. Powers, Jr., Report of Investigation by the Special Investigative Committee of The Board of Directors of Enron Corp. (Feb. 1, 2002). This report uncovered, among other things, pervasive securities fraud by Enron and its officers. The Enron affair became the subject of extensive press coverage and congressional hearings focused on whether securities laws were adequate to protect investors. The collapse of WorldCom in mid-2002 added further fuel to the political firestorm.

Responding to questions from Congress, SEC Chairperson Harvey Pitt testified that in his opinion there was no relationship between the PSLRA and the demise of Enron. See Rachel McTague, Accounting: Pitt Says Don't Change Independence Rules, Favors Much of House Republican Reform Bill, 34 Sec.

Reg. & L. Rep. 488, 489 (BNA) (Mar. 25, 2002) (quoting Chairperson Pitt's statement that "there is no relationship between the collapse of Enron and the Private Securities Litigation Reform Act, absolutely none"). Nonetheless, some members of Congress responded to the Enron and WorldCom scandals by introducing various bills that would repeal PSLRA provisions that disadvantage plaintiffs, expand SEC enforcement powers or both. See, e.g., the Comprehensive Investor Protection Act of 2002, H.R. 3818, proposed by Representative John LaFalce (D-N.Y.) and Richard Gephardt (D-Me.). Although many of the more sweeping repeal proposals in the LaFalce-Gephardt bill were not incorporated into the Sarbanes-Oxley Act of 2002, the very fact that these proposals were made, and taken seriously by some members of Congress, suggests that some parts of the PSLRA might be politically vulnerable in the future.

Section 12(e) of H.R. 3818 would have required auditors who are sued under the federal securities laws to produce documents for the plaintiffs while a motion to dismiss is pending, in effect partially repealing the stay on discovery imposed by Section 21D(b)(3) of the Exchange Act and Section 27(b) of the Securities Act. This would have worked a fundamental change in the litigation landscape, as the discovery stay is widely viewed as one of the PSLRA's most important provisions. See *Steckman v. Hart Brewing, Inc.*, 1996 WL 881659, at *5 (S.D. Cal. 1996) ("One of the salient features of the 1995 Reform Act is the *** automatic discovery stay"). Discovery from auditor defendants would also affect every potential defendant, because audit work papers usually contain extensive documents about an issuer such as correspondence about financial matters, board minutes, internal projections and estimates, and material contracts. Section 12(e) of H.R. 3818 would also have increased the likelihood of auditors being named as defendants in securities-fraud suits in order for plaintiffs to get discovery that could be used against other defendants. In part because of these concerns, this proposal was not incorporated into the final version of the Sarbanes-Oxley Act.

Section 12(a) of H.R. 3818 proposed to repeal part of the PSLRA's proportional liability rules by adding three new sections to the Exchange Act's provisions imposing joint-and-several-liability: (1) any auditor of an issuer's financial statements that failed to detect and report a violation of federal securities laws would become jointly and severally liable for the plaintiffs' whole damages; (2) if an auditor also performed non-auditing work during the fiscal year in which violations occurred, the auditor would also become jointly and severally liable; and (3) if the issuer became insolvent, any defendant against whom a final judgment was entered would become jointly and severally liable. This proposal also failed to make it into the final version of the Sarbanes-Oxley Act.

Section 14 of H.R. 3818 would have amended the Securities Act, Exchange Act, Investment Company Act, and Investment Advisers Act to add a private cause of action for aiding and abetting, in effect overturning *Central Bank v. First Interstate Bank*, 511 U.S. 164, 180 (1994) (finding no civil liability for aiding and abetting under Section 10(b)) of the Exchange Act and Rule 10b-5). Furthermore, Section 14 would have made liable persons whose "omission or failure constituted a breach of a duty owed by such person." This vague provision could have been interpreted to federalize large portions of corporate law and thus overturn *Santa Fe Indus., Inc. v. Green*, 430 U.S. 462, 476 (1977) (requiring misrepresentation or omission of material fact as an element of a violation of Section 10(b) and Rule 10b-5). This proposal also was not incorporated into the Sarbanes-Oxley Act.

The Sarbanes-Oxley Act did, however, grant one important concession to private plaintiffs. Section 804 lengthened the statute of limitations for securities fraud actions from the one year/three year rule imposed by the Supreme Court's decision in *Lampf, Pleva, Lipkind, Prupis & Petigrow v. Gilbertson*, 501 U.S. 350 (1991), to a rule allowing plaintiffs to sue within two years of discovering a fraud or five years of when the fraud took place, whichever is sooner. See discussion of the statute of limitations in Chapter 2.I.

Other provisions of H.R. 3818 would have gone beyond class action litigation and fundamentally altered the framework of securities regulation. Section 8 of H.R. 3818, for example, would have required the SEC to issue new disclosure rules requiring, among other things, issuers to update "information previously disclosed." By contrast, most courts now view the duty to update as a limited one that is triggered only when "statements that, although reasonable at the time made, become misleading when viewed in the context of subsequent events." *Oran v. Stafford*, 226 F.3d 275, 286 (3d Cir. 2000). See also Exchange Act Section 21E(d) ("Nothing in this section shall impose upon any person a duty to update a forward-looking statement"). Section 409 of the Sarbanes-Oxley Act did in fact incorporate part of this proposal by providing that issuers "shall disclose to the public on a rapid and current basis such additional information concerning material changes in the financial condition or operations of the issuer" as the SEC determines by rule is necessary for the protection of investors. Section 409, however, does not require the SEC to promulgate any rules in particular, leaving the "real time" disclosure issue up to the discretion of the SEC. See discussion of the duty to disclose in Chapter 2.A.2.b, supra.

Section 9(b) of H.R. 3818 would have directed the SEC to "establish a risk rating system" and rate issuers based on the risk issuers present to investors. Section 9(c) of H.R. 3818 would have required the SEC to conduct a risk re-evaluation of an issuer at least every three years. This proposal would have brought about an unprecedented shift in the SEC's mission and in the overall approach of the federal securities laws, as every registration statement now contains a disclaimer stating that the SEC has not made a judgment on the merits of the securities offered by that registration statement. These proposals were not incorporated into the Sarbanes-Oxley Act.

Ongoing congressional investigations into the accounting scandals at Enron and WorldCom, as well as other large companies, may spurn further proposals to change rules governing class action securities litigation as well as additional proposals to tighten SEC enforcement and criminal penalties.

## *NOTES AND QUESTIONS*

***1. Meritorious Proposals?*** Which of the proposals H.R. 3818 are in your view worthy of consideration? Which are not? Are some of these proposals likely to create more problems than they solve? To the extent that some of the proposals are good ones, should Congress have adopted them as part of the Sarbanes-Oxley Act? Or is there some benefit to a "wait and see" approach?

*2. Thinking it Through.* Did Congress give the Sarbanes-Oxley Act adequate thought or did it act primarily to grab headlines without thinking through all the implications of the legislation? If Congress was guilty of moving too quickly, has such quick legislative action happened before, in connection with securities litigation?

*3. Empirical Support.* Do the data discussed in the first part of this section support any of these specific proposals? If you find any of the data worrisome, would you make any particular proposals of your own?

## E. PROBLEMS

For each of the following problems, the professor will divide the class (or part of the class while other students work on a different problem) into groups of students who will work as "law firms" assigned to represent either the plaintiffs or one of the defendants in the problem.

The professor will set a date by which the plaintiff's law firm is to serve and file a complaint on behalf of a lead plaintiff and a class of investors against all of the enumerated defendants. The plaintiff's law firm may use as models publicly available complaints (such as those available on the Stanford Law School Securities Class Action Clearinghouse web site), but should keep in mind that complaints differ substantially depending upon the underlying allegations in the action and that some securities class action complaints are not well drafted. Plaintiffs should examine several models of complaints from cases with similar fact patterns to the problem if at all possible.

Plaintiffs may plead facts in their complaint in addition to those stated in the problem, but may not assert any facts that are inconsistent with the facts stated in the problem. Plaintiffs should remember the PSLRA requirement that they plead with specificity. Plaintiffs should, among other things, clearly define the class they purport to represent and the reasons that the lead plaintiff should be allowed to represent the class. Plaintiffs should be careful to meet all of the pleading and procedural requirements imposed on them by the PSLRA.

The complaint should be served by e-mail on one member of the law firm that represents each defendant or group of defendants named in the complaint, and a copy of the complaint should be filed by e-mail with the "court" (the professor).

The professor (acting as judge in the case) will assign a date one or two weeks after service of the complaint by which all defendants are to file and serve separate motions to dismiss (which must be resolved before discovery is allowed under the PSLRA). Each motion to dismiss shall be accompanied by a memorandum of law in support of the motion. For purposes of their motions to dismiss, defendants must accept as true the facts alleged by plaintiffs in their complaints.

Each defendant's motion to dismiss and accompanying memorandum should be served by e-mail on one member of the law firm that represents the plaintiff and on one member of the law firm that represents each of the other defendants named in the complaint. A copy of each motion to dismiss and accompanying memorandum should be filed with the court (by e-mail to the professor).

The professor will set a hearing date on which the professor, acting as judge in the case, will hear the defendants' motions to dismiss. Plaintiffs' counsel will be entitled to submit a brief memorandum of law in opposition to one or more of the defendants' motions to dismiss, provided a copy of this memorandum is served on opposing counsel and filed with the court no later than 24 hours before the hearing date.

On the hearing date, the judge will hear each of the motions to dismiss one at a time. One or two lawyers from each defendant law firm (a member of that firm who did not take a leading role in drafting the motion to dismiss) shall make a brief (5 minute) oral argument to the court in favor of the motion to dismiss. One member of the plaintiffs' law firm (a different member of that firm for each motion) shall briefly (5 minutes) argue against the motion. The defendant's counsel shall be allowed a very brief response (2 minutes). The judge will rule on each motion in open court by dismissing the complaint in whole or in part, with or without leave to amend, and/or by denying the motion to dismiss in whole or in part. The judge shall also make a finding with respect to Rule 11 compliance as required under the PSLRA and shall impose sanctions if a violation of Rule 11 is found.

**Case No. 1. In re American Technologies Securities Litigation**

In the last quarter of 2001 and the first quarter of 2002, numerous news articles discussed the uncertain impact of the terrorist attacks of September 11, 2001 on both the commercial aviation industry and the defense industry. Stock prices for companies doing business in these two sectors of the economy became very volatile.

One such company, American Technologies Corporation (American Technologies), an Exchange Act reporting company listed on the NASDAQ, manufactures computerized aircraft parts and provides technical support for commercial aircraft sold to the major airlines. American Technologies also manufactures computerized aircraft parts and provides technical support for fighter planes and military surveillance aircraft under contract with the U.S. Department of Defense (DOD) and private contractors who assist DOD with production and maintenance of fighter planes and military surveillance aircraft.

After the terrorist attacks of September 11, 2001, the American Technologies directors and senior officers believed that there would likely be a significant slowdown in commercial aviation contracts from major airlines. An internal report prepared for the American Technologies board of directors in December 2001 by a consulting firm that interviewed senior officers of major airlines about their equipment purchasing plans for 2002 projected a 50% drop in orders coming to American Technologies from commercial airlines.

Because of increased concerns about national security, the American Technologies directors believed that orders received by American Technologies from DOD and DOD-related contracts would increase significantly in 2002, but they were not sure by how much. At a board of directors' meeting in early 2002, one director, a retired Air Force General, said he thought DOD and DOD-related orders would double in the next year, but he provided no support for his conclusions.

On March 1, 2002, American Technologies filed a registration statement for the sale of 1 million shares of common stock to the public at $85 per share. The registration statement became effective on April 1, 2002 and the shares were sold to the public through a firm commitment underwriting by Goldperson Socks & Co. On April 1, 2002, American Technologies also mailed its Annual Report to the 500,000 existing shareholders it had before its latest registered public offering.

American Technologies made the following statements about its commercial aviation contracts both in its registration statement and in its Annual Report to shareholders:

> (1) "Despite a temporary slowdown in the commercial airline industry, American Technologies expects to have an annual growth rate in its commercial airline contracts of 10% to 30% over the next several years. This projection is, however, only an estimate and American Technologies could experience a lower growth rate in commercial airline contracts because the post-September 11 slowdown in the commercial aviation industry lasts longer than expected.";
>
> (2) "With experienced management, engineers, scientists and technicians in place, American Technologies is poised to carry the growth and success of 2001 well into the future."

American Technologies made the following statements about its DOD and DOD related contracts both in its registration statement and in its Annual Report to shareholders:

> (1) "With increased concern for national security after September 11, 2001, the DOD is likely to place more orders for computerized aircraft parts and technical support for fighter planes and military surveillance aircraft. We anticipate that these new contracts will be valued at approximately $4 billion in 2002 and that American Technologies will receive at least half of the new contracts awarded in 2002. The result we anticipate is a doubling of our DOD and DOD related contracts over the next year."

On the same day the Annual Report was mailed to shareholders (April 1, 2002), American Technologies also released a statement to its shareholders stating that first quarter earnings were likely to be half of analysts' estimates and that "the lower than anticipated earnings resulted primarily from administrative delays in contract awards by commercial airlines and the resultant increased overhead costs associated with retaining professional staff pending these contract awards," but that American Technologies believed that "conditions in the first quarter of 2002 are temporary and that results during the remainder of 2002 should be in line with analysts' current projections."

American Technologies's filings with the SEC under Section 16(a) of the Exchange Act reveal that several officers and directors of American Technologies were selling their shares in the company during April of 2002.

On May 1, 2002, a senior officer of American Technologies leaked to the Wall Street Journal the news that American Technologies suffered a 70% drop in orders from commercial airlines. Senior managers confirmed that this was indeed true at a press conference the next day and American Technologies stock dropped from $90 per share to $55 per share in a matter of hours.

The next day (May 2, 2002), American Technologies issued a press release stating that despite disappointing results in the commercial airline side of its business, DOD and DOD related contracts had been better than expected, so far exceeding orders for the prior year by 20%. American Technologies stock recovered some of its losses and was trading at $70 per share on May 2, 2002.

On May 3, 2002, American Technologies also announced that it was restating the 2001 revenue and earnings stated in the audited financial statements incorporated into both the registration statement and Annual Report, because $50 million in revenue (and $20 million in profits) had been recognized in the last quarter of 2001 that should have been recognized in the first quarter of 2002. The error—that should have been discovered by the auditors of the 2001 financial statements but was not—resulted from a change in DOD purchasing procedures that lengthened the time for purchase orders to get final DOD approval and a failure by American Technologies to adjust its accounting system for the new DOD procedures. As a result, American booked revenue from DOD contracts several months before revenue from these contracts could properly be recorded under GAAP. Instead of having revenue of $2.55 billion in 2001, American Technologies had revenue of $2.50 billion, and instead of making a profit of $830 million in 2001, American Technologies had a profit of $810 million in 2001. Stock markets reacted to the news with a further decline in American Technologies stock from $70 to $68 per share by the close of the markets on May 3, 2002.

The following groups of defendants in this matter are represented by separate counsel: (i) American Technologies, (ii) the company's inside directors, (iii) the company's outside directors, (iv) the auditors of the financial statements attached to the Annual Report, 10-K and Securities Act registration statement, (v) the underwriters for the public offering, and (vi) the company's outside law firm, Davis Crain & Hart, which worked on the registration statement, annual report and 10-K.

The lead plaintiff is Steve Smith, who owns 100 shares of American Technologies stock that he bought during the class period. Steve owns a cigar store in the basement of the building housing the law firm that represents him in this action.

### Case No. 2. In Re Enron Securities Class Action Litigation

For the facts in this case, plaintiffs may use any facts reported in the major news media or professional publications. All facts alleged in the plaintiff's complaint must also have been reported to have some evidentiary foundation by one or more reputable news sources. Plaintiffs *may not* supplement their pleadings with additional facts of their own choosing.

Plaintiffs' counsel has been asked to represent the Florida State Pension Fund as lead plaintiff in this class action.

The following groups of defendants in this matter are to be represented by separate counsel: (i) Enron, (ii) Enron's inside directors, (iii) Enron's outside directors, (iv) the auditors of Enron's financial statements, (v) Enron's outside lawyers, and (vi) any other defendants named in the plaintiff's complaint.

Students participating in this exercise may examine any complaint, motion to dismiss or other pleading available on a web site or elsewhere, except the actual complaints, motions to dismiss or other pleadings filed in Enron related securities litigation. Every pleading filed with the court in this exercise is to be accompanied by an affidavit signed by counsel stating that no member of counsel's law firm has used actual Enron-related pleadings in connection with this exercise.

**Case No. 3. In Re Microchip, Inc. Securities Litigation**

Microchip, Inc. launched an initial public offering (IPO) in March 2000 at the price of $10 per share. Microchip's registration statement, in its "use of proceeds" section, stated that all of the offering proceeds would be used for research on new technologies for the production of computer microchips. The national accounting firm of Reilly & Whitman audited the financial statements that were included in the registration statement. The lead underwriter was Wilson, Hartley, & Co. The IPO netted $10 million exclusive of costs.

Peter Piper, a retired computer science professor from the University of Illinois, had done extensive reading about Microchip in professional journals and in April 2000 asked his broker Steve Swanson, at Hooker & Faye, if Microchip would be a good investment. Swanson told Piper that Hooker & Faye had been a member of the selling group in the Microchip IPO and that he recommended that Piper buy Microchip stock in the aftermarket where it was now trading for $12 per share. Swanson did not tell Piper, however, that he and other brokers at Hooker & Faye had a month earlier allotted shares from the IPO to a group of favored clients on the condition that these clients purchase additional Microchip stock in the aftermarket at prices higher than the offering price of $10. Swanson also did not reveal that as a result of this "laddering" activity, the current market price of Microchip stock was probably inflated. Piper bought 1000 shares of Microchip stock at $12 per share and upon receiving the prospectus for the Microchip IPO in the mail, disposed of it without reading it.

Microchip's three most senior officials were Jerry Johnson, Peter Passet, and Carol Clarkson who were Chief Executive Officer, President, and Chief Operating Officer respectively. At the time of the IPO, these three officers, all also directors of Microchip, expected that at least 60% of the offering proceeds would be used to satisfy a multi-million dollar past-due account owed to its principal supplier. According to a report from Microchip's Chief Financial Officer, Wilma Wilkins, dated January 2000, the offering proceeds represented the only way to meet this obligation. Ms. Wilkins's report, however, was shown only to Johnson, Passet, and Clarkson, and they did not share it with Microchip's four other directors, all of whom were independent directors not employed by the company.

In April 2000, Microchip paid its supplier $6 million from the IPO proceeds. The other $4 million from the IPO was spent on research on new technologies for the production of computer microchips as described in the use of proceeds section of the prospectus.

After the IPO, Microchip filed periodic forms 10-K and 10-Q as required by the Exchange Act. Between March 2000 and March 2002, none of these reports disclosed that its supplier had received any of the proceeds from the IPO. The financial statements included in these periodic reports, like the financial statements included in the earlier registration statement, were audited by Reilly & Whitman. Microchip's stock declined slowly during 2000 and 2001 from its post-IPO aftermarket price of $12 to a price of $7 per share at the beginning of March, 2002.

On March 10, 2002, Microchip finally disclosed that the company had used 60% of the IPO proceeds to satisfy an obligation owed its supplier. Microchip's stock quickly dropped from a trading price of $7 per share to $2 per share on the same day. The price thereafter tumbled to $1 per share after Suzy Squeal, a former internal auditor for Microchip, announced at a press conference her belief that Johnson, Passet, and Clarkson had intentionally obscured from shareholders and the investing public the payment to the supplier and the consequent diversion of funds from research.

The law firm of Chemmer & Hanskins served as attorneys for Microchip in connection with the preparation of the registration statement for the IPO and the subsequent Exchange Act filings. Plaintiffs' counsel seeks to represent Piper on behalf of a class of similarly situated investors. Defendants include Microchip, its inside directors Johnson, Passet, and Clarkson, its independent directors, the accounting firm of Reilly & Whitman, the investment banking firm of Wilson, Hartley & Co., the brokerage firm of Hooker & Faye, and the law firm of Chemmer & Hanskins.

# Chapter 7

# INSIDER TRADING

" This is not securities litigation. This is cops and robbers. The issue is, 'Did you get the information and did you trade on it.' "

Former U.S. Attorney
Otto G. Obermaier, S.D.N.Y.
quoted in Stephen Labaton and David Leonhardt, Whispers Inside, Thunder Outside: A New Hunt is on for Insider Trading, N.Y. Times at BU14 (June 30, 2002).

The media tends to follow closely allegations of insider trading because the public typically enjoys the drama generated by the government's investigations and prosecutions. But in the year 2002, public interest in the topic of insider trading may have reached an all-time high. Some of this attention has been directed to the corporate insiders of Enron, WorldCom, and other publicly traded companies who sold off millions of dollars in stock in the months preceding the revelation of their company's stock price-cratering accounting scandals. Even more attention, perhaps, has been directed at the home designer-entrepreneur Martha Stewart, and the now famous former chief executive of ImClone Systems, Dr. Samuel Waksal, whose stock trades or attempted trades were the subject of high-profile investigations by the SEC, the Department of Justice (DOJ), and Congress. Most major papers featured as front page news Dr. Waksal's guilty plea to federal charges of securities fraud.

Although it is impossible to deny the "cops and robbers" aspect of investigations and prosecutions for insider trading, it also is important to recognize that insider trading raises complex questions under the federal securities laws. This Chapter highlights such complexities by tracing the development of the law of insider trading, and by posing questions and problems that require application of doctrine to specific facts. Section A discusses early attempts by state courts, Congress, and lower federal courts to deal with the problem of insider trading under the common law and the federal securities laws. Section B then turns to the Supreme Court decisions establishing or endorsing the classical and misappropriation theories of insider trading liability under Rule 10b-5 and examines recent SEC rulemaking that builds on those decisions. Section C focuses on Rule 14e-3's prohibition of insider trading in connection with tender offers and explores whether the rule constitutes a valid exercise of SEC authority. The Insider Trading Sanctions Act of 1984 (ITSA) and the Insider Trading and Securities Fraud Enforcement Act of 1988 (ITSFEA) are discussed in Section D. And Section E highlights the difficulties often faced in cases where proof of insider trading must be established by circumstantial evidence.

As you read and analyze the material in these first five sections, keep in mind the following questions: What, if anything, is wrong with insider trading? Who is harmed by the practice? Does insider trading produce any benefits (other than, of course, the profits to the traders)? Does the offense merit severe sanction? Prison sentences? These fundamental policy issues will be revisited in Section F at the conclusion of the Chapter.

## A. INITIAL EFFORTS TO COMBAT AND CURTAIL INSIDER TRADING

### *1. Insider Trading Under the Common Law*

The earliest litigation in the United States over insider trading took the form of lawsuits filed in state court by shareholders against corporate officers and directors under a theory of fraudulent nondisclosure. Although an affirmative misstatement is generally required for a plaintiff to plead and prove common law fraud, courts have long recognized a number of circumstances under which a defendant's "pure silence" about material facts in a business transaction may constitute fraudulent or deceptive conduct. One such circumstance involves transactions in which the parties stand in a fiduciary relationship.

Common law courts, however, varied widely on the question of whether shareholders stood in a fiduciary relationship with corporate insiders. Under the so-called "majority rule," a traditional insider of a corporation (such as an officer or director) was said to owe fiduciary duties to the corporation itself but not to individual shareholders of the corporation. Thus, in most jurisdictions, corporate insiders were free to remain silent about material facts in transactions with shareholders, and could freely exploit whatever informational advantage they were fortunate enough to possess. See, e.g., *Bawden v. Taylor*, 98 N.E. 941, 942 (Ill. 1912); *Barth v. Fid. & Columbia Trust Co.*, 224 S.W. 351, 356 (Ky. 1920). See also Fletcher Cyc. Corp § 1168.10 (Perm. Ed) (citing cases and concluding that "[t]he 'majority rule' is that directors do not occupy a trust relation with shareholders with respect to their shares because dealing in the corporation's stock is not a corporate function").

The common law "minority rule," in contrast, viewed officers and directors as fiduciaries not only to the corporation but also to its shareholders. Thus, as a fiduciary, a traditional insider was obligated to share with an ignorant shareholder all material facts in his possession prior to consummating a transaction. See, e.g., *Dawson v. Nat'l Life Ins. Co.*, 157 N.W. 929, 938 (Iowa 1916) (recognizing cause of action for fraud in securities trading when corporate officer fails to make "full disclosure of all facts bearing thereon known to such officer and unknown to the shareholder"); *Stewart v. Harris*, 77 P. 277, 281 (Kan. 1904) (holding that "before any director or managing officer *** can rightfully purchase the stock of one not actively engaged in the management of its affairs, such director or managing officer must inform such stockholder of the true condition of the affairs of the corporation").

Other jurisdictions purposefully sidestepped the fiduciary duty issue, and scrutinized acts of insider trading under the so-called "special facts" doctrine, which imposed disclosure duties when one party to a transaction had access to highly significant facts that were unknown to the other party. See, e.g., *Strong v. Repide*, 213 U.S. 419 (1908). However, because it was often a traditional insider's status that provided him with access to "special facts," legal analysis under the minority rule and special facts doctrine often tended to blend together. In *Strong v. Repide*, for example, the Supreme Court granted recission in a case where the plaintiff-shareholder had sold her stock to an agent of the defendant-insider. The company soon after concluded negotiations to sell valuable real estate to the Philippine government, thereby substantially increasing the worth of the company's shares. The Court had no trouble finding that "the negotiations and their probable result were a most material fact affecting the value of the shares of stock of the company." Id. at 432. The Court also found that the plaintiff's agent "would not have sold them at the price he did had he known the actual state of the negotiations as to the lands and that it was the defendant who was seeking to purchase the stock." Id. The Court stated further:

> That the defendant was a director of the corporation is but one of the facts upon which the liability is asserted, the existence of all the others in addition making such a combination as rendered it the plain duty of the defendant to speak. He was not only a director, but he owned three-fourths of the shares of its stock, and was, at the time of the purchase of the stock, administrator general of the company, with large powers, and engaged in the negotiations which finally led to the sale of the company's lands (together with all the other friar lands) to the Government at a price which very greatly enhanced the value of the stock. He was the chief negotiator for the sale of all the lands, and was acting substantially as the agent of the shareholders of his company by reason of his ownership of the shares of stock in the corporation and by the acquiescence of all the other shareholders, and the negotiations were for the sale of the whole of the property of the company. By reason of such ownership and agency, and his participation as such owner and agent in the negotiations then going on, no one knew as well as he the exact condition of such negotiations. No one knew as well as he the probability of the sale of the lands to the Government. No one knew as well as he the probable price that might be obtained on such sale. The lands were the only valuable asset owned by the company. *** Concealing his identity when procuring the purchase of the stock, by his agent, was in itself strong evidence of fraud on the part of the defendant. *** If, under all these facts, he purchased the stock from the plaintiff, the law would indeed be impotent if the sale could not be set aside or the defendant cast in damages for his fraud. ***

Id. at 431-33.

Plaintiffs alleging insider trading under the common law of fraud and deceit had other hurdles to scale, even in those jurisdictions that generally adhered to the minority rule or special facts doctrine. Two principles, in particular, limited a court's ability to impose liability for an insider's fraudulent nondisclosure. First, officers and directors were said to owe shareholders a disclosure duty only in face-to-face securities transactions. The minority rule and the special facts doctrine thus left insider trading in impersonal markets unfettered. See *Goodwin v. Agassiz*, 186 N.E. 659, 660 (Mass. 1933) (refusing to recognize the breach of a disclosure duty when the traditional insider's securities transactions were carried out over the Boston Stock Exchange). The court in *Goodwin* noted that:

> The identity of the buyers and seller of the stock in question in fact was not known to the parties and perhaps could not readily have been ascertained. The defendants caused the shares to be bought through brokers on the stock exchange. They said nothing to anybody as to the reasons actuating them. The plaintiff was no novice. He was a member of the Boston stock exchange and had kept record of sales of [the company] stock. *** He made no inquiries of the defendants or of other officers of the company. The result is that the plaintiff cannot prevail.

Id. at 661-62. The other limiting principle was that traditional insiders were regarded as fiduciaries only with respect to those investors with pre-existing relationships with the corporation. Thus, even in minority rule jurisdictions, there was nothing to prevent corporate insiders from selling their stock to investors who did not already own shares in the corporation. See A.C. Pritchard, *United States v. O'Hagan*: Agency Law and Justice Powell's Legacy for the Law of Insider Trading, 78 B.U. L. Rev. 13, 26 (1998) (noting that "the fiduciary obligation of corporate officers and directors *** does not extend to prospective shareholders who may purchase their shares for the first time when an insider sells").

Mitigating the harshness of these common law limitations on recovery for fraud and deceit, a number of jurisdictions—notably Delaware, see *Brophy v. Cities Service Co.*, 70 A.2d 5, 8 (Del. Ch. 1949) and New York, see *Diamond v. Oreamuno*, 248 N.E.2d 910, 912 (N.Y. 1969)—permitted shareholders to institute derivative actions against officers and directors who had used the corporation's confidential information to reap "secret profits" in securities transactions. The Court in *Diamond* explained its decision in the following manner:

> It is well established, as a general proposition, that a person who acquires special knowledge or information by virtue of a confidential or fiduciary relationship with another is not free to exploit that knowledge or information for his own personal benefit but must account to his principal for any profits derived therefrom. This, in turn, is merely a corollary of the broader principle, inherent in the nature of the fiduciary relationship, that prohibits a trustee or agent from extracting secret profits from his position of trust.
>
> ***[T]he defendants take the position that, although it is admittedly wrong for an officer or director to use his position to obtain trading profits for himself in the stock of his corporation, the action ascribed to them did not injure or damage [the corporation] in any way. Accordingly, the defendants continue, the corporation should not be permitted to recover the proceeds. They acknowledge that, by virtue of the exclusive access which officers and directors have to inside information, they possess an unfair advantage over other shareholders and, particularly, the persons who had purchased the stock from them but, they contend, the corporation itself was unaffected and, for that reason, a derivative action is an inappropriate remedy.
>
> It is true that the complaint before us does not contain any allegation of damages to the corporation but this has never been considered to be an essential requirement for a cause of action founded on a breach of fiduciary duty. This is because the function of such an action, unlike an ordinary tort or contract case, is not merely to compensate the plaintiff for wrongs committed

by the defendant but, as this court declared many years ago "to *prevent* them, by removing from agents and trustees all inducement to attempt dealing for their own benefit in matters which they have undertaken for others, or to which their agency or trust relates."

Just as a trustee has no right to retain for himself the profits yielded by property placed in his possession but must account to his beneficiaries, a corporate fiduciary, who is entrusted with potentially valuable information, may not appropriate that asset for his own use even though, in so doing, he causes no injury to the corporation. The primary concern, in a case such as this, is not to determine whether the corporation has been damaged but to decide, as between the corporation and the defendants, who has a higher claim to the proceeds derived from the exploitation of the information. In our opinion, there can be no justification for permitting officers and directors, such as the defendants, to retain for themselves profits which, it is alleged, they derived solely from exploiting information gained by virtue of their inside position as corporate officials.

In addition, it is pertinent to observe that, despite the lack of any specific allegation of damage, it may well be inferred that the defendants' actions might have caused some harm to the enterprise. Although the corporation may have little concern with the day-to-day transactions in its shares, it has a great interest in maintaining a reputation of integrity, an image of probity, for its management and in insuring the continued public acceptance and marketability of its stock. When officers and directors abuse their position in order to gain personal profits, the effect may be to cast a cloud on the corporation's name, injure stockholder relations and undermine public regard for the corporation's securities. ***

Id. at 912. As you read the *O'Hagan* decision set out in Section B.3 of this Chapter, consider the extent to which the intellectual underpinnings of what is today known as the "misappropriation theory" of insider trading liability can be traced to "secret profits" cases like *Diamond*.

### 2. *A Brief Look at Section 16(b)*

The legislative history of the Exchange Act reveals that the problem of insider trading was very much on the minds of its congressional drafters. Yet, rather than defining the offense of insider trading and prohibiting it outright, Congress chose only to regulate certain trading practices of officers, directors, and shareholders beneficially owning more than 10 percent of issuers with a security registered pursuant to Section 12 of the Exchange Act. The congressional concern with these key "insiders" is reflected in the following passage from the 1934 Report of the Senate Banking and Currency Committee:

> Among the most vicious practices unearthed at the hearings before the subcommittee was the flagrant betrayal of their fiduciary duties by directors and officers of corporations who used their positions of trust and the confidential information which came to them in such positions, to aid them in their market activities. Closely allied to this type of abuse was the unscrupulous employment of inside information by large stockholders who, while not directors and officers, exercised sufficient control over the destinies of their companies to enable them to acquire and profit by information not available to others.

S. Rep. No. 73-1455 at 55 (1934). Section 16 of the Exchange Act constitutes Congress's initial solution to the problem of insider trading.

Section 16(a) imposes a reporting obligation upon every officer or director of a company with an equity security registered under Section 12 of the Exchange Act, as well as every person "who is directly or indirectly the beneficial owner of more than 10 percent of any class of any equity security" so registered. Pursuant to this obligation, such high level insiders must file with the SEC an initial report on Form 3 within ten days of becoming an officer, director, or 10 percent beneficial shareholder of the corporation. When such persons change their beneficial ownership (either through purchases or sales of the company's equity securities), they must file supplementary reports on a Form 4 within two business days. This two business day requirement was a statutory change brought about by the Sarbanes-Oxley Act of 2002. Prior to that legislation, Form 4 reports were required to be filed within ten days of the close of each calendar month in which any additional purchases or sales of the corporation's equity securities had been made. What factors may have prompted Congress to substantially shorten the filing deadline?

To be sure, the mere obligation to report all purchases and sales in a corporation's equity securities is bound to deter some insiders from trading on the basis of confidential corporate information. But Congress intended the principal deterrent for insider trading to stem from Section 16(b), which makes officers, directors, and 10 percent shareholders liable to the corporation, or to shareholders suing on its behalf, for any profits they obtain from "short swing" trading of the corporation's stock. Specifically, Section 16(b) provides that:

> For the purpose of preventing the unfair use of information which may have been obtained by such beneficial owner, director, or officer by reason of his relationship to the issuer, any profit realized by him from any purchase and sale, or any sale and purchase, of any equity security of such issuer (other than an exempted security) *** within any period of less than six months, unless such security *** was acquired in good faith in connection with a debt previously contracted, shall inure to and be recoverable by the issuer, irrespective of any intention on the part of such beneficial owner, director, or officer in entering into such transaction of holding the security *** purchased or of not repurchasing the security *** sold for a period exceeding six months.

The reporting obligation imposed on insiders by Section 16(a) substantially assists the corporation and its shareholders with enforcing the disgorgement provision in Section 16(b).

Obviously, as it relates to insider trading, Section 16(b)'s disgorgement net is both too wide and too narrow: it catches legitimate trades by corporate insiders who lack any knowledge of material nonpublic information, and it allows to slip through those trades that *are* based on inside information when the insider has sold stock that was held for at least six months, or when the insider is patient enough to wait for six months to reap the profit off a new purchase. Indeed, as the Second Circuit recently emphasized, Section 16(b) "operates mechanically, and makes no moral distinctions, penalizing technical violators of pure heart, and bypassing corrupt insiders who skirt the letter of the prohibition." *Magma Power Co. v. Dow Chem. Co.*, 136 F.3d 316, 320-21 (2d Cir. 1998). For the view that Congress had additional objectives in enacting Section 16, see Steve Thel, The Genius of Section 16: Regulating the Management of Publicly Held Companies, 42 Hastings L. J. 391, 399, 414-15 (1991) (contending that "[t]hose who secured the enactment of Section 16 *** were probably more concerned with reforming the way public corporations conduct their business than with the interests of securities traders. *** Section 16 works to focus the attention of corporate managers on corporate business. Automatic forfeiture of short-swing profits eliminates the incentive to speculate for the short swing, and thus helps to keep corporate managers from being distracted from the business of running publicly held companies"). See also Karl S. Okamoto, Rereading Section 16(b) of the Securities Exchange Act, 27 Ga. L. Rev. 183, 205 (1992) (stating that "[s]ince the market will view [an insider's] trading as a signal of information, the insider can manipulate stock prices simply by trading. *** [The six-month limit] serves as the basis for a presumption as to the motivation of the insider trader. If an insider reverses her position within six months, it is more likely that her initial trading was itself a false signal").

Because of its unduly wide and narrow net, Section 16(b) was only somewhat successful in preventing officers and directors from trading corporate stock on the basis of material nonpublic information. But after the SEC promulgated Rule 10b-5 in 1942, another—and very wide—federal regulatory avenue opened. The text of Rule 10b-5 is set out on page 19 in Chapter 2.

### 3. *Insider Trading as a Violation of Rule 10b-5*

Like common law fraud and deceit actions brought by shareholders against traditional insiders, the first Rule 10b-5 cases that permitted shareholders to sue a traditional insider for insider trading involved face-to-face securities transactions. In *Kardon v. Nat'l Gympsum Co.*, 73 F. Supp. 798 (E.D. Penn. 1947), the first decision to recognize a private right of action under Section 10(b) and Rule 10b-5, the court expressly held that "these provisions apply to directors and officers who, in purchasing the stock of the corporation from others, fail to disclose a fact coming to their knowledge by reason of their position, which would materially affect the judgment of the other party to the transaction." Id. at 800. The two plaintiffs in *Kardon* had sold their stock directly to the defendant-insiders who had been in possession of material, nonpublic information.

The scope of Rule 10b-5 expanded quite extraordinarily in 1961 when the Commission decided *In re Cady, Roberts & Co.*, 40 SEC 907 (1961). The Enforcement Division of the SEC brought this landmark case as an administrative broker-dealer disciplinary proceeding against a brokerage firm and a securities broker employed by that firm. The Enforcement Division alleged that the broker had engaged in fraud by selling on the NYSE a company's securities (held in personal and client accounts) on the basis of confidential bad news about a reduction in dividends that had been tipped to the broker by a director of the company. After an administrative hearing, the Commission held that Rule 10b-5 prohibited the tippee-broker's stock sales because "insiders must disclose material facts which are known to them by virtue of their position but which are not known to persons with whom they deal." Id. at 911. The Commission opined that:

> Analytically, the obligation [to disclose or abstain] rests on two principal elements; first, the existence of a relationship giving access, directly or indirectly, to information intended to be available only for a corporate purpose and not for the personal benefit of anyone, and second, the inherent unfairness

> involved where a party takes advantage of such information knowing it is unavailable to those with whom he is dealing.

Id. at 912. Thus, in *Cady, Roberts*, the Commission construed the term "insider" quite broadly to include those persons, such as the tippee-broker before it, who were in positions of access to confidential corporate information. The Commission also construed Rule 10b-5 to support a broad definition of fraud that was not limited by the common law distinction between face-to-face transactions and stock market trading. Even today, commentators continue to be struck by the Commission's groundbreaking decision to bring an administrative enforcement action against the tippee-broker and by the "new corporation law" that was announced in its decision. See Donald C. Langevoort, Rereading *Cady, Roberts*: The Ideology and Practice of Insider Trading Regulation," 99 Colum. L. Rev. 1319, 1320 (1999) (quoting *Cady, Roberts*, 40 SEC at 910).

In the years following *Cady, Roberts*, the Commission continued to expand the scope of the duty to disclose or abstain from securities trading while in possession of material nonpublic information. See, e.g., *In re Investors Mgmt. Co.*, 44 SEC 633 (1971), where the Commission imposed Rule 10b-5 liability against non-insider securities professionals who knew or had reason to know that the information they possessed was confidential.

The view that insider trading over anonymous securities markets constitutes a violation of Rule 10b-5 also won acceptance from the federal courts, particularly in the Second Circuit.

## SEC v. TEXAS GULF SULPHUR CO.

401 F.2d 833 (2d Cir. 1968)

WATERMAN, CIRCUIT JUDGE:

This action was commenced in the United States District Court for the Southern District of New York by the Securities and Exchange Commission (the SEC) pursuant to Sec. 21(e) of the Securities Exchange Act of 1934 (the Act) against Texas Gulf Sulphur Company (TGS) and several of its officers, directors and employees, to enjoin certain conduct *** said to violate Section 10(b) of the Act and Rule 10b-5 (the Rule), promulgated thereunder ***. The complaint alleged (1) that defendants Fogarty, Mollison, Darke, Murray, Huntington, O'Neill, Clayton, Crawford, and Coates had either personally or through agents purchased TGS stock or calls thereon from November 12, 1963 through April 16, 1964 on the basis of material inside information concerning the results of TGS drilling in Timmins, Ontario, while such information remained undisclosed to the investing public generally or to the particular sellers; [and] (2) that defendants Darke and Coates had divulged such information to others for use in purchasing TGS stock or calls[3] or recommended its purchase while the information was undisclosed to the public or to the sellers; ***

---

3. A "call" is a negotiable option contract by which the bearer has the right to buy from the writer of the contract a certain number of shares of a particular stock at a fixed price on or before a certain agreed-upon date.

THE FACTUAL SETTING

This action derives from the exploratory activities of TGS begun in 1957 on the Canadian Shield in eastern Canada. In March of 1959, aerial geophysical surveys were conducted over more than 15,000 square miles of this area by a group led by defendant Mollision, a mining engineer and a Vice President of TGS. The group included defendant Holyk, TGS's chief geologist, defendant Clayton, an electrical engineer and geophysicist, and defendant Darke, a geologist. These operations resulted in the detection of numerous anomalies, i.e., extraordinary variations in the conductivity of rocks, one of which was on the Kidd 55 segment of land located near Timmins, Ontario.

On October 29 and 30, 1963, Clayton conducted a ground geophysical survey on the northeast portion of the Kidd 55 segment which confirmed the presence of an anomaly and indicated the necessity of diamond core drilling for further evaluation. Drilling of the initial hole, K-55-1, at the strongest part of the anomaly was commenced on November 8 and terminated on November 12 at a depth of 655 feet. Visual estimates by Holyk of the core of K-55-1 indicated an average copper content of 1.15% and an average zinc content of 8.64% over a length of 599 feet. This visual estimate convinced TGS that it was desirable to acquire the remainder of the Kidd 55 segment, and in order to facilitate this acquisition TGS President Stephens instructed the exploration group to keep the results of K-55-1 confidential and undisclosed even as to other officers, directors, and employees of TGS. The hole was concealed and a barren core was intentionally drilled off the anomaly. Meanwhile, the core of K-55-1 had been shipped to Utah for chemical assay which, when received in early December, revealed an average mineral content of 1.18% copper, 8.26% zinc, and 3.94% ounces of silver per ton over a length of 602 feet. These results were so remarkable that neither Clayton, an experienced geophysicist, nor four other TGS expert witnesses, had ever seen or heard of a comparable initial exploratory drill hole in a base metal deposit. *** By March 27, 1964, TGS decided that the land acquisition program had advanced to such a point that the company might well resume drilling, and drilling was resumed on March 31.

During this period, from November 12, 1963 when K-55-1 was completed, to March 31, 1964 when drilling was resumed, certain of the individual defendants *** and persons *** said to have received "tips" from them, purchased TGS stock or calls thereon. Prior to these transactions these persons had owned 1135 shares of TGS stock and possessed no calls; thereafter they owned a total of 8235 shares and possessed 12,300 calls.***

When drilling was resumed on March 31, hole K-55-3 was commenced***. Daily progress reports of the drilling of this hole K-55-3 and of all subsequently drilled holes were sent to defendants Stephens and Fogarty (President and Executive Vice President of TGS) by Holyk and Mollison. Visual estimates of K-55-3 revealed an average mineral content of 1.12% copper and 7.93% zinc over 641 of the hole's 876-foot length. On April 7, drilling of a third hole, K-55-4, *** was commenced and mineralization was encountered over 366 of its 579-foot length. Visual estimates indicated an average content of 1.14% copper and 8.24% zinc. Like K-55-1, both K-55-3 and K-55-4 established substantial copper mineralization on the eastern edge of the anomaly. On the basis of these findings relative to the foregoing drilling results, the trial court concluded *** that "There was real evidence that a body of commercially mineable ore might exist." Id. at 281- 82.

On April 8 TGS began with a second drill rig to drill another hole, K-55-6, 300 feet easterly of K-55-1.*** While no visual estimates of its core were immediately available, it was readily apparent by the evening of April 10 that substantial copper mineralization had been encountered over the last 127 feet of the hole's 569-foot length. On April 10, a third drill rig commenced drilling yet another hole, K-55-5 ***. By the evening of April 10 in this hole, too, substantial copper mineralization had been encountered over the last 42 feet of its 97-foot length.

Meanwhile, rumors that a major ore strike was in the making had been circulating throughout Canada. On the morning of Saturday, April 11, Stephens at his home in Greenwich, Conn. read in the New York Herald Tribune and in the New York Times unauthorized reports of the TGS drilling which seemed to infer a rich strike from the fact that the drill cores had been flown to the United States for chemical assay. Stephens immediately contacted Fogarty at his home in Rye, N.Y., who in turn telephoned and later that day visited Mollison at Mollison's home in Greenwich to obtain a current report and evaluation of the drilling progress. The following morning, Sunday, Fogarty again telephoned Mollison, inquiring whether Mollison had any further information and told him to return to Timmins with Holyk, the TGS Chief Geologist, as soon as possible "to move things along." With the aid of one Carroll, a public relations consultant, Fogarty drafted a press release designed to quell the rumors, which release, after having been channeled through Stephens and Huntington, a TGS attorney, was issued at 3:00 P.M. on Sunday, April 12, and which appeared in the morning newspapers of general circulation on Monday, April 13. [The press release was rather gloomy and downplayed the significance to the company of the exploratory activities. Later in the opinion, in a section omitted here but discussed in Chapter 2.B supra, the court held that the company had violated Rule 10b-5 through the issuance of this materially misleading press release.]^^^

Meanwhile, drilling operations continued. By morning of April 13, in K-55-5, the fifth drill hole, substantial copper mineralization had been encountered *** [and] [v]isual estimates revealed an average content of 0.82% copper and 4.2% zinc over a 525-foot section. Also by 7:00 A.M. on April 13, K-55-6 had found mineralization to the 946-foot mark. On April 12 a fourth drill rig began to drill K-55-7 ***

While drilling activity ensued to completion, TGC officials were taking steps toward ultimate disclosure of the discovery. On April 13, a previously-invited reporter for The Northern Miner, a Canadian mining industry journal, visited the drillsite, interviewed Mollison, Holyk and Darke, and prepared an article which confirmed a 10 million ton ore strike. This report, after having been submitted to Mollison and returned to the reporter unamended on April 15, was published in the April 16 issue. A statement relative to the extent of the discovery, in substantial part drafted by Mollison, was given to the Ontario Minister of Mines for release to the Canadian media. Mollison and Holyk expected it to be released over the airways at 11 P.M. on April 15th, but, for undisclosed reasons, it was not released until 9:40 A.M. on the 16th. An official detailed statement, announcing a strike of at least 25 million tons of ore, based on the drilling data set forth above, was read to representatives of American financial media from 10:00 A.M. to 10:10 or 10:15 A.M. on April 16, and appeared over Merrill Lynch's private wire at 10:29 A.M. and, somewhat later than expected, over the Dow Jones ticker tape at 10:54 A.M.

Between the time the first press release was issued on April 12 and the dissemination of the TGS official announcement on the morning of April 16, the only defendants before us on appeal who engaged in market activity were Clayton and Crawford and TGS director Coates. Clayton ordered 200 shares of TGS stock through his Canadian broker on April 15 and the order was executed that day over the Midwest Stock Exchange. Crawford ordered 300 shares at midnight on the 15th and another 300 shares at 8:30 A.M. the next day, and these orders were executed over the Midwest Exchange in Chicago at its opening on April 16. Coates left the TGS press conference and called his broker son-in-law Haemisegger shortly before 10:20 A.M. on the 16th and ordered 2,000 shares of TGS for family trust accounts of which Coates was a trustee but not a beneficiary; Haemisegger executed this order over the New York and Midwest Exchanges, and he and his customers purchased 1500 additional shares.

During the period of drilling in Timmins, the market price of TGS stock fluctuated but steadily gained overall. On Friday, November 8, when the drilling began, the stock closed at 17 3/8 ; on Friday, November 15, after K- 55-1 had been completed, it closed at 18. After a slight decline to 16 3/8 by Friday, November 22, the price rose to 20 7/8 by December 13, when the chemical assay results of K-55-1 were received, and closed at a high of 24 1/8 on February 21 ***. It had reached a price of 26 by March 31, after the land acquisition program had been completed and drilling had been resumed, and continued to ascend to 30 1/8 by the close of trading on April 10, at which time the drilling progress up to then was evaluated for the April 12th press release. On April 13, the day on which the April 12 release was disseminated, TGS opened at 30 1/8, rose immediately to a high of 32 and gradually tapered off to close at 30 7/8. It closed at 30 1/4 the next day, and at 29 3/8 on April 15. On April 16, the day of the official announcement of the Timmins discovery, the price climbed to a high of 37 and closed at 36 3/8. By May 15, TGS stock was selling at 58 1/4.

## I. The Individual Defendants

### *A. Introductory*

Rule 10b-5 on which this action is predicated *** was promulgated pursuant to the grant of authority given the SEC by Congress in Section 10(b) of the Securities Exchange Act of 1934. By that Act Congress purposed to prevent inequitable and unfair practices and to insure fairness in securities transactions generally, whether conducted face-to-face, over the counter, or on exchanges. The Act and the Rule apply to the transactions here, all of which were consummated on exchanges. Whether predicated on traditional fiduciary concepts, see, e.g., *Hotchkiss v. Fisher*, 136 Kan. 530, 16 P.2d 531 (Kan.1932), or on the "special facts" doctrine, see, e.g., *Strong v. Repide*, 213 U.S. 419 (1909), the Rule is based in policy on the justifiable expectation of the securities marketplace that all investors trading on impersonal exchanges have relatively equal access to material information. The essence of the Rule is that anyone who, trading for his own account in the securities of a corporation has "access, directly or indirectly, to information intended to be available only for a corporate purpose and not for the personal benefit of anyone" may not take "advantage of such information knowing it is unavailable to those with whom he is dealing," i.e., the investing public. *Matter of Cady, Roberts & Co.*, 40 SEC 907, 912 (1961). Insiders, as directors or management officers are, of course, by this Rule, precluded from so unfairly dealing, but the Rule is also applicable to one possessing the information who may not be strictly termed an "insider" within the meaning of Sec. 16(b) of the Act. *Cady, Roberts*, supra. Thus, anyone in possession of material inside information must either disclose it to the investing public, or, if he is disabled from disclosing it in order to protect a corporate confidence, or he chooses not to do so, must abstain from trading in or recommending the securities concerned while such inside information remains undisclosed. So, it is here no justification for insider activity that disclosure was forbidden by the legitimate corporate objective of acquiring options to purchase the land surrounding the exploration site; if the information was, as the SEC contends, material, its possessors should have kept out of the market until disclosure was accomplished. *Cady, Roberts*, supra at 911.

### *B. Material Inside Information*

An insider is not, of course, always foreclosed from investing in his own company merely because he may be more familiar with company operations than are outside investors. An insider's duty to disclose information or his duty to abstain from dealing in his company's securities arises only in "those situations which are essentially extraordinary in nature and which are reasonably certain to have a substantial effect on the market price of the security if (the extraordinary situation is) disclosed." Fleischer, Securities Trading and Corporate Information Practices: The Implications of the Texas Gulf Sulphur Proceeding, 51 Va.L.Rev. 1271, 1289 [1965].

Nor is an insider obligated to confer upon outside investors the benefit of his superior financial or other expert analysis by disclosing his educated guesses or predictions. The only regulatory objective is that access to material information be enjoyed equally, but this objective requires nothing more than the disclosure of basic facts so that outsiders may draw upon their own evaluative expertise in reaching their own investment decisions with knowledge equal to that of the insiders.

This is not to suggest *** that the materiality of facts is to be assessed solely by measuring the effect the knowledge of the facts would have upon prudent or conservative investors. *** The speculators and chartists of Wall and Bay Streets are also "reasonable" investors entitled to the same legal protection afforded conservative traders. Thus, material facts include not only information disclosing the earnings and distributions of a company but also those facts which affect the probable future of the company and those which may affect the desire of investors to buy, sell, or hold the company's securities.

In each case, then, whether facts are material within Rule 10b-5 when the facts relate to a particular event and are undisclosed by those persons who are knowledgeable thereof will depend at any given time upon a balancing of both the indicated probability that the event will occur and the anticipated magnitude of the event in light of the totality of the company activity. Here, notwithstanding the trial court's conclusion that the results of the first drill core, K-55-1, were "too 'remote' *** to have had any significant impact on the market, i.e., to be deemed material," 258 F.Supp. at 283, knowledge of the possibility, which surely was more than marginal, of the existence of a mine of the vast magnitude indicated by the remarkably rich drill core located rather close to the surface (suggesting mineability by the less expensive openpit method) within the confines of a large anomaly (suggesting an extensive region of mineralization) might well have affected the price of TGS stock and would certainly have been an important fact to a reasonable, if speculative, investor in deciding whether he should buy, sell, or hold. After all, this first drill core was "unusually good and ... excited the interest and speculation of those who knew about it." 258 F. Supp. at 282.

Our disagreement with the district judge on the issue does not, then, go to his findings of basic fact, as to which the "clearly erroneous" rule would apply, but to his understanding of the legal standard applicable to them. Our survey of the facts found below conclusively establishes that knowledge of the results of the discovery hole, K-55-1, would have been important to a reasonable investor and might have affected the price of the stock.[12] On April 16, The Northern Miner, a trade publication in wide circulation among mining stock specialists, called K- 55-1, the discovery hole, "one of the most impressive drill holes completed in modern times." Roche, a Canadian broker whose firm specialized in mining securities, characterized the importance to investors of the results of K-55-1. He stated that the completion of "the first drill hole" with "a 600 foot drill core is very very significant *** anything over 200 feet is considered very significant and 600 feet is just beyond your wildest imagination." He added, however, that it "is a natural thing to buy more stock once they give you the first drill hole." Additional testimony revealed that the prices of stocks of other companies, albeit less diversified, smaller firms, had increased substantially solely on the basis of the discovery of good anomalies or even because of the proximity of their lands to the situs of a potentially major strike. ***

Finally, a major factor in determining whether the K-55-1 discovery was a material fact is the importance attached to the drilling results by those who knew about it. In view of other unrelated recent developments favorably affecting TGS, participation by an informed person in a regular stock-purchase program, or even sporadic trading by an informed person, might lend only nominal support to the inference of the materiality of the K-55-1 discovery; nevertheless, the timing by those who knew of it of their stock purchases and

---

12. We do not suggest that material facts must be disclosed immediately; the timing of disclosure is a matter for the business judgment of the corporate officers entrusted with the management of the corporation within the affirmative disclosure requirements promulgated by the exchanges and by the SEC. Here, a valuable corporate purpose was served by delaying the publication of the K-55-1 discovery. We do intend to convey, however, that where a corporate purpose is thus served by withholding the news of a material fact, those persons who are thus quite properly true to their corporate trust must not during the period of non-disclosure deal personally in the corporation's securities or give to outsiders confidential information not generally available to all the corporations' stockholders and to the public at large.

their purchases of *short-term* calls—purchases in some cases by individuals who had never before purchased calls or even TGS stock—virtually compels the inference that the insiders were influenced by the drilling results. This insider trading activity, which surely constitutes highly pertinent evidence and the only truly objective evidence of the materiality of the K-55-1 discovery, was apparently disregarded by the court below in favor of the testimony of defendants' expert witnesses, all of whom "agreed that one drill core does not establish an ore body, much less a mine," 258 F.Supp. at 282- 283. Significantly, however, the court below, while relying upon what these defense experts said the defendant insiders *ought* to have thought about the worth to TGS of the K-55-1 discovery, and finding that from November 12, 1963 to April 6, 1964 Fogarty, Murray, Holyk and Darke spent more than $100,000 in purchasing TGS stock and calls on that stock, made no finding that the insiders were motivated by any factor other than the extraordinary K-55-1 discovery when they bought their stock and their calls. No reason appears why outside investors, perhaps better acquainted with speculative modes of investment and with, in many cases, perhaps more capital at their disposal for intelligent speculation, would have been less influenced, and would not have been similarly motivated to invest if they had known what the insider investors knew about the K-55-1 discovery.

Our decision to expand the limited protection afforded outside investors by the trial court's narrow definition of materiality is not at all shaken by fears that the elimination of insider trading benefits will deplete the ranks of capable corporate managers by taking away an incentive to accept such employment. Such benefits, in essence, are forms of secret corporate compensation, see Cary, Corporate Standards and Legal Rules, 50 Calif. L. Rev. 408, 409-10 (1962), derived at the expense of the uninformed investing public and not at the expense of the corporation which receives the sole benefit from insider incentives. Moreover, adequate incentives for corporate officers may be provided by properly administered stock options and employee purchase plans of which there are many in existence. In any event, the normal motivation induced by stock ownership, i.e., the identification of an individual with corporate progress, is ill-promoted by condoning the sort of speculative insider activity which occurred here; for example, some of the corporation's stock was sold at market in order to purchase short-term calls upon that stock, calls which would never be exercised to increase a stockholder equity in TGS unless the market price of that stock rose sharply.

The core of Rule 10b-5 is the implementation of the Congressional purpose that all investors should have equal access to the rewards of participation in securities transactions. It was the intent of Congress that all members of the investing public should be subject to identical market risks,—which market risks include, of course the risk that one's evaluative capacity or one's capital available to put at risk may exceed another's capacity or capital. The insiders here were not trading on an equal footing with the outside investors. They alone were in a position to evaluate the probability and magnitude of what seemed from the outset to be a major ore strike; they alone could invest safely, secure in the expectation that the price of TGS stock would rise substantially in the event such a major strike should materialize, but would decline little, if at all, in the event of failure, for the public, ignorant at the outset of the favorable probabilities would likewise be unaware of the unproductive exploration, and the additional exploration costs would not significantly affect TGS market prices. Such inequities based upon unequal access to knowledge should not be shrugged off as inevitable in our way of life, or, in view of the congressional concern in the area, remain uncorrected.

We hold, therefore, that all transactions in TGS stock or calls by individuals apprised of the drilling results of K-55-1 were made in violation of Rule 10b-5. Inasmuch as the visual evaluation of that drill core (a generally reliable estimate though less accurate than a chemical assay) constituted material information, those advised of the results of the visual evaluation as well as those informed of the chemical assay traded in violation of law. The geologist Darke possessed undisclosed material information and traded in TGS securities. Therefore we reverse the dismissal of the action as to him and his personal transactions. The trial court also found that Darke, after the drilling of K-55-1 had been completed and with detailed knowledge of the results thereof, told certain outside individuals that TGS "was a good buy." These individuals thereafter acquired TGS stock and calls. *** [W]e *** hold that Darke violated Rule 10b-5(3) and Section 10(b) by "tipping" and we remand, pursuant to the agreement of the parties, for a determination of the appropriate remedy. As Darke's "tippees" are not defendants in this action, we need not decide whether, if they acted with actual or constructive knowledge that the material information was undisclosed, their conduct is as equally violative of the Rule as the conduct of their insider source, though we note that it certainly could be equally reprehensible.

With reference to Huntington, the trial court found that he "had no detailed knowledge as to the work" on the Kidd-55 segment. Nevertheless, the evidence shows that he knew about and participated in TGS's land acquisition program which followed the receipt of the K-55-1 drilling results, and that on February 26, 1964 he purchased 50 shares of TGS stock. Later, on March 16, he helped prepare a letter for Dr. Holyk's signature in which TGS made a substantial offer for lands near K-55-1, and on the same day he, who had never before purchased calls on any stock, purchased a call on 100 shares of TGS stock. We are satisfied that these purchases in February and March, coupled with his readily inferable and probably reliable, understanding of the highly favorable nature of preliminary operations on the Kidd segment, demonstrate that Huntington possessed material inside information such as to make his purchase violative of the Rule and the Act.

### *C. When May Insiders Act?*

Appellant Crawford, who ordered the purchase of TGS stock shortly before the TGS April 16 official announcement, and defendant Coates, who placed orders with and communicated the news to his broker immediately after the official announcement was read at the TGS-called press conference, concede that they were in possession of material information. They contend, however, that their purchases were not proscribed purchases for the news had already been effectively disclosed. We disagree.

Crawford telephoned his orders to his Chicago broker about midnight on April 15 and again at 8:30 in the morning of the 16th, with instructions to buy at the opening of the Midwest Stock Exchange that morning. The trial court's finding that "he sought to, and did, 'beat the news,'" 258 F. Supp. at 287, is well documented by the record. The rumors of a major ore strike which had been circulated in Canada and, to a lesser extent, in New York, had been disclaimed by the TGS press release of April 12, which significantly promised the public an official detailed announcement when possibilities had ripened into actualities. The abbreviated announcement to the Canadian press at 9:40 A.M. on the 16th by the Ontario Minister of Mines and the report carried by The Northern Miner, parts of which had sporadically reached New York on the morning of the 16th through reports from Canadian affiliates to a few New York investment firms, are assuredly not the equivalent of the official 10-15 minute announcement which was not released to the American financial press until after 10:00 A.M. Crawford's orders had been placed before that. Before insiders may act upon material information, such information must have been effectively disclosed in a manner sufficient to insure its availibility to the investing public. Particularly here, where a formal announcement to the entire financial news media had been promised in a prior official release known to the media, all insider activity must await dissemination of the promised official announcement.

Coates was absolved by the court below because his telephone order was placed shortly before 10:20 A.M. on April 16, which was after the announcement had been made even though the news could not be considered already a matter of public information. 258 F.Supp. at 288. This result seems to have been predicated upon a misinterpretation of dicta in *Cady, Roberts*, where the SEC instructed insiders to "keep out of the market until the established procedures for public release of the information are *carried out* instead of hastening to execute transactions in advance of, and in frustration of, the objectives of the release," 40 SEC at 915. The reading of a news release, which prompted Coates into action, is merely the first step in the process of dissemination required for compliance with the regulatory objective of providing all investors with an equal opportunity to make informed investment judgments. Assuming that the contents of the official release could instantaneously be acted upon, at the minimum Coates should have waited until the news could reasonably have been expected to appear over the media of widest circulation, the Dow Jones broad tape, rather than hastening to insure an advantage to himself and his broker son-in-law. ***

CONCLUSION

In summary, therefore, we affirm the finding of the court below that appellants Richard H. Clayton and David M. Crawford have violated [Section 10(b)] and Rule 10b-5; we reverse the judgment order entered below dismissing the complaint against appellees Charles F. Fogarty, Richard H. Clayton, Richard D. Mollison, Walter Holyk, Kenneth H. Darke, Earl L. Huntington, and Francis G. Coates, as we find that they have violated [Section 10b-5] and Rule 10b-5. As to these eight individuals we remand so that in accordance with the agreement between the parties the Commission may notice a hearing before the court below to determine the remedies to be applied against them. ***

## NOTES AND QUESTIONS

*1. Silence in Securities Trading vs. Silence in Real Estate Transactions.* The Second Circuit made quite clear in *Texas Gulf Sulphur* that Rule 10b-5 imposed on TGS's insiders a duty to disclose the confidential information about the ore strike or to abstain from trading in the company's shares. The choice to remain silent, then, was clearly an unacceptable alternative when corporate shares were the object of an insider's purchase. But TGS insiders also remained silent about the ore strike when they sought to acquire for the company additional land in close proximity to the original strikes. Was this fair to the potential sellers of the land? Was such silence fraudulent under the common law?

Consider a person's liability for nondisclosure under Section 551 of the Restatement (Second) of Torts (1976), which is set out at pages 60-61 in Chapter 2. What additional information would be relevant in assessing whether the landowners could state a claim for fraud against TGS?

In 1969, when the Ontario High Court of Justice considered claims brought by landowners who had sold property to TGS, the Court had this to say about the company's tactics:

> [O]bviously Texas Gulf could not push the negotiations too hard without causing the prospective vendors to suspect that a discovery had been made, in which event either purchases would have become impossible or prices grossly inflated. Under the circumstances, I believe Texas Gulf did what any prudent mining company would have done to acquire property in which it knew a very promising anomaly lay.

*Leitch GoldMines, Ltd. v. Texas Gulf Sulphur Co.*, 3 D.L.R. 3(d) 161, 184-85 (1969). Rather than chastise the company for its silence, the Court expressed a grudging admiration.

How can potential land sellers protect themselves from disparities of information in transactions with potential buyers? Might such disparities counsel adherence to a rule of caveat emptor in real estate transactions? Do national securities markets lend themselves to a caveat emptor approach? What other factors might justify treating securities transactions differently from real estate or other commercial transactions?

*2. Federal Regulation of Insider Trading Through Rule 10b-5.* As we saw in Chapter 2, the SEC promulgated Rule 10b-5 in 1942 based on its rulemaking powers under Section 10(b) of the Exchange Act. And since then, the contours of the Rule 10b-5 cause of action have been shaped almost entirely by the SEC and the federal judiciary. Moreover, in the context of the regulation of insider trading, the SEC and the courts had to employ particularly creative reasoning because the template for common law fraud did not fit well over insider trading. Was this activism on the part of the SEC and the courts justified? Should Congress have acted to prohibit insider trading outright, rather than acquiesce in its regulation by the SEC and courts under Rule 10b-5? What problems would Congress have encountered in drafting such a prohibition? We will revisit this question in the last subsection of this Chapter.

*3. The Remedy for Insider Trading.* Notice that the Second Circuit found only that the corporate insiders had violated Rule 10b-5 by purchasing stock in TGS (or tipping others) while in possession of material nonpublic information. The court then remanded the case to the district court for imposition of a remedy. On remand, the district judge ordered Holyk, Huntington, Clayton, and Darke to pay to TGS the difference between the average price of TGS stock on April 17, 1964, when news of the ore strike was known to the investing public, and the purchase price of the shares. (Darke also had to pay to TGS the profits that his tippees had derived from sale of TGS stock.) *SEC v. Texas Gulf Sulphur Co.*, 312 F. Supp. 77, 96-97 (S.D.N.Y. 1970). TGS, however, was obliged to hold the money in escrow for five years, subject to disposition in any manner that the court should direct on its own motion, or by application from the SEC or any other interested person. The district court also enjoined defendants Clayton and Crawford from future violations of Rule 10b-5. The Second Circuit later affirmed the district court's order in its entirety. See 446 F.2d 1301 (2d Cir. 1971).

In its affirmance, the Second Circuit rejected the defendants' claims that Section 21(e) of the Exchange Act provided only for injunctive relief and that the required restitution constituted a penalty that could be imposed only in a criminal action brought pursuant to Section 32(a):

> [W]e do not read § 21(e) as restricting the remedies which the SEC can pursue to injunctive relief. *** [I]n other contexts the Supreme Court has upheld the power of the Government without specific statutory authority to seek restitution, and has upheld the lower courts in granting restitution, as an ancillary remedy in the exercise of the courts' general equity powers to afford complete relief. *** Restitution of the profits on these transactions merely deprives the appellants of the gains of their wrongful conduct. Nor does restitution impose a hardship in this case.*** The court's order requires only restitution of the profits made by the violators prior to general knowledge of the ore strike on April 17, 1964, and, in effect, leaves the appellants all the profits accrued after that date. It would severely defeat the purposes of the Act if a violator of Rule 10b-5 were allowed to retain the profits from his violation. ***
>
> As to the requirement that Darke make restitution for the profits derived by his tippees, admittedly more of a hardship is imposed. However, without such a remedy, insiders could easily evade their duty to refrain from trading on the basis of inside information. Either the transactions so traded could be concluded by a relative or an acquaintance of the insider, or implied understandings could arise under which reciprocal tips between insiders in different corporations could be given.

Id. at 1307-08.

Today, courts routinely impose injunctions and orders of disgorgement in insider trading cases in which the SEC has established federal securities law violations, although the funds disgorged typically are paid to the SEC, rather than to the company whose stock was traded. See Rory C. Flynn, SEC Distribution Plans in Insider Trading Cases, 48 Bus. Law. 107 (1992). Moreover, since 1984, the SEC has had the authority to seek a monetary penalty in insider trading cases up to three times the profit gained or loss avoided by the defendant. And, as we will see in the *Chiarella* decision that follows, the government may choose to prosecute an insider trading case criminally and seek the imposition of a prison sentence. Section D of this Chapter explores these remedial issues more fully.

*4. **Implied Private Rights of Action for Insider Trading.*** Could private plaintiffs have asserted an implied right of action under Rule 10b-5 against the TGS insiders who purchased company stock while in possession of the confidential information about the ore strike? Who would have standing to sue? What would have been the plaintiffs' damages? In view of the fact that the TGS insiders purchased their TGS stock over exchanges, could plaintiffs make the requisite showing of causation? That is, wouldn't those shareholders who sold their TGS stock in early April 1964 have done so even if the TGS insiders had abstained from trading?

Federal courts confronted questions like these shortly after *Texas Gulf Sulphur* and began to develop law, particularly in the Second Circuit, that recognized a private right of action for insider trading, at least in circumstances where the defendants were corporate insiders. See, e.g., *Shapiro v. Merrill Lynch, Pierce, Fenner & Smith, Inc.*, 495 F.2d 228, 241 (2d Cir. 1974) (recognizing standing for all persons purchasing shares in company stock from the date of the insiders' sales until disclosure was made by the company); *Wilson v. Comtech Telecomm. Corp.*, 648 F.2d 88, 93 (2d Cir. 1981) (limiting *Shapiro* and restricting the plaintiff class to those investors who traded contemporaneously with the defendants); *Moss v. Morgan Stanley, Inc.*, 719 F.2d 515 (2d Cir. 1983) (denying standing of plaintiffs who sold stock contemporaneously with defendants who had purchased company stock based on information that was stolen from the corporation, because defendants were not fiduciaries of the plaintiffs, and therefore did not owe a duty of disclosure). The Sixth Circuit, however, adopted a harder line on the complicated issues of standing, causation, and damages. See *Fridrich v. Bradford*, 542 F.2d 307, 318 (6th Cir. 1976) (holding that in the absence of proof of a direct causal relationship, shareholders who sold stock over an exchange could not recover from directors who purchased stock based on inside knowledge).

As we will see in Section D, Congress resolved this controversy in 1988 when it added a new Section 20A to the Exchange Act, granting "contemporaneous traders" an express right of action against persons who have violated the federal securities laws through illegal insider trading or tipping. Under Section 20A, those shareholders who sold TGS stock "contemporaneously" with the insiders' purchases would have been entitled to recover damages in the amount of the insiders' illegal profits, offset by any amount paid in disgorgement to the SEC. Why did Congress choose to limit plaintiff's recovery to the amount of defendant's illegal profits?

*5. **"Material Nonpublic Information."*** An insider's obligation under Rule 10b-5 to "disclose or abstain" attaches only when the information can be said to be both "material" and "nonpublic." On what reasoning did the *Texas Gulf Sulphur* court base its decision that the information about the ore findings was material? How does the court's analysis compare to the tests for materiality that were explored in Chapter 2.B—namely the "total mix" formulation from *TSC Indus., Inc. v. Northway*, 426 U.S. 438 (1976) and, for so-called contingent information, the probably/magnitude measure from *Basic Inc. v. Levinson*, 485 U.S. 224 (1988)?

The *Texas Gulf Sulphur* court also concluded that the information used by the insiders in their securities transactions was nonpublic. According to the court, when can information be said to be "public?" The *Texas Gulf Sulphur* standard for determining whether information is public was echoed in *In re Faberge*, 45 SEC 249, 256 (1973) (indicating that information must be disclosed "in a manner calculated to reach the securities market place in general through recognized channels of distribution, and public investors must be afforded a reasonable waiting period to react to the information"). Pursuant to the decisions in *Texas Gulf Sulphur* and *Faberge*, what steps would have to be taken before a company's previously confidential information could be regarded as in the public realm?

There is an alternative theory for determining whether information is public, predicated on the efficient capital markets hypothesis (discussed in Chapter 1.G). The theory postulates that information is "public" when it is known by a sufficient number of securities analysts or other professionals in the financial community. The Second Circuit adopted this theory in *United States v. Libera*, 989 F.2d 596 (2d Cir. 1993), where it maintained that:

> information may be considered public for Section 10(b) purposes even though there has been no public announcement and only a small number of people know of it. The issue is not the number of people who possess it but whether their trading has caused the information to be fully impounded into the price of the particular stock. Once the information is fully impounded in price, such information can no longer be misused by trading because no further profit can be made.

Id. at 601. Why, even today, might the SEC favor the *Texas Gulf Sulphur* approach? Which approach would you favor?

***6. Parity of Information vs. Parity of Access to Information.*** The Second Circuit's approach in *Texas Gulf Sulphur* has often been characterized as "the parity of information" theory of insider trading liability. This characterization, however, is somewhat of a misnomer because the court postulates only an equality *of access* to information, not complete equality of information. The difference is important because, under the equal access approach, those investors who lawfully search out information are clearly entitled to the benefits of their research. See Victor Brudney, Insiders, Outsiders, and Informational Advantages Under the Federal Securities Laws, 93 Harv. L. Rev. 322, 339-41 (1979) (questioning whether an "egalitarian utopia" could even be achieved, and highlighting the values gained by encouraging lawful exploration for relevant corporate and economic information). See also *Chiarella v. United States*, 445 U.S. 222, 252 n. 2 (1980) (Blackmun, J., dissenting) (noting that "there is a significant conceptual distinction between parity of information and parity of *access* to material information" and emphasizing that the "latter gives free rein to certain kinds of informational advantages that the former might foreclose, such as those that result from differences in diligence or acumen").

Do you agree with the Second Circuit's premise in *Texas Gulf Sulphur* that there is a "justifiable expectation of the securities marketplace that all investors trading on impersonal exchanges have relatively equal access to material information?" It is with this premise that the Supreme Court takes issue in the decision that immediately follows.

## B. THE SUPREME COURT SPEAKS ON INSIDER TRADING AND RULE 10b-5

### *1. The Classical Theory of Insider Trading*

### CHIARELLA v. UNITED STATES
445 U.S. 222 (1980)

JUSTICE POWELL:

The question in this case is whether a person who learns from the confidential documents of one corporation that it is planning an attempt to secure control of a second corporation violates § 10(b) of the Securities Exchange Act of 1934 if he fails to disclose the impending takeover before trading in the target company's securities.

I

Petitioner is a printer by trade. In 1975 and 1976, he worked as a "markup man" in the New York composing room of Pandick Press, a financial printer. Among documents that petitioner handled were five announcements of corporate takeover bids. When these documents were delivered to the printer, the identities of the acquiring and target corporations were concealed by blank spaces or false names. The true names were sent to the printer on the night of the final printing.

The petitioner, however, was able to deduce the names of the target companies before the final printing from other information contained in the documents. Without disclosing his knowledge, petitioner purchased stock in the target companies and sold the shares immediately after the takeover attempts were made public. By this method, petitioner realized a gain of slightly more than $30,000 in the course of 14 months. Subsequently, the Securities and Exchange Commission (Commission or SEC) began an investigation of his trading activities. In May 1977, petitioner entered into a consent decree with the Commission in which he agreed to return his profits to the sellers of the shares. On the same day, he was discharged by Pandick Press.

In January 1978, petitioner was indicted on 17 counts of violating § 10(b) of the Securities Exchange Act of 1934 (1934 Act) and SEC Rule 10b-5. After petitioner unsuccessfully moved to dismiss the indictment, he was brought to trial and convicted on all counts.

The Court of Appeals for the Second Circuit affirmed petitioner's conviction. We granted certiorari and we now reverse.

II

***This case concerns the legal effect of the petitioner's silence. The District Court's charge permitted the jury to convict the petitioner if it found that he willfully failed to inform sellers of target company securities that he knew of a forthcoming takeover bid that would make their shares more valuable. In order to decide whether silence in such circumstances violates § 10(b), it is necessary to review the language and legislative history of that statute as well as its interpretation by the Commission and the federal courts.

Although the starting point of our inquiry is the language of the statute, *Ernst & Ernst v. Hochfelder*, 425 U.S. 185, 197 (1976), § 10(b) does not state whether silence may constitute a manipulative or deceptive device. Section 10(b) was designed as a catch-all clause to prevent fraudulent practices. *[Hochfelder]*, 425 U.S., at 202, 206. But neither the legislative history nor the statute itself affords specific guidance for the resolution of this case. When Rule 10b-5 was promulgated in 1942, the SEC did not discuss the possibility that failure to provide information might run afoul of § 10(b).

The SEC took an important step in the development of §10(b) when it held that a broker-dealer and his firm violated that section by selling securities on the basis of undisclosed information obtained from a director of the issuer corporation who was also a registered representative of the brokerage firm. In *Cady, Roberts & Co.*, 40 SEC 907 (1961), the Commission decided that a corporate insider must abstain from trading in the shares of his corporation unless he has first disclosed all material inside information known to him. The obligation to disclose or abstain derives from

> "[a]n affirmative duty to disclose material information[, which] has been traditionally imposed on corporate 'insiders,' particular officers, directors, or controlling stockholders. We, and the courts have consistently held that insiders must disclose material facts which are known to them by virtue of their position but which are not known to persons with whom they deal and which, if known, would affect their investment judgment."

Id., at 911. The Commission emphasized that the duty arose from (i) the existence of a relationship affording access to inside information intended to be available only for a corporate purpose, and (ii) the unfairness of allowing a corporate insider to take advantage of that information by trading without disclosure. Id., at 912, and n. 15.[8]

That the relationship between a corporate insider and the stockholders of his corporation gives rise to a disclosure obligation is not a novel twist of the law. At common law, misrepresentation made for the purpose of inducing reliance upon the false statement is fraudulent. But one who fails to disclose material information prior to the consummation of a transaction commits fraud only when he is under a duty to do so. And the duty to disclose arises when one party has information "that the other [party] is entitled to know because of a fiduciary or other similar relation of trust and confidence between them." [Restatement (Second) of Torts § 551(2)(a) (1976)]. In its *Cady, Roberts* decision, the Commission recognized a relationship of trust and confidence between the

---

8. In *Cady, Roberts*, the broker-dealer was liable under § 10(b) because it received nonpublic information from a corporate insider of the issuer. Since the insider could not use the information, neither could the partners in the brokerage firm with which he was associated. The transaction in *Cady, Roberts* involved sale of stock to persons who previously may not have been shareholders in the corporation. 40 SEC, at 913, and n. 21. The Commission embraced the reasoning of Judge Learned Hand that "the director or officer assumed a fiduciary relation to the buyer by the very sale; for it would be a sorry distinction to allow him to use the advantage of his position to induce the buyer into the position of a beneficiary although he was forbidden to do so once the buyer had become one." Id., at 914, n. 23, quoting *Gratz v. Claughton*, 187 F.2d 46, 49 (CA2 1951).

shareholders of a corporation and those insiders who have obtained confidential information by reason of their position with that corporation. This relationship gives rise to a duty to disclose because of the "necessity of preventing a corporate insider from ... tak[ing] unfair advantage of the uninformed minority stockholders." *Speed v. Transamerica Corp.*, 99 F.Supp. 808, 829 (D.Del.1951).

The federal courts have found violations of § 10(b) where corporate insiders used undisclosed information for their own benefit. E. g., *SEC v. Texas Gulf Sulphur Co.*, 401 F.2d 833 (CA2 1968). The cases also have emphasized, in accordance with the common-law rule, that "[t]he party charged with failing to disclose market information must be under a duty to disclose it." *Frigitemp Corp. v. Financial Dynamics Fund, Inc.*, 524 F.2d 275, 282 (CA2 1975). Accordingly, a purchaser of stock who has no duty to a prospective seller because he is neither an insider nor a fiduciary has been held to have no obligation to reveal material facts. See *General Time Corp. v. Talley Industries, Inc.*, 403 F.2d 159, 164 (CA2 1968).

This Court followed the same approach in *Affiliated Ute Citizens v. United States*, 406 U.S. 128 (1972). ***

Thus, administrative and judicial interpretations have established that silence in connection with the purchase or sale of securities may operate as a fraud actionable under §10(b) despite the absence of statutory language or legislative history specifically addressing the legality of nondisclosure. But such liability is premised upon a duty to disclose arising from a relationship of trust and confidence between parties to a transaction. Application of a duty to disclose prior to trading guarantees that corporate insiders, who have an obligation to place the shareholder's welfare before their own, will not benefit personally through fraudulent use of material, nonpublic information.[12]

III

In this case, the petitioner was convicted of violating § 10(b) although he was not a corporate insider and he received no confidential information from the target company. Moreover, the "market information" upon which he relied did not concern the earning power or operations of the target company, but only the plans of the acquiring company. Petitioner's use of that information was not a fraud under § 10(b) unless he was subject to an affirmative duty to disclose it before trading. In this case, the jury instructions failed to specify any such duty. In effect, the trial court instructed the jury that petitioner owed a duty to everyone; to all sellers, indeed, to the market as a whole. The jury simply was told to decide whether petitioner used material, nonpublic information at a time when "he knew other people trading in the securities market did not have access to the same information."

---

12. "Tippees" of corporate insiders have been held liable under § 10(b) because they have a duty not to profit from the use of inside information that they know is confidential and know or should know came from a corporate insider, *Shapiro v. Merrill Lynch, Pierce, Fenner & Smith, Inc.*, 495 F.2d 228, 237-238 (CA2 1974). The tippee's obligation has been viewed as arising from his role as a participant after the fact in the insider's breach of a fiduciary duty.

The Court of Appeals affirmed the conviction by holding that "*[a]nyone*—corporate insider or not—who regularly receives material nonpublic information may not use that information to trade in securities without incurring an affirmative duty to disclose." Although the court said that its test would include only persons who regularly receive material, nonpublic information, its rationale for that limitation is unrelated to the existence of a duty to disclose.

The Court of Appeals, like the trial court, failed to identify a relationship between petitioner and the sellers that could give rise to a duty. Its decision thus rested solely upon its belief that the federal securities laws have "created a system providing equal access to information necessary for reasoned and intelligent investment decisions." The use by anyone of material information not generally available is fraudulent, this theory suggests, because such information gives certain buyers or sellers an unfair advantage over less informed buyers and sellers.

This reasoning suffers from two defects. First not every instance of financial unfairness constitutes fraudulent activity under § 10(b). See *Santa Fe Industries, Inc. v. Green,* 430 U.S. 462, 474-477 (1977). Second, the element required to make silence fraudulent—a duty to disclose—is absent in this case. No duty could arise from petitioner's relationship with the sellers of the target company's securities, for petitioner had no prior dealings with them. He was not their agent, he was not a fiduciary, he was not a person in whom the sellers had placed their trust and confidence. He was, in fact, a complete stranger who dealt with the sellers only through impersonal market transactions.

We cannot affirm petitioner's conviction without recognizing a general duty between all participants in market transactions to forgo actions based on material, nonpublic information. Formulation of such a broad duty, which departs radically from the established doctrine that duty arises from a specific relationship between two parties, should not be undertaken absent some explicit evidence of congressional intent.

As we have seen, no such evidence emerges from the language or legislative history of § 10(b). Moreover, neither the Congress nor the Commission ever has adopted a parity-of-information rule. Instead the problems caused by misuse of market information have been addressed by detailed and sophisticated regulation that recognizes when use of market information may not harm operation of the securities markets. For example, the Williams Act limits but does not completely prohibit a tender offeror's purchases of target corporation stock before public announcement of the offer. Congress' careful action in this and other areas contrasts, and is in some tension, with the broad rule of liability we are asked to adopt in this case.

Indeed, the theory upon which the petitioner was convicted is at odds with the Commission's view of § 10(b) as applied to activity that has the same effect on sellers as the petitioner's purchases. "Warehousing" takes place when a corporation gives advance notice of its intention to launch a tender offer to institutional investors who then are able to purchase stock in the target company before the tender offer is made public and the price of shares rises. In this case, as in warehousing, a buyer of securities purchases stock in a target corporation on the basis of market information which is unknown to the seller. In both of these situations, the seller's behavior presumably would be altered if he had the nonpublic information. Significantly, however, the Commission has acted to bar warehousing under its authority to regulate tender offers after recognizing that action under §10(b) would rest on a "somewhat different theory" than that previously used to regulate insider trading as fraudulent activity.

We see no basis for applying such a new and different theory of liability in this case. As we have emphasized before, the 1934 Act cannot be read "'more broadly than its language and the statutory scheme reasonably permit.'" *Touche Ross & Co. v. Redington*, 442 U.S. 560, 578, (1979). Section 10(b) is aptly described as a catchall provision, but what it catches must be fraud. When an allegation of fraud is based upon nondisclosure, there can be no fraud absent a duty to speak. We hold that a duty to disclose under § 10(b) does not arise from the mere possession of nonpublic market information. The contrary result is without support in the legislative history of § 10(b) and would be inconsistent with the careful plan that Congress has enacted for regulation of the securities markets. *** The judgment of the Court of Appeals is reversed.

*[The concurring opinions of Justices Stevens and Brennan, and the dissenting opinion of Chief Justice Burger, raise the issue of an alternative "misappropriation theory" of insider trading liability, and are discussed infra at Section B.3]*

JUSTICE BLACKMUN, WITH WHOM JUSTICE MARSHALL JOINS, DISSENTING:

***The Court continues to pursue a course, charted in certain recent decisions, designed to transform § 10(b) from an intentionally elastic "catchall" provision to one that catches relatively little of the misbehavior that all too often makes investment in securities a needlessly risky business for the uninitiated investor. See, e.g., *Ernst & Ernst v. Hochfelder*, 425 U.S. 185, (1976); *Blue Chip Stamps v. Manor Drug Stores*, 421 U.S. 723 (1975). Such confinement in this case is now achieved by imposition of a requirement of a "special relationship" akin to fiduciary duty before the statute gives rise to a duty to disclose or to abstain from trading upon material, nonpublic information. The Court admits that this conclusion finds no mandate in the language of the statute or its legislative history. Yet the Court fails even to attempt a justification of its ruling in terms of the purposes of the securities laws, or to square that ruling with the long-standing but now much abused principle that the federal securities laws are to be construed flexibly rather than with narrow technicality. See *Affiliated Ute Citizens v. United States*, 406 U.S. 128, 151 (1972); *Superintendent of Insurance v. Bankers Life & Casualty Co.*, 404 U.S. 6, 12 (1971); *SEC v. Capital Gains Research Bureau*, 375 U.S. 180, 186 (1963).

I, of course, agree with the Court that a relationship of trust can establish a duty to disclose under § 10(b) and Rule 10b-5. But I do not agree that a failure to disclose violates the Rule only when the responsibilities of a relationship of that kind have been breached. As applied to this case, the Court's approach unduly minimizes the importance of petitioner's access to confidential information that the honest investor no matter how diligently he tried, could not legally obtain. In doing so, it further advances an interpretation of §10(b) and Rule 10b-5 that stops short of their full implications. Although the Court draws support for its position from certain precedent, I find its decision neither fully consistent with developments in the common law of fraud, nor fully in step with administrative and judicial application of Rule 10b-5 to "insider" trading.

The common law of actionable misrepresentation long has treated the possession of "special facts" as a key ingredient in the duty to disclose. See *Strong v. Repide*, 213 U.S. 419, 431-433 (1909); 1 F. Harper & F. James, Law of Torts § 7.14 (1956). Traditionally, this factor has been prominent in cases involving confidential or fiduciary relations, where one party's inferiority of knowledge and dependence upon fair treatment is a matter of legal definition, as well as in cases where one party is on notice that the other is "acting under a mistaken belief with respect to a material fact." *Frigitemp Corp. v. Financial Dynamics Fund, Inc.*, 524 F.2d 275, 283 (CA2 1975); see also Restatement of Torts § 551 (1938). Even at common law, however, there has been a trend away from strict adherence to the harsh maxim *caveat emptor* and toward a more flexible, less formalistic understanding of the duty to disclose. See, e. g., Keeton Fraud—Concealment and Non-Disclosure, 15 Texas L.Rev. 1, 31 (1936). Steps have been taken toward application of the "special facts" doctrine in a broader array of contexts where one party's superior knowledge of essential facts renders a transaction without disclosure inherently unfair. See James & Gray, Misrepresentation—Part II, 37 Md.L.Rev. 488, 526-527 (1978); 3 Restatement (Second) of Torts § 551(e), Comment *l* (1977).

By its narrow construction of § 10(b) and Rule 10b-5, the Court places the federal securities laws in the rearguard of this movement, a position opposite to the expectations of Congress at the time the securities laws were enacted. I cannot agree that the statute and Rule are so limited. The Court has observed that the securities laws were not intended to replicate the law of fiduciary relations. *Santa Fe Industries, Inc. v. Green*, 430 U.S. 462, 474-476 (1977). Rather, their purpose is to ensure the fair and honest functioning of impersonal national securities markets where common-law protections have proved inadequate. Cf. *United States v. Naftalin*, 441 U.S. 768, 775 (1979). As Congress itself has recognized, it is integral to this purpose "to assure that dealing in securities is fair and without undue preferences or advantages among investors."

Indeed, the importance of access to "special facts" has been a recurrent theme in administrative and judicial application of Rule 10b-5 to insider trading. Both the SEC and the courts have stressed the insider's misuse of secret knowledge as the gravamen of illegal conduct. The Court, I think, unduly minimizes this aspect of prior decisions.

*Cady, Roberts & Co.*, 40 SEC 907 (1961), which the Court discusses at some length, provides an illustration. In that case, the Commission *** regarded the insider "relationship" primarily in terms of *access* to nonpublic information, and not merely in terms of the presence of a common-law fiduciary duty or the like. This approach was deemed to be in keeping with the principle that "the broad language of the anti-fraud provisions" should not be "circumscribed by fine distinctions and rigid classifications," such as those that prevailed under the common law. Ibid. The duty to abstain or disclose arose, not merely as an incident of fiduciary responsibility, but as a result of the "inherent unfairness" of turning secret information to account for personal profit. This understanding of Rule 10b-5 was reinforced when *Investors Management Co.*, 44 SEC 633, 643 (1971), specifically rejected the contention that a "special relationship" between the alleged violator and an "insider" source was a necessary requirement for liability.

A similar approach has been followed by the courts. In *SEC v. Texas Gulf Sulphur Co.*, 401 F.2d 833, 848 (CA2 1968) (en banc), the court specifically mentioned the common-law "special facts" doctrine as one source for Rule 10b-5, and it reasoned that the Rule is "based in policy on the justifiable expectation of the securities marketplace that all investors trading on impersonal exchanges have relatively equal access to material information." See also *Lewelling v. First California Co.*, 564 F.2d 1277, 1280 (CA9 1977); *Speed v. Transamerica Corp.*, 99 F.Supp. 808, 829 (D.Del.1951). ***

I believe, and surely thought, that this broad understanding of the duty to disclose under Rule 10b-5 was recognized and approved in *Affiliated Ute Citizens v. United States*, 406 U.S. 128 (1972). That case held that bank agents dealing in the stock of a Ute Indian development corporation had a duty to reveal to mixed-blood Indian customers that their shares could bring a higher price on a non-Indian market of which the sellers were unaware. The Court recognized that "by repeated use of the word 'any,'" the statute and Rule "are obviously meant to be inclusive." Although it found a relationship of trust between the agents and the Indian sellers, the Court also clearly established that the bank and its agents were subject to the strictures of Rule 10b-5 because of their strategic position in the marketplace. The Indian sellers had no knowledge of the non-Indian market. The bank agents, in contrast, had intimate familiarity with the non-Indian market, which they had promoted actively, and from which they and their bank both profited. In these circumstances, the Court held that the bank and its agents "possessed the affirmative duty under the Rule" to disclose market information to the Indian sellers, and that the latter "had the right to know" that their shares would sell for a higher price in another market.

It seems to me that the Court gives *Affiliated Ute Citizens* an unduly narrow interpretation. As I now read my opinion there for the Court, it lends strong support to the principle that a structural disparity in access to material information is a critical factor under Rule 10b-5 in establishing a duty either to disclose the information or to abstain from trading. Given the factual posture of the case, it was unnecessary to resolve the question whether such a structural disparity could sustain a duty to disclose even absent "a relationship of trust and confidence between parties to a transaction." Nevertheless, I think the rationale of *Affiliated Ute Citizens* definitely points toward an affirmative answer to that question. Although I am not sure I fully accept the "market insider" category created by the Court of Appeals, I would hold that persons having access to confidential material information that is not legally available to others generally are prohibited by Rule 10b-5 from engaging in schemes to exploit their structural informational advantage through trading in affected securities. To hold otherwise, it seems to me, is to tolerate a wide range of manipulative and deceitful behavior. [S]ee generally Brudney, Insiders, Outsiders, and Informational Advantages under the Federal Securities Laws, 93 Harv.L.Rev. 322 (1979).

Whatever the outer limits of the Rule, petitioner Chiarella's case fits neatly near the center of its analytical framework. He occupied a relationship to the takeover companies giving him intimate access to concededly material information that was sedulously guarded from public access. The information, in the words of *Cady, Roberts & Co.* was "intended to be available only for a corporate purpose and not for the personal benefit of anyone." Petitioner, moreover, knew that the information was unavailable to those with whom he dealt. And he took full, virtually riskless advantage of this artificial information gap by selling the stocks shortly after each takeover bid was announced. By any reasonable definition, his trading was "inherent[ly] unfai[r]." This misuse of confidential information was clearly placed before the jury. Petitioner's conviction, therefore, should be upheld, and I dissent from the Court's upsetting that conviction.

## *NOTES AND QUESTIONS*

*1.* ***Disclosure Duties at Common Law.*** Does the *Chiarella* Court suggest that disclosure duties under Rule 10b-5 arise only out of pre-existing fiduciary relationships? Is such a suggestion consistent with Section 551(2) of the Restatement of Torts (Second), set out on pages 60-61 of Chapter 2? What may have prompted the Court to focus on the existence of a fiduciary relationship between the parties to a securities transaction?

*2.* **Chiarella's *Departures From the Common Law.*** *Chiarella*'s classical theory was clearly an effort by the Court to curtail the SEC's and the Second Circuit's more expansive approach to insider trading; but it is also important to recognize that *Chiarella* itself construed Rule 10b-5 in a manner that departed from at least two common law limitations on recovery for a fiduciary's silence. What justified those departures?

*3.* ***Identifying Insiders.*** By the very terms of the majority opinion, *Chiarella*'s classical theory of insider trading liability applies to officers, directors, and controlling shareholders of the corporation who trade in the company's stock. Are other employees of the corporation included in this circle? For example, can an attendant in a company's mailroom be viewed as a corporate fiduciary owing disclosure duties to shareholders? Courts have indeed been willing to do so. (Recall the geologists held liable for insider trading in *Texas Gulf Sulphur*.) Is the circle wide enough to include the issuer itself? Again the answer appears to be yes. See, e.g., *Shaw v. Digital Equip. Corp.*, 82 F.3d 1194, 1203 (1st Cir. 1996) (observing that numerous courts "have treated a corporation trading in its own securities as an 'insider' for purposes of the 'disclose or abstain' rule"); *McCormick v. Fund Am. Cos.*, 26 F.3d 869, 876 (9th Cir. 1994) (emphasizing that "the corporate issuer in possession of material nonpublic information, must, like other insiders in the same situation, disclose that information to its shareholders or refrain from trading with them"). But see Deborah A. DeMott, Beyond Metaphor: An Analysis of Fiduciary Obligation, 1988 Duke L.J. 879, 916-21 (1988) (contending that securities issuers do not owe fiduciary duties to their shareholders).

*4.* ***The "Possession vs. Use" Debate.*** Under the classical theory of insider trading liability, is a traditional insider required to abstain from trading securities while that insider is "in possession of" material nonpublic information, or is the insider required to abstain only from trading securities "on the basis of" material nonpublic information? This question is often phrased in terms of whether liability for insider trading under Rule 10b-5 should be determined pursuant to a "knowing possession" test or a "use" test.

For many years, the controversy over the proper test to apply in Rule 10b-5 cases persisted without direct judicial attention, primarily because persons facing substantial monetary penalties and possible prison sentences for alleged insider trading offenses seldom defended themselves by maintaining that although they possessed material nonpublic information, they did not trade securities on the basis of such information. But in *SEC v. Adler,* 137 F.3d 1325 (11th Cir. 1998), and *United States v. Smith*, 155 F.3d 1051 (9th Cir. 1998), two federal courts of appeals squarely confronted this question in the context of insider trading claims against a corporate director (in *Adler*) and a corporate officer (in *Smith*). Both circuits rejected the Commission's "knowing possession" position, holding that Rule 10b-5's disclose or abstain obligation prohibits securities trading only *on the basis of* material nonpublic information. The Second Circuit reached precisely the opposite conclusion in *United States v. Teicher*, 987 F.2d 112 (2d Cir. 1993), but the court's views on the issue of "possession vs. use" constituted dictum rather than a holding. For extensive analysis of these decisions, see Donna M. Nagy, The "Possession vs. Use" Debate in the Context of Securities Trading by Traditional Insiders: Why Silence Can Never Be Golden, 67 U. Cin. L. Rev. 1129 (1999).

Rather than reconciling the circuits' conflicting positions through case-by-case adjudication, the Commission, in August 2000, opted to use its authority under Section 10(b) to promulgate a rule intended to resolve the debate once and for all. The result—Rule 10b5-1—comes close to endorsing a "knowing possession" standard because it focuses liability on whether a person traded securities while "aware" of material nonpublic information. But the rule also contains significant affirmative defenses that allow persons to plan future securities transactions at a time when they are unaware of material nonpublic information, and then have those trades carried out pursuant to such a plan, regardless of whether they may have come into possession of confidential information at the time those trades are actually executed. Specifically, Rule 10b5-1(c)(1) allows persons to avoid liability under Rule 10b-5 by demonstrating that they purchased or sold the securities as part of a written plan, contract, or instruction that "pre-existed" their awareness of material nonpublic information.

What are the principal benefits of Rule 10b5-1? Are there costs or disadvantages? Should the Commission have included affirmative defenses for pre-existing trading plans? Can such defenses be reconciled with *Chiarella*'s "disclose or abstain" rule? With the common law of fraud and deceit?

***5. Financial Institutions and Chinese Walls.*** Financial institutions such as Goldman Sachs, Merrill Lynch, and Morgan Stanley are generally organized into many separate departments, some of which routinely come into contact with material nonpublic information about securities issuers. To prevent confidential information in one sector of the firm (such as an investment banking department) from being imputed to persons working in another sector (such as a trading department), firms typically erect so-called "Chinese Walls." And for decades, the SEC has assured firms that their properly walled-off departments could continue to trade securities for client and proprietary accounts without incurring liability for insider trading. See Ralph C. Ferrara, Donna M. Nagy, and Herbert C. Thomas, Ferrara on Insider Trading and the Wall (2d ed. 2001). Rule 10b5-1(c)(2) now codifies the practice of creating Chinese Walls as a separate affirmative defense available to "non-natural" persons. What must a firm show to invoke this defense?

### *PROBLEM 7-1*

Jonathan Bryant is a Senior Vice President for Chrontonic, Inc., which provides contract manufacturing services to original equipment manufacturers in the electronics industry. He also sits on the company's Board of Directors. For several years, Bryant has received a sizable amount of Chrontonic shares as part of his year-end compensation bonus. In January 2001, his broker and financial adviser recommended that he diversify his stock portfolio by periodically selling some shares in Chrontonic and investing the proceeds in companies outside the electronics industry. Believing this diversification strategy to be a good one, Bryant developed a written plan whereby his broker would sell 1000 shares of Chrontonic stock on January 15, 2001 and the first day of every quarter thereafter. At the time, Bryant was not aware of any material nonpublic information concerning Chrontonic. And in accordance with this plan, sales were made for Bryant's account on January 15, April 15, July 15, and October 15 for the years 2001 and 2002.

During November and December of 2002, Chrontonic began receiving decreased orders from one of its largest customers, Jonners Peripherals ("Jonners"). On January 5, 2003, Chrontonic's CEO informed its Board of Directors that the company was expecting a complete termination in the orders from Jonners due to that company's decision to move much of its manufacturing off-shore. The CEO expressed the view that when this information was disseminated to the public, Chrontonic's stock price was likely to drop substantially. After the Board meeting, Bryant did nothing to alter his broker's standing instructions, and on January 15, 2003, 1000 shares of Chrontonic shares were sold for Bryant's account. A number of other officers and directors of Chrontonic had adhered to similar written trading plans, and shares for their account were also sold pursuant to those plans on January 15, 2003.

On January 17, 2003, Chrontonic issued a press release announcing its cessation of business with Jonners. In response to the press release, the price of Chrontonic stock dropped from $30.50 to $18.25 over the next two trading days. Shareholders of Chrontonic maintain that by selling 1,000 shares of Chrontonic stock before the January 17 press release, Bryant avoided $12,250 in losses. In addition, other officers and directors avoided similar losses, to a combined total of more than $400,000.

Has Bryant violated Rule 10b-5? What if another director had sold Chrontonic stock on January 15, but decided only that morning to trade? Would he have violated Rule 10b-5? What if a third director had been planning to sell a portion of her Chrontonic stock on January 10—the due date for her daughter's college tuition for the second semester? Does the CEO's January 5 announcement to the Board preclude her from selling?

Suppose that, instead of the confidential bad news announced at the board meeting on January 5, the CEO had announced confidential good news that the company would be receiving double its expected orders from Jonners. If Bryant had then called his broker to cancel the sales to occur on January 15, would this have been a violation of Rule 10b-5?

If you were a corporation's general counsel, what advise would you give its officers and directors who wish to set up trading plans like the one developed by Bryant?

### *PROBLEM 7-2*

In January 1997, Brentwood Management LLP ("Brentwood") issued ten-year bonds to finance its acquisition of a shopping center in a downtown area of the city that urban planners had hoped to revitalize. Over the following two years, largely due to effective marketing on the part of Brentwood, many retail stores signed long-term leasing agreements with the company. The shopping center proved to be a very profitable venture for Brentwood in that its goal of maximum occupancy was reached. Indeed, Brentwood even has a "wait list" for any tenant vacancies that might come available. The bonds now trade in a small over-the-counter market.

In January 2001, an employee in Brentwood's marketing department learned from a current tenant that a competing company plans to construct a mega-mall to be located in the near suburbs. The competing company has yet to publicly announce this project because it has not yet finalized its negotiations with the owners of the land on which the mall will be built. Fearing that the construction of the mall will spell doom for the shopping center (and therefore Brentwood), the employee sold his bonds in the market. Under the classical theory of insider trading, has the employee committed a violation of Rule 10b-5?

### 2. *Tippees and Temporary Insiders*

A footnote in *Chiarella*'s majority opinion expressed the view that "tippees" of corporate insiders may incur liability under Rule 10b-5 "because they have a duty not to profit from the use of inside information that they know is confidential and know or should know came from a corporate insider," and that "[t]he tippee's obligation has been viewed as arising from his role as a participant after the fact in the insider's breach of a fiduciary duty." See *Chiarella v. United States*, 445 U.S. 222, 231 n.12 (1980). The Supreme Court elaborated on the scope of tippee liability in the following decision.

## DIRKS v. SEC

463 U.S. 646 (1983)

JUSTICE POWELL:

Petitioner Raymond Dirks received material nonpublic information from "insiders" of a corporation with which he had no connection. He disclosed this information to investors who relied on it in trading in the shares of the corporation. The question is whether Dirks violated the antifraud provisions of the federal securities laws by this disclosure.

I

In 1973, Dirks was an officer of a New York broker-dealer firm who specialized in providing investment analysis of insurance company securities to institutional investors. On March 6, Dirks received information from Ronald Secrist, a former officer of Equity Funding of America. Secrist alleged that the assets of Equity Funding, a diversified corporation primarily engaged in selling life insurance and mutual funds, were vastly overstated as the result of fraudulent corporate practices. Secrist also stated that various regulatory agencies had failed to act on similar charges made by Equity Funding employees. He urged Dirks to verify the fraud and disclose it publicly.

Dirks decided to investigate the allegations. He visited Equity Funding's headquarters in Los Angeles and interviewed several officers and employees of the corporation. The senior management denied any wrongdoing, but certain corporation employees corroborated the charges of fraud. Neither Dirks nor his firm owned or traded any Equity Funding stock, but throughout his investigation he openly discussed the information he had obtained with a number of clients and investors. Some of these persons sold their holdings of Equity Funding securities, including five investment advisers who liquidated holdings of more than $16 million.

While Dirks was in Los Angeles, he was in touch regularly with William Blundell, the Wall Street Journal's Los Angeles bureau chief. Dirks urged Blundell to write a story on the fraud allegations. Blundell did not believe, however, that such a massive fraud could go undetected and declined to write the story. He feared that publishing such damaging hearsay might be libelous.

During the 2-week period in which Dirks pursued his investigation and spread word of Secrist's charges, the price of Equity Funding stock fell from $26 per share to less than $15 per share. This led the New York Stock Exchange to halt trading on March 27. Shortly thereafter California insurance authorities impounded Equity Funding's records and uncovered evidence of the fraud. Only then did the Securities and Exchange Commission (SEC) file a complaint against Equity Funding and only then, on April 2, did the Wall Street Journal publish a front-page story based largely on information assembled by Dirks. Equity Funding immediately went into receivership.

The SEC began an investigation into Dirks' role in the exposure of the fraud. After a hearing by an Administrative Law Judge, the SEC found that Dirks had aided and abetted violations of § 17(a) of the Securities Act of 1933, § 10(b) of the Securities Exchange Act of 1934, and SEC Rule 10b-5 by repeating the allegations of fraud to members of the investment community who later sold their Equity Funding stock. The SEC concluded: "Where 'tippees'—regardless of their motivation or occupation—come into possession of material 'corporate information that they know is confidential and know or should know came from a corporate insider,' they must either publicly disclose that information or refrain from trading." Recognizing, however, that Dirks "played an important role in bringing [Equity Funding's] massive fraud to light," the SEC only censured him.

Dirks sought review in the Court of Appeals for the District of Columbia Circuit. The court entered judgment against Dirks "for the reasons stated by the Commission in its opinion." ***

In view of the importance to the SEC and to the securities industry of the question presented by this case, we granted a writ of certiorari. We now reverse.

II

In the seminal case of *In re Cady, Roberts & Co.*, 40 SEC 907 (1961), the SEC recognized that the common law in some jurisdictions imposes on "corporate 'insiders,' particularly officers, directors, or controlling stockholders" an "affirmative duty of disclosure ... when dealing in securities." Id., at 911, and n. 13. The SEC found that not only did breach of this common-law duty also establish the elements of a Rule 10b-5 violation, but that individuals other than corporate insiders could be obligated either to disclose material nonpublic information before trading or to abstain from trading altogether. In *Chiarella,* we accepted the two elements set out in *Cady Roberts* for establishing a Rule 10b-5 violation: "(i) the existence of a relationship affording access to inside information intended to be available only for a corporate purpose, and (ii) the unfairness of allowing a corporate insider to take advantage of that information by trading without disclosure." 445 U.S., at 227. In examining whether *Chiarella* had an obligation to disclose or abstain, the Court found that there is no general duty to disclose before trading on material nonpublic information, and held that "a duty to disclose under § 10(b) does not arise from the mere possession of nonpublic market information." Id., at 235. Such a duty arises rather from the existence of a fiduciary relationship. See id., at 227-235.

Not "all breaches of fiduciary duty in connection with a securities transaction," however, come within the ambit of Rule 10b-5. *Santa Fe Industries, Inc. v. Green,* 430 U.S. 462, 472 (1977). There must also be "manipulation or deception." Id., at 473. In an inside-trading case this fraud derives from the "inherent unfairness involved where one takes advantage" of "information intended to be available only for a corporate purpose and not for the personal benefit of anyone." *In re Merrill Lynch, Pierce, Fenner & Smith, Inc.,* 43 SEC 933, 936 (1968). Thus, an insider will be liable under Rule 10b-5 for inside trading only where he fails to disclose material nonpublic information before trading on it and thus makes "secret profits." *Cady, Roberts,* [40 SEC], at 916, n. 31.

III

We were explicit in *Chiarella* in saying that there can be no duty to disclose where the person who has traded on inside information "was not [the corporation's] agent, ... was not a fiduciary, [or] was not a person in whom the sellers [of the securities] had placed their trust and confidence." 445 U.S., at 232. Not to require such a fiduciary relationship, we recognized, would "depar[t] radically from the established doctrine that duty arises from a specific relationship between two parties" and would amount to "recognizing a general duty between all participants in market transactions to forgo actions based on material, nonpublic information." Id., at 232, 233. This requirement of a specific relationship between the shareholders and the individual trading on inside information has created analytical difficulties for the SEC and courts in policing tippees who trade on inside information. Unlike insiders who have independent fiduciary duties to both the corporation and its shareholders, the typical tippee has no such relationships.[14] In view of this absence, it has been unclear how a tippee acquires the *Cady, Roberts* duty to refrain from trading on inside information.

A

The SEC's position, as stated in its opinion in this case, is that a tippee "inherits" the *Cady, Roberts* obligation to shareholders whenever he receives inside information from an insider:

> "In tipping potential traders, Dirks breached a duty which he had assumed as a result of knowingly receiving confidential information from [Equity Funding] insiders. Tippees such as Dirks who receive non-public, material information from insiders become 'subject to the same duty as [the] insiders.' *Shapiro v. Merrill Lynch, Pierce, Fenner & Smith, Inc.* 495 F.2d 228, 237 (CA2 1974). *** 21 SEC Docket, at 1410, n. 42.

This view differs little from the view that we rejected as inconsistent with congressional intent in *Chiarella*.[15] ***

In effect, the SEC's theory of tippee liability in both cases appears rooted in the idea that the antifraud provisions require equal information among all traders. This conflicts with the principle set forth in *Chiarella* that only some persons, under some circumstances, will be barred from trading while in

---

14. Under certain circumstances, such as where corporate information is revealed legitimately to an underwriter, accountant, lawyer, or consultant working for the corporation, these outsiders may become fiduciaries of the shareholders. The basis for recognizing this fiduciary duty is not simply that such persons acquired nonpublic corporate information, but rather that they have entered into a special confidential relationship in the conduct of the business of the enterprise and are given access to information solely for corporate purposes. See *SEC v. Monarch Fund*, 608 F.2d 938, 942 (CA2 1979); *In re Investors Management Co.*, 44 SEC 633, 645 (1971); *In re Van Alystne, Noel & Co.*, 43 SEC 1080, 1084-1085 (1969); *In re Merrill Lynch, Pierce, Fenner & Smith, Inc.*, 43 SEC 933, 937 (1968); *Cady, Roberts*, 40 SEC, at 912. When such a person breaches his fiduciary relationship, he may be treated more properly as a tipper than a tippee. See *Shapiro v. Merrill Lynch, Pierce, Fenner & Smith, Inc.*, 495 F.2d 228, 237 (CA2 1974) (investment banker had access to material information when working on a proposed public offering for the corporation). For such a duty to be imposed, however, the corporation must expect the outsider to keep the disclosed nonpublic information confidential, and the relationship at least must imply such a duty.

15. Apparently, the SEC believes this case differs from *Chiarella* in that Dirks' receipt of inside information from Secrist, an insider, carried Secrist's duties with it, while Chiarella received the information without the direct involvement of an insider and thus inherited no duty to disclose or abstain. The SEC fails to explain, however, why the receipt of nonpublic information from an insider automatically carries with it the fiduciary duty of the insider. As we emphasized in *Chiarella*, mere possession of nonpublic information does not give rise to a duty to disclose or abstain; only a specific relationship does that. And we do not believe that the mere receipt of information from an insider creates such a special relationship between the tippee and the corporation's shareholders. ***

possession of material nonpublic information. *** We reaffirm today that "[a] duty [to disclose] arises from the relationship between parties ... and not merely from one's ability to acquire information because of his position in the market." [445 U.S.] at 232-233, n. 14.

Imposing a duty to disclose or abstain solely because a person knowingly receives material nonpublic information from an insider and trades on it could have an inhibiting influence on the role of market analysts, which the SEC itself recognizes is necessary to the preservation of a healthy market. It is commonplace for analysts to "ferret out and analyze information," 21 SEC, at 1406, and this often is done by meeting with and questioning corporate officers and others who are insiders. And information that the analysts obtain normally may be the basis for judgments as to the market worth of a corporation's securities. The analyst's judgment in this respect is made available in market letters or otherwise to clients of the firm. It is the nature of this type of information, and indeed of the markets themselves, that such information cannot be made simultaneously available to all of the corporation's stockholders or the public generally.

B

The conclusion that recipients of inside information do not invariably acquire a duty to disclose or abstain does not mean that such tippees always are free to trade on the information. The need for a ban on some tippee trading is clear. Not only are insiders forbidden by their fiduciary relationship from personally using undisclosed corporate information to their advantage, but they also may not give such information to an outsider for the same improper purpose of exploiting the information for their personal gain. Similarly, the transactions of those who knowingly participate with the fiduciary in such a breach are "as forbidden" as transactions "on behalf of the trustee himself." *Mosser v. Darrow*, 341 U.S. 267, 272 (1951). As the Court explained in *Mosser,* a contrary rule "would open up opportunities for devious dealings in the name of the others that the trustee could not conduct in his own." 341 U.S., at 271. Thus, the tippee's duty to disclose or abstain is derivative from that of the insider's duty. As we noted in *Chiarella,* "[t]he tippee's obligation has been viewed as arising from his role as a participant after the fact in the insider's breach of a fiduciary duty." [445 U.S.] at 230, n. 12.

Thus, some tippees must assume an insider's duty to the shareholders not because they receive inside information, but rather because it has been made available to them *improperly.* And for Rule 10b-5 purposes, the insider's disclosure is improper only where it would violate his *Cady, Roberts* duty. Thus, a tippee assumes a fiduciary duty to the shareholders of a corporation not to trade on material nonpublic information only when the insider has breached his fiduciary duty to the shareholders by disclosing the information to the tippee and the tippee knows or should know that there has been a breach. As Commissioner Smith perceptively observed in *In re Investors Mgmt. Co.:* "[T]ippee responsibility must be related back to insider responsibility by a necessary finding that the tippee knew the information was given to him in breach of a duty by a person having a special relationship to the issuer not to disclose the information...." [44 SEC] at 651 (concurring in the result). Tipping thus properly is viewed only as a means of indirectly violating the *Cady, Roberts* disclose-or-abstain rule.

C

In determining whether a tippee is under an obligation to disclose or abstain, it thus is necessary to determine whether the insider's "tip" constituted a breach of the insider's fiduciary duty. All disclosures of confidential corporate information are not inconsistent with the duty insiders owe to shareholders. In contrast to the extraordinary facts of this case, the more typical situation in which there will be a question whether disclosure violates the insider's *Cady, Roberts* duty is when insiders disclose information to analysts. In some situations, the insider will act consistently with his fiduciary duty to shareholders, and yet release of the information may affect the market. For example, it may not be clear—either to the corporate insider or to the recipient analyst—whether the information will be viewed as material nonpublic information. Corporate officials may mistakenly think the information already has been disclosed or that it is not material enough to affect the market. Whether disclosure is a breach of duty therefore depends in large part on the purpose of the disclosure. This standard was identified by the SEC itself in *Cady, Roberts:* a purpose of the securities laws was to eliminate "use of inside information for personal advantage." 40 SEC, at 912, n. 15. Thus, the test is whether the insider personally will benefit, directly or indirectly, from his disclosure. Absent some personal gain, there has been no breach of duty to stockholders. And absent a breach by the insider, there is no derivative breach. As Commissioner Smith stated in *Investors Management Co.:* "It is important in this type of case to focus on policing insiders and what they do ... rather than on policing information *per se* and its possession...." 44 SEC, at 648 (concurring in the result).

The SEC argues that, if inside-trading liability does not exist when the information is transmitted for a proper purpose but is used for trading, it would be a rare situation when the parties could not fabricate some ostensibly legitimate business justification for transmitting the information. We think the SEC is unduly concerned. In determining whether the insider's purpose in making a particular disclosure is fraudulent, the SEC and the courts are not required to read the parties' minds. Scienter in some cases is relevant in determining whether the tipper has violated his *Cady, Roberts* duty. But to determine whether the disclosure itself "deceive[s], manipulate[s], or defraud[s]" shareholders, *Aaron v. SEC*, 446 U.S. 680, 686 (1980), the initial inquiry is whether there has been a breach of duty by the insider. This requires courts to focus on objective criteria, *i.e.*, whether the insider receives a direct or indirect personal benefit from the disclosure, such as a pecuniary gain or a reputational benefit that will translate into future earnings. Cf. Brudney, Insiders, Outsiders, and Informational Advantages Under the Federal Securities Laws, 93 Harv. L. Rev. 324, 348 (1979) ("The theory ... is that the insider, by giving the information out selectively, is in effect selling the information to its recipient for cash, reciprocal information, or other things of value for himself...."). There are objective facts and circumstances that often justify such an inference. For example, there may be a relationship between the insider and the recipient that suggests a *quid pro quo* from the latter, or an intention to benefit the particular recipient. The elements of fiduciary duty and exploitation of nonpublic information also exist when an insider makes a gift of confidential information to a trading relative or friend. The tip and trade resemble trading by the insider himself followed by a gift of the profits to the recipient.

Determining whether an insider personally benefits from a particular disclosure, a question of fact, will not always be easy for courts. But it is essential, we think, to have a guiding principle for those whose daily activities must be limited and instructed by the SEC's inside-trading rules, and we believe that there must be a breach of the insider's fiduciary duty before the tippee inherits the duty to disclose or abstain. In contrast, the rule adopted by the SEC in this case would have no limiting principle.

IV

Under the inside-trading and tipping rules set forth above, we find that there was no actionable violation by Dirks. It is undisputed that Dirks himself was a stranger to Equity Funding, with no pre-existing fiduciary duty to its shareholders. He took no action, directly or indirectly, that induced the shareholders or officers of Equity Funding to repose trust or confidence in him. There was no expectation by Dirks' sources that he would keep their information in confidence. Nor did Dirks misappropriate or illegally obtain the information about Equity Funding. Unless the insiders breached their *Cady, Roberts* duty to shareholders in disclosing the nonpublic information to Dirks, he breached no duty when he passed it on to investors as well as to the Wall Street Journal.

It is clear that neither Secrist nor the other Equity Funding employees violated their *Cady, Roberts* duty to the corporation's shareholders by providing information to Dirks. The tippers received no monetary or personal benefit for revealing Equity Funding's secrets, nor was their purpose to make a gift of valuable information to Dirks. As the facts of this case clearly indicate, the tippers were motivated by a desire to expose the fraud. In the absence of a breach of duty to shareholders by the insiders, there was no derivative breach by Dirks. Dirks therefore could not have been "a participant after the fact in [an] insider's breach of a fiduciary duty." *Chiarella*, 445 U.S., at 230, n. 12.

V

We conclude that Dirks, in the circumstances of this case, had no duty to abstain from use of the inside information that he obtained. The judgment of the Court of Appeals therefore is reversed.

JUSTICE BLACKMUN, WITH WHOM JUSTICES BRENNAN AND MARSHALL JOIN, DISSENTING:

The Court today takes still another step to limit the protections provided investors by § 10(b) of the Securities Exchange Act of 1934. See *Chiarella v. United States*, 445 U.S. 222, 246 (1980) (dissenting opinion). The device employed in this case engrafts a special motivational requirement on the fiduciary duty doctrine. This innovation excuses a knowing and intentional violation of an insider's duty to shareholders if the insider does not act from a motive of personal gain. Even on the extraordinary facts of this case, such an innovation is not justified. ***

No one questions that Secrist himself could not trade on his inside information to the disadvantage of uninformed shareholders and purchasers of Equity Funding securities. Unlike the printer in *Chiarella,* Secrist stood in a fiduciary relationship with these shareholders. As the Court states, corporate insiders have an affirmative duty of disclosure when trading with shareholders of the corporation. See *Chiarella*, 445 U.S. at 227. This duty extends as well to purchasers of the corporation's securities. Id., at 227, n. 8.

The Court also acknowledges that Secrist could not do by proxy what he was prohibited from doing personally. *Mosser v. Darrow*, 341 U.S. 267, 272 (1951). But this is precisely what Secrist did. Secrist used Dirks to disseminate information to Dirks' clients, who in turn dumped stock on unknowing purchasers. Secrist thus intended Dirks to injure the purchasers of Equity Funding securities to whom Secrist had a duty to disclose. ***

The Court holds, however, that Dirks is not liable because Secrist did not violate his duty; according to the Court, this is so because Secrist did not have the improper purpose of personal gain. In so doing, the Court imposes a new, subjective limitation on the scope of the duty owed by insiders to shareholders. The novelty of this limitation is reflected in the Court's lack of support for it.

The insider's duty is owed directly to the corporation's shareholders. See Langevoort, Insider Trading and the Fiduciary Principle: A Post-*Chiarella* Restatement, 70 Calif. L. Rev. 1, 5 (1982). As *Chiarella* recognized, it is based on the relationship of trust and confidence between the insider and the shareholder. That relationship assures the shareholder that the insider may not take actions that will harm him unfairly. The affirmative duty of disclosure protects against this injury. ***

The fact that the insider himself does not benefit from the breach does not eradicate the shareholder's injury. Cf. Restatement (Second) of Trusts § 205, Comments c and d (1959) (trustee liable for acts causing diminution of value of trust); 3 A. Scott, Law of Trusts § 205, p. 1665 (1967) (trustee liable for any losses to trust caused by his breach). It makes no difference to the shareholder whether the corporate insider gained or intended to gain personally from the transaction; the shareholder still has lost because of the insider's misuse of nonpublic information. The duty is addressed not to the insider's motives, but to his actions and their consequences on the shareholder. Personal gain is not an element of the breach of this duty.

This conclusion is borne out by the Court's decision in *Mosser v. Darrow*, 341 U.S. 267 (1951). There, the Court faced an analogous situation: a reorganization trustee engaged two employee-promoters of subsidiaries of the companies being reorganized to provide services that the trustee considered to be essential to the successful operation of the trust. In order to secure their services, the trustee expressly agreed with the employees that they could continue to trade in the securities of the subsidiaries. The employees then turned their inside position into substantial profits at the expense both of the trust and of other holders of the companies' securities.

The Court acknowledged that the trustee neither intended to nor did in actual fact benefit from this arrangement; his motives were completely selfless and devoted to the companies. [341 U.S.], at 275. The Court, nevertheless, found the trustee liable to the estate for the activities of the employees he authorized. The Court described the trustee's defalcation as "a willful and deliberate setting up of an interest in employees adverse to that of the trust." Id., at 272. The breach did not depend on the trustee's personal gain, and his motives in violating his duty were irrelevant; like Secrist, the trustee intended that others would abuse the inside information for their personal gain.

As *Mosser* demonstrates, the breach consists in taking action disadvantageous to the person to whom one owes a duty. In this case, Secrist owed a duty to purchasers of Equity Funding shares. The Court's addition of the bad-purpose element to a breach of fiduciary duty claim is flatly inconsistent with the principle of *Mosser*. I do not join this limitation of the scope of an insider's fiduciary duty to shareholders. ***

The improper-purpose requirement not only has no basis in law, but it rests implicitly on a policy that I cannot accept. The Court justifies Secrist's and Dirks' action because the general benefit derived from the violation of Secrist's duty to shareholders outweighed the harm caused to those shareholders—in other words, because the end justified the means. Under this view, the benefit conferred on society by Secrist's and Dirks' activities may be paid for with the losses caused to shareholders trading with Dirks' clients.

Although Secrist's general motive to expose the Equity Funding fraud was laudable, the means he chose were not. Moreover, even assuming that Dirks played a substantial role in exposing the fraud, he and his clients should not profit from the information they obtained from Secrist. *** As a citizen, Dirks had at least an ethical obligation to report the information to the proper authorities. The Court's holding is deficient in policy terms not because it fails to create a legal norm out of that ethical norm, but because it actually rewards Dirks for his aiding and abetting.

Dirks and Secrist were under a duty to disclose the information or to refrain from trading on it. I agree that disclosure in this case would have been difficult. I also recognize that the SEC seemingly has been less than helpful in its view of the nature of disclosure necessary to satisfy the disclose-or-refrain duty. The Commission tells persons with inside information that they cannot trade on that information unless they disclose; it refuses, however, to tell them how to disclose. See *In re Faberge, Inc.*, 45 SEC 249, 256 (1973) (disclosure requires public release through public media designed to reach investing public generally). This seems to be a less than sensible policy, which it is incumbent on the Commission to correct. The Court, however, has no authority to remedy the problem by opening a hole in the congressionally mandated prohibition on insider trading, thus rewarding such trading.

In my view, Secrist violated his duty to Equity Funding shareholders by transmitting material nonpublic information to Dirks with the intention that Dirks would cause his clients to trade on that information. Dirks, therefore, was under a duty to make the information publicly available or to refrain from actions that he knew would lead to trading. Because Dirks caused his clients to trade, he violated § 10(b) and Rule 10b-5. Any other result is a disservice to this country's attempt to provide fair and efficient capital markets. I dissent.

## *NOTES AND QUESTIONS*

***1. The "Personal Benefit" Test.*** If a corporate officer breaches her company's well-delineated policy of confidentiality by sharing confidential information with a friend, and if her friend is aware of that breach, should it matter for purposes of Rule 10b-5 liability whether the insider personally benefitted from the breach of this duty?

***2. Tippees and Fiduciary Duties.*** As the *Dirks* Court recognized, the typical tippee stands as a complete stranger to the shareholders of the corporations whose securities are being purchased on the basis of material nonpublic information. Yet the Court extends the classical theory of insider trading to cover these clear outsiders. What policy reasons does the Court provide to justify this departure from the common law?

***3. Identifying Temporary or Constructive Insiders.*** In footnote 14, the *Dirks* Court points out that the "disclose or abstain" rule applies as well to temporary insiders of a corporation, such as attorneys, accountants, and investment bankers, who are provided with confidential corporate information. In the Court's view, these "outsiders may become fiduciaries of the shareholders." Yet other than noting that "the relationship itself must at least imply such a duty [to keep the disclosed information confidential]," *Dirks* does little to shed light on how else one attains this "special status." Lower courts must therefore articulate their own standards. See, e.g., *SEC v. Ingram*, 694 F. Supp. 1437 (C.D. Cal. 1988) (temporary insider status accorded to stockbroker who had assisted the company with finding a merger partner, and who had been invited to attended pre-merger negotiations where there was an absolute expectation of confidentiality); *SEC v. Mayhew*, 916 F. Supp. 123, 129 (D. Conn. 1995) (concluding that SEC had failed to establish that a business consultant was the "functional equivalent of a fiduciary") aff'd without discussion of this issue, 121 F.3d 44 (2d Cir. 1997). *Mayhew* involved a luncheon conversation in which a company executive revealed to a human resources consultant that his company was discussing merger possibilities. The court noted that "there was never any formal agreement" between the consultant's firm and the takeover target, and emphasized that "the fact that [the company executive] expected [the consultant] to keep the substance of the lunch conversation confidential did not, in itself, give rise to a fiduciary duty." Id. at 129-30. Weighing the testimony of both the consultant and the company executive, the court concluded that the consultant's "ambiguous and ambivalent role at the time [of the] lunch when he obtained the insider information was much more akin to the proverbial 'old boys networking' *** lacking indicia of de facto control and dominance resulting from the confidence imposed." Id. at 130. Do you agree?

***4. Securities Analysts and the Problem of Selective Disclosure.*** Issuers and their corporate officials regularly interact with securities analysts, often providing them with publicly available information through telephone conversations, letters, in-person meetings, and other types of communications. In addition, to maintain an active level of interest in their company's securities, corporate officials are often tempted to share with analysts certain information that has yet to be released to the public. This practice of "selective disclosure" may create potential insider trading problems for securities issuers, their officials, and the analysts who cover the company. That is, such selective disclosure raises questions as to whether the issuer and its officials can be characterized as "tippers," and whether the analysts can be characterized as "tippees," engaged in acts and practices prohibited by Rule 10b-5. Such questions, though, are complicated by *Dirks*'s requirement that for tippee liability to be present, the tipper must have acted for a personal benefit.

If a company's CEO informs an analyst of lower than expected quarterly returns, and if that CEO shares this information "to protect and enhance his reputation," does the CEO act with the requisite motivation to trigger tipper liability under *Dirks*? See *SEC v. Stevens*, 48 SEC Docket 739 (Mar. 19, 1991) (consent order sanctioning CEO of Ultrasystems Corporation). Assuming that a "reputational benefit" constitutes sufficient motivation, how likely is that the SEC could demonstrate at trial that this was, in fact, a CEO's motivation? What if a CEO acted solely to bolster favorable publicity about his company? Could an analyst share the negative earnings with his clients and advise them to sell off their shares in the company? Could an analyst sell short the company's stock?

The SEC has taken the position that the practice of selective disclosure "leads to a loss of investor confidence in the integrity of our capital markets." See Selective Disclosure and Insider Trading, Exchange Act Rel. No. 43154, 2000 WL 1201556 at *2 (Aug. 15, 2000). Do you agree?

***5. Regulation FD.*** Regulation FD (which took effect in October 2000) is predicated on the belief that all investors should have access to an issuer's material disclosures at the same time. Regulation FD does not characterize the practice of selective disclosure as a fraudulent act or device under Exchange Act Section 10(b) and Rule 10b-5. Rather, Regulation FD was promulgated pursuant to Exchange Act Section 13(a), which empowers the SEC to regulate the disclosure practices of reporting companies. Although Regulation FD's provisions are somewhat lengthy, it sets forth a basic rule that requires that whenever:

> (1) an issuer, or person acting on its behalf,
>
> (2) discloses material nonpublic information,
>
> (3) to certain enumerated persons (in general, securities market professionals or holders of the issuer's securities who may well trade on the basis of the information),
>
> (4) the issuer must make public disclosure of that same information: (a) simultaneously (for intentional disclosures), or (b) "promptly" (for non-intentional disclosures).

Id. at *6-7 (summarizing Rule 100 of Regulation FD). Accordingly, while Regulation FD does not automatically require covered issuers to promptly disclose all material events as they occur, it does in fact require that when an issuer chooses to disclose material nonpublic information to a person covered by the regulation, "it must do so in a manner that provides general public disclosure, rather than through selective disclosure" to a favored few. Selective Disclosure Release, supra, 2000 WL 1201556 at *7.

If you were a member of the Commission, would you have voted to enact Regulation FD? Why or why not?

### 3. *The Misappropriation Theory*

The government raised the misappropriation theory in its brief to the Supreme Court in *Chiarella*, where it argued that Chiarella had "committed fraud against both the acquiring corporations whose information he converted and the investors who sold him securities in ignorance of forthcoming market events of critical importance." Brief for the Petitioner at 24, *Chiarella v. U.S.*, 445 U.S. 222 (1980) (No. 78-1202). That is, the government contended that Chiarella's "secret conversion of confidential information operated as a fraud on the corporation that entrusted him with that information" and also that his "purchase of securities based on material non-public information obtained by misappropriation constituted fraud on the sellers of those securities." Id. at 28, 38-39. Yet the *Chiarella* majority ruled on the validity of neither version of the misappropriation theory because, in its view, neither had been presented to the jury. Misappropriation theories were, however, discussed at length by a total of five Justices in separate concurring or dissenting opinions.

Chief Justice Burger and Justices Brennan, Blackmun, and Marshall all agreed that Rule 10b-5 liability would be triggered by any person who purchased or sold securities on the basis of material nonpublic information that was improperly obtained or converted for a personal benefit. Thus, four Justices in *Chiarella* endorsed a broad version of the misappropriation theory that recognized a general disclosure obligation owed to any investors with whom a misappropriator trades: "a person who has misappropriated nonpublic information has an absolute duty to disclose that information or to refrain from trading." *Chiarella v. United States*, 445 U.S. 222, 240 (1980) (Burger, J. dissenting). A fifth member of the Court, Justice Stevens, indicated that while he did not accept the existence of a general duty owed to all securities investors on the other side of Chiarella's transactions, "[r]espectable arguments could be made" that Chiarella's actions had defrauded the acquiring companies that had entrusted his employer with confidential tender offer information, and that this fraud occurred " 'in connection with the purchase or sale of any security.' " Justice Stevens's concurring opinion therefore raised the possibility of a narrower version of the misappropriation theory premised on a "fraud on the source" of the misappropriated information. Id. at 238 (Stevens, J., concurring). Yet he thought the Court wise for "leav[ing] the resolution of this issue for another day." Id.

Encouraged by its positive reception from the concurring and dissenting Justices in *Chiarella*, the SEC and the DOJ advanced the misappropriation theory of insider trading liability in instances where the government wished to pursue Section 10(b) and Rule 10b-5 actions against individuals who did not owe fiduciary duties to the shareholders of the companies in which securities transactions had been made. Specifically, the government began to emphasize the argument set forth by Justice Stevens in *Chiarella*, that trading securities based on nonpublic information obtained in breach of a pre-existing duty of confidentiality defrauded the source of the information in connection with the purchase or sale of securities. And the Second Circuit was quick to give this theory a warm embrace. See, e.g., *United States v. Newman*, 664 F.2d 12 (2d Cir. 1981) (affirming criminal conviction in misappropriation case against investment bank employees); *SEC v. Materia*, 745 F.2d 197, 202 (2d Cir. 1984) (affirming injunction and disgorgement in a case against a financial printer involving facts almost identical to those of *Chiarella*); *SEC v. Musella*, 578 F. Supp. 425, 439 (S.D.N.Y. 1984) (enjoining tippees of an administrative staff employee of a law firm who purchased shares of a companies targeted for takeover by the law firm's clients); and *United States v. Carpenter*, 791 F.2d 1024 (2d Cir. 1986), aff'd by an equally divided Court, 484 U.S. 19 (1987) (affirming conviction of Wall Street Journal reporter who had traded on the basis of information in a soon to be released column). Other circuits soon followed. See, e.g., *Rothberg v. Rosenbloom*, 771 F.2d 818 (3d Cir. 1985) (tippee who traded on the basis of confidential merger information obtained from corporate official), rev'd on other grounds after remand, 808 F.2d 252 (3d Cir. 1986); *SEC v. Cherif*, 933 F.2d 403, 410 (7th Cir. 1991) (individual who broke into his former place of employment to steal nonpublic information about his former employer's clients and then used that information to trade securities); *SEC v. Clark*, 915 F.2d 439 (9th Cir. 1990) (employee who tipped and traded in the securities of a company he knew to be a takeover target of his employer).

The unanimity among the federal circuits dissipated in 1995 when the Fourth Circuit decided *United States v. Bryan*, 58 F.3d 933 (4th Cir. 1995) (overturning conviction of state lottery official who had purchased the stock of companies that were slated to receive contracts from the Virginia Lottery Commission). The Eighth Circuit also rejected the misappropriation theory the following year in *United States v. O'Hagan*, 92 F.3d 612, 620 (8th Cir. 1996). The Supreme Court granted certiorari to resolve the split in the federal circuits.

## UNITED STATES v. O'HAGAN

521 U.S. 642 (1997)

JUSTICE GINSBURG:

I

Respondent James Herman O'Hagan was a partner in the law firm of Dorsey & Whitney in Minneapolis, Minnesota. In July 1988, Grand Metropolitan PLC (Grand Met), a company based in London, England, retained Dorsey & Whitney as local counsel to represent Grand Met regarding a potential tender offer for the common stock of the Pillsbury Company, headquartered in Minneapolis. Both Grand Met and Dorsey & Whitney took precautions to protect the confidentiality of Grand Met's tender offer plans. O'Hagan did no work on the Grand Met representation. Dorsey & Whitney withdrew from representing Grand Met on September 9, 1988. Less than a month later, on October 4, 1988, Grand Met publicly announced its tender offer for Pillsbury stock.

On August 18, 1988, while Dorsey & Whitney was still representing Grand Met, O'Hagan began purchasing call options for Pillsbury stock. Each option gave him the right to purchase 100 shares of Pillsbury stock by a specified date in September 1988. Later in August and in September, O'Hagan made additional purchases of Pillsbury call options. By the end of September, he owned 2,500 unexpired Pillsbury options, apparently more than any other individual investor. O'Hagan also purchased, in September 1988, some 5,000 shares of Pillsbury common stock, at a price just under $39 per share. When Grand Met announced its tender offer in October, the price of Pillsbury stock rose to nearly $60 per share. O'Hagan then sold his Pillsbury call options and common stock, making a profit of more than $4.3 million.

The Securities and Exchange Commission initiated an investigation into O'Hagan's transactions, culminating in a 57-count indictment. The indictment alleged that O'Hagan defrauded his law firm and its client, Grand Met, by using for his own trading purposes material, nonpublic information regarding Grand Met's planned tender offer. According to the indictment, O'Hagan used the profits he gained through this trading to conceal his previous embezzlement and conversion of unrelated client trust funds. O'Hagan was charged with 20 counts of mail fraud, in violation of 18 U.S.C. § 1341; 17 counts of securities fraud, in violation of § 10(b) of the Securities Exchange Act of 1934 and SEC Rule 10b-5; 17 counts of fraudulent trading in connection with a tender offer, in violation of § 14(e) of the Exchange Act and SEC Rule 14e-3(a); and 3 counts of violating federal money laundering statutes. A jury convicted O'Hagan on all 57 counts, and he was sentenced to a 41-month term of imprisonment.

A divided panel of the Court of Appeals for the Eighth Circuit reversed all of O'Hagan's convictions. 92 F.3d 612 (1996). ***

II

We address first the Court of Appeals' reversal of O'Hagan's convictions under § 10(b) and Rule 10b-5. Following the Fourth Circuit's lead, see *United States v. Bryan*, 58 F.3d 933, 943-959 (1995), the Eighth Circuit rejected the misappropriation theory as a basis for § 10(b) liability. We hold, in accord with several other Courts of Appeals, that criminal liability under § 10(b) may be predicated on the misappropriation theory.[4]

A

***Liability under Rule 10b-5, our precedent indicates, does not extend beyond conduct encompassed by § 10(b)'s prohibition. See *Ernst & Ernst v. Hochfelder*, 425 U.S. 185, 214 (1976) (scope of Rule 10b-5 cannot exceed power Congress granted Commission under § 10(b)); see also *Central Bank of Denver, N.A. v. First Interstate Bank of Denver, N. A.*, 511 U.S. 164, 173 (1994) ("We have refused to allow [private] 10b-5 challenges to conduct not prohibited by the text of the statute.").

Under the "traditional" or "classical theory" of insider trading liability, § 10(b) and Rule 10b-5 are violated when a corporate insider trades in the securities of his corporation on the basis of material, nonpublic information. Trading on such information qualifies as a "deceptive device" under § 10(b), we have affirmed, because "a relationship of trust and confidence [exists] between the shareholders of a corporation and those insiders who have obtained confidential information by reason of their position with that corporation."

---

4. Twice before we have been presented with the question whether criminal liability for violation of § 10(b) may be based on a misappropriation theory. In *Chiarella v. United States*, 445 U.S. 222, 235-237 (1980), the jury had received no misappropriation theory instructions, so we declined to address the question. In *Carpenter v. United States*, 484 U.S. 19, 24 (1987), the Court divided evenly on whether, under the circumstances of that case, convictions resting on the misappropriation theory should be affirmed.

*Chiarella v. United States*, 445 U.S. 222, 228 (1980). That relationship, we recognized, "gives rise to a duty to disclose [or to abstain from trading] because of the 'necessity of preventing a corporate insider from ... tak[ing] unfair advantage of ... uninformed ... stockholders.'" Id., at 228-229. The classical theory applies not only to officers, directors, and other permanent insiders of a corporation, but also to attorneys, accountants, consultants, and others who temporarily become fiduciaries of a corporation. See *Dirks v. SEC*, 463 U.S. 646, 655, n. 14 (1983).

The "misappropriation theory" holds that a person commits fraud "in connection with" a securities transaction, and thereby violates § 10(b) and Rule 10b-5, when he misappropriates confidential information for securities trading purposes, in breach of a duty owed to the source of the information. Under this theory, a fiduciary's undisclosed, self-serving use of a principal's information to purchase or sell securities, in breach of a duty of loyalty and confidentiality, defrauds the principal of the exclusive use of that information. In lieu of premising liability on a fiduciary relationship between company insider and purchaser or seller of the company's stock, the misappropriation theory premises liability on a fiduciary-turned-trader's deception of those who entrusted him with access to confidential information.

The two theories are complementary, each addressing efforts to capitalize on nonpublic information through the purchase or sale of securities. The classical theory targets a corporate insider's breach of duty to shareholders with whom the insider transacts; the misappropriation theory outlaws trading on the basis of nonpublic information by a corporate "outsider" in breach of a duty owed not to a trading party, but to the source of the information. The misappropriation theory is thus designed to "protec[t] the integrity of the securities markets against abuses by 'outsiders' to a corporation who have access to confidential information that will affect th[e] corporation's security price when revealed, but who owe no fiduciary or other duty to that corporation's shareholders." [Brief for the United States at 14].

In this case, the indictment alleged that O'Hagan, in breach of a duty of trust and confidence he owed to his law firm, Dorsey & Whitney, and to its client, Grand Met, traded on the basis of nonpublic information regarding Grand Met's planned tender offer for Pillsbury common stock. This conduct, the Government charged, constituted a fraudulent device in connection with the purchase and sale of securities.

B

We agree with the Government that misappropriation, as just defined, satisfies § 10(b)'s requirement that chargeable conduct involve a "deceptive device or contrivance" used "in connection with" the purchase or sale of securities. We observe, first, that misappropriators, as the Government describes them, deal in deception. A fiduciary who "[pretends] loyalty to the principal while secretly converting the principal's information for personal gain," Brief for United States 17, "dupes" or defrauds the principal. See Aldave, Misappropriation: A General Theory of Liability for Trading on Nonpublic Information, 13 Hofstra L. Rev. 101, 119 (1984).

We addressed fraud of the same species in *Carpenter v. United States*, 484 U.S. 19 (1987), which involved the mail fraud statute's proscription of "any scheme or artifice to defraud." Affirming convictions under that statute, we said in *Carpenter* that an employee's undertaking not to reveal his employer's confidential information "became a sham" when the employee provided the information to his co-conspirators in a scheme to obtain trading profits. A company's confidential information, we recognized in *Carpenter*, qualifies as property to which the company has a right of exclusive use. The undisclosed misappropriation of such information, in violation of a fiduciary duty, the Court said in *Carpenter*, constitutes fraud akin to embezzlement—"'the fraudulent appropriation to one's own use of the money or goods entrusted to one's care by another.'" Id., at 27. *Carpenter's* discussion of the fraudulent misuse of confidential information, the Government notes, "is a particularly apt source of guidance here, because [the mail fraud statute] (like Section 10(b)) has long been held to require deception, not merely the breach of a fiduciary duty." Brief for United States 18, n. 9.

Deception through nondisclosure is central to the theory of liability for which the Government seeks recognition. As counsel for the Government stated in explanation of the theory at oral argument: "To satisfy the common law rule that a trustee may not use the property that [has] been entrusted [to] him, there would have to be consent. To satisfy the requirement of the Securities Act that there be no deception, there would only have to be disclosure." Tr. of Oral Arg. 12; see generally Restatement (Second) of Agency §§ 390, 395 (1958) (agent's disclosure obligation regarding use of confidential information).[6]

The misappropriation theory advanced by the Government is consistent with *Santa Fe Industries, Inc. v. Green*, 430 U.S. 462 (1977), a decision underscoring that § 10(b) is not an all-purpose breach of fiduciary duty ban; rather, it trains on conduct involving manipulation or deception. See id., at 473-476. In contrast to the Government's allegations in this case, in *Santa Fe Industries*, all pertinent facts were disclosed by the persons charged with violating § 10(b) and Rule 10b-5; therefore, there was no deception through nondisclosure to which liability under those provisions could attach. Similarly, full disclosure forecloses liability under the misappropriation theory: Because the deception essential to the misappropriation theory involves feigning fidelity to the source of information, if the fiduciary discloses to the source that he plans to trade on the nonpublic information, there is no "deceptive device" and thus no § 10(b) violation—although the fiduciary-turned-trader may remain liable under state law for breach of a duty of loyalty.

---

6. Under the misappropriation theory urged in this case, the disclosure obligation runs to the source of the information, here, Dorsey & Whitney and Grand Met. Chief Justice Burger, dissenting in *Chiarella*, advanced a broader reading of § 10(b) and Rule 10b-5; the disclosure obligation, as he envisioned it, ran to those with whom the misappropriator trades. 445 U.S., at 240 ("a person who has misappropriated nonpublic information has an absolute duty to disclose that information or to refrain from trading"); see also id., at 243, n. 4. The Government does not propose that we adopt a misappropriation theory of that breadth.

We turn next to the § 10(b) requirement that the misappropriator's deceptive use of information be "in connection with the purchase or sale of [a] security." This element is satisfied because the fiduciary's fraud is consummated, not when the fiduciary gains the confidential information, but when, without disclosure to his principal, he uses the information to purchase or sell securities. The securities transaction and the breach of duty thus coincide. This is so even though the person or entity defrauded is not the other party to the trade, but is, instead, the source of the nonpublic information. See Aldave, 13 Hofstra L.Rev., at 120 ("a fraud or deceit can be practiced on one person, with resultant harm to another person or group of persons"). A misappropriator who trades on the basis of material, nonpublic information, in short, gains his advantageous market position through deception; he deceives the source of the information and simultaneously harms members of the investing public.

The misappropriation theory targets information of a sort that misappropriators ordinarily capitalize upon to gain no-risk profits through the purchase or sale of securities. Should a misappropriator put such information to other use, the statute's prohibition would not be implicated. The theory does not catch all conceivable forms of fraud involving confidential information; rather, it catches fraudulent means of capitalizing on such information through securities transactions.

The Government notes another limitation on the forms of fraud § 10(b) reaches: "The misappropriation theory would not ... apply to a case in which a person defrauded a bank into giving him a loan or embezzled cash from another, and then used the proceeds of the misdeed to purchase securities." Brief for United States 24, n. 13. In such a case, the Government states, "the proceeds would have value to the malefactor apart from their use in a securities transaction, and the fraud would be complete as soon as the money was obtained." In other words, money can buy, if not anything, then at least many things; its misappropriation may thus be viewed as sufficiently detached from a subsequent securities transaction that § 10(b)'s "in connection with" requirement would not be met.

Justice Thomas' charge that the misappropriation theory is incoherent because information, like funds, can be put to multiple uses misses the point. The Exchange Act was enacted in part "to insure the maintenance of fair and honest markets," and there is no question that fraudulent uses of confidential information fall within § 10(b)'s prohibition if the fraud is "in connection with" a securities transaction. It is hardly remarkable that a rule suitably applied to the fraudulent uses of certain kinds of information would be stretched beyond reason were it applied to the fraudulent use of money.

Justice Thomas does catch the Government in overstatement. Observing that money can be used for all manner of purposes and purchases, the Government urges that confidential information of the kind at issue derives its value *only* from its utility in securities trading. See Brief for United States 10, 21. Substitute "ordinarily" for "only," and the Government is on the mark. ***

The misappropriation theory comports with § 10(b)'s language, which requires deception "in connection with the purchase or sale of any security," not deception of an identifiable purchaser or seller. The theory is also well tuned to an animating purpose of the Exchange Act: to insure honest securities markets and thereby promote investor confidence. See 45 Fed. Reg. 60412 (1980) (trading on misappropriated information "undermines the integrity of, and investor confidence in, the securities markets"). Although informational disparity is inevitable in the securities markets, investors likely would hesitate to venture their capital in a market where trading based on misappropriated nonpublic information is unchecked by law. An investor's informational disadvantage vis-a-vis a misappropriator with material, nonpublic information stems from contrivance, not luck; it is a disadvantage that cannot be overcome with research or skill. See Brudney, Insiders, Outsiders, and Informational Advantages Under the Federal Securities Laws, 93 Harv. L. Rev. 322, 356 (1979) ("If the market is thought to be systematically populated with ... transactors [trading on the basis of misappropriated information] some investors will refrain from dealing altogether, and others will incur costs to avoid dealing with such transactors or corruptly to overcome their unerodable informational advantages.")

In sum, considering the inhibiting impact on market participation of trading on misappropriated information, and the congressional purposes underlying § 10(b), it makes scant sense to hold a lawyer like O'Hagan a § 10(b) violator if he works for a law firm representing the target of a tender offer, but not if he works for a law firm representing the bidder. The text of the statute requires no such result. The misappropriation at issue here was properly made the subject of a § 10(b) charge because it meets the statutory requirement that there be "deceptive" conduct "in connection with" securities transactions. ***

Vital to our decision that criminal liability may be sustained under the misappropriation theory, we emphasize, are two sturdy safeguards Congress has provided regarding scienter. To establish a criminal violation of Rule 10b-5, the Government must prove that a person "willfully" violated the provision. [See Section 32 of the Exchange Act.] Furthermore, a defendant may not be imprisoned for violating Rule 10b-5 if he proves that he had no knowledge of the Rule. See ibid. O'Hagan's charge that the misappropriation theory is too indefinite to permit the imposition of criminal liability thus fails not only because the theory is limited to those who breach a recognized duty. In addition, the statute's "requirement of the presence of culpable intent as a necessary element of the offense does much to destroy any force in the argument that application of the [statute]" in circumstances such as O'Hagan's is unjust. *Boyce Motor Lines, Inc. v. United States*, 342 U.S. 337, 342 (1952). ***

III

*[The Court's discussion regarding the validity of Rule 14e-3(a) appears in Section C of this Chapter]*

IV

Based on its dispositions of the securities fraud convictions, the Court of Appeals also reversed O'Hagan's convictions for mail fraud. Reversal of the securities convictions, the Court of Appeals recognized, "d[id] not as a matter of law require that the mail fraud convictions likewise be reversed." Id., at 627 (citing *Carpenter*, 484 U.S., at 24, in which this Court unanimously affirmed mail and wire fraud convictions based on the same conduct that evenly divided the Court on the defendants' securities fraud convictions). But in this case, the Court of Appeals said, the indictment was so structured that the mail fraud charges could not be disassociated from the securities fraud charges, and absent any securities fraud, "there was no fraud upon which to base the mail fraud charges."

The United States urges that the Court of Appeals' position is irreconcilable with *Carpenter*: Just as in *Carpenter*, so here, the "mail fraud charges are independent of [the] securities fraud charges, even [though] both rest on the same set of facts." Brief for United States 46-47. We need not linger over this matter, for our rulings on the securities fraud issues require that we reverse the Court of Appeals judgment on the mail fraud counts as well. ***

The judgment of the Court of Appeals for the Eighth Circuit is reversed, and the case is remanded for further proceedings consistent with this opinion.

JUSTICE SCALIA, CONCURRING IN PART AND DISSENTING IN PART:

I join Parts I, III, and IV of the Court's opinion. I do not agree, however, with Part II of the Court's opinion, containing its analysis of respondent's convictions under § 10(b) and Rule 10b-5. ***

While the Court's explanation of the scope of § 10(b) and Rule 10b-5 would be entirely reasonable in some other context, it does not seem to accord with the principle of lenity we apply to criminal statutes (which cannot be mitigated here by the Rule, which is no less ambiguous than the statute). See *Reno v. Koray*, 515 U.S. 50, 64-65 (1995) (explaining circumstances in which rule of lenity applies); *United States v. Bass*, 404 U.S. 336, 347-348 (1971) (discussing policies underlying rule of lenity). In light of that principle, it seems to me that the unelaborated statutory language: "[t]o use or employ, in connection with the purchase or sale of any security ... any manipulative or deceptive device or contrivance," § 10(b), must be construed to require the manipulation or deception of a party to a securities transaction.

JUSTICE THOMAS, WITH WHOM CHIEF JUSTICE REHNQUIST JOINS, CONCURRING IN THE JUDGMENT IN PART AND DISSENTING IN PART:

Today the majority upholds respondent's convictions for violating § 10(b) of the Securities Exchange Act of 1934, and Rule 10b-5 promulgated thereunder, based upon the Securities and Exchange Commission's "misappropriation theory." Central to the majority's holding is the need to interpret § 10(b)'s requirement that a deceptive device be "use[d] or employ[ed], in connection with the purchase or sale of any security." Because the Commission's misappropriation theory fails to provide a coherent and consistent interpretation of this essential requirement for liability under § 10(b), I dissent. ***

I do not take issue with the majority's determination that the undisclosed misappropriation of confidential information by a fiduciary can constitute a "deceptive device" within the meaning of § 10(b). Nondisclosure where there is a pre-existing duty to disclose satisfies our definitions of fraud and deceit for purposes of the securities laws. See *Chiarella v. United States*, 445 U.S. 222, 230 (1980).

Unlike the majority, however, I cannot accept the Commission's interpretation of when a deceptive device is "use[d] ... in connection with" a securities transaction. ***

The Commission's construction of the relevant language in § 10(b), and the incoherence of that construction, become evident as the majority attempts to describe why the fraudulent theft of information falls under the Commission's misappropriation theory, but the fraudulent theft of money does not. The majority correctly notes that confidential information "qualifies as property to which the company has a right of exclusive use." It then observes that the "undisclosed misappropriation of such information, in violation of a fiduciary duty, ... constitutes fraud akin to embezzlement—the fraudulent appropriation to one's own use of the money or goods entrusted to one's care by another." So far the majority's analogy to embezzlement is well taken, and adequately demonstrates that undisclosed misappropriation can be a fraud on the source of the information.

What the embezzlement analogy does not do, however, is explain how the relevant fraud is "use[d] or employ[ed], in connection with" a securities transaction. And when the majority seeks to distinguish the embezzlement of funds from the embezzlement of information, it becomes clear that neither the Commission nor the majority has a coherent theory regarding § 10(b)'s "in connection with" requirement.

Turning first to why embezzlement of information supposedly meets the "in connection with" requirement, the majority asserts that the requirement

> "is satisfied because the fiduciary's fraud is consummated, not when the fiduciary gains the confidential information, but when, without disclosure to his principal, he uses the information to purchase or sell securities. The securities transaction and the breach of duty thus coincide."

The majority later notes, with apparent approval, the Government's contention that the embezzlement of funds used to purchase securities would *not* fall within the misappropriation theory. The misappropriation of funds used for a securities transaction is not covered by its theory, the Government explains, because "the proceeds would have value to the malefactor apart from their use in a securities transaction, and the fraud would be complete as soon as the money was obtained." Brief for United States 24, n. 13; see ante (quoting Government's explanation).

Accepting the Government's description of the scope of its own theory, it becomes plain that the majority's explanation of how the misappropriation theory supposedly satisfies the "in connection with" requirement is incomplete. The touchstone required for an embezzlement to be "use[d] or employ[ed], in connection with" a securities transaction is not merely that it "coincide" with, or be consummated by, the transaction, but that it is *necessarily* and *only* consummated by the transaction. Where the property being embezzled has value "apart from [its] use in a securities transaction"—even though it is in fact being used in a securities transaction—the Government contends that there is no violation under the misappropriation theory.

My understanding of the Government's proffered theory of liability, and its construction of the "in connection with" requirement, is confirmed by the Government's explanation during oral argument:

> "[Court]: What if I appropriate some of my client's money in order to buy stock?.....
>
> "[Court]: Have I violated the securities laws?
>
> "[Counsel]: I do not think that you have.
>
> "[Court]: Why not? Isn't that in connection with the purchase of securit[ies] just as much as this one is?
>
> "[Counsel]: It's not just as much as this one is, because in this case it is the use of the information that enables the profits, pure and simple. There would be no opportunity to engage in profit—
>
> "[Court]: Same here. I didn't have the money. The only way I could buy this stock was to get the money. ...
>
> "[Counsel]: The difference ... is that once you have the money you can do anything you want with it. In a sense, the fraud is complete at that point, and then you go on and you can use the money to finance any number of other activities, but *the connection is far less close than in this case, where the only value of this information for personal profit for respondent was to take it and profit in the securities markets by trading on it. . . .*
>
> "[Court]: So what you're saying is, is in this case the misappropriation can only be of relevance, or is of substantial relevance, is with reference to the purchase of securities.
>
> "[Counsel]: Exactly.
>
> "[Court]: When you take the money out of the accounts you can go to the racetrack, or whatever.
>
> "[Counsel]: That's exactly right, and because of that difference, [there] can be no doubt that this kind of misappropriation of property is in connection with the purchase or sale of securities.
>
> "Other kinds of misappropriation of property may or may not, but this is a unique form of fraud, unique to the securities markets, in fact, because *the only way in which respondent could have profited through this information is by either trading on it or by tipping somebody else to enable their trades.*" Tr. of Oral Arg. 16-19 (emphases added).

As the above exchange demonstrates, the relevant distinction is not that the misappropriated information *was* used for a securities transaction (the money example met that test), but rather that it could *only* be used for such a transaction. See also id., at 6-7 (Government contention that the misappropriation theory satisfies "the requisite connection between the fraud and the securities trading, because it is *only* in the trading that the fraud is consummated" (emphasis added)); id., at 8 (same).

The Government's construction of the "in connection with" requirement—and its claim that such requirement precludes coverage of financial embezzlement—also demonstrates how the majority's described distinction of financial embezzlement is incomplete. Although the majority claims that the fraud in a financial embezzlement case is complete as soon as the money is obtained, and before the securities transaction is consummated, that is not uniformly true, and thus cannot be the Government's basis for claiming that such embezzlement does not violate the securities laws. It is not difficult to imagine an embezzlement of money that takes place via the mechanism of a securities transaction—for example where a broker is directed to purchase stock for a client and instead purchases such stock—using client funds—for his own account. The unauthorized (and presumably undisclosed) transaction is the very act that constitutes the embezzlement and the "securities transaction and the breach of duty thus coincide." What presumably distinguishes monetary embezzlement for the Government is thus that it is not *necessarily* coincident with a securities transaction, not that it *never* lacks such a "connection."

Once the Government's construction of the misappropriation theory is accurately described and accepted—along with its implied construction of § 10(b)'s "in connection with" language—that theory should no longer cover cases, such as this one, involving fraud on the source of information where the source has no connection with the other participant in a securities transaction. It seems obvious that the undisclosed misappropriation of confidential information is not necessarily consummated by a securities transaction. In this case, for example, upon learning of Grand Met's confidential takeover plans, O'Hagan could have done any number of things with the information: He could have sold it to a newspaper for publication; he could have given or sold the information to Pillsbury itself; or he could even have kept the information and used it solely for his personal amusement, perhaps in a fantasy stock trading game.

Any of these activities would have deprived Grand Met of its right to "exclusive use," of the information and, if undisclosed, would constitute "embezzlement" of Grand Met's informational property. Under *any* theory of liability, however, these activities would not violate § 10(b) and, according to the Commission's monetary embezzlement analogy, these possibilities are sufficient to preclude a violation under the misappropriation theory even where the informational property *was* used for securities trading. That O'Hagan actually did use the information to purchase securities is thus no more significant here than it is in the case of embezzling money used to purchase securities. In both cases the embezzler *could have* done something else with the property, and hence the Commission's necessary "connection" under the securities laws would not be met.[2] If the relevant test under the "in connection with" language is whether the fraudulent act is *necessarily* tied to a securities transaction, then the misappropriation of confidential information used to trade no more violates § 10(b) than does the misappropriation of funds used to trade. As the Commission concedes that the latter is not covered under its theory, I am at a loss to see how the same theory can coherently be applied to the former. ***

---

2. Indeed, even if O'Hagan or someone else thereafter used the information to trade, the misappropriation would have been complete before the trade and there should be no § 10(b) liability. The most obvious real-world example of this scenario would be if O'Hagan had simply tipped someone else to the information. The mere act of passing the information along would have violated O'Hagan's fiduciary duty and, if undisclosed, would be an "embezzlement" of the confidential information, regardless of whether the tippee later traded on the information.

[T]he majority also points to various policy considerations underlying the securities laws, such as maintaining fair and honest markets, promoting investor confidence, and protecting the integrity of the securities markets. But the repeated reliance on such broad-sweeping legislative purposes reaches too far and is misleading in the context of the misappropriation theory. It reaches too far in that, regardless of the overarching purpose of the securities laws, it is not illegal to run afoul of the "purpose" of a statute, only its letter. The majority's approach is misleading in this case because it glosses over the fact that the supposed threat to fair and honest markets, investor confidence, and market integrity comes not from the supposed fraud in this case, but from the mere fact that the information used by O'Hagan was nonpublic.

As the majority concedes, because "the deception essential to the misappropriation theory involves feigning fidelity to the source of information, if the fiduciary discloses *to the source* that he plans to trade on the nonpublic information, there is no 'deceptive device' and thus no § 10(b) violation." Indeed, were the source expressly to authorize its agents to trade on the confidential information—as a perk or bonus, perhaps—there would likewise be no § 10(b) violation. Yet in either case—disclosed misuse or authorized use—the hypothesized "inhibiting impact on market participation," would be identical to that from behavior violating the misappropriation theory: "Outsiders" would still be trading based on nonpublic information that the average investor has no hope of obtaining through his own diligence.

The majority's statement that a "misappropriator who trades on the basis of material, nonpublic information, in short, *gains his advantageous market position through deception; he deceives the source of the information and simultaneously harms members of the investing public,*" ante (emphasis added), thus focuses on the wrong point. Even if it is true that trading on nonpublic information hurts the public, it is true whether or not there is any deception of the source of the information. Moreover, as we have repeatedly held, use of nonpublic information to trade is not itself a violation of § 10(b). E.g., *Chiarella*, 445 U.S., at 232-233. Rather, it is the use of fraud "in connection with" a securities transaction that is forbidden. Where the relevant element of fraud has no impact on the integrity of the subsequent transactions as distinct from the nonfraudulent element of using nonpublic information, one can reasonably question whether the fraud was used in connection with a securities transaction. And one can likewise question whether removing that aspect of fraud, though perhaps laudable, has anything to do with the confidence or integrity of the market.

The absence of a coherent and consistent misappropriation theory and, by necessary implication, a coherent and consistent application of the statutory "use or employ, in connection with" language, is particularly problematic in the context of this case. The Government claims a remarkable breadth to the delegation of authority in § 10(b), arguing that "the very aim of this section was to pick up unforeseen, cunning, deceptive devices that people might cleverly use in the securities markets." Tr. of Oral Arg. 7. As the Court aptly queried, "[t]hat's rather unusual, for a criminal statute to be that open-ended, isn't it?" Unusual indeed. Putting aside the dubious validity of an open-ended delegation to an independent agency to go forth and create regulations criminalizing "fraud," in this case we do not even have a formal regulation embodying the agency's misappropriation theory. Certainly Rule 10b-5 cannot be said to embody the theory—although it deviates from the statutory language by the addition of the words "any person," it merely repeats, unchanged, § 10(b)'s "in connection with" language. Given that the validity of the misappropriation theory turns on the construction of that language in § 10(b), the regulatory language is singularly uninformative.

Because we have no regulation squarely setting forth some version of the misappropriation theory as the Commission's interpretation of the statutory language, we are left with little more than the Commission's litigating position or the majority's completely novel theory that is not even acknowledged, much less adopted, by the Commission. As we have noted before, such positions are not entitled to deference and, at most, get such weight as their persuasiveness warrants. Yet I find wholly unpersuasive a litigating position by the Commission that, at best, embodies an inconsistent and incoherent interpretation of the relevant statutory language and that does not provide any predictable guidance as to what behavior contravenes the statute. That position is no better than an ad hoc interpretation of statutory language and in my view can provide no basis for liability.***

*[The dissent's discussion regarding the validity of Rule 14e-3(a) appears in Section C of this Chapter.]*

*** With regard to respondent's convictions on the mail fraud counts, my view is that they may be sustained regardless of whether respondent may be convicted of the securities fraud counts.***

As I read the indictment, it does not materially differ from the indictment in *Carpenter v. United States*, 484 U.S. 19 (1987). There, the Court was unanimous in upholding the mail fraud conviction, despite being evenly divided on the securities fraud counts. I do not think the wording of the indictment in the current case requires a finding of securities fraud in order to find mail fraud. Certainly the jury instructions do not make the mail fraud count dependent on the securities fraud counts. Rather, the counts were simply predicated on the same *factual* basis, and just because those facts are legally insufficient to constitute securities fraud does not make them legally insufficient to constitute mail fraud. I therefore concur in the judgment of the Court as it relates to respondent's mail-fraud convictions.

### *NOTES AND QUESTIONS*

*1.* ***"Fraud on the Source" vs. "Fraud on Investors."*** As discussed in the material preceding the *O'Hagan* decision, after *Chiarella*, the SEC and the DOJ gravitated toward Justice Stevens's "fraud on the source" misappropriation theory. What explains that preference? Was a broader misappropriation theory possible in light of the holdings in *Chiarella* and *Dirks*? In other words, could an argument be made that while traders do not owe a general duty to investors in the marketplace to disclose all material nonpublic information or to refrain from trading, traders nonetheless owe all investors a duty of disclosure when they obtained that information through misappropriation or other illegal means? See Donna M. Nagy, Reframing the Misappropriation Theory of Insider Trading Liability: A Post-*O'Hagan* Suggestion, 59 Ohio St. L.J. 1223 (1998) (arguing that the common law of fraud and deceit, the text of Section 10(b), and prior court precedents can all be read to support this broader version of a misappropriation theory).

*2. Rule of Lenity.* Justice Scalia referenced the principle of lenity that is applicable to criminal statutes. What is this principle? In light of the fact that the remedies for Rule 10b-5 violations are both criminal and civil, would it be possible for the misappropriation theory to apply to civil violations but not to criminal violations? What types of problems would this create? These matters will be examined in more detail in Chapter 11.A.2 infra.

*3. Tippee Trading.* The defendant-attorney in *O'Hagan* had misappropriated confidential client information to personally profit from his own securities trading. Accordingly, the Court had no occasion to address directly the application of the misappropriation theory to cases involving tippee trading. Prior to *O'Hagan*, tippees who traded on the basis of misappropriated information were viewed as co-participants in the misappropriator's breach of fiduciary duty. Thus, tippees incurred Rule 10b-5 liability for their own trading when they knew or should have known that their tippers had breached a fiduciary duty owed to the initial source of the information.

Will the SEC encounter problems in cases where the securities are traded by a misappropriator's tippee? In particular, consider whether a tippee's trading would satisfy Section 10(b)'s "in connection with" requirement, as that requirement was explained by the Court in *O'Hagan*. Does the tipper-misappropriator's breach of duty to the source of the information "coincide" with the tippee's securities transaction?

Focusing on this question in *United States v. Falcone*, 257 F.3d 226, 233 (2d Cir. 2001), the Second Circuit acknowledged that "the coincidence of a securities transaction and breach of duty" was not present where a tipper conveyed confidential information to a third party but did not himself trade." The court, however, maintained that "*O'Hagan* did not purport to set forth the sole combination of factors necessary to establish the requisite connection in all contexts." In the court's view, "*O'Hagan*'s requirement that the misappropriated information 'ordinarily' be valuable due to 'its utility in securities trading' appears to be a more generally applicable factor in determining whether section 10(b)'s 'in connection with' requirement is satisfied." Id. at 234. Do you agree with this conclusion?

*4. Identifying Fiduciary-Type Relationships.* Does *O'Hagan* offer insight into the type of relationships that would trigger a duty owed to the source of the information to disclose an intent to trade? What problems are lower courts likely to encounter in defining the scope of this duty? For a decision upholding the misappropriation theory against a psychiatrist who traded stock on the basis of material nonpublic information told to him by a patient, see *United States v. Willis*, 778 F. Supp. 205, 209 (S.D.N.Y. 1991) (emphasizing that "[a] treating psychiatrist's relationship to his patient is a traditional inherently fiduciary relationship"). For a decision upholding the misappropriation theory against a contractor handling the electrical work for a corporation, see *SEC v. Falbo*, 14 F. Supp.2d 508, 523 (S.D.N.Y. 1998) (stating that while not a traditional fiduciary, contractor was nonetheless placed "in a position of trust and confidence" which he violated when he "used for personal benefit information obtained during the course of his association").

Not surprisingly, particularly thorny issues have arisen in the context of misappropriations by family members. See, e.g., *United States v. Reed*, 601 F. Supp. 685 (S.D.N.Y. 1985) (applying misappropriation theory against son who traded on the basis of nonpublic information obtained from father, a corporate director), rev'd in part on other grounds, 773 F.2d 477 (2d Cir. 1985); *United States v. Chestman*, 947 F.2d 551, 568 (2d Cir. 1991) (en banc) (reversing conviction of securities broker on the ground that his alleged tipper did not owe a duty of trust and confidence to his wife who had shared with him confidential information about an upcoming transaction involving the sale of her family's company). Recognizing the uncertainty surrounding this issue, the SEC in 2000 promulgated Rule 10b5-2, which provides that a person trading on the basis of material nonpublic information breaches a duty of "trust and confidence" in any one of three circumstances:

> (1) when the person receiving the information has agreed to maintain that information in confidence;
>
> (2) when the persons involved in the communication "have a history, pattern, or practice of sharing confidences" that results in a reasonable expectation of confidentiality; and
>
> (3) when the person receives such information from a spouse, parent, child or sibling, unless the person can show affirmatively, based on the particular facts and circumstances of that family relationship, that "he or she neither knew nor reasonably should have known that the person who was the source of the information expected that the person would keep the information confidential."

Rule 10b5-2 has yet to be tested in litigation. What issues are likely to be raised by the rule?

### *PROBLEM 7-3*

Which of the following scenarios would constitute a violation of Rule 10b-5 under the misappropriation theory endorsed by the *O'Hagan* Court? Which scenarios lie beyond *O'Hagan*'s reach? Do the "not-reached" scenarios demonstrate a significant weakness in the Court's theory?

1. A computer hacker manages to gain access to the internal e-mail system of the nation's largest biotechnology company. After several days of reading not very interesting confidential e-mails between corporate executives, she stumbles upon a message revealing that company engineers have developed a new wonder drug for treating diabetes. The computer hacker purchases 200 call options on the company, and reaps a tremendous profit when she exercises those options after the drug breakthrough is announced.

2. You are an outside attorney for the nation's largest biotechnology company. You often take work home with you, and on one of those occasions, you inadvertently leave in your living room the notes you took at a recent meeting with your clients. The notes make clear that the

company will soon announce the development of a new wonder drug for treating diabetes. Your unemployed younger brother, who has been staying for the last two weeks as a guest in your home, finds your notes as he is channel surfing through the soap-operas the following day. A bit resentful of your many successes, your brother decides to take for himself a piece of the action, and asks his girlfriend to lend him the money so that he can purchase 500 shares of stock in the company. He tells her he has found a sure way to double that money in less than a week.

3. A taxi driver overhears a conversation between two passengers who appear to be engineers for a large biotechnology company. The passengers discuss the new wonder drug for treating diabetes and their company's anticipated public announcement of this breakthough later in the week. The taxi driver notices on the briefcase of one of the passengers a well known corporate logo. He later opens an investment account with Ameritrade and purchases 1000 shares of that company, whose stock price doubles two days later after the news about the drug is announced to the public.

4. The biotechnology company's assistant director of public relations helps to plan the announcement of the newly developed diabetes drug. The day before the announcement, she resigns her position, and leaves the country for the Caymen Islands. Her resignation letter expresses her unhappiness with the company, and informs her supervisors that she has given her broker instructions to purchase 1000 shares of the company at the opening of the NYSE the next morning. She is confident that the company will do nothing to detract attention from its impending announcement.

5. Instead of resigning and purchasing the stock for herself, the assistant director of public relations for the biotech company secretly sells the information about the newly developed drug to a third party for $100. Two days later, the third party purchases 500 call options on the company. The assistant director continues to perform all other aspects of her job responsibilities quite satisfactorily.

### *PROBLEM 7-4*

Nathan Nottingham was pursuing his MBA degree as an evening student at a prestigious New York business school. He was also a part-time word processor assigned by the temporary agency for which he worked to two Wall Street investment banking firms. As a "temp" for these firms, Nottingham was able to gain access to material nonpublic information regarding numerous merger and acquisition transactions. As is the customary practice on Wall Street, each firm had Nottingham sign a confidentiality agreement which contained an explicit warning that material nonpublic information learned in the course of employment must not be shared with anyone outside the firm and may under no circumstances be used for purposes of personal profit.

In May 2001, Nottingham "met" Adam Appelson, an insurance agent, in an Internet chat room devoted to the performance of a stock in which both had invested and lost money. In the course of their on-line communications,

Nottingham mentioned to Appelson the names of his temporary Wall Street employers. The two then agreed upon a plan to profit from any inside information Nottingham could learn about merger and acquisition transactions being planned by the firm's clients. Specifically, Appelson agreed to give Nottingham one quarter of any profits made by him through the use of the confidential information.

Over the course of the next year, Nottingham and Appelson each had purchased stock in more than 20 companies based on information garnered by Nottingham as a temporary employee. Appelson also shared his profits with Nottingham in accordance with the original agreement.

Nottingham and Appelson were also very generous in providing the confidential merger and acquisition information to their friends and relatives, often sending them e-mails containing "hot stock tips." On April 1, 2002, Appelson sent an e-mail to his brother-in-law Timothy Tyler, who has also an insurance agent, urging him to purchase stock in ABC Corp. because it was a "sure thing." The e-mail did not disclose any additional information, but Tyler was well aware of his brother-in-law's increasingly lavish lifestyle. Tyler then purchased 1000 shares of ABC Corp. for his own account. He also passed this tip on to two of his neighbors, who each bought 1000 shares in the company. When the neighbors asked about the source of the tip, Tyler responded, "you don't want to know." One of these neighbors shared the tip with his dentist, and the dentist purchased 500 shares in ABC.

On April 5, 2002, ABC Corp. announced publicly that it was being acquired by XYZ Corp., a client of one of the Wall Street firms that had employed Nottingham. ABC stock, which was trading at $28 dollars a share prior to the announcement, had skyrocketed to $42 a share by the end of the trading day. On five other occasions during the summer of 2002, Appelson sent an e-mail to his brother-in-law suggesting a "sure thing" stock, and the brother-in-law, his two neighbors, and the neighbors' dentist each purchased a sizable amount of shares in the recommended company. The pattern ceased only when Nottingham was arrested by federal marshals working with the Securities and Commodities Fraud Task Force in the Office of the United States Attorney for the Southern District of New York.

After *O'Hagan*, there is little doubt that Nottingham has engaged in multiple violations of Rule 10b-5 when he purchased for his own account stock in the targets of his employer's client. But is he liable for Appelson's purchases? The brother-in-law's? The neighbors'? The dentist's? When, if ever, is the tipper-tippee relationship too remote to impose liability? What about individual liability on the part of these tippees? Has each of these traders violated Rule 10b-5?

The case on which this problem was loosely based resulted in civil charges against 19 defendants, all who chose to settle with the SEC. See *SEC v. Freeman*, Litigation Release No. 16469, 2000 WL 272268 (March 14, 2000). For an older case discussing and deciding liability for remote tippees, see *SEC v. Musella*, 678 F. Supp. 1060 (S.D.N.Y. 1988).

## C. RULE 14e-3—INSIDER TRADING IN THE CONTEXT OF TENDER OFFERS

As we saw from the *O'Hagan* decision in Section B.3, corporate transactions involving tender offers frequently present particularly tempting opportunities to profit unlawfully from the use of material nonpublic information. Recall that the material nonpublic information to which attorney James O'Hagan had access involved the confidential plans of Grand Metropolitan to launch a tender offer for shares in Pillsbury. Thus, in addition to violations of Section 10(b) and Rule 10b-5, the government charged him with, and the jury convicted him for, illegal trading under Section 14(e) and Rule 14e-3(a). The Supreme Court's analysis of this aspect of the case is set forth below.

### UNITED STATES v. O'HAGAN
521 U.S. 642 (1997)

JUSTICE GINSBURG:

***A sole question is before us as to [O'Hagan's convictions for fraudulent trading in connection with a tender offer, in violation of § 14(e) of the Exchange Act and SEC Rule 14e-3(a)]: Did the Commission, as the Court of Appeals held, exceed its rulemaking authority under § 14(e) when it adopted Rule 14e-3(a) without requiring a showing that the trading at issue entailed a breach of fiduciary duty? We hold that the Commission, in this regard and to the extent relevant to this case, did not exceed its authority.

The governing statutory provision, § 14(e) of the Exchange Act, reads in relevant part:

> "It shall be unlawful for any person ... to engage in any fraudulent, deceptive, or manipulative acts or practices, in connection with any tender offer.... The [SEC] shall, for the purposes of this subsection, by rules and regulations define, and prescribe means reasonably designed to prevent, such acts and practices as are fraudulent, deceptive, or manipulative."

Section 14(e)'s first sentence prohibits fraudulent acts in connection with a tender offer. This self-operating proscription was one of several provisions added to the Exchange Act in 1968 by the Williams Act. The section's second sentence delegates definitional and prophylactic rulemaking authority to the Commission. Congress added this rulemaking delegation to § 14(e) in 1970 amendments to the Williams Act.

Through § 14(e) and other provisions on disclosure in the Williams Act,[14] Congress sought to ensure that shareholders "confronted by a cash tender offer for their stock [would] not be required to respond without adequate informa-

---

14. In addition to § 14(e), the Williams Act and the 1970 amendments added to the Exchange Act the following provisions concerning disclosure: § 13(d) (disclosure requirements for persons acquiring more than five percent of certain classes of securities); § 13(e) (authorizing Commission to adopt disclosure requirements for certain repurchases of securities by issuer); § 14(d) (disclosure requirements when tender offer results in offeror owning more than five percent of a class of securities); § 14(f) (disclosure requirements when tender offer results in new corporate directors constituting a majority).

tion." *Rondeau v. Mosinee Paper Corp.*, 422 U.S. 49, 58 (1975); see *Lewis v. McGraw*, 619 F.2d 192, 195 (C.A.2 1980) ("very purpose" of Williams Act was "informed decisionmaking by shareholders"). As we recognized in *Schreiber v. Burlington Northern, Inc.*, 472 U.S. 1 (1985), Congress designed the Williams Act to make "disclosure, rather than court imposed principles of 'fairness' or 'artificiality,' ... the preferred method of market regulation." Id., at 9, n. 8. Section 14(e), we explained, "supplements the more precise disclosure provisions found elsewhere in the Williams Act, while requiring disclosure more explicitly addressed to the tender offer context than that required by § 10(b)." Id., at 10-11.

Relying on § 14(e)'s rulemaking authorization, the Commission, in 1980, promulgated Rule 14e-3(a). That measure provides:

> (a) If any person has taken a substantial step or steps to commence, or has commenced, a tender offer (the 'offering person'), it shall constitute a fraudulent, deceptive or manipulative act or practice within the meaning of section 14(e) of the [Exchange] Act for any other person who is in possession of material information relating to such tender offer which information he knows or has reason to know is nonpublic and which he knows or has reason to know has been acquired directly or indirectly from:
>
> (1) The offering person,
>
> (2) The issuer of the securities sought or to be sought by such tender offer, or
>
> (3) Any officer, director, partner or employee or any other person acting on behalf of the offering person or such issuer,
>
> to purchase or sell or cause to be purchased or sold any of such securities or any securities convertible into or exchangeable for any such securities or any option or right to obtain or to dispose of any of the foregoing securities, unless within a reasonable time prior to any purchase or sale such information and its source are publicly disclosed by press release or otherwise.

As characterized by the Commission, Rule 14e-3(a) is a "disclose or abstain from trading" requirement. 45 Fed.Reg. 60410 (1980). The Second Circuit concisely described the Rule's thrust:

> "One violates Rule 14e-3(a) if he trades on the basis of material nonpublic information concerning a pending tender offer that he knows or has reason to know has been acquired 'directly or indirectly' from an insider of the offeror or issuer, or someone working on their behalf. Rule 14e-3(a) is a disclosure provision. It creates a duty in those traders who fall within its ambit to abstain or disclose, *without regard to whether the trader owes a pre-existing fiduciary duty* to respect the confidentiality of the information."

*United States v. Chestman*, 947 F.2d 551, 557 (1991) (en banc) (emphasis added)(1992). See also *SEC v. Maio*, 51 F.3d 623, 635 (C.A.7 1995) ("Rule 14e-3 creates a duty to disclose material non-public information, or abstain from trading in stocks implicated by an impending tender offer, *regardless of whether such information was obtained through a breach of fiduciary duty*." (emphasis added)); *SEC v. Peters*, 978 F.2d 1162, 1165 (C.A.10 1992) (as written, Rule 14e-3(a) has no fiduciary duty requirement).

In the Eighth Circuit's view, because Rule 14e-3(a) applies whether or not the trading in question breaches a fiduciary duty, the regulation exceeds the SEC's § 14(e) rulemaking authority. Contra, *Maio*, 51 F.3d, at 634-635(CA7);

*Peters*, 978 F.2d, at 1165-1167 (C.A.10); *Chestman*, 947 F.2d, at 556-563(CA2) (all holding Rule 14e-3(a) a proper exercise of SEC's statutory authority). In support of its holding, the Eighth Circuit relied on the text of § 14(e) and our decisions in *Schreiber* and *Chiarella*.

The Eighth Circuit homed in on the essence of § 14(e)'s rulemaking authorization: "[T]he statute empowers the SEC to 'define' and 'prescribe means reasonably designed to prevent' 'acts and practices' which are 'fraudulent.'" Id., at 624. All that means, the Eighth Circuit found plain, is that the SEC may "identify and regulate," in the tender offer context, "acts and practices" the law already defines as "fraudulent"; but, the Eighth Circuit maintained, the SEC may not "create its own definition of fraud." Ibid.

This Court, the Eighth Circuit pointed out, held in *Schreiber* that the word "manipulative" in the § 14(e) phrase "fraudulent, deceptive, or manipulative acts or practices" means just what the word means in § 10(b): Absent misrepresentation or nondisclosure, an act cannot be indicted as manipulative. See 92 F.3d, at 625 (citing *Schreiber*, 472 U.S., at 7-8, and n. 6). Section 10(b) interpretations guide construction of § 14(e), the Eighth Circuit added, see 92 F.3d, at 625, citing this Court's acknowledgment in *Schreiber* that § 14(e)'s "'broad antifraud prohibition' ... [is] modeled on the antifraud provisions of § 10(b) ... and Rule 10b-5," 472 U.S., at 10; see id., at 10-11, n. 10.

For the meaning of "fraudulent" under § 10(b), the Eighth Circuit looked to *Chiarella*. In that case, the Eighth Circuit recounted, this Court held that a failure to disclose information could be "fraudulent" under § 10(b) only when there was a duty to speak arising out of " 'a fiduciary or other similar relation of trust and confidence.' " *Chiarella*, 445 U.S., at 228 (quoting Restatement (Second) of Torts § 551(2)(a) (1976)). Just as § 10(b) demands a showing of a breach of fiduciary duty, so such a breach is necessary to make out a § 14(e) violation, the Eighth Circuit concluded.

As to the Commission's § 14(e) authority to "prescribe means reasonably designed to prevent" fraudulent acts, the Eighth Circuit stated: "Properly read, this provision means simply that the SEC has broad regulatory powers in the field of tender offers, but the statutory terms have a fixed meaning which the SEC cannot alter by way of an administrative rule." 92 F.3d, at 627.

The United States urges that the Eighth Circuit's reading of § 14(e) misapprehends both the Commission's authority to define fraudulent acts and the Commission's power to prevent them. "The 'defining' power," the United States submits, "would be a virtual nullity were the SEC not permitted to go beyond common law fraud (which is separately prohibited in the first [self-operative] sentence of Section 14(e))." Brief for United States 11; see id., at 37.

In maintaining that the Commission's power to define fraudulent acts under § 14(e) is broader than its rulemaking power under § 10(b), the United States questions the Court of Appeals' reading of *Schreiber*. See Brief for United States at 38-40. Parenthetically, the United States notes that the word before the Schreiber Court was "manipulative"; unlike "fraudulent," the United States observes, " 'manipulative' ... is 'virtually a term of art when used in connection with the securities markets.' " Brief for United States at 38, n. 20 (quoting *Schreiber*, 472 U.S., at 6). Most tellingly, the United States submits, *Schreiber* involved acts alleged to violate the self-operative provision in § 14(e)'s first sentence, a sentence containing language similar to § 10(b). But § 14(e)'s second sentence, containing the rulemaking authorization, the United States points out, does not track § 10(b), which simply authorizes the SEC to proscribe "manipulative or deceptive device[s] or contrivance[s]." Brief for United States 38. Instead, § 14(e)'s rulemaking prescription tracks § 15(c)(2)(D) of the Exchange Act, which concerns the conduct of broker-dealers in over-the-counter markets. See Brief for United States 38-39. Since 1938, § 15(c)(2) has given the Commission authority to "define, and prescribe means reasonably designed to prevent, such [broker-dealer] acts and practices as are fraudulent, deceptive, or manipulative." When Congress added this same rulemaking language to § 14(e) in 1970, the Government states, the Commission had already used its § 15(c)(2) authority to reach beyond common-law fraud. See Brief for United States 39, n. 22.

We need not resolve in this case whether the Commission's authority under § 14(e) to "define ... such acts and practices as are fraudulent" is broader than the Commission's fraud-defining authority under § 10(b), for we agree with the United States that Rule 14e-3(a), as applied to cases of this genre, qualifies under § 14(e) as a "means reasonably designed to prevent" fraudulent trading on material, nonpublic information in the tender offer context.[17] A prophylactic measure, because its mission is to prevent, typically encompasses more than the core activity prohibited. As we noted in *Schreiber*, § 14(e)'s rulemaking authorization gives the Commission "latitude," even in the context of a term of art like "manipulative," "to regulate nondeceptive activities as a 'reasonably designed' means of preventing manipulative acts, without suggesting any change in the meaning of the term 'manipulative' itself." 472 U.S., at 11, n. 11. We hold, accordingly, that under § 14(e), the Commission may prohibit acts not themselves fraudulent under the common law or § 10(b), if the prohibition is "reasonably designed to prevent ... acts and practices [that] are fraudulent."

Because Congress has authorized the Commission, in § 14(e), to prescribe legislative rules, we owe the Commission's judgment "more than mere deference or weight." *Batterton v. Francis*, 432 U.S. 416, 424-426 (1977). Therefore, in determining whether Rule 14e-3(a)'s "disclose or abstain from trading" requirement is reasonably designed to prevent fraudulent acts, we must accord the Commission's assessment "controlling weight unless [it is] arbitrary, capricious, or manifestly contrary to the statute." *Chevron U.S.A. Inc. v.*

---

17. We leave for another day, when the issue requires decision, the legitimacy of Rule 14e-3(a) as applied to "warehousing," which the Government describes as "the practice by which bidders leak advance information of a tender offer to allies and encourage them to purchase the target company's stock before the bid is announced." Reply Brief 17. As we observed in *Chiarella*, one of the Commission's purposes in proposing Rule 14e-3(a) was "to bar warehousing under its authority to regulate tender offers." 445 U.S., at 234. The Government acknowledges that trading authorized by a principal breaches no fiduciary duty. See Reply Brief 17. The instant case, however, does not involve trading authorized by a principal; therefore, we need not here decide whether the Commission's proscription of warehousing falls within its § 14(e) authority to define or prevent fraud.

*Natural Resources Defense Council, Inc.*, 467 U.S. 837, 844 (1984). In this case, we conclude, the Commission's assessment is none of these.

In adopting the "disclose or abstain" rule, the SEC explained:

> The Commission has previously expressed and continues to have serious concerns about trading by persons in possession of material, nonpublic information relating to a tender offer. This practice results in unfair disparities in market information and market disruption. Security holders who purchase from or sell to such persons are effectively denied the benefits of disclosure and the substantive protections of the Williams Act. If furnished with the information, these security holders would be able to make an informed investment decision, which could involve deferring the purchase or sale of the securities until the material information had been disseminated or until the tender offer had been commenced or terminated.

45 Fed. Reg. 60412 (1980).

The Commission thus justified Rule 14e-3(a) as a means necessary and proper to assure the efficacy of Williams Act protections.

The United States emphasizes that Rule 14e-3(a) reaches trading in which "a breach of duty is likely but difficult to prove." Reply Brief 16. "Particularly in the context of a tender offer," as the Tenth Circuit recognized, "there is a fairly wide circle of people with confidential information," *Peters*, 978 F.2d, at 1167, notably, the attorneys, investment bankers, and accountants involved in structuring the transaction. The availability of that information may lead to abuse, for "even a hint of an upcoming tender offer may send the price of the target company's stock soaring." *SEC v. Materia*, 745 F.2d 197, 199 (C.A.2 1984). Individuals entrusted with nonpublic information, particularly if they have no long-term loyalty to the issuer, may find the temptation to trade on that information hard to resist in view of "the very large short-term profits potentially available [to them]." *Peters*, 978 F.2d, at 1167.

"[I]t may be possible to prove circumstantially that a person [traded on the basis of material, nonpublic information], but almost impossible to prove that the trader obtained such information in breach of a fiduciary duty owed either by the trader or by the ultimate insider source of the information." Ibid. The example of a "tippee" who trades on information received from an insider illustrates the problem. Under Rule 10b-5, "a tippee assumes a fiduciary duty to the shareholders of a corporation not to trade on material nonpublic information only when the insider has breached his fiduciary duty to the shareholders by disclosing the information to the tippee and the tippee knows or should know that there has been a breach." *Dirks*, 463 U.S., at 660. To show that a tippee who traded on nonpublic information about a tender offer had breached a fiduciary duty would require proof not only that the insider source breached a fiduciary duty, but that the tippee knew or should have known of that breach. "Yet, in most cases, the only parties to the [information transfer] will be the insider and the alleged tippee." *Peters*, 978 F.2d, at 1167.

In sum, it is a fair assumption that trading on the basis of material, nonpublic information will often involve a breach of a duty of confidentiality to the bidder or target company or their representatives. The SEC, cognizant of the proof problem that could enable sophisticated traders to escape responsibility, placed in Rule 14e-3(a) a "disclose or abstain from trading" command that does not require specific proof of a breach of fiduciary duty. That prescription, we are satisfied, applied to this case, is a "means reasonably designed to prevent" fraudulent trading on material, nonpublic information in the tender offer context. See *Chestman*, 947 F.2d, at 560 ("While dispensing with the subtle problems of proof associated with demonstrating fiduciary breach in the problematic area of tender offer insider trading, [Rule 14e-3(a) ] retains a close nexus between the prohibited conduct and the statutory aims."); accord, *Maio*, 51 F.3d, at 635, and n. 14; *Peters*, 978 F.2d, at 1167. Therefore, insofar as it serves to prevent the type of misappropriation charged against O'Hagan, Rule 14e-3(a) is a proper exercise of the Commission's prophylactic power under § 14(e).

As an alternate ground for affirming the Eighth Circuit's judgment, O'Hagan urges that Rule 14e-3(a) is invalid because it prohibits trading in advance of a tender offer—when "a substantial step ... to commence" such an offer has been taken—while § 14(e) prohibits fraudulent acts "in connection with any tender offer." See Brief for Respondent 41-42. O'Hagan further contends that, by covering pre-offer conduct, Rule 14e-3(a) "fails to comport with due process on two levels": The Rule does not "give fair notice as to when, in advance of a tender offer, a violation of § 14(e) occurs," id., at 42; and it "disposes of any scienter requirement," id., at 43. The Court of Appeals did not address these arguments, and O'Hagan did not raise the due process points in his briefs before that court. We decline to consider these contentions in the first instance. The Court of Appeals may address on remand any arguments O'Hagan has preserved. ***

JUSTICE THOMAS, WITH WHOM CHIEF JUSTICE REHNQUIST JOINS, CONCURRING IN THE JUDGMENT IN PART AND DISSENTING IN PART:

***I find neither of the Commission's justifications for Rule 14e-3(a) acceptable in misappropriation cases. With regard to the Commission's claim of authority to redefine the concept of fraud, I agree with the Eighth Circuit that the Commission misreads the relevant provision of § 14(e).

> "Simply put, the enabling provision of § 14(e) permits the SEC to identify and regulate those 'acts and practices' which fall within the § 14(e) legal definition of 'fraudulent,' but it does not grant the SEC a license to redefine the term." 92 F.3d 612 at 624 (1996).

This conclusion follows easily from our similar statement in *Schreiber v. Burlington Northern, Inc.*, 472 U.S. 1, 11, n. 11 (1985), that § 14(e) gives the "Commission latitude to regulate nondeceptive activities as a 'reasonably designed' means of preventing manipulative acts, without suggesting any change in the meaning of the term 'manipulative' itself."

Insofar as the Rule 14e-3(a) purports to "define" acts and practices that "are fraudulent," it must be measured against our precedents interpreting the scope of fraud. The majority concedes, however, that Rule 14e-3(a) does not prohibit merely trading in connection with fraudulent nondisclosure, but rather it prohibits trading in connection with *any* nondisclosure, regardless of the presence of a pre-existing duty to disclose. The Rule thus exceeds the scope of the Commission's authority to define such acts and practices as "are fraudulent."

Turning to the Commission's second justification for Rule 14e-3(a), although I can agree with the majority that § 14(e) authorizes the Commission to prohibit nonfraudulent acts as a means reasonably designed to prevent fraudulent ones, I cannot agree that Rule 14e-3(a) satisfies this standard.***

In order to be a valid prophylactic regulation, Rule 14e-3(a) must be reasonably designed not merely to prevent *any* fraud, but to prevent persons from engaging in "fraudulent, deceptive, or manipulative acts or practices, *in connection with* any tender offer." Insofar as Rule 14e-3(a) is designed to prevent the type of misappropriation at issue in this case, such acts are not legitimate objects of prevention because the Commission's misappropriation theory does not represent a coherent interpretation of the statutory "in connection with" requirement ***. Even assuming that a person misappropriating information from the bidder commits fraud on the bidder, the Commission has provided no coherent or consistent explanation as to why such fraud is "in connection with" a tender offer, and thus the Commission may not seek to prevent indirectly conduct which it could not, under its current theory, prohibit directly.

Finally, even further assuming that the Commission's misappropriation theory is a valid basis for direct liability, I fail to see how Rule 14e-3(a)'s elimination of the requirement of a breach of fiduciary duty is "reasonably designed" to prevent the underlying "fraudulent" acts. The majority's primary argument on this score is that in many cases "'a breach of duty is likely but difficult to prove.'" Although the majority's hypothetical difficulties involved in a tipper-tippee situation might have some merit in the context of "classical" insider trading, there is no reason to suspect similar difficulties in "misappropriation" cases. In such cases, Rule 14e-3(a) requires the Commission to prove that the defendant "knows or has reason to know" that the nonpublic information upon which trading occurred came from the bidder or an agent of the bidder. Once the source of the information has been identified, it should be a simple task to obtain proof of any breach of duty. After all, it is the bidder itself that was defrauded in misappropriation cases, and there is no reason to suspect that the victim of the fraud would be reluctant to provide evidence against the perpetrator of the fraud. There being no particular difficulties in proving a breach of duty in such circumstances, a rule removing the requirement of such a breach cannot be said to be "reasonably designed" to prevent underlying violations of the misappropriation theory.

What Rule 14e-3(a) was in fact "designed" to do can be seen from the remainder of the majority's discussion of the Rule. Quoting at length from the Commission's explanation of the Rule in the Federal Register, the majority notes the Commission's concern with "'unfair disparities in market information and market disruption.'" In the Commission's further explanation of Rule 14e-3(a)'s purpose—continuing the paragraph partially quoted by the majority—an example of the problem to be addressed is the so-called "stampede effect" based on leaks and rumors that may result from trading on material, nonpublic information. The majority also notes (but does not rely on) the Government's contention that it would not be able to prohibit the supposedly problematic practice of "warehousing"—a bidder intentionally tipping allies to buy stock in advance of a bid announcement—if a breach of fiduciary duty were required.

Given these policy concerns, the majority notes with seeming approval the Commission's justification of Rule 14e-3(a) "as a means necessary and proper to assure the efficacy of Williams Act protections."

Although this reasoning no doubt accurately reflects the Commission's purposes in adopting Rule 14e-3(a), it does little to support the validity of that Rule as a means designed to prevent such behavior: None of the above-described acts involve breaches of fiduciary duties, hence a Rule designed to prevent them does not satisfy § 14(e)'s requirement that the Commission's Rules promulgated under that section be "reasonably designed to prevent" acts and practices that "are fraudulent, deceptive, or manipulative." As the majority itself recognizes, there is no "'general duty between all participants in market transactions to forgo actions based on material, nonpublic information,'" and such duty only "'arises from a specific relationship between two parties.'" Ante, at 2212 (quoting *Chiarella*, 445 U.S., at 233). Unfair disparities in market information, and the potential "stampede effect" of leaks, do not necessarily involve a breach of any duty to anyone, and thus are not proper objects for regulation in the name of "fraud" under § 14(e). Likewise (as the Government concedes, Reply Brief for United States 17), "warehousing" is not fraudulent given that the tippees are using the information with the express knowledge and approval of the source of the information. There simply would be no deception in violation of a duty to disclose under such circumstances.

While enhancing the overall efficacy of the Williams Act may be a reasonable goal, it is not one that may be pursued through § 14(e), which limits its grant of rulemaking authority to the prevention of fraud, deceit, and manipulation. As we have held in the context of § 10(b), "not every instance of financial unfairness constitutes fraudulent activity." *Chiarella*, supra, at 232. Because, in the context of misappropriation cases, Rule 14e-3(a) is not a means "reasonably designed" to prevent persons from engaging in fraud "in connection with" a tender offer, it exceeds the Commission's authority under § 14(e), and respondent's conviction for violation of that Rule cannot be sustained.

### *NOTES AND QUESTIONS*

1. ***Rule 14e-3 and Parity Of Access to Information.*** The SEC promulgated Rule 14e-3 in 1980, a few months after the government's defeat in *Chiarella*. Did the SEC use its rulemaking powers under Section 14(e) to enact the "equal access to information" approach that the Court had rejected in the context of Rule 10b-5 liability? Does Section 14(e) give the SEC the power to (re)define fraud in the context of tender offers?

2. ***"As Applied to Cases of this Genre."*** The *O'Hagan* Court endorsed the validity of Rule 14e-3(a), but only "insofar as it serve[d] to prevent the type of misappropriation charged against O'Hagan." What is meant by this qualification? Does it mean that Rule 14e-3(a)'s validity has been established only in misappropriation cases?

3. ***The Practice of Warehousing.*** The *O'Hagan* Court stated explicitly that the legality of warehousing was an issue left for resolution another day. How does the Court define the practice of warehousing? Why doesn't warehousing constitute fraudulent conduct under Rule 10b-5?

SEC studies done in the 1970s indicated not only that warehousing tactics were often used, but also that such conduct was widespread across many different tender offers with different bidders. The SEC repeatedly pointed to these findings in order to justify its promulgation of Rule 14e-3. See SEC Release No. 33-6022, 44 Fed. Reg. 9956, 9957 (Feb. 15, 1979) ("[T]he Commission is proposing a rule which is designed to curb a serious abuse in tender offer practice by certain persons trading in [target] securities prior to the bidder's announcement of an intention to make a tender offer."). See also id. at 9976-77 ("In some instances, the leaking of the intention to make a tender offer may be deliberate. The [Institutional Investor Study Report] found that bidders frequently gave institutions advance notice in either general or specific terms of proposed tender offers. Whether deliberate or not, the leaking of the bidder's intention to make a tender offer when coupled with trading on such non-public market information is a matter of serious concern to the Commission").

Why would a warehouser tip someone to buy target shares in advance of the public announcement of its tender offer? Since such action may increase the demand for target shares, how would the warehouser benefit from action leading to an upward pressure on the target share price? Who is disadvantaged? Do you think the Supreme Court would be likely to endorse the validity of Rule 14e-3(a) in a case in which the facts directly involved warehousing?

***4. The Substantial Step Requirement.*** Rule 14e-3(a)'s prohibitions apply only when "the offering person" has "taken a substantial step or steps to commence, or has commenced a tender offer." For examples of what constitutes a substantial step, see *SEC v. Mayhew*, 121 F.3d 44, 53 (2d Cir. 1997) (noting that retaining a consulting firm, signing a confidentiality agreement, and holding meetings between company officials constitute "substantial steps"); *SEC v. Maoi*, 51 F.3d 623, 636 (7th Cir. 1995) (officials in a meeting "much more serious than any previous discussion between the parties" satisfies substantial step requirement); *SEC v. Musella*, 578 F. Supp. 425, 443-444 (S.D.N.Y. 1984) (retaining a law firm constitutes a "substantial step"). These cases comport with the SEC definition of "substantial steps" that was set out in the adopting release. See Tender Offers, Exchange Act Release No. 17120, 20 SEC Docket 1241, 1248 n. 23 (Sept. 4, 1980) ("activities which substantially facilitate the offer" engaged in after "the formulation of a plan or proposal to make a tender offer by the offeror or person(s) acting on behalf of the offeror").

***5. Knowledge on the Part of the Defendant.*** For liability to attach under Rule 14e-3(a), must the defendant actually know that substantial steps to commence a tender offer have been taken? On remand from the Supreme Court, the Eighth Circuit Court of Appeals addressed this question in response to a challenge by O'Hagan to the following jury instruction:

> With respect to [the Rule 14e-3(a) counts], you must find that Grand Met had taken one or more substantial steps to commence its tender offer for Pillsbury stock at the time that O'Hagan had purchased the relevant Pillsbury securities. It is not necessary for a bidder to make a tender offer for you to find that substantial steps toward such an offer have been taken or made. *Nor is it necessary that you find that the defendant knew that the substantial steps had been taken.* It is enough that you find one or more substantial steps were in fact taken.

*United States v. O'Hagan*, 139 F.3d 641, 650 (8th Cir. 1998) (quoting Trial Tr. Vol. XII at 39) (emphasis by 8th Circuit). The Eighth Circuit had no trouble with the instruction, maintaining that Rule 14e-3(a) "does not require the defendant to have knowledge of [the substantial steps]. Instead, the defendant need only 'know[ ] or have reason to know' that the material information is 'nonpublic and has been acquired directly or indirectly from' the tender offeror in some way." Id.

Moreover, for liability to attach under Rule 14e-3 (a), must the defendant even know that the information in his possession pertains to a tender offer? See *SEC v. Sargent*, 229 F.3d 68, 78 (1st Cir. 2000) (holding that "there is simply no language in the Rule indicating that a defendant must know that the nonpublic information in his possession relates to a tender offer"). Can a person know or have reason to know that information came from a "tender offeror," if that person is not aware that the information pertained to a tender offer?

### *PROBLEM 7-5*

Reconsider each of the factual scenarios in Problem 7-3 with the following modification: instead of the impending announcement of a new wonder drug for diabetes, assume that the material nonpublic information at issue concerns a tender offer launched by the biotech company. Assume further that all traders had purchased shares of stock in the target. Which scenarios would result in liability under Rule 14e-3(a)? Note how your answers would change once again if the takeover were accomplished through a friendly merger or proxy solicitation rather than through a tender offer.

### *PROBLEM 7-6*

Your spouse received a phone call last night from your next door neighbor asking for a favor. The neighbor was sick in bed with the flu, and she asked your spouse to drive her children to school in the morning. The neighbor hated to put your spouse to that trouble, and told your spouse that her husband was not able to drive to the school himself because his company was being sold and he has been working around the clock throughout the last five days. Your spouse quickly agreed to act as chauffeur and wished your neighbor a speedy recovery. Your spouse then relayed the entire conversation to you.

Because you have lived next door to this couple for the last five years, you are well aware that the "around-the-clock" working husband is a Senior Vice President of Digamax, a medium size company that manufactures compact discs. At this point, your curiosity is peaked, and you surf the Internet to see whether the news about Digamax is public. What you find are several recent references to Digamax in a trade publication indicating that the company is considered by many to be ripe for a takeover.

If you purchase Digamax stock while in possession of the information learned from your neighbor, would you be liable under Rule 14e-3(a)?

### *PROBLEM 7-7*

In the 1980s, Morton Mekko was a well known corporate raider who engineered a number of very high-profile hostile takeovers. After more than a decade of doing only friendly deals, Mekko once again has returned to his old ways and has successfully battled management in four of his last five deals. Mekko often shares his takeover plans with Chris Cransom, a noted Wall Street arbitrageur who has supported Mekko in a number of mutually lucrative ventures. Recently, Mekko called Cransom and told him his plans to launch a tender offer for Greenlawn, Inc. Cransom immediately purchased a sizeable block of shares in the company. Has Mekko and/or Cransom violated Rule 14e-3(a)?

## D. CONGRESS SPEAKS ON INSIDER TRADING—ITSA, ITSFEA, AND SUBSEQUENT LEGISLATION

In enforcing the federal prohibition against insider trading prior to 1984, the SEC had a relatively limited arsenal of enforcement weapons on which to draw, none of which were tailored to insider trading specifically. Thus, enforcement actions brought against persons for insider trading—whether litigated or settled—typically resulted in an injunction against future violations and an order that the defendant disgorge the ill-gotten profit gained or loss avoided from the illegal transactions. (Recall that this was the remedy upheld by the Second Circuit in *Texas Gulf Sulphur.*) Alternatively, if the case involved insider trading by a securities professional—such as a broker-dealer or investment adviser—the SEC could pursue an administrative action, and impose sanctions including censure (as it did in the *Cady, Roberts* and *Dirks* cases), temporary suspension, or a permanent bar from the industry. A final possible enforcement avenue took the case down the path of the criminal law where, as in *Chiarella,* the DOJ could prosecute the defendant in federal court and typically seek a prison sentence. The SEC, however, could only refer matters to the DOJ for criminal prosecutions; as you will be reminded again in Chapters 9 and 11, the SEC does not itself have the power to seek criminal sanctions against violators of the federal securities laws.

Recognizing that these remedies resulted in an unacceptably low level of deterrence, Congress sought to expand the arsenal of remedies available in insider trading cases, first in 1984 with the enactment of the Insider Trading Sanctions Act (ITSA), and then in 1988 when it enacted the Insider Trading and Securities Fraud Enforcement Act (ITSFEA).

ITSA's most important provision accorded the SEC—for the first time ever—the authority to seek in federal district court a civil penalty of up to three times the profit gained or loss avoided through a defendant's illegal insider trading. This penalty, which can be imposed for illegal tipping as well as trading, is clearly in addition to any disgorgement or criminal fine that may also be ordered. ITSA's civil penalty provision is now set out in Section 21A of the Exchange Act:

**Section 21A—Civil penalties for insider trading**

(a) Authority to impose civil penalties

(1) Judicial actions by Commission authorized. Whenever it shall appear to the Commission that any person has violated any provision of this chapter or the rules or regulations thereunder by purchasing or selling a security *** while in possession of material, nonpublic information in, or has violated any such provision by communicating such information in connection with, a transaction

on or through the facilities of a national securities exchange or from or through a broker or dealer, *** the Commission–

> (A) may bring an action in a United States district court to seek, and the court shall have jurisdiction to impose, a civil penalty to be paid by the person who committed such violation; ***

(2) Amount of penalty for person who committed violation. The amount of the penalty which may be imposed on the person who committed such violation shall be determined by the court in light of the facts and circumstances, but shall not exceed three times the profit gained or loss avoided as a result of such unlawful purchase, sale, or communication.

Notice the artful wording that enabled Congress to provide substantial penalties for insider trading without having to define precisely the conduct that is subject to sanction.

ITSA also clarified the law of insider trading as it pertains to options by adding a new Section 20(d) to the Exchange Act. This provision specifies that where trading or tipping on an issuer's securities would violate the Exchange Act, so too would a trade or tip that resulted in the purchase or sale of an option or similar right with respect to that security. Thus, option traders were put on equal footing with shareholders, in terms of their ability to be protected from those with access to material, nonpublic information. Prior to the enactment of Section 20(d), what hurdles may have prevented the government or private plaintiffs from suing those who purchased options on the basis of material, nonpublic information? See *Laventhall v. Gen. Dynamics Corp.*, 704 F.2d 407 (8th Cir, 1983); *O'Connor & Assocs. v. Dean Witter Reynolds, Inc.*, 600 F. Supp. 702 (S.D.N.Y. 1985).

With ITSA in place, the SEC quickly escalated its enforcement efforts with respect to insider trading. Yet a number of high-profile scandals in the mid-1980s primed Congress for action on the SEC's claim that further measures of deterrence and enforcement were needed. The scandals involved the types of facts that eventually found their way into Hollywood movies: extremely wealthy entrepreneurs being led out of their Wall Street offices in handcuffs. But for a while, the scandals themselves were what the public closely watched, and Ivan Boesky, Michael Milkin, Dennis Levine and others soon became well-known villains. Concerned that the scandals represented "far more than the transgressions of a few individuals," Congress set out to send a clear message that "insider trading will not be tolerated in our markets." H.R. Rep. No. 100-910 at 14 (1988).

The legislative response took the form of ITSFEA – the Insider Trading and Securities Fraud Enforcement Act of 1988. One of ITSFEA's most important provisions extended the treble penalty provision in what is now Section 21A to those persons or entities who "control" a person found liable for illegal trading or tipping. Pursuant to Section 21A(a)(1)(B), the SEC may seek a penalty in federal district court against such controlling persons provided it satisfies the following provision:

**Section 21A(b)(1)—Liability of controlling persons**

No controlling person shall be subject to a penalty *** unless the Commission establishes that:

> (A) such controlling person knew or recklessly disregarded the fact that such controlled person was likely to engage in the act or acts constituting the violation and failed to take appropriate steps to prevent such act or acts before they occurred; or
>
> (B) such controlling person knowingly or recklessly failed to establish, maintain, or enforce any policy or procedure required under [Section 15(f) of the Exchange Act or Section 204A of the Investment Advisers Act] and such failure substantially contributed to or permitted the occurrence of the act or acts constituting the violation.

Section 21A(3) provides that a court shall determine the penalty imposed on a controlling person "in light of the facts and circumstances," but that it "shall not exceed the greater of $1,000,000 [now 1.2 million (adjusted for inflation)], or three times the amount of the profit gained or loss avoided as a result of such controlled person's violation." Moreover, in cases where the controlled person's violation involved tipping, the profit gained or loss avoided by the controlled person is to be calculated based on the transactions of the person or persons who directly received the tip from the controlled person. In other words, profits made or losses avoided by so-called remote tippees are disregarded when calculating the maximum penalty for a person found to have controlled a person liable for tipping.

Important questions prompted by this provision include who qualifies as a "control person" and what does it mean to "recklessly" disregard someone's likelihood of engaging in illegal tipping or trading. The legislative history relevant to both questions shows that Congress intended to put economic pressure on employers—particularly, but not exclusively, those on Wall Street—to better supervise those persons who have regular access to material, nonpublic information. But the House Committee Report also makes clear that the case law interpreting that term in Section 20(a) of the Act (see supra Chapter 2.H.3) applies here, such that "control" broadly includes any person "with the power to influence or control the direction of management, policies or activities of another person." H.R. Rep. No. 100-910 at 17 (1988). That said, Congress was not looking to impose a scheme of strict liability for employers in connection with their employees' bad acts, and explicitly provided in Section 21A(b)(2) that no person shall be subject to a penalty "solely by reason of employing another person who is subject to a penalty under such subsection." The House Report further stated that, for a penalty to be imposed, "the Commission must establish that a controlling person objectively disregarded a risk that a controlled person was engaged in violations of the insider trading laws," and that the risk involved "must be such that to disregard it would constitute a gross deviation from the standard of care that a reasonable person would exercise in such a situation." House Report at 18. Notice however, that Section 20(a) provides controlling persons with a "good faith" defense to liability whereas no such defense is provided for controlling persons under Section 21A. Does the recklessness standard in Section 21A(b)(1)(A) effectively ensure that no one acting in good faith could be subject to a penalty under that provision?

Another important provision of ITSFEA added Section 20A to the Exchange Act, a provision that establishes an express private right of action for violations of the federal securities laws involving illegal insider trading or tipping. Note once again how Congress managed to establish a remedy for insider trading without specifically defining the insider trading offense.

**Section 20A—Liability to contemporaneous traders for insider trading**

(a) Private rights of action based on contemporaneous trading. Any person who violates any provision of this chapter or the rules or regulations thereunder by purchasing or selling a security while in possession of material, nonpublic information shall be liable in an action in any court of competent jurisdiction to any person who, contemporaneously with the purchase or sale of securities that is the subject of such violation, has purchased (where such violation is based on a sale of securities) or sold (where such violation is based on a purchase of securities) securities of the same class. ***

(c) Joint and several liability for communicating. Any person who violates any provision of this chapter or the rules or regulations thereunder by communicating material, nonpublic information shall be jointly and severally liable under subsection (a) of this section with, and to the same extent as, any person or persons liable under subsection (a) of this section to whom the communication was directed.

Note also that Section 20A eliminates the need for private plaintiffs to show that the insider trader owed them a disclosure duty. Instead, plaintiffs have to establish merely the existence of a predicate violation—typically, that the defendant violated Rule 10b-5 by trading while in possession of material, nonpublic information. Recall the facts of *United States v. O'Hagan*. Under Section 20A, Pillsbury shareholders and option traders who sold contemporaneously with James O'Hagan's purchases could have sued O'Hagan for damages even though, under the Court's misappropriation theory, it was Grand Metropolitan and the law firm of Dorsey & Whitney who were the actual victims of O'Hagan's fraud. Why should contemporaneous traders who were not defrauded nonetheless be entitled to an insider trader's profits? Do Dorsey & Whitney and Grand Metropolitan have a stronger normative claim for O'Hagan's profits? Would either have had a legal claim against O'Hagan under Section 20A? Could either have sued O'Hagan under the implied right of action under Rule 10b-5?

What does it mean to say that a plaintiff purchased a security contemporaneously with a defendant's sale? Congress chose not to define the term "contemporaneously," preferring instead to rely on the definition that had developed through the case law. Today, most courts agree that a plaintiff trades "contemporaneously" by trading on the same day or no more than a few days after an illegal trade. Just how many days after is an issue of some dispute. Compare *In re Oxford Heath Plans, Inc. Sec. Litig.*, 187 F.R.D. 133, 144 (S.D.N.Y. 1999) (concluding that "[f]ive trading days is a reasonable period between the insider's sales and the plaintiff's purchase to be considered contemporaneous") with *Backman v. Polaroid Corp.*, 540 F. Supp. 667, 671 (D. Mass. 1982) (concluding that purchases two business days after defendant's sales were not contemporaneous) and *Copland v. Grumet*, 88 F. Supp. 2d 326, 338 (D.N.J. 1999) (requiring the plaintiff to have bought the stock "on the same dates on which the defendant's sales took place").

In addition to restricting the right of recovery to persons who trade contemporaneously with (and opposite) the unlawful trade, Congress took other steps to see that the amount of liability to private plaintiffs would not be draconian. First, Section 20A(b)(1) caps the total amount of available damages to "the profit gained or loss avoided in the transaction or transactions that are the subject of the violation." Second, Section 20A(b)(2) provides that any funds that were paid to the SEC as disgorgement may be offset by the "total amount of damages imposed against any person" for the same transaction or transactions. Finally, Section 20A(b)(3) clarifies that "[n]o person shall be liable under this section solely by reason of employing another person who is liable under this section, but the liability of a controlling person under this section shall be subject to [Section 20(a)]." In view of these limitations on liability, is Section 20A a particularly effective deterrent against insider trading? In what types of fact patterns would you most expect to see Section 20A claims asserted?

ITSFEA amended the Exchange Act in other significant ways. It increased the individual criminal fine available under Section 32(a) to a maximum of $1,000,000 and raised the maximum available prison term from 5 to 10 years. For non-natural persons, it increased the maximum criminal fine to 2.5 million. (As you will see when you study criminal enforcement in Chapter 11, the Sarbanes-Oxley Act subsequently amended Section 32(a) to increase the maximum prison sentence to 20 years, and to increase the maximum fine to $5,000,000 for individuals and $25,000,000 for non-natural persons). ITSFEA also added a "bounty program" to Section 21A(e) of the Exchange Act. This provision authorizes the SEC or the Attorney General to pay informants a sum, not to exceed ten percent of the penalty recovered, where an informant's information leads to the imposition of a penalty for illegal trading or tipping.

With the enactment of ITSA and ITSFEA, did Congress achieve its stated objectives? This question, of course, can be answered on a number of levels. To be sure, one measure of success might be the legislation's effect on the types of securities professionals that prompted Congress's intervention in the first place. And there is good reason for congressional satisfaction on this front. Indeed, even one of the SEC's toughest Enforcement Directors has noted that "we have not seen arbitragers and investment banking professionals end up in the caption *** of complaints or charged in criminal cases. *** This is a group of people that understands seeing their name on the front page of the New York Times and the possibility of going to jail." See Micro Cap Fraud, Staffing Issues Top Enforcement Agenda, 29 Sec. Reg. & L. Rep. 1769, 1772 (BNA) (Dec. 19, 1997) (quoting statements by former SEC Enforcement Director William McLucas). Attorneys, legal assistants, and other law firm personnel have also appeared to have heeded the warnings. See, e.g., Crime: Former NY Prosecutor Admits to Insider Trading, Bribery Scheme, 33 Sec. Reg. & L. Rep. 215 (BNA) (February 12, 2001) (reporting guilty plea in criminal case where defendant offered $50,000 to a paralegal at the law firm of Skadden Arps in return for confidential information regarding deals that the law firm was handling; the paralegal refused and reported the offer to Skadden Arps's management, who in turn notified federal authorities). There are, of course notable exceptions. See id. (incredibly, the defendant who pled guilty was formerly a prosecutor for the state of New York). See also *United States v. O'Hagan*, 521 U.S. 642 (1997), supra, Section B.3.

Yet, despite the increased awareness by securities professionals of the perils of insider trading, the number of insider trading cases brought by the government has only increased since the front page scandals noted above. Who, then, are the defendants in today's insider trading cases? According to the SEC, the problem has shifted from "Wall Street to Main Street" in that the "defendants now are more often than not corporate insiders, their family, and friends." See William R. McLucas and Alma M. Angotti, Insider Trading: Is it Back or Did It Ever Really Go Away?, InSights, vol. 9, no. 10, at 1 (Oct. 1995). What lessons can securities counsel draw from this?

---

Since the enactment of ITSA and ITSFEA, Congress has expanded substantially the SEC's arsenal of remedies in enforcement actions for violations of the federal securities laws. In the Securities Enforcement Remedies and Penny Stock Reform Act of 1990 (discussed in Chapter 9.C.1, infra), Congress added new provisions to the Securities Act and Exchange Act which authorized federal courts to impose orders barring individuals from future service as an officer or director of a publicly traded company, upon the SEC's showing that the person committed fraud in violation of Section 10(b) of the Exchange Act or SEC rules thereunder or Section 17(a)(1) of the Securities Act and that the person was "substantially unfit" to serve. Federal courts often imposed this remedy in insider trading cases, although SEC officials contended that the statutory language of "substantial unfitness" courts interpreted in an overly restrictive manner. See Stephen M. Cutler, SEC Director, Division of Enforcement, Remarks at the Glasser LegalWorks 20th Annual Federal Securities Institute (Feb. 15, 2002) (discussing insider trading cases in which federal courts imposed liability for violating Rule 10b-5 but refused to bar defendants from future corporate service).

In the wake of the scandals at Enron and WorldCom, Congress acceded to the SEC's requests to modify this bar order remedy. Under Section 20(e) of the Securities Act and Section 21(d)(2) of the Exchange Act, federal courts may now impose a bar order upon the SEC's showing of an individual's mere "unfitness" to serve. The Act also amended Section 8A of the Securities Act and Section 21C of the Exchange Act to authorize the SEC to impose such bar orders in administrative proceedings. Although only time will tell the extent to which the SEC actually utilizes these additional enforcement weapons, one can certainly expect that insider trading cases will present fact patterns that lead the SEC to seek to impose a greater number of officer and director bars.

The scandals at Enron and WorldCom also prompted Congress to enact its very first express prohibition of insider trading, albeit in a very narrow context. And once again, as with Section 16(b)'s disgorgement provision for short-swing profits (see Section A.2, supra), Congress did so without any regard to whether the trading insiders possess any material nonpublic information. Section 306 of the Sarbanes-Oxley Act, entitled "Insider Trades During Pension Fund Blackout Periods," provides that:

> it shall be unlawful for any director or executive officer of an issuer of any equity security (other than an exempted security), directly or indirectly, to purchase, sell, or otherwise acquire any equity security *** during any blackout period with respect to such equity security if such director or officer acquires such equity security in connection with his or her service or employment as a director or executive officer.

A "blackout period" is defined, subject to certain exceptions, as "any period of more than 3 consecutive business days during which the ability of not fewer than 50 percent of the participants" in an individual account plan (as defined in ERISA) maintained by the issuer, to make trades in the issuer's equity securities "is temporarily suspended by the issuer or by a fiduciary of the plan." See id. at Section 306(a)(4). As a remedy for breaches of its trading prohibition, Section 306(a)(2) provides that an action to recover the profits of the director or executive officer may be instituted at law or in equity in any court of competent jurisdiction by the issuer or on behalf of the issuer if the issuer fails to bring such a suit within 60 days.

Should Congress have used the occasion of the Sarbanes-Oxley Act to legislatively overhaul the regulation of insider trading rather than merely tinker around its peripheral edges? The final section of this Chapter explores the pros and cons of a broad congressional ban on insider trading.

## PROBLEM 7-8

Ben Brittle, a registered representative with the national brokerage firm of Ferris Morton, had been generating tremendous profits, both for his own accounts and for the proprietary accounts that he manages for Ferris Morton. His immediate supervisors had suspected for some time that he is up to no good, but they had no specific evidence of illegal activity. The supervisors shared their suspicions with the Senior Vice President in charge of the Compliance Department, who formulated an enhanced supervisory plan pursuant to which any of the broker's transactions above $5,000 would require pre-approval by the branch manager or assistant manager. When informed of this new procedure, Brittle complained to the Executive Vice President in Charge of Sales, who then pressured the Compliance Director into rescinding the special supervisory measures.

As it turned out, Brittle was one of several people who had been receiving information directly from an analyst who worked at Connelly, Inc., a venture capital firm that recently made a number of highly lucrative acquisitions. One of Connelly's recent deals involved the takeover of Harris Industries. When Connelly first became interested in Harris, its stock had been trading steadily for more than a year in or around $16 a share. Throughout the weeks of negotiations and due diligence, Harris's stock price crept up gradually to $19 a share. Connelly negotiated a friendly deal with management at $21 a share for the 1 million shares outstanding, though it was convinced that the deal could have been consummated at a lower price had Harris continued to trade at the $16 level. The SEC also focused attention on the stock price spike in the days prior to the merger announcement and quickly identified the employee-analyst who was the source of the tips. This employee is cooperating with the SEC and the U.S. Attorney in return for a penalty that will not involve jail time.

The SEC identified Brittle as a tippee who purchased stock in Harris on the basis of the misappropriated information. Brittle agreed to settle the action with the SEC, and consented to a permanent bar from association with a broker-dealer, disgorgement in the sum of $120,000 (representing the profit from the Harris transaction as well as several other ones), and a penalty of $240,000.

Can the SEC bring an action against Ferris Horton? Against officials at Ferris Horton? On what theory? What remedies can it seek?

Can Connolly seek damages under Rule 10b-5 to recoup some of the money it spent in acquiring Harris at the $21 price? Whom can it sue? How would damages be calculated?

What about those who sold stock in Harris on the day that Brittle made his purchases? Do they have an incentive to sue?

## E. LITIGATING INSIDER TRADING CASES—THE PROBLEM OF CIRCUMSTANTIAL EVIDENCE

An overwhelming percentage of enforcement actions brought by the SEC—more than 90%—are settled rather than litigated, and insider trading cases present no exception to this pattern. But what about the one case out of ten that gets litigated? How does the SEC go about proving all of the elements necessary to establish a violation of Rule 10b-5 (or Rule 14e-3)?

Insider trading cases often raise particularly difficult questions of proof because the evidence that one was aware of material nonpublic information at the time of a transaction is often in the sole control of the individual trader or her tipper. If the trader denies such awareness (as is typical in cases brought to trial), and if the suspected tipper denies that information was imparted (or if the suspected tipper cannot be identified), the SEC has no choice but to make its case circumstantially. Sometimes the SEC does so successfully and manages to prove the defendant's awareness by a preponderance of evidence. One such case is *SEC v. Geon Indus., Inc.*, 531 F.2d 39 (2d Cir. 1976), in which Geon's CEO was alleged to have tipped a stockbroker about the company's upcoming merger. Although there was no direct evidence of the tip, the court held that the circumstantial evidence of their telephone conversations followed by substantial stock purchases by the stockbroker supported the trial court's inference that material nonpublic information had passed between them. In so concluding, the court emphasized that the broker had asserted a privilege against self-incrimination and that the CEO had claimed "inability to recall the subject-matter of most of their numerous talks." Id. at 46.

Circumstantial evidence may also be used to establish a defendant's guilt in a criminal insider trading trial. One well-publicized recent example is *U.S. v. McDermott*, 245 F. 3d 133 (2d Cir. 2001), in which the court reviewed a jury's finding that James McDermott, CEO and Chairman of an investment bank, had tipped his "adult film" star girlfriend, Kathryn Gannon, as to to confidential merger information. The court held that "although the government was unable to produce direct evidence" of the tips, "rational minds could have inferred such a conclusion" from the following evidence:

> (1) that McDermott and Gannon were having an affair involving incessant telephone conversations; (2) that Gannon, who was up until this point an amateur trader, opened a trading account funded by monies given to her by McDermott; (3) that during the alleged conspiracy period, Gannon traded twenty-one times in twelve different stocks based upon McDermott's recommendations; (4) that Gannon traded in non-blue chip stocks, many of which were banks subject to non-public negotiations with [McDermott's investment bank]; (5) that Gannon was quite successful in her trading and in the timing of her

> trades; (6) that telephone conversations between Gannon and McDermott coincided with Gannon's trading activity; and (7) that Gannon shared her recommendations with [a third party who acted on those recommendations].

Id. at 138. The court noted specifically that "[c]ircumstantial evidence is a legitimate form of evidence in this Circuit, and in fact-intensive cases such as this, requiring careful examination of trading records and a myriad of public information, the jury is the appropriate body to determine a defendant's guilt or innocence." Id. at 139. Although the court found that the evidence was sufficient to convict McDermott on the insider trading charges, it nonetheless ordered a new trial due to prejudicial errors committed with respect to joining certain conspiracy charges. See id. at 139-40. McDermott subsequently pled guilty to the insider trading charges rather than be retried. See Crime: Former Wall Street Exec. Pleads Guilty to Insider Charges in Lieu of Second Trial, 33 Sec. Reg. & L. Rep. 1003 (BNA) (July 9, 2001). How would you have weighed the circumstantial evidence in the following case?

## SEC v. MORAN

922 F. Supp. 867 (S.D.N.Y. 1996)

NEWMAN, SENIOR JUDGE:

The United States Securities and Exchange Commission, brings this civil securities fraud enforcement action against Frederick Augustus Moran ("Moran Sr."), Frederick Winston Moran ("Moran Jr."), Moran Asset Management Inc. ("Moran Asset"), and Moran & Associates, Inc., Securities Brokerage ("Moran Brokerage"). Specifically, the SEC alleges that Moran Sr., Moran Jr., Moran Asset, and Moran Brokerage engaged in insider trading thereby violating Section 10(b) of the Securities Exchange Act of 1934 ["the Exchange Act"] ***The SEC seeks judgment permanently enjoining each of the defendants from violating the pertinent provisions of the Exchange Act *** disgorgement of all illegal profits, prejudgment interest arising from the alleged insider trading, [and a] payment of three time civil penalties based on the insider trading ***. The defendants deny each of the allegations lodged against them and seek dismissal of the complaint.

***[T]he only issues presented to the court at this juncture are the liability of the defendants for the charges in the complaint. The case was tried to the court in a twelve day bench trial. In conformity with F.R.C.P.Rule 52(a), the following constitutes the court's findings of fact and conclusions of law.

### THE RECORD

In its direct case, the SEC presented eight witnesses: John Reddan, executive vice-president and security analyst for Moran & Associates Securities Brokerage from May 1985 until October 31, 1995; defendant Frederick Winston Moran, a vice-president at Salomon Brothers; defendant Frederick Augustus Moran, president of Moran Asset Management and Moran & Associates Brokerage;[2] Richard Scribner, chief compliance officer for Salomon Brothers, Inc.; Edward Meyercord, vice-president in investment banking for Salomon Brothers; Frank Poli, an attorney, who in 1993 was the head trader for Moran

2. Moran Sr. and Moran Jr. were called as hostile witnesses by the SEC.

Asset Management; Peter D. Crawford, executive director of investor relations and share owner relations for Bell Atlantic Corporation; and Kevin Tarrant, manager of investor relations for Bell Atlantic Corporation. Defendants did not present any witnesses. On rebuttal plaintiff called Raymond Liguori, who was employed as the telecommunication analyst for Salomon Brothers in October 1993. Pursuant to agreement by counsel and F.R.C.P. Rule 32(a)(3)(E), the depositions of Susan Putnam, vice-president of Moran Asset and Moran Brokerage, Katherine Dietze Courage, a director at Salomon Brothers, Richard Holbein, the president of Pension Asset Consulting Associates Inc., and Jennifer Netterville, the investment officer of Louisiana Teacher's Retirement Fund, were admitted into evidence. The parties moved 213 exhibits into evidence.

CONTENTIONS OF THE PARTIES

The SEC alleges that Moran Sr. and his companies acted upon inside information about two cable companies provided by Moran Jr., his son. According to the SEC, Moran Jr. "tipped" Moran Sr. with respect to a merger between Bell Atlantic and Telecommunications Incorporated ("TCI"). This circumstantial case revolves around the fact that Moran Jr., as an employee of Salomon Brothers, was in possession of material, non-public information with respect to the Bell Atlantic-TCI merger. Moran Sr. who had previously been reticent to trade cable stocks, after a series of phone conversations with Moran Jr., made [a] large purchase of Liberty, TCI and other cable company stocks on October 11, 1993, two days before the October 13, 1993 official announcement of the merger. The SEC argues that because Moran Sr. and his companies had lost substantial money and clients as the result of a very unsuccessful prior investment in Chamber Development stock, Moran Sr. needed a "sure winner." Moreover, plaintiff contends that Moran Jr. had a history of violating Salomon Brothers' policies regarding confidential information in order to benefit Moran Sr.'s firms, thereby demonstrating an intent on the part of Moran Jr. to provide his father with confidential information. Finally, plaintiff alleges that because Moran Sr. had previously been bearish on cable, these October 11th stock purchases constituted an aberrant trading pattern for Moran Sr., there were several phone calls between Moran Sr. and Jr., including one for over forty minutes the week before Moran Sr. made the stock purchases, and Moran Sr. faxed to Moran Jr. the Moran "morning meeting notes" specifying the switch in cable policy on the morning of the stock purchases indicates that the defendants traded the cable securities as a result of material, non-public information in violation of the Exchange Act and Rules thereunder. ***

Defendants deny each of the charges. Specifically, Moran Sr. and Moran Jr. respond that Moran Jr. in no way "tipped" any material non-public information with respect to the Bell Atlantic-TCI merger. Defendants maintain that Moran Sr.'s change of heart regarding the cable stocks came about as a result of the actions of Dr. John Malone, a "giant" in the cable industry. Moran Sr. claims that his return to purchasing cable stocks resulted from following Malone's lead. Indeed, defendants additionally point out that news of the impending merger was made public through newspaper articles in the New York Times and the Wall Street Journal. Moran Sr. argues that it was during the weekend of October 9-10, after reading a Wall Street Journal article about a merger between TCI and Liberty, that he made his final decision to begin investment in cable stocks.***

FINDINGS OF FACT

Frederick Augustus Moran ("Moran Sr.") is the president and principal portfolio manager of Moran Asset Management Inc., as well as the president and director of research of Moran & Associates, Inc. Securities Brokerage. Frederick Winston Moran Jr. ("Moran Jr.") is Moran Sr.'s eldest son and has been employed since March 1993 by Salomon Brothers Inc. as an analyst specializing in the cellular telephone and wireless communications industries. In July 1993, while working for Salomon Brothers, Moran Jr. expanded his focus to the cable television industry for Salomon Brothers. Moran Asset Management, Inc. ("Moran Asset") since 1986 has been a registered investment adviser. Moran & Associates, Inc. Securities Brokerage ("Moran Brokerage") since 1987 has been a registered broker-dealer. Moran Sr. and his wife Joan, during the periods in question each owned 50% of the stock of Moran Asset and Moran Brokerage.

The Insider Trading Claim

*Overview of Events*

On October 3, 1993, Moran Jr. was "brought over the wall" at Salomon Brothers with regard to a proposed merger between Telecommunication Incorporated ("TCI") and Bell Atlantic. Moran Jr. was told that the official announcement of the merger would come "within a week to two weeks" (R. 437). On Wednesday, October 6, Moran Jr. was briefed on the details of the proposed Bell Atlantic/TCI merger and told by Edward Meyercord that the announcement was expected to take place early the following week. Moran Jr.'s understanding was that the announcement date "would probably be the 13th, or certainly the 12th, 13th, or 14th" (R. 437). On Thursday, October 7, the Wall Street Journal published an article entitled "TCI Reported In Talks To Buy Liberty Media" (Exhibit 11).

Moran Jr. attended a meeting at Bell Atlantic headquarters in Philadelphia on October 9, 1993. The purpose of the meeting was twofold. First, there were discussions about how to best market the Bell Atlantic/TCI merger. Second, the speech that the president of Bell Atlantic would deliver when the deal was announced was drafted. At this meeting Salomon Brothers representatives, including Moran Jr., learned for the first time that the definitive date of the announcement regarding the merger was October 13. According to Meyercord, "there was a very detailed media plan that was put together and ... there was to be a public announcement in New York City in the morning in which the analyst community would be present" (R. 894). This media plan also set forth October 13 as the date of the public announcement (Exh. 1).

On October 11, 1993 Moran Sr. bought approximately 340,000 and 203,000 shares of TCI and Liberty stock respectively. During the evening of October 12, Moran Jr. told employees of Moran Asset and John Reddan about the merger. The proposed merger of Bell Atlantic and TCI was publicly announced by a press release issued at approximately 7:00 a.m. on October 13.

*Moran Sr.'s Trading Practice*

From 1987 through 1991 Moran Sr. invested at least 35% and as much as 45% of his clients' managed funds in cable television stocks. In 1991, Dr. John Malone, the President and Chief Executive Officer of TCI, the largest cable company in the world, began moving his personal wealth out of TCI, a cable television operator company, and into Liberty, a programing company. Moran Sr. testified that at the time of Malone's transaction, the move did not seem significant "because [Moran Asset's] impression was that [Malone] had exercised only half of his rights and [Moran Sr.] thought that was therefore a case of saying to the world I am not abandoning Liberty and it was something he did with that in mind and he had not exercised all of his rights" (R. 1406-07; 1411 Moran Sr. Exh. CX). At that juncture, Moran Sr. believed that Malone was actually increasing his backing of TCI and therefore Moran Sr. increased his purchases of TCI stocks. In fact, however, Dr. Malone was tendering all of his TCI shares in exchange for increased stocks in Liberty (R. 773, 1413; Moran Sr. Exhs. CW, CQ). From October 25, 1991, when Dr. Malone publicly disclosed his venture into Liberty, and until Liberty recombined with TCI, Liberty's stock price had increased by 3000 percent. During this time Moran Sr. was still a proponent of cable stocks.

Beginning in 1992 Moran Sr.'s view of the cable industry began to change. In addition, Moran Sr. learned on January 7, 1992 that Malone had actually liquidated his TCI holdings to pay for his investment in Liberty. Moran Sr. was further aware that Malone was an outspoken critic of government regulation of the cable industry and predicted a negative impact would result. In response to the problems he believed would result from increased regulation of the cable industry, as well as the discovery that Malone had in fact been divesting himself from TCI holdings, Moran Sr. began selling cable stocks in Moran Asset's client accounts beginning in 1992 (R. 780-82; Exhs. 39-40). On January 8, 1992 Moran Sr. began selling TCI and Comcast stock and within several weeks Moran Asset sold out all its cable stock positions almost completely. According to Moran Sr., the decision to sell was made by him without first consulting Moran Jr. or John Reddan.

In addition to selling TCI stock, Moran Sr. decided to cover the short position he had in Liberty stock. According to Reddan, the short position was closed at a substantial loss. With respect to Moran Sr.'s reaction after these transactions, Reddan testified that "[Moran Sr.] said we've got to learn our lesson here. Malone has a tremendous following. [Moran Sr.] never wanted to go against him again. And it was more—our feeling that Malone's following was more powerful than we had estimated" (R. 775).[8] During 1993, Malone appeared to be moving further into programming and away from cable television. This move was well documented in Moran Brokerage Morning Meeting Notes. Specifically, the notes stated:

---

8. Following Malone with respect to the cable industry is a well recognized practice on Wall Street. Malone had been characterized as "the cable industries most brilliant and creative player," a "multimedia god," and that investing along side Malone "has proved to be profitable," "has continuing merit."

> There is a rumor that TCI will purchase Liberty Media's cable properties. This would mean 1) John Malone would be reducing further his cable interests and moving further into programming inhibits the cable companies ability to pass on programming price increases.

(Morning Meeting Note May 27, 1993, Moran Sr. Exh. K).

> NYT article:—Cable television John Malone is moving further into programming in response to regulatory and technological changes.

(Morning Meeting Note, June 1, 1993, Moran Sr. Exh. L).

> Fortune article: John Malone calls President Clinton a bold face liar. Two possible reasons for this unguarded behavior are: 1) he is so frustrated with what Congress has done to the cable industry, or 2) won't be around to bear the consequences. Recently he has begun to say it is too much trouble for him to be Chairman of both Liberty Media and Telecommunications.

(Morning Meeting Note, June 14, 1993, Moran Sr. Exh, M).

> [Liberty Media is] rumored to be planning to swap its interests in cable system for TCI's interest in programming assets—especially Turner Broadcasting and Discovery Channel. Malone is moving away from cable systems and toward programming.

(Morning Meeting Note, September 20, 1993, Moran Sr. Exh. N).

It is undisputed that from 1992 and into August 1993 Moran Sr. was "bearish" on cable stocks. Indeed, published materials from Moran Brokerage clearly demonstrate Moran Sr.'s unfavorable view of cable stock. In Moran Asset's morning meeting notes from March, April, and June 1993, Moran Sr. predicted that "cable TV stocks, as a group, offer modest upside potential and substantial downside risk," that regulation "was more severe than our forecasted worst case scenario," and that "the focus on technology in cable is causing investors to overlook a serious negative—reregulation" (Exhs. 38 and 45). Included in Moran Sr.'s negative view of the cable television industry was TCI. Aside from completely liquidating all of the Moran Asset's holdings in TCI in 1992, Moran Asset's good relationship with TCI came to an end because according to Reddan, "we had become negative on the cable industry" (R. 61). In the Moran Morning Meeting notes of July 20, 1993, Moran Brokerage concluded that:

> [TCI] Conference call regarding effects of reregulation: effect is somewhat less than expected. Annual revenue is reduced roughly 3% to 4% compared to a 6% to 8% expected.... Even with relatively mild effects, six of TCI's credit agreements will go into technical default. Continue to recommend strength as growth will be very tough over next year.

(Exh. 107). Even as late as September 24, 1993 Moran's morning meeting note stated that "Sumner Redstone's antitrust lawsuit against TCI, Liberty Media and QVC has very serious long term negative implications for those companies. It is likely to ... increase regulatory scrutiny or pressure on those companies" (Exh. 38 at 55; R. 1172-73).

Moran Sr.'s position on cable stocks becomes an issue of dispute between the parties starting in September 1993. The last recommendation to sell cable stocks appeared in Moran Brokerage's morning meeting note for August 26, 1993 (Moran Sr. Exh. BF). While future morning meeting notes, up until the time in question did not include a recommendation to buy cable stocks, the recommendation was the more neutral "hold." According to Reddan, Moran Sr. "began to soften his views in September of 1993, and in October of 1993 he changed his views" (R. 782).

In support of his claim that he was changing his view of cable stocks, Moran Sr. points to the fact that he, along with Susan Putnam, attended a Donaldson Lufkin & Jenrette media conference relating in part to the cable industry from September 20 to September 22, 1993. While there, Moran Sr. learned both that the industry was developing the technology to compete with local telephone companies for long distance access charges by enabling cable companies to carry long distance service over coaxial telephone lines and that Bell Atlantic was permitting cable companies to access its research related to video service over the "twisted pair" copper wires which carry telephone service (R. 1464-1468; Moran Sr. Exh. O). Moran Sr. also learned of technological advances being made by cable companies with respect to their potential long distance capabilities on September 23, 1993 at a Scientific Atlanta meeting. Believing that this innovation could produce an "enormous revenue stream" for cable companies, Moran Sr.'s notes made at the conference read: "Conclusions—sell [local exchange carriers] ... buy cable" (R. 1468-1471; Moran Sr. Exh. P). In fact, Moran Sr. set forth in the Moran Brokerage Morning Meeting Notes of September 24, 1993 that:

> Bottom Line: Of all these competitors, the telcos are in poorest position to compete in video services. Cable companies will enter the long distance telephone business. Cable companies in nine months will attach unit to outside of the home that will reverse amplifiers on existing coax reverse line, will carry the telephone signal. Long distance calls will be offered. AT & T wants the cable companies there to reduce the access charges. Cable companies will be looking at an enormous revenue stream

Moran Sr. Exh. S. Thus, Moran Sr. asserts, the evidence demonstrates that he was now "primed to get back into cable." See Frederick A. Moran's Post Trial Brief, p. 19.

The SEC, on the other hand, argues that the Moran Sr.'s claim that he was turning bullish on cable stocks beginning in August 1993 is contradicted "not only by the morning meeting notes, but also by the testimony of Susan Putnam." See Plaintiff's Proposed Finding of Fact and Conclusions of Law, p. 35. In support of this claim, the SEC points to the morning meeting note of September 24, 1993 addressing the Redstone anti-trust lawsuit against TCI (Exh. 55). In addition, Putnam stated that after seeing a presentation with respect to the Jones Intercable on September 23, 1993, she suggested to Moran Sr. that it might be an "interesting" investment idea (Putnam Deposition, p. 88). Putnam recalled Moran Sr. telling her that "he felt regulation was still a major problem." (Id.). The SEC maintains that this evidence demonstrates that Moran Sr. was not interested in investing in cable. With respect to the other proof relied upon by Moran Sr., the SEC suggests that the very technology Moran Sr. claims he was impressed with, was actually nothing more than innovations which Reddan had been expecting "for some time during the year 1993" (R. 822). Coupled with the fact that Moran did not buy any cable stock after attending the conferences and assigned Scientific Atlanta to Susan Putnam for further study, the SEC concludes that Moran Sr. was still "bearish" on cable.

In resolving this dispute of fact, the court finds that while there is no suggestion that Moran Sr. turned "bullish" on cable stocks in September 1993, there is ample credible evidence that Moran Sr. had begun to soften his view on the cable industry. Indeed, the SEC admits that Moran Sr.'s "firm decided to do more research on the cable phone." SEC Proposed Findings of Fact and Conclusions of Law, p. 36. Additionally, while the conversation with Putnam indicates Moran Sr. was still concerned with regulation of the cable industry, the court will not ignore the documentary evidence with respect to telecommunications, which Moran Sr. would reasonably consider in deciding upon a position to take about cable stocks. Moreover, contrary to Moran Asset's practice since 1992, after August 26, 1993, Moran Morning Meeting Notes no longer included a "sell" recommendation with respect to cable stocks. Significantly, on August 24, 1993, Bell Atlantic won a lawsuit challenging the 1984 Cable Act, which prohibited telephone companies and their affiliates from providing video programming to subscribers in their own telephone service area. While this decision paved the way for competition in the cable television industry, Moran Sr. viewed the "competition as an alternative to regulation" (R. 1459). Knowing that its monopoly status was behind the regulation of the cable industry, Moran Sr. reasoned that "if you had competition in place instead of regulation, you wouldn't need regulation" (R. 1459). Finally, Moran Sr. did not fear the idea of competition in the cable industry because he "had clearly determined the cable companies would be overwhelming winners" (R. 1459). Referring to a report Moran Sr. had previously published he stated, "[a]s far back as 1988 we made that decision" (R. 1459; Moran Sr. Exh. A).

While the SEC argues that "one would most reasonably expect that if the Moran firms were again to take a long position in cable stocks, they would do so either (a) in an orderly fashion; (b) on the basis of careful, detailed and documented research into the fundamentals of cable companies; and/or (c) over an extended period of time," (SEC Proposed Finding of Facts and Conclusions of Law, p. 36), the evidence in this case amply demonstrates that was not the way Moran Sr. typically operated. Reddan testified that "Fred's style is to jump in with both feet. Over the course of our ten-year relationship, we've had many of these disagreements primarily because of a difference in approach. I'm more cautious; Fred is more—acts more decisively" (R. 139). Accordingly, the court finds that the evidence supports defendants' contention that Moran Sr. was softening his view on the cable industry.

*The Alleged Motive and Intent of Moran Jr. to Give and Moran Sr. to Trade Using Material Non-Public Information*

The SEC alleges that because of a very negative experience with Chamber's Development stock, Moran Sr. had a motive to want a "sure thing." In addition, the SEC further claims that Moran Jr.'s conduct[9] demonstrates that

9. The court permitted the SEC to introduce evidence that Moran Jr. provided his father with confidential information from Salomon Brothers in violation of Salomon Brothers' regulation and other information which his father was not entitled to receive. See, Order dated October 30, 1995. The sole purpose that the court allowed this evidence was to the extent that it purported to show Moran Jr.'s state of mind and intent to communicate the material non-public information at issue in this case. See, *United*

he had the intent to provide his father with inside information. Moran Sr. responds that the losses sustained by his venture into Chambers stock were over with, that his company was doing well, and that even if his company were to fold, he could have comfortably retired. Moran Jr. maintains that none of the actions raised by the SEC constitute any breach of securities law or in any way indicates he would act inappropriately to benefit his father's firm.

It is undisputed that the decision by Moran Sr. to invest in Chambers Development Company resulted in significant financial losses for Moran Sr.'s clients as well as his personal account. Shortly after an announcement in March 1992 that Chambers' net income was far less than had been previously reported, Moran Sr. began aggressively purchasing Chambers stock for his clients. By the end of 1992, Moran Sr., Moran Asset, and Moran Brokerage had become the largest or second largest outside shareholder of Chambers. While Moran Asset continued to purchase Chambers stock during 1992, the price of the stock steadily declined. At one point the price of Chamber stock fell approximately 60 percent. Because of the losses being sustained by Moran Sr.'s clients, Reddan testified that beginning in 1992, business began to fall off. Specifically he stated:

> [w]e no longer were beating the market, we were lagging the market and that was beginning to catch up. I think about it, 1990 we had a bad year because several factors, the credit crunch and this was the first wave of cable regulation. '91 we did fairly well, but in '92 we began to lag the market and cumulatively the business wasn't going that well.

(R. 109). In fact, Moran Sr. characterized Chambers as the worst investment experience of his entire business career and in terms of dollars, Chambers represented the largest loss that Moran Sr. had ever suffered on a single stock. Moran Sr. also conceded that one of the reasons that Moran Asset decreased its long position in Turner Broadcasting in 1993, was "because clients were leaving us" (R. 1299).

There is no question that Moran Jr. was aware of the problems the Chambers stock investment was causing for his father. Moran Jr. specifically testified that he had knowledge of his father's big investment in Chambers stock, and that Moran Sr. was suffering losses. Moran Jr. "knew that ... two things were occurring; one, that Chambers was not quite performing up to expectations, and I knew that, given several years of less-than-superior performance, [Moran Sr.] was losing clients" (R. 281). By the beginning of October 1993, Moran Jr. was cognizant of the losses Moran Sr. was sustaining owing to the Chambers stock investment.

Moran Sr. responds that while it is true that the Chambers stock was a bad investment, the bulk of the paper losses in Chambers occurred a full year before the Bell Atlantic merger. While in October 1993 the stock was not doing particularly well, the drop in price of Chambers had reached a plateau. In addition, the firms' financial condition in October 1993 was much better than a

---

*States v. Zackson*, 6 F.3d 911, 921 (2d Cir.1993); Federal R. Evid. 404(b). The introduction of the evidence was not permitted for the purpose of demonstrating that Moran Jr. had a propensity to violate securities law, nor did the court make any such inference when it received this evidence.

year earlier. The firms had no debt, and profits for the quarter ending September 1993 were up more than 60% from a year earlier. Finally, Moran Sr. testified that if he were to retire in October 1993 he could have lived at the same comfort level for the rest of his life. In short, Moran Sr. argues that it would be "ridiculous" to conclude that the losses sustained in Chambers stock had anything to do with his decision to reinvest in cable stocks.

After hearing all of the evidence and examining the documentary exhibits, the court concludes that the losses in Chambers did not put Moran Sr. in any dire position by October 1993. Undoubtedly Chambers was a bad investment causing Moran Sr.'s clients to suffer large monetary losses as the price of the stock plummeted. Certainly because of the losses that were incurred Moran Sr.'s business was negatively affected. However, the evidence is compelling that by October 1993, Moran Sr. had already experienced the worst of the Chambers fallout. While Moran Sr., like any other investor, would desire to pick a winner in the market, there was no special urgency created by the Chambers stock fallout for Moran Sr. to produce a successful stock pick. The court finds that Moran Sr. was in no worse position than any other analyst who seeks to recommend a stock that would significantly increase in value.

The SEC also maintains that Moran Jr. engaged in a pattern of deceptive conduct that indicates he would favor his father's firm even if it meant disclosing confidential material. In support of this assertion, the SEC claims that Moran Jr. was not forthright with Salomon Brothers regarding his directorships and outside business interests, that Moran Jr. through subterfuge allowed Moran Asset to listen in to the TCI conference call, and that Moran Jr. was reprimanded because he improperly sent his research publications to Moran Asset. The SEC asserts that this conduct demonstrates a manifest intent by Moran Jr. to provide special assistance to his father's firms. Moran Jr. counters that the incidents pointed to by the SEC do not even demonstrate wrongdoing on his part, and certainly do not establish an intent to violate the law in order to benefit his father. The court shall address each allegation in turn.

With respect to his position as a director and his trust accounts,[10] the court finds that Moran Jr. did not initially know that he was placed on the board of directors but upon learning of his position, did inform Salomon Brothers about the directorships. Moran Sr. testified that he did not disclose to either of his sons that he had appointed them to the director positions. The fact that Moran Jr. did not participate in running these companies supports the court's conclusion that he had no knowledge of his position. It is not likely that there would have been a need to forge Moran Jr.'s signature on resolutions, if he had been aware that he was on the board of directors. At trial, it was quite clear that the signatures on all the Directors' resolutions that purported to be of Moran Jr. were not genuine. The SEC did not dispute that the resolutions lacked Moran Jr.'s

---

10. The court finds no impropriety with respect to Moran Jr.'s interest in International Tel-Cel. The court credits Moran Jr.'s explanation that he "didn't realize the necessity of disclosing it, as [he] had no involvement in it other than ownership interest" allocated to him by Moran Sr. (R. 351). Significantly, when Salomon Brothers was informed of Moran Jr.'s interest, the compliance department allowed Moran Jr. to maintain his interest in the company (R. 355; 648).

genuine signature and that they were signed without his permission or authority. Moreover, when Moran Jr. learned of his positions, he informed Salomon Brothers and subsequently resigned the positions.

Similarly, with respect to the trust accounts, Moran Sr. specifically confirmed that he did not disclose their existence to Moran Jr. or his other children who were also beneficiaries. Considering this testimony, the Court finds that Moran Jr. was not aware of these trust accounts and consequently, could not disclose his interest to Salomon Brothers. When the existence of these accounts was discovered, Salomon was notified by Moran Jr. and "Salomon Brothers approved [Moran Jr.] being a beneficiary of these trusts and just requested that confirmation statements be sent to Salomon Brothers" (R. 646). Therefore, with respect to the trust accounts and his position as a director, the court finds that the only reason Moran Jr. failed to disclose this information to Salomon Brothers was that he was unaware of his position and status. Hence, the court finds that these holdings do not demonstrate any intent on the part of Moran Jr. to benefit his father or father's firms.

Moran Jr. admits that while using Salomon's office telephone system, he allowed John Reddan to listen to analyst conference calls conducted by TCI after TCI had specifically excluded Reddan and Moran Asset from these calls. Reddan concurred that at his request Moran Jr. gave him access to the conference calls. Moreover, by his own testimony, Moran Jr. concedes that he made no attempt to inform TCI that he was engaging in this practice. In response, Moran Jr. maintains that there was no requirement that TCI be informed as to who was listening in on the calls. More, Moran Jr. attempts to support his conclusion that his actions do not constitute any wrongdoing by pointing out that he did not in any way attempt to conceal from Salomon Brothers that he was allowing Reddan to listen in on these conference calls.

While the court is of the view that Moran Jr.'s actions did not constitute either a violation of law or even Salomon Brothers' policy, Moran Jr.'s actions do demonstrate an intent to help his father's companies beyond any effort he would make for any other firm. While Moran Jr. may not have concealed his actions to Salomon Brothers, the fact that he would allow a member of his father's firms access to a conference call that his father's firm was specifically banned, clearly demonstrates an intent on the part of Moran Jr. to assist his father's firm where he could, even under questionable circumstances. The court finds that Moran Jr. concealed his actions from TCI and that there was no evidence that Moran Jr. ever gave such assistance to any other entity.

The SEC also claims that Moran Jr. was officially reprimanded by Salomon Brothers because he mailed copies of his research publications marked "Internal Use Only" to Moran Asset. Moran Jr. responds that the information contained in the memorandum was not confidential and that he was not reprimanded. As far as Moran Jr. understood, the meeting with the Salomon compliance department was "to advise him of certain aspects of his conduct that the firm—wished to bring to his attention" (R. 873).

The parties agree that on Wednesday October 11 [sic –13], 1993, at approximately 6:30 a.m., Moran Jr. faxed to Moran Asset a summary he prepared which contained his insights as to the proposed Bell Atlantic/TCI transaction (Exh. 5). The document was marked in several areas "For Internal Use Only." Moran Jr. never sought or received approval from anyone at Salomon Brothers to send the document to Moran Asset. Sometime after Moran Jr. used the document to make a presentation at Salomon's morning meeting, the compliance department told Moran Jr. not to put the document on the First Call system, which would have distributed the document to the investment community, because the Salomon involvement in the merger was on an advisory basis. Despite being aware of the decision not to use the First Call system, Moran Jr. did not tell anyone at Salomon Brothers that he had already faxed the document to Moran Asset. When Salomon eventually learned of the fax, Moran Jr. had a meeting with Scribner, the Chief Compliance Officer for Salomon Brothers. At that meeting Moran Jr. was told that "it was contrary to Firm policy for him to have sent "internal use only" material to persons outside of the Firm, and that he must not do it again" (Exh. 6). The SEC characterizes the meeting as a reprimand while Moran Jr. states that he "doesn't know if it qualifies as a reprimand or not" (R. 594). Moreover, Moran Jr. believed that the Internal Use Only designation was "a technical compliance procedure that was used very loosely in this business." See Moran Jr. Post-Trial Brief at 22.

After evaluating all of the evidence, including the testimony of Scribner, the court finds that Moran Jr. was given a "reprimand." Scribner testified that the meeting and subsequent memo was "to advise him of certain aspects of his conduct that the firm wished to—bring to his attention" (R. 873). Scribner explained that the designation of "Internal Use Only" "is that the document on which the—on which that legend appears is not to be distributed outside the firm itself, that is to say, the document, not necessarily—not the information that the document contains" (R. 873). Indeed, other Salomon employees such as Meyercord and Dietze-Courage understood that such a designation meant that the document was not to be distributed to clients or anyone outside the firm (R. 900; Dietze-Courage Deposition, at 59). It is clear that from the tone of the memo regarding Scribner's conversation with Moran Jr. that Salomon Brothers was not pleased that Moran Jr. sent the memo to his father. All of this evidence, coupled with the fact that Scribner warned Moran Jr. not to release such documents again, lead to the unmistakable conclusion that Moran Jr. engaged in a practice that violated Salomon policies in order to benefit his father. Further, there was no evidence that Moran Jr. faxed this document to any other outside parties, other than Moran Asset.

The court notes that the information contained in that memorandum was not confidential. Scribner agreed that there was "absolutely no prohibition for the sales force to discuss the contents of that document with the institutional clients of Salomon Brothers" and that "the prohibition as it stands is merely for the fact of faxing out the document itself rather than the information it contains" (R. 879). Accordingly, after reviewing each of the SEC's allegations regarding Moran Jr.'s conduct, the court finds that the evidence in this case, while not showing an intent on the part of Moran Jr. to violate the law in order to assist his father, nonetheless illustrates Moran Jr.'s willingness to provide information to his father, even if doing so is contrary to the established policies of Salomon Brothers or the wishes of his firm's clients.

*Events From October 3, 1993 to October 11, 1993*

On October 3, 1993, Moran Jr. was officially brought "over the wall" by Salomon Brothers, meaning that he was made aware of the proposed merger between Bell Atlantic and TCI. According to Meyercord, the purpose of involving Moran Jr. was to have him "meet with the company and to discuss how to tell the [merger] story ... to the investment community ... so that he could provide his insight and information on how to tell the story and best position the story to the market place" (R. 893). At that time Moran Jr. was told that "the announcement would come within a week to two weeks" (R. 437).

After being informed about the details of the proposed merger, Moran Jr. left on a previously scheduled business trip to San Francisco. On the night of Monday October 4, Moran Jr. placed two telephone calls from his hotel to the residence of Moran Sr. Upon his return from San Francisco, Moran Jr. reviewed materials relating to the Bell Atlantic/TCI merger plan which he had received in San Francisco. Included in these materials were the details of the merger and an indication that its public announcement would be made in October 1993.

On the morning of October 6, 1993, Moran Jr. attended a meeting at Salomon where he received a full briefing regarding the transaction. During this meeting where Moran Jr. learned the details of the merger, a firm date for the merger's public announcement had not been set. Nonetheless, Moran Jr. was told by Meyercord that the announcement "was going to occur either at the end of the week or in the middle of the following week, and more likely the middle of the following week" (R. 671). Moran Jr. understood that the announcement date "would probably be the 13th, or certainly the 12th, 13th, or 14th" (R. 437). Moran Jr. also received a draft of the press release for the Bell Atlantic/TCI merger which indicated an unspecified announcement day of October 1993. In a telephone conversation that same day, Moran Jr. spoke to either his father or an employee of Moran Asset. Also on October 6, 1993, Furman Selz, a broker dealer issued a report which opined that TCI might reacquire Liberty. Specifically it stated: "To date investing alongside Malone has proved to be profitable. We suspect Liberty might be bought back by TCI. This would make TCI more attractive to a regional Bell investor." In fact, Bell Atlantic sought to acquire Liberty as well as TCI and as a result, TCI and Liberty entered into merger negotiations.

On October 7, the Wall Street Journal published an article entitled "TCI Reported in Talks to Buy Liberty Media" (Exh. 11). In that Wall Street Journal article a Furman Selz analyst speculated that such a merger might "attract a huge investment from a regional Bell phone company." In addition to several brief phone calls between Moran Jr.'s office and Moran Asset as well as Moran Sr.'s home, there was one call where Moran Jr. spoke to Moran Sr. for approximately 43 minutes (R. 720; Exh. 7). Although Moran Jr. remembered that he spoke with Moran Jr. during that period of time, he said "I can't recall the exact specifics, but I believe [Moran Sr.] mentioned something to the effect of Infinity Broadcasting and/or Westwood One during that phone conversation and we talked about that, but I can't remember the specifics of that conversation very well." (R. 427). Moran Jr. further testified that he did not believe there was any discussion of the rumor regarding the rumored TCI/Liberty merger, or the Wall Street Journal article.

Moran Sr. agreed that he had in fact spoken to Moran Jr. during the 43 minute phone conversation. Relative to that conversation, Moran Sr. stated: "To the best of my recollection, my recollection having been helped by two factors, I now believe that I spoke to him about Infinity Broadcasting, and I believe I spoke to him about a party that we were going to have for family and friends at our house sometime in the near future" (R. 1198). Moran Sr. identified the "two factors" stating:

> Well, I studied our buy and sell orders because of this case, and I noticed that we started buying Infinity for the first time I believe it was on October 5th, and I knew Fred followed Infinity, or followed it, and so I believe and I kind of now do recall it, that I talked to him about Infinity, what I thought about it, asked him what he thought about it and so on. The other situation was that, having studied the telephone records and spoken to my wife, I believe—and think it's—let me see—yes, which has to do with my home, perhaps both of those calls were calls to her, or from her—let me see, Frederick A.—yes, that's my wife calling Fred at his office because I had told her to because we were—he wanted her to talk to him about this party that we were going to have, and it had to do with his then fiancee, Michelle, singing at the party and Fred and Michelle coming to the party.

(R. 1198-1199). Moran Sr. also remembered that he did not discuss the rumors regarding the TCI/Liberty merger or the Wall Street Journal Article. October 7, represented the last documented phone conversations between Moran Sr. and Moran Jr. until Monday October 11.

On Friday, October 8, TCI and Liberty announced that they had agreed in principle to a combination of the two companies. An effect of the combination is that John Malone whose holdings in Liberty Stock were valued in excess of $600 million, while his holdings in TCI were $15 million, was diluting his percentage of holdings invested in programming stocks by allocating that wealth to a cable operator. It is undisputed that Moran Sr. did not purchase any TCI or Liberty stock on October 8. In a morning meeting note authored by Reddan, Moran Brokerage reported that "we believe Liberty's real motive is to use TCI's balance sheet to acquire Paramount" (Moran Sr. Exh. AC). This represented the speculation on Wall Street with regard the reasoning behind the merger. Moran Sr. testified that on October 8, he "had no opinion because I really hadn't focused on it" (R. 1482). There was no documented contact between Fred Sr. and Fred Jr. on October 8, 1993.

On Saturday, October 9, 1993, Moran Jr. attended a meeting at Bell Atlantic's headquarters in Philadelphia with co-workers from Salomon Brothers and personnel from Bell Atlantic's Investor Relations Department. Moran Jr.'s purpose in attending the meeting was to discuss the "spin" that would be put on the merger, so as to create the most favorable reaction to the merger from the investment community (R. 912-13). As part of this plan, Bell Atlantic arranged to give advance notice to important members of the investment community "providing notification of a special Bell Atlantic meeting at 8:00 a.m. the following day" through a "blast fax" (Exh. 1). Additionally, it was decided that the Bell's investor relations staff would make phone calls to individual analysts in order to demonstrate the significance of the announcement.

During the weekend of October 9-10, Moran Sr. claims that he began to focus "on what was happening with TCI and Liberty" (R. 1485). After speaking with his wife on October 9th about the possibility of investing in cable stocks, on Sunday October 10th, Moran Sr. telephoned Reddan. Moran Sr. stated that he did not agree with Reddan's view that TCI was acquiring Liberty to help Liberty in its effort to back an acquisition of Paramount. Stating that "my concept was that there were many easier ways to accomplish that [backing of the Paramount acquisition] without having John Malone move all of his wealth from cable—from programming to cable, and I recited the various ways to John [Reddan] that could have been done," Moran Sr. gave his assessment to Reddan (R. 1487). Reddan testified that "at the outset of the conversation I did not agree with him. By the end of the conversation I came around to agree that it represented an endorsement of Telecommunications, Inc. by John Malone and that I thought we should recommend only Telecommunications, Inc. and Liberty Media and we should not recommend other cable television operator stocks or invest in them" (R. 132-33).

Moran Sr. explained to Reddan that beyond Liberty and TCI, the action "was an endorsement of John Malone of the cable TV business and therefore all of the stocks" (R. 1488). Accordingly, Moran Sr. told Reddan that he "wanted to buy all the cable companies and that we were not going to sit by while Malone moved into cable and miss what was happening in the area that had built our reputation and was our forte" (R. 1489). It was the belief of Moran Sr., this was action constituted the appropriate response to Malone's apparent course of conduct. Moran Sr. further explained that "it was a case of following the substance of what John Malone was doing and not limiting [Moran Asset] to the limitation [Malone] had placed on himself of investing only in TCI and Liberty, just like we didn't buy Liberty when he moved into Liberty" (R. 1489). As a result of his analysis, Moran Sr. detailed to Reddan his strategy for buying cable stocks. He testified that "the strategy was to buy almost all the cable TV companies and to move quickly before the rest of Wall Street caught on to what we were doing, because you must understand that everybody was following John Malone, and the logic of my scenario was plain and clear in my opinion, and everybody would end up doing what we were doing, so we wanted to move quickly" (R. 1489). Reddan, while agreeing that there was a basis to buy into TCI and Liberty, urged more caution.

On Monday October 11, 1995 Moran Sr. prepared a written plan to purchase stock in Liberty, TCI and other cable companies for client accounts so that each client would have 25% of its portfolio invested in cable stock (Moran Sr. Exh. W). Prior to the opening of the market, Moran Sr. directed his traders to purchase, through Moran Asset and Moran Brokerage, stock in TCI, Liberty, as well as other cable companies. According to Reddan, Moran Sr. announced to the staff that he had changed his position on cable television operator stocks, and summarized his reasons for doing so. Although Moran Sr. was adamant about his position, Reddan testified that, "there was a general feeling that we should go—everybody was urging caution, and I think that was the feeling of the people in the meeting" (R. 135). In fact, the item in the morning meeting note relating to cable was specifically caption "Fred Moran's Cable TV Industry Comments" because Reddan, who usually co-authored the morning meeting notes, did not agree in total with Moran Sr.'s view. With respect to the Cable TV industry the morning meeting note stated:

> Through the merger of TCI and Liberty Media, John Malone has signaled his plans to transfer the vast majority of his personal wealth, estimated a $700 million, from a company that is roughly half cable TV and half programming, to a company that is very predominantly cable.... Despite the negative of poor government and poor customer relations, the economics of this business are so powerful that they will overshadow the regulatory negative.

(Exh. 41). The morning meeting note was distributed to all of Moran Brokerage's institutional clients. At the opening of the market, Fred Sr. began aggressively purchasing cable stocks, including Liberty and TCI. These stocks were bought for both Moran Sr.'s client accounts and Moran Sr.'s personal and family accounts. His traders were told to be active buyers but don't "chase" stocks which would push the prices higher.

Later on October 11, Moran Asset's Investment Policy Committee ("IPC") held a meeting so that views could be exchanged with respect to the change in strategy. According to Reddan, the purpose "was to talk about the decision to re-recommend the cable television stocks and to invest in those stocks" (R. 143). At the meeting, the general recommendations to Moran Sr. were to adopt a go slow approach and several people wished to engage in more research. The conclusion of the IPC meeting was that "[w]e were going to investigate further change in the cable television industry. We were going to talk to other companies in the cable industry and other investors in cable television" (R. 146). There was no change, however, in the way the stocks were being purchased.[11]

At approximately 3:17 p.m. on October 11, Moran Sr. faxed to Moran Jr. that day's Moran Brokerage Morning Meeting note. Moreover, during the afternoon, Moran Sr. and Moran Jr. spoke via telephone with respect to Moran Sr.'s analysis of cable stocks. Moran Jr.'s recollection of the conversation was that he "was the listener in that conversation. That day [Moran Sr.] called me or I called him and he told me about his change of position on the cable stocks, and basically all I said was your points are well presented or something to that effect" (R. 725). Moran Jr. claimed that he never mentioned Bell Atlantic at any time during the conversation and that the reason he did not respond to Moran Sr.'s inquiry with a "no comment" was because that "could be a signal to [Moran Sr.] that I was working on something, and I purposely avoided signaling anything to him in any way" (R. 725-26). Similarly, Moran Sr. recalled that the conversation regarding the morning meeting note was brief and that Moran Jr. "just said he thought it was well done and that the institutions who [Moran Sr.] sent it to should think well of it, or something to that effect" (R. 1347). While Moran Jr. did not have specific knowledge that Moran Sr.'s new strategy included buying TCI, he testified that "my assumption was that he was probably buying TCI" (R. 459).

On the evening of Tuesday, October 12, Moran Jr. concedes that he spoke to an employee of Moran Asset with respect to the Bell Atlantic proposed

---

11. Although Reddan advocated the "go slow approach," he was not surprised that it was not heeded by Moran Sr. of whom he stated "Fred has a mentality to jump in with both feet and act decisively" (R. 802). Indeed, Reddan testified that he had observed [Moran Sr.] act this way "half a dozen or a dozen times over the course of my ten years" (R. 803).

merger. Moran Jr. testified that he could not remember if he spoke to Kevin Martin or Brian Kelly, and stated:

> What happened is these two gentlemen answered the telephone when I was trying to reach my father and one of them asked me, you know, is something going on, and I said to one of them, I don't remember which one specifically, but I said to them there is, you know, a big deal that's going to be announced tomorrow at the merger of Bell Atlantic and TCI.

(R. 499-500). At the time he disseminated this information, Moran Jr. opined that there was no need to caution either Martin or Kelly because he felt that the information was no longer confidential. Moran Jr. explained that:

> The stock market had already closed, the Wall Street Journal and New York Times were being apprised of the transaction as were the rating agencies, and the announcement would come before the opening of trading the next day, so there would be no way of acting on the information anyway. Plus, they would understand that as professionals in the industry.

(R. 502).

Having failed to reach his father, sometime between 6:30 and 7:00 p.m., Moran Jr. placed a telephone call to Reddan. According to Reddan, the substance of the conversation was that Moran Jr. "told [Reddan] that Bell—there was going to be an announcement in the morning that Bell Atlantic was going to take over Telecommunications, Inc. He asked me if I had heard" (R. 146-47). While Reddan had received a fax from Bell Atlantic which told of an upcoming announcement the next morning, the fax did not include any details such as what the announcement was going to pertain to or if any other parties were involved. Reddan continued, stating that he and Moran Jr. talked a little bit about that, and then Moran Jr. asked me if I knew where his father was" (R. 147). Moran Jr. recalled that he briefed Reddan "on some of the details of the merger at that time" (R. 518). In addition, Moran Jr. left a message on Moran Sr.'s answering machine stating that "there will be a big announcement tomorrow morning essentially creating a merger between Bell Atlantic and TCI" (R. 517).

The reason Moran Jr. believed that the information he disclosed in the evening of October 12 was public was based on his assertion that at the October 9 meeting it was discussed that top investors and the newspapers were to be advised of the transaction prior to the official announcement. When asked who said that the merger was going to be revealed before the public announcement, Moran Jr. stated:

> It was discussed that in general notifying the general public the night of Tuesday, October 12, 1993, that was discussed between Peter Crawford, Kevin Tarrant, Wendy Dietze, Ed Meyercord, Ray Ligouri and myself at the October 12—at the October 9th, 1993 meeting at Bell Atlantic headquarters. Whether they specifically said individual X will notify the Wall Street Journal, I don't remember us discussing that, but they said we will be apprising the investment community in general, which includes the two biggest newspapers.

(R. 506-07). To contradict this assertion by Moran Jr., the SEC called to the stand four of the five individuals Moran Jr. named and offered the deposition of the fifth, and each contradicted Moran Jr.'s recollection.

Specifically, Crawford of Bell Atlantic testified that "there was absolutely no discussion about preannouncing this transaction to any newspapers" (R. 1045). In fact, Crawford continued that Bell Atlantic was "very concerned that there would be no leakage, whether to the investment community or to the newspapers or any other community, for that matter, of the terms and conditions or the announcement itself prior to 7:30 in the morning on the 13th" (R. 1046). After a stipulation that Tarrant would testify on direct to the same facts as Crawford, on redirect Tarrant stated that the policy with respect to media inquiries made on October 12, "would be neither confirm nor deny rumors or choose to comment on that" (R. 1120, 1128). Tarrant stated that the policy was the same until the public announcement on October 13. Katherine Dietze-Courage of Salomon Brothers testified that she did not learn of any Salomon Brothers employees who had disseminated information regarding the merger or disclosed the identities of the companies (Deposition of Katherine Dietze-Courage, at 63). Meyercord and Ligouri of Salomon Brothers each told the court that their understanding of the policies concerning disclosure of the merger details was that public dissemination would take place in the morning on October 13 and that neither of them contacted the newspapers with this information, nor knew of anyone who did so. Further undermining the claim that the information was public in the evening of October 12 is documentary evidence that contradicts Moran Jr.'s recollection. In the story published by the Wall Street Journal on October 13, it was reported that TCI and Bell Atlantic officials would not comment on the rumored merger (Moran Sr. Exh. AL). Moreover, Moran Jr.'s own exhibit, a chronology of events prepared by Bell Atlantic states:

> Calls start coming in to media relations and other Bell Atlantic employees from the New York Times and the Wall Street Journal news reporters indicating that they have some information about the deal and asking for more. Bell Atlantic neither confirms nor denies per routine corporate policy.

(Moran Jr. Exh. AS). Even Reddan, who had already received the blast fax; testified before the court that he did not know the identities of all the parties and the details until he was told by Moran Jr. Thus, the issue of whether the information Moran Jr. passed to Reddan and Moran Asset was still confidential is vehemently contested.

In resolving this factual dispute, the court has examined all of the relevant testimony and documentary evidence. The court finds that the merger details relayed by Moran Jr. on the evening of October 12 were still confidential non- public information. Whether Moran Jr. merely misunderstood the timing of disclosure or intentionally neglected to follow the guidelines, the evidence is overwhelming that the policy was not to disclose the details of the merger to the public as a whole, including the newspapers, until October 13. Every person named by Moran Jr. contradicted his account of the meeting and Moran Jr. was never able to tell the court who specifically authorized disclosure to the public at large on October 12. Therefore, the court is constrained to find that by engaging in these conversations, Moran Jr. disclosed confidential, non-public information.

At 6:36 a.m. on October 13, Moran Jr. sent by fax to Moran Asset a summary of the proposed Bell Atlantic/TCI transaction that he had helped to prepare[13] (R. 153, 464; Exh. 5). This was the same summary Moran Jr. used at Salomon's morning meeting on October 13, to make a presentation. Reddan found this document helpful in interpreting the Bell Atlantic/TCI deal because "it was Fred's [Moran Jr.] analysis of the transaction, and ... took that as a starting point to do our own analysis" (R. 155). Later that morning, but before the market opened, Bell Atlantic, TCI and Liberty announced their agreement in principle to merge. On that day, TCI Class A stock closed up $3.00 per share and Liberty Class A stock rose $2.625 per share (Exh. 24).***

CONCLUSIONS OF LAW

***The SEC alleges that Moran Jr. disclosed material non-public confidential information to Moran Sr., who then purchased stock as a result of that information. There are several possible scenarios proposed by the SEC that it claims constitutes insider trading. Initially, the SEC argues that sometime during the October 7, 1993 forty minute phone call between Moran Jr. and Sr., Moran Jr. disclosed to Moran Sr. material non-public information regarding the merger. The SEC further maintains that the evidence supports its theory that Moran Jr. "tipped" Moran Sr. or relayed additional material non-public information from a public phone during the weekend October 9-10. More, the SEC contends that Moran Jr.'s statements to Moran Sr. during their October 11 telephone conversation constituted a tip of material, non-public information, in that Moran Jr. signaled Moran Sr. that it was advantageous for him to continue to purchase cable stocks. Finally, although not clearly set forth, the SEC implies that Moran Jr.'s disclosure to Reddan and other employees of Moran Asset during the evening of October 12, constituted a violation of Section 10(b) of the Exchange Act and Rule 10b-5 thereunder. For the following reasons, the court finds that the SEC has not proved its claims by a preponderance of the evidence.

To establish that the defendants violated Section 10(b) of the Exchange Act and Rule 10b-5 thereunder, the SEC must show by a preponderance of the evidence that the defendants made improper use of confidential material information in connection with the purchase or sale of securities and that the defendants acted with scienter. *Dirks v. SEC*, 463 U.S. 646, 659-660 (1983); *Aaron v. SEC*, 446 U.S. 680, 695 (1980); *United States v. Carpenter*, 791 F.2d 1024, 1033-34 (2d Cir.1986), aff'd by an evenly divided court, *Carpenter v. United States*, 484 U.S. 19 (1987). A person makes improper use of confidential information when that person obtains material, non-public information intended to be used for a proper purpose and uses it in a breach of a fiduciary duty owed to his employer. *Dirks*, 463 U.S. at 663-64; *United States v. Newman*, 664 F.2d 12, 16-19 (2d Cir.1981).

On October 3, 1993, Moran Jr. was "brought over the wall" with regard to the Bell Atlantic/TCI proposed merger. It is beyond dispute that the information he obtained was confidential and non-public. Indeed, Moran Jr.,

---

13. The summary was marked "For Internal Use Only" and when Salomon learned that Moran Jr. had faxed the document to Moran Asset, Moran Jr. was told that "it was contrary to Firm policy for him to have sent "internal use only" material to persons outside the firm, he must not do so again," and his father's firm should not receive any better treatment than any other firm would ordinarily receive (Exh. 6).

himself, demonstrated that he knew he was in possession of non-public confidential information, specifically testifying that he had admonished two of his research assistants, who had mistakenly seen related information in Moran Jr.'s office, that they had a duty to maintain as strictly confidential the information they had seen. Consequently, as an "insider" Moran Jr. had the requisite fiduciary duty requiring non-disclosure of this material. *SEC v. Texas Gulf Sulphur*, 401 F.2d 833 (2d Cir.1968); *SEC v. Musella*, 748 F.Supp. 1028 (S.D.N.Y.1989), aff'd, 898 F.2d 138 (2d Cir.1990) ("*Musella II*").

A "tippee" inherits the tipper's duty if the tipper disclosed the nonpublic information and the tippee knows or should know of the tipper's breach of duty. *SEC v. Carpenter*, 791 F.2d at 1024; *SEC v. Musella*, 578 F.Supp. 425, 438-39 (S.D.N.Y.1984) ("*Musella I*"). Accordingly, "a tippee who knows or is reckless in not knowing that he was trading on misappropriated non-public information violates Rule 10b-5." *Musella II*, 748 F.Supp. at 1038; see also *Dirks v. SEC*, 463 U.S. at 660; *SEC v. Vaskevitch*, 657 F.Supp. 312, 314 (S.D.N.Y.1987). If Moran Jr. did tip Moran Sr., it would be unfathomable that Moran Sr. would not know or be expected to know that such information was misappropriated by Moran Jr. from his position at Salomon Brothers. Therefore, any resulting stock trades made by Moran Sr. and his companies would subject him to liability as a tippee. Because both Moran Sr. and Jr. would have known that details regarding the merger were confidential misappropriated information, any trading based on a tip would have been made with the requisite scienter necessary to violate federal insider trading statutes. Scienter is established if it is shown that the defendants acted with a "mental state embracing intent to deceive, manipulate, or defraud." *Ernst & Ernst v. Hochfelder*, 425 U.S. 185, 193 (1976); *SEC v. Drexel Burham Lambert*, 837 F.Supp. 587, 608 (S.D.N.Y.1993), aff'd, *SEC v. Posner*, 16 F.3d 520 (2d Cir.1994).

The record further indicates that the information was material. Moran Jr. allegedly informed his father that Liberty and TCI were about to merge, as well as when the announcement was going to take place. The Supreme Court has stated that for actions arising under Federal securities laws, a fact is material "if there is a substantial likelihood that a reasonable [investor] will consider it important in deciding how to [invest]." *Basic Inc. v. Levinson*, 485 U.S. 224, 231 (1988); *TSC Indus., Inc. v. Northway, Inc.*, 426 U.S. 438, 449 (1976); *Azrielli v. Cohen Law Offices*, 21 F.3d 512, 518 (2d Cir.1994); *Sable v. Southmark/Envicon Capital Corp.*, 819 F.Supp. 324, 334 (S.D.N.Y.1993). Here, information of this magnitude was certain to have an effect on cable stocks. Both Moran Jr. and Sr. were specifically knowledgeable about the cable industry. Accordingly, it is beyond peradventure that each defendant would realize the significance of the information regarding the proposed merger and the likely effect that cable stocks would increase in value. Information regarding an impending transaction that is expected to increase the value of a security is certainly of the type that would be considered by a reasonable investor important with respect to deciding how to invest. *SEC v. Shapiro*, 494 F.2d 1301, 1305 (2d Cir.1974); *Musella II*, 748 F.Supp. at 1040.

Hence, the only issue left for the court to resolve with respect to this allegation is whether the SEC has proved by a preponderance of the evidence that Moran Jr. did, in fact, disclose information about the proposed merger to

Moran Sr. before such information was public. As previously stated, if Moran Jr. tipped Moran Sr. as to the proposed merger, they would each be liable for securities violations. The court, however, finds that the evidence does not so prove. With the exception of the claims regarding Moran Jr.'s comments to Moran Sr. about his morning meeting notes and the call to Reddan the evening before the announcement was made, the SEC presented no direct evidence of a tip by Moran Jr. to Moran Sr. The court is mindful that "proof of insider trading can well be made through an inference from circumstantial evidence and not solely upon direct testimonial confession." *SEC v. Singer*, 786 F.Supp. 1158, 1164 (S.D.N.Y.1992). Notwithstanding such recognition, however, if the totality of the evidence suggests an equally or more compelling inference than the SEC's allegation, the plaintiff will not have met its burden of proving its case by preponderance of the evidence. The court finds that the SEC has not established its case.

Surely one possible inference that can reasonably be drawn from the evidence presented in this case is that Moran Sr. purchased cable security stocks based on material non-public information provided to him by Moran Jr. This inference, however, is not the most likely scenario suggested by the proof. The court finds that the testimony and documentary exhibits suggest that Moran Sr. made his stock purchases on October 11, 1993 as a result of following John Malone, the announcement of the TCI/Liberty merger on October 8, and Moran Sr.'s softening position on cable stocks. Moreover, the court also finds that the amount of purchases were not aberrational to Moran Sr.'s style of investing in securities. Further, upon closely examining the SEC assertions, the court declines to accept their proposed inferences regarding the alleged telephone tip, and finds the SEC's argument to be inconsistent. Lastly, the court finds that the statements Moran Jr. made to Moran Sr. with respect to the morning meeting notes on October 11, 1993 do not constitute a tip and that while Moran Jr. may have disclosed non-public information during the evening October 12, 1993, there were no trades made by Moran Sr. as a result of such disclosure. In making this determination, the court relies not only on the testimony of Moran Sr. and Jr., but also that of Reddan, who the court finds completely credible, other workers for Moran Sr., and the voluminous documentary evidence, much of which dates well before October 3, 1993, when Moran Jr. was brought "over the wall."

Contrary to the claims of the SEC, the evidence is overwhelming that Moran Sr. followed Malone. In fact, the record is uncontroverted that the one time Moran Sr. did not react to Malone, he vowed never to be on the wrong side of Malone again. Moran Sr. testified at length as to the power that Malone has over the cable industry. The court credits Moran Sr.'s testimony that he believed Malone to be [the] leader in the cable industry. As previously discussed, there is ample outside evidence such as other broker publications and media articles that lend support to Moran Sr.'s view of Malone. While the SEC is correct that one reason for Moran Sr.'s bearish view on cable was increased government regulation of the industry, another significant reason was that Moran Sr. learned that Malone had liquidated his position in TCI. Reddan testified that concern about regulation and following Malone was virtually "flip sides of the same coin" (R. 781-82). Additionally, Reddan confirmed that Moran Sr. did follow Malone and advised his clients to do the same.

In making its argument that Moran Sr. did not follow Malone, the SEC apparently assumes that "following" Malone is the same as "copying" Malone's investments. Moran Sr. explained, "we don't follow John Malone literally, we follow the substance of what he is doing and then apply it to what makes the most sense given the areas of—the alternative selections that we can make, which are not the same as his because he is limited. As I said before, he chooses to be limited" (R. 1148-49). Moreover, during the period of January 8, 1992 to October 11, 1993, Moran Sr. maintained his holdings in programming, increased his clients' weighting in programming stocks, and purchased most if not all of the Liberty/TCI publicly owned programmers, and followed Malone into the United Kingdom cable television companies (R. 779-781, 1438-39, 1446-51; Exh. 40). The short of the matter is that while Moran Sr. did not simply duplicate investments made by Malone, the evidence before the court nonetheless illustrates a demonstrative pattern of moves made by Moran Sr. that identify his reliance on Malone. Thus, the court finds that Moran Sr. did follow Malone and as discussed at length in the factual section of this opinion, the court finds that by October 1993, Moran Sr. was softening his view on the cable television industry.

The court is therefore presented with circumstantial evidence that indicates Moran Sr. made his investments on October 11, not because of inside information, but rather because he became aware of Malone's actions which indicated that cable stocks would become lucrative. Aside from the testimony of Moran Sr.[20] there is ample evidence which supports Moran Sr.'s innocent explanation of his purchases. The Liberty/TCI merger took place on October 8, 1993. Over the weekend, Reddan testified that Moran Sr. told him about his game plan to invest in cable stocks. Contrary to the SEC argument, Reddan did not disagree with Moran Sr.'s analysis, but urged a "go slow" approach. The court finds no significance that Moran Sr. did not heed Reddan's or his analysts' warnings to go slow, since Moran Sr. typically disregarded such analysis. Additionally, Moran Sr. has a demonstrated history for buying stocks in large quantities. Indeed, his holdings of cable stocks prior to 1992 and investment in Chambers demonstrates that large percentage acquisitions were common place for Moran Sr. By virtue of the evidence as to how Moran Sr. typically engaged in stock purchases, the court finds that the fact that he bought large amounts of cable stocks for himself and clients is not aberrational.

Merely because the defendants present a reasonable inference from the circumstances which suggests no illegality, does not mean that the plaintiff has failed to fulfill its burden. However, the court finds several troubling aspects to the SEC's theory of liability. Initially, the SEC argues an inconsistent position. On the one hand, the SEC argues that Moran Jr. and Sr. should be considered "a sophisticated tipper and tippee," and that would explain why there was no documented contact between October 9 and October 11. See, Plaintiff's Proposed Finding of Fact and Conclusions of Law, p. 21. Since the defendants presumably

20. The SEC reasonably argues that Moran Sr. is now manufacturing a "cover story" to hide the fact that his real reason for investing was inside information. The court certainly takes this possibility into account and accordingly looks to evidence beyond that of Moran Sr.'s testimony.

understood that the SEC's attention would have been drawn by contact during that period, the SEC argues that Moran Sr. and Jr. distanced themselves from each other. On its own this is not an unreasonable proposition, however, under the same theory, the SEC also wants the court to accept that Moran Jr. and Sr. would be foolish enough to give and receive a tip during a 40 minute phone conversation from Moran Jr.'s office to Moran Sr.'s office. A conversation which could be and was documented. Not only that, the SEC asks the court to find that during the time that Moran Sr. was actually engaged in the alleged illegal trade, he would fax his morning meeting notes to Moran Jr., the very morning meeting notes that included the recommendation to buy cable stocks. The court is puzzled as to why Moran Sr. would send these notes to Moran Jr., if as the SEC claims, Moran Sr. was already tipped as to the proposed merger.

Lastly, the SEC asks this court to accept that Moran Jr., "the sophisticated tipper," who had already given the information regarding the merger to his father, would then call his father's firm on the evening before the official announcement and disclose the details of the same merger to at least one employee of Moran Asset and later to Reddan. Considering that Moran Sr. had already made the trades in issue, there is no reason for Moran Jr. to call his father with this information. If he had already tipped his father earlier, as claimed by the SEC, it would have been utterly nonsensical for Moran Jr. to place this call.

The court also has difficulty with the SEC's claim that the fact that there was no documented contact between Moran Sr. and Jr. from October 8 until October 11, is somehow indicative of guilt because it shows that they were attempting to distance themselves from one another or that it was then that the actual tip took place. While this argument is a possible theory, there are other equally possible theories that do not suggest any wrongdoing. One such theory is that the lack of documented contact between Moran Sr. and Jr. was because they truly did not have any contact with each other during that time period. Indeed, the SEC's allegation regarding theoretical secret phone calls from public telephones is nothing more than conjecture which cannot be substituted for evidence. Indeed, even if the court were to assume that there was a tip during that time period or that the defendants were merely attempting to distance themselves, the court is at a loss to explain Moran Sr.'s subsequent fax to Moran Jr. on October 11 and Moran Jr.'s disclosure of the information during the evening of October 12. Certainly, the exchange of this information would be the opposite of distancing. The more logical inference is that there was no tip from Moran Jr. to Moran Sr. in this aspect.

The next claim asserted by the SEC is that Moran Jr.'s statements to Moran Sr. during their October 11 telephone conversation constituted a tip of material, nonpublic information, because it signaled Moran Sr. that it was advantageous to continue purchasing cable stocks. Encouragement to continue to purchase a stock, even if the specific advantageous information is not included in the conversation, and a resulting purchase of the security can be a violation of the prohibition against insider trading. See, *SEC v. Drexel Burnham Lambert, Inc.*, 837 F.Supp. 587, 597-98 (S.D.N.Y.1993), aff'd, *SEC v. Posner*, 16 F.3d 520 (2d Cir.1994); *SEC v. First City Financial Corp.*, 688 F.Supp. 705, 712-13 (D.D.C.1988), aff'd, 890 F.2d 1215 (D.C. Cir.1989). But in this case, the court finds that Moran Jr.'s statements that the morning meeting notes were "well presented" do not constitute a tip for the purposes of the securities law. Moran Jr. testified that he used that response rather than just say no comment because he believed that if he refused to provide an answer, Moran Jr.'s silence would have communicated to his father that there was something imminently about to happen in the cable industry. Specifically Moran Jr. stated, "if I told him no comment that could be a signal to him that I was working on something, and I purposely avoided signaling anything to him in any way" (R. 725-6). Considering that the morning meeting notes did not address any possibility of a merger, it was entirely proper for Moran Jr. to answer the way he did. If he had refused comment, Moran Sr. might then have realized that there was some other aspect to consider. Moreover, considering the conversation took place in the late afternoon after most of the trading was already completed, the conversation between Moran Sr. and Jr., does not appear to be a tip. Additionally, there is no proof that Moran Sr. ever had any hesitancy regarding his purchase of cable stocks. Actually, the evidence demonstrates just the opposite, despite the fact that Moran Sr.'s employees wanted him to slow down, he ignored their requests. Therefore, it is not likely that Moran Sr. was worried about seeking any confirmation from Moran Jr. as to whether the stock purchase was still a good idea. Thus, the court finds that the conversation on October 11, 1993 between Moran Sr. and Jr. does not constitute a violation of the Exchange Act.

The last theory, apparently advanced by the SEC, suggests that Moran Jr.'s October 12th disclosures of the merger details, somehow constituted insider trading. The court rejects this theory. The evidence, in part, leaves no question that the details disclosed by Moran Jr. were material, non-public, and confidential information. The mere disclosure of the information, however, is not sufficient to establish a violation of the Exchange Act. In order to violate § 10(b) of the Exchange Act, the fraud must be "in connection with the purchase or sale of any security registered on a national security exchange or any security not so registered." In this case, the purchases of the securities at issue had previously occurred on October 11. Since it is undisputed that there were no security purchases of cable stock after Moran Jr. disclosed the merger information and prior to the public announcement of the merger, there can be no liability for insider trading. Consequently, since the SEC has not demonstrated by a preponderance of the credible evidence that Moran Sr.'s stock purchases were made as a result of material non-public information disclosed by Moran Jr., the court finds for the defendants with respect to that charge.***

CONCLUSION

The court finds that:

Frederick W. Moran, Frederick A. Moran, Moran Asset Management, and Moran & Associates Securities Brokerage did not violate Section 10(b) of the Exchange Act and Rule 10b-5 thereunder and therefore the court dismisses that claim with prejudice; ***

### *NOTES AND QUESTIONS*

***1. Bench Trial vs. Jury Trial.*** Because the SEC was seeking the imposition of a civil monetary penalty against each of the Morans, the Morans could have asserted a Seventh Amendment right to a trial by jury. Why might the Morans have preferred a bench trial? Did the bench trial offer the SEC any advantages? We will explore more fully the issue of a constitutional right to a jury trial in civil prosecutions by the SEC in Chapter 9.

2. ***SEC and SRO Surveillance.*** The SEC began an investigation of the proposed Bell Atlantic-TCI merger almost immediately following the deal's public announcement. What may have alerted the SEC to the possibility of insider trading? How do you suppose the SEC identified Moran Sr. as a possible insider trader? In addition to Bell Atlantic, TCI, Liberty, and Salomon Brothers, what other entities would most likely have been asked to supply the SEC with information?

Note that the case involving the Morans was one of three SEC enforcement actions brought against persons for insider trading in connection with the Bell Atlantic-TCI merger. In the second case, a member of the board of directors of Liberty was alleged to have told his wife of the proposed merger, who then purchased TCI stock for her own account and advised her son to do the same. After a district judge upheld the validity of the SEC's misappropriation theory as a matter of law, see *SEC v. Lenfest*, 949 F. Supp. 341, (E.D. Pa. 1996), the case was tried to a jury, but the judge issued a directed verdict against the SEC. See *SEC v. Lenfest*, Civil Action No. 95-7597 (E.D. Pa. 1998). The third case was brought against the son of a TCI employee in Denver, who was alleged to have misappropriated information on the proposed deal from his father, avoiding $22,781 in losses on call contracts and making a $14,000 profit. The son settled with the SEC in December 1994, agreeing to pay a civil penalty of $36,781 and to disgorge the sum of $40,113 ($22,781 for losses avoided, $14,000 for gains that would have been realized, and $3,332.72 in prejudgement interest). *SEC v. William K. Fisher*, Litigation Release No. 14362, 58 SEC Docket 1309 (Dec. 20, 1994).

3. ***Constructing the Circumstantial Case.*** Do you agree with the trial judge that the 40 minute phone call on Thursday, October 7 was done too openly and conspicuously to support the inference that an illegal tip was communicated between Moran Jr. and Moran Sr.? Speculate as to what types of facts may have provided stronger support for this inference. What if the SEC had been able to introduce evidence of a call from a pay phone to the Moran Sr. residence on Sunday, October 10, the evening prior to Moran Sr.'s stock purchases?

Consider the SEC's evidence regarding Moran Sr.'s prior investments and trading practices. What types of documents would the SEC have been likely to seek from Moran Sr.? How did the SEC attempt to establish that Moran Sr. had been reticent about cable stocks prior to his purchases in TCI and Liberty? Did the SEC's contention that Moran Sr. needed a "sure thing" to recover from his substantial losses in Chamber Development strengthen or detract from its case?

Consider also the SEC's contention that Moran Jr. had violated Salomon Brothers' procedures on a number of occasions. From where did the SEC likely get evidence to support this contention? For what purpose was this evidence admitted at trial?

*4. Violations of the Advisers Act and the Exchange Act.* Although the trial judge dismissed the SEC's Rule 10b-5 allegations against both of the Morans, the trial judge held Moran Sr. and Moran Asset liable for violating Sections 204, 206(2), and 207 of the Investment Advisers Act of 1940 and Rule 204-1(b)(1) thereunder. The trial judge also imposed liability for Moran Sr.'s and Moran Brokerage's violation of Section 15(b) of the Exchange Act and Rule 15b3-1 thereunder. *SEC v. Moran*, 922 F. Supp 867, 902 (S.D.N.Y. 1996) (*Moran I*). The Section 206(2) of the Advisers Act violations were based on Moran Sr.'s breach of fiduciary duty through a negligent decision to allocate purchases of Liberty stock to his personal and family trading accounts rather than to the accounts of his client. *Moran I*, 922 F. Supp. at 897-98. For these violations, the court ordered disgorgement in the amount of $9,551, a permanent injunction against both Moran Sr. and Moran Asset, and a civil penalty of $5,000 and 25,000, respectively. See *SEC v. Moran*, 944 F. Supp. 286, 295-96 (S.D.N.Y. 1996) (*Moran II*). With respect to the other violations of the Advisers Act, and the violations of the Exchange Act, the court found that Moran Asset had willfully failed to amend its Forms ADV, and Moran Brokerage had willfully failed to amend its Form BD, to reflect the fact that Moran's Sr.'s wife and two sons held directorships. *Moran I*, 922 F. Supp. at 900-01. For these violations, the court ordered permanent injunctions against Moran Sr., Moran Asset, and Moran Brokerage, and imposed a civil penalty of $20,000, $25,000, and $25,000 respectively. *Moran II*, 944 F. Supp. at 298.

*5. Collateral Consequences.* After the trial judge announced his initial decision in the case brought against both of the Morans, Moran Sr. shared these sentiments with reporters: "I feel beaten up, bloodied, worn-out. All I want to do at this point is go in a corner and hide for fear that [the SEC] will come back and beat me up some more." He is also reported to have said that the Advisers Act and Exchange Act violations found by the judge were "administrative nonsense." See Frances A. McMorris, Moran and Son are Cleared in Insider Case, Wall St. J. at B2 (Apr. 3, 1996). Moran Sr. commented that "[T]he hurt will never go away. [The SEC] knew from the beginning they had no evidence against us.... They didn't care. They proceeded to destroy my business and my son's career. It cost us over $1 million in legal fees." Sharon Walsh, Securities Analyst, Father Cleared of Insider Trading, Both Men Critical of SEC's High-Profile Case, Wash. Post at G3 (April 3, 1996). Press reports note that Moran Sr.'s firm managed $540 million in assets when the SEC began its investigations, but had only $4 million under management when the judge's decision was announced. Id. Reports further state that Moran Sr.'s profit figures alleged by the SEC were based on "'paper' estimates of how much the stock position gained in value on the day the takeover bid was announced." See Jeffrey Taylor & Amy J. Schatz, SEC Accuses Moran and His Son of Insider Trading, Wall St. J. at B8 (June 16, 1995). Most of the TCI and Liberty stock was not "sold for several months and eventually resulted in a substantial loss after the takeover deal later collapsed." Id. With respect to Moran Jr., it was reported that Salomon Brothers suspended him from dealing with clients when the SEC filed its complaint, and that while the firm kept him on the payroll and paid for much of his legal fees, "the firm has been essentially pushing him out." John M. Higgins, Judge Clears Morans on Insider Trading, Multichannel News (April 1996), 1996 WL 13824595. See also Walsh, supra, Wash. Post. at G3. In view of all this, did the government extract a significant penalty from both of the Morans notwithstanding the judge's findings and official sanctions? Based on your review of the circumstantial evidence, would you have taken this case to trial?

***6. Suspicious Trading as Proof of Possession.*** What if SEC officials are convinced that a person traded securities based on material nonpublic information but have no evidence to establish that the defendant had access to that information at the time of the trades? It is well established that suspicious trading activity (in terms of timing and/or amount) can provide circumstantial evidence of possession. But can it ever, by itself, support such an inference? At least one court has concluded that the answer is no. See *SEC v. Truong*, 98 F. Supp. 2d 1086, 1097 (N.D. Cal. 2000) ("[a]llowing the SEC to tell a jury that 'because the [defendant's] trading was suspicious, the [defendant] must have possessed some material nonpublic information,' would relieve the SEC of its burden to identify the information, prove its materiality, and prove possession and use by the [defendant]"). Would facts showing mere access to material nonpublic information, when coupled with evidence of suspicious trading, support such an inference? Was this basically the SEC's argument in *Moran*?

***7. Using Circumstantial Evidence to Establish Scienter.*** Even in cases in which it is easy to establish that the defendant was aware of material, nonpublic information at the time of his trade, liability under Rule 10b-5 will attach only if it can also be shown that the defendant acted with "scienter," a "mental state embracing intent to deceive, manipulate, or defraud." *Ernst & Ernst v. Hochfelder*, 425 U.S. 185, 193-94 n. 12 (1976). As we have seen, this showing is generally made in insider trading cases through proof that the defendant knew, or was reckless in not knowing, that the information in his possession was both material and nonpublic. And in cases in which a tip has been given, the defendant-tippee must also have known or should have known that the tipped information stemmed from a breach of duty on the part of the tipper. Not surprisingly, the government often uses evidence of uncharacteristically large, speculative, or otherwise suspicious trading in proving the defendant's scienter. See, e.g., *SEC v. Warde*, 151 F.3d 42, 48 (2d Cir. 1998) (noting that co-defendants tipper and tippee "engaged in uncharacteristic, substantial and exceedingly risky investments in [ ] warrants shortly after speaking with one another, suggesting that they discussed not only the inside information, but also the best way to profit from it"); *SEC v. Willis*, 777 F. Supp. 1165, 1173 (S.D.N.Y. 1991) (stating that scienter was plead sufficiently with allegation in complaint concerning "the volume and timing of the trading"); *SEC v. Musella*, 748 F. Supp. 1028, 1039 (S.D.N.Y. 1989) (inferring scienter in part from "the amounts involved and the financing of the trades"). From what other types of facts can a defendant's scienter be inferred?

## F. POLICY RATIONALES FOR FEDERAL REGULATION OF INSIDER TRADING AND THE SEARCH FOR A DEFINITION

All of the preceding material in this Chapter relates to the question of *how* the federal securities laws operate to prevent, detect, and remedy offenses involving insider trading. What follows are various arguments as to *why* insider trading should—or should not—be subject to federal prohibition and why the offense of insider trading should—or should not—be specifically defined. While the chosen excerpts shed much light on the most important policy concerns, they intended to provide only a flavor of what is out there in a very rich universe of insider trading literature.

### 1. *The Policy Debate Over the Harms and Benefits of Insider Trading*

#### a. *Insider Trading and its Effects on Corporate Management*

## IN DEFENSE OF INSIDER TRADING

**by Henry G. Manne**

Harv. Bus. Rev. 113-19 (Nov.- Dec. 1966)

In April 1965, when the Securities and Exchange Commission announced its action against executives of the Texas Gulf Sulphur Company for alleged violations of rules against insider trading, there was an outcry of public indignation against the defendants. It was as though men who were highly respected members of the community had suddenly been found out in heinous crime.

But this is only one more manifestation of a long and persistent trend. The main push came with the Pecora hearings in Congress in 1933-1934, where the activities of prominent executives who conceded playing some part in insider trading were characterized as "immoral," "unscrupulous," "unfair," a "betrayal of fiduciary duties," and a "vicious practice." Since that time, leading academic figures, lawyers, businessmen, and spokesmen for the SEC with almost boring uniformity, have castigated insider trading as being costly to shareholders and giving unfair and undeserved gains to insiders. The tone of most discussions on this subject suggests that there is no doubt whatever: insider trading is a sin, and the war against it is a holy one.

But, as in most holy wars, self-righteousness and hypocrisy may be the true order of the day. In the entire literature on insider trading there does not exist one careful analysis of the subject. Lawyers have been having a field day arguing about the meaning of words or the reach of the last case or any of a thousand technical and legal issues. Unfortunately, however, most lawyers do not have the skills to develop a careful economic analysis of the subject, and economists have offered no assistance. The tone of debate has remained essentially moralistic and question-begging. Logic has been totally lost to emotion.

It is very likely, however, that unless businessmen, commentators, and the courts wake up, far more than logic will be lost. For the current attack on insider trading may prove to be a fundamental attack on free capital markets and entrepreneurial capitalism. It would be a shame to lose the battle by default. ***

This article constitutes at least a starting point for logical analysis of the subject. In particular, I shall argue that insider trading is the best, if not the only, method of adequately compensating corporate innovators ***

### Stimulus to Innovation

***I should begin this discussion with some explanation of what is meant by the "entrepreneurial function." The term is used here in a technical, economic sense, and the function differs in critical respects from that performed by managers:

*Entrepreneur—An Innovator.* Fundamentally the entrepreneur is a man who finds a new product or a new way to make or sell an old one. He may reorganize corporate administration, or he may be responsible for the merger of two companies. He may be a corporate promoter, or he may perform the job of selecting and guiding the managers. In short, he is the individual responsible for having or taking a new idea and causing it to be put into effect. A critical part of this definition is the "new idea," but there is no payoff unless the idea is put into effect successfully.

Since the value of an entrepreneur's contribution cannot be known until it has been made, there is rarely any way of appraising his services in advance. This is undoubtedly why early economists, including Adam Smith, did not see the entrepreneurial function as being distinct from the capitalist's function, for in the eighteenth century one was generally required to risk his own money to prove the value of his innovation. The return for successful innovation looks, superficially at least, like the return to the owner of capital.

Today, however, a sizable portion of economic literature, introduced principally by the late Joseph A. Schumpeter of Harvard University, has been built on the distinction between the entrepreneur and the capitalist, though it has not yet had a great impact on popular thinking.

*Manager—A Technician.* The management function is, in the pure sense, simply to administer a business along lines already determined. Though it may be extraordinarily complex and highly paid, the manager's job is basically that of a technician. As soon as he begins to reorganize the existing arrangement, then and only then is the executive performing an innovational or entrepreneurial activity, rather than a management function. Again the distinction between functions remains even though the same individual performs both. As Schumpeter commented, it is "just as rare for anyone always to remain an entrepreneur through the decades of his active life as it is for a businessman never to have a moment in which he is an entrepreneur, to however modest a degree."[2]

Reward for Performance

In return for performing its function, management receives its compensation, generally termed by economists the "wage." This wage is simply the market price for managerial skills. No one knowingly pays more or takes less. Similarly, the capitalist receives "interest," which, whatever the legal form might be called, is the economic return to him. It may be relatively certain, as in the case of bonds, or it may be very indefinite, as with speculative securities; but its economic nature remains the same. Although the degrees of risk may vary greatly, interest is the price that has to be paid for the use of money over time.

---

2. Joseph Alois Schumpeter, The Theory of Economic Development, translated by Redvers Opie (Cambridge, Harvard University Press, 1934), p.78.

But in the sense that wages and interest are the market return for capital and management, there is no such thing as a market price for entrepreneurial skills. In fact, almost by definition, it is impossible to value entrepreneurial activities *before they have paid off in some other form.* Economic theorists do, however, have a word for the entrepreneurial return; it is termed "profit," although that particular usage of the word has not received popular acceptance. But, aside from having a word for it, we have little knowledge about the particular form that this "profit" may take, or even whether it can redound to the benefit of entrepreneurs in large corporations. ***

Compensation Not Enough

To provide an effective incentive, entrepreneurial compensation has to be available when the benefits are realized by the corporation, and it must vary with the value of the contribution. Since neither of these eventualities can ordinarily be predicted in advance, most existing compensation plans are inadequate for the task. Obviously, salary is inappropriate. The amount of salary has to be decided on in advance, it does not allow for distinguishing the manager who only manages from one who also innovates, and it is not flexible enough to reward particular contributions.

At first glance the bonus does seem to answer most of these objections. However, most bonuses today are formulated in advance and depend on total profits rather than individual contributions. Bonus plans are incentive devices, but they probably tend to generate managerial improvements, such as small cost-cutting, rather than radical innovations. The bonus plan, as opposed to the special bonus, will not serve the entrepreneur's purpose.

The special bonus can, of course, be used to reward great innovations, though there are legal restrictions if authorization is not established in advance. But the main drawback is that the true value of a particular contribution, in the form of higher profits, may not be known for many years. So there frequently are gross disparities in judgment between the bonus committee and the executive as to the latter's true worth. This misjudgment may become even more serious if the innovation has caused the price of the stock to rise but has not yet affected profits, though the stock price rise is precisely what the entrepreneur should be rewarded for.

In addition, the entrepreneurial type who is motivated by the possibility of "getting rich quick" probably does not like the idea of negotiating his reward after his contribution has been made. This distinction is like that between a patent system and a system of bonuses or government awards for inventions. Few will be found to argue that the latter system encourages as much invention as the former.

Stock options also add some incentive to efficiency for managers, but it is doubtful that they can serve the needs of the entrepreneur for massive reward for great innovations. The difficulty should be obvious. The number of shares to be optioned to various executives normally has to be determined in advance of any entrepreneurial innovation. If the options are granted after the innovation, they are the same as the special bonus, except that payment is made in the form of a free call on corporate stock rather than in the form of cash. Stock options undoubtedly add greatly to incentive, but they may still promise too little to entrepreneurial types with ambition, enthusiasm, and a large measure of self-confidence.

Incentives from Trading

On the other hand, free trading by insiders in a company's securities meets the objections mentioned for other compensation schemes and has special advantages of its own. Perhaps this can best be seen by comparing systems of compensation for patentable and nonpatentable innovations.

Basically the patent system is designed to allow inventors to receive an appropriate reward for successful innovations by preventing others from copying and participating in profits which we might say were not earned by them. The granting of a temporary monopoly to the patentee assures two goals: (1) it excludes the would-be interloper; (2) it provides the patentee with a substantial reward for his idea, although that reward will vary with the economic importance of the invention.

The patent system seems to work reasonably well, but only for patentable ideas. How can we guarantee a similar reward to inventors of nonpatentable ideas? In this area our legal system has been rather weak and ineffective; it has developed few really successful techniques for the protection of such ideas. Most businessmen recognize that secrecy and speed of marketing are the two principal devices for realizing substantial profits for their companies from nonpatentable innovations—secrecy to keep competitors away and speed because they cannot be kept away for long. But nothing in this scheme provides any protection or reward for the individual who has an important, nonpatentable idea which he personally is in no position to exploit.

For the man who has not founded his own business to exploit his idea—historically the traditional course for an entrepreneur—trading in the stock market on inside information provides a reward system, and is the only effective device available for the entrepreneur who is employed by a large corporation.

Insider trading allows any individual who works for a publicly traded corporation to play the entrepreneurial role, a very important advantage. Individuals can, in effect, sell their own ideas without the necessity of having large amounts of capital available. The increase in stock price, though not perfect, will provide as accurate a gauge of the value of the innovation as can be found, and it will leave little room for argument about an individual's worth.

Large corporations will be able to compete more effectively for entrepreneurial talent with closely owned companies, since they can now hold out the promise of very great rewards for the successful innovator. The image of corporate executives as gray bureaucrats can and should be erased. Large corporations can furnish as much romance, excitement, and opportunity for rapid economic and social advancement as any other avenues pursued today. But if corporations get hung up on foolish moralizing, such as characterizes most discussions of insider trading, they cannot hope to compete successfully or to survive the subtle attacks of government agencies.

If there really is an economic service or function that can be termed entrepreneurship, then we must have some way of compensating it. The cases are legion of new corporate managers bringing in fresh, imaginative, but often untested ideas. If these individuals were to be limited to the same compensation as their dull unimaginative, and overly conservative predecessors, what incentive would they have to innovate? Their salaries, bonuses, and pensions are usually secure, and few large companies face imminent bankruptcy. Their stock options and bonus plans will give some motivation to improve things, but not to take very great personal risks. For the true entrepreneur, the possibility of great riches will elicit more risk-taking activities and enterprise than will the possibility of smaller though more certain gain.

It might also be added that this promise attracts a different type of personality as well, one with which successful American businessmen have traditionally been proud to identify—the self-made, rags-to-riches, "Horatio Alger" hero. There is still room for such characters in the large modern corporation.***

---

Critics of Professor Manne's "management compensation" argument—and through the years there have been many—respond chiefly that insider trading is a particularly poor method of compensating managers because:

- it tempts managers to engage in overly risky projects because greater trading profits can be extracted in companies with more volatile stock prices. See Frank Easterbrook, Insider Trading, Secret Agents, Evidentiary Privileges, and the Production of Information, 1981 Sup. Ct. Rev. 309, 323;
- it allows managers to profit from bad news and negative corporate developments as well as the good (thus creating perverse incentives on the part of management). See Richard A. Posner and Kenneth E. Scott, Economics of Corporation Law and Securities Regulation 154 (1980).
- it encourages company officials and employees to keep secrets from each other thereby decreasing the firm's internal operational efficiency. See Robert J. Haft, The Effect of Insider Trading Rules on the Internal Efficiency of the Large Corporation, 80 Mich. L. Rev. 1051 (1982);
- it allows for rewards to all managers—even those who shirk responsibilities and are largely unproductive. See Iman Anabtawi, Note, Toward a Definition of Insider Trading, 41 Stan. L. Rev. 377, 392-93 (1989); and
- it hides from corporate shareholders the total benefits that are being received by management. See Robert C. Clark, Agency Costs Versus Fiduciary Duties 55, in Principals and Agents: The Structure of Business (John W. Pratt & Richard J. Zeckhauser eds., 1985).

b. *The Effects of Insider Trading on Stock Market Price Efficiency*

In addition to its value as potential compensation for managers, the practice of insider trading has also been defended on the theory that it contributes to efficiency in stock market pricing. Professors Dennis Carlton and Daniel Fischel, two of the most prominent proponents of this "stock market efficiency" theory, advance the following argument:

> Since the firm's shareholders value the ability to control information that flows to the stock market, they may also value insider trading because it gives the firm an additional method of communicating and controlling information. If insiders trade, the share price will move closer to what it would have been had the information been disclosed. How close will depend on the amount of "noise" surrounding the trade. The greater the ability of market participants to identify insider trading, the more information such trading will convey. At the extreme, trading by insiders is as fully revealing as complete disclosure. But since insiders will limit the size of their positions because of risk aversion and will camouflage their trading to some degree, they convey less information by trading than that conveyed by (credible) full disclosure.
>
> Several reasons explain why communicating information through insider trading may be of value to the firm. Through insider trading, a firm can convey information it could not feasibly announce publicly because an announcement would destroy the value of the information, would be too expensive, not believable, or-owing to the uncertainty of the information-would subject the firm to massive damage liability if it turned out ex post to be incorrect. Conversely, firms also could use insider trading to limit the amount of information to be reflected in price. Controlling the number of traders who have access to information may be easier than controlling how much information gets announced over time. In other words, announcement of information need not be continuous, while trading on inside information can be. Thus, insider trading gives firms a tool either to increase or to decrease the amount of information that is contained in share prices.

Dennis W. Carlton and Daniel R. Fischel, The Regulation of Insider Trading, 35 Stan. L. Rev. 857, 868 (1983).

Critics of the "stock market efficiency" defense point out that insider trading is a highly inefficient way to impound information into a company's stock price. As Professor James Cox has argued:

> [c]ertainly price changes will occur more quickly and efficiently through disclosure of the material nonpublic information than through the manager's use of personal resources and time to trade in his firm's stock. The insider's trading simply has too much "noise" associated with it to be an efficient substitute for a clarion corporate announcement.

James D. Cox, Insider Trading and Contracting: A Critical Response to the "Chicago School," 1986 Duke L.J. 628, 646. Moreover, although widespread trading among insiders and their tippees would be more likely than individual and isolated trading to produce a signaling effect, as noted above, such widespread trading would expose the company to substantial risks in its internal operations.

Arguments about stock price efficiency have also been launched from the other direction. For example, Professor Schotland and others have argued that a ban on insider trading promotes efficiency by eliminating the personal profit incentive that otherwise would come from delaying disclosure of corporate events:

> Allowing any trading on undisclosed material information makes improper delay of disclosure more likely. We must not forget that if disclosure is improperly delayed, we cannot find out until all or at least some of the harm is done, and often we will not find out at all. To ensure timely disclosure—an end to which the SEC and the self-regulatory bodies are equally dedicated—it is obvious that we must avoid encouraging motivations for improper delay, however subconscious they may be. If we abandon restraints on insider trading, we tempt insiders to delay disclosure so that they can buy more shares or arrange financing for more buying; we also invite the timing of disclosure to get maximum market response. *** It is difficult enough to time disclosure properly for corporate reasons, without adding an extraneous, easily avoidable conflict of interest.

Roy Schotland, Unsafe at Any Price: A Reply to Manne, Insider Trading and the Stock Market, 53 Va. L. Rev. 1425, 1448-49 (1967).

Moreover, some argue that insider trading contributes to inefficient stock prices because it forces specialists and market makers to protect themselves by widening the spreads between their bid and ask prices. This argument was summarized succinctly by amici urging the Supreme Court's endorsement of the misappropriation theory:

> Trading in organized securities markets is usually effected through specialized intermediaries (e.g., market makers in dealer markets or specialists on the exchanges), who determine a bid-ask spread at which they trade with public customers. The width of the spread between the prices at which intermediaries will buy or sell (the bid-ask spread) is essentially a measure of the efficiency of the market for a security. While dealers and specialists are the initial victims of those who trade on misappropriated material nonpublic information, they pass this injury along to public customers through a widened bid-ask spread. To the extent it is foreseeable that people will trade with misappropriated material nonpublic information, intermediaries must protect themselves in advance by widening the bid-ask spread. Thus trading by those who misappropriate material nonpublic information for personal profit necessarily injures all public customers by decreasing the price at which they can sell to intermediaries (the bid) and increasing the price at which they can buy from intermediaries (the ask). Indeed, customers trading other securities will also be injured, because dealers cannot anticipate which securities will be traded by those in possession of material nonpublic information and will consequently widen the bid-ask spread for all securities that may be the subject of such information.

Amicus Curiae Brief of North Amer. Sec. Administrators Ass'n., Inc. and Law Professors in Support of Petitioner, at 8, *United States v. O'Hagan*, 521 U.S. 642 (1997) (No. 96-842).

### c. *Identifying the "Victims" of Insider Trading*

Clearly, one of the most contentious issues in the policy debate over insider trading involves the identification of actual victims. To be sure, the persons on the other side of an insider's transactions would not have traded at that same time and price had they known of the material nonpublic information in the insider's possession. But can these persons properly be thought of as "victims" of the insider trader? If such an insider had obeyed the law and simply abstained from trading, these contemporaneous traders would still have traded in ignorance, and still would have suffered financial damage when the company revealed the material nonpublic information. Thus, in this sense, it is difficult to regard those who traded with the insider as the victims of his unlawful act.

The above excerpt from the *O'Hagan* brief argues that everyone is in one sense a victim of insider trading to the extent that we all must trade in less efficient securities markets. Professor William Wang's "law of conservation of securities" provides an even more precise identification of the victims of insider trading.

## STOCK MARKET INSIDER TRADING: VICTIMS, VIOLATORS AND REMEDIES—INCLUDING AN ANALOGY TO FRAUD IN THE SALE OF A USED CAR WITH A GENERIC DEFECT

**by William K.S. Wang**

45 Vill. L. Rev. 27, 28-38 (2000)

*** The presence of victims is important to the [insider trading] debate. Analogous to this issue is the controversy about regulating pornography. Some argue that pornography is a victimless crime. Others contend that pornography increases sex crimes or undermines respect for women. Whether pornography has victims does not resolve the question of how to regulate it. Nevertheless, society is more likely to regulate pornography strictly if it has victims. Similarly, whether insider trading is a victimless crime does not resolve the question of how to regulate it. Nevertheless, society is more likely to regulate insider trading strictly if it has victims.

In fact, each *act* of stock market insider trading has *specific* victims. This part of the Article will discuss the victims of the *act* of insider trading. These victims are those who would be better off, but for the *act* of insider trading. This part of the Article will not focus on the victims of the *nondisclosure* accompanying a stock market insider trade.

Assume that the outstanding number of shares of a company remains constant between the time of the insider trade and public disclosure. Let us focus on the shares outstanding at the time of public disclosure.

With an insider *purchase* of stock, the insider has more of that issue at public disclosure. Someone else must have less. That someone is worse off because of the insider trade.

With an insider *sale* of shares, the insider has less of that issue at public disclosure. Someone else must have more. That someone is worse off because of the insider trade.

Paraphrasing "the law of conservation of mass-energy," I call this phenomenon "the law of conservation of securities." I label as "trade victims" those harmed by the phenomenon of the "law of conservation of securities."

Who are those harmed by the phenomenon of the "law of conservation of securities"? The victims are those whose transactions were either preempted or induced by the insider trade. To paraphrase Milton Friedman, there is no such thing as a free insider trade.

To explain preempted and induced traders, I shall use an analogy to used cars. The used automobile market is roughly comparable to the securities market. Over the counter dealers, stock exchange specialists and large block positioning firms often trade stock for their own account with the public. All these market-makers are somewhat like used car dealers.

Many commentators assume that stock exchange transactions are anonymous. This is an oversimplification, at least with large block trades between an institutional investor and a block positioner. In fact, if Prudential Life Insurance Company wants to sell a large block of IBM stock, Prudential may sell to Goldman Sachs, a block positioner. Prudential and Goldman Sachs know each other's identity before, during and after the trade.

They could even ask each other questions before the transaction. At least conceivably, Goldman Sachs could ask Prudential: "Do you have any material, nonpublic information about IBM?" At least conceivably, Prudential might lie in response. In other words, much trading in New York Stock Exchange listed shares has aspects of face-to-face dealing. This strengthens the analogy between stock market and used car transactions.

To illustrate how induced and preempted stock traders are harmed by insider trading under the law of conservation of securities, I shall use two analogies to used car trading:

(1) the *solitary* defect hypothetical, and

(2) the *generic* defect hypothetical.

In the solitary defect hypothetical, only one automobile is a lemon. In contrast, in the generic defect situation, many individuals are buying and selling cars, *all* the same year model and *all* with the same defect. Even a slight change in price may dissuade or induce trading. Stock market insider trading resembles the *generic* defect used car hypothetical.

The *generic* defect used car analogy will demonstrate two points: First, each act of stock market insider trading has one or more particular victims. Second, these victims are anonymous. They exist, but, practically, cannot be identified.

I shall start with the *solitary* defect used car hypothetical. Suppose Mr. Greedie owns a 1998 Cadillac. He discovers that his particular automobile has a major defect. He goes to a car dealer and sells the car for the going price, $25,000.

Assume in the alternative that:

(1) the dealer does not ask Greedie about any defect, or

(2) the dealer asks Greedie about defects, and Greedie *lies*.

The dealer discovers the defect and is stuck with a lemon. The victim of Greedie's sale is clearly the dealer.

Suppose the dealer does not discover the defect and resells the car to Mr. Public Buyer. This resale is illustrated in Figure 1 below:

FIGURE 1:
SOLITARY DEFECT HYPOTHETICAL
(ONLY GREEDIE'S 1998 CADILLAC HAS DEFECT)

| GREEDIE ————> | DEALER ————> | MR. PUBLIC BUYER, |
|---|---|---|
| SELLS LEMON TO | SELLS SAME LEMON TO | THE VICTIM |

Assume that Mr. Public Buyer is now stuck with a lemon. Who is the victim of Greedie's sale? Only *one* 1998 Cadillac is a lemon. If Greedie had not sold his lemon to the dealer, the dealer would not have been able to resell the lemon to Mr. Public Buyer. The victim of Greedie's sale is Mr. Public Buyer.

Now, I shall turn to the generic defect example. (This hypothetical is analogous to stock market insider trading.)

Suppose Mr. Greedie is an employee of General Motors. Through his job at GM, Greedie receives material, nonpublic information that *all* 1998 Cadillacs have a major defect. By coincidence, Greedie personally owns a 1998 Cadillac. He immediately sells his Cadillac to a car dealer for the going price, $25,000.

Again, assume in the alternative that:
(1) the dealer does not ask Greedie about any defect, or
(2) the dealer asks Greedie about defects, and Greedie *lies*.

When GM announces the news of the defect to the public, the price of the 1998 Cadillac falls by $10,000. Greedie is clearly better off.

Who is the victim of Greedie's sale? Who in the universe would be better off had Greedie not sold? Is it the car dealer who bought the Cadillac? The answer is not necessarily.

Suppose, *without changing its prices*, the dealer resold Greedie's Cadillac to Mr. Public Buyer before announcement of the defect. Mr. Public Buyer is stuck with the lemon after the announcement.

Nevertheless, Mr. Public Buyer is also not necessarily the victim of Greedie's sale. *All* 1998 Cadillacs are lemons, although only Greedie knows this. Had Mr. Public Buyer not bought Greedie's car, he might have purchased *another* 1998 Cadillac.

These transactions are illustrated in Figure 2 below:

FIGURE 2:
GENERIC DEFECT HYPOTHETICAL
(ALL 1998 CADILLACS HAVE THE SAME DEFECT)

| GREEDIE ————> | DEALER ————> | MR. PUBLIC BUYER, |
|---|---|---|
| SELLS LEMON TO | WITH *NO CHANGE IN PRICE*, DEALER SELLS SAME LEMON TO | NOT NECESSARILY THE VICTIM |

What is the difference between this *generic* defect hypothetical and the *solitary* defect hypothetical? In the *solitary* defect hypothetical, Greedie's car was the only one with the defect. In the *solitary* defect hypothetical, had Greedie not sold his Cadillac, and had Mr. Public Buyer bought another 1998 Cadillac, Mr. Public Buyer would have been *better off.*

In the *generic* defect hypothetical, *all* 1998 Cadillacs have the same defect. Innocent individuals without Greedie's information compete with Greedie to sell 1998 Cadillacs with the same defect. Had Greedie *not* sold his Cadillac, and had Mr. Public Buyer bought another 1998 Cadillac instead of Greedie's, Mr. Public Buyer would have been *equally worse off.*

This phenomenon has prompted some commentators to conclude that each act of insider trading has *no* specific victims. This conclusion is wrong.

In the *generic defect* example, the insider trade has a specific victim. Identifying this victim is easier if we assume that the dealer does not sell Greedie's automobile to Mr. Public Buyer and still owns Greedie's car at the time of public disclosure (as illustrated in Figure 3 below).

FIGURE 3:

THE VICTIM IN THE GENERIC DEFECT HYPOTHETICAL (ASSUME THAT DEALER STILL OWNS GREEDIE'S CAR AT TIME OF PUBLIC DISCLOSURE)

| | |
|---|---|
| GREEDIE ————> | DEALER, |
| SELLS LEMON TO | MAY OR MAY NOT BE VICTIM DEPENDING ON SIZE OF INVENTORY AT DISCLOSURE |
| DEALER MAY *LOWER PRICES,* AND | *MAY* INDUCE MR. POTENTIAL TO BUY ANOTHER 1998 CADILLAC (INDUCED BUYER); |
| OR | *MAY* DISSUADE MS. MARGINAL FROM SELLING (PREEMPTED SELLER) |

Even if the dealer still owns Greedie's car at the time of the public announcement of the defect, the dealer is not necessarily the victim of Greedie's sale. Prior to public disclosure, the dealer *may* have passed the harm to someone else.

The dealer desires a certain inventory level. Because of Greedie's sale, the dealer's inventory of 1998 Cadillacs increased. The dealer sets a price at which it will purchase a car *from* the public. The dealer sets a *higher* price at which it will sell *to* the public. In an attempt to reduce inventory, the dealer may have slightly reduced both its buying and selling prices for 1998 Cadillacs.

Assume that Mr. Potential was interested in purchasing a 1998 Cadillac. The lower price *may* have induced him to buy *another* 1998 Cadillac (other than Greedie's) from the dealer. All 1998 Cadillacs have the same defect. As an induced purchaser, Mr. Potential may be the victim of Greedie's sale.

Alternatively, assume that Ms. Marginal owned a 1998 Cadillac and was thinking about selling her automobile. The lower price *may* have dissuaded her from selling the car to the dealer. She may still hold the car at the time of the public announcement of the defect. As a *preempted* seller, Ms. Marginal may be the victim of Greedie's sale.

What is the difference between this generic defect hypothetical and the solitary defect hypothetical? In the *solitary* defect situation, Greedie's automobile was the only one with the defect. In the *solitary* defect hypothetical, if the dealer owned Greedie's particular car at discovery of the defect, the dealer was worse off. *The size of the dealer's total inventory of 1998 Cadillacs at discovery of the solitary defect was not relevant.*

In the *generic* defect hypothetical, *all* 1998 Cadillacs have the defect. The size of the dealer's inventory of 1998 Cadillacs at public disclosure is crucial. The size of the inventory determines the dealer's damage.

The dealer is only worse off as a result of Greedie's sale if his sale causes the dealer's inventory at disclosure to be higher than it otherwise would have been. Initially, Greedie's sale increased the dealer's inventory. Nevertheless, the dealer may have *decreased* its inventory by lowering prices. The dealer *may* have shifted the harm to a preempted seller or induced buyer.

In practice, identifying the preempted seller or induced buyer is impossible. In order to identify the victim, one must determine the prices the dealer would have charged absent Greedie's sale. Then, one must ascertain how the public would have reacted to these prices. This information is unknowable. Nevertheless, the victim still exists.

At the time of the defect's announcement, there are a fixed number of 1998 Cadillacs. If Greedie has one less Cadillac at the time of the announcement, someone else must have one more. That someone is the victim of Greedie's sale. I call this "the law of conservation of used automobiles."

If the sale of one car on inside information to the car dealer causes even a slight lowering of the dealer's prices for 1998 Cadillacs, that decline may dissuade or induce a transaction. If the dealer's prices do not change (or if the price declines fail to dissuade or induce a trade), the loss falls on the automobile dealer (an induced buyer). Under the "law of conservation of used automobiles," Greedie's sale *must* induce a purchase or preempt a sale.

Only one victim exists: either a preempted seller, like Ms. Marginal, or an induced buyer, like Mr. Potential or the dealer. The loss is not spread among a large number of victims. The price decline after disclosure falls on this *one* victim; that loss corresponds to Greedie's gain.

The law of conservation of used automobiles is similar to the law of conservation of *securities*. Each stock market insider trade has one or more specific victims, either induced and/or preempted traders.

One may make the following objection. Suppose an innocent individual fortuitously sells *stock* in advance of an announcement of adverse, material information. Under the law of conservation of securities, does not this innocent sale also cause harm? Does not this innocent sale either preempt a sale or induce a purchase? The answer is yes.

Clearly, society will not impose liability on traders who *unknowingly*, fortuitously make advantageous trades prior to public disclosure. Therefore, causing harm under the law of conservation of securities is not *sufficient* in itself to impose liability.

Unlike innocent traders, however, stock market insider traders *knowingly* profit by taking advantage of others. This difference alone may or may not be sufficient to impose liability. (Suppose an analyst discovers material nonpublic information about a corporation through diligent outside research with no contact with company employees. If the analyst's firm traded on this information, the transaction would harm preempted or induced traders. Nevertheless, the analyst and the firm might not be liable. )

One analogy is to but-for causation and proximate causation. The law of conservation of securities demonstrates that the insider trade is a *but-for* cause of injury to specific victims. Whether the insider trade is a *proximate* cause of harm is a separate issue. Nevertheless, if the insider trade is not even a but-for cause of injury, liability is much less likely. As mentioned earlier, as with pornography, whether insider trading has victims, affects, but does not resolve the question of how strictly to regulate it.

The analysis above deals with the specific ex post victims of a stock market insider trade. What are *some* of the broader possible adverse effects of insider trading?

If the public becomes aware of insider trading, the prices of stocks generally may decline (although estimating the risk may be difficult). If the employees of a *particular* corporation acquire a reputation for trading on nonpublic information, that specific company's stock may decline in price. *Such declines would increase the cost of capital of particular companies or of publicly traded corporations generally.*

Ex ante, these price decreases might partially compensate new buyers for the risk of being victims of stock market insider trading (although, as mentioned earlier, estimating the risk would be difficult). Nevertheless, ex post the harm of insider trading would not be spread equally. An insider trade has arbitrary, but specific victims. These victims are *disproportionately* harmed by the trade. (Some victims, preempted buyers, may never own stock in the issuer.)

Even ex ante, a decline in the price of all publicly traded stocks (or of a particular stock) would not adequately compensate all investors for the risk of being victims of a stock market insider trade. This risk of harm is associated with the act of trading (or of *almost* trading, in the case of a preempted trader). Consequently, the risk varies with the frequency of one's trades (or "near trades").

Even if the return on all publicly traded stocks (or of a particular stock) were slightly higher because of the risk of harm from insider trading, the higher return would not adequately compensate *frequent* traders for incurring that risk. Nor would risk-averse investors who trade *often* be able to diversify away the risk of becoming a victim.

In short, ex post, victims of a stock market insider trade are *disproportionately* injured even if they originally purchased their stock at a price that accurately reflected the possibility of insider trading. Even ex ante, frequent traders definitely suffer harm from insider trading.

To analogize, suppose apartment rents in one neighborhood are slightly lower because a small percentage of arbitrarily chosen residents will be mugged and/or assaulted. Ex post, the unfortunate victims suffer disproportionately and are only minimally compensated by the lower rents. Ex ante, residents who take walks often are not adequately compensated because they take more risk than others. ***

---

### d. *Investor Confidence in Securities Markets*

As we saw in Section C of this Chapter, the policy argument that has seemed to carry the day with at least a majority of the Supreme Court is that insider trading "'undermines the integrity of, and investor confidence in, the securities markets.'" See *O'Hagan* at 658 (quoting the Government's brief). See also id. at 653 ("the misappropriation theory is ... designed to protec[t] the integrity of the securities markets against abuses by 'outsiders' to a corporation who have access to confidential information that will affect th[e] corporation's security price when revealed"); id. at 658 (observing that "investors likely would hesitate to venture their capital in a market where trading based on misappropriated nonpublic information is unchecked by law").

Congress also invoked investor confidence and market integrity arguments as the principal justification for enhancing the sanctions available to the government in insider trading cases. See H. Rep. No. 98-355, ITSA, at 2 (noting that "[c]apital formation and our nation's economic growth and stability depend on investor confidence in the fairness and integrity of our capital markets" and that "[i]nsider trading threatens these markets by undermining the public's expectations of honest and fair securities markets where all participants play by the same rules"). These congressional sentiments were echoed four years later with the enactment of ITSFEA:

> [T]he far greater number of commentators support efforts to curb insider trading, viewing such efforts as crucial to the capital formation process that depends on investor confidence in the fairness and integrity of our securities markets. Insider trading damages the legitimacy of the capital market and diminishes the public's faith. The investing public has a legitimate expectation that the prices of actively traded securities reflect publicly available information about the issuer of such securities. *** [T]he small investor will be—and has been—reluctant to invest in the market if he feels it is rigged against him.

H. Rep. No. 100-910 at 8.

Critics of the "investor confidence/market integrity" rationale have a variety of counter arguments. Some highlight its lack of empirical support. See, e.g., Dennis S. Karjala, Statutory Regulation of Insider Trading in Impersonal Markets, 1982 Duke L.J. 627, 629 (noting that a formula to measure loss of investor confidence does not exist). Others argue that the rationale is undercut by the experiences of other countries such as Japan, India, and Hong Kong, all of which have very active stock markets but insider trading prohibitions and enforcement provisions that are quite lax. See Jonathan R. Macey, Insider Trading: Economics, Politics, and Policy 44 (1991); Stephen M. Bainbridge, Incorporating State Law Fiduciary Duties into the Federal Insider Trading Prohibition, 52 Wash. & Lee L. Rev. 1189, 1243 n. 226 (1995). It is also argued that if insider trading were legal, investors could easily protect themselves by discounting the price they are willing to pay for shares in companies that allow insider trading. In other words, "if the existence of insider trading is known, *** outsiders will not be disadvantaged because the price they pay will reflect the risk of insider trading." Carlton & Fischel, supra, 35 Stan. L. Rev. at 881.

#### e. *Fairness and Morality*

Of course, there are those who urge the regulation of insider trading principally as a matter of fairness and morality. Indeed, as a former Chairman of the SEC once remarked: "[t]he American people see it, bluntly, as a form of cheating." Arthur Levitt, A Question of Integrity: Promoting Investor Confidence By Fighting Insider Trading, Vital Speeches of the Day, Vol. LXIV, 354, 355 (April 1, 1998). See also Robert C. Clark, Corporate Law 271 (1986) (bemoaning that "many people, including judges and legislators, feel no need to say anything [other than] *** it is simply *** unfair for some investors (insiders and their tip[p]ees) to have preferential access to information").

But there have also been very thoughtful arguments against insider trading advanced from perspectives of fairness and morality. Professor Kim Lane Scheppele, for example, uses "contractarian ethics" to support her "equality of access" approach to the regulation of insider trading, an approach similar to the one advanced by Justice Blackmun in his dissent in *Chiarella*. Professor Scheppele explains that:

> Equal access to information is the moral concept on which a prohibition on insider trading would be grounded. When one person has special knowledge and nonetheless trades with those who do not, the offense is not just that a secret is kept. The offense lies in the fact that the secret is withheld under conditions in which those with whom the secret-keeper trades cannot discover the information as easily (or, *** as legally) as those who have the secret information. The target of the secret and the secret-keeper do not have *equal access* to information, and that is the problem.
>
> Consider the following hypothetical. If an insider were to trade with another insider, few would have moral qualms about the transaction. Under those circumstances, the two parties to the deal would be on equal footing; such equality of access to information underwrites the moral argument about secret-keeping. But the contractarian argument reveals what is wrong when insiders trade with those who do not have *access* to knowledge equal to theirs (not equal knowledge), particularly where the insiders trade using deep secrets. People would not agree to be part of a system where their disadvantage in access to knowledge could be turned into disadvantages in the distribution of other resources. They might be willing to take their chances on a system that required them to work as hard as anyone else at acquiring this knowledge, but they would not be willing to enter into transactions with people who are clearly advantaged relative to them at the starting point. When insiders trade with people who are in no position, or a distinctly disadvantageous position, to acquire the information that the insiders now want to use, the insiders should have an obligation to disclose the information or refrain from trading with these unequal trading partners.

> This obligation should extend not just to those unproblematically thought to be insiders, like officers and directors employed by a particular firm, but also to anyone whose position gives them special *access* to knowledge that others cannot acquire. In the complicated world of corporate transactions, an insider should be considered to be any person whose position allows access to information unavailable to those with whom the insider is interacting. This does not mean that all traders must have equal information; rather, all traders should face *roughly equal search costs* in locating relevant information. Without such a level playing field at the start, it is unlikely that rational consenters would agree to such rules in advance. After all, why should one sign onto a system in which one may be permanently disadvantaged? It is the *structural* imbalance in access to information, as Justice Blackmun started to argue in *Chiarella*, that gives rise to the duty to disclose. This argument is grounded not only in existing equitable rules about fair dealing that courts have long invoked in determining fraud, but also in contractarian ethics.

Kim Lane Scheppele, "It's Just Not Right:" The Ethics of Insider Trading, 56 Law & Contemp. Probs. 123, 162-63 (Summer 1993).

Reasoned moral arguments against the practice of insider trading can also be found in Alan Strudler and Eric W. Orts, Moral Principle in the Law of Insider Trading, 78 Tex. L. Rev. 375, 383 (1999) (maintaining that the "hard problems in insider trading law are paradigmatically moral, such as whether nondisclosure of material nonpublic information deprives a participant in a public securities market of the ability to make an autonomous choice, or whether an inside securities trader uses information that is stolen, converted to an improper use, or otherwise morally tainted").

*f. Protecting Private Property*

One additional policy justification for the regulation of insider trading merits our close attention. It involves the very valuable role that information plays in our society and the harms that would flow from a legal system's failure to protect a corporation's right to the information it produces.

## INSIDER TRADING REGULATION: THE PATH DEPENDENT CHOICE BETWEEN PROPERTY RIGHTS AND SECURITIES FRAUD

**by Stephen M. Bainbridge**

52 S.M.U. L. Rev. 1589, 1606-08 (1999)

*** There is a growing consensus that the federal insider trading prohibition is more easily justified as a means of protecting property rights in information than as a way of protecting investors. As I have elsewhere defended in some detail, a property rights-based approach to insider trading regulation, a brief recapitulation will suffice here. Consider the prototypical insider trading transaction, in which an insider trades in her employer's stock on the basis of information learned solely because of her position with the firm. The property right must be assigned to either the corporation or the inside trader. A rule allowing insider trading assigns the property right to the insider, while a rule prohibiting insider trading assigns it to the corporation.

The rationale for assigning the property right to the firm is precisely the same as the rationale for prohibiting patent infringement or theft of trade secrets: protecting the economic incentive to produce socially valuable information. As the theory goes, the readily appropriable nature of information makes it difficult for the developer of a new idea to recoup the sunk costs incurred in developing it. For example, if an inventor develops a better mousetrap, he cannot profit on that invention without selling mousetraps and thereby making the new design available to potential competitors. Assuming both the inventor and his competitors incur roughly equivalent marginal costs to produce and market the trap, the competitors will be able to set a market price at which the inventor will likely be unable to earn a return on his sunk costs. *Ex post*, the rational inventor should ignore his sunk costs and go on producing the improved mousetrap. *Ex ante*, however, the inventor will anticipate that he will be unable to generate positive returns on his up-front costs, and therefore will be deterred from developing socially valuable information. As Judge Ralph Winter explained in his separate opinion in *United States v. Chestman*:

> Information is ... expensive to produce, and, because it involves facts and ideas that can be easily photocopied or carried in one's head, there is a ubiquitous risk that those who pay to produce information will see others reap the profit from it. Where the profit from an activity is likely to be diverted, investment in that activity will decline. If the law fails to protect property rights in commercial information, therefore, less will be invested in generating such information. [947 F.2d 551, 576-77 (2d Cir. 1991) (Winter, J., concurring in part and dissenting in part)]

Accordingly, society provides incentives for inventive activity by using the patent system to give inventors a property right in new ideas. By preventing competitors from appropriating the idea, the patent allows the inventor to charge monopolistic prices for the improved mousetrap, thereby recouping his sunk costs. Trademark, copyright, and trade secret law are all justified on similar grounds.

Granted, this argument may not provide quite as compelling a justification for the insider trading prohibition as it does for the patent system. Legalizing insider trading would likely have a much smaller impact on the corporation's incentive to develop new information than would, say, legalizing patent infringement. It seems plausible, however, that insider trading will have at least some impact on the incentive to produce new information. Again, Judge Winter explains:

> [I]nsider trading creates a risk that information will be prematurely disclosed by such trading, and the corporation will lose part or all of its property in that information. Although trades by an insider may rarely affect market price, others who know of the insider's trading may notice that a trader is unusually successful, or simply perceive unusual activity in a stock and guess the information and/or make piggyback trades. A broker who executes a trade for [an insider] may well draw relevant conclusions. Or, as in the instant matter, the trader . . . may tell his or her broker about the inside information, who may then trade on his or her account, on clients' accounts, or may tell friends and relatives. One inside trader has publicly attributed his exposure in part to the fact that the bank through which he made trades piggybacked on the trades, as did the broker who made the trades for the bank. Once activity in a stock reaches an unusual stage, others may guess the reason for the trading—the corporate secret. Insider trading thus increases the risk that confidential information acquired at a cost may be disclosed. If so, the owner of the

> information may lose its investment. [947 F. 2d 551, 577-78 (2d Cir. 1991) (Winter, J., concurring in part and dissenting in part].

Even if one is skeptical that insider trading poses the sort of threats Winter identifies, the affirmative case for assigning the property right to the corporation is demonstrably stronger than the one for assigning it to the insider, as I have explained elsewhere. The law, therefore, should assume (although the assumption may sometimes be wrong) that assigning the property right to the firm maximizes the social incentives for the production of valuable new information.

There are essentially two ways of assigning a property right to information: (1) allowing the owner to enter into transactions without disclosing the information; or (2) prohibiting others from using the information. In effect, the federal insider trading prohibition vests a property right of the latter type in the owner of nonpublic information. To be sure, enforcement of the insider trading prohibition differs rather dramatically from enforcement of, say, trespassing laws. In context, however, the prohibition's enforcement mechanisms are not inconsistent with a property rights analysis. Where public policy argues for giving someone a property right, but the costs of enforcing such a right would be excessive, the state often uses its regulatory powers as a substitute for granting a property right. Insider trading poses such a situation. Private enforcement of the insider trading laws is rare and usually parasitic on public enforcement proceedings. Indeed, *** the very nature of insider trading makes public regulation essential precisely because private enforcement is almost impossible. The insider trading prohibition's regulatory nature thus need not preclude a property rights-based analysis.

---

In addition to Professor Bainbridge, other notable law and economics scholars, including Judge Frank Easterbrook and Professor Jonathan Macey, have endorsed the private property rationale for regulating insider trading. But the rationale has also been criticized:

> The property rights theory appeals to those who believe that securities regulation should be predicated on principles of economics, rather than on principles of fairness. However, the federal securities laws were based on the principle that when an issuer goes public, investors are entitled to information about its business and affairs. The easiest criticism of the property rights theory is that when Congress passed and subsequently amended the Exchange Act, it was concerned about fairness and the protection of investors, not the protection of property rights in information held by issuers and traders. Protecting the source of confidential information is illogical when the parties injured by traders possessing informational advantages are those who purchase or sell securities without access to the material information. Further, the property rights theory seems to be concerned with interests in information that are generally protected by state law. The federal securities laws impose disclosure duties on issuers, bidders, and other market participants and the insider trading laws should be viewed as a means to enforce the investing public's right to this information.

Roberta S. Karmel, Outsider Trading on Confidential Information—A Breach in Search of a Duty, 20 Cardozo L. Rev. 83, 112-13 (1998). More specifically, Professor Karmel proposes that:

> the ban on insider trading be related to the disclosure obligations of issuers, bidders, and other market participants under the federal securities laws, as a means to enforce those obligations and accelerate the release of material information. Although the ban is regulatory, its necessity arises from gaps in the disclosure system administered by the SEC, gaps that can only be filled by the disclose or abstain doctrine.

Id. at 113. Professor Karmel contends that this link between the insider trading prohibition and the mandatory disclosure provision in the federal securities laws "seems self-evident." Yet, in her view, "the SEC, the courts, and the commentators seem to have become so bogged down in the details of the misappropriation theory, as well as other theories, that they have overlooked [this] basic rationale ***." Id. at 133. For additional critique of the property rights rationale, see Kimberly D. Krawiec, Fairness, Efficiency, and Insider Trading: Deconstructing the Coin of the Realm in the Information Age, 95 Nw. U.L. Rev. 443 (2001) (situating insider trading regulation within the larger body of intellectual property law).

### 2. *The Debate Over a Statutory Definition of Insider Trading*

Despite numerous calls to do so, Congress has not provided a statutory definition of insider trading. Some of its reasons for failing to act are set forth in the material that follows.

## U.S. HOUSE REPORT, ENERGY AND COMMERCE COMMITTEE INSIDER TRADING SANCTIONS ACT OF 1984

No. 98-355 at 13-14
September 15, 1983

Because insider trading is pursued under the broad anti-fraud provisions of the federal securities laws, some witnesses suggested that the Committee should add to the legislation specific language defining the scope of the violation for purposes of the triple penalty provided by the legislation. They suggested that judicial interpretations have not provided clear boundaries of acceptable conduct and that the case-by-case approach, while appropriate for a remedial sanction such as an injunction, would not be appropriate for the civil penalty provided under the legislation.

Others testified that a definition of insider trading would not be desirable. For example, Arnold S. Jacobs testified that hundreds of cases clarify the insider trading prohibition of Rule 10b-5. He noted that: "As with any broad anti-fraud remedy, the fringes of what constitutes the prohibited act are occasionally fuzzy. This, however, does not justify placing a definition in the bill; unscrupulous traders would skirt around any definition constructed." He warned: "Even if H.R. 559 were redrafted to include a caveat that any definition of insider trading contained in H.R. 559 is not to be applied to private rights of action or actions by the SEC for injunctions, it is highly probable that any definition in H.R. 559 (although limited by its terms to the triple-profit sanctions) would become the definition for all purposes of the federal securities laws...."

The Committee believes that the law with respect to insider trading is sufficiently well-developed at this time to provide adequate guidance. Further, the Committee believes that the Commission has used its broad rulemaking authority to respond to marketplace developments; that the adoption of a statutory definition could reduce flexibility; and that any new definition which might be adopted would be likely to create new ambiguities, thereby increasing rather than limiting uncertainty.

The deliberations of the American Law Institute and the American Bar Association Securities Law Committee in drafting the Proposed Federal Securities Code are also instructive on this point. Those deliberations were publicly and democratically conducted over a period of 12 years under conditions where every segment of the securities bar was thoroughly involved. The result was sections 1602(a)(1) and 1603 of the Code as supplemented by definitional and remedial provisions. The conclusion was that hard-core insider trading could be vaguely defined in section 1603 but that all other types of questionable conduct involving illicit misappropriation of market and insider information must be left to the courts which must determine whether the particular conduct amounts to a "fraudulent act" or a "misrepresentation" under Section 1602(a)(1). Comment 3(d) to section 1603 states, after full analysis, "this area must be left to further judicial development."

Hence, evidence seems to show that any effort to define insider trading would result in, at best, a slightly less generalized rule than 10b-5 and, at worst, a rule that leaves gaping holes, previously referred to in hearings on the Code as "large enough to drive a truck through."

Further, the clarification made to the scope of the persons liable for the penalty answers the definitional concerns of some commentators. Finally, the Committee believes that the adoption of a definition (which would inevitably affect to some degree the substantive law) is not necessary to achieve the basic purpose of the bill: to increase the sanctions available under the law as it now exists and as it continues to evolve.

Since the seminal cases of *In re Cady, Roberts & Co.*, and *SEC v. Texas Gulf Sulphur Co.*, it has been clear that trading by corporate officials and employees on information gained in their employment violates fiduciary duties and violates the federal securities laws. These cases and their progeny do not, however, proscribe legitimate business communications. The Committee does not intend that the legislation reach legitimate business transactions.

## U.S. HOUSE REPORT, ENERGY AND COMMERCE COMMITTEE INSIDER TRADING AND SECURITIES FRAUD ENFORCEMENT ACT

No. 100-910 at 10-11
September 9, 1988

The Committee clearly has recognized the continuing concern over a definition of insider trading. The securities bar and the Congress have debated this issue for a number of years, including during consideration of the adoption of the Insider Trading Sanctions Act of 1984. During this Congress, such definitional questions have been the focus of much attention in Senate inquiries on this subject.

While cognizant of the importance of providing clear guidelines for behavior which may be subject to stiff criminal and civil penalties, the Committee nevertheless declined to include a statutory definition in this bill for several reasons. First, the Committee believed that the court-drawn parameters of insider trading have established clear guidelines for the vast majority of traditional insider trading cases, and that a statutory definition could potentially be narrowing, and in an unintended manner facilitate schemes to evade the law. Second, the Committee did not believe that the lack of consensus over the proper delineation of an insider trading definition should impede progress on the needed enforcement reforms encompassed within this legislation. Accordingly, the Committee does not intend to alter the substantive law with respect to insider trading with this legislation. The legal principles governing insider trading cases are well- established and widely-known.

---

Consider this relatively recent call by one of your casebook authors for a congressional definition of insider trading.

## DON'T ASK, JUST TELL: INSIDER TRADING AFTER *UNITED STATES V. O'HAGAN*

**by Richard W. Painter, Kimberly D. Krawiec, and Cynthia A. Williams**

84 Va. L. Rev. 153, 211-12, 219-228 (1998)

Virtually every other country that has joined the United States in prohibiting trading on the basis of material, nonpublic information has done so through statutes that define with specificity such terms as "insider" and "inside information" as well as the circumstances in which trading is prohibited. The United Kingdom, for example, enacted a specific prohibition in 1980, Italy did so in 1991, and Germany followed in 1994. The United States stands alone in allowing judges to develop a common law prohibition against insider trading, and now against trading on the basis of misappropriated information, from a general antifraud statute that does not even mention insiders, inside information, insider trading, or misappropriation. The Supreme Court's analysis, or perhaps lack of analysis, of Section 10(b) in *Chiarella*, *Dirks*, and now *O'Hagan*, makes a compelling case that the United States should abandon its common law approach to trading on material, nonpublic information and follow Europe***

[A]s the Commission has begun more vigorously to enforce insider trading prohibitions over the last fifteen years, and as the penalties for such trading have been enhanced, the ABA's Task Force on the Regulation of Insider Trading and others have called on Congress to specify when trading on material, nonpublic information is illegal, so far without success.

In spite of its reluctance to act, Congress may be the best institution to make these determinations. Trading on inside and misappropriated information is a complex area of law that has engendered an outpouring of scholarship and disagreement. Much of the disagreement arises from a lack of consensus among scholars, regulators, and judges about the purpose to be served by regulation. The numerous possible purposes include protection of investors, prevention of unfair information asymmetries in trading transactions, promotion of confidence in the market, promotion of disclosure, prevention of fraud, protection of proprietary information, enforcement of fiduciary duties, or some combination of the foregoing purposes. As Professor Louis Loss and Dean Joel Seligman have emphasized, a legislative determination "could address a fundamental question that the Supreme Court believed that it could not: whether a legislative approach ought to be limited to a fraud rubric?"[264] A legislative determination, like a formal SEC rulemaking procedure, also offers the advantage of public participation to develop a consensus on the purposes of the regulation.

Moreover, Congress can define prohibited trading on material, nonpublic information in a systematic way, in the context of the federal securities laws as a whole, so the development of the law will not depend on the serendipity of what cases happen to arise after *O'Hagan*. To be sure, Congress's failure to define insider trading in 1988, even after the SEC finally endorsed a proposed definition, does not bode well for congressional action now, notwithstanding *O'Hagan*. And yet there are any number of approaches Congress could take that would have the benefits of logical consistency and clarity not now found in this area of law.

For instance, Congress could establish a pre-*United States v. Chiarella* equality of access approach, even for outsiders, and then carve out exceptions, if necessary, for securities analysts and perhaps others who are perceived to benefit securities markets through their use of nonpublic information. This is the approach Joel Seligman advocated after *Dirks v. Securities and Exchange Commission* and *Chiarella*.[269] His proposal suggested a general prohibition on trading while in possession of material, nonpublic information modeled on the *Securities and Exchange Commission v. Texas Gulf Sulphur Co.* approach, with certain provisions to "harmonize the new standard with other parts of the securities law." [Id. at 1138]. Those provisions included 1) an exception for potential acquirers prior to their acquisition of five percent of the target, necessary to parallel the Williams Act; 2) a legitimization of the "Chinese wall" defense for securities firms, whereby traders can continue to buy and sell the securities of issuers that have provided their underwriting departments with material, nonpublic information, so long as firm procedures are adequate to prevent information from leaking from the underwriters to the traders; 3) recognition that securities analysts could continue to search out immaterial,

---

**264**. Louis Loss & Joel Seligman, 8 Securities Regulation 3763 (3d ed. 1991). The "alternative approach would involve simply prohibiting certain undesirable practices the same way that wash sales and certain short sales are prohibited." Id.

**269**. Joel Seligman, "The Reformulation of Federal Securities Law Concerning Nonpublic Information," 73 Geo. L.J. 1083 (1985).

nonpublic information and make recommendations on the basis of that information; and 4) permission for "stock or options exchange specialists, market-makers or floor traders to trade while in possession of material nonpublic information about trading activity on the floor of an exchange to the extent . . . permitted by section 11 of the Securities Exchange Act or Stock Exchange rules." [Id.]

A somewhat narrower approach was suggested by Professor Victor Brudney: a ban on trading based on "unerodable informational advantages."[276] Professor Brudney recognized that allocative efficiency goals are furthered by providing incentives for outsiders to search for relevant corporate and economic information; thus people ought to be able to benefit from the informational advantages that their searches provide by freely trading on such advantages. Professor Brudney's suggestion therefore does not follow a pure equality of access approach. Yet he argued that the law should "deny an informational advantage to those who seek to use otherwise nonpublic information which they are precluded by legal restrictions from disclosing to public investors" or which the public cannot lawfully acquire, notwithstanding diligent effort. [Id. at 355-56].

Professor Jill Fisch has suggested a still narrower approach, one that focuses on the duties of insiders to the market, particularly disclosure duties.[280] Her proposal concentrates on defining the insider class, since the harm to be prevented by insider trading regulation is "not only superior access to information but also the opportunity [by insiders] to manipulate the timing and quality of [market] disclosure" to capitalize on informational advantages. [Id. at 239-40] Professor Fisch's insiders would include "primary insiders" such as officers, directors, and ten percent stockholders, and "secondary insiders" such as lower-level employees and outsiders such as lawyers and investment bankers who have irregular access to material, nonpublic information. Both categories would be prohibited from trading or tipping while in possession of material, nonpublic information obtained by virtue of their status as an insider.

In addition, Congress could look either to the detailed codes adopted in Great Britain and Germany or to the insider trading provisions of the Federal Securities Code, developed over ten years by the ALI under the guidance of Louis Loss, but never enacted into law.[285] Professor Loss's Code set out a specific provision prohibiting insider trading, while recognizing that Section 10(b)'s broad antifraud analogue stood available as a backstop in the event a particular egregious case did not fall within the parameters of the insider trading section. Section 1603 of the Securities Code endorsed an abstain or disclose rule for

---

**276.** Victor Brudney, "Insiders, Outsiders, and Informational Advantages Under the Federal Securities Laws," 93 Harv. L. Rev. 322, 326-39 (1979).

**280.** Jill E. Fisch, "Start Making Sense: An Analysis and Proposal for Insider Trading Regulation," 26 Ga. L. Rev. 179, 238-39 (1991).

**285.** Fed. Sec. Code §§ 1602, 1603 (1978).

insiders who know "fact[s] of special significance" concerning the issuer or the security, while defining insiders broadly, to include any "person who, by virtue of his relationship or former relationship to the issuer, knows a fact of special significance about the issuer or the security in question that is not generally available." This formulation does not ground liability by reference to a fiduciary relationship or a relationship of trust and confidence with the issuer. Rather, any passage of material, inside information, coupled with any relationship with the issuer, suffices as a basis to impose a duty to abstain from trading. This provision thus avoids the complexities inherent in importing a separate body of law—that of fiduciary duty—into the insider trading prohibition. Moreover, this formulation more directly addresses concerns of inappropriate information asymmetries among investors than does the misappropriation theory. The latter does not reach outsiders' trading on inside information in the absence of a fiduciary relationship, nor under *O'Hagan,* does it reach outsiders who disclose to the principal their intention to trade. Although Section 1603 is animated by policy concerns closer to the equality of access theory, by imposing disclosure duties only on insiders, even as broadly defined, Section 1603 specifically disclaims complete equality of access among investors.

Congress may conclude, however, that Section 1603 is only a starting place. As Professor Loss recognized, a category of outsiders remains, who are not reached by Section 1603's definition. Congress may determine that:

> It would be convenient to have a new category of 'quasi-insider' that would cover people like (i) judges' clerks who trade on information in unpublished opinions, (ii) Federal Reserve Bank employees who trade with knowledge of an imminent change in the margin rate, [and] (iii) printers of tender offer literature who buy the target company's stock . . . [Id. §1603 cmt. d.]

Professor Loss was concerned that this quasi-insider category would be difficult to define. Perhaps, though, with Section 1603 as a starting point, and given the existence of Rule 14e-3 in the tender offer context, Congress could work to define the quasi-insider category with substantially more precision than the courts have used in defining the misappropriation theory. Indeed, the fact that this quasi-insider category is difficult to define with precision is a strong argument for Congress to undertake the task rather than leave it to the courts.

One aspect of the ALI approach, which was echoed in 1985 by the ABA Task Force on Regulation of Insider Trading, is avoiding reliance on the law of fraud altogether, and instead simply prohibiting specific types of conduct.[294] This approach recognizes that the misuse of informational advantages is an analytically different problem than fraud, and that regulating the former through an approach designed for the latter is problematic:

---

**294.** See Committee on Federal Regulation of Securities, American Bar Association, Report of the Task Force on Regulation of Insider Trading: Part I: Regulation Under the Antifraud Provisions of the Securities Exchange Act of 1934, 41 Bus. Law. 223, 253 (1985).

Because section 10(b) of the 1934 Act is an antifraud rather than an unfair-trading provision, any rulemaking initiative based on section 10(b), whether an expansion of present rule 10b-5 or a new rule aimed specifically at abuse of informational advantages like rule 14e-3, may be subject to some of the same problems that have accompanied development of the case law under rule 10b-5.

...

... If, as the task force believes, more specific guidance is required as to what conduct is forbidden, then a legislative definition based on legislative policy determinations is highly desirable, if not essential....

... Both proposals [set out by the Task Force] depart from the fraud-based framework of section 10(b) and the *Chiarella* and *Dirks* decisions, and instead directly regulate trading and tipping regardless of whether such conduct may be characterized as "fraud." [Id. at 253]

The Task Force suggested two alternative statutes, one very specific and comprehensive, the other much simpler. Yet under both approaches the prohibited conduct was directly defined and regulated, rather than relying upon the analytic construct of fraud. Similarly, in response to those legislative proposals by the Task Force (introduced in the Senate in 1987), the SEC ultimately, if reluctantly, supported a statutory definition that departed from the fraud construct towards direct regulation of certain prohibited conduct.

Finally, Congress could develop a statutory definition of the proscribed conduct based on a theory of property rights in information, and clearly define the relationship between the property rights in information and the trading transaction necessary to give rise to liability. Jonathan Macey has advocated this approach, defining the primary concern of prohibitions on trading on material, nonpublic information as the misuse of corporate property (information).[300] Given this view of the harm to be prevented, Macey has argued that companies should be permitted to allow insiders to trade on proprietary company information.

Regardless of which proposal Congress adopts, it might consider bifurcating criminal liability from civil liability and SEC enforcement actions, in order to allow broader liability in the civil context while setting clear, very specific standards for the imposition of criminal sanctions. For example, Congress could empower the Commission to designate which categories of professionals and other fiduciaries could be held criminally liable for trading on misappropriated information and which categories would be subject only to civil liability to contemporaneous traders under Section 20A.

The above ideas are not meant to be exhaustive. Indeed, some commentators have suggested that insider trading should be legalized entirely. It may even be the case that as securities trading becomes more sophisticated,

---

**300**. Jonathan R. Macey, Insider Trading: Economics, Politics, and Policy, 67 (1991).

global, and instantaneous, any regulatory regime aimed at illegal informational advantages will become increasingly difficult to enforce in all but the most egregious cases. When an American can buy call options in Switzerland on securities traded in Japan, it may not be possible to detect unusual trading patterns that suggest illegal trading on material, nonpublic information. Perhaps in light of these realities, the expanded, real-time disclosure of corporate information that Professor Langevoort has suggested may be the most effective means to achieve the regulatory goals of investor protection and fundamental fairness.[304] The point of this wide-ranging enumeration of possible legislative approaches is not to advocate any one idea. Rather, the point is to suggest that the proper institution to consider these and other suggestions and to make the necessary policy choices is Congress. Absent congressional action, the definition of illegal trading on proscribed informational advantages will remain incomplete, unsystematic, and analytically unsatisfying, particularly after *O'Hagan*.

---

The preceding arguments for a congressional definition of insider trading were made prior to the SEC's adoption of Rule 10b5-1 and Rule 10b5-2. Do these new rules lessen the need for a congressional definition? Or have they only compounded the problem? How difficult would it be to draft a statutory prohibition of insider trading?

When faced with this challenge in 1989, the European Community issued to its Member States its first directive aimed at coordinating insider trading regulations. See Council Directive 89/592/EEC of 13 November 1989, Coordinating Regulations of Insider Dealing, OJ 1989 L334/30. On May 7, 2002, European Union finance ministers agreed in principle to a new common set of rules, as set forth in the following pages. Should Congress enact a version of this Directive? What if the Directive's prohibitions against insider trading were only a floor upon which the SEC could build through its rulemaking powers?

---

304. Donald C. Langevoort, Toward More Effective Risk Disclosure for Technology-Enhanced Investing, 75 Wash. U. L.Q. 753 (1997) (analyzing the problems of risk disclosure in public disclosure documents, and suggesting that, in an electronic disclosure environment, annual and quarterly filings should be replaced with a company file that is required to be relatively accurate and up-to-date on a real-time basis).

## PROPOSAL FOR A DIRECTIVE OF THE EUROPEAN PARLIAMENT AND OF THE COUNCIL ON INSIDER DEALING AND MARKET MANIPULATION

May 30, 2001

OJ 2001 C240E/265

***

### Article 1

For the purposes of this Directive:

(1) 'Inside information' shall mean information which has not been made public of a precise nature relating to one or more issuers of financial instruments or to one or more financial instruments, which, if it were made public, would be likely to have a significant effect on the price of those financial instruments or on the price of related derivative financial instruments.

***

### Article 2

1. Member States shall prohibit any natural or legal person who possesses inside information from taking advantage of that information by acquiring or disposing of it for his own account or for the account of a third party, either directly or indirectly, financial instruments to which that information relates.

The first subparagraph shall apply regardless of whether such person has obtained that information:

(a) by virtue of his membership of the administrative, management or supervisory bodies of the issuer, or

(b) by virtue of his holding in the capital of the issuer, or

(c) by virtue of his having access to the information through the exercise of his employment, profession or duties.

2. Where the person referred to in paragraph 1 is a company or other type of legal person, the prohibition laid down in that paragraph shall also apply to the natural persons who take part in the decision to carry out the transaction for the account of the legal person concerned.

3. The prohibition laid down in paragraph 1 shall apply to any acquisition or disposal of financial instruments.

### Article 3

Member States shall prohibit any person subject to the prohibition laid down in Article 2 who possesses inside information from:

(a) disclosing that inside information to any third party unless such disclosure is made in the normal course of the exercise of his employment, profession or duties;

(b) recommending or procuring a third party, on the basis of that inside information, to acquire or dispose of financial instruments to which that information relates.

### Article 4

Member States shall also impose the prohibitions provided for in Articles 2 and 3 on any person other than those persons referred to in those Articles who with full knowledge of the facts possesses inside information.

***

### Article 8

1. The prohibitions of this Directive shall not apply to trading in own shares in 'buy back' programmes nor to the stabilisation of a financial instrument provided such trading is carried out under agreed conditions.

2. The Commission shall determine these technical conditions in accordance with the procedure referred to in Article 17 (2).

***

### Article 13

Member States shall provide that all persons who work or who have worked for the competent authority, as well as auditors and experts instructed by the competent authority, shall be bound by the obligation of professional secrecy. Information covered by professional secrecy may not be divulged to any person or authority except by virtue of provisions laid down by law.

***

# Chapter 8

# MARKET MANIPULATION

The term "market manipulation," according to the Supreme Court, "connotes intentional or willful conduct designed to deceive or defraud investors by controlling or artificially affecting the price of securities." *Ernst & Ernst v. Hochfelder*, 425 U.S. 185, 199 (1976). That definition, however, raises many more questions than it settles. For example, what, precisely, does it mean to "control" the price of a security? And how is it possible to ascertain whether a security is trading at an "artificial" price? Even more basically, what is the difference between an artificially and a non-artificially priced security?

Courts must necessarily struggle with these questions because the terms "manipulation" and "manipulative" appear in, but are not defined by, the federal securities laws. As we have seen in previous chapters, Section 10(b) of the Exchange Act accords the SEC broad authority to proscribe the use of "any manipulative or deceptive device or contrivance" in connection with the purchase or sale of securities, and Section 14(e) of the Exchange Act specifically prohibits "fraudulent, deceptive, or manipulative acts or practices" in connection with tender offers. The terms are also set out in the titles of Section 9 ("Manipulation of Security Prices") and Section 10 ("Regulation of the Use of Manipulative and Deceptive Devices") of the Exchange Act. As we shall see in this Chapter, Section 9 pertains to securities registered on national exchanges, and proscribes a number of particular practices designed to create the appearance of active securities trading (e.g., washed sales and matched orders). A catchall provision in Section 9(a)(2) makes it unlawful for any person to effect a transaction that creates actual or apparent active securities trading "for the purpose of inducing the purchase or sale of such security by others." Section 10(a) authorizes the SEC to regulate short sales of securities registered on national securities exchanges and stop-loss orders pertaining to such securities. A final important provision is Section 15(c) of the Exchange Act, prohibiting "manipulative, deceptive or other fraudulent" conduct by broker-dealers in the over-the-counter markets. Taken together, these statutory sections evidence a strong congressional concern that the federal securities markets be free of conduct that interferes with the "natural" forces of supply and demand.

The types of manipulative conduct and schemes that have captured the attention of securities regulators have varied markedly over time. When the federal securities laws were first enacted in 1933 and 1934, Congress's desire to eradicate manipulative activity from the securities markets was propelled, in large part, by testimony and reports of stock pools and other conspiratorial trading schemes thought to have contributed to the stock market crash a few years earlier. Typically, the pools operated to effectuate a series of transactions in a particular security that created the illusion of rapidly rising prices, and the operators would then systematically unload the security to the unsuspecting public before the price dropped and their scam was exposed. Boiler room operations became the concern in the 1950s, and securities regulators sought to slow down, or put out of business altogether, those unscrupulous broker-dealers who used high pressure (and generally misleading) sales tactics over the telephone to generate market activity in stocks of fledgling companies. In the 1980s, with the scandals that made Michael Milken, Ivan Boesky, and Dennis Levine virtually household names, attention was focused on Wall Street and the staggering profits that could be generated in the securities markets through manipulative activity. In contrast to these high-flying defendants, many of today's market manipulation cases involve far more ordinary types of characters—auto mechanics, tree trimmers, and even law school students—who have managed to use the Internet to perpetrate wide-spread schemes at a speed and in a manner that would have been unimaginable only a decade ago. Practices on Wall Street also continue to occupy the enforcement agenda of the SEC, the Department of Justice (DOJ), the NYSE, the NASD, and State Attorneys General and blue sky regulators, all of which, in October 2002, agreed to join forces to investigate and prosecute some of the nation's largest investment banks and brokerage firms. These investigations have focused on whether such firms engaged in fraud and market manipulation in the late 1990s through questionable IPO allocation practices and conflicts of interest affecting securities analysts' research reports.

Reflecting the various types of market manipulation cases that the SEC pursues through the initiation of enforcement actions and, though less frequently, through criminal referrals to the DOJ, this Chapter is organized into three sections: Section A, which focuses on manipulation in the context of so-called "fictitious" securities transactions; Section B, which centers on actual trading activity that is alleged to have been motivated by a manipulative purpose; and Section C, which focuses on misleading recommendations and material misstatements about particular securities—conduct that forms the basis of schemes known as "pump and dumps." Section C also discusses conflicts of interest on Wall Street. Issues relating to private actions for market manipulation are discussed in notes following the primary material.

## A. PRACTICES THAT CREATE THE APPEARANCE OF ACTIVE TRADING

On three separate occasions, the Supreme Court has emphasized that manipulation is "virtually a term of art when used in connection with securities markets." See *Ernst & Ernst v. Hochfelder*, 425 U.S. 185, 199 (1976), *Sante Fe Indus., Inc. v. Green*, 430 U.S. 462, 476 (1977), and *Schreiber v. Burlington Northern, Inc.*, 472 U.S. 1, 6 (1985). It has also stated that the "term refers generally to practices, such as wash sales, matched orders, or rigged prices, that are intended to mislead investors by artificially affecting market activity." *Schreiber*, 472 U.S. at 6 (quoting *Sante Fe*, 430 U.S. at 476).

As you read the following SEC enforcement action alleging market manipulation in violation of Section 10(b) and Rule 10b-5, consider the ways in which the defendants' actions could be said to have intentionally misled investors.

## SEC v. U.S. ENVIRONMENTAL, INC.

155 F.3d 107 (2d Cir. 1998)

WALKER, JR., CIRCUIT JUDGE:

Plaintiff-appellant Securities and Exchange Commission ("SEC") appeals from the [district court order] dismissing, pursuant to Fed.R.Civ.P. 12(b)(6), the SEC's claim that defendant-appellee John Romano engaged in market manipulation in violation of Section 10(b) of the Securities Exchange Act of 1934 and Rule 10b-5 thereunder.

We hold that Romano can be primarily liable under § 10(b) for following a stock promoter's directions to execute stock trades that Romano knew, or was reckless in not knowing, were manipulative, even if Romano did not share the promoter's specific overall purpose to manipulate the market for that stock. We therefore vacate the order of the district court and remand for further proceedings.

*Background*

The following facts are taken exclusively from the SEC's amended complaint, which on a motion to dismiss at the pleading stage must be read in the light most favorable to the SEC.

Romano was employed as a trader and registered representative of defendant Castle Securities Corporation ("Castle"), a securities broker-dealer. Castle agreed to participate in a scheme whereby it and other defendants, including Romano, would manipulate upward the price of the stock of U.S. Environmental, Inc. ("USE"). At the direction of stock promoter Mark D'Onofrio ("D'Onofrio"), certain of the defendants or their nominees traded USE shares among themselves "for the purpose of creating the appearance of an actual market for trading USE shares" and thus raising USE's stock price.

The complaint alleges that

> Romano knowingly or recklessly participated in and furthered a market manipulation by:
>
> (a) effecting offers, purchases, and sales of USE securities in return for promises of risk-free profit for engaging in such trades;
>
> (b) effecting directed and controlled trades of USE securities;
>
> (c) effecting "wash sales" and "matched orders"; and
>
> (d) effecting trades involving undisclosed nominees.

Wash sales are "transactions involving no change in beneficial ownership" and matched orders are "orders for the purchase [or] sale of a security that are entered with the knowledge that orders of substantially the same size, at substantially the same time and price, have been or will be entered by the same or different persons for the sale/purchase of such security." *Ernst & Ernst v. Hochfelder*, 425 U.S. 185, 205 n.25 (1976). The complaint states further that

> Romano agreed to advise D'Onofrio continuously as Castle received buy and sell orders for USE shares during each trading day. Romano agreed to execute trades as directed by D'Onofrio, and Romano also agreed to move, or adjust, the price Castle quoted for USE shares at D'Onofrio's direction. In return,

D'Onofrio assured Romano that Castle would receive a profit on the transactions D'Onofrio directed.

In a typical manipulative transaction,

> (a) D'Onofrio would direct a buy order from one of the ... brokerage accounts controlled by the D'Onofrio group [consisting of stock promoters Ramon N. D'Onofrio, Richard Kirschbaum, and D'Onofrio] to a market maker other than Castle;
>
> (b) D'Onofrio would arrange in advance that the other market maker would contact Romano at Castle to buy the same number of shares;
>
> (c) D'Onofrio would alert Romano that the other market maker would be calling Romano for stock;
>
> (d) D'Onofrio, specifying number of shares and price, would instruct Romano to sell shares of USE to the other market maker; and
>
> (e) D'Onofrio would supply Castle with the specified number of shares at a discount, enabling Romano to complete the transaction at a price at which both Castle and the other market maker received a risk-free profit on the transaction, as had been prearranged with Castle ... and Romano.

Romano, Castle, and the D'Onofrio group "intentionally engaged" in such "manipulative conduct ... between September 1989 and December 1989." As a result of these manipulative trades, the price of USE stock rose from $.05 to approximately $5.00 per share in this period. In June or early July 1990, Castle sold approximately 15,000 shares of USE stock to retail customers at $6.00 per share. Between September 1989 and August 1990, Castle made a profit of approximately $175,000 as a result of its market-making activity for USE.

The SEC then commenced the instant action, alleging that defendants violated various provisions of the securities laws in connection with their manipulation of USE stock and other aspects of an illegal scheme involving USE. Romano moved, pursuant to Fed R. Civ. P. 12(b)(6), to dismiss the SEC's manipulation claim under Section 10(b) of the Securities Exchange Act of 1934 and Rule 10b-5 thereunder. The district court granted the motion on the sole ground that the SEC had failed to allege that Romano was a "primary violator[ ]," as required by the Supreme Court in *Central Bank of Denver, N.A. v. First Interstate Bank of Denver, N.A.*, 511 U.S. 164, 191 (1994). Rather, the district court held that Romano was alleged only to be an aider/abettor of securities violations, because Romano "follow[ed] directions from D'Onofrio in carrying out buy or sell orders" and "did not himself make wash sales, match orders, or use undisclosed nominees to artificially affect the price of securities."[a] ***

---

a Ed. Note—At the conclusion of its opinion, the court observed that although Section 20(e) of the Exchange Act, enacted after the Supreme Court's decision in *Central Bank,* now provides the SEC with the authority to assert aiding and abetting claims under Section 10(b), there was some question as to whether the SEC could bring aiding and abetting claims based on conduct occurring before Section 20(e) was on the books. The court did not address this alternative ground for vacating the district court's dismissal order because the SEC did not make this argument before the district court or on appeal.

*Discussion*

In reviewing the district court's dismissal of the SEC's claim pursuant to Fed.R.Civ.P. 12(b)(6), we are "required to accept the material facts alleged in the complaint as true" and will vacate the dismissal "unless it appears beyond doubt that the plaintiff can prove no set of facts in support of [its] claim which would entitle [it] to relief." Our review is *de novo.*

Romano's principal contention on appeal, with which the district court agreed, is that he cannot be primarily liable under § 10(b) for following a stock promoter's directions to execute trades that Romano knew, or was reckless in not knowing, were manipulative, where Romano did not share the promoter's ultimate "manipulative ... purpose" to raise the stock price. We disagree.

*** In *Central Bank,* the Supreme Court held that private civil liability under § 10(b) applies only to those who "engage in the manipulative or deceptive practice," but not to those "who aid and abet the violation." 511 U.S. at 167. The Court observed that "[a]iding and abetting is a method by which courts create secondary liability in persons *other than* the violator [or violators] of the statute." Id. at 184. We have noted further that a primary violator is one who "participated in the fraudulent scheme" or other activity proscribed by the securities laws. *SEC v. First Jersey Secs., Inc.,* 101 F.3d 1450, 1471 (2d Cir.1996).

Under the foregoing standards, we believe that, as alleged in the complaint, Romano falls well within the boundaries of primary liability. *** We [therefore] disagree with the district court's view that "[e]ven if Romano knew that [the buyers and sellers] were D'Onofrio and undisclosed nominees of D'Onofrio, and hence knew that D'Onofrio was manipulating USE stock, [Romano] did not himself manipulate USE stock because he did not himself have a manipulative purpose." ***

*A. Scienter*

Of course, to establish Romano's liability under § 10(b), the complaint must as a threshold matter allege that Romano acted with sufficient scienter. The complaint's allegation that Romano "knowingly or recklessly participated in and furthered a market manipulation by ... effecting 'wash sales' and 'matched orders'" and that he "intentionally engaged" in "manipulative conduct" is plainly sufficient to satisfy that requirement. It is well-settled that knowledge of the proscribed activity is sufficient scienter under § 10(b). See *Ernst & Ernst,* 425 U.S. at 197 ("[t]he words 'manipulative or deceptive' ... strongly suggest that § 10(b) was intended to proscribe knowing or intentional misconduct")*; SEC v. Lorin,* 76 F.3d 458, 460 (2d Cir.1996) (per curiam) (affirming liability against defendant who "knew of the manipulation agreement and knowingly participated in carrying it out")*;* cf. Restatement (Second) of Torts, § 8A (1965) ("If the actor knows that the consequences are certain, or substantially certain, to result from his act, and still goes ahead, he is treated by the law as if he had in fact desired to produce the result."). Therefore, the allegation that Romano executed trades that he knew were for a manipulative purpose sufficiently alleged scienter in a manner supporting § 10(b) liability.

Although we need not rely on this point, we also note that the complaint's claim that Romano recklessly participated in the manipulation also alleges sufficient scienter. See *San Leandro Emergency Med. Group Profit Sharing Plan v. Philip Morris Cos.,* 75 F.3d 801, 813 (2d Cir.1996) ("In order to establish scienter ..., [it is sufficient that] the plaintiffs ... identify circumstances indicating conscious or reckless behavior by the defendants"); see also Louis Loss & Joel Seligman, Securities Regulation, Vol. VIII, ch.9, § B(6), at 3665-67 n. 521 (3d ed.1991) (noting holdings of eleven circuits that recklessness can constitute sufficient scienter); cf. *Ernst & Ernst,* 425 U.S. at 193 n. 12 (leaving open question whether "reckless behavior" is sufficient to establish § 10(b) liability).

Moreover, as long as Romano, with scienter, effected the manipulative buy and sell orders, Romano's personal motivation for manipulating the market is irrelevant in determining whether he violated § 10(b). Even if Romano were motivated by a desire to obtain compensation rather than by a desire to change USE's market price, as D'Onofrio was, Romano is liable under § 10(b) if, with scienter, he effected the manipulative trades.

B. *Primary Violator or Aider and Abettor*

It is plain to us that the complaint alleged Romano to be a primary violator. Romano "participated in the fraudulent scheme," *First Jersey Secs.,* 101 F.3d at 1471, i.e., the manipulation of USE's stock, by effecting the very buy and sell orders that artificially manipulated USE's stock price upward. Indeed, if the trader who executes manipulative buy and sell orders is not a primary violator, it is difficult to imagine who would remain liable after *Central Bank.*

*** [I]t is of no relevance that D'Onofrio, not Romano, masterminded the USE stock manipulation and that D'Onofrio's group "directed" Romano to effect the illegal trades. *** The Supreme Court in *Central Bank* never intended to restrict § 10(b) liability to supervisors or directors of securities fraud schemes while excluding from liability subordinates who also violated the securities laws. In sum, the complaint alleges that Romano is primarily liable under § 10(b) and Rule 10b-5 for the manipulation of USE stock. ***

### *NOTES AND QUESTIONS*

***1. Manipulation as a Sub-Category of Fraud.*** When a defendant's conduct involves securities trading that is designed to create the impression that multiple buyers and sellers are actively engaging in securities transactions, is the separate concept of market manipulation even necessary to state a claim under Section 10(b) and Rule 10b-5? See Daniel R. Fischel and David J. Ross, Should the Law Prohibit "Manipulation" in Financial Markets?, 105 Harv. L. Rev. 503, 510-11 (1991) (contending that fictitious transactions—such as wash sales and matched orders—are "a form of fraud by conduct" and that "the concept of manipulation for this category of cases is superfluous"). Can fictitious trades be analogized to material misrepresentations in connection with the purchase or sale of a security? What assumptions underlie this analogy? Decide whether you agree with the following statement:

> When an outsider, a member of the public, reads the price quotations of a stock listed on an exchange, he is justified in supposing that the quoted price is an appraisal of the value of that stock due to a series of actual sales between various persons dealing at arm's length in a free and open market on the

> exchange, and so represents a true chancering of the market value of that stock thereon under the process of attrition due to supply operating against demand.

*United States v. Brown*, 5 F. Supp. 81, 85 (S.D.N.Y. 1933), aff'd on other grounds, 79 F.2d 321 (2d Cir. 1935).

***2. Section 9(a) of the Exchange Act.*** Although it is Section 9(a)(1) of the Exchange Act that expressly prohibits wash sales and matched orders, most market manipulation cases involving these so-called fictitious trading practices are brought by the SEC under the more generally worded provisions in Section 10(b) and Rule 10b-5. One basic reason is that Section 9's prohibitions extend only to practices involving securities listed on national securities exchanges. In *US Environmental*, for instance, the allegedly manipulated security—USE—was traded in the over-the-counter market. But what if the securities of USE were listed on the New York Stock Exchange? Given the allegations in its complaint, would the SEC have been able to satisfy the other elements necessary to state a claim against Romano under Section 9(a)(1)? What about under the catch-all provisions in Section 9(a)(2), which reads as follows:

> **Section 9(a).** It shall be unlawful for any person, directly or indirectly, by the use of the mails or any means or instrumentality of interstate commerce, or of any facility of any national securities exchange, or for any member of a national securities exchange—***
>
> (2) To effect, alone or with one or more other persons, a series of transactions in any security registered on a national securities exchange *** with respect to such security creating actual or apparent active trading in such security, or raising or depressing the price of such security, for the purpose of inducing the purchase or sale of such security by others.

***3. Section 9(e)'s Private Right of Action.*** Under Section 9(e) of the Exchange Act, any person who "willfully participates in any act or transaction" in violation of Section 9 shall be liable "to any person who shall purchase or sell any security at a price which was affected by such act or transaction" for "the damages sustained as a result of any such act or transaction." The provision also authorizes courts, in their discretion, "to assess reasonable costs, including reasonable attorneys' fees, against either party litigant." Although Section 9(e) constitutes one of only a few express private remedies in the Exchange Act, it is generally viewed as "a dead letter so far as producing recoveries is concerned." 9 Louis Loss & Joel Seligman, Securities Regulation 4280 (3d ed. 1992). What accounts for the dearth in cases?

## *PROBLEM 8-1*

Recent press reports indicate that the SEC staff is considering filing securities fraud and market manipulation charges against at least two of the nation's largest investment banks for conduct described as "laddering"—improperly tying the allocation of shares in an initial public offering (IPO) to a client's willingness to buy additional shares of the same company at higher prices once the stock begins trading in the secondary market. As the Wall Street Journal noted,

> [i]f true, such alleged laddering tactics would have stimulated additional demand for technology-company IPOs during the stock-market bubble of the

> late 1990s, *** contributing to the huge first-day IPO price gains that eventually worsened losses suffered by individual investors who bought once trading began.

Randall Smith, SEC "Laddering" Inquiry Reaches Two Firms, Wall Street Journal at C1 (November 6, 2002).

Press reports further indicate that laddering allegations are at the center of more than 300 class action complaints against 55 investment banks that are pending in federal court in the Southern District of New York. The lawsuits allege that, through the practice of laddering,

> banks were able to artificially inflate the market for these new [IPO] stocks, drawing in unwitting outside investors. The fund managers would then get out, leaving individual investors holding the bag when the stocks later fell off their artificially created high.

Tamara Loomis, Judge to Weigh Dismissal of IPO Litigation, N.Y. L.J. at 1 (Oct. 24, 2002).

Assume that the SEC and private plaintiffs have garnered evidence supporting the claim that laddering occurred in connection with IPOs by specifically identified companies. Under which provisions of the federal securities laws might the investment banks be liable? What arguments would you anticipate that the banks would make by way of defense?

## B. ACTUAL TRADING CONDUCTED FOR A MANIPULATIVE PURPOSE

Recall that in *US Environmental*, the Second Circuit held that a broker's personal motivation for executing sell and buy orders was irrelevant because the trades themselves were manipulative acts proscribed by Section 10(b) and Rule 10b-5. The following decision demonstrates the very important role that motive plays in a market manipulation case in which the defendant has engaged in bona fide, arms-length, securities transactions.

### UNITED STATES v. MULHEREN

938 F.2d 364 (2d Cir. 1991)

MCLAUGHLIN, CIRCUIT JUDGE:

In the late 1980's a wide prosecutorial net was cast upon Wall Street. Along with the usual flotsam and jetsam, the government's catch included some of Wall Street's biggest, brightest, and now infamous—Ivan Boesky, Dennis Levine, Michael Milken, Robert Freeman, Martin Siegel, Boyd L. Jeffries, and Paul A. Bilzerian—each of whom either pleaded guilty to or was convicted of crimes involving illicit trading scandals. Also caught in the government's net was defendant-appellant John A. Mulheren, Jr., the chief trader at and general partner of Jamie Securities Co. ("Jamie"), a registered broker-dealer.

Mulheren was charged in a 42-count indictment handed-up on June 13, 1989. The indictment alleged that he conspired to and did manipulate the price on the New York Stock Exchange (the "NYSE") of the common stock of Gulf & Western Industries, Inc. ("G & W" or the "company") in violation of [Section 10(b) of the Exchange Act and Rule 10b-5] *** by purchasing 75,000 shares of

G & W common stock on October 17, 1985 for the purpose of raising the price thereof to $45 per share (Counts One through Four) ***.

***[A jury found Mulheren guilty and he] was sentenced to concurrent terms of one year and one day imprisonment, a $1,681,700 fine and a $200 special assessment.

This appeal thus focuses solely on the convictions concerning Mulheren's alleged manipulation of G & W common stock. The government sought to prove that on October 17, 1985, Mulheren purchased 75,000 shares of G & W common stock with the purpose and intent of driving the price of that stock to $45 per share. This, the government claimed, was a favor to Boesky, who wanted to sell his enormous block of G & W common stock back to the company at that price. Mulheren assails the convictions on several grounds.

First, Mulheren claims that the government failed to prove beyond a reasonable doubt that when he purchased the 75,000 shares of G & W common stock on October 17, 1985, he did it for the sole purpose of raising the price at which it traded on the NYSE, rather than for his own investment purposes. Second, Mulheren argues that even if his sole intent had been to raise the price of G & W stock, that would not have been a crime because, he claims, (1) he neither misrepresented any fact nor failed to disclose any fact that he was under a duty to disclose concerning his G & W purchases; (2) his subjective intent in purchasing G & W stock is not "material"; and (3) he did not act for the purpose of deceiving others. ***

Although we harbor doubt about the government's theory of prosecution, we reverse on Mulheren's first stated ground because we are convinced that no rational trier of fact could have found the elements of the crimes charged here beyond a reasonable doubt.

BACKGROUND

Reviewing the evidence "in the light most favorable to the government, and construing all permissible inferences in its favor," the following facts were established at trial.

In 1985, at the suggestion of his long-time friend, Carl Icahn, a prominent arbitrageur and corporate raider, Ivan Boesky directed his companies to buy G & W stock, a security that both Icahn and Boesky believed to be "significantly undervalued." Between April and October 1985, Boesky's companies accumulated 3.4 million shares representing approximately 4.9 percent of the outstanding G & W shares. According to Boesky, Icahn also had a "position of magnitude."

On September 5, 1985, Boesky and Icahn met with Martin Davis, the chairman of G & W. At the meeting, Boesky expressed his interest in taking control of G & W through a leveraged buyout or, failing that, by increasing his position in G & W stock and securing seats on the G & W board of directors. Boesky told Davis that he held 4.9 percent of G & W's outstanding shares. Davis said he was not interested in Boesky's proposal, and he remained adamant in subsequent telephone calls and at a later meeting on October 1, 1985.

At the October 1, 1985 meeting, which Icahn also attended, Boesky added a new string to his bow: if Davis continued to reject Boesky's attempts at control, then G & W should buy-out his position at $45 per share. At that time, G & W was, indeed, reducing the number of its outstanding shares through a repurchase program, but, the stock was trading below $45 per share. Davis stated that, although he would consider buying Boesky's shares, he could not immediately agree to a price. Icahn, for his part, indicated that he was not yet sure whether he would sell his G & W stock.

During—and for sometime before—these negotiations, Mulheren and Boesky also maintained a relationship of confidence and trust. The two had often shared market information and given each other trading tips. At some point during the April-October period when Boesky was acquiring G & W stock, Mulheren asked Boesky what he thought of G & W and whether Icahn held a position in the stock. Boesky responded that he "thought well" of G & W stock and that he thought Icahn did indeed own G & W stock. Although Boesky told Mulheren that G & W stock was "a good purchase and worth owning," Boesky never told Mulheren about his meetings or telephone conversations with Davis because he considered the matter "very confidential." Speculation in the press, however, was abound. Reports in the August 19, 1985 issue of *Business Week* and the September 27, 1985 issue of the *Wall Street Journal* indicated that Boesky and Icahn each owned close to five percent of G & W and discussed the likelihood of a take-over of the company. Mulheren, however, testifying in his own behalf, denied reading these reports and denied knowing whether Boesky and Icahn held positions in G & W.

On October 3, 1985, two days after his meeting with Boesky and Icahn, Davis met with Mulheren. Mulheren stated that he had a group of investors interested in knowing whether G & W would join them in acquiring CBS. According to Davis, Mulheren also volunteered that he could be "very helpful in monitoring the activities of Ivan Boesky [in G & W stock;] [Mulheren] knew that [Davis] considered Mr. Boesky adversarial;" and Mulheren agreed with Davis' unflattering assessment of Boesky. In a telephone conversation sometime between this October 3 meeting and a subsequent meeting between the two on October 9, 1985, Mulheren told Davis that he believed that Boesky did not own any G & W securities. Mulheren also said that he did not own any G & W stock either. When Davis and Mulheren met again on October 9, they spoke only about Mulheren's CBS proposal.

In the meantime, Boesky continued to press Davis to accept his proposals to secure control of G & W. When Boesky called Davis after their October 1, 1985 meeting, Davis "told [Boesky] as clearly as [he] could again that [G & W] had no interest whatsoever in doing anything with [Boesky]." Boesky then decided to contact his representative at Goldman, Sachs & Co. to arrange the sale of his massive block of stock to G & W. Boesky advised Goldman, Sachs that G & W common stock was not trading at $45 per share at the time, "but that should it become 45," he wanted to sell. A Goldman, Sachs representative met with Davis shortly thereafter regarding the company's repurchase of Boesky's G & W shares.

Sometime after the close of the market on October 16, 1985, Boesky called Davis, offering to sell his block of shares back to G & W at $45 per share.

NYSE trading had closed that day at $44 3/4 per share, although at one point during that day it had reached $45. Davis told Boesky that the company would buy his shares back, but only at the "last sale"—the price at which the stock traded on the NYSE at the time of the sale—and that Boesky should have his Goldman, Sachs representative contact Kidder Peabody & Co. to arrange the transaction.

After this conversation with Davis, but before 11:00 a.m. on October 17, 1985, Boesky called Mulheren. According to Boesky's testimony, the following, critical exchange took place:

> Boesky: Mr. Mulheren asked me if I liked the stock on that particular day, and I said yes, I still liked it. At the time it was trading at 44 3/4 . I said I liked it; however, I would not pay more than 45 for it and it would be great if it traded at 45. The design for the comment—
>
> DEFENSE COUNSEL MR. PUCCIO: Objection to the "design of the comment." I would ask [ ] only for the conversation.
>
> A.U.S.A. GILBERT: What if anything did he say to you?
>
> BOESKY: I understand.

Shortly after 11:00 a.m. on October 17, 1985, Jamie (Mulheren's company) placed an order with Oliver Ihasz, a floor broker, to purchase 50,000 shares of G & W at the market price. Trading in G & W had been sluggish that morning (only 32,200 shares had traded between 9:30 a.m. and 11:03 a.m.), and the market price was holding steady at $44 3/4 , the price at which it had closed the day before. At 11:04 a.m., Ihasz purchased 16,100 shares at $44 3/4 per share. Unable to fill the entire 50,000 share order at $44 3/4 , Ihasz purchased the remaining 33,900 shares between 11:05 a.m. and 11:08 a.m. at $44 7/8 per share.

At 11:09 a.m., Ihasz received another order from Jamie; this time, to purchase 25,000 shares of G & W for no more than $45 per share. After attempting to execute the trade at $44 7/8, Ihasz executed the additional 25,000 share purchase at $45 per share at 11:10 a.m. In sum, between 11:04 a.m. and 11:10 a.m., Jamie purchased a total of 75,000 shares of G & W common stock, causing the price at which it traded per share to rise from $44 3/4 to $45. At 11:17 a.m., Boesky and Icahn sold their G & W stock—6,715,700 shares between them—back to the company at $45 per share. Trading in G & W closed on the NYSE on October 17, 1985 at $43 5/8 per share. At the end of the day, Jamie's trading in G & W common stock at Mulheren's direction had caused it to lose $64,406.

## DISCUSSION

A convicted defendant, of course, bears "a very heavy burden" to demonstrate that the evidence at trial was insufficient to prove his guilt beyond a reasonable doubt. "A jury's verdict will be sustained if there is *substantial evidence,* taking the view most favorable to the government, to support it." Where "'*any* rational trier of fact could have found the essential elements of the crime,' the conviction must stand."

On this appeal, however, we are reminded that "in America we still respect the dignity of the individual, and [a defendant] ... is not to be imprisoned except on definite proof of a specific crime." To that end, it is "imperative that we not rend the fabric of evidence and examine each shred in isolation; rather, the reviewing court 'must use its experience with people and events in weighing the chances that the evidence correctly points to guilt against the possibility of innocent or ambiguous inference.'"

The government's theory of prosecution in this case is straightforward. In its view, when an investor, who is neither a fiduciary nor an insider, engages in securities transactions in the open market with the sole intent to affect the price of the security, the transaction is manipulative and violates Rule 10b-5.[2] Unlawful manipulation occurs, the argument goes, even though the investor has not acted for the "purpose of inducing the purchase or sale of such security by others," an element the government would have had to prove had it chosen to proceed under the manipulation statute, § 9(a)(2). Mulheren was not charged with violating § 9(a)(2). When the transaction is effected for an investment purpose, the theory continues, there is no manipulation, even if an increase or diminution in price was a foreseeable consequence of the investment.

Although we have misgivings about the government's view of the law, we will assume, without deciding on this appeal, that an investor may lawfully be convicted under Rule 10b-5 where the purpose of his transaction is solely to affect the price of a security. The issue then becomes one of Mulheren's subjective intent. The government was obligated to prove beyond a reasonable doubt that when Mulheren purchased 75,000 shares of G & W common stock on October 17, 1985, he did it with the intent to raise its price, rather than with the intent to invest. We conclude that the government failed to carry this burden.

In order to convict, the government had to demonstrate, in the first place, that Mulheren was aware that Boesky had a stake in G & W. In proof of knowledge, the government makes three arguments.

First, the government suggests that Boesky himself told Mulheren of his G & W positions. Boesky, however, never so testified; and the greatest puzzle in this record is why that critical question was never directly put to Boesky.

Second, the government relies on the speculation reported in the media, specifically the *Wall Street Journal* and *Business Week,* and the rumors floating on Wall Street that Boesky and Icahn owned substantial positions in G & W. There was no evidence, however, that Mulheren read these articles or heard these rumors. On the contrary, Mulheren flatly denied knowing of their existence. Moreover, knowledge of a rumor, particularly one on Wall Street, can hardly substitute for knowledge of a fact.

Third, the government contends that Mulheren's knowledge of Boesky's position is evident in the October 3, 1985 meeting between Davis and Mulheren.

---

2. The government also appears to argue in the alternative that the violation occurs not by simply engaging in a securities transaction with the intent to affect the price of a security, but rather by failing to disclose that subjective intent to the market. The government contends that all investors are under a "general duty" not to manipulate; thus, absent disclosure of an intent to manipulate, Rule 10b-5 is violated. We express no view on this theory.

In that meeting, Mulheren told Davis that he knew that Davis and Boesky had an "adversarial" relationship and Mulheren "understood" Davis' "position" and offered to help Davis "in any way he could" to "monitor" Boesky's G & W transactions. While this evidence, taken in isolation, might create an inference that Mulheren knew of Boesky's G & W holdings (as the source of the Boesky-Davis adversarial relationship), the rest of Davis' testimony casts a considerable shadow on the inference. Davis went on to testify that in a telephone conversation sometime between their October 3 and October 9 meetings Mulheren stated that he did not believe Boesky owned any G & W stock at all. By this time, of course, Boesky had already told Davis (at their September 5 meeting) that he owned 4.9 percent of G & W's outstanding shares. Given that Mulheren was at the time attempting to curry favor from Davis in connection with Mulheren's CBS proposal, it was hardly in Mulheren's best interest to lie to Davis by telling him that Boesky owned *no* shares, if in fact Mulheren knew that Boesky owned 3.4 million shares. In sum, the evidence of Mulheren's knowledge that Boesky had an interest in G & W rests on a very slender reed.

Even were we to conclude otherwise, however, the convictions still could not be sustained. Assuming that Mulheren knew that Boesky held a substantial position in G & W stock, the government nevertheless failed to prove that Mulheren agreed to and then purchased the 75,000 shares for the sole purpose of raising the price at which G & W common stock traded.

The strongest evidence supporting an inference that Mulheren harbored a manipulative intent, is the telephone conversation between Boesky and Mulheren that occurred either late in the day on October 16 or before 11:00 a.m. on October 17, 1985. In discussing the virtues of G & W stock, Boesky told Mulheren that he "would not pay more than 45 for it and it would be great if it traded at 45." To this Mulheren replied "I understand." The meaning of this cryptic conversation is, at best, ambiguous, and we reject the government's contention that this conversation "*clearly* conveyed Boesky's request that the price of the stock be pushed up to $45 ... [and Mulheren's] agreement to help." Boesky never testified (again, he was not asked) what he meant by his words.[4]

We acknowledge that, construed as an innocent tip—*i.e.* G & W would be a "great" buy at a price of $45 or below—the conversation appears contradictory. It seems inconsistent for Boesky to advise, on one hand, that he would not pay more than $45, yet on the other to exclaim that it would be a bargain ("great") at $45. The conversation does not make any more sense, however, if construed as a request for illicit manipulation. That Boesky put a limit on the price he would pay for the stock ("I would not pay more than 45 for it") seems inconsistent with a request to drive up the price of the stock. If a conspiracy to manipulate for his own selfish benefit had been Boesky's intent, and if Davis were poised to repurchase the shares at the "last sale," Boesky would obviously have preferred to see Mulheren drive the trading in G & W stock to a price above $45. In this regard, it is noteworthy that there was *no* evidence whatever that Mulheren knew of Boesky's demand to get $45 per share from G & W.

4. Defense counsel objected after Boesky testified "[t]he design of the comment...." No ruling was made on the objection and the government—for reasons known only to itself—abandoned further inquiry into Boesky's state of mind.

Moreover, during the four to six weeks preceding this conversation, Mulheren repeatedly asked Boesky what he thought of G & W—evincing Mulheren's predisposition (and Boesky's knowledge thereof) to invest in the company. In fact, Mulheren took a position in G & W when he shorted a broker 25,000 shares of G & W after the market closed on October 16.

Clearly, this case would be much less troubling had Boesky said "I want you to bring it up to 45" or, perhaps, even, "I'd like to see it trading at 45." But to hang a conviction on the threadbare phrase "it would be great if it traded at 45," particularly when the government does not suggest that the words were some sort of sinister code, defies reason and a sense of fair play. Any doubt about this is dispelled by the remaining evidence at trial.

First, and perhaps most telling, is that Jamie *lost* over $64,000 on Mulheren's October 17th transactions. This is hardly the result a market manipulator seeks to achieve. One of the hallmarks of manipulation is some profit or personal gain inuring to the alleged manipulator. See, e.g., *Baum v. Phillips, Appel & Walden, Inc.*, 648 F. Supp. 1518, 1531 (S.D.N.Y. 1986), aff'd per curiam, 867 F.2d 776 (2d Cir. 1989); *Walck v. American Stock Exchange, Inc.*, 565 F. Supp. 1051, 1065-66 (E.D. Pa. 1981), aff'd, 687 F.2d 778 (3rd Cir. 1982); *SEC v. Commonwealth Chemical Securities, Inc.*, 410 F. Supp. 1002, 1013 (S.D.N.Y.1976), aff'd in part, modified on other grounds, 574 F.2d 90 (2d Cir. 1978).

Second, the unrebutted trial testimony of the G & W specialist demonstrated that if raising the price of G & W to $45 per share was Mulheren's sole intent, Mulheren purchased significantly more shares (and put Jamie in a position of greater risk) than necessary to achieve the result. The G & W specialist testified that at the time Jamie placed its second order, 5,000 shares would "definitely" have raised the trading price from $44 7/8 to $45 per share. Yet, Jamie bought 25,000 shares.

Although there was no evidence that Mulheren received a *quid pro quo* from Boesky for buying G & W stock, the government, nevertheless, claims that Mulheren had a "strong pecuniary interest" in accommodating Boesky in order to maintain the close and mutually profitable relationship they enjoyed. With this argument the government is hoist with its own petard. Precisely because of this past profitable relationship, the more reasonable conclusion is that Mulheren understood Boesky's comment as another tip—this time to buy G & W stock. Indeed, there was no evidence that Boesky had ever asked Mulheren to rig the price of a stock in the past.

None of the traditional badges of manipulation are present in this case. Mulheren conspicuously purchased the shares for Jamie's account in the open market. Compare *United States v. Scop*, 846 F.2d 135, 137 (matched orders through fictitious nominees) (2d Cir.1988); *United States v. Gilbert*, 668 F.2d 94, 95 (2d Cir. 1981) (matched orders and wash sales); *United States v. Minuse*, 114 F.2d 36, 38 (2d Cir. 1940) (fictitious accounts, matched orders, wash sales, dissemination of false literature). The government argues that Mulheren's deceptive intent can be inferred from the fact that (1) he purchased the G & W shares through Ihasz, a floor broker whom the government claims was used only infrequently by Jamie; and (2) Ihasz never informed anyone that the purchases were made for Jamie. These arguments are factually flawed.

There was no evidence that there was anything unusual about Ihasz's execution of the trades. Oliver Ihasz testified that Jamie was a customer of his company. There was no testimony that his company was used infrequently, or that Mulheren's request was in any way out of the ordinary. Nor is there anything peculiar about the fact that Ihasz disclosed only the name of the clearing broker and not Jamie, as the purchaser, when he executed the trade. As Ihasz testified, in an open market transaction, the only information the floor broker provides to the seller is the name of the clearing broker, not the ultimate buyer. Jamie was conspicuously identified as the ultimate buyer of the G & W securities on Ihasz's order tickets, where it is supposed to appear.

The government also argues that manipulative intent can be inferred from the fact that Mulheren's purchase on October 17, 1985 comprised 70 percent of the trading in G & W common stock during the period between the opening of the market and 11:10 a.m. Such market domination, the government contends, is indicative of manipulation. While we agree, as a general proposition, that market domination is a factor that supports a manipulation charge, the extent to which an investor controls or dominates the market at any given period of time cannot be viewed in a vacuum. For example, if only ten shares of a stock are bought or sold in a given hour and only by one investor, that investor has created 100 percent of the activity in that stock in that hour. This alone, however, does not make the investor a manipulator. The percent of domination must be viewed in light of the time period involved and other indicia of manipulation. Taken in this context, the cases upon which the government relies, *United States v. Gilbert,* 668 F.2d 94 (2d Cir. 1981); *United States v. Stein,* 456 F.2d 844 (2d Cir. 1972); *In re Delafield & Delafield,* [1967- 69 Transfer Binder] Fed. Sec. L. Rep. (CCH) § 77, 648 (SEC 1969), are readily distinguishable.

*Gilbert,* for example, involved the manipulation of the shares of Conrac Corporation where, over a *one-year period,* the defendant's trading constituted more than 50 percent of the overall trading. See *United States v. Gilbert,* [1981-82 Transfer Binder] Fed. Sec. L. Rep. (CCH) § 98, 244, at 91,602, 91,605, 1981 WL 1662 (S.D.N.Y.1981), *aff'd,* 668 F.2d at 95. In *Stein,* the manipulator's transactions accounted for 28.8 percent of the daily exchange volume of transactions in Buckeye Corporation stock over a *four month period.* When domination is sustained over such an extended period of time, evidence of manipulation is strong. But, if the percentage of control be measured in terms of minutes or hours, anyone could find himself labeled as a manipulator.

*In re Delafield & Delafield* is the only case that gives us pause. There, the respondents entered into a consent decree with the Securities and Exchange Commission concerning allegations that they had manipulated the Class A common stock of the Mary Carter Paint Company by selling 17,600 shares of the stock between 2:00 p.m. and the close of the market on January 9, 1968. Respondents' transactions represented 83 percent of the transactions in the stock during that period. Significantly, however, the sales "were effected in the name of two foreign banks to conceal the identity" of the true seller. No such chicanery exists here. Thus, in the absence of other indicia of manipulation—and there are none—the fact that Mulheren dominated the market between 9:30 a.m. and 11:10 a.m. on October 17, 1985 (noting that Mulheren's purchases represented a small fraction of the total October 17th activity in G & W stock) carries little weight.

The government also urges that Mulheren's manipulative intent—as opposed to investment intent—can be inferred from certain of Mulheren's actions after his purchase of the G & W shares. For example, Mulheren sold G & W call options in the afternoon of October 17, 1985 that were designed to create a hedge in the event of a drop in the price of stock. Had Mulheren known, however, that Boesky and Icahn were going to unload 6.7 million shares of G & W stock—which had the inevitable effect of driving the price down—surely Mulheren would have had the foresight to write the options *before* Boesky and Icahn had a chance to sell. That Mulheren wrote the options in the afternoon suggests only that he was attempting to mitigate his losses.

Finally, the government contends that the fact that Mulheren continued to do favors for Boesky after G & W repurchased Boesky and Icahn's shares is inconsistent with his claim that he was "duped" by Boesky into purchasing the 75,000 G & W shares. We disagree. First, the evidence of "favors" rests largely on the unproven "stock parking" charges. Second, Mulheren's conduct after his G & W purchases is equally consistent with that of a sophisticated businessman who turns the other cheek after being slapped by the hand that usually feeds him.

We acknowledge that this case treads dangerously close to the line between legitimate inference and impermissible speculation. We are persuaded, however, that to come to the conclusion it did, "the jury must have engaged in false surmise and rank speculation." At best, Mulheren's convictions are based on evidence that is "at least as consistent with innocence as with guilt," and "on inferences no more valid than others equally supported by reason and experience." Accordingly, the judgments of conviction are reversed and Counts One through Four of the indictment are dismissed.

## *NOTES AND QUESTIONS*

***1. The Government's Legal Theories.*** The *Mulheren* court expressed "misgivings" about the government's argument that a person violates Rule 10b-5 by trading securities in the open market with the sole purpose of affecting the price of a security. The court also noted, but "expressed no view" on, the government's alternative theory that Rule 10b-5 is violated by the failure to disclose the subjective "manipulative" intent behind one's trading decisions.

The government's latter argument found acceptance with another Second Circuit panel in *United States v. Regan*, 937 F.2d 823 (2d Cir. 1991), a case decided less than two weeks before *Mulheren*. At trial, the government alleged, and ultimately convinced a jury, that Lee Newberg, a bond trader at Drexel, Burnham, Lambert (Drexel) had sought to depress the price of C.O.M.B. common stock by arranging with Charles Zarzecki, a trader at the arbitrage firm of Princeton/Newport (PN), to sell short a substantial amount of C.O.M.B. stock. Drexel had agreed to underwrite a $25 million dollar offering of convertible bonds for C.O.M.B., and a lower C.O.M.B. stock price would have enabled Drexel to command a higher interest rate for the convertible bonds and therefore make issue more easy to sell. In effecting the short sales, Zarzecki did not disclose that PN was the short seller or that "Drexel was the moving party behind the entire deal." Id. at 829.

The bond traders argued on appeal that because they did not stand in a fiduciary relationship with the parties on the other side of their short sales, they were free to remain silent about their motivations for trading, even if they did engage in short sales with the hope of affecting the market price of C.O.M.B. stock. The court rejected this argument, and affirmed the jury's finding that Section 10(b) and Rule 10b-5 had been violated. The following constitutes the court's analysis on this issue:

> In enacting section 10(b), "Congress meant to prohibit the full range of ingenious devices that might be used to manipulate securities prices." *Santa Fe Indus. v. Green*, 430 U.S. 462, 477 (1977). *** The plan conceived by Newberg and Zarzecki fits comfortably within this "full range" of wrongful acts. "Failure to disclose that market prices are being artificially depressed operates as a deceit on the market place and is an omission of a material fact." *United States v. Charnay*, 537 F.2d 341, 351 (9th Cir. 1976). Appellants' argument that a fiduciary relationship must exist before liability can be found is without merit. The case of *Chiarella v. United States*, 445 U.S. 222 (1980), upon which appellants rely involved trading on the basis of nonpublic information; here, appellants are charged with market manipulation.

*Regan*, 937 F.2d at 829.

Did the *Regan* court come to terms with the defendants' argument? To be sure, *Chiarella* was an insider trading case, but the Supreme Court's holding that silence may operate as a fraud under Rule 10b-5 only if there is a duty to speak has never been limited to that narrow context. See, e.g., *Basic Inc. v. Levinson*, 485 U.S. 224, 239 n. 17 (1988) (stating that "[s]ilence, absent a duty to disclose, is not misleading under Rule 10b-5"). (See also Chapter 2.A.2 supra.) What, if anything, is special about manipulative conduct that imposes a duty to disclose "subjective motivations?"

Does the government stand on firmer footing when it asks courts to view manipulation not as a disclosure violation but as a form of active conduct that serves to deceive investors? In its brief to the Supreme Court opposing Zarzecki's petition for certiorari, the DOJ argued that the traders "engaged in affirmative conduct designed to deceive investors by creating an artificial market price for C.O.M.B. stock." Brief for the U.S. in Opposition at 10-11, *Zarzecki v. U.S.*, 504 U.S. 940 (1992) (No. 91-1233). Leaving aside the uncertainty surrounding the meaning of "artificial," is this argument otherwise consistent with the Supreme Court's view that manipulative acts require either misrepresentation or nondisclosure? See *Schreiber*, 472 U.S. at 8 ("[a]ll three species of misconduct, i.e., 'fraudulent, deceptive, or manipulative,' listed by Congress are directed at failures to disclose"); *Santa Fe*, 430 U.S. at 477 ("nondisclosure is generally essential to the success of a manipulative scheme"). Recall in *Schreiber* the plaintiff-shareholder's allegation that the original hostile tender offer's replacement with the friendly one had the effect of "artificially" lowering the market price of El Paso's stock. See Chapter 5.B.1. Why couldn't the friendly tender offer have been characterized as "affirmative conduct designed to deceive investors by creating an artificial market price for El Paso stock?"

*2. Artificial v. Non-artificial Prices.* Professors Fischel and Ross have recognized that the task of defining the difference between artificial and non-artificial securities prices is an exceedingly difficult one. Consider their analysis:

> One possible definition is that any price change that results from trading designed to produce such a price change is an artificial price. This definition is unsatisfactory because trading with the purpose of producing a price change is not necessarily harmful. Consider *** the example of an issuer that purchases its own shares to signal investors that the shares are undervalued. In this example, the trading moves prices in the correct direction and thus the resulting price change should not be labeled "artificial."
>
> An alternate approach is to focus on whether the trading moves prices closer to or away from their correct level. But what is the "correct level"? One possibility is the price that reflects long-run conditions of supply and demand. Manipulation could then be defined as trades that "do not move price more quickly in the direction that reflects long-run conditions of supply and demand." *** But this definition is also unsatisfactory. What if the trades do not move prices at all or move prices in the direction that reflects short-run conditions of supply and demand? Most importantly, what happens if the trades move prices in one direction because the trader genuinely believes that prices will move in this direction, but the trader turns out to be wrong and prices ultimately move in the opposite direction? Trading based on a genuine belief that prices will ultimately move in the direction of the trades is the essence of nonmanipulative trading.
>
> To avoid the need to distinguish between short-run and long-run conditions of supply and demand, the correct level of prices could be defined as the level prices would be if all relevant information were publicly disclosed. But this definition is also unhelpful. "All relevant information" includes not only the information possessed by the trader, but also the trades themselves. If prices move in response to trades, the price cannot be said to be "artificial" unless the trades are defined as illegitimate in some way. Once again we are faced with the problem of circularity—improper trades are trades that produce an artificial price and artificial price is defined as a price produced by improper trades.
>
> Defining manipulation by reference to whether the trades move prices closer to their correct level has another flaw: it jeopardizes property rights in information. Absent a fiduciary relationship or other special circumstance, traders do not have a duty to disclose the information they possess that motivates their trades. Disclosure would cause the information to lose its value and thus eliminate the incentive to acquire the information in the first place. Without such an incentive, no one would search for information and securities markets—which depend on new information to cause price changes—would be destroyed. But trades, as well as disclosures, can reveal information. The more information the trade reveals, the closer the trade comes to a direct disclosure, which decreases the trader's ability to capture the value of the private information in his possession. For markets to exist, therefore, trades cannot be fully revealing. Traders must be allowed to disguise their trades to avoid disclosing the information they possess to other traders. Accordingly, manipulation cannot be defined as trading that does not move prices closer to their "correct" level. Such a definition would deny traders the ability to disguise their trades to capture the value of the information they possess.

> Thus, there is no objective definition of manipulation. The only definition that makes any sense is subjective—it focuses entirely on the intent of the trader. Manipulative trades could be defined as profitable trades made with "bad" intent—in other words, trades that meet the following conditions: (1) the trading is intended to move prices in a certain direction; (2) the trader has no belief that the prices would move in this direction but for the trade; and (3) the resulting profit comes solely from the trader's ability to move prices and not from his possession of valuable information. Traders who trade with "good" intent—for the purpose of moving prices in the direction they believe prices will move—are not engaged in manipulation. Similarly, traders with private information who disguise their trades with the effect that prices do not move in the correct direction, or even move in the wrong direction, also trade with "good" intent and thus are not engaged in manipulation because their ultimate profit is attributable to the private information they possess.

Daniel R. Fischel and David J. Ross, Should the Law Prohibit "Manipulation" in Financial Markets?, 105 Harv. L. Rev. 503, 508-10 (1991).

***3. Proving "Bad Intent" With Circumstantial Evidence.*** *Mulheren* reveals some of the problems that the government (or a private plaintiff) will typically encounter when it seeks to prove that actual stock trades were made with "bad intent." Indeed, because "it is impossible to probe into the depths of a man's mind, it is necessary in the usual case (that is, absent an admission) that the finding of manipulative purpose be based on inferences drawn from circumstantial evidence." *In re Federal Corp.*, Release No. 34-3909, 25 SEC 227, 230 (Jan. 29, 1947).

In *Regan*, the government prosecutors were fortunate to have a recording of the conversation between the Drexel and PN bond traders, wherein Newberg told Zarzecki about the upcoming Drexel underwriting of C.O.M.B.'s convertible bonds and said:

> The stock is sixteen bid, up from fifteen and three eighths.
>
> I don't want this thing to be sixteen bid.
>
> I want, y-y- you know, to get rid of it, y—, ah, you know. I want, I want it down to at least fifteen and three quarters and hopefully lower. Umm ..., I wouldn't mind you selling a little bit first. And um ..., you're indemnified, uh, you know, my—, it's, y—, you know what I'm saying.

Information, *United States v. Drexel Burnham Lambert, Inc.* (S.D.N.Y. Mar. 29, 1989) (89 Cr. 41) at 22-23 (quoted in Lewis D. Lowenfels and Alan R. Bromberg, Securities Market Manipulations: An Examination and Analysis of Domination and Control, Frontrunning, and Parking, 55 Alb. L. Rev. 293, 352 (1991)). While hardly an unequivocal "smoking gun," the recorded conversation certainly did much to bolster the government's case that the bond traders' sole intent in shorting the C.O.M.B stock was to depress the price for Drexel's benefit in the upcoming bond offering.

Can you identify other areas of law—apart from federal securities law—where the legality of a person's conduct turns exclusively on a person's subjective motivations? In such cases, what types of facts would support a claim that the law was violated?

***4. Manipulative Activity Designed to Restore Value.*** What if a person sincerely believes that others in the market are acting to artificially affect the price of a security and therefore trades with the ultimate goal of *restoring* the stock's price to its "true" value? For example, there was evidence in *Regan* that Drexel believed that C.O.M.B. was itself manipulating—"levitat[ing]," to use the court's term—the price of its common stock into a higher range. *Regan,* 937 F.2d at 829. If Drexel acted with the purpose of counteracting C.O.M.B's activity, is it fair to say that the bond traders acted with the requisite "bad intent?" The court in *United States v. Hall,* 48 F. Supp.2d 386, 387 (S.D.N.Y. 1999) had this to say about "correcting" the market:

> A fraudulent scheme to manipulate is unlawful, even if the defendant is trying in his mind to correct the market. Even assuming Hall was genuinely trying to bring the price of HealthTech stock up to where he believed it should be, the ends do not justify the means and he could not seek to do so through unlawful means.

Assuming that the defendant's trades did not involve wash sales, matched orders, or other such fictitious trading practices, does *Hall* reach a sound conclusion?

***5. The Costs and Benefits of Market Manipulation.*** In *Mulheren,* among other evidence, the Second Circuit found "most telling" that Mulheren's firm lost over $64,000 on the G & W stock purchases and concluded that "this is hardly the result a market manipulator seeks to achieve." Given the government's contention that Mulheren's trading was motivated by a desire to assist Boesky, shouldn't the economic inquiry have been on the profit made by Boesky? Professor Steve Thel points out that the 1/4 point rise in the price of G & W due to Mulheren's trading resulted in Boesky receiving about $850,000 more for his 3.4 million shares than he would have received had Mulheren not effected the trades. And if the overall benefit of the alleged manipulation scheme is measured to include the increase in value for Carl Icahn's shares, the profit earned through the Mulheren trades becomes $1,678,925. See Steve Thel, $850,000 in Six Minutes—The Mechanics of Securities Manipulation, 79 Cornell L. Rev. 219, 255 (1994).

***6. "Real" Trades Revisited.*** In *Markowski v. SEC,* 274 F.3d 525 (D.C. Cir. 2001), the court affirmed an SEC order sustaining a disciplinary action taken by the NASD against Michael Markowski, the Chairman, CEO, and majority shareholder of Global America, Inc (then an NASD member firm that specialized in emerging growth companies), and Joseph Riccio, Global's trader. The order imposed liability under Rule 10b-5 for manipulating the stock market. Specifically, in connection with an initial public offering of Mountaintop Corporation underwritten by Global, Markowski and Riccio were found to have artificially supported the price of Mountaintop securities by "(1) maintain[ing] high bid prices for Mountaintop securities, and (2) absorb[ing] all unwanted securities into inventory, thereby preventing sales from depressing market prices." Id. at 527. The D.C. Circuit had this to say about the defendants' argument that "because Global's bids and trades in this case were 'real'—they involved real customers, real transactions, and real money—the trades cannot be classified as an unlawful manipulation":

> Liability for manipulation wholly independent of fictitious transactions in fact raises interesting questions. Without such transactions, the core of the offense can be obscure. It may be hard to separate a "manipulative" investor

from one who is simply over-enthusiastic, a true believer in the object of investment. Both may amass huge inventories and place high bids, even though there are scant objective data supporting the implicit estimate of the stock's value. Legality would thus depend entirely on whether the investor's intent was "an investment purpose" or "solely to affect the price of [the] security." *United States v. Mulheren*, 938 F.2d 364, 368 (2d Cir.1991). Given the typical ambiguity of intent, commentators have suggested that imposing liability may chill investors from transactions that actually contribute to the efficiency of securities markets. Daniel R. Fischel & David J. Ross, "Should the Law Prohibit 'Manipulation' in Financial Markets?," 105 Harv. L. Rev. 503, 523 (1991) (expressing concerns about the manipulation doctrine's over-deterrence effects); see also *Mulheren*, 938 F.2d at 368 (expressing misgivings about basing 10b-5 violations purely on whether or not a "transaction is effected for an investment purpose").

Commentators have also suggested that where manipulative behavior is solely defined in terms of the actor's purpose, it may well be self-deterring as a general matter, so that any need for an external sanction is slight. Purely "trade-based" manipulation schemes, in which the manipulator simply buys a security in order to induce higher prices and then sells to take advantage of the price change, are likely to fail. First, it is difficult unilaterally to cause price to rise. Second, it is even more difficult to sell subsequently at a price high enough to cover both purchase costs *and* transaction costs. For one thing, if the actor's purchases are such as to give the market a material upward thrust, his later sales may equivalently drive it down. See Fischel & Ross, supra, at 512-19. But see Steve Thel, "$850,000 in Six Minutes—The Mechanics of Securities Manipulation," 79 Cornell L. Rev. 219 (1994) (suggesting that manipulators may profit from very small, short-lived price changes).

These arguments, however, are of little use to Markowski and Riccio. Whatever the practical concerns, we cannot find the Commission's interpretation to be unreasonable in light of what appears to be Congress's determination that "manipulation" can be illegal solely because of the actor's purpose. See *Chevron U.S.A., Inc. v. Natural Resources Defense Council, Inc.*, 467 U.S. 837, 843-44(1984). Section 9(a)(2) of the Securities Exchange Act manifests this idea by declaring it unlawful

> [t]o effect ... a series of transactions in any security registered on a national securities exchange creating actual or apparent active trading in such security or raising or depressing the price of such security, for the purpose of inducing the purchase or sale of such security by others.

Id. This provision is quite separate from the subsections of § 9 prohibiting manipulation through fraudulent devices such as wash sales, [Exchange Act Section 9(a)(1)(A)], matched sales, id. at [Section 9(a)(1)(B)-(C)], and false statements, id. at [Section 9(a)(4)]. Given Congress's clear endorsement for sanctions against this sort of manipulation, the Commission's inclusion of it within the phrase "manipulative ... device" in § 10(b) cannot have been unreasonable.

The Commission's interpretation is also consistent with its rules governing an issuer's purchases of its own securities. See Securities Exchange Act of 1934, Rule 10b-18. Issuer repurchases are perfectly real transactions. But the Commission has created a safe harbor measured in terms of timing, volume, and price; purchases outside the safe harbor are subject to possible enforcement action as manipulations. See Purchases of Certain Equity Securities by the Issuer and Others; Adoption of Safe Harbor, 47 Fed. Reg. 53,333 (1982).

> Further, to the extent that the case against liability for "trade-based" manipulation depends on its inherently self-deterring character, petitioners' situation may be distinguishable. The activity in Mountaintop furthered an external purpose. At least in the short term, Global supported Mountaintop's price not to profit from later sales of Mountaintop, but to maintain customer interest in Global generally and to sustain confidence in its other securities. As James Shanley, Global's chief operating officer, testified, petitioner Riccio explained his refusal to lower his bid price: "If we do that on one stock, they [presumably, holders of Global's stocks] will hit us on all the stocks." Thus, the prospects of losing some money on Mountaintop in the short run would not deter Global from manipulating—if that cost was worth the benefit of keeping its customers and preserving confidence in its other stocks.

Id. at 528-29. Was *Markowski's* reasoning sound?

### *PROBLEM 8-2*

Frank Franklin is a very sophisticated investor who has recently reduced his work schedule as an architect so that he can spend more time at home researching companies and "day-trading" his stock portfolio through his on-line investment account. On many mornings throughout the last several months, Frank has bought substantial amounts of low priced stocks in companies that he believes the market is overlooking and, therefore, undervaluing. Frank has noticed that his early morning trading often seems to spark others' interest in his selected stock, such that he can make a reasonable profit by selling off his holdings at the close of the business day. Are there any aspects of Frank's day-trading strategy that could be considered manipulative? Could the government prove that his actions were in violation of the federal securities laws? Should it try?

Would your answer change if, after he purchased his chosen stocks, Frank routinely sent postings to on-line bulletin boards stating that "now is the time to buy X stock" or "I strongly recommend X stock"?

## C. MISLEADING RECOMMENDATIONS AND MATERIAL MISSTATEMENTS DESIGNED TO AFFECT MARKET PRICES

### *1. Scalping and "Pump and Dumps"*

The SEC's complaint that follows this prefatory material charges a Georgetown law student with Rule 10b-5 violations in connection with a stock scalping scheme that was conducted over the Internet with the assistance of three other law students. Although sometimes viewed and prosecuted as a type of insider trading (see discussion of *Carpenter v. United States* in Chapter 7), scalping can be more generally described as the practice of recommending the purchase of a security to a group of investors while one is selling, or intending to sell, that security at the same time. To be sure, the scalper is purchasing securities on the basis of the nonpublic information that he is about to publicize a positive recommendation about a security. But unlike the typical insider trading case, the scalper controls—indeed creates—the very information that, when released, is bound to affect the security's market price. Accordingly, when recommendations are made for the avowed purpose of profiting from their effect, the practice of scalping can be viewed as a type of market manipulation. Once again, then, the role of motive is key.

The Supreme Court first considered the legality of scalping in *SEC v. Capital Gains Research Bureau, Inc.*, 375 U.S. 180 (1963), a case which involved recommendations issued by the publishers of a monthly investment report who were registered investment advisers. The SEC argued, and the Court agreed, that the advisers had committed acts which "operat[ed] as a fraud or deceit" in violation of Section 206 of the Investment Advisers Act of 1940. Id. at 181. The Court focused specifically on the advisers' failure to disclose to their clients their "practice of purchasing shares of a security for [their] own account shortly before recommending that security for long-term investment and then immediately selling the shares at a profit upon the rise in the market price following the recommendation." Id. at 181. In the Court's view, it did not matter whether the advisers' "advice was 'honest' in the sense that they believed it was sound and did not offer it for the purpose of furthering personal pecuniary objectives." Id. at 200. Rather, the Court found in the legislative history an intent "to eliminate, *or at least to expose*, all conflicts of interest which might incline an investment adviser—consciously or unconsciously—to render advice which was not disinterested." Id. at 191-192 (emphasis added). Absent from the case was any suggestion that the investment advisers had sought to intentionally manipulate the market.

An inquiry into the unlawfulness of scalping becomes a bit more complex when we depart from the context of recommendations by investment advisers or broker-dealers who clearly owe fiduciary duties of disclosure to their clients. Yet in *Zweig v. Hearst Corp.*, 594 F.2d 1261 (9th Cir.1979), the court had little trouble concluding that a newspaper columnist had violated Rule 10b-5 when he touted a stock in his column without disclosing that he had recently purchased 5,000 shares of that stock from the issuer at a discounted price and intended to sell the stock after the column's publication. (The plaintiff's case was no doubt strengthened when he was able to show that the columnist had written similar columns about 21 other securities which he had purchased shortly before and had sold shortly after each column was published.) In finding an omission of a material fact in violation of Rule 10b-5, the court concluded that "[c]olumnists *** ordinarily have no duty to disclose facts about their personal financial affairs ***" but that here "the defendant assumed those duties when, with knowledge of the stock's market and an intent to gain personally, he encouraged purchases of the securities in the market." Id. at 1268. Although the facts of the case may well have supported it, the court in *Zweig* did not consider the theory that the newspaper columnist had violated Rule 10b-5 by engaging in acts that were intended to have a manipulative effect on the market.

The *Zweig* court's conclusion that the failure to disclose an intention to scalp violates Rule 10b-5 was reached prior to the Supreme Court's holding in *Chiarella* that silence, absent a duty to disclose, is not actionable as fraud under Rule 10b-5. Is *Zweig's* conclusion still valid? At least one court has answered affirmatively, at least in the context where, like a newspaper columnist, the defendant was found to have stood in a relationship of trust and confidence with the recipients of his stock recommendations. See *SEC v. Gun Soo Oh Park (a.k.a."Tokyo Joe")*, 99 F. Supp.2d 889 (N.D. Ill. 2000) (refusing to dismiss Rule 10b-5 scalping allegations against defendant, a former burrito vendor and present-day "internet guru," who operated a stock-pick and investment advice website for fee-paying subscribers).

Consider the allegations in the following complaint:

## SEC v. DOUGLAS W. COLT
## COMPLAINT
## CV-1:00CV00423 (D.C.D.C) (EGS)

March 2, 2000

Plaintiff Securities and Exchange Commission ("the Commission") alleges:

### NATURE OF THE ACTION

1. During February and March 1999, defendant Douglas Colt, a student at a Washington, D.C. area law school, carried out an illegal scheme to manipulate the price of four stocks using a free subscription internet website called "Fast-Trades.com."

2. Through his scheme centered on recommending stocks, Colt drove up the short-term price for each stock by as much as 700%. By trading in advance of the stock recommendations, Colt generated more than $345,000 in total profits for himself, four individuals who assisted him in the scheme, and two of Colt's friends. At times, some of them garnered profits exceeding 500% within one hour. Within a few hours after the recommendations were disseminated to subscribers, the price of each of the four stocks decreased significantly from its intraday high.

3. Colt targeted low priced, thinly traded stocks knowing that his trades and trades by subscribers would artificially increase the price of the stocks selected. For each of the four manipulated stocks, Colt and the other participants collectively purchased a significant volume of the selected stock -in three cases more than 150% of the total average daily volume [the average number of shares bought and sold each day for approximately 200 business days immediately preceding the selection of the stock by the Fast-Trades.com website]. For all four stock selections, Fast-Trades purchases were made shortly before the website disseminated the recommendations to its subscribers.

4. After making these purchases and before the recommendations to purchase the stock were e-mailed to subscribers, Colt and the other participants entered sell limit orders or had orders entered on their behalf. Colt expected that unwitting subscribers would buy the recommended stock. Colt further expected that the purchases would drive the price higher still, triggering the sell limit orders. This is precisely what happened.

5. Subscriber purchases were essential to the scheme. Thus, Colt constantly needed to maintain and expand Fast-Trades subscriber rolls. To attract new subscribers, Colt recruited and trained his roommates, Kenneth Terrell and Jason Wyckoff, along with Adam Altman—all law school classmates—to help him promote the site by posting false and misleading messages on hundreds of publicly accessible internet message boards. These messages disguised the authors' connection with the site and misrepresented the investment success they achieved from following Fast-Trades' recommendations. Partly through these postings, the subscriber base grew to more than 9,000 people over a two month period.

6. Colt also included a false "track record" on the Fast-Trades.com website, where he touted the performance of several stocks that he claimed were past Fast-Trades selections. In fact, several of these stocks had not been selected by Fast-Trades.

7. The Fast-Trades.com website also contained a misleading disclaimer crafted by Colt, Terrell, Wyckoff and Altman that misrepresented their trading intentions to their subscribers. The disclaimer stated that Fast-Trades representatives "may" trade Fast-Trades selections "at any time." In fact, for each of the four stocks, Colt had already purchased the selected stock *and* entered sell limit orders before Fast-Trades even distributed the selection to its subscribers.

8. By engaging in the transactions, acts, practices and courses of business alleged herein, defendant Colt violated the antifraud provisions of the federal securities laws.

## JURISDICTION

9. The Commission brings this action pursuant to Section 21(d)(1) of the Securities Exchange Act of 1934 ("Exchange Act").

10. This Court has jurisdiction of this action pursuant to Section 27 of the Exchange Act.

11. The defendant, directly or indirectly, has engaged in, and unless restrained and enjoined by this Court will continue to engage in, transactions, acts, practices, and courses of business that violate Section 10(b) of the Exchange Act and Rule 10b-5 promulgated thereunder.

12. In connection with the transactions, acts, practices, and courses of business described in this Complaint, the defendant, directly or indirectly, has made use of the means and instrumentalities of interstate commerce, of the mails, and/or of the facilities of national securities exchanges.

## THE DEFENDANT

13. Defendant Douglas Colt, age 24, is a permanent resident of Colorado Springs, Colorado, and a third-year law student at a Washington, D.C. area law school. During the time of the violations alleged herein, Colt resided in Arlington, Virginia, in an apartment he shared with two law school classmates, Kenneth Terrell and Jason Wyckoff.

## CLAIM FOR RELIEF

Violations of Section 10(b) of the Exchange Act
and Rule 10b-5 Promulgated Thereunder

## COLT LAYS THE GROUNDWORK FOR THE FAST-TRADES.COM SCHEME

14. Douglas Colt began trading stocks in the summer of 1998, when he opened a margin account at Charles Schwab & Co. Through 1998 and early 1999, he predominantly traded technology and penny stocks, holding most positions for only a few days or weeks. In total, he bought and sold approximately thirteen positions before he began making recommendations on the Fast-Trades website.

Colt's trading in these thirteen stocks yielded a total net profit of approximately $24.

15. In late January 1999, Colt created Fast-Trades.com, an internet stock selection subscription website. Fast-Trades offered a free "six month trial period," which the website represented was a "limited time" offer, and no subscriber ever paid a fee. Subscribers received the stock selections from Fast-Trades in one of two ways: either through a password protected area of the Fast-Trades website that allowed subscribers to learn the selection twenty-four hours before it was available to the public; or by having the selection e-mailed to them at the same time it became available to subscribers on the website.

16. The website consisted of an introduction page describing the site, a page that allowed visitors to the site to register as subscribers, and a page listing the current stock selection and providing information about the company selected, and displaying a disclaimer. The introduction page also included a "track record" that listed alleged previous stock picks, the highest price the stock reached after that pick, and a "stable high" price purportedly showing a price at which the stock settled after Fast-Trades selected it.

17. The "track record" of alleged previous stock picks that Colt included on the Fast-Trades website was materially false and misleading. In his posted track record, Colt included the names and short term performance of some stocks that had never been selected by Fast-Trades. He did this in order to artificially enhance Fast-Trades stock-picking credibility with potential subscribers. In fact, in an April 27, 1999 online message board posting, Colt revealed his understanding of this part of the scheme when he accused a competing stock picking website of doing the same thing. Using an alias, Colt attacked the other website's track record, calling it an "extremely fraudulent practice." Colt noted that on the first day the competing site appeared, "they somehow had a `track record' of about five picks." The posting continued: "Hmmm ... think they just made those up so that investors would be fooled into thinking [the unrelated stock picking website] actually knew something about picking stocks? You bet."

18. Colt created the website and selected all of Fast-Trades' recommendations, purportedly after researching various companies. Colt's "research," however was illusory. In an April 29, 1999 online message board posting criticizing an unrelated stock picking website, and again using an alias, Colt set forth an eleven-point blueprint for a price manipulation scheme. Colt's blueprint posting stated: screen for thinly traded stocks in the $1 to $2 range; get rid of all the oil and gas stocks because "they're not trendy"; modify the screen to find companies that have shown revenue increases in the last quarter, "so you can justify this gem to the world"; of the remaining stocks, look for one with very low average volume and low float; pull together information from optimistic company press releases; "throw in some bull*** about the company being an internet wonder"; "buy a bunch of this garbage stock"; "tell your idiot subscribers about how great the stock is, and, like sheep, they will run out and buy it"; "dump the shares you bought a few hours ago to all of these suckers"; "watch the stock steadily tank for the next month"; and "laugh all the way to the bank."

19. Before investing, Colt conducted a test to determine what impact dissemination of his stock recommendation would have on the market. On February 1,

1999, Colt recommended the test selection, Electrosource, Inc. (ticker: ELSI). Colt observed ELSI's price increase by thirty-five percent after the selection was announced.

COLT ENLISTS HIS ROOMMATES TO JOIN FAST-TRADES

20. During the 1998-99 academic year, Colt shared an apartment with two other law students, Kenneth Terrell and Jason Wyckoff. Shortly after Colt started the Fast-Trades website in late January, Colt offered his roommates the opportunity to participate in Fast-Trades. Colt told them he had posted a selection on the website and monitored the market to see how his selection affected the stock. If they agreed to help, Colt would allow them to trade on Fast-Trades selections through his account.

21. Terrell and Wyckoff agreed to participate with Colt, and during February and March 1999, the two spent numerous hours posting materially false and misleading messages on several hundred different Yahoo! internet message boards promoting the site to potential subscribers. Colt's roommates each gave Colt money to purchase shares on their behalf in Colt's brokerage account. Neither Terrell nor Wyckoffhad any prior experience investing in stocks.

THE FAST-TRADES.COM SCHEME

22. After observing the upward price movement stemming from his recommendation of Electrosource, Colt began purchasing stock in advance of Fast-Trades selections. From February 16 through March 10, Colt, one or more Fast-Trades participants, and as many as two friends purchased shares in the next four Fast-Trades selections before they were provided to subscribers. As the chart below illustrates, participants in the Fast-Trades scheme and their two friends collectively purchased an increasing number of shares with each selection.

| Security | Fast-Trades Related Purchases | Avg. Daily Volume | % of Avg. Daily Volume |
|---|---|---|---|
| Apache Medical | 5,000 | 11,694 | 43% |
| Option Care | 24,000 | 13,823 | 174% |
| American Education | 36,283 | 3,454 | 1050% |
| Artecon | 51,512 | 33,341 | 154% |

23. For all four stock selections, Fast-Trades purchases drove up the price and volume of the stock selected even before the selection was sent out to subscribers. Non-subscribing investors who observed the increase in price and volume of the selected stock and purchased shares—both before and after the release of the stock pick—also helped create a price increase. The rising price usually triggered the sell limit orders that Colt and the other Fast-Trades participants who traded had previously entered. Colt, his mother Joanne Colt (who was a participant in the Fast-Trades scheme), Terrell and Wyckoff monitored the run up by watching real time market quotes.

COLT, TERRELL AND WYCKOFF PURCHASE AMSI ON FEBRUARY 16

24. Apache Medical Systems, Inc. (ticker: AMSI) was the first Fast-Trades selection in which Fast-Trades participants traded. The AMSI selection was sent out to subscribers at approximately 2:45 p.m. on February 16, 1999.

25. Less than an hour before sending out the selection, Colt purchased 5,000 shares at $1.0625 per share in his account: 4,000 for himself and 500 each for his two roommates. Colt then entered a sell limit order of $4.00 per share just before the message recommending the stock was sent to subscribers. Colt set the sell limit order based on his observing the extent of the price movement on ELSI.

26. Colt's purchase of 5,000 shares spurred an increase in the price and volume of AMSI stock. Colt's purchase represented more than 40% of the 11,700 share total average daily volume of AMSI. In addition, between 2:25 p.m., the time that Colt's purchase was reported, and 2:45 p.m., when the Fast-Trades selection was sent out, an additional 44,600 shares of AMSI were traded, and the price rose to $1.50, a 41% increase over a twenty minute period.

27. After the Fast-Trades selection was sent to subscribers, the trading volume and price of AMSI increased significantly. The stock had a reported one day trading volume of 1,085,600 shares and reached an intraday high of $7.9375 per share—a price movement of $6.875, more than 600% higher than the price of Colt's first purchase. As the price of AMSI rose far above Colt's $4.00 sell limit price, Colt, watching the real-time price movement on a computer, chased the market, raising his sell price twice in a matter of minutes just after the selection went out to subscribers. Colt finally set his sell limit price at $6.00 per share, and his order was filled in 1000 share lots at prices ranging from $6.00 up to $7.75 per share. In the end, Colt, Terrell and Wyckoff reaped a collective profit of $27,937.50 on their AMSItrading in just thirty minutes. Within just a few hours after the recommendation was distributed to subscribers, the price of AMSI collapsed. Within a few days, AMSI was back to trading within pennies of its price at the time the recommendation was disseminated.

COLT, TERRELL, WYCKOFF AND
JOANNE COLT PURCHASE OPTN ON FEBRUARY 24

28. Fast-Trades' next selection was Option Care, Inc. (ticker: OPTN). The OPTN selection went out to subscribers shortly after 11:00 a.m. on February 24, 1999. Through his account, Colt purchased twice as many shares—10,000—of OPTN as he had of AMSI. Colt purchased these shares at a price of $1.625: 8000 for himself and 1,000 for each of his two roommates, just minutes before he sent out the selection to subscribers. Colt then entered a sell limit order of $5.00 for the shares—more than 200% above his purchase price. Colt believed that there was a "strong possibility" that OPTN would increase in price after the selection was announced.

29. Before Colt's 10,000 share purchase around 11:00 a.m., there were no trades in OPTN on February 24. The 10,000 share purchase represented approximately 70% of the roughly 14,000 share total average daily volume of OPTN.

30. After the Fast-Trades selection went out to subscribers, the price and volume of OPTN climbed rapidly. On February 24, OPTN had a reported one day trading volume of 1,290,100 shares and reached an intraday high of $5.875—a

price movement of $4.25, more than 250% higher than the price of Colt's first purchase. Colt's sell limit order was filled at $5.375 shortly after the Fast-Trades announcement. Colt, Terrell and Wyckoff reaped a collective profit of $37,500. Within just a few hours after the recommendation was distributed to subscribers, the price of OPTN collapsed. Within a few days, OPTN was back to trading within pennies of its price at the time the recommendation was disseminated.

31. Joanne Colt, the defendant's mother, purchased 14,000 shares of OPTN in the same manner as other subscribers: she waited until she received the Fast-Trades e-mail, then placed her purchase orders. Joanne Colt lost more than $24,000 in approximately twenty-five minutes trading on the recommendation from the Fast-Trades website. After losing more than $24,000 in one day trading in OPTN, Joanne Colt withdrew $15,000 from her individual retirement account at a penalty and borrowed $11,000 from her life insurance policy to replace her losses and accumulate funds in her brokerage account to use to buy the next Fast-Trades selection.

COLT, THE PARTICIPANTS, AND FRIENDS PURCHASE AEDU ON MARCH 5

32. The next Fast-Trades selection was American Education Corporation (ticker: AEDU), which Fast-Trades sent to subscribers at approximately 2:45 p.m. on March 5. The total average daily volume for AEDU as of that date was approximately 3,500 shares. Starting around four hours before the selection was sent out, Colt purchased a total of 19,000 AEDU shares in his account: 10,000 for himself, 4,000 each for his two roommates, and 1,000 for Adam Altman, another law school classmate who had agreed to become a participant in Fast-Trades. The shares were purchased in six separate market orders at ascending prices: the first 1,000 shares were purchased at $1.25, while the last 3,000 shares were purchased at $1.62. Colt then entered a sell limit order at $6.50 per share.

33. At Colt's direction, one of his friends, another fellow law student, purchased an additional 2,000 shares. Colt then instructed this friend to enter a sell limit order at $5.00 per share. Both Colt's and his friend's sell orders were entered before the message recommending AEDU was sent to subscribers.

34. Shortly before sending out the AEDU selection, Colt told Joanne Colt that AEDU would be the March 5 selection. Joanne Colt then called her friend. Joanne Colt then purchased 10,750 shares of AEDU and quickly placed sell limit orders staggered between $4.50 and $7.00 per share. Joanne Colt's friend—who had not purchased a stock on the open market in approximately eight years—purchased 4,533 shares, and quickly entered sell limit orders ranging from $4.00 to $5.00 per share.

35. These purchases spurred a dramatic increase in the price and volume of AEDU stock. The 36,283 shares bought by Fast-Trades participants and their friends represented over 1000% of the 3,500 share total average daily volume of AEDU. On March 5 there was only one trade reported for 1,000 shares at $1.25 per share before Colt and the others began buying. From 10:47 a.m., Douglas Colt's first trade, through the 2:45 p.m. dissemination of the Fast-Trades recommendation, over 100,000 shares of AEDU changed hands, and the price of AEDU rose to $1.625, a 30% increase in three and a half hours of trading.

36. Moreover, Colt knew that his purchases, along with those of the other Fast-Trades participants and friends, were impacting the price of AEDU, because as his multiple purchase orders were filled over the course of the day, he paid progressively higher prices for the stock. Colt paid $1.25 for his first 1,000 shares at around 10:45 a.m., and paid incrementally higher prices until his last purchase of 3,000 shares at 2:19 p.m. at $1.625 per share.

37. After Fast-Trades recommended AEDU to subscribers, the price and volume of the stock rose dramatically. On March 5, AEDU had a reported one day trading volume of 842,600 shares and reached an intraday high of $10.00—a price movement of $8.75, 700% higher than the price at Colt's first purchase. Colt's account reaped a profit of $41,093.75, and Colt's friend made a profit of $3,500. Joanne Colt made $59,984.37, and her friend made $15,899. Within just a few hours, the price of AEDU collapsed, plummeting several dollars. Within a few days, AEDU was back to trading within pennies of its price at the time the recommendation was disseminated.

COLT, THE PARTICIPANTS, AND
FRIENDS ALL PURCHASE ARTE ON MARCH 10

38. The fourth and final Fast-Trades selection purchased by Colt and the other participants was Artecon, Inc. (ticker: ARTE). The ARTE selection went out to subscribers at approximately 11:30 a.m. on March 10. Starting an hour and twenty minutes before the selection was sent out, Colt used six separate orders to purchase a total of 18,282 ARTE shares in his account: 9,282 for himself, 4,000 each for his two roommates, and 1,000 for the other law student. Colt's friend also purchased 4,000 shares at Colt's direction.

39. Colt also telephoned Joanne Colt and told her about ARTE, and Joanne Colt immediately called her friend. Joanne Colt purchased 17,500 shares and her friend purchased 11,730 shares, increasing the total number of shares purchased by the group to 51,512. All entered sell limit orders before the recommendation went out to subscribers.

40. These purchases of ARTE spurred an increase in the price and volume of ARTE stock. The purchases of 51,512 shares by Fast-Trades participants and their friends represented over 150% of the 33,000 share total average daily volume of ARTE. On March 10, before Colt began buying ARTE, only 800 shares changed hands and the price remained steady at $1.125 per share. From 10:11 a.m., when Colt's first trade was reported, until 11:30 when the recommendation went out, total trading volume of ARTE increased to 164,500 shares and the price rose to $1.375, a 22% increase in two hours.

41. As with his AEDU trading, Colt could see the effect of his purchases on the market because over the course of his purchases he paid progressively more for ARTE shares. Colt's first purchase of ARTE was at $1.125, but over the next eighty minutes Colt made ARTE purchases at $1.1875 and then $1.25 a share, and by the time of his last purchase before the selection was announced he paid $1.375 per share.

42. After the Fast-Trades recommendation went out to subscribers, the price and volume of ARTE went higher still. On March 10, ARTE had a reported one day trading volume of 4,581,000 shares and reached an intraday high of $6.00—a

price movement of $4.875, more than 400% higher than the price of Colt's first purchase. The orders by Fast-Trades participants and their two friends were filled shortly after the recommendation went out. Douglas Colt's account reaped a profit of $66,516.36, Colt's friend made $15,474.37, Joanne Colt made $47,081.25, and her friend made $34,937. Within just a few hours after the recommendation, the price of ARTE collapsed, plummeting several dollars. Within a few days, ARTE was back to trading within pennies of its price at the time the recommendation was disseminated.

COLT AND OTHER PARTICIPANTS
POST MESSAGES ON THE INTERNET

43. As part of the Fast-Trades scheme, Colt, Terrell, Wyckoff and Altman posted hundreds of false or misleading messages on internet message boards. The vast majority of these messages were advertisements used to promote the Fast-Trades website to attract new subscribers. The purpose of these messages was to build the subscriber base by inducing readers of the message boards to visit the website, to review its recommendations and to become subscribers, so that they would in turn purchase Fast-Trades selected stocks and help drive up the price of the selection. Colt, Terrell, Wyckoff and later, Altman, all made such postings. Colt taught each of them how to create on-line "identities," and how to post messages to internet message boards at financial websites such as Yahoo.com and RagingBull.com.

44. Colt instructed them not to disclose their affiliation with Fast-Trades and to use multiple identities in order to enhance the credibility of their messages. Colt also instructed them to misrepresent substantive information, such as their investment successes from following Fast-Trades recommendations, to draw readers of the message boards to the Fast-Trades site.

45. For example, a February 9, 1999, posting by Colt to the Electrosource message bulletin board contains false information regarding his age and geographic location, conveys that he was not a participant in Fast-Trades when in fact he was, and misrepresents that Colt had made profits from Fast-Trades' recommendation of Electrosource, when in fact he had not traded in the stock.

46. Through these and hundreds of other postings containing false or misleading information, Colt expected to induce individuals to visit the Fast-Trades website and become subscribers so that they would then purchase Fast-Trades selections and drive up the price of the selected stocks. At Colt's direction, Wyckoff, Terrell and Altman all made numerous false or misleading postings similar to Colt's that failed to disclose their identities or their ties to Fast-Trades, and misrepresented their trading activity or success in trading Fast-Trades selections.

47. In addition to these "advertising" postings, Colt also posted messages on the internet defending Fast-Trades against investors who accused the site of price manipulation. In those messages, Colt misrepresented his identity and geographic location, and argued that Fast-Trades' activities were lawful. Indeed, Colt tried to discourage individuals from informing the SEC about the Fast-Trades scheme, at times taunting those who posted internet messages stating that they were going to contact the SEC about the website.

THE DISCLAIMER ON THE FAST-TRADES.COM WEBSITE

48. From the first time Fast-Trades published a recommendation, it included a disclaimer on the webpage that purported to describe the trading intentions of Fast-Trades representatives. This disclaimer was revised after the AMSI selection. With the first selection the participants traded in, Apache Medical Systems on February 16, the disclaimer stated: "We may buy or sell our picks at any time." After that selection, Colt, Terrell, and Wyckoff, along with the new participant Altman, revised various aspects of the disclaimer, including the portion addressing their trading in Fast-Trades selections. From that point on, through the remaining three selections they traded in, the disclaimer read, in relevant part: "FastTrades representatives may, and in many cases do, invest or hold positions in the companies that FastTrades recommends; FastTrades representatives reserve the right to buy or sell securities recommended by FastTrades at any time."

49. Both versions were materially misleading as to the real trading intent or trading activities of the participants. By the time the subscribers received the Fast-Trades recommendation, the Fast-Trades participants already had purchased shares in the recommended stock, and already had placed orders to sell the stock, which they expected to be filled by the increase in price and volume caused by the purchases of their own subscribers. If Fast-Trades had accurately disclosed their trading intentions, subscribers would have been able to deduce that the only reason Colt offered his "free" service was so he could further influence the market price movement initiated by his purchase of the recommended stock just before the announcement. In this way, Colt could condition the market and then profit at the expense of his subscribers by executing pre-set sales of the recommended stock at inflated prices to a market which was likely to include subscribers.

50. By reason of the foregoing, Douglas Colt violated Section 10(b) of the Exchange Act and Rule 10b-5 thereunder.

PRAYER FOR RELIEF

WHEREFORE, the Commission respectfully requests that this Court:

I.

Issue a Final Judgment of Permanent Injunction permanently restraining and enjoining Douglas Colt from violating Section 10(b) of the Exchange Act and Rule 10b-5 thereunder.

II.

Issue a Final Judgment requiring Colt to disgorge all illicit profits from the manipulative scheme alleged herein, with prejudgment interest.

III.

Issue a Final Judgment requiring Colt to pay appropriate civil penalties pursuant to Section 21(d)(3)(A) of the Exchange Act.

IV.

Grant such other relief as this Court may deem just and appropriate.

Dated: March 2, 2000

Respectfully submitted.

______________________________

Attorneys for Plaintiff
SECURITIES AND EXCHANGE COMMISSION

---

### *NOTES AND QUESTIONS*

***1. Settlement with the SEC.*** Simultaneously with the filing of the Complaint set out above, Douglas Colt, "without admitting or denying the allegations," consented to the entry of a final judgment permanently enjoining him from committing or causing any violation or future violation of Section 10(b) and Rule 10b-5. Pursuant to this settlement, the SEC waived payment of disgorgement and prejudgment interest based on Colt's "demonstrated financial inability to pay" and did not seek the imposition of a civil monetary penalty. *Douglas M. Colt*, Litigation Release No. 16461, 71 SEC Docket 1951 (March 2, 2000).

At the same time it settled its case against Douglas Colt, the SEC also entered an administrative order and "without admitting or denying the Commission's findings," Kenneth Terrell, Jason Wyckoff, Adam Altman and Joanne Colt consented to an Order directing them to cease and desist from committing or causing any violation and any future violation of Section 10(b) of the Exchange Act and Rule 10b-5, and ordering Terrell, Wyckoff and Joanne Colt to pay disgorgement of all illicit profits with prejudgment interest. See *In re Kenneth Terrell, Jason Wyckoff, Adam Altman and Joanne Colt*, Release No. 34-42483, 2000 WL 248549 (March 2, 2000). As in its settlement with Douglas Colt, based on Terrell's, Wyckoff's and Joanne Colt's "demonstrat[ed] financial inability to pay," the Commission waived payment of disgorgement and prejudgment interest.

A number of commentators expressed surprise at the SEC's willingness to resolve these actions without at least insisting on the recovery of the "ill-gotten gains." Some have even questioned whether it reflects the SEC's doubts of the merits of its case. See Ellen Rosen, SEC May Lack Basis to Bar Stock Touting, Nat'l L. J. at A1 (March 20, 2000) (quoting Professor John Coffee's statements that "[t]he facts justify the fraud prosecution, but the settlement is so weak [that it appears to express] the SEC's own doubts of the merits" and that it is "rare to quantify ill-gotten gains with no attempt to get restitution"). Is it likely that the SEC's enforcement action could have been resolved at the summary judgment stage? Based on the allegations in the complaint, what difficulties would you expect the SEC to have faced at trial? Consider the "legal discussion" from the SEC's administrative order:

> Colt effected a series of transactions and through the Fast-Trades.com website disseminated stock recommendations without completely and accurately describing those transactions in the website's disclaimer. Those transactions

> created actual trading activity causing the price of the selected stocks to increase. Colt's purpose was to induce the purchase of the Fast-Trades.com stock recommendation by both subscribers and non-subscribers. Colt's purchases, recommendations and misleading statements and omissions about his trading in the recommended stocks were material to reasonable investors deciding whether to purchase the securities recommended by the Fast-Trades.com website. As a result of his conduct, Colt violated Section 10(b) of the Exchange Act and Rule 10b-5, thereunder, and Terrell, Wyckoff, Altman and Joanne Colt knew or should have known that their acts or omissions to act would contribute to such violations.

*In re Kenneth Terrell,* supra, 2000 WL 248549 at *9. Can you identify both the stronger and the weaker aspects of the SEC's legal theories?

*2. The SEC's Cyberforce.* There is little doubt that the SEC regarded the *Colt* case as an old wine in a new bottle. In announcing the settlement, Richard H. Walker, Director of the SEC's Division of Enforcement, emphasized that "[t]he Internet has replaced the boiler room as the stock manipulator's tool of choice" and that "[i]ts low cost and ease of use has attracted a new breed of persons seeking to profit at the expense of innocent investors." See SEC News Digest 2000-40 (March 2, 2000). Reflecting a similar theme, the SEC's administrative order cautioned that the "type of activity involved in [the Colt] case *** was a variation of a "pump and dump" scheme," and maintained that the only novelty was in "the way that internet technology was used to promote the stocks and deceive investors." The publicity surrounding the *Colt* case was clearly used by the SEC to send the message that "[a]ttempts to deceive investors or disrupt the securities markets, whether such schemes are perpetrated on the internet or by more traditional means, will not be tolerated." *In re Kenneth Terrell,* supra, 2000 WL 248549 at *10.

The *Colt* case constitutes only one of the more than 200 Internet-related enforcement actions that have been brought by the SEC in recent years. The agency began its surveillance of the Internet in 1995 with a very small task force; today, the SEC has in place an "Office of Internet Enforcement" (OIE), which coordinates the activities of the "CyberForce"—a group of over 250 SEC attorneys, investigators, and accountants who are charged with responsibility for Internet surveillance. Specifically, the OIE:

- identifies areas of surveillance;
- formulates investigative procedures;
- provides strategic and legal guidance to Enforcement staff nationwide;
- conducts Internet investigations and prosecutions (a task it shares with the entire Enforcement staff);
- performs training for Commission staff and outside agencies and;
- serves as a resource on Internet matters for the entire Commission.

"Internet Enforcement Program," described on the SEC's web site at www.sec.gov/enforce/intrela.htm. (Chapter 9.A contains a general discussion of the SEC's Division of Enforcement.) In addition to surveillance efforts by the SEC, the OIE also works to coordinate Internet-related efforts with various U.S. Attorneys, the FBI and the self-regulatory organizations that form the Intermarket Surveillance Group.

The OIE has also conducted a number of "Internet sweeps"—described in a speech by SEC Commissioner Laura Unger as "a relatively new enforcement technique involving the simultaneous investigation of numerous individuals, broker-dealers or issuers, with multiple actions being announced on the same day for maximum deterrent effect." See Speech by SEC Commissioner Laura S. Unger, Empowering Investors in an Electronic Age, IOSCO Annual Conference, May 17, 2000. These Internet sweeps have generated extensive media coverage, and have highlighted to the investing public what might seem to be the rather obvious risks of acting on investment advice from strangers over the Internet.

To be sure, market manipulation has not been the only type of fraudulent activity swept up by the SEC's recent attention to the Internet. But the SEC maintains that of the many types of fraud, "market manipulations are by far the most prevalent on the Internet." Unger Speech, supra. In addition to the classic "pump and dump" scheme alleged to have been perpetrated by the law students, can you identify other types of manipulative conduct that is facilitated by widespread usage of the Internet?

***3. Not a Minor Problem.*** The following quotations, from an adoring father and a frustrated SEC Enforcement Director, represent what are no doubt polar opinions as to the legality—and indeed morality—of Jonathan Lebed's stock trading practices:

> "I'm more proud of him now than ever. He's a smart boy and he's done a good job.... He earned it. He did a lot of work. He didn't sit behind a garage smoking pot or stealing wheels off a car."
>
> *Greg Lebed (60 Minutes, CBS television broadcast, Oct. 22, 2000).*
>
> "I wonder how many investors who've lost money as a result of Jonathan's manipulations would agree with this sentiment. A hubcap is worth about $20. Smoking pot—as harmful and foolish as it may be—does not injure innocent bystanders. Securities manipulation, by contrast, deprives people of hard-earned dollars needed for retirement, education and the like. So Mr. Lebed is right in saying his son's conduct is different from smoking pot or stealing hubcaps. It's worse."
>
> *Richard Walker, Director, SEC Division of Enforcement, "Regulation vs. Enforcement in an On-Line World," Speech Delivered to the Bond Market Association, October 25, 2000.*

As many will readily recall, Jonathan Lebed undoubtedly stands as one of the country's most famous stock traders, having been the subject of a featured story in the New York Times Magazine (see Michael Lewis, Jonathan Lebed's Extracurricular Activities, Feb. 25, 2001 at 26) in addition to the segment on 60 Minutes noted above.

Though probably few need to be reminded, the SEC charged Lebed with numerous violations of Rule 10b-5. The case was settled (without admission or denial of liability) rather than litigated, with the SEC issuing an Order requiring Lebed to cease and desist from further violations and to pay $272,826, an amount said to constitute the ill-gotten gains from his Internet schemes. See *In re Jonathan G. Lebed*, Release No. 34-43307, 2000 WL 1353040 (Sept. 20, 2000).

According to the SEC, on eleven separate occasions between August 1999 and February 2000, Lebed had

> purchased large blocks of thinly traded microcap stocks and, within hours of making such purchases, sent numerous false and/or misleading messages, or "spam," over the Internet touting the stocks he had just purchased. Lebed then sold all of these shares, usually within 24 hours, profiting from the increased price his messages had caused.

Id. at *1. The SEC's Order sets out the following as a "representative transaction":

> On January 5, 2000, Lebed purchased 18,000 shares of [Man Sang Holdings, Inc. (ticker symbol "MSHI")] at prices ranging from $1.375 to $2.00 per share. The trading volume on December 30, 1999 was 100 shares with a closing price of $1.125 per share. On January 5, 2000, the volume was 60,700 shares at a closing price of $1.8125. At 11:46 p.m. on January 5, 2000, Lebed posted messages on Yahoo!Finance message boards claiming that MSHI was "the most undervalued stock in history" and would be trading at more than $20 per share "very soon." On January 6, 2000, in response to the messages posted by Lebed, the volume of trading skyrocketed to 1,074,900 shares at a high of $4.6875 per share. On that date, Lebed sold all 18,000 shares of MSHI at prices ranging from $3.8125 to $4.00 per share. His net profit was $34,959. MSHI issued no press releases and there was no news in the marketplace during this time period to account for the rise in price and volume.
>
> Three weeks later, Lebed again manipulated the price of MSHI stock. From January 27, 2000, the date he purchased MSHI and posted his spams touting the stock (again predicting a price of $20 "very soon"), until the following day, January 28, 2000, the date he liquidated his entire position, the volume of the stock increased from 71,500 to 1,879,000 shares, and the price jumped from $2.25 to a high of $5.125. Both the price and volume were 52-week highs. Lebed realized a net profit of $37,901.

Id. at *2.

With respect to the MSHI transactions set out above, what legal arguments might have been made in Lebed's defense against Rule 10b-5 liability? In this regard, consider the so-called puffery exception to the element of materiality discussed in Chapter on page 66. Consider also the Supreme Court's conclusion in *Virginia Bankshares* as to when statements of opinion may be found to be materially misleading. See page 41. In his Internet postings, did Lebed have a duty to disclose his substantial holdings in the recommended stocks? Why or why not?

---

### 2. *Conflicts of Interest on Wall Street*

Do securities analysts engage in fraud or market manipulation when they publish "buy" recommendations in research reports to brokerage firm customers while simultaneously holding the view that those recommended stocks are "dogs," "crap," or "junk?" What if it could be shown that these analysts intentionally misled investors about the quality of the stocks in order to win lucrative investment banking business for their firms?

As we will see from the discussion of so-called parallel investigations and proceedings in Chapter 9.F.2, these questions and many related ones have risen to the top of recent enforcement agendas for the SEC, DOJ, State Attorneys General and blue sky regulators, NYSE and NASD. Indeed, throughout the 2002-03 time period, newspapers were filled with weekly, and often daily, accounts of the various investigations into securities analysts' conflicts of interest. (It therefore may be useful to read pages 755-60 of the casebook here.)

The topic of conflicts of interest on Wall Street also received much attention from Congress in the months preceding the Sarbanes-Oxley Act of 2002. As noted in the Senate Report:

> The Committee [on Banking, Housing, and Urban Affairs] heard persuasive testimony that a serious problem exists regarding conflicts of interest between Wall Street stock analysts and their employing brokerage firms, on the one hand, and the public companies that the stock analysts cover on the other hand. Growing knowledge of these conflicts is harming the integrity and credibility to the public of stock analyst recommendations. ***
>
> The Committee feels that it is critical to restore investor confidence in this area. The bill is intended to prevent certain pressures on analysts which could compromise their objectivity and to provide disclosure to investors of certain conflicts of interest that can also influence the objectivity of the analyst in preparing a research report.

Senate Report 107-205, 107th Cong. 2d Session, Committee on Banking, Housing, and Urban Affairs, July 3, 2002 at 32-33.

Responding to these concerns, Section 501 of the Sarbanes-Oxley Act adds a new Section 15D to the Exchange Act:

**Section 15D—Securities Analysts And Research Reports**

(a) Analyst protections—The Commission, or upon the authorization and direction of the Commission, a registered securities association or national securities exchange, shall have adopted, not later than 1 year after the date of enactment of this section [enacted July 30, 2002], rules reasonably designed to address conflicts of interest that can arise when securities analysts recommend equity securities in research reports and public appearances, in order to improve the objectivity of research and provide investors with more useful and reliable information, including rules designed—

(1) to foster greater public confidence in securities research, and to protect the objectivity and independence of securities analysts, by—

(A) restricting the prepublication clearance or approval of research reports by persons employed by the broker or dealer who are engaged in investment banking activities, or persons not directly responsible for investment research, other than legal or compliance staff;

(B) limiting the supervision and compensatory evaluation of securities analysts to officials employed by the broker or dealer who are not engaged in investment banking activities; and

(C) requiring that a broker or dealer and persons employed by a broker or dealer who are involved with investment banking activities may not, directly or indirectly, retaliate against or threaten to retaliate against any securities analyst employed by that broker or dealer or its affiliates as a result of an adverse, negative, or otherwise unfavorable research report that may adversely affect the present or prospective investment banking relationship of the broker or dealer with the issuer that is the subject of the research report, except that such rules may not limit the authority of a broker or dealer to discipline a securities analyst for causes other than such research report in accordance with the policies and procedures of the firm;

(2) to define periods during which brokers or dealers who have participated, or are to participate, in a public offering of securities as underwriters or dealers should not publish or otherwise distribute research reports relating to such securities or to the issuer of such securities;

(3) to establish structural and institutional safeguards within registered brokers or dealers to assure that securities analysts are separated by appropriate informational partitions within the firm from the review, pressure, or oversight of those whose involvement in investment banking activities might potentially bias their judgment or supervision; and

(4) to address such other issues as the Commission, or such association or exchange, determines appropriate.

(b) Disclosure—The Commission, or upon the authorization and direction of the Commission, a registered securities association or national securities exchange, shall have adopted, not later than 1 year after the date of enactment of this section [enacted July 30, 2002], rules reasonably designed to require each securities analyst to disclose in public appearances, and each registered broker or dealer to disclose in each research report, as applicable, conflicts of interest that are known or should have been known by the securities analyst or the broker or dealer, to exist at the time of the appearance or the date of distribution of the report, including—

(1) the extent to which the securities analyst has debt or equity investments in the issuer that is the subject of the appearance or research report;

(2) whether any compensation has been received by the registered broker or dealer, or any affiliate thereof, including the securities analyst, from the issuer that is the subject of the appearance or research report, subject to such exemptions as the Commission may determine appropriate and necessary to prevent disclosure by virtue of this paragraph of material non-public information regarding specific potential future investment banking transactions of such issuer, as is appropriate in the public interest and consistent with the protection of investors;

(3) whether an issuer, the securities of which are recommended in the appearance or research report, currently is, or during the 1-year period preceding the date of the appearance or date of distribution of the report has been, a client of the registered broker or dealer, and if so, stating the types of services provided to the issuer;

(4) whether the securities analyst received compensation with respect to a research report, based upon (among any other factors) the investment banking revenues (either generally or specifically earned from the issuer being analyzed) of the registered broker or dealer; and

(5) such other disclosures of conflicts of interest that are material to investors, research analysts, or the broker or dealer as the Commission, or such association or exchange, determines appropriate.

Many of the rules required under new Section 15D of the Exchange Act were proposed by the NASD and NYSE and approved by the SEC in May 2002, more than two months before the enactment of the Sarbanes-Oxley Act. See Commission Approves Rules to Address Analyst Conflicts, SEC Press Release 2002-63, May 8, 2002. Note also that in February 2003, the SEC voted to adopt Regulation Analyst Certification (Regulation AC) which will require "research analysts to certify the truthfulness of the views they express in research reports and public appearances, and to disclose whether they have received any compensation related to the specific recommendations or views expressed in those reports and appearances." SEC Press Release 2003-21, Feb. 6, 2003.

Do you think the enactment of Section 15D reflects a congressional judgment that manipulative activity was pervasive in the stock market in the late 1990s? Assuming that such conflicts of interest were pervasive, does that necessarily mean that the practices were manipulative?

## *PROBLEM 8-3*

Susan Shore is a securities analyst with Shaker Hanley, a Wall Street investment bank/brokerage firm with an international reputation. A few years ago, Susan's firm acquired a stake in a start-up business, Betatech, by obtaining shares in exchange for financial services. Betatech later made the decision to go public and, not surprisingly, Shaker Hanley acted as the lead underwriter in the IPO. The firm's shares in Betatech were subject to a 180 day lock-up period which was to expire on July 23, 2001.

On July 20, 2001, Susan issued a favorable research report on Betatech and rated the stock a "strong buy." The report was contained in Shaker's monthly newsletter to clients, the back page of which contained disclaimers reading: "The firm and/or affiliates and employees have or may have a long or short position or holding in the securities, options on securities, or other related investments of issuers mentioned herein" and "The firm may have, within the last three years, served as manager or co-manager of a public offering of or makes markets in the securities of any or all of the companies mentioned." The following day, Susan appeared on WallStreet Beat, a cable TV show, where she repeated her favorable view of Betatech and her "strong buy" recommendation.

Betatech's shares steadily rose in value on July 20, 21st, and 22nd, and Shaker Hanley reaped a substantial profit when it sold its shares on July 23rd. Has Susan, Betatech, or Shaker Hanley violated the federal securities laws? On what theory?

## *PROBLEM 8-4*

Assume that there is evidence to show that a high-profile securities analyst upgraded his recommendation of a publicly traded company's stock in order to win a favor from that company's CEO—a favor that involved using the CEO's influence as a member of the board of directors of an elite private preschool to gain admission for the securities analyst's children. Could the SEC pursue enforcement action against the securities analyst? On what theory?

Cf. Charles Gasparino, Citigroup Investigation Now Leads To Door of Elite Nursery School, Wall St. J. at A1 (Nov. 14, 2002).

# Chapter 9

# SEC ENFORCEMENT OF THE FEDERAL SECURITIES LAWS

Although in any given year the sheer volume of enforcement proceedings initiated by the SEC pales in comparison to the volume of private securities litigation, familiarity with the SEC's enforcement process is essential to representing corporate clients. One reason is that, regardless of whether enforcement action is actually initiated, SEC investigations have a tremendous impact on the persons or companies involved. Indeed, as we have seen from our previous study of insider trading and market manipulation, investigations by the SEC are often long and detailed, typically demanding significant amounts of time and attention on the part of numerous people. And Congress has given the SEC broad powers to investigate whether the federal securities laws have been, are being, or are likely to be violated. A second reason is that once securities law violations have been established, the SEC has at its disposal a wide arsenal of enforcement remedies, most of which are not available in private litigation. These remedies run the gamut from an order by the Commission to "cease and desist," to the imposition of substantial monetary penalties by a federal district court judge, to a broker-dealer disciplinary proceeding that results in a permanent suspension. SEC officials also have the power to refer securities law violations to the Department of Justice (DOJ) for criminal prosecution. One cannot represent a corporate client effectively without being well versed in the possible enforcement stakes—including the sanctions that may be imposed by courts or directly by the SEC and the collateral consequences that may flow from them.

This Chapter is divided into six sections. Section A provides a brief introduction to the SEC's Division of Enforcement, the division that is generally responsible for investigating and litigating suspected violations of the federal securities laws. Section B then explores the investigatory process in more detail and highlights some procedural issues that often arise in the course of investigations. It also examines the process by which an investigation may result in a consensual settlement with the SEC. Section C turns to the important topic of remedies and looks at how, and in what fora, such remedies may be employed, and Section D focuses on litigation with the SEC. Section E shifts attention to the enforcement powers of the self-regulatory organizations (SROs) in the securities industry, with particular emphasis on the National Association of Securities Dealers, Inc. (NASD) and the New York Stock Exchange, Inc. (NYSE). The Chapter concludes with Section F, which examines the law governing so-called parallel proceedings—concurrent or subsequent investigations and litigation that may be conducted by the SEC, federal criminal prosecutors, the SROs, and/or state officials.

Securities enforcement issues are also subject to extensive examination in Chapter 10 (focusing on the new enforcement regimes for attorneys and accountants created by the Sarbanes-Oxley Act of 2002) and Chapter 11 (focusing on criminal enforcement). In addition, international securities enforcement is discussed in Chapter 12 (focusing on international securities fraud).

## A. THE SEC's DIVISION OF ENFORCEMENT

The SEC's Division of Enforcement investigates possible violations of the federal securities laws, recommends action to the Commission when appropriate, negotiates settlements on behalf of the Commission, and litigates in federal court or in administrative proceedings before the agency. The Division also refers cases to the DOJ, and the various U.S. Attorney's offices throughout the country, when criminal prosecution for securities law violations appears to be warranted. Of all the SEC's Divisions, it is the Enforcement Division that is the most visible to the public, in large part due to the publicity that typically surrounds its investigations and prosecutions.

The Division is composed of more than 600 attorneys, accountants, and other professionals ("the staff"), most of whom are based at the SEC's headquarters in Washington, D.C. Additional staff members in the SEC's five regional offices and six district offices also pursue enforcement matters within their respective jurisdictions. The Division is headed by a Director who is appointed by the SEC's Chairperson. There are also at least two Associate Directors of Enforcement, typically each of whom is supported by one or more Assistant Directors and a number of Branch Chiefs. Branch Chiefs, in turn, are generally the direct supervisors of the many staff attorneys, analysts, and accountants who perform the day-to-day work on ongoing investigations and cases. The Division also has its own Chief Counsel.

Along with capturing the lion's share of public attention, the Enforcement Division also receives far more funding than any other division of the SEC. For fiscal year 2002, the Commission requested, and Congress and the President approved, a total of $439 million in funding for the SEC, more than one-third of which was allocated to the Division of Enforcement. For fiscal year 2003, as part of its swift and sweeping reaction to the corporate and accounting scandals at Enron, WorldCom, and other publicly traded companies, Congress nearly doubled the SEC's appropriations, with legislation authorizing an appropriation of $776 million. The SEC's Division of Enforcement will once again be the largest beneficiary, because Congress specifically earmarked much of this new funding for the enhancement of the SEC's investigative and enforcement efforts. See Section 601 of the Sarbanes-Oxley Act (providing specific funding for enhanced information technology and for the addition of at least 200 attorneys, accountants, and other professionals to the SEC's staff).

Not surprisingly, the SEC has been quick to point out that all monies received by the Division of Enforcement will be very well spent. In the SEC's 2001 Annual Report, the Enforcement Division reported that it:

- Obtained orders in SEC judicial and administrative proceedings requiring securities law violators to disgorge illegal profits of approximately $478 million. Civil penalties ordered in SEC proceedings totaled approximately $44 million.

- Obtained emergency relief from federal courts, in the form of temporary restraining orders (TROs) to halt ongoing fraudulent conduct, in 42 actions.
- Halted trading in two securities of issuers about which there was inadequate public disclosure.

2001 Annual Report at 1.

The SEC's 2001 Annual Report also documents the number and general types of enforcement actions initiated over the past five years:

**Enforcement Actions Initiated**

| | FY97 | FY98 | FY99 | FY00 | FY01 |
|---|---|---|---|---|---|
| Civil Injunctive Actions | 189 | 214 | 198 | 223 | 205 |
| Administrative Proceedings | 285 | 248 | 298 | 244 | 248 |
| Contempt Proceedings | 14 | 15 | 29 | 36 | 31 |
| Reports of Investigation | 1 | 0 | 0 | 0 | 0 |
| Total | 489 | 477 | 525 | 503 | 484 |

See 2001 Annual Report at 1. The chart set forth below and on the following page provides additional information about the types of enforcement cases initiated by the Commission in the fiscal year of 2001.

**ENFORCEMENT CASES INITIATED BY THE COMMISSION DURING FISCAL YEAR 2001 IN VARIOUS PROGRAM AREAS**

*(Each case initiated has been included in only one category listed below, even though many cases involve multiple allegations and may fall under more than one category. The number of defendants and respondents is noted parenthetically.)*

| Program Area in Which a Civil Action or Administrative Proceeding Was Initiated | Civil Actions | Administrative Proceedings | Total | % of Total Cases |
|---|---|---|---|---|
| Securities Offering Cases | 56 (258) | 39 (57) | 95 (315) | 20% |
| Broker-dealer Cases | | | | |
| (a) Fraud Against Customer | 6 (8) | 26 (47) | 32 (55) | 7% |
| (b) Failure to Supervise | 0 (0) | 6 (8) | 6 (8) | 1 % |
| (c) Government/Municipal Securities | 3 (15) | 1 (1) | 4 (16) | 1% |
| (d) Books & Records | 1 (1) | 5 (6) | 6 (7) | 1% |
| (e) Other | 3 (12) | 14 (31) | 17 (43) | 4% |
| Total Broker-Dealer Cases | 13 (36) | 52 (93) | 65 (129) | 13% |

| Program Area in Which a Civil Action or Administrative Proceeding Was Initiated | Civil Actions | Administrative Proceedings | Total | % of Total Cases |
|---|---|---|---|---|
| Issuer Financial Statement and Reporting Cases | | | | |
| (a) Issuer Financial Disclosure | 38 (106) | 65 (77) | 103 (183) | 21% |
| (b) Issuer Reporting Other | 3 (7) | 6 (10) | 9 (17) | 2% |
| Total Issuer Financial Statement and Reporting Cases | 41 (113) | 71 (87) | 112 (200) | 23% |
| Other Regulated Entity Cases | | | | |
| (a) Investment Advisers | 10 (17) | 28 (35) | 38 (52) | 8% |
| (b) Investment Companies | 1 (1) | 2 (2) | 3 (3) | 1% |
| (c) Transfer Agent | 2 (3) | 3 (5) | 5 (8) | 1% |
| Total Other Regulated Entity Cases | 13 (21) | 33 (42) | 46 (63) | 9% |
| Insider Trading Cases | 47 (101) | 10 (14) | 57 (115) | 12% |
| Market Manipulation Cases | 17 (60) | 23 (44) | 40 (104) | 8% |
| Delinquent Filings | | | | |
| (a) Issuer Reporting | 3 (3) | 3 (3) | 6 (6) | 1% |
| (b) Forms 3 & 4 | 2 (2) | 6 (7) | 8 (9) | 2% |
| Total Delinquent Filings Cases | 5 (5) | 9 (10) | 14 (15) | 3% |
| Contempt Proceedings | 31 (41) | 0 (0) | 31 (41) | 6% |
| Touting | 9 (22) | 11 (16) | 20 (38) | 4% |
| Miscellaneous Cases | 2 (5) | 1 (2) | 3 (7) | 1% |
| Fraud Against Regulated Entities | 1 (1) | 0 (0) | 1 (1) | 0% |
| Corporate Control | 1 (1) | 0 (0) | 1 (1) | 0% |
| GRAND TOTAL | 236 (664) | 249 (365) | 485 (1029) | 100% |

2001 Annual Report at 134 (Table 1).

As captured in the front page headlines of most major newspapers, the SEC's Enforcement Division has been keep even busier in 2002 with investigations into the corporate and accounting scandals at Enron, WorldCom, Sunbeam, Waste Management, Adelphia, and numerous other publicly traded companies. And while the dollar amounts of the fraud involved in those scandals has been staggering, the amounts that the SEC will seek to recoup through disgorgement, and the civil penalties that the SEC will seek to impose, will be equally so. The SEC can also be expected to bring high profile enforcement actions against not only the companies plagued by the scandals but also the corporate officials in those companies that helped to perpetrate them.

## B. SEC INVESTIGATIONS

Investigations by the SEC staff are often described as "the heart of the securities enforcement practice." The following analysis by experienced defense counsel offers several reasons why.

### SEC INVESTIGATIONS: THE HEART OF SEC ENFORCEMENT PRACTICE
### by Richard M. Phillips, Glenn R. Reichardt, Michael J. Missal, and Robyn J. Lipton *in* The Securities Enforcement Manual: Tactics and Strategies (1997)

***First, the staff typically conducts a comprehensive investigation before recommending enforcement action by the Commission. The investigation often involves extensive document production and the testimony of numerous witnesses. By the time the staff recommends an enforcement action, it usually has amassed a great deal of evidence and has developed a detailed theory of the alleged liability of the targets of the staff's investigation. At the conclusion of its investigation, the staff will normally invite a potential target of its enforcement recommendation to file a Wells Submission, in which counsel can argue why the Commission ought not institute a public enforcement proceeding. The ability to prepare a persuasive Wells Submission will depend on the factual record developed during the staff's investigation. Accordingly, the best opportunity to influence the outcome of an SEC investigation occurs **during** the staff's investigation, rather than **after** its completion.

Second, for most persons who are confronted by an SEC enforcement action, the staff's investigation will represent their only "day in court" because the vast majority of cases brought by the Commission are settled at the time or shortly after they are instituted. SEC investigations generally are confidential, whereas formal enforcement proceedings are matters of public record. The publicity associated with the institution of a public enforcement proceeding can cause more reputational and business damage than the formal sanctions that may ultimately be imposed as a result of the proceeding. Thus, a primary focus of defense counsel during an SEC investigation is to persuade the Commission not to initiate a public enforcement proceeding, to reduce the gravity of the charges made in an enforcement proceeding, or to lay the foundation for a satisfactory settlement in which the client accepts certain findings and sanctions without admitting or denying any wrongdoing.

Third, the witnesses called to testify or produce documents in SEC investigations greatly exceed in number the defendants named in enforcement actions that result from those investigations. Thus, the number of firms and individuals requiring representation will be greatest at the investigatory stage. The investigatory stage is also a time when many issues will arise regarding joint representation, e.g., whether one law firm can represent both a securities firm and its individual officers or employees. Often, to avoid potential conflicts of interest, firms and individuals will retain separate counsel during the investigatory stage.

Finally, SEC enforcement actions are expensive and difficult to defend successfully. More often than not, the SEC prevails in litigated enforcement actions, not only in administrative proceedings before the SEC's own administrate law judges, but also in court. Accordingly, in most cases the subjects of an SEC investigation and their counsel devote their efforts toward developing a favorable record during the staff's investigation; they do not delay their defense in the hope or expectation of a successful result in a formal enforcement proceeding.

The SEC's Rules of Practice applicable to investigations do not explicitly provide for an active role for counsel representing the subjects of an investigation. Nevertheless, experienced counsel typically have ample opportunity to influence an investigation's outcome. Through a proactive approach with the staff, counsel can often allay the staff's concerns and otherwise help to shape the staff's investigative conclusions. Moreover, through negotiating reasonable accommodations and developing a professionally credible relationship with the staff, counsel can influence the scope and time frame for the production of documents as well as the number of witnesses and the nature and location of their testimony.

To have the maximum impact, counsel must be closely involved in an investigation from its outset. An investigation generally should not be treated like discovery in a civil case, in which the presumed strategy often is "the less said, the better." Instead, in many cases the most effective strategy is to present the client's defense at every stage of the investigation. Such an approach requires a thorough evaluation of the client's case at an early stage. This evaluation will help determine whether to: (a) present the client's defenses to the staff in an aggressive fashion by freely furnishing information even beyond that requested, or (b) take a more defensive "sit back and wait" approach, furnishing to the staff only the minimum information necessary to comply with the staff's subpoenas.

If the first strategy is chosen, the potential target will want to present its affirmative defenses to the staff's factual allegations and legal theories through discussions with the staff, document production, testimony and, if necessary, through Wells Submissions and post-Submission discussions with the staff. If, on the other hand, a "sit back and wait" strategy is appropriate, the potential target of the investigation may provide only the minimum information required and may rely heavily on privileges, such as the attorney-client privilege and the privilege against self-incrimination, to limit the evidence that might be used against the potential target in subsequent proceedings.

While the nature of each client's defense will depend upon the particular circumstances of each investigation, anyone with potential exposure should approach an SEC investigation with the same careful attention and preparation that he or she would devote to the defense of civil litigation. Otherwise counsel will not be in a position to counteract and dispel the staff's prosecutorial suspicions—suspicions that may be assisted by the often misguided inclination of other potential targets to deflect the staff's attention from themselves by pointing fingers at others.

Of course, each investigation varies in scope and tone, depending upon the severity of the potential violations being investigated, the reputation of the parties under investigation, the interest of the press or the Congress in the subject matter of the investigation, the culture and priorities of the particular

SEC office (i.e., headquarters or a regional office) in which the investigation originates, and the personalities of the individual staff members actually conducting the investigation. Nevertheless, there are certain characteristics that are common to many staff investigations.***

---

### *1. The Investigatory Process*

The above excerpt emphasizes the enormous sweep of the SEC's investigatory powers. The source of these broad powers can be found in each of the six securities acts administered and enforced by the SEC, all of which authorize the Commission to investigate past, ongoing, or prospective violations of the federal securities laws, the SEC rules or regulations promulgated thereunder, and the rules and regulations of the various SROs. See Sections 20(a) and 8(e) of the Securities Act; Sections 21(a)(1) and (2) of the Exchange Act; Section 209(a) of the Advisers Act; Section 42(a) of the Investment Company Act; Section 18(a) of the Public Utility Holding Company Act; and Section 321(a) of the Trust Indenture Act. Section 21(a)(1) of the Exchange Act provides an example:

> The Commission may, in its discretion, make such investigations as it deems necessary to determine whether any person has violated, is violating, or is about to violate any provision of this title, the rules or regulations thereunder, the rules of a national securities exchange or registered securities association of which such person is a member or a person associated with a member, [and] *** is authorized in its discretion, to publish information concerning any such violations, and to investigate any facts, conditions, practices, or matters which it may deem necessary or proper to aid in the enforcement of such provisions, in the prescribing of rules and regulations under this title, or in securing information to serve as a basis for recommending further legislation concerning the matters to which this title relates.

The conduct of these investigations is governed by the SEC's Rules of Informal and Other Procedures, 17 C.F.R. §§ 202.1 et seq. (particularly § 202.5(a)-(f), which governs enforcement activities) and the SEC's Rules Relating to Investigations, 17 C.F.R. §§ 203.1-203.8. The SEC's Rules of Practice, 17 C.F.R. § 201.100 et seq., also has some relevance in the investigatory phase.

Courts have routinely emphasized Congress's intent to grant federal agencies broad discretion in the conduct of their investigations and have generally refused to interfere in judgments by SEC officials that investigations are warranted. A decision often cited is *United States v. Morton Salt Co.*, 338 U.S. 632 (1950), where the Supreme Court stated that:

> Even if one were to regard the request for information in this case as caused by nothing more than official curiosity, nevertheless, law-enforcing agencies have a legitimate right to satisfy themselves that corporate behavior is consistent with the law and the public interest *** [I]t is sufficient if the inquiry is within the authority of the agency, the demand is not too indefinite and the information sought is reasonably relevant.

Id. at 652. See *SEC v. Brigadoon Scotch Distributing* Co., 480 F.2d 1047, 1052-53 (2d Cir. 1973) (emphasizing that "[t]he Commission must be free without undue interference or delay to conduct an investigation which will adequately develop a factual basis for a determination as to whether particular activities come within the Commission's regulatory authority"); *Treats Int'l Enter., Inc. v. SEC*, 828 F. Supp. 16, 19 (S.D.N.Y. 1993) (refusing to enjoin SEC investigation where the agency had shown "some good faith basis for investigating"). For an exceptional decision in which a court displayed a willingness to second-guess SEC officials, see *SEC v. Wheeling-Pittsburgh Steel Corp.*, 648 F. 2d 118 (3d Cir. 1981). In this very famous case, Wheeling-Pittsburgh put forth compelling evidence that SEC subpoenas of company officials resulted from pressure by Senator Lowell Weicker who was in turn acting under pressure from Wheeling-Pittsburgh's leading competitor. The mere fact that the SEC was investigating Wheeling-Pittsburgh could have been very damaging to the company, because Senator Weicker had introduced a bill in Congress that would have barred any corporation that was under investigation by the SEC from receiving federal loan guarantees. It appeared that both the Senator and the competitor knew that Wheeling-Pittsburgh was seeking a loan guarantee from the Department of Commerce.

Section 202.5(a) of the SEC's Informal and Other Procedures suggests some of the far more typical sources of SEC investigations, noting specifically that "complaints received from members of the public, communications from Federal or State agencies, examination of filings made with the Commission, or otherwise" may trigger an inquiry by the staff. Other likely sources of SEC investigations include:

- market surveillance and internet surveillance units in the Division of Enforcement;
- referrals from other offices and divisions within the SEC (such as Corporation Finance and Market Regulation);
- periodic inspections of broker-dealers, investment advisers, and investment companies by the SEC or SROs;
- press accounts of troubled companies and other news stories;
- complaints from disgruntled customers and whistleblowing employees;
- referrals from foreign governments;
- referrals from the SROs; and
- informants (including those seeking bounties in insider trading cases).

And even the smallest of leads can trigger a major investigation. For example, officials from the Fort Worth District office of the SEC have credited a Wall Street Journal article on Enron's financial woes as the initial source of its investigation into Enron's alleged violations of the federal securities laws. See Brenda S. Jeffreys, Extra Funds, Political Pressure Help Once-Strapped Office Rise to Enforcement Challenge, Tex. Law. at 1 (Sept. 16, 2002).

As with Enron, SEC investigations most often begin with a preliminary inquiry, which may be conducted by the staff without any need to obtain the approval of the Commissioners. On other occasions, however, the staff may launch an investigation with a "formal order of investigation" that is issued by the Commission. Both types of investigations are non-public, except in the very rare instances where the Commission authorizes otherwise.

Valuable insight into the SEC's investigatory process can be drawn from the following article by two leading defense attorneys. The first co-author once served as the SEC's General Counsel; the second served as Senior Counsel in the Enforcement Division.

## SEC ENFORCEMENT PROCEEDINGS: STRATEGIC CONSIDERATIONS FOR WHEN THE AGENCY COMES CALLING

**by Ralph C. Ferrara and Philip S. Khinda**

51 Admin. L. Rev. 1143, 1148-1165 (1999)

****The Informal Inquiry*

When the SEC learns of possible violations of the federal securities laws, it generally conducts a preliminary investigation. The enforcement staff will usually refer to such a preliminary matter as an informal inquiry or, less frequently, as an "MUI," an abbreviation for "matter under inquiry."

The enforcement staff uses the informal inquiry to conduct a preliminary review of certain facts and circumstances that it believes may involve violative conduct. The staff will generally review documents and other information in order to determine whether further investigation is warranted. At a minimum, the staff will need to obtain background information regarding the subject matter and activities that prompted its inquiry. In a preliminary investigation, "no process is issued or testimony compelled." [17 C.F.R. § 202.5(a)] The success of a preliminary investigation depends almost entirely on the voluntary cooperation of the individuals or entities approached by the SEC staff.

In an initial meeting or telephone call, the SEC staff may identify certain corporate personnel or officers with whom they wish to speak, either through an in-person or telephone interview or under oath. The enforcement staff's policy regarding requests for information from corporate personnel is to direct its inquiries to the corporate general counsel's office, or to outside counsel if the staff has been so notified.

The staff may ask that the company voluntarily produce or supply particular information from corporate records, such as schedules, indexes, or chronologies. The staff may also present counsel with a request list seeking documents relevant to particular subjects. To the extent that the recipient of such a request intends to supply any information to the staff, counsel should review all of the same considerations it would in producing information pursuant to a subpoena, particularly with respect to confidentiality.

In evaluating these considerations, counsel should bear in mind that a refusal to provide such information, or an extended delay in doing so, may serve as the basis for the enforcement staff's seeking to obtain a formal order of investigation (and, in turn, subpoena power) from the Commission to further its fact-finding efforts.

If the SEC staff seeks to examine a witness during the course of an informal inquiry, counsel should request that it be done via an interview rather than through testimony, i.e., not under oath and without the use of a court reporter. Interviews are generally preferable whenever parallel proceedings or litigation exists or is likely, as such discussions with the staff will not generate witness transcripts (as would be the case with formal testimony) that may be discoverable and later used to challenge the witness or otherwise impair the witness's or the company's defense in other actions.

During preliminary inquiries and formal investigations, the staff occasionally may wish or agree to interview a witness "informally"—that is, not in the presence of a court reporter or stenographer. If the staff does so, it will usually begin the session with a number of notices and warnings that should be considered carefully. The witness should be told (1) that the conversation is voluntary; (2) whether or not a formal order has been granted by the Commission; (3) that he or she has the right to have counsel present during the interview; (4) that the staff will be taking notes during the interview that will be subject to the SEC's routine uses for such information; and (5) that, although the witness is not under oath, he or she should understand that knowingly and willfully providing false information to the staff in connection with such an inquiry is a crime.

Whether a witness provides testimony voluntarily or agrees to be interviewed by the staff, here as in a formal proceeding, the staff will provide the witness and/or counsel with a standard form setting forth several important notices, warnings, and routine uses applicable to any information provided to the staff. Any information given to the SEC may be forwarded to a number of government and regulatory entities, among others.

While noting that compliance with its requests is voluntary at this point, the SEC staff may nevertheless insist that the witness appear to testify. A voluntary appearance before the staff should be treated in the same manner as one required by subpoena in a formal investigation, discussed below. Procedurally, the testimony will differ from its formal counterpart only in that a notary public (the court reporter or stenographer), rather than a member of the enforcement staff, will administer the oath and the witness will be informed that he or she may decline to answer any question. It is important to bear in mind that a witness's refusal to answer questions may serve as the basis for a staff recommendation seeking a formal order of investigation.

****The Formal Investigation*

If the enforcement staff's concerns are not resolved through the informal inquiry, it may request that the Commission authorize a formal investigation. The regulations suggest, but do not require, that a formal investigation occur after the completion of a preliminary investigation. [See 17 C.F.R.§ 202.5]

***It is important to bear in mind that the commencement of an SEC investigation initiates only a fact-finding proceeding and not an adjudication. The Supreme Court has held that an SEC investigation is "an administrative investigation [which] adjudicates no legal rights." [*SEC v. O'Brien, Inc.*, 467 U.S. 735, 742 (1984)]. It is also important to note that, unlike criminal investigations, SEC investigations do not have formal targets or subjects. Rather, the enforcement staff will assert that it has made no final judgments regarding the potential liability of any individual or entity involved in an investigation, although its actions may suggest otherwise.

The SEC initiates a formal investigation with the entry of an "Order Directing Private Investigation and Designating Officers to Take Testimony," generally referred to as a formal order. Formal orders are granted based on the Commission's review of the recommendations made by the Division of Enforcement. In its recommendation, the enforcement staff will generally describe the facts and circumstances that have raised concerns, the potential securities law violations, and its need for subpoena power to further its investigative efforts. Counsel and their clients should understand that the Division of Enforcement does not need to persuade the Commission that violations have in fact occurred. Rather, it is often sufficient to claim that they may have occurred, may be occurring, or may be about to occur. Indeed, in certain types of inquiries, the issuance of a formal order seems to be a routine matter.

Although the graduation of an informal SEC inquiry to a formal investigation may be of little legal consequence, it represents a significant milestone in the agency's enforcement process. Specifically, a formal investigation represents a certain degree of entrenchment on the part of the enforcement staff with respect to the matter, both with regard to its resolve in exploring further and as a matter of internal administrative practice. A formal investigation has a sense of importance and perhaps an impetus, as compared with an informal inquiry, that will be harder to stop.

Moreover, even when a formal investigation that will not yield an enforcement action has wound down, it often develops an inertia that is difficult to overcome. Administrative practices within the SEC may add to this apparent sense of permanence. The closure of a formal investigation requires the staff to prepare a memorandum that accounts for all of the actions it took in exploring the issues that raised concern and explains why further investigation is unwarranted. This closing memorandum must then be reviewed and approved by one or more senior members of the Division of Enforcement staff, usually an Assistant Director, among others. In contrast, an informal inquiry may be closed without written explanation by a Branch Chief, the lowest level supervisor within the Division.

The formal order of investigation is itself an important document that should be reviewed carefully by counsel. Drafted by the Division of Enforcement, the order generally outlines the scope of the investigation that the Commission has authorized. The order also delegates to members of the enforcement staff designated as officers of the SEC the power to issue subpoenas *ad testificandum* and *duces tecum* and to administer oaths. A formal order is generally a blend of general boilerplate recitations and specific language dealing with the conduct and concerns that prompted the inquiry.

Structurally, the formal order of investigation usually consists of six sections: the caption, a recitation of information from the SEC's "public files," a staff report, a statement of purpose and order, a designation of officers, and authentications. Two of these sections are of special importance. The first two paragraphs of the "purpose and order" section should contain a list of the specific statutory provisions that are given as grounds for ordering the commencement of a formal investigative proceeding. In addition, the "staff report" section of the formal order summarizes facts relating to each potential statutory violation.

Although these descriptions are usually general, they may be helpful in determining the enforcement staff's factual awareness and areas of interest.

Copies of the formal order are furnished to parties upon request only with the approval of the appropriate staff member, generally the Assistant Director overseeing the matter, who find such production to be consistent with both the protection of privacy of the persons involved in the investigation, and the unimpeded conduct of the investigation. The release of a copy of the formal order is usually limited to individuals and entities contacted by the staff and/or their respective counsel.

*1. SEC Subpoenas*

The subpoena power granted by the Commission provides the Division of Enforcement with its most important tool in conducting formal investigations. Under the Commission's revised Rules of Practice, the general service provisions of Rule 150 apply to the issuance of subpoenas for the purposes of an investigation. [See 17 C.F.R. §§ 201.150, 201.232(c), 203.8] Such service may be made in person, through the United States mail, via courier or express delivery, or by facsimile. The reach of an SEC subpoena is nationwide. *** In practice, however, the staff is free to, and often does, negotiate the location of witness testimony before and after a subpoena is issued based on the particular circumstances of the witness and the case. When not taking place at its Washington, D.C. headquarters, SEC testimony generally is taken at one of the Commission's regional or district offices or in an available federal office building.***

*2. Producing Documents in Response to an SEC Subpoena*

If a corporation determines that it will comply with a subpoena for documents, it will benefit from a number of preliminary considerations. Practical considerations for the production of documents in response to an SEC subpoena are, in most respects, the same as those for production in response to a grand jury or judicially-issued subpoena. A discussion or meeting with the SEC staff—like one with opposing counsel or a meeting with a criminal prosecutor—provides an opportunity to propose a procedure for making documents available to the staff and potentially to limit the scope of its requests.

A threshold question for counsel is whether the staff should be invited to examine original documents or, alternatively, whether copies of requested materials should be reproduced and delivered to the staff. The staff will generally accept copies in lieu of original records with the understanding that the originals will be preserved and that the reproduction costs will be borne by the recipient of the subpoena.

***Ordinarily, off-site review of documents by the SEC staff is highly preferable for the recipient of a subpoena. The delivery of relevant documents to the SEC (or to outside counsel's office) eliminates the disruption and possible inadvertent contacts of an on-site visit. In addition, off-site review of photocopies provides a superior procedure for organizing documents, identifying the documents produced, withholding documents on grounds of privilege, and preventing inadvertent loss or misplacement of original documents. The location and arrangement of original documents can be accurately described when groups of documents are correctly marked and their sources identified.

Before any records are made available to the SEC staff, they should be reviewed carefully to determine whether any applicable legal privilege, such as the attorney-client privilege or work product doctrine, might shield them from production. In addition, any production of documents to the SEC should be made in compliance with its various rules regarding confidentiality [to third parties].

*3. Witness Examinations*

Formal investigations invariably involve the taking of testimony by the members of the staff of the Commission's Division of Enforcement who have been designated as officers of the Commission for the purposes of the investigation in question. Such testimony may be required by a subpoena *ad testificandum* (requiring only that the witness appear) or a subpoena *duces tecum* (requiring that the witness appear in connection with the production of certain documents).

Pursuant to Rule 7(b) of the SEC's Rules Relating to Investigations [17 C.F.R. §203.7(b)], witnesses are entitled to be "accompanied, represented, and advised" by counsel of their choice in connection with any formal investigative proceedings at which the witness personally appears. The right to counsel affords the witness the right to consult his or her attorney before, during, and after the examination. During the examination, the attorney may also question the witness briefly to clarify his or her answers, and the attorney may take summary notes during the examination for the witness's subsequent use.

Following an opening statement by the staff, counsel should use an invitation to make an opening statement to place any relevant assertion or request to the staff on the record. Some practitioners use this opportunity to assert a statement of the witness's rights. Others reserve making such assertions until they are given an opportunity to clarify the record, generally towards the close of the proceeding.

If multiple witnesses are called to appear, corporate counsel should consider certain preliminary issues. The backdrop for these considerations is the SEC's sequestration rule, which provides that witnesses and their counsel be sequestered at the discretion of any of the enforcement staff members designated as officers of the Commission. In other words, a witness's testimony is generally closed to other witnesses and counsel.

Outside counsel may not represent both the corporation and its officers if differing or divergent interests are present. Similarly, counsel cannot represent multiple witnesses if such conflicting interests appear. Counsel bears the responsibility of determining at the outset of the engagement whether a possible conflict exists.***

Counsel for the corporation may request the SEC staff's permission to attend the examination of a company officer, director, or employee not represented by corporate counsel, but no right to do so has been recognized by the courts. Counsel for the corporation is most likely to be permitted to appear as co-counsel on behalf of the witness in the witness's capacity as a corporate employee, officer, and/or director in addition to the witness's personal counsel.

Witnesses should be prepared for testimony before the SEC in accordance with counsel's usual witness preparation practice, with certain considerations given added emphasis. The customary instructions should underscore the witness's obligation to testify truthfully, and review features typical of SEC examinations. Questioning in the course of an investigation may be primarily in the format of cross-examination and may focus the witness's attention largely upon documents. Witnesses should be given the practical advice that their demeanor and attitude—whether captured in a transcribed record or not—may influence the recommendations of the staff with respect to further enforcement inquiries or actions.

Similarly, any statement made in the presence of the staff may be used for any purpose it chooses. Even if a statement is made after a staff member advises that communications are "off the record" and is not recorded by the court reporter, the statement may be used for the same purposes as statements made on the record. In short, statements made in the presence of the staff are never "off the record." Such communications, even if not transcribed, may influence the recommendation of the staff with respect to an enforcement action. They may also implicate the United States Code provision that provides criminal penalties for knowingly and willfully providing false information to a government agent. [18 U.S.C. § 1001]

A witness's speculation and surmise are especially dangerous as other witnesses, whose testimony and identity will not be known, may be called to testify on the same matters. Further, counsel for the witness will not have had the opportunity to cross-examine these other witnesses. Although this right is available in court and in administrative proceedings, it is not generally available during investigations.

Irrespective of the issues being pursued, the SEC staff will routinely ask the witness a series of personal questions regarding, among other things, biographical and educational background; employment history; personal securities brokerage accounts and trading activity; corporate offices held; the location of bank accounts and loans; residence(s); telephone number(s); telephone calling card and credit card numbers; and prior testimony in securities-related and fraud-related proceedings. Counsel may be successful in limiting some of these lines of questioning insofar as the witness's personal conduct or contacts are not at issue. ***

*[4.] Confidentiality Considerations*

Anyone who supplies information to the SEC (whether in the form of documents or testimony) should carefully comply with its rules regarding confidentiality. These rules provide a procedure for requesting that information not be released in response to a request under the Freedom of Information Act (FOIA), the statute that provides for public access to documents held by the federal government. [5 U.S.C. § 552; 17 C.F.R. § 200.83]. Confidentiality may be requested for documentary or oral information (to the extent that oral information is memorialized in writing) submitted to the SEC, and applies to information produced pursuant to subpoena as well as information produced voluntarily. The two general grounds for a request are personal privacy and business confidentiality, although other reasons are permitted by law.

## *NOTES AND QUESTIONS*

***1. Cooperating with the SEC.*** Because SEC staff members conducting an informal investigation lack the power to subpoena documents or testimony, a client's initial inclination may well be to refuse to voluntarily produce any requested material. Yet experienced defense counsel often advise that cooperation with the SEC staff generally constitutes a superior strategy. What, precisely, is meant by the term "cooperation?" Does it involve more than producing voluntarily what the staff could otherwise obtain only through its subpoena power? What benefits are to be gained from cooperation? What are some drawbacks? Are there particular types of cases where the cooperation strategy would seem clearly preferable? Are there particular types of cases where that strategy may be counter-productive? For discussion of the possible "credit" that the SEC may give for a company's cooperation, see Report of Investigation Pursuant to Section 21(a) of the Securities Exchange Act of 1934 and Commission Statement on the Relationship of Cooperation to Agency Enforcement Decisions, Exchange Act Release No. 44969, 76 SEC Docket 220 (Oct. 23, 2001), which is set out in subsection 2 infra.

Note also the excerpt by Phillips et al., supra, which expresses the view that an SEC investigation "should not be treated like discovery in a civil case, in which the presumed strategy is 'the less said the better.'" Upon what are these differences based? Acting on this view, what advice might you give in preparing your client (or clients) for interviews or testimony with the SEC staff? Are there particular types of cases where "the less said" strategy may well be the superior one?

***2. Multiple Representations.*** Assume you represent a corporation that has received an SEC subpoena for documents with an accompanying letter indicating that the staff intends to subpoena testimony from a number of the corporation's top officials in the upcoming months. What are some of the factors you should consider in determining whether your ethical responsibilities permit you to engage in multiple representations? State professional responsibility rules, such as the following two rules from the ABA's Model Rules of Professional Conduct, will play a key role in your analysis.

### ABA MODEL RULE 1.13: ORGANIZATION AS CLIENT

(a) A lawyer employed or retained by an organization represents the organization acting through its duly authorized constituents. ***

(d) In dealing with an organization's directors, officers, employees, members, shareholders or other constituents, a lawyer shall explain the identity of the client when the lawyer knows or reasonably should know that the organization's interests are adverse to those of the constituents with whom the lawyer is dealing.

(e) A lawyer representing an organization may also represent any of its directors, officers, employees, members, shareholders or other constituents, subject to the provisions of Rule 1.7. If the organization's consent to the dual representation is required by Rule 1.7, the consent shall be given by an appropriate official of the organization other than the individual who is to be represented, or by the shareholders.

**ABA MODEL RULE 1.7: CONFLICT OF INTEREST: CURRENT CLIENTS**

(a) Except as provided in paragraph (b), a lawyer shall not represent a client if the representation involves a concurrent conflict of interest. A concurrent conflict of interest exists if:

(1) the representation of one client will be directly adverse to another client; or

(2) there is a significant risk that the representation of one or more clients will be materially limited by the lawyer's responsibilities to another client, a former client or a third person or by a personal interest of the lawyer.

(b) Notwithstanding the existence of a concurrent conflict of interest under paragraph (a), a lawyer may represent a client if:

(1) the lawyer reasonably believes that the lawyer will be able to provide competent and diligent representation to each affected client;

(2) the representation is not prohibited by law;

(3) the representation does not involve the assertion of a claim by one client against another client represented by the lawyer in the same litigation or other proceeding before a tribunal; and

(4) each affected client gives informed consent, confirmed in writing.

For a decision concluding that a single law firm could continue its simultaneous representation of a brokerage firm and 47 registered representatives under investigation by the SEC for securities fraud, see *In the Matter of Merrill Lynch, Pierce, Fenner & Smith, Inc.*, [1973-74 Transfer Binder] Fed. Sec. L. Rep. ¶ 79,608, 83,630 at 83,633 (Ullman, ALJ) (Dec. 6, 1973) (maintaining that "where it is not clear that a conflict of interests will occur between two or more clients of an attorney, the informed consent of the client or clients whose interests more likely would suffer in the event a conflict should develop can provide justification for the continuation of multiple representations"). From the clients' perspective, what are some of the advantages and disadvantages of engaging in a multiple representation on such a large scale? For additional discussion of this issue, see Richard W. Painter, Advance Waiver of Conflicts, 13 Geo. J. Legal Ethics 289 (2000); Marc I. Steinberg & Timothy U. Sharpe, Attorney Conflicts of Interest: The Need for a Coherent Framework, 66 Notre Dame L. Rev. 1 (1990). See also Karl A. Groskaufmanis, Ethics for Securities Lawyers, 111 PLI/NY 219 (Nov. 2001).

*3. **Tell the Truth.*** It should go without saying that counsel representing clients under investigation by the SEC should do everything in their power to encourage their clients to tell the truth to SEC officials under all sets of circumstances, no matter how formal or seemingly informal the interview or testimony. Among other reasons, counsel can emphasize that: (a) it is the morally right thing to do; (b) the truth typically comes out eventually; (c) making knowingly false statements to a federal official is a crime in and of itself under 18 U.S.C. § 1001; and (d) lying to the SEC is one of the surest ways of turning even the most routine civil securities infraction into a criminal case. For elaboration on the latter point, see Phyllis Diamond, SEC Official Outlines Factors Triggering Criminal Referrals, 28 Sec. Reg. & L. Rep. 970 (BNA) (Aug.9, 1996) (discussing statement by SEC Southeast Regional Director that "while there is no 'checklist' of factors that will turn a civil investigation into a criminal action, failing to be truthful to the Securities and Exchange Commission staff during a civil investigation is increasingly likely to trigger a Justice Department referral").

*4. **Obstruction of Justice.*** Whereas concerns about truth telling are typically directed to targets and witnesses in SEC investigations, it is critical that all of the potential participants in an SEC investigation—including targets, witnesses, and their agents (particularly attorneys and accountants)—be aware of the broad sweep of the federal laws against the obstruction of justice. One clear example of the enormous liability risks for obstructing justice is the verdict issued against the accounting firm of Arthur Andersen, LLP, for document destruction and other actions taken in connection with the SEC's investigation into the collapse of Enron, a long-time audit client of the firm.

On June 15, 2002, Arthur Andersen was found guilty by a unanimous jury on the charge of obstruction of justice, in violation of 18 U.S.C. § 1512(b), which authorizes criminal liability for anyone who "knowingly, intentionally and corruptly persuades another person to (a) withhold records, documents or other records from an official proceeding; or (b) alter, destroy or mutilate, or conceal an object with the intent to impair the object's *** availability for use in an official proceeding." The company was sentenced to five years probation and fined $500,000—the maximum penalty allowed under the law. See Andersen Sentenced to 5 Years Probation, Wall St. J. at C3 (Oct. 17, 2002).

Reacting specifically to the conduct involved in the Arthur Andersen case, as well as more generally to the scandal ridden atmosphere that prompted new legislation, Congress included in the Sarbanes-Oxley Act of 2002 a number of provisions designed to facilitate the government's ability to gather evidence in the wake of suspicions that federal law may have been violated. Most broadly, Section 802 of the Act creates the new crime of "Destruction, Alteration, or Falsification of Records in Federal Investigations and Bankruptcy":

> Whoever knowingly alters, destroys, mutilates, conceals, covers up, falsifies, or makes a false entry in any record, document, or tangible object with the intent to impede, obstruct, or influence the investigation or proper administration of any matter within the jurisdiction of any department or agency of the United States or any case filed under title 11, or in relation to or contemplation of any such matter or case, shall be fined under this title, imprisoned not more than 20 years, or both.

18 U.S.C. § 1519. How do the elements of this crime compare to the elements of the crime with which Arthur Andersen was charged (and convicted)?

In light of the federal laws against obstruction of justice, what specific advice would you give to clients at the outset of an investigation by the SEC? What suggestions would you give an attorney who is advising a client under investigation?

*5. **New Federal Protection for Corporate Whistleblowers.*** In addition to ensuring greater access to potentially incriminating corporate documents and evidence, the Sarbanes-Oxley Act of 2002 also provides government investigators greater access to potential witnesses of corporate wrongdoing by according employees who cooperate with government investigations broad protection against retaliatory acts by their employees. The Act protects corporate whistleblowers in two ways. First, the Act creates a private civil action for employees of publicly traded companies who believe that they have been retaliated against for providing information to a federal agency or Congress about suspected fraud. See Section 806 of the Sarbanes-Oxley Act, to be codified at 18 U.S.C. § 1514A. Section 1107 of the Act also creates a new crime for "Retaliation Against Informants":

> Whoever knowingly, with the intent to retaliate, takes any action harmful to any person, including interference with the lawful employment or livelihood of any person, for providing to a law enforcement officer any truthful information relating to the commission or possible commission of any Federal offense, shall be fined under this title or imprisoned not more than 10 years, or both.

18 U.S.C. § 1513(e). How do these new provisions affect the advice that you would give a corporate client who is under investigation by the SEC?

6. ***Applicable Privileges.*** As in depositions or document discovery conducted under the Federal Rules of Civil Procedure, persons subject to an SEC subpoena or an SEC request for testimony or documents possess constitutional and other legal rights to withhold such testimony or materials. What types of privileges might you expect to see asserted in the course of an SEC investigation? What are some of the consequences that flow from a client's decision to assert an applicable privilege?

7. ***SEC Investigations and the Duty to Disclose.*** When a company learns that it is under investigation by the SEC, must it disclose this information to its shareholders? Does it matter whether the investigation takes the form of a preliminary inquiry or a formal investigation authorized by the Commission? Even absent a legal duty, should it disclose the investigation? Consider the important judgments—both legal and business—that must be made by the issuer. What role should an attorney play in assisting a corporate client with this decision?

8. ***The Power to Subpoena Documents and Testimony.*** SEC subpoenas are not self-enforcing. This means that if a subpoena recipient fails to produce documents or fails to attend scheduled testimony, the SEC must take the subsequent step of applying for a judicial order to enforce the subpoena. The SEC may bring this action by filing a motion and an "order to show cause" in the federal district court where the investigation is being conducted or in any jurisdiction where the subpoenaed party resides. See, e.g., Exchange Act Section 21(c). Such actions are conducted as "summary proceedings" under Rule 81(a)(3) of the Federal Rules of Civil Procedure (i.e., there is no complaint and no discovery), and the burden of proof is on the opposing party to demonstrate why the judge should not enforce the SEC subpoena. As we saw earlier, courts are typically reluctant to second guess the SEC's broad investigatory power, and only in the most extraordinary cases will they refuse to use their judicial power to enforce an agency subpoena of non-privileged materials.

In cases involving valid claims of privilege, persons or companies under investigation by the SEC may also file objections to an SEC motion seeking judicial enforcement of a subpoena to a third party. However, because SEC investigations are generally confidential, the investigation's target may not even be aware that the agency has called for documents or testimony. This situation is illustrated in the following case.

## SEC v. JERRY T. O'BRIEN, INC.

467 U.S. 735 (1984)

JUSTICE MARSHALL:

The Securities and Exchange Commission (SEC or Commission) has statutory authority to conduct nonpublic investigations into possible violations of the securities laws and, in the course thereof, to issue subpoenas to obtain relevant information. The question before us is whether the Commission must notify the "target" of such an investigation when it issues a subpoena to a third party.

I

This case represents one shard of a prolonged investigation by the SEC into the affairs of respondent Harry F. Magnuson and persons and firms with whom he has dealt. The investigation began in 1980, when the Commission's staff reported to the Commission that information in their possession tended to show that Magnuson and others had been trading in the stock of specified mining companies in a manner violative of the registration, reporting, and antifraud provisions of the Securities Act of 1933 and the Securities Exchange Act of 1934. In response, the Commission issued a Formal Order of Investigation authorizing employees of its Seattle Regional Office to initiate a "private investigation" into the transactions in question and, if necessary, to subpoena testimony and documents "deemed relevant or material to the inquiry."

Acting on that authority, members of the Commission staff subpoenaed financial records in the possession of respondent Jerry T. O'Brien, Inc. (O'Brien), a broker-dealer firm, and respondent Pennaluna & Co. (Pennaluna). O'Brien voluntarily complied, but Pennaluna refused to disgorge the requested materials. Soon thereafter, in response to several inquiries by O'Brien's counsel, a member of the SEC staff informed O'Brien that it was a "subject" of the investigation.

O'Brien, Pennaluna, and their respective owners promptly filed a suit in the District Court for the Eastern District of Washington, seeking to enjoin the Commission's investigation and to prevent Magnuson from complying with subpoenas that had been issued to him.[3] Magnuson filed a cross-claim, also seeking to block portions of the investigation. O'Brien then filed motions seeking authority to depose the Commission's officers and to conduct expedited discovery into the Commission's files.

The District Court denied respondents' discovery motions and soon thereafter dismissed their claims for injunctive relief. The principal ground for

3. The principal bases of O'Brien's suit were that the SEC's Formal Order of Investigation was defective, that the investigation did not have a valid purpose, that the Commission should have afforded the subjects of the investigation a chance to comment upon it, and that the issues around which the case revolved had been litigated and settled in another proceeding. Complaint 9-15.

the court's decision was that respondents would have a full opportunity to assert their objections to the basis and scope of the SEC's investigation if and when the Commission instituted a subpoena enforcement action. The court did, however, rule that the Commission's outstanding subpoenas met the requirements outlined in *United States v. Powell*, 379 U.S. 48 (1964), for determining whether an administrative summons is judicially enforceable. Specifically, the District Court held that the Commission had a legitimate purpose in issuing the subpoenas, that the requested information was relevant and was not already in the Commission's possession, and that the issuance of the subpoenas comported with pertinent procedural requirements.

Following the District Court's decision, the SEC issued several subpoenas to third parties. In response, Magnuson and O'Brien renewed their request to the District Court for injunctive relief, accompanying the request with a motion, pursuant to Rule 62(c) of the Federal Rules of Civil Procedure, for a stay pending appeal. For the first time, respondents expressly sought notice of the subpoenas issued by the Commission to third parties. Reasoning that respondents lacked standing to challenge voluntary compliance with subpoenas by third parties, and that, in any subsequent proceeding brought by the SEC, respondents could move to suppress evidence the Commission had obtained from third parties through abusive subpoenas, the District Court denied the requested relief.

A panel of the Court of Appeals for the Ninth Circuit affirmed the District Court's denial of injunctive relief with regard to the subpoenas directed at respondents themselves, agreeing with the lower court that respondents had an adequate remedy at law for challenging those subpoenas. However, the Court of Appeals reversed the District Court's denial of respondents' request for notice of subpoenas issued to third parties. In the Court of Appeals' view, "targets" of SEC investigations "have a right to be investigated consistently with the *Powell* standards." To enable targets to enforce this right, the court held that they must be notified of subpoenas issued to others.

The Court of Appeals denied the Commission's request for rehearing and rejected its suggestion for rehearing en banc. ***

We granted certiorari because of the importance of the issue presented. We now reverse.

II

***No provision in the complex of statutes governing the SEC's investigative power expressly obliges the Commission to notify the "target" of an investigation when it issues a subpoena to a third party. If such an obligation is to be imposed on the Commission, therefore, it must be derived from one of three sources: a constitutional provision; an understanding on the part of Congress, inferable from the structure of the securities laws, regarding how the SEC should conduct its inquiries; or the general standards governing judicial enforcement of administrative subpoenas enunciated in *United States v. Powell*, 379 U.S. 48 (1964), and its progeny. Examination of these three potential bases for the Court of Appeals' ruling leaves us unpersuaded that the notice requirement fashioned by that court is warranted.

A

Our prior cases foreclose any constitutional argument respondents might make in defense of the judgment below. The opinion of the Court in *Hannah v. Larche*, 363 U.S. 420 (1960), leaves no doubt that neither the Due Process Clause of the Fifth Amendment nor the Confrontation Clause of the Sixth Amendment is offended when a federal administrative agency, without notifying a person under investigation, uses its subpoena power to gather evidence adverse to him. The Due Process Clause is not implicated under such circumstances because an administrative investigation adjudicates no legal rights, id., at 440-443, and the Confrontation Clause does not come into play until the initiation of criminal proceedings, id., at 440, n. 16. These principles plainly cover an inquiry by the SEC into possible violations of the securities laws.

It is also settled that a person inculpated by materials sought by a subpoena issued to a third party cannot seek shelter in the Self-Incrimination Clause of the Fifth Amendment. The rationale of this doctrine is that the Constitution proscribes only *compelled* self-incrimination, and, whatever may be the pressures exerted upon the person to whom a subpoena is directed, the subpoena surely does not "compel" anyone else to be a witness against himself. *Fisher v. United States*, 425 U.S. 391, 397 (1976); *Couch v. United States*, 409 U.S. 322, 328-329 (1973). If the "target" of an investigation by the SEC has no Fifth Amendment right to challenge enforcement of a subpoena directed at a third party, he clearly can assert no derivative right to notice when the Commission issues such a subpoena.

Finally, respondents cannot invoke the Fourth Amendment in support of the Court of Appeals' decision. It is established that, when a person communicates information to a third party even on the understanding that the communication is confidential, he cannot object if the third party conveys that information or records thereof to law enforcement authorities. *United States v. Miller*, 425 U.S. 435, 443 (1976). Relying on that principle, the Court has held that a customer of a bank cannot challenge on Fourth Amendment grounds the admission into evidence in a criminal prosecution of financial records obtained by the Government from his bank pursuant to allegedly defective subpoenas, despite the fact that he was given no notice of the subpoenas. Id., at 443, and n. 5. See also *Donaldson v. United States*, 400 U.S. 517, 522 (1971) (Internal Revenue summons directed to third party does not trench upon any interests protected by the Fourth Amendment). These rulings disable respondents from arguing that notice of subpoenas issued to third parties is necessary to allow a target to prevent an unconstitutional search or seizure of his papers.

B

The language and structure of the statutes administered by the Commission afford respondents no greater aid. The provisions vesting the SEC with the power to issue and seek enforcement of subpoenas are expansive. ***

More generally, [these] statutes vest the SEC with "power to make such rules and regulations as may be necessary or appropriate to implement [their] provisions...." 15 U.S.C. §§ 77s(a), 78w(a)(1). Relying on this authority, the SEC has promulgated a variety of rules governing its investigations, one of which provides that, "[u]nless otherwise ordered by the Commission, all formal investigative proceedings shall be non-public." 17 CFR § 203.5 (1983). In other words, the Commission has formally adopted the policy of not routinely informing anyone, including targets, of the existence and progress of its investigations. To our knowledge, Congress has never questioned this exercise by the Commission of its statutory power. And, in another context, we have held that rulemaking authority comparable to that enjoyed by the SEC is broad enough to empower an agency to "establish standards for determining whether to conduct an investigation publicly or in private." *FCC v. Schreiber*, 381 U.S. 279, 292 (1965).

It appears, in short, that Congress intended to vest the SEC with considerable discretion in determining when and how to investigate possible violations of the statutes administered by the Commission. We discern no evidence that Congress wished or expected that the Commission would adopt any particular procedures for notifying "targets" of investigations when it sought information from third parties.

The inference that the relief sought by respondents is not necessary to give effect to congressional intent is reinforced by the fact that, in one special context, Congress has imposed on the Commission an obligation to notify persons directly affected by its subpoenas. In 1978, in response to this Court's decision in *United States v. Miller*, supra, Congress enacted the Right to Financial Privacy Act, 92 Stat. 3697, 12 U.S.C. § 3401 et seq. That statute accords customers of banks and similar financial institutions certain rights to be notified of and to challenge in court administrative subpoenas of financial records in the possession of the banks. The most salient feature of the Act is the narrow scope of the entitlements it creates. Thus, it carefully limits the kinds of customers to whom it applies, §§ 3401(4), (5), and the types of records they may seek to protect, § 3401(2). A customer's ability to challenge a subpoena is cabined by strict procedural requirements. For example, he must assert his claim within a short period of time, § 3410(a), and cannot appeal an adverse determination until the Government has completed its investigation, § 3410(d). Perhaps most importantly, the statute is drafted in a fashion that minimizes the risk that customers' objections to subpoenas will delay or frustrate agency investigations. Thus, a court presented with such a challenge is required to rule upon it within seven days of the Government's response, § 3410(b), and the pertinent statutes of limitations are tolled while the claim is pending, § 3419. Since 1980, the SEC has been subject to the constraints of the Right to Financial Privacy Act. When it made the statute applicable to the SEC, however, Congress empowered the Commission in prescribed circumstances to seek *ex parte* orders authorizing it to delay notifying bank customers when it subpoenas information about them, thereby further curtailing the ability of persons under investigation to impede the agency's inquiries.

Considerable insight into the legislators' conception of the scope of the SEC's investigatory power can be gleaned from the foregoing developments. We know that Congress recently had occasion to consider the authority of the SEC and other agencies to issue and enforce administrative subpoenas without notifying the persons whose affairs may be exposed thereby. In response, Congress enacted a set of carefully tailored limitations on the agencies' power, designed "to strike a balance between customers' right of privacy and the need of law enforcement agencies to obtain financial records pursuant to legitimate investigations." H.R. Rep. No. 95-1383, p. 33 (1978). The manner in which Congress dealt with this problem teaches us two things. First, it seems apparent that Congress assumed that the SEC was not and would not be subject to a general obligation to notify "targets" of its investigations whenever it issued administrative subpoenas. Second, the complexity and subtlety of the procedures embodied in the Right to Financial Privacy Act suggest that Congress would find troubling the crude and unqualified notification requirement ordered by the Court of Appeals.

C

The last of the three potential footings for the remedy sought by respondents is some other entitlement that would be effectuated thereby. Respondents seek to derive such an entitlement from a combination of our prior decisions. Distilled, their argument is as follows: A subpoena issued by the SEC must comport with the standards set forth in our decision in *United States v. Powell*, 379 U.S., at 57-58.[18] Not only the recipient of an SEC subpoena, but also any person who would be affected by compliance therewith, has a substantive right, under *Powell*, to insist that those standards are met. A target of an SEC investigation may assert the foregoing right in two ways. First, relying on *Reisman v. Caplin*, 375 U.S. 440, 445 (1964), and *Donaldson v. United States*, 400 U.S., at 529, the target may seek permissive intervention in an enforcement action brought by the Commission against the subpoena recipient. Second, if the recipient of the subpoena threatens voluntarily to turn over the requested information, the target "might restrain compliance" by the recipient, thereby forcing the Commission to institute an enforcement suit. See *Reisman v. Caplin*, supra, 375 U.S., at 450. A target can avail himself of these options only if he is aware of the existence of subpoenas directed at others. To ensure that ignorance does not prevent a target from asserting his rights, respondents conclude, the Commission must notify him when it issues a subpoena to a third party.

There are several tenuous links in respondents' argument. Especially debatable are the proposition that a target has a substantive right to be investigated in a manner consistent with the *Powell* standards and the assertion

---

18. The holding of *Powell* was that the Commissioner of Internal Revenue need not demonstrate probable cause in order to secure judicial enforcement of a summons issued pursuant to § 7602 of the Internal Revenue Code. The Court then went on to sketch the requirements that the Commissioner would be obliged to satisfy:

> "He must show that the investigation will be conducted pursuant to a legitimate purpose, that the inquiry may be relevant to that purpose, that the information sought is not already within the Commissioner's possession, and that the administrative steps required by the Code have been followed.... [A] court may not permit its process to be abused. Such an abuse would take place if the summons had been issued for an improper purpose, such as to harass the taxpayer or to put pressure on him to settle a collateral dispute, or for any other purpose reflecting on the good faith of the particular investigation."

379 U.S., at 57-58. *** Because of the manner in which we dispose of this case, we have no occasion to pass upon respondents' characterization or application of our decision in *Powell*.

that a target may obtain a restraining order preventing voluntary compliance by a third party with an administrative subpoena. Certainly we have never before expressly so held. For the present, however, we may assume, *arguendo*, that a target enjoys each of the substantive and procedural rights identified by respondents. Nevertheless, we conclude that it would be inappropriate to elaborate upon those entitlements by mandating notification of targets whenever the Commission issues subpoenas.

Two considerations underlie our decision on this issue. First, administration of the notice requirement advocated by respondents would be highly burdensome for both the Commission and the courts. The most obvious difficulty would involve identification of the persons and organizations that should be considered "targets" of investigations. The SEC often undertakes investigations into suspicious securities transactions without any knowledge of which of the parties involved may have violated the law. To notify all potential wrongdoers in such a situation of the issuance of each subpoena would be virtually impossible. The Commission would thus be obliged to determine the point at which enough evidence had been assembled to focus suspicion on a manageable subset of the participants in the transaction, thereby lending them the status of "targets" and entitling them to notice of the outstanding subpoenas directed at others. The complexity of that task is apparent. Even in cases in which the Commission could identify with reasonable ease the principal targets of its inquiry, another problem would arise. In such circumstances, a person not considered a target by the Commission could contend that he deserved that status and therefore should be given notice of subpoenas issued to others. To assess a claim of this sort, a district court would be obliged to conduct some kind of hearing to determine the scope and thrust of the ongoing investigation. Implementation of this new remedy would drain the resources of the judiciary as well as the Commission.

Second, the imposition of a notice requirement on the SEC would substantially increase the ability of persons who have something to hide to impede legitimate investigations by the Commission. A target given notice of every subpoena issued to third parties would be able to discourage the recipients from complying, and then further delay disclosure of damaging information by seeking intervention in all enforcement actions brought by the Commission. More seriously, the understanding of the progress of an SEC inquiry that would flow from knowledge of which persons had received subpoenas would enable an unscrupulous target to destroy or alter documents, intimidate witnesses, or transfer securities or funds so that they could not be reached by the Government. Especially in the context of securities regulation, where speed in locating and halting violations of the law is so important, we would be loathe to place such potent weapons in the hands of persons with a desire to keep the Commission at bay.

We acknowledge that our ruling may have the effect in practice of preventing some persons under investigation by the SEC from asserting objections to subpoenas issued by the Commission to third parties for improper reasons. However, to accept respondents' proposal "would unwarrantedly cast doubt upon and stultify the [Commission's] every investigatory move," *Donaldson v. United States*, 400 U.S., at 531. Particularly in view of Congress' manifest disinclination to require the Commission to notify targets whenever it seeks information from others, we refuse so to curb the Commission's exercise of its statutory power.

III

Nothing in this opinion should be construed to imply that it would be improper for the SEC to inform a target that it has issued a subpoena to someone else. But, for the reasons indicated above, we decline to curtail the Commission's discretion to determine when such notice would be appropriate and when it would not. Accordingly, the judgment of the Court of Appeals is reversed, and the case is remanded for further proceedings consistent with this opinion.

### *NOTES AND QUESTIONS*

*1. **Balancing Burdens.*** Do you agree with the Court that requiring notice to the target of a third party subpoena would impose an undue administrative burden on the SEC? Did the Court give adequate consideration to the legitimate concerns of persons who become subject to SEC investigations? What potentially negative consequences to the target could be avoided were the SEC required to provide such notice? Is there anything unique about the securities industry that, from the target's perspective, makes "secret investigations" by the SEC particularly harmful? See Therese Maynard, *SEC v. Jerry T. O'Brien, Inc.:* Has the Supreme Court Overruled *United States v. Powell?*, 18 Loy. L.A. L. Rev. 643, 645-46 (1985). Has the SEC's recent experience with Enron and its auditor Arthur Andersen bolstered the case for investigative secrecy?

*2. **Lessons to Draw.*** Does the Court's decision in *O'Brien* impact the advice that you would give clients who wish to retain agents, such as accountants or consultants, to provide assistance with matters where confidentiality is key? Assuming that an engagement letter will be executed, what specific provisions can be included to ensure that your client is not surprised by an agent's release of its information to a government agency such as the SEC?

---

### *2. Concluding an SEC Investigation*

As with the commencement of formal investigations, the commencement of enforcement actions against persons or companies that may have violated the federal securities laws cannot be initiated by the staff of the Enforcement Division. Rather, if the staff believes that enforcement action is warranted, a recommendation to that effect must be made to the Commission. This recommendation typically includes the staff's analysis of the facts and the law, and their views with respect to appropriate sanctions. Even in instances where a person or company is willing to settle and consent to a sanction that is also acceptable to the SEC staff, such a settlement can be accepted only by the Commission. As we shall see, the Commission extends simultaneous authorization to a large percentage of enforcement actions and settlements.

Important aspects of the process by which the Commission considers staff recommendations are described in the following excerpt. At the time of its publication, the article's first co-author was the Director of the SEC's Enforcement Division.

## A PRACTITIONER'S GUIDE TO THE SEC'S INVESTIGATIVE AND ENFORCEMENT PROCESS

**by William R. McLucas, J. Lynn Taylor, and Susan A. Mathews**[a]

70 Temple L. Rev. 53, 111-116 (1997)

*** A. *Staff Recommendation*

At the conclusion of an investigation, the staff may determine to take no action or to recommend that the Commission bring enforcement proceedings. The staff is not required to inform a witness or an individual or entity whose activities were under scrutiny if the investigation is terminated without action. The staff may, in its discretion, use a "closing letter" to advise a witness that its investigation has been terminated.

Historically, the staff issued these letters only when counsel made a request for such a communique. Recognizing that the uncertainty of the status of an investigation may have adverse consequences for individuals and businesses, the staff changed its practice. Currently, the staff notifies individuals and entities whose activities were under scrutiny of the termination of an investigation. If an investigation is terminated without the staff recommending or the Commission authorizing an action, the staff will notify those persons and entities: (1) named in the formal order of investigation or (2) provided with a Wells submission notification. Other persons or entities involved in the investigation, such as those subpoenaed or whose activities were under scrutiny, also may request such notification. Notification of the termination of an investigation is not an exoneration or an indication that no enforcement action ultimately may result from the staff's investigation. Rather, such notification simply means that the staff has completed its investigation and is not, as of the date of the letter, recommending enforcement action to the Commission.

If the staff determines that remedial action is necessary as a result of its investigation, it will make a recommendation to the Commission that identifies the proposed defendants or respondents, states the evidentiary and legal bases supporting the claimed violations, and sets forth a proposed remedy and the rationale therefor. The staff, at the time that it makes its recommendation, will forward to the Commission any Wells Submissions received from proposed defendants.

*B. Wells Submissions* ***

In Securities Act Release 5310, the Commission discussed its discretionary practice "of permitting persons involved in an investigation to present a statement to [the Commission] setting forth their interests and position." [Sec. Act Rel. No. 5310 (Sept. 27, 1972)]. In order to advise the public of its practice,

---

a. The Securities and Exchange Commission, as a matter of policy, disclaims responsibility for any private publication by any of its employees. The views expressed herein are those of the authors and do not necessarily reflect the views of the Commission or its staff. See 17 C.F.R. § 200.735-4(e).

the Wells Committee procedure was set forth in the Commission's regulations relating to Informal and Other Procedures. [17 C.F.R.§ 202.5(c).]

In Release 5310, the Commission indicated that interested persons may find it useful to discuss the matter under investigation with the staff. To that end, the Commission stated that the staff, in its discretion, may advise prospective defendants of the general nature of the investigation and violations contemplated by the staff and permit the proposed defendant to submit a response to the allegations within a time frame determined by the staff. The Commission viewed the submissions from the proposed defendants to be of the greatest benefit when addressing questions of policy or law. The Commission indicated that it did not view a discussion of factual disagreements between the staff and proposed defendants as particularly useful. Notwithstanding the language of the Release, many Wells Submissions do address factual issues, evidentiary matters, and the inference and/or weight to be given the evidence, and they often highlight factual disagreements with the staff's position. Generally, unless circumstances otherwise warrant, the staff will describe in its Wells notice the proposed enforcement recommendation, and provide a summary of the evidence and legal theories on which the staff relies.

The Wells Submission practice has not created, nor has the Commission employed, any formal, pre-proceeding notification or solicitation procedure. Release 5310 was not intended to, and did not, confer any rights upon the subjects of Commission investigations. While there is no requirement that the Commission provide a Wells notice to persons or entities which may be the subject of an enforcement recommendation by the staff, and although no due process rights attach to this practice, the staff generally provides the opportunity for such a submission as an investigation nears completion. The Commission, however, does not provide such an opportunity when there are concerns about dissipation of assets, destruction of documents, or any other situations which may require the Commission to act quickly to protect the public interest.

***Strategic Considerations in Making Wells Submissions

A substantial number of proposed respondents and defendants do make Wells Submissions. The submissions are evaluated carefully, not only by the Commissioners and by the enforcement staff, but also by other offices and divisions within the Commission which may have an interest in the matters involved in the case. While statistics are not maintained on the number of successful submissions, the Commission staff often has modified its recommendations, or dropped individuals altogether, after evaluating a submission. The Commission has done likewise in considering whether to authorize an enforcement action. The following points regarding Wells Submissions bear noting:

(a) A submission may highlight factual and legal deficiencies in a proposed enforcement action.

(b) The Division of Enforcement takes the position that a submission may be utilized subsequently as an admission or for impeachment purposes.

(c) Submissions may be particularly helpful in analyzing the role of "peripheral" defendants or persons charged with "aiding and abetting" violations.

(d) Novel, unique, or unusual policy issues may be highlighted, especially the nature of relief sought and the statutory provisions alleged to have been violated.

(e) A concise submission is likely to be more effective than a lengthy discourse. Currently, Commission policy is that Wells Submissions should be limited to no more than 40 pages.

(f) The Commission's current policy is that a videotaped statement by counsel of no more than twelve minutes may be submitted in lieu of a written Wells Submission. A transcript of the videotaped statement also should be submitted.

(g) A submission must be timely. In general, a one-month period for the submission of Wells statements is permitted, although the time frame may vary somewhat depending upon the complexity of a case. Extensions of time are granted in certain circumstances, but should not be counted upon as they are not granted as a matter of course. ***

In general, after the completion of an enforcement proceeding, Wells Submissions may become available under the FOIA [Freedom of Information Act] unless

i) Disclosure would "constitute an unwarranted invasion of personal privacy" [or] "disclose the identity of a confidential source"; [5 U.S.C. § 552(b)(7)(C), (D)]

(ii) It is likely that additional proceedings may be brought, even if a particular enforcement action has been concluded;

(iii) Disclosure would deprive a person of a fair trial or impartial adjudication in proceedings other than the Commission's action; [5 U.S.C. § 552(b)(7)(B)] or

(iv) Disclosure would disclose Commission investigative techniques or procedures; [5 U.S.C. § 552(b)(7)(E)]

Notwithstanding the above, it is important to note that § 552 of the Administrative Procedures Act contemplates disclosure of "any reasonably segregable portion of a record" and thus, disclosure of nonexempt portions of a Wells Submission may be appropriate. Further, considerations of personal privacy do not apply to Wells Submissions made solely on behalf of a corporate entity. ***

### *NOTES AND QUESTIONS*

***1. The Costs and Benefits of Drafting a Wells Submission.*** The above excerpt highlights some strategic considerations in deciding whether to prepare a Wells submission on a client's behalf. Can you identify some of the other potential advantages and disadvantages of preparing a Wells submission? Are there particular types of cases where a Wells submission on behalf of a client may be particularly harmful? Particularly useful? For additional guidance, see

Kenneth B. Winer & Samuel J. Winer, Effective Representation in the SEC Wells Process, 34 Rev. Sec. & Comm. Reg. 59 (2001).

*2. Commission Adoption of Staff Recommendations.* SEC staff members work long and hard in gathering the facts, analyzing the law, and preparing the memorandum that is eventually presented to the Commission along with a recommendation that enforcement action be instituted against the subject of a pending investigation. Note also that the Commission may have already considered at least some of the facts and violations alleged in that memorandum in situations where they had previously issued formal orders of investigation. Could it therefore be argued that the Commission has an inherent bias that favors its staff in deciding whether to institute enforcement action? Should the Commissioners view the facts and the law presented by the enforcement staff at the prosecutorial stage any differently from how they view those facts and law when sitting in an adjudicative capacity? For an insightful essay focusing on the Commission's role as prosecutor, see Roberta S. Karmel, Creating Law at the Securities and Exchange Commission: The Lawyer as Prosecutor, 61 Law & Contemp. Probs. 33 (1998). Note in particular former Commissioner Karmel's observation that "[i]t is psychologically and politically difficult to decline to institute a case involving bad facts or to accept a questionable settlement." Id. at 41.

---

What factors does the staff consider when determining whether to recommend to the Commission the initiation of an enforcement action? What factors do the staff and the Commission consider in determining an appropriate sanction? The following Report, issued by the Commission pursuant to its authority under Section 21(a) of the Exchange Act, provides a rare glimpse into the SEC's internal decisionmaking process.

## REPORT OF INVESTIGATION PURSUANT TO SECTION 21(a) OF THE SECURITIES EXCHANGE ACT OF 1934 AND COMMISSION STATEMENT ON THE RELATIONSHIP OF COOPERATION TO AGENCY ENFORCEMENT DECISIONS

Exchange Act Release No. 44969 (Oct. 23, 2001)

Today, we commence and settle a cease-and-desist proceeding against Gisela de Leon-Meredith, former controller of a publicly traded company's subsidiary. [Release No. 34-44970 (October 23, 2001)] Our order finds that Meredith caused the parent company's books and records to be inaccurate and its periodic reports misstated, and then covered up those facts. We are not taking action against the parent company, given the nature of the conduct and the company's responses. Within a week of learning about the apparent misconduct, the company's internal auditors had conducted a preliminary review and had advised company management who, in turn, advised the Board's audit committee, that Meredith had caused the company's books and records to be inaccurate and its financial reports to be misstated. The full Board was advised and authorized the company to hire an outside law firm to conduct a thorough inquiry. Four days later, Meredith was dismissed, as were two other employees who, in the company's view, had inadequately supervised Meredith; a day later, the company disclosed publicly and to us that its financial statements would be restated. The price of the company's shares did not decline after the announcement or after the restatement was published. The company pledged and gave complete cooperation to our staff. It provided the staff with all information relevant to the underlying violations. Among other things, the company produced the details of its internal investigation, including notes and transcripts of interviews of Meredith and others; and it did not invoke the attorney-client privilege, work product protection or other privileges or protections with respect to any facts uncovered in the investigation

The company also strengthened its financial reporting processes to address Meredith's conduct—developing a detailed closing process for the subsidiary's accounting personnel, consolidating subsidiary accounting functions under a parent company CPA, hiring three new CPAs for the accounting department responsible for preparing the subsidiary's financial statements, redesigning the subsidiary's minimum annual audit requirements, and requiring the parent company's controller to interview and approve all senior accounting personnel in its subsidiaries' reporting processes.

Our willingness to credit such behavior in deciding whether and how to take enforcement action benefits investors as well as our enforcement program. When businesses seek out, self-report and rectify illegal conduct, and otherwise cooperate with Commission staff, large expenditures of government and shareholder resources can be avoided and investors can benefit more promptly. In setting forth the criteria listed below, we think a few caveats are in order:

First, the paramount issue in every enforcement judgment is, and must be, what best protects investors. There is no single, or constant, answer to that question. Self-policing, self-reporting, remediation and cooperation with law enforcement authorities, among other things, are unquestionably important in promoting investors' best interests. But, so too are vigorous enforcement and the imposition of appropriate sanctions where the law has been violated. Indeed, there may be circumstances where conduct is so egregious, and harm so great, that no amount of cooperation or other mitigating conduct can justify a decision not to bring any enforcement action at all. In the end, no set of criteria can, or should, be strictly applied in every situation to which they may be applicable.

Second, we are not adopting any rule or making any commitment or promise about any specific case; nor are we in any way limiting our broad discretion to evaluate every case individually, on its own particular facts and circumstances. Conversely, we are not conferring any "rights" on any person or entity. We seek only to convey an understanding of the factors that may influence our decisions.

Third, we do not limit ourselves to the criteria we discuss below. By definition, enforcement judgments are just that—judgments. Our failure to mention a specific criterion in one context does not preclude us from relying on that criterion in another. Further, the fact that a company has satisfied all the criteria we list below will not foreclose us from bringing enforcement proceedings that we believe are necessary or appropriate, for the benefit of investors.

In brief form, we set forth below some of the criteria we will consider in determining whether, and how much, to credit self-policing, self-reporting, remediation and cooperation—from the extraordinary step of taking no enforcement action to bringing reduced charges, seeking lighter sanctions, or including mitigating language in documents we use to announce and resolve enforcement actions.

1. What is the nature of the misconduct involved? Did it result from inadvertence, honest mistake, simple negligence, reckless or deliberate indifference to indicia of wrongful conduct, willful misconduct or unadorned venality? Were the company's auditors misled?

2. How did the misconduct arise? Is it the result of pressure placed on employees to achieve specific results, or a tone of lawlessness set by those in control of the company? What compliance procedures were in place to prevent the misconduct now uncovered? Why did those procedures fail to stop or inhibit the wrongful conduct?

3. Where in the organization did the misconduct occur? How high up in the chain of command was knowledge of, or participation in, the misconduct? Did senior personnel participate in, or turn a blind eye toward, obvious indicia of misconduct? How systemic was the behavior? Is it symptomatic of the way the entity does business, or was it isolated?

4. How long did the misconduct last? Was it a one-quarter, or one-time, event, or did it last several years? In the case of a publicly traded company, did the misconduct occur before the company went public? Did it facilitate the company's ability to go public?

5. How much harm has the misconduct inflicted upon investors and other corporate constituencies? Did the share price of the company's stock drop significantly upon its discovery and disclosure?

6. How was the misconduct detected and who uncovered it?

7. How long after discovery of the misconduct did it take to implement an effective response?

8. What steps did the company take upon learning of the misconduct? Did the company immediately stop the misconduct? Are persons responsible for any misconduct still with the company? If so, are they still in the same positions? Did the company promptly, completely and effectively disclose the existence of the misconduct to the public, to regulators and to self-regulators? Did the company cooperate completely with appropriate regulatory and law enforcement bodies? Did the company identify what additional related misconduct is likely to have occurred? Did the company take steps to identify the extent of damage to investors and other corporate constituencies? Did the company appropriately recompense those adversely affected by the conduct?

9. What processes did the company follow to resolve many of these issues and ferret out necessary information? Were the Audit Committee and the Board of Directors fully informed? If so, when?

10. Did the company commit to learn the truth, fully and expeditiously? Did it do a thorough review of the nature, extent, origins and consequences of the conduct and related behavior? Did management, the Board or committees consisting solely of outside directors oversee the review? Did company employees or outside persons perform the review? If outside persons, had they done other

work for the company? Where the review was conducted by outside counsel, had management previously engaged such counsel? Were scope limitations placed on the review? If so, what were they?

11. Did the company promptly make available to our staff the results of its review and provide sufficient documentation reflecting its response to the situation? Did the company identify possible violative conduct and evidence with sufficient precision to facilitate prompt enforcement actions against those who violated the law? Did the company produce a thorough and probing written report detailing the findings of its review? Did the company voluntarily disclose information our staff did not directly request and otherwise might not have uncovered? Did the company ask its employees to cooperate with our staff and make all reasonable efforts to secure such cooperation?

12. What assurances are there that the conduct is unlikely to recur? Did the company adopt and ensure enforcement of new and more effective internal controls and procedures designed to prevent a recurrence of the misconduct? Did the company provide our staff with sufficient information for it to evaluate the company's measures to correct the situation and ensure that the conduct does not recur?

13. Is the company the same company in which the misconduct occurred, or has it changed through a merger or bankruptcy reorganization?

We hope that this Report of Investigation and Commission Statement will further encourage self-policing efforts and will promote more self-reporting, remediation and cooperation with the Commission staff. We welcome the constructive input of all interested persons. We urge those who have contributions to make to direct them to our Division of Enforcement. The public can be confident that all such communications will be fairly evaluated not only by our staff, but also by us. We continue to reassess our enforcement approaches with the aim of maximizing the benefits of our program to investors and the marketplace.

## *NOTES AND QUESTIONS*

*1. A Typical Case?* Note the quick and decisive actions taken by officials at Seaboard Corporation, the publicly traded company that was the subject of the SEC's Section 21(a) report. All within a two week period, Seaboard officials conducted an internal inquiry which confirmed the subsidiary's inaccurate financial statements; terminated the subsidiary's former controller and two of her supervisors; and notified the public and the SEC that the company would be restating its financial statements. The report also reveals that Seaboard's stock price was unaffected by the restatement of its financial statements and that the company had taken steps to strengthen its financial reporting processes. In view of these facts, can Seaboard's "enforcement story" be considered a typical one? In particular, how likely is it that the discovery and revelation of material errors in an issuer's financial statements will have no impact on that issuer's stock price? Is this a report about a company's cooperation or merely an instance where enforcement action against the parent company would serve no identifiable public good?

*2. Waiver of Privilege.* In footnote 3 of its Report, the Commission stated that "[i]n some cases, the desire to provide information to the Commission staff may cause companies to consider choosing not to assert the attorney-client privilege, the work product protection and other privileges, protections and exemptions with respect to the Commission." Recognizing that these privileges, protections and exemptions "serve important social interests," the Commission stated that it "does not view a company's waiver of a privilege as an end in itself, but only as a means (where necessary) to provide relevant and sometimes critical information to the Commission staff."

What risks are associated with a client's decision to waive vis-a-vis the SEC otherwise applicable privileges such as attorney-client or work product protections? In particular, can a client waive a privilege in an SEC investigation or proceeding and then reassert that privilege in litigation brought by third parties? There is a split of authority on this issue of "selective" or "limited" waiver. Compare *Westinghouse Elec. Corp. v. Republic of the Philippines*, 951 F.2d 1414 (3d Cir. 1991) (waiver to SEC in the course of investigation waives privilege to all third parties) and *In re Subpoena Duces Tecum,* 738 F.2d 1367 (D.C. Cir. 1984) (same) with *Diversified Indus., Inc. v. Meredith,* 572 F.2d 596 (8th Cir. 1977) (holding that a corporation participating in the SEC's voluntary disclosure program retains a privilege as to all third party litigants, and noting that "[t]o hold otherwise may have the effect of thwarting the developing procedure of corporations to employ independent outside counsel to investigate and advise them in order to protect stockholders, potential stockholders and customers"). Consider also the decision in *In re Steinhardt Partners*, 9 F.3d 230 (2d Cir. 1993). There the court ruled that voluntary disclosure of work product to the SEC waived the privilege for all parties but left open the possibility that limited waiver may be appropriate where the SEC has explicitly agreed with the disclosing party to maintain the confidentiality of the disclosed materials. Id. at 236. Are the policy reasons behind the doctrine of selective disclosure compelling ones? As a matter of course, should the SEC enter into confidentiality agreements to encourage voluntary disclosure? What concerns are raised by the SEC's willingness to enter into these agreements?

*3. Real Time Enforcement.* Within a few weeks of issuing the Section 21(a) report in the Seaboard Corporation matter, SEC Chairperson Harvey Pitt emphasized that its "Statement on Cooperation" was an integral part of a broader initiative by the Commission to move toward "real time enforcement." As Chairperson Pitt explained:

> This is a serious new policy we are following so that we can better protect investors by acting quickly and effectively. It means we seek to learn of potential violations quickly and, where investor interests are being disserved or abused, take immediate action to undo the effects of any violative conduct. Faster enforcement will help prevent continued fleecing of the investing public and the dissipation of assets, and will allow us to use court-supervised methods to learn what other unlawful acts may have been committed.
>
> ***Among other things, our Staff has been directed to look for creative ways to segment cases, so that wrongdoing can be publicly identified, and interim relief can be imposed that might effectively prevent the dissipation of significant amounts of investor funds.

SEC Chairperson Harvey L. Pitt, Remarks at the PLI 33rd Annual Institute on Securities Regulation (November 8, 2001). What additional benefits flow from making "real time enforcement" a top Commission priority? Does the Commission's emphasis on "real time enforcement" pose particular concerns?

*4. Section 21(a) Reports.* Section 21(a) authorizes the SEC "to publish information" concerning its investigations of possible violations of the federal securities laws. The Commission tends to use its authority under this provision to articulate novel legal theories or standards of conduct. By including its views in a report, rather than in an SEC order resolving an enforcement action, the Commission is able to draw public attention without placing the agency in the uncomfortable position of applying its views retroactively to justify the imposition of a sanction. The vehicle of a Section 21(a) report also eliminates the need to hold a hearing to establish the violation and forecloses any judicial review of the theories and standards articulated in the report.

On several occasions, the SEC has issued reports of investigations that address the roles and responsibilities of boards of directors in ensuring their company's compliance with the federal securities laws. See Report of Investigation Pursuant to Section 21(a) of the Securities Exchange Act of 1934 Concerning the Conduct of Certain Former Officers and Directors of W.R. Grace & Co., Exchange Act Release No. 39157, 65 SEC Docket 1240 (Sept. 30, 1997); Report of Investigation in the Matter of the Cooper Companies, Inc. as it Relates to the Conduct of Cooper's Board of Directors, Exchange Act Release No. 35082, 58 SEC Docket 591 (Dec. 12, 1994); Report of Investigation In the Matter of Stirling Homex Corporation Relating to Activities of the Board of Directors of Stirling Homex Corporation, Exchange Act Release No. 11516, 7 SEC Docket 298 (July 2, 1975); Report of Investigation In the Matter of Nat'l Tel. Co., Relating to Activities of the Outside Directors of Nat'l Tel. Co., Exchange Act Release 14380, 13 SEC Docket 1393 (Jan. 16, 1978). In each of these reports, the SEC subjected the board to substantial criticism for their lax procedures and inadequate diligence in overseeing management. Assuming that the subjects of the report could have prevented or at least cut short the period of management's misconduct, why might the SEC have nonetheless been reluctant to officially sanction those directors?

As we will see in Section C of this Chapter, in 1990 Congress gave the SEC broad authority to issue "cease and desist" orders, a vehicle that allows the SEC to settle with the party under investigation and thereby publicize its views concerning conduct that may not warrant the imposition of a federal court-ordered injunction. Does the ready availability of this congressionally authorized sanction raise an issue as to the SEC's continued use of Section 21(a) reports?

*5. Creating Law Through the Initiation of Enforcement Actions.* The SEC has many vehicles available for creating rules and standards that become a part of the federal securities laws. One vehicle—and undoubtedly the most obvious one—is to promulgate rules and regulations under either specific or general rulemaking authorization from Congress. For example, the Commission has issued a number of rules that establish criteria for so-called limited offerings and private offerings under the Securities Act. See, e.g., Regulation D, Rules 504, 505, 506.

The SEC may also create new law through litigated proceedings, either directly through adjudicating administrative proceedings or indirectly through initiating civil enforcement actions in federal district court. In *SEC v. Chenery Corp.*, 332 U.S. 194 (1947), the Supreme Court recognized that announcing new regulatory interpretations in the course of a litigated proceeding would necessarily have a retroactive effect on respondents. But the court made clear that "the choice made between proceeding by general rule or by individual, ad hoc litigation is one that lies primarily in the informed discretion of the administrative agency." Id. at 203. What are some of the advantages and disadvantages of creating law through the SEC enforcement process? Can you identify contexts in which the SEC seems drawn to this litigation approach? Can you identify other contexts where the SEC initially created law through litigation but later clarified the law through explicit rulemaking? For elaboration of some of the advantages of "ad hoc litigation," see William R. McLucas et al., Common Sense, Flexibility, and Enforcement of the Federal Securities Laws, 51 Bus. Law. 1221, 1222-23 (1996) (emphasizing that "the SEC has tried to adopt a reasoned, common sense application of the basic requirements of the federal securities laws to new market conditions as they have evolved over the years"). For in-depth analysis of some disadvantages, see Roberta S. Karmel, Regulation by Prosecution: The Securities and Exchange Commission vs. Corporate America 96 (1982) (strongly disfavoring prosecutorial strategies for developing law, in part because "[o]ther regulated persons who will become subject to that regulatory policy do not have the opportunity to object or to comment upon the new interpretation or rule, as they would have in a rulemaking proceeding").

---

### *3. Consent Decrees and Settlements with the SEC*

An overwhelming number of SEC enforcement actions are resolved through a consensual settlement (often termed a "consent decree") between the party charged with securities law violations and the SEC. Indeed, more than 90% of the SEC's enforcement actions are resolved in this manner, though the timing of the settlement may vary. Invariably, the party's "Offer of Settlement" as well as the resulting Order will make clear that the party has consented to the imposed sanction "without either admitting or denying the allegations in the Commission's complaint" (in actions pursued in district court) or "without either admitting or denying the Commission's findings of fact and conclusions of law" (in actions pursued administratively). As we shall see in subsequent sections of this Chapter, many variables determine whether the SEC brings and settles an enforcement action in federal district court or as an administrative proceeding, including the types of remedies available in each of those fora. For example, if the settlement in an insider trading case includes the payment of a civil monetary penalty pursuant to Section 21A of the Exchange Act, that Section requires the SEC to bring and settle the enforcement action in federal district court. We shall also see that SEC settlements are often the highly preferred avenue for parties charged with securities law violations because litigating with the SEC and losing may collaterally estop a defendant from re-litigating facts and issues in related actions filed by private plaintiffs.

In many cases, even before the Commission has authorized enforcement action, the staff of the Enforcement Division negotiates the terms of an SEC settlement and presents its recommendation for enforcement to the Commission together with the party's offer of settlement as a "package" for approval and authorization. Upon giving such authorization, the Commission issues a release that announces to the public the enforcement action and its resolution. The discussions that lead to this type of early settlement must generally be initiated by defense counsel. That is, although the staff is typically responsive to the settlement overtures made by defense counsel, they are generally reluctant to initiate the settlement dialogue themselves without prior authorization from the Commission. See 17 C.F.R. § 202.5(f) (providing that "[i]n the course of the Commission's investigations, *** the staff, *with appropriate authorization*, may discuss with persons involved the disposition of such matters by consent, by settlement, or in some other manner") (emphasis added).

A significant and increasing number of settlements occur after the Commission has authorized an enforcement action but before it files a complaint in court or commences an administrative proceeding. A smaller, but still sizable, number of settlements occur after the staff files its complaint in federal district court or issues an order instituting administrative proceedings. As one might expect, only a few cases are settled on the courthouse steps.

What benefits might flow from deciding to negotiate an offer of settlement with the SEC staff before the Commission has authorized enforcement action? What are some drawbacks? Note that even in cases where an early settlement is pursued, counsel should still consider preparing of a Wells Submission. A well-drafted Wells Submission—setting out both the facts and the law from the client's perspective—will often be a useful starting point in discussions with the staff. Then, once an agreement in principle is reached with the staff, the offer of settlement, the Wells Submission (or a modified version), and the staff's recommendation memorandum can be presented to the Commission simultaneously.

The following excerpt sheds significant light on a rather basic question: why are most SEC enforcement actions settled and not litigated? The Task Force was chaired by Harvey L. Pitt almost a decade before he became SEC Chairperson.

## REPORT OF THE TASK FORCE ON SEC SETTLEMENTS PREPARED BY THE SUBCOMMITTEE ON CIVIL LITIGATION AND SEC ENFORCEMENT MATTERS OF THE FEDERAL REGULATION OF SECURITIES COMMITTEE OF THE ABA'S SECTION ON BUSINESS LAW

47 Bus. Law. 1083, 1092-1094 (1992)

*** Although settlement of pending claims is a common method of resolving disputes between private parties as well as between private parties and the government, such as the SEC, the two processes differ in a number of significant respects. In a wholly private settlement, the plaintiff generally is motivated by a desire to maximize its own individual position vis-a-vis the defendant. Any effect upon non-parties is, at best, a tangential concern. In the case of a "public" plaintiff, however, and certainly in the case of the SEC, the agency's position reflects a strong public interest dimension. Unlike private litigants, the agency is motivated by an inherent desire to affect the rights and interests of the public and of particular parties and/or interest groups who are not directly involved in the proceeding to be settled.

As a result, the respondent and the SEC generally approach a settlement with differing, although not necessarily opposing, objectives. The respondent will seek a minimal sanction pursuant to the statutory provision which suggests the lowest degree of culpability. The respondent also will seek the elimination of any inflammatory language from the release issued by the Commission upon settlement of the enforcement proceeding (the "Settlement Release" or "Release"). The Commission, on the other hand, may feel compelled to impose a harsh sanction and, moreover, to "send a message" to industry participants through a strongly worded Release which applies the relevant law to as broad a range of conduct as possible.

Both the Commission and the respondent possess considerable incentive to reach a settlement rather than become embroiled in lengthy litigation. The caseload of the SEC is enormous, and its resources are limited. Nevertheless, it is clear that the Commission will litigate the cases it deems necessary to vindicate important principles. In order to utilize its Staff efficiently, the SEC must choose with particularity those matters it will pursue, and which matters it will litigate. Thus, if the Commission chooses to take action against a company or an individual, the odds are high that the SEC views its position as strong. Litigation risks the certainty of a result (since the SEC could and does lose) while occupying the time of personnel who otherwise could be conducting other investigations. To litigate all of these cases would burden the Commission tremendously. ***

As great an incentive as the Commission has to avoid the demands of full-blown judicial litigation, the incentive of respondents to do the same is, perhaps, even greater. For the private party, litigation is extremely expensive. It creates a drain on both financial and human resources. These tangible costs of litigation, and the related, intangible costs (including the harm to the individual's and/or company's reputation with customers and others in the business environment, the ability to obtain employment or to recruit new employees and the uncertainty resulting from prolonged litigation), provide a powerful incentive to settle a pending charge.

In addition to these relatively direct costs of litigation, other, less obvious, costs exist for the respondent. Personal costs, including harm from adverse publicity resulting from having been accused of wrongdoing, should not be overlooked. In addition, regardless of the final disposition of the matter, many respondents still must coexist with the Commission. Thus, the company or individual accused of a violation may be reluctant to earn a reputation for being uncooperative by resisting, even when it does not believe it is in the wrong. Finally, although the collateral consequences of settling an action with the SEC can be significant, a negative outcome in litigation will likely open up the Commission's findings to discovery in private litigation and may even eliminate the respondent's right to deny the relevant conduct in such proceedings.

With both sides hoping for settlement, the process by which settlements are finalized becomes particularly sensitive. The divergence in the parties' marginal propensity towards settlement creates uneven bargaining power, with the Commission holding the upper hand. Short of an unacceptable sanction or inflammatory language, many respondents will consent to the violation(s) the Commission wants to allege, including an expansive enunciation of the applicable legal principles, in return for a few cosmetic changes in the settlement documents.

For these reasons, with the likelihood that the settlement documents and the SEC's public release describing the settlement will be viewed as precedent in subsequent SEC cases, and particularly with the advent of increased actions and higher consequences resulting from the Remedies Act, the language of settlement documents and the procedures in the settlement process become increasingly significant. ***

## *NOTES AND QUESTIONS*

*1. **Neither Admitting nor Denying Liability.*** The SEC's willingness to allow parties to settle without either "admitting or denying" the allegations in the complaint or administrative order clearly promotes settlements. This terminology, however, imposes significant restraints on the settling parties long into the future. Indeed, SEC rules provide "that in any civil lawsuit brought by it or in any administrative proceeding of an accusatory nature pending before it, it is important to avoid creating, or permitting to be created, an impression that a decree is being entered or a sanction imposed, when the conduct alleged did not, in fact, occur." 17 C.F.R. § 202.5(e). Thus, the SEC has announced a "policy not to permit a defendant or respondent to consent to a judgment or order that imposes a sanction while denying the allegations in the complaint or order for proceedings." Id. And enforcement staff officials have stated their view that a settling party's subsequent public denial of such allegations constitutes an abrogation of the express terms of settlement, such that the SEC "will not hesitate to seek to vacate a settled proceeding if the terms of the settlement are breached by the defendant or counsel." See William R. McLucas and John Polise, A Critical Examination of the SEC's Enforcement Process, InSights at 3 (Jan. 1994). In light of the foregoing, what advice would you give to a client about how to respond to an inquiry from the press about his or her SEC settlement?

*2. **The Settlement Documents.*** Settlements of SEC enforcement actions are matters of public record, and the actual settlement documents are relatively easy to obtain: most complaints filed in federal district court are posted on the SEC's website, and SEC orders in administrative proceedings can be accessed through the website as well as through databases on Westlaw and Lexis. Although the specific terms of the settlement generally protect the settling party from third party claims of collateral estoppel (see Section D.2.c infra), private litigants, business competitors, and members of the media can all be expected to take particular interest in such documents. In anticipation of this heavy public scrutiny, defense counsel typically reviews draft settlement documents with painstaking care and often negotiates about the precise wording with the SEC staff. Can you identify other important points or issues involving the settlement documents that defense counsel might wish to negotiate?

*3. **Undertakings.*** As we have seen, a party's settlement with the SEC may include one or more "undertakings," which are prospective, and typically remedial, acts and measures not specifically authorized by statutory provisions. (Section C of this Chapter provides extensive detail of the SEC's statutory remedies.) Both defense counsel and the SEC staff have been very creative in crafting such undertakings, which over the years have included the retention of independent consultants or committees to conduct reviews of the party's operations, the adoption of internal training programs for company personnel, and the appointment of new officers and directors or the removal of existing ones. See ABA Committee on Federal Regulation of Securities, Report of the Task Force on SEC Settlements, 47 Bus. Law. 1083, 1128-30 (1992). The Task Force specifically endorsed this vehicle for "creative relief" in SEC settlements, emphasizing that it "can offer both the Commission and the defendant the opportunity to tailor a settlement to the unique needs of the case at hand." Id. at 1127. Does this settlement practice raise concerns? What are the consequences if a settling party fails to adequately fulfill an undertaking to which he agrees?

*4. **It Ain't Over 'Til it's Over.*** As the excerpt from the Task Force Report on SEC Settlements makes clear, a powerful incentive for settling rather than litigating an enforcement action with the SEC is the desire for closure by the subject of an investigation. In light of the following provision from Rule 202.5(f) of the Commission's "Informal and Other Procedures," what advice regarding "closure" would you provide to your client before he or she makes a decision to settle an enforcement action with the SEC?

> It is the policy of the Commission [that the disposition of any investigation, civil lawsuit, or administrative proceeding] may not, expressly or impliedly, extend to any criminal charges that have been, or may be, brought against any such person or any recommendation with respect thereto. Accordingly, any person involved in an enforcement matter before the Commission who consents, or agrees to consent, to any judgment or order does so solely for the purpose of resolving the claims against him in that investigative, civil, or administrative matter and not for the purpose of resolving any criminal charges that have been, or might be, brought against him. This policy reflects the fact that neither the Commission nor its staff has the authority or responsibility for instituting, conducting, settling, or otherwise disposing of criminal proceedings. That authority and responsibility are vested in the Attorney General and representatives of the Department of Justice.

How would the SEC's enforcement program be affected if, after the settlement and public announcement of an SEC action, the DOJ initiated criminal investigations or proceedings routinely? Periodically? Seldomly? Note also that in addition to subsequent criminal proceedings, parties that settle with the SEC must also consider their status vis-a-vis the self-regulatory organizations such as the NYSE or the NASD as well as with state securities regulators and state bar or other professional organizations.

Assume that a client will consent to a settlement with the SEC only if it is part of a "global settlement" resolving all potential federal and state actions for the same underlying conduct. Is such a settlement possible? What would be some of the risks in pursuing this strategy?

*5. **Creating New Law Through Settled Proceedings.*** Concerns about the SEC's "regulation by prosecution" have already been discussed in this Chapter. Does the creation of new law through *settled* proceedings raise additional issues? Note that the ABA Task Force on SEC Settlements emphasized the likelihood that settlement documents and SEC releases will be viewed as "precedent" in subsequent cases. The Report further pointed out that SEC administrative orders in settled cases actually take the form of opinions by the Commission and contain lengthy findings of fact and conclusions of law. As such, they are particularly susceptible to being quoted in subsequent orders and judicial opinions as statements of "the law." See Task Force Report, supra, 47 Bus. Law. at 1148-49. Consider this view of one commentator, who was also a member of the Task Force:

> If a respondent elects not to settle, the SEC initiates an action almost immediately and seeks penalties even greater than those offered in the settlement. As a practical matter, respondents confront a Hobbesian choice: to accept whatever severe penalties are being imposed to conclude the matter or to face the uncertainty and expense that will result from a decision to resist. Consequently, the SEC has tremendous leverage in fashioning the final outcome of the case. Interested persons such as industry representatives play no role in shaping the content of an individual settled order even though that order establishes how the SEC expects persons similarly situated to the respondents to conduct themselves in the future.

Anne C. Flannery, Time for Change: A Re-Examination of the Settlement Policies of the Securities and Exchange Commission, 51 Wash. & Lee L. Rev. 1015, 1018 (1994). Should settled cases be viewed as precedent stating the law? Even if one is troubled by this practice, is there a feasible way to avoid it?

The SEC's use of settlements to create new law has also drawn sharp criticism from former SEC Commissioner Roberta Karmel. During her tenure, Commissioner Karmel objected particularly to the SEC's practice of issuing Section 21(a) reports that contain a subject's admission of misconduct as well as his agreement to specific undertakings:

> In my view, publication by the Commission under Section 21(a) of a negotiated statement by a person under investigation setting forth admissions and undertakings constitutes, in effect, a sanction. Moreover, the publication would not necessarily announce a Commission determination as to whether or not the facts set forth in the submitted statements constitute a violation of the securities laws. I do not believe the imposition of a sanction is proper unless the Commission makes such a determination and then announces it. It is wrong for a government prosecutor to impose sanctions based on factual admissions, as contrasted to violations of law. If the Commission is unwilling to authorize administrative or injunctive proceedings based on the facts uncovered in an enforcement investigation, it should exercise its prosecutorial discretion by simple terminating the investigation.
>
> I appreciate *** the need for administrative flexibility and the public policy favoring the settlement of cases. Nevertheless, I believe that flexibility can only go so far as a statute reasonably permits and that extra caution with respect to those limitations must be taken when the prosecutorial function is involved. The appropriate channel for enhancement of the Commission's law enforcement capability is a request to Congress for additional administrative jurisdiction, rather than the formulation of a new administrative remedy.

The Commission's Practice Relating to Reports of Investigations and Statements Submitted to the Commission Pursuant to Section 21(a) of the Securities Exchange Act of 1934, Exchange Act Release No. 15664, 17 SEC Docket 18, 20

(Mar. 21, 1979). As you read the following materials, consider whether Congress may have answered this objection when it enacted the Securities Enforcement Remedies and Penny Stock Reform Act of 1990.

## C. CIVIL REMEDIES FOR VIOLATIONS OF THE SECURITIES LAWS

"What can the SEC do to me?" "How much money will I have to pay?" "Will an action be filed in federal court?" "Can my case be resolved administratively?" "What collateral consequences result from a finding that I violated the securities laws?" "What effects can SEC sanctions have in private litigation?"

The above questions, and questions like them, have been posed to counsel by concerned clients since the SEC's creation in 1934. Yet, while the questions may not have changed, their answers certainly have, as Congress has added more and more to the SEC's arsenal of enforcement remedies.

As originally contemplated, violations of the federal securities laws were to be remedied principally through the filing of civil injunctive actions in federal district court. To this end, each of the six federal securities statutes authorized the SEC to seek injunctive relief. Any additional relief sought in court by the SEC came not from provisions in the federal securities laws but from the exercise of the considerable equitable powers possessed by federal district judges. Congress had also authorized the SEC to pursue relief administratively, but only against specific categories of regulated persons, such as broker-dealers, investment advisers, and reporting companies. Regulated persons could be subject to an array of sanctions ranging from censure, to temporary suspensions, to permanent bars from the industry (in the case of securities professionals), and orders to comply (in the case of publicly traded companies).

The modern landscape is quite different. We have already seen that 1984 was an important year, since it was then that Congress for the first time authorized the SEC to seek civil monetary penalties in insider trading cases. But an even more drastic sea change occurred six years later, when Congress passed and the President signed the "Securities Enforcement Remedies and Penny Stock Reform Act of 1990" (the "Remedies Act"). This legislation significantly enhanced the remedies previously available by authorizing the SEC to seek civil monetary penalties in federal district courts for virtually any violation of the federal securities laws and, in cases involving securities fraud, judicial orders barring individuals from service as corporate officers and directors upon a showing of "substantial unfitness" to serve. The Remedies Act also broadened considerably the SEC's administrative remedies, providing for the imposition of cease-and-desist orders against anyone found to have violated—or to have caused someone else to violate—the federal securities laws. It also allowed the SEC to impose civil monetary penalties in administrative proceedings brought against certain securities professionals, including broker-dealers, investment advisers, and their associated personnel.

Congress further expanded the SEC's enforcement arsenal in the Sarbanes-Oxley Act of 2002. First, the Act facilitated the SEC's ability to obtain officer and director bar orders in federal court by changing the former "substantial unfitness" standard to one of mere "unfitness." Congress also acceded to the SEC's request for new authority to impose bar orders in administrative proceedings without any judicial involvement. Second, in an effort to provide an even more solid foundation for remedies that had been traditionally viewed as part of a federal court's equitable authority, the Act authorized the SEC to seek and federal courts to impose "any equitable relief that may be appropriate or necessary for the benefit of investors." Third, the Act authorized court-ordered temporary asset freezes to prevent publicly traded companies under investigation by the SEC from making "extraordinary payments" to any of its directors, officers, agents, or employees. The Act also authorized courts, in an SEC injunctive action, to bar persons from participating in penny stock offerings if their alleged misconduct related to an offering of penny stock. In addition, the Act contained two significant expansions of SEC enforcement power that will be dealt with extensively in Chapter 10: authority for the SEC to censure, suspend, or deny any person the privilege of appearing or practicing before the Commission; and the establishment of a new self-regulatory body, the "Public Company Accounting Oversight Board," over which the SEC has significant control.

The chart on the next several pages sketches out this modern landscape and highlights the most important types of judicial and administrative relief available to the SEC. The cases and notes that follow provide a closer inspection of the statutory framework and demonstrate some of the complex determinations that must be made by courts and the SEC in fashioning appropriate remedies. The significant collateral consequences of SEC sanctions are explored at the end of this section.

| *Judicial Relief Available* | *Statutory Authority* | *Brief Overview* |
|---|---|---|
| Preliminary Injunctions & Temp. Restraining Orders | Exchange Act § 21(d)<br>Securities Act § 20(d)<br>Advisers Act § 209(d)<br>Inv. Company Act § 42(d) | SEC may seek a preliminary injunction or TRO against "any person" who may be violating or about to violate any provision of the federal securities laws |
| Temporary Asset Freezes | Exchange Act § 21C(c) | SEC may request court to temporarily freeze assets to prevent a publicly traded company from making "extraordinary payments" to corporate officials |
| Permanent Injunctions | Exchange Act § 21(d)<br>Securities Act § 20(d)<br>Advisers Act § 209(d)<br>Inv. Company Act § 42(d) | SEC must establish a securities law violation and demonstrate a reasonable likelihood that the defendant will engage in future violations |

| ***Judicial Relief Available*** | ***Statutory Authority*** | ***Brief Overview*** |
|---|---|---|
| Equitable Relief—Including Disgorgement | Exchange Act § 21(d)(5) | In any action instituted by the SEC under the federal securities laws, the SEC may seek and any federal court may grant "any equitable relief that may be appropriate or necessary for the benefit of investors" |
| Civil Monetary Penalties | Exchange Act § 21(d)(3)<br>Securities Act § 20(d)<br>Advisers Act § 209(e)<br>Inv. Company Act § 42(e) | SEC may seek monetary penalties against "any" person for "any" violation of the securities laws or the violation of a cease and desist order issued by the SEC; penalty must be "in the public interest," to be calculated in accordance with a three-tiered structure |
| Civil Monetary Penalties in Insider Trading Cases | Exchange Act § 21A(a) | SEC may seek penalty of up to three times the profit gained or loss avoided by any person who has engaged in illegal insider trading or tipping |
| Bar Orders Against Future Service as an Officer or Director of a Publicly Traded Company | Exchange Act § 21(d)(2)<br>Securities Act § 20(e) | Court may bar defendant from future corporate service where SEC establishes a violation of Exchange Act § 10(b) or any rule thereunder, or Securities Act § 17(a)(1), where the SEC has demonstrated "unfitness to serve" |
| Bar Orders Against Future Participation in Penny Stock Offerings | Exchange Act § 21(d)(6) | In an injunctive proceeding initiated by the SEC, court may bar defendant in penny stock offering if defendant's misconduct involved an offering of penny stock |

| *Admin. Relief Available* | *Statutory Authority* | *Brief Overview* |
|---|---|---|
| Permanent Cease-and-Desist Orders | Exchange Act § 21C(a)<br>Securities Act § 8A(a)<br>Advisers Act § 203(k)(1)<br>Inv. Company Act § 9(f)(1) | SEC, after notice and opportunity for a hearing, may publish findings and issue order against "any person" found to have violated "any provision" of the federal securities laws or to have caused any such violation. The SEC may also order the respondent to "comply" with the relevant provision and/or to take steps to ensure future compliance |
| Accounting & Disgorgement | Exchange Act § 21B(e)<br>Securities Act § 8A(e)<br>Advisers Act § 203(k)(5)<br>Inv. Company Act § 9(e) | Where a violation has been shown in any permanent cease-and-desist proceeding, or in any action in which the SEC may impose a monetary penalty, the SEC may order the retention of an accountant to calculate the profit from the unlawful activity, and may order the payment of that profit |
| Disciplinary proceedings against broker-dealers and their associated persons | Exchange Act § 15(b)(4) and § 15(b)(6) | Instituted for violations of the securities laws, or a person's "failure to reasonably supervise" another person who has violated the securities laws. Possible sanctions, after notice and the opportunity for a hearing, include censures, temporary suspensions, or permanent bars |
| Disciplinary proceedings against investment advisers and their associated persons | Advisers Act §§ 203(e) & 203(f) | Same as above |
| Disciplinary proceedings against persons associated with investment companies | Inv. Company Act § 9(b) | Instituted for "willful" violations of the securities laws. After notice and opportunity for a hearing, sanctions may include baring person from future employment or service with a registered investment company |

| *Admin. Relief Available* | *Statutory Authority* | *Brief Overview* |
|---|---|---|
| Civil Monetary Penalties Against Certain Securities Professionals | Exchange Act § 21B<br>Advisers Act § 203(i)<br>Inv. Company Act § 9(d) | SEC, after notice and hearing, may impose monetary penalties according to a three-tiered structure for "willful" violations of the securities laws by certain regulated persons including broker-dealers, investment advisers, and their associated persons. Penalties may also be imposed against such persons for "failure to reasonably supervise" |
| Temporary Cease-and-Desist Orders | Exchange Act § 21C(c)<br>Securities Act § 8A(c)<br>Advisers Act § 203(k)(3)<br>Inv. Company Act § 9(f)(3) | In extraordinary cases, SEC may issue orders ex parte against the regulated persons specified in the statutes |
| Orders to comply with filing and other reporting obligations imposed by Sections 12, 13, 14, or 15(d) of the Exchange Act | Exchange Act § 15(c)(4) | After notice and opportunity for a hearing, and a finding that one has failed to comply or caused another person's failure to comply with the relevant statutory provision, an order may be issued requiring respondent to "comply, or take steps to effect compliance with [the relevant] provision *** upon such terms and conditions and within such time as the Commission may specify" |
| Summary Suspensions of Exchange Trading or OTC Trading | Exchange Act §§ 12(k) & 15(c)(5) | Extraordinary remedy to be used for periods of limited duration |
| Stop Orders to Suspend Effectiveness of Registration Statement | Securities Act § 8(d) | SEC may issue a stop order if it finds, after notice and opportunity for a hearing, that a registration statement is false or misleading |

| *Admin. Relief Available* | *Statutory Authority* | *Brief Overview* |
|---|---|---|
| Proceedings Against Professionals Who Practice Before the Commission | Exchange Act § 4C<br>17 C.F.R. § 201.102(e) | The SEC may suspend or bar a person from future practice, if, after notice and opportunity for a hearing, it is established that the person violated the federal securities laws or that the person "engaged in unethical or improper professional conduct" |

### 1. *Judicial Remedies*

## SEC v. FIRST CITY FINANCIAL CORP.

890 F.2d 1215 (D.C. Cir. 1989)

SILBERMAN, CIRCUIT JUDGE:

Section 13(d) of the Securities Exchange Act of 1934 requires any person who has directly or indirectly obtained the beneficial ownership of more than 5 percent of any registered equity security to disclose within 10 days certain information to the issuer, the exchanges on which the security trades, and to the Securities and Exchange Commission ("SEC").[1] The SEC charged appellants, First City Financial Corporation, Ltd. ("First City") and Marc Belzberg, with deliberately evading section 13(d) and its accompanying regulations in their attempted hostile takeover of Ashland Oil Company ("Ashland") by filing the required disclosure statement after the 10 day period. The district court concluded that appellants had violated the statute; it then enjoined them from further violations of section 13(d) and ordered them to disgorge all profits derived from the violation. We think that the district court's findings were not clearly erroneous and that the injunction and disgorgement orders were lawful and appropriate remedies for appellants' violations. We therefore affirm.

I.

The SEC's case is based on its contention that on March 4, 1986 Marc Belzberg, a vice-president of First City, telephoned Alan ("Ace") Greenberg, the Chief Executive Officer of Bear Stearns, a large Wall Street brokerage firm, and asked Greenberg to buy substantial shares of Ashland for First City's account. Appellants claim that Greenberg "misunderstood" Belzberg: the latter intended only to recommend that Bear Stearns buy Ashland for its own account.

---

1. Section 13(d) of the Act provides in pertinent part:

> Any person who, after acquiring directly or indirectly the beneficial ownership of any equity security ... is directly or indirectly the beneficial owner of more than 5 per centum of such class shall, within ten days after such acquisition, send to the issuer of the security at its principal executive office, ... to each exchange where the security is traded, and file with the Commission, a statement containing ... the following information, and such additional information, as the Commission may prescribe ... as necessary or appropriate in the public interest or for the protection of investors.

First City is a diversified Canadian corporation founded and controlled by the Belzberg family and engaged in, among other things, investing in the publicly-traded securities of United States corporations. Samuel Belzberg, Marc's father, is the Chairman and Chief Executive Officer of the company. Samuel Belzberg and his two brothers own at least 70 percent of the stock of First City. Marc Belzberg managed the company's fifteen-person New York City subsidiary. The New York office apparently evaluated potential investments for the parent First City.

On February 3, 1986, a New York stockbroker, Alan D. Alan, wrote a letter to Samuel Belzberg describing Ashland as a "sensational business opportunity" and stating that "the circumstances and timing could hardly be better for the '*Sam Belzberg Effect.*' " (emphasis in original). In a second letter sent several days later, Alan presented Samuel Belzberg with additional financial information on Ashland, including its break-up valuation. After Marc Belzberg received copies of this information, he instructed two financial analysts in the New York office to begin to study Ashland and its component divisions. Armed with their favorable preliminary analysis, on February 11 Marc and Samuel Belzberg purchased 61,000 shares of Ashland stock for First City using Goldman Sachs, another large Wall Street investment banking house. Throughout the month, First City also steadily acquired large blocks of Ashland stock through Katz-Goldring, Alan's smaller brokerage firm. By February 26, First City had accumulated more than 1.3 million shares, approximately 4.8 percent of Ashland's total outstanding stock. Around the same time, Marc Belzberg discontinued purchasing Ashland stock through Katz-Goldring and began acquiring shares through Greenberg at Bear Stearns. Greenberg had enjoyed a longstanding business relationship with First City and Samuel Belzberg. Additional purchases of approximately 53,000 shares of Ashland stock through Greenberg between February 26 and 28 pushed First City's holdings to 1.4 million shares, or just over 4.9 percent of all Ashland stock.

During this period, First City employed several commonly accepted measures to maintain the secrecy of its purchases, since public knowledge that First City was acquiring a large stake in Ashland would likely drive up the price of the stock. For instance, First City bought the Ashland stock through nominee accounts established at Katz-Goldring specifically for the Ashland purchases. Confirmations of the stock purchases were mailed under the nominee name to the home of Robi Blumenstein, an officer in First City's New York subsidiary.

On Friday, February 28, First City received a favorable report from Pace Consultants, a Texas consulting firm hired to assess Ashland's petroleum-related businesses. Pace valued these segments of Ashland at $726 million. The following Monday, on March 3, Pace revised its estimate upward to $844 million. The next day, on March 4, Marc Belzberg telephoned Greenberg and engaged him in a short conversation that would be the centerpiece of this litigation. At his deposition Greenberg described the conversation in the following manner:

> [Marc Belzberg] called me and said something to the effect that—something like, "It wouldn't be a bad idea if you bought Ashland Oil here," or something like that. And I took that to mean that we were going to do another put and call arrangement that we had done in the past.... I was absolutely under the impression I was buying at their risk and I was going to do a put and call.

While Greenberg interpreted Marc Belzberg's call as an order to purchase Ashland stock on behalf of First City, Marc Belzberg later claimed that he intended only to recommend that Greenberg buy stock for himself, that is, for Bear Stearns, and that Greenberg apparently misunderstood Belzberg. Immediately after the phone call, Greenberg purchased 20,500 Ashland shares. If purchased for First City, those shares would have pushed First City's Ashland holdings above 5 percent and triggered the beginning of the 10 day filing period of section 13(d). In that event, First City would have been obliged to file a Schedule 13D disclosure statement on March 14 with the SEC.

Between March 4 and 14, Greenberg purchased an additional 330,700 shares of Ashland stock for First City costing more than $14 million. Greenberg called Marc Belzberg periodically during those ten days to discuss various securities, including Ashland. In these conversations, Greenberg reported to Marc Belzberg the increasing number of Ashland shares Greenberg had accumulated. According to Greenberg, Belzberg replied to these reports by saying, "'Fine, keep going,' or something to that effect." Greenberg also characterized Belzberg's response as "grunt[ing]" approvingly. Belzberg did not squarely deny that testimony; he testified that he, Belzberg, said "uh-huh, I think it's cheap." Over the March 15-16 weekend, Marc Belzberg met with his father and uncles in Los Angeles to discuss Ashland. On Sunday, March 16, Samuel Belzberg decided that First City should continue to buy Ashland stock. Marc Belzberg then advised his father that Greenberg had accumulated a block of Ashland shares that "First City could acquire quickly." Samuel Belzberg later testified that he had no prior knowledge of the Greenberg purchases.

Returning to New York the next morning, March 17, Marc Belzberg called Greenberg and arranged a written put and call agreement for the 330,700 shares Bear Stearns had accumulated. During that conversation, Marc Belzberg did not mention a price to Greenberg. Several days later, Marc Belzberg received the written agreement with a "strike price," or the price Bear Stearns was charging First City, of $43.96 per share. This price was well below the then market price of $45.37; thus, the total March 17 put and call price was almost $500,000 below market. Marc Belzberg apparently expressed no surprise that Bear Stearns was charging almost half a million dollars less than market value. He later testified that he believed that Bear Stearns was acting as a "Santa Claus" and that Greenberg was giving him "a bit of a break" to gain more business from First City in the future.

When Blumenstein, the officer responsible for ensuring First City's compliance with the federal securities laws, noticed the strike price, he immediately met with Marc Belzberg. Blumenstein recognized that the computation of the price reflected only the cost to Bear Stearns of acquiring the stock over the two week period before the written agreement (plus interest and commission), thus creating an inference that First City was the beneficial owner of the securities before March 17. After Blumenstein outlined the problem to Belzberg, the two men called Greenberg on a speakerphone. Belzberg later testified, "I informed Mr. Greenberg [during that conversation] that the letter [the written agreement] was incorrect, that I didn't care what the price of the stock was that he bought for himself, I didn't care what day he made the trades for himself, that I was buying stock from him as of today." Belzberg then testified that Greenberg said, "[Y]ou're right, the letter's wrong, I didn't read it before it went out, throw it out and I will send you a corrected copy." Greenberg, however, testified that Belzberg referred only to an error in the calculation of interest and not to the date on which First City acquired the stock. At the end of the conversation, Belzberg suggested he pay $44.00 per share, 4 cents per share higher than the original strike price but still $1.36, or a total of nearly $450,000, below the market price. At trial, Belzberg admitted to picking the $44 figure "out of the air" and that he "did not want the price [he] was paying to relate to [Greenberg's] cost." Between March 17 and 25, on Marc Belzberg's instructions, Greenberg bought another 890,100 Ashland shares on behalf of First City using several put and call agreements.

After these purchases, Samuel Belzberg sent a letter to Ashland's management, informing them of First City's holdings in their stock and proposing a friendly takeover of the company. Ashland rejected the offer, and on the morning of March 25 the company issued a press release disclosing that First City held between 8 and 9 percent of Ashland's stock. Almost immediately, the price of Ashland stock rose 10 percent to $52.25. The next day, on March 26, First City filed the Schedule 13D disclosure statement required by section 13(d). The statement indicated that First City had accumulated 9 percent of Ashland stock and intended to launch a tender offer for the remaining shares at $60 per share. The market price of Ashland stock then rose to $55, peaking at $55.75 per share the next day.

At Ashland's urging, the Kentucky legislature passed legislation hampering First City's ability to obtain financing for the tender offer. Soon thereafter, First City abandoned the attempted tender offer. On March 31, Ashland agreed to buy back First City's shares for $51 per share, or $134.1 million, resulting in a $15.4 million profit for First City. In return, First City agreed not to purchase any Ashland shares for the next 10 years.

Around the time of the buy-back agreement, the SEC began an informal inquiry into the timeliness of First City's Schedule 13D filing and requested that both First City and Bear Stearns provide a detailed chronology of events describing their contacts with each other relating to the Ashland purchases. After deposing Greenberg and Marc Belzberg, the SEC filed a civil complaint against Marc Belzberg and First City, alleging that they crossed the 5 percent threshold on March 4 but filed the required disclosure statement on March 26, twelve days past the section 13(d) deadline.

The district court found that Marc Belzberg and First City entered into an informal put and call agreement on March 4 and then deliberately violated the 10 day filing requirement of section 13(d). The district court, in an extensive opinion, relied primarily on First City's acknowledged ultimate purpose to take over Ashland, Greenberg's understanding of his March 4 telephone conversation with Marc Belzberg, the subsequent conversations between Belzberg and Greenberg, and the suspicious price of the March 17 written agreement. The court discounted Marc Belzberg's "misunderstanding" explanation as "self-serving, inconsistent with his later actions and [not] squar[ing] with the objective evidence." Belzberg, to put it bluntly, was not credited. The court also refused to consider Greenberg's later testimony that there might have been an "honest misunderstanding" since Greenberg reached that conclusion based only on Belzberg's suggestions and statements.

The district court permanently enjoined appellants from future violations of section 13(d) because they violated the statute deliberately, showed no "remorse," and were engaged in a business which presented opportunities to violate the statute in the future. The court also ordered appellants to disgorge approximately $2.7 million, representing their profits on the 890,000 shares of Ashland stock acquired between March 14 and 25. The court reasoned that appellants were able to purchase these shares at an artificially low price due to their failure to make the section 13(d) disclosure on March 14. Appellants *** contend that the district court abused its discretion in ordering the injunction and disgorgement remedies. ***

Appellants challenge the injunction the district court granted as unwarranted on the facts of this case. Since a district judge has wide latitude in fashioning a remedy, we will not disturb the trial court's remedial choice unless there is no reasonable basis for the decision. See *United States v. W.T. Grant Co.*, 345 U.S. 629, 634 (1953); *SEC v. Bausch & Lomb, Inc.*, 565 F.2d 8, 18 (2d Cir.1977). Appellants claim such an abuse of discretion here because the SEC did not show "that there [was] a *reasonable likelihood* of further violation[s] in the future." *SEC v. Savoy Indus.*, 587 F.2d 1149, 1168 (D.C. Cir.1978) (emphasis in original); see also *SEC v. Bausch & Lomb, Inc.*, 565 F.2d at 18.

Under our *Savoy Industries* test, the district judge should consider whether a defendant's violation was isolated or part of a pattern, whether the violation was flagrant and deliberate or merely technical in nature, and whether the defendant's business will present opportunities to violate the law in the future. See *Savoy Indus.*, 587 F.2d at 1168; *Commonwealth Chem.*, 574 F.2d at 100; *SEC v. National Student Mktg.*, 457 F.Supp. 682, 715-16 (D.D.C. 1978). No single factor is determinative; instead, the district court should determine the propensity for future violations based on the totality of circumstances. See *SEC v. Youmans,* 729 F.2d 413, 415 (6th Cir. 1984); *SEC v. Bausch & Lomb, Inc.,* 565 F.2d at 18.

Appellants raise two troubling points about the injunction order. First, in explaining the injunction the district court said, "[T]here is also a public perception that defendants have been recent and active participants in heated takeover battles and unfriendly mergers." Justifying an injunction, even in part, in terms of propitiating public sentiment, is objectionable as a matter of law. Second, the district court misconstrued our precedents in suggesting that another basis for justifying the injunction was appellants' "lack of remorse." See *SEC v. Savoy Indus.*, 587 F.2d 1149, 1168 (D.C. Cir. 1978). The district court compared Belzberg's "unrepentant demeanor" with defendants in other cases who "express[ ] immediate and vociferous remorse for [their] errors." The government's appellate brief compounds this mistake by urging us to consider, as further evidence of lack of remorse, appellants' *counsel's* arguments and appellants' willingness to pursue this case on appeal. The securities laws do not require defendants to behave like Uriah Heep in order to avoid injunctions. They are not to be punished because they vigorously contest the government's accusations. We think "lack of remorse" is relevant only where defendants have previously violated court orders, see *SEC v. Koenig,* 469 F.2d 198, 202 (2d Cir.

1972), or otherwise indicate that they did not feel bound by the law, see *Savoy Indus.*, 587 F.2d at 1168. As such, it is really only another indication as to whether it is "reasonably likely" that future violations will occur in the absence of an injunction.

The district court, then, appeared to rely in part on two inappropriate factors to support the injunction. Typically we would remand to the district court under these circumstances for reconsideration of the injunction. We do not do so here, however, because we have made an independent determination that the injunction is appropriate, i.e. a reasonable likelihood of future violations exist. Appellants do not even deny that their business will offer many opportunities in the future to violate the securities laws. Instead, appellants quarrel primarily with the district court's determination that Belzberg *deliberately* violated section 13(d). As our prior discussion—particularly our appraisal of Belzberg's testimony—should make clear, we think the district court's determination as to Belzberg's state of mind is not subject to serious challenge. That this is First City's first section 13(d) violation is no bar to the issuance of an injunction. See *SEC v. National Student Mktg. Corp.*, 360 F.Supp. 284, 299 (D.D.C. 1973) (stating that a single violation may justify an injunction if committed willfully and knowingly); see also *SEC v. Bausch & Lomb, Inc.*, 565 F.2d 8, 18 (2d Cir. 1977) (approving injunctions for single acts in some circumstances). ***

The district court directed disgorgement of profits, and appellants' challenge to this aspect of the order presents an issue of first impression—whether federal courts have the authority to employ that remedy with respect to section 13(d) violations and whether it is appropriate in this sort of case. Appellants also claim that the amount ordered disgorged is excessive. We reject both arguments and affirm the district court's order on these issues as well.

Appellants, by claiming that Congress did not explicitly authorize a monetary remedy for section 13(d) violations, misapprehend the source of the court's authority. Disgorgement is an equitable remedy designed to deprive a wrongdoer of his unjust enrichment and to deter others from violating the securities laws. See *SEC v. Tome*, 833 F.2d 1086, 1096 (2d Cir. 1987); *SEC v. Blavin*, 760 F.2d 706, 713 (6th Cir. 1985); *SEC v. Texas Gulf Sulphur Co.*, 446 F.2d 1301, 1307 (2d Cir. 1971). "Unless otherwise provided by statute, all the inherent equitable powers of the District Court are available for the proper and complete exercise of that jurisdiction." *Porter v. Warner Holding Co.*, 328 U.S. 395, 398 (1946); see also *Mitchell v. Robert DeMario Jewelry, Inc.*, 361 U.S. 288, 291-92 (1960). We see no indication in the language or the legislative history of the 1934 Act that even implies a restriction on the equitable remedies of the district courts. See *Mills v. Electric Auto-Lite Co.*, 396 U.S. 375, 391 (1970). Disgorgement, then, is available simply because the relevant provisions of the Securities Exchange Act of 1934, sections 21(d) and (e), vest jurisdiction in the federal courts.

Indeed, appellants concede that disgorgement is rather routinely ordered for insider trading violations despite a similar lack of specific authorizations for that remedy under the securities law. But they seek to distinguish section 13(d) violations as a "technical" transgression of reporting rules that really do not cause injury. In contrast, they argue, insider trading under modern theory is tantamount to theft; an actual injury is inflicted on the individual or institution entitled to confidentiality. Section 13(d), however, is the pivot of the entire Williams Act regulation of tender offers. To be sure, some may doubt the usefulness of that statute generally or the section 13(d) requirement specifically, but it is hardly up to the judiciary to second-guess the wisdom of Congress' approach to regulating takeovers. Suffice it for us to note that section 13(d) is a crucial requirement in the congressional scheme, and a violator, it is legislatively assumed, improperly benefits by purchasing stocks at an artificially low price because of a breach of the duty Congress imposed to disclose his investment position. The disclosure of that position—a holding in excess of 5 percent of another company's stock—suggests to the rest of the market a likely takeover and therefore may increase the price of the stock. Appellants circumvented that scheme, and the theory of the statute, by which we are bound, is that the circumventions caused injury to other market participants who sold stock without knowledge of First City's holdings. We therefore see no relevant distinction between disgorgement of inside trading profits and disgorgement of post-section 13(d) violation profits.

There remains, of course, the question of how the court measures those illegal profits. Appellants vigorously dispute the $2.7 million figure that the district court arrived at by simply calculating all of the profits First City realized (in its eventual sale back to Ashland) on the 890,000 shares First City purchased between March 14 and 25. The SEC's claim to disgorgement, which the district court accepted, is predicated on the assumption that had First City made its section 13(d) disclosure on March 14, at the end of the statutory 10 day period, the stock it purchased during the March 14-25 period would have been purchased in a quite different and presumably more expensive market. That hypothetical market would have been affected by the disclosure that the Belzbergs had taken a greater than 5 percent stake in Ashland and would soon propose a tender offer.

Since disgorgement primarily serves to prevent unjust enrichment, the court may exercise its equitable power only over property causally related to the wrongdoing. The remedy may well be a key to the SEC's efforts to deter others from violating the securities laws, but disgorgement may not be used punitively. See *SEC v. Blatt*, 583 F.2d 1325, 1335 (5th Cir. 1978); *SEC v. Manor Nursing Centers, Inc.*, 458 F.2d 1082, 1104 (2d Cir. 1972). Therefore, the SEC generally must distinguish between legally and illegally obtained profits. Appellants assert that the hypothetical market between March 14-25 that the SEC urged and the district court accepted was simplistic, quite unrealistic, and so *de facto* punitive. It did not take into account other variables—besides the section 13(d) disclosure—which caused the post-March 25 price of the stock to rise above that which prevailed during the March 14-25 period. At trial appellants' expert witness testified that four independent factors combined to increase the stock price to the level it reached on March 25 and that these factors were not present on March 14, when the defendants should have disclosed. He identified these factors as: (1) the Belzbergs by the 25th held between 8 and 9 percent of Ashland, (2) the Belzbergs had prior to the 25th communicated to Ashland the size of their holdings, (3) Ashland publicly disclosed the Belzbergs' position on the 25th before the 13(d) disclosure, and (4) by the 25th, rumors swirled of an imminent takeover bid at $55 per share. In an attempt to hypothesize how the Belzbergs would have acted—had they disclosed on March 14—and how the market would have responded to those actions, the witness presented three alternative scenarios that in his view more accurately measured the impact of the nondisclosure and which yielded disgorgement figures of zero, $496,050, and $864,588. Perhaps not surprisingly, appellants' witness testified that the most realistic scenario required no disgorgement at all.[23]

If exact information were obtainable at negligible cost, we would not hesitate to impose upon the government a strict burden to produce that data to measure the precise amount of the ill-gotten gains. Unfortunately, we encounter imprecision and imperfect information. Despite sophisticated econometric modelling, predicting stock market responses to alternative variables is, as the district court found, at best speculative. Rules for calculating disgorgement must recognize that separating legal from illegal profits exactly may at times be a near-impossible task. See, e.g., *Elkind v. Liggett & Myers, Inc.,* 635 F.2d 156, 171 (2d Cir.1980).

Accordingly, disgorgement need only be a reasonable approximation of profits causally connected to the violation. ***

Although the SEC bears the ultimate burden of persuasion that its disgorgement figure reasonably approximates the amount of unjust enrichment, we believe the government's showing of appellants' actual profits on the tainted transactions at least presumptively satisfied that burden. Appellants, to whom the burden of going forward shifted, were then obliged clearly to demonstrate that the disgorgement figure was not a reasonable approximation. Defendants in such cases may make such a showing, for instance, by pointing to intervening events from the time of the violation. In *SEC v. MacDonald,* 699 F.2d 47 (1st Cir.1983) (en banc), the First Circuit reversed a district court order requiring the defendant to disgorge all profits from an illegal insider trade when the defendant had held on to the stock for more than a year. The court restricted the amount to a figure based on the price of the stock "a reasonable time after public dissemination of the inside information." Id. at 55. Similarly, the Second Circuit in *SEC v. Manor Nursing Centers, Inc.,* 458 F.2d 1082 (2d Cir.1972), refused to extend the disgorgement remedy to income subsequently earned on the initial illegal profits. In those cases, the defendant demonstrated a clear break in or considerable attenuation of the causal connection between the illegality and the ultimate profits.

Here, appellants took a different approach using a sophisticated expert witness. As we noted, they maintained that the post-March 25 price was

---

23. The expert witness concluded that disgorgement was unnecessary because if First City had disclosed on March 14, as the SEC claims it should have, we should assume that the 890,000 shares actually bought in the March 17-25 period (the 10-day window in Belzberg's view) would have been purchased in the lawful March 4-14 10-day window. Since Ashland prices were lower in the March 4-14 period than during March 17-25, the witness believed that no disgorgement was appropriate. This analysis, however, does not consider the impact of buying these 890,000 shares within this 10-day period—in addition to the 330,000 shares the Belzbergs actually purchased then—which presumably would have itself pushed up the price.

influenced by four other independent factors besides the belated section 13(d) disclosure, so even if First City had disclosed on March 14, the price would not have run up then to the extent it did after March 25. The difficulty we see with appellants' argument is that none of the four factors are independent of the section 13(d) disclosure determination. Thus, although by March 25 First City had accumulated 8-9 percent of Ashland, whereas on March 14 it had slightly over 5 percent (and although the market might react more strongly to the higher figure), we do not see why we should not assume that First City would have acquired 8-9 percent before March 14—if they knew they had to disclose on the earlier date. Second, it seems likely that First City would have notified Ashland's management on March 13 if they had planned to disclose on the next day, just as they did on March 25. Third, Ashland's premature disclosure of First City's holdings (prior to the section 13(d) notice) would likely have also occurred. And finally, the March 25 market takeover rumors were probably associated with all of the above activity, which is inextricably linked with the impending section 13(d) notice. We therefore agree with the district court that appellants' efforts to hypothesize both the takeover efforts of a First City that complied with section 13(d) and the market reaction to that are impossibly speculative.

Placing the burden on the defendants of rebutting the SEC's showing of actual profits, we recognize, may result, as it has in the insider trader context, in actual profits becoming the typical disgorgement measure. But the line between restitution and penalty is unfortunately blurred, and the risk of uncertainty should fall on the wrongdoer whose illegal conduct created that uncertainty. See *SEC v. MacDonald,* 699 F.2d 47, 55 (1st Cir. 1983) (en banc); *Elkind v. Liggett & Myers, Inc.,* 635 F.2d 156, 171 (2d Cir. 1980).

***We [therefore] uphold the permanent injunction and disgorgement orders. Accordingly, the judgment of the district court is affirmed.

---

## SEC v. PATEL

61 F.3d 137 (2d Cir. 1995)

MINER, CIRCUIT JUDGE:

Defendant-appellant Ratilal K. Patel appeals from a judgment entered in the United States District Court for the Southern District of New York (Patterson, J.) in an action brought against him by plaintiff-appellee Securities and Exchange Commission ("SEC") for violations of federal securities laws. The judgment permanently enjoins Patel from future violations, orders him to disgorge $453,203 in illegal profits plus prejudgment interest and bars him from serving as an officer or director of any publicly traded company. On appeal, Patel contends *** that the district court considered improper factors in barring him permanently from serving as an officer or director of any publicly traded company.

### BACKGROUND

The parties have no dispute regarding the factual background of this case. Patel was a founder, director and senior vice president for research and development of Par Pharmaceutical, Inc. ("Par"), a manufacturer of generic drugs. In November of 1987, Par submitted to the Food and Drug Administration ("FDA") an Abbreviated New Drug Application ("the Application") for a generic version of the drug known as Maxzide, which is used for the treatment of hypertension. The Application falsely represented that Par's generic Maxzide, of which sodium bicarbonate was an ingredient, had been tested in bioequivalency studies required by the FDA. This misrepresentation came in the form of a certificate of analysis for sodium bicarbonate. The certificate was backdated to conceal the fact that the bioequivalency studies were performed with a formulation of Maxzide that did not contain the sodium bicarbonate. Patel knew that the Application was false and, in February and March of 1988, sold 75,000 shares of common stock in Par. The average sale price was approximately $21.00 per share, and Patel realized a total of $1,576,358. It was not until July 24, 1989 that Par publicly disclosed that it was recalling its Maxzide tablets.

Par had experienced a number of adverse events before it revealed its problems with Maxzide. In July of 1988, a congressional subcommittee (the Dingell Subcommittee), which had begun an investigation into the generic pharmaceutical industry, focused on Par. A subcommittee subpoena for Par records was served on July 5, 1988, and the press later reported that Par was involved in the Dingell Subcommittee's inquiry into allegations of bribes and payoffs to FDA officials. It seems certain that this information had a negative impact on the price of Par's stock. Another, more serious, decline in the price of the stock occurred in October of 1988, following Par's announcement that it was a target of a grand jury investigation into various improprieties, including bribery, in the generic drug industry.

In April of 1989, the press reported that Ashok Patel, another Senior Vice President of Par, had resigned his position with Par and had agreed to plead guilty to unspecified charges. Later that month, the press reported the indictment of two FDA officials on bribery charges, in an article that referred to Par, Ashok Patel and Dilip Shah. Shah later resigned from the Board of Directors of a Par subsidiary known as Quad Pharmaceuticals, Inc. In May of 1989, the Dingell Subcommittee held public hearings in connection with its investigation into the generic drug approval process. The following month, there were negative press reports on the relationship between FDA officials and Ashok Patel and Dilip Shah. Thereafter, on July 11, it was reported that a third FDA employee had been criminally charged and, on July 17, it was reported that Par had agreed to plead guilty to a charge of providing an unlawful gratuity to an FDA employee. As was to be expected, all the negative news resulted in depressions in the price of Par stock.

When Par announced on July 24, 1989 that it was recalling its Maxzide product and suspending all shipments of the drug, it also announced that it had intentionally furnished a false report to the FDA during a recent inspection; that Ratilal Patel was taking a leave of absence from the company; that its vice president for regulatory affairs and its executive vice-president were taking leaves of absence from the Board of Directors; and that the company was postponing its annual shareholders' meeting in light of the ongoing investigation. Following that announcement, the price of Par stock closed on July 24 at $8.375 per share, down $1.625 from the $10 closing price on Friday, July 21, the previous trading day. On July 25, the next trading day, the stock closed at $7.125 per share. The total decline from the July 21 closing price was $2.875 or 28.75%. On July 26, 1989, the third day after the disclosure, Par stock rallied from $7.125 to close at $7.625.

On September 8, 1989, Patel resigned as a director and senior vice president of Par and as a director of its subsidiary, Quad Pharmaceuticals, Inc. In March of 1992, he settled a securities fraud class action claim with the payment of 500,000 shares of Par stock valued at approximately $3,000,000. In January of 1993, Patel pled guilty to conspiracy to defraud the FDA in connection with the generic Maxzide Application and thereafter was sentenced to a 27-month term of imprisonment, two years of supervised release and a $25,000 fine.

The enforcement action giving rise to this appeal was commenced by the filing of a complaint by the SEC on July 7, 1993. In the complaint, the SEC alleged violations by Patel of various antifraud provisions of the federal securities laws: Section 17(a) of the Securities Act of 1933, Section 10(b) of the Securities Exchange Act of 1934, and Rule 10b-5 promulgated thereunder. Injunctive relief was sought, along with disgorgement of "avoided losses" plus prejudgment interest, assessment of civil penalties under the provisions of the Insider Trading Sanctions Act of 1984, [Exchange Act Section 21A], and an order barring Patel from ever serving as an officer or director of a publicly traded company. Following a motion for summary judgment by the SEC, Patel conceded that he had violated the antifraud provisions and agreed that a permanent injunction against future violations would be appropriate. The district court denied the relief sought under the Insider Trading Sanctions Act but ordered the disgorgement of Patel's avoided losses plus interest in accordance with the computation suggested by the SEC. The district court also imposed a lifetime bar against Patel's service as an officer or director of any publicly traded company. As he did in the district court, Patel here challenges *** the permanent employment ban imposed upon him.

DISCUSSION

****Injunction Against Service as Officer and Director*

For violations of the antifraud provisions of the securities laws,

> the court may prohibit, conditionally or unconditionally, and permanently or for such period of time as it shall determine, any person who violated [the applicable provisions] from acting as an officer or director [of a publicly traded company] if the person's conduct demonstrates substantial unfitness to serve as an officer or director....

[Securities Act Section 20(e); Exchange Act Section 21(d)(2)].

In permanently enjoining Patel from serving as an officer or director of any publicly traded company at the behest of the SEC, the district court necessarily determined that Patel was substantially unfit to hold such positions. The court identified six factors that it considered in resolving the issue of substantial unfitness: "(1) the 'egregiousness' of the underlying securities law violation; (2) the defendant's 'repeat offender' status; (3) the defendant's 'role' or position when he engaged in the fraud; (4) the defendant's degree of scienter; (5)

the defendant's economic stake in the violation; and (6) the likelihood that misconduct will recur." These factors were suggested in a law review article by Jayne W. Barnard entitled When is a Corporate Executive "Substantially Unfit to Serve"?, 70 N.C.L.Rev. 1489, 1492-93 (1992).

Applying the factors suggested by Professor Barnard, the district court found: that Patel's violations were not egregious in comparison with those of others and in view of the size of the loss avoided; that Patel was a first-time offender; that in his position as officer and director of Par, Patel allowed the false Application to be submitted and obstructed the FDA investigation of the Application by providing a "switched sample" of Maxzide to an FDA inspector; that Patel "showed some scienter in his actions, although he did not engage in clandestine trading"; that he was the sole economic beneficiary of his insider trading; and that, because he was a founder of Par and abused his position as officer and director, "the likelihood of future misconduct is sufficient to warrant the imposition of the injunctive relief requested."

Patel contends that the district court improperly applied the factors it considered "by 'mixing' Patel's 'insider trading' with Par's submission of the false [application] to the FDA." He further contends that, although his "conduct in the Maxzide affair gave rise to his 'insider' knowledge, it was not part of any 'scheme' to commit the securities law violation[s], and is not relevant to an analysis of his conduct" in respect of the violations. Patel claims that the district court's application of the six-factor test results in an almost even "split" between those factors that cut in his favor and those factors that cut against him. Moreover, Patel thinks that the district court should have taken into account the fact that criminal sanctions were imposed upon him and that he voluntarily settled the class action suit brought against him.

The district court properly considered Patel's involvement in the "Maxzide affair" as part and parcel of his conduct in the securities law violations. His deception of the FDA, although perhaps not originally designed to obtain profits or avoid losses in the sale of his stock, set in motion the scheme that culminated in his breach of fiduciary duties and in the resultant detriment to investors. Also, the district court properly took into account the six factors that it identified in evaluating substantial unfitness. These factors are useful in making the unfitness assessment, although we do not mean to say that they are the only factors that may be taken into account or even that it is necessary to apply all these factors in every case. A district court should be afforded substantial discretion in deciding whether to impose a bar to employment in a publicly traded company.

We do find a problem in this case, however, with the district court's finding regarding the likelihood of future misconduct, which is always an important element in deciding whether the substantial unfitness found justifies the imposition of a lifetime ban. The only findings that the district court made in this regard were that "Patel was a founder of Par and used his position as an officer and director to engage in misconduct." This is merely a general statement of events and can in no way justify the prediction that future misconduct will occur.

Moreover, we think that it was error for the district court to say that the likelihood of future misconduct based on the foregoing statement "is sufficient to warrant the imposition of the injunctive relief requested." The loss of livelihood and the stigma attached to permanent exclusion from the corporate suite certainly requires more. In a case in which we approved lifetime banishment as a common law remedy, we noted that the defendants "had committed securities law violations with a 'high degree of scienter' and that their past securities law violations and lack of assurances against future violations demonstrated that such violations were likely to continue." [*SEC v.*] *Posner*, 16 F.3d [520, 521-22 (2d Cir. 1994)]. Although it is not essential for a lifetime ban that there be past violations, we think that it is essential, in the absence of such violations, that a district court articulate the factual basis for a finding of the likelihood of recurrence.

Finally, we take note of the fact that the governing statute provides that a bar on service as an officer or director that is based on substantial unfitness may be imposed "conditionally or unconditionally" and "permanently or for such period of time as [the court] shall determine." We take these provisions to suggest that, before imposing a permanent bar, the court should consider whether a conditional bar (e.g., a bar limited to a particular industry) and/or a bar limited in time (e.g., a bar of five years) might be sufficient, especially where there is no prior history of unfitness. In this connection, we do not think that it would be improper for the district court to take into account any prior punishment that may have been imposed in a criminal proceeding. If the district court decides that a conditional ban or a ban limited in time is not warranted, it should give reasons why a lifetime injunction is imposed.

CONCLUSION

We affirm the judgment to the extent that it enjoins future securities law violations and orders the disgorgement of avoided losses. We reverse so much of the judgment as imposes a lifetime injunction on Patel's service as an officer or director of any publicly traded company, and we remand for further consideration of the issue in accordance with the foregoing.

### *NOTES AND QUESTIONS*

*1. Injunctions—"Mild Prophylactic" or "Drastic Remedy?"* Although viewed at one time as a "mild prophylactic," *SEC v. Capital Gains Research Bureau, Inc.*, 375 U.S. 180, 193 (1963), a court-ordered injunction against future securities law violations is today widely recognized to be a rather "drastic remedy." *Aaron v. SEC*, 446 U.S. 680, 703 (1980) (Burger, C.J., concurring). What is it about an injunction that makes it more than a mere slap on the wrist? Aren't defendants obliged to obey the law in the future even in the absence of a court-ordered injunction?

*2. Injunctions—The Operative Standard.* Because the federal securities laws provide the SEC with a statutory basis for obtaining permanent injunctive relief, see, e.g., Exchange Act Section 21(d), the SEC does not have to satisfy the traditional test for equitable relief, which generally requires the plaintiff to plead and prove irreparable injury and inadequacy of remedies at law. Instead, courts may grant "permanent or temporary injunction[s] or restraining order[s]" upon "a proper showing." According to *First Financial*, what evidence must the SEC put forth to make this "proper showing?" In cases where the SEC establishes an underlying violation of the securities laws, how likely is it that courts will refuse to enjoin a defendant from future violations? For examples of such instances, see *SEC v. Ginsburg*, 2002 WL 1835810 at *4-*6 (S.D. Fla. 2002) (finding defendant liable for insider trading in violation of Rule 10b-5 and ordering disgorgement of profits and penalty of $1 million but denying injunction because defendant "did not engage in egregious or recurrent behavior"); *SEC v. Pros Int'l, Inc.*, 994 F.2d 767 (10th Cir. 1993) (holding that the lower court did not abuse its discretion in denying motion for injunction, since there was no showing that the defendant-accountant intended to defraud investors, accountant did not profit from transaction, and it was unlikely that future violations of securities laws would occur). See also Daniel J. Morrissey, SEC Injunctions, 68 Tenn. L. Rev. 427, 467-470 (2001); Daniel F. Levy, The Impact of the Remedies Act on the SEC's Ability to Obtain Injunctive Relief, 44 Am. U. L. Rev. 645, 656-69 (1994).

***3. Preliminary Injunctions, Temporary Restraining Orders, and Temporary Asset Freezes.*** In addition to permanent relief, Section 21(d) of the Exchange Act authorizes the SEC to seek both preliminary injunctions and temporary restraining orders. In what types of cases would the SEC be likely to seek these remedies? What standards should govern their issuance?

In *SEC v. Unifund SAL*, 910 F.2d 1028 (2d Cir. 1990), the Second Circuit held that the SEC's requests for preliminary or temporary relief must be judged against a "likelihood of success" standard. However, pointing to the "very serious consequences" that may flow from such relief, the court emphasized that district judges, exercising their equitable discretion, should "bear in mind the nature of the preliminary relief the Commission is seeking, and should require a more substantial showing of likelihood of success, both as to violation and risk of recurrence, whenever the relief sought is more than preservation of the status quo." Id. at 1039. In applying this standard to the relief ordered by the lower court in a case involving allegations of insider trading, the Second Circuit affirmed (with modifications) a temporary asset freeze, which was imposed to preserve the SEC's "opportunity to collect funds that may be yet ordered disgorged." Id. at 1041. But the Second Circuit reversed the lower court's order of a preliminary injunction, finding that the SEC had not produced sufficient evidence to warrant a remedy that "accomplishes significantly more than preserving the status quo." Id. at 1040. Among other deficiencies, the court noted that the SEC had yet to establish the identity of the tipper, and had yet to demonstrate that the defendants had breached a fiduciary duty in trading on the material nonpublic information. Id.

New authority for temporary asset freezes was among the remedies made available to the SEC in the Sarbanes-Oxley Act of 2002. Specifically, the Act added a new Section 21C(c)(3)(A)(i) to the Exchange Act:

> Whenever, during the course of a lawful investigation involving possible violations of the Federal securities laws by an issuer of publicly traded securities or any of its directors, officers, partners, controlling persons, agents, or employees, it shall appear to the Commission that it is likely that the issuer will make extraordinary payments (whether compensation or otherwise) to any of the foregoing persons, the Commission may petition a Federal district court

> for a temporary order requiring the issuer to escrow, subject to court supervision, those payments in an interest-bearing account for 45 days.

Without the SEC's initiation of an enforcement proceeding charging a violation of the federal securities laws, the order may be extended only up to an additional 45 days, provided the SEC establishes "good cause." Exchange Act Section 21C(c)(3)(A)(iv). The order, however, may continue subject to court approval if a violation of the federal securities laws is charged, though an issuer or other affected person has the right to petition the court for review. See Exchange Act Section 21C(c)(3)(B)(i).

Consider the ways in which this new provision authorizing temporary asset freezes is actually more limiting than the provision for temporary restraining orders in Section 21(d). What constraints, if any, does this new authority place on the general equitable powers of federal courts (particularly as now bolstered by new Section 21(d)(5), which authorizes federal courts to grant "any equitable relief that may be appropriate or necessary for the benefit of investors")? Would you expect to see the SEC make significant use of its specific authority to seek temporary asset freezes in instances where it appears likely that an issuer may make extraordinary payments to corporate officials?

*4. **The Permanence of Permanent Injunctions.*** Unless specifically limited in duration (a relatively rare occurrence), court-ordered injunctions against future violations of the federal securities laws are permanent. That said, SEC injunctions may be modified or even dissolved by a subsequent court on a defendant's petition, though the granting of such relief is also a rare occurrence. Indeed, both the SEC and courts routinely point to *United States v. Swift & Co.*, 286 U.S. 106, 119 (1932), which held that the appropriate standard for vacating an injunction is "[n]othing less than a clear showing of grievous wrong evoked by new and unforeseen conditions." See, e.g., *SEC v. Blinder, Robinson & Co.*, 855 F.2d 677, 680 (10th Cir. 1988) (confirming that *Swift* articulates the applicable standard and emphasizing the necessity of clear proof of "unforeseen conditions" flowing from the injunction). Yet there have been occasions when a court's power "to do equity" resulted in modification or dissolution. See, e.g., *SEC v. Warren*, 583 F.2d 115, 121-22 (3d Cir. 1978) (dissolving injunction imposed five years earlier pursuant to a consent decree, finding that the defendant's unlawful conduct was "a single isolated offense in an esoteric area of the law *** and never again renewed," and which caused him "personal humiliation and business embarrassment"). As a matter of policy, would you favor a change in the law to provide for automatic dissolution of SEC injunctions after a certain number of years? After five years? Ten years? Twenty? For additional discussion and suggested standards, see Marc I. Steinberg, SEC and Other Permanent Injunctions—Standards for Their Imposition, Modification, and Dissolution, 66 Cornell L. Rev. 27 (1980).

*5. **Officer and Director Bars.*** Section 20(e) of the Securities Act and Section 21(d)(2) of the Exchange Act specifically identify the statutory provisions that, if violated, may be remedied through a court order barring a person from future service as an officer or director of a publicly traded company. What are these provisions and why did Congress impose this limitation? As we saw in *Patel*, Congress originally conditioned the availability of this remedy on the SEC's showing of "a substantial unfitness to serve." Did the factors enumerated by the *Patel* court (prompted by Professor Barnard's law review article) provide sufficient standards? How would you have decided Patel's appeal based on these (or other) factors?

Note the recent amendments to Securities Act Section 20(e) and Exchange Act Section 21(d)(2), which now authorize federal courts to issue officer and director bar orders upon the lesser showing of a person's "unfitness" to serve. The legislative history of the Sarbanes-Oxley Act reflects congressional agreement with the SEC's argument that "the 'substantial unfitness' standard for imposing bars [was] inordinately high, causing courts to refrain from imposing bars even in cases of egregious misconduct." Sen. Rep. 107-205, at 27 (July 3, 2002). Do these amendments entail a congressional judgment that *Patel* was wrongly decided? Was Congress's decision to do away with the "substantial unfitness" standard a wise one? Should Professor Barnard's six-factor test continue to play a role in a judge's analysis of whether to order a bar under the new standard of "unfitness?"

Note also that prior to the passage of the Remedies Act, courts on a number of occasions had issued consent decrees enjoining defendants from future corporate service. Such equitable relief was also ordered in litigated proceedings, though less frequently. See, e.g., *SEC v. Posner*, 16 F.3d 520 (2d Cir. 1994) (holding that order enjoining officers from acting as officers or directors of any publicly traded company was within the district court's well-established equitable power). Do Section 20(e) of the Securities Act and Section 21(d)(2) of the Exchange Act merely provide statutory authorization for a remedy that could otherwise be ordered through the exercise of a federal court's equitable powers?

The officer and director bar remedy was in fact one of the more controversial aspects of the Remedies Act, in part because it called into question the interplay between the federal securities laws and state corporate law. Consider, for example, how this remedy impacts the corporate shareholder franchise and who, in fact, should determine the minimum qualifications for director and officer service. On this point, in his testimony before Congress, then-SEC Chairperson Richard Breeden stated the following:

> The Commission recognizes that corporate governance issues are generally regulated by state law. The purpose of the corporate bar provisions is not to establish federal standards governing the qualifications of corporate officers or directors. Rather, the purpose of this provision is to protect public investors from persons who have already demonstrated a propensity to abuse a position of corporate trust. Where a person's conduct is such that the disclosure provisions of the federal securities laws, even when supplemented by the coercive power of a federal court injunction, are insufficient to protect investors from further loss, the availability of such a provision is necessary. ***

Written Testimony of Chairperson Richard C. Breeden, Securities and Exchange Commission, Before the Subcomm. on Securities of the Comm. on Banking, Housing and Urban Affairs Concerning S. 647, The "Securities Law Enforcement Remedies Act of 1989," at 63 (Feb. 1, 1990). Do you agree? Have the massive financial frauds by publicly traded companies such as Enron and WorldCom created a need for even greater use of the bar order remedy? Congress apparently thought so, since it granted the SEC the new authority to issue such bar orders in administrative proceedings. See Section 1105 of the Sarbanes-Oxley Act (adding a new Section 8A(f) to the Securities Act and a new Section 21C(f) to the Exchange Act). Was this a wise decision?

*6. Civil Monetary Penalties.* The SEC's ability to seek monetary penalties in virtually any federal court case involving virtually any violation of the federal securities laws was another controversial aspect of the Remedies Act. In enacting these penalty provisions, Congress sought to achieve the clear goal of deterring future securities law violations:

> The Committee believes that the money penalties proposed in this legislation are needed to provide financial disincentives to securities law violations other than insider trading*** Absent a criminal prosecution or a private suit for damages *** even the defendant who makes a deliberate decision to violate the law and causes significant harm to the markets does not risk any monetary sanction more severe than an order of disgorgement. Disgorgement merely requires the return of wrongfully obtained profits; it does not result in any actual economic penalty or act as a financial disincentive to engage in securities fraud. A violator who avoids detection is able to keep the profits resulting from illicit activities. Currently, even a violator who is caught is required merely to give back his gains with interest, leaving him no worse off financially than if he had not violated the law. The Committee therefore concluded that authority to seek or impose substantial money penalties, in addition to the disgorgement of profits, is necessary for the deterrence of securities law violations that otherwise may provide great financial returns to the violator.

H.R. Rep. No. 101-616, reprinted in 1990 U.S.C.C.A.N. 1379, 1384-86. Did the Committee make a strong case for this remedy? Can you identify the arguments that were raised by those in opposition? Is it appropriate for the SEC to seek sanctions that deter future violations through a form of punishment? See Mary M. Cheh, Constitutional Limits on Using Civil Remedies to Achieve Criminal Law Objectives: Understanding and Transcending the Criminal-Civil Law Distinction, 42 Hastings L.J. 1325, 1355 (1991) (stating that "when it comes to deterrence, civil and criminal remedies are essentially indistinguishable and interchangeable"). See also Kenneth Mann, Punitive Civil Sanctions: The Middleground Between Criminal and Civil Law, 101 Yale L.J. 1795, 1803-10 (1992). For specific discussion and analysis as to how the SEC has used the monetary penalty remedy, see Arthur B. Laby & W. Hardy Callcott, Patterns of SEC Enforcement Under the 1990 Remedies Act: Civil Monetary Penalties, 58 Alb. L. Rev. 5 (1994).

Had the defendants in the *First Financial* case been "eligible" for a civil monetary penalty, would you expect the SEC to have sought and a court to have imposed such a penalty? Note that the Remedies Act civil penalty provisions require a "proper showing" for the ordering of a penalty. Would the SEC's evidence support such a showing? From your review of the three tiers in Exchange Act Section 21(d)(3)(B), what would you estimate to be the maximize amount of a possible penalty against the *First Financial* defendants?

*7. Disgorgement and Other Equitable Relief.* As is reflected in both *First Financial* and *Patel*, the equitable remedy of disgorgement is likely to be sought and ordered in almost any case in which the SEC is able to prove that a defendant has wrongfully profited from a violation of the securities laws. Both cases also reflect the SEC's routine decision to seek, and the federal courts' routine decisions to order, the defendant to pay "pre-judgment interest" on the amount subject to disgorgement. Can the ordering of pre-judgment interest be described as remedial?

As we have seen from the material on SEC settlements, a number of courts have also used their equitable power to approve consent decrees that impose "creative relief" such as additional reporting requirements, the prohibition of exercising voting control, the appointment of additional independent directors on a corporate board, and the appointment of "corporate overseers" to ensure compliance with federal securities laws. See Section B.3 supra. Yet the argument was often made that Congress's enactment of specific statutory remedies in the Remedies Act should restrict a court's ability to fashion additional equitable remedies and that it was particularly inappropriate for courts to order "creative relief" in the absence of the defendant's express agreement. See ABA Committee on Federal Regulation of Securities, Report of the Task Force on SEC Settlements, 47 Bus. Law. 1083, 1127 (1992) (stating that "there should be no question that these unauthorized remedies are appropriate solely in the context of settled enforcement matters"). How does new Section 21(d)(5) of the Exchange Act factor into this debate?

8. ***"Show Me the Money."*** Prior to the Sarbanes-Oxley Act of 2002, the SEC typically distributed disgorgement monies obtained through enforcement action to investors injured by a defendant's wrongful conduct, provided that such persons could be identified. Civil monetary penalties, on the other hand, were directed to the U.S. Treasury. In a provision of the Sarbanes-Oxley Act entitled "Fair Funds for Investors," Congress altered this scheme by specifying that in any judicial or administrative action brought by the SEC under the federal securities laws, any amounts disgorged and any civil penalties imposed "shall, on the motion or at the direction of the Commission, be added to and become part of the disgorgement fund for the benefit of the victims of such violation." Section 308(a) of the Sarbanes-Oxley Act. The Act further authorizes the SEC to add to this fund any "gifts, bequests and devises of property, both real and personal." Id. at Section 308(b).

What logistical problems do you foresee with the SEC's ability to carry out Congress's rather clear intention that victims of securities fraud be made as whole as possible? Consider, for example, the $12 million in disgorgement that former Enron official Michael J. Kopper agreed to pay as part of his guilty plea in the criminal case and related civil settlement with the SEC. According to press reports, "[p]rosecutors said all the money would be distributed by the SEC to injured investors, but added no details about who would qualify or how it would be doled out." Mitchell Pacelle, Ex-Executive's Guilty Plea Sets Stage for Battle Between Banks and SEC, Wall St. J. at C13 (Aug. 27, 2002). But Enron's unsecured creditors quickly filed an action in federal bankruptcy court, claiming an entitlement to the disgorged funds. The bankruptcy judge then issued a temporary injunction barring transfer of the funds. See id. Who has greater entitlement to that money—the company (that Koppers admitted to defrauding) or the shareholders (who lost substantial amounts of money as the value of Enron stock crashed)?

---

### 2. *Administrative Remedies*

## RIZEK v. SEC

215 F.3d 157 (1st Cir. 2000)

LYNCH, CIRCUIT JUDGE:

Al Rizek was a vice president of PaineWebber Incorporated of Puerto Rico. Over a ten-month period in 1993 he churned the accounts of five customers, causing losses of approximately $195,000 on accounts with average balances that totaled about $700,000. This violated Section 10(b) of the Securities Exchange Act of 1934 and Rule 10b-5. Although his customers indicated that they had conservative investment objectives, Rizek pursued the extremely risky strategy of trading U.S. Treasury bonds in an attempt to take advantage of short-term fluctuations in the market. He magnified the risk by trading the accounts on margin.

In 1999, the Securities and Exchange Commission ordered that Rizek be permanently barred from the securities industry, cease and desist from violations, pay a civil penalty of $100,000, and disgorge over $120,000. In doing so, the SEC departed from the recommendations of its own Administrative Law Judge, who would have imposed a disgorgement of over $275,000, but only a two-year suspension. See generally *In re Al Rizek,* Exchange Act Release No. 41,725, 70 SEC Docket 705 (Aug. 11, 1999), available in 1999 WL 600427.

Rizek, by petition for review of the SEC order, challenges the permanent bar order and the civil penalty; he does not challenge the findings that he excessively traded the accounts. The essence of his argument is that the SEC was wrong in finding he had the degree of scienter required for such a sanction: while his investment strategy may have been wrong, he had a good faith belief in it, he meant no harm, and he is remorseful. From this he argues that a permanent bar from the industry where he has supported himself and his family for fifteen years is arbitrary and capricious, and so should be reversed. He also urges that this court adopt a rule that when the Commission imposes a permanent bar, the most drastic sanction available, it must show that a less drastic remedy would not suffice to protect the public.

We decline that invitation and affirm the Commission order.

I.

There is very little dispute about the underlying facts, which we take from the record before the Commission. The parties disagree, however, as to the conclusions that may be drawn from those facts.

The five customers in question—Eddie Figueroa, Jorge Donato, Jose Acevedo, Hector Torres Nadal, and Herminio R. Cintron—opened their accounts with Rizek in 1990 and 1991. Only Donato and Cintron had some prior experience investing in securities. Acevedo and Torres had purchased CDs or similar investment products, while Figueroa had previously kept his money in a savings account.

Four of the customers' new account forms listed "speculation" last among possible investment objectives, while Rizek's record of Torres's account does not mention speculation at all. Donato told Rizek that he was primarily interested in long-term bonds and the "safety of [his] investment." Acevedo testified that he was looking for a long-term investment; he was not willing to speculate or risk any of his principal. Cintron was planning for his retirement and his children's education; he testified that he was looking for "something that was safe"; Torres was also saving for retirement and described himself as "very cautious" and interested in "something that was protected and secure." Figueroa testified that he was willing to take "any type of risk," but that Rizek had counseled him that "given the small amount of money that [he] had, the most convenient thing was to put most of the savings into some safe investments and devote a small amount to moderate type of risk." ***

In early 1993, Rizek recommended a strategy of short-term trading of zero-coupon bonds to certain of his customers, including the five whose accounts are at issue here. Zero-coupon bonds are U.S. government instruments that accumulate interest until maturity, rather than paying interest periodically. The value of a zero-coupon bond is very sensitive to changes in interest rates. Rizek recommended that his customers purchase the bonds on margin, which significantly increased the face value amounts of the trades, thus magnifying the potential gains and losses. Purchasing on margin meant that the customers had to make monthly margin interest payments to PaineWebber; it also placed them at risk of being forced to sell at a loss to meet a margin call.

The SEC Division of Enforcement's expert witness testified that there was no economic logic to Rizek's trading strategy of swapping zero-coupon bonds, because bond prices move in parallel with each other. The expert stated that only a "very sophisticated, experienced investor" could have understood Rizek's strategy and its risks. On the other hand, Rizek's expert witness testified that trading zero-coupon bonds was an "accepted trading strategy," but conceded that Rizek's customers would have had to be able to tolerate "aggressive risk" for the strategy to have been appropriate for them.

Figueroa, Torres, and Cintron testified that they always followed Rizek's investment recommendations, while Donato said that he followed them "ninety-nine percent" of the time. Acevedo testified that he could not remember refusing any of Rizek's recommendations during the relevant period.

During the fifteen-month period from January 1993 to March 1994, the five accounts had average monthly balances of approximately $50,000; $85,000; $86,000; $165,000; and $312,000. During this time, Rizek carried out approximately $24 million in transactions on the accounts, generating tens of thousands of dollars in commissions and margin interest fees. For example, Rizek effected $1.6 million in transactions on the account with the $50,000 average balance, incurring average annual commissions of about $16,000 and interest fees of over $5,000. On the largest account, Rizek carried out $9.3 million in transactions, which generated average annual commissions of more than $82,000 and interest fees of over $30,000. All told, Rizek's strategy led to losses of approximately $195,000 on the five accounts, which had average monthly balances totaling about $700,000.

II.

A sanctions order of the Commission must be upheld unless the order is a "gross abuse of discretion." *A.J. White & Co. v. SEC,* 556 F.2d 619, 624 (1st Cir. 1977).

Congress has charged the Commission with protecting the investing public. See *Pierce v. SEC,* 239 F.2d 160, 163 (9th Cir. 1956) ("The Commission is given the duty to protect the public. What will protect the public must involve, of necessity, an exercise of discretionary determination."). And so the question of the appropriate remedy is "peculiarly a matter for administrative competence." *American Power & Light Co. v. SEC,* 329 U.S. 90 (1946). As a result, the Commission's sanctions must be affirmed unless "unwarranted in law or ... without justification in fact." *American Power & Light,* 329 U.S. at 112-13.

Rizek contends that his conduct was at most negligent and naive. He says that the violations involved only five of his 400 customers; that his strategy relied on predictions from Paine Webber's chief economist; and that he stopped investing in zero-coupon bonds when his customers began to lose money. He also points to the fact that he has given assurances against future violations. Rizek claims that the bar is improperly punitive in nature and not meant to protect the investing public.

Rizek argues that this court should follow *Steadman v. SEC,* 603 F.2d 1126 (5th Cir. 1979), aff'd on other grounds, 450 U.S. 91 (1981). Rizek claims *Steadman* held that a court should not affirm a permanent bar, the most drastic sanction available, unless the SEC has shown that no lesser remedy will suffice to protect the public interest.

We think Rizek's argument confuses two concepts. We understand *Steadman* to articulate no more than the well-established rule that agencies must sufficiently articulate the grounds of their decisions so that appellate courts are able to perform their function of judicial review meaningfully. The Supreme Court made this point about the need for adequate SEC findings in *SEC v. Chenery Corp.,* 318 U.S. 80, 94 (1943) ( "[T]he orderly functioning of the process of review requires that the grounds upon which the administrative agency acted be clearly disclosed and adequately sustained."). This court has made the point in various contexts involving judicial review of administrative actions, and at times has remanded to the agency when it has not provided such an explanation.

To say that the Commission must adequately set forth its grounds is far different from saying that the agency's discretion as to remedy is curtailed by judge-made rules, such as a rule that a permanent bar may be imposed only if the agency has explained to the satisfaction of a court why no lesser remedy will do. *** Section 15(b)(6)(A) of the Securities Exchange Act authorizes the Commission to issue a permanent bar if it finds that such a bar "is in the public interest." Considerable deference should be given the Commission's ultimate judgment about what will best protect the public.

We also note that the term "permanent bar" is more than a bit of a misnomer. It does not literally mean that the sanctioned person may never reenter the securities industry. In fact, there are two routes back in. First, Rizek may later apply to the SEC for consent to associate with an entity that is not a member of a self-regulatory organization such as the National Association of Securities Dealers (NASD). See SEC Rule of Practice 193, 17 C.F.R. § 201.193(a). Second, Rizek may find a NASD member firm willing to employ him, and that firm may apply to NASD to have Rizek become associated with it. See By-Laws of The National Association of Securities Dealers, Inc., art. III, § 3(d). NASD's approval of any such application is subject to whatever further action the Commission may take. See id., art. III, § 3(f). This is a remarkably porous definition of a permanent bar.

The Commission said it was imposing a permanent bar on Rizek because of the egregiousness of his violation; because there was little basis to credit his claim of remorse (he was remorseful about the losses, but not about using the strategy which caused the losses); and because Rizek, who was at the time president of his own investment company, posed a substantial threat to public investors.

The activity was egregious. These five clients were unsophisticated in the world of investing and trusted Rizek to handle their savings conservatively. In some instances these were their life savings, their funds for retirement, or their funds for educating their children. On average balances in the five accounts totaling $700,000, Rizek engaged in over $24 million in transactions over a ten month period. The transaction costs equaled roughly 40% of the account balances; one customer lost about 50% of his account. While his customers lost $195,000, Rizek received about $125,000 in commissions.

There is no doubt that Rizek churned the accounts. Churning is commonly said to have three elements: (1) control of the customer's account by the broker, either explicit or de facto; (2) excessive trading in light of the customer's investment objectives; and (3) scienter—the required state of mind for liability under Section 10(b) and Rule 10b-5. See *Tiernan v. Blyth, Eastman, Dillon & Co.*, 719 F.2d 1, 2 (1st Cir. 1983). Rizek focuses on the third element. ***

Rizek argues that while the Commission may have been entitled to find that he had the degree of scienter needed to establish a churning violation, a greater degree of scienter is needed to justify the sanctions imposed. There is no statutory basis to distinguish between the scienter needed to establish a violation for which a sanction may be imposed administratively and the scienter needed to warrant a particular penalty. At most, Rizek's argument goes to the Commission's exercise of its discretion. And the Commission found that even if Rizek had a good faith belief in the efficacy of his strategy, "he had no justification for recommending it to unsophisticated customers who were incapable of making an independent judgment, when he knew that the extremely high risk was directly contrary to the customers' conservative investment objectives." That finding is adequate support for the remedy.

In any event, this case involves churning plus. The Commission also found that "Rizek was well aware that he had acted improperly in recommending his strategy, and tried to conceal his conduct from his firm." Id. Rizek both misled his firm's management and attempted to mislead the Commission. Paine Webber management had become concerned about Rizek's trading strategy and questioned him about it at four meetings. Rizek responded by giving the firm a list of clients whose strategies, he said, had changed so that "speculation" was now a high ranking objective. In addition, at the hearings before the ALJ, Rizek testified that he had called all of the customers in November 1993 and all of them agreed to the reordering of their investment objectives. But the facts were to the contrary: none of the customers testified that Rizek had sought or received their permission to change their investment objectives. There was ample evidence to support the Commission's conclusion that Rizek acted willfully and recklessly.

Under these circumstances, there is simply no viable argument that the permanent bar was an abuse of discretion, or that it was punitive and not meant to protect the investing public.

III.

Rizek also challenges the imposition of a $100,000 civil penalty. Under Section 21B(b) of the Act, there is a three-tiered system for assessing civil penalties, ranging from a first tier penalty of $5,000 to a third tier penalty of $100,000. See [Exchange Act Section 21B(b)]. The requirements for imposition of the third tier penalty are set forth at [Exchange Act Section 21B(b)(3)]:

> (3) Third tier
>
> Notwithstanding paragraphs (1) and (2), the maximum amount of penalty for each such act or omission shall be $100,000 for a natural person or $500,000 for any other person if—
>
> > (A) the act or omission described in subsection (a) of this section involved fraud, deceit, manipulation, or deliberate or reckless disregard of a regulatory requirement; and
> >
> > (B) such act or omission directly or indirectly resulted in substantial losses or created a significant risk of substantial losses to other persons or resulted in substantial pecuniary gain to the person who committed the act or omission.

In turn, the statute sets forth six factors which the Commission may consider in assessing monetary penalties:

> (1) whether the act or omission for which such penalty is assessed involved fraud, deceit, manipulation, or deliberate or reckless disregard of a regulatory requirement;
>
> (2) the harm to other persons resulting either directly or indirectly from such act or omission;
>
> (3) the extent to which any person was unjustly enriched, taking into account any restitution made to persons injured by such behavior;
>
> (4) whether such person previously has been found by the Commission, another appropriate regulatory agency, or a self-regulatory organization to have violated the Federal securities laws, State securities laws, or the rules of a self-regulatory organization, has been enjoined by a court of competent jurisdiction from violations of such laws or rules, or has been convicted by a court of competent jurisdiction of violations of such laws or of any felony or misdemeanor described in [Exchange Act Section 15(b)(4)(b)];
>
> (5) the need to deter such person and other persons from committing such acts or omissions; and

(6) such other matters as justice may require.

[Exchange Act Section 21B(c)] To the extent Rizek argues he is unable to pay the penalty, we note that he did not raise the argument before the Commission, and so it is waived. See [Exchange Act Section 25(c)(1)]. For the same reasons there was no abuse of discretion in the permanent bar order, there was no abuse of discretion in the imposition of the civil penalty.

We affirm the Commission's order.

---

## IN THE MATTER OF JEFFRY L. FELDMAN
## Administrative Proceeding File No. 3-8063
## Release No. 33-7014 / September 20, 1993

## FINDINGS AND CEASE AND DESIST ORDER PURSUANT TO SECTION 8A OF THE SECURITIES ACT OF 1933

### I.

By Order dated May 27, 1993, the Commission instituted administrative proceedings pursuant to Section 8A of the Securities Act of 1933 ("Securities Act") against Jeffry Feldman ("Feldman") to determine whether Feldman caused violations of Sections 5(a) and 5(c) of the Securities Act. Feldman has submitted an Offer of Settlement which the Commission has determined to accept. Solely for the purpose of these proceedings and any other proceeding brought by or on behalf of the Commission or to which the Commission is a party, Feldman consents to the issuance of these Findings and Cease and Desist Order Pursuant to Section 8A of the Securities Act of 1933 ("Order"), without admitting or denying the matters set forth herein.

### II.

### FACTS

Based on the foregoing, the Commission finds the following:

*A. Respondent*

Feldman, age 46, is admitted to practice law in the State of New York. Feldman is a partner with the New York law firm of Dunn & Zuckerman. Feldman's practice consists of commercial law, bankruptcy, commercial litigation and banking law.

*B. The Pakistani Banks Proposed to Offer and Sell Foreign Exchange Bearer Certificates*

In 1985, the Islamic Republic of Pakistan ("Pakistan") formulated a plan to offer rupee denominated foreign exchange bearer certificates ("FEBC"), issued and guaranteed by Pakistan, in foreign countries, including the United States. The offer and sale of FEBCs was administered by the State Bank of Pakistan, Pakistan's central bank, and carried out in the United States through the United States branches of nationalized Pakistani commercial banks.

In June 1985, the Karachi headquarters offices of three Pakistani commercial banks, National Bank of Pakistan, Habib Bank, Ltd., and United

Bank, Ltd., informed their New York offices about the proposal to offer and sell FEBCs in the United States. The Karachi offices requested that the New York offices determine what legal or regulatory restrictions applied to the sale and purchase of the FEBCs, including restrictions imposed by "exchange or securities authorities," and make arrangements to comply with any applicable regulations.

*C. Feldman Was Asked to Determine the Applicability of the Federal Securities Laws to the FEBCs*

Officials of the New York offices of the Pakistani banks sought to fulfill the directives of their Karachi offices by seeking the advice of counsel and through independent inquiries to state and federal regulatory agencies. In June or July of 1985, officials of each of the New York offices of the Pakistani banks began to communicate with Feldman, whose law firm had a long-established relationship with the Pakistani banks.

The New York offices of the Pakistani banks requested that Feldman identify all regulatory barriers to the offer and sale of the FEBCs in New York and take the steps necessary to comply with regulatory requirements. To assist Feldman in evaluating the regulatory obstacles, the Pakistani banks provided Feldman with numerous documents describing the characteristics of the FEBC program.

Feldman understood that the Pakistani banks wanted him to determine the applicability of the federal securities laws to the offer and sale of the FEBCs. Neither Feldman nor any other member of Dunn & Zuckerman had any background in the practice of law relating to the offer and sale of securities.

In addition to engaging the services of Feldman, in July 1985, an officer of the National Bank of Pakistan (the "Bank Officer") independently contacted the Commission both by telephone and by letter concerning the proposed program. In a letter dated July 8, 1985, the Bank Officer described the FEBC program and asked the Commission to confirm that it would have "no objection to the proposed sale of the Bonds."

On July 19, 1985, a staff member of the Division of Corporation Finance responded orally to that inquiry. The staff member informed the Bank Officer that registration on Schedule B was required. On July 23, 1985, Feldman received a handwritten note from the Bank Officer informing him about the staff member's conclusion regarding registration on Schedule B and stating that "[w]e have to know precisely which forms need to be filed with the SEC." Despite these circumstances, Feldman took no steps to effect registration of the FEBCs with the Commission.

*D. Feldman Told the Pakistani Banks That the Offer and Sale of the FEBCs Did Not Need to Be Registered*

The only measure taken by Feldman on behalf of the Pakistani banks to comply with regulatory requirements was submitting applications to the New York Superintendent of Banks seeking permission for the New York branches to exercise fiduciary powers to sell and encash the FEBCs. These applications were submitted for each of the three banks between September 3, 1985, and January 21, 1986.

National Bank of Pakistan's application to the New York Superintendent of Banks was approved in November 1985, Habib Bank's in January 1986, and United Bank's in February 1986. Once the first application for the exercise of fiduciary powers was approved by the New York Superintendent of Banks, Feldman began telling the Pakistani banks that they had no obligation to take the additional step of registering the offer of the FEBCs with the Commission. In December 1985, Feldman wrote to the legal department of Habib Bank in Karachi stating that the activities of selling and purchasing FEBCs "do not involve what can be considered securities" and recommending that "no further action be taken with those agencies [SEC and New York State securities authorities] for the time being." In January 1986, Feldman again told the Karachi office that the offer and sale of the FEBCs did not require Commission "authorization." Feldman made identical statements to the other two Pakistani banks. Feldman had no basis for his statement that the FEBCs were not securities and thus exempt from the registration requirements of Section 5.

*E. Feldman Took No Notice of Further Indications That The Offer and Sale of the FEBCs Must Be Registered*

In March 1986, after the New York offices of the Pakistani commercial banks had begun selling the FEBCs, the Washington, D.C. branch of the National Bank of Pakistan submitted an application to the Office of the Comptroller of the Currency ("OCC") to obtain permission to sell the FEBCs in Washington, D.C. The OCC responded with a letter warning that "[t]he Certificates may be securities subject to registration under the securities laws" and that "[i]f the Certificates are securities, the branch may be subject to registration with the Securities and Exchange Commission as a broker-dealer." The OCC sent a copy of this letter to the New York Superintendent of Banks.

In a letter to Feldman dated June 26, 1986, the Bank Officer enclosed a copy of the OCC letter and requested that Feldman draft responses both to the OCC and the New York Superintendent of Banks. As requested, Feldman wrote to the New York State Superintendent of Banks, in a letter dated July 1, 1986, arguing that the bearer certificates were analogous to certificates of deposit that were not required to be registered under the federal securities laws. Feldman's letter also stated that "the National Bank of Pakistan did, in fact, request the Securities & Exchange Commission to comment upon the prospective activities of the Bank in connection with the sale/encashment of Foreign Exchange Bearer Certificates" and that "[t]o date, no written response has been received from the Securities & Exchange Commission." Feldman did not inform the Superintendent of Banks that, as he knew, the National Bank of Pakistan had received an oral response in July 1985 in which Commission staff stated that registration on Schedule B was required.

Feldman did not respond to the OCC. Instead, on August 12, 1986, Feldman wrote another officer of the New York office of the National Bank of Pakistan, warning that registration of the FEBCs with the Commission would be "cumbersome, time consuming and expensive," and recommending that the National Bank of Pakistan "make no further attempt to obtain authorization to transact the sale of Foreign Exchange Bearer Certificates by the Washington, D.C. Branch." Feldman warned that, in light of the OCC letter, which indicated that the offering of FEBCs may need to be registered with the Commission, pursuing the application would only "open a 'can of worms' which may adversely affect the ongoing activities of the State Bank of Pakistan in continuing sale of Foreign Exchange Bearer Certificates [in New York] pursuant to State Banking Law authorization."

As a consequence of Feldman's actions, more than $8 million of FEBCs were offered and sold in the United States without registration from 1986 through March 1992. Sales of the FEBCs were halted in April 1992.

III.

OPINION

Feldman aided and abetted the Pakistani banks' violations of Section 5 of the Securities Act. See, e.g., *Metge v. Baehler*, 762 F.2d 621, 624 (8th Cir.1985); *Woodward v. Metro Bank of Dallas*, 522 F.2d 84, 94-95 (5th Cir.1975) (discussing standards for aiding and abetting liability). The first element of aiding and abetting liability—a primary violation of Section 5—is clearly established. The FEBCs were securities the offer and sale of which was required to be registered with the Commission. Section 5(a) of the Securities Act prohibits any person, directly or indirectly, from selling a security in interstate commerce unless a registration statement is in effect as to such security. Section 5(c) of the Securities Act prohibits the offer or sales of a security unless a registration statement has been filed as to the security. A security is defined to include a "note" or "evidence of indebtedness" or "bond." [Securities Act Section 2(1)]. On their face, the FEBCs come within the definition of a security. Each FEBC represented a promise by the issuing entity, Pakistan, to repay the principal amount, plus accrued interest at a specified rate, within a specified time period or on demand.

The offer and sale of FEBCs did not fall within any exemption from the registration requirements of Section 5. For example, the FEBCs were not exempt as government-issued securities. Section 3(a)(2) of the Securities Act exempts from registration only securities issued or guaranteed by the United States government or by state or local governments. Nor were the FEBCs exempt pursuant to Sections 3(a)(2) or 3(a)(5) of the Securities Act as securities or certificates of deposit issued or guaranteed by a financial institution because the FEBCs were issued by the government of Pakistan and not by a financial institution. Furthermore, the FEBCs were not certificates of deposit because the purchase of a FEBC did not create a deposit in the Pakistani commercial banks on behalf of the purchaser. Rather, the Pakistani commercial banks were to remit the proceeds to the government of Pakistan and receive a one percent sales commission from the State Bank of Pakistan for FEBCs sold at each U.S. branch.

Feldman substantially assisted the Pakistani banks' violations of Section 5 of the Securities Act. The Pakistani banks relied on Feldman to inform them of what obligations, if any, they had under the federal securities laws with respect to their offer and sale of FEBCs. Feldman substantially contributed to the Pakistani banks' violations of Section 5 because the banks did not register the FEBC offering after Feldman told them repeatedly that they did not have to do so. Feldman persisted in his erroneous position even though he had been put on notice by the Commission staff of the need for registration. Feldman knew when he told the Pakistani banks that the offering and sale of FEBCs did not need to be registered that the Commission staff had expressed a contrary view to the Bank Officer. Feldman did not do anything to resolve this discrepancy.

Soon after the sales of FEBCs commenced, Feldman was confronted with additional indications that his conclusion was wrong when the OCC informed one of the Pakistani banks that the FEBCs may be securities subject to registration with the Commission. Instead of addressing the OCC's concerns, Feldman told the Pakistani bank simply to abandon its plans to sell the FEBCs at the Washington, D.C. branch, since any further contact with the OCC could "open a 'can of worms' that could "adversely affect" the banks' ongoing unregistered sales of FEBCs. Although he knew that the Bank Officer had spoken with a member of the Commission staff, who had indicated that registration was required on Schedule B in connection with the offering, he informed the New York banking authorities who learned of the OCC's concerns only that "to date, no written response" had been received from the Commission concerning the need to register the offering of FEBCs.

IV.

FINDINGS

Based on the above, the Commission finds that Feldman aided and abetted and caused violations of Sections 5(a) and 5(c) of the Securities Act.

V.

ORDER

Accordingly, it is hereby ordered, pursuant to Section 8A of the Securities Act, that Feldman permanently cease and desist from committing or causing any violation of, and committing or causing any future violation of, Section 5 of the Securities Act.

### *NOTES AND QUESTIONS*

***1. Permanent Cease-and-Desist Orders.*** Consider how the addition of administrative cease-and-desist authority has affected the SEC's enforcement program. Prior to 1990, when the Commission believed that enforcement action was warranted against a non-regulated person or entity, what remedies were available? What policy goals were served by including cease-and-desist authority in the Remedies Act? Note that the Remedies Act also empowers the Commission to seek an accounting and disgorgement in any permanent cease-and-desist proceeding. See, e.g., Exchange Act Section 21C(e).

Note the text of Exchange Act Section 21C(a), which sets out the Commission's authority for issuing cease-and-desist orders in connection with violations of the Exchange Act or rules and regulations thereunder. The authority that this Section gives the Commission is wide-ranging:

> In addition to ordering a person to cease and desist from committing or causing violations or future violations, the Commission is also authorized to order a person to comply with a provision or to take steps to effect compliance. The Commission may also prescribe specific terms and conditions that a person must observe in order to effect compliance and may specify the time frame

> within which compliance must be effected. Thus, the Commission is authorized to require a person to take action to correct an existing condition resulting from a violation and to specify the steps to be taken. Most importantly, the Commission may issue orders requiring a person to comply in the future with, or requiring the person to take steps to effect future compliance with, a provision, rule or regulation with respect to any security, any issuer or any other person. The Commission may order such relief permanently, or for such period as it determines appropriate. For example, the Commission may direct a corporate respondent to add directors and to form specific committees to monitor certain corporate activities, or to resolicit proxies obtained by deficient proxy materials. Similarly, the Commission could order a brokerage firm to retain counsel to conduct a review of the firm's compliance with applicable provisions.

Ralph C. Ferrara et al., Hardball! The SEC's New Arsenal of Enforcement Weapons, 47 Bus. Law. 33, 58-59 (1991). Is the statutory text of Section 21C(a) broad enough to enable the SEC and the courts to circumvent the statutory requirements of other administrative or judicial remedies? Ferrara points out, for example, that if the Commission were to use its authority to direct a respondent corporation to terminate an officer in order to effect compliance with an Exchange Act reporting provision, "the Commission would undermine the Congressional determination to vest in the district courts the power to enter orders suspending or barring persons from serving as an officer or director based only upon a violation of the antifraud provisions or proof of *** unfitness." See id. at 59. What checks operate on the SEC's ability to use its cease and desist authority in this way?

2. ***Permanent Cease-and-Desist Orders—The Operative Standard.*** Must the Commission find a likelihood of future violations in order to impose a permanent cease-and-desist order? In order words, should a cease-and-desist order be analogized to a court-ordered injunction, in that both remedies are forward-looking?

In a recent enforcement action against the accounting firm of KPMG, the Commission decided that, although there must be "some" risk of future violations, the amount of risk "need not be very great," since "[a]bsent evidence to the contrary, a finding of violation raises a sufficient risk of future violation." *In the Matter of KPMG Peat Marwick LLP,* Exchange Act Release No. 43862, 2001 WL 47245 at *24 (Jan. 19, 2001).

The Commission then went on to hold that it would consider a laundry list of "traditional factors" in deciding whether a cease-and-desist order is an appropriate sanction:

> Along with the risk of future violations, we will continue to consider our traditional factors in determining whether a cease-and-desist order is an appropriate sanction based on the entire record. Many of these factors are akin to those used by courts in determining whether injunctions are appropriate, including the seriousness of the violation, the isolated or recurrent nature of the violation, the respondent's state of mind, the sincerity of the respondent's assurances against future violations, the respondent's recognition of the wrongful nature of his or her conduct, and the respondent's opportunity to commit future violations. In addition, we consider whether the violation is recent, the degree of harm to investors or the marketplace resulting from the violation, and the remedial function to be served by the cease-and-desist order

> in the context of any other sanctions being sought in the same proceedings. This inquiry is a flexible one and no one factor is dispositive. This inquiry is undertaken not to determine whether there is a "reasonable likelihood" of future violations but to guide our discretion.

Id. at * 26. Moreover, in a footnote, the Commission observed:

> "In some instances, we may also consider the function that a cease-and-desist order serves in alerting the public that a respondent has violated the securities laws."

Id. at n.148.

On review, the D.C. Circuit questioned whether "a single violation" would suffice to show that there was "some" risk of a future violation, but the court ultimately concluded that a remand was unnecessary because the Commission's findings of fact had included multiple violations. *KPMG v. SEC*, 289 F.3d 109 (D.C. Cir. 2002).

***3. Causing vs. Aiding and Abetting Liability.*** Contrast Section 21C(a)'s provision for enforcement action against persons who "cause" another person's Exchange Act violation with the SEC's authority to pursue "aiders and abetters" under Exchange Act Section 20(e). Specifically, what is the mental state necessary to trigger liability under each provision? Could Feldman have been subject to enforcement action under Section 20(e)? From your review of the facts, is it likely that Feldman "knowingly" rendered substantial assistance to the Pakistani banks? Could a district court enjoin a person under Section 20(e) based on conduct that is merely reckless?

In the *KPMG* order noted above, the Commission made a number of factual findings, including that KPMG's lack of independence as an outside auditor had caused its client to violate Section 13(a) of the Exchange Act and Rule 13a-1 thereunder, which require every issuer with securities registered pursuant to Section 12 to include financial statements certified by independent auditors in their annual reports. The Commission further found that KPMG had acted negligently in determining that it was independent from its client and, among other sanctions, it issued a cease-and-desist order in connection with KPMG's having "caused" its client's primary violations. See *In the Matter of KPMG Peat Marwick LLP,* Exchange Act Release No. 43862, 2001 WL 47245 (Jan. 19, 2001).

In its petition for review to the D.C. Circuit, KPMG challenged, among numerous other issues, the propriety of a negligence standard under Section 21C, particularly for accountants who are also subject to professional discipline under SEC Rule 102(e). In denying this petition, the D.C. Circuit emphasized that "the Commission was virtually compelled by Congress' choice of language in enacting Section 21C to interpret the phrase 'an act or omission the person *knew or should have known* would contribute to such violation' as setting a negligence standard." *KPMG, LLP v. SEC*, 289 F.3d 109, 120 (D.C. Cir. 2002) (emphasis in original).

As a matter of policy, should the Commission make a practice of initiating cease-and-desist proceedings against attorneys and accountants for conduct that may constitute a single act of negligence? What would be some of the costs and benefits of such a practice? Note that we will revisit this issue in our discussion of Rule 102(e) in Chapter 10.

*4. **Ex Parte Orders.*** The Remedies Act also empowers the SEC to issue temporary cease-and-desist orders against certain regulated entities and associated persons, and such orders may be issued ex parte if the Commission "determines that notice and hearing prior to entry would be impractical or contrary to the public interest." Exchange Act Section 21C(c)(1); Securities Act Section 8A(c)(1). What types of facts would justify the imposition of such temporary relief? As originally proposed to Congress by the Commission, the SEC's authority to issue temporary cease-and-desist orders would have extended to any person. Was Congress's decision to limit this authority to regulated entities and persons a wise one? Note that in the Sarbanes-Oxley Act of 2002, Congress amended Section 21C(c)(2) to include a "registered public accounting firm" among the entities which may be subject to ex parte orders.

*5. **Civil Monetary Penalties.*** The *Rizek* court considered the SEC's authority under Exchange Act Section 21B to assess a monetary penalty in a broker-dealer proceeding brought pursuant to Exchange Act Sections 15(b)(4) and (6). Contrast the administrative remedy in Section 21B with the judicial remedy in Section 21(d)(3). Besides the fact that the former is available in only certain administrative proceedings against securities professionals, what other differences do you see?

In the wake of Enron, WorldCom, and other massive financial frauds in 2001-02, the SEC asked Congress for the power to impose civil penalties on publicly traded companies and their officers and directors in administrative proceedings. See Chairperson Harvey Pitt, Written Testimony Concerning Accounting and Investor Protection Issues Raised by Enron and Other Public Companies, Before the Sen. Comm. on Banking, Housing and Urban Affairs, March 21, 2002. Although it acceded to many SEC requests in the Sarbanes-Oxley Act, Congress failed to authorize such additional enforcement authority. Was this a wise decision?

*6. **Collateral Bar Orders.*** The *Rizek* court also reviewed the SEC's decision to permanently bar Rizek from "association with any broker, dealer, member of a national securities exchange, or member of a registered securities association." *In re Al Rizek,* Exchange Act Release No. 41725, 70 SEC Docket 705 (Aug. 11, 1999). Note how the D.C. Circuit inaccurately characterized this sanction as a permanent bar "from the securities industry." This overly broad characterization has significance because, until relatively recently, the SEC's ability to impose so-called "collateral bars" (or industry-wide bars) was a hotly contested issue. The controversy was resolved in *Teicher v. SEC,* 177 F.3d 1016 (D.C. Cir. 1999), where the respondent securities brokers had challenged an SEC order permanently barring them from the entire securities industry (including from association with investment advisers), rather than specifically from the "broker-dealer" industry. The D.C. Circuit held in favor of the respondents, finding that the Commission's "collateral bar" had exceeded its authority under Section 15(b)(6) of the Exchange Act. Emphasizing particular provisions in the Investment Advisers Act as well as the separate provisions in the Exchange Act that extend to broker-dealers and municipal securities dealers, the court reasoned that "Congress's thrice repeated use of a nexus requirement focused on a single branch of the industry seems to us to underscore a congressional determination to create separate sets of sanctions, each triggered by an individual's satisfying the industry-specific nexus." Id. at 1020.

7. ***Administrative Proceedings Under Exchange Act Section 15(c)(4).*** Section 15(c)(4) of the Exchange Act provides an administrative remedy where the Commission finds a failure to comply with Sections 12, 13, 14, or 15(d) of the Exchange Act or any rule or regulation thereunder. A remedy is also available against any person "who was a cause of the failure [of another person] to comply due to an act or omission the person knew or should have known would contribute to the failure to comply." Specifically, after notice and an opportunity for a hearing, the Commission may issue an order requiring the respondent "to comply, or to take steps to effect compliance with [the relevant] provision *** upon such terms and conditions and within such time as the Commission may specify."

In *In re George C. Kern, Jr.*, Exchange Act Release No. 29356, 49 SEC Docket 422 (June 21, 1991), the Commission upheld an administrative law judge's finding that George Kern, a highly respected securities lawyer and partner at the New York firm of Sullivan & Cromwell, had caused his corporate client's violation of Exchange Act Section 14(d)(4) and Rule 14d-9(b), which require the target of a tender offer to promptly disclose to the SEC any material changes in the information provided in the target's initial SEC filing. Yet the Commission refused to issue the relief requested by the Enforcement Division, which was an order that would require Kern to comply, and to take steps to see that his future clients comply, with Section 14(d). The staff's suggested order was phrased broadly in terms of future compliance because Kern's client in the tender offer dispute was no longer in business. In rejecting the Division's recommendation, the Commission held that it lacked the power under Section 15(c)(4) to issue such an order of "general compliance." Instead, it pointed to legislative history indicating that the provision was to be used "primarily as a means of compelling issuers to correct false or inaccurate periodic reports."

The tender offer events underlying the violations by Kern's corporate client occurred in 1986. Had these violations occurred a decade later, what enforcement remedies wold have been available to the SEC? Would it surprise you to learn that the SEC now invokes Section 15(c)(4) only on rare occasions?

---

### 3. *Collateral Consequences of SEC Sanctions*

SEC sanctions must be evaluated with reference to their possible collateral consequences. The following excerpt draws a useful comparison between court-ordered injunctions and administrative cease-and-desist orders.

## SEC CEASE-AND-DESIST ORDERS

**by Andrew M. Smith**

51 Admin. L. Rev. 1197, 1217-1225 (1999)

****Direct Effects: Enforcement of Order if Violated*

The direct effect of an injunction is that it compels the person charged by it to obey the law, or be found in contempt of the court issuing the injunction. Being found in contempt of court might carry with it fines, imprisonment, or other civil and criminal penalties.

A cease-and-desist order is a command from the SEC to refrain from violating the securities laws. If violated, the SEC can seek an injunction requiring compliance with the order. In addition, the SEC can bring an action in a federal court for a civil money penalty.

In the injunctive proceeding, the SEC would be required to show the violation of its order and a reasonable likelihood that its order will be violated in the future. The SEC would not be required to prove the violation that was the subject of the underlying cease-and-desist order. Contempt proceedings could be initiated if this subsequent injunction were violated. ***

Because a violation of an injunction subjects one immediately to contempt proceedings, the direct consequences of an injunction generally are more serious than those of a cease-and-desist order. However, the SEC's option to seek money penalties for violations of cease-and-desist orders, might work to make such violations more serious under certain circumstances.

****Additional SEC Disciplinary Action*

Another collateral effect of an injunction is that it might subject one to further SEC disciplinary action, including a bar from the securities industry or from practicing before the SEC. Exchange Act sections 15(b)(4)(C) and 15(b)(6)(A) authorize the SEC to censure, suspend, or bar broker-dealers and associated persons who have been enjoined from committing securities violations. Investment Advisers Act sections 203(e) and 203(f) authorize the SEC to censure, suspend, or bar investment advisers and associated persons who have been enjoined from committing securities violations. While there is no analogous provision authorizing the SEC to place limitations on persons who have been sanctioned administratively, these laws do allow the SEC to censure, suspend, or bar broker-dealers, investment advisers, and associated persons who have "willfully violated" the securities laws or who have "willfully aided, abetted, counseled, commanded, induced, or procured" such a violation. There is no authority on whether these provisions would allow the SEC to bootstrap a suspension, censure, or bar from a cease-and-desist order imposed in an administrative hearing. Presumably, however, if the public interest warranted, the SEC could find a "willful" violation and censure, suspend, or bar a person under Exchange Act section 15(b) or Investment Advisers Act section 203 in the initial proceeding, in addition to imposing upon him a cease-and-desist order.

*i. Disciplinary Action Against Professionals*

Commission Rule of Practice 102(e) provides that attorneys, accountants, engineers, and other professionals who are "found by the [SEC] ... to have engaged in unethical or improper professional conduct; or [t]o have willfully violated, or willfully aided and abetted" securities violations may be suspended or barred by the SEC from appearing or practicing before it. The SEC also may temporarily suspend any person permanently enjoined from committing securities violations or found by the SEC in an administrative proceeding to have violated the securities law or to have aided and abetted violations of the securities laws. In other words, for the purposes of Rule 102(e), cease-and-desist orders and injunctions appear to be equally serious.

*ii. Investment Company Act Restrictions*

A person who is enjoined from violating the securities laws automatically becomes ineligible to serve as an employee, officer, director, investment adviser, or depositor of an investment company or as an underwriter of an open- end investment company, unit investment trust, or face-amount certificate company. [See Investment Company Act Section 9(a)] While there is no analogous provision making ineligible persons who have been sanctioned administratively, this law allows the SEC to prohibit persons who have "willfully violated" the securities laws or who have "willfully aided, abetted, counseled, commanded, induced, or procured" such a violation from serving as an employee, officer, director, investment adviser, underwriter, or depositor of an investment company. [Investment Company Act Section 9(b)]

*iii. Statutory Disqualification*

A person enjoined from securities violations also becomes subject to a "statutory disqualification." [Exchange Act Section 3(a)(39)(F)] Self-regulatory organizations, i.e., the NASD, securities exchanges, and clearing agencies, may deny membership to any person subject to a statutory disqualification. Moreover, they *shall* deny such membership when ordered to do so by the SEC. Persons subject to SEC cease-and-desist orders are not subject automatically to a statutory disqualification, although, like Exchange Act section 15(b)(4) and Investment Company Act section 9(b), persons who have "willfully violated" the securities laws or who have "willfully aided, abetted, counseled, commanded, induced, or procured" such a violation are subject to a statutory disqualification.

****Other Sanctions*

*i. Unavailability of Registration Exemptions*

An injunction also disqualifies an issuer of securities from taking advantage of certain exemptions from the securities registration process. For instance, Regulation A provides that its exemption shall be denied to any issuer that has been enjoined from engaging in a practice involving the making of a false filing with the SEC, and to any issuer with a director, officer, general partner, promoter, or ten percent shareholder who has been enjoined from committing certain securities violations. Regulation A does not include restrictions on issuers that are subject to SEC cease-and-desist orders or on issuers with a director, officer, general partner, promoter, or ten percent shareholder who is subject to an SEC cease-and-desist order.

*ii. Disclosure of Violation*

An injunction must be disclosed in many instances, with concomitant damage to one's reputation. For instance, disclosure is required if one has been enjoined from violating the securities laws within the last five years and (1) one is a director or officer of a publicly traded company, or is nominated to become a director or officer of a publicly traded company; (2) one is bidding to acquire a publicly traded company; (3) one becomes a five-percent shareholder of a publicly traded company; or (4) one engages in a going-private transaction. Each of these disclosures also must be made, however, when a person is subject to a cease-and-desist order issued by the SEC. For instance, Regulation S-K requires disclosure whenever a person has been found by the SEC to have violated a federal or state securities or commodities law, and the judgment has not been reversed, suspended, or vacated.

Both an injunction and a cease-and-desist order also must be disclosed on a Form U-4, the form filed by broker-dealers with the National Association of Securities Dealers (NASD) to register associated persons. Form ADV, for registration with the SEC as an investment adviser, also requires disclosures of both injunctions and cease-and-desist orders.

*iii. Nasdaq Delisting*

The NASD has broad discretion to delist from Nasdaq the securities of an issuer, where the NASD "deems it necessary to prevent fraudulent and manipulative acts and practices, to promote just and equitable principles of trade, or to protect investors and the public interest." [NASD Sec. Dealers Man. (CCH) Rule 4330(a)(3)] Presumably, the NASD could use this authority to delist or refuse to list the securities of an issuer who has associated with it a person who has been enjoined from violating the securities laws, and, by the same token, an issuer who has associated with it a person who is subject to an SEC cease-and-desist order.

*iv. State Disciplinary Action*

The laws of many, if not all, states, allow the securities administrator of the state to suspend or revoke the broker, dealer, or investment adviser registration of any person who has been enjoined by a "court of competent jurisdiction" from "engaging in ... any aspect of the securities business." While these same laws also provide that a state securities administrator may suspend or revoke the broker, dealer, or investment adviser registration of any person who 'is the subject of an order entered by [the SEC] denying or revoking' such registration, they generally do not specifically address cease-and-desist orders entered by the SEC. However, there are several notable exceptions to this general rule—at least 17 state codes provide that the state securities administrator may suspend or revoke the registration of a person who is the subject of an SEC cease-and-desist order.

Many state laws also provide that licensing authorities may deny, suspend, or revoke non-securities professional licenses where the licensee has been enjoined from committing securities violations or is subject to an SEC cease-and-desist order. For instance, Arizona law provides that the state real estate commissioner may deny, suspend, or revoke the real estate license of any person who has "violated any federal or state law, regulation or rule that relates to real estate or securities or that involves forgery, theft, extortion, fraud, substantial misrepresentation, [or] dishonest dealings." Under this law, the effect of a securities violation, whether sanctioned by an injunction or by a cease-and-desist order, would be the same. It appears, however, that the effect on a non-securities license of any civil violation of the securities laws would be limited, given that states tend to deny, suspend, or revoke licenses on the basis of factors relevant to the licensee's character and fitness to practice that particular profession. ***

### *NOTES AND QUESTIONS*

1. ***The Power of the Press.*** Although the regulatory consequences of SEC sanctions may often be grave, consider also the impact of an SEC release reporting a settlement or announcing a judicial or administrative decision. In assessing the consequences of SEC settlements, the ABA Task Force specifically noted that:

> Although publicity is not necessarily a legal consequence collateral to the settlement, in many circumstances, publicity can be the most devastating of all collateral consequences and should not be overlooked or treated as insignificant by the Commission or practitioners. Often, information about the settling party that has never before been released becomes public, such as an officer or director's involvement with other United States or foreign entities, his or her personal financial condition, or business or personal relationships. Persons and entities previously eager to do business with the settling party may refuse to do so upon hearing of the settlement or may, while continuing to do business, cause the working relationship to be affected. Lenders may consider the settlement a negative factor in determining whether to provide financing. Even personal relationships may become strained because, although the settling party would not have admitted wrongdoing when entering the settlement, the party would have rejected the opportunity to be pronounced innocent by a factfinder. These significant consequences should not be ignored when examining the legal consequences that also may result from settlement with the Commission.

ABA Committee on Federal Regulation of Securities, Report of the Task Force on SEC Settlements, 47 Bus. Law. 1083, 1149-50 (1992). What constraints do SEC rules impose on a settling party's ability to respond to media inquiries about the reasons for settlement?

2. ***Litigation and Evidentiary Consequences.*** As we shall see in Section D.2.c of this Chapter, the Supreme Court's decision in *Parklane Hosiery Co. v. Shore*, 439 U.S. 322 (1979), imposes significant collateral consequences on those that litigate with the SEC and lose. Indeed, after *Parklane*, such defendants face the risk that principles of collateral estoppel will be invoked in subsequent private litigation to prevent them from re-litigating those issues of fact and law that were necessarily determined in the prior proceeding with the SEC. And even when collateral estoppel is inapplicable, such as where the defendant has settled and has "neither admitted nor denied liability," sanctions imposed by a court or the SEC, as well as any findings relating thereto, may be admissible as evidence in subsequent litigation. For what purposes may a court admit such evidence? What arguments can a defendant make to exclude such evidence?

## *PROBLEM 9-1*

*(Based on the facts from the third problem in Chapter 6)*

Microchip, Inc. launched an initial public offering (IPO) in March 2000 at the price of $10 per share. Microchip's registration statement, in its "use of proceeds" section, stated that all of the offering proceeds would be used for research on new technologies for the production of computer microchips. The national accounting firm of Reilly & Whitman audited the financial statements that were included in the registration statement. The lead underwriter was Wilson, Hartley, & Co. The IPO netted $10 million exclusive of costs.

Hooker & Faye had been a member of the selling group in the Microchip IPO. In the months following the public offering, office managers at Hooker & Faye encouraged their brokers to recommend to clients the purchase of Microchip stock in the aftermarket. Hooker & Faye also featured Microchip as the "stock of the month" in its April 2000 investment newsletter. Steve Swanson and Emma Emerald were among the Hooker & Faye brokers that participated in the hyping of Microchip. Both brokers were particularly aggressive in soliciting their clients to buy Microchip, which was trading in the aftermarket at $12 per share. However, neither broker—nor any other broker at Hooker—revealed to those clients that in March 2000, a small group of favored clients had been allotted shares from the Microchip IPO on the condition that they purchase additional Microchip stock in the aftermarket at prices higher than the offering price of $10. The brokers also did not reveal to their present clients that as a result of this "laddering" activity with the favored clients, the current market price of Microchip stock was probably inflated.

Microchip's three most senior officials were Jerry Johnson, Peter Passet, and Carol Clarkson who were Chief Executive Officer, President, and Chief Operating Officer respectively. At the time of the IPO, these three officers, all also directors of Microchip, expected that at least 60% of the offering proceeds would be used to satisfy a multi-million dollar past-due account owed to its principal supplier. According to a report from Microchip's Chief Financial Officer, Wilma Wilkins, dated January 2000, the offering proceeds represented the only way to meet this obligation. Ms. Wilkins's report, however, was shown only to Johnson, Passet, and Clarkson, and they did not share it with Microchip's four other directors, all of whom were independent directors not employed by the company.

In April 2000, Microchip paid its supplier $6 million from the IPO proceeds. The other $4 million from the IPO was spent on research on new technologies for the production of computer microchips as described in the use of proceeds section of the prospectus.

After the IPO, Microchip filed periodic forms 10-K and 10-Q as required by the Exchange Act. Between March 2000 and March 2002, none of these reports disclosed that its supplier had received any of the proceeds from the IPO. The financial statements included in these periodic reports, like the financial statements included in the earlier registration statement, were audited by Reilly & Whitman. Microchip's stock declined slowly during 2000 and 2001 from its post-IPO aftermarket price of $12 to a price of $7 per share at the beginning of March, 2002.

On March 10, 2002, Microchip finally disclosed that the company had used 60% of the IPO proceeds to satisfy an obligation owed its supplier. Microchip's stock quickly dropped from a trading price of $7 per share to $2 per share on the same day. The price thereafter tumbled to $1 per share after Suzy Squeal, a former internal auditor for Microchip, announced at a press conference her belief that Johnson, Passet, and Clarkson had intentionally obscured from shareholders and the investing public the payment to the supplier and the consequent diversion of funds from research. She also voiced a suspicion that the funds had been unavailable to pay the supplier in March 2000 because all three officers and directors had been embezzling from the company for years.

Assume that all of the above facts and suspicions have been confirmed by SEC staff members in the course of an informal investigation. What enforcement alternatives are available to the SEC? Against whom can enforcement actions be instituted? What remedies would the SEC be most likely to seek?

## D. LITIGATING WITH THE SEC

Although the overwhelming majority of enforcement actions initiated by the SEC are settled, approximately one in ten are litigated, either in an administrative proceeding or in federal court. As we have seen, the choice of whether to pursue an action through the SEC's administrative process or a federal court rests entirely with the Commission. Often, a case that the staff would have been willing to settle administratively with, for example, the issuance of a cease-and-desist order, may be litigated as an injunctive action in federal district court with the SEC also seeking the imposition of a monetary penalty. (Under these circumstances, the added threat of a federal court action coupled with a possible injunction and monetary fine constitute additional costs to the party in refusing to settle.) Other types of litigated actions—particularly those against regulated entities such as broker-dealers, investment advisers, and investment companies—are almost always brought administratively, in part because of the wide array of sanctions that Congress has empowered the Commission to impose.

This section first describes the process of litigation with the SEC—in both administrative proceedings and in federal court. It then examines three issues common to both types of enforcement proceedings: burdens of proof, statutes of limitations, and collateral estoppel.

### 1. *The Litigation Process*

#### *a. SEC Administrative Proceedings*

Although administrative proceedings vary widely depending on the particular type that is instituted by the SEC—for example, stop order proceedings against publicly traded companies are very different from disciplinary proceedings brought against broker-dealers—there are certain shared characteristics. First, administrative proceedings are governed by the Commission's Rules of Practice. See 17 C.F.R. § 201.100 et seq. Second, they typically are initiated with the Commission's issuance of an "Order of Proceedings" that specifies the charges against the "respondent" and there is typically a 20 day period for the respondent to file an answer. See § 201.220(b). Third, administrative proceedings that require evidentiary hearings are generally conducted by administrative law judges (ALJs), who are employees of the Commission. ALJs address pre-hearing motions, see § 201.221(c)(5), supervise the limited process of discovery, see § 201.230, evaluate the testimony and cross-examinations of the witnesses presented by the enforcement staff and the respondent, see § 201.326, and render a written decision, see § 201.360, often after the receipt of post-hearing briefs submitted by both the respondent and the staff, see § 201.340(c). In an evidentiary hearing conducted by an ALJ, neither the Federal Rules of Civil Procedure nor the Federal Rules of Evidence apply. Such a hearing is thus very different from a hearing in federal district court.

The initial decision issued by the ALJ generally includes findings of fact and conclusions of law (supported by reasons for those findings and conclusions) and a recommended sanction. This initial decision is final unless either party files a petition for review with the Commission within the time limit specified by the ALJ, generally not to exceed 21 days from the date of decision. See 17 C.F.R. §§ 201.360(b), 201.410. The Commission may also order review on its own initiative. See § 201.411(c). On review, the Commission may affirm, reverse, modify, or set aside the ALJ's initial decision, or may remand the case to the ALJ for further proceedings, and may make "any findings or conclusions that in its judgment are proper and on the basis of the record." § 201.411(a). In other words, the Commission's authority on review is *de novo*. If no review is sought, or if the Commission declines review where it has discretion to do so, see § 201.411(b), the Commission issues a final order which sets the date on which the sanction recommended by the ALJ, if any, takes effect. See § 201.360(e).

Some have argued that conflict inheres in the Commission's quasi-judicial function of adjudicating administrative proceedings that it itself has authorized. Even in the Commission's very early years, it was thought that "there is something abhorrent in the idea that any single group may make laws, may act as a public prosecutor in enforcing those laws, and may then determine the guilt or innocence of the person it has accused." Roland L. Redmond, The Securities Exchange Act of 1934: An Experiment in Administrative Law, 47 Yale L.J. 622, 636-37 (1938). Do you agree? Is the conflict, if any, ameliorated by the availability of judicial review?

In this regard, consider that each of the federal securities laws provides for judicial review of a final order by the Commission in the United States Court of Appeals for the circuit in which the respondent resides or has his principal place of business or in the District of Columbia Circuit. See, e.g., Section 25(a)(1) of the Exchange Act. The statutes specify that an appeal must be commenced within sixty days after the entry of the Commission's final order, see, e.g., id., and that the SEC's factual findings, if supported by substantial evidence, are conclusive. See, e.g., Section 25(a)(4) of the Exchange Act. A respondent may seek circuit court review of an administrative proceeding only if she has already pursued and exhausted all administrative remedies available.

### b. *Federal Court Proceedings*

At first blush it may seem, from a private litigant's perspective, that litigating in federal court is a superior alternative to the administrative process because the fact finder—whether judge or jury—is very much independent of the

SEC. But consider whether this independence comes with a level of formality that is often avoided in an administrative hearing. What are the consequences when the SEC (literally) makes a federal case out of a suspected securities law violation? In this regard, consider even seemingly simple things, such as the fact that, in federal court, the SEC files a "complaint" against a "defendant" in an action captioned "SEC v. *defendant.*" How does this differ from the administrative nomenclature? Consider also the fact that the Federal Rules of Civil Procedure and the Federal Rules of Evidence now apply. In what ways would this benefit a defendant? Are there ways in which this constitutes a tactical disadvantage?

As we have seen from the preceding Section of this Chapter, enforcement actions initiated by the SEC in federal court are typically filed as injunctive actions pursuant to provisions in one or more of the federal securities laws. See, e.g., Section 21(d)(1) of the Exchange Act. The action commences with the filing of the SEC's complaint, which in cases alleging fraud, must meet the particularity requirements of Rule 9(b) of the Federal Rules of Civil Procedure. In most cases, this is hardly a hurdle because the SEC typically files complaints of considerable length and detail, often described by defense counsel as "speaking complaints."

Although both pre-trial and trial practice with the SEC follows a similar course with the same rules as private litigation, it would be extremely unwise to regard the SEC as an ordinary litigant. Consider this view from the defense counsel's perspective:

> First, the Commission, as a law enforcement agency, enters many courts on an important public mission and with an aura of credibility, advantages not often held by private plaintiffs. Second, its investigative powers give the Commission substantial advantages when seeking a TRO or preliminary injunction. The Commission usually goes to court with the benefit of many months and sometimes several years of "discovery" through the investigative process. Even the best funded and best prepared of defendants often can assemble only a few pieces of the mosaic that the staff has had months or years to complete. The Commission also enjoys immunity from certain legal defenses and tactics that may be available in private actions. Finally, the Commission now holds a wide array of flexible "remedies" to rectify and punish violations of the law.

Jeffrey B. Maletta, Litigating SEC Injunctive Actions: The SEC's Traditional Enforcement Mechanism, in the Securities Enforcement Manual: Tactics and Strategies 204 (Richard M. Philips, ed., 1997).

As with private litigation, the defendant in an SEC injunctive action may file any number of pre-trial motions, including motions to dismiss under Fed. R. Civ. P. 12(b)(6) and motions for summary judgment under Rule 56. The SEC also frequently submits motions for summary judgment, or partial summary judgment, in cases where it is the law rather than the facts that are in dispute. Unresolved issues of material fact must proceed to trial.

Because SEC injunctive actions are "equitable" in nature, they are typically tried before a judge. However, in cases where the SEC is seeking the imposition of a civil monetary penalty, a defendant may invoke a Seventh Amendment right to a trial by jury. As the Supreme Court made clear in *Tull v. United States*, 481 U.S. 412 (1987), this right applies only to the determination of the defendant's liability; the determination of the penalty amount occurs in a subsequent phase conducted by a judge. What tactical considerations may influence a defendant's choice between a bench trial or a jury trial? In penalty cases where the defendant chooses not to assert the jury right, can this right be asserted by the SEC?

### 2. *Legal Issues in SEC Litigation*

#### *a. Burden of Proof*

As this next decision and the notes that follow make clear, controversy has surrounded the issue of the SEC's burden of proof at trial and in administrative hearings. Although at one time it appeared that a higher standard should govern in at least some actions brought by the Commission, today there is little doubt that "preponderance of the evidence" is the standard that the SEC must meet in virtually all of its civil litigation.

## STEADMAN v. SEC

450 U.S. 91 (1981)

JUSTICE BRENNAN:

In administrative proceedings, the Securities and Exchange Commission applies a preponderance-of-the-evidence standard of proof in determining whether the antifraud provisions of the federal securities laws have been violated. The question presented is whether such violations must be proved by clear and convincing evidence rather than by a preponderance of the evidence.

I

In June 1971, the Commission initiated a disciplinary proceeding against petitioner and certain of his wholly owned companies. The proceeding against petitioner was brought pursuant to § 9(b) of the Investment Company Act of 1940 and § 203(f) of the Investment Advisers Act of 1940. The Commission alleged that petitioner had violated numerous provisions of the federal securities laws in his management of several mutual funds registered under the Investment Company Act.

After a lengthy evidentiary hearing before an Administrative Law Judge and review by the Commission in which the preponderance-of-the-evidence standard was employed, the Commission held that between December 1965 and June 1972, petitioner had violated antifraud, reporting, conflict of interest, and proxy provisions of the federal securities laws. Accordingly, it entered an order permanently barring petitioner from associating with any investment adviser or affiliating with any registered investment company, and suspending him for one year from associating with any broker or dealer in securities.

Petitioner sought review of the Commission's order in the United States Court of Appeals for the Fifth Circuit on a number of grounds, only one of which is relevant for our purposes. Petitioner challenged the Commission's use of the preponderance-of-the-evidence standard of proof in determining whether he had violated antifraud provisions of the securities laws. He contended that, because of the potentially severe sanctions that the Commission was empowered to impose and because of the circumstantial and inferential nature of the evidence that might be used to prove intent to defraud, the Commission was required to weigh the evidence against a clear-and-convincing standard of proof. The Court of Appeals rejected petitioner's argument, holding that in a disciplinary proceeding before the Commission violations of the antifraud provisions of the securities laws may be established by a preponderance of the evidence. Because this was contrary to the position taken by the United States Court of Appeals for the District of Columbia Circuit, see *Whitney v. SEC*, 604 F.2d 676 (1979); *Collins Securities Corp. v. SEC*, 562 F.2d 820 (1977), we granted certiorari to resolve the conflict. We affirm.

II

Where Congress has not prescribed the degree of proof which must be adduced by the proponent of a rule or order to carry its burden of persuasion in an administrative proceeding, this Court has felt at liberty to prescribe the standard, for "[i]t is the kind of question which has traditionally been left to the judiciary to resolve." *Woodby v. INS*, 385 U.S. 276, 284 (1966). However, where Congress has spoken, we have deferred to "the traditional powers of Congress to prescribe rules of evidence and standards of proof in the federal courts" absent countervailing constitutional constraints. *Vance v. Terrazas*, 444 U.S. 252, 265 (1980). For Commission disciplinary proceedings initiated pursuant to [Section 9(b) of the Investment Company Act and Section 203(f) of the Investment Advisers Act] we conclude that Congress has spoken, and has said that the preponderance-of-the-evidence standard should be applied.

The securities laws provide for judicial review of Commission disciplinary proceedings in the federal courts of appeals and specify the scope of such review. Because they do not indicate which standard of proof governs Commission adjudications, however, we turn to § 5 of the Administrative Procedure Act (APA), 5 U.S.C. § 554, which "applies ... in every case of adjudication required by statute to be determined on the record after opportunity for an agency hearing," except in instances not relevant here. Section 5(b) makes the provisions of § 7, 5 U.S.C. § 556, applicable to adjudicatory proceedings. The answer to the question presented in this case turns therefore on the proper construction of § 7.

The search for congressional intent begins with the language of the statute. Section 7(c) states in pertinent part:

> Except as otherwise provided by statute, the proponent of a rule or order has the burden of proof. Any oral or documentary evidence may be received, but the agency as a matter of policy shall provide for the exclusion of irrelevant, immaterial, or unduly repetitious evidence. A sanction may not be imposed or rule or order issued except on consideration of the whole record or those parts thereof cited by a party and supported by and *in accordance with* the reliable, probative, and *substantial evidence.* (Emphasis added.)

The language of the statute itself implies the enactment of a standard of proof. By allowing sanctions to be imposed only when they are "in accordance with ... *substantial* evidence," Congress implied that a sanction must rest on a *minimum quantity* of evidence. The word "substantial" denotes quantity. The phrase "in accordance with ... substantial evidence" thus requires that a decision be based on a certain quantity of evidence. Petitioner's contention that the phrase "reliable, probative, and substantial evidence" sets merely a standard of *quality* of evidence is, therefore, unpersuasive.

The phrase "in accordance with" lends further support to a construction of § 7(c) as establishing a standard of proof. *** [This section] provides that an agency may issue an order only if that order is "supported by and *in accordance with* ... substantial evidence" (emphasis added). The additional words "in accordance with" suggest that the adjudicating agency must weigh the evidence and decide, based on the weight of the evidence, whether a disciplinary order should be issued. The language of § 7(c), therefore, requires that the agency decision must be "in accordance with" the weight of the evidence, not simply supported by enough evidence " 'to justify, if the trial were to a jury, a refusal to direct a verdict when the conclusion sought to be drawn from it is one of fact for the jury.' " *Consolo v. FMC*, 383 U.S. 607, 620 (1966), quoting *NLRB v. Columbian Enameling & Stamping Co.*, 306 U.S. 292, 300 (1939). Obviously, weighing evidence has relevance only if the evidence on each side is to be measured against a standard of proof which allocates the risk of error. See *Addington v. Texas*, 441 U.S. 418, 423 (1979). *** Thus, petitioner's argument that § 7(c) merely establishes the scope of judicial review of agency orders is unavailing.

While the language of § 7(c) suggests, therefore, that Congress intended the statute to establish a standard of proof, the language of the statute is somewhat opaque concerning the precise standard of proof to be used. The legislative history, however, clearly reveals the Congress' intent. The original Senate version of § 7(c) provided that "no sanction shall be imposed ... except as supported by relevant, reliable, and probative evidence." S. 7, 79th Cong., 1st Sess. (1945). After the Senate passed this version, the House passed the language of the statute as it reads today, and the Senate accepted the amendment. Any doubt as to the intent of Congress is removed by the House Report, which expressly adopted a preponderance-of-the-evidence standard:

> [W]here a party having the burden of proceeding has come forward with a prima facie and substantial case, he will prevail unless his evidence is discredited or rebutted. In any case the agency must decide 'in accordance with the evidence.' Where there is evidence pro and con, the agency must weigh it and decide *in accordance with the preponderance*. In short, these provisions require a conscientious and rational judgment on the whole record in accordance with the proofs adduced." H.R. Rep. No. 1980, 79th Cong., 2d Sess., 37 (1946) (emphasis added)

Nor is there any suggestion in the legislative history that a standard of proof higher than a preponderance of the evidence was ever contemplated, much less intended. Congress was primarily concerned with the elimination of agency decisionmaking premised on evidence which was of poor quality—irrelevant, immaterial, unreliable, and nonprobative—and of insufficient quantity—less than a preponderance. See id., at 36-37 and 45; S. Doc. No. 248, 79th Cong., 2d Sess., 320-322 and 376-378 (1946); n. 21, *supra*.

The language and legislative history of § 7(c) lead us to conclude, therefore, that § 7(c) was intended to establish a standard of proof and that the standard adopted is the traditional preponderance-of-the-evidence standard.

III

Our view of congressional intent is buttressed by the Commission's longstanding practice of imposing sanctions according to the preponderance of the evidence. As early as 1938, the Commission rejected the argument that in a proceeding to determine whether to suspend, expel, or otherwise sanction a brokerage firm and its principals for, *inter alia*, manipulation of security prices in violation of § 9 of the Securities Exchange Act of 1934 a standard of proof greater than the preponderance-of-the-evidence standard was required. *In re White*, 3 S.E.C. 466, 539-540 (1938). Use of the preponderance standard continued after passage of the APA, and persists today. E.g., *In re Cea*, 44 S.E.C. 8, 25 (1969); *In re Pollisky*, 43 S.E.C. 458, 459-460 (1967). The Commission's consistent practice, which is in harmony with § 7(c) and its legislative history, is persuasive authority that Congress intended that Commission disciplinary proceedings, subject to § 7 of the APA, be governed by a preponderance-of-the- evidence standard. See *Andrus v. Sierra Club*, 442 U.S. 347, 358 (1979); *United States v. National Association of Securities Dealers, Inc.*, 422 U.S. 694, 719 (1975); *Skidmore v. Swift & Co.*, 323 U.S. 134, 140 (1944).

In *Vermont Yankee Nuclear Power Corp. v. Natural Resources Defense Council, Inc.*, 435 U.S. 519, 524 (1978), we stated that § 4 of the APA established the "maximum procedural requirements which Congress was willing to have the courts impose upon agencies in conducting rulemaking procedures." In § 7(c), Congress has similarly expressed its intent that adjudicatory proceedings subject to the APA satisfy the statute where determinations are made according to the preponderance of the evidence. Congress was free to make that choice, *Vance v. Terrazas*, 444 U.S., at 265-266, and, in the absence of countervailing constitutional considerations, the courts are not free to disturb it.

JUSTICE POWELL, WITH WHOM JUSTICE STEWART JOINS, DISSENTING:

The Securities and Exchange Commission (SEC), acting under the antifraud provisions of the Investment Company Act of 1940 and the Investment Advisers Act of 1940, has imposed severe sanctions on petitioner. He has been barred permanently from practicing his profession and also forced to divest himself of an investment at a substantial loss. In making its findings of fraud and imposing these penalties, the SEC applied the "preponderance of the evidence" standard of proof. ***

The SEC acted in this case under § 9(b) of the Investment Company Act of 1940 and § 203(f) of the Investment Advisers Act of 1940. Sanctions imposed under these sections are the functional equivalent of penalties for fraud. At common law, it was plain that allegations of fraud had to be proved by clear and convincing evidence. E.g., *Addington v. Texas*, 441 U.S. 418, 424 (1979); *Woodby v. INS*, 385 U.S. 276, 285, n. 18 (1966); *Weininger v. Metropolitan Fire Insurance Co.*, 359 Ill. 584, 598 (1935); *Bank of Pocahontas v. Ferimer*, 161 Va. 37, 40-41 (1933); *Bowe v. Gage*, 127 Wis. 245, 251 (1906). Congress enacted the Investment Company and Investment Advisers Acts against this common-law background. There is no evidence that Congress, when it adopted these Acts, intended to authorize the SEC to abandon the then-applicable standard of proof in fraud adjudications. See *Whitney v. SEC*, 604 F.2d 676 (1979); *Collins Securities Corp. v. SEC*, 562 F.2d 820 (1977).

The APA, upon which the Court relies, did not become law for some seven years after the enactment of the two statutes under which the SEC imposed these penalties. Again, the Court points to no specific evidence that

Congress intended the APA to supplant the burden-of-proof rule generally applicable when the securities laws were enacted. Thus, the APA—the *general* statute applicable only where a *specific* statute is not—should have no bearing on the proof burden in this case.

I imply no opinion on the question whether the evidence supports the SEC's allegations against petitioner. It is clear, however, that the SEC's finding of fraud and its imposition of harsh penalties have resulted in serious stigma and deprivation. Cf. *Addington v. Texas,* supra.[1] In the absence of any specific demonstration of Congress' purpose, we should not assume that Congress intended the SEC to apply a lower standard of proof than the prevailing common-law standard for similar allegations. With all respect, it seems to me that the Court's decision today lacks the sensitivity that traditionally has marked our review of the Government's imposition upon citizens of severe penalties and permanent stigma.

## *NOTES AND QUESTIONS*

***1. Civil Proceedings vs. Criminal Proceedings.*** Consider Justice Powell's reference in the footnote of his dissenting opinion to the "beyond a reasonable doubt" standard of the criminal law. Given some of the severe sanctions that Congress has authorized the SEC to seek against securities law violators, does it make sense to distinguish a person's rights based on whether enforcement is civil or criminal? In addition to the higher burden of proof, what additional protections—constitutional or otherwise—attach only to criminal proceedings? As a matter of policy, should any of these be extended to defendants/respondents in litigation with the SEC? How much should turn on whether a sanction is deemed to be "remedial" or "punitive"? How much should turn on the technical description of a sanction as criminal or civil? In this regard, consider the Supreme Court's decision in *Hudson v. United States* discussed in Section F.3 infra. Consider also the material in Section D.2.b infra dealing with whether statutes of limitations are applicable to enforcement actions brought by the Commission.

***2. Burden of Proof in SEC Injunctive Actions.*** *Steadman* established preponderance of the evidence as the standard of proof in administrative proceedings brought by the Commission. Does this standard apply as well in enforcement actions brought by the Commission in federal court?

Although there have been a few twists in the road in the past, today one can expect that in seeking injunctive relief in federal court, the SEC will be held to a preponderance of the evidence standard. That there was ever any controversy is somewhat surprising in light of the Supreme Court's clear statement in *SEC v. C.M. Joiner Leasing Corp.*, 320 U.S. 344, 355 (1943), that "[w]here *** proof is offered in a civil action *** a preponderance of the evidence will establish the case." *Joiner* was an injunctive action brought by the SEC for

---

1. Petitioner has practiced the profession of investment adviser for many years. He has been forever barred from resuming that profession. Many penalties imposed under our criminal laws—such as monetary fines and probation—are far less severe, and yet these can be imposed only under the "beyond a reasonable doubt" standard of the criminal law.

violations of Section 17(a) of the Securities Act. The issue arose again in *Herman & MacLean v. Huddleston*, 459 U.S. 375 (1983), which involved a private action for damages under Rule 10b-5. Because the latter action involved allegations of fraud, the Fifth Circuit maintained that clear and convincing evidence was the appropriate standard of proof. The Supreme Court disagreed, noting that "[a] preponderance-of-the-evidence standard allows both parties to 'share the risk of error in roughly equal fashion,' " id. at 390, and that the plaintiffs should recover if "they prove that it is more likely than not that they were defrauded." Id. Courts routinely cite *Herman & MacLean* in the context of Section 10(b) injunctive actions brought by the Commission. See, e.g., *SEC v. Lorin*, 877 F. Supp. 192, 195 (S.D.N.Y. 1995), aff'd in part, vacated in part on other grounds, 76 F.3d 458 (2d Cir. 1996); *SEC v. Musella*, 678 F. Supp. 1060, 1063 (S.D.N.Y. 1988).

***3. Loss of Livelihood.*** In *SEC v. Moran*, 922 F. Supp. 867, 887-88 (S.D.N.Y. 1996), an insider trading case that we studied in Chapter 7, the court considered the defendants' claim that because "they [were] subjected to money damages, an injunction, and loss of livelihood in [a] wholly circumstantial case, the higher standard proof, clear and convincing evidence, is necessitated." In so doing, the court noted that:

> Historically, there are relatively few areas of the law which impose upon the plaintiff the burden of proving its case by clear and convincing evidence. Those examples are limited to cases in which the defendant faces a judgement which could potentially impose penalties such as loss of liberty, deportation, termination of parental rights, or deprivation of ability to engage in ones livelihood. See e.g., *Santosky v. Kramer*, 455 U.S. 745 (1982) (proceeding to terminate parental rights); *Addington v. Texas*, [441 U.S. 418, 427 (1979)] (due process requires that in a commitment proceeding the state must "justify confinement by proof more substantial than a mere preponderance of the evidence"); *Woodby v. INS*, [385 U.S. 276, 285-86 (1966)] (deportation proceedings governed by clear and convincing standard); *In re Ryder*, 263 F.Supp. 360, 361 (E.D.Va.), aff'd, 381 F.2d 713 (4th Cir.1967) (disbarment proceeding governed by clear and convincing standard).

*Moran*, 922 F. Supp. at 889. The court further cited to *Collins Sec. Corp. v. SEC*, 562 F.2d 820, 825-26 (D.C. Cir. 1977) where the D.C. Circuit had stated that the clear and convincing standard would govern an action brought by the SEC seeking revocation of a defendant's broker and dealer registration, expulsion from membership in NASD, and barring association with any other broker or dealer. See *Moran*, 922 F. Supp. at 889.

The *Moran* court ultimately rejected the defendants' request for a higher proof burden, distinguishing the injunctive relief sought against the insider trading defendants from the relief of a permanent bar sought against the securities broker in *Collins*. See id. at 889 (stating that "there is significant difference between a defendant who will in fact be deprived of his livelihood and one who will 'effectively' be deprived"). But in so doing, the *Moran* court seemed to assume that *Collins*' "loss of livelihood" rationale for a clear and convincing standard survives the Supreme Court's decision in *Steadman*. Does it?

### b. *Statutes of Limitations*

With the single exception of the five year period specified in Section 21A(d)(5) for civil monetary penalties in insider trading cases, the federal securities laws do not specify any statutes of limitations for enforcement actions brought by the SEC. And the SEC's unequivocal and long-standing position had been that no such statute of limitations should be implied. The SEC's position met with complete success the few times it was litigated, until 1995, when the D.C. Circuit decided *Johnson v. SEC*, the principal case that follows.

Prior to *Johnson*, the most important case to consider this statute of limitations issue was *SEC v. Rind*, 991 F.2d 1486 (1993). The underlying conduct at issue involved the well-publicized collapse of ZZZZ Best Company ("Z Best"). In August 1990, more than three years after Z Best's declaration of bankruptcy, the SEC filed a civil injunction action against Rind and thirteen other defendants. Because twelve of these defendants had consented to judgments against them and another one defaulted, Rind was the only defendant left in the case.

The SEC's complaint alleged that Rind had concocted a fraudulent transaction (from which he gained at least $700,000 in profits) which allowed Z Best to overstate its assets vastly, thereby enabling the company to raise millions of dollars in capital. The SEC sought a permanent injunction prohibiting Rind from violating Securities Act Section 17(a), Exchange Act Section 10(b), and Rule 10b-5 in the future and requiring disgorgement of his unlawful gains. Rind sought dismissal on the ground that the SEC must adhere to the same one year/ three year limitations rule applicable to private plaintiffs by the Supreme Court's decision in *Lampf, Pleva, Lipkind, Prupis & Petigrow v. Gilbertson*, 501 U.S. 350 (1991). The district court had granted the SEC's motion to strike that defense but certified the question for interlocutory appeal.

In rejecting Rind's arguments, the Ninth Circuit drew a stark contrast between private actions for securities fraud and enforcement actions brought by the SEC, emphasizing that:

> [T]he Commission sues as part of its statutory mandate to enforce the federal securities laws. As such, civil enforcement actions promote economic and social policies independent of the claims of individual investors. The fact that disgorgement involves money does not change the nature of the remedy. The Commission seeks disgorgement in order to deprive the wrongdoer of his or her unlawful profits and thereby eliminate the incentive for violating the securities laws. The theory behind the remedy is deterrence and not compensation. Indeed, a district court may grant the Commission's request for disgorgement even where no injured investors can be identified. In light of the important public function served by Commission enforcement activity, we therefore cannot conclude, as did the Court in *Lampf*, that the express time limits for private claims "accommodate a balance of interests very similar to that at stake here."

*Rind*, 991 F.2d Id. at 1490.

Having determined that the Supreme Court's decision in *Lampf* did not establish a statute of limitations for SEC enforcement actions, the Ninth Circuit next considered whether such a limitations period should nonetheless be implied. Although the court observed that Congress's silence regarding a statute of limitations often has been interpreted to require "borrowing" from analogous state statutes, the court pointed to the exception that:

> [s]tate limitations periods do not bind the United States when it sues to vindicate a public right or interest, absent a clear showing of congressional intent to the contrary. This doctrine, which has its origins in the ancient principle that time does not run against the king, finds its modern justification in the policy that public rights, revenues, and property should not be forfeited due to the negligence of public officials. See *Guaranty Trust Co. v. United States,* 304 U.S. 126, 132 (1938).

*Rind,* 991 F.2d at 1491. The court then stated that:

> When the Commission sues to enforce the securities laws, it vindicates public rights and furthers the public interest. The public character of Commission action is reflected in the introduction to the 1934 Act: "[T]ransactions in securities ... are affected with a national public interest which makes it necessary to provide for regulation and control of such transactions." Congress entrusted the Commission with the vital mission of ensuring the honesty and fairness of the capital markets. "The entire purpose and thrust of a [Commission] enforcement action is to expeditiously safeguard the public interest by enjoining securities violations. The claims asserted in such an action stem from, and are colored by, the intense public interest in [Commission] enforcement of these laws." *SEC v. Asset Management Corp.,* 456 F. Supp. 998, 1000 (S.D. Ind. 1978). ***

*Rind,* 991 F.2d at 1491.

The court further emphasized the central role that disgorgement plays in the enforcement of the securities laws and the complexity of many of the securities fraud cases pursued by the Commission. It noted specifically that "[b]y deterring violations of the securities laws, disgorgement actions further the Commission's public policy mission of protecting investors and safeguarding the integrity of the markets." Id. at 1491. It also observed that "the Commission must expend considerable time and energy investigating alleged violations of the securities laws" and that "securities fraud may involve multiple parties and transactions of mind-boggling complexity." Id. at 1492. Quoting the Supreme Court's decision in *Occidental Life Ins. Co. v. EEOC,* 432 U.S. 355, 367 (1977), it therefore concluded that "[p]lacing strict time limits on Commission enforcement actions *** would quite plainly 'frustrate or interfere with the implementation of national policies.'" *Rind,* 991 F.2d at 1492.

As you read the following decision, consider whether it signals a potential turning of the tide.

## JOHNSON v. SEC

87 F.3d 484 (D.C. Cir. 1996)

WALD, CIRCUIT JUDGE:

*** In this case, we decide that a Securities and Exchange Commission ("SEC") proceeding resulting in a censure and a six-month disciplinary suspension of a securities industry supervisor was a proceeding "for the enforcement of any civil fine, penalty, or forfeiture, pecuniary or otherwise," within the meaning of [the five-year statute of limitations in 28 U.S.C. ] § 2462.

Accordingly we grant petitioner Patricia A. Johnson's petition for review and vacate the SEC's order imposing sanctions on her.

I. BACKGROUND

Patricia A. Johnson was the branch manager of PaineWebber, Inc.'s Beverly Hills, California office from November 1984 to April 1991. Among the employees she supervised was David Zetterstrom, an account representative who allegedly stole more than $114,000 from his customers between 1987 and 1988 by writing unauthorized checks against their accounts. Though Johnson was unaware of these thefts, she had received other complaints about Zetterstrom's handling of customer accounts which eventually led her to place him on probation, and then fire him, on June 10, 1988. Three days after he was fired, Zetterstrom committed suicide.

After terminating Zetterstrom's employment, Johnson further investigated his activities and learned for the first time that he had stolen clients' funds. PaineWebber began an internal audit, and notified the SEC, which began its own investigation in June 1988. More than five years later, on October 26, 1993, the SEC brought formal charges against Johnson, alleging that she had "failed reasonably to supervise [Zetterstrom] ... within the meaning of Section 15(b)(4)(E) of the Exchange Act." Order Instituting Public Administrative Proceedings. The SEC alleged that Johnson had allowed Zetterstrom to issue checks drawn from his customers' accounts without first obtaining from them the required letters of authorization, and that Johnson—even after preliminary evidence of Zetterstrom's wrongdoing had come to light—had allowed him continued access to customers' funds, thereby facilitating his thievery.

In the administrative proceedings, Johnson conceded that Zetterstrom had stolen money from his customers, but disputed the SEC's allegation that her supervision of him was unreasonable. In addition, Johnson claimed that the SEC's action was barred by the general five-year statute of limitations of 28 U.S.C. § 2462:

> Except as otherwise provided by Act of Congress, an action, suit or proceeding for the enforcement of any civil fine, penalty, or forfeiture, pecuniary or otherwise, shall not be entertained unless commenced within five years from the date when the claim first accrued....

The SEC denied Johnson's motion to dismiss under § 2462, holding in February 1994 that "[s]ection 2462 does not apply to Commission administrative proceedings." The SEC's position, however, was severely undercut less than two weeks later when this court decided [*3M Co. v. Browner*, 17 F.3d 1453 (D.C.Cir.1994)] rejecting the view that § 2462 applies only to *judicial* proceedings and holding that § 2462 applies to administrative proceedings as well. 17 F.3d at 1457.

Notwithstanding the *3M* decision, an SEC Administrative Law Judge ("ALJ") held hearings and issued a decision in Johnson's case, finding that she had failed reasonably to supervise Zetterstrom, and imposing a six-month "supervisory suspension" on her. Johnson petitioned the SEC for review of the ALJ's decision, again seeking dismissal based on the statute of limitations.

Evaluating Johnson's second petition in light of *3M*, the SEC articulated another theory for rejecting her claim, holding this time that § 2462 should not apply because the "proceeding before us does not seek to impose a *civil penalty*, but rather to determine the appropriate *remedial action*. The intent of Johnson's suspension is to protect the public from future harm at her hands." Opinion of the Commission at 11. Finally, the SEC affirmed the ALJ's finding that Johnson had failed reasonably to supervise Zetterstrom, and issued an order saying:

> On the basis of the Commission's opinion issued this day, it is ordered that Patricia A. Johnson be, and hereby is, censured and suspended from acting in a supervisory capacity with any broker or dealer for six months. ***

II. DISCUSSION

The sole question in this case is whether the SEC proceeding which resulted in the sanctions imposed on Johnson was "an action, suit, or proceeding for the enforcement of any civil fine, penalty, or forfeiture, pecuniary or otherwise" within the meaning of 28 U.S.C. § 2462. Because § 2462 is a statute of general applicability rather than one whose primary administration has been delegated to the SEC, we interpret it *de novo*.

A. *The Meaning of "Penalty" Under* § 2462

The term "penalty" is nowhere defined in § 2462, so we must be guided here by the Supreme Court's common-sense rule that "[c]ourts properly assume, absent sufficient indication to the contrary, that Congress intends the words in its enactments to carry 'their ordinary, contemporary, common meaning.' " *Pioneer Inv. Servs. Co. v. Brunswick Assoc. Ltd. Partnership*, 507 U.S. 380, 388 (1993).

In common usage, a penalty is "the suffering in person, rights or property which is annexed by law or judicial decision to the commission of a crime or public offense." Webster's Third New International Dictionary 1668 (1976). For at least a century, legal dictionaries have similarly defined penalty. See Black's Law Dictionary 1020 (5th ed.1979) ("A punishment imposed by statute as a consequence of the commission of an offense."); Ballentine's Law Dictionary 948 (1930) ("An exaction in the nature of a punishment for the nonperformance of an act, or for the performance of an unlawful act, and involving the idea of punishment, whether enforced by a civil or criminal action or proceeding."); 2 Burrill's Law Dictionary (1871) ("A punishment; a punishment imposed by statute as a consequence of the commission of a certain act."); 2 Bouvier's Law Dictionary 323 (1866) ("By penalty is understood, also, the punishment inflicted by law for its violation....").

In *Huntington v. Attrill*, 146 U.S. 657 (1892), the Supreme Court addressed the question of whether a judgment in a state court was "penal," and thus could not be enforced in another state under the Constitution's Full Faith and Credit Clause. The Court explained that "[p]enal laws, strictly and properly, are those imposing punishment for an offense committed against the state.... The test whether a law is penal, in the strict and primary sense, is whether the wrong sought to be redressed is a wrong to the public, or a wrong to the individual...." 146 U.S. at 667-68. Put another way, the question of whether a law is penal depends on whether its purpose "is to punish an offense against the public justice of the State, or to afford a private remedy to a person injured by the wrong." Id. at 673-74.

Thus where a legal action is essentially private in nature, seeking only compensation for the damages suffered, it is not an action for a penalty. ***

In many other situations the courts have reaffirmed that a sanction which only remedies the damage caused by the defendant does not trigger the protections of § 2462. ***

In sum, we conclude that a "penalty," as the term is used in § 2462, is a form of punishment imposed by the government for unlawful or proscribed conduct, which goes beyond remedying the damage caused to the harmed parties by the defendant's action.

B. *The Sanctions Here*

We turn next to the specific sanctions imposed here, asking whether the suspension of a supervisor or broker fits within this definition of penalty.

At the outset, we agree with the SEC that the test for whether a sanction is sufficiently punitive to constitute a "penalty" within the meaning of § 2462 is an objective one, not measured from the subjective perspective of the accused (which would render virtually every sanction a penalty). It is obviously not enough that the person subjected to a sanction feels pain or finds the sanction disagreeable; as the Supreme Court has pointed out, "even remedial sanctions carry the sting of punishment." *United States v. Halper*, 490 U.S. 435, 447 n. 7 (1989).***

Here, the sanctions imposed by the SEC—censure and a six-month suspension—clearly resemble punishment in the ordinary sense of the word. The SEC not only restricted Johnson's ability to earn a living as a supervisor during her six-month suspension, but the suspension was also likely to have longer-lasting repercussions on her ability to pursue her vocation. Suspended brokers must forever after disclose the sanction, and it becomes part of their permanent public file. See Form ADV, 17 C.F.R. § 279.1, Part I, Item 11(C)(4) (must disclose whether SEC has "entered an order denying, suspending, or revoking the applicant's ... registration"). Congress has also required securities associations such as the National Association of Securities Dealers to set up a toll-free number for investors and other members of the public to check whether brokers or other brokerage employees have been subject to disciplinary actions. See 15 U.S.C. § 78o-3(i). These collateral consequences of the censure and suspension, while not the central determinant in whether a sanction reaches penalty status, do suggest its punishment-like qualities.

This sanction would less resemble punishment if the SEC had focused on Johnson's current competence or the degree of risk she posed to the public. Despite the SEC's claims to the contrary, however, it is evident that the sanctions here were not based on any general finding of Johnson's unfitness as a supervisor, nor any showing of the risk she posed to the public, but rather were based on Johnson's alleged failure reasonably to supervise Zetterstrom, as required by section 15(b) of the Securities Exchange Act of 1934 ("Exchange Act"). The SEC initiated these proceedings with an indictment-like document entitled "Order Instituting Public Administrative Proceedings Pursuant to

Sections 15(b) and 19(h) of the Securities Exchange Act of 1934," which alleged, *inter alia,* that:

> C. From approximately August 1987 through June 1988, a registered representative in PaineWebber's Beverly Hills branch office willfully violated Section 17(a) of the Securities Act of 1933 ..., Section 10(b) of the Securities Exchange Act of 1934 ... and Rule 10b-5 thereunder in that he misappropriated funds from the accounts of customers without their knowledge or consent.
>
> D. During the period from approximately August 1987 through June 1988, Johnson failed reasonably to supervise the registered representative described in paragraph C above with a view to preventing his violations of Section 17(a) of the Securities Act, Section 10(b) of the Exchange Act and Rule 10b-5 thereunder.

Consistent with this charge, the SEC inquiry appears to have focused almost exclusively on Johnson's failure reasonably to supervise, not her current competence or risk to the public.

Although the ALJ held two days of hearings, with three witnesses and 22 exhibits, the SEC cites not a single piece of evidence in the record explicitly supporting its finding that suspension of Johnson was necessary due to Johnson's current unfitness to be a supervisor. In its final order of more than 11 single-spaced pages, the SEC included only one conclusory paragraph concerning the sanction:

> We believe the sanctions of censure and six months suspension from acting in a supervisory capacity with any broker or dealer imposed by the law judge to be warranted. Johnson displayed a lack of hands-on involvement with her staff and a lack of responsiveness to serious violations by a registered representative under her supervision. Her deficiencies permitted further violations to occur. Accordingly, we affirm the law judge's sanctions against Johnson.

This statement, which justifies the sanction solely in view of Johnson's past misconduct, belies the SEC's assertion in this litigation that the sanctions were imposed not as punishment for past dereliction, but primarily because of Johnson's present danger to the public.[9] To the contrary, we conclude that any inquiry into Johnson's current competence or the danger she posed to the public (and the SEC cites to no such inquiry) was at most *pro forma*. In substance, this proceeding was directed toward one thing only—determining whether Johnson had failed reasonably to supervise Zetterstrom within the meaning of the Exchange Act—and the resultant sanction was inflicted on Johnson for that failure.

C. *Exception for Statutes Protecting the Public?*

The SEC argues nonetheless that a license suspension should not constitute punishment or a penalty where the government's purpose is to protect the public. See, e.g., *Hawker v. New York*, 170 U.S. 189, 200 (1898) (law barring convicted felons from practicing medicine did not violate *ex post facto* clause); *Ex parte Wall*, 107 U.S. 265, 287 (1883) (disbarment of attorney could proceed

---

9. If the SEC really viewed Johnson as a clear and present danger to the public, it is inexplicable why it waited *more than five years* to begin the proceedings to suspend her.

without grand jury indictment or jury trial); *United States v. Stoller*, [78 F.3d 724 (1st Cir. 1996)] (debarment of individual from banking industry did not violate double jeopardy clause); *DiCola v. FDA*, 77 F.3d 504, 507 (D.C.Cir.1996) (exclusion of an individual from further activities in the pharmaceutical industry was "solely remedial" and thus did not constitute punishment for double jeopardy or *ex post facto* purposes).

While these cases do hold that a license suspension—if motivated by a *bona fide* goal of protecting the public—may not be punishment in various *constitutional* contexts, they do not control the question of whether license suspension is a *penalty for purposes of § 2462.*[10] In the constitutional cases cited by the SEC, the chief concern has been whether a putatively civil or regulatory sanction is in actuality a back-door form of punishment, such that certain constitutional protections should be triggered. Accordingly, the main focus of these cases has been on whether the law imposing the sanctions has an overall remedial *purpose* of protecting the public (with the sanctions being the reasonable means of achieving that purpose). In interpreting § 2462, however, the court's concern is not whether Congress legislated the sanction as part of a regulatory scheme to protect the public, but rather whether the sanction is itself a form of punishment of the individual for unlawful or proscribed conduct, going beyond compensation of the wronged party.

Thus in *Meeker* [*v. Lehigh Valley R.R.*I, 236 U.S. 412, 423 (1915)], the sanction was "strictly remedial" because it only required the defendant to return overcharges to the plaintiff, and did not impose any punishment. Similarly, where the effect of the SEC's action is to restore the *status quo ante,* such as through a proceeding for restitution or disgorgement of ill-gotten profits, § 2462 will not apply. See, e.g., *SEC v. Lorin*, 869 F. Supp. 1117, 1122-23 (S.D.N.Y. 1994) (reading *Meeker* to support proposition that disgorgement is not a "fine, penalty, or forfeiture" within the meaning of § 2462 since such sanction is "strictly remedial").

The sanctions imposed here, however, are certainly not "remedial" in the sense that term is used in *Meeker* and its progeny, for they are not directed toward correcting or undoing the effects of Johnson's allegedly faulty supervision. Unlike restitution or disgorgement, the sanctions here do not attempt to restore the stolen funds to their rightful owner. To the contrary, the sanctions in this case impose a punishment for Johnson's violation of a standard laid down in the Exchange Act, and qualify therefore as a "penalty" within the meaning of § 2462.

D. *Public Policy Exception?*

Finally, the SEC suggests that we should narrowly construe "penalty" in this case, in light of the fact that its proceedings "serve[ ] public policy by preserving public rights, revenues and interests," SEC Brief at 33. While we do

---

10. The SEC's own position on what constitutes a penalty appears to vary with the context. In *SEC v. Telsey*, 144 B.R. 563 (Bankr.S.D.Fla.1992), the court agreed with the SEC that disgorgement orders are not dischargeable in bankruptcy because they have a deterrent purpose and thus *are* a "fine, penalty, or forfeiture." The SEC never explains why the position it took in *that* case should not apply here as well.

not doubt the public importance of SEC proceedings, the Supreme Court has admonished us that:

> Whatever prejudice there may have been in ancient times against statutes of limitations, it is a cardinal principle of modern law and of this court, that they are to be treated as statutes of repose, and are not to be construed so as to defeat their obvious intent to secure the prompt enforcement of claims during the lives of the witnesses, and when their recollection may be presumed to be still unimpaired. [14]

*Campbell v. City of Haverhill*, 155 U.S. 610, 617 (1895). The SEC also directs us toward cases which serve up maxims about the need for strict construction of statutes of limitation, *see* SEC Brief at 32. But as we pointed out in *3M*, 17 F.3d at 1457, such cases—including their maxims—are unpersuasive, as they run counter to the Supreme Court's basic position on the subject, first stated by Chief Justice Marshall:

> In a country where not even treason can be prosecuted, after a lapse of three years, it would scarcely be supposed, that an individual would remain for ever liable to a pecuniary forfeiture.

*Adams v. Woods*, 6 U.S. (2 Cranch) 336, 341 (1805).

Finally, any public policy concerns in this case are greatly attenuated because § 2462 applies "[e]xcept as otherwise provided by Act of Congress," and thus Congress, should it believe a five-year statute of limitations is too burdensome in any particular situation, can simply put in a longer limitations period. We therefore find no reason based on public policy or general concerns about statutes of limitation to depart from the "ordinary, contemporary, common meaning" of the word "penalty," as a sanction imposed by the government for unlawful or proscribed conduct which goes beyond remedying the damage caused to the harmed party.

## III. CONCLUSION

We find that the five-year statute of limitations set forth in § 2462 does apply to SEC proceedings under section 15(b) of the Securities and Exchange Act of 1934 which seek to censure and suspend a securities supervisor. Accordingly, we grant Johnson's petition for review, and vacate the SEC's order imposing sanctions on her.

## *NOTES AND QUESTIONS*

1. ***Distinctions and Differences.*** Can the D.C. Circuit's decision in *Johnson* be reconciled with the Ninth Circuit's decision in *Rind?* Are there circumstances under which an SEC action for injunctive relief could be considered an action for a penalty? Note the *Johnson* court's footnote highlighting the SEC's characterization of disgorgement as a "penalty" for purposes of the "no discharge" provisions in the bankruptcy code. Are there other circumstances under which disgorgement may be viewed as a penalty? In this regard, note

---

14. In addition, the SEC argues that enforcing § 2462 would "hobble efforts to prevent future harm to the public." SEC Brief at 33. It is equally likely, however, that once the SEC has delayed more than five years in proceeding against a broker it considers a grave threat to the public, the bulk of the harm has already been done.

that the *Johnson* court cited with approval the district court's holding in *SEC v. Lorin* that § 2462 does not apply to SEC actions for disgorgement.

***2. Balancing the Public Interest.*** The *Rind* court emphasized that its refusal to impose a "borrowed" statute of limitations on the SEC accorded with the common law doctrine *nullum tempus occurrit regi* (time does not run against the king). As a matter of policy, should there be an outside time limit in which the SEC must act to use its enforcement powers under the federal securities laws? Would such a limit jeopardize the SEC's ability to protect the public? What would be an appropriate limit? Five years? Less? More?

*c. Collateral Estoppel*

As we noted previously, one explanation for the overwhelming number of enforcement actions resolved through consensual settlement is the potential collateral estoppel ramifications of litigating with the SEC and losing. The following case vividly illustrates why collateral estoppel constitutes such a serious collateral consequence.

## PARKLANE HOSIERY CO. v. SHORE

439 U.S. 322 (1979)

JUSTICE STEWART:

This case presents the question whether a party who has had issues of fact adjudicated adversely to it in an equitable action may be collaterally estopped from relitigating the same issues before a jury in a subsequent legal action brought against it by a new party.

The respondent brought this stockholder's class action against the petitioners in a Federal District Court. The complaint alleged that the petitioners, Parklane Hosiery Co., Inc. (Parklane), and 13 of its officers, directors, and stockholders, had issued a materially false and misleading proxy statement in connection with a merger. The proxy statement, according to the complaint, had violated §§ 14(a), 10(b), and 20(a) of the Securities Exchange Act of 1934, as well as various rules and regulations promulgated by the Securities and Exchange Commission (SEC). The complaint sought damages, rescission of the merger, and recovery of costs.

Before this action came to trial, the SEC filed suit against the same defendants in the Federal District Court, alleging that the proxy statement that had been issued by Parklane was materially false and misleading in essentially the same respects as those that had been alleged in the respondent's complaint. Injunctive relief was requested. After a 4-day trial, the District Court found that the proxy statement was materially false and misleading in the respects alleged, and entered a declaratory judgment to that effect. The Court of Appeals for the Second Circuit affirmed this judgment.

The respondent in the present case then moved for partial summary judgment against the petitioners, asserting that the petitioners were collaterally estopped from relitigating the issues that had been resolved against them in the action brought by the SEC. The District Court denied the motion on the ground that such an application of collateral estoppel would deny the petitioners their Seventh Amendment right to a jury trial. The Court of Appeals for the Second

Circuit reversed, holding that a party who has had issues of fact determined against him after a full and fair opportunity to litigate in a nonjury trial is collaterally estopped from obtaining a subsequent jury trial of these same issues of fact. The appellate court concluded that "the Seventh Amendment preserves the right to jury trial only with respect to issues of fact, [and] once those issues have been fully and fairly adjudicated in a prior proceeding, nothing remains for trial, either with or without a jury." [*Shore v. Parklane Hosiery Co.*, 565 F.2d 815, 819 (2d Cir. 1977)], at 819. Because of an inter-circuit conflict, we granted certiorari.

I

The threshold question to be considered is whether, quite apart from the right to a jury trial under the Seventh Amendment, the petitioners can be precluded from relitigating facts resolved adversely to them in a prior equitable proceeding with another party under the general law of collateral estoppel. Specifically, we must determine whether a litigant who was not a party to a prior judgment may nevertheless use that judgment "offensively" to prevent a defendant from relitigating issues resolved in the earlier proceeding.[4]

A

Collateral estoppel, like the related doctrine of res judicata,[5] has the dual purpose of protecting litigants from the burden of relitigating an identical issue with the same party or his privy and of promoting judicial economy by preventing needless litigation. *Blonder-Tongue Laboratories, Inc. v. University of Illinois Foundation,* 402 U.S. 313, 328-329. Until relatively recently, however, the scope of collateral estoppel was limited by the doctrine of mutuality of parties. Under this mutuality doctrine, neither party could use a prior judgment as an estoppel against the other unless both parties were bound by the judgment. Based on the premise that it is somehow unfair to allow a party to use a prior judgment when he himself would not be so bound, the mutuality requirement provided a party who had litigated and lost in a previous action an opportunity to relitigate identical issues with new parties.

By failing to recognize the obvious difference in position between a party who has never litigated an issue and one who has fully litigated and lost, the mutuality requirement was criticized almost from its inception. Recognizing the validity of this criticism, the Court in *Blonder-Tongue Laboratories, Inc. v. University of Illinois Foundation, supra*, abandoned the mutuality requirement,

4. In this context, offensive use of collateral estoppel occurs when the plaintiff seeks to foreclose the defendant from litigating an issue the defendant has previously litigated unsuccessfully in an action with another party. Defensive use occurs when a defendant seeks to prevent a plaintiff from asserting a claim the plaintiff has previously litigated and lost against another defendant.

5. Under the doctrine of res judicata, a judgment on the merits in a prior suit bars a second suit involving the same parties or their privies based on the same cause of action. Under the doctrine of collateral estoppel, on the other hand, the second action is upon a different cause of action and the judgment in the prior suit precludes relitigation of issues actually litigated and necessary to the outcome of the first action. 1B J. Moore, Federal Practice ¶ 0.405[1], pp. 622-624 (2d ed. 1974).

at least in cases where a patentee seeks to relitigate the validity of a patent after a federal court in a previous lawsuit has already declared it invalid. The "broader question" before the Court, however, was "whether it is any longer tenable to afford a litigant more than one full and fair opportunity for judicial resolution of the same issue." 402 U.S., at 328. The Court strongly suggested a negative answer to that question. ***

B

The *Blonder-Tongue* case involved defensive use of collateral estoppel—a plaintiff was estopped from asserting a claim that the plaintiff had previously litigated and lost against another defendant. The present case, by contrast, involves offensive use of collateral estoppel—a plaintiff is seeking to estop a defendant from relitigating the issues which the defendant previously litigated and lost against another plaintiff. In both the offensive and defensive use situations, the party against whom estoppel is asserted has litigated and lost in an earlier action. Nevertheless, several reasons have been advanced why the two situations should be treated differently.

First, offensive use of collateral estoppel does not promote judicial economy in the same manner as defensive use does. Defensive use of collateral estoppel precludes a plaintiff from relitigating identical issues by merely "switching adversaries." Thus defensive collateral estoppel gives a plaintiff a strong incentive to join all potential defendants in the first action if possible. Offensive use of collateral estoppel, on the other hand, creates precisely the opposite incentive. Since a plaintiff will be able to rely on a previous judgment against a defendant but will not be bound by that judgment if the defendant wins, the plaintiff has every incentive to adopt a "wait and see" attitude, in the hope that the first action by another plaintiff will result in a favorable judgment. Thus offensive use of collateral estoppel will likely increase rather than decrease the total amount of litigation, since potential plaintiffs will have everything to gain and nothing to lose by not intervening in the first action.

A second argument against offensive use of collateral estoppel is that it may be unfair to a defendant. If a defendant in the first action is sued for small or nominal damages, he may have little incentive to defend vigorously, particularly if future suits are not foreseeable. Allowing offensive collateral estoppel may also be unfair to a defendant if the judgment relied upon as a basis for the estoppel is itself inconsistent with one or more previous judgments in favor of the defendant Still another situation where it might be unfair to apply offensive estoppel is where the second action affords the defendant procedural opportunities unavailable in the first action that could readily cause a different result.[15]

---

15. If, for example, the defendant in the first action was forced to defend in an inconvenient forum and therefore was unable to engage in full scale discovery or call witnesses, application of offensive collateral estoppel may be unwarranted. Indeed, differences in available procedures may sometimes justify not allowing a prior judgment to have estoppel effect in a subsequent action even between the same parties, or where defensive estoppel is asserted against a plaintiff who has litigated and lost. The problem of unfairness is particularly acute in cases of offensive estoppel, however, because the defendant against whom estoppel is asserted typically will not have chosen the forum in

C

We have concluded that the preferable approach for dealing with these problems in the federal courts is not to preclude the use of offensive collateral estoppel, but to grant trial courts broad discretion to determine when it should be applied. The general rule should be that in cases where a plaintiff could easily have joined in the earlier action or where, either for the reasons discussed above or for other reasons, the application of offensive estoppel would be unfair to a defendant, a trial judge should not allow the use of offensive collateral estoppel.

In the present case, however, none of the circumstances that might justify reluctance to allow the offensive use of collateral estoppel is present. The application of offensive collateral estoppel will not here reward a private plaintiff who could have joined in the previous action, since the respondent probably could not have joined in the injunctive action brought by the SEC even had he so desired. Similarly, there is no unfairness to the petitioners in applying offensive collateral estoppel in this case. First, in light of the serious allegations made in the SEC's complaint against the petitioners, as well as the foreseeability of subsequent private suits that typically follow a successful Government judgment, the petitioners had every incentive to litigate the SEC lawsuit fully and vigorously. Second, the judgment in the SEC action was not inconsistent with any previous decision. Finally, there will in the respondent's action be no procedural opportunities available to the petitioners that were unavailable in the first action of a kind that might be likely to cause a different result.[19]

We conclude, therefore, that none of the considerations that would justify a refusal to allow the use of offensive collateral estoppel is present in this case. Since the petitioners received a "full and fair" opportunity to litigate their claims in the SEC action, the contemporary law of collateral estoppel leads inescapably to the conclusion that the petitioners are collaterally estopped from relitigating the question of whether the proxy statement was materially false and misleading.

---

the first action. See [Restatement (Second) of Judgments] § 88(2) and Comment *d*.

**19**. It is true, of course, that the petitioners in the present action would be entitled to a jury trial of the issues bearing on whether the proxy statement was materially false and misleading had the SEC action never been brought—a matter to be discussed in Part II of this opinion. But the presence or absence of a jury as factfinder is basically neutral, quite unlike, for example, the necessity of defending the first lawsuit in an inconvenient forum.

II

The question that remains is whether, notwithstanding the law of collateral estoppel, the use of offensive collateral estoppel in this case would violate the petitioners' Seventh Amendment right to a jury trial.***[20]

"[T]he thrust of the [Seventh] Amendment was to preserve the right to jury trial as it existed in 1791." *Curtis v. Loether*, 415 U.S. 189, 193. At common law, a litigant was not entitled to have a jury determine issues that had been previously adjudicated by a chancellor in equity.

***The petitioners contend that since the scope of the Amendment must be determined by reference to the common law as it existed in 1791, and since the common law permitted collateral estoppel only where there was mutuality of parties, collateral estoppel cannot constitutionally be applied when such mutuality is absent.

The petitioners have advanced no persuasive reason, however, why the meaning of the Seventh Amendment should depend on whether or not mutuality of parties is present. A litigant who has lost because of adverse factual findings in an equity action is equally deprived of a jury trial whether he is estopped from relitigating the factual issues against the same party or a new party. In either case, the party against whom estoppel is asserted has litigated questions of fact, and has had the facts determined against him in an earlier proceeding. In either case there is no further factfinding function for the jury to perform, since the common factual issues have been resolved in the previous action. Cf. *Ex parte Peterson*, 253 U.S. 300, 310 ("No one is entitled in a civil case to trial by jury, unless and except so far as there are issues of fact to be determined").

The Seventh Amendment has never been interpreted in the rigid manner advocated by the petitioners. On the contrary, many procedural devices developed since 1791 that have diminished the civil jury's historic domain have been found not to be inconsistent with the Seventh Amendment. See *Galloway v. United States*, 319 U.S. 372, 388-393 (directed verdict does not violate the Seventh Amendment); *Gasoline Products Co. v. Champlin Refining Co.*, 283 U.S. 494, 497-498 (retrial limited to question of damages does not violate the Seventh Amendment even though there was no practice at common law for setting aside a verdict in part); *Fidelity & Deposit Co. v. United States*, 187 U.S. 315, 319-321 (summary judgment does not violate the Seventh Amendment). ***

The law of collateral estoppel, like the law in other procedural areas defining the scope of the jury's function, has evolved since 1791. Under the rationale of the *Galloway* case, these developments are not repugnant to the Seventh Amendment simply for the reason that they did not exist in 1791. Thus if, as we have held, the law of collateral estoppel forecloses the petitioners from relitigating the factual issues determined against them in the SEC action, nothing in the Seventh Amendment dictates a different result, even though

20. The Seventh Amendment provides: "In Suits at common law, where the value in controversy shall exceed twenty dollars, the right to jury trial shall be preserved...."

because of lack of mutuality there would have been no collateral estoppel in 1791. ***

## NOTES AND QUESTIONS

*1. Stacking the Decks for Settlement?* Key to the Supreme Court's decision in *Parklane Hosiery* was that the issues to be precluded from the private litigation had already been "fully and fairly" adjudicated in the defendant's prior proceeding with the SEC. What if the Parklane defendants had entered into a settlement with the SEC and agreed to be bound by a consent decree ordering an injunction and disgorgement? Could principles of collateral estoppel preclude such defendants from relitigating liability in a subsequent action brought by private plaintiffs? At least in the typical case where a settlement with the SEC has been entered into "for purposes of this proceeding only" and "without admitting or denying" the SEC's allegations, the answer is almost assuredly no. See, e.g., *In re Cenco Inc. Sec. Litig.*, 529 F. Supp. 411, 413-15 (N.D. Ill. 1982). See also ABA Committee on Federal Regulation of Securities, Report of the Task Force on SEC Settlements, 47 Bus. Law. 1083, 1155 (1992) (emphasizing that "SEC settlement documents should have no collateral estoppel effect").

The conclusion that settlements with the SEC lack collateral estoppel effect also captured the attention of Justice Rehnquist, who wrote the sole dissent in *Parklane Hosiery*. Justice Rehnquist chastised the majority for ruling in a way that could "coerc[e] defendants to agree to consent orders or settlements in agency enforcement actions in order to preserve their right to jury trial in the private actions." 439 U.S. at 355-56 (Rehnquist, J., dissenting). Thus, in his view, "for no compelling reason," the majority had "simply added a powerful club to the administrative agencies' arsenals that even Congress was unwilling to provide them." Id. at 356. How would the *Parklane* majority likely respond?

*2. Collateral Estoppel Ramifications of SEC Administrative Proceedings.* Although the defendants in *Parklane* were estopped from relitigating the factual and legal issues that had been necessarily determined in a prior injunctive action brought by the SEC in federal district court, the doctrine of collateral estoppel is also potentially applicable to adverse findings made in the course of an SEC administrative proceeding. Support for this conclusion dates back more than 35 years, to the Supreme Court's statement in *United States v. Utah Constr. & Mining Co.*, 384 U.S. 394, 422 (1966), that "[w]hen an administrative agency is acting in a judicial capacity and resolves disputed issues of fact properly before it which the parties have had an adequate opportunity to litigate, the courts have not hesitated to apply *res judicata* to enforce repose." See also *Univ. of Tenn. v. Elliott*, 478 U.S. 788, 797 (1986) (endorsing the practice of applying "principles of issue preclusion to the fact-finding of administrative bodies acting in a judicial capacity"). Although there has yet to be a litigated case directly on point, commentators generally advise respondents in SEC proceedings to weigh heavily this possibility in calculating the consequences of litigation. See, e.g., Andrew M. Smith, SEC Cease-and-Desist Orders, 51 Admin. L. Rev. 1197, 1219-20 (1999) (stating that "an SEC cease-and-desist order might easily be given nonmutual offensive preclusive effect"). See also Edmund H. Kerr & Robert J. Stillman, Collateral Estoppel Implications of SEC Adjudications, 42 Bus. Law. 441 (1987).

*3. Collateral Estoppel in SEC Litigation.* The SEC often invokes the doctrine of collateral estoppel to prevent a defendant in a civil case from relitigating issues that were "fully and fairly" decided in a criminal trial. See, e.g., *SEC v. Grossman*, 887 F. Supp. 649 (S.D.N.Y. 1995), aff'd, 101 F.3d 109 (2d Cir. 1996). The SEC has also successfully argued for collateral estoppel in cases in which the defendant has resolved the prior criminal action through a guilty pleas. See *Palmisano* (set out in Section F.2 of this Chapter). See also *SEC v. McCaskey*, 2001 WL 1029053 (S.D.N.Y. 2001). Should the SEC be able to use collateral estoppel to preclude a defendant in a subsequent civil action from relitigating issues resolved in a prior sentencing proceeding? See *SEC v. Monarch Funding Corp.*, 192 F.3d 295 (2d Cir. 1999) (rejecting the use of collateral estoppel but declining to adopt a bright-line rule).

*4. The Importance of Jury Trials.* As noted above, Justice Rehnquist was the sole dissenter from the Court's opinion in *Parklane*, arguing strongly that the defendant's Seventh Amendment right to a jury trial would be violated by the application of collateral estoppel. In his view, "developments in the judge-made doctrine of collateral estoppel, however salutary, cannot, consistent with the Seventh Amendment, contract in any material fashion the right to a jury trial that a defendant would have enjoyed in 1791." 439 U.S. at 347 (Rehnquist, J., dissenting).

Justice Rehnquist also maintained that notwithstanding the Seventh Amendment, it was highly "unfair" to apply estoppel in this case because the company never had the opportunity to have the facts determined by a jury. Thus, based on the majority's own standards for the use of non-mutual offensive collateral estoppel, Justice Rehnquist would not have applied the doctrine to estop the company from relitigating in front of a jury the issues determined in the SEC's injunctive action.

Justice Rehnquist reasoned that "the use of offensive collateral estoppel in this case runs counter to the strong federal policy favoring jury trials." Id. at 351. He also argued that "the opportunity for a jury trial in the second action could easily lead to a different result from that obtained in the first action before the court," id. at 353, and took particular issue with the majority's footnote 19:

> [T]hose who drafted the Declaration of Independence and debated so passionately the proposed Constitution during the ratification period, would indeed be astounded to learn that the presence or absence of a jury is merely "neutral," whereas the availability of discovery, a device unmentioned in the Constitution, may be controlling. It is precisely because the Framers believed that they might receive a different result at the hands of a jury of their peers than at the mercy of the sovereign's judges, that the Seventh Amendment was adopted. And I suspect that anyone who litigates cases before juries in the 1970's would be equally amazed to hear of the supposed lack of distinction between trial by court and trial by jury. ***
>
> Contrary to the majority's supposition, juries can make a difference, and our cases have, before today at least, recognized this obvious fact. Thus, in *Colgrove v. Battin*, [413 U.S. 149, 157 (1973),] we stated that "the purpose of the jury trial in . . . civil cases [is] to assure a fair and equitable resolution of factual issues." And in *Byrd v. Blue Ridge Rural Electrical Cooperative*, [356 U.S. 525, 537 (1958),] the Court conceded that "the nature of the tribunal which tries issues may be important in the enforcement of the parcel of rights making

> up a cause of action or defense .... It may well be that in the instant personal-injury case the outcome would be substantially affected by whether the issue of immunity is decided by a judge or a jury." Jurors bring to a case their common sense and community values; their "very inexperience is an asset because it secures a fresh perception of each trial, avoiding the stereotypes said to infect the judicial eye." H. Kalven & H. Zeisel, The American Jury 8 (1966).

*Parklane Hosiery*, 439 U.S. at 354-55 (Rehnquist, J., dissenting). Are you persuaded that the use of collateral estoppel against Parklane would have been unfair?

## E. SROs AS ENFORCERS OF THE FEDERAL SECURITIES LAWS

Although Congress established the SEC as the principal enforcer of its newly created federal securities laws, even in 1934, Congress clearly envisioned that the stock exchanges—particularly the New York Stock Exchange (NYSE)—would continue to play a major role in regulating the conduct of exchange members and their associated persons. Four years later, the National Association of Securities Dealers (NASD) was added to this scheme of self-regulation, when Congress enacted the Maloney Act of 1938, which extended federal regulation to the non-exchange, or over-the-counter (OTC), market.

### 1. *Self-Regulation and SEC Oversight*

The legislative history that immediately follows reflects a decision by Congress in 1975 to significantly change many of the aspects of self-regulation that had existed in the decades prior. As you read the material, consider the role that Congress expects the SROs to play in the enforcement of the federal securities laws. Do these congressional expectations help to answer whether actions by SROs involve "government action?" Consider the various contexts in which this question may be raised.

## P.L. 94-29, SECURITIES ACTS AMENDMENTS OF 1975 SENATE REPORT (BANKING, HOUSING AND URBAN AFFAIRS COMMITTEE)

No. 94-75, Apr. 14, 1975 (To accompany S. 249)

The Committee on Banking, Housing and Urban Affairs *** reports favorably upon S. 249 as amended and recommends without objection that the bill do pass.***

A. NATIONAL MARKET SYSTEM AND SELF-REGULATORY ORGANIZATIONS ***

Because of the unique system of self-regulation in the securities industry, the principal markets for securities, i.e., the exchanges, are also the principal regulators of the activities of broker-dealers using those markets. Meaningful reform of this country's securities trading mechanisms will, therefore, be impossible unless there is also a reform of the method and manner by which the self-regulatory organizations operate and in the way that the SEC oversees the performance of their regulatory responsibilities.

Accordingly, S. 249 would significantly amend the provisions of the Exchange Act dealing with the powers of the self-regulatory organizations and the oversight authority of the SEC with respect to these organizations. The Committee believes that self-regulation should be preserved in the securities industry, but it also believes that the self-regulatory organizations must display a greater responsiveness to their statutory obligations and to the need to coordinate their functions and activities. In the new regulatory environment created by this bill, self-regulation would be continued, but the SEC would be expected to play a much larger role than it has in the past to ensure that there is no gap between self-regulatory performance and regulatory need and, when appropriate, to provide leadership for the development of a more coherent and rational regulatory structure to correspond to and to police effectively the new national market system. ***

II. SELF-REGULATION AND SEC OVERSIGHT***

S. 249 contains a number of provisions which would clarify the scope of the self-regulatory responsibilities of national securities exchanges and registered securities associations (which are defined in section 3(a)(26) as "self-regulatory organizations") and the manner in which they are to exercise those responsibilities. The bill would also clarify and strengthen the Commission's oversight role with respect to the self-regulatory organizations.

The Committee has found a common and serious misunderstanding of the nature and limits of the concept of self-regulation. All too frequently, the view is expressed that self-regulation is an arrangement whereby the exchanges and the NASD, rather than the federal government, police the conduct and strengthen the professional standards of securities firms. In other words, self-regulation is thought to mean that the securities industry regulates itself and therefore is not regulated by the government. Such a conception of self-regulation is seriously misleading in that it fails to recognize the essential and continuing role of the federal government. Industry regulation and government regulation are not alternatives, but complementary components of the self-regulatory process.

In enacting the Exchange Act, the Congress balanced the limitation and dangers of permitting the securities industry to regulate itself against "the sheer ineffectiveness of attempting to assure [regulation] directly through the government on a wide scale." The result was a unique pattern of regulation combining both industry and government responsibility. The fundamental pattern established in 1934 has not been essentially changed since then:

> The SEC has the authority and responsibility to assure compliance by all broker-dealers with the legal requirements of the Exchange Act and of the rules which the SEC is authorized to promulgate under the Exchange Act.
>
> Industry organizations, i.e., the exchanges and the NASD, are delegated governmental power in order to enforce, at their own initiative, compliance by members of the industry with both the legal requirements laid down in the Exchange Act and ethical standards going beyond those requirements.
>
> The SEC is charged with supervising the exercise of this self-regulatory power in order to assure that it is used effectively to fulfill the responsibilities assigned to the self-regulatory agencies, and that it is not used in a manner inimical to the public interest or unfair to private interests.

In an effort to emphasize the fact that both the industry and the government have regulatory responsibilities under the Exchange Act, it has become commonplace to refer to the "partnership" between the self-regulatory organizations and the SEC, or to the "cooperative" character of the regulatory system. The Committee concurs in the need to emphasize the mutual regulatory responsibilities of the industry and the SEC. However, it believes care should be exercised, lest the use of phrases such as "partnership" and "cooperative regulation" lead to the impression that the industry and the government fulfill the same function in the regulatory framework or that they enjoy the same order of authority or deserve the same degree of deference, whether by firms, courts or the Congress. The self-regulatory organizations exercise authority subject to SEC oversight. They have no authority to regulate independently of the SEC's control.

The self-regulatory roles of the exchanges and the NASD have been major elements of the regulatory scheme of the Exchange Act since 1934 and 1938, respectively. Although self-regulation has not always performed up to expectations, on the whole it has worked well, and the Committee believes it should be preserved and strengthened. S. 249 is designed to accomplish this, not only by clarifying regulatory responsibilities at all levels but also by assuring that the self-regulatory organizations follow effective and fair procedures, that their activities are not anticompetitive and that the Commission's oversight powers are ample and its responsibility to correct self-regulatory lapses is unmistakable. The intent of the bill is not to diminish the role of self-regulation but to strengthen the total regulatory fabric.

## A. THE CONCEPT OF MEMBERSHIP

The concept of "membership"—i.e., voluntary association with an industry organization—is fundamental to the self-regulatory system established by the Exchange Act. However, because of certain changes in the operation of the markets a change in the definition of "member" appears desirable.***

Section 3(a)(3) as amended by the bill would redefine "member" to mean any natural person permitted to effect transactions without the services of a broker and any registered broker or dealer with which such a natural person is associated, any registered broker or dealer permitted to designate as a representative such a natural person and any registered broker or dealer which agrees to be regulated by such exchange and with respect to which the exchange undertakes to enforce compliance with its rules and the Exchange Act. An exchange's or association's undertaking to regulate a broker or dealer would not be discretionary with respect to persons qualified for membership. In other words, if a person meets the requirements for membership he must be admitted. (Sections 6(b)(2) and 15A(b)(3)). And with respect to a person admitted, i.e., a member, an exchange or association must enforce compliance with its rules, the Exchange Act, and the rules and regulations thereunder. (Section 19(g)). ***

## B. PROCEDURAL STANDARDS FOR SELF-REGULATORY ACTION

The self-regulatory organizations exercise government power, and they do so in basically three ways which may adversely affect the interests of particular persons: (1) by imposing a disciplinary sanction, broadly defined, on a member or person affiliated with a member, (2) by denying membership to an applicant, and (3) by requiring members to cease doing business entirely or in specified ways with a particular non-member or with respect to a particular security.

The self-regulatory organizations must exercise governmental-type powers if they are to carry out their responsibilities under the Exchange Act. When a member violates the Act or a self-regulatory organization's rules, the organization must be in a position to impose appropriate penalties or to revoke relevant privileges. Similarly, a self-regulatory organization must be able to prevent an unqualified person from obtaining access to facilities and business opportunities by denying membership. And members' transactions and relationships with non-members must be regulated, as the Supreme Court pointed out in the *Silver* case, in order that "... contact with an unreliable non-member [does not] injure the member or the member's customer on whose behalf the contract is made and [thus] ultimately imperil the future status of the [self-regulatory organization] by sapping public confidence." [*Silver v. New York Stock Exch.*, 373 U.S. 341, 356 (1963)].

Recognizing that the self-regulatory organizations utilize governmental-type powers in carrying out their responsibilities under the Exchange Act highlights the fact that these organizations must be required to conform their activities to fundamental standards of due process.

The Exchange Act presently requires that the NASD's disciplinary actions be conducted in accordance with rules which provide "a fair and orderly procedure," including the obligation that the self-regulatory organization bring "specific charges," give notice, provide an opportunity for hearing, and identify in any adverse determination the act or practice which constitutes the violation of a "specific rule or rules." [Section 19(d)(1)]. The Exchange Act also provides for Commission review of NASD disciplinary actions both on the Commission's own motion and by petition of an aggrieved person. [Section 19(d)(2)]. In contrast to the provisions under which the NASD must operate, the Exchange Act contains no requirements as to an exchange's disciplinary procedures and no provision for Commission review of an exchange's enforcement actions. Sections 6(b)(7), 15A(b)(8), 19(d) and 19(e) would eliminate these statutory anomalies and establish uniform standards to which both exchange and NASD rules would be required to conform and in accordance with which SEC review would be available.

The Exchange Act presently requires that in a proceeding to determine whether an applicant is to be denied membership, the NASD must notify the applicant of "the specific grounds for denial ... which are under consideration;" give him an opportunity to be heard on those grounds; keep a record; and set forth in the determination "the specific grounds upon which the denial ... is based." [Section 15(h)(2)]. The Exchange Act also provides for Commission review of the NASD's denial of a membership application on its own motion and by petition of an aggrieved person. [Section 19(d)(2)]. There are no comparable provisions with respect to an exchange's procedure for denial of a membership application or Commission review thereof.

The Committee is well aware of the historical differences between "membership" in an exchange and in the NASD. The limited number of "seats" on an exchange, as contrasted with the availability of NASD membership to all qualified brokers and dealers, is only the most obvious of these differences. However, the Committee does not believe that the substantive differences in the two concepts of membership justify any less attention to procedural fairness in the case of the exchanges than in that of the NASD. Sections 6(b)(7), 15A(b)(8), 19(d) and 19(f) would establish the same procedural requirements and review rights for exchange and NASD actions concerning membership applications.

With respect to non-members, the Committee believes the Exchange Act should be amended to require all self-regulatory agencies to adopt procedures which will afford constitutionally adequate due process to non-members directly affected by self-regulatory action. The bill would accomplish this in Sections 6(b)(7) and 15A(b)(8) by establishing a formal procedure that must be followed before a self-regulatory organization could take any action directly affecting a non-member. Sections 19(e) and 19(f) would establish a right to obtain review of such an action by the appropriate regulatory agency as defined in Section 3(a)(34).

With respect to all three types of quasi-adjudicatory self-regulatory proceedings—the disciplining of a member, the denial of membership, and the limitation or prohibition of a person's access to requested services—the Committee believes that final action should be open to public scrutiny. ***Accordingly, Section 19(d) would require the self- regulatory organizations to file with the appropriate regulatory agency for the self-regulatory organization, and with the appropriate regulatory agency for the member, participant, applicant or other person affected (if other than the appropriate regulatory agency for the self-regulatory organization), notice of all final quasi-adjudicatory actions affecting members and nonmembers. That agency would have the power to prescribe the information to be included in the notices, and it would be required to make all notices available for public inspection. [Section 19(d)(1)].

## C. SCOPE OF SELF-REGULATORY AUTHORITY

***Under the bill the scope of the rule-making authority and responsibility of all self-regulatory organizations would be defined in terms of purposes and standards rather than subject matters. The purposes to be served by self-regulatory rules would be expressed affirmatively and negatively (what the rules must be, and what they may not be, designed to accomplish). New Sections 6(b)(5) and 15A(b)(6) would require the rules of any self-regulatory organization to be designed to prevent fraudulent and manipulative acts and practices, to promote just and equitable principles of trades, to foster cooperation and coordination with persons engaged in regulating, clearing, settling, processing information with respect to, and facilitating transactions in securities, to remove impediments to and perfect the mechanism of a national market system, and, in general, to protect investors and the public interest. Similarly, by reason of the same sections, a self-regulatory organization's rules must not be designed to permit unfair discrimination between customers, issuers, brokers, or dealers or to regulate, by virtue of any authority conferred by the Exchange Act, matters not related to the purposes of the Exchange Act or the administration of such self-regulatory organization.

Under procedures established by the bill whereby self-regulatory rule changes would have to be justified to and reviewed by the Commission after opportunity for public comment, the Commission's action in approving any such change would constitute a determination by the Commission that the rule was within the permitted purposes, and in conformity with the specified standards, of the Exchange Act. [Section 19(b)]. ***

## D. SELF-REGULATORY RULE-MAKING

The Exchange Act says very little about the internal decision-making processes of the self-regulatory organizations. These bodies do not act just like Government agencies, whose procedures and functions are derived from, and often prescribed by, statutes rather than from the decisions of those who choose to become members, and the Committee believes the distinction is essential to the concept of self-regulation. This does not mean that the decision-making processes of the self-regulatory bodies cannot be improved. Quite to the contrary, but in the Committee's view it would be self-defeating to saddle the self-regulatory organizations with the wholly panoply of Governmental administrative procedure.

One of the advantages of self-regulation is the flexibility and informality of its decision-making procedures. Further, self-regulatory organizations differ as to their membership, regulatory responsibilities, and economic power. It would be difficult to prescribe a single "proper" decision-making procedure appropriate to the circumstances of every self-regulatory organization, and it is doubtful that any such formal procedure would better serve the goal of effective securities regulation than the present practice of encouraging each organization to develop procedures which best serve its needs and those of public investors.

The increased use of public governors, providing an opportunity for public comment on proposed rule changes, and the delegation of increased authority to professional staffs are only some of the positive steps that are being taken by the self-regulatory organizations in the area of policy formation. The Committee encourages the self-regulatory organization to continue their healthy experimentation and innovation with regard to decision-making processes, keeping in mind at all times that they were quasi-public organizations, not private clubs, and that one of their principal goals is the prevention of inequitable and unfair practices and the advancement of the public interest.

Without qualifying its general support for preserving flexibility in self-regulatory decision-making, the Committee believes there are several respects in which the rule-making processes of the self-regulatory organizations should be improved by legislation.

First, although all self-regulatory organizations are required to file proposed rule changes with the SEC, there is no requirement that they file an explanation or justification for their proposals. In order to facilitate expeditious Commission review and evaluation of such proposals and to assure informed public comment on them, Section 19(b)(1) would require all self-regulatory organizations to file with the SEC in connection with any proposed rule change a "concise general statement of the basis and purpose" of the proposed rule change. It is the Committee's intention in adopting this standard to hold the self-regulatory organizations to the same standards of policy justification that the Administrative Procedure Act imposes on the SEC.

Second, the Committee believes interested persons should have a meaningful opportunity to obtain accurate information about proposed changes in self-regulatory rules and to comment on the need or justification for these changes. Section 19(b)(1) would require the SEC to give notice and provide an opportunity for interested persons to participate in the process of reviewing a proposed change in a self-regulatory organization's rules. In addition, this section would require that all comments and all correspondence between the SEC and the self-regulatory agency concerning the proposal be available for public inspection. Section 19(b)(2) would give the SEC sufficient flexibility to fashion a proceeding appropriate to the particular self-regulatory proposal being considered. In many, perhaps most, situations, notice and an opportunity for written comment would be sufficient and there would undoubtedly be few, if any, comments. In cases in which fundamental policy issues are involved, however, oral hearings or publicly announced conferences might be most appropriate.

Third, the Exchange Act at present creates the anomalous situation whereby an exchange, which may not lawfully do business until its rules have undergone official scrutiny in relation to statutory standards, is free to change those rules at any time thereafter without similar advance scrutiny or approval. Section 19(b)(2) would fill this regulatory gap by providing that, subject to certain exceptions specified in Section 19(b)(3), no change in the rules of any self-regulatory organization may become effective until the SEC finds it to be consistent with the registration requirements for the organization and the purposes of the Exchange Act. The Committee believes the Commission has a responsibility to see that self-regulatory rules are fully responsive to regulatory needs. By explicitly providing that the Commission's oversight authority encompasses major self-regulatory policies, the bill would make this responsibility clear and substantially decrease the possibility of slippage between regulatory need and self-regulatory performance.***

E. SEC TO CHANGE SELF-REGULATORY RULES

*** Under the bill, the SEC would have uniform authority to "abrogate, add to, or delete from" any self-regulatory organization's rules. (Section 19(c)). Moreover, where the Commission has exercised its rulemaking authority under Section 19(c) of the Exchange Act to abrogate, add to, or delete from the rules of any self-regulatory organization, any rule of a self-regulatory organization inconsistent with such Commission rule adopted pursuant to Section 19(c) shall be null and void.

***[T]here has been a continuing controversy as to the precise scope of the SEC's power to amend the rules of a self-regulatory organization. The bill would give the SEC clear authority to amend any self-regulatory organization's rules in any respect consistent with the objectives of the Exchange Act (Section 19(c)).

***[T]here is also a controversy over the procedures that the SEC must follow in order to force a change in the rules of a self-regulatory organization. In recognition of the quasi-legislative, policy-making nature of an SEC determination to require such a change, Section 19(c) would provide that the Commission's action shall be by "rule". Accordingly, the basic procedures the Commission would be required to follow are specified in the Administrative Procedure Act (5 U.S.C. § 553) for rulemaking not on the record. The bill would, however, also require the Commission to (1) provide all interested persons an opportunity to present their views in person as well as in writing; (2) keep a transcript of all oral presentations; and (3) publish a statement of its reasons for taking the action it did, including an identification of the facts, if any, it has relied upon in reaching its conclusion. (Section 19(c)). ***

F. COORDINATION OF SELF-REGULATORY RESPONSIBILITIES

***[T]he Committee believes the SEC can do a great deal more than it has in the past to foster the development of a more rational self-regulatory framework. The Committee agrees with the recommendation of the Commission's Advisory Committee on Enforcement Policies and Practices that "the Commission should play an affirmative role in allocating inspection and enforcement responsibilities among the self-regulatory organizations...." Further, as the Advisory Committee on Broker-Dealer Reports and Registration Requirements recommends: "... for reporting purposes each broker-dealer [should] be assigned to a designated principal self-regulator or government regulator who will be responsible for determining the broker-dealer's operating and financial status." Section 17(d) would provide the SEC with unquestioned authority to accomplish these objectives. It is the Committee's hope that the SEC would use this authority to lay the foundation for a restructured self-regulatory system appropriate to the national market system.

***Section 19(g) would obligate a self-regulatory organization "absent any reasonable justification or excuse" to enforce compliance by its members or participants with applicable provisions of the Exchange Act and its own rules. In Section 19(h)(1), the SEC or other appropriate regulatory agency would be authorized to sanction any self-regulatory organization which fails to enforce compliance by its members "without reasonable justification or excuse." The Committee believes the standard in these Sections appropriately defines the responsibility of the self-regulatory organizations. Such organizations should never be placed in the position of being insurers of their members' compliance. They do, however, have an obligation to enforce applicable provisions of the Exchange Act and their own rules which they should not be permitted to avoid except for good cause.

G. SEC ENFORCEMENT POWERS

***The SEC's "reserved control" over the self-regulatory organizations is of several sorts ranging from the draconian remedy of suspending or withdrawing registration to highly flexible rulemaking authority. Although it has become commonplace to refer to the SEC's oversight authority as a "big stick" or a "shotgun behind the door," the Committee found the SEC also has available certain, albeit limited, powers to act in specific ways to correct identified instances of inappropriate self-regulatory activity.

The Commission's oversight responsibility with respect to the self-regulatory agencies is to insure that they exercise their delegated governmental power effectively to meet regulatory needs in the public interest and that they do not exercise that delegated power in a manner inimical to the public interest or unfair to private interests. To the degree that there may have been undue deference to the self-regulatory organizations because of the cumbersomeness of the oversight mechanisms or the unavailability of appropriately focused remedies, the Committee believes the Exchange Act should be amended to correct the problem. However, the Committee also believes that the successful performance of the Commission's oversight task necessarily involves the willingness to take steps to assure that the self-regulatory agencies comply with and advance the policies of the Exchange Act. This willingness to act can be encouraged by legislation but it cannot be compelled.

In order to enhance the oversight powers of the Commission and the other appropriate regulatory agencies, as defined in Section 3(a)(34), and to provide them with greater regulatory flexibility, the bill would significantly increase the regulatory options available to them to deal with perceived self-regulatory shortcomings.

First, Section 19(h)(1) would authorize them, by order and upon appropriate findings, to censure and place restrictions on the activities, functions, and operations of a self-regulatory agency. These powers are in addition to suspension and deregistration and are intended to provide more usable sanctions than the SEC's traditional "big stick."

Second, Section 19(h)(1) would also expand and make uniform the grounds on which the Commission may sanction a self-regulatory organization. The appropriate regulatory agency would be able to take appropriate action directly against any self-regulatory organization upon a finding that it had failed to enforce its own rules or failed to enforce the Exchange Act or the rules thereunder.

Third, Section 19(h)(4) would authorize the appropriate regulatory agency to censure or remove from office any officer or director of a self-regulatory organization who had willfully failed to enforce compliance with the Exchange Act, the rules thereunder, or the organization's own rules.

Fourth, Sections 21(e) and 21(f) would empower the SEC to apply to a federal court for an order to (1) enjoin the violation of the rules of a self-regulatory organization, (2) command a member of a self-regulatory organization to comply with the rules of such organization, or (3) command a self-regulatory organization to enforce compliance by its members with the Exchange Act, the rules thereunder, and the organization's own rules. Before exercising a power described in (1) or (2), it must appear to the commission (1) that the self-regulatory organization was unable or unwilling to take appropriate action or (2) that such action is otherwise necessary in the public interest or for the protection of investors.

The Committee expects the additional enforcement powers provided by the bill to lead to an increased willingness on the part of the Commission to take formal action where needed to assure adequate self-regulatory performance. Although the Congress cannot mandate such a willingness, the Committee has no reason to believe that the Commission and the other agencies granted regulatory authority under S. 249 would not be responsive to such an explicit expression of congressional intent. It is important, however, for the Congress to monitor the performance of the Commission and the other regulatory agencies with oversight responsibilities with respect to self-regulatory organizations. Section 23(b) would require the Commission and the other regulatory agencies in their annual report to the Congress to describe fully their activities with respect to the self-regulatory organizations. The SEC would be required to include in its annual reports information as to (1) its program for inspecting the self-regulatory organizations; (2) the expenses and operations of each self-regulatory organization in connection with performance of its responsibilities under the Exchange Act; (3) the development of a national market system and a national system for clearance and settlement; (4) steps the Commission has taken toward the discontinuance of the physical movement of securities certificates in connection with the settlement of securities transactions and any recommendations for legislation to eliminate the use of securities certificates; (5) the number of exemptions requested from provisions of the Exchange Act, the number granted, and the basis for exemptions granted; (6) the Commission's regulatory activities with respect to municipal securities dealers and brokers for which it is not the appropriate regulatory agency; *** and (8) the time elapsed between the Commission's receipt and its publication of reports filed pursuant to Section 13(f) of the Exchange Act.

## H. JUDICIAL REVIEW

The bill would substantially revise Section 25 of the Exchange Act concerning judicial review of SEC action. ***

The Exchange Act now establishes a procedure for review of SEC "orders" in the Court of Appeals. *** The bill would (1) simplify and clarify the provisions relating to the review of Commission orders and (2) establish a statutory review procedure for certain SEC rules, including those approving and disapproving self-regulatory actions.

The changes with respect to review of SEC orders are included in Section 25(a). These changes are intended to codify existing law and would not alter in any fundamental respect the availability of court review of orders or the manner in which such review is exercised. ***[They are also] designed to create a more logical and realistic review procedure without impairing the due process protections presently afforded parties to administration adjudications before the SEC.

The bill's major innovation in the area of judicial review relates to SEC rule-making. *** Section 25(b), as amended by the bill, would give to any person adversely affected a right to preenforcement review in the Court of Appeals of any rule promulgated under Sections 6, [19(h)(2)], 11, 11A, 15(c)(5)- (6), 15A, 17, 17A or 19 of the Exchange Act—i.e., any provision directly relating to the operation or regulation of the national market system, a national clearing system, or the SEC's oversight of the self-regulatory organizations.

By establishing a scheme for the preenforcement review of rules, the Committee believes the bill would expedite final resolution of the major policy determinations the Commission will be called upon to make with respect to the national market system and the rationalization of the self-regulatory system. The changes, however, are not intended to change the existing law with respect to finality or standing in connection with pre-enforcement review of agency rule-making. The Court of Appeals appears to provide the most appropriate forum for this review in light of the fact that the District Court's fact finding function is rarely necessary and the questions subject to review are likely to end up in the higher court anyway. ***

## *NOTES AND QUESTIONS*

*1. The Benefits and Costs of Self-Regulation.* What factors help to explain why self-regulation in the securities industry is a workable alternative to regulation by the government? Should there be serious concerns about the proverbial "fox guarding the chicken coop?" In what types of regulatory matters or areas would we most expect to see rigorous enforcement by the SROs? In what areas or matters might rigorous enforcement be the most compromised? Are there concerns that may be unique to particular SROs?

*2. SEC Involvement in Self-Regulation.* How would you characterize the SEC's relationship to SROs such as the NYSE and the NASD? How did Congress characterize that relationship when it enacted the 1975 amendments to the Exchange Act? How does the SEC's involvement in self-regulation relate to the question of whether SROs are private actors or state actors? Note that this question will be revisited in the material that follows the decision in *United States v. Solomon.*

*3. Voluntary Association?* As we will see, courts that refuse to recognize SRO action as state action often emphasize that SROs are private organizations in which membership is voluntary. Is this a fair characterization? What result if a broker-dealer chooses not to be a member of the NYSE? What result if a broker-dealer chooses not to be a member of the NASD—currently the only national securities association registered with the SEC? In this regard, consider the following statement on the home page of the NASD's website:

> Under federal law, virtually every securities firm doing business with the US public is a member of this private, not-for-profit organization. Roughly 5,400 brokerage firms, over 92,000 branch offices and more than 675,000 registered securities representatives come under our jurisdiction.

www.nasd.com (visited last on Jan. 7, 2003).

*4. SEC Enforcement Action Against the NASD.* Section 19(g) of the Exchange Act authorizes the SEC to pursue enforcement actions against an SRO for any failure to comply with the Exchange Act or the rules and regulations of the SRO. Acting pursuant to this provision, in 1996, the SEC brought an administrative enforcement action against the NASD, alleging primarily that the NASD failed to carry out its obligations to oversee the Nasdaq market and the anticompetitive conduct of its members. In settling the action without admitting or denying the SEC's findings, the NASD consented to a censure and agreed to spend at least $100 million during the next five years to enhance its oversight functions of enforcement, surveillance, and examination. The NASD also agreed to reorganize into two new subsidiaries: NASD Regulation, Inc., which was to have primary responsibility for regulatory matters, and the Nasdaq Stock Market, Inc. See *In re National Ass'n of Sec. Dealers, Inc.*, Release No. 37358, 62 SEC Docket 1346 (Aug. 8, 1996); Report Pursuant to Section 21(a) of the Securities Exchange Act Regarding the NASD and the Nasdaq Market, Release No. 37542, 62 SEC Docket 1385 (Aug. 8, 1996). The NASD's merger with the American Stock Exchange (AMEX) in 1998 resulted in the creation of a new subsidiary, the Nasdaq-AMEX Market Group, Inc. Further reorganization occurred in 2000, when the NASD sold Nasdaq, and again in June 2002, when the NASD announced its intention to separate from the AMEX, reflecting its current "singular regulatory focus on investor protection and market integrity." NASD Press Release, NASD Board Approves New Divisional Structure (June 7, 2002). The new organizational structure eliminates subsidiaries and divides the NASD into three operating divisions: Regulatory Policy and Oversight, with primary responsibility for rulemaking, member regulation, market surveillance, and enforcement; Regulatory Services and Operations, with responsibility for market operations and information systems; and Dispute Resolution, with responsibility for arbitration and mediation of investor and industry disputes.

*5. A Single SRO for the Securities Industry?* In a speech delivered in 1999, former SEC Chairperson Arthur Levitt raised the possibility of combining forces to create a single SRO for the securities industry, a model that "regulates all markets, alleviates conflicts and reduces redundancy, paperwork, and operational costs." SEC Chairperson Arthur Levitt, Speech or Dynamic Markets, Timeless Principles (Sept. 23, 1999). He also raised a second model "where each market would maintain the regulatory and surveillance function solely for its own market—but member regulation, sales practices, and all other aspects of intermarket trading would be overseen by a single SRO." Id. Consider the advantages that these models have over the multiple SRO system that is now in place? What would be some of the disadvantages? How do the NYSE's plans to demutualize factor into the debate?

---

### 2. *SRO Investigations and Disciplinary Proceedings*

As you read the following material, consider the similarities and differences between SEC and SRO-initiated investigations and enforcement proceedings. In particular, consider how the SROs are able to fulfill their obligations under Sections 6(b)(7) and 15A(b)(8) of the Exchange Act to provide "a fair procedure for the disciplining of members and persons associated with members."

## MONEY PENALTIES: SECURITIES AND FUTURES REGULATORS COLLECT MANY FINES BUT NEED TO BETTER USE INDUSTRYWIDE DATA

**United States General Accounting Office**
**Report to Congressional Committees**
GAO/GGD-99-8, November 1998

***SRO disciplinary cases usually begin as a result of a customer complaint, compliance examination, market surveillance activity, regulatory filings, or even an item reported in the press. SROs generally have enforcement authority over only their members and employees. An SRO's enforcement or regulation division is responsible for investigating and prosecuting disciplinary cases. The enforcement or regulation division is to investigate possible violative activity and prepare a memorandum outlining the facts and evidence found by its investigation. The disciplinary committee, SRO staff, or other authorizing entity is to review the matter and decide whether to issue a formal complaint against the alleged violator. If they issue a complaint, a written statement of charges is to be sent to the alleged violator to which he or she may be required to respond in writing, either admitting or denying each charge. Upon receiving this response, the enforcement staff is to schedule a hearing before a hearing panel. In the hearing, the enforcement staff, acting as prosecutor, and the respondent can present evidence and witnesses. The hearing panel must then examine the evidence and witnesses. The hearing panel must then examine the evidence and decide on each charge and the appropriate sanction. A written statement of the panel's decision and sanctions is to be sent to the respondent.

SRO disciplinary cases also can be settled with the respondent agreeing to sanctions without admitting or denying liability. SRO officials told us that settlements are common and are often preferred because they enable the SRO to conserve investigative and legal resources and still remedy violations.

In 1997, SEC approved an NASD proposal that cases be heard by a hearing panel presided over by a professional hearing officer assisted by two securities industry professionals, instead of being heard by members of NASD district business conduct committees. The hearing panel's decisions may be appealed to NASD's National Adjudicatory Council (formerly called the National Business Conduct Committee), [and thereafter to the] SEC, and the federal [circuit] courts. [At the NYSE, cases are heard by a hearing panel presided over by a hearing officer (who is an officer and employee of the NYSE) and at least two securities industry professionals who are not NYSE employees. NYSE hearing panel decisions may be appealed to the NYSE's Board of Directors, and thereafter to the SEC, and the federal circuit courts. Hearings at the other major stock exchanges follow a similar course.] ***

---

The above referenced GAO Report documents that during the four year period between 1992 and 1996, the NASD closed 4,076 cases against member firms and associated persons, imposing a total dollar amount in fines of $113,857,938. See id. at 13. The Report also documents that the three major stock exchanges—the NYSE, AMEX, and Chicago Board Options Exchange (CBOE)—closed 713 cases in this same time period, imposing a total dollar amount in fines of $14,238,473. See id. at 11.

Other useful statistics about NASD, NYSE, AMEX, and CBOE disciplinary actions are compiled by the ABA's Securities Litigation Subcommittee on SRO Matters. The subcommittee's most recently published report includes the monetary penalties imposed by these SROs in 1996, and reports the following additional sanctions for the single year of 1996:

> [T]he NASD expelled, barred or suspended 612 individuals and firms as follows: 394 individuals barred; 204 individuals suspended; 7 firms expelled; and 7 firms suspended. ***
>
> [T]he NYSE imposed permanent bars in 28 cases. It also imposed 22 bars for failure to cooperate with Division of Enforcement investigations. In 1996, over 50% of the bars or suspensions in NYSE disciplinary actions were for one year or longer (including the 22 bars in failure to cooperate cases that virtually always extend beyond one year). ***
>
> The AMEX imposed either a bar or a suspension in nine cases in 1996 (two of which were permanent bars, and two others were bars for three or more years***). ***

> The CBOE imposed a bar in 6 cases in 1996 (1 of which was a permanent bar).
> ***

Subcommittee on SRO Matters, Am. Bar Ass'n, SRO Disciplinary Action 1996 (1998).

Additional information on sanctions, and the SRO disciplinary process in general, can be found in T. Grant Callery & Anne H. Wright, NASD Disciplinary Proceedings: Recent Developments, 48 Bus. Law. 791 (1993) and David P. Doherty, et al., The Enforcement Role of the New York Stock Exchange, 85 Nw. U. L. Rev. 637 (1991).

---

As the following decision makes clear, major consequences turn on whether SROs are characterized as private—rather than state—actors.

## UNITED STATES v. SOLOMON

509 F.2d 863 (2d Cir. 1975)

FRIENDLY, CIRCUIT JUDGE:

In mid-April 1973 Arthur Levine and Sol Leit, the chairman and president of Weis Securities, Inc. (Weis), a brokerage and investment banking firm which was a member of the New York Stock Exchange (NYSE), notified the Exchange that the firm was in financial difficulty and that there might have been certain "bookkeeping inadequacies" which had resulted in an understatement by as much as $2.5 million of its reported operating losses over the prior several months. Despite the officers' urging that NYSE refrain, at least temporarily, from sending in examiners, NYSE commenced a full investigation on the following day. During the next two weeks, a number of financial irregularities were discovered in Weis' accounts, including an understatement of losses and bank loans. In accordance with its statutory duty, NYSE advised the Securities and Exchange Commission (SEC) of the probable violations of its rules and regulations and began transmitting, on an almost daily basis, reports containing the results of its investigatory activities and contemplated actions.

On May 17, Alan C. Solomon, who as a Weis officer and director was an allied member of NYSE, was summoned to appear before the Department of Member Firms and testify. Article XIV of NYSE's Constitution provided:

> Whenever it is adjudged in a proceeding under this Article that a member, allied member or approved person has been required by the Board or any committee, officer or employee of the Exchange authorized thereby ... to furnish information to or to appear and testify before or to cause any such employee to appear and testify before the Board or any such committee, officer, or employee and has refused or failed to comply with such requirement, such member or allied member may be suspended or expelled and such approved person may have his approval withdrawn.

Accompanied by his then counsel, Solomon appeared and was questioned at some length, first off the record and then on the record. The chief interrogator was Dennis Pape, special counsel to NYSE. According to an affidavit by Solomon, he "was aware of the provisions of Article XIV of the New York Stock Exchange Constitution which empowered the Exchange to suspend me if I refused to cooperate and answer all the questions put to me during the May 17th interrogation." He averred also that "Mr. Pape and his cohorts in the off-the-record discussions which preceded their formal interrogation, also reminded me of the sanction of suspension which would be imposed if I did not testify." Under questioning Solomon admitted that he had originated the idea of seeking to create an appearance of a better financial situation for Weis by "taking a position in Pan American convertible bonds 4 1/2's 1986, which were selling at around 52, and misevaluating them as Pan Am's 4 1/2's 1984, which were selling around 80."

Two days prior to Solomon's testimony before the Department of Member Firms, the SEC entered an order of investigation and on May 16 served a subpoena requiring NYSE to turn over all material developed in its investigation. NYSE immediately submitted depositions already taken; considering the subpoena to be a continuing one, it later furnished Solomon's. On a complaint by the SEC alleging that Weis did not have sufficient capital under the Securities Exchange Act and the implementing rules of the Commission and NYSE and had been filing false financial reports with both bodies in an effort to conceal this, Weis was placed in receivership at the end of May by the District Court for the Southern District of New York. That action was followed in July by an eighteen count indictment, in the same court, of five of Weis' officers and directors, including Solomon.

The indictment charged in part a conspiracy to violate and a number of substantive violations of the recordkeeping and reporting regulations promulgated by the SEC under § 17(a) of the Securities Exchange Act. Each of the other defendants pleaded guilty to at least one substantive count and three to the conspiracy count as well. After a bench trial on stipulated facts which included a transcript of his deposition before the Department of Member Firms, Solomon was found guilty on one substantive count of creating and maintaining false books and records. With the Government's agreement the other counts were dismissed with prejudice. The judge placed him on a supervised probation program for a year and imposed a $5,000 fine.

The sole point on appeal is the use, both before the grand jury and at trial, of Solomon's self-incriminating testimony to the Department of Member Firms, allegedly in violation of *Garrity v. New Jersey*, 385 U.S. 493 (1967). The complete deposition containing his admissions had been presented to the grand jury and constituted an important basis for the indictment. Solomon's present counsel moved to dismiss the indictment and to suppress use of the testimony or any of its fruits at trial. The judge denied the motion both before and again after an evidentiary hearing. ***[On appeal] Solomon again claims that the indictment should have been dismissed since the allegedly tainted testimony is claimed to have been the only evidence before the grand jury on the count on which he was convicted; alternatively he seeks a reversal and remand for a hearing to determine whether the Government possesses sufficient evidence not derived directly or derivatively through investigation from the deposition testimony to justify a retrial. We do not reach the question of remedy since we find no taint.

I.

The United States suggests, in an elaborate footnote to its brief, that we could affirm without reaching the question whether interrogation by NYSE is to be deemed governmental action. The most appealing basis asserted is the lack of any evidence that Solomon claimed his privilege against self- incrimination. Even when the inquiry is by a body having power to compel testimony, the rule is "that when an *ordinary witness* is on the stand and an incriminating fact, relevant to the issue, is desired to be proved through him, the question may be asked, and it is for him then to say, in terms which the court may reasonably be expected to understand to be a claim of privilege, that he will exercise the option given him by the law," 8 Wigmore, Evidence § 2268 at 402 (McNaughton rev. 1961) (emphasis in original); per contra with respect to the accused in a criminal case, id. at 406. The former principle, which governs a witness before a grand jury, or a Congressional investigating committee, would seem clearly applicable here. When Solomon appeared before the Department of Member Firms he was a subject of investigation for possible future NYSE disciplinary proceedings, not a person accused of crime.

The first problem with taking this smooth road to affirmance is that except for a possible ground of distinction noted below the same reasoning would have led to a result in *Garrity* opposite to that reached by the Supreme Court. There the New Jersey Deputy Attorney General had advised the defendants, who at the time were still only unindicted witnesses, of the privilege, but had added that this was "limited to the extent that you as a police officer once sworn and asked questions pertaining to your office and your conduct therein, if you refuse to answer, you may then be subject to a proceeding to have you removed from the department." *State v. Naglee*, 44 N.J. 209, 212 (1965); the officers then proceeded to answer without protest. Although the State's brief before the Supreme Court did not argue the point that appellants had not claimed their privilege, the Court was surely aware of the usual necessity for this in the case of an ordinary witness. Insofar as the decision rested on a violation of the privilege, the Court evidently considered an exception to that principle to be required when invocation of the privilege was clogged by *certain* forfeiture of office and pension rights and permanent disability from future state employment. *** We thus prefer to place decision on the basic ground that interrogation by the New York Stock Exchange in carrying out its own legitimate investigatory purposes does not trigger the privilege against self-incrimination or, at least under the circumstances here, render Solomon's statement involuntary.

II.

Most of the provisions of the Fifth Amendment, in which the self-incrimination clause is embedded, are incapable of violation by anyone except government in the narrowest sense. No private body, however close its affiliations with the government, can hold a person "to answer for a capital or otherwise infamous crime" without an indictment, or subject a person "for the same offense to be twice put in jeopardy of life or limb." No one can take property for public use except the government or a person on whom the government has expressly bestowed that power. Solomon argues, however, that the remaining provision of the Fifth Amendment, the due process clause, has been extended in some instances to action by private persons having certain types of connection with the government, see, e.g., *Burton v. Wilmington Parking Authority*, 365 U.S. 715 (1961); that NYSE has close connections with the government; and that the self-incrimination clause as explicated in *Garrity* should therefore apply.

There is no need for us to add to the extensive discussion of the history of the privilege against self-incrimination in 8 Wigmore, Evidence § 2250, and Professor Leonard W. Levy's The Origins of the Fifth Amendment (1968). Whatever differences in the precise details of its origin and historic scope may exist among scholars, there can be no doubt that the privilege was in large part developed to protect the individual in what was thought to be an unequal contest with the state. The Supreme Court has frequently referred to Wigmore's statement, 8 Evidence § 2251 at 317:

> The privilege contributes toward a fair state-individual balance by requiring the government to leave the individual alone until good cause is shown for disturbing him and by requiring the government in its contest with the individual to shoulder the entire load.

*Murphy v. Waterfront Commission*, 378 U.S. 52, 55 (1968); *Tehan v. United States ex rel. Shott*, 382 U.S. 406, 415 (1966). The Court has also said that the origin and history of the Fourth Amendment "clearly show that it was intended as a restraint upon the activities of sovereign authority, and was not intended to be a limitation upon other than governmental agencies ...", *Burdeau v. McDowell*, 256 U.S. 465, 475 (1921). Relying in part on that statement and the fact that *Burdeau* itself dismissed a self-incrimination claim, we have held the same to be true of the self-incrimination clause of the Fifth, in the context, quite pertinent here, of the application of *Miranda v. Arizona*, 384 U.S. 436 (1966), to interrogation by private security guards at a pier. *United States v. Antonelli*, 434 F.2d 335 (2 Cir. 1970). Accord *United States v. Birnstihl*, 441 F.2d 368 (9 Cir. 1971) (per curiam) (store security officer); *United States v. Casteel*, 476 F.2d 152 (10 Cir. 1973) (employees of private security firm).

Solomon argues that despite all this, interrogation by NYSE must be deemed the equivalent of interrogation by the United States because the Exchange has become in effect the arm of the Government in administering portions of the Securities Exchange Act. He relies on various provisions of the Act, such as the reporting requirements of § 17(a) and the regulations thereunder and the many other powers over exchanges and their members conferred on the SEC by § 19(a), (b), see *Gordon v. New York Stock Exchange, Inc.*, 498 F.2d 1303, 1306-1307 (2 Cir. 1974). Particular emphasis is placed on *Silver v. New York Stock Exchange*, 373 U.S. 341, 350-353 (1963), where, after discussing the proved inadequacies of "ungoverned self-regulation" by the exchanges and the consequent need for government supervision, the Court said:

> The pattern of governmental entry, however, was by no means one of total displacement of the exchanges' traditional process of self-regulation. The intention was rather, as Mr. Justice Douglas said, while Chairman of the SEC, one of "letting the exchanges take the leadership with Government playing a residual role. Government would keep the shotgun, so to speak, behind the door, loaded, well oiled, cleaned, ready for use but with the hope it would never have to be used." Douglas, Democracy and Finance (Allen ed. 1940), 82. ***

Thus arose the federally mandated duty of self-policing by exchanges.

Solomon misconceives the thrust of the Act and the Court's discussion of it. The exchanges' "traditional process of self-regulation" was not displaced. See H.R.Rep. No. 1383, 73d Cong., 2d Sess. 15 (1934); S.Rep. No. 792, 73d Cong., 2d Sess. 13 (1934) (stressing the broad responsibility left with the exchanges to administer their own affairs). Rather the SEC was given the power and the duty to make sure that the responsibility was diligently and effectively used. See *Gordon v. New York Stock Exchange*, supra, 498 F.2d at 1306-1307, and sources cited therein. NYSE's inquiry into Weis was in pursuance of its own interests and obligations, not as an agent of the SEC. It is not enough to create an agency relationship that Solomon's conduct violated both a rule of NYSE, thereby subjecting him to disciplinary action by that body, and federal law, with consequent liability to civil and criminal enforcement proceedings by the Government.

***[W]e see no principled basis whereby acceptance of Solomon's argument could be confined to interrogation by stock exchanges; this is but one of many instances where government relies on self-policing by private organizations to effectuate the purposes underlying federal regulating statutes. Under the Commodity Exchange Act, § 5, 7 U.S.C.§ 7, boards of trade have self-policing functions quite similar to those of stock exchanges under the Securities Exchange Act. Airline and steamship conferences have elaborate enforcement machinery to bring to light the charging of less than prescribed rates, the payment of more than agreed commissions to travel and freight agents, or violations of any of the many other regulations concerning the conduct of their members. Whether or not the agreements provide explicitly for suspension or expulsion for refusal to furnish needed records or testimony, a member is aware that any such refusal will likely involve this or some other heavy penalty and will have methods of making this known to refractory employees. One purpose of the provision of the Elkins Act, 32 Stat. 847 (1903), as amended, 49 U.S.C. § 41(2), imposing criminal liability on shippers and carriers for railroad rebates resulting from "the act, omission, or failure of any officer, agent, or other person acting for or employed by any common carrier, or shipper, acting within the scope of his employment" was surely to enlist the aid of the carriers and shippers in policing their employees; clearly a refusal to answer an employer's questions about a rebate on the ground of self-incrimination would lead to discharge, and an employee discharged on that account would be unlikely to gain employment elsewhere in the industry at least for some time. We cite these only as examples that come readily to mind; there would be a complete breakdown in the regulation of many areas of business if employers did not carry most of the load of keeping their employees in line and have the sanction of discharge for refusal to answer what is essential to that end. ***

We find no basis for a different conclusion in the many "state action" cases in wholly different contexts cited by Solomon's counsel. Analysis of the particular constitutional provision at issue must be among the first, if not the very first, step in the process of "sifting facts and weighing circumstances" needed to attribute "true significance" to "the nonobvious involvement of the State in private conduct" dictated by *Burton v. Wilmington Parking Authority*, supra, 365 U.S. at 722. It is one thing to say that the exclusion of blacks is no more permissible for a restaurant which is a lessee of a state parking authority than it would be for the authority itself; it would be altogether different to say that a lease of state property carries the privilege against self-incrimination on its back. Nothing in *Burton* remotely suggests that if the proprietor of the Eagle Coffee Shoppe had interrogated a waiter suspected of snatching a patron's purse, under the same kind of threat that refusal to answer would lead to discharge and a report to a restaurant trade association as would be made by other employers, the answer could not be used in evidence at a criminal trial. We need not here decide whether stock exchanges may be subject to some due process requirements for certain types of action as stated in dictum in *Intercontinental Industries, Inc. v. American Stock Exchange*, 452 F.2d 935, 941 (5 Cir. 1971) (delisting of corporation's stock), *Crimmins v. American Stock Exchange, Inc.*, 346 F.Supp. 1256, 1259 (S.D.N.Y. 1972) (disciplinary hearing), and *Villani v. New York Stock Exchange*, 348 F.Supp. 1185, 1188 n.1 (S.D.N.Y. 1972), aff'd sub nom. *Sloan v. New York Stock Exchange*, 489 F.2d 1 (2 Cir. 1973) (same), although the recent decision in *Jackson v. Metropolitan Edison Co.*, 419 U.S. 345 (1974), would suggest the need for some caution on this score. We deal here with special factors concerning the privilege against self-incrimination and, although we do not think this decisive, even with that only in a preliminary investigation rather than a formal disciplinary proceeding.

III.

There remains for consideration the ground of involuntariness on which *Garrity* may have been rested. This interpretation of *Garrity* seems to have been accepted in *United States ex rel. Sanney v. Montanye*, [500 F.2d 411 (2d Cir. 1974)], although the majority there held that the economic threat to Sanney—discharge from a job as driver's assistant which he had held for one or two days—was not sufficiently serious to bring the case within the *Garrity* doctrine. Both *Garrity* and *Sanney* are distinguishable from this case. In *Garrity* there was clearly government action. Similarly, the *Sanney* court found that the private employer was "admittedly acting as an agent for the police". While it therefore could perceive no consequence from the fact that the coercive threat was conveyed in that manner "rather than through a person on the public payroll", it repeatedly stressed that government action was involved, 500 F.2d at 415. Here, as we have concluded above, it was not.

It is settled law that the common law rule excluding confessions induced by a threat is limited to inducement by "a person in authority"; what is generally required is "a legal interest in the prosecution" and "not the mere existence of actual control or influence growing out of the social or commercial relations of the persons." 3 Wigmore, Evidence, § 829 at 443 (Chadbourn rev. 1970). There is more debate about what "a legal interest in the prosecution" means. Under the leading English case a master or mistress is deemed "a person in authority" for purposes of the rule excluding involuntary confessions when and only when the offense concerns him or her. *R. v. Moore*, 2 Den.C.C. 522 (1852). *** Most American courts have opted for a "middle way" in which "[t]he injured person, or the master of a servant, is not regarded as necessarily having a control sufficient to vitiate confessions made by his inducement ..." and "[e]ach case is decided upon its own circumstances, and the actual state of the relation between him [the master] and the confessor is inquired into with reference to the probable strength of the inducement", 3 Wigmore, supra § 830 at 446-47 and cases cited in n.5.

Whatever may be the ultimate solution of the question how far coercion by non-governmental sources can ever demand exclusion as distinguished from consideration by the fact-finder, in the instant case, on this issue of involuntariness in fact we find the distinction [from] *Garrity* *** to be important. There the penalty for a claim of a right to remain silent was mandatory dismissal from office, loss of accrued pension benefits and permanent disability from state or municipal employment. Here there was no certainty what penalty NYSE would prescribe if Solomon refused to speak. It seems plain to us that Solomon, who had conferred with counsel and had his lawyer present during the off-the-record and the later on-the-record interrogation, decided it would be to his advantage to make a clean breast of falsifications that were bound to be discovered, or, indeed, very likely had been, rather than add another item to the case against him. To be sure, Solomon's position was not a particularly pleasant one. But the rule excluding involuntary confessions does not protect against hard choices when a person's serious misconduct has placed him in a position where these are inevitable. Of course, if there were any question whether Solomon was responsible for the false entries in Weis' books, he would have been entitled to have a trier of the facts consider whether the circumstances under which he admitted having conceived the plan affected the reliability of his statement. But there was none. It would be a wholly unwarranted extension of the principle with respect to involuntary confessions to include Solomon's statement to the Exchange.

### *NOTES AND QUESTIONS*

*1. **The Relevance of the 1975 Exchange Act Amendments.*** Note that the *Solomon* decision preceded the 1975 amendments to the Exchange Act set out in the previous subsection of this Chapter. Had this legislation been in place at the time, would it likely have changed Judge Friendly's analysis in any significant respect?

*2. **Refusals to Testify and Failures to Cooperate.*** To what extent did Judge Friendly base his determination as to the voluntariness of Solomon's confession on the ground that there was "no certainty" about the consequences of failing to testify in an NYSE investigation? Today, there is little doubt that a person's refusal to testify or cooperate in an SRO investigation typically results in a permanent suspension from association with a member organization. See, e.g., *John D. Goldsmith*, NYSE Hearing Panel Decision No. 96-60 (July 25, 1996) (censuring and barring the registered representative from employment or association with a member firm until he complies with NYSE's request to testify, and imposing a permanent bar if refusal extends beyond one year). See also John Falvey & Stephanie Gibson, The NASD's Invitation to Testify: An Offer You Can't Refuse, 16 No. 6 White-Collar Crime Rep. 1 (June 2002) (maintaining that a client's "refusal to testify will likely mean expulsion"). Courts, however, routinely cite to *Solomon* when declining to recognize a Fifth Amendment privilege in an SRO proceeding. See, e.g., *D.L. Cromwell Invs., Inc. v. NASD Regulation, Inc.*, 279 F.3d 155, 161-63 (2d Cir. 2002) (affirming district court's refusal to order injunction barring NASD from compelling testimony as part of civil securities fraud investigation); *United States v. Shvarts*, 90 F. Supp. 2d 219, 222 (E.D.N.Y. 2000) (denying self-incrimination privilege because "[i]t is beyond cavil that the NASD is not a government agency; it is a private, not-for-profit corporation. It was not created by statute. None of its directors *** are government officials or appointees. It receives no government funding ***, [and] its actions cannot be imputed to the government."); *Datek Sec. Corp. v. Nat'l Ass'n of Sec. Dealers, Inc.*, 875 F. Supp. 230, 234 (S.D.N.Y. 1995) (holding that "[p]laintiffs' claim to have raised a substantial constitutional question *** fails because [defendant] is not a governmental actor subject to the Fifth Amendment"). In contrast, persons under investigation by the SEC may assert their Fifth Amendment rights and refuse to testify, though the fact finder in civil litigation is entitled to draw a negative inference from this assertion.

*3.* ***Immunity for SRO Officials.*** A number of courts have recognized that SROs perform a quasi-governmental role in enforcing the federal securities laws and have held SRO officials—or the SRO itself—subject to absolute immunity for damages in private actions. See, e.g., *D'Alessio v. NYSE,* 258 F.3d 93, 105 (2d Cir. 2001) (stating that "[t]he NYSE, as a SRO, stands in the shoes of the SEC in interpreting the securities laws for its members and in monitoring compliance with those laws. It follows that the NYSE should be entitled to the same immunity enjoyed by the SEC when it is performing functions delegated to it under the SEC's broad oversight authority"); *Barbara v. NYSE,* 99 F.3d 49, 59 (2d Cir. 1996) (holding that "absolute immunity is particularly appropriate in the unique context of the self-regulation of the national securities exchanges," where the NYSE "performs a variety of regulatory functions that would, in other circumstances, be performed by [the SEC]"); *Austin Mun. Sec., Inc. v. Nat'l Ass'n of Sec. Dealers, Inc.*, 757 F.2d 676, 690-91 (5th Cir. 1985) (stating that the "NASD disciplinary officers serve as surrogates for the SEC, and should receive the same immunity their principles [sic] possess"). See also *D'Alessio*, supra, 258 F.3d at 105 (quoting lower court's statement that "according the NYSE absolute immunity when it performs regulatory functions that would otherwise be performed by the SEC 'is a matter not simply of logic but of intense practicality, since, in the absence of such immunity, the [NYSE's] exercise of its quasi-governmental functions would be unduly hampered by disruptive and recriminatory lawsuits' "). Are these cases reconcilable with *Solomon* and its progeny?

*4.* ***The Supreme Court and Controversies Over State Action.*** In *Brentwood Academy v. Tenn. Secondary School Athletic Ass'n*, 531 U.S. 288, 291 (2001), a closely divided Supreme Court found that a nominally private statewide association that regulated interscholastic athletic competition engaged in state action when it enforced a rule against a member school, in light of the "pervasive entwinement of state school officials in the structure of the association." Other decisions have held that a challenged activity may be state action when it results from the government's exercise of "coercive power," *Blum v. Yaretsky*, 457 U.S. 991, 1004 (1982), when the government provides "significant encouragement, either overt or covert," id., or when a private actor operates as a "willful participant in joint activity with the State or its agents," *Lugar v. Edmondson Oil Co.,* 457 U.S. 922, 941 (1982). The Supreme Court has also recognized a nominally private entity as a state actor when it has been delegated a public function by the government, *West v. Atkins*, 487 U.S. 42, 56 (1988), when it is "entwined with governmental policies," or when government is "entwined in [its] management or control." *Evans v. Newton*, 382 U.S. 296, 299, 301 (1966). The *Brentwood* Court also drew attention to *Lebron v. Nat'l R.R.*

*Passenger Corp.*, 513 U.S. 374 (1995), where the Supreme Court recognized Amtrak as a federal state actor for constitutional purposes: "regardless of its congressional designation as private, it was organized under federal law to attain governmental objectives and was directed and controlled by federal appointees." *Brentwood*, supra, 531 U.S. at 296. Based on many of these Supreme Court precedents, a number of scholars have taken the controversial position that "when enforcing federal law, as they are required to do under the Exchange Act, SROs are state actors *** [and] should be subject to the same constitutional limitations as the Commission or any other government agency." Richard L. Stone & Michael A. Perino, Not Just a Private Club: Self Regulatory Organizations as State Actors When Enforcing Federal Law, 1995 Colum. Bus. L. Rev. 453, 455. Do you agree?

***5. Temporary Cease-and-Desist Authority for the NASD.*** The NASD has formally requested the SEC to grant it authority to impose temporary cease-and-desist orders that could be used "to halt misconduct while it is happening, rather than proceed[ing] on the normal enforcement timetable." Rachel McTague, NASDR Speeds Pace of Enforcement Cases, Seeks Temporary Cease-and Desist Power, 34 Sec. Reg. & L. Rep. 264, 264 (BNA) (Feb. 18, 2002). According to the NASD's Executive Vice President of Enforcement, the temporary cease-and-desist authority would be used in "egregious cases where there is a risk of investor loss." Id. Moreover, under the proposed procedures, the respondent would have to be represented by counsel and could not be sanctioned ex parte. Should the SEC grant the NASD this new power?

## F. PARALLEL PROCEEDINGS

The phrase "parallel proceedings" is frequently used to describe concurrent or successive civil and criminal investigations or prosecutions by the SEC and the DOJ, though the phrase can take on an even broader construct if state officials or SRO officials become involved. Because the federal securities laws specifically provide for both civil and criminal enforcement, and because federal securities laws often have state blue sky analogues, such parallel proceedings are a relatively common occurrence and raise complicated issues for both potential defendants and government prosecutors. The first subsection focuses on general issues raised by multiple investigations, and the second places some of these issues in the context of recent high profile investigations into the activities of securities analysts and investment banks. The final subsection explores the issues of multiple sanctions and prosecutions in light of the Double Jeopardy Clause of the Fifth Amendment.

### *1. Multiple Investigations of the Same Conduct or Activities*

### SEC v. DRESSER INDUSTRIES, INC.

628 F.2d 1368 (D.C. Cir. 1980) (en banc)

WRIGHT, CHIEF JUDGE:

Dresser Industries, Inc. (Dresser) appeals from a decision of the District Court requiring obedience to a subpoena *duces tecum* issued by the Securities and Exchange Commission (SEC) on April 21, 1978, and denying Dresser's motion to quash the subpoena. The subpoena was issued in connection with an SEC investigation into Dresser's use of corporate funds to make what are euphemistically called "questionable foreign payments," and into the adequacy of Dresser's disclosures of such payments under the securities laws.

The principal issue facing this *en banc* court is whether Dresser is entitled to special protection against this SEC subpoena because of a parallel investigation into the same questionable foreign payments now being conducted by a federal grand jury under the guidance of the United States Department of Justice (Justice). Dresser argues principally that the SEC subpoena abuses the civil discovery process of the SEC for the purpose of criminal discovery and infringes the role of the grand jury in independently investigating allegations of criminal wrongdoing. On November 19, 1979 a panel of this court issued a decision affirming the District Court but, with Judge Robb dissenting, attaching a condition prohibiting the SEC from providing Justice with the information received from Dresser under this subpoena. Because of the importance of this issue to enforcement of the regulatory laws of the United States, this court voted to vacate the panel opinions and rehear the case *en banc*.

## I. BACKGROUND

### A. *Origin of the Investigations*

Illegal and questionable corporate payments surfaced as a major public problem in late 1973, when several major scandals implicated prominent American corporations in improper use of corporate funds to influence government officials in the United States and foreign countries. The exposure of these activities disrupted public faith in the integrity of our political system and eroded international trust in the legitimacy of American corporate operations abroad.[3] SEC investigation revealed that many corporate officials were falsifying financial records to shield questionable foreign and domestic payments from exposure to the public and even, in many cases, to corporate directors and accountants. Since the completeness and accuracy of corporate financial reporting is the cornerstone of federal regulation of the securities markets, such falsification became a matter of grave concern to the SEC.

Beginning in the spring of 1974 the SEC brought a series of injunctive actions against certain American corporations. It obtained consent decrees prohibiting future violations of the securities laws and establishing internal corporate procedures for investigation, disclosure, and prevention of illegal corporate payments. However, the problem of questionable foreign payments proved so widespread that the SEC devised a "Voluntary Disclosure Program"

3. The Senate Committee on Banking, Housing, and Urban Affairs reported in May 1977:

> Recent investigations by the SEC have revealed corrupt foreign payments by over 300 U.S. companies involving hundreds of millions of dollars. These revelations have had severe adverse effects. Foreign governments friendly to the United States in Japan, Italy, and the Netherlands have come under intense pressure from their own people. The image of American democracy abroad has been tarnished. Confidence in the financial integrity of our corporations has been impaired. The efficient functioning of our capital markets has been hampered.

S. Rep. No. 114, 95th Cong., 1st Sess. 3 (1977).

to encourage corporations to conduct investigations of their past conduct and make appropriate disclosures without direct SEC coercion. Participation in the Voluntary Disclosure Program would not insulate a corporation from an SEC enforcement action, but the Commission would be less likely to exercise its discretion to initiate enforcement actions against participants. The most important elements of the Voluntary Disclosure Program were (1) an independent committee of the corporation would conduct a thorough investigation into questionable foreign and domestic payments made by the corporation; (2) the committee would disclose the results of this investigation to the board of directors in full; (3) the corporation would disclose the substance of the report to the public and the SEC on Form 8-K; and (4) the corporation would issue a policy statement prohibiting future questionable and illegal payments and maintenance of false or incomplete records in connection with them. Except in "egregious cases" the SEC would not require that public disclosures include specific names, dates, and places. Rather, the disclosures might be "generic" in form. Thus companies participating in the Voluntary Disclosure Program would ordinarily be spared the consequences to their employees, property, and business that might result from public disclosure of specific instances of foreign bribery or kickbacks. However, companies participating in the Voluntary Disclosure Program had to agree to grant SEC requests for access to the final report and to the unexpurgated underlying documentations.

B. *The Dresser Investigations*

On January 27, 1976 an attorney and other representatives of Dresser met with members of the SEC staff to discuss a proposed filing. At the meeting Dresser agreed to conduct an internal inquiry into questionable foreign payments, in accordance with the terms of the Voluntary Disclosure Program. The next day Dresser submitted a Form 8-K describing, in generic terms, one questionable foreign payment. On November 11, 1976 Dresser filed a second Form 8-K reporting the results of the internal investigation. On February 10, 1977 the company supplemented this report with a third Form 8-K concerning a questionable payment not reported in the earlier reports. The reports concerned Dresser's foreign activities after November 1, 1973. All disclosures were in generic, not specific, terms.

As part of its general monitoring program the SEC staff requested access to the documents underlying Dresser's report. On July 15, 1977 Dresser refused to grant such access. The company argued that allowing the staff to make notes or copies might subject its documents to public disclosure through the Freedom of Information Act. Dresser stated that such disclosure could endanger certain of its employees working abroad. During the ensuing discussions with the staff Dresser attempted to impose conditions of confidentiality upon any SEC examination of its documents, but the staff did not agree. Instead, it issued a recommendation to the Commission for a formal order of investigation in the Dresser case. This recommendation was predicated on the staff's conclusions that Dresser:

1. may have used corporate funds for non-corporate purposes;
2. may have made false and misleading statements concerning the existence of and circumstances surrounding material obligations

of Dresser to certain foreign governments and to other entities; and

3. may have made false entries and caused false entries to be made upon the books and records of Dresser, and its affiliates and subsidiaries with respect to, among other things, payments to foreign government officials.

Moreover, the staff reported that Dresser's proxy soliciting materials, reports, and statements may have been misleading with respect to the potential risks involved in its conduct of business through questionable foreign payments, and may have included false statements in connection with such payments. Dresser vigorously opposed issuance of an order of investigation.

Meanwhile, the Department of Justice had established a task force on transnational payments to investigate possible criminal violations arising from illegal foreign payments. Two SEC attorneys participated in the task force. In the summer of 1977 the Justice task force requested access to SEC files on the approximately 400 companies, including Dresser, that had participated in the Voluntary Disclosure Program. Pursuant to Commission authorization the SEC staff transmitted all such files to the Justice task force in August 1977. After its preliminary investigation of the Form 8-K's submitted by Dresser under the Voluntary Disclosure Program, Justice presented Dresser's case to a grand jury in the District of Columbia on January 25, 1978.

Before any summons or subpoena had issued in either the SEC or the grand jury investigation, Dresser filed suit in the Southern District of Texas against the SEC and Justice to enjoin any further investigation of it by either agency. While Dresser's suit was pending in the Southern District of Texas, the District of Columbia grand jury subpoenaed Dresser's documents on April 21, 1978. At roughly the same time the SEC issued a formal order of private investigation, authorizing the staff to subpoena the documents and to obtain other relevant evidence. Pursuant to that order the staff issued a subpoena *duces tecum*, returnable on May 4, 1978. This subpoena covered substantially the same documents and materials subpoenaed by the grand jury, and more. Dresser did not respond to the subpoena.

On May 1, 1978 the District Court in Houston, Texas dismissed Dresser's suit against Justice without opinion. Three days later, after the period for compliance with its subpoena had lapsed, the SEC applied to the District Court for the District of Columbia for enforcement. In the meantime, Dresser had appealed the adverse judgment in the Texas action to the Fifth Circuit, and sought interim relief. On May 5 Judge Coleman of the Fifth Circuit enjoined further prosecution of the SEC subpoena enforcement action until after the District Court for the Southern District of Texas had ruled on Dresser's action against the SEC. Judge Coleman also obtained a stipulation from Justice that Justice would not require Dresser or its agents to appear before the grand jury until after the Company had filed a motion to quash the grand jury subpoena in the District of Columbia and had received a ruling on such motion.

On May 8, 1978 Dresser filed a motion to quash the grand jury subpoena in the District Court for the District of Columbia. On May 19 the District Court (Parker, J.) denied Dresser's motion to quash, but imposed a protective order requiring strict confidentiality in accordance with Rule 6(e) of the Federal Rules of Criminal Procedure. In imposing the protective order the court stated that the "concern of Dresser and especially its employees is not illusory and should not be lightly considered." This was in reference to Dresser's argument that public disclosures of the names, places, and dates connected with its questionable foreign payments could endanger the lives of its employees in certain turbulent foreign countries. Dresser thereafter complied with this grand jury subpoena.

On May 26, 1978 the Southern District of Texas dismissed Dresser's action against the SEC without reaching the merits. Dresser appealed to the Fifth Circuit and on June 8 obtained an order from the court that:

> Until the appeal in this case shall have been decided in this court, and except for proceedings before the Grand Jury in the District of Columbia, the Securities and Exchange Commission, its officers and employees, are enjoined to preserve inviolate the confidentiality of any information obtained by the subpoena here in issue. This order is not intended to interfere with pending proceedings in the District of Columbia to enforce the SEC subpoenas.

On June 2, 1978 the District Court for the District of Columbia issued an order to Dresser to show cause why it should not be required to appear, give testimony, and produce records in obedience to the SEC subpoena. On June 7 Dresser filed a motion for leave to obtain discovery from the SEC concerning the agency's alleged bad faith and attempted abuse of the judicial process, and on June 13 filed a motion to quash the SEC subpoena.

The District Court (Flannery, J.) denied Dresser's motion to compel discovery on June 16, without opinion. Judge Flannery explained in court that he had carefully examined the papers filed by Dresser, that discovery is rarely necessary in subpoena enforcement cases, and that he did not think this was an appropriate case for it. Then, on June 30, 1978, the District Court (Flannery, J.) issued a memorandum opinion and order rejecting all of Dresser's objections to the SEC subpoena and requiring Dresser to comply with the subpoena within ten days after notice from the SEC. *** This appeal followed.

Meanwhile, the United States Court of Appeals for the Fifth Circuit affirmed the decisions of the District Court for the Southern District of Texas dismissing Dresser's actions against Justice and the SEC in that court, largely on ripeness grounds. *Dresser Industries, Inc. v. United States*, 596 F.2d 1231 (5th Cir. 1979). Accordingly, the interlocutory injunction requiring the SEC to preserve inviolate the confidentiality of Dresser's materials pending a decision on appeal was dissolved.

Having set forth the complicated procedural history of this case, we turn now to the principles that govern parallel administrative and criminal proceedings concerning the same conduct.

## II. GENERAL PRINCIPLES

### A. *Parallel Investigations*

The civil and regulatory laws of the United States frequently overlap with the criminal laws, creating the possibility of parallel civil and criminal proceedings, either successive or simultaneous. In the absence of substantial prejudice to the rights of the parties involved, such parallel proceedings are unobjectionable under our jurisprudence. As long ago as 1912 the Supreme Court recognized that under one statutory scheme—that of the Sherman Act—a transaction or course of conduct could give rise to both criminal proceedings and civil suits. *Standard Sanitary Manufacturing Co. v. United States*, 226 U.S. 20, 52 (1912). The Court held that the government could initiate such proceedings either "simultaneously or successively," with discretion in the courts to prevent injury in particular cases. Id. It explained:

> The Sherman Act provides for a criminal proceeding to punish violations and suits in equity to restrain such violations, and the suits may be brought simultaneously or successively. The order of their bringing must depend upon the Government; the dependence of their trials cannot be fixed by a hard and fast rule or made imperatively to turn upon the character of the suit. Circumstances may determine and are for the consideration of the court. An imperative rule that the civil suit must await the trial of the criminal action might result in injustice or take from the statute a great deal of its power. ***

Id.

The Supreme Court returned to this theme in *United States v. Kordel*, 397 U.S. 1 (1970). In that case the Food and Drug Administration (FDA) investigated a company and certain of its officers in connection with possible violations of the Federal Food, Drug, and Cosmetic Act, 21 U.S.C.§ 301 et seq. *** Before the company had responded [to interrogatories issued by the FDA in connection with a civil seizure proceeding,] the FDA notified it that the agency was contemplating a criminal proceeding against it in connection with the same alleged violations of the statute. The company therefore moved to stay civil proceedings or, in the alternative, to extend the time for answering the interrogatories until after disposition of the criminal proceedings. The District Court denied this motion. *** After it received the answers, the Department of Health, Education, and Welfare formally recommended criminal prosecution to the Justice Department. Justice obtained an indictment, and subsequently convictions. The case reached the Supreme Court upon appeal of the convictions of several of the company's officers.

The officers in *Kordel* argued that use of the civil discovery process to compel answers to interrogatories that could be used to build the government's case in a parallel criminal proceeding "reflected such unfairness and want of consideration for justice" as to require reversal. 397 U.S. at 11. The Supreme Court did not agree. The Court noted that the government had not brought the civil action "solely to obtain evidence for its criminal prosecution," id. at 11-12, or without notice to the defendants that it contemplated a criminal action, id. at 12. Moreover, the defendant was not unrepresented by counsel, id., and had no reason to fear "prejudice from adverse pretrial publicity or other unfair injury," id. Nor were there any other "special circumstances" suggesting that the parallel proceedings were unconstitutional or improper. Id. In the absence of such "special circumstances" the Court recognized that prompt investigation of both civil and criminal claims can be necessary to the public interest. It said:

> The public interest in protecting consumers throughout the Nation from misbranded drugs requires prompt action by the agency charged with responsibility for administration of the federal food and drug laws. But a rational decision whether to proceed criminally against those responsible for the misbranding may have to await consideration of a fuller record than that before

> the agency at the time of the civil seizure of the offending products. It would stultify enforcement of federal law to require a governmental agency such as the FDA invariably to choose either to forgo recommendation of a criminal prosecution once it seeks civil relief, or to defer civil proceedings pending the ultimate outcome of a criminal trial.

Id. at 11.

The Constitution, therefore, does not ordinarily require a stay of civil proceedings pending the outcome of criminal proceedings. See *Baxter v. Palmigiano*, 425 U.S. 308 (1976). Nevertheless, a court may decide in its discretion to stay civil proceedings, postpone civil discovery, or impose protective orders and conditions "when the interests of justice seem[ ] to require such action, sometimes at the request of the prosecution, *** sometimes at the request of the defense[.]" *United States v. Kordel*, supra, 397 U.S. at 12 n.27. The court must make such determinations in the light of the particular circumstances of the case.

Other than where there is specific evidence of agency bad faith or malicious governmental tactics, the strongest case for deferring civil proceedings until after completion of criminal proceedings is where a party under indictment for a serious offense is required to defend a civil or administrative action involving the same matter. The noncriminal proceeding, if not deferred, might undermine the party's Fifth Amendment privilege against self-incrimination, expand rights of criminal discovery beyond the limits of Federal Rule of Criminal Procedure 16(b), expose the basis of the defense to the prosecution in advance of criminal trial, or otherwise prejudice the case.[20] If delay of the noncriminal proceeding would not seriously injure the public interest, a court may be justified in deferring it. *** In some such cases, however, the courts may adequately protect the government and the private party by merely deferring civil discovery or entering an appropriate protective order. *Gordon v. FDIC*, 427 F.2d 578, 580-581 (D.C.Cir.1970). The case at bar is a far weaker one for staying the administrative investigation. No indictment has been returned; no Fifth Amendment privilege is threatened; Rule 16(b) has not come into effect; and the SEC subpoena does not require Dresser to reveal the basis for its defense.

B. *SEC Investigations*

The case at bar concerns enforcement of the securities laws of the United States, especially the Securities Act of 1933 and the Securities Exchange Act of 1934. These statutes explicitly empower the SEC to investigate possible infractions of the securities laws with a view to both civil and criminal enforcement, and to transmit the fruits of its investigations to Justice in the event of potential criminal proceedings. The '34 Act provides in relevant part: "The Commission may, in its discretion, make such investigations as it deems necessary to determine whether any person has violated, is violating, or is about to violate any provision of this chapter[.]" Section 21(a) of the '34 Act. This

---

20. In some cases the government seeks postponement of the noncriminal proceeding, to prevent the criminal defendant from broadening his rights of criminal discovery against the government. E.g., *Campbell v. Eastland*, 307 F.2d 478 (5th Cir. 1962).

investigative authority includes the power to administer oaths and affirmations, subpoena witnesses, take evidence, and require production of any books, papers, correspondence, memoranda, or other records which the SEC deems relevant or material. Id., Section 21(b). If it determines that a person "is engaged or is about to engage in acts or practices constituting a violation" of the Act, the SEC may bring an action in federal district court to enjoin such acts or practices. Id., Section 21(d). Under the same subsection of the '34 Act the SEC may "transmit such evidence as may be available concerning such acts or practices *** to the Attorney General, who may, in his discretion, institute the necessary criminal proceedings under this chapter." Id. The '33 Act is to similar effect. See Sections 19(b), 20(a), (b) of the '33 Act.

Effective enforcement of the securities laws requires that the SEC and Justice be able to investigate possible violations simultaneously. Dissemination of false or misleading information by companies to members of the investing public may distort the efficient workings of the securities markets and injure investors who rely on the accuracy and completeness of the company's public disclosures. If the SEC suspects that a company has violated the securities laws, it must be able to respond quickly: it must be able to obtain relevant information concerning the alleged violation and to seek prompt judicial redress if necessary. Similarly, Justice must act quickly if it suspects that the laws have been broken. Grand jury investigations take time, as do criminal prosecutions. If Justice moves too slowly the statute of limitations may run, witnesses may die or move away, memories may fade, or enforcement resources may be diverted. See *United States v. Fields*, 592 F.2d 638, 646 (2d Cir. 1978). The SEC cannot always wait for Justice to complete the criminal proceedings if it is to obtain the necessary prompt civil remedy; neither can Justice always await the conclusion of the civil proceeding without endangering its criminal case. Thus we should not block parallel investigations by these agencies in the absence of "special circumstances" in which the nature of the proceedings demonstrably prejudices substantial rights of the investigated party or of the government. See *United States v. Kordel*, supra, 397 U.S. at 11-13. ***

In essence, Dresser has launched this attack on the parallel SEC and Justice proceedings in order to obtain protection against the bare SEC proceeding, which it fears will result in public disclosure of sensitive corporate documents. The prejudice Dresser claims it will suffer from the parallel nature of the proceedings is speculative and undefined if indeed Dresser would suffer any prejudice from it at all. Any entitlement to confidential treatment of its documents must arise under the laws pertaining to the SEC; the fortuity of a parallel grand jury investigation cannot expand Dresser's rights in this SEC enforcement action. ***

## IV. COOPERATION BETWEEN SEC AND JUSTICE

In its initial decision in this case a panel of this court *** affirmed the District Court and ordered enforcement of the SEC subpoena. Out of a concern that the SEC subpoena might somehow "subvert the limitations of criminal discovery," however, the panel, with one judge dissenting, modified the terms of the subpoena enforcement order. It required that "once the Justice Department initiates criminal proceedings by means of a grand jury, the SEC may not provide the Justice Department with the fruits of the Commission's civil discovery gathered after the decision to prosecute." We affirm the judgment of the District Court and reject the panel's modification.

First, we note that no party to this case had suggested or requested a modification such as that imposed by the panel majority, either in the District Court or in this court. In supplemental briefs submitted to the *en banc* court both the SEC and Justice vigorously oppose the modification, while Dresser's support for it is lukewarm at most. Dresser had argued that the SEC investigation is flatly prohibited[.] *** The reactions of the parties, therefore, suggest that the panel's modification might serve more to impede securities law enforcement than to protect the interests of Dresser.

Second, we note that there is no support for the panel's modification in either the relevant statutes or legislative history. Both the '33 Act and the '34 Act—and other statutes related to securities law enforcement as well—expressly authorize the SEC to "transmit such evidence as may be available *** to the Attorney General, who may, in his discretion, institute the necessary criminal proceedings under this subchapter." Section 20(b) of the '33 Act; Section 21(d) of the '34 Act. The statutes impose no limitation on when this transmittal may occur. The parties have not cited any portions of the legislative histories of these Acts relevant to this question, nor have we found any. But the SEC and Justice find considerable support for their interpretation in the legislative history of the Foreign Corrupt Practices Act of 1977.

The Foreign Corrupt Practices Act outlaws corporate bribery of foreign officials and associated inaccurate or misleading financial recordkeeping. In passing the statute Congress recognized the role of the SEC in combatting such practices under the '33 and '34 Acts, and sought to "strengthen the Commission's ability to enforce compliance with the existing requirements [sic] of the securities laws[.]" S.Rep.No. 114, 95th Cong., 1st Sess. 12 (1977). Both the Senate and the House reports on the bill acknowledged the SEC's dual investigative role in preparing cases for civil and criminal enforcement actions. They also recognize the necessity of close cooperation between the SEC and Justice in preparing such cases. ***

Although the legislative history of the Foreign Corrupt Practices Act is not directly probative of congressional intent governing the '33 and '34 Acts, these statements by the 95th Congress are nevertheless entitled to some weight. The remarks in the committee reports concerning the investigative practices of the SEC and Justice were not intended to change, but to reaffirm, past practice. This indicates that Congress understands and approves of the "close working relationship" between the agencies in their investigative capacities. Since such a "close working relationship" will govern the activities of the agencies in enforcing the laws against questionable foreign payments under the new statute, it would be impractical for us to attempt to screen the agencies from each other when they are investigating the same sort of offense under the former statutes.

Congress manifestly did not intend that the SEC be forbidden to share information with Justice at this stage of the investigation. Under the panel majority's theory of the case the SEC would be foreclosed from sharing the fruits of its investigation with Justice as soon as Justice begins its own investigation through a grand jury. Only by waiting until the close of the SEC proceeding before initiating its own grand jury investigation could Justice obtain access to the evidence procured by the SEC. In view of Congress' concern that the agencies share information "at the earliest stage of any investigation in order to insure that the evidence needed for a criminal prosecution does not become stale," S.Rep.No. 114, supra, at 12, and that the agencies avoid "a costly duplication of effort," H.R.Rep.No. 640, supra, at 9, it would be unreasonable to prevent a sharing of information at this point in the investigation.

Third, we note that there is little or no judicial precedent for the panel's modification. The only support adduced by the panel opinion is a District Court opinion in *SEC v. Gilbert*, 79 F.R.D. 683 (S.D.N.Y.1978). In that case, which arose on the defendant's request for a protective order under the discovery rules of the Federal Rules of Civil Procedure—as contrasted to an investigative subpoena enforcement proceeding as in this case—the court ordered the SEC "not to furnish the U.S. Attorney specially with any information procured in the course of discovery in this case." Id. at 687. The court offered no authority for this order nor, indeed, any reason for its application. While we recognize the similarity of *Gilbert* to this case in many respects, its lack of reasoning and its distinguishable procedural posture make it but weak authority.

In fact, the reasoning of the Supreme Court in [*United States v. LaSalle Nat'l Bank*, 437 U.S. 298 (1978)] is contrary to that of the panel in two respects, and should govern this case in lieu of *Gilbert*. The *LaSalle* Court considered, and explicitly rejected, the course adopted by the panel majority: "[I]t is unrealistic to attempt to build a partial information barrier between the two branches of the executive." *United States v. LaSalle Nat'l Bank*, supra, 437 U.S. at 312. More fundamentally, the *LaSalle* Court conceived of the controversy before it as an analysis of the good or bad faith of the IRS investigation. A bad faith investigation, in the Court's conception, is one conducted solely for criminal enforcement purposes. See id. at 307-308, 316, & 316 n.18. Where the agency has a legitimate noncriminal purpose for the investigation, it acts in good faith under the *LaSalle* conception even if it might use the information gained in the investigation for criminal enforcement purposes as well. In the present case the SEC plainly has a legitimate noncriminal purpose for its investigation of Dresser. It follows that the investigation is in good faith, in the absence of complicating factors. There is, therefore, no reason to impose a protective order such as that imposed by the panel majority.

Finally, we note that the panel's modification would serve no compelling purpose, and might interfere with enforcement of the securities laws by the SEC and Justice. As the Second Circuit has said, the procedure permitting the SEC to communicate with Justice during the preliminary stages of an investigation has "significant advantages." *United States v. Fields*, supra, 592 F.2d at 646:

> Allowing early participation in the case by the United States Attorney minimizes statute of limitations problems. The more time a United States Attorney has, the easier it is for him to become familiar with the complex facts of a securities fraud case, to prepare the case, and to present it to a grand jury before expiration of the applicable statute of limitations. Earlier initiation of criminal proceedings moreover is consistent with a defendant's right to a speedy trial. ***

Id. The panel's modification would "interfere with this commendable example of inter-agency cooperation," id., to the detriment of securities law enforcement and in contravention of the will of Congress. On the other side of the balance, the panel's concern for preserving the limitations on criminal discovery is largely irrelevant at this stage of the proceedings, as Dresser agrees. Thus this would be an inappropriate situation to impose a "prophylactic" rule against cooperation between the agencies. We believe the courts can prevent any injustice that may arise in the particular circumstances of parallel investigations in the future. We decline to adopt the position of the panel majority. ***

EDWARDS, CIRCUIT JUDGE, CONCURRING:

I concur in the opinion of the court in this case. I wish to point out, however, that I do not read the court's opinion as expressing any view as to the proper outcome in a case of this sort *once an indictment has issued.* Once an indictment has issued, the policy interest expressed in *United States v. LaSalle National Bank,* 437 U.S. 298, 312 (1978), concerning the impermissibility of broadening the scope of criminal discovery through the summons authority of an agency, may come into play. I express no opinion as to whether or not the summons authority of a government agency may continue once an indictment has been issued or, if it may, whether protective conditions need be placed on the exercise of that power. These issues raise questions which are not presented here. The resolution of these questions, therefore, must await another day.

## *NOTES AND QUESTIONS*

***1. Horizontal Proceedings vs. Vertical Proceedings.*** The *Dresser* case involved what we may term "horizontal proceedings"—concurrent or successive proceedings initiated by different agencies in the federal government. The phrase "vertical proceedings" can be used to connote multiple layers of investigations/prosecutions by different authorities, such as multiple proceedings brought by the federal government (the SEC and/or the DOJ), state officials (often involving many different states acting under both criminal and civil authority), and SROs (often the NASD and the NYSE). Coordination is typically easiest among the various agencies of the federal government. As a matter of policy, should coordination be encouraged among all others with regulatory authority? How could such coordination be accomplished?

***2. Enforcement Actions by SROs.*** Is there reason for concern that the SEC or the DOJ could instruct an SRO to launch an investigation of a broker-dealer or associated person because of the fewer constitutional constraints that would be imposed on SRO officials? In this regard, consider the parallel investigations conducted by the DOJ and the NYSE in the *Solomon* case set out in the previous section of this Chapter. Would you feel differently about the outcome of the case if there were evidence that the DOJ had asked the NYSE to initiate the investigation and to seek testimony from potential targets? Is this simply a variation of the concerns raised (and dismissed) in *Dresser*?

***3. Administrative Subpoenas Post-Indictment.*** Note that the *Dresser* court did not consider whether the SEC may issue and enforce a subpoena after the return of a criminal indictment. Yet Judge Edwards wrote separately to express his concern with this possibility. On what was his concern based? In such cases, what, specifically, should be done?

### 2. *Multiple State, Federal, and SRO Enforcement Proceedings Against Securities Analysts and Investment Banks*

In 2002, New York State Attorney General Eliot Spitzer brought several high-profile enforcement proceedings against major Wall Street investment banks and brokerage firms. These proceedings, labeled a "crusade" by some observers, investigated and in some cases criminally charged investment bankers, brokers and analysts suspected of various types of misconduct that Spitzer labeled fraudulent. See, e.g., Robin Sidel, Sorry, Wrong Number: Some Untimely Analyst Advice on WorldCom Raises Eyebrows, Wall St. J. at A12 (June 27, 2002) (stating that "Spitzer has launched an all-out crusade to eradicate conflicts of interests on Wall Street"). Most important for purposes of the material discussed in this section, these state investigations and enforcement proceedings involved conduct that the SEC also could have investigated and prosecuted, and indeed in some instances the same conduct was concurrently the subject of ongoing SEC investigations. Controversy continues over whether state investigations and proceedings are a useful supplement to the enforcement activities of an understaffed and underfinanced SEC, or whether they pose an unacceptable risk of either interfering with SEC enforcement activity or unduly burdening the targeted companies and individuals.

The first area investigated by Attorney General Spitzer was conflicts of interest of Wall Street stock analysts, many of whom were employed by broker-dealers that do substantial investment banking business with the same companies that these analysts evaluate in reports circulated to investors. The Attorney General first probed whether Merrill Lynch & Co. misled investors about the quality of stocks in order to win lucrative investment banking business. The allegations, mainly of undisclosed conflicting interests, arose from Merrill's investment banking relationship with companies its analysts covered. The analysts' evaluation of certain stocks was "supposedly independent and objective investment advice [which] was tainted and biased by the desire to aid [the] investment banking business." See Press Release, Merrill Lynch Stock Rating System Found Biased by Undisclosed Conflicts of Interest, Office of New York State Attorney General Eliot Spitzer (April 8, 2002).

The Attorney General asked for and received a court order compelling Merrill and its employees to produce documents relating to the allegations. After probing that materials, Spitzer's office publicly revealed e-mail messages from Merrill analysts, written in late 2000, that described some stocks as "dogs," "crap" or "junk." The Attorney General maintained that, in that same time period, those stocks had been aggressively promoted to the investing public by the very same analysts, including former star analyst Henry Blodget, who gave the stocks "buy" or "accumulate" ratings in reports circulated to investors. See Charles Gasparino, Wall Street Has Unlikely New Cop: Spitzer, Wall St. J. at C1 (Apr. 25, 2002).

After 10 months of investigation, the Attorney General's office was ready to indict Merrill for criminal violations of the antifraud provisions of New York's securities law, the Martin Act. Merrill then hired former NYC Mayor Rudolph Giuliani, himself a former United States Attorney who had prosecuted high-profile insider trading cases in the 1980s, to represent the company in reaching a settlement with the Attorney General's office.

On May 21, 2002, the Attorney General announced a settlement with Merrill Lynch, whereby the company agreed to:

- Sever the link between compensation for analysts and investment banking. ***
- Prohibit investment banking input into analysts' compensation. *** Merrill is forbidden from soliciting or considering any information concerning the amount of investment banking revenue received from clients [and from its analysts] from being evaluated by investment bankers.
- Create a new investment review committee responsible for approving all research recommendations with strict standards and independence from investment banking and the analysts themselves.
- Establish a monitor to ensure compliance with the agreement.
- Require that upon discontinuation of research coverage of a company, Merrill will issue a report disclosing the termination of coverage and the rationale for such termination, and will notify investors that the last rating should no longer be relied upon.
- Disclose in Merrill's research reports whether it has received or is entitled to receive any compensation from a covered company over the past 12 months.
- Pay a $100 million penalty. ***

Spitzer, Merrill Lynch Reach Unprecedented Agreement to Reform Investment Practices, Press Release, Office of the New York State Attorney General Eliot Spitzer (May 21, 2002). Merrill Lynch was also required to issue a statement of contrition for failing to adopt policies and procedures that adequately addressed the risks of conflicting interests. Id.

Attorney General Spitzer then turned attention to other targets, focusing particularly on the research that analysts did on the now bankrupt WorldCom, Inc. For example, Salomon Smith Barney's highly paid analyst Jack Grubman gave WorldCom stock a "buy" rating from 1997 through April of 2002. Spitzer's investigation of Grubman sought to uncover whether he (and other analysts) improperly or fraudulently promoted shares of WorldCom, and whether they were influenced by Grubman's close relationship with WorldCom's ex-CEO and former CFO. See Richard A. Oppel, Jr., Turmoil at WorldCom: Wall Street, N.Y. Times (June 27, 2002). In April 2002, Spitzer subpoenaed documents from Salomon's offices, related to Grubman's research.

The Attorney General investigated how Salomon became one of three lead underwriters of AT&T Corp's $10.62 billion stock offering for its wireless-phone unit. The investigation centered on whether AT&T chairman C. Michael Armstrong had asked Citigroup CEO Sanford Weill to prevail upon Grubman to upgrade his rating on AT&T stock. See Charles Gasparino, Inquiry Into Salomon Widens to Include Possible Weill Role, Wall St. J. at A1 (Aug. 23, 2002). Citigroup is the parent company of Salomon Smith Barney.

With respect to analysts' conflicts of interest, Spitzer also investigated Credit Suisse First Boston, Morgan Stanley Dean Witter & Co., Goldman Sachs Group Inc., UBS AG's Paine Webber Group Inc., Bear Stearns Co., and Lazard Freres. See Charles Gasparino, Merrill Lynch Investigation Widens: Probe of Conflicts of Interest of Analysts Is Expanded to Other Wall Street Firms, Wall St. J. at C4 (Apr. 11, 2002).

A second area on which the Attorney General focused, in addition to the conduct of research analysts, was abuses in connection with underwriters' distribution of shares in initial public offerings (IPOs). Spitzer's investigation of Salomon, for example, included investigation into allocation of IPO shares to favored customers in order to attract investment banking business. As the Attorney General explained in a radio interview:

> What is emerging now is that the practice of allocating IPO shares based upon the notion that you wanted to keep CEO clients happy was pervasive. And part of what has been emerging on the Street is that the practices were not isolated to one bank or one rogue operator, but that there was a certain way of doing business, and so that dynamic is one that has been problematic to regulators and prosecutors.

All Things Considered: Investment Banking Probe (National Public Radio broadcast, Sept. 20, 2002).

A third area investigated by Spitzer resulted in the indictment of five individuals alleged to have defrauded the public through the sale of securities in private placements. The securities sold by the indicted individuals were of worthless shell companies through Westminster Holdings, Ltd, a corporation "purporting to be a Wall Street 'investment banking firm.'" Press Release, Office of New York State Attorney General Eliot Spitzer, Officers of Fraudulent Investment Bank Face 62-Court Indictment in IPO Scheme (June 10, 2002). The indicted individuals face charges such as grand larceny, scheme to defraud, issuing false financial statements, and violation New York's General Business Law.

More specifically, the indictment alleged that the defendants described Westminster Holdings, Ltd. as an established investment bank with over 25 years of experience in corporate finance transactions, when actually Westminster Holdings, Ltd. was a newly-formed company managed by Robert Moses who was barred from the securities industry only a few years before. The investors were persuaded to purchase shares in companies claimed by the defendants to be privately owned start-ups which would complete a reverse merger or an IPO soon. The defendants also were alleged to have persuaded the investors that the investment was a no-risk or small-risk investment and that the investors could get back their money if the companies did not go public or merge within a year. The indictment alleged further that the defendants "pressured investors to withdraw money from their retirement and IRA accounts or to borrow money if necessary with promises of returns within 90 days." Id.

While all of this was going on at the state level, the SEC and the SROs began to investigate much of the same alleged misconduct, and were specifically targeting many of the same securities analysts and investment banks as Spitzer. See Charles Gasparino & Scot J. Paltrow, SEC Joins Pack, Opens Inquiry Into Analysts, Wall St. J. at C1 (Apr. 26, 2002) (reporting that the SEC had opened a "formal inquiry" that will be conducted with the NYSE and NASD). And on September 23, 2002, the NASD announced a $5 million settlement with Salomon Smith Barney in connection with its issuance of materially misleading research reports in 2001 on Winstar Communications and the filing of a complaint against Jack Grubman and his assistant Christine Gochuico, who authored the reports. The NASD's News Release made clear that the settlement resolves only the investigation into the Winstar reports "and does not address other, larger Salomon-related research analyst investigations currently underway by NASD and other regulators." Press Release, NASD, Salomon Smith Barney Fined $5 Million for Issuing Misleading Research Reports on Winstar (September 23, 2002).

## *NOTES AND QUESTIONS*

*1.* ***Should There Be a Top Cop?*** Which, if any, of Attorney General Spitzer's investigations would have been better carried out by the SEC, assuming it had the resources and will to do so? Absent a large scale investigation by the SEC, did it make sense for Spitzer to investigate and prosecute? When the SEC made and announced a decision to investigate, should state authorities have closed their investigations and allowed the SEC to take over? Should the SROs have deferred to SEC enforcement efforts?

*2.* ***Calls for Federal Preemption.*** In early 2002, Congress considered legislation that would preempt state investigations of a wide range of conduct in connection with nationally traded securities. After the collapse of WorldCom, and as Spitzer's investigations gained political support, this preemption idea was abandoned. Should Congress legislate that only the SEC can investigate certain conduct? If so, which types of conduct?

*3.* ***Risks of Agency Capture.*** Are state investigations and enforcement actions a useful check on potential "capture" of SEC and SRO regulators by the securities industry? See Jonathan R. Macey, Administrative Agency Obsolescence and Interest Group Formation: A Case Study of the SEC at Sixty, 15 Cardozo L. Rev. 909, 922 (1994) (expressing concern that "[t]he predictable phenomenon of agency 'capture' by special interest groups has led to [SEC] subsidies to favored constituencies, particularly securities analysts, institutional investors, market professionals (traders and market makers), and retail brokerage firms"). Was the SEC's relatively slow pace in pursuing the conflicts of interest issue a possible example of agency capture? What about the SROs? What alternative explanations may be offered? For analysis challenging some of Professor Macey's contentions, see David L. Ratner, The SEC at Sixty: A Reply to Professor Macey, 16 Cardozo L. Rev. 1765, 1776 (1995) (arguing that "[u]nlike the regulators of banks, thrift institutions, and insurance companies, which have acted principally as protectors and advocates for their constituents, the SEC has frequently been at loggerheads with some of the most powerful organizations in the securities industry").

*4.* ***All's Well That Ends Well?*** On October 3, 2002, the SEC, N.Y. Attorney General Spitzer, the NYSE, the NASD, and the North American Securities Administrators Association (NASAA) announced, with much fanfare, "a joint initiative to wrap up their various investigations into research analysts' practices and initial public offering (IPO) allocations." Rachel McTague & Kip

Betz, Cooperative Spirit Prevails as Regulators Join Together to Resolve Analyst, IPO Cases, 34 Sec. Reg. & L. Rep. 1622 (BNA) (Oct. 7, 2002). And with even more fanfare, on December 20, 2002, the SEC announced that a "global settlement" had been agreed to "in principle" with the nation's top investment firms. SEC Press Release 2002-179, SEC, NY Attorney General, NASD, NASAA, NYSE and State Regulators Announce Historic Agreement to Reform Investment Practices (December 20, 2002). According to the Press Release, the terms of the proposed agreement include:

- The insulation of research analysts from investment banking pressure. Firms will be required to sever the links between research and investment banking, including analyst compensation for equity research, and the practice of analysts accompanying investment banking personnel on pitches and road shows. This will help ensure that stock recommendations are not tainted by efforts to obtain investment banking fees.
- A complete ban on the spinning of Initial Public Offerings (IPOs). Brokerage firms will not allocate lucrative IPO shares to corporate executives and directors who are in the position to greatly influence investment banking decisions.
- An obligation to furnish independent research. For a five-year period, each of the brokerage firms will be required to contract with no less than three independent research firms that will provide research to the brokerage firm's customers. An independent consultant ("monitor") for each firm, with final authority to procure independent research from independent providers, will be chosen by regulators. This will ensure that individual investors get access to objective investment advice.
- Disclosure of analyst recommendations. Each firm will make publicly available its ratings and price target forecasts. This will allow for evaluation and comparison of performance of analysts.
- Settled enforcement actions involving significant monetary sanctions.

Id. The Press Release also contained the following chart documenting the fines, monies toward investor restitution, and escrow funds for investor education that were agreed to in principle by the regulators and investment firms. As these figures reveal, the agreement that was reached totals more than $1.4 billion.

| Name of Firm | Retrospective Relief ($ millions) | Independent Research ($ millions) | Investor Education ($ millions) |
|---|---|---|---|
| Bear Stearns & Co. LLC | 50 | 25 | 5 |
| Credit Suisse First Boston Corp. | 150 | 50 | 0 |
| Deutsche Bank | 50 | 25 | 5 |
| Goldman Sachs | 50 | 50 | 10 |
| J.P. Morgan Chase & Co. | 50 | 25 | 5 |
| Lehman Brothers, Inc. | 50 | 25 | 5 |
| Merrill Lynch & Co., Inc. | 100* | 75 | 25 |
| Morgan Stanley | 50 | 75 | 0 |
| Salomon Smith Barney, Inc. | 300 | 75 | 25 |
| UBS Warburg LLC | 50 | 25 | 5 |
| Total | 900 | 450 | 85 |

*Payments made in prior settlement of Research Analyst conflicts.

Noting that the global settlement remained subject to approval by the full Commission, SEC Chairperson Harvey L. Pitt remarked that "[t]his cooperative agreement in principle *** is a tribute to the wonderful cooperative efforts of the NYSE, the NASD, the NYAG and the states in the public interest." Id.

What practical problems might arise for the SEC, SROs, and state regulators as they seek to finalize this global settlement with the investment firms? See, e.g., Charles Gasparino, Analyst Pack is Held Up by Words, Wall St. J. at C1 (January 18, 2003) (reporting a "showdown" between the NASD and the New York Attorney General's Office over "tough wording" in the final report). Do you anticipate that similar "global settlements" will be reached with individual analysts and other investment firm officials?

---

### 3. *Multiple Prosecutions and Sanctions and the Double Jeopardy Clause*

The Double Jeopardy Clause of the Fifth Amendment protects defendants against multiple criminal prosecutions and multiple criminal punishments for the same offense. We have already seen that while Congress has given the SEC the authority to seek in federal court, or impose in administrative proceedings, a wide array of sanctions, the SEC's arsenal of enforcement remedies is entirely a civil one. Does this end the inquiry for purposes of the constitutionality of multiple prosecutions and sanctions by both the SEC and DOJ for the same securities law violations?

In *United States v. Halper*, 490 U.S. 435, 448-49 (1989), the Supreme Court held that "a defendant who already has been punished in a criminal prosecution may not be subjected to an additional civil sanction to the extent that the second sanction may not fairly be characterized as remedial, but only as a deterrent or retribution." *Halper,* which involved first criminal and then civil sanctions brought under the Federal False Claims Act, opened the door to constitutional challenges in cases where the remedy sought by the SEC arguably could be characterized as punitive. The Court's holding in *Halper* also implicated double jeopardy concerns in cases where the SEC obtained a civil monetary penalty against a defendant and the Department of Justice subsequently sought to initiate a criminal prosecution. See, e.g., *United States v. Marcus Schloss & Co.*, 724 F. Supp. 1123, 1126-27 (S.D.N.Y. 1989) (holding that imposition of civil monetary penalty under Exchange Act Section 21A did not preclude, on double jeopardy grounds, criminal prosecution for insider trading where the defendant's consent order entered into with the SEC was agreed to with knowledge of an ongoing grand jury investigation). The court in *Marcus Schloss,* however, did not answer the more difficult question of whether the imposition of an unconsented to civil penalty for insider trading would bar the imposition of a subsequent criminal prosecution and penalty.

Less than a decade after deciding *Halper*, a majority of the Supreme Court found its analysis "unworkable" and "disavow[ed]" its reasoning in *Hudson v. United States*, 522 U.S. 93, 96, 102 (1997). The following case discusses *Hudson.*

## SEC v. PALMISANO

135 F.3d 860 (2d Cir. 1998)

KEARSE, CIRCUIT JUDGE:

Defendant pro se Joseph C. Palmisano appeals from so much of a judgment of the United States District Court for the District of Vermont, Franklin S. Billings, Jr., Judge, as orders him, in this civil enforcement action brought by the Securities and Exchange Commission ("SEC"), to disgorge approximately $9.2 million and to pay an additional civil penalty of $500,000, for violations of the Securities Act of 1933 ("Securities Act"), the Securities Exchange Act of 1934 ("Exchange Act"), and SEC Rule 10b-5. On appeal, Palmisano contends principally that the disgorgement order and the civil penalty violate the Double Jeopardy Clause of the Fifth Amendment because he had been punished for the same conduct in a criminal proceeding. For the reasons set forth below, we modify the judgment in one respect and, as modified, we affirm.

### I. BACKGROUND

Prior to 1994, Palmisano was an attorney who specialized in bankruptcy law. From at least December 1987 through November 1992, he operated a fraudulent Ponzi-type scheme in which he induced some 90 persons to invest with him a total of approximately $7.9 million. Palmisano solicited investments from his clients and others for the avowed purpose of purchasing property of bankrupt or distressed companies, which would then be sold at a profit. He represented that the invested funds would be placed in a separate escrow account, and he told some investors that their investments involved "no risk" to principal and would produce tax-free returns of 20-30 percent per year. In fact, there was no reasonable basis for these representations. Palmisano did not invest the money as promised but instead used it for his own personal purposes and used some investors' money to make distributions to other investors in order to perpetuate the scheme.

Palmisano gave his investors various written instruments representing their investments. At the time, there was no registration statement in effect with the SEC.

In July 1994, the United States filed a 40-count indictment charging Palmisano with a variety of criminal conduct in connection with the above scheme. The present civil enforcement action was filed by the SEC on the same day. The civil complaint alleged the sale of unregistered securities, in violation of §§ 5(a) and (c) of the Securities Act, and the sale of securities by means of fraud and misrepresentation, in violation of § 17(a) of the Securities Act, and of § 10(b) of the Exchange Act, and Rule 10b-5. It requested principally that the district court enjoin Palmisano from violating the securities laws, order disgorgement of all gains he derived from his unlawful conduct, and impose a monetary penalty on him pursuant to the remedial provisions added to the Securities Act and the Exchange Act by the Securities Enforcement Remedies and Penny Stock Reform Act of 1990 ("Remedies Act").

In the criminal case, Palmisano pleaded guilty in September 1995 to 44 counts of a 45-count superseding indictment, including counts of mail fraud, wire fraud, money laundering, and securities fraud. The securities fraud counts were based on the same conduct that was alleged in the civil complaint. Following his plea of guilty, Palmisano was sentenced principally to 188 months' imprisonment, to be followed by a five-year term of supervised release, and was ordered to make restitution to his victims in the amount of $3,779,868.49. In addition, property involved in Palmisano's money-laundering violation, to wit, $700,000 and all interest and proceeds traceable thereto, was ordered forfeited to the United States.

In the meantime, the SEC had moved for summary judgment in the present civil action, and its motion had not been decided when Palmisano pleaded guilty in the criminal case. Following the entry of the guilty plea, the SEC argued that it was entitled to summary judgment in this case on the ground of collateral estoppel. The magistrate judge to whom the summary judgment motion was referred recommended granting the motion on that ground. Although Palmisano objected on the basis that the facts of the criminal and civil actions were different, and on other grounds not at issue here, the district court granted the motion on the basis of the collateral estoppel effect of Palmisano's plea of guilty to the securities fraud charges.

Judgment was entered in the present action, enjoining Palmisano from future securities law violations, ordering him to disgorge approximately $9.2 million, comprising $6,169,291.98 in unlawful gains plus $2,989,086.42 in prejudgment interest, and ordering him to pay a $500,000 civil penalty.

## II. DISCUSSION

Palmisano has appealed from so much of the judgment as imposes the $9.2 million disgorgement obligation and the $500,000 civil penalty, contending principally that each of those sanctions, in light of the punishment imposed in his criminal case, violates his right to be free from double jeopardy. ***[W]e conclude that [Palmisano's contentions] are without merit.

*A. The Possibility of Overlapping Remedies*

***[T]here is one aspect of the present judgment that warrants consideration here. The present judgment does not indicate how the disgorgement ordered is to be affected by Palmisano's payment of the restitution ordered in the criminal proceeding, which raises the possibility that the total amount that Palmisano is to pay in disgorgement and restitution could exceed his unlawful gains. The SEC, in its brief on this appeal, has conceded that payments by Palmisano to his victims pursuant to the restitution order in the criminal case should be credited toward the disgorgement ordered here: "Defendant is only required to give back the proceeds of his securities fraud once. Thus, to the extent he pays back the victims of his securities fraud as a result of the criminal restitution order, those payments should be credited towards the disgorgement award." (SEC brief on appeal at 13 n. 11.)

We conclude that that acknowledged limitation should be specified in the present judgment. Accordingly, we modify the judgment to provide that to the extent that Palmisano pays or has paid restitution as ordered in the criminal judgment, such payments will offset his disgorgement obligation under the present judgment.

*B. The Principal Double Jeopardy Contentions*

Palmisano's principal double jeopardy arguments are that because he was subjected to sanctions in his criminal case, his right to be free from double jeopardy is violated by the requirements in this action for disgorgement and payment of a civil fine. In support of these arguments, he relies primarily on *United States v. Halper,* 490 U.S. 435 (1989), which held that civil penalties constitute punishment within the meaning of the Double Jeopardy Clause if they are "overwhelmingly disproportionate" to the harm suffered by the government. *Id.* at 449. Even assuming that Palmisano's contentions could have been viewed as valid under *Halper*, they are plainly meritless in light of *Hudson v. United States,* [118 S.Ct. 488] (1997), in which the Supreme Court largely "disavow[ed] the method of analysis used in *United States v. Halper,*" *Hudson v. United States,* 118 S.Ct. at 491, and reaffirmed the traditional rule that the Double Jeopardy Clause prohibits multiple sanctions for the same offense only if those sanctions are "*criminal* punishments," 118 S.Ct. at 493 (emphasis in original). Under the traditional analysis, there was no double jeopardy here.

In protecting an already-punished person against further punishments, the Double Jeopardy Clause does not prohibit the imposition of all additional sanctions "that could, in common parlance, be described as punishment," 118 S.Ct. at 493; rather it "protects only against the imposition of multiple *criminal* punishments for the same offense" in successive proceedings, id. Whether a particular punishment is criminal or civil is, at least initially, a matter of statutory interpretation. See, e.g., id.; *Helvering v. Mitchell,* 303 U.S. 391, 399 (1938). Thus, the first question the court must ask is "whether the legislature, 'in establishing the penalizing mechanism, indicated either expressly or impliedly a preference for one label or the other.'" *Hudson v. United States,* 118 S.Ct. at 493 (quoting *United States v. Ward,* 448 U.S. 242, 248 (1980)). If the court determines that the legislature has indicated an intention to establish a sanction that is civil, the court must then ask whether the statutory scheme is "so punitive either in purpose or effect," as to "transfor[m] what was clearly intended as a civil remedy into a criminal penalty." *Hudson v. United States,* 118 S.Ct. at 493. Congress's designation of a penalty as civil is entitled to considerable deference. Such a designation will not be overborne unless the statute, considered on its face and without reference to the level of sanction imposed in the particular case, see, e.g., *Hudson v. United States,* 118 S.Ct. at 493; *Kennedy v. Mendoza-Martinez,* 372 U.S. 144, 169 (1963), is clearly so punitive as to "render [it] criminal despite Congress' intent to the contrary," *United States v. Ursery,*116 S.Ct. 2135, 2148 (1996). " '[O]nly the clearest proof' " of its punitive character "will suffice to override legislative intent and transform" a sanction labeled "civil" into one that is criminal. *Hudson v. United States,* 118 S.Ct. at 493 (quoting *United States v. Ward,* 448 U.S. at 249, 100 S.Ct. at 2641).

The test to be used in determining whether a sanction is so punitive in nature as to transform what was intended as a civil remedy into a criminal penalty, and thus subject to the Double Jeopardy Clause's bar on multiple punishments, is the same inquiry that is used in determining whether other criminal proceeding protections apply. See *Hudson v. United States,* 118 S.Ct. at 493 (citing *United States v. Ward,* 448 U.S. at 248 (addressing Fifth Amendment privilege against self-incrimination), and *Kennedy v. Mendoza-Martinez,* 372 U.S. at 167 (addressing Fifth and Sixth Amendment rights to "criminal trial and all its incidents, including indictment, notice, confrontation, jury trial, assistance of counsel, and compulsory process for obtaining witnesses")). Thus, consideration of the seven factors set out in *Kennedy v. Mendoza-Martinez* is appropriate:

> (1) "[w]hether the sanction involves an affirmative disability or restraint"; (2) "whether it has historically been regarded as a punishment"; (3) "whether it comes into play only on a finding of *scienter*"; (4) "whether its operation will promote the traditional aims of punishment—retribution and deterrence"; (5) "whether the behavior to which it applies is already a crime"; (6) "whether an alternative purpose to which it may rationally be connected is assignable for it"; and (7) "whether it appears excessive in relation to the alternative purpose assigned."

*Hudson v. United States,* 118 S.Ct. at 493 (quoting *Kennedy v. Mendoza-Martinez,* 372 U.S. at 168-69).

This seven-factor list, though not exhaustive, provides "useful guideposts," *Hudson v. United States,* 118 S.Ct. at 493, and no single factor is dispositive, see, e.g., id. at 494. For example, the nature of the sanction cannot turn solely on whether the conduct at issue is also a crime, for it is well established that " 'Congress may impose both a criminal and a civil sanction in respect to the same act or omission,' " *United States v. Ursery,* 116 S.Ct. at 2149. Thus, in *Ursery,* the Court ruled that the property forfeitures authorized in 18 U.S.C. § 981(a)(1)(A) and 21 U.S.C. § 881(a)(6) in order to "require disgorgement of the fruits of illegal conduct," 116 S.Ct. at 2145, are properly classified as civil penalties, not as criminal punishment. See id. at 2149 (the "goal of ensuring that persons do not profit from their illegal acts" is "nonpunitive"). Nor does the nature of the sanction turn solely on whether it has a goal of deterrence. Although deterrence is a traditional purpose of criminal punishment, that purpose "is insufficient to render a sanction criminal, as deterrence 'may serve civil as well as criminal goals.'" *Hudson v. United States,* 118 S.Ct. at 496. In the context of the banking industry, for example, government regulation in the form of monetary sanctions to deter fraud and self-dealing is designed to, *inter alia,* foster public confidence and promote the stability of the banking industry, and the *Hudson* Court noted that "[t]o hold that the mere presence of a deterrent purpose renders such sanctions 'criminal' for double jeopardy purposes would severely undermine the Government's ability to engage in effective regulation." 118 S.Ct. at 496. Thus, the Court concluded that administratively imposed monetary penalties for violation of banking regulations are properly classified as civil, not criminal, sanctions. See id.

Applying these principles to the sanctions imposed in the present case for violations of the securities laws, we note that the threshold matter of Congress's intent clearly favors classifying disgorgement and the fines at issue here as civil. The penalties provided for in the Remedies Act are expressly designated as civil: the subsections authorizing the fines are labeled "[m]oney penalties in civil actions," and within those provisions the fine is referred to as a "civil penalty." [Securities Act Section 20(d); Exchange Act Section 21(d)(3)]. Further, although disgorgement is not specifically provided for in the securities statutes, Congress has expressly endorsed that sanction, see, e.g., H.R. Rep. No. 101-616, at 13 (1990) (Remedies Act authorizes courts "to order the payment of civil money penalties, *in addition to disgorgement*" (emphasis added)). The disgorgement remedy, which has long been upheld as within the general equity powers granted to the district court by § 22(a) of the Securities Act and § 27 of the Exchange Act has not been considered a criminal sanction.

Turning to the seven factors that guide the second step of the double jeopardy inquiry, we conclude that neither disgorgement nor the monetary penalties set out in the Remedies Act are so punitive in purpose or effect as to override Congress's intent to provide for civil penalties. Although disgorgement and the Remedies Act fines apply to conduct that may also be prosecuted under a criminal statute, and they possess some characteristics common to criminal laws, such as requiring scienter and effecting deterrence, see, e.g., H.R. Rep. No. 101-616, at 17 (Remedies Act "would greatly increase deterrence"), neither disgorgement nor money penalties have historically been viewed as punishment. Rather, the "payment of fixed or variable sums of money" is a sanction that has long been recognized as civil. *Hudson v. United States,* 118 S.Ct. at 496. Moreover, such monetary sanctions do not involve an "affirmative disability or restraint," as that term is normally understood, see id.; certainly neither approaches the type of restraint involved in imprisonment.

In addition, these remedies have a clear rational purpose other than punishment. Disgorgement, like the forfeitures discussed in *Ursery,* is designed in part to ensure that the defendant not profit from his illegal acts, a goal that is nonpunitive. Further, the deterrence of securities fraud serves other important nonpunitive goals, such as encouraging investor confidence, increasing the efficiency of financial markets, and promoting the stability of the securities industry. All of these goals are advanced by the structure of the Remedies Act, which establishes three levels of fines; each tier sets maximum dollar amounts (distinguishing between individuals and corporations), with the proviso that a fine may exceed that tier's stated dollar maximum in order to match the defendant's unlawful gains. See [Securities Act Section 20(d)(2); Exchange Act Section 21(d)(3)(B)]. The first tier of fines applies to all securities law violations; the second provides higher maximum fines for violations that involved fraud; and the third provides the highest maximums for violations that involved fraud and "resulted in substantial losses or created a significant risk of substantial losses to other persons." Id. The linkage of the size of the potential fine to the level of the violator's scienter, the risk of loss to others, and the amount of the defendant's unlawful profits minimizes the possibility that a fine will be excessive in relation to Congress's nonpunitive goals.

We conclude that there is little indication, and certainly not the "clearest proof," required under *Hudson*, that disgorgement and the fines provided by the Remedies Act are criminal punishments. The Double Jeopardy Clause is therefore inapplicable. ***

## *NOTES AND QUESTIONS*

1. **Halper *vs.* Hudson.** As *Palmisano* made clear, *Hudson* slammed shut the double jeopardy door that may have been opened by *Halper*. As a matter of constitutional policy, which analysis is superior? Which framework is more workable?

2. **Palmisano *vs.* Johnson.** Can the Second Circuit's decision in *Palmisano* be easily reconciled with the D.C. Circuit's observation in *Johnson v. SEC* (a statutes of limitations case set out in Section D.2 supra) that many SEC sanctions are imposed for punitive, rather than remedial, purposes? What result in *Palmisano* had the defendant been subject to a prior criminal fine in addition to jail time, restitution, and forfeiture? Could a district judge grant the SEC's request to impose a civil penalty?

3. ***The Justifications for Multiple Sanctions.*** Even if multiple criminal and civil sanctions are permissible as a constitutional matter, what policy interests are served by their imposition? SEC officials have suggested at least one possible justification:

> If we have caught someone who has defrauded scores of poor elderly couples and deprived them of millions of dollars in life's savings, even if we have won on the civil side and made him disgorge his profits and enjoined him from ever doing it again—even if we have made him pay severe penalties—it does not mean he should be absolved of the punishment and condemnation due him as a criminal. On the other hand, if we are unable to prove every element on the criminal side, at least we have the civil system as a backstop for correction and deterrence.

Thomas C. Newkirk & Ira L. Brandriss, The Advantages of a Dual System: Parallel Streams of Civil and Criminal Enforcement of the U.S. Securities Laws, Remarks at the 16th International Symposium on Economic Crime (Sept. 19, 1998). Recognizing the important "backstop" role served by civil enforcement, is there nonetheless a compelling justification for parallel civil sanctions *after* a defendant has been prosecuted and convicted in a criminal action?

4. ***Multiple Sanctions Imposed by an SRO and the SEC.*** In *Jones v. SEC*, 115 F.3d 1173 (4th Cir. 1997), the Fourth Circuit held that the SEC could affirm sanctions upon a registered representative imposed by the NASD (a censure, a three-day suspension, and a $22,500 fine) and then, with respect to the same misconduct, impose on that representative its own additional

sanctions (a permanent injunction, a censure, and a suspension totaling 30 months). The representative had argued that the SEC was precluded from so doing based on the following three points:

> (1) because the SEC has a right to review, modify, and cancel (but not increase) the NASD's sanction and did not do so, it is now bound by its decision not to do so under principles of res judicata; (2) to permit the SEC to increase the NASD's sanction through a separate proceeding violates the Maloney Act which recognizes the NASD as a quasi-public regulatory body whose sanctions the SEC may not increase, see [Exchange Act Section 19(e)]; and (3) the SEC's sanction is a second penalty for the same conduct that violates the Fifth Amendment's Double Jeopardy Clause.

Id. at 1177. Assuming that the court's decision was correct as a matter of law, should the SEC make a practice of affirming SRO sanctions against an individual or entity and then further penalizing that individual or entity by adding its own sanctions for the same misconduct?

# Chapter 10

# ENFORCEMENT ISSUES INVOLVING ATTORNEYS AND ACCOUNTANTS

---

This Chapter examines the recently expanded role of the federal government in regulating attorneys engaged in securities law practice and accountants responsible for the auditing of companies required to file reports with the SEC. The statutory basis for this expansion is the Sarbanes-Oxley Act of 2002, and its lightening rod was, of course, the financial and corporate governance scandals at Enron, WorldCom and many other companies.

Until this landmark legislation was enacted at the end of July 2002, securities attorneys were regulated principally by state bar associations. These bar associations (along with the American Bar Association (ABA)) usually howled in protest in those rare instances when the SEC stated what it believed to be the professional responsibilities of securities lawyers. Congress intervened in 2002 because of the widely-held belief that lawyer malfeasance had played a role in numerous securities fraud scandals, and also because of concerns expressed by academics and others that bar association rules were ambiguous and overly deferential to attorney discretion. Specifically, Section 307 of the Sarbanes-Oxley Act mandates that the SEC promulgate rules of professional conduct for securities lawyers, including a rule that would require an attorney for a securities issuer to report securities law violations to the client's board of directors. In January 2003, the SEC fulfilled this requirement by adopting new Rule 205.

As for accountants, prior to July 2002 they were regulated primarily by independent organizations such as the American Institute of Certified Public Accountants (AICPA) and the Financial Accounting Standards Board (FASB). The SEC also promulgated rules defining minimum accounting standards and "independence" requirements for auditors of reporting companies. But after the malfeasance of auditors was blamed for the collapses of Enron and WorldCom, as well as for a large number of other earnings restatements in the early 2000s, the Sarbanes-Oxley Act established a new independent board to regulate auditors under the supervision of the SEC—the Public Company Accounting Oversight Board (PCAOB). That Act also specified nine types of non-audit services which can no longer be provided contemporaneously by the auditor of a public company, and charged the PCAOB with enforcement of these new independence requirements.

This Chapter is divided into three sections. Section A addresses the SEC's regulation of attorneys and accountants under Rule 102(e) of its Rules of Practice, an SEC rule in existence since 1935, and now codified in the Sarbanes-

Oxley Act as a new Section 4C of the Exchange Act. Section B focuses on the professional obligations of securities attorneys. After reading the most famous Rule 102(e) proceeding ever brought against attorneys, you will be asked how an attorney faced with those same facts today should respond based on SEC rules promulgated under the Sarbanes-Oxley Act. Finally, Section C explores the new regime for auditors of public companies.

## A. SEC DISCIPLINE OF PROFESSIONALS UNDER RULE 102(e)

As discussed above, the SEC's power to discipline attorneys and accountants was until very recently codified only in the SEC's own Rules of Practice. SEC Rule 102(e) provides, in part, that:

> The Commission may censure a person or deny, temporarily or permanently, the privilege of appearing or practicing before it in any way to any person who is found by the Commission after notice of and opportunity for hearing in the matter:
>
> (i) Not to possess the requisite qualifications to represent others; or
>
> (ii) To be lacking in character or integrity or to have engaged in unethical or improper professional conduct; or
>
> (iii) To have willfully violated, or willfully aided and abetted the violation of any provision of the Federal securities laws, or the rules and regulations thereunder.[a] ***

17 C.F.R. § 201.102(e)(1).

Rule 102(f) ensures that Rule 102(e) enforcement has a very broad reach by providing that:

> For the purposes of these Rules of Practice, practicing before the Commission shall include, but shall not be limited to:
>
> (1) Transacting any business with the Commission; and
>
> (2) The preparation of any statement, opinion or other paper by any attorney, accountant, engineer or other professional or expert, filed with the Commission in any registration statement, notification, application, report or other document with the consent of such attorney, accountant, engineer or other professional or expert.

17 C.F.R. § 201.102(f).

Prior to July 2002, there was some question as to Rule 102(e)'s validity. On the one hand, the SEC argued, and courts agreed without exception, that Rule 102(e) constitutes a proper exercise of the SEC's general authority under the federal securities laws "to make such rules and regulations as may be necessary or appropriate *** for the execution of [its] functions ***." See, e.g., *Touche Ross & Co. v. S.E.C.*, 609 F.2d 570, 577 (2d Cir. 1979) (quoting Exchange Act Section 23(a) and citing to its analogues in Section 19 of the Securities Act, Section 20 of the Public Utility Holding Company Act, Section 319 of the Trust Indenture Act, Section 38 of the Investment Company Act, and Section 211 of the Investment Advisers Act). In explicitly rejecting the assertion that the

---

**a.** Ed. Note—In 1995, the SEC renumbered its Rules of Practice, such that former Rule 2(e) became present Rule 102(e).

Commission lacked authority to promulgate Rule 2(e), the *Touche Ross* court stated that:

> Although there is no express statutory provision authorizing the Commission to discipline professionals appearing before it, Rule 2(e), promulgated pursuant to its statutory rulemaking authority, represents an attempt by the Commission to protect the integrity of its own processes. It provides the Commission with the means to ensure that those professionals, on whom the Commission relies heavily in the performance of its statutory duties, perform their tasks diligently and with a reasonable degree of competence. As such the Rule is "reasonably related" to the purposes of the securities laws. *Mourning v. Family Publications Service, Inc.*, [411 U.S. 356 (1973)]. Moreover, we hold that the Rule does not violate, nor is it inconsistent with, any other provision of the securities laws. We therefore sustain the validity of the Rule as a necessary adjunct to the Commission's power to protect the integrity of its administrative procedures and the public in general.

Id. at 582. For additional cases upholding the validity of Rule 102(e), see *Davy v. SEC*, 792 F.2d 1418, 1421-22 (9th Cir. 1986) (concluding that the Commission had statutory authority to adopt Rule 102(e)); *Checkosky v. SEC*, 23 F.3d 452, 456 (D.C. Cir. 1994) (""There can be little doubt that the Commission, like any other institution in which lawyers or other professionals participate, has authority to police the behavior of practitioners before it"") (Silberman, J., quoting *Polydoroff v. ICC*, 773 F.2d 372, 374 (D.C. Cir. 1985)).

Yet others, including a former SEC Commissioner, took the position that Rule 102(e) exceeded the agency's general rulemaking authority. In the case of *In re Keating, Muething & Klekamp*, 47 S.E.C. 95 (1979), then SEC Commissioner (now Professor) Roberta Karmel, wrote a scathing dissent to the Commission's order imposing sanctions on a law firm for its failure to carry out its professional responsibilities with respect to certain SEC filings by a law firm client, stating that:

> in my opinion, it is improper for an independent federal administrative agency to impose sanctions which are not specified by Congress. In addition, the potential corruption of justice when an administrative agency with significant prosecutorial responsibilities has the power to sanction an adversary representing and advising a client persuades me that the Commission should not exercise disciplinary power against attorneys.

Id. at 111. Section 602 of the Sarbanes-Oxley Act of 2002 puts an end to this debate by codifying Rule 102(e) in what is now Section 4C of the Exchange Act.

Over the last few decades, the SEC has applied Rule 102(e) to attorneys and accountants in very different ways. Indeed, as we will see, the SEC traditionally has initiated Rule 102(e) proceedings against attorneys only following a judicial or administrative finding that the attorney has violated the federal securities laws. Yet the SEC has used Rule 102(e) rather routinely to discipline accounting firms and individual accountants for "unethical and improper professional conduct" and to set standards of conduct for the accounting profession. Moreover, although for most of its history the rule was silent as to the requisite state of mind necessary for liability, the SEC had long maintained that negligent conduct could trigger Rule 102(e) discipline of an accountant. Attorneys, however, were traditionally subject to Rule 102(e) discipline only when they acted intentionally.

In 1998, in response to the D.C. Circuit's unambiguous demand for clearer standards regarding state of mind in *Checkosky v. SEC*, 139 F.3d 221 (D.C. Cir. 1998), the SEC amended Rule 102(e) to clarify its operative standard for disciplining members of the accounting profession. To that end, Rule 102(e)(1) now contains a subpart (iv) that provides:

> With respect to persons licensed to practice as accountants, "improper professional conduct" under § 201.102(e)(1)(ii) means:
>
> (A) Intentional or knowing conduct, including reckless conduct, that results in a violation of applicable professional standards; or
>
> (B) Either of the following two types of negligent conduct:
>
> > (1) A single instance of highly unreasonable conduct that results in a violation of applicable professional standards in circumstances in which an accountant knows, or should know, that heightened scrutiny is warranted.
> >
> > (2) Repeated instances of unreasonable conduct, each resulting in a violation of applicable professional standards, that indicate a lack of competence to practice before the Commission.

In new Section 4C(b) of the Exchange Act, Congress adopted this definition of "improper professional conduct" in toto, making it applicable "[w]ith respect to any registered public accounting firm or associated person." (The Sarbanes-Oxley Act's new registration requirement for accounting firms is discussed in Section C below).

Significantly, neither Section 4C of the Exchange Act nor Rule 102(e) itself supplies a state of mind for other professionals. Thus, whether the same standard of negligence or a different higher standard shall apply to lawyers and other professionals is left to ad hoc adjudication in an SEC enforcement proceeding or to future SEC rulemaking.

### *NOTES AND QUESTIONS*

1. ***The Impact of Sanctions.*** How would a temporary or permanent suspension under Section 4C/Rule 102(e) impact the professional life of a certified public accountant? A lawyer? How would it impact an accounting firm? A law firm? How do the sanctions available under Section 4C/Rule 102(e) compare with the remedies available in enforcement actions brought against professionals for "causing" or "aiding and abetting" their clients' violations of the securities laws? (For a review of these remedies, see Chapter 9.C supra.)

2. ***Protecting the Integrity of the SEC's Processes.*** In addition to the statutory remedies in the federal securities laws, what other avenues might be available to the SEC to, in the words of the court in *Touche Ross*, "protect the integrity of its own processes?" What are the advantages and disadvantages of the SEC's use of these other avenues?

3. ***"Practice Before the Commission."*** Note the definition in Rule 102(f) of "practice before the Commission." What issues might be raised by its breadth? Would you favor a narrowing of this definition? Why or why not? Note also that neither Rule 102(e) nor Rule 102(f) contains a requirement that a professional's "unethical or improper professional conduct" necessarily relate to his or her representation of a client before the SEC. Should the SEC

nonetheless have to demonstrate such a nexus before imposing disciplinary sanctions under Section 4C / Rule 102(e)?

**4. *State of Mind.*** Do you agree with the SEC's decision to apply to accountants the standard of negligence set forth in Rule 102(e)(1)(iv)? The accounting profession lobbied the SEC vigorously for a scienter standard. Would this have been preferable? SEC Commissioner Norman Johnson clearly thought so, and went as far as to argue that his fellow Commissioners exceeded their rulemaking authority by amending Rule 102(e) to impose a standard of negligence:

> The Standard exceeds the Commission's authority in several ways. It improperly gives the Commission de facto substantive regulatory authority over the accounting profession, and it arrogates to the Commission authority to enforce the securities laws that is reserved to the federal courts. Accountants, like attorneys, are members of "ancient professions," regulated according to rigorous ethical rules enforced by professional societies and state licensing boards. I simply do not believe that we should recast negligent violations of an accounting standard as improper professional conduct under the Commission's Rules of Practice. That is not an appropriate role for the Commission. Difficult ethical and professional responsibility concerns are generally matters most appropriately dealt with by professional organizations or, in certain cases, malpractice litigation. Nor do I believe that mere misjudgments or negligence establishes either professional incompetence warranting Commission disciplinary action or the likelihood of future danger to the Commission's processes.

Amendment to Rule 102(e) of the Commission's Rules of Practice, Release No. 33-7593, 1998 WL 729201 at *28 (Oct. 19, 1998) (Commissioner Johnson, dissenting). Of course, any doubt over the SEC's authority to issue Rule 102(e)(1)(iv)'s standard of negligence for accountants has now been removed through Congress's inclusion of that language in Exchange Act 4C(b).

Should the standard governing "improper professional conduct" for accountants be applied to determinations involving attorneys and other professionals? Why or why not? As we will see from the Commission's opinion in *In Re Carter & Johnson,* set out in this Chapter's next section, the Commission offered the following justification for requiring scienter in order to impose "aiding and abetting" liability on an attorney under Rule 2(e)(1)(iii):

> If a securities lawyer is to bring his best independent judgment to bear on a disclosure problem, he must have the freedom to make innocent—or even, in certain cases, careless—mistakes without fear of legal liability or loss of the ability to practice before the Commission. Concern about his own liability may alter the balance of his judgment in one direction as surely as an unseemly obeisance to the wishes of his client can do so in the other. While one imbalance results in disclosure rather than concealment, neither is, in the end, truly in the public interest. Lawyers who are seen by their clients as being motivated by fears for their personal liability will not be consulted on difficult issues.

*In re Carter & Johnson,* 47 S.E.C. 471, 504 (1981). And at least until recently, the Commission appeared to adopt the similar view that scienter was required to establish that an attorney had engaged in "improper professional conduct" under Rule 102(e)(1)(ii). Assuming this to have been the standard for securities attorneys in the past, should it continue into the future?

***5. Evidentiary Privileges as a Hindrance to Rule 102(e) Proceedings.*** The initiation of a Rule 102(e) enforcement proceeding against an attorney or an accountant is feasible only if the SEC can obtain the evidence necessary to prosecute. However, communications between lawyers and clients are generally subject to the attorney-client privilege, and lawyers' work papers are often protected from compelled production by the work product privilege. Thus, in order for the SEC to effectively prosecute a lawyer for violating Rule 102(e), the Commission may have to obtain a waiver from the client, perhaps as part of settling an enforcement proceeding against the client.

On the other hand, no evidentiary privilege applies to information disclosed to an accountant from a client. See *Couch v. United States*, 409 U.S. 322, 335 (1973) ("no confidential accountant-client privilege exists under federal law, and no state-created privilege has been recognized in federal cases"). Audit work papers also are not protected by a work product privilege, as the Supreme Court recognized in *United States v. Arthur Young & Co.*, 465 U.S. 805, 817-18 (1984), when it stated that:

> the attorney work-product doctrine was founded upon the private attorney's role as the client's confidential adviser and advocate***. An independent certified public accountant performs a different role.*** To insulate from disclosure a certified public accountant's interpretations of the client's financial statements would be to ignore the significance of the accountant's role as a disinterested analyst charged with public obligations.

As a practical matter, the fact that evidentiary privileges surround the attorney-client relationship but not the accountant-client relationship tends to make it easier for the SEC to bring enforcement proceedings, including Rule 102(e) discipline proceedings, against accountants than against attorneys.

## B. ETHICAL AND PROPER CONDUCT FOR SECURITIES ATTORNEYS

### 1. *The Legal Landscape Before the Sarbanes-Oxley Act*

As discussed above, the professional conduct of lawyers has historically been regulated by state bar associations, which adopt codes similar to the model ethics codes of the American Bar Association (ABA). Most state codes are based on the ABA's Model Rules of Professional Conduct (last revised in 2003), and a minority of states (most notably New York) base their codes on the ABA's earlier Model Code of Professional Responsibility while making selective changes to some provisions.

The ABA Model Rules make it clear that a lawyer may not assist a client in committing a securities law violation or counsel the client to commit such a violation and that the lawyer may not affirmatively make misrepresentations either to the SEC or to investors (for example, in an opinion letter). In this regard, Model Rule 1.2(d) provides that a lawyer shall not knowingly assist a client in, or counsel a client to engage in, a crime or fraud. Model Rule 4.1 further states that, in the course of representing a client a lawyer shall not knowingly "make a false statement of material fact or law to a third person."

The ABA Model Rules are not as clear, however, in describing the appropriate response of the lawyer to illegal acts and misrepresentations by the client or by an agent of the client, particularly if the client is a corporation or other organization. The rule that speaks to this situation most directly is ABA Model Rule 1.13:

**ABA MODEL RULE 1.13: ORGANIZATION AS CLIENT**

> (a) A lawyer employed or retained by an organization represents the organization acting through its duly authorized constituents.
>
> (b) If a lawyer for an organization knows that an officer, employee or other person associated with the organization is engaged in action, intends to act or refuses to act in a matter related to the representation that is a violation of a legal obligation to the organization, or a violation of law which reasonably might be imputed to the organization, and is likely to result in substantial injury to the organization, the lawyer shall proceed as is reasonably necessary in the best interest of the organization. In determining how to proceed, the lawyer shall give due consideration to the seriousness of the violation and its consequences, the scope and nature of the lawyer's representation, the responsibility in the organization and the apparent motivation of the person involved, the policies of the organization concerning such matters and any other relevant considerations. Any measures taken shall be designed to minimize disruption of the organization and the risk of revealing information relating to the representation to persons outside the organization. Such measures may include among others:
>
> (1) asking for reconsideration of the matter;
>
> (2) advising that a separate legal opinion on the matter be sought for presentation to appropriate authority in the organization; and
>
> (3) referring the matter to higher authority in the organization, including, if warranted by the seriousness of the matter, referral to the highest authority that can act on behalf of the organization as determined by applicable law.
>
> (c) If, despite the lawyer's efforts in accordance with paragraph (b), the highest authority that can act on behalf of the organization insists upon action, or a refusal to act, that is clearly a violation of law and is likely to result in substantial injury to the organization, the lawyer may resign in accordance with Rule 1.16 [Declining or Terminating Representation]. ***

Although the Rule does not explicitly require a lawyer to report fraud "to the highest authority in the organization," the commentary to Rule 1.13 states that if asking the constituent to reconsider the matter fails, "it may be *reasonably necessary* for the lawyer to take steps to have the matter reviewed by a higher authority in the organization." Id. at comment 3 (emphasis added). But see Roger C. Cramton, Enron and the Corporate Lawyer: A Primer on Legal and Ethical Issues, 58 Bus. Law. 143, 154-156 (2002) (noting that the current rule is "ambiguous," and that "[m]any lawyers view the provision only as giving the lawyer discretion to choose among a number of options ***").

The ABA Model Rules are even less precise in specifying when lawyers for an organization may disclose confidential information to sources outside that organization. Here, the principal authority is Model Rule 1.6:

**ABA MODEL RULE 1.6: CONFIDENTIALITY OF INFORMATION**

> (a) A lawyer shall not reveal information relating to the representation of a client unless the client gives informed consent, the disclosure is impliedly

authorized in order to carry out the representation or the disclosure is permitted by paragraph (b).

(b) A lawyer may reveal information relating to the representation of a client to the extent the lawyer reasonably believes necessary:

(1) to prevent reasonably certain death or substantial bodily harm;

(2) to secure legal advice about the lawyer's compliance with these Rules;

(3) to establish a claim or defense on behalf of the lawyer in a controversy between the lawyer and the client, to establish a defense to a criminal charge or civil claim against the lawyer based upon conduct in which the client was involved, or to respond to allegations in any proceeding concerning the lawyer's representation of the client; or

(4) to comply with other law or a court order.

To be sure, Model Rule 1.6 mandates strict confidentiality with no exceptions for disclosures necessary to prevent a client's financial fraud. Yet, as one commentator recently pointed out: "[b]uried in the comments, and inconsistent with the black-letter text of the Rule, is language permitting a lawyer to 'disaffirm documents'—such as legal opinions prepared for a client—'that are being, or will be, used in furtherance of the fraud, even though such a "noisy" withdrawal may have the collateral effect of inferentially revealing client confidences.' " Cramton, supra, 58 Bus. Law. at 156 (quoting ABA Comm. on Ethics and Professional Responsibility, Formal Op. 366 (1992)).

Professor Cramton further noted that the strict confidentiality stance in the text of Model Rule 1.6 is in fact a minority position:

> The vast majority of U.S. jurisdictions *** have not adopted Model Rule 1.6 as recommended by the ABA. Forty-one states permit a lawyer to disclose confidential information to prevent a client's criminal fraud; four of those states require a lawyer to make such a disclosure; and only nine states and the District of Columbia may be viewed as forbidding a lawyer to reveal such information. ***

Cramton, supra, 58 Bus. Law. at 157.

Despite the preeminence of state bar associations in regulating lawyers, the SEC has long claimed a corresponding right to set professional standards for securities lawyers under Rule 102(e) as well as through enforcement actions for aiding and abetting a client's violation of Rule 10b-5. Yet the SEC has rarely exercised that right. One notable exception is *SEC v. National Student Mktg. Corp.*, 457 F. Supp. 682 (D.D.C. 1978). In that case, which the SEC brought under Rule 10b-5, attorneys representing National Student Marketing ("National") had discovered that National's proxy materials had overstated earnings but nonetheless had allowed a merger between National and another company to go forward without resoliciting approval of the merger from the shareholders of both companies based on corrected information. The court held that the attorneys aided and abetted their client's fraud because the attorneys neglected their duty to protest their client's decision to go ahead with the merger. The court emphasized that '[t]heir silence was not only a breach of this duty to speak, but in addition lent the appearance of legitimacy to the closing." Id. at 713. The court, however, failed to comment specifically on what seemed to be the SEC's position: that the lawyers for both corporations had a professional responsibility to alert the SEC to the fraud intended by their clients.

The case below documents another instance where the SEC sought to establish professional standards for securities lawyers, this time in the context of a Rule 2(e) proceeding. As you read the Commission's very lengthy opinion, consider whether it clearly explains what was expected of the securities attorneys or whether it simply raises additional questions.

## IN RE CARTER & JOHNSON

47 S.E.C. 471 (1981)

William R. Carter and Charles J. Johnson, Jr., respondents, appeal from the initial decision of the Administrative Law Judge in this proceeding brought under Rule 2(e) of the Commission's Rules of Practice. In an opinion dated March 7, 1979, the Administrative Law Judge found that, in connection with their representation of National Telephone Company, Inc. during the period from May 1974 to May 1975, Carter and Johnson willfully violated and willfully aided and abetted violations of Sections 10(b) and 13(a) of the Securities Exchange Act of 1934 (the "Exchange Act") and Rules 10b-5, 12b-20 and 13a-11 thereunder and that they engaged in unethical and improper professional conduct. In light of these findings, the Administrative Law Judge concluded that Carter and Johnson should be suspended from appearing or practicing before the Commission for periods of one year and nine months, respectively.

For the reasons stated more fully below, we reverse the decision of the Administrative Law Judge with respect to both respondents. We have concluded that the record does not adequately support the Administrative Law Judge's findings of violative conduct by respondents. Moreover, we conclude that certain concepts of proper ethical and professional conduct were not sufficiently developed, at the time of the conduct here at issue, to permit a finding that either respondent breached applicable ethical or professional standards. In addition, we are today giving notice of an interpretation by the Commission of the term "unethical or improper professional conduct," as that term is used in Rule 2(e)(1)(ii). This interpretation will be applicable prospectively in cases of this kind. ***

### III.

### RESPONDENTS' CONDUCT

*A. National Telephone Company.* The conduct at issue in these proceedings occurred in connection with respondents' legal representation of National Telephone Company, Inc. ("National") during the period from mid-1974 through mid-1975. National, a Connecticut corporation with its principal offices located in East Hartford, Connecticut, was founded in 1971 to lease sophisticated telephone equipment systems to commercial customers pursuant to long-term (5- to 10-year) leases. National enjoyed an impressive growth rate in its first three years, increasing its total assets from $320,123 to $19,028,613 and its net income from $2,390 to $633,485 during this period. At the same time, the company's backlog grew from $66,000 to $2,610,000 and the value of equipment leases written by it increased from $255,422 to $13,292,549.

The architect of National's meteoric rise was Sheldon L. Hart, one of its founders and, at all times relevant to these proceedings, its controlling stockholder. From its incorporation until his resignation on May 24, 1975, Hart was National's chief executive officer, chairman of the board of directors, president and treasurer. National's chief in-house counsel was Mark I. Lurie who, assisted by Brian Kay, was one of respondents' principal contacts with the company.

In large measure, National was a prisoner of its own success. As is commonly the case with equipment leasing companies, the greater part of National's costs in connection with a new lease, including equipment, marketing and installation expenses, was incurred well before rental payments commenced. Since rental payments were National's only significant source of revenues, the company's cash flow situation worsened with each new lease, and continued growth and operations could only be sustained through external financing. Between 1971 and 1973, National managed to obtain needed capital from an initial public offering of stock under Regulation A, short-term loans from local banks, and an offering of convertible debentures in September of 1973.

National's last successful effort to secure significant outside financing resulted in the execution, in May and June of 1974, of a $15 million credit agreement (the "Credit Agreement") with a group of five banks. Although the Credit Agreement was not closed (in amended form) until December 1974, the banks were willing to advance substantial sums to National under a variety of demand arrangements prior to the closing. *** Unfortunately, funds available under the Credit Agreement, as amended, were not sufficient to finance National's expansion and operations much beyond the closing, and the pressure on National's cash flow continued.

National finally ran out of time in July of 1975, after being unable to secure sufficient external financing after the closing of the Credit Agreement. On July 2, 1975, National was forced to file a petition for an arrangement under Chapter XI of the Bankruptcy Act; in March of 1976 this proceeding was converted into a reorganization under Chapter X of the Bankruptcy Act.

On November 26, 1975, the Commission authorized a formal investigation into the facts and circumstances surrounding National's collapse in order to determine whether any violations of the federal securities laws had occurred. This investigation covered the involvement of respondents, as well as of their law firm.

An injunctive proceeding was initiated by the Commission on January 16, 1978, in the United States District Court for the District of Columbia, against Hart, Lurie, the company's management directors, the company's independent auditors and others, alleging violations of the antifraud and reporting provisions of the Exchange Act, and the rules thereunder. That action has now been settled by all named defendants, without admitting or denying the allegations in the complaint, through issuance of permanent injunctions against future violations of the federal securities laws and the ordering of certain ancillary equitable relief. Also on January 16, 1978, the Commission issued a Report of Investigation, pursuant to Section 21(a) of the Exchange Act, discussing the conduct of National's outside directors in failing to ensure that the company timely disclosed the matters discussed herein, as well as a release discussing the role of National's independent auditors in the alleged accounting deficiencies.

*B. Respondents and Their Law Firm.* Carter, an attorney admitted to practice in the State of New York, was born in 1917. He received his law degree from Harvard Law School and has been working for the law firm now known as Brown, Wood, Ivey, Mitchell & Petty ("Brown, Wood") since 1945, having become a partner of the firm in 1954. Carter's principal areas of practice have been securities, general corporate and antitrust law.

Johnson, also admitted to practice as an attorney in the State of New York, as well as in the State of Connecticut, was born in 1932. He received his legal education at Harvard Law School and joined Brown, Wood's predecessor firm in 1956, becoming a partner in 1967. Johnson's principal areas of practice have been corporate and securities law.

Kenneth M. Socha worked with Carter and Johnson on a variety of legal matters affecting National, including all of the matters which are the basis of these proceedings. Socha joined Brown, Wood as an associate in 1970 and continued in that capacity during all periods relevant to these proceedings.[31]

Brown, Wood first came to Hart's attention in April of 1973 when Socha and a Brown, Wood partner who has since left the firm represented an underwriter in a proposed financing by National that was never consummated. After this financing failed to materialize, Hart requested Brown, Wood to represent National as special counsel in the preparation and filing of the Form S-1 registration statement for National's 1973 debenture offering.

During 1974 and 1975, Brown, Wood, principally through Carter, Johnson and Socha, provided a wide range of legal services to National, including the preparation of a Form S-8 registration statement, proxy materials and an annual report for the company's 1974 annual stockholders meeting, other Commission filings, press releases and communications to National's stockholders. Johnson was charged with the overall coordination of Brown, Wood's legal efforts on National's behalf and was generally kept aware of progress on all significant projects. In March of 1974, after another Brown, Wood partner left the firm, Johnson asked Carter to assist Socha in working on the Credit Agreement. Thereafter Carter assumed primary responsibility for that project.

In July of 1974, Johnson was elected secretary of National, agreeing to serve in such capacity at Hart's urging. Although his principal duty as secretary was to attend meetings of the board of directors and prepare appropriate minutes, Johnson testified that he attended a total of only four meetings during this period. *** The National board of directors held at least three additional meetings during Johnson's tenure as secretary at which he was not present. ***

31. Socha was not named as a respondent in these proceedings or in any other Commission action relating to National's activities. Given his role in the representation of National during the period here at issue, however, a discussion of Socha's activities is essential to an understanding of the relevant facts; nevertheless, nothing we say today is intended to reflect adversely on Socha's activities in this regard.

*C. Chronology of National's Final Year: May 1974 to May 1975.* In order fully to appreciate respondents' role in the events at issue here, it is necessary to set forth the following rather lengthy description of the 12 months immediately preceding public disclosure of the circumstances that led to National's bankruptcy. Except as may be noted below, the record contains ample evidence to support the conclusion that both respondents were aware of the facts and circumstances described.

*1. May to August 1974: National Executes a $15 Million Credit Agreement; the Annual Report Projections; the Continuing Need for Additional Financing.* National's story lies in its unrelenting need to secure ever greater amounts of outside financing. As explained above, given the nature of its leasing business, the more installations the company contracted for, the greater became the gap between internally generated cash flow and the soaring needs of front-end equipment installation costs. As early as 1973, National had begun to explore the availability of longterm debt to supplement its earlier public equity and debt offerings and to replace existing, expensive short-term indebtedness.

In May and June of 1974, negotiations with a consortium of five banks, in which Carter, Johnson and Socha were all participants, culminated in the execution of the Credit Agreement, which was dated as of April 30, 1974. The Credit Agreement provided for an interim revolving loan of up to $15 million, evidenced by rolling 90-day notes, until November 29, 1974, at which time National had the option to convert the principal amount then outstanding into six-year term notes. As discussed below, the Credit Agreement (as amended) was not formally closed until December 20, 1974, in part because National was unable to satisfy the closing conditions relating to its liquidity and debt-to-net-worth ratios. Ultimately the banks agreed to waive these conditions.

Since the Credit Agreement contemplated that the loans thereunder would be secured by substantially all of National's assets, it was necessary for National to transfer these assets to Systems, a transfer which in turn required the approval of National's stockholders. In order to secure this approval, National called its annual stockholders meeting for June 27, 1974, and Brown, Wood was asked to prepare the proxy materials for this meeting. Carter and Johnson also participated in the preparation of National's 1974 Annual Report. These proxy materials, along with National's 1974 Annual Report, were sent to National's stockholders on June 17 and filed with the Commission on June 19.

In urging approval of the asset transfers necessitated by the Credit Agreement, National's proxy statement disclosed that

> [t]he future growth and operations of the Company are dependent upon its ability to obtain financing such as is supplied by the Credit Agreement.

National's 1974 Annual Report contained projections of future lease installations which showed, by each quarter, a doubling of annual installations from approximately $13.3 million in fiscal 1974 to approximately $27 million in fiscal 1975. In response to a specific request from Hart, Carter advised National orally and in writing that, in light of Securities Act Release No. 5362 (Feb. 2, 1973), a copy of which Carter sent to Hart, it was permissible to include projections in the Annual Report, but that the assumptions underlying the projections should also be disclosed. Hart ignored this advice and the Annual Report was distributed without assumptions. This incident is the first example in the record of Hart's uncooperative reaction to respondents' advice concerning the disclosure demands of the federal securities laws.

National's management, as well as Carter and Johnson, were well aware that the company would need substantial outside financing in addition to that provided by the Credit Agreement to realize the Annual Report projections. As early as the July 1 meeting of National's board of directors the company had already borrowed $10 million of the $15 million which would be available under the Credit Agreement. At that meeting, which was attended by Johnson in his new capacity as corporate secretary, Hart announced that National needed at least $17 million in new financing to achieve the new lease installation projections in the Annual Report. After Hart reported to the meeting on the various alternatives being explored for additional funds, the directors focused on the importance of this issue to the continuing growth and viability of the company. The minutes of that meeting reflect the board's conclusion that "it [was] essential ... to continue to explore all appropriate means for obtaining financing for the Corporation's operations." ***

It is clear that National did not want for opportunities to disclose to its stockholders the continuing financial squeeze in which it found itself. After the Credit Agreement was signed, the first of these opportunities arose on or about June 18, when Hart sent a one-page letter to the company's stockholders announcing the declaration of a 3% stock dividend, payable in three equal installments of 1% each on August 1, September 3 and October 1, 1974. The record does not specifically reflect whether respondents were aware of or consulted on this letter before it was sent, although it may be inferred that Brown, Wood received a copy at the same time National's stockholders did, by virtue of the fact that the law firm was on National's general mailing list.

As the summer of 1974 wore on, both the severity of and concern for National's financial predicament intensified, fueled in large measure by the deteriorating credit markets. At an August 19 meeting of National's board of directors—the second board meeting attended by Johnson—Hart once again reported on his continuing attempts to raise more capital. ***

*2. September to December 1974: National's Growing Cash Crisis; Preparations for the Closing under the Credit Agreement.* By early fall of 1974, National's cash needs outstripped its existing financing sources and a severe cash crisis ensued. A meeting between National and its bankers was held on September 11, 1974; neither respondent was present. By that date, National had already received from the bank group more than $13.2 million of the $15 million contemplated by the Credit Agreement, which had yet to be closed. Moreover, in the preceding months, National had borrowed an additional $1.5 million from two of the lending banks, an amount that was not originally contemplated by the pending agreement, thus bringing the total funds already advanced by the banks to something approximating the $15 million provided for under the original agreement.

At the September 11 meeting with the banks, Hart indicated that the projected equity offering had been ruled out by National's investment bankers, due to deteriorating market conditions. He further reported that National's cash flow problems had caused the company voluntarily to institute a "wind-down" program, effective September 1. As he described it, this program, projected to last five months, was a severe retrenchment, designed to protect the banks' existing investment. Under it, National would limit its operations to the conversion of present inventory—approximately $5 million—into installed systems under new leases, phase out further marketing and installation efforts and reduce the company to a "pure maintenance organization." Hart requested an increase in the total amount of the banks' planned loan from $15 to $21 million in order to finance this wind-down program. The banks, however, hesitated, agreeing only that no decision would be made on lending National additional funds until the pending $15 million Credit Agreement was closed.

Hart, in fact, had lied to the banks. No wind-down program had been instituted or, as it turned out, would be until almost eight months later, in May of 1975. There is, however, no evidence in the record that respondents were, or ever became, aware of Hart's September 11, 1974 deception.

Despite the tenor of the September 11 meeting with the banks and the representations Hart had made concerning the wind-down of the company's operations, the day after the meeting Hart once again sent out an optimistic letter to stockholders and others. The letter gave no hint of National's precarious financial situation, stating rather that August had been "an outstanding month." ***

At the October 15, 1974 meeting of National's board of directors, attended by Johnson, there was a further discussion of National's "tight cash position," its inability to secure additional credit despite vigorous efforts, and its continued need for external financing. By that time, National had already increased its borrowings from the bank group from $13.2 million (the September 11 figure) to $14.3 million of the initially planned $15 million loan, with the additional $1.5 million in separate loans from two of the banks still outstanding. Hart stated to the board that he had discussed with the banks a "contingency plan" for the orderly "wind-down" of National's sales activities, but apparently did not disclose to the board or to Johnson who was present that he had falsely represented to the banks that such a program was already being implemented.

The board of directors became increasingly concerned about the company's financial situation recognizing that a curtailment of National's operations and a termination of its sales would soon become necessary unless significant additional financing were obtained, and that one of the major impediments to obtaining such financing was the failure to close the Credit Agreement. The board therefore instructed Hart to take immediate steps to close the Credit Agreement.

Two days later, on October 17, National issued a press release reporting its results for the second fiscal quarter ended September 30, 1974. The release, which respondents did not prepare or review, but which they did receive after the fact, disclosed a substantial increase in lease installations, net income and earnings per share over the corresponding fiscal quarter in 1973, but once again made no mention of the financial crisis then facing the company. Thus the gap between National's public posture and the private realities continued to widen.

The banks' position and the concerned reaction of National's board of directors made closing the Credit Agreement the first order of the day for National. As a result, on October 18, respondents both attended a meeting with various representatives of National and the lending banks to discuss what remained to be done to close the Credit Agreement. The extent of the company's unsecured borrowings, its unsuccessful efforts to obtain other financing and its past due operating expenses were also discussed, along with the steps the company had purportedly taken to curtail operations. Significantly, a wind-down plan—this time characterized as a "contingency" plan—was also discussed, with Hart again asking the banks to increase the Credit Agreement coverage by $6 million to fund such a plan, in order to protect their existing $15 million investment.

In light of his presence at the July 1, August 19 and October 15 board meetings, as well as the October 18 bank meeting, Johnson was well aware of National's cash crisis, its continuing failure to obtain needed financing and its purported "wind-down" program. This, in addition to the well-known depressed state of the credit markets and the fact that National had projected, confirmed and continued to report, without obviously relevant qualifications, rapidly growing sales and earnings, undoubtedly prompted Johnson to instruct Socha to draft a disclosure letter to National's stockholders approximately two days after the October 18 bank meeting.

The proposed stockholders letter, which was reviewed by both Carter and Johnson and sent to the company in early November, was a candid summary of National's financial predicament, noting that National would "in the near future" have to obtain significant financing in addition to the Credit Agreement. It concluded:

> The Company's efforts to obtain additional financing have been adversely affected by tight credit conditions, increased interest costs, a generally unfavorable equity market and certain factors that are peculiar to its business such as the negative cash flow described above. In view of these factors the Company has determined that it would be prudent to curtail its sales operations and, therefore, to emphasize liquidity rather than growth until such time as additional debt or equity financing can be obtained.

Johnson subsequently told Lurie that this was the type of communication "that a company ... interested in keeping its stockholders advised on a regular basis should be making." Despite this advice, National's management declined to issue the letter. Neither respondent elected to pursue the matter.

During this period, Hart continued his efforts to develop further outside sources of financing for National. Carter was informed by Hart and others about negotiations concerning numerous such potential sources for financing that were in various stages of completion.

*** [O]n November 26, a draft of an amendment to the Credit Agreement (the "Amendment"), prepared by the banks' counsel, White & Case, but worked on and reviewed by Carter, treated the wind-down plan as an attached exhibit. The November 26 draft of the Amendment also reflected a new total commitment of $21 million—indicating that Hart's $6 million request had been agreed to—but provided that National had to implement the plan to wind-down its operations, and thus terminate sales, if it desired to borrow more than $17 million.[41]

It is important to note, at this point, that both Carter and Johnson must have been aware that, if National were to implement the wind-down plan, the company would have no reasonable opportunity to meet the projections of $27 million in lease installations which were set forth in the 1974 Annual Report and indirectly reconfirmed the company's September 12 letter to its stockholders. The wind-down plan, which Socha summarized in a December 2 memorandum to Johnson, provided that National would not be permitted to enter into any further leases. Obviously, under these circumstances, the company's sales and earnings growth would be halted—short of projected levels.

In early December, Socha received from National a draft of the company's quarterly report to its stockholders for the second fiscal quarter ended September 30, 1974. The report contained a series of graphs, illustrating the successful results of National's operations, but once again made no mention of the dire financial straights in which the company found itself in December. Such an omission was especially significant in light of the disclosure recommendations which Brown, Wood had by then made to National. When Socha inquired whether the use of the graphs had been cleared by Johnson, Lurie informed him that they had. This was not true, as Johnson noted on the copy of the draft report circulated to him by Socha. The quarterly report was mailed as proposed, and neither respondent ever spoke with the company's management about the disclosure problems it presented or about Lurie's misrepresentation to Socha.

It thus appears that, by early December, Carter and Johnson were both fully aware that (1) National was experiencing a cash crisis severe enough to threaten the continued viability of the company if further financing could not be found, (2) when closed, the Credit Agreement, as modified by the Amendment, would not provide the necessary additional financing, (3) National's earlier projections could no longer be achieved if the Credit Agreement's wind-down plan were to be implemented, and (4) National's management was unreceptive when confronted with respondents' advice to disclose the company's financial problems.

With this background, National and respondents moved on to the final preparations for the closing under the Credit Agreement and the Amendment.

*3. December 1974 to January 1975: The Lease Maintenance Plan; the Closing; Related Public Disclosure.* In the final days leading to the closing, National's "wind-down" plan was renegotiated somewhat and finally emerged with a new name, the lease maintenance plan ("LMP"). All the witnesses speaking to the question agreed that the term "lease maintenance plan" had no generally accepted meaning in the industry and that they had never used or heard this term before. Moreover, the terms "wind-down plan," "contingency

---

**41.** Carter wrote a note on his copy of the November 26 draft questioning the amount of new financing that would be available with a limit of $17 million, since over $15 million was already outstanding in bank borrowings. Carter did not follow up on this question.

plan," and "lease maintenance plan," were all intended to refer to the same thing.

The need to revise the original wind-down plan emerged when the consulting firm hired by National to evaluate the plan reported to the banks that, in its original form, the plan was neither feasible nor in the best interests of the banks. Rather, the independent consultants advised that the best course would be to allow National limited continuing growth, financed with additional bank borrowings, and that a wind-down should be implemented only as a last resort and only if the company were unable to obtain additional outside financing.

At a meeting held on December 11, with Carter and representatives of National and the banks present, final details of the Amendment were negotiated. A draft of the Amendment dated December 13, 1974, which was prepared by White & Case, contemplated an arrangement under which the banks would permit Systems to borrow up to $19 million at any time on or before April 30, 1975. These borrowings were to be secured by the telephone leases and equipment transferred to Systems by National and guaranteed by National. If either (1) National and/or Systems attempted to borrow in excess of $19 million from the existing bank group or (2) National failed to meet a specified liquidity test, National and Systems were required to implement the LMP. Their failure to do so in accordance with the provisions of the LMP was an event of default under the Credit Agreement, as modified by the Amendment (the "Amended Credit Agreement"), and resulted in all outstanding indebtedness under that Agreement becoming due and payable upon demand.

The December 13 draft of the Amendment for the first time contained a reference to a "lease maintenance plan" and indicated that the LMP was to be attached as an exhibit to the Amendment. The effect of the implementation of the LMP on National's operations and growth would obviously be both dramatic and devastating. Indeed, as one expert called by respondents testified, the LMP was a "sort of a holding pattern short of bankruptcy or levy by the creditors." The LMP required National to terminate all sales activities, dismiss all sales personnel, and limit its operations to those necessary to service existing leases. In effect, the company would be transformed into a mere service agency, maintaining existing leases, but writing no new ones. Moreover, the final $2 million of the funds to be provided by the banks was only available until June 30, 1975 and could only be used to implement the LMP, principally by financing the installation of equipment already in inventory to complete existing orders. ***

On December 19, the day immediately preceding the closing under the Amended Credit Agreement, at a day-long pre-closing meeting, Hart told Carter that he did not want the terms of the LMP made public or filed with the Commission. Although Carter testified that he could not recall the reason for this request, he speculated that Hart sought not to publicize the LMP because he was concerned that the disclosure of the LMP's effects on the company's business would have a negative impact on the morale of National's sales personnel. After reading the LMP, Carter advised Hart that the LMP would have to be filed with the Commission if it were an exhibit to the Amendment, as originally had been contemplated. However, Carter added that the LMP need not be filed with the Commission or publicized if it were not an exhibit but rather merely referred to in the Amendment. Hart agreed, and the Amendment was modified to delete the LMP as an exhibit.

Also at the December 19 pre-closing conference, Carter reviewed and extensively revised a press release prepared by National announcing the closing of the Amended Credit Agreement. The revised press release was reviewed by all parties at the meeting, including the company's management. No one raised any objections to the revisions proposed by Carter.

On December 20, the Amended Credit Agreement was closed and National immediately borrowed $18 million from the banks. Of this amount, over $16.8 million was used to repay existing demand indebtedness based on advances the banks had made to National since the original Credit Agreement had been signed six months earlier. All or virtually all of the remainder was used to pay various operating expenses which National had already incurred. ***

Immediately after the closing, National issued the press release that Carter had redrafted the day before. The release stated, in its entirety:

> *PRESS RELEASE—FOR IMMEDIATE RELEASE*
> EAST HARTFORD, CONN., DECEMBER 20, 1974
>
> National Telephone Company today announced the execution of a $6,000,000 extension of a $15,000,000 Credit Agreement with a group of banks headed by Bankers Trust Company of New York. Included in the $21 million is a contingency fund of $2 million which is available until June 30, 1975 and which may be utilized by the Company only for the purpose of funding a lease maintenance program in the event additional financing is not otherwise available.
>
> Of the $21 million, the Company has borrowed $18 million pursuant to a seven-year term loan, of which approximately $16,500,000 was used to repay outstanding short-term loans. The balance will be used for general operating expenses. Participating in the loans are Bankers Trust Company of New York, Mellon Bank N.A. of Pittsburgh, Central National Bank of Cleveland, The Connecticut Bank and Trust Company and The Hartford National Bank and Trust Company of Hartford, Connecticut.

The press release did not discuss either of the following matters each of which was then within knowledge of Carter and Johnson.

> (1) The precise nature and effects on National's business of the LMP and the likelihood that National would be required to implement the LMP within a short period of time; and
>
> (2) The substantial limitations placed on National's operations by the Amended Credit Agreement.

It is also apparent from the record that the press release's statement indicating that the balance of the financing remaining after the repayment outstanding bank debt "will be used for general operating expenses" was misleading, in light of the substantial overdue obligations of National then existing.

The second major item of public disclosure concerning the closing was a stockholders' letter mailed, without respondents' knowledge, by National on or about December 23. This letter, which was issued in the face of Socha's advice to National that no further public statements should be issued concerning the Amended Credit Agreement unless such statements were cleared by Brown, Wood, contained numerous misstatements and omissions, including the following:

> (1) The letter indicated that the company "was stronger now than ever before in its history" and that it had "a greater availability of capital, expanding productivity and growing earnings" and was "looking forward to an outstanding year in calendar 1975."
>
> (2) The letter indicated that the entire additional $6 million loan to National could be used for future operating expenses.
>
> (3) The letter made no reference to National's repayment of existing bank loans and other pre-existing debts with the proceeds of the financing, its continuing cash needs and shortages, or the LMP.

Respondents first learned of the letter on December 27, when Brian Kay, who was aware that National had ignored Socha's advice that all public disclosure should be reviewed by them, voluntarily telephoned Socha and dictated the letter to him. Socha thought that the letter's description of the Amended Credit Agreement was "seriously inadequate" and immediately gave a copy of it to Johnson. Carter, too, was consulted. While respondents felt that the letter did not make "adequate disclosure" with respect to the Amended Credit Agreement, they concluded that, when read together with the earlier December 20 press release which Carter had revised, it was not materially false or misleading, and that no corrective action by National was therefore required. Johnson later did, however, orally express his dissatisfaction with the letter to Lurie.

With the close of 1974, the record reveals that respondents were in the uncomfortable position of attempting to provide disclosure advice to an aggressive client whose unreceptive management actively frustrated the giving of advice and ignored what advice managed to get through. It is in the context of this attitude that respondents and National moved into the new year, with the final efforts to save the company and the resulting sharp needs to attend to the company's public disclosure obligations.

*4. January to March 1975: National's December 1974 Form 8-K; the Triggering of the LMP; Disclosure Pressures from the Banks.* On January 9, 1975, National filed a current report on Form 8-K for the month of December 1974, reporting on the closing under the Amended Credit Agreement. This document was drafted by Carter, who accepted full responsibility for it.

The Amended Credit Agreement, which was attached to the Form 8-K as an exhibit, made frequent reference to the LMP. And the 8-K itself stated that $2 million of National's recent $21 million loan arrangement was "a contingency fund available until June 30, 1975 only for the purpose of financing a lease maintenance program in the event additional financing is not otherwise available." As previously requested by Hart, however, the LMP itself was not included as an exhibit to the Agreement or the filing; nor was the term "lease maintenance plan" specifically defined or the effects which it would have on the company discussed.

Between the January 9, 1975 filing of National's form 8-K and mid-March, National's financial condition deteriorated even further, to a degree requiring the implementation of the LMP. In addition, the gap between National's public disclosure posture and its private financial condition continued to widen and National's board of directors was becoming increasingly uncomfortable with the situation. ***

On March 17—***over six weeks after the LMP had in fact been triggered—Brown, Wood was informed for the first time, by the *banks'* lawyers, White & Case, that events requiring implementation of the LMP had occurred. The White & Case lawyers had received a telephone call from a vice president of one of the banks informing them of this fact and reporting that no public disclosure had been made by National. The bank vice president also sought White & Case's advice on how to respond to trade creditors of National who were making inquiries to the banks about the company.

During their March 17 conversation, the White & Case lawyers advised Carter that National and its counsel, Brown, Wood, had the responsibility to determine what disclosure, if any, would be appropriate under the circumstances, and they sought assurances that, if proper disclosure were deemed necessary, it would be forthcoming. Carter, who admittedly considered the triggering of the LMP clearly material, assured White & Case that, if what they said were true, Brown, Wood would contact National and "get a statement out." ***

On the following day, March 18, Carter telephoned Lurie and informed him of the call from the White & Case lawyers. Lurie neither confirmed nor denied that the LMP had been triggered. Rather, he dissembled, stating that the situation was "tight," but adding that, "if they were careful, they would be all right." Carter advised Lurie that, if the LMP had indeed been triggered, the fact should be disclosed publicly, although he did not press Lurie for a definite answer on whether the LMP had in fact been triggered, or on whether National's management was in fact implementing the LMP as required by the Amended Credit Agreement.

Carter informed Johnson both of the telephone call from the banks' lawyers and the subsequent conversations with Lurie. While Johnson's first reaction was to find out what the facts were, neither he nor anyone else at Brown, Wood sought to verify the facts by contacting anyone at National. Nor did they seek to contact anyone outside of National, such as the consulting firm, which they knew had been charged by the parties with responsibility for monitoring National's compliance with the terms of the Amended Credit Agreement.

*5. April to May 1975: Respondents' Disclosure Advice; National's Board Acts; Hart's Resignation; Public Disclosure.* In early April, Carter and Johnson once again discussed the need to disclose National's obligation to implement the LMP. As a result of a conversation with Hart, Johnson had become "morally certain" that National was required to implement the LMP, and that the failure to do so would result in National's being in default under the Amended Credit Agreement, although he did not believe, nor did Carter, that Hart intended to implement the LMP even though it was required.

On April 21, in response to a comment letter from the Commission's staff, National filed an amendment to its current report on Form 8-K for the month of December 1974. Carter participated in the preparation of that amendment, which concerned technical matters not at issue here. As was the case with the original Form 8-K, the nature of the LMP was not described, even though, by this time, both respondents had been told—and, indeed, believed—that National was obligated to implement the LMP, both understood that it had not done so and both knew that the failure to do so in the circumstances was an event of default under the Amended Credit Agreement.

On April 23, 1975 both respondents met with Hart and advised him in no uncertain terms that immediate disclosure was required. In response to Hart's protestations that National would soon obtain additional financing, respondents advised him that these hopes, as well as any negotiations for a waiver of the LMP by the banks, did not serve to excuse National's legal obligation to make prompt disclosure.

Shortly before the April 23 meeting, the vice president of one of the lending banks had written to Hart requesting, among other things, a "written response from your counsel regarding [National's] obligation to make public disclosure regarding significant transactions which may have transpired during the last several months, particularly with regard to the implementing of the lease maintenance plan." Presumably as a result of this request, Hart telephoned Johnson on April 28—only five days after having received the unambiguous and forceful advice that disclosure was required—to request that Johnson issue a legal opinion for the banks to the effect that disclosure of the triggering of the LMP was *not* necessary. Johnson testified that he replied as follows:

> I'm incredulous. I just can't believe this. You sat in my office last week and I told you as clearly and positively and precisely as I could that my advice was that you should disclose that you had gone into the lease maintenance mode.

Ultimately, Hart responded to the bank's request for an opinion of counsel with a letter from National stating that no disclosure had been made because, "in the opinion of the company," none was required.

In late April, after the telephone encounter with Hart described above, Johnson instructed Socha to draft a disclosure document for National to issue, either in its next report to the Commission or in a special letter to the stockholders. In doing so, Johnson specified that the draft should be one that would be "acceptable to a person as emotionally involved as Hart." Both respondents reviewed and approved the draft prepared by Socha and it was forwarded to Hart on or about May 1, with the suggestion that Hart call Carter or Johnson about it.

The proposed document indicated that, under the Amended Credit Agreement, National was required to cease writing new leases when its borrowings exceeded $19 million; that the company was seeking a waiver of this requirement by the banks, as well as new financing; that the company was hopeful that both of these efforts would succeed; and that the company had curtailed its sales operations because it had not obtained essential additional financing. National did not issue this disclosure document in any form and the record does not indicate any response to Brown, Wood's disclosure advice. Neither respondent questioned anyone at the company about management's failure to make the suggested disclosure.

On May 9, Kay called Socha to seek his approval of a draft of the company's proposed current report on Form 8-K for the month of April. Socha reiterated Brown, Wood's earlier advice that disclosure should be made concerning National's present status under the Amended Credit Agreement and of the event of default that resulted from the company's failure to implement the LMP. Although Kay agreed to include the suggested disclosure, the report actually filed with the Commission did not contain any such disclosure, because Lurie would not permit it.

On May 12, *** Socha called Kay and asked for a copy of the company's April Form 8-K. Kay replied that Lurie would not permit him to mail a copy to Brown, Wood or to the Commission. The April Form 8-K was eventually filed with the Commission on May 15, 1975. Socha testified that he was required to obtain a copy of it from the Commission. ***

The internal and external tensions which had been developing around National came to a head on Saturday afternoon, May 24, at [a] special meeting of the board of directors in Hartford, Connecticut. Johnson was there, acting as secretary, having been asked to attend by Hart. Also present at the meeting was independent counsel who had been consulted by the outside directors and asked to attend the meeting in the expectation that Johnson would not be there. It was at this meeting that the outside directors learned for the first time that, for over a month, Brown, Wood had been recommending disclosure and Johnson read a draft of the letter which Brown, Wood had sent to Hart on May 1, disclosing that the LMP had been triggered and its effect on the company. One of the nonmanagement directors testified that he had no prior indication that Brown, Wood had been recommending this disclosure to Hart and that when he heard the letter read by Johnson he "was shocked to the core."

At the May 24 meeting, Hart resigned each of his corporate offices, although he remained a director of the company, Johnson prepared a press release which was unanimously approved by the Board and it was decided that Brown, Wood would continue as company counsel. Johnson, however, resigned as secretary of the company.

The press release prepared by Johnson during the May 24 meeting announced that National would immediately curtail the writing of new leases, and described the management changes and the company's need for outside financing. It also expressed the company's hope that its growth structure could be resumed in the future. The release made no mention of the fact that the company had defaulted under the Amended Credit Agreement. The release was made public on May 27, 1975.

*6. May to July 1975: The Events Following Public Disclosure.* Following the disclosure contained in the May 27 press release and the company's subsequent current report on Form 8-K for the month of May 1975, the market price for National's common stock declined from the $13 bid, $14 asked range to the $3 bid, $4 asked range and the market for the company's common stock became virtually nonexistent. On July 2, National initiated proceedings for an arrangement under the bankruptcy laws. Among the creditors in the resulting proceeding was Brown, Wood, which submitted a claim for legal fees in excess of $200,000.

IV.

AIDING AND ABETTING[a]

[The Commission next reviewed the ALJ's findings that Carter and Johnson had "aided and abetted" National's violations of Sections 10(b) and 13(a) of the Exchange Act and Rules 10b-5, 12b-20 and 13a-11 thereunder. There were essentially two theories underlying those findings. First, the ALJ found that Carter and Johnson had aided and abetted National's violations by participating in the drafting of the December 20, 1974 press release and the Form 8-K filed with the SEC. Second, the ALJ found that Carter and Johnson had aided and abetted National's continuing fraud by "failing to ensure that the required disclosures were made or to communicate to National's board of directors concerning management's refusal to make such disclosures." In connection with both theories, the Commission observed that "the crucial inquiry in a Rule 2(e) proceeding against a lawyer inevitably tends to focus on the awareness or the intent element of the offense of aiding and abetting." The Commission therefore held explicitly that a "finding of *willful aiding and abetting* within the meaning of Rule 2(e)(1)(iii) requires a showing that respondents were aware or knew that their role was part of an activity that was improper or illegal."

With respect to the ALJs first rationale for the "aiding and abetting" finding, the Commission agreed with the ALJ's determination that "National's failure to disclose the nature of the LMP in the December 20 press release and the December Form 8-K constituted a violation of Sections 10(b) and 13(a) of the Exchange Act and Rules 10b-5, 12b-20 and 13a-11 thereunder." The Commission also agreed that the respondents were "deeply involved" in National's disclosure activities and participated in the drafting of these documents. Yet the Commission reversed the ALJ's finding because the evidence did not show definitively that Carter and Johnson had fully appreciated the materiality of the LMP at the time the December press release and the Form 8-K were prepared. In reaching this conclusion, the Commission reasoned that:

> If a securities lawyer is to bring his best independent judgment to bear on a disclosure problem, he must have the freedom to make innocent—or even, in certain cases, careless—mistakes without fear of legal liability or loss of the ability to practice before the Commission. Concern about his own liability may alter the balance of his judgment in one direction as surely as an unseemly obeisance to the wishes of his client can do so in the other. While one imbalance results in disclosure rather than concealment, neither is, in the end, truly in the public interest. Lawyers who are seen by their clients as being motivated by fears for their personal liability will not be consulted on difficult issues.

The Commission also took issue with respect to the ALJ's second rationale, which focused on Carter and Johnson's repeated instances of silence

---

**a.** Ed. Note—The following discussion summarizes and, where indicated, quotes from Part IV of the Commission's opinion.

and inaction subsequent to the press release and SEC filing in December 1974. Although it agreed with the ALJ's conclusion that National had "violated the federal securities laws through its continued failure to make adequate disclosures in public statements and Commission filings regarding its deteriorating cash position, its inability to meet earlier growth projections, the triggering of the LMP, and the impact the LMP would have on National," it reversed the ALJ's ultimate finding because it was "unable to infer that respondents intended to aid the violations by not acting." Here the Commission emphasized that:

> Our review of the record, which includes respondents' periodic exhortations to Hart to improve the quality of National's disclosure, leads us to believe that respondents did not intend to assist the violations by their inaction or silence. Rather, they seemed to be at a loss for how to deal with a difficult client.

The Commission concluded that:

> Association of a law firm with a client lends an air of legitimacy and authority to the actions of a client. There are occasions when, but for the law firms's association, a violation could not have occurred. Under those circumstances, if the firm were cognizant of how it was being used and acquiesced, or if it gained some benefit from the violation beyond that normally obtained in a legal relationship, inaction would probably give rise to an inference of intent. This, however, is not such a case, and we find that respondents did not intend to assist the violation by their inaction.]

## V.

## ETHICAL AND PROFESSIONAL RESPONSIBILITIES

*A. The Findings of the Administrative Law Judge.* The Administrative Law Judge found that both respondents "failed to carry out their professional responsibilities with respect to appropriate disclosure to all concerned, including stockholders, directors and the investing public ... and thus knowingly engaged in unethical and improper professional conduct, as charged in the Order." In particular, he held that respondents' failure to advise National's board of directors of Hart's refusal to disclose adequately the company's perilous financial condition was itself a violation of ethical and professional standards referred to in Rule 2(e)(1)(ii).

Respondents argue that the Commission has never promulgated standards of professional conduct for lawyers and that the Commission's application in hindsight of new standards would be fundamentally unfair. Moreover, even if it is permissible for the Commission to apply—without specific adoption or notice—generally recognized professional standards, they argue that no such standards applicable to respondents' conduct existed in 1974-75, nor do they exist today.

We agree that, in general, elemental notions of fairness dictate that the Commission should not establish new rules of conduct and impose them retroactively upon professionals who acted at the time without reason to believe that their conduct was unethical or improper. At the same time, however, we perceive no unfairness whatsoever in holding those professionals who practice before us to generally recognized norms of professional conduct, whether or not such norms had previously been explicitly adopted or endorsed by the Commission. To do so upsets no justifiable expectations, since the professional is already subject to those norms.

The ethical and professional responsibilities of lawyers who become aware that their client is engaging in violations of the securities laws have not been so firmly and unambiguously established that we believe all practicing lawyers can be held to an awareness of generally recognized norms. We also recognize that the Commission has never articulated or endorsed any such standards. That being the case, we reverse the Administrative Law Judge's findings under subparagraph (ii) of Rule 2(e)(1) with respect to both respondents. Nevertheless, we believe that respondents' conduct raises serious questions about the obligations of securities lawyers, and the Commission is hereby giving notice of its interpretation of "unethical or improper professional conduct" as that term is used in Rule 2(e)(1)(ii). The Commission intends to issue a release soliciting comment from the public as to whether this interpretation should be expanded or modified.

*B. Interpretive Background.* Our concern focuses on the professional obligations of the lawyer who gives essentially correct disclosure advice to a client that does not follow that advice and as a result violates the federal securities laws. ***

While precise standards have not yet emerged, it is fair to say that there exists considerable acceptance of the proposition that a lawyer must, in order to discharge his professional responsibilities, make all efforts within reason to persuade his client to avoid or terminate proposed illegal action. Such efforts could include, where appropriate, notification to the board of directors of a corporate client. ***

We are mindful that, when a lawyer represents a corporate client, the client—and the entity to which he owes his allegiance—is the corporation itself and not management or any other individual connected with the corporation. [ABA E.C. 5-18] Moreover, the lawyer should try to "insure that decisions of his client are made only after the client has been informed of relevant considerations." [ABA E.C. 7-8] These unexceptionable principles take on a special coloration when a lawyer becomes aware that one or more specific members of a corporate client's management is deciding not to follow his disclosure advice, especially if he knows that those in control, such as the board of directors, may not have participated in or been aware of that decision. Moreover, it is well established that no lawyer, even in the most zealous pursuit of his client's interests, is privileged to assist his client in conduct the lawyer knows to be illegal. [ABA D.R. 7-102(A)(7)] The application of these recognized principles to the special role of the securities lawyer giving disclosure advice, however, is not a simple task.

The securities lawyer who is an active participant in a company's ongoing disclosure program will ordinarily draft and revise disclosure documents, comment on them and file them with the Commission. He is often involved on an intimate, day-to-day basis in the judgments that determine what will be disclosed and what will be withheld from the public markets. When a lawyer serving in such a capacity concludes that his client's disclosures are not adequate to comply with the law, and so advises his client, he is "aware," in a literal sense, of a continuing violation of the securities laws. On the other hand, the lawyer is only an adviser, and the final judgment—and, indeed, responsibility—as to what course of conduct is to be taken must lie with the client. Moreover, disclosure issues often present difficult choices between multiple shades of gray, and while a lawyer's judgment may be to draw the disclosure obligation more broadly than his client, both parties recognize the degree of uncertainty involved.

The problems of professional conduct that arise in this relationship are well-illustrated by the facts of this case. In rejecting Brown, Wood's advice to include the assumptions underlying its projections in its 1974 Annual Report, in declining to issue two draft stockholders letters offered by respondents and in ignoring the numerous more informal urgings by both respondents and Socha to make disclosure, Hart and Lurie indicated that they were inclined to resist any public pronouncements that were at odds with the rapid growth which had been projected and reported for the company.

If the record ended there, we would be hesitant to suggest that any unprofessional conduct might be involved. Hart and Lurie were, in effect, pressing the company's lawyers hard for the minimum disclosure required by law. That fact alone is not an appropriate basis for a finding that a lawyer must resign or take some extraordinary action. Such a finding would inevitably drive a wedge between reporting companies and their outside lawyers; the more sophisticated members of management would soon realize that there is nothing to gain in consulting outside lawyers.

However, much more was involved in this case. In sending out a patently misleading letter to stockholders on December 23 in contravention of Socha's plain and express advice to clear all such disclosure with Brown, Wood, in deceiving respondents about Johnson's approval of the company's quarterly report to its stockholders in early December and in dissembling in response to respondents' questions about the implementation of the LMP, the company's management erected a wall between National and its outside lawyers—a wall apparently designed to keep out good legal advice in conflict with management's improper disclosure plans.

Any ambiguity in the situation plainly evaporated in late April and early May of 1975 when Hart first asked Johnson for a legal opinion flatly contrary to the express disclosure advice Johnson had given Hart only five days earlier, and when Lurie soon thereafter prohibited Kay from delivering a copy of the company's April 1975 Form 8-K to Brown, Wood.

These actions reveal a conscious desire on the part of National's management no longer to look to Brown, Wood for independent disclosure advice, but rather to embrace the firm within Hart's fraud and use it as a shield to avoid the pressures exerted by the banks toward disclosure. Such a role is a perversion of the normal lawyer-client relationship, and no lawyer may claim that, in these circumstance, he need do no more than stubbornly continue to suggest disclosure when he knows his suggestions are falling on deaf ears.

C. "*Unethical or Improper Professional Conduct.*" The Commission is of the view that a lawyer engages in "unethical or improper professional conduct" under the following circumstances: When a lawyer with significant responsibilities in the effectuation of a company's compliance with the disclosure requirements of the federal securities laws becomes aware that his client is engaged in a substantial and continuing failure to satisfy those disclosure requirements, his continued participation violates professional standards unless he takes prompt steps to end the client's noncompliance. The Commission has determined that this interpretation will be applicable only to conduct occurring after the date of this opinion.

We do not imply that a lawyer is obliged, at the risk of being held to have violated Rule 2(e), to seek to correct every isolated disclosure action or inaction which he believes to be at variance with applicable disclosure standards, although there may be isolated disclosure failures that are so serious that their correction becomes a matter of primary professional concern. It is also clear, however, that a lawyer is not privileged to unthinkingly permit himself to be co-opted into an ongoing fraud and cast as a dupe or a shield for a wrong-doing client.

Initially, counselling accurate disclosure is sufficient, even if his advice is not accepted. But there comes a point at which a reasonable lawyer must conclude that his advice is not being followed, or even sought in good faith, and that his client is involved in a continuing course of violating the securities laws. At this critical juncture, the lawyer must take further, more affirmative steps in order to avoid the inference that he has been co-opted, willingly or unwillingly, into the scheme of non-disclosure.

The lawyer is in the best position to choose his next step. Resignation is one option, although we recognize that other considerations, including the protection of the client against forseeable prejudice, must be taken into account in the case of withdrawal. [See, e.g. ABA D.R. 2-110; ABA E.C. 2-32.] A direct approach to the board of directors or one or more individual directors or officers may be appropriated; or he may choose to try to enlist the aid of other members of the firm's management. What is required, in short, is some prompt action[77] that leads to the conclusion that the lawyer is engaged in efforts to correct the underlying problem, rather than having capitulated to the desires of a strong-willed, but misguided client.

Some have argued that resignation is the only permissible course when a client chooses not to comply with disclosure advice. We do not agree. Premature resignation serves neither the end of an effective lawyer-client relationship nor, in most cases, the effective administration of the securities laws. The lawyer's continued interaction with his client will ordinarily hold the greatest promise of corrective action. So long as a lawyer is acting in good faith and exerting reasonable efforts to prevent violations of the law by his client, his professional obligations have been met. In general, the best result is that which

---

77. In those cases where resignation is not the only alternative, should a lawyer choose not to resign, we do not believe the action taken *must be successful* to avoid the inference that the lawyer had improperly participated in his client's fraud. Rather, the acceptability of the action must be considered in the light of all relevant surrounding circumstances. Similarly, what is "prompt" in any one case depends on the situation then facing the lawyer.

promotes the continued, strong-minded and independent participation by the lawyer.

We recognize, however, that the "best result" is not always obtainable, and that there may occur situations where the lawyer must conclude that the misconduct is so extreme or irretrievable, or the involvement of his client's management and board of directors in the misconduct is so thoroughgoing and pervasive that any action short of resignation would be futile. We would anticipate that cases where a lawyer has no choice but to resign would be rare and of an egregious nature.[78]

D. *Conclusion.*

As noted above, because the Commission has never adopted or endorsed standards of professional conduct which would have applied to respondents' activities during the period here in question, and since generally accepted norms of professional conduct which existed outside the scope of Rule 2(e) did not, during the relevant time period, unambiguously cover the situation in which respondents found themselves in 1974-75, no finding of unethical or unprofessional conduct would be appropriate. That being the case, we reverse the findings of the Administrative Law Judge under Rule 2(e)(1)(ii). In future proceedings of this nature, however, the Commission will apply the interpretation of subparagraph (ii) of Rule 2(e)(1) set forth in this opinion. ***

## *NOTES AND QUESTIONS*

1. ***Affirmative Duty to Halt a Client's Noncompliance.*** Does the Commission's opinion in *Carter & Johnson* effectively impose an affirmative duty on securities lawyers to halt their client's noncompliance with the federal securities laws? Consider the facts as detailed in *Carter & Johnson* and assume that the standards for "ethical and professional" conduct announced in Part V of the opinion had previously been articulated. What should Carter and Johnson have done differently? When in the chronology of events was action advisable? When was action required?

2. ***Disclosing Client Confidences to Prevent Fraud.*** As noted in our discussion of state rules of professional responsibility, states vary considerably as to whether a lawyer can disclose to sources outside the corporation that the client is about to engage in conduct that constitutes securities fraud. At one end of the spectrum is ABA Model Rule 1.6 and Rule 1.6 of the District of Columbia, which provide that a lawyer *may not* reveal such a fraud. Most states (including Georgia, Illinois, Ohio, and New York) adopt a middle position—consistent with an earlier ABA Model Code provision (Disciplinary Rule 4-101)—that a lawyer *may* disclose such confidential information if necessary to prevent the client from committing a crime. At the other end of spectrum, New Jersey, Florida, Virginia, and Wisconsin provide that a lawyer *must* disclose

78. This case does not involve, nor do we here deal with, the additional question of when a lawyer, aware of his client's intention to commit fraud or an illegal act, has a professional duty to disclose that fact either publicly or to an affected third party. Our interpretation today does not require such action at any point, although other existing standards of professional conduct might be so interpreted. See, e.g., ABA D.R. 7-102(B).

client confidences to prevent criminal acts. Thus, New Jersey's Rule of Professional Conduct 1.6(b) requires an attorney

> [to reveal confidential information relating to the representation of a client] *** to the proper authorities, as soon as, and to the extent the lawyer reasonably believes necessary, to prevent the client:
>
> (1) from committing a criminal, illegal or fraudulent act that the lawyer reasonably believes is likely to result in *** substantial injury to the financial interest or property of another;
>
> (2) from committing a criminal, illegal or fraudulent act that the lawyer reasonably believes is likely to perpetrate a fraud upon a tribunal.

Of these many possibilities, which is the best rule? Does your answer change if your role is typically that of a client? A lawyer? An investor? Should it change?

*3. **Noisy Withdrawals.*** As Professor Cramton pointed out in his post-Enron primer, supra, 58 Bus. Law. at 143, even in the minority of jurisdictions that prohibit lawyers from revealing information necessary to prevent a client's financial fraud in accordance with Model Rule 1.6, lawyers may (and often must) withdraw from representation on account of the client's conduct. And a comment to Rule 1.6 provides the lawyer a way to suggest to third parties the reasons for such withdrawal:

> Neither this rule nor Rule 1.8(b) nor Rule 1.16(d) prevents the lawyer from giving notice of the fact of withdrawal, and the lawyer may also withdraw or disaffirm any opinion, document, affirmation, or the like.

Comment to Rule 1.6, paragraph 16. How is the "noisy withdrawal" permitted under the comment to Model Rule 1.6 different from outright disclosure? What factors should a lawyer consider in determining whether to make a noisy withdrawal?

*4. **Independence vs. Interdependence.*** In an article that includes substantial analysis of the facts and issues raised in *Carter & Johnson*, one of your co-authors has contrasted the view that lawyers and their clients are "morally independent" with the view that they are "morally interdependent." Ultimately, he concludes that:

> As monitors of corporate conduct and as dealmakers designing transactions, lawyers often participate in their clients' conduct to an extent that a distinction between the lawyers' acts and those of clients is difficult if not impossible to make. In such cases, the moral independence theory is no longer tenable, and lawyers are morally responsible for at least some of their clients' actions.
>
> Lawyers have important obligations to their clients, but also to others who may be harmed by clients. Although balancing these obligations may be difficult, moral action requires recognizing and making choices, not opting out of choices by denial. Lawyers who acknowledge their moral interdependence with clients may change the way they choose their clients and the type of advice they give. Clients will also be more likely to trust, and follow the advice of, lawyers whose conception of their moral responsibilities corresponds with functions they actually perform.

Richard W. Painter, The Moral Interdependence of Corporate Lawyers and their Clients, 67 S. Cal. L. Rev. 507, 583-84 (1994). Does moral responsibility for client conduct translate into moral responsibility to do something about that conduct? At what point should a moral responsibility—what the morally righteous attorney would do—translate into a legal responsibility? Who should be charged with making this determination—the SEC, Congress, or state bar associations?

*5. **The SEC's Rule 102(e) Retreat with Respect to Lawyers.*** The SEC's case against Carter and Johnson, brought over twenty years ago, was the last enforcement action brought by the SEC against a lawyer or law firm for "improper professional conduct." After an outcry from the legal profession against the *Carter & Johnson* proceeding, the SEC went so far as to announce that:

> With respect to attorneys, the Commission generally has not sought to develop or apply independent standards of professional conduct. The great majority of Rule 2(e) proceedings against attorneys involve allegations of violations of the law (not of professional standards); thus, the Commission, as a matter of policy, generally refrains from using its administrative forum to conduct de novo determinations of the professional obligation of attorneys.

Disciplinary Proceedings Involving Professionals Appearing or Practicing Before the Commission, Exchange Act Release No. 25893, 41 SEC Docket 465 (July 13, 1988). Why did the SEC retreat from Rule 102(e) proceedings against lawyers but not from similar proceedings against accountants? Are some of the justifications for SEC regulation of accountants lacking when it comes to lawyers?

*6. **Other SEC Enforcement Proceedings Against Lawyers.*** After *Carter & Johnson*, the SEC pursued several enforcement actions against attorneys who it believed were substantially responsible for their clients' securities law violations. Some of these cases involved allegedly negligent legal advice involving the securities laws. See, e.g., *In the Matter of Jeffry Feldman*, Release No. 33-7014, 55 SEC Docket 9, 12 (September 20, 1993) (consent order issued under Securities Act Section 8A against lawyer for three Pakistani banks who "caused" violations of Securities Act's registration provisions by incorrectly advising his client that offering of rupee-denominated foreign exchange bearer certificates did not have to be registered prior to sale in the U.S.), set out in Chapter 9.C.2. Recall also that before the 1990 Remedies Act added "cease and desist" authority to the SEC's arsenal of enforcement weapons, the SEC brought, but eventually dismissed, a high-profile enforcement action under Exchange Act Section 15(c)(4) against an attorney for "causing" a client's violation of the tender offer rules. See *In Re George C. Kern, Jr.*, Exchange Act Release No. 29356, 49 SEC Docket 422 (June 21, 1991) (reversing administrative law judge's order and holding that the Commission lacked the power under Section 15(c)(4) to issue an order of "general compliance"). See Note 7 in Chapter 9 on page 693.

The SEC has also initiated enforcement actions against lawyers who knowingly engaged in actions that substantially assisted a client's securities law violations. See e.g., *SEC v. Fehn*, 97 F.3d 1276 (9th Cir. 1996) (enjoining attorney under Section 20(e) for aiding and abetting violations of Rule 10b-5 and other Exchange Act provisions that were committed by the company that retained him, discussed in Note 4 on pages 218-219 supra.

Finally, in-house lawyers at brokerage firms—who may often act in the supervisory chain of command—face potential disciplinary sanctions under Exchange Act Section 15(b)(4)(E). See Report Under Exchange Act Section 21(a) in the Matter of John H. Gutfreund, Thomas W. Strauss & John W. Meriwether, Exchange Act Release No. 31554, 52 SEC Docket 2849 (Dec. 3, 1992). Although Salomon Brothers' chief legal officer Donald M. Feuerstein repeatedly advised C.E.O. Gutfreund to report unauthorized U.S. Treasury auction bids by trader Paul Mozer to the Federal Reserve, Gutfreund did not do so. The Commission did not initiate enforcement action against Feuerstein. But in its report on the conduct of other top Salomon officials, the Commission concluded that Feuerstein was Mozer's "supervisor" for purposes of Section 15(b)(4)(E) and as such was obligated to take appropriate steps to deal with Mozer's misconduct. These steps, the SEC suggested, consisted of approaching senior management, but if that failed, they included: (i) approaching the board of directors, (ii) resigning, or (iii) disclosing the misconduct to regulators (within the bounds permitted by the rules of professional responsibility).

### 2. *The Enron Scandal and Questions of Professional Responsibility*

## TESTIMONY BY SUSAN P. KONIAK PROFESSOR OF LAW, BOSTON UNIVERSITY SCHOOL OF LAW, FEBRUARY 6, 2002

## U.S. SENATE COMMITTEE ON THE JUDICIARY ACCOUNTABILITY ISSUES: LESSONS LEARNED FROM ENRON'S FALL

***Twelve years ago in a court opinion dealing with some aspects of the Lincoln Savings and Loan fraud, Judge Stanley Sporkin wrote:

> Where ... were the ... accountants and attorneys...? [W]ith all the professional talent involved (both accounting and legal), why [didn't] at least one professional ... [act] to stop the overreaching that took place in this case?

[*Lincoln Sav. & Loan Ass'n v. Wall*, 743 F. Supp. 901, 920 (D.D.C. 1990)]

Now, there is Enron. And we are here asking the same questions, Judge Sporkin and others were asking 12 years ago. To paraphrase Pete Seeger, "When will [we] ever learn?" ***

All too often lawyers act as if they were wearing magic caps—hats that transport them to some alternative reality, a law free zone, in which they are free to do anything and everything for the person or entity paying the lawyers' fees—hats that transport them to a magic land where lawyers need not fear that law will come crashing down on them. "It may hit the client, but it will never hit me." There are no such magic caps. But the scant attention that has thus far been paid to the role of lawyers in this mess suggests that the myth of the magic cap has spread far and wide.***

The mere fact that there are always lawyers around when securities fraud is taking place does not mean that lawyers cause securities fraud nor does it demonstrate that they are always in a position to discover it or stop it from taking place. They aren't. In plain English, fraud, as I tell my students year in and year out, is lying to someone to get them to give you their stuff. Fraud-doers are by definition liars (sneaks, cheats) and many are slick enough at lying to fool a room full of experienced lawyers. On the other hand, not all fraud-doers are quite that slick, and I dare say when it comes to securities fraud being slick enough to keep it from one's lawyers for a significant period of time takes some considerable degree of skill. Don't get me wrong, even a sophisticated and careful lawyer may not be able to detect a complex and well crafted scheme to defraud others in connection with the sale or purchase of securities. But then again many a sophisticated lawyer is not careful, at least, not about detecting securities fraud, and all too many sophisticated lawyers are all too willing to turn a blind eye.***

To make this as simple as possible a lawyer has done wrong and is likely to be in significant legal trouble when three things are true. One, the client is breaking the law. Two, the lawyer has enough facts in front of her to have been able to figure out, with the exercise of reasonable care, that number one is true. And three, with number one and number two in place, the lawyer either acts to help the client to break the law or does nothing to stop the client from breaking the law in those instances (which are not as few as some would like to think) when the lawyer has a duty to intervene.

Using the three part test I have just laid out, we can gauge the universe of lawyers who might be in trouble by asking which clients are we likely, in the end, to discover were breaking the law? [I'm] assuming [that] Enron will be in that category; possibly Arthur Andersen, possibly the partnerships that appear to have been part of what now appears to be a fraudulent scheme, some investors in those partnerships, maybe some investment banks. And while that list may include some innocent parties, it is at least as likely to have left out some individuals and entities who we will later discover were involved in violations of law.

The lawyers for any of the individuals or entities that turn out to be on the "broke the law" list constitute the universe of lawyers who need to start worrying. Vinson & Elkins was Enron's outside counsel, but other law firms may have represented Enron during what may have been its crime spree and might have been in a position to have figured out that Enron was breaking the law and to have helped it to do so. Enron's in-house counsel were certainly in a position to satisfy all three parts of the test I set forth above, as were Andersen's in-house counsel, and any outside law firms who may have advised Andersen on Enron related-questions during the years Andersen was auditing and advising Enron. ***

But as my list of potential law breakers was designed to emphasize, the lawyers who may be in trouble for assisting their clients' unlawful conduct (assuming those clients turn out to have broken the law) does not end with lawyers representing Enron and Andersen.

Now, we move to question two: Did any of the lawyers for clients who were breaking the law have enough facts in front of them to have figured out with the exercise of reasonable care that law breaking was going on? Well, the

Powers report[a] strongly suggests that if Enron was breaking the law, its in-house counsel and Vinson & Elkins had enough facts in front of them to have figured it out, had they been exercising reasonable care. I hasten to add that does not make either in-house counsel or outside counsel, guilty of any crime, but it does leave them in legal jeopardy in malpractice actions brought on Enron's behalf by the Trustee in bankruptcy or whomever ultimately emerges as the new management or entity in control of Enron.

To take just one example detailed in the Powers report, knowing that the Board had waived Enron's conflict of interest rules (and possibly having advised that it was a good idea to do so), it does not appear that any lawyer (within or outside) Enron bothered to worry much about the "procedures" that were supposed to prevent bad things from happening to Enron due to the conflicting roles its CFO was not licensed to play. The Powers report says whatever procedures were supposed to be in place, not only failed miserably but were not designed well enough to do anything but fail. It was Enron's lawyers who should have designed better procedures, or at least, monitored whatever procedures were designed to see to it that they had some reasonable chance of working. I do not know whether this was within the scope of Vinson & Elkins retainer, but in-house counsel was apparently not paying all this much mind. Some lawyer or group of lawyers appears to have been hopelessly careless on this matter. Indeed, it seems to me that a reasonably careful lawyer would have strongly advised the board not to waive the conflict rules in the first place, especially not as to the company's CFO.

The fact that agents within Enron, including senior management, may have been actively engaged in fraud does not, in most states, relieve the lawyer from a claim of negligence for having failed to take steps to have saved her client, the corporation, from harm (legal and financial) that these wrongdoing agents may have been causing. Again, if a careful lawyer would not have discerned that agents within the client corporation were acting unlawfully, which includes breaching their duties to the corporation by self-dealing or taking actions that would leave the corporation open to a multitude of civil lawsuits and possibly criminal charges, the lawyer should not be found liable. The liability of the lawyer will turn on how many red flags were in front of him, indicating ongoing fraud. The Powers report suggests there were signs aplenty. A company's lawyers can avoid liability for negligence, but not if they are careless about detecting wrongdoing by the CEO or CFO or other senior management, and only if they take steps to bring any signs of serious wrongdoing to the attention of the board and advise management and the board that the wrongdoing must stop. The Powers report suggests that that did not happen, although we have yet to hear from the lawyers involved.

Malpractice, is of course a matter of state law. But extreme negligence amounting to reckless disregard of the fact that corporate actors are engaged in

a. Ed. Note—In October 2001, as Enron's corporate scandal was nearing public exposure, the Board of Directors established a Special Investigation Committee, which was chaired by outside director William C. Powers, Jr., Dean of University of Texas School of Law. The Committee's Report of February 1, 2002 has become known as the "Powers Report," and is available at 2002 WL 198018.

securities fraud has long been a matter of federal law, although that may no longer be the case. Before the mid-1990s, federal securities law, as interpreted by the courts, provided that lawyers could be sued by shareholders in a derivative action and by the SEC for failing to take steps to stop securities fraud that those lawyers had to be deaf, dumb and blind not to have detected (i.e., fraud the lawyers recklessly ignored or to which the lawyers deliberately closed their eyes). This was "aiding and abetting" securities fraud. It should be the law [for private securities fraud actions] today, but for a number of reasons it isn't. That should change.

Before getting to why it should change. Let me explain why it is necessary for federal law to punish lawyer recklessness when state law allows a malpractice action for negligence and thus by definition presumably deters recklessness as well, both by leaving lawyers liable for less serious carelessness (negligence) and by providing punitive damages when that negligence gets out of control and rises to the level of recklessness.

First, there is the fact plain for all to see: the existence of state negligence actions has not proven to be an effective deterrent, possibly because lawyers bet on the fraud-doers staying in control of the corporation through fraud and thus there being no "clean, new" management with an interest in suing them. Possibly because lawyers believe that the wrongdoing of high corporate officials will somehow be attributed to the corporation in such a way as to bar a negligence suit or that even if such a suit may legally proceed, a jury will be loathe to hit the lawyers hard when management was so dirty itself. Perhaps, some state tort law reform, e.g., laws capping damages, have rendered it worthwhile for lawyers to risk a negligence suit when the fees to be reaped are high enough to pay whatever damages may be imposed (discounted by the risk that the negligence may go undiscovered or unprosecuted).

Perhaps it is as simple as lawyers believing (and being trained to act) as if the agents for their clients were their clients, making it much more difficult to internalize the notion that there is a client out there that doesn't know what's going on. Perhaps (and I believe there is something to this) the elimination of private causes of action against lawyers for aiding and abetting liability, the changes to RICO, restrictions on joint and several liability in many actions against lawyers, and other changes in federal law have encouraged lawyers to overlook that something as relatively trivial as negligently failing to take action to stop a fraud could still offend the law at all. ***

Lawyers are notorious for never "knowing" their clients are guilty. That inability is built into the ethos of the bar, which still takes its shape from the paradigm of the lawyer as advocate, And by and large, as to lawyers charged with defending clients in court, that ethos is okay. We do not want lawyers to substitute their judgment of the client's guilt for that of the jury or that of the judge. Although I hasten to add that this "no judging" attitude sometimes leads to abuse in courtrooms too, as when litigators believe they have a license in civil and criminal cases to assist perjury on the ground that they are incapable of "knowing" what the truth of the matter is. That caveat made, in general it is appropriate that the trial lawyer leave "judging" the client to the finder of fact. That's what trials are for.

But none of that applies to the lawyer who is not litigating a matter after the alleged wrong has occurred, but rather one who enters the scene before or during the client's wrongdoing—the lawyer in the role of a facilitator of the client's transactions. Indeed, very few lawyers practice in court compared to the number whose daily work is to facilitate transactions. The transaction or office lawyer, as distinguished from her trial colleagues, must understand what the client is doing and whether that is within or without the law. Otherwise, there is simply no reason for the lawyer being there.

But transaction lawyers share the ethic of trial lawyers that makes it difficult to believe, difficult to "know" that their clients are breaking the law. Complicating that problem is the fact that every good transaction lawyer understands, what every good lawyer knows, the lines of the law are almost always fuzzy at the edges. It is simply not easy to "know for sure" when those lines have been crossed, particularly when clients want to walk on the wild side and expect their lawyers to support that behavior. The lawyer who seems too quick to judge his client is likely to be replaced rapidly with one much more willing to "believe" that his client is right.

Letting lawyers know that there is a price to be paid for failing to "know" what the facts in front of the lawyer plainly suggest—that the client is committing fraud—is absolutely necessary. Without that we create a world in which fraud doers can count on high-priced and savvy lawyers to help them with their schemes, as long as the fraud doer never directly admits to the lawyer precisely what he is up to. This is not a world we should encourage. It is a world our law should try to erase.

In 1964, Judge Friendly said this about the importance of holding lawyers and accountants liable when they recklessly disregarded evidence of their client's securities fraud:

> Congress did not mean that every mistake of law or misstatement of fact should subject an attorney or an accountant to criminal liability simply because more skilled practitioners would not have made them. But Congress equally could not have intended that men holding themselves out as members of these ancient professions should be able to escape criminal liability on a plea of ignorance when they have shut their eyes to what was plainly to be seen or have represented a knowledge they knew they did not possess.

[*United States v. Benjamin*, 328 F.2d 854, 863 (2d Cir. 1964)]

Congress should change the securities laws to make clear once again that such recklessness on the part of lawyers and accountants is enough to subject a lawyer to a private suit for money damages from those the lawyer's recklessness has helped to harm. Such recklessness is rightly thought of as "criminal," given the learning, privileged position, substantial financial rewards and expertise that come with being a securities lawyer. And if it's rightly thought of as criminal when such privileged folks behave recklessly, it should be a civil wrong as well.

Were the lawyers who represented Enron negligent? Were they reckless? Did they actually know, what we now suspect, that Enron through its agents was committing securities fraud? I can tell you this much I am highly doubtful that they "knew," if "knowing" means subjectively believing that Enron was breaking the law. I am sure they convinced themselves that however close to the legal line Enron was, it had not crossed it. I am sure they refused to see and took no steps to actively ferret out, facts that would have burst that bubble—facts that would have made it difficult to maintain their "belief" that nothing was rotten in the state of Denmark. Hard as I am on lawyers, I can hardly blame them. The law as "reformed" by Congress invited them to act that way. If they "knew" I am sure that it was only in the sense that it may have crossed their mind, but any agile legal mind can formulate a doubt about whether something is "illegal" to chase those occasional bogey-men away.

But the facts (as we know them so far) do seem to suggest that at least some of Enron's lawyers and likely some of the lawyers for other actors in this drama went way beyond negligence. According to the Powers report there were not just red flags all over the place but cannons booming and music playing, all with the same message: Enron's financial condition is way different than what it (with its lawyers' help and its accountants' blessings) was leading everyone to believe. A jury need not accept a lawyer's denial of knowledge. It is perfectly free to infer that with so many major clues, some of these lawyers did "know," no matter what they were telling themselves or what they tell the jury under oath. That is, a jury can decide not to believe the lawyer, assuming a court allows the case to get to the jury, something Congress's reforms discourage judges from doing in cases when "actual knowledge" is in doubt.

But whatever happens or doesn't happen to the lawyers in Enron, there is every reason to believe that there will be securities fraud in our future and every reason to believe that its success will depend in part on lawyer's being asleep at the wheel or acting with reckless abandon. Keep in mind that in the past, as will be the case here—assuming lawyers are found to have substantially assisted fraud at Enron—the lawyers who have done wrong were (and will be) members of our finest law firms, not some nobodies from nowhere. The bar can complain all it wants about federal encroachment on self-regulation, but one thing should be abundantly clear by now: Without the discipline that fairly certain and substantial liability brings, the bar will not reform itself. Lawyers need law at least as much, if not more, than everyone else. You do neither the bar nor anyone else a favor by leaving them behind the curtain trusting in their magic caps.***

If Enron was the Emerald City, no matter what individual or groups of individuals end up to have been standing behind the curtain playing the Wizard of Oz (be it Enron's CEO, its CFO, some or all of its board of directors or whomever), I guarantee you one thing: A lawyer was standing beside them making sure the curtain stayed drawn and all the bells and whistles were hooked up and operating to fool Dorothy, the brainless scarecrow and the cowardly lion. ***

## *NOTES AND QUESTIONS*

*1. **Recognizing Securities Fraud.*** Do you agree with Professor Koniak's statement that "lawyers are notorious for never 'knowing' that their clients are guilty"? What reforms does she propose in order to give lawyers a greater incentive to more readily recognize fraudulent actions by their clients? Do you agree with Professor Koniak's recommendations?

*2. Magic Caps.* Recall the facts set out in the *Carter & Johnson* opinion. Does Professor Koniak's theory of "magic caps" ring true? What examples, if any, might illustrate this phenomenon?

*3. Professional Independence.* In their analysis of lawyers' roles in the Enron scandal, Professor Deborah Rhode and Paul Paton draw attention to "the financial incentives created by Vinson & Elkins' dependence on Enron-related work and employment opportunities." They note, in particular, that

> [i]n 2001, Enron was Vinson & Elkins' largest client, accounting for more than seven percent of the law firm's revenues. Both Enron's general counsel and deputy general counsel at the time were former Vinson & Elkins partners; an additional twenty or so Vinson & Elkins attorneys reportedly had taken jobs at Enron since 1991.

Deborah L. Rhode & Paul D. Paton, Lawyers, Ethics, and Enron, 8 Stan. J. of Law, Bus. & Fin. 9, 25 (2002).

As we will see, in the aftermath of Enron and WorldCom, Congress made the independence of auditors a high legislative priority. Should similar attention be paid to the independence of lawyers? Is reliance on general rules of professional responsibility enough? In answering no, Professor Rhode and Mr. Paton maintain:

> Increased competition from within and outside the bar has led to increased pressure on firms to favor responsiveness to client demands over broader societal concerns. Allegiance to management's short-term financial interests may compromise obligations to the broader public, as well as to the entity itself, which is, at least in theory, the lawyer's client.
>
> The challenges of maintaining independent judgment are compounded in a competitive market where powerful clients can shop for expedient rather than ethical advice. Yet while resisting client pressures can carry financial risks, so, too, can satisfying their demands. In the long run, firms' reputational interests are not well served by assisting conduct that cuts ethical corners. ***

Id. at 26.

*4. Reporting Up the Corporate Ladder.* Although the ABA has for years been considering a proposed amendment to Model Rule 1.13 that would require lawyers for a corporation to report ongoing or prospective illegal conduct "up the corporate ladder" to the client's board of directors, the ABA has yet to adopt the amendment. See Cramton, supra, 58 Bus. Law. at 155 (citing Richard W. Painter, Proposal to Amend Model Rule 1.13 (Organization as Client) (reprinted in Prof. Law. 10 (Spring 1998)). See also Richard W. Painter & Jennifer E. Duggan, Lawyer Disclosure of Corporate Fraud: Establishing a Firm Foundation, 50 SMU L. Rev. 225 (1996) (proposing that Congress amend the Exchange Act to require a lawyer representing an issuer to report known securities law violations and other illegal acts first to senior management and then, if necessary, to the client's full board of directors).

In the wake of allegations against lawyers at Enron and other corporations rocked by scandal, the SEC received various recommendations for change. The most publicized proposal came from a group of forty law professors (including your casebook authors) who urged the SEC to add to Rule 102(e) a requirement that lawyers representing securities issuers must report known securities law violations to senior management and then, if necessary, to the issuer's board of directors. The law professors emphasized that their proposed requirement was substantially less demanding than the requirement imposed on accountants by Section 10A of the Exchange Act, which requires the reporting of illegal acts to the client's directors as well as to the SEC if senior management fails to take remedial action. See Letter dated March 7, 2002 from Richard W. Painter, et al. to Harvey Pitt, Chairperson of the Securities and Exchange Commission. The ABA, however, lobbied the SEC against the proposed requirement and the SEC responded by declaring that federal professional responsibility standards for lawyers should be mandated, if at all, by Congress rather than by the SEC. See Letter dated March 28, 2002 from David Becker, General Counsel, Securities and Exchange Commission, to Richard W. Painter (citing Painter & Duggan, supra).

In the summer of 2002, Senators John Edwards (D N.C.), Mike Enzi (R WY), and John Corzine (D N.J.) responded to Mr. Becker's invitation by sponsoring the provision that became Section 307 of the Sarbanes-Oxley Act. As we shall see, Section 307 requires the SEC to promulgate rules requiring a lawyer for an issuer to report to the board of directors "evidence" of fraud rather than "knowledge" of fraud, a standard even stricter than that proposed by the law professors. Section 307 also requires that the new rule cover breaches of fiduciary duty as well as securities law violations, whereas the mandatory reporting in the law professors' proposal extended only to violations of the securities laws.

### *3. Section 307 of the Sarbanes-Oxley Act and SEC Rules Thereunder*

As pointed out in Section A above, Section 602 of the Sarbanes-Oxley Act adds a new Section 4C to the Exchange Act which gives the SEC the power that it has long asserted under Rule 102(e)—to discipline professionals appearing and practicing before it. Accordingly, the SEC now has very clear statutory authority to discipline lawyers who represent issuers, broker-dealers, underwriters, investment advisers, and other persons involved in securities transactions.

But Section 307 of the Act goes substantially further by requiring the SEC to promulgate professional responsibility rules for attorneys representing securities issuers, including one rule in particular:

**Section 307. Rules of Professional Responsibility for Attorneys**

Not later than 180 days after the date of enactment of this Act, the Commission shall issue rules, in the public interest and for the protection of investors, setting forth minimum standards of professional conduct for attorneys appearing and practicing before the Commission in any way in the representation of issuers, including a rule—

(1) requiring an attorney to report evidence of a material violation of securities law or breach of fiduciary duty or similar violation by the company or any agent thereof, to the chief legal counsel or the chief executive officer of the company (or the equivalent thereof); and

(2) if the counsel or officer does not appropriately respond to the evidence (adopting, as necessary, appropriate remedial measures or sanctions with

respect to the violation), requiring the attorney to report the evidence to the audit committee of the board of directors of the issuer or to another committee of the board of directors comprised solely of directors not employed directly or indirectly by the issuer, or to the board of directors.

In response to this directive, on November 21, 2002, the SEC published for comment a proposed rule that generated vigorous debate. Set out below is the significantly modified final rule, which the SEC adopted a little more than two months later. See Final Rule: Implementation of Standards of Professional Conduct for Attorneys, Exchange Act Release No. 47276 (Jan. 29, 2003). As you read through this lengthy rule, consider some of the questions and issues that are bound to be raised as securities attorneys assess their new duties and responsibilities under it.

## STANDARDS OF PROFESSIONAL CONDUCT FOR ATTORNEYS APPEARING AND PRACTICING BEFORE THE COMMISSION IN THE REPRESENTATION OF AN ISSUER

17 C.F.R. § 205—Effective date: August 5, 2003

### § 205.1 Purpose and scope

This part sets forth minimum standards of professional conduct for attorneys appearing and practicing before the Commission in the representation of an issuer. These standards supplement applicable standards of any jurisdiction where an attorney is admitted or practices and are not intended to limit the ability of any jurisdiction to impose additional obligations on an attorney not inconsistent with the application of this part. Where the standards of a state or other United States jurisdiction where an attorney is admitted or practices conflict with this part, this part shall govern.

### § 205.2 Definitions

For purposes of this part, the following definitions apply:

(a) *Appearing and practicing* before the Commission:

(1) Means:

(i) Transacting any business with the Commission, including communications in any form;

(ii) Representing an issuer in a Commission administrative proceeding or in connection with any Commission investigation, inquiry, information request, or subpoena;

(iii) Providing advice in respect of the United States securities laws or the Commission's rules or regulations thereunder regarding any document that the attorney has notice will be filed with or submitted to, or incorporated into any document that will be filed with or submitted to, the Commission, including the provision of such advice in the context of preparing, or participating in the preparation of, any such document; or

(iv) Advising an issuer as to whether information or a statement, opinion, or other writing is required under the United

States securities laws or the Commission's rules or regulations thereunder to be filed with or submitted to, or incorporated into any document that will be filed with or submitted to, the Commission; but

(2) Does not include an attorney who:

(i) Conducts the activities in paragraphs (a)(1)(i) through (a)(1)(iv) of this section other than in the context of providing legal services to an issuer with whom the attorney has an attorney-client relationship; or

(ii) Is a non-appearing foreign attorney.

(b) *Appropriate response* means a response to an attorney regarding reported evidence of a material violation as a result of which the attorney reasonably believes:

(1) That no material violation, as defined in paragraph (i) of this section, has occurred, is ongoing, or is about to occur;

(2) That the issuer has, as necessary, adopted appropriate remedial measures, including appropriate steps or sanctions to stop any material violations that are ongoing, to prevent any material violation that has yet to occur, and to remedy or otherwise appropriately address any material violation that has already occurred and to minimize the likelihood of its recurrence; or

(3) That the issuer, with the consent of the issuer's board of directors, a committee thereof to whom a report could be made pursuant to §§ 205.3(b)(3), or a qualified legal compliance committee, has retained or directed an attorney to review the reported evidence of a material violation and either:

(i) Has substantially implemented any remedial recommendations made by such attorney after a reasonable investigation and evaluation of the reported evidence; or

(ii) Has been advised that such attorney may, consistent with his or her professional obligations, assert a colorable defense on behalf of the issuer (or the issuer's officer, director, employee, or agent, as the case may be) in any investigation or judicial or administrative proceeding relating to the reported evidence of a material violation.

(c) *Attorney* means any person who is admitted, licensed, or otherwise qualified to practice law in any jurisdiction, domestic or foreign, or who holds himself or herself out as admitted, licensed, or otherwise qualified to practice law.

(d) *Breach of fiduciary duty* refers to any breach of fiduciary or similar duty to the issuer recognized under an applicable federal or state statute or at common law, including but not limited to misfeasance, nonfeasance, abdication of duty, abuse of trust, and approval of unlawful transactions.

(e) *Evidence of a material violation* means credible evidence, based upon which it would be unreasonable, under the circumstances, for a prudent and competent attorney not to conclude that it is reasonably likely that a material violation has occurred, is ongoing, or is about to occur.

(f) *Foreign government issuer* means a foreign issuer as defined in 17 CFR 230.405 eligible to register securities on Schedule B of the Securities Act of 1933.

(g) *In the representation of an issuer* means providing legal services as an attorney for an issuer, regardless of whether the attorney is employed or retained by the issuer.

(h) *Issuer* means an issuer (as defined in section 3 of the Securities Exchange Act of 1934), the securities of which are registered under section 12 of that Act, or that is required to file reports under section 15(d) of that Act, or that files or has filed a registration statement that has not yet become effective under the Securities Act of 1933, and that it has not withdrawn, but does not include a foreign government issuer. For purposes of paragraphs (a) and (g) of this section, the term "issuer" includes any person controlled by an issuer, where an attorney provides legal services to such person on behalf of, or at the behest, or for the benefit of the issuer, regardless of whether the attorney is employed or retained by the issuer.

(i) *Material violation* means a material violation of an applicable United States federal or state securities law, a material breach of fiduciary duty arising under United States federal or state law, or a similar material violation of any United States federal or state law.

(j) *Non-appearing foreign attorney* means an attorney:

(1) Who is admitted to practice law in a jurisdiction outside the United States;

(2) Who does not hold himself or herself out as practicing, and does not give legal advice regarding, United States federal or state securities or other laws (except as provided in paragraph (j)(3)(ii) of this section); and

(3) Who:

(i) Conducts activities that would constitute appearing and practicing before the Commission only incidentally to, and in the ordinary course of, the practice of law in a jurisdiction outside the United States; or

(ii) Is appearing and practicing before the Commission only in consultation with counsel, other than a non-appearing foreign attorney, admitted or licensed to practice in a state or other United States jurisdiction.

(k) *Qualified legal compliance committee* means a committee of an issuer (which also may be an audit or other committee of the issuer) that:

(1) Consists of at least one member of the issuer's audit committee (or, if the issuer has no audit committee, one member from an equivalent committee of independent directors) and two or more members of the issuer's board of directors who are not employed, directly or indirectly, by the issuer and who are not, in the case of a registered investment

company, "interested persons" as defined in section 2(a)(19) of the Investment Company Act of 1940;

(2) Has adopted written procedures for the confidential receipt, retention, and consideration of any report of evidence of a material violation under §§ 205.3;

(3) Has been duly established by the issuer's board of directors, with the authority and responsibility:

(i) To inform the issuer's chief legal officer and chief executive officer (or the equivalents thereof) of any report of evidence of a material violation (except in the circumstances described in §§205.3(b)(4));

(ii) To determine whether an investigation is necessary regarding any report of evidence of a material violation by the issuer, its officers, directors, employees or agents and, if it determines an investigation is necessary or appropriate, to:

(A) Notify the audit committee or the full board of directors;

(B) Initiate an investigation, which may be conducted either by the chief legal officer (or the equivalent thereof) or by outside attorneys; and

(C) Retain such additional expert personnel as the committee deems necessary; and

(iii) At the conclusion of any such investigation, to:

(A) Recommend, by majority vote, that the issuer implement an appropriate response to evidence of a material violation; and

(B) Inform the chief legal officer and the chief executive officer (or the equivalents thereof) and the board of directors of the results of any such investigation under this section and the appropriate remedial measures to be adopted; and

(4) Has the authority and responsibility, acting by majority vote, to take all other appropriate action, including the authority to notify the Commission in the event that the issuer fails in any material respect to implement an appropriate response that the qualified legal compliance committee has recommended the issuer to take.

(l) *Reasonable* or *reasonably* denotes, with respect to the actions of an attorney, conduct that would not be unreasonable for a prudent and competent attorney.

(m) *Reasonably believes* means that an attorney believes the matter in question and that the circumstances are such that the belief is not unreasonable.

(n) *Report* means to make known to directly, either in person, by telephone, by e-mail, electronically, or in writing.

### § 205.3 Issuer as client

(a) *Representing an issuer.* An attorney appearing and practicing before the Commission in the representation of an issuer owes his or her professional and ethical duties to the issuer as an organization. That the attorney may work with and advise the issuer's officers, directors, or employees in the course of representing the issuer does not make such individuals the attorney's clients.

(b) *Duty to report evidence of a material violation.*

(1) If an attorney, appearing and practicing before the Commission in the representation of an issuer, becomes aware of evidence of a material violation by the issuer or by any officer, director, employee, or agent of the issuer, the attorney shall report such evidence to the issuer's chief legal officer (or the equivalent thereof) or to both the issuer's chief legal officer and its chief executive officer (or the equivalents thereof) forthwith. By communicating such information to the issuer's officers or directors, an attorney does not reveal client confidences or secrets or privileged or otherwise protected information related to the attorney's representation of an issuer.

(2) The chief legal officer (or the equivalent thereof) shall cause such inquiry into the evidence of a material violation as he or she reasonably believes is appropriate to determine whether the material violation described in the report has occurred, is ongoing, or is about to occur. If the chief legal officer (or the equivalent thereof) determines no material violation has occurred, is ongoing, or is about to occur, he or she shall notify the reporting attorney and advise the reporting attorney of the basis for such determination. Unless the chief legal officer (or the equivalent thereof) reasonably believes that no material violation has occurred, is ongoing, or is about to occur, he or she shall take all reasonable steps to cause the issuer to adopt an appropriate response, and shall advise the reporting attorney thereof. In lieu of causing an inquiry under this paragraph (b), a chief legal officer (or the equivalent thereof) may refer a report of evidence of a material violation to a qualified legal compliance committee under paragraph (c)(2) of this section if the issuer has duly established a qualified legal compliance committee prior to the report of evidence of a material violation.

(3) Unless an attorney who has made a report under paragraph (b)(1) of this section reasonably believes that the chief legal officer or the chief executive officer of the issuer (or the equivalent thereof) has provided an appropriate response within a reasonable time, the attorney shall report the evidence of a material violation to:

(i) The audit committee of the issuer's board of directors;

(ii) Another committee of the issuer's board of directors consisting solely of directors who are not employed, directly or indirectly, by the issuer and are not, in the case of a registered investment company, "interested persons" as defined in section 2(a)(19) of the Investment Company Act of 1940 (15 U.S.C. 80a-

2(a)(19)) (if the issuer's board of directors has no audit committee); or

(iii) The issuer's board of directors (if the issuer's board of directors has no committee consisting solely of directors who are not employed, directly or indirectly, by the issuer and are not, in the case of a registered investment company, "interested persons" as defined in section 2(a)(19) of the Investment Company Act of 1940 (15 U.S.C. 80a-2(a)(19))).

(4) If an attorney reasonably believes that it would be futile to report evidence of a material violation to the issuer's chief legal officer and chief executive officer (or the equivalents thereof) under paragraph (b)(1) of this section, the attorney may report such evidence as provided under paragraph (b)(3) of this section.

(5) An attorney retained or directed by an issuer to investigate evidence of a material violation reported under paragraph (b)(1), (b)(3), or (b)(4) of this section shall be deemed to be appearing and practicing before the Commission. Directing or retaining an attorney to investigate reported evidence of a material violation does not relieve an officer or director of the issuer to whom such evidence has been reported under paragraph (b)(1), (b)(3), or (b)(4) of this section from a duty to respond to the reporting attorney.

(6) An attorney shall not have any obligation to report evidence of a material violation under this paragraph (b) if:

(i) The attorney was retained or directed by the issuer's chief legal officer (or the equivalent thereof) to investigate such evidence of a material violation and:

(A) The attorney reports the results of such investigation to the chief legal officer (or the equivalent thereof), and

(B) Except where the attorney and the chief legal officer (or the equivalent thereof) each reasonably believes that no material violation has occurred, is ongoing, or is about to occur, the chief legal officer (or the equivalent thereof) reports the results of the investigation to the issuer's board of directors, a committee thereof to whom a report could be made pursuant to paragraph (b)(3) of this section, or a qualified legal compliance committee; or

(ii) The attorney was retained or directed by the chief legal officer (or the equivalent thereof) to assert, consistent with his or her professional obligations, a colorable defense on behalf of the issuer (or the issuer's officer, director, employee, or agent, as the case may be) in any investigation or judicial or administrative proceeding relating to such evidence of a material violation, and the chief legal officer (or the equivalent thereof) provides reasonable and timely reports on the progress and outcome of such proceeding to the issuer's board of directors, a committee thereof to whom a report could be made pursuant to paragraph (b)(3) of this section, or a qualified legal compliance committee.

(7) An attorney shall not have any obligation to report evidence of a material violation under this paragraph (b) if such attorney was retained or directed by a qualified legal compliance committee:

(i) To investigate such evidence of a material violation; or

(ii) To assert, consistent with his or her professional obligations, a colorable defense on behalf of the issuer (or the issuer's officer, director, employee, or agent, as the case may be) in any investigation or judicial or administrative proceeding relating to such evidence of a material violation.

(8) An attorney who receives what he or she reasonably believes is an appropriate and timely response to a report he or she has made pursuant to paragraph (b)(1), (b)(3), or (b)(4) of this section need do nothing more under this section with respect to his or her report.

(9) An attorney who does not reasonably believe that the issuer has made an appropriate response within a reasonable time to the report or reports made pursuant to paragraph (b)(1), (b)(3), or (b)(4) of this section shall explain his or her reasons therefor to the chief legal officer (or the equivalent thereof), the chief executive officer (or the equivalent thereof), and directors to whom the attorney reported the evidence of a material violation pursuant to paragraph (b)(1), (b)(3), or (b)(4) of this section.

(10) An attorney formerly employed or retained by an issuer who has reported evidence of a material violation under this part and reasonably believes that he or she has been discharged for so doing may notify the issuer's board of directors or any committee thereof that he or she believes that he or she has been discharged for reporting evidence of a material violation under this section.

(c) *Alternative reporting procedures for attorneys retained or employed by an issuer that has established a qualified legal compliance committee.*

(1) If an attorney, appearing and practicing before the Commission in the representation of an issuer, becomes aware of evidence of a material violation by the issuer or by any officer, director, employee, or agent of the issuer, the attorney may, as an alternative to the reporting requirements of paragraph (b) of this section, report such evidence to a qualified legal compliance committee, if the issuer has previously formed such a committee. An attorney who reports evidence of a material violation to such a qualified legal compliance committee has satisfied his or her obligation to report such evidence and is not required to assess the issuer's response to the reported evidence of a material violation.

(2) A chief legal officer (or the equivalent thereof) may refer a report of evidence of a material violation to a previously established qualified legal compliance committee in lieu of causing an inquiry to be conducted

under paragraph (b)(2) of this section. The chief legal officer (or the equivalent thereof) shall inform the reporting attorney that the report has been referred to a qualified legal compliance committee. Thereafter, pursuant to the requirements under §§ 205.2(k), the qualified legal compliance committee shall be responsible for responding to the evidence of a material violation reported to it under this paragraph (c).

(d) *Issuer confidences.*

(1) Any report under this section (or the contemporaneous record thereof) or any response thereto (or the contemporaneous record thereof) may be used by an attorney in connection with any investigation, proceeding, or litigation in which the attorney's compliance with this part is in issue.

(2) An attorney appearing and practicing before the Commission in the representation of an issuer may reveal to the Commission, without the issuer's consent, confidential information related to the representation to the extent the attorney reasonably believes necessary:

(i) To prevent the issuer from committing a material violation that is likely to cause substantial injury to the financial interest or property of the issuer or investors;

(ii) To prevent the issuer, in a Commission investigation or administrative proceeding from committing perjury, proscribed in 18 U.S.C. 1621; suborning perjury, proscribed in 18 U.S.C. 1622; or committing any act proscribed in 18 U.S.C. 1001 that is likely to perpetrate a fraud upon the Commission; or

(iii) To rectify the consequences of a material violation by the issuer that caused, or may cause, substantial injury to the financial interest or property of the issuer or investors in the furtherance of which the attorney's services were used.

### § 205.4 Responsibilities of supervisory attorneys

(a) An attorney supervising or directing another attorney who is appearing and practicing before the Commission in the representation of an issuer is a supervisory attorney. An issuer's chief legal officer (or the equivalent thereof) is a supervisory attorney under this section.

(b) A supervisory attorney shall make reasonable efforts to ensure that a subordinate attorney, as defined in §§ 205.5(a), that he or she supervises or directs conforms to this part. To the extent a subordinate attorney appears and practices before the Commission in the representation of an issuer, that subordinate attorney's supervisory attorneys also appear and practice before the Commission.

(c) A supervisory attorney is responsible for complying with the reporting requirements in §§ 205.3 when a subordinate attorney has reported to the supervisory attorney evidence of a material violation.

(d) A supervisory attorney who has received a report of evidence of a material violation from a subordinate attorney under §§205.3 may report such evidence to the issuer's qualified legal compliance committee if the issuer has duly formed such a committee.

### § 205.5 Responsibilities of a subordinate attorney

(a) An attorney who appears and practices before the Commission in the representation of an issuer on a matter under the supervision or direction of another attorney (other than under the direct supervision or direction of the issuer's chief legal officer (or the equivalent thereof)) is a subordinate attorney.

(b) A subordinate attorney shall comply with this part notwithstanding that the subordinate attorney acted at the direction of or under the supervision of another person.

(c) A subordinate attorney complies with §§ 205.3 if the subordinate attorney reports to his or her supervising attorney under §§ 205.3(b) evidence of a material violation of which the subordinate attorney has become aware in appearing and practicing before the Commission.

(d) A subordinate attorney may take the steps permitted or required by §§ 205.3(b) or (c) if the subordinate attorney reasonably believes that a supervisory attorney to whom he or she has reported evidence of a material violation under §§ 205.3(b) has failed to comply with §§ 205.3.

### § 205.6 Sanctions and discipline

(a) A violation of this part by any attorney appearing and practicing before the Commission in the representation of an issuer shall subject such attorney to the civil penalties and remedies for a violation of the federal securities laws available to the Commission in an action brought by the Commission thereunder.

(b) An attorney appearing and practicing before the Commission who violates any provision of this part is subject to the disciplinary authority of the Commission, regardless of whether the attorney may also be subject to discipline for the same conduct in a jurisdiction where the attorney is admitted or practices. An administrative disciplinary proceeding initiated by the Commission for violation of this part may result in an attorney being censured, or being temporarily or permanently denied the privilege of appearing or practicing before the Commission.

(c) An attorney who complies in good faith with the provisions of this part shall not be subject to discipline or otherwise liable under inconsistent standards imposed by any state or other United States jurisdiction where the attorney is admitted or practices.

(d) An attorney practicing outside the United States shall not be required to comply with the requirements of this part to the extent that such compliance is prohibited by applicable foreign law.

### § 205.7 No private right of action

(a) Nothing in this part is intended to, or does, create a private right of action against any attorney, law firm, or issuer based upon compliance or noncompliance with its provisions.

(b) Authority to enforce compliance with this part is vested exclusively in the Commission.

### NOTES AND QUESTIONS

*1. Applying Rule 205 to* **Carter & Johnson.** Assume the up-the-ladder reporting rule now required under Rule 205 were applicable to the facts of *Carter & Johnson.* How would you answer the following questions:

a. At what point in the representation did Carter and Johnson have "evidence" of a securities law violation requiring them to report to the chief legal officer or chief executive officer of National Telephone? Did they satisfy this requirement?

b. At what point should Carter and Johnson have taken their concerns to the full board of directors of National Telephone? Is it clear that they did so too late? Would they have clearly violated the rule by waiting as long as they did?

c. What other rules of professional responsibility do you believe the SEC ought to promulgate that would guide lawyers in a similar situation? For example, should Carter and Johnson have been required to resign from the representation at any point? Should they have been required to inform the SEC that they were renouncing any work product that they had done for National Telephone?

*2. Noisy Withdrawals.* There will be instances in which a report to the client's board of directors required by Rule 205 will not succeed in persuading the client to respond appropriately to a violation. Under these circumstances, should the lawyer be *required* to make a report outside the board to the SEC, just as auditors are required to do under Section 10A of the Exchange Act? Should the lawyer be *required* to withdraw from the representation, but not to report?

As noted above, the version of Rule 205 that the SEC adopted in January 2003 differs in a number of important respects from the rule it had proposed two months earlier. Most significantly, the final version did not require an attorney to make a "noisy withdrawal" in situations where the attorney reasonably believes that the issuer's directors have either made no response or have not made an appropriate response to his or her report of violations. Rather, the SEC opted to go ahead only with the up-the-ladder reporting requirements (as it had to do under Section 307 of the Sarbanes-Oxley Act) and to propose for further comment the noisy withdrawal provision. See Final Rule, Exchange Act Release No. 47276, supra. See also Proposed Rule: Implementation of Standards of Professional Conduct for Attorneys, Exchange Act Release No. 34-47282 (Jan. 29, 2003). The proposed rule would add the following new sub-section to Rule 205:

> **Proposed Rule 205.3(d)(1).** *Notice to the Commission where there is no appropriate response within a reasonable time.*
>
> (1) Where an attorney who has reported evidence of a material violation under paragraph 3(b) of this section rather than paragraph 3(c) of this section does not receive an appropriate response, or has not received a response in a reasonable time, to his or her report, and the attorney reasonably believes that a material

violation is ongoing or is about to occur and is likely to result in substantial injury to the financial interest or property of the issuer or of investors:

(i) An attorney retained by the issuer shall:

(A) Withdraw forthwith from representing the issuer, indicating that the withdrawal is based on professional considerations;

(B) Within one business day of withdrawing, give written notice to the Commission of the attorney's withdrawal, indicating that the withdrawal was based on professional considerations; and

(C) Promptly disaffirm to the Commission any opinion, document, affirmation, representation, characterization, or the like in a document filed with or submitted to the Commission, or incorporated into such a document, that the attorney has prepared or assisted in preparing and that the attorney reasonably believes is or may be materially false or misleading;

(ii) An attorney employed by the issuer shall:

(A) Within one business day, notify the Commission in writing that he or she intends to disaffirm some opinion, document, affirmation, representation, characterization, or the like in a document filed with or submitted to the Commission, or incorporated into such a document, that the attorney has prepared or assisted in preparing and that the attorney reasonably believes is or may be materially false or misleading; and

(B) Promptly disaffirm to the Commission, in writing, any such opinion, document, affirmation, representation, characterization, or the like; and

(iii) The issuer's chief legal officer (or the equivalent) shall inform any attorney retained or employed to replace the attorney who has withdrawn that the previous attorney's withdrawal was based on professional considerations.

See id. The SEC also proposed a new Rule 205.3(d)(2), which would apply to situations in which the reported material violation has already occurred and is not ongoing. Without specifying any particular time frames, proposed Rule 205.3(d)(2) states that attorneys "may" take the very same steps that would have been required under proposed Rule 205.3(d)(1) if the violation had been ongoing or about to occur. Id.

Should the SEC adopt the above provisions for "noisy withdrawals"? In its January 2003 release, the SEC also proposed for comment an alternative to the noisy withdrawal provision that would require the securities issuer (rather than its attorney) to report to the SEC the attorney's written notice of withdrawal or failure to receive an appropriate response. In connection with this alternative proposal, the SEC proposed to amend Forms 8-K, 20-F, and 40-F to require issuers to disclose to the public an attorney's written notice of withdrawal within two business days of that notice. The alternative proposal would also permit (but would not require) an attorney to inform the SEC of his or her withdrawal in situations where the issuer fails to make the required reports.

See id. (proposing alternative Rule 205.3(e) and Rule 205.3(f)). Which would you prefer to see adopted: the proposed rule mandating an attorney's noisy withdrawal or the alternative rule mandating issuer reporting? Does your answer change depending on whether you are usually an attorney? A client? An investor? Should it change?

*3. Multiple Representations and Conflicts of Interest.* Recall the discussion of multiple representations in the context of investigations or enforcement proceedings by the SEC. See Chapter 9.B. supra. Could the SEC use its authority under Section 307 of the Sarbanes-Oxley Act to regulate conflicts and potential conflicts that may arise when a lawyer simultaneously represents issuers and individual corporate officials?

Multiple representations may raise particularly troubling questions in the context of an IPO where, in many cases, the insider shareholders are for practical purposes also clients of the lawyer representing the issuer. Full disclosure of the issuer's relationship with its principals is generally required in the issuer's registration statement, yet there may be certain information that the principals do not want publicly disclosed. Also, if there is a secondary offering by the principals as well as, or instead of, a primary offering by the issuer, the principals may have a personal interest in closing the deal despite defects in the issuer's disclosure. Assuming it has the authority to do so, should the SEC adopt rules to address potential conflicts precipitated by multiple representations in the IPO context? Should it do so in other contexts?

*4. Compensation of Counsel.* Recently, law firms have moved away from hourly billing for securities and transactional work to alternative billing arrangements. These arrangements presumably create added incentives for the lawyers to perform high quality work, conform client payment obligations more closely to client cash flows, and more accurately reflect the value to the client of the legal work. These new methods include taking equity in lieu of fees, contingent fees, and premium billing. See generally Donald C. Langevoort, When Lawyers and Law Firms Invest in Their Corporate Clients' Stock, 80 Wash. U. L.Q. 569 (2002); Poonam Puri, Taking Stock of Taking Stock, 87 Cornell L. Rev. 99 (2001). See also Richard W. Painter, Irrationality and Cognitive Bias at a Closing in Arthur Solmssen's *The Comfort Letter*, 69 Fordham L. Rev. 1111 (2000) (criticizing contingent fee arrangements in transactional work, including the $35 million fee that Cravath Swaine and Moore was paid by Time-Warner, contingent on the closing of Time-Warner's merger with AOL). As part of its effort to discern minimum standards of professional responsibility for securities lawyers, should the SEC consider what, if any, effect these various payment methods have on the quality of representation provided to a corporate client?

## *PROBLEM 10-1*

Cintron, Inc., a Delaware corporation engaged in energy trading, is planning a public offering of common stock. Cintron is an Exchange Act reporting company and does not have a Qualified Legal Compliance Committee (as described in Rule 205.2(k)). Davis, Sullivan & Moore ("DSM"), a New York law firm, represents Cintron in connection with the preparation of a registration statement for the offering. Larry Silver is the partner at DSM in charge of the

Cintron stock offering and has been responsible for the firm's representation of Cintron in other securities-related matters over the past five years. Peter Black is a third-year associate at DSM and works for Silver on the Cintron registration statement. The lead underwriter for the stock offering is Gardner, Smith & Co. ("GS"), and the lead underwriter's counsel is another New York law firm, Cromwell & Wardwell ("C&W"). Susan Williams is the C&W partner in charge of representing GS in the Cintron transaction.

Cintron has been engaging in numerous deceitful accounting practices, including disguising substantial losses in off-balance-sheet entities. Up until two weeks before the scheduled closing date for the Cintron stock offering, none of the lawyers involved in the transaction was aware of the problem. Neither were Cintron's auditors at the accounting firm of Batter & Notly.

Two weeks before the Cintron stock offering, however, Sarah Stevens, a junior employee in Cintron's accounting department, sent an e-mail to Peter Black and to Susan Williams, alerting them both to credible evidence of accounting fraud at Cintron. Stevens's allegations, if true, would mean that Cintron's registration statement for the proposed offering, already filed with the SEC and about to become effective, would be materially misleading.

a. What are Peter Black's professional obligations under the SEC's rules of professional responsibility for attorneys?

b. Assume that Peter Black directs Larry Silver's attention to the problem. What are Larry Silver's professional obligations under the SEC's rules of professional responsibility for attorneys?

c. What are Susan Williams's professional obligations under the SEC's rules of professional responsibility for attorneys?

d. Assume that Larry Silver brings this problem to the attention of Cintron's directors but that they refuse to do anything about it and insist on proceeding with the stock offering. What is Larry Silver required to do next? What is he permitted to do?

e. Assume that Susan Williams brings this problem to the attention of GS's directors but that they refuse to do anything about it and insist on proceeding with the Cintron stock offering. What is Susan Williams required to do next? What is she permitted to do?

f. How would the answers to any of the above questions change if Cintron had a Qualified Legal Compliance Committee?

g. With respect to Silver, Black, and DSM, how would your answers to the above questions change if DSM were not a New York law firm, but instead a London law firm? Assume that DSM (i) represented Cintron principally in connection with its compliance with listing requirement for sale of securities under U.K. law and (ii) did not advise Cintron on United States securities laws but did assist Cintron with preparation of documents that Cintron incorporated into securities filings both in the U.S. and in the U.K.

h. How would your answers to the above questions change if Cintron was *not* subject to the reporting requirements of the Exchange Act and was planning a private placement of stock rather than a public offering? Assume that the private placement memorandum that was distributed to investors included several materially misleading statements.

i. If any of the above lawyers fail to meet their professional obligations under the SEC's rules or state rules of professional responsibility, to what extent are they exposed to civil liability? To whom are they possibly liable and under what law?

## C. THE REGULATION OF ACCOUNTANTS UNDER THE SARBANES-OXLEY ACT

The accounting profession has long been governed by internal standards of professional conduct such as the American Institute of Certified Public Accountants (AICPA), Code of Professional Conduct (1995). Rule 202 of the AICPA Code requires an AICPA member to comply with auditing and other standards "promulgated by bodies designated by [the AICPA council]." Rule 203 states that a member shall not express an opinion or state affirmatively that financial statements are presented in conformity with GAAP [Generally Accepted Accounting Principles] or claim that he "is not aware of any material modifications that should be made," if such financial statements materially depart from promulgated standards. Rule 301 prohibits a member from disclosing "any confidential client information without the specific consent of the client." However, Rule 301 is not intended to relieve a member of professional obligations under Rules 202 or 203, or to limit the member's duty "to comply with a validly issued and enforceable subpoena or summons." Nor should Rule 301 be interpreted to prevent an AICPA member from exchanging information with a recognized "investigative or disciplinary body." Id., Rule 301. Although the AICPA Code does not ordinarily require the auditor to disclose its findings to persons other than the client itself, such a duty might arise under some circumstances. For example, disclosure to the SEC is required when an issuer reports changes in auditors to the SEC on Form 8-K. Disclosure of confidential client information is also mandatory in response to a successor auditor who makes an inquiry in accordance with applicable rules.

Congress stepped in for the first time to tighten professional standards for accountants in 1995 when it enacted the Private Securities Litigation Reform Act (PSLRA), which added Section 10A to the Exchange Act. Section 10A places an affirmative duty on auditors to report illegal acts first to a client's senior management and then, if the illegal acts are not rectified, directly to the client's board of directors and to the SEC. As pointed out in Chapter 2.G.2, however, the PSLRA introduced a proportionate liability scheme in private litigation for damages under the Exchange Act. This change reduced auditors' exposure to civil liability for accounting fraud and thus may have encouraged them to be less careful.

After auditors were implicated in a large number of accounting frauds in the early 2000s, including the collapses of Enron and WorldCom, Congress responded by introducing sweeping new regulation of the accounting profession under the Sarbanes-Oxley Act of 2002. The provisions of that Act dealing with accountants are discussed in the Senate Report that follows.

## U.S. SENATE REPORT
## COMMITTEE ON BANKING, HOUSING, AND URBAN AFFAIRS
## TO ACCOMPANY S. 2673
## JULY 3, 2002

***TITLE I—PUBLIC COMPANY ACCOUNTING OVERSIGHT BOARD

Title I of the bill creates a Public Company Accounting Oversight Board (the "Board"), to provide for more effective oversight of the part of the nation's accounting industry that audits public companies. ***

The new Board may, subject to review by the Securities and Exchange Commission (the "SEC" or the "Commission"), establish, adopt, or modify auditing, quality control, ethics, and independence standards for public company audits, inspect accounting firms, investigate potential violations of applicable rules relating to audits, and impose sanctions if those violations are established. The Board will have authority only with respect to audits of public companies. It has no jurisdiction over the work of accountants in auditing other companies. ***

*A. Appointment and operation of board* [Section 101 of the Sarbanes-Oxley Act]

The successful operation of the Board depends upon its independence and professionalism. The Board will have five members, each of whom must have a demonstrated commitment to the interests of investors, as well as an understanding of the financial disclosures required of public companies, and the responsibilities for those disclosures, under the federal securities laws [Section 101(e)(1)]. Three members of the Board will have a general background, and two members will have an accountancy background. (The Board's Chairperson may have an accountancy background, but if so, he or she may not have been a practicing accountant for at least five years prior to appointment to the Board.)

Board members are to be appointed by the SEC after consultation with the Federal Reserve Board and the Department of the Treasury. [Section 101(e)(4)] They will serve full-time, for five-year (staggered) terms, with a two-term limit. To further assure their independence, Board members may engage in no other business activities of any nature, or receive any payments from any accounting firms (except for standard retirement payments) or other persons. In addition, former Board members will be subject to a one-year "cooling off" period at the end of their Board service, during which time they may not work for an accounting firm registered with the Board.

It is essential that the Board have a strong, well-trained, and experienced staff, of sufficient size to carry out its responsibilities. A number of witnesses emphasized, for example, that inspections must no longer be left to "peer reviews" of one accounting firm by another. The bill makes it plain, as the Committee intends, that the Board is to provide for staff salaries that are fully competitive with those for comparable private-sector self-regulatory, accounting, technical, supervisory, or related staff or management positions.[12] ***

*B. Registration of accounting firms* [Section 102]

Accounting firms that audit public companies must register with the Board, no later than six months after the SEC determines that the Board is ready to begin operation. It is unlawful for a firm that has not registered to continue to audit public companies. [Section 102(a)]

Conditioning eligibility to audit public companies on registration with the Board is the linchpin of the Board's authority. Suspension or revocation of registration renders a firm unable to continue its public company audit practice.

As part of its registration process, each accounting firm must execute a consent to comply with any requests, within the Board's authority, for documents or testimony made in the course of the Board's operation. The firm must also agree to obtain (and ultimately, if necessary, to enforce) similar consents from the firm's partners and employees, who are subject to the Board's investigative and disciplinary jurisdiction. [Section 102(b)(3)]

Certain necessary information is to accompany the registration materials (including a list of the firm's accountants who perform public company audits), and the Board will determine within 45 days of receipt whether an application is complete and the applicant can be registered. Basic registration information is to be public, but each accounting firm may protect from public disclosure information that it reasonably identifies as proprietary or that is otherwise protected by law. Each registrant is to file a report annually to update the required information.

The Board is to assess a registration fee, and an annual fee, to recover the costs of processing and reviewing applications and annual reports. [Section 102(f)]

*C. Auditing, quality control, ethics, and independence standards and rules* [Section 103]

The bill requires the Board to establish or adopt auditing, quality control, and ethics standards for the audit of public companies.***

The Board's standard-setting authority, however, is neither intended nor structured to exclude practicing accountants from participation in the standard-setting process. The Board may adopt as part of its rules (and modify as appropriate for that purpose, at the time of adoption or thereafter), any portion of a statement of auditing, quality control, or ethics standards that meets the bill's statutory tests and that is proposed (i) by a professional group of accountants (designated by a rule of the Board for that purpose), or (ii) by one or more advisory groups of practicing accountants or other interested parties convened by the Board. (Pre-existing standards of designated professional groups of

12. The Board itself will be a corporation created under the D.C. Nonprofit Corporation Act. It will be neither an agency nor establishment of the federal government, and its members and employees are not to be deemed to be federal officers or employees by reason of their Board service. [Section 101(b)]

accountants may be adopted during the Board's transitional period.) [Section 103(a)] The Board is to cooperate on an ongoing basis with the designated professional groups of accountants noted above, with its own advisory groups, and with other interested groups (and the accounting profession and the investing public at large), in examining the need for changes in any standards subject to Board authority. [Section 103(c)] It is to recommend issues for inclusion on the agendas of these groups, take other steps to facilitate the standard-setting process, and respond in a timely fashion to requests for changes in the standards. Finally, rules are open to comment by accountants and any other interested persons in a public process before they are approved either by the Board or, ultimately, by the SEC. ***

*Particular Standards Required by the Bill.* Although the Board's power to establish or adopt auditing and related standards extends to the full range of those standards, the bill specifies certain provisions that must be part of the standards. These include (i) preparation, and maintenance for at least seven years, by public company auditors of audit work papers and related information in sufficient detail to support each audit's conclusions, (ii) "second partner" review and approval of each public company audit report and its issuance, and (iii) inclusion in each audit report of a description of the auditor's testing of the public company's systems for compliance with the requirements of section 13(b)(2) of the Securities Exchange Act and of the company's controls over its receipts and expenditures, together with specific notation of any significant defects or material noncompliance of which the auditor should know on the basis of such testing. [Section 103(a)(2)(A)] In addition, the quality control standards adopted by the Board must address an accounting firm's monitoring of ethics and independence; internal and external consulting on audit issues; audit supervision; hiring, development, and advancement of audit personnel; acceptance and continuance of engagements; and internal inspection. [Section 103(a)(2)(B)

*Auditor Independence.* The Board is also authorized to issue rules to implement the provisions of title II of the bill relating to auditor independence. That authority is discussed in greater detail in connection with title II, below.

*D. Inspections of registered accounting firms* [Section 104]

***The Board is to inspect the operations of each registered accounting firm, in order to assess compliance of that firm, and of its partners and employees, with the new statute, the Board's rules, and professional accounting standards. Initially, firms that audit more than 100 public companies are to be inspected each year, and firms that audit 100 or fewer public companies are to be inspected at least every three years. [Section 104(b)] The Board is given the power to adjust these inspection schedules if it finds different schedules to be consistent with the bill's purposes, the protection of investors, and the public interest.

During an inspection, the Board is to review particular audit engagements (that it selects) of a firm and the firm's general quality control systems and policies, as well as to perform such other testing of the firm's audit, supervisory, and quality control procedures as is necessary or appropriate. The Board is specifically given authority to require firms to retain their records for inspection purposes regardless of whether retention of those records is otherwise required.

After each inspection, the Board will prepare an inspection report, which will be available for comment in draft form by the firm under inspection. Quality control defects found by the Board may be disposed of simply by corrective action, but specific violations identified during inspections may form the basis for a more formal investigation or disciplinary action by the Board and are to be reported, if appropriate, to the SEC and relevant state accountancy boards; final inspection reports are to be sent to the SEC and relevant state accountancy boards in any event. [Section 104(c) and (g)] The reports will also be made public, subject to appropriate protection of confidential or proprietary information. However, firms will be given 12 months to correct defects in their quality control systems, to the satisfaction of the Board, before portions of the reports dealing with those defects are added to the public record. [Section 104(g)(2)]

*E. Investigations and disciplinary proceedings* [Section 105]

Committee witnesses stressed that the Board must possess investigative and disciplinary authority. Arthur Levitt, who served as Chairman of the SEC during most of the 1990s, told the Committee that:

> We need a truly independent oversight body that has the power not only to set the standards by which audits are performed, but also to conduct timely investigations that cannot be deferred for any reason and to discipline accountants.

Robert Glauber, the Chairman and CEO of the National Association of Securities Dealers, explained that:

> Any form of private-sector regulation must be empowered to effectively enforce the rules: [it must possess] the ability to levy meaningful fines, place conditions on continued participation in the industry, suspend, and where appropriate, banish those who misbehave from the industry. This "ultimate sanction" is both a powerful deterrent for would-be violators and an important investor protection.

***In response, the bill grants the Board broad authority to investigate any act or practice, or omission, by a registered accounting firm, or its associated persons, that may violate the new statute, the Board's rules, professional accounting standards, or the portions of the Federal securities laws (and SEC rules) relating to the preparation and issuance of audit reports and the obligations and liabilities of accountants with respect to those reports.

The Board's rules are to prescribe fair investigative and disciplinary procedures. [Section 105(a)] It may, under those rules, require testimony or the production of audit work papers and other documents from (and may inspect the records of) registered firms or their associated persons, and it may suspend or revoke the registration of a firm, or suspend or bar from further association with a firm an "associated person," for non-cooperation with a Board investigation, subject to review of that action by the SEC.[18] [Section 105(b)(3)(A)]

Committee witnesses also emphasized that information gathered by Board investigators should be "privileged from outsiders" during the investigative process. Under the bill, any information gathered in the course of an investigation is to be confidential and privileged for all purposes (including civil discovery), unless and until particular information is presented in connection with a public proceeding. However, the Board may disclose investigative information, if it determines that such disclosure is "necessary to accomplish the purposes of the Act or to protect investors," to the SEC, any federal financial supervisor (if the investigation pertains to an institution under the latter's supervision), the Attorney General, and, with the SEC's permission, to state attorneys general, in connection with criminal investigations, or state accountancy boards. (The Board may also refer an investigation to the SEC or other agencies to which disclosure of information is permitted.) [Section 105(b)(4)]

A full range of sanctions is available if the Board finds that a registered firm (or its partners or employees) has violated one or more of the rules within the Board's investigative jurisdiction. Potential sanctions include revocation or suspension of an accounting firm's registration, or of the ability of particular individuals to remain associated with that firm or become associated with any other registered accounting firm (effectively barring the subject of the sanction from participating in audits of public companies), substantial civil money penalties,[19] required professional education or training, and censure; the breadth of these sanctions is intended to encourage flexible and appropriate action, designed to correct if possible. [Section 105(c)(4)] The Board's ability to suspend or bar an associated person from the auditing of public companies, and its ability to impose civil money penalties above a certain amount, is limited to situations involving intentional, knowing, or reckless conduct, or repeated negligent conduct. [Section 105(c)(5)]

An important provision of the bill permits the Board to impose sanctions upon a registered accounting firm for failure reasonably to supervise a partner or employee who is found to have violated applicable rules. The terms for liability for failure to supervise are similar to those that apply to broker-dealers under section 15(b)(4) of the Securities Exchange Act of 1934; they permit an accounting firm to defend itself from supervisory liability by showing that its internal control procedures were reasonable and were operating fully in the situation at issue. [Section 105(c)(6)]

The Board's determination that a violation has occurred and that a sanction should be imposed may be appealed to the Commission (as described

---

18. The Board may request, but not require, the testimony of, or production of documents, in the possession of any other person (for example, an audit firm's client). Its rules may provide for procedures to seek issuance of a subpoena from the SEC to any person.

19. Fines imposed by the Board are to be used to fund a scholarship program for students in undergraduate or graduate programs in accounting. [See Section 109(c)(2)]

below). Disciplinary sanctions must be reported to the Commission, appropriate state or foreign boards of accountancy, and the public (once any stay of enforcement pending appeal has been lifted). [Section 105(d)]

*F. Foreign public accounting firms* [Section 106]

***[A]ccounting firms organized under the laws of countries other than the United States that issue audit reports for public companies subject to the U.S. securities laws are covered by the bill in the same manner as domestic accounting firms, subject to the exemptive authority of both the Board and the SEC. (Registration under the bill will not in itself provide a basis for subjecting a foreign accounting firm to U.S. jurisdiction other than with respect to controversies between such a firm and the Board.) ***

*G. SEC Oversight of the Board* [Section 107]

The Board is subject to SEC oversight and review to assure that the Board's policies are consistent with the administration of the federal securities laws, and to protect the rights of accounting firms and individuals subject to the Board's jurisdiction. Oversight also allows the public an important forum for commenting on Board rules relating to auditing, quality control, and related standards.

The rules for SEC oversight of the Board are generally the same as those that apply to SEC oversight of the National Association of Securities Dealers, under section 19 of the Securities Exchange Act. Thus, the Board's proposed rules will be filed with the SEC and published by the SEC for public comment; SEC approval is necessary in most cases before rules of the Board take effect, and the SEC may itself abrogate or amend Board rules (as well as disapprove proposed Board rules). [Section 107(b)(4)] (Transitional rules are to be separately approved by the SEC at the time of the SEC's determination that the Board is ready to begin operation.) Disciplinary sanctions imposed by the Board are subject to SEC review and may be canceled or modified (or in some cases enhanced) by the SEC. [Section 107(c)(2)] The SEC can relieve the Board of any responsibility to enforce any provision of the bill, or censure or limit operations of the Board, or remove a Board member, for cause. [Section 107(d)] Finally, the bill makes clear that any violations of its terms will constitute a violation of the Securities Exchange Act itself for purposes of the SEC's enforcement (including injunctive and cease-and-desist) authority under that Act, so that the SEC may proceed under the bill's provisions directly if appropriate.

*H. Accounting principles* [Section 108]

Since 1973, the SEC has generally required public companies operating in the United States to prepare their financial statements in accordance with "principles, standards, and practices" promulgated by the Financial Accounting Standards Board (the "FASB") in the absence of specific SEC pronouncements on particular accounting questions. The bill seeks to formalize the SEC's reliance on the FASB and, as discussed below, to strengthen the independence of the FASB by assuring its funding and eliminating any need for it to seek contributions from accounting firms or companies whose financial statements must conform to FASB's rules. ***

*I. Funding* [Section 109]

The Committee's witnesses overwhelmingly agreed that both the Board and the FASB required guaranteed sources of funding, in order to protect their independence. Several witnesses testified to the problems various attempts at oversight of auditors had encountered when voluntary funding was withheld. With respect to the FASB, Michael Sutton, a former SEC Chief Accountant, testified to the Committee that "[t]o restore confidence in our standards setters, we should take immediate steps to secure independent funding for the FASB—funding that does not depend on contributions from constituents that have a stake in the outcome of the process."

Under the bill, public companies are required to pay "accounting support fees" to support the annual budgets of the Board and the FASB. [Section 109(c)] (The Board's budget will be subject to approval by the SEC.) Amounts payable by public companies to either body will generally be allocated among those companies based on relative average annual monthly market capitalization for the 12 months prior to the year to which the support fee relates; both the Board and the FASB are permitted to differentiate among various classes of public companies in allocating fees.

TITLE II—AUDITOR INDEPENDENCE

The issue of auditor independence is at the center of this legislation. Public confidence in the integrity of financial statements of publicly-traded companies is based on belief in the independence of the auditor from the audit client. As noted above, each of the country's federal securities laws requires comprehensive financial statements that must be prepared, in the words of the Securities Act of 1933, by "an *independent* public or certified accountant."

The statutory independent audit requirement has two sides. It grants a franchise to the nation's public accountants—their services, and only their services, and certification, must be secured before an issuer of securities can go to market, have the securities listed on the nation's stock exchanges, or comply with the reporting requirements of the securities laws. This is a source of significant private benefit to the public accountants.

But the franchise is conditional. It comes in return for the CPA's assumption of a public duty and obligation. As a unanimous Supreme Court noted nearly 20 years ago:

> In certifying the public reports that collectively depict a corporation's financial status, the independent auditor assumes a *public* responsibility. *** [That auditor] owes ultimate allegiance to the corporation's creditors and stockholders, as well as to the investing public. This 'public watchdog' function demands that the accountant maintain total independence from the client at all times and requires complete fidelity to the public trust.

*United States* v. *Arthur Young,* 465 U.S. 805, 817–18 (1984) (emphasis added).

*** There is arguably an inherent conflict in the fact that an auditor is paid by the company for which the audit is being performed. That conflict is implicit in the relationship between the auditor and the audit client. In the last 15 years, however, the rapid growth in management consulting services offered by the major accounting firms has created a second, more substantial conflict that has eroded the independence that the auditor must bring to the audit function.

According to the SEC, 55 percent of the average revenue of the big five accounting firms came from accounting and auditing services in 1988. Twenty-two percent of the average revenue came from management consulting services. By 1999, those figures had fallen to 31 percent for accounting and auditing services, and risen to 50 percent for management consulting services. Recent data reported to the SEC showed on average public accounting firms' non-audit fees comprised 73 percent of their total fees, or $2.69 in non-audit fees for every $1.00 in audit fees. At the same time, the frequency of financial restatements by public companies has dramatically increased. From 1990–97, the number of public company financial restatements averaged 49 per year, but jumped to an average of 150 per year in 1999 and 2000.

For these reasons, the bill includes a number of provisions directed to the issue of auditor independence.

*A. Services outside the scope of practice of auditors* [Section 201, adding Section 10A(g) to the Exchange Act]

A number of the witnesses who testified before the Committee during the course of the hearings, as well as other informed observers, argued that the growth in the non-audit consulting business done by the large accounting firms for their audit clients has so compromised the independence of the audits that a complete prohibition is required on the provision of consulting services by accounting firms to their audit clients. ***

The Committee considered adopting a complete prohibition on non-audit services by accounting firms for their audit clients, but instead decided on a somewhat more flexible approach.***

The bill provides that it shall be unlawful for a public accounting firm registered with the Board which performs an audit for a public company to provide, contemporaneously with the audit, the following non-audit services:

(1) bookkeeping or other services related to the accounting records or financial statements of the audit client;

(2) financial information systems design and implementation;

(3) appraisal or valuation services, fairness opinions, or contribution-in-kind reports;

(4) actuarial services;

(5) internal audit outsourcing services;

(6) management functions or human resources;

(7) broker or dealer, investment adviser, or investment banking services;

(8) legal services and expert services unrelated to the audit; and

(9) any other services that the Board determines, by regulation, is impermissible.

[Section 102(a), Exchange Act Section 10A(g)]

The Board may, on a case-by-case basis, exempt any person, issuer, public accounting firm, or transaction from the prohibition on the provision of non-audit services to the extent that such exemption is necessary or appropriate in the public interest and is consistent with the protection of investors. [Section 201(b)] A registered public accounting firm may engage in any non-audit service, including tax services, that is not on the list for an audit client only if the activity is approved in advance by the audit committee of the issuer. [Section 201(a), Exchange Act Section 10A(h)] No limitations are placed on accounting firms in providing non-audit services to public companies which they do not audit or to any nonpublic companies. ***

In summary, the bill adopts a strong, balanced approach to assure that in return for the significant private benefits conferred on accounting firms by our securities laws, they maintain their independence from the companies they audit and fulfill their "public trust."

*B. Audit committee pre-approval of audit and non-audit services* [Section 202, Exchange Act Section 10A(i)]

The legislation requires that audit services, as well as non-audit services other than those proscribed by the bill, must be pre-approved by the audit committee of the public company's board of directors. The Committee heard testimony on the role that the audit committee of a public company should play in connection with the engagement of an auditor to provide audit and non-audit services contemporaneously. ***

After studying this issue, the Committee believes the protection of investors warrants a requirement that a public company's audit committee approve in advance the services that the auditor will provide to such company (if those services are not explicitly prohibited under the bill). Accordingly, the bill requires the audit committee of a public company to pre-approve all of the services, both audit and non-audit, provided to that company by a registered public accounting firm. The bill does not require an issuer's audit committee to pre-approve non-audit services provided by an accounting firm that is not auditing the issuer.

*C. Audit partner rotation* [Section 203, Exchange Act Section 10A(j)]

The Committee heard testimony from numerous witnesses on whether, in order to maintain the objectivity of its audits, an issuer should be required to rotate its audit firm after a number of consecutive years. ***

The Committee determined that the possibility of requiring audit firm rotation merits further study. The bill directs the U.S. General Accounting Office ("GAO") to analyze the merits and potential effects of requiring mandatory rotation of auditors, and to report its analysis to Congress within one year. [Section 207]

While the bill does not require issuers to rotate their accounting firms, the Committee recognizes the strong benefits that accrue for the issuer and its shareholders when a new accountant "with fresh and skeptical eyes" evaluates the issuer periodically. Accordingly, the bill requires a registered public accounting firm to rotate its lead partner and its review partner on audits so that neither role is performed by the same accountant for the same issuer for more than five consecutive years. ***

*D. Disclosure of Accounting Issues* [Section 204, Exchange Act Section 10A(k)]

The Committee believes that it is important for the audit committee to be aware of key assumptions underlying a company's financial statements and of disagreements that the auditor has with management. The audit committee should be informed in a timely manner of such disagreements, so that it can independently review them and intervene if it chooses to do so in order to assure the integrity of the audit.

Accordingly, the bill requires a registered independent public accounting firm performing an audit for a public company to report in a timely manner to that company's audit committee (1) the critical accounting policies and practices to be used; (2) all alternative treatments of financial information within GAAP (generally accepted accounting principles) that have been discussed with management; (3) any accounting disagreements between the auditor and management; and (4) other material written communications between the auditor and management.

*E. Cooling off period* [Section 206, Exchange Act Section 10A(*l*)]

The Committee received extensive testimony on whether to impose a cooling off period between an accountant's employment by an auditor and his or her employment by an issuer.***

The Committee considered various options, including imposing a cooling off period of one, two, or three years, and applying a cooling off period to all employees who worked for the auditor, regardless of whether they worked on the audit of a particular issuer and regardless of the position they would take with that issuer, or applying a cooling off period only to certain groups of employees.

The Committee decided to impose a one-year cooling off period that would apply to an employee of the accounting firm who worked on the issuer's audit and subsequently seeks to be employed by that issuer in a senior management capacity. Thus, the bill provides that an accounting firm may not provide audit services for a public company if that company's chief executive officer, controller, chief financial officer, chief accounting officer, or other individual serving in an equivalent position, was employed by the accounting firm during the one year before the start of the audit services. ***

*F. The bill does not create state regulatory standards* [Section 209]

Titles I and II are designed to apply only to accounting firms that audit public companies. They are not designed to apply to audits of private companies. Nonetheless, some have raised the concern that the bill could lead state regulatory authorities to impose similar requirements for audits of private companies.

The bill indicates clearly that Congress does not intend that state regulatory authorities should find this Act controlling in their regulation of non-registered accountants. The bill states that it is the intention of the Act that, in supervising non-registered accounting firms, state regulatory authorities should make an independent determination of the proper standards, and should not presume the standards applied by the Board under this bill to be applicable to small- and medium-sized non-registered accounting firms. ***

### NOTES AND QUESTIONS

1. ***SEC Attention to the "Numbers Game."*** Arthur Andersen's role in the collapse of Enron, as well as other high-profile accounting scandals in the early 2000s, brought never before seen public scrutiny to the accounting profession. Yet concerns about accountants' ethics or, even more precisely, the ethics of auditors, were building throughout the 1990s. This momentum is evidenced in part by former SEC Chairperson Arthur Levitt's vow to bring an end to "the numbers game," and by former SEC Enforcement Division Director Richard Walker's pledge to make "combating financial fraud [his] number one priority." See Speech of SEC Chairperson Arthur Levitt, The Numbers Game, (Sept. 28, 1998); SEC Enforcement: Accounting Fraud is Top Priority, Enforcement Officials Tell CPAs, 30 Sec. Reg. & L. Rep. 1757 (BNA) (Dec. 11, 1998). Many of the reforms suggested by Chairperson Levitt, however, were never able to get off the ground. Why might this have been so? Do reforms mandated by Congress send an even more powerful message to the industry? What if the specific reforms are dictated by the Public Company Accounting Oversight Board (the "Board" or the "PCAOB") rather than by Congress or the SEC?

2. ***The PCAOB and the State Action Doctrine.*** As we saw in Chapter 9.E in connection with SRO enforcement in the securities industry, academics and litigants often have challenged the characterization of the NASD and NYSE as "private actors." Courts, however, have generally refused to view the NASD and NYSE as "state actors," at least insofar as the challenge involved a broker's claim of a Fifth Amendment privilege against self-incrimination. See e.g., *United States v. Solomon*, 509 F.2d 863 (2d Cir. 1975), set out in Chapter 9.E.2 supra. What are the similarities between the PCAOB and the NASD or NYSE? What are the principal differences? In the event of litigation challenging PCAOB action as state action, are these differences likely to affect a court's analysis?

What weight should be given to Section 101(b) of the Sarbanes-Oxley Act, which states that "[t]he Board shall not be an agency or establishment of the United States Government," and that "[n]o member or person employed by, or agent for, the Board shall be deemed to be an officer or employee of or agent for the Federal Government by reason of such service"? In answering this question, consider the Supreme Court's analysis in *Lebron v. Nat'l RR. Pass. Corp.*, 513 U.S. 374 (1995). There the Court confronted Amtrak's authorizing statute, which declared that Amtrak "will not be an agency or establishment of the United States Government." Id. at 391 (quoting 84 Stat. 1330). The Court held as follows:

> [I]t is not for Congress to make the final determination of Amtrak's status as a Government entity for purposes of determining the constitutional rights of citizens affected by its actions. If Amtrak is, by its very nature, what the Constitution regards as the Government, congressional pronouncement that it is not such can no more relieve it of its First Amendment restrictions than a similar pronouncement could exempt the Federal Bureau of Investigation from the Fourth Amendment. The Constitution constrains governmental action "by whatever instruments or in whatever modes that action may be taken." *Ex parte*

> *Virginia*, 100 U.S. 339, 346-347 (1880). And under whatever congressional label. As we said of the Reconstruction Finance Corporation in deciding whether debts owed it were owed the United States Government: "That the Congress chose to call it a corporation does not alter its characteristics so as to make it something other than what it actually is...." *Cherry Cotton Mills, Inc. v. United States*, 327 U.S. 536, 539 (1946).

*Lebron*, supra, 513 U.S. at 392-93.

If a court concluded that actions by the PCAOB constituted state action, which provisions of the Sarbanes-Oxley Act would be most susceptible to constitutional challenge? In this regard, consider the manner in which PCAOB members are appointed. Consider also the consents that must be executed by partners and employees of an accounting firm as part of the registration process.

***3. The Reach of the PCAOB's Authority.*** The Senate Report suggested that auditors may have overlooked so many accounting frauds in the late 1990s and early 2000s, in part because of the way that accounting firms compensate their partners for obtaining and keeping large clients. And the audit partner rotation rule in new Exchange Act Section 10A(j) was designed to address this problem. Should the PCAOB also regulate compensation systems in firms that audit public companies? How so? Should audit fees be fixed by the PCAOB rather than by private agreement between auditor and client? Would the Board need additional statutory authorization to regulate such fees? Consider also that some European jurisdictions require public companies to rotate their auditors every few years. Should the Board adopt such a requirement? Does it have the statutory authorization to do so?

***4. Reducing the Incidence of Securities Fraud.*** Did the scandals at Enron and WorldCom result from the failure of auditing standards? Congress apparently thought so, but others disagree and question whether the PCAOB will be able to modify accounting standards to prevent abuses:

> [O]ne can find few instances of independent auditors colluding with companies to defraud investors. Instead, auditors were usually defrauded in almost all instances. Although imposing more stringent audit standards on auditors might reduce attempts by some to defraud auditors, we must acknowledge that tougher standards will not necessarily prevent fraud. In implementing the goals of [the Sarbanes-Oxley Act], the PCAOB needs to make certain that individual accountants and their firms are not unduly burdened by and even punished for their clients' acts. Moreover, the Act fails to take into consideration the significant additional costs companies will have to bear to pay for additional internal and external audit services, as well as fees payable to fund the PCAOB. Although discovering financial fraud in early stages is undoubtedly beneficial to all, it is still too early to see whether this effort will actually effectively prevent fraud.

Neil H. Aronson, Preventing Future Enrons: Implementing the Sarbanes-Oxley Act of 2002, 8 Stan. J. L. Bus. & Fin. 127, 135 (2002). Which provisions in the Sarbanes-Oxley Act are designed specifically to bolster an auditor's ability to discover fraud in its early stages?

***5. Ancillary Services for Auditing Clients.*** In the 1990s, the SEC sought to increase the independence of accountants by restricting an auditing firm's ability to provide ancillary services such as consulting to auditing clients of the firm. The SEC, however, received heavy pressure from various members of Congress not to restrict these ancillary services. The tide then turned after the Enron collapse, and Section 10A(g) of the Exchange Act now imposes restrictions almost identical to those that the SEC had been considering years before. How likely is it that ancillary services will distort incentives to provide a truly independent audit? Are there ways in which providing ancillary services to an audit client might improve the quality of an audit? What types of ancillary services, if any, are likely to be given Board approval pursuant to the exemptive authority provided by Section 201(b) of the Sarbanes-Oxley Act?

***6. SEC Rules Regarding Auditor Independence.*** Section 208 of the Sarbanes-Oxley Act required the Commission, not later than 180 days after the Act's enactment, to "issue final regulations to carry out each of the subsections (g) through (*l*) of Section 10A" of the Exchange Act. In January 2003, the SEC adopted rules consistent with this directive. These new rules:

> revise the Commission's regulations related to the non-audit services that, if provided to an audit client, would impair an accounting firm's independence; require that an issuer's audit committee pre-approve all audit and non-audit services provided to the issuer by the auditor of an issuer's financial statements; prohibit certain partners on the audit engagement team from providing audit services to the issuer for more than five or seven consecutive years, depending on the partner's involvement in the audit, except that certain small accounting firms may be exempted from this requirement; prohibit an accounting firm from auditing an issuer's financial statements if certain members of management of that issuer had been members of the accounting firm's audit engagement team within the one-year period preceding the commencement of audit procedures; require that the auditor of an issuer's financial statements report certain matters to the issuer's audit committee, including "critical" accounting policies used by the issuer; and require disclosures to investors of information related to audit and non-audit services provided by, and fees paid to, the auditor of the issuer's financial statements. In addition, under the final rules, an accountant would not be independent from an audit client if an audit partner received compensation based on selling engagements to that client for services other than audit, review and attest services.

Final Rule: Strengthening the Commission's Requirements Regarding Auditor Independence, Exchange Act Release No. 47265, 2003 WL 183801 at *1 (Jan. 28, 2003). The rules become effective on May 6, 2003.

# Chapter 11

# CRIMINAL ENFORCEMENT

The Department of Justice (DOJ) has exclusive authority over criminal enforcement of the federal securities laws. In bringing securities prosecutions, the DOJ typically operates through U.S. Attorney's Offices throughout the United States.

While criminal securities actions are more numerous than they used to be, they have changed in another respect as well. Indeed, prior to the 1980s, criminal securities actions rarely posed novel questions of substantive securities law. Rather, they typically involved the application of well-settled principles previously established in SEC or private actions. See, e.g., *United States v. Gleason,* 616 F.2d 2, 28 (2d Cir. 1979) (applying civil precedent on the meaning of materiality); *United States v. Cook,* 573 F.2d 281, 283 (5th Cir. 1978) (applying civil precedent on extraterritoriality); *United States v. Charnay*, 537 F.2d 341, 348-49 (9th Cir. 1976) (applying civil precedent as to what constitutes manipulation). But beginning in the 1980s, the DOJ became more willing to bring securities actions with the capacity to break new legal ground. See, e.g., *Chiarella v. United States,* 445 U.S. 222 (1980) (government favors broad view of the duty to abstain or disclose to hold "outsider" liable for insider trading); *Carpenter v. United States,* 484 U.S. 19 (1987) (government urges acceptance of the misappropriation theory of insider trading); *United States v. O'Hagan,* 521 U.S. 642 (1997) (same). See also *United States v. Bingham,* 992 F.2d 975, 976 (9th Cir. 1993) (government supports adoption of two per se rules regarding materiality); *United States v. Chestman,* 947 F.2d 551, 569 (2d Cir. 1991) (government favors liberal definition of the trust relationship that is critical to the misappropriation theory); *United States v. Holtzclaw,* 950 F. Supp. 1306, 1313-14 (S.D. W. Va. 1997) (government favors a definition of the term "investment contract" as to which the circuits are divided), aff'd in part, vacated in part on other grounds, 131 F.3d 137 (4th Cir. 1997).

What accounts for the enhanced use of criminal securities actions? There are at least two (by no means mutually exclusive) explanations. One is that in the wake of the insider trading scandals that beset Wall Street in the 1980s, the DOJ became intrigued by substantive securities law issues. See Harvey L. Pitt & Karen L. Shapiro, Securities Regulation by Enforcement: A Look Ahead at the Next Decade, 7 Yale J. on Reg. 149, 219-20 (1990). The other is the perception that criminal securities actions are a potent deterrent. See John C. Coffee, Jr., Does "Unlawful" Mean "Criminal"? Reflections on the Disappearing Tort/Crime Distinction in American Law, 71 B.U. L. Rev. 193, 238 (1991) ("public authorities get a bigger bang for the buck" with criminal actions).

Congress expressed confidence in the deterrent impact of criminal securities actions with its enactment of the Sarbanes-Oxley Act of 2002.

Precipitated by the scandals at Enron, WorldCom, and other large companies, that Act sets forth new securities crimes and in addition provides stiffer penalties for some securities crimes already on the books.

To be sure, federal judges lack the discretion simply to impose the stiffer penalties that are now authorized. Rather, they must conform their sentences to the guidelines adopted by the United States Sentencing Commission. See generally *Mistretta v. United States,* 488 U.S. 361 (1989) (upholding the constitutionality of the sentencing guidelines); Matthew J. Berman et al., Sentencing Guidelines, 90 Geo. L. J. 1753 (2002). Consistent with this reality, the Sarbanes-Oxley Act directs the Sentencing Commission to "promptly review the sentencing guidelines applicable to securities and accounting fraud and related offenses" and to "ensure that the sentencing guidelines and policy statements reflect the serious nature of securities, pension, and accounting fraud and the need for aggressive and appropriate law enforcement action to prevent such offenses." Section 1104 of the Sarbanes-Oxley Act.

This Chapter is divided into four sections. Section A examines crimes created by the Securities Act and the Exchange Act, while Section B examines crimes created by the Sarbanes-Oxley Act. Sections C and D address two other criminal statutes which come into play when securities transactions are at issue—the federal mail and wire fraud statutes (Section C) and the Racketeer Influenced and Corrupt Organizations Act (Section D). For all of these statutes, criminal enforcement authority lies with the DOJ, to which the Commission frequently refers cases that it deems worthy of prosecution.

As you read this Chapter, ask yourself whether the new crimes created by the Sarbanes-Oxley Act are apt to reduce the likelihood that debacles such as those at Enron and WorldCom will occur again. In this regard, note that convictions require proof beyond a reasonable doubt. See *In re Winship,* 397 U.S. 358, 361-62 (1970).

More generally, consider to what extent the criminalizing of securities violations represents an effective means of taming corporate misconduct. Some scholars argue that when merely economic crimes are criminalized, the criminal sanction tends to lose its stigma. See Sanford H. Kadish, Some Observations on the Use of Criminal Sanctions in Enforcing Economic Regulations, 30 U. Chi. L. Rev. 423, 437 (1963). Other scholars reply that the public regards as criminal whatever society brands as criminal. See Harry V. Ball & Lawrence M. Friedman, The Use of Criminal Sanctions in the Enforcement of Economic Legislation: A Sociological View, 17 Stan. L. Rev. 197, 216 (1965). Might both of these positions be valid simultaneously? See John C. Coffee, Jr., Hush!: The Criminal Status of Confidential Information After *McNally* and *Carpenter* and the Enduring Problem of Overcriminalization, 26 Am. Crim. L. Rev. 121, 149 (1988).

## A. THE SECURITIES ACT AND THE EXCHANGE ACT

The only criminal provision in the Securities Act is Section 24, which reads as follows:

> Any person who willfully violates any of the provisions of this act, or the rules and regulations promulgated by the Commission under authority thereof, or any person who willfully, in a registration statement filed under this Act, makes any

> untrue statement of a material fact or omits to state any material fact required to be stated therein or necessary to make the statements therein not misleading, shall upon conviction be fined not more than $10,000 or imprisoned not more than five years, or both.

Observe that Section 24 piggybacks onto the Securities Act's substantive provisions and rules, authorizing criminal liability when one of those provisions or rules is "willfully" violated.

The same piggybacking approach is evident in Section 24's counterpart, Section 32(a) of the Exchange Act. As you read Section 32(a), note its use of "willfully and knowingly" as well as "willfully" and also its final clause (known as the "no knowledge" clause):

> Any person who willfully violates any provision of this Act (other than section 30A), or any rule or regulation thereunder the violation of which is made unlawful or the observance of which is required under the terms of this Act, or any person who willfully and knowingly makes, or causes to be made, any statement in any application, report, or document required to be filed under this Act or any rule or regulation thereunder or any undertaking contained in a registration statement as provided in subsection (d) of section 15 of this Act or by any self-regulatory organization in connection with an application for membership or participation therein or to become associated with a member thereof, which statement was false or misleading with respect to any material fact, shall upon conviction be fined not more than $5,000,000 or imprisoned not more than 20 years, or both, except that when such person is a person other than a natural person, a fine not exceeding $25,000,000 may be imposed; but no person shall be subject to imprisonment under this section for the violation of any rule or regulation if he proves that he had no knowledge of such rule or regulation.

The penalties set forth in Section 32(a) are the product of an amendment enacted as part of the Sarbanes-Oxley Act. Prior to that Act, Section 32(a) authorized fines for a natural person of not more than $1,000,000 and imprisonment for not more than 10 years; other defendants could be fined no more than $2,500,000. (The Sarbanes-Oxley Act left untouched the criminal penalties set forth in Section 24 of the Securities Act).

As Sections 24 and 32(a) make apparent, a defendant can be convicted under the Securities Act or the Exchange Act only if he commits his violation "willfully." We begin with the meaning of "willfully," and then consider the provisions and rules the violation of which can give rise to criminal liability.

### *1. The Requirement that the Defendant Act "Willfully"*

While both the Securities Act and the Exchange Act condition criminal liability on proof that the defendant acted "willfully," neither Act defines that term. The legislative history of each is likewise silent. To be sure, the term "willfully" is commonplace in federal criminal statutes. See Sharon L. Davies, The Jurisprudence of Willfulness: An Evolving Theory of Excusable Ignorance, 48 Duke L. J. 341, 420-27 (1998) (listing such statutes). But the term has no generally accepted definition that can simply be imported into the Securities Act or the Exchange Act. Cf. *Bryan v. United States,* 524 U.S. 184, 191 (1998) (describing "willfully" as a "word of many meanings" (quoting *Spies v. United States,* 317 U.S. 492, 497 (1943))).

The following decision provides a definition of "willfully" for purposes of Section 32(a) of the Exchange Act. Consider not only the definition but how the court arrived at it.

## UNITED STATES v. PELTZ

433 F.2d 48 (2d Cir. 1970)

FRIENDLY, CIRCUIT JUDGE:

After trial in the District Court ***, Philip Peltz, an attorney, was convicted on the four counts of an indictment ***. Count One charged that Peltz had conspired with an employee of the Securities and Exchange Commission to defraud the United States and the Commission of their rights to have their business conducted impartially and according to law and to have the securities laws administered impartially and according to their terms ***. Counts Three and Four charged willful violations of § 10(b) of the Securities Exchange Act of 1934 and *** Rule 10b-5 in that Peltz had told two brokerage houses that sales of the common stock of Georgia Pacific Corporation which he had ordered were long whereas in fact they were short. Count Five charged that Peltz willfully violated § 10(a), relating to short sales, and the Commission's Rule 10a-1(a). The court imposed four concurrent one-year sentences, three months of which were to be served in prison; the remainder of the term was suspended as to each count.

The first count charged that from about January 1, 1966, Peltz had conspired with others, including an employee of the SEC, to obtain confidential inside information about matters under consideration by the Commission and use such information for private profit. Specific mention was made of the Georgia Pacific Corporation and Peltz' sales of its stock. The proof identified the employee as Murray B. Weiner, a branch chief of the SEC's corporation finance division.

Essential background was furnished by the testimony of Ira Pearce, who at the time was a branch chief of the SEC's trading and markets division and whose integrity was not in question. On or about March 11, 1966, Pearce had recommended that the SEC bring suit against Georgia Pacific because the company had apparently been purchasing its own securities through a pension fund it controlled, thereby influencing the market for its own stock in violation of the securities laws. *** During April Weiner asked Pearce about the current status of the matter, and Pearce kept him posted as to the target date for the filing of the action. ***

On April 7, Peltz telephoned a registered representative at Bache & Co., told him he was thinking of selling 1,000 shares of Georgia Pacific which he owned because he had heard there was a lawsuit pending against the company, and directed him to sell the shares at no less than a specific price. In fact, Peltz did not own the shares at that time. On the same day, he instructed a registered representative at Loeb, Rhoades & Co. to sell 2,000 shares allegedly belonging to his mother but, according to the proof, not in fact owned by her. Four days later Weiner asked a former SEC attorney to recommend a broker for Peltz; the attorney suggested a representative at Sterling, Grace & Co., with whom Peltz placed sell orders for 300 shares as long sales. The proof again was that Peltz did not own these shares. All of Peltz' sales instructions were carried out. He made various excuses for not delivering the shares on the settlement dates but, after the SEC suit was announced and the price of Georgia Pacific fell, he borrowed enough money to enable him to cover his short sales and make a tidy profit.

The most damaging testimony against Peltz was given by a friend, Norman Horwitz, an attorney with experience in securities matters, and Horwitz' wife, Sheila, who in April 1966 was his fiancee. According to them, Peltz indicated that he had a "contact" at the SEC who had previously given him information about several companies that were to be or had been investigated by the agency. On April 14, Peltz told them, in Sheila's apartment in New York City, that he had obtained information from his "contact" at the SEC concerning proposed action against Georgia Pacific and had sold several thousand shares, but that he was having trouble "buying in" because the SEC had not made its announcement and the price of the stock had not yet dropped. Peltz then accompanied Horwitz to the latter's office and placed a call to a number identified as Weiner's residence in Maryland. After completing the call, he declared that "Everything is okay, it's going to be released in a day or two, they're working on the final papers." *** Early in May, Peltz expressed concern about being watched by the FBI and, in answer to an inquiry whether he had paid money, said he had not but "expected this fellow would be in shortly" and hoped to avoid paying or seeing him. ***

I.

*[The court in this part rejects Peltz's challenges to his conviction for conspiracy].*

II.

*** Section 32(a) of the Securities Exchange Act *** makes criminal any willful violation of any provision of the act or any rule or regulation thereunder the violation of which is made unlawful. Section 10(b) of the Act and *** Rule 10b-5 thereunder *** admittedly qualify under this test. The Government's submission was that by Peltz' assertions to Loeb, Rhoades & Co. and to Bache & Co. with respect to ownership of the stock of Georgia Pacific whose sale he directed, he willfully and knowingly made untrue statements of material facts and engaged in acts that would operate as a fraud or deceit in connection with the sale of a security.

Prima facie this would seem entirely clear. The immediate consequence of the lies was that the brokerage houses did not demand the 70% collateral required by the then applicable regulation of the Federal Reserve Board for short sales. As a result the firms were exposed to risk of serious loss when, as turned out to be the case, Peltz did not deliver the stock on the normal settlement date. Also, as we shall see, the lies caused the brokerage firms to violate § 10(a) and Rule 10a-1 relating to the price at which short sales can lawfully be made. Even though these violations of the margin and short sale rules were unwitting, the brokers were subject to possible disciplinary proceedings by the New York Stock Exchange. Despite the caveat in *SEC v. Capital Gains Research Bureau, Inc.*, 375 U.S. 180, 192 n. 40 (1963), we see no more reason for requiring proof of actual (as distinguished from potential) injury in a criminal prosecution than in a suit for an injunction in a securities fraud case.

Indeed, Peltz does not so contend. His position is rather that there can be no criminal liability for violations of § 10(b) and Rule 10b-5 "where the fraud was not related to the investment value of securities." Recognizing our decision in *A. T. Brod & Co. v. Perlow*, 375 F.2d 393, 397 (2 Cir. 1967), that the placing of purchase orders with the intent to pay only if the securities had appreciated by the settlement date gave rise to civil liability under the statute and the rule, he argues that the same words must have a narrower application in criminal prosecutions. We are not convinced of this, Herlands, Criminal Aspects of the Securities Exchange Act of 1934, 21 Va.L.Rev. 139, 162 (1934), nor do we believe that Peltz' formulation would be appropriate if any narrowing were to be done. Short selling without compliance with the margin and short sale price rules can have a materially larger adverse effect on the public than a seller's hoodwinking a buyer into an unfortunate purchase of a few hundred shares.

III.

Section 10(a) of the Securities Exchange Act of 1934 makes it unlawful "for any person, directly or indirectly, by the use *** of any facility of any national securities exchange" to effect a short sale of any security registered on a national securities exchange in contravention of such rules and regulations as the Commission may prescribe as necessary in the public interest or for the protection of investors. The Commission's Rule 10a-1(a), sometimes called the "down-tick" rule, provides:

> No person shall, for his own account or for the account of any other person, effect on a national securities exchange a short sale of any security (1) below the price at which the last sale thereof, regular way, was effected on such exchange, or (2) at such price unless such price is above the next preceding different price at which a sale of such security, regular way, was effected on such exchange.***

The Government established that Rule 10a-1(a) had been violated in the case of 1700 of the 3000 Georgia Pacific shares Peltz ordered to be sold on April 7, 1966.

Peltz' first contention, that the statute and rule apply only to brokers and dealers, requires little discussion. The statute speaks of "any person" and the intention to go beyond the "person" actually arranging the trade is made manifest by the phrase "directly or indirectly." The rule is even clearer in covering the person for whose account the sale is made as well as the person making it. We thus would have no doubt that a customer explicitly instructing a broker to make a short sale in contravention of Rule 10a-1(a) would be as much subject to criminal liability as the broker who carried out the instruction.

However, there was no evidence that Peltz gave any such instruction and we must confront the issue whether a customer "willfully" violates Rule 10a-1(a) when he deliberately makes a false statement to a broker that he owns securities directed to be sold and there is a resulting violation of the rule, because the broker, having no reason to think that the rule was applicable, failed to take the precautions that would prevent such a violation. ***

The language makes one point entirely clear. A person can willfully violate an SEC rule even if he does not know of its existence. This conclusion follows from the difference between the standard for violation of the statute or a rule or regulation, to wit, "willfully," and that for false or misleading statements, namely, "willfully and knowingly." It follows also from the proviso whereby lack of knowledge of a rule or regulation prevents imprisonment but not a fine.[7] All this was pointed out in a penetrating article written by the late Judge Herlands many years before his appointment to the federal bench, Criminal Law Aspects of the Securities Exchange Act of 1934, supra, 21 Va. L. Rev. at 148-149.

Decision that the Government need not prove knowledge of Rule 10a-1(a)[8] in order to establish criminal liability still leaves the question what mental state it must prove. The Herlands article concluded it was necessary only that "the prosecution establishes a realization on the defendant's part that he was doing a wrongful act," 21 Va. L. Rev. at 149. We accept this with the qualifications, doubtless intended by the author, that the act be wrongful under the securities laws and that the knowingly wrongful act involve a significant risk of effecting the violation that has occurred. See A.L.I. Model Penal Code, § 2.03 (1962); Study Draft of a New Federal Criminal Code, § 305 (1970).

On this analysis the court was clearly justified in submitting the § 10(a) counts to the jury under proper instructions. There was ample evidence that Peltz was aware "he was doing a wrongful act," namely, telling the brokers he was long when he knew he was not. His false statements, negating the facts that would have induced the brokers to take the requisite steps to avoid a violation of 10a-1(a), created a serious risk that such a violation would occur, as it did.

The conviction on all four counts is affirmed.

## *NOTES AND QUESTIONS*

***1. Did Congress Drop the Ball?*** The requirement that the defendant commit her violations "willfully" is an essential precondition to criminal liability under both the Securities Act and the Exchange Act. Why did Congress not provide a definition of this critical term?

***2. The Sufficiency of Recklessness.*** Some courts have adopted the definition of "willfully" upheld in *Peltz*. See, e.g., *United States v. Dixon*, 536 F.2d 1388, 1396 (2d Cir. 1976). A number of other courts, however, have held

---

7. Peltz made no effort to bring himself within this proviso.

8. Horwitz testified that on at least three occasions Peltz called him to ask "whether or not selling stock without labelling it a short sale was crime; whether it had to be done on an up tick or not." However, these calls appear to have been some weeks after the sales of April 7. Although "the subsequent existence of a fact supports the inference of its earlier existence, when the subsequent condition is one which ordinarily would not exist unless it had also existed at the earlier time," *United States v. Consolidated Laundries Corp.*, 291 F.2d 563, 569 (2 Cir. 1961), we are not at all sure that the inference here would be sufficiently strong to support a conviction if the Government was required to prove knowledge of the regulation beyond a reasonable doubt. Peltz' inquiries may well have stemmed from his concern arising from an FBI investigation.

that "willfully" can mean merely recklessly. See, e.g., *United States v. DeSantis*, 134 F.3d 760, 764 (6th Cir. 1998) (defining "willfully" to mean recklessly or knowingly for purposes of Section 32(a)); *United States v. Amick*, 439 F.2d 351, 369 (7th Cir. 1971) (holding proof of recklessness sufficient for conviction under the Securities Act). Recall that every federal appeals court to consider the issue has held that recklessness satisfies the scienter requirement under Section 10(b) of the Exchange Act and Rule 10b-5. See Chapter 2.D.1 supra. Is it important to differentiate between the state of mind requirements of civil and criminal actions? If so, why? Does the definition of "willfully" provided by *Peltz* create such a differentiation?

*3.* ***"Willfully" vs. "Knowingly."*** The *Peltz* court took the position that "willfully" must have a different meaning from "knowingly," a term which also appears in Section 32(a). Professor Loss and Dean Seligman disagree with *Peltz* on this point. They argue that "knowingly" in Section 32(a) is "redundant" of "willfully." 10 Louis Loss & Joel Seligman, Securities Regulation 4758-59 (3d rev. ed. 1996). Which position do you find more persuasive?

*4.* ***The Securities Act vs. the Exchange Act.*** The *Peltz* court gave two reasons for concluding that a defendant can act "willfully" while nonethless being unaware of the illegality of his conduct. One reason had to do with Section 32(a)'s "no knowledge" clause, while the other involved the necessity of distinguishing between "willfully" and "knowingly." Consider that Section 24 of the Securities Act contains neither a "no knowledge" clause nor the term "knowingly." What (if anything) does this suggest about how to define "willfully" for purposes of Section 24? Cf. *United States v. English,* 92 F.3d 909, 915 (9th Cir. 1996) (declining to define "willfully" in Section 24 to require knowledge of illegality based on analysis of case law); *United States v. Brown,* 578 F.2d 1280, 1284 (9th Cir. 1978) (noting that the absence of a "no knowledge" clause in Section 24 increases the difficulty of interpreting that Section). More generally, should courts use the same definition of "willfully" regardless of whether the Securities Act or the Exchange Act is at issue?

*5.* ***Different Definitions For Different Securities Crimes?*** Should courts define "willfully" differently depending upon the nature of the securities crime involved? Consider the relevance of *Ratzlaf v. United States,* 510 U.S. 135 (1994). At issue in *Ratzlaf* was whether to affirm a conviction for "willfully" violating the antistructuring provision of the Currency and Foreign Transactions Reporting Act (CFTRA) without proof that the defendant knew his conduct was illegal. Like the Securities Act and the Exchange Act, CFTRA sets forth a willfulness requirement in one provision (Section 5322) that is a prerequisite to criminal liability for violations of other provisions. To determine how to define "willfully" for purposes of the crime of antistructuring, the Court found relevant judicial definitions of "willfully" that had been used in connection with other CFTRA crimes. See id. at 141-42. The Court explained that "willfully" had to have the same meaning regardless of which crime was involved:

> A term appearing in several places in a statutory text is generally read the same way each time it appears. We have even stronger cause to construe a *single* formulation *** the same way each time it is called into play. See *United States v. Aversa*, 984 F.2d 493, 498 (CA1 1993) (en banc) ("Ascribing various meanings to a single iteration of [§ 5322(a)'s willfulness requirement]—

> reading the word differently for each code section to which it applies—would open Pandora's jar. If courts can render meaning so malleable, the usefulness of a single penalty provision for a group of related code sections will be eviscerated and ... almost any code section that references a group of other code sections would become susceptible to individuated interpretation.")

Id. at 143. Does *Ratzlaf* preclude different definitions of "willfully" for different securities crimes?

***6. Emasculating the "No Knowledge" Clause.*** Lower courts have long construed Section 32(a)'s "no knowledge" clause in a fashion that blunts its usefulness for criminal defendants. Consider the following explanation for why the clause is inapplicable to defendants convicted of violating Rule 10b-5:

> [The no knowledge clause] was adopted to ensure that no person could be imprisoned for the violation of a standard contained in a rule of which he had no knowledge. It is equally clear, however, that Congress intended to charge every man with knowledge of the standards prescribed in the securities acts themselves. It would frustrate the intent of Congress to permit a person whose conduct is expressly prohibited by statute to attempt to prove no knowledge of a parallel rule provision. Allowing these defendants to invoke the "no knowledge" clause would have precisely this effect. The conduct here admitted by defendants is prohibited by two provisions of the securities acts. Section 17(a) of the Securities Act of 1933 prohibits securities fraud in language almost identical with the language of Rule 10b-5. Moreover, the fraudulent activity to which defendants have pled guilty, price manipulation, is expressly prohibited by § 9(a)(2) of the 1934 Act. ***

*United States v. Lilley,* 291 F. Supp. 989, 992-93 (S.D. Tex. 1968). Is *Lilley's* analysis persuasive? If not, why do you suppose it has largely carried the day? In this connection, one commentator has observed that courts may resist regarding the "no knowledge" clause "as an expression of an important governmental policy, at least in a system in which the rules are regularly published and available under the Federal Register Act." Joseph E. Murphy, The Duty of the Government to Make the Law Known, 51 Fordham L. Rev. 255, 281 n. 180 (1982).

In *United States v. O'Hagan,* 521 U.S. 642, 665-66 (1997), the Supreme Court described the "no knowledge" clause as a "sturdy safeguard[ ]" for criminal defendants. Was this empty rhetoric or did the Court have an interpretation of the clause in mind different from that endorsed by *Lilley*?

***7. The "No Knowledge" Clause and Mr. Peltz.*** The *Peltz* court observed that the defendant had "made no effort to bring himself within" the "no knowledge" clause. Why do you suppose that he did not try, at least with respect to his conviction for violating Rule 10a-1?

***8. The Relevance of Strict Construction.*** Notice that the *Peltz* court declined to construe Rule 10b-5 more narrowly than it would have in a civil action. We will explore the pros and cons of so doing in the subsection of this Chapter immediately following.

### *PROBLEM 11-1*

Endring Corporation, now bankrupt, engaged in a fraudulent scheme of massive proportions that duped the market and caused huge investor losses. During the time the scheme was ongoing, Lyle was Endring's CEO. Lyle insisted that he was unaware of the fraud. He claimed that he relied on subordinates as well as on outside law and accounting firms to handle disclosure matters so that he could focus his attention on Endring's overall direction and other "big picture" items.

Several months before the fraud at Endring was uncovered, Lyle received a letter from the CFO's principal assistant (Verity), who had an extensive accounting background. In her letter, Verity warned that Endring "could soon implode" and advised Lyle to put tough questions to the CFO. When Lyle asked the CFO (Farrell) to comment on Verity's letter, Farrell dismissed the letter out of hand and claimed that Verity was upset about having been passed over for a recent promotion. Lyle did nothing further about Verity's letter. He later explained this failure to act as a function of the faith that he had in Farrell.

The DOJ is considering prosecuting Lyle under Rule 10b-5 for his involvement in the scheme in which Endring engaged. Would the DOJ have difficulty establishing that Lyle acted "willfully"?

### 2. *The Violations That Give Rise to Criminal Liability*

As has already been noted, a defendant can be convicted for violating the Securities Act or the Exchange Act only if he acted "willfully." Two questions arise concerning the violations that can trigger criminal liability.

The first question is whether criminal liability can rest on the violation of any provision or rule or only on certain ones. Notice that Section 24 encompasses willful violations of "any of the provisions" of the Securities Act or its "rules and regulations," whereas Section 32(a) encompasses willful violations of "any provisions of this Act ***, or any rule or regulation thereunder the violation of which is made unlawful or the observance of which is required under the terms of this Act." According to the late Judge Herlands, on whom the *Peltz* court relied in developing its definition of "willfully," Section 32(a) calls for a "distinction *** between those rules and regulations which are mentioned, in general terms, by the statute, in connection with specific subjects, and the great mass of comparatively minor administrative rules and regulations whose violation or observance is not expressly mentioned in the body of the statute." William B. Herlands, Criminal Law Aspects of the Securities Exchange Act of 1934, 21 Va. L. Rev. 139, 172 (1934). Do you agree? Why doesn't Section 24 of the Securities Act call for the same distinction? Would a court be entitled to read such a limitation into Section 24 by implication?

The second question involves how to interpret the provision or rule that the defendant allegedly violated. Indeed, suppose that the provision or rule contains an ambiguity (whether on its face or as applied) and that the ambiguity is not resolvable through analysis of statutory language or legislative history. Is it appropriate to select the interpretation that best furthers the underlying statutory policies (whether of the Securities Act or Exchange Act in general or the provision or rule in particular)? Or is it necessary to apply strict construction (sometimes called the rule of lenity) in recognition of the prison sentence and opprobrium that the defendant may face if convicted? The Supreme Court has sent conflicting signals on this issue.

In *United States v. Naftalin,* 441 U.S. 768 (1979), the Court came down on the side of strict construction. At issue in *Naftalin* was whether Section 17(a)(1) of the Securities Act prohibits fraud against brokers as well as fraud against investors. After holding the Section to encompass fraud against brokers, the Court announced that it would have applied strict construction had the statutory language been ambiguous:

> This is a criminal case, and we have long held that " 'ambiguity concerning the ambit of criminal statutes should be resolved in favor of lenity,' " *United States v. Culbert,* 435 U.S. 371, 379 (1978), quoting *Rewis v. United States,* 401 U.S. 808, 812 (1971), and that a defendant may not " 'be subjected to a penalty unless the words of the statute plainly impose it.' " *United States v. Campos-Serrano,* 404 U.S., 293, 297 (1971), quoting *Keppel v. Tiffin Savings Bank,* 197 U.S. 356, 362 (1905). In this case, however, the words of the statute do "plainly impose it."

Id. at 778-79.

Yet in *United States v. O'Hagan,* 521 U.S. 642 (1997), the Court eschewed strict construction under circumstances in which *Naftalin* would seemingly have required it. Recall that in *O'Hagan* (which you read in Chapter 7), the Court concluded that Section 10(b) and Rule 10b-5 encompassed the misappropriation theory of insider trading and upheld a conviction under the Rule that had been premised on this theory. The Court did not claim that the misappropriation theory followed from statutory language or legislative history. Rather, it adopted this theory based on an analysis of the Exchange Act's policies. See id. at 658-59. Justice Scalia dissented because of the Court's failure to apply the rule of lenity and resolve the ambiguity in the defendant's favor. See id. at 679. See generally Richard W. Painter et al., Don't Ask, Just Tell: Insider Trading After *United States v. O'Hagan,* 84 Va. L. Rev. 153, 196-99 (1998) (arguing that the Court should have applied the rule of lenity).

To cure fair warning problems that might arise from its approach to statutory construction, the *O'Hagan* Court relied on the fact that a defendant must act "willfully" in order to be convicted:

> To establish a criminal violation of Rule 10b-5, the Government must prove that a person "willfully" violated the provision. *** [T]he statute's "requirement of the presence of culpable intent as a necessary element of the offense does much to destroy any force in the argument that application of the [statute]" in circumstances such as O'Hagan's is unjust. *Boyce Motor Lines, Inc. v. United States,* 342 U.S. 337, 342 (1952).

521 U.S. at 665-66.

## *NOTES AND QUESTIONS*

*1. **"Willfully" and Fair Warning.*** The *O'Hagan* Court did not specify the definition of "willfully" that would suffice to cure fair warning problems. According to Professor Anthony Amsterdam, such a definition would require "not only a knowing what is done but a knowing that what is done is unlawful or, at least, so wrong that it is probably unlawful." Anthony G. Amsterdam, Note, The Void for Vagueness Doctrine in the Supreme Court, 109 U. Pa. L. Rev. 67, 87 n. 98 (1960). Is the definition of "willfully" offered by *Peltz* consistent or inconsistent?

*2. **Strict Construction Under Siege.*** If a court construes an ambiguous securities provision strictly in a criminal action, would the same interpretation automatically apply in a later civil action involving the same provision? Or can a provision be read differently in different enforcement contexts? Compare *United States v. Chestman,* 947 F.2d 551, 567-70 (2d Cir. 1991) (rejecting, for purposes of a criminal prosecution, a liberal interpretation of the relationship of trust that is critical to the misappropriation theory, but suggesting that such an interpretation might apply in a civil action) with *SEC v. Burns,* 614 F. Supp. 1360, 1367 (S.D. Cal. 1985) (suggesting the necessity of reading Rule 10b-6 strictly in a civil action if strict construction would be necessary in a criminal action), aff'd, 816 F.2d 471 (9th Cir. 1987) and *Drasner v. Thomson McKinnon Sec., Inc.,* 433 F. Supp. 485, 499 (S.D.N.Y. 1977) (concluding that Regulation T of the Exchange Act must be read the same way in civil and criminal actions). Suppose that strict construction of the federal securities laws was commonplace. What consequences would follow? See generally Margaret V. Sachs, Harmonizing Civil and Criminal Enforcement of Federal Regulatory Statutes: The Case of the Securities Exchange Act of 1934, 2001 U. Ill. L. Rev. 1025.

*3. **The Irrelevance of Standing and Reliance Requirements.*** In criminal actions under the Securities Act or the Exchange Act, the standing requirements relevant to private actions do not apply. See, e.g., *United States v. O'Hagan,* 521 U.S. 642, 664-65 (1997) (holding Rule 10b-5's purchaser-seller requirement inapplicable in a criminal action). Nor does criminal liability require "identification of or reliance by a particular victim." *United States v. Haddy,* 134 F.3d 542, 551 (3d Cir. 1998).

*4. **Filing Crimes.*** Section 24 of the Securities Act and Section 32(a) of the Exchange Act criminalize not only the willful violation of statutory provisions and rules but also the filing with the SEC of certain fraudulent documents. The filing crimes created by the two acts are not identical, however. What are the differences between them? See Arthur F. Mathews, Criminal Prosecutions Under the Federal Securities Laws and Related Statutes: The Nature and Development of SEC Criminal Cases, 39 Geo. Wash. L. Rev. 901, 906 (1971). The DOJ often forgoes these filing crimes in favor of 18 U.S.C. § 1001(a), a false statement statute of general application that encompasses both writings and oral statements. See, e.g., *United States v. Bilzerian,* 926 F.2d 1285, 1299-1301 (2d Cir. 1991) (applying Section 1001(a) to the filing of Schedules 13D and 14D-1); *United States v. Lang,* 766 F. Supp. 389, 394 (D. Md. 1991) (applying Section 1001(a) to the filing of Form 10-Q). Congress enacted the statute that is now Section 1001(a) a mere twelve days after enacting the Exchange Act. In so doing, did it intend to supplant the filing crimes in the Securities Act and the Exchange Act?

*5. **Aiding and Abetting and Conspiracy.*** The DOJ has authority to prosecute the aiding and abetting of Securities Act and Exchange Act crimes pursuant to 18 U.S.C. § 2:

> Whoever commits an offense against the United States or aids, abets, counsels, commands, induces or procures its commission, is punishable as a principal.

18 U.S.C. § 2(a). See, e.g., *United States v. Flynn*, 196 F.3d 927, 929 (8th Cir. 1999); *United States v. Brown*, 555 F.2d 336, 338 (2d Cir. 1977). Moreover, the DOJ can also charge defendants with conspiracy to commit a securities crime pursuant to 18 U.S.C. § 371:

> If two or more persons conspire either to commit any offense against the United States, or to defraud the United States, or any agency thereof in any manner for any purpose, and one or more of such persons do any act to effect the object of the conspiracy, each shall be fined under this title or imprisoned not more than five years, or both. ***

See, e.g., *United States v. Russo,* 74 F.3d 1383, 1388 (2d Cir. 1996); *United States v. Vasilios,* 598 F.2d 387, 389 (5th Cir. 1979). (In the next section of this Chapter, we will contrast this provision with the conspiracy provision enacted as part of the Sarbanes-Oxley Act).

***6. Statute of Limitations.*** The Securities Act and the Exchange Act do not contain a special statute of limitations for criminal actions. Therefore, the general five year federal criminal limitations period set forth in 18 U.S.C. § 3282 controls. See, e.g. *United States v. O'Hagan,* 139 F.3d 641, 650-51 (8th Cir. 1998); *United States v. United Med. & Surgical Supply Corp.,* 989 F.2d 1390, 1398 (4th Cir. 1993).

### *PROBLEM 11-2*

Ted, a dealer in a municipal bond offering, made a $200,000 kickback payment through intermediaries to Ralph, an employee of a county municipal securities authority. Ted mistakenly concluded that he owed Ralph an additional $50,000 under the kickback agreement. Thus, about two months after the bond offering had closed, Ted asked Ralph to concoct a false invoice for $50,000 worth of work related to the bond issue. Ralph obliged and Ted paid him the additional $50,000. Hence Ted's records concerning that payment were false.

Based on that false record, the government indicted Ted for violating Section 15B(c)(1) of the Exchange Act. That section prohibits municipal securities dealers from "induc[ing] or attempt[ing] to induce the purchase or sale of any municipal security in contravention of any rule of the Municipal Securities Rulemaking Board." Ted was charged with violating Rule G-8, which requires municipal securities dealers to make and keep accurate records of all receipts and disbursements of cash "with respect to transactions in municipal securities."

Ted made a motion to dismiss the indictment. He argued that Rule G-8 was inapplicable to him because the bond issue had closed by the time the false record was created. The government countered that "bond transactions like the one at issue here are routinely followed by post-closing balancing payments, adjustments of accounts and financial statements, whose accuracy is so germane to the transaction itself that if the records are false the whole transaction is tainted, the statute is invoked, and a crime committed."

There is no case law (or other precedent) concerning how to construe Rule G-8. Should the court dismiss the indictment?

Cf. *United States v. Rudi,* 927 F. Supp. 686 (S.D.N.Y. 1996).

## B. THE SARBANES-OXLEY ACT

The Sarbanes-Oxley Act augmented the DOJ's arsenal by creating several new crimes (listed below), the first two of which will occupy our attention:

> *(i) a new crime of securities fraud.* Section 807 of the Sarbanes-Oxley Act, enacted as 18 U.S.C. § 1348;
>
> *(ii) a new crime involving false certification of financial reports.* Section 906 of the Sarbanes-Oxley Act, enacted as 18 U.S.C. § 1350;
>
> *(iii) several new crimes involving record tampering.* Section 802 of the Sarbanes-Oxley Act creates two crimes, one entitled "destruction, alteration, or falsification of records in federal investigations and bankruptcy," enacted as 18 U.S.C. § 1519, and the other entitled "destruction of corporate audit records," enacted as 18 U.S.C. § 1520. In addition, Section 1102 of the Sarbanes-Oxley Act creates a crime entitled "tampering with a record or otherwise impeding an official proceeding," enacted as 18 U.S.C. § 1512 (c).

Note also that Section 902 of the Sarbanes-Oxley Act provides that "[a]ny person who attempts or conspires to commit any offense under this chapter shall be subject to the same penalties as those prescribed for the offense, the commission of which was the object of the attempt or conspiracy." 18 U.S.C. § 1349. How does this provision compare with 18 U.S.C. § 371, the conspiracy provision set forth supra in note 5 on page 845? What is the relationship between these two provisions?

### 1. *The New Crime of Securities Fraud*

Section 807 of the Sarbanes-Oxley Act creates a new crime of securities fraud involving the securities of publicly traded companies. This crime, enacted as 18 U.S.C. § 1348, reads as follows:

**Section 1348. Securities Fraud**

> Whoever knowingly executes, or attempts to execute, a scheme or artifice—
>
> (1) to defraud any person in connection with any security of an issuer with a class of securities registered under section 12 of the Securities Exchange Act of 1934 or that is required to file reports under section 15(d) of the Securities Exchange Act of 1934; or
>
> (2) to obtain, by means of false or fraudulent pretenses, representations, or promises, any money or property in connection with the purchase or sale of any security of an issuer with a class of securities registered under section 12 of the Securities Exchange Act of 1934 or that is required to file reports under section 15(d) of the Securities Exchange Act of 1934;
>
> shall be fined under this title, or imprisoned not more than 25 years, or both.

18 U.S.C. § 1348. Subsection (1) of Section 1348 is the principal focus of the notes, questions, and problems that immediately follow. Subsection (2) is

addressed mainly in connection with the mail and wire fraud statutes in Section C of this Chapter.

### *NOTES AND QUESTIONS*

***1. Location, Location, Location.*** Why do you suppose that Congress added this new securities crime to Title 18 rather than to the federal securities laws?

***2. Rule 10b-5 Compared.*** Consider the crime established by Section 1348(1). Does it amount to Rule 10b-5 in different packaging? If not, what are the differences? If so, what was the point?

***3. The Requirement that the Defendant Act "Knowingly."*** What is the difference between "knowingly" in Section 1348 and "willfully," the state of mind requirement for crimes under the Securities Act and the Exchange Act? Are courts entitled to import their definitions of "willfully" from the latter two Acts into Section 1348? If not, how should courts define knowingly"?

***4. The Relevance of Strict Construction.*** What role should strict construction play in the construction of Section 1348?

***5. Publicly Traded Companies Only.*** Why do you suppose that Congress limited the new crime of securities fraud to the securities of issuers with a class of securities registered pursuant to Section 12 or those required to file reports under Section 15(d)? Was this a good idea?

***6. Comparative Attractiveness.*** In what respects is Section 1348(1) apt to be more attractive to prosecutors than are crimes under the Securities Act and the Exchange Act?

### *PROBLEM 11-3*

Return to Problem 11-1. Assume that the DOJ is contemplating prosecuting Lyle under Section 1348(1). Would he satisfy the state of mind requirement?

### *PROBLEM 11-4*

Return to Problem 11-2. Can the DOJ charge Ted with violating Section 1348(1)?

### *PROBLEM 11-5*

Imdrone, Inc., is a drug company that had spent years fueling the market's interest in miraclex, a treatment for certain potent cancers. Optimism concerning the effectiveness of miraclex rested largely on a few small clinical trials. In 2001, Imdrone applied to the Food and Drug Administration for permission to market miraclex.

On December 20, 2001, an FDA official told the company that it had made its decision on the application and that the official announcement would come on December 28. On December 21, the Imdrone general counsel issued a company-wide blackout on trading in Imdrone stock.

Overcome by curiosity, Imdrone's president (Watson) telephoned a friend at the FDA on December 22. The friend told Watson that "things looked very bad" for miraclex. Watson thereupon called his broker that same day and directed her to sell his considerable block of Imdrone stock. She refused, citing the blackout on trading.

Can Watson be charged with violating Section 1348(1)?

### 2. *The New Crime of Failing to Certify Financial Reports*

Section 906 of the Sarbanes-Oxley Act requires CEOs and CFOs of reporting companies to certify the periodic financial reports that their companies file with the SEC and in addition criminalizes the making of false certifications. Enacted as 18 U.S.C. § 1350, the new certification crime reads as follows:

**18 U.S.C. § 1350. Failure of corporate officers to certify financial reports**

> (a) Certification of periodic financial reports.—Each periodic report containing financial statements filed by an issuer with the Securities Exchange Commission pursuant to section 13(a) or 15(d) of the Securities Exchange Act of 1934 shall be accompanied by a written statement by the chief executive officer and chief financial officer (or equivalent thereof) of the issuer.
>
> (b) Content.—The statement required under subsection (a) shall certify that the periodic report containing the financial statements fully complies with the requirements of section 13(a) or 15(d) of the Securities Exchange Act of 1934 and that information contained in the periodic report fairly presents, in all material respects, the financial condition and results of operations of the issuer.
>
> (c) Criminal penalties.—Whoever—
>
>> (1) certifies any statement as set forth in subsections (a) and (b) of this section knowing that the periodic report accompanying the statement does not comport with all the requirements set forth in this section shall be fined not more than $1,000,000 or imprisoned not more than 10 years, or both; or
>>
>> (2) willfully certifies any statement as set forth in subsections (a) and (b) of this section knowing that the periodic report accompanying the statement does not comport with all the requirements set forth in this section shall be fined not more than $5,000,000, or imprisoned not more than 20 years, or both.

18 U.S.C. § 1350.

### *NOTES AND QUESTIONS*

1. ***The Meaning of "Fairly Presents."*** Look closely at the requirement in Section 1350(b) that the CEO and CFO certify that the "information contained in the periodic report *fairly present*[ ] in all material respects, the financial condition and results of operations of the issuer." (emphasis added). Does "fairly present" refer simply to the absence of material omissions and misrepresentations? In answering this question, consider the possible relevance of Section 302 of the Sarbanes-Oxley Act. That Section calls upon the SEC to adopt rules requiring CEOs and CFOs of reporting companies to certify that each annual and quarterly report "does not contain any untrue statement of a material fact or omit to state a material fact necessary in order to make the statements made, in light of the circumstances under which such statements were made, not misleading" and also that "the financial statements, and other

financial information included in the report, fairly present in all material respects the financial condition and results of operations."

*2. Operations vs. Financial Operations.* Consider the reference in Section 1350(b) to the issuer's "financial condition and results of operations." Does "results of operations" refer to financial operations only?

*3. The Relevance of Strict Construction.* Would it be appropriate to resolve the questions posed in notes 1 and 2 by adopting a strict construction approach?

*4. CEOs and CFOs Beware.* What steps should CEOs and CFOs take to insure that they do not incur criminal liability under Section 1350?

*5. What's in a Title?* Note that Section 1350 is entitled "failure of corporate officers to certify financial reports." Does this provision cover the CEO or CFO who fails altogether to certify a report?

*6. "Willfully" Again.* What is the difference (if any) between "willfully" in Section 1350 and "knowingly" in Section 1348? Are courts entitled to equate "willfully" in Section 1350 with "willfully" in Section 24 of the Securities Act and Section 32(a) of the Exchange Act?

## C. THE MAIL AND WIRE FRAUD STATUTES

Enacted in 1872, the mail fraud statute is renowned for its versatility. Indeed, the mail fraud statute was used to prosecute securities violations prior to the enactment of the federal securities laws. See *United States v. Maze,* 414 U.S. 395, 406 (1974) (Burger, C.J., dissenting). In its current form it reads as follows:

> Whoever, having devised or intending to devise any scheme or artifice to defraud, or for obtaining money or property by means of false or fraudulent pretenses, representations, or promises, or to sell, dispose of, loan, exchange, alter, give away, distribute, supply, or furnish or procure for unlawful use any counterfeit or spurious coin, obligation, security, or other article, or anything represented to be or intimated or held out to be such counterfeit or spurious article, for the purpose of executing such scheme or artifice or attempting so to do, places in any post office or authorized depository for mail matter, any matter or thing whatever to be sent or delivered by the Postal Service, or deposits or causes to be deposited any matter or thing whatever to be sent or delivered by any private or commercial interstate carrier, or takes or receives therefrom, any such matter or thing, or knowingly causes to be delivered by mail or such carrier according to the direction thereon, or at the place at which it is directed to be delivered by the person to whom it is addressed, any such matter or thing, shall be fined under this title or imprisoned not more than 20 years, or both. If the violation affects a financial institution, such person shall be fined not more than $1,000,000 or imprisoned not more than 30 years, or both.

18 U.S.C. § 1341. For discussions of the evolution of the mail fraud statute, see John C. Coffee, Jr., The Metastasis of Mail Fraud: The Continuing Story of the Evolution of a White-Collar Crime, 21 Am. Crim. L. Rev. 1 (1983); Jed S. Rakoff, The Federal Mail Fraud Statute (Part I), 18 Duq. L. Rev. 771 (1980).

The wire fraud statute, enacted in 1952, currently reads as follows:

> Whoever, having devised or intending to devise any scheme or artifice to defraud, or for obtaining money or property by means of false or fraudulent pretenses, representations, or promises, transmits or causes to be transmitted by means of wire, radio, or television communication in interstate or foreign commerce, any writings, signs, signals, pictures, or sounds for the purpose of executing such scheme or artifice, shall be fined under this title or imprisoned not more than 20 years, or both. If the violation affects a financial institution, such person shall be fined not more than $1,000,000 or imprisoned not more than 30 years, or both.

18 U.S.C. § 1343. While wire fraud prosecutions have been less numerous than mail fraud prosecutions, the former could grow in number given the increasing importance of the Internet.

The prison terms of up to twenty years authorized by the mail and wire fraud statutes result from an amendment to those statutes that was enacted as part of the Sarbanes-Oxley Act. Prior to that Act, the mail and wire fraud statutes authorized imprisonment for up to five years.

Conviction under either the mail fraud or wire fraud statute requires proof of three elements: (i) a scheme to defraud; (ii) the defendant's participation in the scheme with the intent to defraud; and (iii) the use of the mails or wires in furtherance of the scheme. See, e.g., *United States v. Syme*, 276 F.3d 131,142 n. 3 (3d Cir. 2002); *United States v. Davuluri*, 239 F.3d 902, 906 (7th Cir. 2001). Courts have interpreted these elements liberally.

Thus, in the view of a number of courts, the intent requirement can be satisfied by proof of recklessness. See, e.g., *United States v. Coyle*, 63 F.3d 1239,1243 (3d Cir. 1995); *United States v. Gay*, 967 F.2d 322, 326 (9th Cir. 1992). But see *United States v. Guadagna*, 183 F.3d 122, 129 (2d Cir. 1999) (requiring a " 'conscious knowing intent to defraud' " (quoting *United States v. Leonard*, 61 F.3d 1181,1187 (5th Cir. 1995))). Does the text of the mail and wire fraud statutes explicitly impose an intent requirement? Even if the answer is no, there is a presumption of an intent requirement when liability is criminal. See *Posters 'N' Things, Ltd. v. United States*, 511 U.S. 513, 522-23 (1994); *United States v. United States Gypsum Co.*, 438 U.S. 422, 436-37 (1978).

Moreover, the use of the mails or wires does not have to be an "essential element" of the scheme but only "incident to an essential part of" it. *Pereira v. United States*, 347 U.S. 1, 8 (1954). See also *Schmuck v. United States*, 489 U.S. 705, 715 (1989) (noting that a mailing need not itself be fraudulent in order to provide a basis for prosecution). Indeed, the defendant need not herself have used the mails or wires so long as she has "knowledge that the use of the mails [or wires] will follow in the ordinary course of business, or where such use can reasonably be foreseen." *Pereira v. United States*, 347 U.S. at 9. Can a defendant avoid being prosecuted for mail fraud by using Federal Express?

The Supreme Court addressed the "scheme to defraud" element in the two decisions that follow. As you read them, be alert to interfaces with the federal securities laws.

## CARPENTER v. UNITED STATES

484 U.S. 19 (1987)

JUSTICE WHITE:

Petitioners Kenneth Felis and R. Foster Winans were convicted of violating § 10(b) of the Securities Exchange Act of 1934 and Rule 10b-5. They were also found guilty of violating the federal mail and wire fraud statutes, 18 U.S.C. §§ 1341, 1343 ***

I

In 1981, Winans became a reporter for the Wall Street Journal (the Journal) and in the summer of 1982 became one of the two writers of a daily column, "Heard on the Street." That column discussed selected stocks or groups of stocks, giving positive and negative information about those stocks and taking "a point of view with respect to investment in the stocks that it reviews." [*United States v. Winans*, 612 F. Supp. 827, 830 (SDNY 1985). Winans regularly interviewed corporate executives to put together interesting perspectives on the stocks that would be highlighted in upcoming columns, but, at least for the columns at issue here, none contained corporate inside information or any "hold for release" information. Id., at 830, n. 2. Because of the "Heard" column's perceived quality and integrity, it had the potential of affecting the price of the stocks which it examined. The District Court concluded on the basis of testimony presented at trial that the "Heard" column "does have an impact on the market, difficult though it may be to quantify in any particular case." Id., at 830.

The official policy and practice at the Journal was that prior to publication, the contents of the column were the Journal's confidential information. Despite the rule, with which Winans was familiar, he entered into a scheme in October 1983 with Peter Brant and petitioner Felis, both connected with the Kidder Peabody brokerage firm in New York City, to give them advance information as to the timing and contents of the "Heard" column. This permitted Brant and Felis and another conspirator, David Clark, a client of Brant, to buy or sell based on the probable impact of the column on the market. Profits were to be shared. The conspirators agreed that the scheme would not affect the journalistic purity of the "Heard" column, and the District Court did not find that the contents of any of the articles were altered to further the profit potential of petitioners' stock-trading scheme. Id., at 832, 834-835. Over a 4-month period, the brokers made prepublication trades on the basis of information given them by Winans about the contents of some 27 "Heard" columns. The net profits from these trades were about $690,000.

In November 1983, correlations between the "Heard" articles and trading in the Clark and Felis accounts were noted at Kidder Peabody and inquiries began. Brant and Felis denied knowing anyone at the Journal and took steps to conceal the trades. Later, the Securities and Exchange Commission began an investigation. Questions were met by denials both by the brokers at Kidder Peabody and by Winans at the Journal. As the investigation progressed, the conspirators quarreled, and on March 29, 1984, Winans and Carpenter went to the SEC and revealed the entire scheme. This indictment and a bench trial followed. Brant, who had pleaded guilty under a plea agreement, was a witness for the Government.

The District Court found, and the Court of Appeals agreed, that Winans had knowingly breached a duty of confidentiality by misappropriating prepublication information regarding the timing and contents of the "Heard" column, information that had been gained in the course of his employment under the understanding that it would not be revealed in advance of publication and that if it were, he would report it to his employer. It was this appropriation of confidential information that underlay both the securities laws and mail and wire fraud counts. ***

In affirming the mail and wire fraud convictions, the Court of Appeals ruled that Winans had fraudulently misappropriated "property" within the meaning of the mail and wire fraud statutes and that its revelation had harmed the Journal. It was held as well that the use of the mail and wire services had a sufficient nexus with the scheme to satisfy §§ 1341 and 1343. ***

The Court is evenly divided with respect to the convictions under the securities laws and for that reason affirms the judgment below on those counts. For the reasons that follow, we also affirm the judgment with respect to the mail and wire fraud convictions.

II

Petitioners assert that their activities were not a scheme to defraud the Journal within the meaning of the mail and wire fraud statutes;[6] and that in any event, they did not obtain any "money or property" from the Journal, which is a necessary element of the crime under our decision last Term in *McNally v. United States,* 483 U.S. 350 (1987). We are unpersuaded by either submission and address the latter first.

We held in *McNally* that the mail fraud statute does not reach "schemes to defraud citizens of their intangible rights to honest and impartial government," id., at 355, and that the statute is "limited in scope to the protection of property rights." Id., at 360. Petitioners argue that the Journal's interest in prepublication confidentiality for the "Heard" columns is no more than an intangible consideration outside the reach of § 1341; nor does that law, it is urged, protect against mere injury to reputation. This is not a case like *McNally,* however. The Journal, as Winans' employer, was defrauded of much more than its contractual right to his honest and faithful service, an interest too ethereal in itself to fall within the protection of the mail fraud statute, which "had its origin in the desire to protect individual property rights." *McNally,* supra, at 359, n. 8. Here, the object of the scheme was to take the Journal's confidential business information—the publication schedule and contents of the "Heard" column—and its intangible nature does not make it any less "property" protected by the mail and wire fraud statutes. *McNally* did not limit the scope of § 1341 to tangible as distinguished from intangible property rights.

---

6. The mail and wire fraud statutes share the same language in relevant part, and accordingly we apply the same analysis to both sets of offenses here.

Both courts below expressly referred to the Journal's interest in the confidentiality of the contents and timing of the "Heard" column as a property right, and we agree with that conclusion. Confidential business information has long been recognized as property. See *Dirks v. SEC,* 463 U.S. 646, 653, n. 10 (1983); *Board of Trade of Chicago v. Christie Grain & Stock Co.,* 198 U.S. 236, 250- 251 (1905). *** The Journal had a property right in keeping confidential and making exclusive use, prior to publication, of the schedule and contents of the "Heard" column. *Christie Grain,* supra. ***

Petitioners' arguments that they did not interfere with the Journal's use of the information or did not publicize it and deprive the Journal of the first public use of it miss the point. The confidential information was generated from the business, and the business had a right to decide how to use it prior to disclosing it to the public. Petitioners cannot successfully contend *** that a scheme to defraud requires a monetary loss, such as giving the information to a competitor; it is sufficient that the Journal has been deprived of its right to exclusive use of the information, for exclusivity is an important aspect of confidential business information and most private property for that matter.

We cannot accept petitioners' further argument that Winans' conduct in revealing prepublication information was no more than a violation of workplace rules and did not amount to fraudulent activity that is proscribed by the mail fraud statute. Sections 1341 and 1343 reach any scheme to deprive another of money or property by means of false or fraudulent pretenses, representations, or promises. As we observed last Term in *McNally,* the words "to defraud" in the mail fraud statute have the "common understanding" of " 'wronging one in his property rights by dishonest methods or schemes,' and 'usually signify the deprivation of something of value by trick, deceit, chicane or overreaching.' " 483 U.S., at 358 (quoting *Hammerschmidt v. United States,* 265 U.S. 182, 188 (1924)). The concept of "fraud" includes the act of embezzlement, which is " 'the fraudulent appropriation to one's own use of the money or goods entrusted to one's care by another.' " *Grin v. Shine,* 187 U.S. 181, 189 (1902). ***

We have little trouble in holding that the conspiracy here to trade on the Journal's confidential information is not outside the reach of the mail and wire fraud statutes, provided the other elements of the offenses are satisfied. The Journal's business information that it intended to be kept confidential was its property; the declaration to that effect in the employee manual merely removed any doubts on that score and made the finding of specific intent to defraud that much easier. Winans continued in the employ of the Journal, appropriating its confidential business information for his own use, all the while pretending to perform his duty of safeguarding it. In fact, he told his editors twice about leaks of confidential information not related to the stock-trading scheme, demonstrating both his knowledge that the Journal viewed information concerning the "Heard" column as confidential and his deceit as he played the role of a loyal employee. Furthermore, the District Court's conclusion that each of the petitioners acted with the required specific intent to defraud is strongly supported by the evidence.

Lastly, we reject the submission that using the wires and the mail to print and send the Journal to its customers did not satisfy the requirement that those mediums be used to execute the scheme at issue. The courts below were quite right in observing that circulation of the "Heard" column was not only anticipated but an essential part of the scheme. Had the column not been made available to Journal customers, there would have been no effect on stock prices and no likelihood of profiting from the information leaked by Winans.

The judgment below is affirmed.

### *NOTES AND QUESTIONS*

1. ***Testing the Limits of the Court's Theory.*** Suppose Winans had shared the columns with his friends, expecting them to trade, but the friends became conscience-stricken and did not do so. Could he still have been prosecuted for mail fraud consistent with the Court's opinion? Cf. John C. Coffee, Jr., Hush!: The Criminal Status of Confidential Information After *McNally* and *Carpenter* and the Enduring Problem of Overcriminalization, 26 Am. Crim. L. Rev. 121, 131 (1988).

2. ***Fraud on the Wall Street Journal vs. Fraud on Investors.*** Why did the Court deem the victim of the fraud to be the Wall Street Journal rather than the investors who traded without knowing what Winans and his friends knew? One commentator has argued that the answer lies with certain Supreme Court securities decisions:

> The Court was driven to focus on Winans's mere taking of information, rather than its profitable use, in part because of constraints created by decisions under the securities laws. Since fraud requires deception, there must be a deceived party to establish the mail fraud violation. The investors who sold to or bought from Winans could not play that role. Under *Chiarella* and *Dirks*, Winans owed no duty of disclosure under the securities laws to these shareholders. He had acquired no nonpublic information about their companies through an insider's breach of duty. *** Accordingly, the investors were not the victims of a fraud. But if the investors were not defrauded, then the victim had to be the Journal.

Michael Dreeben, Insider Trading and Intangible Rights: The Redefinition of the Mail Fraud Statute, 26 Am. Crim. L. Rev. 181, 204-05 (1988). Do you agree with this analysis?

3. ***What About Fair Warning?*** Could the *Carpenter* defendants have challenged their convictions on the ground that they lacked fair warning of the wrongfulness of their conduct?

4. ***Nullifying* McNally.** By concluding that the mail fraud statute embraced fraudulent deprivations of intangible property rights, the *Carpenter* Court limited *McNally v. United States,* 483 U.S. 350 (1987), which held that the mail fraud statute did not reach fraudulent deprivations of the intangible right to honest government service. See id. at 358-61. Following *Carpenter,* Congress overturned *McNally* entirely by enacting the following supplement to the mail fraud and wire fraud statutes:

> For the purposes of this chapter, the term "scheme or artifice to defraud" includes a scheme or artifice to deprive another of the intangible right of honest services.

18 U.S.C. § 1346. Prosecutors occasionally rely upon Section 1346 in the context of securities transactions. See, e.g., *United States v. ReBrook,* 58 F.3d 961, 966

(4th Cir. 1995) (appeal by state attorney convicted of depriving state's citizens of honest services when he traded on material nonpublic information obtained through his position).

*5. **The Sarbanes-Oxley Act and the New Crime of Securities Fraud.*** Revisit 18 U.S.C. § 1348, the new crime of securities fraud created by the Sarbanes-Oxley Act that was set out on page 846 of this Chapter. Could the *Carpenter* defendants have been prosecuted under subsection (2) of Section 1348 if it had been on the books at the time? What are the similarities and differences between subsection (2) of Section 1348 and the mail and wire fraud statutes?

---

In the decision that follows, the Supreme Court addressed whether the mail fraud and wire fraud statutes require proof that the fraud was material in nature.

## NEDER v. UNITED STATES

527 U.S. 1 (1999)

CHIEF JUSTICE REHNQUIST:

*** In the mid-1980's, petitioner Ellis E. Neder, Jr., an attorney and real estate developer in Jacksonville, Florida, engaged in a number of real estate transactions financed by fraudulently obtained bank loans. ***

Neder was indicted on, among other things, 9 counts of mail fraud, in violation of 18 U.S.C. § 1341; 9 counts of wire fraud, in violation of § 1343; 12 counts of bank fraud, in violation of § 1344; and 2 counts of filing a false income tax return, in violation of 26 U.S.C. § 7206(1). The fraud counts charged Neder with devising and executing various schemes to defraud lenders in connection with the land acquisition and development loans, totaling over $40 million. The tax counts charged Neder with filing false statements of income on his tax returns. ***

In accordance with then-extant Circuit precedent and over Neder's objection, the District Court instructed the jury that, to convict on the tax offenses, it "need not consider" the materiality of any false statements "even though that language is used in the indictment." App. 256. The question of materiality, the court instructed, "is not a question for the jury to decide." Ibid. The court gave a similar instruction on bank fraud, and subsequently found, outside the presence of the jury, that the evidence established the materiality of all the false statements at issue. In instructing the jury on mail fraud and wire fraud, the District Court did not include materiality as an element of either offense. ***

The Court of Appeals for the Eleventh Circuit affirmed the conviction. It held that the District Court erred under our intervening decision in *United States v. Gaudin,* 515 U.S. 506 (1995), in failing to submit the materiality element of the tax offense to the jury. It concluded, however, that the error was subject to harmless-error analysis and, further, that the error was harmless because "materiality was not in dispute," and thus the error "'did not contribute to the verdict obtained,'" ibid. (quoting *Yates v. Evatt,* 500 U.S. 391, 403 (1991)). The Court of Appeals also held that materiality is not an element of the mail fraud, wire fraud, and bank fraud statutes, and thus the District Court did not err in failing to submit the question of materiality to the jury.

We granted certiorari to resolve a conflict in the Courts of Appeals on two questions: (1) whether, and under what circumstances, the omission of an element from the judge's charge to the jury can be harmless error, and (2) whether materiality is an element of the federal mail fraud, wire fraud, and bank fraud statutes.

II

*** Neder was tried before an impartial judge, under the correct standard of proof and with the assistance of counsel; a fairly selected, impartial jury was instructed to consider all of the evidence and argument in respect to Neder's defense against the tax charges. Of course, the court erroneously failed to charge the jury on the element of materiality, but that error did not render Neder's trial "fundamentally unfair," as that term is used in our cases. ***

*** In *Chapman* v. *California,* 386 U.S. 18 (1967), we set forth the test for determining whether a constitutional error is harmless. That test, we said, is whether it appears "beyond a reasonable doubt that the error complained of did not contribute to the verdict obtained." Id., at 24.

To obtain a conviction on the tax offense at issue, the Government must prove that the defendant filed a tax return "which he does not believe to be true and correct as to every material matter." 26 U.S.C. § 7206(1). In general, a false statement is material if it has "a natural tendency to influence, or [is] capable of influencing, the decision of the decisionmaking body to which it was addressed." *United States v. Gaudin,* 515 U.S., at 509 (quoting *Kungys v. United States,* 485 U.S. 759, 770 (1988)). In a prosecution under § 7206(1), several courts have determined that "any failure to report income is material." *United States v. Holland,* 880 F.2d 1091, 1096 (CA9 1989). Under either of these formulations, no jury could reasonably find that Neder's failure to report substantial amounts of income on his tax returns was not "a material matter."

At trial, the Government introduced evidence that Neder failed to report over $5 million in income from the loans he obtained. The failure to report such substantial income incontrovertibly establishes that Neder's false statements were material to a determination of his income tax liability. *** We think it beyond cavil here that the error "did not contribute to the verdict obtained." *Chapman,* supra, at 24. ***

III

We also granted certiorari in this case to decide whether materiality is an element of a "scheme or artifice to defraud" under the federal mail fraud (18 U.S.C. § 1341), wire fraud (§ 1343), and bank fraud (§ 1344) statutes. The Court of Appeals concluded that the failure to submit materiality to the jury was not error because the fraud statutes do not require that a "scheme to defraud" employ *material* falsehoods. We disagree.

Under the framework set forth in *United States v. Wells,* 519 U.S. 482 (1997), we first look to the text of the statutes at issue to discern whether they require a showing of materiality. In this case, we need not dwell long on the text because, as the parties agree, none of the fraud statutes defines the phrase "scheme or artifice to defraud," or even mentions materiality. Although the mail fraud and wire fraud statutes contain different jurisdictional elements (§ 1341 requires use of the mails while § 1343 requires use of interstate wire facilities), they both prohibit, in pertinent part, "any scheme or artifice to defraud" or to obtain money or property "by means of false or fraudulent pretenses, representations, or promises." The bank fraud statute, which was modeled on the mail and wire fraud statutes, similarly prohibits any "scheme or artifice to defraud a financial institution" or to obtain any property of a financial institution "by false or fraudulent pretenses, representations, or promises." Thus, based solely on a "natural reading of the full text," id., at 490, materiality would not be an element of the fraud statutes.

That does not end our inquiry, however, because in interpreting statutory language there is a necessary second step. It is a well-established rule of construction that " '[w]here Congress uses terms that have accumulated settled meaning under ... the common law, a court must infer, unless the statute otherwise dictates, that Congress means to incorporate the established meaning of these terms.' " *Nationwide Mut. Ins. Co. v. Darden,* 503 U.S. 318, 322 (1992) (quoting *Community for Creative Non-Violence v. Reid,* 490 U.S. 730, 739 (1989)). Neder contends that "defraud" is just such a term, and that Congress implicitly incorporated its common-law meaning, including its requirement of materiality,[5] into the statutes at issue.

The Government does not dispute that both at the time of the mail fraud statute's original enactment in 1872, and later when Congress enacted the wire fraud and bank fraud statutes, actionable "fraud" had a well-settled meaning at common law. Nor does it dispute that the well-settled meaning of "fraud" required a misrepresentation or concealment of *material* fact. Indeed, as the sources we are aware of demonstrate, the common law could not have conceived of "fraud" without proof of materiality. See *BMW of North America, Inc. v. Gore,* 517 U.S. 559, 579 (1996) ("[A]ctionable fraud requires a *material* misrepresentation or omission" (citing Restatement (Second) of Torts § 538 (1977); W. Keeton, D. Dobbs, R. Keeton, & D. Owen, Prosser and Keeton on Law of Torts § 108 (5th ed.1984))). Thus, under the rule that Congress intends to incorporate the well-settled meaning of the common-law terms it uses, we cannot infer from the absence of an express reference to materiality that Congress intended to drop that element from the fraud statutes. On the contrary, we must *presume* that

---

5. The Restatement instructs that a matter is material if:

> (a) a reasonable man would attach importance to its existence or nonexistence in determining his choice of action in the transaction in question; or
>
> (b) the maker of the representation knows or has reason to know that its recipient regards or is likely to regard the matter as important in determining his choice of action, although a reasonable man would not so regard it.

Restatement (Second) of Torts § 538 (1977).

Congress intended to incorporate materiality " 'unless the statute otherwise dictates.' " *Nationwide Mut. Ins.*, supra, at 322.[7]

The Government attempts to rebut this presumption by arguing that the term "defraud" would bear its common-law meaning only if the fraud statutes "indicated that Congress had codified the crime of false pretenses or one of the common-law torts sounding in fraud." Brief for United States 37. Instead, the Government argues, Congress chose to unmoor the mail fraud statute from its common-law analogs by punishing, not the completed fraud, but rather any person "having devised or intending to devise any scheme or artifice to defraud." Read in this light, the Government contends, there is no basis to infer that Congress intended to limit criminal liability to conduct that would constitute "fraud" at common law, and in particular, to *material* misrepresentations or omissions. Rather, criminal liability would exist so long as the defendant *intended* to deceive the victim, even if the particular means chosen turn out to be immaterial, *i.e.*, incapable of influencing the intended victim.

The Government relies heavily on *Durland v. United States*, 161 U.S. 306 (1896), our first decision construing the mail fraud statute, to support its argument that the fraud statutes sweep more broadly than common-law fraud. But *Durland* was different from this case. There, the defendant, who had used the mails to sell bonds he did not intend to honor, argued that he could not be held criminally liable because his conduct did not fall within the scope of the common-law crime of "false pretenses." We rejected the argument that "the statute reaches only such cases as, at common law, would come within the definition of 'false pretenses,' in order to make out which there must be a misrepresentation as to some existing fact and not a mere promise as to the future." Id. at 312. Instead, we construed the statute to "includ[e] everything designed to defraud by representations as to the past or present, or suggestions and promises as to the future." Id. at 313. Although *Durland* held that the mail fraud statute reaches conduct that would not have constituted "false pretenses" at common law, it did not hold, as the Government argues, that the statute encompasses more than common-law fraud.

In one sense, the Government is correct that the fraud statutes did not incorporate *all* the elements of common-law fraud. The common-law requirements of "justifiable reliance" and "damages," for example, plainly have no place in the federal fraud statutes. See, e.g., *United States v. Stewart*, 872 F.2d 957,

---

7. The Government argues that because Congress has provided express materiality requirements in other statutes prohibiting fraudulent conduct, the absence of such an express reference in the fraud statutes at issue " 'speaks volumes.' " Brief for United States 35. These later enacted statutes, however, differ from the fraud statutes here in that they prohibit both "false" and "fraudulent" statements or information. Because the term "false statement" does not imply a materiality requirement, *United States v. Wells*, 519 U.S. 482, 491 (1997), the word "material" limits the statutes' scope to material falsehoods. Moreover, these statutes cannot rebut the presumption that Congress intended to incorporate the common-law meaning of the term "fraud" in the mail fraud, wire fraud, and bank fraud statutes. That rebuttal can only come from the text or structure of the fraud statutes themselves.

960 (CA10 1989) ("[Under the mail fraud statute,] the government does not have to prove actual reliance upon the defendant's misrepresentations"); *United States v. Rowe,* 56 F.2d 747, 749 (CA2 1932) (L. Hand, J.) ("Civilly of course the [mail fraud statute] would fail without proof of damage, but that has no application to criminal liability"). By prohibiting the "scheme to defraud," rather than the completed fraud, the elements of reliance and damage would clearly be inconsistent with the statutes Congress enacted. But while the language of the fraud statutes is incompatible with these requirements, the Government has failed to show that this language is inconsistent with a materiality requirement.

Accordingly, we hold that materiality of falsehood is an element of the federal mail fraud, wire fraud, and bank fraud statutes. Consistent with our normal practice where the court below has not yet passed on the harmlessness of any error, we remand this case to the Court of Appeals for it to consider in the first instance whether the jury-instruction error was harmless. ***

## *NOTES AND QUESTIONS*

***1. Seeking a Definition.*** Does *Neder* define materiality for purposes of the mail and wire fraud statutes? According to some courts, *Neder* adopted the definition from the Restatement of Torts. See, e.g., *United States v. Richards,* 204 F.3d 177, 191-92 (5th Cir. 2000). According to other courts, *Neder* adopted the definition provided by *United States v. Gaudin,* 515 U.S. 506, 509 (1995)—having "a natural tendency to influence, or [is] capable of influencing, the decision of the decisionmaking body to which it was addressed." See, e.g., *United States v. Gee,* 226 F.3d 885, 891 (7th Cir. 2000). Still others apparently conclude that *Neder* did not ratify a specific definition of materiality, thereby permitting them to utilize pre-*Neder* definitions. See, e.g., *United States v. Autuori,* 212 F.3d 105, 118 (2d Cir. 2000). Which reading of *Neder* (if any) do you find the most plausible?

***2. The Relevance of* Carpenter.** In the wake of *Neder,* one court applied the following pre-*Neder* definition of materiality: " 'To be material, the information withheld either must be of some independent value or must bear on the ultimate value of the transaction.' " *United States v. Autuori,* 212 F.3d 105, 118 (2d Cir. 2000) (quoting *United States v. Mittelstaedt,* 31 F.3d 1208, 1217 (2d Cir. 1994)). The court that originated this definition derived it from the Supreme Court's *Carpenter* decision. See *United States v. Mittelstaedt,* 31 F.3d 1208, 1217 (2d Cir. 1994). Do you agree that *Carpenter* provides such a definition? From the standpoint of policy, is the *Autuori-Mittelstaedt* definition preferable to those described in note 1?

***3. Securities Law to the Rescue?*** You will recall from previous Chapters that under the Securities Act and the Exchange Act, a fact is material when there is "a substantial likelihood that, under all the circumstances, the omitted fact would have assumed actual significance in the deliberations of the reasonable shareholder." *TSC Indus., Inc. v. Northway, Inc.,* 426 U.S. 438, 449 (1976). See generally Chapter 2.B.1. Is a court entitled to import this definition of materiality into a mail or wire fraud prosecution involving a securities transaction? Would the *Northway* definition be useable (with minor changes such as substituting "reasonable person" for "reasonable shareholder") if a securities transaction were not involved?

As you also know from Chapter 2, materiality jurisprudence under the federal securities laws does not end with the *Northway* definition. Aspects of that jurisprudence might be useful in the resolution of materiality questions under the mail and wire fraud statutes regardless of whether the *Northway* definition is itself specifically embraced. For example, can a court import into a mail or wire fraud prosecution the probability/magnitude test for contingent information from *Basic Inc. v. Levinson*, 485 U.S. 224 (1988), which you read earlier in Chapter 2.B.2? Can it import the bespeaks caution doctrine (see generally Chapter 2.B.3.b) or the puffery doctrine (see note 3 of Chapter 2.B.1)? Do the answers to these questions turn on whether the cases involve securities transactions?

*4. Possible Conservative Tilt.* Does *Neder* presage a new conservative tilt in the Court's approach to the mail and wire fraud statutes? Cf. *Cleveland v. United States,* 531 U.S. 12, 24-25 (2000) (endorsing strict construction of the mail fraud statute partly on the ground that mail fraud is a predicate act for purposes of the Racketeer Influenced and Corrupt Organizations Act).

*5. Statute of Limitations.* There is no statute of limitations specifically applicable to the federal mail and wire fraud statutes. Therefore, the general federal criminal limitations period of 5 years set forth in 18 U.S.C. § 3282 is applicable. See, e.g., *United States v. Bach,* 172 F.3d 520, 521 (7th Cir. 1999); *United States v. Bouyea,* 152 F.3d 192, 195 (2d Cir. 1998).

### *PROBLEM 11-5*

Joe developed a technique for bilking the elderly out of their retirement savings. In a mass mailing to residents of retirement communities, Joe urged them to bring an end to their financial worries by buying stock in Stupendix, Inc. (which in fact did not exist). The mailing declared: "Become a Stupendix shareholder now and see your money double in two weeks! Triple in three weeks!" A number of recipients of this letter sent Joe cash (or checks), but did not hear from Joe again (much less reap the promised profits). Joe was indicted under the mail fraud statute as well as under the Sarbanes-Oxley Act's new crime of securities fraud set forth in 18 U.S.C. § 1348(2). On what grounds can he challenge his indictment? Is he likely to prevail on his challenge?

Cf. *United States v. Davis,* 226 F.3d 346 (5th Cir. 2000).

### *PROBLEM 11-6*

Clown, Inc., a reporting company under the Exchange Act, is a toy manufacturer and distributor with $100 million in yearly sales. Beginning approximately five years ago, the company's president (Felix) directed his assistant (Jane) to sell Clown merchandise to specified merchants for cash in off-the-books transactions. Over the years, these transactions (which were implemented through the use of e-mail) generated a total of $100,000. The existence of these transactions was disclosed neither to the accountants nor to the shareholders. If Felix were indicted under the wire fraud statute, could he mount a successful challenge? Suppose he were charged instead with violating 18 U.S.C. § 1348(2)?

Cf. *United States v. Siegel,* 717 F.2d 9 (2d Cir. 1983).

## D. RACKETEER INFLUENCED AND CORRUPT ORGANIZATIONS ACT

In 1970, Congress enacted the Racketeer Influenced and Corrupt Organizations Act ("RICO") in order to combat organized crime. Prevented by the First Amendment of the Constitution from criminalizing mere membership in organized crime, Congress created a complex new set of crimes premised on offenses (including mail, wire, and securities fraud) in which it believed that organized crime frequently engaged. See 18 U.S.C. §§ 1961-1968. RICO authorizes prison terms of up to twenty years (see Section 1963(a)) as well as the freezing of the defendant's assets prior to trial (see id.).

By far the most frequently invoked RICO offense is Section 1962(c), which is our focus. That Section reads as follows:

> It shall be unlawful for any person employed by or associated with any enterprise engaged in, or the activities which affect, interstate or foreign commerce, to conduct or participate, directly or indirectly, in the conduct of such enterprise's affairs through a pattern of racketeering activity or collection of an unlawful debt.

18 U.S.C. § 1962(c). We examine Section 1962(c)'s constituent elements—(1) racketeering activity; (2) pattern; (3) enterprise; and (4) "conduct[ing] or participat[ing] *** in the conduct of" the enterprise. We conclude our study of RICO by looking briefly at the limits on the RICO private action imposed by the Private Securities Litigation Reform Act of 1995.

RICO is a difficult statute to interpret for several reasons. One is its complexity and strangeness. Indeed, note that terms such as "racketeering activity," "pattern," and "enterprise" are hardly common law classics.

A second reason that RICO is difficult to interpret is that it has a liberal construction clause, which reads as follows: "The provisions of this Title shall be liberally construed to effectuate its remedial purposes." Section 904(a) of RICO, 84 Stat. 947. It is not immediately self-evident how to square the liberal construction clause with the rule of lenity (or strict construction) that normally applies in the criminal context. See generally David Kurzweil, Note, Criminal and Civil RICO: Traditional Canons of Statutory Interpretation and the Liberal Construction Clause, 30 Colum. J. L. & Soc. Probs. 41 (1996). Although it is an integral part of the RICO statute enacted by Congress, the liberal construction clause did not make its way into the United States Code. That fact does not affect its status as law, however.

A third reason that RICO is difficult to interpret has to do with the multiple types of RICO actions. Indeed, RICO is enforceable not only through criminal actions but also through civil actions (brought by either the DOJ or private parties). Must care be taken to construe RICO in a manner that is suitable for all enforcement contexts? Or can RICO be interpreted differently depending on the form of enforcement? This question—which you encountered previously in connection with the federal securities laws—has provoked conflicting commentary. Compare Bryan T. Camp, Dual Construction of RICO: The Road Not Taken in *Reves,* 51 Wash. & Lee L. Rev. 61, 95-96 (1994) (arguing that "[t]o deal with RICO's abundant ambiguities, courts should adopt a doctrine of dual construction, resolving the ambiguities according to a different and more restrictive standard in private civil cases than in cases where the government is either plaintiff or prosecutor") with Matthew C. Blickensderfer, Note, Unleashing RICO, 17 Harv. J. L. & Pub. Pol'y 867, 878 n. 66 (1994) (maintaining that RICO must be interpreted uniformly regardless of the form of enforcement). As you proceed with this Chapter, consider the advantages and disadvantages of "dual construction." Is it plausible to favor "dual construction" under RICO but not under the federal securities laws?

### *1. Racketeering Activity*

A critical element of the offense created by Section 1962(c) is "racketeering activity." RICO provides a definition of "racketeering activity" in Section 1961(1). That definition has six sub-parts, denominated A through F. Sub-part D reads as follows:

> any offense involving fraud connected with a case under title 11 (except a case under section 157 of this title), fraud in the sale of securities, or the felonious manufacture, importation, receiving, concealment, buying, selling, or otherwise dealing in a controlled substance or listed chemical (as defined in section 102 of the Controlled Substances Act), punishable under any law of the United States.

18 U.S.C. § 1961(1)(D). The other sub-parts include various state crimes such as murder and kidnaping (sub-part A); an amalgam of federal crimes from Title 18 of the United States Code, including mail fraud and wire fraud (sub-part B); certain crimes involving labor organizations and union funds (sub-part C); crimes under the Currency and Foreign Transactions Reporting Act (sub-part E); and certain crimes under the Immigration and Nationality Act (sub-part F).

### *NOTES AND QUESTIONS*

***1. Invitation to Expansiveness?*** Notice that sub-part D references specific statutory provisions of the United States Code in connection with bankruptcy fraud and drug crimes but contains no such references in connection with "fraud in the sale of securities." By such drafting, did Congress invite expansive interpretations of the phrase "fraud in the sale of securities"?

***2. Rule 10b-5 as RICO Securities Fraud.*** What is the relationship between RICO's "fraud in the sale of securities" and Rule 10b-5's fraud "in connection with the purchase or sale of any security"? Consider whether you agree with the following view:

> Had Congress intended RICO to be coextensive with § 10(b), it certainly knew how to do so. However, "fraud in the sale of securities" is quite limited in comparison to the broader language Congress used in § 10(b), which prohibits fraud "in connection with the purchase or sale of any security." The "in connection with" language *** does not limit liability to defendants who sold or bought from the plaintiffs. Thus, under the "in connection with" requirement, a defendant may be held liable even though he was not a party to a securities transaction. This concept arises directly out of the "in connection with" language. The language *** "fraud in the sale of securities" *** is much less susceptible to such an interpretation ***.
>
> *** The court's conclusion is that the phrase "fraud in the sale of securities" *** must be read to mean *** that only fraud that occurs as part of the actual securities transaction is a predicate act under that provision. In this case, it is not alleged that defendants sold any securities to plaintiffs. Instead,

> plaintiffs claim that defendants' issuance of misleading statements caused them to buy their shares *on the open market* at artificially inflated prices. Therefore, defendants have not committed "fraud in the sale of securities" *** and plaintiffs have not stated a RICO claim based on defendants' alleged securities fraud.

*In re Par Pharm., Inc. Sec. Litig.,* 733 F. Supp. 668, 683-84 (S.D.N.Y 1990). But see *Pandick, Inc. v. Rooney,* 632 F. Supp. 1430, 1434 (N.D. Ill. 1986) (making no distinction between RICO's "in" language and Rule 10b-5's "in connection with" language). Moreover, does "fraud in the sale of securities" embrace fraud in the *purchase* of securities? Cf. *Pandick,* supra, 632 F. Supp. at 1434 (giving an affirmative answer). To resolve these questions, what role (if any) should be played by RICO's liberal construction clause? By the rule of lenity?

*3.* ***Other Federal Securities Provisions Involving Omissions and Misrepresentations.*** To what extent (if at all) does "fraud in the sale of securities" embrace violations of Section 17(a) of the Securities Act? What about Section 14(a) and Rule 14a-9 of the Exchange Act or Section 14(e) of that Act? What about 18 U.S.C. § 1348 (the crime of securities fraud created by the Sarbanes-Oxley Act) and 18 U.S.C. § 1350 (the certification crime created by the Sarbanes-Oxley Act)?

*4.* ***Duties to Register or Report.*** Does RICO's "fraud in the sale of securities" encompass violations of the registration and reporting requirements of the Securities Act and the Exchange Act? Compare *First Pacific Bancorp, Inc. v. Bro,* 847 F.2d 542, 546 (9th Cir. 1988) (finding that failures to file under Sections 13(d) and 14(a) of the Exchange Act do not qualify as RICO securities fraud) with *United States v. Eisenberg,* 773 F. Supp. 662, 725-26 (D.N.J. 1991) (finding that failure to report beneficial ownership in a registration statement qualifies as RICO securities fraud where it was part of "an affirmative scheme to defraud"). Is it arguable that the registration and reporting requirements should be classified as fraud (at least for purposes of RICO) because the ultimate function of these requirements is to prevent fraud on investors?

*5.* ***State of Mind.*** Proof that a defendant engaged in a particular act of racketeering activity entails proof that she satisfied that activity's required state of mind. See, e.g., *United States v. Blinder,* 10 F.3d 1468, 1477 (9th Cir. 1993). What state of mind requirement is called for by "fraud in the sale of securities *** punishable under any law of the United States"? Consider the comments of Justice O' Connor:

> The embracing words "offense ...punishable under any law of the United States" plainly signify the elements necessary to bring a criminal prosecution. To the extent that RICO's reference to an "offense" involving fraud in the sale of securities" encompasses conduct that violates § 10(b), the relevant predicate is defined not by §10(b) itself, but rather by § 32(a) of the 1934 Act, which authorizes criminal sanctions against any person who willfully violates the Act or rules promulgated thereunder. ***

*Holmes v. Securities Investor Protection Corp.,* 503 U.S. 258, 280 (1992) (O'Connor, J., concurring in part and concurring in the judgment). Recall the lack of consensus regarding how to define "willfully" in Section 32(a) of the Exchange Act. See supra Section A of this Chapter. Therefore, it is not surprising to see uncertainty about the appropriate definition of "willfully" to import into RICO. Compare *Friedlob v. Trs. of Alpine Mut. Fund Trust,* 905 F. Supp. 843, 858 (D. Colo. 1995) (finding that a RICO defendant acts "willfully" where he acts " 'deliberately and intentionally and his acts, statements, or omissions are not the result of innocent mistake, negligence, inadvertence, or other innocent conduct' " (quoting *In re Colonial Ltd. P'ship Litig.*, 854 F. Supp. 64, 106 (D. Conn. 1994))) with *In re Integrated Res. Real Estate Ltd. P'ships Sec. Litig.,* 850 F. Supp. 1105, 1145 n. 56 (S.D.N.Y. 1994) (finding that a RICO defendant acts "willfully" when he acts "knowingly and willfully" and "with actual knowledge of the illegal activities").

***6. Giving the Federal Securities Laws Their Due.*** Courts deciding RICO cases involving "fraud in the sale of securities" may be called upon to construe the federal securities laws. Is it likely that courts will give those laws (and their accompanying policies) short shrift when construing them in the RICO context? Are constructions of the federal securities laws that emerge from the RICO context applicable outside the RICO context?

---

### 2. *Pattern*

Under Section 1962(c), the "racketeering activity" must constitute a "pattern." RICO says only that a " 'pattern of racketeering activity' requires at least two acts of racketeering activity" within a ten year period. 18 U.S.C. § 1961(5). Consider the gloss that the Supreme Court placed on "pattern" in the following decision.

## H.J. INC. v. NORTHWESTERN BELL TELEPHONE CO.

492 U.S. 229 (1989)

JUSTICE BRENNAN:

The Racketeer Influenced and Corrupt Organizations Act (RICO or Act) imposes criminal and civil liability upon those who engage in certain "prohibited activities." Each prohibited activity is defined in 18 U.S.C. § 1962 to include, as one necessary element, proof either of "a pattern of racketeering activity" or of "collection of an unlawful debt." "Racketeering activity" is defined in RICO to mean "any act or threat involving" specified state-law crimes, any "act" indictable under various specified federal statutes, and certain federal "offenses," 18 U.S.C. § 1961(1); but of the term "pattern" the statute says only that it "requires at least two acts of racketeering activity" within a 10-year period, 18 U.S.C. § 1961(5). We are called upon in this civil case to consider what conduct meets RICO's pattern requirement.

I

*** Petitioners, customers of respondent Northwestern Bell Telephone Co., filed this putative class action in 1986 in the District Court *** . Petitioners alleged violations of §§ 1962(a), (b), (c), and (d) by Northwestern Bell and the other respondents—some of the telephone company's officers and employees, various members of the Minnesota Public Utilities Commission (MPUC), and other unnamed individuals and corporations—and sought an injunction and treble damages under RICO's civil liability provisions, §§ 1964(a) and (c).

The MPUC is the state body responsible for determining the rates that Northwestern Bell may charge. Petitioners' five-count complaint alleged that between 1980 and 1986 Northwestern Bell sought to influence members of the MPUC in the performance of their duties—and in fact caused them to approve rates for the company in excess of a fair and reasonable amount—by making cash payments to commissioners, negotiating with them regarding future employment, and paying for parties and meals, for tickets to sporting events and the like, and for airline tickets. Based upon these factual allegations, petitioners alleged in their first count a pendent state-law claim, asserting that Northwestern Bell violated the Minnesota bribery statute, Minn. Stat. § 609.42 (1988), as well as state common law prohibiting bribery. They also raised four separate claims under § 1962 of RICO. Count II alleged that, in violation of § 1962(a), Northwestern Bell derived income from a pattern of racketeering activity involving predicate acts of bribery and used this income to engage in its business as an interstate "enterprise." Count III claimed a violation of § 1962(b), in that, through this same pattern of racketeering activity, respondents acquired an interest in or control of the MPUC, which was also an interstate "enterprise." In Count IV, petitioners asserted that respondents participated in the conduct and affairs of the MPUC through this pattern of racketeering activity, contrary to § 1962(c). Finally, Count V alleged that respondents conspired together to violate §§ 1962(a), (b), and (c), thereby contravening § 1962(d).

The District Court granted respondents' Federal Rule of Civil Procedure 12(b)(6) motion, dismissing the complaint for failure to state a claim upon which relief could be granted. The court found that "[e]ach of the fraudulent acts alleged by [petitioners] was committed in furtherance of a single scheme to influence MPUC commissioners to the detriment of Northwestern Bell's ratepayers." It held that dismissal was therefore mandated by the Court of Appeals for the Eighth Circuit's decision in *Superior Oil Co. v. Fulmer*, 785 F.2d 252 (1986), which the District Court interpreted as adopting an "extremely restrictive" test for a pattern of racketeering activity that required proof of "multiple illegal schemes." The Court of Appeals for the Eighth Circuit affirmed the dismissal of petitioners' complaint, confirming that under Eighth Circuit precedent "[a] single fraudulent effort or scheme is insufficient" to establish a pattern of racketeering activity, and agreeing with the District Court that petitioners' complaint alleged only a single scheme. Two members of the panel suggested in separate concurrences, however, that the Court of Appeals should reconsider its test for a RICO pattern. Most Courts of Appeals have rejected the Eighth Circuit's interpretation of RICO's pattern concept to require an allegation and proof of multiple schemes, and we granted certiorari to resolve this conflict. We now reverse.

II

*** We begin, of course, with RICO's text, in which Congress followed a "pattern [of] utilizing terms and concepts of breadth." *Russello v. United States*, 464 U.S. 16, 21 (1983). As we remarked in *Sedima* [*S.P.R.L. v. Imrex Co.*, 473 U.S. 479, 496 n.14 (1985)] the section of the statute headed "definitions," 18 U.S.C. § 1961, does not so much define a pattern of racketeering activity as state a minimum necessary condition for the existence of such a pattern. Unlike other provisions in § 1961 that tell us what various concepts used in the Act "mean,"

18 U.S.C. § 1961(5) says of the phrase "pattern of racketeering activity" only that it "requires at least two acts of racketeering activity, one of which occurred after [October 15, 1970,] and the last of which occurred within ten years (excluding any period of imprisonment) after the commission of a prior act of racketeering activity." It thus places an outer limit on the concept of a pattern of racketeering activity that is broad indeed.

Section 1961(5) does indicate that Congress envisioned circumstances in which no more than two predicates would be necessary to establish a pattern of racketeering—otherwise it would have drawn a narrower boundary to RICO liability, requiring proof of a greater number of predicates. But, at the same time, the statement that a pattern "requires at least" two predicates implies "that while two acts are necessary, they may not be sufficient." *Sedima,* 473 U.S., at 496, n. 14. Section 1961(5) concerns only the minimum *number* of predicates necessary to establish a pattern; and it assumes that there is something to a RICO pattern *beyond* simply the number of predicate acts involved. The legislative history bears out this interpretation, for the principal sponsor of the Senate bill expressly indicated that "proof of two acts of racketeering activity, without more, does not establish a pattern." 116 Cong. Rec. 18940 (1970) (statement of Sen. McClellan). Section § 1961(5) does not identify, though, these additional prerequisites for establishing the existence of a RICO pattern.

In addition to § 1961(5), there is the key phrase "pattern of racketeering activity" itself, from § 1962, and we must "start with the assumption that the legislative purpose is expressed by the ordinary meaning of the words used." *Richards v. United States,* 369 U.S. 1, 9 (1962). In normal usage, the word "pattern" here would be taken to require more than just a multiplicity of racketeering predicates. A "pattern" is an "arrangement or order of things or activity," 11 Oxford English Dictionary 357 (2d ed. 1989), and the mere fact that there are a number of predicates is no guarantee that they fall into any arrangement or order. It is not the number of predicates but the relationship that they bear to each other or to some external organizing principle that renders them "ordered" or "arranged." The text of RICO conspicuously fails anywhere to identify, however, forms of relationship or external principles to be used in determining whether racketeering activity falls into a pattern for purposes of the Act.

It is reasonable to infer, from this absence of any textual identification of sorts of pattern that would satisfy § 1962's requirement, in combination with the very relaxed limits to the pattern concept fixed in § 1961(5), that Congress intended to take a flexible approach, and envisaged that a pattern might be demonstrated by reference to a range of different ordering principles or relationships between predicates, within the expansive bounds set. For any more specific guidance as to the meaning of "pattern," we must look past the text to RICO's legislative history, as we have done in prior cases construing the Act.

The legislative history *** shows that Congress indeed had a fairly flexible concept of a pattern in mind. A pattern is not formed by "sporadic activity," S. Rep. No. 91-617, p. 158 (1969), and a person cannot "be subjected to the sanctions of title IX simply for committing two widely separated and isolated criminal offenses," 116 Cong. Rec. at 18940 (1970) (Sen. McClellan). Instead, "[t]he term 'pattern' itself requires the showing of a relationship" between the predicates, ibid., and of " 'the threat of continuing activity,' " ibid., quoting S. Rep. No. 91-617, supra at 158. "It is this factor of *continuity plus relationship* which combines to produce a pattern." 116 Cong. Rec., at 18940 (emphasis added). RICO's legislative history reveals Congress' intent that to prove a pattern of racketeering activity a plaintiff or prosecutor must show that the racketeering predicates are related, *and* that they amount to or pose a threat of continued criminal activity.

B

For analytic purposes these two constituents of RICO's pattern requirement must be stated separately, though in practice their proof will often overlap. The element of relatedness is the easier to define, for we may take guidance from a provision elsewhere in the Organized Crime Control Act of 1970 (OCCA), of which RICO formed Title IX. OCCA included as Title X the Dangerous Special Offender Sentencing Act, 18 U.S.C. § 3575 *et seq.* (now partially repealed). Title X provided for enhanced sentences where, among other things, the defendant had committed a prior felony as part of a pattern of criminal conduct or in furtherance of a conspiracy to engage in a pattern of criminal conduct. As we noted in *Sedima,* supra, at 496, n. 14, Congress defined Title X's pattern requirement solely in terms of the *relationship* of the defendant's criminal acts one to another: "[C]riminal conduct forms a pattern if it embraces criminal acts that have the same or similar purposes, results, participants, victims, or methods of commission, or otherwise are interrelated by distinguishing characteristics and are not isolated events." § 3575(e). We have no reason to suppose that Congress had in mind for RICO's pattern of racketeering component any more constrained a notion of the relationships between predicates that would suffice.

RICO's legislative history tells us, however, that the relatedness of racketeering activities is not alone enough to satisfy § 1962's pattern element. To establish a RICO pattern it must also be shown that the predicates themselves amount to, or that they otherwise constitute a threat of, *continuing* racketeering activity. As to this continuity requirement, § 3575(e) is of no assistance. It is this aspect of RICO's pattern element that has spawned the "multiple scheme" test adopted by some lower courts, including the Court of Appeals in this case. But although proof that a RICO defendant has been involved in multiple criminal schemes would certainly be highly relevant to the inquiry into the continuity of the defendant's racketeering activity, it is implausible to suppose that Congress thought continuity might be shown *only* by proof of multiple schemes. The Eighth Circuit's test brings a rigidity to the available methods of proving a pattern that simply is not present in the idea of "continuity" itself; and it does so, moreover, by introducing a concept—the "scheme"—that appears nowhere in the language or legislative history of the Act.[3] We adopt a less inflexible approach that seems to us to derive from a

3. Nor does the multiple scheme approach to identifying continuing criminal conduct have the advantage of lessening the uncertainty inherent in RICO's pattern component, for " 'scheme' is hardly a self-defining term." *Barticheck v. Fidelity Union Bank/First National State,* 832 F.2d, at 39. A "scheme" is in the eye of the beholder,

commonsense, everyday understanding of RICO's language and Congress' gloss on it. What a plaintiff or prosecutor must prove is continuity of racketeering activity, or its threat, *simpliciter*. This may be done in a variety of ways, thus making it difficult to formulate in the abstract any general test for continuity. We can, however, begin to delineate the requirement.

"Continuity" is both a closed- and open-ended concept, referring either to a closed period of repeated conduct, or to past conduct that by its nature projects into the future with a threat of repetition. See *Barticheck v. Fidelity Union Bank/First National State,* 832 F.2d 36, 39 (CA3 1987). It is, in either case, centrally a temporal concept—and particularly so in the RICO context, where *what* must be continuous, RICO's predicate acts or offenses, and the *relationship* these predicates must bear one to another, are distinct requirements. A party alleging a RICO violation may demonstrate continuity over a closed period by proving a series of related predicates extending over a substantial period of time. Predicate acts extending over a few weeks or months and threatening no future criminal conduct do not satisfy this requirement: Congress was concerned in RICO with long-term criminal conduct. Often a RICO action will be brought before continuity can be established in this way. In such cases, liability depends on whether the *threat* of continuity is demonstrated. See S. Rep. No. 91-617, at 158.

Whether the predicates proved establish a threat of continued racketeering activity depends on the specific facts of each case. Without making any claim to cover the field of possibilities—preferring to deal with this issue in the context of concrete factual situations presented for decision—we offer some examples of how this element might be satisfied. A RICO pattern may surely be established if the related predicates themselves involve a distinct threat of long-term racketeering activity, either implicit or explicit. Suppose a hoodlum were to sell "insurance" to a neighborhood's storekeepers to cover them against breakage of their windows, telling his victims he would be reappearing each month to collect the "premium" that would continue their "coverage." Though the number of related predicates involved may be small and they may occur close together in time, the racketeering acts themselves include a specific threat of repetition extending indefinitely into the future, and thus supply the requisite threat of continuity. In other cases, the threat of continuity may be established by showing that the predicate acts or offenses are part of an ongoing entity's regular way of doing business. Thus, the threat of continuity is sufficiently established where the predicates can be attributed to a defendant operating as part of a long-term association that exists for criminal purposes. Such associations include, but extend well beyond, those traditionally grouped under the phrase "organized crime." The continuity requirement is likewise satisfied where it is shown that the predicates are a regular way of conducting defendant's ongoing legitimate business (in the sense that it is not a business that

---

since whether a scheme exists depends on the level of generality at which criminal activity is viewed. ***

exists for criminal purposes), or of conducting or participating in an ongoing and legitimate RICO "enterprise."[4]

The limits of the relationship and continuity concepts that combine to define a RICO pattern, and the precise methods by which relatedness and continuity or its threat may be proved, cannot be fixed in advance with such clarity that it will always be apparent whether in a particular case a "pattern of racketeering activity" exists. The development of these concepts must await future cases, absent a decision by Congress to revisit RICO to provide clearer guidance as to the Act's intended scope. ***

IV

We turn now to the application of our analysis of RICO's pattern requirement. Because respondents prevailed on a motion under Federal Rule of Civil Procedure 12(b)(6), we read the facts alleged in the complaint in the light most favorable to petitioners. ***

Petitioners' complaint alleges that at different times over the course of at least a 6-year period the noncommissioner respondents gave five members of the MPUC numerous bribes, in several different forms, with the objective—in which they were allegedly successful—of causing these commissioners to approve unfair and unreasonable rates for Northwestern Bell. RICO defines bribery as a "racketeering activity," 18 U.S.C. § 1961(1), so petitioners have alleged multiple predicate acts.

Under the analysis we have set forth above, and consistent with the allegations in their complaint, petitioners may be able to prove that the multiple predicates alleged constitute "a pattern of racketeering activity," in that they satisfy the requirements of relationship and continuity. The acts of bribery alleged are said to be related by a common purpose, to influence commissioners in carrying out their duties in order to win approval of unfairly and unreasonably high rates for Northwestern Bell. Furthermore, petitioners claim that the racketeering predicates occurred with some frequency over at least a 6-year period, which may be sufficient to satisfy the continuity requirement. Alternatively, a threat of continuity of racketeering activity might be established at trial by showing that the alleged bribes were a regular way of conducting Northwestern Bell's ongoing business, or a regular way of conducting or participating in the conduct of the alleged and ongoing RICO enterprise, the MPUC.

The Court of Appeals thus erred in affirming the District Court's dismissal of petitioners' complaint for failure to plead "a pattern of racketeering

4. Insofar as the concurrence seems to suggest that very short periods of criminal activity that do *not* in any way carry a threat of continued criminal activity constitute "obvious racketeer[ing]" to which Congress intended RICO, with its enhanced penalties, to apply, we have concluded that it is mistaken, and that when Congress said predicates must demonstrate "continuity" before they may form a RICO pattern, it expressed an intent that RICO reach activities that amount to or threaten long-term criminal activity.

activity." The judgment is reversed, and the case is remanded for further proceedings consistent with this opinion.

JUSTICE SCALIA, WITH WHOM THE CHIEF JUSTICE, JUSTICE O'CONNOR, AND JUSTICE KENNEDY JOIN, CONCURRING IN THE JUDGMENT.

*** Elevating to the level of statutory text a phrase taken from the legislative history, the Court counsels the lower courts: " 'continuity plus relationship.' " (emphasis deleted). This seems to me about as helpful to the conduct of their affairs as "life is a fountain." Of the two parts of this talismanic phrase, the relatedness requirement is said to be the "easier to define," ibid., yet here is the Court's definition, *in toto:* " '[C]riminal conduct forms a pattern if it embraces criminal acts that have the same or similar purposes, results, participants, victims, or methods of commission, or otherwise are interrelated by distinguishing characteristics and are not isolated events,' " This definition has the feel of being solidly rooted in law, since it is a direct quotation of 18 U.S.C. § 3575(e). Unfortunately, if normal (and sensible) rules of statutory construction were followed, the existence of § 3575(e)—which is the definition contained in another title of the Act that was explicitly *not* rendered applicable to RICO—suggests that *whatever* "pattern" might mean in RICO, it assuredly *does not* mean that. "[W]here Congress includes particular language in one section of a statute but omits it in another section of the same Act, it is generally presumed that Congress acts intentionally and purposely in the disparate inclusion or exclusion." *Russello v. United States,* 464 U.S. 16, 23 (1983). But that does not really matter, since § 3575(e) is utterly uninformative anyway. It hardly closes in on the target to know that "relatedness" refers to acts that are related by "purposes, results, participants, victims, ... methods of commission, *or* [just in case that is not vague enough] *otherwise.*" Is the fact that the victims of both predicate acts were women enough? Or that both acts had the purpose of enriching the defendant? Or that the different coparticipants of the defendant in both acts were his coemployees? I doubt that the lower courts will find the Court's instructions much more helpful than telling them to look for a "pattern"—which is what the statute already says.

The Court finds "continuity" more difficult to define precisely. "Continuity," it says, "is both a closed- and open-ended concept, referring either to a closed period of repeated conduct, or to past conduct that by its nature projects into the future with a threat of repetition." I have no idea what this concept of a "closed period of repeated conduct" means. Virtually all allegations of racketeering activity, in both civil and criminal suits, will relate to past periods that are "closed" (unless one expects plaintiff or the prosecutor to establish that the defendant not only committed the crimes he did, but is still committing them), and all of them *must* relate to conduct that is "repeated," because of RICO's multiple-act requirement. I had thought, initially, that the Court was seeking to draw a distinction between, on the one hand, past repeated conduct (multiple racketeering acts) that is "closed-ended" in the sense that, in its totality, it constitutes only one criminal "scheme" or "episode"—which would not fall within RICO unless in its nature (for one or more of the reasons later described by the Court) it threatened future criminal endeavors as well—and, on the other hand, past repeated conduct (multiple racketeering acts) that constitutes several separate schemes—which is alone enough to invoke RICO.

But of course that cannot be what it means, since the Court rejects the "multiple scheme" concept, not merely as the *exclusive* touchstone of RICO liability, but in all its applications, since it "introduc[es] a concept ... that appears nowhere in the language or legislative history of the Act," and is so vague and "amorphous" as to exist only "in the eye of the beholder." Moreover, the Court tells us that predicate acts extending, not over a "substantial period of time," but only over a "few weeks or months and threatening no future criminal conduct" do not satisfy the continuity requirement. Since the Court has rejected the concept of separate criminal "schemes" or "episodes" as a criterion of "threatening future criminal conduct," I think it must be saying that at least a few months of racketeering activity (and who knows how much more?) is generally for free, as far as RICO is concerned. The "closed period" concept is a sort of safe harbor for racketeering activity that does not last *too* long, no matter how many different crimes and different schemes are involved, so long as it does not otherwise "establish a threat of continued racketeering activity," ibid. A gang of hoodlums that commits one act of extortion on Monday in New York, a second in Chicago on Tuesday, a third in San Francisco on Wednesday, and so on through an entire week, and then finally and completely disbands, cannot be reached under RICO. I am sure that is not what the statute intends, but I cannot imagine what else the Court's murky discussion can possibly mean. ***

It is, however, unfair to be so critical of the Court's effort, because I would be unable to provide an interpretation of RICO that gives significantly more guidance concerning its application. It is clear to me from the prologue of the statute, which describes a relatively narrow focus upon "organized crime," that the word "pattern" in the phrase "pattern of racketeering activity" was meant to import some requirement beyond the mere existence of multiple predicate acts. Thus, when § 1961(5) says that a pattern "requires at least two acts of racketeering activity" it is describing what is needful but not sufficient. (If that were not the case, the concept of "pattern" would have been unnecessary, and the statute could simply have attached liability to "multiple acts of racketeering activity"). But what that something more is, is beyond me. As I have suggested, it is also beyond the Court. Today's opinion has added nothing to improve our prior guidance, which has created a kaleidoscope of Circuit positions, except to clarify that RICO may in addition be violated when there is a "threat of continuity." It seems to me this increases rather than removes the vagueness. There is no reason to believe that the Courts of Appeals will be any more unified in the future, than they have in the past, regarding the content of this law.

That situation is bad enough with respect to any statute, but it is intolerable with respect to RICO. *** RICO, since it has criminal applications as well, must, even in its civil applications, possess the degree of certainty required for criminal laws. No constitutional challenge to this law has been raised in the present case, and so that issue is not before us. That the highest Court in the land has been unable to derive from this statute anything more than today's meager guidance bodes ill for the day when that challenge is presented.

However unhelpful its guidance may be, however, I think the Court is correct in saying that nothing in the statute supports the proposition that predicate acts constituting part of a single scheme (or single episode) can never support a cause of action under RICO. Since the Court of Appeals here rested its decision on the contrary proposition, I concur in the judgment of the Court reversing the decision below.

### *NOTES AND QUESTIONS*

***1. Closed Period Continuity—How Much Time is Enough?*** The Court held that "[p]redicate acts extending over a few weeks or months and threatening no future criminal conduct" do not constitute closed period continuity. How much longer would be long enough? See, e.g., *United States v. Pelullo,* 964 F.2d 193, 209 (3d Cir. 1993) (19 months sufficient); *Primary Care Investors, Seven, Inc. v. PHP Healthcare Corp.,* 986 F.2d 1208, 1215-16 (8th Cir. 1993) (11 months insufficient) (collecting cases). On what basis should the line be drawn?

***2. Closed Period Continuity and the Centrality of Time.*** In determining whether closed period continuity is present, should time be the exclusive consideration? Compare *Fleet Credit Corp. v. Sion,* 893 F.2d 441, 446-47 (1st Cir. 1990) (giving affirmative answer where defendant committed predicate offenses over a "substantial period of time") with *Resolution Trust Corp. v. Stone,* 998 F.2d 1534, 1543 (10th Cir. 1993) (giving a negative answer). Courts that look at other factors typically take into account "the number of victims, the number of racketeering acts, the variety of racketeering acts, whether the injuries caused were distinct, the complexity and size of the scheme, and the nature or character of the enterprise or unlawful activity." Id. at 1543-44. Does *HJ* preclude consideration of some (or all) of these factors in evaluating closed period continuity? What about taking into account the threat of continuing criminal activity? Compare *Tabas v. Tabas,* 47 F.3d 1280, 1295 (3d Cir. 1995) (finding it appropriate to do so) with *Kehr Packages, Inc. v. Fidelcor, Inc.,* 926 F.2d 1406, 1421 (3d Cir. 1991) (Alito, J., concurring in part and dissenting in part) (finding it inappropriate to do so).

***3. Assessing Open-Ended Continuity.*** The Court indicated that open-ended continuity can turn on whether "the predicate acts or offenses are part of an ongoing entity's regular way of doing business." Are the factors mentioned in note 2 relevant to open-ended continuity as well? Cf. *Tabas v. Tabas,* 47 F.3d 1280, 1296 n. 21 (3d Cir. 1995) (answering this question in the affirmative).

***4. The Merits of Separateness.*** Does *H.J.* suggest the need to retain open-ended continuity and closed period continuity as separate categories? Would it be a good idea to maintain their separateness?

***5. Void for Vagueness?*** In his concurrence, Justice Scalia encouraged defendants to mount vagueness challenges to the pattern requirement. Such challenges have not met with success. See, e.g., *United States v. Glecier,* 923 F.2d 496, 497 n. 1 (7th Cir. 1991). See generally Joseph E. Bauerschmidt, Note, "Mother of Mercy—Is this the End of RICO?"—Justice Scalia Invites Constitutional Void-for-Vagueness Challenges to RICO "Pattern," 65 Notre Dame. L. Rev. 1106 (1990).

### 3. *The Enterprise*

Under Section 1962(c), the defendant must be "employed by or associated with" a RICO "enterprise." RICO defines an "enterprise" as "includ[ing] any individual, partnership, corporation, association, or other legal entity, and any union or group of individuals associated in fact although not a legal entity." § 1961(4). In *United States v. Turkette,* 452 U.S. 576 (1981), the Supreme Court held that this definition "no more excludes criminal enterprises than it does legitimate ones" and therefore encompasses a criminal gang. Id. at 580-81. Moreover, the Court made the following observations concerning the necessary relationship between the RICO enterprise and the pattern of racketeering activity:

> In order to secure a conviction under RICO, the Government must prove both the existence of an "enterprise" and the connected "pattern of racketeering activity." The enterprise is an entity, for present purposes a group of persons associated together for a common purpose of engaging in a course of conduct. The pattern of racketeering activity is, on the other hand, a series of criminal acts as defined by the statute. The former is proved by evidence of an ongoing organization, formal or informal, and by evidence that the various associates function as a continuing unit. The latter is proved by evidence of the requisite number of acts of racketeering committed by the participants in the enterprise. While the proof used to establish these separate elements may in particular cases coalesce, proof of one does not necessarily establish the other. The "enterprise" is not the "pattern of racketeering activity;" it is an entity separate and apart from the pattern of activity in which it engages. The existence of an enterprise at all times remains a separate element which must be proved by the Government.

Id. at 583.

### *NOTES AND QUESTIONS*

*1. **Establishing an Association-In-Fact-Enterprise.*** When an enterprise is a corporation or other legal entity, it typically has a structure wholly apart from the pattern of racketeering activity in which it engages. Suppose, however, that the enterprise is an association-in-fact, as in *Turkette.* Under these circumstances, must the enterprise have an identifiable structure that is distinct from the pattern of racketeering activity? The courts are divided. See *Chang v. Chen,* 80 F.3d 1293, 1297-1300 (9th Cir. 1996) (collecting cases). Cf. *United States v. Bledsoe,* 674 F.2d 647, 665 (8th Cir. 1982) (rejecting for lack of sufficient structure an association of agricultural cooperatives that engaged in fraudulent securities transactions); *In re Rexplore, Inc. Sec. Litig.,* 671 F. Supp. 679, 689-90 (N.D. Cal. 1987) (rejecting for lack of sufficient structure an association of defendants who engaged in wire and securities fraud). Consider the following argument against requiring proof of an identifiable structure:

> [O]n the issue of structure and its ascertainability, the slope is slippery, and the district court appropriately avoided the slope's edge. Since Congress intended the term "enterprise" to include both legal and criminal enterprises, and because the latter may not observe the niceties of legitimate organizational structures, we refuse to import an "ascertainable structure" requirement into jury instructions.

*United States v. Patrick,* 248 F.3d 11, 19 (1st Cir. 2001). Is this position consistent with *Turkette?* Is it sound as a matter of policy?

*2. Association-in-Fact vs. Legal Entity.* Assume that the DOJ has the option of naming as the enterprise either a legal entity or an association-in-fact with an identifiable structure. Which would it be more likely to choose?

*3. Differentiating the Enterprise from the "Person."* Section 1962(c) differentiates between the "enterprise" and the "person" who is the defendant. The Supreme Court has held that the "enterprise" and the "person" are sufficiently distinct when the enterprise is a corporation with a single shareholder and that shareholder is the defendant: "The corporate owner/employee, a natural person, is distinct from the corporation itself, a legally different entity with different rights and responsibilities due to its different legal status." *Cedric Kushner Promotions, Ltd. v. King,* 533 U.S. 158, 163 (2001). Can the enterprise be a sole proprietorship and the defendant the sole proprietor? In a decision prior to *Cedric,* Judge Posner suggested that the answer turns on whether the proprietorship has employees:

> A sole proprietorship is a recognized legal entity, and, provided it has any employees, is in any event a "group of individuals associated in fact." Since *** the enterprises to which the statute refers include criminal enterprises, and not just legitimate enterprises penetrated or looted by criminals, it would be passing strange to exclude proprietorships. After all, we do not suppose that "Murder, Inc." was really a corporation.***
>
> There would be a problem if the sole proprietorship were strictly a 1-man show. *** [Y]ou cannot associate with yourself, any more than you can conspire with yourself, just by giving yourself a *nom de guerre.* *** But Suter had several people working for him; this made his company an enterprise, and not just a one-man-band. ***

*McCullough v. Suter,* 757 F.2d 142, 143-44 (7th Cir. 1985). Cf. *Guidry v. Bank of LaPlace,* 954 F.2d 278, 283 (5th Cir. 1992) (finding Section 1962(c) inapplicable to a proprietorship with no employees). Are *McCullough* and *Guidry* consistent with *Cedric*? Can the corporation be the "person" and the enterprise be an association of the corporation and its employees?

---

### 4. *Conducting or Participating in the Conduct of the Enterprise*

Under Section 1962(c), the defendant must "conduct or participate, directly or indirectly, in the conduct of " the RICO enterprise. The Supreme Court construed this language in the decision that follows.

## REVES v. ERNST & YOUNG

507 U.S. 170 (1993)

JUSTICE BLACKMUN:

This case requires us once again to interpret the provisions of the Racketeer Influenced and Corrupt Organizations (RICO) chapter of the Organized Crime Control Act of 1970. Section 1962(c) makes it unlawful "for any person employed by or associated with any enterprise engaged in, or the activities of which affect, interstate or foreign commerce, to conduct or participate, directly or indirectly, in the conduct of such enterprise's affairs through a pattern of racketeering activity...." The question presented is whether one must participate in the operation or management of the enterprise itself to be subject to liability under this provision.

I

The Farmer's Cooperative of Arkansas and Oklahoma, Inc. (Co-Op), began operating in western Arkansas and eastern Oklahoma in 1946. To raise money for operating expenses, the Co-Op sold promissory notes payable to the holder on demand. Each year, Co-Op members were elected to serve on its board. The board met monthly but delegated actual management of the Co-Op to a general manager. In 1952, the board appointed Jack White as general manager.

In January 1980, White began taking loans from the Co-Op to finance the construction of a gasohol plant by his company, White Flame Fuels, Inc. By the end of 1980, White's debts to the Co-Op totaled approximately $4 million. In September of that year, White and Gene Kuykendall, who served as the accountant for both the Co-Op and White Flame, were indicted for federal tax fraud. At a board meeting on November 12, 1980, White proposed that the Co-Op purchase White Flame. The board agreed. One month later, however, the Co-Op filed a declaratory action against White and White Flame in Arkansas state court alleging that White actually had sold White Flame to the Co-Op in February 1980. The complaint was drafted by White's attorneys and led to a consent decree relieving White of his debts and providing that the Co-Op had owned White Flame since February 15, 1980.

White and Kuykendall were convicted of tax fraud in January 1981. Harry Erwin, the managing partner of Russell Brown and Company, an Arkansas accounting firm, testified for White, and shortly thereafter the Co-Op retained Russell Brown to perform its 1981 financial audit. Joe Drozal, a partner in the Brown firm, was put in charge of the audit and Joe Cabaniss was selected to assist him. On January 2, 1982, Russell Brown and Company merged with Arthur Young and Company, which later became respondent Ernst & Young.

One of Drozal's first tasks in the audit was to determine White Flame's fixed-asset value. After consulting with White and reviewing White Flame's books (which Kuykendall had prepared), Drozal concluded that the plant's value at the end of 1980 was $4,393,242.66, the figure Kuykendall had employed. Using this figure as a base, Drozal factored in the 1981 construction costs and capitalized expenses and concluded that White Flame's 1981 fixed-asset value was approximately $4.5 million. Drozal then had to determine how that value should be treated for accounting purposes. If the Co-Op had owned White Flame from the beginning of construction in 1979, White Flame's value for accounting purposes would be its fixed-asset value of $4.5 million. If, however, the Co-Op had purchased White Flame from White, White Flame would have to be given its fair market value at the time of purchase, which was somewhere between $444,000 and $1.5 million. If White Flame were valued at less than $1.5 million, the Co-Op was insolvent. Drozal concluded that the Co-Op had owned White Flame from the start and that the plant should be valued at $4.5 million on its books.

On April 22, 1982, Arthur Young presented its 1981 audit report to the Co-Op's board. In that audit's Note 9, Arthur Young expressed doubt whether the investment in White Flame could ever be recovered. Note 9 also observed that White Flame was sustaining operating losses averaging $100,000 per month. Arthur Young did not tell the board of its conclusion that the Co-Op always had owned White Flame or that without that conclusion the Co-Op was insolvent.

On May 27, the Co-Op held its 1982 annual meeting. At that meeting, the Co-Op, through Harry C. Erwin, a partner in Arthur Young, distributed to the members condensed financial statements. These included White Flame's $4.5 million asset value among its total assets but omitted the information contained in the audit's Note 9. Cabaniss was also present. Erwin saw the condensed financial statement for the first time when he arrived at the meeting. In a 5-minute presentation, he told his audience that the statements were condensed and that copies of the full audit were available at the Co-Op's office. In response to questions, Erwin explained that the Co-Op owned White Flame and that the plant had incurred approximately $1.2 million in losses but he revealed no other information relevant to the Co-Op's true financial health.

The Co-Op hired Arthur Young also to perform its 1982 audit. The 1982 report, presented to the board on March 7, 1983, was similar to the 1981 report and restated (this time in its Note 8) Arthur Young's doubt whether the investment in White Flame was recoverable. The gasohol plant again was valued at approximately $4.5 million and was responsible for the Co-Op's showing a positive net worth. The condensed financial statement distributed at the annual meeting on March 24, 1983, omitted the information in Note 8. This time, Arthur Young reviewed the condensed statement in advance but did not act to remove its name from the statement. Cabaniss, in a 3-minute presentation at the meeting, gave the financial report. He informed the members that the full audit was available at the Co-Op's office but did not tell them about Note 8 or that the Co-Op was in financial difficulty if White Flame were written down to its fair market value.

In February 1984, the Co-Op experienced a slight run on its demand notes. On February 23, when it was unable to secure further financing, the Co-Op filed for bankruptcy. As a result, the demand notes were frozen in the bankruptcy estate and were no longer redeemable at will by the noteholders.

II

On February 14, 1985, the trustee in bankruptcy filed suit against 40 individuals and entities, including Arthur Young, on behalf of the Co-Op and certain noteholders. The District Court certified a class of noteholders, petitioners here, consisting of persons who had purchased demand notes between February 15, 1980, and February 23, 1984. Petitioners settled with all defendants except Arthur Young. The District Court determined before trial that the demand notes were securities under both federal and state law. The court then granted summary judgment in favor of Arthur Young on the RICO claim. The District Court applied the test established by the Eighth Circuit in *Bennett v. Berg*, 710 F.2d 1361, 1364 (en banc) (1983), that § 1962(c) requires "some participation in the operation or management of the enterprise itself."

The court ruled: "Plaintiffs have failed to show anything more than that the accountants reviewed a series of completed transactions, and certified the Co-Op's records as fairly portraying its financial status as of a date three or four months preceding the meetings of the directors and the shareholders at which they presented their reports. We do not hesitate to declare that such activities fail to satisfy the degree of management required by *Bennett v. Berg*."

The case went to trial on the state and federal securities fraud claims. The jury found that Arthur Young had committed both state and federal securities fraud and awarded approximately $6.1 million in damages. The Court of Appeals reversed, concluding that the demand notes were not securities under federal or state law. On writ of certiorari, this Court ruled that the notes were securities within the meaning of § 3(a)(10) of the Securities Exchange Act of 1934. *Reves v. Ernst & Young,* 494 U.S. 56, 70 (1990).

On remand, the Court of Appeals affirmed the judgment of the District Court in all major respects except the damages award, which it reversed and remanded for a new trial. The only part of the Court of Appeals' decision that is at issue here is its affirmance of summary judgment in favor of Arthur Young on the RICO claim. Like the District Court, the Court of Appeals applied the "operation or management" test articulated in *Bennett v. Berg* and held that Arthur Young's conduct did not "rise to the level of participation in the management or operation of the Co-Op." ***

III

"In determining the scope of a statute, we look first to its language. If the statutory language is unambiguous, in the absence of 'a clearly expressed legislative intent to the contrary, that language must ordinarily be regarded as conclusive.' " *United States v. Turkette,* 452 U.S. 576, 580 (1981), quoting *Consumer Product Safety Comm'n v. GTE Sylvania, Inc.,* 447 U.S. 102, 108 (1980). Section 1962(c) makes it unlawful "for any person employed by or associated with any enterprise ... to conduct or participate, directly or indirectly, in the conduct of such enterprise's affairs through a pattern of racketeering activity...."

The narrow question in this case is the meaning of the phrase "to conduct or participate, directly or indirectly, in the conduct of such enterprise's affairs." The word "conduct" is used twice, and it seems reasonable to give each use a similar construction. As a verb, "conduct" means to lead, run, manage, or direct. Webster's Third New International Dictionary 474 (1976). Petitioners urge us to read "conduct" as "carry on," so that almost any involvement in the affairs of an enterprise would satisfy the "conduct or participate" requirement. But context is important, and in the context of the phrase "to conduct ... [an] enterprise's affairs," the word indicates some degree of direction.

The dissent agrees that, when "conduct" is used as a verb, "it is plausible to find in it a suggestion of control." The dissent prefers to focus on "conduct" as a noun, as in the phrase "participate, directly or indirectly, in the conduct of [an] enterprise's affairs." But unless one reads "conduct" to include an element of direction when used as a noun in this phrase, the word becomes superfluous. Congress could easily have written "participate, directly or indirectly, in [an] enterprise's affairs," but it chose to repeat the word "conduct." We conclude, therefore, that as both a noun and a verb in this subsection "conduct" requires an element of direction.

The more difficult question is what to make of the word "participate." This Court previously has characterized this word as a "ter [m] ... of breadth." *Russello* [*v. United States*, 464 U.S. 16, 21-22 (1983).] Petitioners argue that Congress used "participate" as a synonym for "aid and abet." That would be a term of breadth indeed, for "aid and abet" "comprehends all assistance rendered by words, acts, encouragement, support, or presence." Black's Law Dictionary 68 (6th ed. 1990). But within the context of § 1962(c), "participate" appears to have a narrower meaning. We may mark the limits of what the term might mean by looking again at what Congress did *not* say. On the one hand, "to participate ... in the conduct of ... affairs" must be broader than "to conduct affairs" or the "participate" phrase would be superfluous. On the other hand, as we already have noted, "to participate ... in the conduct of ... affairs" must be narrower than "to participate in affairs" or Congress' repetition of the word "conduct" would serve no purpose. It seems that Congress chose a middle ground, consistent with a common understanding of the word "participate"—"to take part in." Webster's Third New International Dictionary 1646 (1976).

Once we understand the word "conduct" to require some degree of direction and the word "participate" to require some part in that direction, the meaning of § 1962(c) comes into focus. In order to "participate, directly or indirectly, in the conduct of such enterprise's affairs," one must have some part in directing those affairs. Of course, the word "participate" makes clear that RICO liability is not limited to those with primary responsibility for the enterprise's affairs, just as the phrase "directly or indirectly" makes clear that RICO liability is not limited to those with a formal position in the enterprise,[4] but *some* part in directing the enterprise's affairs is required. The "operation or management" test expresses this requirement in a formulation that is easy to apply.

## IV

### A

This test finds further support in the legislative history of § 1962. ***

In their comments on the floor, Members of Congress consistently referred to subsection (c) as prohibiting the *operation* of an enterprise through a pattern of racketeering activity and to subsections (a) and (b) as prohibiting the *acquisition* of an enterprise. Representative Cellar, who was chairman of the House Judiciary Committee that voted RICO out in 1970, described § 1962(c) as proscribing the "conduct of the affairs of a business by a person acting in a *managerial* capacity, through racketeering activity." 116 Cong. Rec. 35196 (1970) (emphasis added).

---

4. For these reasons, we disagree with the suggestion of the Court of Appeals for the District of Columbia Circuit that § 1962(c) requires "*significant control* over or within an enterprise." *Yellow Bus Lines, Inc. v. Drivers, Chauffeurs & Helpers Local Union 639,* 913 F.2d 948, 954 (1990) (en banc) (emphasis added).

Of course, the fact that Members of Congress understood § 1962(c) to prohibit the operation or management of an enterprise through a pattern of racketeering activity does not necessarily mean that they understood § 1962(c) to be limited to the operation or management of an enterprise. It is clear from other remarks, however, that Congress did not intend RICO to extend beyond the acquisition or operation of an enterprise. *** [C]ritics of the bill raised concerns that racketeering activity was defined so broadly that RICO would reach many crimes not necessarily typical of organized crime. See 116 Cong. Rec. 18912-18914, 18939-18940 (1970) (remarks of Sen. McClellan). Senator McClellan reassured the bill's critics that the critical limitation was not to be found in § 1961(1)'s list of predicate crimes but in the statute's other requirements, including those of § 1962:

> The danger that commission of such offenses by other individuals would subject them to proceedings under title IX [RICO] is even smaller than any such danger under title III of the 1968 [Safe Streets] [A]ct, since commission of a crime listed under title IX provides only one element of title IX's prohibitions. Unless an individual not only commits such a crime but engages in a pattern of such violations, and uses that pattern to obtain or operate an interest in an interstate business, he is not made subject to proceedings under title IX.

116 Cong. Rec., at 18940.

Thus, the legislative history confirms what we have already deduced from the language of § 1962(c)—that one is not liable under that provision unless one has participated in the operation or management of the enterprise itself.

B

RICO's "liberal construction" clause does not require rejection of the "operation or management" test. Congress directed, by § 904(a) of Pub.L. 91-452, 84 Stat. 947, that the "provisions of this title shall be liberally construed to effectuate its remedial purposes." This clause obviously seeks to ensure that Congress' intent is not frustrated by an overly narrow reading of the statute, but it is not an invitation to apply RICO to new purposes that Congress never intended. Nor does the clause help us to determine what purposes Congress had in mind. Those must be gleaned from the statute through the normal means of interpretation. The clause " 'only serves as an aid for resolving an ambiguity; it is not to be used to beget one.' " *Sedima, S.P.R.L. v. Imrex Co.,* 473 U.S. 479, 492, n. 10 (1985), quoting *Callanan v. United States,* 364 U.S. 587, 596 (1961). In this case it is clear that Congress did not intend to extend RICO liability under § 1962(c) beyond those who participate in the operation or management of an enterprise through a pattern of racketeering activity.[8]

V

Petitioners argue that the "operation or management" test is flawed because liability under § 1962(c) is not limited to upper management but may extend to "any person employed by or associated with [the] enterprise." We

8. Because the meaning of the statute is clear from its language and legislative history, we have no occasion to consider the application of the rule of lenity. We note, however, that the rule of lenity would also favor the narrower "operation or management" test that we adopt.

agree that liability under § 1962(c) is not limited to upper management, but we disagree that the "operation or management" test is inconsistent with this proposition. An enterprise is "operated" not just by upper management but also by lower rung participants in the enterprise who are under the direction of upper management.[9] An enterprise also might be "operated" or "managed" by others "associated with" the enterprise who exert control over it as, for example, by bribery.

The United States also argues that the "operation or management" test is not consistent with § 1962(c) because it limits the liability of "outsiders" who have no official position within the enterprise. The United States correctly points out that RICO's major purpose was to attack the "infiltration of organized crime and racketeering into legitimate organizations," S. Rep. No. 91-617, at 76, but its argument fails on several counts. First, it ignores the fact that § 1962 has four subsections. Infiltration of legitimate organizations by "outsiders" is clearly addressed in subsections (a) and (b), and the "operation or management" test that applies under subsection (c) in no way limits the application of subsections (a) and (b) to "outsiders." Second, § 1962(c) is limited to persons "employed by or associated with" an enterprise, suggesting a more limited reach than subsections (a) and (b), which do not contain such a restriction. Third, § 1962(c) cannot be interpreted to reach complete "outsiders" because liability depends on showing that the defendants conducted or participated in the conduct of the "*enterprise's* affairs," not just their *own* affairs. Of course, "outsiders" may be liable under § 1962(c) if they are "associated with" an enterprise and participate in the conduct of *its* affairs—that is, participate in the operation or management of the enterprise itself—but it would be consistent with neither the language nor the legislative history of § 1962(c) to interpret it as broadly as petitioners and the United States urge.

In sum, we hold that "to conduct or participate, directly or indirectly, in the conduct of such enterprise's affairs," § 1962(c), one must participate in the operation or management of the enterprise itself.

## VI

*** In this case, it is undisputed that Arthur Young relied upon existing Co-Op records in preparing the 1981 and 1982 audit reports. The AICPA's professional standards state that an auditor may draft financial statements in whole or in part based on information from management's accounting system. See [1 CCH AICPA Professional Standards, SAS No. 1, § 110.02 (1982)]. It is also undisputed that Arthur Young's audit reports revealed to the Co-Op's board that the value of the gasohol plant had been calculated based on the Co-Op's investment in the plant. Thus, we only could conclude that Arthur Young participated in the operation or management of the Co-Op itself if Arthur

9. At oral argument, there was some discussion about whether low-level employees could be considered to have participated in the conduct of an enterprise's affairs. We need not decide in this case how far § 1962(c) extends down the ladder of operation because it is clear that Arthur Young was not acting under the direction of the Co-Op's officers or board.

Young's failure to tell the Co-Op's board that the plant should have been given its fair market value constituted such participation. We think that Arthur Young's failure in this respect is not sufficient to give rise to liability under § 1962(c).

The judgment of the Court of Appeals is affirmed.

JUSTICE SOUTER, WITH WHOM JUSTICE WHITE JOINS, DISSENTING:

In the word "conduct," the Court today finds a clear congressional mandate to limit RICO liability under 18 U.S.C. § 1962(c) to participants in the "operation or management" of a RICO enterprise. What strikes the Court as clear, however, looks at the very least hazy to me, and I accordingly find the statute's "liberal construction" provision not irrelevant, but dispositive. But even if I were to assume, with the majority, that the word "conduct" clearly imports some degree of direction or control into § 1962(c), I would have to say that the majority misapplies its own "operation or management" test to the facts presented here. I therefore respectfully dissent.

The word "conduct" occurs twice in § 1962(c), first as a verb, then as a noun.

> It shall be unlawful for any person employed by or associated with any enterprise engaged in, or the activities of which affect, interstate or foreign commerce, to conduct or participate, directly or indirectly, in the conduct of such enterprise's affairs through a pattern of racketeering activity or collection of unlawful debt.

18 U.S.C. § 1962(c).

Although the Court is surely correct that the cognates should receive consistent readings, and correct again that "context is important" in coming to understand the sense of the terms intended by Congress, the majority goes astray in quoting only the verb form of "conduct" in its statement of the context for divining a meaning that must fit the noun usage as well. Thus, the majority reaches its pivotal conclusion that "in the context of the phrase 'to conduct ... [an] enterprise's affairs,' the word indicates some degree of direction." Ibid. To be sure, if the statutory setting is so abbreviated as to limit consideration to the word as a verb, it is plausible to find in it a suggestion of control, as in the phrase "to conduct an orchestra." (Even so, the suggestion is less than emphatic, since even when "conduct" is used as a verb, "[t]he notion of direction or leadership is often obscured or lost; e.g. an investigation is *conducted* by all those who take part in it." 3 Oxford English Dictionary 691 (2d ed. 1989) (emphasis in original).

In any event, the context is not so limited, and several features of the full subsection at issue support a more inclusive construction of "conduct." The term, when used as a noun, is defined by the majority's chosen dictionary as, for example, "carrying forward" or "carrying out," Webster's Third New International Dictionary 473 (1976), phrases without any implication of direction or control. The suggestion of control is diminished further by the fact that § 1962(c) covers not just those "employed by" an enterprise, but those merely "associated with" it, as well. And associates (like employees) are prohibited not merely from conducting the affairs of an enterprise through a pattern of racketeering, not merely from participating directly in such unlawful conduct, but even from indirect participation in the conduct of an enterprise's affairs in such a manner. The very breadth of this prohibition renders the majority's reading of "conduct" rather awkward, for it is hard to imagine how the "operation or management" test would leave the statute with the capacity to reach the indirect participation of someone merely associated with an enterprise. I think, then, that this contextual examination shows "conduct" to have a long arm, unlimited by any requirement to prove that the activity includes an element of direction. But at the very least, the full context is enough to defeat the majority's conviction that the more restrictive interpretation of the word "conduct" is clearly the one intended.[1]

What, then, if we call it a tie on the contextual analysis? The answer is that Congress has given courts faced with uncertain meaning a clear tiebreaker in RICO's "liberal construction" clause, which directs that the "provisions of this title shall be liberally construed to effectuate its remedial purposes." We have relied before on this "express admonition" to read RICO provisions broadly, see *Sedima, S.P.R.L. v. Imrex Co.*, 473 U.S. 479, 497-498 (1985), and in this instance, the "liberal construction" clause plays its intended part, directing us to recognize the more inclusive definition of the word "conduct," free of any restricting element of direction or control.[2] Because the Court of Appeals employed a narrower reading, I would reverse.

Even if I were to adopt the majority's view of § 1962(c), however, I still could not join the judgment, which seems to me unsupportable under the very "operation or management" test the Court announces. If Arthur Young had confined itself in this case to the role traditionally performed by an outside auditor, I could agree with the majority that Arthur Young took no part in the management or operation of the Farmer's Cooperative of Arkansas and Oklahoma, Inc. (Co-Op). But the record on summary judgment, viewed most favorably to Reves, shows that Arthur Young created the very financial statements it was hired, and purported, to audit. Most importantly, Reves adduced evidence that Arthur Young took on management responsibilities by

---

1. The Court attempts to shore up its interpretation with an examination of relevant legislative materials. The legislative history demonstrates only that when Members of Congress needed a shorthand method of referring to § 1962(c), they spoke of prohibiting "the operation" of an enterprise through a pattern of racketeering activity. As Arthur Young points out, "operation" is essentially interchangeable with "conduct"; each term can include a sense of direction, but each is also definable as "carrying on" or "carrying out." There is no indication that the congressional shorthand was meant to attend to the statutory nuance at issue here. As the Court concedes, "[T]he fact that Members of Congress understood § 1962(c) to prohibit the operation or management of an enterprise through a pattern of racketeering activity does not necessarily mean that they understood § 1962(c) to be limited to the operation or management of an enterprise."

2. The majority claims that without an element of direction, the word "conduct," when it appears as a noun, becomes superfluous. Given the redundant language Congress has chosen for § 1962(c), however, any consistent reading of "conduct" will tend to make one of its two appearances superfluous.

deciding, in the first instance, what value to assign to the Co-Op's most important fixed asset, the White Flame gasohol plant, and Arthur Young itself conceded below that the alleged activity went beyond traditional auditing. Because I find, then, that even under the majority's "operation or management" test the Court of Appeals erroneously affirmed the summary judgment for Arthur Young, I would (again) reverse.

For our purposes, the line between managing and auditing is fairly clear. ***

*** [M]anagement chooses the assertions to appear in financial statements; the auditor "simply expresses an opinion on the client's financial statements." Brief for Respondent 30. These standards leave no doubt that an accountant can in no sense independently audit financial records when he has selected their substance himself. See *In re Thomas P. Reynolds Securities, Ltd.*, Exchange Act Release No. 29689 (Sept. 16, 1991) ("A company may, of course, rely on an outside firm to prepare its books of account and financial statements. However, once an accounting firm performs those functions, it has become identified with management and may not perform an audit").

The evidence on summary judgment, read favorably to Reves, indicates that Arthur Young did indeed step out of its auditing shoes and into those of management, in creating the financial record on which the Co-Op's solvency was erroneously predicated. ***

Arthur Young realized it could not rely on White Flame's 1980 financial statement, which had been prepared by a convicted felon (who also happened to be the Co-Op's former accountant), and an internal memo that appears in the record shows that Arthur Young had a number of serious questions about White Flame's cost figures for the plant. Nonetheless, Arthur Young "essentially invented" a cost figure that matched, to the penny, the phoney figure that Kuykendall, White Flame's convicted accountant, had created. With this "invented" cost figure in hand, Arthur Young then proceeded to decide, again without consulting management, when the Co-Op had acquired White Flame. Although the Co-Op's 1980 financial statement indicated an acquisition of White Flame in February 1980, as did a local court decree, Arthur Young "adopted a blatant fiction—that the Co-Op [had] owned the entire plant at its inception in May, 1979—in order to justify carrying the asset on [the Co-Op's] books at its total cost, as if the Co-Op had built it from scratch." App. 137. Apparently, the idea that the Co-Op had owned the gasohol plant since 1979 was reflected nowhere in the Co-Op's books, and Arthur Young was solely responsible for the Co-Op's decision to treat the transaction in this manner.[5]

5. The majority asserts, as an "undisputed" fact, "that Arthur Young relied upon Co-Op records in preparing the 1981 and 1982 audit reports." In fact, however, the District Court found that Reves had presented evidence sufficient to show that Arthur Young "essentially invented" a cost figure for White Flame (after examining White Flame records created by Kuykendall). Since the Co-Op's 1980 financial statement indicated that the Co-Op had advanced White Flame only $4.1 million through the end of 1980, Arthur Young could not have relied on the Co-Op's records in concluding that the plant's value was nearly $4.4 million at the end of 1980. The District Court also found sufficient evidence in the record to support the conclusion that Arthur Young had created the

Relying on this fiction, the unreality of which it never shared with the Co-Op's board of directors, let alone the membership, Arthur Young prepared the Co-Op's 1981 financial statement and listed a fixed- asset value of more than $4.5 million for the gasohol plant. Arthur Young listed a similar value for White Flame in the Co-Op's financial statement for 1982. By these actions, Arthur Young took on management responsibilities, for it thereby made assertions about the fixed-asset value of White Flame that were derived, not from information or any figure provided by the Co-Op's management, but from its own financial analysis. ***

The evidence petitioners presented in opposing the motion for summary judgment demonstrated Arthur Young's "participation" in this broad sense. By assuming the authority to make key decisions in stating the Co-Op's own valuation of its major fixed asset, and by creating financial statements that were the responsibility of the Co-Op's management, Arthur Young crossed the line separating "outside" auditors from "inside" financial managers. Because the majority, like the Court of Appeals, affirms the grant of summary judgment in spite of this evidence, I believe that it misapplies its own "operation or management" test, and I therefore respectfully dissent.

## *NOTES AND QUESTIONS*

***1. Plain Language?*** The majority found it "clear" that Section 1962(c) limits liability to participants in the operation or management of the enterprise. Do you agree? Suppose that a majority of justices had found the statutory language ambiguous. Under these circumstances, would application of the liberal construction clause have been appropriate? Or would it instead have been appropriate to apply strict construction, on the theory that whatever interpretation emerged must be suitable for criminal actions as well as civil actions?

***2. Applying the Operation or Management Test to Arthur Young.*** Why wasn't Arthur Young's involvement in the Co-Op's affairs sufficient to satisfy the "operation or management test"? One commentator has suggested that the Court would have found the test satisfied "[h]ad the auditors prepared the misleading summaries or had the plaintiffs' claim for relief relied on misleading statements made by a representative of the accounting firm (rather than a failure to disclose information), or had a representative of the accounting firm made misleading statements at the board meeting." Michael Vitiello, More Noise from the Tower of Babel: Making "Sense" Out of *Reves v. Ernst & Young*,

---

"blatant fiction" that the Co-Op had owned White Flame from its inception, despite overwhelming evidence to the contrary in the Co-Op's records. See App. 137-138; see also 937 F.2d, at 1317 ("In concluding that the Co-Op had always owned White Flame, [Arthur Young] ignored a great deal of information suggesting exactly the opposite"). The evidence indicates that it was creative accounting, not reliance on the Co-Op's books, that led Arthur Young to treat the Co-Op as the plant's owner from the time of its construction in 1979 (a conclusion necessary to support Arthur Young's decision to value the plant at total cost). Not even the decree procured in the friendly lawsuit engineered by White and his lawyers treated the Co-Op as building the plant, or as owning it before February 1980.

56 Ohio St. L.J. 1363, 1382 (1995). Do you agree? Is the Court correct in its assertion that the operation or management test is "easy to apply"?

*3. The Association-In-Fact-Enterprise Revisited.* Would the *Reves* plaintiffs have stood a better chance of success if they had alleged that Arthur Young was the "person" who directed the affairs of an entity comprised of the Co-Op, Arthur Young, and Jack White? Cf. Daniel R. Fischel & Alan O. Sykes, Civil RICO After *Reves*: An Economic Commentary, 1993 Sup. Ct. Rev. 157, 194 (raising this question).

*4. Applying the Operation or Management Test to Lower Rung Employees.* The Court acknowledged that liability under Section 1962(c) encompasses not only outsiders and "upper management" but also "lower rung participants in the enterprise who are under the direction of upper management." Does the liability of such lower rung participants turn on the application of the operation or management test? Cf. *United States v. Allen,* 155 F.3d 35, 42 (2d Cir. 1998) (observing that *Reves* "[l]eft unclear *** whether *** lower rung participants must themselves play some 'direct[ing]' role, or need only be acting under the direction of upper management"). Consider the following view:

> *Reves* is a case about the liability of *outsiders* who may assist the enterprise's affairs. Special care is required in translating *Reves'* concern with "horizontal" connections–focusing on the liability of an outside adviser–into the "vertical" question of how far RICO liability may extend within the enterprise but down the organizational ladder.

*United States v. Oreto,* 37 F.3d 739, 750 (1st Cir. 1994) (concluding that "one may 'take part in' the conduct of an enterprise by knowingly implementing decisions, as well as by making them"); *Napoli v. United States,* 32 F.3d 31, 36 (2d Cir. 1994) (looking at whether insiders "had participated in the core activities that constituted the affairs" of the enterprise). But cf. *Fidelity Funding of Cal., Inc. v. Reinhold,* 79 F. Supp.2d 110, 128 (E.D.N.Y 1997) (looking to whether the insider defendants had "discretionary authority"). Are *Oreto* and *Napoli* consistent with *Reves*? What about *Fidelity*? Are different standards for insider and outsider liability consistent with the language of Section 1962(c)? Is such a distinction sound as a matter of policy?

*5. What Must the Defendant Know?* In order to operate or manage the enterprise, must the defendant have knowledge of the acts of racketeering activity in which the enterprise has engaged? Consider the following view:

> The key to deciding whether the amended complaint states a RICO claim against Friedlander Gaines lies in the terms "conduct" or "participate." These terms are not defined in the RICO statute. However, in common usage they imply at least a general awareness or knowledge of the activity one "conducts" or in which one "participates." A person that assists another in some unknown activity does not conduct the activity and is not a participant.

*Andreo v. Friedlander, Gaines, Cohen, Rosenthal & Rosenberg,* 660 F. Supp. 1362, 1370 (D. Conn. 1987) Do you agree? Does *Reves* shed any light on what the defendant must know?

*6. The Operation or Management Test and RICO Conspiracy.* Consider whether the operation or management test also applies to RICO's conspiracy provision, which reads as follows: "It shall be unlawful for any person to conspire to violate any of the provisions of subsections (a),(b), or (c) of this section." 18 U.S.C. § 1962(d). The courts are divided on this issue:

> To date five circuit courts have addressed whether the management and control test set forth in *Reves* applies to a RICO conspiracy. The Second, Seventh, and Eleventh Circuits have held that *Reves'* management and control test does not apply to a RICO conspiracy, concluding that "*Reves* addressed only the extent of conduct or participation necessary to violate a substantive provision of the statute; the holding in that case did not address the principles of conspiracy law undergirding § 1962(d)." *United States v. Quintanilla,* 2 F.3d 1469, 1484-85 (7th Cir. 1993); accord *United States v. Starrett,* 55 F.3d 1525, 1547 (11th Cir. 1995); *Napoli v. United States,* 45 F.3d 680, 683-84 (2d Cir. 1995). The Third and Ninth Circuits, however, have held that the *Reves'* management and control test must necessarily apply to a RICO conspiracy because to hold otherwise would render *Reves* nugatory. See *Neibel v. Trans World Assurance Co.,* 108 F.3d 1123, 1128 (9th Cir. 1997); *United States v. Antar,* 53 F.3d 568, 581 (3d Cir. 1995).

*United States v. Posada-Rios,*158 F.3d 832, 857 (5th Cir. 1998). Why would declining to apply the operation and management test to RICO conspiracy "render *Reves* nugatory"?

*7. **Statute of Limitations.*** RICO does not provide a statute of limitations for criminal liability. Accordingly, RICO prosecutions are governed by the general five year statute of limitations for criminal offenses set forth in 18 U.S.C. § 3282. See *Agency Holding Corp. v. Malley Duff & Assocs., Inc.,* 483 U.S. 143, 155-56 (1987); *United States v. Vogt,* 910 F.2d 1184, 1195 (4th Cir. 1990).

### *PROBLEM 11-7*

Sam did legal work for Plex, Inc. while an associate at a large law firm. After several years at the firm, Sam left to set up his own firm, with Plex as his sole client. After consulting with Sam, Plex's president (Hugh) decided that Plex would make a private offering. In his work on that offering, Sam suggested to Hugh that the private placement memorandum be drafted so as to hide certain highly risky aspects of the business. Hugh accepted this suggestion. Does Sam operate or manage Plex for purposes of RICO? Would it make a difference if Sam were also a member of the Plex board of directors?

### *PROBLEM 11-8*

Lincoln, Inc., a technology firm and reporting company under the Exchange Act, made a $10 million registered offering in January 2001. The announced purpose of the offering was to raise money to expand the business. But the actual intent was to use half the money raised to pay off accumulated debts. This intent was carried out, but the company made no public acknowledgment as to the actual use of the proceeds. Indeed, in consecutive SEC filings from March 2001 through November 2002, Lincoln misrepresented how the proceeds from the offering had been used.

The perpetrators of the scheme to misrepresent the true use of the proceeds were the five inside directors and the outside accountant (Mary). Mary is senior vice president of the accounting firm of Triplecheck, Inc., having served as a vice president of Lincoln from 1999-2000.

Can prosecutors bring a RICO action based on these facts? Who should be the defendant? The enterprise? What difficulties would the prosecution be likely to encounter?

### 5. *Private RICO Securities Actions*

Until 1995, private plaintiffs suing for fraud under the Securities Act and the Exchange Act would typically add a RICO allegation to their complaints. In addition to providing for recovery of treble damages and attorneys' fees and costs, civil RICO afforded plaintiffs an attractive vehicle for circumventing many of the limitations embedded in the federal securities laws. For example, RICO allowed them to sidestep the purchaser-seller requirement, see *Holmes v. Securities Investor Protection Corp.*, 503 U.S. 258, 285-86 (1992) (O' Connor, J., concurring in part and concurring in the judgment); the elimination of aiding and abetting liability, see, e.g., *Jaguar Cars, Inc. v. Royal Oaks Motor Car Co.*, 46 F.3d 258, 270 (3d Cir. 1995); and the Exchange Act's requirement of exclusive federal jurisdiction, see *Tafflin v. Levitt*, 493 U.S. 455 (1990). That RICO made possible such circumventions generated widespread dismay, as did the perception that securities defendants were being coerced into settling dubious RICO claims so as to avoid being labeled racketeers.

Congress responded to these concerns in the Private Securities Litigation Reform Act (PSLRA). That Act amended Section 1964(c) of RICO—the provision authorizing private actions—by stating that for such actions (but not for government actions) an act of racketeering activity does not encompass "conduct that would have been actionable as fraud in the purchase or sale of securities." Moreover, the Conference Report accompanying the legislation expressed Congress's desire that plaintiffs be barred from pleading other offenses (wire or mail fraud, for example) as acts of racketeering activity if those offenses embrace conduct prohibited by the federal securities laws. H.R. Conf. Rep. No. 104-369 at 47 (1995). Courts have displayed a willingness to give effect to this statement in the legislative history. See, e.g., *Bald Eagle Area Sch. Dist. v. Keystone Fin.*, 189 F.3d 321, 329 (3d Cir. 1999).

The PSLRA does, however, permit a plaintiff to assert civil RICO claims against a defendant who, in connection with the fraud, has previously been convicted of a criminal securities law violation. See Section 1964(c). Accordingly, a plaintiff's use of civil RICO for a claim predicated on securities fraud is now entirely dependent on a federal prosecutor's ability to convict a defendant of a crime involving securities fraud. But since criminal prosecutions are by no means infrequent, the civil RICO weapon may well continue to serve as a weapon in the private plaintiff's arsenal. See generally J. Scott Colesanti, The Private Securities Litigation Reform Act of 1995: Did the "Rushed Debate" Really Spell the End of Securities Claims and RICO?, 26 Sec. Reg. L. J. 139, 150-51 (1998) (discussing the conviction exception).

# Chapter 12

# INTERNATIONAL SECURITIES FRAUD

---

The federal securities laws do not specify whether (or to what extent) their fraud provisions apply to transactions that cross national boundaries. Courts attribute this silence to Congress's failure in the 1930s to anticipate the eventual internationalization of the securities markets. See, e.g., *Zoelsch v. Arthur Andersen & Co.*, 824 F.2d 27, 30 (D.C. Cir. 1987) (observing that "[t]he web of international connections in the securities market was then not nearly as extensive or complex as it has become"); *Bersch v. Drexel Firestone, Inc.*, 519 F.2d 974, 993 (2d Cir. 1975) (noting that "[t]he Congress that passed these extraordinary pieces of legislation in the midst of the depression could hardly have been expected to foresee the development of off-shore funds thirty years later").

That Congress in the 1930s was unaware of internationalized securities markets is, however, hard to square with either the history of the period or the text of the federal securities laws as originally enacted. Securities markets were highly internationalized in the 1920s until overtaken by world depression at the close of that decade. See Margaret V. Sachs, The International Reach of Rule 10b-5: The Myth of Congressional Silence, 28 Colum. J. Transnat'l L. 677, 691-94 (1990). By 1933, United States investors holding foreign securities had incurred substantial losses. See id. at 693-94. Consistent with Congress's awareness of these facts, the Securities Act explicitly required foreign securities issuers to register offerings made in the United States. See id. at 702-03. Moreover, Title II of that Act, called the Foreign Bondholders Act, directly addressed the plight of United States investors holding defaulted foreign securities. See id. at 706-08. But if Congress knew about internationalized markets, what accounts for its silence concerning the extraterritorial reach of the fraud provisions? Did it simply drop the ball? Did it expect the courts to resolve the matter?

Congress's lack of specificity carried no consequences so long as securities markets were essentially domestic. But beginning in the 1960s, internationalization of these markets began again to take hold, infusing federal securities fraud actions with numerous permutations of foreign elements—foreign plaintiffs and defendants, foreign securities, foreign securities exchanges, and negotiations and trades that had occurred (wholly or partly) in foreign countries.

Courts thus had to decide which (if any) of these actions they were entitled to hear. They did so by articulating jurisdictional principles that turn on where effects are felt and events occur as well as on the nationality and residence of the injured investors and the securities issuer. Today courts struggle to accommodate these principles to the twenty-first century, where effects are often felt in many places simultaneously, where Internet communications are hard to pinpoint geographically, and where multinational corporations (not to mention law firms and accounting firms) and individuals with dual citizenship defy easy alignment with a single country. Increasing globalization and technical advances are apt to make this undertaking more difficult in the years to come. Consider the following prediction regarding changes likely to occur within the present decade:

> Internet communication will involve the highly programmed, artificially intelligent cyber-agent (or Bot), which will perform many securities transactions for principals who will have greatly decreased involvement. These Bots will have extensive information about the background, assets, and preferences of their principals and will be equipped with enormous amounts of artificial intelligence, including analytical tools, computational abilities and the like. They will scour the cybersecurities marketplace and conduct transactions in multiple languages.
>
> *** The marketplace that these Bots can scour will be increasingly globalized and centralized ***. In about five years, there will be three or four global exchanges, trading in securities from a multitude of different nations. *** Bots will determine which markets are most reliable and efficient. Moreover, the investor's Bot will not be dealing with human intermediaries on the other side of transactions but with sophisticated systems and highly programmed sale Bots.

ABA Global Cyberspace Jurisdiction Project, Achieving Legal and Business Order in Cyberspace: A Report on Global Jurisdiction Issues Created By the Internet, 55 Bus. Law. 1801, 1932 (2000).

This Chapter is divided into four sections. Section A considers the principles of extraterritorial jurisdiction developed by courts. Section B examines whether these principles can be trumped by contracts that select the forum and the applicable substantive law. Section C addresses the forum non conveniens doctrine, while Section D discusses the Commission's efforts to combat international securities fraud.

## A. THE PRINCIPLES OF EXTRATERRITORIAL JURISDICTION DEVELOPED BY COURTS

Lower federal courts have developed two principal tests for determining whether they have subject matter jurisdiction over international securities fraud actions. One test focuses on domestic effects, and the other on domestic conduct. After examining these tests, we consider the utility of drawing upon the Restatement (Third) of Foreign Relations Law to advance the jurisdictional analysis.

### 1. *Jurisdiction Based Upon Domestic Effects*

## SCHOENBAUM v. FIRSTBROOK

405 F.2d 200 (2d Cir. 1968)

LUMBARD, CHIEF JUDGE:

Plaintiff, an American shareholder of Banff Oil Ltd., a Canadian corporation, brought this shareholder derivative action to recover under Section 10(b) *** and Rule 10b-5 for damages to the corporation resulting from the sales, in Canada, of Banff treasury stock to defendants Aquitaine of Canada, Ltd., and Paribas Corporation. Plaintiff alleged that the defendant corporations and Banff's directors, who are the individual defendants in this action, conspired to defraud Banff by making Banff sell treasury shares at the market price which the defendants, who had inside information not yet disclosed to the public, knew did not represent the true value of the shares. ***

Banff is a Canadian corporation and conducts all of its operations within Canada. Its common stock is registered with the SEC and traded upon both the American Stock Exchange and the Toronto Stock Exchange. In February 1964, Aquitaine Company of Canada, Ltd., acquired Control of Banff through a tender offer to Banff shareholders in the United States and Canada. Aquitaine is a wholly owned subsidiary of a French corporation, Societe National des Petroles d'Aquitaine, which in turn is a subsidiary of Enterprises for Research and Activities in Petroleum (ERAP), a French governmental oil agency.

In March 1964, Banff and Aquitaine entered into an agreement to conduct joint oil explorations. In October 1964, Banff entered into a "farmout agreement" with Socony Mobil under which Banff and Aquitaine would receive a 50% interest in 160,000 acres in the Rainbow Lake area of Alberta, Canada, in return for paying the total cost of drilling two exploratory wells. The Rainbow area is a desolate wilderness region over 100 miles from the nearest allweather road or railway. At least sixteen wells had previously been drilled in the general vicinity by six different oil companies, and all had been abandoned as failures. Because of the difficulty of conducting explorations in this region and the highly speculative prospects for success Socony Mobil was willing to give up a half interest merely for drilling two test wells.

Banff received a 5% interest and Aquitaine received a 45% interest, pursuant to their joint exploration agreement, with the drilling costs to be paid 10% by Banff and 90% by Aquitaine. On December 11, 1964 Banff's Board of Directors, the three Aquitaine representatives abstaining, voted to offer to sell 500,000 shares of Banff treasury stock to Aquitaine at the current market price allegedly for the purpose of financing Banff's share of the exploration expenses. On January 5, 1965, Aquitaine's president wrote to Banff that "our Chairman and Managing Director *** has agreed to your *** proposal." On January 26, Banff issued a press release announcing that Aquitaine "intended to purchase" 500,000 shares of common stock at the price of $1.35 per share, the closing price on the Toronto Stock Exchange on December 11, 1964. Actual delivery of the shares took place March 16, 1965.

Exploration in the Rainbow area commenced toward the end of 1964. On February 6, 1965, the test well flowed oil to the surface on a drillstem test.

This information was released to the public on February 8. The well reached total depth on March 17, 1965, the day after delivery on the Aquitaine purchase. On March 18, Banff issued a press release indicating that the discovery well was completed and that no further information would be disclosed in the immediate future. A further release on April 20 explained that the company was taking advantage of the Alberta law permitting it to withhold information on its discovery for one year to reduce competition from other companies in bidding on government oil lands in the discovery area. The release stated "The Board feels that this discovery is of great significance to the company but it is too early to have any idea of the areal extent."

After the discovery, further exploration activity was undertaken. In September 1965, a press release announced the formation of a company, in which Banff has a 3 1/3% interest and Aquitaine has a 30% interest, to build a pipeline into the area. To finance its activities, Banff's Board of Directors authorized negotiation of sales of treasury shares of common stock at $6.75 per share or more. Paribas Corporation—a Delaware corporation doing business in New York and a wholly owned subsidiary of Banque de Paris et des Pays-Bas, a French banking institution—negotiated a purchase of 270,000 shares of Banff Common at $7.30 per share, the current price on the Toronto Stock Exchange, on behalf of Banque de Paris et des Pays-Bas pour le Grand Duche de Luxembourg, another subsidiary of Banque de Paris. The issue was to be placed with "ten European professional investors." A verbal offer was made by Paribas on November 19, 1965. A written offer was mailed by Paribas from New York and was accepted by Banff in Canada on November 22. Payment and delivery took place in Canada January 24, 1966. ***

The complaint alleged that "For some time prior to February 6, 1965, Aquitaine and the other defendants knew Banff had exceptionally valuable oil properties located in the Rainbow Lake area in Alberta, Canada." It alleged that the Aquitaine purchase of 500,000 treasury shares at $1.35 per share took place March 15, 1965, and that the Paribas purchase of 270,000 shares at $7.30 on January 24, 1966 was on behalf of "affiliates, business associates and friends" of Aquitaine and its parent companies, and that defendants withheld information until March 16, 1966 in order to purchase the treasury shares at an artificially low market price, paying to Banff about $10,000,000 less than the stock's fair market value. ***

*Subject Matter Jurisdiction*

*** The district court concluded that the Act has no extraterritorial application, and that therefore no liability arose under the Act with regard to the sales in question, which took place in Canada between foreign buyers and sellers. The court found nothing to rebut the presumption that the Act was intended to apply only to transactions within the territorial limits of the United States. It also stated that the presumption was reinforced by the "specific mandate" of Section 30(b) ***.

We disagree with the district court's conclusion. We believe that Congress intended the Exchange Act to have extraterritorial application in order to protect domestic investors who have purchased foreign securities on American exchanges and to protect the domestic securities market from the effects of improper foreign transactions in American securities. In our view, neither the usual presumption against extraterritorial application of legislation nor the specific language of Section 30(b) show Congressional intent to preclude application of the Exchange Act to transactions regarding stocks traded in the United States which are effected outside the United States, when extraterritorial application of the Act is necessary to protect American investors. ***

The Act seeks to regulate the stock exchanges and the relationships of the investing public to corporations which invite public investment by listing on such exchanges. H.R. Rep. No. 1383, 73rd Cong., 2d Sess. (1934).

Banff common stock is registered and traded on the American Stock Exchange. To protect United States shareholders of Banff common stock, Banff is required to comply with the provisions of the Securities Exchange Act concerning financial reports to the SEC; proxy solicitation, § 14, and reports of insider holdings, § 16. Similarly, the anti-fraud provision of § 10(b) *** reaches beyond the territorial limits of the United States and applies when a violation of the Rules is injurious to United States investors. "Acts done outside a jurisdiction, but intended to produce and producing detrimental effects within it, justify a state in punishing the cause of the harm as if [the actor] had been present at the [time of the detrimental] effect, if the state should succeed in getting him within its power." *Strassheim v. Daily*, 221 U.S. 280, 285 (1911). ***

The provision contained in Section 30(b) does not alter our conclusion that the Exchange Act has extraterritorial application. In our view, while Section 30(b) was intended to exempt persons conducting a business in securities through foreign securities markets from the provisions of the Act, it does not preclude extraterritorial application of the Exchange Act to persons who engage in isolated foreign transactions.

Section 30, entitled "Foreign Securities Exchanges," deals with the extent to which the Act applies to persons effecting securities transactions through foreign exchanges.[3] Section 30(a) empowers the SEC to regulate all brokers and dealers who use the mails or interstate commerce, for the purpose of effecting a transaction in American securities on exchanges outside the United States. It was intended to prevent evasion of the Act through transactions on foreign exchanges. See Hearings on S. Res. 89 (72d Cong.), and S. Res.

---

3. Section 30. (a) It shall be unlawful for any broker or dealer, directly or indirectly, to make use of the mails or of any means or instrumentality of interstate commerce for the purpose of effecting on an exchange not within or subject to the jurisdiction of the United States, any transaction in any security the issuer of which is a resident of or is organized under the laws of, or has its principal place of business in, a place within or subject to the jurisdiction of the United States, in contravention of such rules and regulations as the Commission may prescribe as necessary or appropriate in the public interest or for the protection of investors or to prevent the evasion of this title.

(b) The provisions of this title or of any rule or regulation thereunder shall not apply to any person insofar as he transacts a business in securities without the jurisdiction of the United States, unless he transacts such business in contravention of such rules and regulations as the Commission may prescribe as necessary or appropriate to prevent the evasion of this title.

56 and S. Res. 97 (73d Cong.) before the Committee on Banking and Currency, 73d Cong., 2d Sess, part 15, pp. 6569, 6578-79 (1934).

Section 30(b) states that the Act does not apply in the absence of SEC rule to prevent evasion of the Act to "any person insofar as he transacts a business in securities without the jurisdiction of the United States." The language of § 30(b) must be construed in light of the purpose of the subsection, and the definitions of terms contained in § 3(a) of the Act.

The purpose of this subsection is to permit persons in the securities business to conduct transactions in securities outside of the United States without complying with the burdensome reporting requirement of the Act and without being subject to its regulatory provisions, except insofar as the Commission finds it necessary and appropriate to regulate such transactions to prevent evasion of the Act. It is also designed to take the Commission out of the business of regulating foreign security exchanges unless the Commission deems regulation necessary to prevent evasion of the domestic regulatory scheme.[4] The exemption relieves the Commission of the impossible task of enforcing American securities law upon persons whom it could not subject to the sanctions of the Act for actions upon which it could not bring its investigatory powers to bear.

If § 30(b) had been meant to exempt every transaction by any person outside of the United States it would have been drafted to state that the Act does not apply to "any transaction in any security outside the jurisdiction of the United States," a phrase used in § 30(a). The drafters used the phrase "any person insofar as he transacts a business in securities without the jurisdiction of the United States" in § 30(b) because it is a term which would exempt the business transactions not only of brokers and dealers but also of banks. The term "brokers and dealers," used in § 30(a), could not be used because the definitions of "broker" and "dealer" in §§ 3(a)(4) and 3(a)(5) specifically exclude "banks" as defined in § 3(a)(6). It is precisely the terminology that appears in § 30(b), when construed in light of § 3(a)(4) and (5) that exempts brokers and dealers and banks otherwise subject to the Act insofar as they conduct transactions not subject to § 30(a) outside the United States, even though their United States transactions are subject to the Act. ***

We find that the language and purpose of § 30(b) show that it was not meant to exempt transactions that are conducted outside the jurisdiction of the United States unless they are part of a "business in securities." Indeed, since Congress found it necessary to draft an exemptive provision for certain foreign transactions and gave the Commission power to make rules that would limit this exemption, the presumption must be that the Act was meant to apply to those foreign transactions not specifically exempted.

We hold that the district court has subject matter jurisdiction over violations of the Securities Exchange Act although the transactions which are alleged to violate the Act take place outside the United States, at least when the

4. The SEC has not promulgated any rules or regulations under § 30.

transactions involve stock registered and listed on a national securities exchange, and are detrimental to the interests of American investors.

However, the district court found that the only harm alleged was to the foreign corporation on whose behalf plaintiff brought the action. We do not agree. A fraud upon a corporation which has the effect of depriving it of fair compensation for the issuance of its stock would necessarily have the effect of reducing the equity of the corporation's shareholders and this reduction in equity would be reflected in lower prices bid for the shares on the domestic stock market. This impairment of the value of American investments by sales by the issuer in a foreign country, allegedly in violation of the Act, has in our view, a sufficiently serious effect upon United States commerce to warrant assertion of jurisdiction for the protection of American investors and consideration of the merits of plaintiff's claim. ***

## *NOTES AND QUESTIONS*

1. ***Assumption of Risk?*** Should the court have declined jurisdiction on the theory that when United States investors buy stock in a foreign company, they assume the risk that foreign fraud remedies will be sufficient to protect them? Cf. Stephen J. Choi & Andrew T. Guzman, The Dangerous Extraterritoriality of American Securities Law, 17 Nw. J. Int'l L. & Bus. 207, 220-21 (1996). Does your answer turn on whether the investors purchased their shares on the American Stock Exchange or on the Toronto Stock Exchange?

2. ***The Puzzle of Section 30(b).*** According to the court, Section 30(b) establishes a "presumption *** that the [Exchange] Act was meant to apply to those foreign transactions not specifically exempted." Is Congress likely to have intended such a presumption if it was unaware of internationalized securities markets? Why is there no counterpart to Section 30(b) in the Securities Act?

3. ***Exporting Our Conceptions of Fraud.*** While every country prohibits fraud, there is no universally accepted definition of the term and thus activities constituting securities fraud in the United States may not be illegal in other countries. See, e.g., *Pinker v. Roche Holdings, Ltd.*, 292 F.3d 361, 372 & n. 4 (3d Cir. 2002) (noting that not every country regards the omission of information as fraudulent and acknowledging the plaintiff's argument that the fraud-on-the-market theory is "unique to American law"); Franklin A. Gevurtz, The Globalization of Insider Trading Prohibitions, 15 Transnat'l Law. 63, 68-89 (2002) (describing the range of insider trading prohibitions worldwide). The result is that those acting outside the United States in compliance with local fraud law may nonetheless violate the federal securities laws if their activities produce effects in this country. Consider *In the Matter of E. On AG,* Exchange Act Release 43372, 73 SEC Docket 974 (Sept. 28, 2000), an administrative action against a major German industrial holding company whose shares were listed on the New York Stock Exchange. Acting in its adjudicative capacity, the Commission concluded that the company had intentionally and repeatedly falsely denied its involvement in merger negotiations and that these denials (issued in both German and English) violated Rule 10b-5 since the merger negotiations were far enough along to qualify as material under *Basic Inc. v. Levinson,* 485 U.S. 224 (1988). (The *Basic* decision is set out in Chapter 2.B

supra). The false denials did not violate German law, however, as the Commission acknowledged in its cease-and-desist order:

> The Commission recognizes that disclosure practices and laws regarding the existence of merger negotiations may differ in other jurisdictions. Where jurisdictional requirements are met, however, there is no safe harbor for foreign issuers from violations of the antifraud provisions of the U.S. federal securities laws. The Commission will not apply a different standard with respect to foreign issuers commenting on merger discussions or negotiations. When a foreign issuer voluntarily avails itself of the opportunities in the U.S. capital markets, it must adhere to the U.S. federal securities laws.

73 SEC Docket at 978. Should United States courts confine their extraterritorial reach to fraud actions involving activities that would constitute fraud in at least most other countries?

4. ***The Requirement of a National Exchange.*** The *Schoenbaum* court upheld effects jurisdiction "at least" where the securities at issue were listed on a national securities exchange. If the goal is to protect domestic investors and domestic markets, why distinguish between securities traded on an exchange and those traded over the counter? In deciding whether to make this distinction, should a court take account of the anticipated shift from national exchanges to global exchanges described at the beginning of this Chapter? Would effects jurisdiction ever be appropriate in connection with securities sold in a private offering? On the latter question, see Robert W. Hillman, Cross-Border Investment, Conflict of Laws, and the Privitization of Securities Law, 55 Law & Contemp. Probs. 331, 353-54 (1992) .

5. ***The Nature of the Required Effects.*** The Second Circuit revisited effects jurisdiction in *Bersch v. Drexel Firestone, Inc.*, 519 F.2d 974 (2d Cir. 1975), a fraud action under the Securities Act and the Exchange Act that involved public offerings by a Canadian corporation (IOS) whose shares were not listed on any United States securities exchange. The purchasers consisted largely of foreign nationals residing outside the United States along with a small number of United States citizens (some resident and others non-resident). The district court had premised jurisdiction on the affidavit of a University of Pennsylvania finance professor, who stated that " '[t]he false and misleading prospectus issued in connection with the Public Offering impaired investors' confidence and trust and contributed to a steep decline in the purchase of United States securities by foreigners' with attendant adverse effects on the balance of payments and the price of American securities generally." Id. at 987-88. Disagreeing with the district court, the Second Circuit held that these effects were insufficient for jurisdictional purposes:

> [W]e do not doubt that the collapse of IOS after the offering had an unfortunate financial effect in the United States. Nevertheless we conclude that the generalized effects described by Professor Mendelson would not be sufficient to confer subject matter jurisdiction over a damage suit by a foreigner under the anti-fraud provisions of the securities laws.
>
> This branch of plaintiff's argument goes back to Mr. Justice Holmes' statement in *Strassheim v. Daily*, 221 U.S. 280, 284-85 (1911) ***:
>
>> Acts done outside a jurisdiction, but intended to produce and producing detrimental effects within it, justify a state in punishing the cause of

> the harm as if he had been present at the effect, if the state should succeed in getting him within its power.
>
> *** This principle *** does not support subject matter jurisdiction if there was no intention that the securities should be offered to anyone in the United States, simply because in the long run there was an adverse effect on this country's general economic interests or on American security prices. Moderation is all. *** These considerations are particularly pertinent in view of the limitations in § 17(a) of the 1933 Act to acts in "the offer or sale of any securities" and in § 10(b) of the 1934 Act to acts "in connection with the purchase or sale of any security." This means to us that there is subject matter jurisdiction of fraudulent acts relating to securities which are committed abroad only when these result in injury to purchasers or sellers of those securities in whom the United States has an interest, not where acts simply have an adverse effect on the American economy or American investors generally. ***

Id. at 988-89. Who are investors "in whom the United States has an interest"? Should the touchstone for jurisdiction be the immediacy of the harm to such investors rather than the substantiality of that harm? Does *Bersch* appear to sanction the exercise of effects jurisdiction where the securities in question are traded over-the-counter?

***6. Intending to Reach United States Investors.*** Sometimes a court must determine the appropriateness of effects jurisdiction when the injured investors are predominantly (but not exclusively) foreign nationals. In *IIT v. Vencap, Ltd.*, 519 F.2d 1001 (2d Cir. 1975), the Second Circuit concluded that there was no effects jurisdiction in the situation where "300 American investors, owning only some .5% of a foreign investment trust *** and the shares of which apparently were not intended to be offered to American residents or citizens." Id. at 1017. Later, in *Consolidated Gold Fields PLC v. Minorco, S.A.*, 871 F.2d 252 (2d Cir. 1989), the same court upheld effects jurisdiction "where American residents represent[ed] 2.5% of Gold Fields' shareholders" and the domestic effects were "direct and foreseeable." Id. at 262. Do these decisions suggest a pivotal role for scienter in international securities fraud actions? To what extent is the scienter analysis likely to center on a head count of defrauded United States investors?

***7. The Necessity of Personal Jurisdiction.*** To adjudicate a federal securities fraud action, courts must have not only subject matter jurisdiction but also personal jurisdiction. The personal jurisdiction inquiry involves concepts familiar to you from your civil procedure course—whether each defendant purposefully availed herself of the United States securities market so as to establish the minimum national contacts that render the exercise of personal jurisdiction consistent with due process standards. See, e.g., *Pinker v. Roche Holdings, Ltd.*, 292 F.3d 361, 368-71 (3d Cir. 2002) (citing relevant Supreme Court decisions and upholding personal jurisdiction over a Swiss corporation in a Rule 10b-5 action). Increasingly, courts must decide whether a defendant established such national contacts through her use of the Internet. In making this determination, the following framework is frequently cited as an analytical tool:

> [T]he likelihood that personal jurisdiction can be constitutionally exercised is directly proportionate to the nature and quality of commercial activity that an entity conducts over the Internet. This sliding scale is consistent with well

> developed personal jurisdiction principles. At one end of the spectrum are situations where a defendant clearly does business over the Internet. If the defendant enters into contracts with residents of a foreign jurisdiction that involve the knowing and repeated transmission of computer files over the Internet, personal jurisdiction is proper. E.g. *CompuServe, Inc. v. Patterson*, 89 F.3d 1257 (6th Cir. 1996). At the opposite end are situations where a defendant has simply posted information on an Internet Web site which is accessible to users in foreign jurisdictions. A passive Web site that does little more than make information available to those who are interested in it is not grounds for the exercise of personal jurisdiction. E.g. *Bensusan Restaurant Corp. v. King*, 937 F.Supp. 295 (S.D.N.Y.1996). The middle ground is occupied by interactive Web sites where a user can exchange information with the host computer. In these cases, the exercise of jurisdiction is determined by examining the level of interactivity and commercial nature of the exchange of information that occurs on the Web site. E.g. *Maritz, Inc. v. Cybergold, Inc.*, 947 F.Supp. 1328 (E.D.Mo.1996).

*Zippo Mfg. Co. v. Zippo Dot Com, Inc.*, 952 F. Supp. 1119, 1124 (W.D. Pa. 1997). Is the *Zippo* framework likely to prove useful in resolving personal jurisdiction questions involving the Internet of the future as described at the beginning of this Chapter?

---

## 2. *Jurisdiction Based Upon Domestic Conduct*

The seminal decision involving jurisdiction based mainly upon domestic conduct is *Leasco Data Processing Equip. Corp. v. Maxwell*, 468 F.2d 1326 (2d Cir. 1972). In *Leasco*, foreign defendants allegedly conspired to cause the Netherlands Antilles subsidiary of a United States corporation to buy the stock of Permagon Press, Ltd. (a British corporation) at an inflated price on the London Stock Exchange. Pergamon, controlled by defendant Robert Maxwell, a British citizen, was not traded in any organized United States securities market. Writing for the Second Circuit, Judge Friendly reasoned that even assuming that the "critical misrepresentations" occurred in England, earlier misrepresentations in the United States provided a sufficient basis for subject matter jurisdiction:

> On what is now before us it is impossible to say that conduct in the United States was not "an essential link," *Mills v. Electric Auto-Lite Co.*, 396 U.S. 375, 385 (1970), in leading Leasco into the contract of June 17, 1969. And that contract, signed in the United States, was "an essential link" in inducing Leasco to make the open-market purchases, whether these were triggered by a call from London to New York, as Leasco contends, or by a conversation in England, as defendants assert. Putting the matter in another way, if defendants' fraudulent acts in the United States significantly whetted Leasco's interest in acquiring Pergamon shares, it would be immaterial, from the standpoint of foreign relations law, that the damage resulted, not from the contract whose execution Maxwell procured in this country, but from interrelated action which he induced in England or, for that matter, which Leasco took there on its own. ***
>
> This brings us to appellants' *** line of defense *** that the purchaser was not an American but a Netherlands Antilles corporation. ***
>
> *** But even if Leasco N.V. is the beneficial owner, it would be elevating form over substance to hold that this entails a conclusion that the

> purchases did not have a sufficient effect in the United States to make § 10(b) apply. Whether Leasco N.V. is merely a financial conduit, as plaintiffs assert, or was planned to conduct an active business, as some of the SEC filings indicate, it was wholly-owned and its debt securities were guaranteed by Leasco and were convertible with Leasco common stock. We see no need to enter into the debate whether, as defendants contend and plaintiffs deny, Leasco obtained substantial tax and other advantages through the incorporation of Leasco N.V. and the use of the latter to acquire the Permagon shares. Whatever may be the rule where the defrauded American investor chooses, deliberately and unilaterally, to have the purchase consummated abroad by a foreigner, here the situation was quite different. The Maxwell group expressly agreed in its written contract that Leasco could "at its election" have the offer made "by a wholly-owned subsidiary of Leasco or a wholly-owned subsidiary of such subsidiary," "providing Leasco shall remain responsible for the due performance" of the obligation to acquire the shares. This clause specifically covered Leasco N.V., which was part and parcel of Leasco in every realistic sense. In acceding to this provision the defendants themselves recognized that Leasco, the United States company, remained at all times intimately involved in the transaction; the foreign entity was accepted by both sides as the *alter ego* of the American. The case is quite different from another hypothetical we posed at argument, namely, where a German and a Japanese businessman met in New York for convenience, and the latter fraudulently induced the former to make purchases of Japanese securities on the Tokyo Stock Exchange. ***

Id. at 1335, 1337-38.

### *NOTES AND QUESTIONS*

*1. The Importance of the German/Japanese Hypothetical.* The court distinguished the facts of *Leasco* from those of a hypothetical involving German and Japanese businesspeople. What light does this hypothetical shed on the court's conclusion regarding jurisdiction?

*2. Identifying Corporate Nationality.* The court treated the defrauded foreign subsidiary as in substance a United States corporation. Are you persuaded by the court's analysis on this point? Consider *MCG, Inc. v. Great W. Energy Corp.*, 896 F.2d 170 (5th Cir. 1990), in which a United States company not listed on any United States exchange used the London Stock Exchange to make a stock offering that excluded United States purchasers from participation. Certain United States corporations formed a Hong Kong shell corporation in order to participate in the offering. They thereafter brought a Rule 10b-5 action that claimed that they had been defrauded in connection with their purchases. The Fifth Circuit found that it did not have subject matter jurisdiction over the action:

> The policy concerns that have resulted in the extension of subject matter jurisdiction are not implicated where, as here, the "foreign" purchaser seeking protection is a mere "shell" created to avoid the obligations of the securities laws. Having gone to such lengths to structure a transaction not burdened by the securities laws, plaintiffs cannot expect to wrap themselves in their protective mantle when the deal sours. Cf. *Royal Air Properties, Inc. v. Smith*, 312 F.2d 210, 213-14 (9th Cir. 1962) ("The purpose of the Securities Exchange Act is to protect the innocent investor, not one who loses his innocence and then waits to see how his investment turns out before he decides to invoke the provisions of the Act."). We do not view this as the type of transaction towards which "Congress would have wished the precious resources

> of the United States courts and law enforcement agencies to be devoted...." *Bersch*, 519 F.2d at 985.

Id. at 175-76. Are *MCG* and *Leasco* harmonizable? A growing number of United States corporations are reincorporating for tax reasons in Bermuda and the Caymen Islands. Should these companies (or their United States subsidiaries) be treated as de facto United States entities if they bring fraud actions under the federal securities laws?

***3. The Significance of Judge Friendly.*** The Second Circuit issued most of the foundational opinions on jurisdiction over international securities fraud actions and the majority of these were authored by Judge Friendly. See 10 Louis Loss & Joel Seligman, Securities Regulation 5100 & n. 2 ( 3d ed. rev. 1996). Judge Friendly's opinions on this subject were influenced in a number of respects by Professor Louis Loss of Harvard Law School, the leading twentieth century scholar of securities law. See Margaret V. Sachs, Judge Friendly and the Law of Securities Regulation: The Creation of a Judicial Reputation, 50 SMU L. Rev. 777, 794-96, 800-02 (1997).

---

Following *Leasco*, courts in various circuits have upheld subject matter jurisdiction based upon domestic conduct, but divide over the nature of the conduct that must be shown. The following decision describes this division of authority.

## KAUTHAR SDN BHD v. STERNBERG

149 F.3d 659 (7th Cir. 1998)

RIPPLE, CIRCUIT JUDGE:

*** This case centers on a $38 million investment made by Kauthar in a company called Rimsat, Ltd. Kauthar is a Malaysian corporation with its principal place of business in Kuala Lumpur, Malaysia. Rimsat, whose principal place of business is in Fort Wayne, Indiana, was incorporated in the Caribbean island nation of Nevis for the purpose of providing satellite communications services to customers within the Pacific Rim region. These satellite communications were to be provided using satellites that Rimsat had contracted to purchase from a Russian satellite company. The satellites were to be placed in geosynchronous (or geostationary) orbit positions ("GSOs") that were leased to Rimsat by a company called Friendly Islands Satellite Communications, Ltd., doing business as "Tongasat." Tongasat is incorporated in the Pacific Rim Kingdom of Tonga.

Apparently, there is a limited number of GSOs available in the world because satellites may not be put in too close proximity to one another or else communications interference occurs. Satellites in geosynchronous orbit, by definition, stay essentially in the same spot over the earth and on the same equatorial plane. Consequently, the number of these spots in space is finite and, as with all scarce resources for which there is demand, they are valuable. *** Rimsat's apparent plan was to make its fortune by buying relatively inexpensive Russian communications satellites, leasing GSOs from Tongasat and selling satellite communications services.

Not surprisingly, such a venture is highly capital-intensive. Rimsat and various of the individual defendants involved in forming Rimsat and Tongasat sought investors for this project. Kauthar allegedly was convinced, on the basis of various communications and meetings, that Rimsat was a worthy investment, and it sank $38 million into the venture through a purchase of Rimsat stock. Kauthar effected this purchase by wiring funds to Rimsat's bank in Fort Wayne, Indiana.

In January 1995, several of Rimsat's creditors forced Rimsat into bankruptcy by filing a petition for involuntary bankruptcy in the United States Bankruptcy Court for the Northern District of Indiana. Six weeks later, when Kauthar realized that its equity stake in Rimsat was worthless, it brought this suit. Essentially, Kauthar alleged in its complaint that all of the parties involved in soliciting its investment in Rimsat intentionally misled Kauthar about the investment. Kauthar specifically points to a document that it terms a "prospectus" that was disseminated by Rimsat to outline the company's investment and business plans. In its 113-page amended complaint, Kauthar identifies alleged misrepresentations contained in the prospectus in addition to other misrepresentations and omissions it alleges were made in the course of dealings. ***

II

DISCUSSION

*** The district court determined that the securities violations alleged by Kauthar *** were beyond the ambit of statutory protection because they involved transnational securities transactions without a sufficient connection to the United States. Specifically, the district court held that Kauthar's allegations satisfied neither the "effects" nor the "conduct" analyses employed by federal courts to decide whether the securities acts cover a particular transnational securities transaction. We review this question of law de novo.

Courts have struggled for many years to define with meaningful precision the extent to which the antifraud provisions of the securities laws apply to securities transactions that are predominantly extraterritorial in nature but have some connection to the United States. The courts that have addressed the issue have noted that the question is a difficult one because Congress has given little meaningful guidance on the issue. In addition, resort to the legislative history of the securities acts does little to illuminate Congress' intent in this area. See, e.g., *Zoelsch v. Arthur Andersen & Co.*, 824 F.2d 27, 30 (D.C.Cir.1987). In fact, some courts have admitted candidly that, in fashioning an approach to the issue of extraterritorial application of the securities laws, policy considerations and the courts' best judgment have been utilized to determine the reach of the federal securities laws.[6] ***

---

6. *See Robinson* [*v. TCI/US West Communications, Inc.*, 117 F.3d 900, 905 (5th Cir. 1997)] (describing the court's task of determining jurisdiction as " 'fill[ing] the void' created by a combination of congressional silence and the growth of international commerce since the Exchange Act was passed"); *Continental Grain (Australia) Pty. Ltd. v. Pacific Oilseeds, Inc.*, 592 F.2d 409, 416 (8th Cir.1979) (recognizing that its decision "in favor of finding subject matter jurisdiction is largely based upon policy

Although the circuits that have confronted the matter seem to agree that there are some transnational situations to which the antifraud provisions of the securities laws are applicable, agreement appears to end at that point. Identification of those circumstances that warrant such regulation has produced a disparity in approach, to some degree doctrinal and to some degree attitudinal, as the courts have striven to implement, in Judge Friendly's words, "what Congress would have wished if these problems had occurred to it." *Bersch v. Drexel Firestone, Inc.*, 519 F.2d 974, 993 (2d Cir. 1975).

These efforts have produced two basic approaches to determining whether the transaction in question ought to be subject to American securities fraud regulation. These two approaches (we think that "test" is too inflexible a term to characterize the present state of the case law) focus on whether the activity in question has had a sufficient impact on or relation to the United States, its markets or its citizens to justify American regulation of the situation. Specifically, one approach focuses on the domestic conduct in question, and the other focuses on the domestic effects resulting from the transaction at issue.[8]

When focusing on the effects, the courts seek to determine whether actions " 'occurring in foreign countries ha[ve] caused foreseeable and substantial harm to interests in the United States.' " *Mak v. Wocom Commodities Ltd.*, 112 F.3d 287, 289 (7th Cir.1997) (quoting *Tamari v. Bache & Co. (Lebanon) S.A.L.*, 730 F.2d 1103, 1108 (7th Cir. 1984). Several cases have examined the type and severity of the harm that must be suffered domestically in order to enable an exercise of jurisdiction. This case, however, affords us no occasion to explore this approach; the record does not reveal sufficient effect on domestic interests to justify its invocation here.

In contrast with the effects analysis, which examines actions occurring outside of the United States, the conduct analysis focuses on actions occurring in this country as they "relate[ ] to the alleged scheme to defraud." *Tamari*, 730 F.2d at 1107. The chronic difficulty with such a methodology has been describing, in sufficiently precise terms, the sort of conduct occurring in the United States that ought to be adequate to trigger American regulation of the transaction. Indeed, the circuits that have confronted the matter have articulated a number of methodologies.

---

considerations"); [*SEC v.*] *Kasser*, [548 F.2d 109, 116 (3d Cir. 1977)] (stating that "it should be recognized that this case in a large measure calls for a policy decision").

8. The general approach of the courts has been to assume that the securities laws are applicable if either approach so indicates. See *Robinson*, 117 F.3d at 905; *Zoelsch*, 824 F.2d at 30; *Tamari v. Bache & Co.* (Lebanon) S.A.L., 547 F.Supp. 309, 311 (N.D.Ill.1982). We note, however, that the Second Circuit, from which these analytical approaches of conduct and effects originated, has recently stated that they need not "be applied separately and distinctly from each other" and that, in fact, "an admixture or combination of the two often gives a better picture of whether there is sufficient United States involvement to justify the exercise of jurisdiction by an American court." *Itoba Ltd.* [*v. Lep Group, PLC*, 54 F.3d 118, 122 (2d Cir. 1995)] 54 F.3d at 122. Since the aim of this inquiry is to measure the degree of United States involvement in the transaction in question, the joint assessment of conduct and effects seems appropriate because it permits a more comprehensive assessment of the overall transactional situation.

The predominant difference among the circuits, it appears, is the degree to which the American-based conduct must be related causally to the fraud and the resultant harm to justify the application of American securities law. At one end of the spectrum, the District of Columbia Circuit appears to require that the domestic conduct at issue must itself constitute a securities violation. See *Zoelsch*, 824 F.2d at 31 ("[J]urisdiction will lie in American courts where the domestic conduct comprises all the elements of a defendant's conduct necessary to establish a violation of section 10(b) and Rule 10b-5.").[10] At the other end of the spectrum, the Third, Eighth and Ninth Circuits, although also focusing on whether the United States-based conduct caused the plaintiffs' loss, to use the Fifth Circuit's words, "generally require some lesser quantum of conduct." *Robinson v. TCI/US West Communications, Inc.*, 117 F.3d 900, 906 (5th Cir.1997). In *SEC v. Kasser*, 548 F.2d 109, 114 (3d Cir. 1977), the Third Circuit stated that the conduct came within the scope of the statute if "at least some activity designed to further a fraudulent scheme occurs within this country." The Eighth Circuit, in *Continental Grain (Australia) Pty. Ltd. v. Pacific Oilseeds, Inc.*, 592 F.2d 409, 421 (8th Cir.1979), held that the antifraud provisions were applicable when the domestic conduct "was in furtherance of a fraudulent scheme and was significant with respect to its accomplishment." The Ninth Circuit adopted the Continental Grain approach in *Grunenthal GmbH v. Hotz*, 712 F.2d 421, 425 (9th Cir.1983).

Our colleagues in the Second and Fifth Circuits have set a course between the two extremes that we have just discussed. That approach requires a higher quantum of domestic conduct than do the Third, Eighth and Ninth Circuits. See *Robinson v. TCI/US West Communications Inc.*, 117 F.3d 900, 905-06 (5th Cir.1997). The Second Circuit has stated that foreign plaintiffs' suits under the antifraud provisions of the securities laws, such as Kauthar's, will be "heard only when substantial acts in furtherance of the fraud were committed within the United States." *Psimenos v. E.F. Hutton & Co., Inc.*, 722 F.2d 1041, 1045 (2d Cir.1983).[12] Furthermore, if the United States-based

---

**10.** Indeed, in *Zoelsch*, the court expressed doubt "that an American court should ever assert jurisdiction over domestic conduct that causes loss to foreign investors." 824 F.2d at 32. In adopting this restrictive approach, the District of Columbia Circuit claimed to adopt expressly the Second Circuit's methodology. See id. at 33. We share the reservations of the Fifth Circuit as to whether the District of Columbia Circuit accurately portrayed the Second Circuit's jurisprudence. See *Robinson*, 117 F.3d at 905 n. 10. Rather, we believe that the Fifth Circuit more accurately mirrored the Second Circuit's approach, which it articulated as: "Where (as here) the alleged fraud is in connection with a sale of securities to a foreigner outside the United States, the federal securities laws apply only if acts or culpable failures to act within the United States directly caused the plaintiff's loss." *Robinson*, 117 F.3d at 905.

**12.** In *Psimenos*, a case brought under the Commodity Exchange Act, the Greek plaintiff alleged fraud in the defendant's managers' handling of his commodities transactions. Although the court noted that "most of the fraudulent misrepresentations alleged in the complaint occurred outside the United States," it found the conduct analysis was satisfied because a pamphlet emanating from the defendant's New York office indicated that the managers would be supervised and because the alleged fraud was completed "by trading domestic futures contracts on American commodities

activities were merely preparatory in nature, or if the " 'bulk of the activity was performed in foreign countries,' " jurisdiction will not exist. Id. at 1046 (quoting *IIT v. Vencap, Ltd.*, 519 F.2d 1001, 1018 (2d Cir.1975)). In addition, only "where conduct 'within the United States directly caused' the loss will a district court have jurisdiction over suits by foreigners who have lost money through sales abroad." Id. (quoting *Bersch v. Drexel Firestone, Inc.*, 519 F.2d 974, 993 (2d Cir. 1975)).

Although this court has not had occasion to articulate an approach to the extraterritorial application of the securities laws, we have employed these concepts with respect to analogous actions brought under the Commodity Exchange Act. See *Mak*, 112 F.3d at 288-89; *Tamari*, 730 F.2d at 1107 & n. 11. In that context, we have stated that "[w]hen the conduct occurring in the United States is material to the successful completion of the alleged scheme, jurisdiction is asserted based on the theory that Congress would not have intended the United States to be used as a base for effectuating the fraudulent conduct of foreign companies." *Tamari*, 730 F.2d at 1108. We think that our approach under the Commodities Act ought to be followed with respect to the securities laws and, although stated more generally, that it represents the same midground as that identified by the Second and Fifth Circuits. In our view, the absence of all but the most rudimentary Congressional guidance counsels that federal courts should be cautious in determining that transnational securities matters are within the ambit of our antifraud statutes. Nevertheless, we would do serious violence to the policies of these statutes if we did not recognize our Country's manifest interest in ensuring that the United States is not used as a "base of operations" from which to "defraud foreign securities purchasers or sellers." *Kasser*, 548 F.2d at 116. This interest is amplified by the fact that we live in an increasingly global financial community. The Second and Fifth Circuit's iterations of the test embody a satisfactory balance of these competing considerations. This analytical pattern will enable the courts to address situations in which the United States is being used as a launching pad for fraudulent international securities schemes. At the same time, it will cause us to refrain from adjudicating disputes which have little in the way of a significant connection to the United States.

We believe, therefore, that federal courts have jurisdiction over an alleged violation of the antifraud provisions of the securities laws when the conduct occurring in the United States directly causes the plaintiff's alleged loss in that the conduct forms a substantial part of the alleged fraud and is material to its success. This conduct must be more than merely preparatory in nature; however, we do not go so far as to require that the conduct occurring domestically must itself satisfy the elements of a securities violation.

We turn now to an application of these principles to Kauthar's allegations. Kauthar argues that a host of alleged general activities undertaken by various of the defendants constitutes conduct that was part of the scheme to

---

exchanges." 722 F.2d at 1044, 1046. Other cases have indicated that effecting transactions on exchanges in America is sufficient conduct in the United States to satisfy the conduct test. See, e.g., *Tamari*, 730 F.2d at 1108.

defraud Kauthar and to solicit Kauthar's investment in Rimsat. Kauthar alleges that various documents containing fraudulent misrepresentations and omissions were prepared in the United States and were sent to it by wire and by the United States mail in an effort to obtain Kauthar's investment. Kauthar also alleges that phone calls were made from Fort Wayne, Indiana, and from San Diego, California, for the same purpose. Kauthar further alleges that the defendants had meetings and phone conversations in the United States to discuss the deceptive information contained in the prospectus and to "ultimately agree upon a plan to obtain equity funding from Kauthar by means of false and deceptive statements of fact." Thus, according to the complaint, the United States was utilized as a base of operations from which to launch the defendants' fraudulent scheme to defraud Kauthar. Moreover, Kauthar also alleges a set of specific acts that, in combination with those already mentioned, satisfy the conduct analysis. Specifically, Kauthar alleges that it wired the payment for the Rimsat securities, over $38 million, in six installments to Rimsat's bank account in Fort Wayne, Indiana. Therefore, Kauthar has alleged that the defendants conceived and planned a scheme to defraud Kauthar in the United States, that they prepared materials in support of the scheme to solicit the payment in the United States and sent those materials from the United States via the United States mail, and that they received in the United States the fraudulently solicited payment for the securities—he final step in the alleged fraud. We think these allegations sufficient to bring the alleged conduct within the ambit of the securities laws. We are therefore constrained to disagree respectfully with the district court's contrary conclusion. ***

## *NOTES AND QUESTIONS*

*1. **Domestic Conduct and Defrauded Foreign Investors.*** In *SEC v. Kasser,* 548 F.2d 109 (3d Cir. 1977), the only victim of the fraud was a Canadian corporation wholly-owned by the Canadian Province of Manitoba. The Third Circuit upheld jurisdiction based on domestic conduct and articulated the following rationales for so doing:

> First, to deny such jurisdiction may embolden those who wish to defraud foreign securities purchasers or sellers to use the United States as a base of operations. *** We are reluctant to conclude that Congress intended to allow the United States to become a "Barbary Coast," as it were, harboring international securities "pirates."
>
> Also, we are concerned that a holding of no jurisdiction might induce reciprocal responses on the part of other nations. Some countries might decline to act against individuals and corporations seeking to transport securities frauds to the United States. Such parties may well be outside the ambit of the power of our courts. For foreign nations to adopt the position that the defendants are urging this Court to take would enable defrauders beyond the reach of our courts to escape with impunity. By finding jurisdiction here, we may encourage other nations to take appropriate steps against parties who seek to perpetuate frauds in the United States. ***
>
> As a final policy justification ***, we register the opinion that the antifraud provisions of the 1933 and 1934 Acts were designed to insure high standards of conduct in securities transactions within this country in addition to protecting domestic markets and investors from the effects of fraud. ***

Id. at 116. Another rationale for upholding jurisdiction based on domestic conduct is that "under many circumstances, the country where the conduct occurs is in a far better position to investigate and enforce the law more effectively or at lower cost than those countries where the harm is felt, especially when the harm is relatively diffused." Donald C. Langevoort, *Schoenbaum* Revisited: Limiting the Scope of Antifraud Protection in an Internationalized Securities Marketplace, 55 Law & Contemp. Probs. 241, 247 (1992). Which (if any) of these rationales do you find persuasive? Do other rationales occur to you as well? What attracts foreign investors to our courts and securities laws? Why not open the federal courthouse doors whenever foreign investors are defrauded by transactions linked in any way to the United States? Who is better positioned to determine how widely to open those doors to foreign investors—Congress or the courts?

*2. **Assessing the Circuit Split.*** Consider the three positions outlined in *Kauthar* concerning the nature of the domestic conduct required for subject matter jurisdiction. Which position strikes you as preferable? To what extent does your answer follow from your choice of rationale(s) in the preceding note?

*3. **Identifying "Merely Preparatory" Conduct.*** Following the lead of the Second Circuit, the *Kauthar* court held that domestic conduct provides a predicate for jurisdiction only when it "forms a substantial part of the alleged fraud and is material to its success" and not when it is "merely preparatory in nature." Is this distinction apt to be self-evident? Cf. *IIT v. Vencap, Ltd.*, 519 F.2d 1001, 1017-18 (2d Cir. 1975) (Friendly, J.) (acknowledging that "the distinction is a fine one" but maintaining that "the line has to be drawn somewhere if the securities laws are not to apply in every instance where something has happened in the United States").

In identifying conduct that is "merely preparatory," the nationality of the issuer may make a difference. Consider *IIT v. Cornfeld*, 619 F.2d 909 (2d Cir. 1980), a Rule 10b-5 action involving a foreign investment trust which bought debentures issued by the wholly-owned foreign subsidiary of a United States company. Judge Friendly upheld jurisdiction based upon domestic conduct after deeming the security to be "essentially *** American":

> [A] consequence of the KRCC debentures being essentially of an American security is that the activities occurring in the United States, which on their surface may appear similar to those held in *Bersch* to be "merely preparatory" and thus insufficient to have "directly caused" loss to foreigners, assume a different aspect. *** The *Bersch* prospectus was mainly drafted in Europe because that was where IOS' records and principals were. Here the prospectus was wholly drafted in the United States because the offering *** was of securities of an American based corporation. Similarly, while there was some domestic accounting work in *Bersch*, most of the field work was and in the nature of things had to be done abroad. Here all the accounting work was and had to be done in the United States. Similarly the fact that the prospectuses in *Bersch* were printed in Europe while those in this case *** were printed in the United States, while not of particular significance in and of itself, reflects the fact that in *Bersch* the work on the prospectuses had mainly been done in Europe, so that Europe was the natural place for printing, whereas here most of the work had been done in the United States and there was no reason to ship the prospectus elsewhere for printing. In sum, while many of the acts in the United States in this case were similar to those in *Bersch*, the relativity is

> entirely different because of the lack here of the foreign activity so dominant in *Bersch*. Determination whether American activities "directly" caused losses to foreigners depends not only on how much was done in the United States but also on how much (here how little) was done abroad.

Id at 920-21. How (if at all) does this analysis illuminate the result in *Kauthar*?

*4. Conduct and Effects Combined.* Following the reasoning of the Second Circuit in *Itoba, Ltd. v. Lep Group PLC*, 54 F.3d 118 (2d Cir. 1995), the *Kauthar* court deemed it "appropriate" to rest jurisdiction on a combination of conduct and effects. Is such a combination approach likely to expand appreciably the extraterritorial reach of the fraud provisions?

*5.* **Bersch's** *Three Categories of Domestic Conduct.* Recall *Bersch v. Drexel Firestone, Inc.*, 519 F.2d 974 (2d Cir. 1975), which you encountered in note 5 on pages 895-96 following the *Schoenbaum* decision. In *Bersch*, United States citizens (some resident and others non-resident) joined numerous foreign investors in alleging fraud in connection with public offerings by a Canadian corporation not listed on any United States exchange. For the resident United States citizens, Judge Friendly premised jurisdiction on their receipt in the United States of fraudulent prospectuses mailed from Europe. See id. at 991. He then contrasted the level of domestic conduct required when resident United States citizens are defrauded with the levels of domestic conduct required when fraud is perpetrated on non-resident United States citizens or non-resident foreign nationals:

> While merely preparatory activities in the United States are not enough to trigger application of the securities laws for injury to foreigners located abroad, they are sufficient when the injury is to Americans so resident. ***
>
> We have *** concluded that the anti-fraud provisions of the federal securities laws:
>
> (1) Apply to losses from sales of securities to Americans resident in the United States whether or not acts (or culpable failures to act) of material importance occurred in this country; and
>
> (2) Apply to losses from sales of securities to Americans resident abroad if, but only if, acts (or culpable failures to act) of material importance in the United States have significantly contributed thereto; but
>
> (3) Do not apply to losses from sales of securities to foreigners outside the United States unless acts (or culpable failures to act) within the United States directly caused such losses.
>
> Other fact situations, such as losses to foreigners from sales to them within the United States, are not before us. We freely acknowledge that if we were asked to point to language in the statutes, or even in the legislative history, that compelled these conclusions, we would be unable to respond. ***

Id. at 992-93. Cf. *Europe and Overseas Commodity Traders, S.A. v. Banque Parabas London*, 147 F.3d 118, 128 n.12 (2d Cir. 1998) (reaffirming *Bersch* but maintaining that "U.S. residence of individual investors—not American nationality—must be the focus").

The District of Columbia Circuit has reserved the question of whether to adopt the first of the three *Bersch* categories set forth above:

> Because Blackwell and his codefendants operated to a significant degree from within the United States *** when they defrauded United States investors, we need not decide today whether to adopt the *Bersch* test for extraterritorial jurisdiction. Instead, we hold only that when a resident of the United States is allegedly defrauded in the United States in connection with the sale of securities, the courts of the United States have jurisdiction under the 1934 Act.

*SEC v. Banner Fund Int'l*, 211 F.3d 602, 609 (D.C. Cir. 2000). Does the first *Bersch* category constitute too low a standard? Does the distinction between the second and third categories violate equal protection? Cf. *Gruenthal GmbH v. Hotz*, 712 F.2d 421, 426 n. 9 (9th Cir. 1983) (observing that "the Second Circuit's apparent application of different tests depending on the nationality of the plaintiff may raise constitutional questions"). Into which *Bersch* category (if any) does *Leasco* fit?

---

### 3. *The Restatement (Third) of Foreign Relations Law*

In deciding whether to exercise subject matter jurisdiction over a federal securities fraud action, courts sometimes consult the Restatement (Third) of Foreign Relations Law. Consider the following decision.

## EUROPE AND OVERSEAS COMMODITY TRADERS, S.A. v. BANQUE PARIBAS LONDON

147 F.3d 118 (2d Cir. 1998)

OAKES, SENIOR CIRCUIT JUDGE:

Europe and Overseas Commodity Traders, S.A. ("EOC"), a Panamanian corporation, appeals from a final judgment dismissing EOC's complaint ***. EOC's sole business is the investment of its capital in securities and other ventures. It is wholly owned by Alan Carr, a citizen of Canada. Defendant-Appellees are Banque Paribas ("Paribas"), Paribas Global Bond Futures Fund, S.A. (the "Fund"), Paribas Asset Management Ltd. ("PAM"), and John Arida, a U.K. national who works as an account manager in the London, England, office of Paribas. Paribas is a French bank; the Fund is organized under the laws of Luxembourg; and PAM is a Bahamian corporation which manages the Fund.

The transaction underlying this dispute is entirely foreign inasmuch as there is no U.S. party, but not, strictly speaking, wholly extraterritorial in that EOC alleges that an offer to sell foreign securities was made over the telephone and facsimile to its sole shareholder and agent, Alan Carr, who was in Florida, and both parties agree that orders to purchase securities were placed from Florida. We therefore address the question whether phone calls and facsimiles to a person on U.S. soil provide enough of a connection to the United States to implicate the registration and fraud provisions of U.S. securities laws, and give us jurisdiction thereunder. ***

I.

*Facts*

*** EOC's account at Paribas was established in London in 1992. The "Non-discretionary Investment Agreement" between EOC and Paribas was executed on October 22, 1992, by EOC directors Ian F. Leger and Herbert W. Marvelly. In this agreement, EOC gave a corporate registration address in Panama and a mailing address in Monaco. The company also represented that its directors' meetings take place in Monaco, and named an agent for service of process in England.

In October of 1993, Carr was visiting England, as he often does in the autumn. Arida, on October 7, there informed him that a substantial amount of cash had accumulated in EOC's account, and offered to recommend an attractive investment opportunity for the money. Carr says he expressed interest in the proposal, but explained to Arida that he was preparing to leave for Florida on the 9th and that he would be happy to hear more after his arrival.

In a series of telephone conversations which began on October 14, Carr and Arida resumed their discussion of EOC's investment in the Fund as planned after Carr's arrival in Florida. The parties agree that each party initiated at least some of these calls. Carr claims that these conversations with Arida were their first significant discussion of the Fund. Carr also alleges that Arida misled him by conveying the following facts, which EOC now claims are not accurate: (a) the Fund was overseen by Paribas's proprietary trading desk; (b) the investors' capital in the Fund was traded along with Paribas's own capital; and (c) the Fund traded securities based primarily on technical as opposed to fundamental considerations. In reliance on these statements, Carr says that from Florida he ordered EOC's first purchase of shares of the Fund on October 18, 1993. He also alleges that these representations were repeated on the occasion of each of his subsequent six purchases which, together with the October 18 purchase, totaled some $1,800,000. ***

For reasons discussed next, even accepting as true EOC's allegations that the initial offer to sell Fund shares occurred while Carr was in Florida, the transactions between EOC and Paribas did not implicate the prescriptive jurisdiction of the federal securities laws.

II.

*Discussion****

A. *Registration Under the 1933 Act.*

*[The court held that the transaction was not subject to the Securities Act's registration requirements and that therefore subject matter jurisdiction could not be grounded on this basis.]* ***

C. *Antifraud Provisions.*

*** [T]the antifraud provisions of the securities laws have been held to reach beyond the registration requirement of the 1933 Act. Our conclusion with respect to registration does not therefore eliminate the possibility that jurisdiction could be found under § 10(b) of the 1934 Act *** and Rule 10b-5.[10]

---

**10.** The complaint also alleged a violation of the fraud provision of § 12 of the 1933 Act. Appellant's brief to this court does not advance this provision as a basis for our assertion of jurisdiction apart from § 10(b), or cite us to any case considering § 12 as a distinct basis for asserting jurisdiction over a foreign transaction. Accordingly, we do not

Congress's power to impose civil penalties for fraud in predominately foreign securities transactions is limited only by the Due Process Clause of the Fifth Amendment. In a long line of decisions stretching back to *Schoenbaum* [*v. Firstbrook*, 405 F2d 200 (2d Cir. 1968)] this circuit has recognized that the federal securities laws do not reach this constitutional limit. We have looked for conduct, see, e.g., *Leasco* [*Data Processing Equip. Corp. v. Maxwell*, 468 F.2d 1326, 1333-34 (2d Cir. 1972)]; effects, see, e.g., *Schoenbaum*, 405 F.2d at 206-09; or a combination thereof, see, e.g., *Itoba* [*Ltd. v. Lep Group PLS*, 54 F.3d 118, 122 (2d Cir. 1995)] in the United States to arrive at "our best judgment as to what Congress would have wished if these problems [of extraterritorial application] had occurred to it." *Bersch* [*v. Drexel Firestore, Inc.*, 519 F.2d 974, 993 (2d Cir. 1975)].

Perhaps the most difficult cases under the conduct test have concerned activity in the United States that causes, or plays a substantial part in causing, harm to foreign interests overseas. By contrast, as stated above, the effects test concerns the impact of overseas activity on U.S. investors and securities traded on U.S. securities exchanges.[12] See *Fidenas AG v. Compagnie Internationale Pour L'Informatique CII Honeywell Bull S.A.*, 606 F.2d 5, 9-10 (2d Cir. 1979); *Itoba*, 54 F.3d at 124. Telephone calls and facsimile transmissions conveying offers to sell securities and investment information could be characterized as either conduct or effects in the United States.

If evaluated as an effect, the U.S. interest affected by this transaction is indiscernible for reasons already discussed: the plaintiff is a Panamanian corporation; the individual who placed the purchase orders, and who ultimately suffered any losses, is a Canadian citizen; the securities are not traded on a U.S. exchange; and no effect on a U.S. affiliated company is alleged by EOC. There is, thus, no U.S. entity that Congress could have wished to protect from the machinations of swindlers. Cf. *IIT v. Vencap, Ltd.*, 519 F.2d 1001, 1017 (2d Cir. 1975) (declining jurisdiction under the effects test over an allegedly fraudulent sale of foreign securities to a British investment trust with 300 U.S. investors who formed .2% of the trust's fundholders).

---

address the question, beyond concluding that § 12 does not reach further than § 10(b). ***

12. As formulated in *Bersch*, the effects test concerns sales to "Americans resident in the United States." 519 F.2d at 993. We agree with the opinion expressed by Judge Motley in *O'Driscoll v. Merrill Lynch, Pierce, Fenner & Smith, Inc.*, 1983 WL 1360, *3 (S.D.N.Y. Sept. 8, 1983) that "the United States would have a greater interest in protecting foreigners residing within its borders than foreigners resident abroad" and that, for this reason, U.S. residence of individual investors—not American nationality—must be the focus of the effects test. Indeed, as Judge Motley noted, *O'Driscoll*, 1983 WL 1360 at *4, since alienage is a protected class under the Constitution, *Graham v. Richardson*, 403 U.S. 365 (1971), limiting the effects test to citizen investors would be constitutionally suspect. Plaintiff EOC is, however, a foreign corporation, and even Carr was only vacationing in the United States. We see no reason that the U.S. interest in protecting transients, who benefit from the protection of their own national governments, should be as great as that in protecting resident aliens.

The analysis becomes somewhat more difficult when we turn to the conduct test. The conduct test in this circuit has been stated in two parts as follows:

> the anti-fraud provisions of the federal securities laws ... [a]pply to losses from sales of securities to Americans resident abroad if, but only if, acts (or culpable failures to act) of material importance in the United States have significantly contributed thereto; but ... [d]o not apply to losses from sales of securities to foreigners outside the United States unless acts (or culpable failures to act) within the United States directly caused such losses.

*Bersch,* 519 F.2d at 993. Or, alternatively, we have said more simply that activity in the United States that is "merely preparatory" to a securities fraud elsewhere will not implicate our antifraud laws. *Itoba,* 54 F.3d at 122 (citing *Bersch*). EOC's allegations do not fit neatly into either of the two categories outlined in *Bersch.* Clearly, EOC is not a U.S. entity: even were we to look through the Panamanian corporate identity, its owner, a Canadian citizen, is still foreign. Yet, on the other hand, EOC alleges solicitation and sale of securities within the United States, and the second *Bersch* category is specifically limited to sales outside the United States. EOC's claim, thus, falls in yet another category which, although identified, was not addressed in *Bersch:* "losses to foreigners from sales to them within the United States." EOC's is a novel factual pattern not squarely governed by any of our decisions to date.

The facts alleged by EOC, nonetheless, satisfy the requirement that U.S. activity directly cause the harm to the foreign interest, which has in the past been the key element of litigation involving the conduct test. Or, stated in the alternative language we have sometimes used, Arida's communications into the United States were more than "mere preparation" for the fraud. EOC alleges that Arida solicited, offered to sell, and accepted a purchase order for securities from Carr when he was in Florida. Carr also says he relied upon the allegedly misleading information given to him from abroad while he was present in the United States, and such reliance was the direct cause of the loss sustained by EOC. The difficult question raised by EOC's allegations is whether Arida's communications to Carr in Florida may be considered activity within the United States for the purpose of the antifraud provisions of the security laws sufficient to support the jurisdiction of this court under the 1934 Act. We believe that they were not.

Although phone calls (or any other communications into the United States) soliciting or conveying an offer to sell securities ordinarily would be sufficient to support jurisdiction, it would be inconsistent with the law of this circuit to accept jurisdiction over this dispute, because the surrounding circumstances show that no relevant interest of the United States was implicated. In other words, a series of calls to a transient foreign national in the United States is not enough to establish jurisdiction under the conduct test without some additional factor tipping the scales in favor of our jurisdiction. Without such added weight, the exercise of prescriptive jurisdiction by Congress would be unreasonable within the meaning of the Restatement of Foreign

Relations [hereinafter Restatement] §§ 416(2) and 403 (1987),[15] and is particularly so when the transaction is clearly subject to the regulatory jurisdiction of another country with a clear and strong interest in redressing any wrong. We do not think Congress intended to make the securities laws have such a broad reach or to make U.S. courts available for such suits.

In the past, we have found jurisdiction over a predominantly foreign securities transaction under the conduct test when, in addition to communications with or meetings in the United States, there has also been a transaction on a U.S. exchange, economic activity in the U.S., harm to a U.S. party, or activity by a U.S. person or entity meriting redress. All of these factors are absent from EOC's allegations. *AVC Nederland B.V. v. Atrium Inv. Partnership,* 740 F.2d 148 (2d Cir. 1984), which Judge Friendly indicated was a very close case, id. at 154, provides the strongest support of EOC's position, but does not go far enough. *Nederland* concerned the sale of an interest in a partnership formed by Dutch nationals[17] for the purpose of investing in U.S. real estate. Plaintiff-purchaser was also Dutch. Much of the negotiation during which the alleged misrepresentations were made occurred in the United States, but the deal was concluded abroad. Even though the consummation of the allegedly fraud-tainted sale occurred outside the United States, Judge Friendly's opinion found jurisdiction, after considering the many factors listed in § 403(2) of Tentative Draft No.2 of the current Restatement. Id. Specifically, the opinion found the extent of the activity within the regulating state and the economic activity connecting both the plaintiff and defendants to the United States weighed in favor of jurisdiction. Presumably, although the opinion does not say as much, it considered the U.S. real estate investments, which were the purpose of the partnership and the subject of the alleged fraud, to be economic activity connecting the parties to the United States within the meaning of § 403(2)(b) of the Tentative Draft. In any event, we find *Nederland* distinguishable for this

---

15. Section 416 of the Restatement addresses "Jurisdiction to Regulate Activities Related to Securities." Subsection (2) of 416 provides:

> Whether the United States may exercise jurisdiction to prescribe with respect to transactions or conduct other than those addressed in Subsection (1) depends on whether such exercise of jurisdiction is reasonable in the light of § 403, in particular
>
> (a) whether the transaction or conduct has, or can reasonably be expected to have, a substantial effect on a securities market in the United States for securities of the same issuer or on holdings in such securities by United States nationals or residents;
>
> (b) whether representations are made or negotiations are conducted in the United States;
>
> (c) whether the party sought to be subjected to the jurisdiction of the United States is a United States national or resident, or the persons sought to be protected are United States nationals or residents.

Section 403 includes a longer list of generally-applicable factors relevant to the question whether the exercise of prescriptive jurisdiction is reasonable.

17. The seller was a partnership of two Dutchmen formed under Georgia law, but the court considered it a Dutch entity. *Nederland,* 740 F.2d at 154.

reason. The sales by Paribas to EOC have no similar connection to the United States: EOC invested in Europe; and Paribas's offices in and any other connections to the United States have no relevance to these transactions. We therefore find that the slight additional factor of economic activity in the United States, which "tipped the balance" in favor of jurisdiction in *Nederland,* is absent from EOC's case.

In this case, there is no U.S. party to protect or punish, despite the fact that the most important piece of the alleged fraud—reliance on a misrepresentation—may have taken place in this country. Congress may not be presumed to have prescribed rules governing activity with strong connections to another country, if the exercise of such jurisdiction would be unreasonable in the light of established principles of U.S. and international law. See Restatement § 403. And, the answer to the question of what jurisdiction is reasonable depends in part on the regulated subject matter. Id. cmt. c. ("[R]egulation by the United States of the labor relations of a foreign vessel that regularly calls on the United States may be unreasonable; regulation of the vessel's safety standards may not be unreasonable.")

This case illustrates the kind of circumstances in which it is unreasonable to prescribe rules of conduct with respect to securities fraud, even when a misrepresentation is made in the United States and reliance occurs on U.S. soil. Section 10(b), although it sounds in the common law tort of fraud, is part of a regulatory system that serves the public interest of the United States in much the same way as banking and currency regulations. This apparent purpose of protecting and regulating an entire system led this court to extend, through the use of the effects test, the antifraud provisions of these laws to activity not ordinarily within the "presumptive" scope of legislation. See *Equal Employ. Opp. Comm'n v. Arabian American Oil Co.,* 499 U.S. 244, 248 (1991) (legislation presumptively territorial); *Zoelsch* [*v. Arthur Andersen & Co.,* 824 F.2d 27, 31 (D.C. Cir. 1987)] (same) (collecting cases).[19] The very considerations that have led this court to conclude that Congress meant for the securities antifraud laws to reach beyond our shores to certain fraudulent activities abroad militate against finding subject matter jurisdiction over EOC's complaint. It would be ironic if a foreign party seeking redress in a U.S. court could sidestep the effect requirement by stretching our notions of conduct in the United States to include telephone calls from abroad to an agent/owner of that party here fortuitously. The situation is entirely different from the difficult cases under the conduct test in which a U.S. person or entity is the source of misleading information causing harm elsewhere. The U.S. interest in punishing an English malfeasor working at a French bank branch in London who caused no harm here is not apparent.

---

**19.** After adopting the Second Circuit's "conduct" test for the extraterritorial application of U.S. securities fraud laws, Judge Bork's opinion in *Zoelsch* noted "the test we adopt here does provide jurisdiction whenever any individual is defrauded in this country, regardless of whether the offer originates somewhere else, for the actual consummation of securities fraud in the United States in and of itself would constitute domestic conduct that satisfies all the elements of liability." *Zoelsch,* 824 F.2d at 33 n. 4. We agree with this general statement, but think it inapplicable when, as here, there is no U.S. citizen, resident or other identifiable U.S. interest concerned.

We therefore hold that the alleged solicitation, offer to sell, and purchases occurring while Carr was present in Florida did not bring this otherwise entirely foreign transaction within the antifraud provisions of U.S. securities law. ***

The decision of the district court dismissing plaintiff EOC's complaint for lack of subject matter jurisdiction is affirmed.

## *NOTES AND QUESTIONS*

*1. **Wisdom from the Restatement.*** How much weight did the court attach to the Restatement in deciding to deny jurisdiction? Could the Restatement provisions cited by the court have also provided support for upholding jurisdiction?

*2. **Retrenchment?*** The court found the domestic conduct insufficient because there was no "additional factor tipping the scales," such as "a transaction on a U.S. exchange, economic activity in the U.S., harm to a U.S. party, or activity by a U.S. person or entity meriting redress." Under what circumstances must the scales be tipped? Cf. *In re Gaming Lottery Sec. Litig.*, 58 F. Supp.2d 62, 74-75 (S.D.N.Y. 1999) (posing the question). Did the court raise the level of domestic conduct that must be shown when foreign investors are defrauded?

*3. **The Distinction Between Fraud and Registration.*** According to the court, the extraterritorial reach of the fraud provisions is wider than that of the Securities Act's registration requirement. Accord *Consol. Gold Fields PLC v. Minorco, SA,* 871 F.2d 252, 262 (2d Cir. 1989); *Bersch v. Drexel Firestone, Inc.,* 519 F.2d 974, 986 (2d Cir. 1975). Why should this be the case?

*4. **Vexatious Private Litigation.*** Recall especially from your study of Rule 10b-5 in Chapter 2 the judicial (as well as congressional) perception that much private securities fraud litigation is vexatious—that is, filed largely for its settlement value and irrespective of merit. Why is this concern largely absent from decisions involving the extraterritorial reach of the fraud provisions?

## *PROBLEM 12-1*

Gabrielle, Inc., a French corporation with offices only in France, manufactures a perfume that is popular in the United States. The company's shares are traded on various French exchanges but not on any organized United States securities market. Gabrielle launched a public offering from its Internet web site, which prominently announced that the offering was not open to United States investors. But United States investors nonetheless purchased five percent of the shares in the offering by utilizing fictitious European addresses. Gabrielle had constructive knowledge that at least one of these addresses might not be genuine but did not pursue the matter. Subsequent to their purchases, some of the United States investors concluded that the web site's offering materials fraudulently misstated the company's earnings. These investors have filed a Rule 10b-5 action against Gabrielle. Would a federal district court have subject matter jurisdiction over their action?

## *PROBLEM 12-2*

Pizzazz, Inc. is a soft drink manufacturer incorporated in the United States and headquartered in Chicago. Its wholly-owned subsidiary (Fizz, Inc.), incorporated in Canada and headquartered in Toronto, is responsible for the vast majority of Pizzazz's profits. Toronto is also the location of Pizzazz's main computer (server). Pizzazz stock is traded over the counter in the United States and also on the Toronto Stock Exchange. Eliza, a United States citizen, is a senior vice president of Pizzazz who regularly spends large amounts of time in Toronto in connection with Fizz's activities there.

While in Toronto last spring, she prepared the first draft of a press release that announced a new upsurge in Fizz's profitability. She finalized the draft upon her return in Chicago and then posted it on Pizzazz's web site. The press release (which contained fraud) was downloaded by Canadian investors in Canada, who then purchased Pizzazz stock on the Toronto Stock Exchange. Once the fraudulent nature of the press release became publicly known, these Canadian investors sued Pizzazz under Rule 10b-5 in a United States federal district court. Would the court have subject matter jurisdiction over the action?

### *PROBLEM 12-3*

Europa, Inc. is a Belgian corporation whose stock is traded on a Belgian exchange as well as on the New York Stock Exchange. Anna, a citizen of both Belgium and the United States who lives six months a year in each country, purchased Europa stock in Belgium. Thereafter, she brought a fraud-on-the-market action against Europa in a United States district court. According to Anna, fraudulent reports filed by Europa with the SEC artificially inflated the market price. Anna acknowledged that she did not read the SEC reports prior to investing. Would the court have subject matter jurisdiction over Anna's lawsuit?

Cf. *Baan Co. Sec. Litig.*, 103 F. Supp.2d 1 (D.D.C. 2000).

## B. CHOICE OF LAW AND CHOICE OF FORUM CLAUSES

Suppose that a United States investor bought securities pursuant to a contract providing that any fraud actions resulting from the purchase would be litigated in a specified foreign country in accordance with that country's laws. Suppose further that the investor thereafter filed a federal securities fraud action against the seller in a United States federal district court and that the court had subject matter jurisdiction under the principles set out in Section A of this Chapter. If the seller made a motion to dismiss based on the contract, would the court be obliged to grant it?

To decide such a motion, the court must consider Section 29(a) of the Exchange Act and/or its Securities Act counterpart, Section 14. Section 29(a) provides as follows:

> Any condition, stipulation, or provision binding any person to waive compliance with any provision of this title or of any rule or regulation thereunder, or of any rule of an exchange required thereby shall be void.

See also Section 14 ("Any condition, stipulation, or provision binding any person acquiring any security to waive compliance with any provision of this title or of the rules and regulations of the Commission shall be void"). In the decision that follows, the court held choice of law and choice of forum clauses enforceable, these antiwaiver provisions notwithstanding.

## LIPCON v. UNDERWRITERS AT LLOYD'S, LONDON

148 F.3d 1285 (11th Cir. 1998)

KRAVITCH, SENIOR CIRCUIT JUDGE:

In this appeal, we are confronted with the important question of whether the anti-waiver provisions of the United States securities laws preclude enforcement of certain choice-of-law and forum-selection clauses ("choice clauses") in international agreements. Although we recognize that it is a close question, we follow the weight of circuit authority and conclude that the choice clauses are enforceable despite the anti-waiver provisions. In addition, we conclude that the agreements in this case satisfy scrutiny for fundamental fairness and do not contravene public policy. *** Accordingly, we affirm the district court's decision to dismiss the Lipcons' complaint against Lloyd's.

I.

Lloyd's [London (Lloyd's)] is a large insurance market in which more than three hundred Underwriting Agencies compete for underwriting business. Pursuant to the British Lloyd's Acts of 1871 and 1982, Lloyd's oversees and regulates the competition for underwriting business in the insurance market; according to the *amicus curiae* brief of the British Government, Lloyd's "has statutory powers granted by Parliament to regulate the affairs of the international insurance market in London...." Lloyd's itself, however, does not accept premiums or insure risks. Instead, Underwriting Agencies, which act as syndicates, compete for the insurance business. Each Underwriting Agency is controlled by a Managing Agent, who is responsible for the financial status of its agency. The Managing Agent must attract not only underwriting business from brokers but also the capital with which to insure the risks that are underwritten.

Managing Agents recruit "Names" to provide the underwriting capital. A Name becomes a Member of the Society of Lloyd's through a series of agreements, proof of financial means, and the deposit of an irrevocable letter of credit in favor of Lloyd's. By becoming a Member, a Name obtains the right to participate in the Lloyd's Underwriting Agencies. The Names, however, do not deal directly with Lloyd's or with the Managing Agents. Instead, the Names are represented by Members' Agents, who, pursuant to agreement, act as fiduciaries for the Names. Upon becoming a Name, an individual selects the underwriting agencies in which he wishes to participate. The Names generally join more than one underwriting agency in order to spread their risks across different types of insurance. In large part because of the experience of the Members' Agents, Names generally rely on the advice of their Members' Agents in deciding in which syndicates to invest. Selecting well is of the utmost financial importance because a Name is responsible for his share of an agency's losses.

In addition to providing the indicia of financial security mentioned above, to become a Name one must travel to England to acknowledge the attendant risks of participating in a syndicate by signing a standard-form "General Undertaking." The General Undertaking is a two-page document containing the choice clauses that form the basis for this dispute. The choice clauses provide:

> The rights and obligations of the parties arising out of or relating to the Member's membership of, and/or underwriting of insurance business at, Lloyd's and any other matter referred to in this Undertaking shall be governed by and construed in accordance with the laws of England.
>
> Each party hereto irrevocably agrees that the courts of England shall have exclusive jurisdiction to settle any dispute and/or controversy of whatsoever nature arising out of or relating to the Member's membership of, and/or underwriting of insurance business at, Lloyd's and that accordingly any suit, action or proceeding ... arising out of or relating to such matters shall be brought in such courts....

Irmgard and Mitchell Lipcon are Names who entered into underwriting agreements, and Charles and Barbara Lipcon, who signed letters of credit to provide collateral for the Names, are their spouses. Irmgard and Mitchell first became Names in 1983 and 1984, respectively, and in 1986 signed a revised General Undertaking that contains the choice clauses set out above.

After it became clear that the Names would be responsible for massive losses for asbestos and pollution claims, appellants brought suit in United States District Court for the Southern District of Florida alleging that: (1) Lloyd's actively sought investors from the United States to fill an urgent need to build up capital; (2) concealed information regarding the possible consequences of the risks undertaken; and (3) deliberately and disproportionately exposed the Names to massive liabilities for which sufficient underwriting capital or reinsurance was not available. The Lipcons stated claims under the Securities Act of 1933, §§ 5, 12(1), & 15; the Securities Exchange Act of 1934, §§ 10(b) & 20; the Racketeer Influenced and Corrupt Organizations Act ("RICO"); and various provisions of Florida law. The district court granted the motion to dismiss brought by Lloyd's, finding that the choice clauses are enforceable and preclude litigation arising out of the Lipcons' agreement with Lloyd's in United States courts. ***

II.

*** We note at the outset that although this circuit has not yet ruled on the validity of the Lloyd's choice clauses at issue in this case, we do not write on a clean slate. Thus far, the Second, Fourth, Fifth, Sixth, Seventh, Ninth, and Tenth Circuits have addressed the enforceability of the precise choice clauses that we confront today, and although the reasoning of those courts has not been uniform, all seven courts of appeals have concluded that the clauses are valid and enforceable.

B.

Appellants' first argument is that the choice clauses, which make United States law inapplicable to disputes arising between them and Lloyd's, are unenforceable under the anti-waiver provisions of the United States securities laws. The Securities Act of 1933 provides: "Any condition, stipulation, or provision binding any person acquiring any security to waive compliance with any provision of this subchapter or of the rules and regulations of the Commission shall be void." 15 U.S.C. § 77n. The Securities Exchange Act of 1934 contains a similar provision. See 15 U.S.C. § 78cc(a). *** According to the Securities and Exchange Commission ("SEC"), which filed an *amicus curiae* brief, "These provisions are essential to the enforcement of the securities laws in that they prevent persons from avoiding their obligations under those laws through the simple expedient of requiring investors to waive their rights under those laws as a condition to engaging in securities transactions."

The district court rejected appellants' and the SEC's argument that the anti- waiver provisions categorically render unenforceable the choice clauses in the Lipcons' contract. Instead, the district court reviewed the clauses under the framework for evaluating choice provisions in international agreements first announced in *M/S Bremen v. Zapata Off-Shore Co.*, 407 U.S. 1 (1972). In *Bremen*, an admiralty case that did not involve the securities laws, the Court enforced a choice-of-forum clause that required litigation in the courts of London. Because "[w]e cannot have trade and commerce in world markets and international waters exclusively on our terms, governed by our laws, and resolved in our courts," id. at 9, the Court concluded that forum-selection clauses in international agreements "are prima facie valid and should be enforced unless enforcement is shown by the resisting party to be 'unreasonable' under the circumstances," id. at 10. Although the contract at issue in *Bremen* provided for a forum in which to litigate, as opposed to the substantive law that would apply to, any dispute, the Court noted that the choice-of-forum clause likely would have the effect of a choice-of-law clause:

> [I]t is the general rule in English courts that the parties are assumed, absent contrary indications, to have designated the forum with the view that it should apply its own law.... It is therefore reasonable to conclude that the forum choice clause was also an effort to obtain certainty as to the applicable substantive law.

Id. at 14 n.15.

In giving content to *Bremen* 's "strong showing" standard for invalidating international choice-of-forum clauses, courts have announced that those provisions will be found "unreasonable under the circumstances," *Bremen*, 407 U.S. at 10, and thus unenforceable only when: (1) their formation was induced by fraud or overreaching; (2) the plaintiff effectively would be deprived of its day in court because of the inconvenience or unfairness of the chosen forum; (3) the fundamental unfairness of the chosen law would deprive the plaintiff of a remedy; or (4) enforcement of the provisions would contravene a strong public policy. See *Carnival Cruise Lines, Inc. v. Shute*, 499 U.S. 585, 594-95 (1991). Applying this test (hereinafter "the *Bremen* test"), the district court concluded that the choice clauses in this case are enforceable.

Appellants and the SEC contend that the *Bremen* test is inapplicable when Congress has spoken directly as to whether it is permissible to waive United States statutory remedies. They argue that to apply the *Bremen* test—which requires courts to assess public policy—is tantamount to treating "the anti-waiver provisions [of the securities laws] as merely reflecting a Congressional direction to the courts to decide whether 'the public policies incorporated into' the securities laws would be undermined." ***

Although appellants' argument finds strong support in the plain language of the anti-waiver provisions, which facially admit of no exceptions, precedent and policy considerations compel us to conclude that *Bremen* 's framework for evaluating choice clauses in international agreements governs this case. We turn first to an examination of Supreme Court precedent.

In *Scherk v. Alberto-Culver Co.,* 417 U.S. 506 (1974), "the Supreme Court explicitly relied on *Bremen* in a case involving a securities transaction." *Richards v. Lloyd's of London,* 135 F.3d 1289, 1293 (9th Cir.1998). *Scherk* involved an international transaction to sell a company, where that transaction was based upon a contract that included arbitration and choice-of-law clauses that provided for the application of Illinois law by an arbitrator in France. When the deal soured, one of the parties challenged the enforceability of the arbitration provision. In enforcing the provisions, the Court relied in large part upon the nature of international agreements:

> [I]n the absence of the arbitration provision considerable uncertainty existed at the time of the agreement, and still exists, concerning the law applicable to the resolution of disputes arising out of the contract. Such uncertainty will almost inevitably exist with respect to any contract touching two or more countries, each with its own substantive laws and conflict-of-laws rules. A contractual provision specifying in advance the forum in which disputes shall be litigated and the law to be applied is, therefore, an almost indispensable precondition to achievement of the orderliness and predictability essential to any international business transaction.

*Scherk,* 417 U.S. at 516.

We recognize that *Scherk* differed from the case before us in that the choice clause before the Court in *Scherk* provided, by designating Illinois law as the governing law, for the application of United States securities law, see id. at 519 n.13, and thus that the Court in *Scherk* had no opportunity to decide if an international choice-of-law provision is enforceable if it conflicts with the anti-waiver provisions of the United States securities laws. Nevertheless, the Court's statement in *Scherk* that a choice-of-forum clause is "an almost indispensable precondition to achievement of the orderliness and predictability essential to any international business transaction," 417 U.S. at 516, combined with the Court's observation that a forum-selection clause "might also be viewed as implicitly selecting the law of that place to apply to that transaction," id. at 519 n.13, indicates that international agreements—even those that render United States securities law inapplicable—are *sui generis.*[14]

Appellants nevertheless point our attention to a line of Supreme Court cases that they contend indicate the Court's disapproval of choice provisions that waive the substantive protections of United States law. ***

Appellants claim that the Court in *Mitsubishi Motors Corp. v. Soler Chrysler-Plymouth,* 473 U.S. 614 (1985), indicated its unwillingness to permit

---

14. We think it clear that the agreement in this case is "truly international," *Scherk,* 417 U.S. at 515, as that term was used in *Scherk.* In this case, the parties to the agreement are from different countries, the negotiations leading up to the agreement took place in the United States whereas the closing took place in England, and the subject matter of the transaction concerned investment in an international insurance market.

choice provisions to eliminate United States statutory remedies. In *Mitsubishi,* the Court held that the Sherman Act did not render unenforceable a forum-selection provision in an international agreement, because "[b]y agreeing to arbitrate a statutory claim, a party does not forgo the *substantive* rights afforded by the statute; it only submits to their resolution in an arbitral, rather than a judicial, forum." Id. at 628 (emphasis added). Appellants rely in particular on the Court's statement that "in the event the choice-of-forum and choice-of-law clauses operated in tandem as a prospective waiver of a party's right to pursue the statutory remedy for antitrust violations, we would have little hesitation in condemning the agreement as against public policy." Id. at 637 n.19. In *Mitsubishi,* however, the Court was not confronted with the scope of the anti-waiver provisions of the United States securities laws. More important, the Court in *Mitsubishi* recognized and affirmed *Scherk*'s policy of treating international commercial agreements as *sui generis.* See *Mitsubishi,* 473 U.S. at 629 .

Appellants rely as well upon *Shearson/American Express, Inc., v. McMahon,* 482 U.S. 220 (1987), in which the Court held that the anti-waiver provision of the Securities Exchange Act of 1934 did not render an arbitration agreement unenforceable, because "[b]y its terms, [section 78cc(a)] only prohibits waiver of the *substantive* obligations imposed by the Exchange Act." Id. at 288 (emphasis added). *McMahon,* however, involved the enforceability of an arbitration clause in a *domestic* securities agreement. Although appellants contend that *McMahon* makes clear the Court's categorical unwillingness to permit waiver of the substantive remedies of the securities laws, we do not think that *McMahon* controls the case before us. As stated above, the Court consistently has treated "truly international agreements," *Scherk,* 417 U.S. at 515, differently than domestic transactions, which indisputably are subject to the anti-waiver provisions of the securities laws, see *McMahon,* 482 U.S. at 230.

Supreme Court precedent thus suggests that the enforceability of choice clauses in international agreements should be determined by a framework designed specifically for the international commercial context. Because the Supreme Court has not ruled on whether the anti-waiver provisions of the United States securities laws categorically render unenforceable choice-of-law clauses in international agreements, however, we turn to policy considerations.

2.

Underlying the Supreme Court's conclusions in *Bremen* and *Scherk* were two main concerns: (1) ensuring "the orderliness and predictability [that are] essential to any international business transaction," *Scherk,* 417 U.S. at 516; and (2) furthering international comity, see *Scherk,* 417 U.S. at 516; *Bremen,* 407 U.S. at 9.

To conclude that the anti-waiver provisions of the United States securities laws categorically preclude sophisticated parties from entering into international agreements—agreements that by definition involve parties and subject matter that would be subject to the laws of more than one nation if the parties did not contract *ex ante* for provisions governing choice of forum and choice of law—would undermine both policies upon which *Bremen* and *Scherk* were based. As the Ninth Circuit has observed, appellants' assertion that the statutory anti-waiver provisions categorically invalidate the choice clauses in the agreement with Lloyd's would, if correct, expand the reach of United States securities law to "any and all such transactions, no matter how remote from the United States." *Richards v. Lloyd's of London,* 135 F.3d 1289, 1293 (9th Cir.1998).

We also find in the content of the *Bremen* test itself support for our conclusion that the anti-waiver provisions of the United States securities laws do not preclude application of the *Bremen* test to determine the validity of the choice clauses. A court will invalidate a choice clause in an international agreement when "enforcement would contravene a strong public policy of the forum in which the suit is brought...." *Bremen,* 407 U.S. at 15. Thus, "[i]n *Bremen* itself, the Supreme Court contemplated that a forum selection clause may conflict with relevant statutes." *Richards,* 135 F.3d at 1293.

Although we do not deny that there is some force to appellants' argument that the anti-waiver provisions preclude application of the *Bremen* test, we believe that to invalidate the choice provisions for that reason in effect would be to conclude that "the reach of the United States securities laws [is] unbounded," *Richards,* 135 F.3d at 1293, and to ignore the Supreme Court's caveat that "[w]e cannot have trade and commerce in world markets and international waters exclusively on our terms, governed by our laws, and resolved in our courts," *Bremen,* 407 U.S. at 9. Because we are unwilling so to conclude, we hold that the anti-waiver provisions of the United States securities laws do not categorically render unenforceable the Lloyd's choice clauses, and we join the seven other courts of appeals that have addressed the issue in holding that the *Bremen* test controls our resolution of the enforceability of the Lloyd's choice clauses.

### III.

Appellants contend on appeal that even if the anti-waiver provisions of the United States securities laws do not *per se* invalidate the choice clauses, the district court erred in concluding that the *Bremen* test was satisfied and that the choice clauses in this case are enforceable. We disagree and conclude that the district court correctly applied the *Bremen* test.

As noted supra, section II.B, forum-selection and choice-of-law clauses "are presumptively valid where the underlying transaction is fundamentally international in character." *Roby v. Corporation of Lloyd's,* 996 F.2d 1353, 1362 (2d Cir. 1993). " This presumption of validity may be overcome, however, by a clear showing that the clauses are 'unreasonable under the circumstances.' " *Roby,* 996 F.2d at 1363 (quoting *Bremen,* 407 U.S. at 10). Choice clauses will be found "unreasonable under the circumstances," *Bremen,* 407 U.S. at 10), and thus unenforceable only when: (1) their formation was induced by fraud or overreaching; (2) the plaintiff effectively would be deprived of its day in court because of the inconvenience or unfairness of the chosen forum; (3) the fundamental unfairness of the chosen law would deprive the plaintiff of a remedy; or (4) enforcement of such provisions would contravene a strong public policy. See *Carnival Cruise Lines, Inc. v. Shute,* 499 U.S. 585, 594-95 (1991); *Bremen,* 407 U.S. at 15-18; Appellants contend that the choice clauses in this case are unreasonable under the first, third, and fourth *Bremen* factors.

A.

Appellants first contend that the choice clauses were the product of fraud and overreaching. The only specific allegation in the complaint of fraud is that Lloyd's "tricked and fraudulently induced [the Lipcons] to sign on or about Nov. 5, 1986 a forum selection clause" by making "fraudulent statements" that included the following:

> The purpose, in both instances, is to bring the agreements into line with ... the new Lloyd's legislation.
>
> * * * * * *
>
> The new Premiums Trust Deed will incorporate some new provisions which are mainly of a technical nature, and will not affect you greatly on a day to day basis.

Appellants contend that allegation of these statements is sufficient to invalidate the choice clauses.

In *Scherk,* the Court stated:

> In *The Bremen* we noted that forum-selection clauses "should be given full effect" when "a freely negotiated private international agreement [is] unaffected by fraud...." This qualification *** means that an arbitration or forum-selection clause in a contract is not enforceable if the *inclusion of that clause in the contract* was the product of fraud or coercion.

417 U.S. at 519 n.14 (emphasis in original). By requiring the plaintiff specifically to allege that the choice clause itself was included in the contract due to fraud in order to succeed in a claim that the choice clause is unenforceable, courts may ensure that more general claims of fraud will be litigated *in the chosen forum,* in accordance with the contractual expectations of the parties.

We conclude that the allegations in the Lipcons' complaint are insufficient to satisfy *Scherk* 's rigorous standard for pleading fraud. The first alleged statement by Lloyd's (or, presumably, by an agent of Lloyd's)—that "[t]he purpose, in both instances, is to bring the agreements into line with ... the new Lloyd's legislation"[16]—is in no way fraudulent or misleading. Indeed, the General Undertaking, which the Lipcons signed on the day that Lloyd's allegedly made this statement, specifically provides that "[t]hroughout the period of his membership of Lloyd's the Member shall comply with the provisions of Lloyd's acts 1871-1982 [and] any subordinate legislation made or to be made thereunder...." ***

The second allegedly fraudulent statement—that "[t]he new Premiums Trust Deed will incorporate some new provisions which are mainly of a technical nature, and will not affect you greatly on a day to day basis"—likewise fails to satisfy *Scherk* 's standard. Appellants contend that the insertion of the choice clauses in the General Undertaking was a change of more than simply "a technical nature" and that the statement thus was misleading and fraudu-

---

**16.** It is not clear what the phrase "in both instances" refers to, but we assume *arguendo* that the phrase refers at least in part to the General Undertaking, as well as to the choice clauses specifically.

lent. *** An allegation that the Lipcons were induced—even fraudulently induced—to make changes in the Premiums Trust Deed is insufficient to support a claim that the choice clauses, which are contained in a *separate* agreement (the General Undertaking), were induced by fraud. ***

B.

Appellants also contend that the remedies provided by English law are inadequate. They argue that no cause of action exists under the laws of England analogous to an action under Section 12(1) of the Securities Act of 1933 for securities registration violations. Appellants also contend that their remedies under English law for misrepresentations made in connection with the sale of a security are inferior to those available under Section 12(2) of the Securities Act of 1933 because Section 14 of the Lloyd's Act of 1982 immunizes Lloyd's from any claims under the English Misrepresentations Act, absent a showing of bad faith. Finally, appellants assert that Lloyd's is immune from liability under England's Financial Services Act of 1986, which provides private remedies for fraud in connection with securities transactions, and that unlike United States securities law, English law does not recognize controlling person liability.

We have little doubt that "the United States securities laws would provide [appellants] with a greater variety of defendants and a greater chance of success due to lighter scienter and causation requirements...." *Roby,* 996 F.2d at 1366. We will not invalidate choice clauses, however, simply because the remedies available in the contractually chosen forum are less favorable than those available in the courts of the United States. Instead, we will declare unenforceable choice clauses only when the remedies available in the chosen forum are so inadequate that enforcement would be fundamentally unfair. See *Carnival Cruise Lines, Inc. v. Shute,* 499 U.S. 585, 595 (1991); *Roby,* 996 F.2d at 1360-61; *Riley v. Kingsley Underwriting Agencies, Ltd.,* 969 F.2d 953, 958 (10th Cir.1992).

Like the seven other courts of appeals that have addressed this issue, we hold that English law provides remedies adequate to address the complaints of the aggrieved Names. Although Section 14 of the Lloyd's Act of 1982 exempts Lloyd's, its officers, and its employees from liability under the English Misrepresentations Act, no other entities within Lloyd's—such as the Members' Agents and Managing Agents, both of whom owe a fiduciary duty to the Names—are exempt. In addition, even Lloyd's itself is not immune from liability if appellants can make a credible showing of bad faith. We therefore conclude that the contractually chosen law is not fundamentally unfair and thus does not provide a basis upon which to deny enforcement of the choice clauses.

C.

Appellants argue that enforcement of the choice clauses would contravene a strong public policy, namely the policy expressed in the anti-waiver provisions of the United States securities laws that substantive remedies be available for securities violations. We already have rejected appellants' argument that the anti-waiver provisions categorically render invalid the choice clauses. We now must decide whether enforcement of the choice clauses, which would require appellants to litigate in England under

English remedies, would undermine the public policies more generally expressed in the United States securities laws. In so doing, we are mindful that at least one commentator has criticized the decisions of some other courts of appeals on the ground that the public policy inquiry "necessitates an exploration of foreign legal regimes about which U.S. courts are likely to know little or nothing" and requires courts to "determine which of two incommensurables is greater." See D. Hall, Note, No Way Out: An Argument Against Permitting Parties to Opt Out of U.S. Securities Laws in International Transactions, 97 Colum. L.Rev. 57, 83 (1997). ***

In *Roby* and *Bonny,* the Second and Seventh Circuits, respectively, concluded that "[t]he framers of the securities laws were concerned principally with reversing the common law rule favoring 'caveat emptor,' " *Roby,* 996 F.2d at 1364, and accordingly that the United States securities laws embody the policies of "insuring full and fair disclosure by issuers and deterring the exploitation of United States investors," *Bonny* [*v. Society of Lloyd's,* 3 F.3d 156, 161 (7th Cir. 1993)]. Appellants and the SEC do not disagree that the securities laws were intended to ensure disclosure and deter exploitation, but they argue that the Second and Seventh Circuits, as well as the district court in this case, ignored the compensatory function of private actions under the securities laws.

We agree with the SEC that private actions under the securities laws "serve as an important means of providing recompense to investors who have been harmed by wrongdoers." We are more confident than the SEC, however, that the compensatory policy underlying United States securities law will be vindicated by litigation in English courts under English law; this is especially so given our conclusion that English law provides adequate remedies to appellants in this case. Because we conclude that "the available remedies and potential damage recoveries suffice to deter deception of American investors[,] to induce the disclosure of material information to investors," *Bonny,* 3 F.3d at 162, and to provide redress to aggrieved Names, we hold that the choice clauses satisfy the public-policy prong of the *Bremen* test. We thus conclude that the district court did not err in finding that the choice clauses are enforceable. ***

The judgment of the district court is affirmed.

## *NOTES AND QUESTIONS*

***1. Giving the Antiwaiver Provisions Their Due.*** Did the court give appropriate weight to Section 29(a) of the Exchange Act and Section 14 of the Securities Act? Consider whether you agree with the view of a judge dissenting from a decision similar to *Lipcon*:

> Courts should not employ amorphous public policy to emasculate plain statutory language. ***
>
> The majority turns this *** inside out, by holding that underlying antiwaiver public policy eviscerates specific antiwaiver statutory provisions. Disregarding this express prohibition to assess whether enforcement of the choice clauses contravenes the underlying policy against waiver is akin to overlooking the plain language of a statute to consider its legislative history, a clearly disfavored method of statutory interpretation.

*Richards v. Lloyd's of London,* 135 F.3d 1289, 1298 (9th Cir. 1998) (Thomas, J., dissenting).

2. ***The Adequacy of Foreign Law.*** The court deemed English remedies "adequate," despite their being "less favorable" to the plaintiffs than federal securities law remedies would have been. When would foreign remedies be "so inadequate that enforcement would be found unfair"? How about when an investor wishes to bring a class action but the foreign forum in question has no class action mechanism?

3. ***Should Congress Eliminate the Antiwaiver Provisions?*** Congress's elimination of the anti-waiver provisions would probably increase the use of choice of law and choice of forum clauses. Should Congress take this step? If so, should the anti-waiver provisions be eliminated altogether or only as applied to international securities transactions (however they might be defined)?

### *PROBLEM 12-4*

Sam, a citizen and resident of the United States, is an unsophisticated investor who purchased over the Internet the stock of Maxx, Inc., a German firm, upon being favorably impressed with Maxx's web site. The web site announced that all securities fraud litigation against Maxx would be heard in German courts under German law. Sam later concluded that the web site had misrepresented Maxx's earnings prospects. He filed a Rule 10b-5 action in a federal district court in a circuit with a decision equivalent to *Lipcon*. Maxx moved to dismiss on the ground that Sam could bring the action only in Germany. Should the court grant the motion? How (if at all) would your answer change if Germany did not recognize the illegality of fraud committed on the Internet?

### *PROBLEM 12-5*

Fred purchased securities from Lorraine in a transaction that was in all respects domestic. Their contract provided that any disputes resulting from the purchase would be heard in the state courts of Idaho in accordance with Idaho law. Fred thereafter sued Lorraine for securities fraud in a federal district court, whereupon Lorraine moved to dismiss based on the contract. Assume that the circuit in which the action was filed already has on the books a decision equivalent to *Lipcon*. How should the court rule on the motion?

## C. THE FORUM NON CONVENIENS DOCTRINE

In two decisions issued in 1947, the Supreme Court upheld the common law doctrine of forum non conveniens. See *Gulf Oil Corp. v. Gilbert,* 330 U.S. 501 (1947); *Koster v. Lumbermens Mut. Cas. Co.,* 330 U.S. 518, 524 (1947). This doctrine allows federal courts to dismiss federal actions in favor of a foreign forum "when an alternative forum has jurisdiction to hear the case, and when trial in the chosen forum would 'establish ... oppressiveness and vexation to a defendant ... out of all proportion to plaintiff's convenience,' or when the 'chosen forum [is] inappropriate because of considerations affecting the court's own administrative and legal problems.'" *Piper Aircraft Co. v. Reyno,* 454 U.S. 235, 241 (1981), quoting *Koster,* supra, 330 U.S. at 524. Applying this doctrine, federal courts have dismissed fraud actions brought under the federal securities laws. See, e.g., *Robinson v. TCI/US West Communications, Inc.,* 117 F.3d 900 (5th Cir. 1997) (concluding that "the district court did not err in deciding that this case belongs in England"); *Howe v. Goldcorp Invs., Ltd.*, 946 F.2d 944 (1st Cir. 1991) (Breyer, J.) (affirming dismissal in favor of Canada); *Dragon Capital Partners L.P. v. Merrill Lynch Capital Servs., Inc.*, 949 F. Supp. 1123 (S.D.N.Y. 1997) (dismissing action in favor of Hong Kong).

To be sure, the plaintiff's choice of a United States forum is in general less likely to oppress a foreign defendant today than in 1947, when international travel and communication were relatively difficult and multinational corporations were quite unusual. Cf. *Fitzgerald v. Texaco, Inc.*, 521 F.2d 448, 456 (2d Cir. 1975) (Oakes, J., dissenting) (noting that "one may wonder whether the entire doctrine of *forum non conveniens* should not be reexamined in light of the transportation revolution"); id. at 456 n. 3 (noting that "[t]he whole doctrine might also be reexamined in light of *** the use of multinational subsidiaries to conduct international business"). As you read the following decision and accompanying materials, ask yourself whether the forum non conveniens doctrine merits reformulation.

## ALFADDA v. FENN

159 F.3d 41 (2d Cir. 1998)

MCLAUGHLIN, CIRCUIT JUDGE:

Saudi European Investment Corporation ("SEIC") is incorporated in the Netherlands Antilles to invest Saudi Arabian capital in "Western markets." SEIC's stock is not publicly traded. Until 1989, its principal asset was Saudi European Bank ("SE Bank"), a French-licensed bank, headquartered in Paris. Although SEIC maintained an office in New York, and SE Bank had a branch there, SEIC's operations were indisputably based in France; and it dealt almost exclusively with money from Saudi Arabia. Both SEIC and SE Bank were run by the Chairman of SEIC, Jamal Radwan.

Under its Deed of Incorporation, SEIC was authorized at its founding to issue 40,000 voting shares. It initially issued only 20,000 shares, which were sold in its first offering in 1979. Following a 30:1 split in 1983, there were 600,000 issued shares outstanding and 600,000 more authorized, but unissued, shares.

In 1984, SEIC sought to raise $60 million in capital through a private stock offering of its remaining 600,000 authorized shares. These shares were offered pursuant to a Subscription Agreement and Private Placement Memorandum ("PPM"), which made certain representations about SEIC's financial condition and business plan. The PPM represented that the 1984 offering would consist of 600,000 voting shares to be sold for $100 each and that if the offering was oversubscribed, nonvoting shares would then be issued. Finally, the PPM provided that none of the shares would be sold in the United States. The PPM was prepared for SEIC in the United States by Ronald Reilly, the president of a Texas corporation retained by SEIC to help it raise money.

A number of wealthy Saudi businessmen purchased 600,000 shares in SEIC's 1984 private offering. However, after the 1984 offering closed, Radwan converted certain SEIC "capital notes" (which were essentially stock options) into shares of SEIC voting stock. The existence of the capital notes was not disclosed in the PPM.

Radwan owned 600,000 of the capital notes, which he converted into 600,000 shares of SEIC stock by paying SEIC $33 per share. Radwan then sold the shares to Charles Keating's now infamous Lincoln Savings and Loan for $100 per share. The effect, of course, was that SEIC had now sold 1.2 million voting shares, rather than the 600,000 shares originally contemplated. SEIC, however, did not disclose the sale of the extra shares in the PPM. Moreover, Radwan's sale to Keating contradicted the PPM's representation that shares would not be sold in the United States.

Around 1988, SE Bank began to stumble. A number of French banks with ties to the Middle East had failed in the late 1980's; and the French government began to fear that SE Bank would also fail. In 1988 and 1989, the Governor of the Bank of France requested that SEIC shareholders deposit funds into SE Bank to solve its liquidity problems. However, no shareholders responded. In November 1989, the French government ordered Radwan either to sell the bank to new investors or face the involuntary liquidation of SE Bank. Radwan chose to sell the bank.

The Commission Bancaire, France's banking regulatory authority, became an active player in the sale of SE Bank. Prospective purchasers were required to obtain the Commission Bancaire's approval of a plan to stabilize the bank to avoid future liquidity crises. After an audit of the bank's condition, it was sold for approximately $3.4 million. The new owners injected $9.8 million into SE Bank and rechristened it Societe de Banque Privee, S.A. ("SBP"). As a result of the sale, SEIC shareholders lost all equity in SE Bank.

Soon after the sale of SE Bank, the new entity, SBP, became embroiled in several American lawsuits arising out of SEIC's and Radwan's dealings with Charles Keating. SBP was sued in several investor class actions. The United States' Resolution Trust Company also sued SBP as the successor to SE Bank. To insulate SBP from these claims, French banking authorities reorganized SBP and placed SE Bank's former American holdings in an entity called Societe d'Analyses et d'Etudes Bretonneau ("Bretonneau"). Soon after the spin-off, Bretonneau's banking license was revoked by French authorities and its only business then became the liquidation of SE Bank's former American business.

In July 1987, Abdulrahman Sharbatly, a Saudi investor, filed a criminal complaint in the French *Tribunal de Grande Instance* against Radwan and SEIC, alleging that the misrepresentations contained in the PPM constituted fraud under French penal law. He also filed a civil complaint against Radwan and SEIC involving the same transactions. Under the French criminal code, a private party may bring a civil action for damages (*action civile* ) based on a criminal offense, and may initiate a criminal prosecution if the state fails to do so.

One year later, Abdulrahman Al-Turki and Abdullatif Alissa, who also invested in SEIC, filed separate criminal complaints against SEIC with the *Tribunal de Grande Instance.* The Saudi investors charged that "unknown persons" associated with SEIC concealed the existence of Radwan's convertible capital notes and misrepresented in the PPM both the number of shares to be sold in the 1984 offering and the financial condition of SEIC in 1984.

The French examining magistrate indicted Radwan for the crime of "swindling" under Article 405 of the French Penal Code. In October 1994, the *Tribunal Correctionnel* in Paris acquitted Radwan of the criminal charges, and the Court of Appeals for Paris later affirmed the acquittal.

In April 1989, while the French actions were proceeding, Al-Turki, Saad Alissa, Abdullatif Alissa, Abdulaziz Alfadda, Abdullah Abbar, Yusif Bin Ahmed Kanoo (a Saudi Arabian partnership), and Ahmed Zainy filed a civil complaint against Radwan and SEIC in the Court of First Instance in Curacao, Netherlands Antilles. The plaintiff-shareholders alleged that they purchased SEIC shares in 1984 on the basis of the defendants' misrepresentations regarding SEIC's capital structure.

In September 1989, part of the litigation now before us started. Alfadda, Abbar, Abdulla Kanoo, Abdulaziz Kanoo, Yusif Bin Ahmed Kanoo, and Zainy sued Radwan, SEIC, SE Bank, SBP, Bretonneau, Richard Fenn (Vice-Chairman of SEIC), Alef Bank, S.A., and Alef Investment Corporation N.V. in the United States District Court for the Southern District of New York (McKenna, J.) (the "*Alfadda* action"). The investors alleged that the defendants violated Section 10(b) of the Securities Exchange Act of 1934 and the Racketeer Influenced and Corrupt Organizations Act ("RICO") by: (1) misrepresenting SEIC's value at the time of the 1984 offering; (2) diluting SEIC's stock by selling too many shares in 1984; (3) failing to disclose the existence of the capital notes held by Radwan; and (4) misappropriating SEIC funds (the "SEIC claims"). Plaintiffs also alleged New York state common law claims for fraud and breach of fiduciary duty.

In 1990, Judge McKenna dismissed the *Alfadda* action for lack of subject matter jurisdiction because the claims had no connection to the United States. This Court reversed Judge McKenna, finding that the action had a sufficient connection to this country because of the sales to Keating's Lincoln Savings and Loan. *Alfadda v. Fenn,* 935 F.2d 475, 478 (2d Cir.1991).

On July 5, 1990, Al-Turki, Sharbatly, and the Alissas filed yet another complaint against the *Alfadda* defendants in the United States District Court for the Southern District of New York (the "*Al-Turki* action"). The *Al-Turki* plaintiffs alleged that Fenn, Radwan, SEIC, SE Bank, Alef Investment Corporation N.V., and Alef Bank, S.A. violated RICO by manipulating SBP's assets during SBP's restructuring to prevent plaintiffs from obtaining damages on the SEIC claims (the "SBP claims"). The *Al-Turki* and *Alfadda* actions were consolidated before Judge McKenna.

In 1992, after the *Alfadda* action was remanded to Judge McKenna, the defendants moved for dismissal of the consolidated actions on the ground of *forum non conveniens.* Judge McKenna denied the motion, concluding that although France might be a more convenient forum, the balance of interests did not tilt particularly in its favor. The parties then conducted significant discovery for three years under the supervision of Magistrate Judge Katz.

In 1996, defendants again moved to dismiss the consolidated cases on *forum non conveniens* grounds. This time Judge McKenna granted the motion, reasoning that the suit had little connection to the United States and that France would be a more convenient forum. *** Plaintiffs now appeal, arguing, *inter alia,* that Judge McKenna misapplied the doctrine of *forum non conveniens.*

DISCUSSION

I. *Forum Non Conveniens*

Plaintiffs argue that, given the massive discovery and preparation that went into this suit, application of the *forum non conveniens* doctrine was inappropriate. We disagree.

Our review of a *forum non conveniens* dismissal is severely cabined. See *Piper Aircraft Co. v. Reyno,* 454 U.S. 235, 257 (1981). "[T]he decision lies wholly within the broad discretion of the district court and should be reversed only if that discretion has been clearly abused." *Peregrine Myanmar Ltd. v. Segal,* 89 F.3d 41, 46 (2d Cir. 1996) A *forum non conveniens* analysis proceeds in two steps.

First, the court must determine that there is an adequate alternative forum somewhere. See *Piper,* 454 U.S. at 254 n. 22. An alternative forum is adequate if: (1) the defendants are subject to service of process there; and (2) the forum permits "litigation of the subject matter of the dispute." *Piper,* 454 U.S. at 254 n. 22. That the law of the foreign forum differs from American law "should ordinarily not be given conclusive or even substantial weight" in assessing the adequacy of the forum. Id. at 247.

Having concluded that an adequate alternative forum does exist, the court must then weigh the public and private interests identified in *Gulf Oil Corp. v. Gilbert,* 330 U.S. 501, 508-09 (1947), to determine which forum "will be most convenient and will best serve the ends of justice." *Peregrine Myanmar,* 89 F.3d at 46. If a district court focuses on all the *Gilbert* factors before dismissing a case on *forum non conveniens* grounds, we accord its decision "substantial deference." See *Piper,* 454 U.S. at 257.

The public interests include: (1) having local disputes settled locally; (2) avoiding problems of applying foreign law; and (3) avoiding burdening jurors with cases that have no impact on their community.

The private interests include: (1) ease of access to evidence; (2) the cost for witnesses to attend trial; (3) the availability of compulsory process; and (4) other factors that might shorten trial or make it less expensive. See *Piper,* 454 U.S. at 241; *Gilbert,* 330 U.S. at 508.

In assessing convenience, "[t]here is ordinarily a strong presumption in favor of the plaintiff's choice of forum." *Murray v. British Broad. Corp.,* 81 F.3d 287, 290 (2d Cir. 1996); see *Piper,* 454 U.S. at 255 ("strong presumption in favor of the plaintiff's choice of forum"). Thus, dismissal usually is not appropriate unless "the balance of convenience tilts strongly in favor of trial in the foreign forum." *R. Maganlal & Co. v. M.G. Chem. Co.,* 942 F.2d 164, 167 (2d Cir. 1991). However, this presumption is weaker when the plaintiff is foreign. See *Piper,* 454 U.S. at 255-56 ("the presumption applies with less force when the plaintiff or real parties in interest are foreign").

Neither side challenges Judge McKenna's conclusion that France is an adequate alternative forum. The only issue, therefore, is whether Judge McKenna properly weighed the *Gilbert* factors.

A. *Public Interest Factors*

1. Gilbert *Factors*

Judge McKenna properly concluded that the *Gilbert* public interest factors weigh strongly in favor of France as a forum. First, the interest in having local disputes settled locally weighs heavily against the United States as a forum. This case involves a dispute between a Netherlands Antilles corporation and Saudi Arabian shareholders over the conduct of a French bank. Thus, France has a far greater interest in this litigation than the United States.

The complications of applying foreign law do not weigh in favor of either forum. In adjudicating plaintiffs' RICO and securities laws claims, an American court would apply American law. If the case is transferred to France, however, French law would apply and a consideration of American law would be unnecessary. While plaintiffs will not be able to avail themselves of the benefits of United States securities and racketeering laws in the French forum, "*forum non conveniens* dismissal is not trumped simply because the foreign forum will apply different substantive law than an American court." *Capital Currency Exch., N.V. v. National Westminster Bank PLC,* 155 F.3d 603, 609-10 (2d Cir. 1998). Moreover, the difference in applicable substantive law is properly considered when assessing whether an adequate alternative forum exists, an issue that plaintiffs do not challenge on appeal. See *Piper,* 454 U.S. at 254-55.

The interest in protecting jurors from sitting on cases with no relevance to their own community weighs heavily in favor of France. This suit involves not only plaintiffs' investment in a Netherlands Antilles holding company that owned a French-licensed bank, but also a challenge to a bank restructuring ordered and supervised by French banking authorities. Thus, French jurors have a more significant interest in this case than American jurors. See *Scottish Air Int'l, Inc. v. British Caledonian Group, PLC,* 81 F.3d 1224, 1233-34 (2d Cir. 1996) (Great Britain had greater interest in litigation involving inquiry into internal affairs of British corporation).

2. *Interest in Application of Domestic Law*

Plaintiffs argue that the United States has a significant interest in applying RICO and securities laws to international transactions. Plaintiffs assert that in dismissing the action, Judge McKenna should have considered this significant public interest, and that this interest weighs heavily in favor of the United States as a forum. ***

Plaintiffs' initial argument, that *forum non conveniens* dismissal is never appropriate when a plaintiff alleges a federal securities or racketeering cause of action, is clearly wrong. We have specifically held to the contrary. *PT United Can Co. v. Crown Cork & Seal Co.,* 138 F.3d 65, 74 (2d Cir. 1998) (RICO); *Allstate* [*Life Ins. Co. v. Linter Group Ltd.*, 994 F.2d 996, 1001 (2d Cir. 1993)] (securities).

We also reject plaintiffs' alternative contention that the United States' interest in applying its own securities and RICO laws to the international financial transaction at issue made the Southern District a more convenient forum. We recognize that this argument finds some support in our previous decisions, at least in regard to securities actions. In *Allstate,* we noted that "United States courts have an interest in enforcing United States securities laws." *Allstate,* 994 F.2d at 1002; cf. *Alfadda v. Fenn,* 935 F.2d 475, 478 (2d Cir. 1991) (United States had a sufficient interest in seeing its securities and RICO laws applied to justify exercising *subject matter jurisdiction* over plaintiffs' claims).

However, we made clear that this interest is merely one consideration to be weighed in the totality of the *Gilbert* analysis. *Allstate,* 994 F.2d at 1002 ("[T]his [interest] alone does not prohibit [United States courts] from dismissing a securities action on the ground of forum non conveniens."); Because the traditional *Gilbert* public interest factors weigh heavily in favor of France, we do not agree that the United States' interest in applying its securities and RICO laws rendered Judge McKenna's decision to dismiss on the grounds of *forum non conveniens* an abuse of discretion.

B. *Private Interests*

1. *Traditional Private Interest Factors*

Judge McKenna correctly concluded that the private interests involved in this case also strongly favor litigating in France. First, *all* the defendants and *nearly all* the documentary evidence are located in France. See *Blanco v. Banco Industrial de Venezuela S.A.,* 997 F.2d 974, 982-83 (2d Cir. 1993). In addition, the cost for witnesses to attend trial will be significantly lessened if trial is held in France because almost all the entities involved are based there. See *Blanco,* 997 F.2d at 982. Moreover, France is much closer to Saudi Arabia, so it will presumably be easier for the plaintiffs to travel there. See *Schertenleib v. Traum,* 589 F.2d 1156, 1165 (2d Cir. 1978) (Geneva more convenient forum when "[a]ll of the prospective witnesses, apart from [the defendant], either are Swiss or reside in European countries").

Finally, compulsory process is available in France to secure the live testimony of necessary foreign witnesses outside the reach of United States process. See, e.g., *Schertenleib,* 589 F.2d at 1165 (inability to bring witness to United States for live cross-examination before fact-finder "[p]erhaps the most significant problem" making litigation in United States court inappropriate). The ability to secure witness testimony takes on added importance in this action because "where, as here, appellants have alleged fraud, live testimony of key witnesses is necessary so that the trier of fact can assess the witnesses' demeanor." *Allstate,* 994 F.2d at 1001.

2. *Pretrial Discovery*

Plaintiffs' major argument on the *Gilbert* factors is that significant discovery was conducted, and has been completed, in the Southern District of New York. Plaintiffs contend that the extent of completed discovery weighs heavily in favor of the United States as a forum because: (1) Judge McKenna and Magistrate Judge Katz acquired unusual familiarity with this action in the course of resolving approximately 15 discovery disputes; (2) plaintiffs would be forced to recommence discovery in France since Judge McKenna's previous order precluding the use of discovery in the French *action civile* prevents the parties from using the existing discovery material in a subsequent French civil proceeding; and (3) plaintiffs' financial investment in translating documents from French to English and videotaping depositions of witnesses outside the reach of United States process would be wasted. We are not persuaded. ***

*** Although an issue of first impression in this Court, the Third, Fifth, and Tenth Circuits have concluded that the extent of completed discovery in the American forum is a relevant—but not necessarily dispositive—consideration in assessing convenience. See *Lony v. E.I. Du Pont de Nemours & Co.*, 935 F.2d 604, 613-14 (3d Cir. 1991); *Schexnider v. McDermott Int'l, Inc.*, 817 F.2d 1159, 1163 (5th Cir. 1987); *Gates Learjet Corp. v. Jensen*, 743 F.2d 1325, 1335 (9th Cir. 1984).

There appears to be some disagreement, largely of academic interest, as to whether the extent of completed discovery should be considered a public or a private interest under the *Gilbert* analysis. Compare *Schexnider*, 817 F.2d at 1163 (public interest) with *Gates*, 743 F.2d at 1329 (private interest) *and Lony*, 935 F.2d at 613-14 (discovery "goes to both private concerns ... and public ones"). We see little need to address this quibble, or even whether it should be considered at all in the *Gilbert* analysis. Assuming, *arguendo*, that the extent of completed discovery is relevant—whether as a public or private interest—we do not believe that it tips the balance towards an American forum. The traditional public and private interest factors weigh heavily in favor of France. Completing discovery within the Southern District and investing financial resources in order to facilitate trial in the United States does not sufficiently tip the scales of the *Gilbert* balance, especially since plaintiffs are free to use the existing discovery material to whatever extent the French tribunal will permit.

We do not read Judge McKenna's prior order as preventing the parties from using discovery materials in a future civil proceeding. Judge McKenna ordered that "[n]o discovery obtained in the present action is to be used in the litigations pending in France or the Netherlands Antilles." The order barred the use of discovery in any *pending* action. It does not bar the use of such material in a *future* civil litigation.

Finally, none of the plaintiffs are United States citizens and the *Gilbert* factors strongly favor France as a forum. Thus, we apply a weaker presumption in favor of plaintiffs' forum, and that presumption has been overcome. See *Piper*, 454 U.S. at 255-56. ***

## CONCLUSION

Balancing the *Gilbert* factors favors France as a forum. Given the deferential standard of review applicable in *forum non conveniens* inquiries, we find no abuse of discretion in dismissing on *forum non conveniens* grounds. ***

## *NOTES AND QUESTIONS*

***1. Forum Non Conveniens vs. Subject Matter Jurisdiction.*** As the court mentioned, an earlier decision in this same case had upheld subject matter jurisdiction based on domestic conduct. That earlier decision necessarily found that the United States had an interest in the litigation. In deciding whether to grant the forum non conveniens motion, did the court give sufficient consideration to the interest of the United States recognized by the earlier decision? See Lonny S. Hoffman & Keith A. Rowley, Forum Non Conveniens in Federal Statutory Cases, 49 Emory L.J. 1137, 1187-90 (2000).

2. ***The Adequacy of the Foreign Forum.*** As the court noted, a forum non conveniens dismissal requires an "adequate" alternative forum. How should adequacy be defined for these purposes? Consider the observations of a federal district court:

> [T]his Court has two concerns with the adequacy of Belgium as a forum for this class action securities action: Belgium's lack of a class action mechanism and its failure to recognize the fraud-on-the-market theory. Increased difficulty in proceeding as a class in a foreign forum does not, without more, render that forum inadequate. See *Howe v. Goldcorp Investments, Ltd.*, 946 F.2d 944, 952 (1st Cir. 1991) (in securities fraud action against Canadian corporation, holding that "greater difficulty" in meeting class action requirements deemed "beside the point" of adequacy inquiry). The complete lack of a class action mechanism is, however, an important factor to be weighed in determining the adequacy of an alternative forum. See *Bodner v. Banque Paribas*, 114 F. Supp.2d 117, 132 (E.D.N.Y. 2000); but see *Aguinda v. Texaco, Inc.*, 142 F. Supp.2d 534, 541 (S.D.N.Y. 2001) (in tort action, absence of class action procedure "does not ordinarily render a foreign forum 'inadequate' "). The Court has found no cases, and counsel has cited none, where a court has dismissed a securities fraud class action on forum non conveniens grounds where the plaintiff class has purchased stock on the American exchange and no class action remedy was available in the alternative forum.
>
> As for the fraud-on-the-market theory, courts have so far been reluctant to find a forum inadequate based on the lack of a recognized fraud-on-the-market doctrine. See *In re CINAR Corp. Sec. Litig.*, 186 F. Supp.2d 279, 298 (E.D.N.Y. 2002) (declining to find inadequacy of forum based solely on lack of a recognized fraud-on-the-market doctrine). When combined with the lack of a fraud-on-the-market theory, however, the lack of a class action mechanism creates virtually insurmountable concerns regarding the adequacy of the foreign forum. See *Derensis v. Coopers & Lybrand Chartered Accountants*, 930 F. Supp. 1003, 1007-09 (D.N.J. 1996) (deeming Canada an inadequate forum because it failed to recognize fraud-on-the-market theory and had just enacted a limited, and undeveloped, class action procedure). Dismissal in favor of Belgium would force each of the thousands of the United States purchasers to file separate actions in Belgium and demonstrate individual reliance on the misstatements. This is a remedy "so clearly inadequate or unsatisfactory that it is no remedy at all." *Piper Aircraft* [*v. Reyno*, 545 U.S. 239, 254 (1981)].

*In re Lernout & Hauspie Sec. Litig.*, 208 F. Supp. 2d 74, 91-92 (D. Mass. 2002). Do you agree that the lack of a class action mechanism in the foreign forum should not constitute inadequacy by itself? Why are courts generally hesitant to deem a foreign forum "inadequate"? Cf. id. at 92 (ruling that "even if Belgium were an adequate forum, when some deference is given to plaintiffs' choice of forum, defendants fail to demonstrate that the balance of public and private factors compels dismissal in favor of Belgium"). Should the definition of adequacy be the same regardless of whether the issue arises in a forum non conveniens motion or in a motion to enforce choice of law and choice of forum clauses as seen in Section B of this Chapter?

*3. The Importance of Motives.* In a decision after *Alfadda,* the Second Circuit stressed the importance of examining the plaintiff's motive in choosing the forum as well as the defendant's motive in contesting the forum:

> We *** understand the Supreme Court's teachings on the deference due to plaintiff's forum choice as instructing that we give greater deference to a plaintiff's forum choice to the extent that it was motivated by legitimate reasons, including the plaintiff's convenience and the ability of a U.S. resident plaintiff to obtain jurisdiction over the defendant, and diminishing deference to a plaintiff's forum choice to the extent that it was motivated by tactical advantage. ***
>
> Courts should be mindful that, just as plaintiffs sometimes choose a forum for forum-shopping reasons, defendants also may move for dismissal under the doctrine of *forum non conveniens* not because of genuine concern with convenience but because of similar forum-shopping reasons. District courts should therefore arm themselves with an appropriate degree of skepticism in assessing whether the defendant has demonstrated genuine inconvenience and a clear preferability of the foreign forum. ***

*Iragorri v. United Techs. Corp.,* 274 F.3d 65, 73-75 (2d Cir. 2001). Does focusing on the motives of the parties make the forum non conveniens doctrine more coherent?

*4. The Motives of Class Action Plaintiffs.* Should less significance be accorded the forum choice of plaintiffs who represent a class? What would be the reasons for so doing? The Second Circuit initially refused to attach less significance to a class action plaintiff's forum choice. See *DiRienzo v. Philip Serv. Corp.,* 232 F.3d 49, 62-63 (2d Cir. 2000) (reversing the district court on this point). But after granting a petition for rehearing, the Second Circuit issued a new decision:

> The district court in the case at hand, relying on *Koster v. (American) Lumbermens Mutual Casualty Co.,* 330 U.S. 518 (1947), gave less weight to the plaintiffs' choice of forum because they sued in a representative capacity. In our prior decision the majority disagreed with the district court's interpretation of *Koster,* but we now vacate that portion of the opinion. For even were the district court correct, *Iragorri* posits that defendants' motion to dismiss should also be viewed with greater skepticism.
>
> Affording less deference to representative plaintiffs does not mean they are deprived of all deference in their choice of forum. ***

*DiRienzo v. Philip Serv. Corp.,* 294 F.3d 21, 28 (2d Cir. 2002). What do you understand the court's new position to be? Why is the question seemingly so difficult for the court to answer?

*5. The Relevance of Comity.* Consider how (if at all) the evaluation of "public interests" in forum non conveniens analysis should be affected by the Supreme Court's decision in *Hartford Fire Ins. Co. v. California,* 509 U.S. 764 (1993), which made no explicit reference to forum non conveniens. In *Hartford Fire,* an antitrust action against various domestic and English insurance businesses, certain defendants argued in favor of dismissal based on "international comity." Id. at 797. The Supreme Court rejected this argument:

> [E]ven assuming that in a proper case a court may decline to exercise Sherman Act jurisdiction over foreign conduct ***, international comity would not counsel against exercising jurisdiction in the circumstances alleged here.
>
> The only substantial question in this litigation is whether "there is in fact a true conflict between domestic and foreign law." *Societe Nationale Industrielle Aerospatiale v. United States Dist. Court for Southern Dist. of Iowa*, 482 U.S. 522, 555 (1987) (Blackmun, J., concurring in part and dissenting in part). The London reinsurers contend that applying the Act to their conduct would conflict significantly with British law, and the British Government, appearing before us as *amicus curiae*, concurs. They assert that Parliament has established a comprehensive regulatory regime over the London reinsurance market and that the conduct alleged here was perfectly consistent with British law and policy. But this is not to state a conflict. "[T]he fact that conduct is lawful in the state in which it took place will not, of itself, bar application of the United States antitrust laws," even where the foreign state has a strong policy to permit or encourage such conduct. Restatement (Third) Foreign Relations Law § 415, Comment j. No conflict exists, for these purposes, "where a person subject to regulation by two states can comply with the laws of both." Restatement (Third) Foreign Relations Law § 403, Comment e. Since the London reinsurers do not argue that British law requires them to act in some fashion prohibited by the law of the United States, see Reply Brief for Petitioners Merrett Underwriting Agency Management Ltd. et al. in No. 91-1128, pp. 7-8, or claim that their compliance with the laws of both countries is otherwise impossible, we see no conflict with British law. See Restatement (Third) Foreign Relations Law § 403, Comment e, § 415, Comment j. ***

Id. at 798-99.

### *PROBLEM 12-6*

Mary, a citizen of both the United States and England, filed a Rule 10b-5 action in a federal district court against (mainly) English defendants. The defendants initially made a motion to dismiss for lack of subject matter jurisdiction but the court concluded that it had such jurisdiction based on domestic conduct. The defendants then moved for dismissal on forum non conveniens grounds, citing their own convenience along with the location of some of the witnesses. In opposing the defendants' motion, Mary argued that she cannot afford to litigate the action in England because contingency fee arrangements would not be available there. Should the court deny the defendants' motion based on Mary's financial situation?

Cf. *Murray v. British Broad. Corp.,* 81 F.3d 287 (2d Cir. 1996).

## D. INTERNATIONAL SECURITIES FRAUD AND THE SEC

The SEC regularly brings judicial and administrative actions involving international securities fraud, relying on the principles set out in Section A of this Chapter. See, e.g., *SEC v. Banner Fund Int'l,* 211 F.3d 602 (D.C. Cir. 2000); *SEC v. Stroud,* Lit. Release No. 17057, 75 SEC Docket 823 (June 29, 2001). The SEC has not, however, supplemented the case law by issuing rules and releases.

To be sure, it has issued rules and releases on the extraterritorial reach of provisions that do not involve fraud. But these stress their inapplicability when fraud is at issue and defer to the case law addressed in Section A of this Chapter. See, e.g., Statement of the Commission Regarding Use of the Internet

Web Sites to Offer Securities, Solicit Securities Transactions, or Advertise Investment Services Off-Shore, Securities Act Release 7516 (March 23, 1998), 66 SEC Docket 1869, 1870 and n. 5 (noting that "[t]his interpretation does not address the anti-fraud and anti-manipulation provisions of the securities laws, which continue to reach all Internet activities that satisfy the relevant jurisdictional tests"); Regulation S—Rules Governing Offers and Sales Made Outside the United States Without Registration Under the Securities Act of 1933, Preliminary Note 1 (stating that Regulation S does not apply to the fraud provisions of the federal securities laws).

In addition to its judicial and administrative actions, the SEC combats international securities fraud by collaborating with other countries. In 2001, the SEC responded to 483 requests for enforcement assistance from foreign authorities regarding securities investigations and made 364 requests to foreign authorities for enforcement assistance. See SEC Annual Report 2001 at 17. The SEC's collaboration with other countries takes a number of additional forms as well.

The SEC is a member of the International Organization of Securities Commissions (IOSCO), the principal organization for cooperation among securities regulators in different countries. Founded in 1974 and composed of more than 170 members, IOSCO makes recommendations and proposes guidelines on topics ranging from record-keeping to the Internet. See, e.g. Report of the Technical Committee, Securities Activity on the Internet (September 1998) (recognizing the necessity of international cooperation to Internet investigations). Although IOSCO's recommendations are non-binding, the SEC considers its involvement in the organization to be a substantial part of its international securities regulation. See Isaac C. Hunt, Jr., It's a Small World After All: The SEC's Role in Securities Regulation Globalization, 51 Admin. L. Rev. 1105, 1106-07 (1999).

Moreover, the SEC benefits from treaties between the United States and other countries that call for mutual legal assistance on crimes, including securities crimes. These Mutual Legal Assistance Treaties (called MLATs) are negotiated through diplomatic channels and require Senate ratification. Virtually all MLATs have a "dual criminality requirement"—each country must recognize the criminality of the violation for which assistance is sought. The SEC's ability to use these treaties stems from the fact that the federal securities laws may be enforced in criminal as well as civil actions. See Michael D. Mann, et al., International Agreements and Understandings for the Production of Information and Other Mutual Assistance, 29 Int'l Law. 780, 781 (1995).

The SEC has also negotiated "Memoranda of Understanding" (or MOUs) with securities regulators in other countries. MOUs are bilateral non-binding agreements that facilitate the exchange of information and cooperation in securities investigations. MOUs do not require Senate ratification, have no dual criminality requirement, and are generally considered to be more flexible than MLATs. MOUs vary widely in terms of the range of securities violations that they embrace. A list of the MOUs negotiated by the members of IOSCO is available at www.IOSCO.org/mou/index.

Congress has enacted several provisions that facilitate adoption of MOUs and MLATs. Section 21(a)(2) of the Exchange Act authorizes the Commission to investigate violations of foreign law. Moreover, Section 24(d) of that Act creates an exception from the Freedom of Information Act for certain records received by the Commission from foreign securities regulators.

Principal obstacles to international securities enforcement efforts include bank secrecy laws and blocking statutes. Bank secrecy laws protect the confidentiality of bank customers and are waivable by those customers. Cf. *SEC v. Thorn*, 2001 WL 1678787 at *6 (S.D. Ohio 2001) (noting that the defendant's investments were protected by Swiss bank secrecy laws). Blocking statutes, on the other hand, impose penalties for providing information to foreign investors. They are intended to protect national interests rather than individual interests and hence individuals cannot waive them. Cf. *SEC v. Elfindepan, SA*, 169 F. Supp.2d 420, 426-27 (M.D.N.C. 2001) (discussing Costa Rican blocking statute). For a discussion of bank secrecy laws and blocking statutes, see Caroline A.A. Greene, Note, International Securities Law Enforcement: Recent Advances in Assistance and Cooperation, 27 Vand. J. Transnat'l L. 635, 664-71 (1994).

### *NOTES AND QUESTIONS*

***1. The Virtues of Rules.*** Are there aspects of international securities fraud litigation that would benefit from SEC rulemaking?

***2. Criminal Enforcement Compared.*** Criminal prosecutions of international securities fraud are by no means unknown. See, e.g., *United States v. Cook*, 573 F.2d 281 (5th Cir. 1978). They nonetheless are quite unusual. Why would this be the case?

# Chapter 13

# SECURITIES ARBITRATION

---

Arbitration is the principal means of resolving disputes between investors and their brokers. To open an account with a brokerage firm, an investor signs an agreement containing a so-called mandatory pre-dispute arbitration clause. As its name suggests, that clause compels arbitration of all future disputes between the investor and the firm or its brokers. Such clauses have become so routine that today the absence of such a clause from an investor-broker agreement would be highly unusual.

Mandatory arbitration of investor-broker disputes is a relatively recent phenomenon. As we will see, turning points occurred in 1987, when the Supreme Court upheld an agreement to arbitrate an Exchange Act claim and again in 1989, when the Court upheld an agreement to arbitrate a Securities Act claim.

Not surprisingly, there has been a steady increase in the number of securities cases filed in arbitration since 1990. Consider the following statistics for NASD-Dispute Resolution, Inc. (NASD-DR), a division of the National Association of Securities Dealers (NASD) and the forum for more than ninety percent of securities arbitrations (including those filed with the American Stock Exchange, the Municipal Securities Rulemaking Board, and the Philadelphia Stock Exchange):

**Arbitration Cases Filed**

| Year | Cases | Year | Cases |
|---|---|---|---|
| 1990 | 3,617 | 1997 | 5,997 |
| 1991 | 4,150 | 1998 | 4,938 |
| 1992 | 4,379 | 1999 | 5,608 |
| 1993 | 5,421 | 2000 | 5,558 |
| 1994 | 5,586 | 2001 | 6,915 |
| 1995 | 6,058 | 2002 | 7,704 |
| 1996 | 5,631 | | |

NASD Dispute Resolution Statistics, available at www.nasdadr.com/statistics.asp (Jan. 21, 2003)

The balance of securities arbitrations are filed mainly with the stock exchanges, principally with the Arbitration Department of the New York Stock Exchange (NYSE), which by itself accounts for eight percent of the total securities arbitrations filed. Recall from Chapter 1 that the NASD and the stock exchanges are self-regulatory organizations (SROs) subject to SEC oversight. It is no accident that SROs are the predominant forums for securities arbitration. Indeed, few brokerage firms allow investors to choose a non-SRO forum, such as the American Arbitration Association (AAA).

Mandatory arbitration of investor-broker disputes has been controversial. Supporters maintain that arbitration is a fair, efficient, and economical means of dispute resolution. They also note that judges often recommend arbitration as a form of alternative dispute resolution in a wide spectrum of civil cases. Critics, however, contend that investors can be protected only when there is a trial conducted by a judge, based on the rules of evidence (not applicable in arbitration), with a right to appeal (which, as we will see, is highly limited in arbitration). Critics further complain that the system has an inherent pro-broker bias, since brokerage firms comprise the membership of SROs, where almost all securities arbitrations are conducted.

The debate over mandatory securities arbitration encompasses every aspect of the arbitration process. Who determines the issues subject to arbitration? To what extent are arbitrators bound by substantive securities law? Do arbitration procedures favor brokers? Should arbitrators have the authority to award punitive damages? Is there adequate judicial review of arbitration decisions?

This Chapter explores these questions in four sections. Section A examines the relationship between the Federal Arbitration Act and the federal securities laws. Section B focuses on the process of securities arbitration. Section C addresses the role that courts continue to play in securities arbitration. Section D provides data and observations concerning how investors fare in arbitration.

## A. THE RELATIONSHIP BETWEEN THE FEDERAL ARBITRATION ACT AND THE FEDERAL SECURITIES LAWS

For many years, courts struggled with the following question: when an investor agrees to arbitrate disputes with her broker, does she waive the right to sue the broker for violations of the federal securities laws? The answer to this question turns on the relationship between the federal securities laws and the Federal Arbitration Act of 1925 ("Arbitration Act"). That relationship is not self-evident, and the Supreme Court had viewed the relationship differently at different times.

The Arbitration Act declares arbitration agreements "valid, irrevocable, and enforceable, save upon such grounds as exist at law or in equity for the revocation of any contract." 9 U.S.C. § 2. The Act was intended to "revers[e] centuries of judicial hostility to arbitration agreements ***, to allow parties to avoid 'the costliness and delays of litigation,' and to place arbitration agreements 'upon the same footing as other contracts.' " *Scherk v. Alberto-Culver Co.*, 417 U.S. 506, 510-11 (1974) (quoting H.R. Rep. No. 96, 68th Cong., 1st Sess. 1, 2 (1924)).

In *Wilko v. Swan,* 346 U.S. 427 (1953), the Supreme Court upheld an investor's right to sue his broker under what is now Section 12(a)(2) of the Securities Act, notwithstanding an arbitration agreement between them. In so holding, the Court focused on Section 14 of the Securities Act, which declares "void" "[a]ny condition, stipulation or provision binding any person acquiring any security to waive compliance with any provision" of that Act:

> This arrangement to arbitrate is a "stipulation," and we think the right to select the judicial forum is the kind of "provision" that cannot be waived under § 14 of the Securities Act. *** While a buyer and seller of securities, under some circumstances, may deal at arm's length on equal terms, it is clear that the Securities Act was drafted with an eye to the disadvantages under which buyers labor. ***
>
> When the securities buyer, prior to any violation of the Securities Act, waives his right to sue in courts, he gives up more than would a participant in other business transactions. The security buyer has a wider choice of courts and venue. He thus surrenders one of the advantages the Act gives him and surrenders it at a time when he is less able to judge the weight of the handicap the Securities Act places upon his adversary.
>
> Even though the provisions of the Securities Act, advantageous to the buyer, apply, their effectiveness in application is lessened in arbitration as compared to judicial proceedings. *** This case requires subjective findings on the purpose and knowledge of an alleged violator of the Act. They must be not only determined but applied by the arbitrators without judicial instruction on the law. As their award may be made without explanation of their reasons and without a complete record of their proceedings, the arbitrators' conception of the legal meaning of such statutory requirements as "burden of proof," "reasonable care" or "material fact" cannot be examined. Power to vacate an award is limited. *** [T]he interpretations of the law by the arbitrators in contrast to manifest disregard are not subject, in the federal courts, to judicial review for error in interpretation. *** As the protective provisions of the Securities Act require the exercise of judicial direction to fairly assure their effectiveness, it seems to us that Congress must have intended § 14 to apply to waiver of judicial trial and review.

Id. at 434-37. In the wake of *Wilko*, lower federal courts likewise refused to order arbitration of Exchange Act claims on the ground that Section 29(a) of the Exchange Act is largely identical to Section 14 of the Securities Act. See, e.g., *Merrill Lynch Pierce Fenner & Smith, Inc. v. Moore,* 590 F.2d 823, 827-29 (10th Cir. 1978).

The Supreme Court abandoned *Wilko* in stages. By a 5-4 vote, the Court held a Rule 10b-5 claim to be arbitrable on the ground that the agreement containing the arbitration clause was "truly international." *Scherk v. Alberto-Culver Co.*, 417 U.S. 506, 515 (1974). The Court thereafter mandated arbitration of state law securities claims despite their pendency to a Rule 10b-5 claim that would eventually be litigated. See *Dean Witter Reynolds, Inc. v. Byrd*, 470 U.S. 213, 223 (1985). The Court's abandonment of *Wilko* culminated in the following decision, which again split the Court 5-4.

## SHEARSON/AMERICAN EXPRESS, INC. v. McMAHON
482 U.S. 220 (1987)

JUSTICE O' CONNOR:

This case presents two questions regarding the enforceability of predispute arbitration agreements between brokerage firms and their customers. The first is whether a claim brought under § 10(b) of the Securities Exchange Act of 1934 (Exchange Act) must be sent to arbitration in accordance with the terms of an arbitration agreement. The second is whether a claim brought under the Racketeer Influenced and Corrupt Organizations Act (RICO) must be arbitrated in accordance with the terms of such an agreement.

### I

Between 1980 and 1982, respondents Eugene and Julia McMahon, individually and as trustees for various pension and profit-sharing plans, were customers of petitioner Shearson/American Express Inc. (Shearson), a brokerage firm registered with the Securities and Exchange Commission (SEC or Commission). Two customer agreements signed by Julia McMahon provided for arbitration of any controversy relating to the accounts the McMahons maintained with Shearson. The arbitration provision provided in relevant part as follows:

> "Unless unenforceable due to federal or state law, any controversy arising out of or relating to my accounts, to transactions with you for me or to this agreement or the breach thereof, shall be settled by arbitration in accordance with the rules, then in effect, of the National Association of Securities Dealers, Inc. or the Boards of Directors of the New York Stock Exchange, Inc. and/or the American Stock Exchange, Inc. as I may elect." 618 F.Supp. 384, 385 (1985).

In October 1984, the McMahons filed an amended complaint against Shearson and petitioner Mary Ann McNulty, the registered representative who handled their accounts, in the United States District Court for the Southern District of New York. The complaint alleged that McNulty, with Shearson's knowledge, had violated § 10(b) of the Exchange Act and Rule 10b-5, by engaging in fraudulent, excessive trading on respondents' accounts and by making false statements and omitting material facts from the advice given to respondents. The complaint also alleged a RICO claim, and state law claims for fraud and breach of fiduciary duties.

Relying on the customer agreements, petitioners moved to compel arbitration of the McMahons' claims pursuant to § 3 of the Federal Arbitration Act. The District Court granted the motion in part. The court first rejected the McMahons' contention that the arbitration agreements were unenforceable as contracts of adhesion. It then found that the McMahons' § 10(b) claims were arbitrable under the terms of the agreement, concluding that such a result followed from this Court's decision in *Dean Witter Reynolds Inc. v. Byrd,* 470 U.S. 213 (1985), and the "strong national policy favoring the enforcement of arbitration agreements." The District Court also held that the McMahons' state law claims were arbitrable under *Dean Witter Reynolds Inc. v. Byrd,* supra. It concluded, however, that the McMahons' RICO claim was not arbitrable "because of the important federal policies inherent in the enforcement of RICO by the federal courts."

The Court of Appeals affirmed the District Court on the state law and RICO claims, but it reversed on the Exchange Act claims. ***

*** The [C]ourt [of Appeals] *** acknowledged that *Scherk v. Alberto-Culver Co.*, 417 U.S. 506 (1974), and *Dean Witter Reynolds Inc. v. Byrd*, supra, had "cast some doubt on the applicability of *Wilko* to claims under § 10(b)." The Court of Appeals nevertheless concluded that it was bound by the "clear judicial precedent in this Circuit," and held that *Wilko* must be applied to Exchange Act claims.

We granted certiorari to resolve the conflict among the Courts of Appeals regarding the arbitrability of § 10(b) and RICO claims.

II

The Federal Arbitration Act provides the starting point for answering the questions raised in this case. ***

The Arbitration Act *** establishes a "federal policy favoring arbitration," *Moses H. Cone Memorial Hospital v. Mercury Construction Corp.*, 460 U.S. 1, 24 (1983), requiring that "we rigorously enforce agreements to arbitrate." *Dean Witter Reynolds Inc. v. Byrd*, supra, 470 U.S., at 221. This duty to enforce arbitration agreements is not diminished when a party bound by an agreement raises a claim founded on statutory rights. As we observed in *Mitsubishi Motors Corp. v. Soler Chrysler-Plymouth, Inc.*, "we are well past the time when judicial suspicion of the desirability of arbitration and of the competence of arbitral tribunals" should inhibit enforcement of the Act " 'in controversies based on statutes.' " 473 U.S., at 626-627, quoting *Wilko v. Swan*, supra, 346 U.S., at 432. Absent a well-founded claim that an arbitration agreement resulted from the sort of fraud or excessive economic power that "would provide grounds 'for the revocation of any contract,' " 473 U.S. at 627, the Arbitration Act "provides no basis for disfavoring agreements to arbitrate statutory claims by skewing the otherwise hospitable inquiry into arbitrability." Ibid.

The Arbitration Act, standing alone, therefore mandates enforcement of agreements to arbitrate statutory claims. Like any statutory directive, the Arbitration Act's mandate may be overridden by a contrary congressional command. The burden is on the party opposing arbitration, however, to show that Congress intended to preclude a waiver of judicial remedies for the statutory rights at issue. See id., at 628. If Congress did intend to limit or prohibit waiver of a judicial forum for a particular claim, such an intent "will be deducible from [the statute's] text or legislative history," ibid., or from an inherent conflict between arbitration and the statute's underlying purposes. See id., at 632-637.

To defeat application of the Arbitration Act in this case, therefore, the McMahons must demonstrate that Congress intended to make an exception to the Arbitration Act for claims arising under RICO and the Exchange Act, an intention discernible from the text, history, or purposes of the statute. ***

III

When Congress enacted the Exchange Act in 1934, it did not specifically address the question of the arbitrability of § 10(b) claims. The McMahons contend, however, that congressional intent to require a judicial forum for the resolution of § 10(b) claims can be deduced from § 29(a) of the Exchange Act, which declares void "[a]ny condition, stipulation, or provision binding any person to waive compliance with any provision of [the Act]."

First, we reject the McMahons' argument that § 29(a) forbids waiver of § 27 of the Exchange Act. Section 27 provides in relevant part:

> The district courts of the United States ... shall have exclusive jurisdiction of violations of this title or the rules and regulations thereunder, and of all suits in equity and actions at law brought to enforce any liability or duty created by this title or the rules and regulations thereunder.

The McMahons contend that an agreement to waive this jurisdictional provision is unenforceable because § 29(a) voids the waiver of "any provision" of the Exchange Act. The language of § 29(a), however, does not reach so far. What the antiwaiver provision of § 29(a) forbids is enforcement of agreements to waive "compliance" with the provisions of the statute. But § 27 itself does not impose any duty with which persons trading in securities must "comply." By its terms, § 29(a) only prohibits waiver of the substantive obligations imposed by the Exchange Act. Because § 27 does not impose any statutory duties, its waiver does not constitute a waiver of "compliance with any provision" of the Exchange Act under § 29(a).

We do not read *Wilko v. Swan,* 346 U.S. 427 (1953), as compelling a different result. In *Wilko,* the Court held that a predispute agreement could not be enforced to compel arbitration of a claim arising under § 12(2) of the Securities Act. The basis for the ruling was § 14 of the Securities Act, which, like § 29(a) of the Exchange Act, declares void any stipulation "to waive compliance with any provision" of the statute. At the beginning of its analysis, the *Wilko* Court stated that the Securities Act's jurisdictional provision was "the kind of 'provision' that cannot be waived under § 14 of the Securities Act." This statement, however, can only be understood in the context of the Court's ensuing discussion explaining why arbitration was inadequate as a means of enforcing "the provisions of the Securities Act, advantageous to the buyer." Ibid. The conclusion in *Wilko* was expressly based on the Court's belief that a judicial forum was needed to protect the substantive rights created by the Securities Act: "As the protective provisions of the Securities Act require the exercise of judicial direction to fairly assure their effectiveness, it seems to us that Congress must have intended § 14 ... to apply to waiver of judicial trial and review." *Wilko* must be understood, therefore, as holding that the plaintiff's waiver of the "right to select the judicial forum" was unenforceable only because arbitration was judged inadequate to enforce the statutory rights created by § 12(2). ***

The second argument offered by the McMahons is that the arbitration agreement effects an impermissible waiver of the substantive protections of the Exchange Act. Ordinarily, "[b]y agreeing to arbitrate a statutory claim, a party does not forgo the substantive rights afforded by the statute; it only submits to their resolution in an arbitral, rather than a judicial, forum." *Mitsubishi Motors*

*Corp. v. Soler Chrysler-Plymouth, Inc.*, 473 U.S., at 628. The McMahons argue, however, that § 29(a) compels a different conclusion. Initially, they contend that predispute agreements are void under § 29(a) because they tend to result from broker overreaching. They reason, as do some commentators, that *Wilko* is premised on the belief "that arbitration clauses in securities sales agreements generally are not freely negotiated." See, e.g., Sterk, Enforceability of Agreements to Arbitrate: An Examination of the Public Policy Defense, 2 Cardozo L. Rev. 481, 519 (1981). According to this view, *Wilko* barred enforcement of predispute agreements because of this frequent inequality of bargaining power, reasoning that Congress intended for § 14 generally to ensure that sellers did not "maneuver buyers into a position that might weaken their ability to recover under the Securities Act." The McMahons urge that we should interpret § 29(a) in the same fashion.

We decline to give *Wilko* a reading so far at odds with the plain language of § 14, or to adopt such an unlikely interpretation of § 29(a). The concern that § 29(a) is directed against is evident from the statute's plain language: it is a concern with whether an agreement "waive[s] compliance with [a] provision" of the Exchange Act. The voluntariness of the agreement is irrelevant to this inquiry: if a stipulation waives compliance with a statutory duty, it is void under § 29(a), whether voluntary or not. Thus, a customer cannot negotiate a reduction in commissions in exchange for a waiver of compliance with the requirements of the Exchange Act, even if the customer knowingly and voluntarily agreed to the bargain. Section 29(a) is concerned, not with whether brokers "maneuver[ed customers] into" an agreement, but with whether the agreement "weaken[s] their ability to recover under the [Exchange] Act." 346 U.S., at 432. The former is grounds for revoking the contract under ordinary principles of contract law; the latter is grounds for voiding the agreement under § 29(a).

The other reason advanced by the McMahons for finding a waiver of their § 10(b) rights is that arbitration does "weaken their ability to recover under the [Exchange] Act." Ibid. That is the heart of the Court's decision in *Wilko*, and respondents urge that we should follow its reasoning. *Wilko* listed several grounds why, in the Court's view, the "effectiveness [of the Act's provisions] in application is lessened in arbitration." First, the *Wilko* Court believed that arbitration proceedings were not suited to cases requiring "subjective findings on the purpose and knowledge of an alleged violator." *Wilko* also was concerned that arbitrators must make legal determinations "without judicial instruction on the law," and that an arbitration award "may be made without explanation of [the arbitrator's] reasons and without a complete record of their proceedings." Finally, *Wilko* noted that the "[p]ower to vacate an award is limited," and that "interpretations of the law by the arbitrators in contrast to manifest disregard are not subject, in the federal courts, to judicial review for error in interpretation." *Wilko* concluded that in view of these drawbacks to arbitration, § 12(2) claims "require[d] the exercise of judicial direction to fairly assure their effectiveness."

As Justice Frankfurter noted in his dissent in *Wilko*, the Court's opinion did not rest on any evidence, either "in the record ... [or] in the facts of which [it could] take judicial notice," that "the arbitral system ... would not afford the plaintiff the rights to which he is entitled." Instead, the reasons given in *Wilko* reflect a general suspicion of the desirability of arbitration and the competence of arbitral tribunals—most apply with no greater force to the arbitration of securities disputes than to the arbitration of legal disputes generally. It is difficult to reconcile *Wilko's* mistrust of the arbitral process with this Court's subsequent decisions involving the Arbitration Act. See, e.g., *Dean Witter Reynolds Inc. v. Byrd,* 470 U.S. 213 (1985); *Scherk v. Alberto-Culver Co.,* 417 U.S. 506 (1974).

Indeed, most of the reasons given in *Wilko* have been rejected subsequently by the Court as a basis for holding claims to be nonarbitrable. In *Mitsubishi,* for example, we recognized that arbitral tribunals are readily capable of handling the factual and legal complexities of antitrust claims, notwithstanding the absence of judicial instruction and supervision. Likewise, we have concluded that the streamlined procedures of arbitration do not entail any consequential restriction on substantive rights. Id., at 628. Finally, we have indicated that there is no reason to assume at the outset that arbitrators will not follow the law; although judicial scrutiny of arbitration awards necessarily is limited, such review is sufficient to ensure that arbitrators comply with the requirements of the statute. See id., at 636- 637, and n. 19.

The suitability of arbitration as a means of enforcing Exchange Act rights is evident from our decision in *Scherk.* Although the holding in that case was limited to international agreements, the competence of arbitral tribunals to resolve § 10(b) claims is the same in both settings. ***

Thus, the mistrust of arbitration that formed the basis for the *Wilko* opinion in 1953 is difficult to square with the assessment of arbitration that has prevailed since that time. This is especially so in light of the intervening changes in the regulatory structure of the securities laws. Even if *Wilko's* assumptions regarding arbitration were valid at the time *Wilko* was decided, most certainly they do not hold true today for arbitration procedures subject to the SEC's oversight authority.

In 1953, when *Wilko* was decided, the Commission had only limited authority over the rules governing self-regulatory organizations (SROs)—the national securities exchanges and registered securities associations—and this authority appears not to have included any authority at all over their arbitration rules. See Brief for Securities and Exchange Commission as *Amicus Curiae* 14-15. Since the 1975 amendments to § 19 of the Exchange Act, however, the Commission has had expansive power to ensure the adequacy of the arbitration procedures employed by the SROs. No proposed rule change may take effect unless the SEC finds that the proposed rule is consistent with the requirements of the Exchange Act, 15 U.S.C. § 78s(b)(2); and the Commission has the power, on its own initiative, to "abrogate, add to, and delete from" any SRO rule if it finds such changes necessary or appropriate to further the objectives of the Act, 15 U.S.C. § 78s(c). In short, the Commission has broad authority to oversee and to regulate the rules adopted by the SROs relating to customer disputes, including the power to mandate the adoption of any rules it deems necessary to ensure that arbitration procedures adequately protect statutory rights.

In the exercise of its regulatory authority, the SEC has specifically approved the arbitration procedures of the New York Stock Exchange, the American Stock Exchange, and the NASD, the organizations mentioned in the arbitration agreement at issue in this case. We conclude that where, as in this case, the prescribed procedures are subject to the Commission's § 19 authority, an arbitration agreement does not effect a waiver of the protections of the Act. While *stare decisis* concerns may counsel against upsetting *Wilko*'s contrary conclusion under the Securities Act, we refuse to extend *Wilko*'s reasoning to the Exchange Act in light of these intervening regulatory developments. The McMahons' agreement to submit to arbitration therefore is not tantamount to an impermissible waiver of the McMahons' rights under § 10(b), and the agreement is not void on that basis under § 29(a).

The final argument offered by the McMahons is that even if § 29(a) as enacted does not void predispute arbitration agreements, Congress subsequently has indicated that it desires § 29(a) to be so interpreted. According to the McMahons, Congress expressed this intent when it failed to make more extensive changes to § 28(b), in the 1975 amendments to the Exchange Act. Before its amendment, § 28(b) provided in relevant part:

> Nothing in this chapter shall be construed to modify existing law (1) with regard to the binding effect on any member of any exchange of any action taken by the authorities of such exchange to settle disputes between its members, or (2) with regard to the binding effect of such action on any person who has agreed to be bound thereby, or (3) with regard to the binding effect on any such member of any disciplinary action taken by the authorities of the exchange. 48 Stat. 903.

The chief aim of this provision was to preserve the self-regulatory role of the securities exchanges, by giving the exchanges a means of enforcing their rules against their members. In 1975, Congress made extensive revisions to the Exchange Act intended to "clarify the scope of the self-regulatory responsibilities of national securities exchanges and registered securities associations ... and the manner in which they are to exercise those responsibilities." S. Rep. No. 94-75, p. 22 (1975). In making these changes, the Senate Report observed: "The self-regulatory organizations must exercise governmental-type powers if they are to carry out their responsibilities under the Exchange Act. When a member violates the Act or a self-regulatory organization's rules, the organization must be in a position to impose appropriate penalties or to revoke relevant privileges." Id., at 24.

The amendments to § 28 reflect this objective. Paragraph (3) of § 28(b) was deleted and replaced with new § 28(c), which provided that the validity of any disciplinary action taken by an SRO would not be affected by a subsequent decision by the SEC to stay or modify the sanction. At the same time, § 28(b) was expanded to ensure that all SROs as well as the Municipal Securities Rulemaking Board had the power to enforce their substantive rules against their members. Section 28(b), as amended, provides:

> Nothing in this chapter shall be construed to modify existing law with regard to the binding effect (1) on any member of or participant in any self- regulatory organization of any action taken by the authorities of such organization to settle disputes between its members or participants, (2) on any municipal securities dealer or municipal securities broker of any action taken pursuant to a procedure established by the Municipal Securities Rulemaking Board to settle

> disputes between municipal securities dealers and municipal securities brokers, or (3) of any action described in paragraph (1) or (2) on any person who has agreed to be bound thereby.

Thus, the amended version of § 28(b), like the original, mentions neither customers nor arbitration. It is directed at an entirely different problem: enhancing the self-regulatory function of the SROs under the Exchange Act.

The McMahons nonetheless argue that we should find it significant that Congress did *not* take this opportunity to address the general question of the arbitrability of Exchange Act claims. Their argument is based entirely on a sentence from the Conference Report, which they contend amounts to a ratification of *Wilko's* extension to Exchange Act claims. The Conference Report states:

> The Senate bill amended section 28 of the Securities Exchange Act of 1934 with respect to arbitration proceedings between self-regulatory organizations and their participants, members, or persons dealing with members or participants. The House amendment contained no comparable provision. The House receded to the Senate. It was the clear understanding of the conferees that this amendment did not change existing law, as articulated in *Wilko v. Swan,* 346 U.S. 427 (1953), concerning the effect of arbitration proceedings provisions in agreements entered into by persons dealing with members and participants of self-regulatory organizations. H.R. Conf. Rep. No. 94-229, p. 111 (1975).

The McMahons contend that the conferees would not have acknowledged *Wilko* in a revision of the Exchange Act unless they were aware of lower court decisions extending *Wilko* to § 10(b) claims and intended to approve them. We find this argument fraught with difficulties. We cannot see how Congress could extend *Wilko* to the Exchange Act without enacting into law any provision remotely addressing that subject. And even if it could, there is little reason to interpret the Report as the McMahons suggest. At the outset, the committee may well have mentioned *Wilko* for a reason entirely different from the one postulated by the McMahons—lower courts had applied § 28(b) to the Securities Act, and the committee may simply have wished to make clear that the amendment to § 28(b) was not otherwise intended to affect *Wilko's* construction of the Securities Act. Moreover, even if the committee were referring to the arbitrability of § 10(b) claims, the quoted sentence does not disclose what committee members thought "existing law" provided. The conference members might have had in mind the two Court of Appeals decisions extending *Wilko* to the Exchange Act, as the McMahons contend. See *Greater Continental Corp. v. Schechter,* 422 F.2d 1100 (CA2 1970); *Moran v. Paine, Webber, Jackson & Curtis,* 389 F.2d 242 (CA3 1968). It is equally likely, however, that the committee had in mind this Court's decision the year before expressing doubts as to whether *Wilko* should be extended to § 10(b) claims. See *Scherk v. Alberto-Culver Co.,* 417 U.S., at 513 ("[A] colorable argument could be made that even the semantic reasoning of the *Wilko* opinion does not control [a case based on § 10(b)]"). Finally, even assuming the conferees had an understanding of existing law that all agreed upon, they specifically disclaimed any intent to change it. Hence, the *Wilko* issue was left to the courts: it was unaffected by the amendment to § 28(b). This statement of congressional inaction simply does not support the proposition that the 1975 Congress intended to engraft onto unamended § 29(a) a meaning different from that of the enacting Congress.

We conclude, therefore, that Congress did not intend for § 29(a) to bar enforcement of all predispute arbitration agreements. In this case, where the SEC has sufficient statutory authority to ensure that arbitration is adequate to vindicate Exchange Act rights, enforcement does not effect a waiver of "compliance with any provision" of the Exchange Act under § 29(a). Accordingly, we hold the McMahons' agreements to arbitrate Exchange Act claims "enforce[able] ... in accord with the explicit provisions of the Arbitration Act." *Scherk v. Alberto-Culver Co.*, supra, at 520.

IV

*[The Court held that the McMahons' agreement to arbitrate their RICO claim was enforceable.]*

JUSTICE BLACKMUN, WITH WHOM JUSTICE BRENNAN AND JUSTICE MARSHALL JOIN, CONCURRING IN PART AND DISSENTING IN PART:

I concur in the Court's decision to enforce the arbitration agreement with respect to respondents' RICO claims and thus join Parts I, II, and IV of the Court's opinion. I disagree, however, with the Court's conclusion that respondents' § 10(b) claims also are subject to arbitration.

*** In today's decision *** the Court effectively overrules *Wilko* by accepting the Securities and Exchange Commission's newly adopted position that arbitration procedures in the securities industry and the Commission's oversight of the self-regulatory organizations (SROs) have improved greatly since *Wilko* was decided. The Court thus approves the abandonment of the judiciary's role in the resolution of claims under the Exchange Act and leaves such claims to the arbitral forum of the securities industry at a time when the industry's abuses towards investors are more apparent than ever. ***

II

There are essentially two problems with the Court's conclusion that predispute agreements to arbitrate § 10(b) claims may be enforced. First, the Court gives *Wilko* an overly narrow reading so that it can fit into the syllogism offered by the Commission and accepted by the Court, namely, (1) *Wilko* was really a case concerning whether arbitration was adequate for the enforcement of the substantive provisions of the securities laws; (2) all of the *Wilko* Court's doubts as to arbitration's adequacy are outdated; (3) thus *Wilko* is no longer good law. Second, the Court accepts uncritically petitioners' and the Commission's argument that the problems with arbitration, highlighted by the *Wilko* Court, either no longer exist or are not now viewed as problems by the Court. This acceptance primarily is based upon the Court's belief in the Commission's representations that its oversight of the SROs ensures the adequacy of arbitration.

A

*** The Court in *Wilko* recognized the policy of investor protection in the Securities Act. *** In the Court's view, the express language, legislative history, and purposes of the Securities Act all made predispute agreements to arbitrate § 12(2) claims unenforceable despite the presence of the Arbitration Act.[9]

Accordingly, the Court seriously errs when it states that the result in *Wilko* turned only on the perceived inadequacy of arbitration for the enforcement of § 12(2) claims. It is true that the *Wilko* Court discussed the inadequacies of this process and that this discussion constituted one ground for the Court's decision. The discussion, however, occurred *after* the Court had concluded that the language, legislative history, and purposes of the Securities Act mandated an exception to the Arbitration Act for these securities claims. ***

In light of a proper reading of *Wilko,* the pertinent question then becomes whether the language, legislative history, and purposes of the Exchange Act call for an exception to the Arbitration Act for § 10(b) claims. The Exchange Act waiver provision is virtually identical to that of the Securities Act. More importantly, the same concern with investor protection that motivated the Securities Act is evident in the Exchange Act, although the latter, in contrast to the former, is aimed at trading in the secondary securities market. See *Ernst & Ernst v. Hochfelder,* 425 U.S. 185, 195 (1976). We have recognized that both Acts were designed with this common purpose in mind. See id., at 206. ***

In sum, the same reasons that led the Court to find an exception to the Arbitration Act for § 12(2) claims exist for § 10(b) claims as well. It is clear that *Wilko,* when properly read, governs the instant case and mandates that a predispute arbitration agreement should not be enforced as to § 10(b) claims.

B

Even if I were to accept the Court's narrow reading of *Wilko,* as a case dealing only with the inadequacies of arbitration in 1953, I do not think that this case should be resolved differently today so long as the policy of investor protection is given proper consideration in the analysis. Despite improvements in the process of arbitration and changes in the judicial attitude towards it, several aspects of arbitration that were seen by the *Wilko* Court to be inimical to the policy of investor protection still remain. Moreover, I have serious reservations about the Commission's contention that its oversight of the SROs' arbitration procedures will ensure that the process is adequate to protect an investor's rights under the securities Acts.

---

9. In discussing the similar nonwaiver provision under the Exchange Act, § 29(a), the Court now suggests that it can be read only to mean that an investor cannot waive security-investment personnel's "compliance" with a duty under the statute. The Court implies that the literal language of § 29(a) does not apply to an investor's waiver of his own action. It appears, however, that in *Wilko* the Court understood the nonwaiver provision *also* to mean that, at least in the predispute context, an investor could not waive *his* compliance with the provision for dispute resolution in the courts. This reading of the antiwaiver provision makes sense in terms of the policy of investor protection. To counteract the inherent superior position of the securities-industry professional, up to and including the time when a dispute might occur between a broker and the investor, Congress intended to place the investor on "a different basis from other purchasers." Construing § 14 not to allow the investor to waive his right to a judicial forum in the predispute setting serves this congressional purpose of maintaining the investor in a special position. ***

As the Court observes, in *Wilko* the Court was disturbed by several characteristics of arbitration that made such a process inadequate to safeguard the special position in which the Securities Act had placed the investor. ***

The Court today appears to argue that the *Wilko* Court's assessment of arbitration's inadequacy is outdated, first, because arbitration has improved since 1953, and second, because the Court no longer considers the criticisms of arbitration made in *Wilko* to be valid reasons why statutory claims, such as those under § 10(b), should not be sent to arbitration. It is true that arbitration procedures in the securities industry have improved since *Wilko's* day. Of particular importance has been the development of a code of arbitration by the Commission with the assistance of representatives of the securities industry and the public. See Uniform Code of Arbitration, Exh. C, Fifth Report of the Securities Industry Conference on Arbitration 29 (Apr.1986) (Fifth SICA Report).

Even those who favor the arbitration of securities claims do not contend, however, that arbitration has changed so significantly as to eliminate the essential characteristics noted by the *Wilko* Court. Indeed, proponents of arbitration would not see these characteristics as "problems," because, in their view, the characteristics permit the unique "streamlined" nature of the arbitral process. As at the time of *Wilko,* preparation of a record of arbitration proceedings is not invariably required today. Moreover, arbitrators are not bound by precedent and are actually discouraged by their associations from giving reasons for a decision. See R. Coulson, Business Arbitration—What You Need to Know 29 (3d ed. 1986) ("Written opinions can be dangerous because they identify targets for the losing party to attack"). Judicial review is still substantially limited to the four grounds listed in § 10 of the Arbitration Act and to the concept of "manifest disregard" of the law.

The Court's "mistrust" of arbitration may have given way recently to an acceptance of this process, not only because of the improvements in arbitration, but also because of the Court's present assumption that the distinctive features of arbitration, its more quick and economical resolution of claims, do not render it inherently inadequate for the resolution of statutory claims. See *Mitsubishi Motors Corp. v. Soler Chrysler-Plymouth, Inc.,* 473 U.S., at 633. Such reasoning, however, should prevail only in the absence of the congressional policy that places the statutory claimant in a special position with respect to possible violators of his statutory rights. As even the most ardent supporter of arbitration would recognize, the arbitral process *at best* places the investor on an equal footing with the securities-industry personnel against whom the claims are brought.

Furthermore, there remains the danger that, *at worst,* compelling an investor to arbitrate securities claims puts him in a forum controlled by the securities industry. This result directly contradicts the goal of both securities Acts to free the investor from the control of the market professional. The Uniform Code provides some safeguards but despite them, and indeed because of the background of the arbitrators, the investor has the impression, frequently justified, that his claims are being judged by a forum composed of individuals sympathetic to the securities industry and not drawn from the public. ***

More surprising than the Court's acceptance of the present adequacy of arbitration for the resolution of securities claims is its confidence in the Commission's oversight of the arbitration procedures of the SROs to ensure this adequacy. *** The Court, however, fails to acknowledge that, until it filed an *amicus* brief in this case, the Commission consistently took the position that § 10(b) claims, like those under § 12(2), should not be sent to arbitration, that predispute arbitration agreements, where the investor was not advised of his right to a judicial forum, were misleading, and that the very regulatory oversight upon which the Commission now relies could not alone make securities-industry arbitration adequate. It is most questionable, then, whether the Commission's recently adopted position is entitled to the deference that the Court accords it.

The Court is swayed by the power given to the Commission by the 1975 amendments to the Exchange Act in order to permit the Commission to oversee the rules and procedures of the SROs, including those dealing with arbitration. ***

*** The Commission does not pretend that its oversight consists of anything other than a general review of SRO rules and the ability to require that an SRO adopt or delete a particular rule. It does not contend that its "sweeping authority," Brief 16, includes a review of specific arbitration proceedings. It thus neither polices nor monitors the results of these arbitrations for possible misapplications of securities laws or for indications of how investors fare in these proceedings. Given, in fact, the present constraints on the Commission's resources in this time of market expansion, it is doubtful whether the Commission could undertake to conduct any such review. ***

JUSTICE STEVENS, CONCURRING IN PART AND DISSENTING IN PART:

Gaps in the law must, of course, be filled by judicial construction. But after a statute has been construed, either by this Court or by a consistent course of decision by other federal judges and agencies, it acquires a meaning that should be as clear as if the judicial gloss had been drafted by the Congress itself. This position reflects both respect for Congress' role, see *Boys Market, Inc. v. Retail Clerks,* 398 U.S. 235, 257-258 (1970) (Black, J., dissenting), and the compelling need to preserve the courts' limited resources, see B. Cardozo, The Nature of the Judicial Process 149 (1921).

During the 32 years immediately following this Court's decision in *Wilko v. Swan,* 346 U.S. 427 (1953), each of the eight Circuits that addressed the issue concluded that the holding of *Wilko* was fully applicable to claims arising under the Securities Exchange Act of 1934. This longstanding interpretation creates a strong presumption, in my view, that any mistake that the courts may have made in interpreting the statute is best remedied by the Legislative, not the Judicial, Branch. ***

For this reason, I respectfully dissent from the portion of the Court's judgment that holds *Wilko* inapplicable to the 1934 Act. Like Justice Blackmun, however, I join Parts I, II, and IV of the Court's opinion.

## *NOTES AND QUESTIONS*

*1. **The Import of Section 29(a).*** The majority opinion and Justice Blackmun's opinion divide, among other things, over whether Section 29(a) of the Exchange Act prohibits enforcement of arbitration agreements. Which view of this Section do you find more persuasive?

*2. **Divining Congress's Intent.*** The majority opinion maintained that Congress's 1975 Conference Report did not amount to an endorsement of *Wilko*. Do you agree? If Congress agreed with *Wilko*, what should it have done to make its views known? If, on the other hand, Congress disagreed with *Wilko*, why didn't it overturn the decision through amendment of the federal securities laws and/or the Arbitration Act?

*3. **Burying*** **Wilko.** Two years after *McMahon*, the Supreme Court explicitly reversed *Wilko* in a decision involving the Securities Act. See *Rodriguez v. Shearson/Am. Express, Inc.*, 490 U.S. 477 (1989) (requiring investors to arbitrate claims under what is now Section 12(a)(2) of the Securities Act). Like *McMahon*, *Rodriguez* divided the Court 5-4.

*4. **The Better Decisionmaker.*** Which is better positioned to decide whether investors and the public would benefit from mandatory securities arbitration—Congress or the courts? Which of these is likely to be more receptive to the preferences and interests of the securities industry? What weight should be given to these preferences and interests?

*5. **The Question of Voluntariness.*** In what sense (if any) do the McMahons and other investors "voluntarily" agree to arbitrate disputes with their brokers? As previously noted, the contract that an investor signs upon opening a brokerage account typically contains a mandatory pre-dispute arbitration clause. Yet many investors are not fully aware of the import of this clause and others do not know even that their brokerage contract contains such a clause.

After *McMahon*, a number of states took steps to preserve access to the courts for customers of brokerage firms. One such state was Massachusetts, which in 1988 adopted regulations (i) barring brokerage firms from requiring customers to sign pre-dispute arbitration agreements as a condition of opening an account; (ii) requiring that prospective customers receive notice of the prohibition against such agreements; and (iii) compelling complete disclosure in writing of the legal significance of such agreements. See *Sec. Indus. Ass'n. v. Connolly*, 883 F.2d 1114, 1117 (1st Cir. 1989). The First Circuit struck down these regulations, however, on the ground that they were preempted by the Arbitration Act. See id. at 1123. That court explained:

> The Commonwealth may well be correct that PDAAs [pre-dispute arbitration agreements] ought to be arrived at with greater negotiation and disclosure between broker-dealers and customers than currently takes place. That judgment, however, is not the Commonwealth's to make, at least in its current embodiment, for it singles out arbitration in an impermissible way. The states are forbidden from critical scrutiny expressed in a fashion which might mask historic hostility toward arbitration. Congress sought to avoid having that possibility come to fruition, choosing instead to emphasize and endorse arbitral

> efficiencies. That value judgment was within the congressional domain—and only Congress, not the states, may create exceptions to it.
>
> That is not to say, of course, that a state must permit broker-dealers to sail as close to the wind as their consciences (or lack thereof) might permit. Massachusetts has a plenitude of lawful weapons in its ethical armamentarium to preserve the integrity of the securities business as conducted in the Commonwealth and to protect consumers. But because the Regulations treat standard-form PDAAs in the securities industry more severely than standard-form contracts are generally treated under Massachusetts law, and because the policies underlying the Regulations, and their method of enforcement, conflict with the national policy favoring arbitration, the state scheme is too discommoding to the federal plan. The Regulations are, therefore, preempted.

Id. at 1124.

The question whether investors should be free to litigate rather than arbitrate their disputes with their brokers was also addressed by an Arbitration Policy Task Force appointed by the NASD and led by former SEC Chairperson David Ruder. The Task Force issued a report which supported the continued use by brokerage firms of mandatory pre-dispute arbitration clauses but noted that more should be done to educate investors about securities arbitration and its consequences. See Report of the Arbitration Policy Task Force to the Board of Governors, National Association of Securities Dealers, Inc. [1995-96 Transfer Binder] Fed. Sec. L. Rep. (CCH) ¶ 85,735 (Jan. 1996) [hereinafter Ruder Report]. What steps could brokers take to educate their customers? Should brokers be required to take such steps? Why or why not?

## B. THE PROCESS OF SECURITIES ARBITRATION

In 1977, in response to an SEC initiative, the Securities Industry Conference on Arbitration (SICA) was established in order to bring uniformity to the arbitration process. Pursuant to its mandate, the SICA developed the Uniform Code of Arbitration and over the years has revised it. Members of SICA have included SRO representatives, the public, and the Securities Industry Association, a trade association for the securities industry.

Each SRO that serves as an arbitration forum has adopted its own variation of the Code with the consent of the SEC. As *McMahon* noted, the SEC must approve all SRO rules and rule changes in accordance with the procedures set out in Section 19(b) of the Exchange Act. The SEC also conducts periodic inspections of SRO arbitration programs.

SICA produced the following description of arbitration procedures, available at the web sites of the two leading forums for securities arbitrations: NASD-DR and the NYSE. See www.nasdadr.com/arb_procedures.asp and www.nyse.com/pdfs/arb_procedures.pdf. As you read the description, consider the ways in which securities arbitration differs from securities litigation.

## SECURITIES INDUSTRY CONFERENCE ON ARBITRATION ARBITRATION PROCEDURES

March 15, 2001[a]

*** Arbitration of disputes with broker/dealers has long been used as an alternative to the courts because it is devised as a prompt and inexpensive means of resolving complicated issues. There are certain laws governing the conduct of an arbitration proceeding that must be considered by those planning to use arbitration to resolve the dispute. Most importantly, perhaps, is the fact that an arbitration award is final and binding, subject to review by a court only on a very limited basis. Parties should recognize, too, that in choosing arbitration as a means of resolving a dispute, they generally give up their right to pursue the matter through the courts.

### What Disputes Are Eligible For Arbitration?

*** Under the Uniform Code a controversy is not eligible for submission to arbitration if six or more years have elapsed from the date of the event giving rise to the dispute. The arbitrators also may dismiss a claim barred by shorter applicable state or federal statutes of limitations.***

Even after a customer has signed the agreement to arbitrate, the customer may request either the sponsoring organization or the arbitrators to permit that customer to proceed with his or her claim in court. The customer should be aware, however, that in most cases the sponsoring organization and the arbitrators will retain jurisdiction and proceed with the arbitration.

The Uniform Code states that a claim submitted as a class action shall not be eligible for arbitration. The rule also sets forth the circumstances where a claim encompassed by a putative or certified class action may or may not be eligible to be filed in arbitration. For further guidance you should refer to the rule and discuss its application to a particular case with the staff of the SRO where you intend to file your claim.

### Who Are The Arbitrators?

Arbitrators are impartial persons who are knowledgeable in securities industry disputes. Each sponsoring organization maintains a roster of individuals whose professional qualifications and experience qualify them for service as arbitrators. The arbitrators are not employees of the sponsoring organization and they, not the sponsoring organization, will decide your dispute. The arbitrators do, however, receive an honorarium from the SROs.

Under the Uniform Code, cases will be decided by one or three arbitrators, depending on the amount in dispute. Unless a customer elects otherwise, the majority of the members of such panels are individuals referred to as "public arbitrators" who are neither associated with nor employed by a broker/dealer or securities industry organization. ***

---

a. ©2001 National Association of Securities Dealers, Inc. (NASD, Inc.). Reprinted with permission from NASD, Inc.

The Director of Arbitration (Director) will inform the parties of the names and business affiliations of the selected arbitrators, their employment histories for the last 10 years, as well as any conflict information disclosed pursuant to the Uniform Code. Some parties are interested in previous awards issued by prospective arbitrators. Each sponsoring organization has developed procedures to make available information on customer awards issued since May 1989.

**Can I Be Represented By An Attorney?**

Parties have an absolute right to be represented by an attorney and may do so at any stage of the arbitration. Parties should be aware that, even if they do not elect to be represented by counsel, the other party may have an attorney, and they can assume that broker/dealers will be represented by an attorney.

Any party represented by counsel should notify the Director of the counsel's name and address either in the Statement of Claim or the Statement of Answer or by a separate written notice. After such notification, communications concerning the case will be addressed to the counsel. ***

**How Is Arbitration Begun?**

To begin arbitration, the prospective claimant must do the following:

(1) ***Statement Of Claim***—File with the Director a typewritten or printed document stating the claim. This document should set forth the details of the dispute, including all relevant dates and names, in a clear, concise, and chronological fashion and should conclude by indicating what relief (e.g., money damages in a specific amount, performance of a particular agreement, interest, etc.) is requested. The claimant should attach copies of documents and supporting materials as exhibits to the Statement of Claim. The claimant should provide sufficient copies for each party, the arbitrators, and the SRO.

(2) ***Small-Claims Procedures***—If the amount of the claim is $25,000 or less (at some SROs $10,000 or less), the claim will be processed under the Simplified Arbitration Procedures. In customer disputes, unless the customer requests a hearing, the claim will be decided solely on the basis of the parties' written submissions. The arbitrator, however, also may request a hearing or require a party to submit additional documentation. Parties may ask to submit additional documents to an arbitrator who is deciding the case without a hearing.

(3) ***Service Of Pleadings***—After the initial Statement of Claim is served by the Director, it is each party's responsibility to provide every other party directly with any further pleadings, motions, or correspondence. In addition, it is each party's responsibility to simultaneously provide sufficient copies directly to the sponsoring SRO for the arbitrators and its files. Service of the filings and correspondence on the sponsoring SRO and the other parties should be made on the same date and by the same means (i.e., via overnight mail, facsimile, etc.)

(4) ***Counsel***—State whether the claimant will be represented by an attorney and, if so, the attorney's name, address, and telephone number.

(5) ***Location***—State where the claimant wants the case to be heard and the reasons for that choice. The decision as to the location of the initial hearing is made by the Director. Consideration generally will be given to a number of factors, including the convenience of the parties, the availability of necessary records or witnesses, and the availability of qualified arbitrators. In customer cases, the hearing will generally be in a major urban area near where the customer resided when the dispute arose unless the parties agree to a different location after the case is filed.

(6) ***Complex Cases***—In appropriate cases, parties may request special services such as mediation, findings of facts and conclusions of law, expedited hearings, and the appointment of arbitrators with special qualifications. Parties seeking special or additional services should advise the sponsoring SRO at the earliest time possible. Additional fees may be charged for these services. In many complex cases, the parties may desire block scheduling of hearing dates. To the greatest extent possible, such cases will be scheduled in three-day blocks.

(7) ***Arbitrators***—The proposed panel will be composed of a majority of persons from outside the securities industry. If a customer would like a panel consisting of a majority of arbitrators from the securities industry, he or she should indicate that preference in writing when filing the claim.

(8) ***Uniform Submission Agreement***—Complete and return three signed copies of the Uniform Submission Agreement provided by the sponsoring organization. The claimant should provide sufficient copies for each party, the arbitrators, and the SRO. *** By signing the Uniform Submission Agreement, the claimant agrees to submit the dispute to arbitration and to abide by the decision (the "award") of the arbitrators. The claimant also agrees to be bound by the decision of the arbitrators with regard to any counterclaim (a claim against the claimant) permitted under these procedures that may be brought by an opposing party. Once a Uniform Submission Agreement has been signed, the procedures and timing set out in the Uniform Code become operative and binding. Generally, parties may not withdraw the Uniform Submission Agreement and Claim without the consent of either the other parties or the arbitrators.

(9) ***Filing Fees And Deposits***—Include a check or money order made payable to the sponsoring organization for the appropriate non-refundable filing fee and hearing session deposit. Where multiple hearing sessions are scheduled or conducted the arbitrators are authorized to require additional hearing session deposits by one or more parties. Additional deposits also may be required to be made for prehearing conferences with an arbitrator and for the postponement of a scheduled hearing date after the arbitrators have been selected. The arbitrators will determine in the final award if these deposits will be returned or assessed to another party. See the arbitration rules of the sponsoring SRO for the definition of a hearing session, as well as the appropriate fee and deposit.

(10) ***Disclosure Of Arbitration Award***—At some sponsoring organizations, customers must state in writing whether they either permit or decline to permit the inclusion of their names in the public version of the award. Check with your SRO for specific guidance.

(11) ***Incomplete Filing Of A Claim***—A filing may be returned if it does not comport with the rules. The Statement of Claim, with exhibits, Uniform Submission Agreement, and non-refundable filing fee and hearing session deposit should be submitted to the Director of the sponsoring organization at the address listed at the end of this pamphlet. All pleadings, correspondence, and exhibits after the claim is served must be sent to all parties directly with sufficient additional copies sent to the Director for the arbitrators and for the sponsoring organization.

**What Happens After the Claim is Filed?**

*** Generally, following the receipt of the claim, the respondent has 20 calendar days in the case of a small-claim arbitration and 20 business days in all other arbitrations to provide an answer, unless an extension of time has been granted by the Director. It is within the discretion of the Director to grant such extensions even over the objection of a party. However, the Director will consider the objection when determining the length of the extension. Remember to review the rules of the sponsoring organizations for the time to serve and file answers, and for the procedure in granting extensions of time to answer.

Under NASD rules, respondents in non-small claim customer cases have 45 calendar days from the receipt of a claim to serve and file answers. Although a claimant may agree to a respondent's request to extend the time to answer, the Director will only grant such extensions in extraordinary circumstances.

The respondent may assert a related counterclaim as part of its answer, or may file a claim against a third party; that is, a claim against another person who may bear responsibility for any of the alleged damages. Generally, a claim is considered to be related if it pertains to the customer's account at the broker/dealer. In support of its defense or counterclaim, the respondent should attach copies of documents and supporting materials to its answer.

The respondent also should send to each party an executed Uniform Submission Agreement and a copy of the respondent's answer and any counterclaim. The respondent's executed Uniform Submission Agreement and answer shall also be filed with the Director, with additional copies for the arbitrator(s) along with any deposit required under the Schedule of Fees. On receipt of an answer containing a counterclaim, the claimant has 10 calendar days in the case of a small-claim arbitration and 10 business days in all other arbitrations to file a reply to any counterclaim. The claimant also should send to each party a copy of the reply to a counterclaim. The reply also shall be filed with the Director with additional copies for the arbitrators. ***

**Appointment of the Arbitrators**

*** Under the NASD arbitrator selection rules, an automated process called the Neutral List Selection System (NLSS) generates lists of arbitrators for parties to either strike or rank according to their preference. NLSS generates these lists by sorting and searching for arbitrators according to public and non-public classification, geographic hearing location, rotation, conflict of interest, and upon request, subject-matter knowledge. Once the parties rank the arbitrators, staff uses NLSS to consolidate party rankings and appoint the arbitrators.

At other sponsoring organization, the Director may appoint an arbitrator or a panel of arbitrators, subject to challenges by the parties. The New York Stock Exchange (NYSE) offers parties, upon their agreement, the option of selecting how arbitrators are selected.

The Director will notify the parties of the names, current affiliations, and 10 years' business histories of the proposed arbitrators. In addition, parties will be informed of any information disclosed pursuant to the Uniform Code and the Code of Ethics for Arbitrators by any arbitrator. The arbitrators will be informed of the names of the parties to the dispute, counsel, witnesses, and the nature of the issues raised. If any arbitrator determines that he or she cannot render a fair and impartial award, the Director will appoint a substitute arbitrator.***

**Can I Challenge An Arbitrator?**

Under the Uniform Code a party has an absolute right to challenge arbitrators (strike an arbitrator from the list(s)) without giving a reason. This is called a peremptory challenge. This right may be exercised by filing a written notice of a challenge with the Director within the time period set in the rules. In addition, each party is entitled to an unlimited number of challenges for cause. ***

**What Are Challenges For Cause?**

Pursuant to the Uniform Code, an arbitrator is required to disclose any direct or indirect financial or personal interest in the outcome of the arbitration as well as any existing or past financial, business, professional, family, or social relationships that are likely to affect impartiality. Persons requested to serve as arbitrators should disclose any such relationships that they have with any party or its counsel, or with any individual whom they have been told or have reason to believe will be a witness. They should also disclose any such relationship involving members of their families or their current employers, partners, or business associates. Pursuant to the Code, arbitrators are requested to make reasonable efforts to identify these relationships. In addition, parties should advise the Director if they are aware of any similar relationships involving a party, counsel, or a potential witness.

A challenge for cause to a particular arbitrator will be granted where it is reasonable to infer an absence of impartiality, the presence of bias, or, the existence of some interest on the part of the arbitrator in the outcome of the arbitration. The interest or bias should be direct, definite, and capable of reasonable demonstration, rather than remote or speculative. ***

**How Do I Prepare For A Hearing?**

***Under the Uniform Code, the parties shall, at least 20 calendar days prior to the first scheduled hearing date, serve on each other copies of documents (including graphs, charts, and recordings) they intend to present at the hearing and identify witnesses they intend to present at the hearing. This time frame may be modified by agreement of the parties or at the discretion of the arbitrators. Failure to comply with this requirement may result in the arbitrators excluding any document not exchanged or witnesses not identified. Arbitrators will consider such action at the request of a party. If all parties agree, they may submit exhibits in addition to those in the Statement of Claim to the Director for forwarding to the arbitrators prior to the hearing. ***

The parties should cooperate in the voluntary exchange of documents and information to expedite the arbitration. Any request for documents or other information should be specific, relate to the matter in controversy, and afford the party to whom the request is made a reasonable period of time to respond without interfering with the time set for the hearing. Document production and information exchange is to be accomplished within the time set forth in the Uniform Code. ***

In October 1999, NASD made available a Discovery Guide (Guide) for use in customer cases. The Guide was the result of a consensus reached by a multi-partisan task force convened by NASD. Although the Guide is not incorporated into the Code, it does provide expanded guidance to the parties and the arbitrators, and is aimed at expediting the arbitration process. ***

At the written request of a party or an arbitrator, or at the discretion of the Director, a prehearing conference will be scheduled. The Director will set the time and place of a prehearing conference and appoint either a staff person or an arbitrator to preside. The prehearing conference may be held by telephone, by written submission, or in person. Under the rules, there are timetables for parties either to produce requested information or to object to the production requests. If a prehearing conference without an arbitrator does not resolve the outstanding issues, those information-request disputes or issues will be referred to a single arbitrator prior to the first hearing. Where possible, each party should submit to the SRO in advance of the prehearing conference a concise outline of the outstanding issues to be resolved by the single arbitrator.

The single arbitrator has the authority to issue subpoenas, direct appearances of witnesses and production of documents, set deadlines for compliance, and issue other rulings that would expedite the arbitration proceedings or enable a party to prepare its case. Parties should be aware that arbitrators may sanction a party that fails to comply with these hearing orders.

To the extent possible, testimony and documentary evidence should be exchanged voluntarily by the parties without the use of subpoenas. If a subpoena is necessary, the arbitrators and any counsel of record have such power of subpoena as may be provided by the law of the state where the hearing will be held or by the Federal Arbitration Act. All parties must be given a copy of the subpoena on its issuance. If a party has an attorney, the attorney should answer all questions concerning subpoenas. Parties without attorneys may request that the Director ask the arbitrators to issue a subpoena. If possible the request should be in writing, should set forth why the subpoena is necessary and what efforts the requesting party made to obtain the appearance of witnesses and the production of documents without the use of the subpoena, and should include a copy of the subpoena which the arbitrators are requested to issue. If the arbitrators issue a subpoena, the requesting party has the obligation of serving the subpoena on the opposing party and bearing the costs involved as provided by law of the state where the hearing will be held or by federal law. The requesting party may need to employ the services of a professional process server to serve the subpoena. ***

In addition to the subpoena process, in some instances the arbitrators have the power to direct the appearance of persons employed in the securities industry and the production of records in the possession or control of such persons. If the parties request the arbitrators to use this power, they may be required to bear all reasonable expenses in connection with such appearance or production. All such requests should be made in advance of the hearing.***

**How Are The Hearings Conducted?**

Under the Uniform Code, the Director schedules the date of the first hearing. The parties will be notified in writing of the date and location of the initial hearing at least 15 business days in advance. A verbatim record is kept of the proceedings. A party that elects to have the record transcribed shall bear the cost of such transcript unless the arbitrators direct otherwise or the parties agree to split the costs. At the hearing, the parties must present their respective cases by testimony and documentary evidence to the arbitrators. Claimants should document carefully the issues involved and their proof of damages, and explain to the arbitrators how much in money damages is being claimed and how they arrived at that figure. All hearings will be conducted by the arbitrators in the manner they determine will most expeditiously permit full presentation of the evidence of the parties. ***

**How Are The Parties Notified Of The Arbitrators' Decision?**

When the arbitrators have reached their decision and have signed an award, copies will be sent to the parties by the SRO. The award shall be in writing and signed by a majority of the arbitrators. The award may be entered by the prevailing party as a judgment in any court of competent jurisdiction.

Arbitrators shall endeavor to render an award within 30 business days from the date the record is closed.***

**What If I Don't Get Paid?**

Brokers must pay arbitration awards within 30 days of receipt, unless they file in court a motion to vacate. ***

Investors who haven't been paid within 30 days of receipt of the award should notify the SRO that issued the award. Under the Constitution, Rules, and Bylaws of the SROs, the membership or registration of a member can be suspended or canceled if the member does not comply with an arbitration award, unless the member has made a timely motion to vacate or modify the award (see below). ***

Arbitration awards are also enforceable under federal and state laws. For example, under the Federal Arbitration Act, (9 U.S.C. sec. 1 et seq.) and every state arbitration law, a party has one year from when the award was issued to move to confirm the arbitration award. By this summary process, an arbitration award is turned into a court judgment that can be enforced like any other judgment. The arbitration statutes provide very limited grounds for attacking arbitration awards, such as fraud, arbitrator misconduct, arbitrators exceeding their authority, or arbitrator bias. It is usually difficult to overturn an arbitration award. The typical time frame for mounting a challenge to an award is three months from when the award was issued. ***

The awards will be made publicly available. Arbitrators are not required to write opinions or provide reasons for the award. A party, however, may request an opinion. This request should be made no later than the hearing date. Some sponsoring organizations delete from the public version of awards information that identifies either the arbitrators or the parties. The decision of the arbitrators is final; that is, the decision is subject to review by a court only on a very limited basis.

**Important**: It should be kept in mind that the arbitrators' decision will be based solely and exclusively on the documents and related material provided by the parties to a dispute. In the case of a hearing, the decision will be based on both the documents and testimony presented at the hearing. It is therefore important that a party's case be carefully and thoroughly prepared. As noted, this may be done either with or without the assistance of counsel. Such preparation will ensure that all relevant facts and evidence will be presented by the parties and, thus, considered by the arbitrators. Arbitrators are not allowed to reconsider a decision because new evidence has been found after the award was rendered.

In addition, it is the responsibility of the parties to submit briefs for any novel theories of recovery and/or requests for special damages. In some cases, arbitrators may require even parties without lawyers to support their claims by reference to the relevant law. ***

## *NOTES AND QUESTIONS*

1. ***Arbitration vs. Litigation.*** What are the differences between arbitration and litigation? Should arbitration be made more like litigation, even if doing so decreases arbitration's efficiency? Who would be more apt to favor making arbitration more like litigation—investors or brokers?

2. ***Punitive Damages.*** Arbitrators are entitled to award punitive damages in connection with state law securities claims to the extent that the state law in question so permits. Perhaps surprisingly, brokerage firms cannot waive punitive damages by agreement with their customers. Not only would any such waiver have to be clear and unambiguous. See *Mastrobuono v. Shearson Lehman Hutton, Inc.*, 514 U.S. 52 (1995) (holding that an Illinois couple had not waived their right to seek punitive damages even though they had signed an arbitration agreement calling for application of the law of New York, which disallowed punitive damages in arbitration). In addition, SRO rules prohibit even a clear and unambiguous waiver of punitive damages in customer agreements signed after 1989. See, e.g., NASD Conduct Rule 3110(f)(4) (prohibiting an arbitration agreement from "includ[ing] any condition which *** limits the ability of the arbitrators to make any award").

Arbitrators in fact rarely award punitive damages, but even their theoretical availability has stirred considerable debate. According to former SEC Chairperson David Ruder:

> Arguments for and against punitive damages are forceful. Proponents of punitive damages argue that punitive damages should be available in arbitration if they are available in a judicial forum and that punitive damages provide important curbs on customer abuse by brokerage firms. The firms, on the other hand, argue that punitive damages are inappropriate in an arbitration

> system that does not provide a right to trial by jury, has no written opinions, and has limited rights to appeal.

David S. Ruder, Elements of a Fair and Efficient Securities Arbitration System, 40 Ariz. L. Rev. 1101, 1107 (1998). For these reasons, the NASD Task Force chaired by Ruder recommended a compromise: limiting punitive damage awards in arbitration to "the lesser of two times compensatory damages or 750,000." Ruder Report, supra, at 87,431. Should the NASD—or the Uniform Code—adopt this change?

One commentator has observed that "[p]rocedures designed to ensure that arbitral awards of punitive damages comport with due process *** necessarily impede the goals of, and the incentives to, arbitration." Karl Neudorfer, Note, Defining Due Process Down: Punitive Awards and Mandatory Arbitration of Securities Disputes, 15 Ohio St. J. on Disp. Resol. 207, 252 (1999). Why would this be the case? See also Thomas J. Stipanowich, Punitive Damages and the Consumerization of Arbitration, 92 Nw. U. L. Rev. 1 (1997); Richard E. Speidel, Punitive Damages and the Public Interest Model of Securities Arbitration: A Response to Professor Stipanowich, 92 Nw. U. L. Rev. 99 (1997).

*3.* ***Decisions without Explanations.*** Should arbitrators have to explain their decisions? What would be the advantages and disadvantages of requiring them to do so? Consider the following:

> Since the 1980s, securities disputes have been resolved in a conference room rather than a courtroom. Consequently, the number of reported court decisions has decreased dramatically and case law concerning the broker-customer relationship is frozen in time. Without judicial interpretation this body of law may not properly develop.
>
> Without disclosing the rationale behind an award, brokers do not have the benefit of knowing what constitutes a violation. Similarly, customers are unaware of their evidentiary burden.
>
> Securities arbitrators should be required to submit well-reasoned opinions to expose problems and concerns in the securities industry to policy makers. Such information is crucial to determine whether a securities or arbitration law needs to be amended, repealed, or reformed.

Marilyn Blumberg Cane and Marc J. Greenspon, Securities Arbitration: Bankrupt, Bothered & Bewildered, 7 Stan. J. of Law. Bus. & Fin. 131, 152 (2002). Do you agree with this recommendation? Might your answer be affected by the nature of the securities claims that are typically arbitrated? In this regard, take the following chart into account:

**Controversies Involved in Arbitration Cases**

| Types of Controversy* | 1998 | 1999 | 2000 | 2001 | 2002 |
|---|---|---|---|---|---|
| Margin Calls | 39 | 104 | 284 | 375 | 366 |
| Churning | 552 | 665 | 473 | 784 | 824 |
| Unauthorized Trading | 824 | 915 | 611 | 884 | 930 |
| Failure to Supervise | 956 | 1,097 | 1,270 | 1,968 | 2,633 |
| Negligence | 869 | 1,329 | 1,867 | 2,275 | 2,522 |
| Omission of Facts | 579 | 474 | 476 | 692 | 1,178 |
| Breach of Fiduciary Duty | 1,655 | 2,093 | 2,489 | 3,458 | 4,236 |
| Unsuitability | 1,104 | 1,311 | 900 | 1,524 | 2,644 |
| Misrepresentation | 1,578 | 1,482 | 1,321 | 1,895 | 2,623 |
| Online Trading** | ___ | 55 | 214 | 155 | 95 |

*Each case can be coded to contain up to four controversy types. Therefore the columns in this table cannot be totaled to determine the number of cases served in a year.

** Online Trading was first tracked in 1999.

NASD Dispute Resolution Statistics, available at www.nasdadr.com/statistics.asp (Jan. 21, 2003).

4. ***Class Actions.*** As you read in the SICA's description of arbitration procedures, the Uniform Code prohibits the arbitration of class actions. What policy reasons underlie this prohibition? From an investor's standpoint, when might a class action be especially useful? Should the Uniform Code be amended to permit arbitration of class actions? Should arbitration of class actions be required?

5. ***Qualifications and Training of Arbitrators.*** To qualify as a NASD-DR arbitrator, a person needs only five years of "full-time, paid business or professional experience." NASD-DR, Become an Arbitrator, available at www.nasdadr.com/arbbrochure.htm.asp. Moreover, NASD-DR desires to "recruit arbitrators diverse in culture, profession, and background." Id. Although a law degree is not a requirement, many arbitrators are lawyers.

Whether arbitrators receive sufficient training is a matter of some controversy:

> Virtually no training materials, written or oral, are devoted to educating arbitrators about areas of substantive law they may face in a typical customer dispute. ***
>
> *** Arbitrators are expected to achieve an equitable resolution of the dispute before them but they may not ignore the law. However, without ample training or legal briefing by the parties on each relevant issue, how can arbitrators know what the law is or how to apply it?

Barbara Black and Jill Gross, Making it up as They Go Along: The Role of Law in Securities Arbitration, 23 Cardozo L. Rev. 991, 1028-30 (2002). What would be the advantages and disadvantages of instituting a more formalized system that provided arbitrators with training in substantive securities law?

***6. Beyond Customer vs. Broker.*** Although most disputes in securities arbitration are initiated by customers against their brokers, arbitration is a two-way street. In recent years, a number of brokers have initiated arbitration against their customers for repayment of margin credit (i.e., money loaned by a brokerage firm to a customer based on the value of the customer's portfolio). See Walter Hamilton, Some Investors Face Flip Side of Arbitation, L.A. Times, at C1 (June 20, 2001).

Moreover, this two-way street intersects with an altogether different avenue: virtually all individual securities brokers agree to arbitrate their employment disputes upon signing Form U-4, the uniform application for work in the securities industry. See also NASD Code of Arbitration Procedure 10101 (mandating "the arbitration of any dispute, claim, or controversy arising out of or in connection with the business of any member of the Association, or arising out of the employment of associated person(s) with any member"). What additional concerns does mandatory arbitration raise in the employment context? For two opposing views on the subject, see Beth E. Sullivan, Note, The High Cost of Efficiency: Mandatory Arbitration in the Securities Industry, 26 Fordham Urb. L.J. 311 (1999) and Stuart J. Kaswell (General Counsel, Securities Industry Association), Written Statement Before the Senate Committee on Banking, Housing, and Urban Affairs, available at www.sia.com/testimony/html/stuart_testimony.html (July 31, 1998).

Consider in particular the problems that may arise when the claim to be arbitrated involves employment discrimination. These problems prompted congressional hearings as well as a decision by the NASD and NYSE to amend Form U-4 to exempt statutory employment discrimination claims from the mandatory arbitration requirements. See, e.g., Order Granting Approval to NASD Rule Change Relating to the Arbitration of Employment Discrimination Claims, Exchange Act Release No. 40109, 67 SEC Docket 824 (June 22, 1998). Note, however, that the change in Form U-4 does not affect the enforceability of a mandatory arbitration clause in the broker's employment contract with the brokerage firm. See Russell D. Feingold, Mandatory Arbitration: What Process is Due?, 39 Harv. J. on Legis. 281, 292 (2002) (advocating legislation that would preserve access to courts in employment discrimination cases and arguing that the "practice of mandatory, binding arbitration does not comport with the purpose and spirit of our nation's civil rights and sexual harassment laws"). Would you favor legislation that would allow brokers to litigate their claims of employment discrimination?

***7. Arbitration vs. Mediation.*** Various SROs, including the NASD and the NYSE, sponsor mediation services. Institution of these services came about because of the perception that arbitration had become less efficient (on account of its growing similarity to litigation).

Mediation differs from arbitration in several respects—it is voluntary and non-binding and does not involve a proceeding resembling a trial. If mediation does not resolve the dispute, the parties can submit to arbitration (or to a court in the unlikely event that arbitration of the dispute is not mandatory). Mediation can also be initiated at any stage during the arbitration process and both processes can occur concurrently.

The NASD mediation process begins with a session in which the mediator and the parties all have the opportunity to make opening statements. The mediator then holds individual meetings with each party that focus on settlement expectations and possible settlement offers. If a mutually acceptable resolution is reached, the parties sign a written settlement agreement. Even if mediation does not produce a settlement, the improved lines of communication often result in more efficient arbitration. For a complete description of the process, see NASD Mediation: an Alternate Path to Resolving Securities Disputes," available at www.nasdadr.com/med_alt path.asp

Compare the following data on arbitration and mediation:

**Summary Arbitration Statistics December 2002**

**Number of Cases Closed through December:**

| 2002 | 2001 | 2000 |
|---|---|---|
| 5,957 | 5,582 | 5,473 |

**Turnaround Time (in months) through December:**

| | 2002 | 2001 | 2000 |
|---|---|---|---|
| **Overall** | 13.7 | 13.0 | 12.8 |
| **Hearing Decisions** | 16.5 | 16.5 | 16.7 |
| **Simplified Decisions** | 7.5 | 9.2 | 10.0 |

**Summary Mediation Statistics December 2002**

**Mediation Cases in Agreement through December:**

| 2002 | 2001 | 2000 |
|---|---|---|
| 936 | 880 | 1,186 |

**Mediation Cases Closed through December:**

| | 2002 | 2001 | 2000 |
|---|---|---|---|
| **Cases Closed** | 1,360 | 1,262 | 1,262 |
| **Percent Settled** | 82% | 77% | 77% |

**Turnaround Time (in Days) through December:**

| 2002 | 2001 | 2000 |
|---|---|---|
| 129 | 122 | 99 |

NASD Dispute Resolution Statistics, available at www.nasdadr.com/statistics.asp (Jan. 21, 2003).

## C. THE REMAINING JUDICIAL ROLE IN ARBITRATION

Even though mandatory pre-dispute arbitration clauses are enforceable, courts are by no means out of the picture altogether (class actions aside). First, there is the matter of arbitrability. Second, there is the matter of judicial review.

### *1. Arbitrability*

An investor must arbitrate only where (i) she signed an agreement containing a mandatory pre-dispute arbitration clause and (ii) that clause encompasses the dispute at issue. But who decides whether these requirements (called matters of arbitrability) have been satisfied—the arbitrators or the courts? Does federal or state law control the outcome? Consider the following decision.

**FIRST OPTIONS OF CHICAGO, INC. v. KAPLAN**
514 U.S. 938 (1995)

JUSTICE BREYER:

In this case we consider two questions about how courts should review certain matters under the federal Arbitration Act: (1) how a district court should review an arbitrator's decision that the parties agreed to arbitrate a dispute, and (2) how a court of appeals should review a district court's decision confirming, or refusing to vacate, an arbitration award.

The case concerns several related disputes between, on one side, First Options of Chicago, Inc., a firm that clears stock trades on the Philadelphia Stock Exchange, and, on the other side, three parties: Manuel Kaplan; his wife, Carol Kaplan; and his wholly owned investment company, MK Investments, Inc. (MKI), whose trading account First Options cleared. The disputes center on a "workout" agreement, embodied in four separate documents, which governs the "working out" of debts to First Options that MKI and the Kaplans incurred as a result of the October 1987 stock market crash. In 1989, after entering into the agreement, MKI lost an additional $1.5 million. First Options then took control of, and liquidated, certain MKI assets; demanded immediate payment of the entire MKI debt; and insisted that the Kaplans personally pay any deficiency. When its demands went unsatisfied, First Options sought arbitration by a panel of the Philadelphia Stock Exchange.

MKI, having signed the only workout document (out of four) that contained an arbitration clause, accepted arbitration. The Kaplans, however, who had not personally signed that document, denied that their disagreement with First Options was arbitrable and filed written objections to that effect with the arbitration panel. The arbitrators decided that they had the power to rule on the merits of the parties' dispute, and did so in favor of First Options. The Kaplans then asked the Federal District Court to vacate the arbitration award, and First Options requested its confirmation. The court confirmed the award. Nonetheless, on appeal the Court of Appeals for the Third Circuit agreed with the Kaplans that their dispute was not arbitrable; and it reversed the District Court's confirmation of the award against them. ***

II

The first question—the standard of review applied to an arbitrator's decision about arbitrability—is a narrow one. To understand just how narrow, consider three types of disagreement present in this case. First, the Kaplans and First Options disagree about whether the Kaplans are personally liable for MKI's debt to First Options. That disagreement makes up the *merits* of the dispute. Second, they disagree about whether they agreed to arbitrate the merits. That disagreement is about the *arbitrability* of the dispute. Third, they disagree about *who should have the primary power to decide the second matter.* Does that power belong primarily to the arbitrators (because the court reviews their arbitrability decision deferentially) or to the court (because the court makes up its mind about arbitrability independently)? We consider here only this third question.

Although the question is a narrow one, it has a certain practical importance. That is because a party who has not agreed to arbitrate will normally have a right to a court's decision about the merits of its dispute (say, as here, its obligation under a contract). But, where the party has agreed to arbitrate, he or she, in effect, has relinquished much of that right's practical value. The party still can ask a court to review the arbitrator's decision, but the court will set that decision aside only in very unusual circumstances. See, e.g., 9 U.S.C. § 10 (award procured by corruption, fraud, or undue means; arbitrator exceeded his powers); *Wilko v. Swan,* 346 U.S. 427, 436-437 (1953) (parties bound by arbitrator's decision not in "manifest disregard" of the law), overruled on other grounds, *Rodriguez de Quijas v. Shearson/American Express, Inc.,* 490 U.S. 477 (1989). Hence, who—court or arbitrator—has the primary authority to decide whether a party has agreed to arbitrate can make a critical difference to a party resisting arbitration.

We believe the answer to the "who" question (*i.e.,* the standard-of-review question) is fairly simple. Just as the arbitrability of the merits of a dispute depends upon whether the parties agreed to arbitrate that dispute, see, e.g., *Mastrobuono v. Shearson Lehman Hutton, Inc.,* [514 U.S. 52], 57 (1995); *Mitsubishi Motors Corp. v. Soler Chrysler-Plymouth, Inc.,* 473 U.S. 614, 626 (1985), so the question "who has the primary power to decide arbitrability" turns upon what the parties agreed about *that* matter. Did the parties agree to submit the arbitrability question itself to arbitration? If so, then the court's standard for reviewing the arbitrator's decision about *that* matter should not differ from the standard courts apply when they review any other matter that parties have agreed to arbitrate. See *AT& T Technologies, Inc. v. Communications Workers,* 475 U.S. 643, 649 (1986) (parties may agree to arbitrate arbitrability). That is to say, the court should give considerable leeway to the arbitrator, setting aside his or her decision only in certain narrow circumstances. See, e.g., 9 U.S.C. § 10. If, on the other hand, the parties did *not* agree to submit the arbitrability question itself to arbitration, then the court should decide that question just as it would decide any other question that the parties did not submit to arbitration, namely, independently. These two answers flow inexorably from the fact that arbitration is simply a matter of contract between the parties; it is a way to resolve those disputes—but only those disputes—that the parties have agreed to submit to arbitration.

We agree with First Options, therefore, that a court must defer to an arbitrator's arbitrability decision when the parties submitted that matter to arbitration. Nevertheless, that conclusion does not help First Options win this case. That is because a fair and complete answer to the standard-of-review question requires a word about how a court should decide whether the parties have agreed to submit the arbitrability issue to arbitration. And, that word makes clear that the Kaplans did not agree to arbitrate arbitrability here.

When deciding whether the parties agreed to arbitrate a certain matter (including arbitrability), courts generally (though with a qualification we discuss below) should apply ordinary state-law principles that govern the formation of contracts. See, e.g., *Mastrobuono,* at 62-63, and n. 9; *Volt Information Sciences, Inc. v. Board of Trustees of Leland Stanford Junior Univ.*, 489 U.S. 468, 475-476 (1989); G. Wilner, 1 Domke on Commercial Arbitration § 4:04, p. 15 (rev. ed. Supp.1993) (hereinafter Domke). The relevant state law here, for example, would require the court to see whether the parties objectively revealed an intent to submit the arbitrability issue to arbitration. See, e.g., *Estate of Jesmer v. Rohlev,* 241 Ill.App.3d 798, 803, (1993) (law of the State whose law governs the workout agreement); *Burkett v. Allstate Ins. Co.*, 368 Pa. 600, 608 (1987) (law of the State where the Kaplans objected to arbitrability).

This Court, however, has (as we just said) added an important qualification, applicable when courts decide whether a party has agreed that arbitrators should decide arbitrability: Courts should not assume that the parties agreed to arbitrate arbitrability unless there is "clea[r] and unmistakabl[e]" evidence that they did so. *AT & T Technologies,* supra, at 649. In this manner the law treats silence or ambiguity about the question "*who* (primarily) should decide arbitrability" differently from the way it treats silence or ambiguity about the question "*whether* a particular merits-related dispute is arbitrable because it is within the scope of a valid arbitration agreement"—for in respect to this latter question the law reverses the presumption. See *Mitsubishi Motors,* supra, at 626 ("'[A]ny doubts concerning the scope of arbitrable issues should be resolved in favor of arbitration'") (quoting *Moses H. Cone Memorial Hospital v. Mercury Constr. Corp.,* 460 U.S. 1, 24-25 (1983)).

But, this difference in treatment is understandable. The latter question arises when the parties have a contract that provides for arbitration of some issues. In such circumstances, the parties likely gave at least some thought to the scope of arbitration. And, given the law's permissive policies in respect to arbitration, see, e.g., *Mitsubishi Motors,* supra, at 626, one can understand why the law would insist upon clarity before concluding that the parties did *not* want to arbitrate a related matter. On the other hand, the former question—the "who (primarily) should decide arbitrability" question—is rather arcane. A party often might not focus upon that question or upon the significance of having arbitrators decide the scope of their own powers. Cf. Cox, Reflections Upon Labor Arbitration, 72 Harv. L. Rev. 1482, 1508-1509 (1959). And, given the principle that a party can be forced to arbitrate only those issues it specifically has agreed to submit to arbitration, one can understand why courts might hesitate to interpret silence or ambiguity on the "who should decide arbitrability" point as giving the arbitrators that power, for doing so might too often force unwilling parties to arbitrate a matter they reasonably would have thought a judge, not an arbitrator, would decide. Ibid.

On the record before us, First Options cannot show that the Kaplans clearly agreed to have the arbitrators decide (*i.e.,* to arbitrate) the question of arbitrability. First Options relies on the Kaplans' filing with the arbitrators a written memorandum objecting to the arbitrators' jurisdiction. But merely arguing the arbitrability issue to an arbitrator does not indicate a clear willingness to arbitrate that issue, *i.e.,* a willingness to be effectively bound by the arbitrator's decision on that point. To the contrary, insofar as the Kaplans were forcefully objecting to the arbitrators deciding their dispute with First Options, one naturally would think that they did *not* want the arbitrators to have binding authority over them. This conclusion draws added support from (1) an obvious explanation for the Kaplans' presence before the arbitrators (*i.e.,* that MKI, Mr. Kaplan's wholly owned firm, was arbitrating workout agreement matters); and (2) Third Circuit law that suggested that the Kaplans might argue arbitrability to the arbitrators without losing their right to independent court review, *Teamsters v. Western Pennsylvania Motor Carriers Assn.,* 574 F. 2d 783, 786-788 (1978).

First Options makes several counterarguments: (1) that the Kaplans had other ways to get an independent court decision on the question of arbitrability without arguing the issue to the arbitrators (*e.g.,* by trying to enjoin the arbitration, or by refusing to participate in the arbitration and then defending against a court petition First Options would have brought to compel arbitration); (2) that permitting parties to argue arbitrability to an arbitrator without being bound by the result would cause delay and waste in the resolution of disputes; and (3) that the Arbitration Act therefore requires a presumption that the Kaplans agreed to be bound by the arbitrators' decision, not the contrary. The first of these points, however, while true, simply does not say anything about whether the Kaplans intended to be bound by the arbitrators' decision. The second point, too, is inconclusive, for factual circumstances vary too greatly to permit a confident conclusion about whether allowing the arbitrator to make an initial (but independently reviewable) arbitrability determination would, in general, slow down the dispute resolution process. And, the third point is legally erroneous, for there is no strong arbitration-related policy favoring First Options in respect to its particular argument here. After all, the basic objective in this area is not to resolve disputes in the quickest manner possible, no matter what the parties' wishes, but to ensure that commercial arbitration agreements, like other contracts, "'are enforced according to their terms,'" *Mastrobuono,* at 54 (quoting *Volt Information Sciences,* 489 U.S., at 479), and according to the intentions of the parties, *Mitsubishi Motors,* 473 U.S., at 626. That policy favors the Kaplans, not First Options.

We conclude that, because the Kaplans did not clearly agree to submit the question of arbitrability to arbitration, the Court of Appeals was correct in finding that the arbitrability of the Kaplan/First Options dispute was subject to independent review by the courts.

III

We turn next to the standard a court of appeals should apply when reviewing a district court decision that refuses to vacate or confirms an arbitration award. Although the Third Circuit sometimes used the words "*de novo* " to describe this standard, its opinion makes clear that it simply believes (as do all Circuits but one) that there is no *special* standard governing its review of a district court's decision in these circumstances. Rather, review of, for example, a district court decision confirming an arbitration award on the ground that the parties agreed to submit their dispute to arbitration should proceed like review of any other district court decision finding an agreement between parties, e.g., accepting findings of fact that are not "clearly erroneous" but deciding questions of law *de novo.*

One Court of Appeals, the Eleventh Circuit, has said something different. Because of federal policy favoring arbitration, that court says that it applies a specially lenient "abuse of discretion" standard (even as to questions of law) when reviewing district court decisions that confirm (but not those that set aside) arbitration awards. See, e.g., *Robbins v. Day,* 954 F.2d, at 681-682. First Options asks us to hold that the Eleventh Circuit's view is correct.

We believe, however, that the majority of Circuits is right in saying that courts of appeals should apply ordinary, not special, standards when reviewing district court decisions upholding arbitration awards. For one thing, it is undesirable to make the law more complicated by proliferating review standards without good reasons. More importantly, the reviewing attitude that a court of appeals takes toward a district court decision should depend upon "the respective institutional advantages of trial and appellate courts," not upon what standard of review will more likely produce a particular substantive result. *Salve Regina College v. Russell,* 499 U.S. 225, 231-233 (1991). The law, for example, tells all courts (trial and appellate) to give administrative agencies a degree of legal leeway when they review certain interpretations of the law that those agencies have made. See, e.g., *Chevron U.S.A. Inc. v. Natural Resources Defense Council, Inc.,* 467 U.S. 837, 843-844 (1984). But no one, to our knowledge, has suggested that this policy of giving leeway to agencies means that a court of appeals should give *extra* leeway to a district court decision that upholds an agency. Similarly, courts grant arbitrators considerable leeway when reviewing most arbitration decisions; but that fact does not mean that appellate courts should give *extra* leeway to district courts that uphold arbitrators. ***

We conclude that the Court of Appeals used the proper standards for reviewing the District Court's arbitrability determinations. ***

## *NOTES AND QUESTIONS*

***1. Deciding Whether Arbitrability is at Issue.*** *Kaplan* established the presumption that courts decide matters of arbitrability. But what is an arbitrability matter in the first place? Consider the following analysis:

> [I]f the parties have (1) entered into a valid arbitration agreement *** and (2) the arbitration agreement covers the subject matter of the underlying dispute between them ***, then we will presume that the parties have made a commitment to have an arbitrator decide all the remaining issues necessary to

> reach a decision on the merits of the dispute. Put differently, the signing of a valid agreement to arbitrate the merits of the subject matter in dispute presumptively pushes the parties across the "arbitrability" threshold; we will then presume that other issues relating to the substance of the dispute or the procedures of arbitration are for the arbitrator. But, if the parties clearly and unmistakably provide that an issue is one of "arbitrability"—*i.e.*, that the issue is a threshhold matter that must be determined before any adjudicative power will be granted to the arbitrator—then the court must respect that clear expression of intent and decide that threshold issue, rather than compelling arbitration.***

*Painewebber, Inc. v. Elahi*, 87 F.3d 589, 599 (1st Cir. 1996). Is this analysis implicit in *Kaplan* or does it break new ground?

2. ***How Clear is the "Clear and Unmistakable" Standard?*** As *Kaplan* noted, *AT&T Techs., Inc. v. Communication Workers*, 475 U.S. 643, 649 (1986), held that the parties' intent to arbitrate arbitrability must be "clear and unmistakable." Could *Kaplan* have been more specific regarding its own application of this standard? What problems are lower courts likely to have in applying this standard? What facts are relevant for purposes of deciding a party's "clear and unmistakable" intent to arbitrate a matter of arbitrability?

3. ***Eligibility as An Issue of Arbitrability.*** Recall that under the Uniform Code, a dispute is eligible for arbitration so long as the underlying event occurred no more than six years earlier. Who decides whether this requirement has been satisfied—the court or the arbitrators? The Supreme Court has answered this question as follows:

> *** [W]e find that the applicability of the NASD time limit rule is a matter presumptively for the arbitrator, not for the judge. The time limit rule closely resembles the gateway questions that this Court has found not to be "questions of arbitrability." E.g., *Moses H. Cone Memorial Hospital* [*v. Mercury Constr. Corp.*, 460 U.S. 1, 24-25 (1983)] (referring to "waiver, delay, or a like defense"). Such a dispute seems an "aspec[t] of the [controversy] which called the grievance procedures into play." [*John Wiley & Sons, Inc. v. Livingston*, 376 U.S. 543, 559 (1964) (holding that an arbitrator should decide whether the first two steps of a grievance procedure were completed, where these steps are prerequisites to arbitration)].
>
> Moreover, the NASD arbitrators, comparatively more expert about the meaning of their own rule, are comparatively better able to interpret and to apply it. In the absence of any statement to the contrary in the arbitration agreement, it is reasonable to infer that the parties intended the agreement to reflect that understanding. Cf. [*First Options of Chicago, Inc. v. Kaplan*, 514 U.S. 938, 944-945 (1995)]. And for the law to assume an expectation that aligns (1) decisionmaker with (2) comparative expertise will help better to secure a fair and expeditious resolution of the underlying controversy—a goal of arbitration systems and judicial systems alike.
>
> We consequently conclude that the NASD's time limit rule falls within the class of gateway procedural disputes that do not present what our cases have called "questions of arbitrability." And the strong pro-court presumption as to the parties' likely intent does not apply.

*Howsam v. Dean Witter Reynolds, Inc.*, 123 S.Ct. 588, 592-93 (2002). See generally Barbara Black, Securities Arbitration Is Not Supposed To Be So

Complicated: Arbitrability, the Eligibility Rule, and Whose Law Decides, 30 Sec. Reg. L. J. 134 (2002).

4. ***State and Federal Law Together.*** *Kaplan* accorded a role to both federal and state law in resolving questions of arbitrability. What is the role of each? Is there any actual or perceived unfairness in treating investors with identical arbitration agreements differently depending on their states of residence?

5. ***Brokers and the Courts.*** Brokerage firms (rather than investors) are responsible for most attempts to involve the courts in arbitration. See Norman S. Poser, Making Securities Arbitration Work, 50 SMU L. Rev. 277, 289 (1996). Why would this be so?

### *PROBLEM 13-1*

Mary bought securities from Frank, an independent securities broker, who had authority to sell certain securities on behalf of Duncan, Inc., a member of the NASD. Mary has concluded that Frank defrauded her in connection with her purchase in violation of Rule 10b-5 and she would like to hold Duncan responsible in arbitration. Mary did not enter into an arbitration agreement with Frank and she signed no agreement of any sort with Duncan.

NASD rules require members to arbitrate "[a]ny dispute, claim, or controversy *** between a customer and a member and/or associated person arising in connection with the business of such member or in connection with the activities of such associated persons *** upon demand of the customer." NASD rules define an "associated person" as "a sole proprietor, partner, officer, director or branch manager of a member, or other natural person occupying a similar status or performing similar functions, or a natural person engaged in the investment banking or securities business who is directly or indirectly controlling or controlled by a member."

Can Mary require Duncan to arbitrate her claim? Who decides that question?

Cf. *John Hancock Life Ins. Co. v. Wilson,* 254 F.3d 48 (2d Cir. 2001).

### 2. *Judicial Review*

The Arbitration Act gives courts authority to vacate arbitration decisions only in four narrow situations: "(1) where the award was procured by corruption, fraud, or undue means; (2) where there was evident partiality or corruption in the arbitrators ***; (3) where the arbitrators were guilty of misconduct ***; or (4) where the arbitrators exceeded their powers." 9 U.S.C. § 10(a)(1-4). Most courts have held that an additional (albeit limited) ground for vacating arbitration decisions is "manifest disregard of the law." See *Montes v. Shearson Lehman Bros., Inc.,* 128 F.3d 1456, 1460 (11th Cir. 1997) (collecting cases). The manifest disregard standard originated in the Supreme Court's decision in *Wilko v. Swan,* 346 U.S. 427 (1953), rev'd on other grounds, *Rodriquez de Quijas v. Shearson/Am. Express, Inc.,* 490 U.S. 477 (1989), the relevant portion of which appears in the *Wilko* excerpt at the beginning of Section A of this Chapter.

To vacate an arbitration decision based on manifest disregard, a court must conclude "both that (1) the arbitrators knew of a governing legal principle yet refused to apply it or ignored it altogether, and (2) the law ignored by the arbitrators was well defined, explicit, and clearly applicable to the case." *Greenberg v. Bear Stearns & Co.*, 220 F.3d 22, 28 (2d Cir. 2000) (quoting *DiRussa v. Dean Witter Reynolds, Inc.*, 121 F.3d 818, 821 (2d Cir. 1997)).

### *NOTES AND QUESTIONS*

*1.* ***Egregious but Unintentional.*** Why shouldn't the manifest disregard standard encompass an egregious legal error that the arbitrators committed unintentionally? Consider the following view:

> If "manifest disregard" means only a legal error, *** then arbitration cannot be final. Every arbitration could be followed by a suit, seeking review of legal errors, serving the same function as an appeal within a unitary judicial system. That would prevent the parties from achieving the principal objectives of arbitration: swift, inexpensive, and conclusive resolution of disputes. If "manifest disregard" means not just any legal error but rather a "clear" error (one about which there is *** "no reasonable debate"), again arbitration could not be final, and the post-arbitration litigation would be even more complex than a search for simple error—for how blatant a legal mistake must be to count as "clear" or "manifest" error lacks any straightforward answer.

*George Watts & Son, Inc. v. Tiffany & Co.*, 248 F.3d 577, 579 (7th Cir. 2001). Do you agree? Does the phraseology "manifest disregard" presuppose a focus on the arbitrators' intent?

*2.* ***Decisions without Explanations Revisited.*** Recall that arbitrators do not have to give reasons for their decisions. What is the impact on judicial review?

*3.* ***Sufficient or Insufficient.*** In *McMahon,* you may remember, the Supreme Court asserted that "[judicial] review is sufficient to ensure that arbitrators comply with the requirements of the statute." Do you agree?

*4.* **Wilko's *Flicker.*** Consider the fact that the manifest disregard standard emanates from dictum in *Wilko*, a Supreme Court decision that has otherwise been reversed. Is *Wilko*'s continuing influence in this respect inappropriate or merely ironic? What significance (if any) should be attached to *Kaplan*'s reference to the manifest disregard standard?

### *PROBLEM 13-2*

Decide whether either of the following arbitrators' decisions warrants reversal based on manifest disregard of the law:

*a.* Following a closing argument by the customer's attorney that misrepresented the law, the arbitrators awarded the customer substantial damages. The arbitrators' decision did not indicate why damages had been awarded. The legal and factual basis for the award was tenuous at best.

*b.* In her closing argument to the arbitrators, the customer's attorney stated as follows: "You have to choose between following the legal technicalities and doing what is fair. In this case, fairness and the law point in very different directions." The arbitrators quoted this statement in their decision (which awarded the customer substantial damages) but did not indicate whether they found the statement persuasive. The decision did not otherwise refer to the closing arguments or offer an explanation for the award. The legal and factual basis for the award was tenuous at best.

Cf. *Montes v. Shearson Lehman Bros., Inc.*, 128 F.3d 1456 (11th Cir. 1997).

## D. SECURITIES ARBITRATION IN PERSPECTIVE

In the wake of the Supreme Court's decision in *McMahon*, many worried that securities arbitration would favor brokers. Indeed, not only do brokers comprise the membership of the NASD and the NYSE, the leading forums for securities arbitration. In addition, a broker must be a member of a registered national securities association in order to trade in the over-the-counter market, and the NASD is the only association so registered with the SEC. See Chapter 9.E supra. Moreover, in order to execute a trade on a stock exchange, a broker must be a member, or be affiliated with a member, of that exchange. See id.

Was the anxiety over pro-broker bias misplaced? In 1992, in response to a request from Congress, the U.S. General Accounting Office (GAO) conducted a study relating to the SRO arbitration process. The study, involving the time period from January 1989 through June 1990, found no indication of pro-industry bias in arbitration decisions at SRO-sponsored forums. Specifically, the GAO report stated:

> Statistical analysis of decisions in cases initiated by investors at all arbitration forums—industry and nonindustry—showed that the forum in which the decision was made was not a factor affecting investors' chances of receiving awards. The results of securities arbitration at all industry-sponsored forums were similar to each other and to the results of securities arbitration at AAA ***. Decision outcomes varied depending on several factors, such as attorney representation and claim size. The analysis also showed that when broker-dealers initiated the claims, arbitrators' decisions usually favored the broker-dealers and that these cases usually involved well-documented investors' debt to the broker-dealer.
>
> In addition to cases decided by arbitrators, the disputing parties settled about one-third to one-half of the cases we reviewed without requiring arbitrator's decisions. Our analysis of these cases showed that several factors, such as attorney representation and claim size, influenced whether the parties were able to settle their cases.
>
> ***At the four SRO-sponsored forums—Amex, CBOE, NASD, and NYSE—arbitrators decided in favor of investors in a combined average of about 59 percent of the cases in which investors filed claims against broker-dealers. Also, investors receiving awards got an overall average of about 61 percent of the amount they claimed. *** Our multivariate analysis showed that the forum in which a case was arbitrated was not a factor that affected whether investors received an award or the proportion of any award the investor received.
>
> ***[A]rbitrators decided in favor of the investor in a combined average of *** 60 percent of the cases at the AAA. ***[W]hen investors received an award, they were awarded ***about 57 percent of their claim at AAA.

U.S. General Accounting Office, Securities Arbitration: How Investors Fare 35, 38-39 (May 1992).

The GAO conducted a follow-up study in 2000, yielding these additional conclusions:

> In 1992, we reported that 59 percent of investors received favorable decisions in cases arbitrated from January 1989 through June 1990. This percentage declined to an average of about 51 percent for cases decided from 1992 through 1996 and increased to 56 percent in 1997 and 57 percent in 1998. Similarly, we reported in 1992 that investors who had favorable decisions received an average of 61 percent of the dollar amount they claimed. This percentage declined to an average of about 51 percent during 1992 through 1998, ranging from a low of 46 percent in 1994 to a high of 57 percent in 1997.
>
> Regulatory officials attribute the decline in arbitration results favoring investors to a corresponding increase in the percentage of cases settled. These officials said the higher percentage of cases that are settled tends to reduce the percentage of arbitration award decisions in which investors might receive favorable awards because broker-dealers are more likely to try to settle cases that they think they might lose. We estimate that between 1992 and 1998, the percentage of cases settled ranged from 43 percent in 1992 to 50 percent or greater for the years 1993 through 1998, reaching a high of 60 percent in 1997. In 1992, we reported that settlements occurred in 44 percent of SRO cases and 33 percent of AAA cases. ***
>
> In 1992, we [also] compared SRO-sponsored arbitration results to those at AAA, as an indication of the fairness of the arbitration process. We found no significant differences in case outcomes. We could not make the same comparison for this report because AAA's securities caseload declined significantly from what we reported in 1992 and, therefore, AAA's results no longer provided as meaningful a comparison to SRO-sponsored forums.

U.S. General Accounting Office, Securities Arbitration: Actions Needed to Address Problem of Unpaid Awards 23-24, 29-30 (June 2000). As the title of the report reflects, the GAO expressed principal concern in the area of award payment and recommended to the SEC a number of regulatory steps necessary to address the problem of unpaid rewards.

Notwithstanding the GAO's conclusion as to the lack of pro-broker bias, should the SEC and the SROs encourage (or perhaps even require) brokerage firms to permit the use of arbitration forums outside the securities industry, such as the AAA? If such an alternative forum were available, would investors be more likely to perceive the system as fair? See Joel Seligman, The Quiet Revolution: Securities Arbitration Confronts the Hard Questions, 33 Hous. L. Rev. 327, 344-346 (1996). Would you expect many investors to choose a forum outside the securities industry? Note that industry-sponsored forums generally have substantially lower fees because they are partially subsidized by the SROs.

As you contemplate the impact on investors of the current system of arbitration, consider also the following observations by two law professors who co-direct a securities arbitration clinic:

> [A]rbitration panels, on more than an occasional basis, are reaching decisions favorable to investors even where the "law is clear" that there is no basis for imposing liability on the broker. These results may be explained by the arbitrators being swayed by the equities: innocent, unsophisticated investors generate sympathy from arbitrators, in the form of an award, for tragic, seemingly avoidable losses, despite the well-established law that suggests no liability by the brokers. ***

Barbara Black & Jill I. Gross, Making It Up As They Go Along: The Role of Law in Securities Arbitration, 23 Cardozo L. Rev. 991, 1040 (2002). See also Lewis

D. Lowenfels & Alan R. Bromberg, Beyond Precedent: Arbitral Extensions of Securities Law, 57 Bus. Law. 999 (2002). Are there specific attributes of securities arbitration that contribute to this "making it up" phenomenon? Is this phenomenon to be deplored or celebrated? Do you think investors are widely aware of it?

Finally, note that those who predicted that *McMahon* would produce calamity could not have foreseen the Private Securities Litigation Reform Act of 1995. How is that Act relevant to assessing whether securities arbitration is good for investors? On this question, see Marc I. Steinberg, Securities Arbitration: Better for Investors Than the Courts?, 62 Brook. L. Rev. 1503, 1506-08 (1996).

Should securities arbitration be expanded beyond the brokerage context to encompass other private securities claims as well? For an argument that the SEC should move in this direction, along with particular proposals for so doing, see Steven A. Ramirez, Arbitration and Reform in Private Securities Litigation: Dealing with the Meritorious as Well as the Frivolous, 40 Wm. & Mary L. Rev. 1055 (1999).

# Index

References are to Pages

**Accountants**
Auditor independence, 826-32
Public Company Accounting Oversight Board, 820-32
SEC's authority to regulate, 768-73

**Aiding and abetting liability**
criminal actions, 844-45
private Rule 10b-5 actions, 207-220
SEC actions, 219, 691-92, 790-91
state law, 220

**Analysts**, 15, 487-88, 613-16, 755-60

**Arbitration**
*Chapter 13*
arbitrability, 965-71
eligibility, 970-71
employment disputes in securities industry, 963
judicial review, 971-73
judicial role, 965-73
mediation, 963-64
process and procedure, 952-64
punitive damages, 960-61

**Attorneys**
class actions, plaintiffs' attorneys, 398-402, 434-35
multiple representations, 631-32, 817
primary liability of, 225
professional obligations of securities attorneys, 773-819
SEC's authority to regulate, 768-773, 805-19

**Bars to serving as officers or directors**, 521, 676-78

**Blue sky laws**, 2, 14, 15
*See also* Preemption, Securities Litigation Uniform Standards Act, State Law

**Bespeaks caution doctrine**, 75-79, 315

**Burden of proof**
criminal actions, 14, 706, 834
private actions, 14, 23, 269
SEC actions, 14, 702-707

**Causation**
Rule 10b-5, 147-193
Rule 14a-9, 338-362
*See also* Loss causation, Negative causation, Reliance

**Cease-and-desist orders**, 689-91, 744

**Choice of forum clauses**, 914-24

**Choice of law clauses**, 914-24

**Class actions**
*Chapter 6*
counsel, selection of, 399-400, 401-02
damages, 202-04, 433-34
discovery stays, 402-03
empirical data, 427-36
lead plaintiff, selection of, 398-99, 400-01
PSLRA and, 395-404
Rule 11 violations, 404-16
settlements, disclosure of proposed, 403-04
SLUSA and, 419-27
Sarbanes-Oxley Act and, 439-42

**Collateral bar orders**, 692-93

**Collateral estoppel**, 651, 654, 716-23

**Comity**, 933-34

**Conduct as basis for jurisdiction**
*See* International securities fraud

**Concurrent jurisdiction**, 317

**Conflicts of Interest**
analysts, 613-16, 755-60

**Conspiracy**
criminal actions, 844-46
Rule 10b-5, 219-220

**Contribution**
Rule 10b-5, 204
Section 11, 291
Section 12(a)(2), 310

**Controlling person liability**
culpable participation, 233-34
defense, statutory, 234
definitions, controlling person, 233
insider trading and, 517-18
Rule 10b-5 and, 226-35
SEC, right to utilize, 226
Section 11 and, 316
Section 12(a)(2) and, 316

**Criminal enforcement**
*Chapter 11*

burden of proof, 14, 706, 834
Department of Justice, 13-14
federal securities laws, 834-49
aiding and abetting, 844-45
conspiracy, 844-46
knowingly, 840, 847
lenity, 843
no knowledge clause, 841
Sarbanes-Oxley Act, crimes created by 846-49
statute of limitations, 845
violations of, 842-45
willfully, 835-45
Mail and wire fraud, 849-60
intent, 850
jurisdictional means, 850
materiality, 855-60
scheme to defraud, 849-60
statute of limitations, 860
Racketeer Influenced & Corrupt Organizations Act (RICO), 861-887
conspiracy, 885-86
enterprise, 873-74
operation and management test, 874-86
pattern, 864-72
private RICO actions, 887
racketeering activity, 862-64
state of mind, 863-64, 885
statute of limitations, 886

**Damages**
class actions, 202-04, 433-34
market overreactions, statutory correction for, 201
out of pocket measure, 194, 201
punitive damages, 194, 960-61
rescission, 194, 314
Rule 10b-5, 193-206
Rule 14a-9, 344
Section 11, 287-91
Section 12(a)(2), 314-15
Section 14(e), 389-90

**Department of Justice**, 13-14
*See also* Criminal enforcement

**Discovery stays**, 10, 23, 114, 128, 317, 402-03

**Duty to disclose**
common law and, 60-61
correct, duty to, 58-60
line-item and real time disclosure requirements, 52-56
materiality, relation to, 61-62
omitted forecasts and, 79
Regulation FD, 56-57
Rule 10b-5 and, 52-64
update, duty to, 57-58

**Duty to correct**, 58-60

**Duty to update**, 57-58

**Effects as basis for jurisdiction**
*See* International securities fraud

**Efficient capital markets hypothesis**
generally, 16-17
fraud-on-the-market, 164-71
materiality and, 65-66, 333-34
nonpublic information and, 467

**Exclusive federal jurisdiction**, 317, 378

**Extraterritoriality**
*See* International securities fraud

**Forum non conveniens**, 924-34

**Forward-looking statements**
bespeaks caution doctrine, 75-79
Rule 10b-5 and, 74-86
statutory safe harbor for, 79-86, 315-16, 327, 388

**Fraud-created-the-market**, *See* Reliance

**Friendly, Judge**, 899

**Implied private action, recognition of**
Rule 10b-5
generally, 19-20
insider trading, 466
Rule 14a-9, 8, 328-32
Section 14(e), 378-82
Section 17(a), non-recognition of, 322-25
Williams Act, generally, 367

**"In connection with" requirement**, 86-101

**In pari delicto**, 180-81

**Indemnification**, 205-06

**Insider trading**
*Chapter 7*
bounty program, 520
Chinese walls, 476-77
circumstantial evidence of, 523-49
classical theory, 468-78
common law and, 449-52
materiality, 466
misappropriation theory, 489-505
nonpublic information, 466-67
possession vs. use, 475-76
penalties, monetary, 516-18
private action for, 466, 518-20
remedies, 516-23
Rule 10b5-1, 476
Rule 10b5-2, 502-03
Rule 14e-3, 506-16

Sarbanes-Oxley Act, 521-22
Section 16(b), 452-54
tender offers, 506-16
tippees and temporary insiders, 478-488

**Insurance**, 205-06

**International securities fraud**
*Chapter 12*
choice of law clauses, 914-24
choice of forum clauses, 914-24
conduct as basis for jurisdiction, 897-914
effects as basis for jurisdiction, 890-97
forum non conveniens, 924-34
personal jurisdiction, 896-97
Restatement (Third), Foreign Relations Law, 907-13
SEC enforcement, 934-36

**Joint and several liability**, 204, 291

**Justifiable reliance**, 172-81, 389

**Lenity**, 843

**Loss causation,** 181-93

**Lost state remedies**
Rule 10b-5, 32-43
Rule 14a-9, 345-62

**Mail fraud**, *See* Criminal enforcement

**Manipulation**
*Chapter 8*
conflicts of interest as, 613-16
generally, 23
intent, proving bad, 596
laddering, 584-85
practices creating appearance of active trading, 579-85
pump and dumps, 599-613
scalping, 599-613
Section 9(a), 584
Section 9(e), 584
trading conducted for manipulative purpose, 585-99

**Materiality**
bespeaks caution doctrine, 75-79
defined, 64-67
duty to disclose, relation to, 61-62
efficient market hypothesis, relation to, 65-66, 333-34
forward-looking statements, *See* Forward looking statements
hindsight bias, 73
mail fraud, 855-61
probability/magnitude test, 73
puffery, 21, 66, 315, 613
Rule 10b-5, 64-86
Rule 14a-9, 332-34
Sections 11 and 12 , 315-16
Section 14(e), 387-88
soft information, 67-74
wire fraud, 855-61

**Measure of damages**. *See* Damages

**Mediation**, 963-64

**Memoranda of understanding**, 935

**Misappropriation theory**, *See* Insider trading

**Mutual legal assistance treaties**, 935

**Negative causation**, 286-91, 314-15
*See also* Causation

**Parallel proceedings**, 744-67
double jeopardy clause, 760-67
multiple enforcement proceedings, 755-60
multiple investigations, 744-55

**Pleading**
discovery stays, 10, 114, 128
Exchange Act, 22-23, 113-33, 337
group pleading, 129-30
Securities Act, 316-17

**Preemption**, 317, 419-27
*See also* State law, Blue sky law

**Primary liability**, 220-26

**Punitive damages**. *See* Damages

**Proportionate liability**, 204-05

**Proxy fraud**. *See* Rule 14a-9

**Public Company Accounting Oversight Board**, 820-32

**Puffery**, 21, 66, 315, 613

**Pump and dumps**, 599-613

**Purchaser-seller requirement**, 133-46

**Reasonable care defense**, 311-14

**Reasonable reliance**, 172-81
*See also* Justifiable reliance

**Regulation AC**, 616

**Regulation FD**, 56-57, 488

**Reliance**

justifiable reliance, 172-81, 389
presumptions of reliance
fraud-created-the-market, 164-71
fraud-on-the-market, 153-64
efficient market, necessity of, 160
justifiable reliance and, 172-79
Rule 10b-5 and, 21, 153-64
truth-on-the-market, 21, 159
omissions, 147-53
Rule 10b-5 and, 147-81
Rule 14a-9 and, 345
Section 11 and, 262
Section 12(a)(2) and, 292
Section 14(e) and, 388-89
*See also* causation, justifiable reliance

**Reporting companies**, 7-8

**Rescission**
*See* Damages

**Respondeat superior**, 235-36

**Restatement (Third) of Foreign Relations Law of the United States**, 907-13

**Rule 10b-5**
*Chapter 2*
aiding and abetting liability, 207-20
bespeaks caution doctrine, 75-79
causation, 147-93
controlling person liability *See* controlling person liability
corporate mismanagement, 32-43
damages *See* Damages
deception 23-64
silence as, 47-64
duty to correct, 58-60
duty to disclose, 52-64
duty to update, 57-58
express private actions, overlap with, 254-59
forward-looking statements, 74-86
fraud-created-the-market, 164-71
fraud-on-the-market, 153-64
generally, 6
"in connection with" requirement, 86-101
joint and several liability, 204
justifiable reliance, 172-81
loss causation, 181-93
lost state remedies, 32-43
manipulation, 23, 578-616
materiality, 64-86
pleading *See* Pleading
primary liability, 220-26
proportionate liability, 204-05
puffery, 21, 66, 613
purchaser-seller requirement, 133-46
reliance, 147-81
respondeat superior, 235-36
scienter, 102-33
silence as deception, 47-64
statute of limitations *See* Statute of limitations

**Rule 14a-9**, 8
*Chapter 4*
causation, 338-62
equitable relief, 344
implied private action, recognition of 328-32
lost state remedies, 346-62
materiality, 332-34
reliance, 345
state of mind, 334-38

**Rule 14e-3**, 506-16

**Rule 102(e)**, 769-776

**Rule 205**, 806-17
proposed revisions, 815-16

**Sarbanes-Oxley Act**
accountants, SEC's authority, 768-773
analysts, 614-16
attorneys, SEC's authority, 768-73, 805-19
crimes created by, 846-49
disclosure obligations created by, 53-54
generally, 10-11
Public Company Accounting Oversight Board, 820-32
remedies, SEC, 657-58
statute of limitations, private fraud actions, 237

**Scienter**
*See* State of mind

**Secondary liability**
*See* Aiding and abetting liability; Conspiracy; Controlling person liability; Respondeat superior

**Securities analysts**. *See* Analysts

**Section 9(a), Exch. Act**, 7, 584

**Section 9(e), Exch. Act**, 259, 584

**Section 10(b), Exch. Act**, *See* Rule 10b-5

**Section 11, Securities Act**
concurrent jurisdiction, 317
contribution, 291
controlling person liability, 316
damages, 286-91
due diligence defenses, 269-86
forward-looking statements, 315-16
generally, 5-6, 262-92
joint and several liability, 291

materiality, 315-16
negative causation, 286-91
pleading, 316-17
standing to sue, 263-69
statute of limitations, 316
tracing, 263-69

**Section 12(a)(2), Securities Act**
and aftermarket, 302
by means of a prospectus or oral communication, 292-303
concurrent jurisdiction, 317
contribution, 310
controlling person liability, 316
damages, 314-15
forward-looking statements, 315-16
generally, 5-6, 291-92
materiality, 315-16
negative causation, 314-15
pleading, 316-17
public offerings and, 300-01
reasonable care defense, 311-14
seller, definition of, 303-11
statute of limitations, 316

**Section 14(a), Exch. Act**, *See* Rule 14a-9

**Section 14(e), Exch. Act**
*Chapter 5*
damages, 389-90
forward-looking statements, 388
generally, 8-9
insider trading and Rule 14e-3, 506-16
materiality, 387-88
misrepresentation or nondisclosure, necessity of, 370-78
reliance, 388-89
scienter, 388
SEC's rulemaking authority, 391, 506-16
standing to sue, 378-82
*See also* Tender offers

**Section 16(b), Exch. Act**, 452-54

**Section 17(a), Securities Act**, 7, 320-25
implied action, non-recognition of, 322-25
scienter, 321-22

**Section 18(a), Exch. Act**, 258-59

**Securities & Exchange Commission (SEC)**

**SEC enforcement**
*Chapters 9, 10*
accountants, 768-73, 819-32
administrative remedies, 680-93
aiding and abetting, 219, 691, 791-92
attorneys, 768-73, 806-19
burden of proof, 702-07
cease-and-desist orders, 689-91, 744
collateral bar orders, 692-93
collateral estoppel, 651, 654, 716-34
consent decrees and settlements, 651-57
controlling person liability, right to utilize, 226
division of enforcement, 13, 618-20
international securities fraud, 934-36
investigations, 621-657
judicial remedies, 662-79
litigating with the SEC, 699-723
officer and director bars, 521, 676-78
parallel proceedings, 744-67
remedies, chart, 658-62
rulemaking authority, 391, 506-16
sanctions, collateral consequences of, 693-99
self-regulatory organizations, 723-44
statute of limitations, 708-16
Wells submissions, 643-45

**Securities Litigation Uniform Standards Act (SLUSA)**, 14-15, 419-27

**Self-regulatory organizations**, 9, 723-44

**Standing to sue**
Rule 10b-5, 133-46
Section 11, 263-69
Section 14(e), 378-82

**State action doctrine**, 736-44, 830-31

**State law**
aiding and abetting liability, 220
disclosure duties, 60-61
enforcement proceedings, 755-60
generally, 14-15
insider trading, 449-52
merit approach, 3
state of mind, 112
tender offer litigation, 392-99
*See also* Blue sky law, Preemption

**State of mind**
criminal enforcement, federal securities laws, 835-42
joint and several liability, 204
mail fraud, 850
RICO (criminal), 863-64, 885
Rule 14a-9, 334-38
scienter
corporate scienter, 112
pleading, 113-33, 430-31
Rule 10b-5, 102-33
Section 17(a), 321-22
substantive standard, 102-13
state law, 112
willfully, 835-42
wire fraud, 850
*See also* pleading

**Statute of limitations**
criminal enforcement of federal securities laws, 845
mail fraud, 860

RICO, 886
Rule 10b-5 (private), 236-54
SEC, 708-16
Sections 11 and 12, 316
wire fraud, 860

**Tender offers**
generally, 8-9, 363-69
insider trading, 506-16
litigation under state law, 392-94
warehousing, 513-14
*See also* Section 14(e)

**Truth-on-the-market**, 21, 159

**Warehousing**, 513-14

**Wells submission**, 643-45

**Whistleblowers**, 633-34

**Willfully**, *See* Criminal enforcement, State of mind

**Wire fraud**. *See* Mail and wire fraud